W9-CCI-548

LEVELED BOOKS FOR READERS, GRADES 3–6

A Companion Volume to *Guiding Readers and Writers*

GAY SU PINNELL

IRENE C. FOUNTAS

HEINEMANN
PORTSMOUTH NH

Heinemann
A division of Reed Elsevier Inc.
361 Hanover Street
Portsmouth, NH 03801–3912
www.heinemann.com

Offices and agents throughout the world

The authors and publisher wish to thank those who have generously given permission to reprint borrowed material:

Amazing Spiders by Alexandra Parson. Copyright © 1990. Reprinted by permission of D.K. Publishers, Inc.

Bridge to Terabithia. Copyright © 1977 by Katherine Paterson. Used by permission of HarperCollins Publishers.

Caves by Lisa A. Klobuchar. Published by Rigby in 1998. Reprinted by permission.

The Chocolate Flier. Text and illustrations written by Margaret Beames and illustrated by Mark Eastland Stevens. Copyright © 1999 by Shortland Publications, Inc. Reprinted by permission of the Wright Group/McGraw Hill, 19201 120th Ave., Suite #100, Bothell, WA 98011. 1-800-523-2371.

Dad. Copyright © by Beverley Randell. Used by permission of Nelson Thomson Learning.

Dear Mr. Henshaw. Text Copyright © 1983 by Beverly Cleary. Used by permission of HarperCollins Publishers.

The Diary of a Young Girl, The Definitive Edition by Anne Frank. Otto H. Frank & Mirjam Pressler, editors. Translated by Susan Massotty. Copyright © 1995 by Doubleday, a division of Bantam Doubleday Dell Publishing Group, Inc. Used by permission of Doubleday, a division of Random House, Inc.

Dicey's Song by Cynthia Voigt. Copyright © 1982 by Cynthia Voigt. Reprinted with the permission of Atheneum Books for Young Readers, an imprint of Simon & Schuster Children's Publishing

Fig Pudding by Ralph Fletcher. Copyright © 1995 by Ralph Fletcher. Used by permission of Marian Reiner for the author. Reprinted by permission of Clarion Books/Houghton Mifflin Company. All rights reserved.

Fighting Ground. Copyright © 1984 by Avi Wortis. Used by permission of HarperCollins Publishers.

The Giver. Copyright © 1993 by Lois Lowry. Reprinted by permission of Houghton Mifflin Co. All rights reserved.

Hairy Little Critters by Buck Wilde. First published in 1997 by Shortland Publications Ltd. Reprinted by permission of Rigby.

Harriet Beecher Stowe and the Beecher Preachers by Jean Fritz. Copyright © 1994 by Jean Fritz. Used by permission of G.P. Putnam's Sons, an imprint of Penguin Putnam Books for Young Readers, a divison of Penguin Putnam Inc.

Harriet Tubman. Recorded by the permission of Russell & Volkening as agents for the author. Copyright © 1955 by Ann Petry, renewed in 1983 by Ann Petry.

Helen Keller: Courage in the Dark by Johann Hurwitz. Text copyright © 1997 by Johanna Hurwitz. Illustrations copyright © 1997 by Neverne Covington. Used by permission of Random House Children's Books, a division of Random House, Inc.

The Hero and the Crown by Robin McKinley. Text copyright © 2000 by Robin McKinley. Used by permission of HarperCollins Publishers.

Henry and Mudge and the Best Day of All. Text copyright © 1995 by Cynthia Rylant. Illustration copyright © 1995 by Sucie Stevenson. Reprinted with the permission of Simon and Schuster Books for Young Readers, an imprint of Simon and Schuster Children's Publishing Division,

Insects, written by Bettina Bird and Joan Short, from Mondo's BOOKSHOP Literacy Program. Text copyright © 1988 by Bettina Bird and Joan Short, reprinted by permission of Mondo Publishing, 980 Avenue of the Americas, New York, New York 10018. All rights reserved.

Looking at Insects by David Glover. Published by Rigby in 1998. Reprinted by permission.

Man Out at First by Matt Christopher. Copyright © 1993 by Matthew F. Christopher (text); copyright © 1993 by Ellen Beier (illustrations). By permission of Little, Brown and Company (Inc.).

Maps and Codes. Written by Lisa Burton, David Chang, and Sandra Iverson. Illustrated by Madeline Beasley, Geoffrey Cox, Marjory Gardner, Kelvin Hawley, Nicolas van Pallant, and Linette Porter. Copyright © 1999 by Lands End Publishing, Inc. Reprinted by permission of the Wright Group/McGraw Hill, 19201 120th Ave., Suite #100, Bothell, WA 98011. 1-800-523-2371.

Mieko and the Fifth Treasure by Eleanor Coerr, calligraphy by Cecil H. Uyehara. Copyright © 1993 by Eleanor Coerr. Used by permission of G.P. Putnam's Sons, an imprint of Penguin Putnam Books for Young Readers, a division of Penguin Putnam Inc.

Mouse Tales. Copyright © 1972 by Arnold Lobel. Used by permission of HarperCollins Publishers.

Nate the Great and the Tardy Tortoise by Marjorie Weinman Sharmat and Craig Sharmat. Copyright © 1995 by Marjorie Weinman Sharmat and Craig Sharmat. Illustrations copyright © 1995 by Marc Simont. Used by permission of Random House Children's Books, a division of Random House, Inc.

Pinky and Rex and the Spelling Bee by James Howe, illustrated by Melissa Sweet. Text copyright © 1991 James Howe. Illustrations copyright © 1991 by Melissa Sweet. Reprinted with the permission of Atheneum Books for Young Readers, an imprint of Simon & Schuster Children's Publishing Division.

Seeds by Gail Saunders-Smith, published by Pebble Books, an imprint of Capstone Press © 1998. For information on Pebble Books, please call 1-800-747-4992.

Shoeshine Girl. Copyright © 1975 by Clyde Robert Bulla. Illustrations copyright © 1975 by Leigh Grant. Used by permission of HarperCollins Publishers.

The View From Saturday by E.L. Konigsburg. Copyright © 1996 by E.L. Konigsburg. Reprinted with the permission of Atheneum Books for Young Readers, an imprint of Simon & Schuster Children's Publishing Division.

The Watsons Go to Birmingham 1963 by Christopher Paul Curtis. Copyright © 1995 by Christopher Paul Curtis. Used by permission of Dell Publishing, a division of Random House, Inc.

We Shall Not Be Moved by Joan Dash. Copyright © 1996 by Joan Dash. Reprinted by permission of Scholastic, Inc.

What Happens When You Recycle? by Joan Heilman. Published by Rigby in 1998. Reprinted by permission.

Where the Red Fern Grows by Wilson Rawls. Copyright © 1961 by Sophie S. Rawls, Trustee, or successor Trustee(s) of the Rawls Trust, dated July 31, 1991. Copyright © 1961 by The Curtis Publishing Company. Used by permission of Random House Children's Books, a division of Random House, Inc.

Yang the Youngest and His Terrible Ear. Copyright © 1992 by Lensey Namioka. Used by permission of Lensey Namioka. All rights are reserved by the author. Illustrations copyright © 1992 by Kees de Kiefte Used by permission of Little, Brown and Company Inc.

Stealing Home: The Story of Jackie Robinson by Barry Denenberg. Copyright ©1990 by Barry Denenberg. Reprinted by permission of Scholastic Inc. Photo of Jackie Robinson used by permission of AP/Wide World Photos.

Library of Congress Cataloging-in-Publication Data is on file with the Library of Congress

ISBN: 0-325-00307-6

Editor: Lois Bridges
Production: Michael Cirone
Cover design: Cat and Mouse Design/Catherine Hawkes
Manufacturing: Louise Richardson
Photography: Mark Morelli; photograph on page XX courtesy of Woodland Heights Elementary School
Composition: Uppercase Production and Design
Printed in the United States of America on acid-free paper

06 05 04 03   ML   4 5 6

To

Susan E. Hundley,

a collector and lover of books

CONTENTS

ACKNOWLEDGMENTS

Teachers and books make a difference in the lives of children. We have particularly enjoyed the creation of this book. We had the pleasure of reading and rereading thousands of wonderful books. But even more gratifying was the opportunity we had to talk with hundreds of teachers and students across the country who, over the past several years, have reviewed and provided invaluable feedback on books.

We especially appreciate the teams of teachers who reviewed and leveled books and engaged with us in dialogue that moved our thinking forward in analyzing the characteristics of texts. This process has helped all of us to become more knowledgeable about helping students develop a reading process.

Our colleagues at Ohio State and Lesley University are a continual source of learning for us and we thank them for their feedback and support. At OSU, we thank Diane DeFord for her work with intermediate teachers. We also express appreciation to Joan Wiley, Pat Scharer, Andrea McCarrier, Jonda McNair, Lynda Mudre, Justina Henry, Sharon Gibson, Peg Gwyther, and Paige Fullterton, who are doing excellent work with primary teachers. At Lesley University, we thank Jill Eurich, Margaret Crosby, Toni Czekanski and Helen Sisk for their work with intermediate teachers and Carol Woodworth for her patience and meticulous attention to the book collection. We also express appreciation to the primary team, including Diane Powell, Meredith Neville and Leslie Ryan.

Our Reading Recovery colleagues, as always, provide a wonderful example for us in matching books to readers. We thank Emily Rodgers, Susan Fullerton, and Carol Lyons at Ohio State and Eva Konstantellou at Lesley University. We also thank Joanne Bartlam and Jane Williams for their valuable guidance in gathering data to document the literacy achievement of intermediate students.

It is always a pleasure to work with the Heinemann team on the production of a book. We thank them for all they do to make our work available to teachers in a high quality way. We express special appreciation to our editor, Lois Bridges, who always offers timely, succinct, and wise advice and whose editing skills are monumental. Michael Cirone's special attention to the details and artistry of layout and design were a valuable contribution to this volume. We thank them both for patience and problem-solving. As well, we express special thanks to Michael Gibbons and Lesa Scott, whose encouragement and advice has been so important in the process.

We would also like to acknowledge our friend Salli Oddi for sharing her expertise on the range of wonderful books for intermediate readers. We also thank our teams at OSU and Lesley, especially Jennifer Gleason, Natalia Zuazo, Nora Menzi, Julie Skogsbergh, Polly Taylor, and Sharon Freeman. To our families, especially Catherine Fountas and Elfrieda Pinnell, we express appreciation for their continued patience and support for our commitment to our professional work. We thank Ron Melhado for lending technical expertise to the organization and production of the work. As always we thank him and Ron Heath for humor, patience, and love during the preparation of this book.

Finally, we have dedicated this book to Susan E. Hundley, a courageous woman who loved children, teachers, and books. As a collector of wonderful books for children, she treated each beautiful book she acquired as a treasure. Early on, she became interested in how books can be viewed from the perspective of a reading process and found special joy in her leveling work with teachers. In our years of friendship and collegial work, she was unfailingly generous in contributing her insights about texts. We will miss her always.

INTRODUCTION

Students in the upper elementary grades, swept up in a period of rapid growth and emotional change, vary in just about every way possible. Their experiences during these maturing years will influence the rest of their lives. What kinds of readers will these students become? Will they read voluntarily? Will they develop well-defined tastes? Will they use reading as a tool for learning and for successful achievement throughout their lives? Will they find that reading opens new worlds to them? And will reading be an essential part of their lives—one that brings them joy and an enthusiastic, ever-evolving dedication to learning?

These questions are as yet unresolved for most elementary students. They are still developing as readers and forming their tastes, attitudes, and habits. For this reason, knowing books and knowing how to use them skillfully in classroom instruction is a professional responsibility of paramount importance for teachers.

In the upper elementary grades, we work with readers who are competent and skilled but are reluctant to read; we teach readers who struggle but want to learn; and we respond to struggling readers who are so daunted by reading that they avoid it at all costs. We also work with students who read voraciously, are highly skilled, and view reading as one of the important pleasures in their lives. As teachers, we find ways to reach, nurture, and support all of these readers.

In our book *Guiding Readers and Writers, Grades 3–6: Teaching Comprehension, Genre, and Content Literacy* (2001) we describe a comprehensive language and literacy framework designed to help students develop a broad and integrated range of reading, writing, and language abilities. We stress the profound interconnectedness of reading and writing, and we describe a variety of texts that are used in different ways to support students' development.

In *Leveled Books for Readers, Grades 3–6*, we focus on the texts you will need to support a rich environment for literacy teaching and learning, beginning with a description of the most effective ways to use books. The rest of the book describes a gradient of leveled texts and its uses. A gradient of text is a powerful tool for teachers as they engage students in group instruction, known as guided reading, or as they guide students' book choices for independent reading.

A good classroom program brings students into contact with many different kinds of books. We want our students to become familiar with a wide range of genres, authors, topics, styles, formats. They will hear some texts read aloud and relish the opportunity to think deeply about them as they discuss and debate the meaning with others. Other texts they may share with a partner or delve into on their own, with teacher support, as they pursue specific information for a research project.

Leveled texts serve a particular instructional purpose. In guided reading, you select books from leveled collections (either in a school bookroom or a classroom storage area that is not accessible to students) for small groups of students. Books read in guided reading are within students' control but offer a few instructional challenges. Because of your teaching, students read these books with a high level of success and at the same time expand their reading abilities.

In this book we focus mainly on books that students choose to read for themselves, with guidance from the teacher. The books are attractively arranged by topic, author, genre, or series. Your knowledge of book levels helps you unobtrusively guide choices, suggest books, and teach students to decide for themselves whether the book is easy, just right, or challenging for them. Knowing book levels also enables you to put aside some interesting books at an appropriate level for students who are struggling with the more difficult texts and having trouble making choices.

"Leveling" is not an exact science. There are many variables to take into account in determining text difficulty. A text's demands and supports cannot be reduced to a mathematical formula. The concepts of "easier" and "harder" must always be understood in relation to the complex and interrelated text factors that we describe in this volume; what's more, myriad student factors impact text readability as well. The readability of a text is influenced by the background knowledge required of the reader to understand the text, the reader's facility with word solving, the number of complex sentences embedded in the text, and so on. The specialized process of determining text difficulty is a challenge worthy of our time because the more we learn about texts, the better we understand their demands on the individual readers we teach—the first step in matching books to readers.

Book collections continually evolve. You build your collection slowly over time as you test books with students. We hope our gradient and book list will help you select texts that are "just right" for your readers.

Our list of individual titles includes books by many publishers: no one source could supply the wide variety that upper elementary students need. We have included many series books, which offer students the familiarity that helps them bring background knowledge to their reading and make connections among texts. In addition, series books are very popular with students; if they like one book in a series, they are likely to read more. Often, if students are introduced to one book in a series in guided reading, they choose to read many more books in that series independently.

We have also included a wide range of trade books because we believe quality children's literature must be part of guided and independent reading to the greatest extent possible. We have taken care to include a variety of genres so that in their elementary years students can build a foundation for wide reading as adults.

The fourteen chapters that precede the book list will help you use the list as a support for instruction and also help you acquire books. In the first chapter, we describe selecting and using books in a comprehensive language and literacy program. In Chapter 2, we explore the concept of a text gradient and discuss the process of leveling books.

Chapter 3 provides information about text characteristics—how they support and challenge readers. The basic concept of "readability" is explored here, along with some descriptions of tools. The heart of the leveling process is analyzing text features. In Chapter 4, we discuss how we analyze text features to create the gradient of text included in this book, and in Chapter 5, we further develop that concept by discussing a high-quality leveled collection.

Chapters 6, 7, and 8, provide level-by-level descriptions, with page layouts and prototype texts. These chapters will help you analyze and level texts on your own. We recommend that you and your colleagues use these chapters as a base for extended discussions about the texts in your collection. Undoubtedly, you will find good

texts that are not included in this representative list.

Over time, as you consider your own students and their backgrounds, you will do an excellent job of leveling your own books. The real advantage of this work, of course, is that you will not only learn about texts and their demands, you will think deeply about your students and the reading process. Colleagues who work together as they assemble and continually evaluate a leveled book collection find that their skills increase. They can more easily select "short reads," such as journal articles, for guided reading. They also become more skillful at introducing texts and using them to teach processing strategies.

In Chapter 9 we address instruction in guided and independent reading. We also describe the classroom library, because the way you organize books for student selection impacts their interest in reading. Chapters 10, 11, and 12 describe collections. In Chapter 11, we describe a classroom collection for guided reading; in Chapter 12, we describe a school bookroom. In both of these chapters, we recommend numbers of texts for basic and extended collections.

Chapters 13 and 14 focus on acquiring books to support your students' extensive reading. We provide a guide to proposal writing as well as suggestions on how to use book clubs, gifts, and cost-effective planning.

Our earlier book *Matching Books to Readers: Using Leveled Books in Guided Reading, K–3* (1999) lists 7,500 titles for the primary grades. This book extends the list for grades 3–6. For you convenience, the list is provided three ways—by title, level, and genre. We also provide ordering information, including lists of publishers and addresses.

Book leveling begins with an in-depth analysis of the text by teams of experts who are experienced in teaching guided reading as well as in analyzing features of texts. The true test, of course, is using the texts with students over time. We have included a form, Evaluation Response for Text Gradient (see Appendix 3), to gather more information about the books on our list. We want teachers in many different geographic areas to test the books and provide feedback based on their deeper analysis as they use the books with students. We invite you to send feedback to us at any time. As this book is revised, we will take your comments and suggestions into consideration.

G.S.P.
I.C.F.

CHAPTER ONE

SELECTING AND USING BOOKS IN THE LITERACY PROGRAM

In Patricia Polacco's *The Bee Tree*, Mary Ellen gets tired of reading and goes with her grampa to chase a bee to its tree. They capture the sweet honey and then share this wonderful moment:

> "Now child, I am going to show you what my father showed me, and his father before," he said quietly.
>
> He spooned the honey onto the cover of one of her books. "Taste," he said, almost in a whisper.
>
> Mary Ellen savored the honey on her book.
>
> "There is such sweetness inside of that book too!" he said thoughtfully. "Such things . . . adventure, knowledge and wisdom. But these things do not come easily. You have to pursue them. Just like we ran after the bees to find their tree, so you must also chase these things through the pages of a book!"

As teachers, we want our students, like Mary Ellen, to lead literate lives and discover for themselves that adventure, knowledge, and wisdom. Like this young child running after the honey, we want them to read voluntarily and view literacy as essential to their lives. For most children not everything about learning to read comes easily, but we want the dream to be always within their reach. It will take repeated efforts on their part and ours to reach the necessary levels of competence; we want these efforts to be successful, the kind that become their own reward.

Good readers think of themselves as readers, and read voluntarily, voraciously, and regularly. They read a wide variety of material with confidence and enjoyment. They read for many purposes—to become informed, to improve their lives, to escape to other worlds, to learn about themselves, to revel in adventures, and to understand others who are distant in time, space, and culture. They collect books, talk about books, and recommend books to their friends. They have favorite books and favorite authors. They know their tastes and preferences but are willing to try something new. They remember what they read, reflect on the ideas and experiences they've gained from books, and make connections between and among books. They read actively, bringing their imagination and past experiences to bear on their reading; and they read critically, evaluating what they read for objectivity, completeness, authenticity, and quality. All of these characteristics are part of being a reader, and developing those characteristics is the goal of the literacy program in the upper elementary grades.

Within a broad language and literacy framework designed to support student learning in reading, writing, and word study, books assume a key role in five instructional contexts: interactive read-aloud, independent reading, guided reading, literature study, and investigations or research. A teacher's understanding of leveled books is particularly helpful in independent and guided reading.

Goals of a Language and Literacy Program

We don't normally learn to do something well if we don't like doing it. A high-quality literacy program is designed to help students expand their reading skill and at the same time build their interest in and love for books. Becoming the good reader we describe above requires thousands of hours of engaged reading. It means coming to know authors and illustrators in a variety of genres, developing readerly tastes, and gaining a wide range of skills while refining literate knowledge and finely honed confidence as a reader.

Components of the Language/Literacy Framework

The integrated elements of a comprehensive language and literacy framework work together to develop broad-based and effective reading, writing, thinking, and speaking skills.

As shown in Figure 1–1, we conceptualize this framework within three blocks of time, which may be scheduled anywhere within the school day. The broad range of instructional approaches coordinated within this framework is presented in detail, with many examples, in *Guiding Readers and Writers, Grades 3–6: Teaching Comprehension, Genre, and Content Literacy* (Fountas and Pinnell 2001). Here, we include a brief overview in order to provide a context for using leveled texts.

Language/Word Study

The language and word study block consists of a number of instructional techniques from which you may select according to the needs of your students and the curriculum in your district. Because these are essentially separate components, you can also "scatter" them across the day. Language/word study is a real help in planning the other blocks, and you may well be able to find thirty to sixty minutes in which to coordinate these activities. Most teachers place higher priority on large, uninterrupted blocks of time for reading workshop and writing workshop and use smaller time segments for the types of activities in this block. Activities such as handwriting or current events may fit conveniently within a five- or ten-minute "space"—between music and lunch, for example. Some of the language/word study activities are text based; that is, they involve books and other kinds of texts. Some involve work on individual words. They all include learning more about oral and written language, and generally include the whole class in a community meeting.

Here are brief descriptions of these activities:

■ In *interactive read-alouds*, you read to *and discuss* with students a large range of high-quality fiction, nonfiction, and poetry. By reading texts aloud, you provide the opportunity for students to notice literary elements, build vocabulary and background knowledge, and expand their comprehension of books that may be too difficult for many of them to process entirely on their own. The term *interactive*

A Comprehensive Language and Literacy Framework for the Intermediate Grades	
Language/Word Study	
30–60 minutes	*Select from:* ❖ Interactive Read-Aloud ❖ Modeled/Shared Reading ❖ Modeled/Shared Writing ❖ Poetry Sharing/Response ❖ Readers' Theater/Process Drama ❖ Choral Reading ❖ Interactive Vocabulary ❖ Interactive Edit ❖ Handwriting ❖ Current Events ❖ Test Reading & Writing ❖ Word Study
Reading Workshop	
60 minutes	❖ Independent Reading ❖ Guided Reading ❖ Literature Study
Writing Workshop	
60 minutes	❖ Independent Writing ❖ Guided Writing ❖ Investigations

Figure 1–1. A Comprehensive Language and Literacy Framework for the Intermediate Grades

characterizes the quality of the learning: as you read, you are, in effect, having a brief conversation with students about the text. This conversation supports their understanding.

■ In *modeled/shared reading*, the entire group either follows along as you read aloud (making comments about your thinking as you go) or reads a text together. You support the reading and engage the students in processing it.

■ In *modeled/shared writing,* you demonstrate writing for the group or act as their scribe as you guide them in composing a common text related to an experience, a piece of literature, or a subject in the curriculum. Modeled/shared writing is a chance to let students in on the problem solving that writers do relative to word choice, organization, punctuation, spelling, etc.

■ In *poetry sharing/response,* you or the students read and discuss poetry. Often, they select poems to read or they memorize and recite a special favorite. The focus is on talking about what appeals to individuals about poems or what students notice about the writing.

■ In *readers' theater and process drama,* students assume roles based on problems or issues they have encountered in their content area study or literature. In readers' theater, two or more students read a piece of writing aloud, usually taking roles as the characters. The piece is first selected and practiced and then performed. Process drama is less about performance and more about assuming identities and roles over time. It usually involves reading and research and may involve writing, but the emphasis is on living through a vicarious experience that helps students understand the world and themselves at a new level.

■ *Choral reading* is the rehearsed recitation of written language, either prose or poetry. It may grow from shared reading of texts as students read particular parts in unison or solo and work to use their voices to show their interpretations.

■ In *interactive vocabulary* students study word meanings. A short, focused lesson helps students solve the meaning of new words or associate words by their meanings. You may make a chart to help students remember the lesson as they work.

■ In an *interactive edit,* you focus briefly on the conventions of language (capitalization, punctuation, grammar, spelling, word choice) by asking students to consider a few sentences that require editing.

■ *Handwriting* is a quick lesson on any aspect of handwriting, followed by focused practice.

■ *Current events* is a way of helping students build interest in the world about them. A brief discussion of current events every week creates the habit of noticing issues relative to the environment or science or politics. Students can prepare brief presentations on current events, and you can also provide guidelines for talking and writing about them.

■ In *test reading and writing,* you acquaint your students with the "genre" of tests, because tests often require them to use language in tricky and unexpected ways. You lead quick, lively practice sessions in which you help the students solve representative test items and support their work with demonstration and conversation.

■ *Word study* is the systematic process whereby you help students learn the rules and principles of phonics and spelling. You present a minilesson on any spelling pattern, rule, or concept that will help students understand a specific spelling principle, then have the students apply the principle (often by manipulating magnetic letters or letter tiles). The word study system described in detail in Pinnell and Fountas 1999 involves five days of planned activity. In a minilesson exploring a particular principle on day 1, students are guided to select six, seven, or eight words that exemplify an important principle, and the same amount from their words-to-learn list. On day 1, they write their words on a study card and then make them with magnetic letters. On day 2, they use "look, say, cover, write, check," an established word-study technique. Day 3 is a buddy check; after a practice test, students highlight parts of words that they do not know accurately and study them. On day 4, students make connections between the words they are studying and many other words; the connections may involve a visual pattern, they may be meaning-related, or they may relate to letter-sound relationships. On day 5 there is a test that is checked by the teacher.

Components of the language/word study block together help students understand how written language works. In interactive edit, modeled/shared writing, interactive vocabulary, handwriting, and word study, they look closely at the details of written language by studying words and word parts. Word study connections, as well as vocabulary, contribute to reading comprehension. Interactive read-aloud, modeled/shared reading, poetry sharing/response, readers' theater and process drama, choral reading, and test reading and writing (as genre study) contribute overall to students' ability to process and understand continuous texts.

Reading Workshop

The reading workshop block is a laboratory in which students engage in the kind of reading that real readers do. They learn how to work together as a community as they talk, read, and write about topics that interest them. They take responsibility for their own growth in reading. During reading workshop, students are engaged in one of three activities, described below.

INDEPENDENT READING

The reading workshop block begins with a whole-group meeting during which you:

◼ Give a brief "book talk"—introduce a new book or point out books you think students will find interesting. Students may jot down interesting titles on their Reading Interests list in their reading response journal.

◼ Present a minilesson on some aspect of reading that most students need to work on.

Following the book talk and minilesson, students read independently and silently for about forty minutes, usually texts they've selected themselves. Occasionally they also write in their response journals. During any given week they are to produce one thoughtful letter to you, which you answer. (You can manage this by responding to one fourth of the class each day, Monday through Thursday.) If you have an unusually large class, you may want to respond every two weeks to each reader. The questions and comments you pose in this written interaction prompts students to think deeper about texts. While the students are reading and/or writing, you confer with individuals, supporting their understanding, stretching their thinking, and making observations that will guide your teaching.

At the end of the reading workshop block, you and the students meet again to revisit the minilesson, share insights and experiences, or call attention to specific points from reading response journals. This meeting is brief—every student won't share his or her thinking every day—but it is a way to wrap things up.

Maintaining the proper classroom atmosphere during independent reading is important. Students read silently without talking to one another. The only sounds are whispered conferences between teacher and individual students or the low voices of students work-

Figure 1–2. A Student in Independent Reading

ing in small groups with the teacher. The idea is to provide a time for sustained, engaged reading every day (or four out of the five days, devoting one day to reading and writing poetry).

GUIDED READING

While students are reading independently and silently, you can pull together a small group for guided reading. Guided reading is small-group instruction designed to expand students' ability to process a text with understanding and fluency. The students in the group are at a similar stage in their development of reading strategies and have similar needs. They read about the same level of text with accuracy and understanding. These kinds of groupings are flexible and change often, making them different from traditional reading groups. Guided reading groups may be assembled for particular concepts or purposes; they may also be ongoing as you introduce texts that gradually increase the challenge to students.

You select a text that offers the small, temporary, homogenous group of students opportunities for problem solving and new learning. The text should be one that is within students' control, *with teacher support*. A gradient of increasing difficulty, discussed further in Chapter 2, helps you select appropriate texts. The selection is always made with the particular readers in mind, however.

As indicated in Figure 1–4, guided reading lessons have a consistent structure: (1) the teacher introduces the text (or a unified part of it); (2) students read the text silently, sometimes with teacher support and interaction; (3) teacher and students revisit the text after reading to discuss the meaning; (4) specific processing strategies are taught; (5) the meaning of the text is extended [optional]; and (6) word work takes place [optional]. Guided reading with upper elementary students needs variety. It must include both fiction and nonfiction texts; some that are long, and some that are short (see Figure 1–5). Indeed, one of the goals of guided reading is to broaden students' repertoires as readers.

The introduction supports students' comprehension and problem solving as they each read the text independently. You may introduce an entire text (a longer chapter book, for example), and assign students a unified part of it, or you may introduce one section at a time and have students read and discuss each section over consecutive days. You will also often use "short reads" (to include articles or short stories) for guided reading lessons.

While the students are reading, you may want to sample some oral reading so that you can monitor individual processing. This is not necessary in every lesson. For the most part, students should be reading a text silently. You can also prompt problem solving or draw attention to some aspect of the text that will help a student increase his reading powers. You can demonstrate effective reading strategies and prompt students to use those you have already taught them. These brief interactions give you a great deal of information:

Figure 1–3.   A Guided Reading Group

■ Whether the text is appropriate.
■ What aspects of the text students are reading fluently.
■ Strategies in which students need further instruction.
■ Whether the group's next selection should be more difficult, easier, or at about the same level.
■ Whether to revise group membership.
■ How well the reader is understanding the text.

After reading, you revisit the text with students to discuss what they have understood. They may talk about characters and why they do what they do or may discuss the plot and why it was exciting, interesting, or scary. They may offer opinions or make hypotheses and return to the text to cite evidence. You will also want to do some specific teaching based on your observations of students'

Structure of Guided Reading

❖ Introducing the text

❖ Reading the text silently, with conferring

❖ Discussing and revisiting the text to discuss the meaning

❖ Teaching for processing strategies

❖ Extending meaning [optional]

❖ Word work [optional]

Figure 1–4.   Structure of Guided Reading

Variety of Texts in Guided Reading

❖ Realistic fiction

❖ Historical fiction

❖ Fantasy and science fiction

❖ Traditional literature—folktales, fables, myths, legends

❖ Biography

❖ Informational books

Figure 1–5. Variety of Texts in Guided Reading

reading behavior over time. These teaching points provide explicit instruction that will expand students' reading ability at the word or text level.

You may want to extend the meaning of some texts through additional discussion or writing. Occasionally, you may use a graphic organizer to help students connect or compare ideas and concepts. If students need to develop stronger control of letters, sounds, and words, at the end of the guided reading lesson you introduce very explicit word work geared precisely to what they need to know. You might use magnetic letters or a dry-erase whiteboard to explore words and how they are related structurally (endings, beginnings, middle parts, letter clusters, syllables) (see Pinnell & Fountas 1999).

LITERATURE STUDY

Literature study groups (book clubs) may also meet while the rest of the class is involved in independent, silent reading. In contrast to guided reading, literature study is intended to involve students in mixed, or heterogeneous groups. Groups are brought together to engage in extended discussion of an age-appropriate text. Literature study is variously called *book club, literature circle, literature discussion group,* or *response group.* Whatever the name, the purpose is to enable readers to develop a deeper understanding of the texts they read. Literature study helps students become aware of the writer's craft in structuring and organizing a text as well as using language.

Literature study may be structured around the texts you use for interactive read-aloud; or students may select a text they want to discuss, set a time for discussion and then read it during independent and home reading; or you may select a text and assign it to a group; or you may give a brief book talk on a number of choices, ask students to sign up for their first, second, and third choices, and configure the groups based on these lists.

You'll want to set up assigned reading/writing tasks as well as meeting times. After that your role is to facilitate literature discussion groups and teach students effective routines for interaction and in-depth discussion. You want the students to talk to one another, not just answer your questions; your role is to "lift" the discussion by modeling thoughtful responses and helping students get to the significant, worthwhile issues in high quality texts. There may also be written responses or a culminating project.

Text difficulty should not be a factor in keeping students from reading their first choice. Even if a text is too hard for a student to read independently, she can still understand and discuss it after listening to it on tape or hearing it read by the teacher, a parent, or a buddy.

MANAGING INTERRELATIONSHIPS WITHIN THE READING WORKSHOP

The three components of reading workshop are interconnected. Sometimes one moves into another. For example, students may read most of a text in guided reading and finish it independently. A literary text used

Figure 1–6. A Literature Study Group

for guided reading may become the text for an in-depth literature discussion. Students who have read a certain text in their independent reading (and responded to it in their journal) may sign up to discuss it as a work of literature. Even if students are reading a different text in each of the three settings, there will be related concepts and intertextual connections. Students in literature study who are exploring flashback as a literary device may offer examples from books in their independent reading. Students who encounter an author in guided reading may be prompted to remember a text that they discussed during literature study.

Since students are reading at least thirty minutes every day in reading workshop and thirty minutes each evening for homework, *and* they are reading texts they can read with ease and fluency, they are expected to get through a lot of material. On average, students complete about one chapter book or several shorter books in a week. Students can keep more than one book going at a time, although you will want to minimize the number of books being read. When you are planning to begin work with a group of students in guided reading, let them know they should finish up their independent book as home reading.

Writing Workshop

The structure for writing workshop is similar to that for reading workshop. The block consists of independent writing, guided writing, and investigations.

INDEPENDENT WRITING

In independent writing, students work on the various phases of their own projects. At the beginning of the writing workshop block, you may provide a brief "writer's talk," providing insights into the way professional writers work, and you may take a "status of the class" to find out the progress each student is making on his writing piece(s). Then, you provide a minilesson on some aspect of writing. The minilesson may focus on:

- Management and procedures for the writing workshop (how to move from the writer's notebook to a discovery draft, how to report progress, and so on).
- Useful strategies and skills (for example, how to proofread your work or use punctuation effectively).
- The craft of writing and the introduction of specific techniques that help students develop as writers

(for example, how to write with voice or use literary language such as metaphor).

Next, students work silently and independently on their own pieces of writing while you confer with individual students. The independent writing period ends with a brief large-group share as well as an evaluation of how the workshop went that day.

GUIDED WRITING

While most students are writing independently, you bring together small, temporary groups of writers who need a focused look at particular skills and strategies or aspects of craft. This approach allows you, very efficiently, to focus on what one group needs without wasting the time of others. The particular groupings will be based on your observations of students *while they are writing* and your evaluation of their written drafts.

INVESTIGATIONS

Investigations are inquiry projects that allow students to explore topics in depth. Both reading and writing are usually involved; students usually work individually but may work in pairs or small groups from time to time. Investigations are a way to integrate content areas; students may be researching subjects related to science, social studies, or any other area—even literature itself. You provide guidelines, a structure, and a timeline for projects; you also provide instruction and meet with individuals and groups as needed. Projects involve reading and writing informational texts and utilizing technology.

The Classroom Collection

The classroom library supports all the activities defined as components of the language and literacy framework. You will want a broad and varied collection of books that:

1. Expand students' literary experiences.
2. Support investigations and inquiry.
3. Support guided and independent reading.

Only the third category will be "leveled" for the teacher's use. A rich classroom collection will include beautifully illustrated picture books, many kinds of novels, informational books, magazines and journals, newspapers, and other kinds of reading material.

Books to Expand Students' Literature Experience Through Interactive Read-Aloud

You will want a good variety of books to read to students. A lot of high-quality illustrated fiction and non-fiction appropriate for intermediate students is available. These picture books can usually be finished in a single setting. The illustrations offer further opportunity for students to interpret the texts and add to the enjoyment. Using picture books you can:

- Model the range of possibilities in the craft of writing.
- Explore language.
- Provide information on a topic.
- Introduce a variety of new genres (such as biography or question/ answer books).
- Increase students' knowledge of an author's or illustrator's style.
- Build up a group of texts students can compare with one another and with the texts they encounter in guided and independent reading.

Many picture books are available in paperback, but you should also have lots of hardbound editions. Covered with clear plastic (which you can order through library supply catalogs), these volumes will last for many years. Properly and accessibly displayed, picture books invite students to read. If you can, store these books on shelves so that the covers face out, making it easier for students to find and revisit them (see Figure 1–7). Also, students can flip through a number of titles kept in a basket, looking at the covers easily, without having to pull out each one from a shelf.

You will also want to read some carefully selected chapter books. Texts that offer rich opportunities for discussion and follow-up will extend students' ability to understand and read longer texts. You won't want to eat up your interactive read-aloud time with just a few long texts over the course of the year, however. It's best to vary the experiences and explore as many different texts as possible. You will also want to read poetry aloud and have students read poetry for them-selves. Poetry and prose texts can also form the basis for shared reading and choral reading.

Books to Expand Students' Literary Experiences Through Independent Reading and Literature Study

All students need the opportunity to select their own books and build their tastes as readers. Reading aloud, independent reading, and literature study offer the chance to deeply experience books. Students need to learn how to:

- Select books.
- Vary their reading repertoire.
- Compare books.
- Know the kinds of books they like.
- Consciously work to expand their tastes.
- Get to know a range of authors, illustrators, and genres.
- Talk with others about books.

Book talks given by you (and by your students after they learn how to do it) raise students' interest in high-quality books. As with the picture books, make books available to students in a variety of ways.

As shown in Figure 1–8, you can place books in tubs by author and topic. Other teachers organize books in tubs labeled by category:

- Biographies, historical fiction, science fiction.
- Books by certain authors or illustrators.

Figure 1–7. Picture Books Displayed in a Classroom

■ Short stories.
■ Books about a specific topic (the human body, space).
■ Newbery Medal and Honor books.

You can also make a rack of "book recommendations" by inviting students to make selections and including some of your own (see Figure 1–9). However you go about it, displaying books invites students to examine them and place them on their Reading Interests list.

Books to Support Inquiry

You will want to have a wide variety of books that help students expand their understanding of specific content areas. We have mentioned that many beautifully illustrated picture books provide information in interesting ways. Of special note are a series of books by Seymour Simon. *The Brain* (1997), for example, shows detailed, close-up photographs of the brain and spinal cord.

Figure 1–8. Books in Baskets by Categories

Reference books on various topics should also be part of the classroom collection. These books are not intended to be read from beginning to end but for readers to look up the information they need. Informational texts to support inquiry can be placed in the center in which they will be used. For example books on the human body or rocks can be located in the science center. Topics that are included in the required curriculum may be clustered together and labeled. Even if students can't read everything in these informational texts, you can help them find the information they need; they can wrestle with a small section in an attempt to answer a particular question. You will want to have resources such as dictionaries, encyclopedias, and thesauruses handy as well.

You will also want to have a good supply of magazines as part of the classroom collection. Excellent resources such as *Cobblestone* ("The History Magazine for Young People"), *Cricket* magazine, *Dragonfly*, or *Ranger Rick* do not go out of date quickly. You can save these magazines and make them available throughout the year.

The Role of Leveled Books

Leveled books have an important role, particularly in guided reading. Being aware of book levels can also help you support and inform students' independent reading selections.

Independent Reading

Students select their own books for independent reading based on their interests, but they are also expected to monitor and make judgments about books that are appropriate for them at this point in time. For example, for each book they read, they should indicate in their reading response journal whether it was E (easy), JR (just right), or C (challenging). (See Fountas and Pinnell 2001.) This act requires that they think about their own reading and learn to make good choices. In your minilessons, you teach them how to make these judgments.

Remember, this judgment should be broad and general. You wouldn't want to narrow a student's choice to a particular level; however, knowing the approximate levels of books students choose gives you information. If a

Figure 1–9.   Display of Student-Recommended Books on Rack

texts they can control, they will gradually increase the level of texts they can process successfully. You should expect the level of independent reading to move up as the guided reading lessons help students improve their processing powers.

Guided Reading

The primary use for a leveled book collection is to support your instruction in guided reading. Knowing the gradient of difficulty will help you select texts that are just right for your students. You still need to analyze the text with the particular group of readers in mind, but having a ballpark level helps streamline the process. Your introduction to the text fine-tunes the selection.

Successful instruction in guided reading helps students expand their reading strategies by applying them to increasingly challenging texts. Selecting the right book goes a long way in assuring that the instruction is helpful to students. In addition, the gradient of text is a way to track their progress. By recording reading levels at regular intervals, you keep track of progress over time. (And as we explain in Chapter 2, you can identify benchmarks that provide a record of reading progress over several years of school.)

Value of a Leveled Book Set

You will build your leveled book set over time as you acquire more books, and more copies of those books, at various levels. This collection is quite economical because you will never have to replace it (as you would if you adopt a new textbook). Rather, the collection grows gradually but steadily, as you add titles to the levels you need most. The leveled book set assists you as a teacher by:

■ Making it easier to select appropriate books to use with groups in guided reading.
■ Helping you assess and record students' progress over time.
■ Providing a set of good reading materials that does not need to be replaced but can simply be expanded over time.
■ Helping you guide individuals when they select books for independent reading.
■ Providing ways to match books to readers so that the reading they do at home will be successful.
■ Providing a "ladder" that students can use to gradually increase their reading abilities.

student is reading and understanding a level L book, and rates it as "just right," the text you select for her guided reading group should be at least level L. If a student is struggling with a text that you know is an L, you can guide him toward choices below that level. On occasion, you may want to organize a basket of books for one or two readers who are struggling to find books that they can read. The point is not to make the student aware of the "level" but to narrow the choice so they can be successful in selecting texts. You need not label the baskets, but show it to the students who will benefit from it.

It is extremely important that students' independent reading be within their control. They should be able to read these texts with ease and fluency so that they can concentrate on their responses and interpretations. Only by successfully processing texts they understand can they build reading power. Over time, because they are participating in guided reading and spending a great deal of time reading and reflecting on

Summary

The books in the classroom library are not leveled; however, a leveled set of books for reading instruction is essential. Your knowledge and skill in using books underlies the success of your literacy program. Some books will expand children's knowledge of literature; others will support their research projects in content areas; still others are critical to expanding their reading strategies and skills (still essential for intermediate students even though they have learned the basic processes).

Suggestions for Professional Development

1. Assess your classroom library by answering these ten questions. Put your estimates or inventory results in writing so you can refer to it later.
   a. What is the variety of books that expand students' knowledge of literature? Do I have a range of both fiction and nonfiction?
   b. Do I have a good collection of picture books suitable for reading aloud to intermediate students? (A good list of fiction and nonfiction picture books is included in Fountas and Pinnell 2001.)
   c. Do I have a good collection of books to support students' inquiry?
   d. Do I have a good collection of leveled books? Which levels do I need most for this group of students? How many titles do I have at each level, and how many copies of each title? Is the collection adequate to support guided reading?
   e. Do I have enough books so that students have good choices in independent reading?
   f. Are the titles for independent reading at the appropriate levels for the students in my class? Are they interesting to students in my class?
   g. Do my book displays allow students to find and replace books easily?
   h. Do my book displays invite readers?
   i. Do my book displays help readers think about categories for reading?
   j. Do my book displays help readers notice books that they will want to read?

2. This beginning evaluation will help you target areas where you want to expand your collection of books. When resources become available, you will be ready! Chances are, you will find that your collection of leveled books is inadequate. In this case, you will find it profitable to join forces with your colleagues in the upper elementary grades.

3. The school librarian is a key person in advising you on your classroom collection. Ask the librarian to act as a consultant as you evaluate your classroom collection. There may be ways to collaborate with her in supplementing the collection.

4. Meet with colleagues to compare and discuss your evaluations of your classroom collections. Discuss building a leveled "school collection" that all of you can share. After all, while you need many single copies for students' independent reading, you need only a few multiple copies of a text at any given time. Sharing with other teachers is economical. Also, you will learn from building a collection with your colleagues.

5. With colleagues, make a plan for improving your classroom collections. Set actions and deadlines to assure that you move forward.

CHAPTER TWO

LEVELING BOOKS: WHY AND HOW

You need a large and varied collection of books to foster variety and quality in students' reading. As your students read widely and develop a sophisticated understanding of texts and how they 'work', they extend and refine their comprehension strategies. In order to use these books most effectively, you need to determine accessibility to readers at different points in their development as they learn how to meet the demands of different kinds of texts. Looking closely at a book's characteristics, you consider: *How easy or how difficult will this text be for readers? What makes it easy or hard? What are the challenges and supports?*

Using Books for Different Purposes

If we expect students to read voluntarily and with ease and understanding, the texts we present to them must be accessible. Accessibility is provided in two ways—by teacher selection and by instruction. Sometimes you read a text *to* students and then discuss it. At other times, you introduce them to important topics and support them as they do research. You guide their independent reading choices, then listen to individual students read and talk with them about their reading. In your minilessons in writing workshop, you make connections between reading and writing.

It is thus essential to have a reliable guide to text difficulty.

A Gradient of Text

To support your work in guided reading, we recommend using a gradient of text. You can create your own gradient or use one that you have found reliable in the past. Or you can follow the guidelines in this book, leveling and adding books to our list as you read and use them with students. We strongly recommend, however, that you and your colleagues select a gradient, work together to understand it, and use only that gradient in your school. Be aware of the text characteristics used to determine the gradient. Having many different leveling systems in play at the same time makes it quite difficult to communicate across classrooms and grade levels about the complexity of texts.

Definition

A gradient of text is a defined continuum of characteristics related to the level of support and challenge that a reader meets in a text. Terms like *easy* and *hard* are not helpful to teachers in the upper elementary grades. Texts are easy or hard with regard to a wide range of factors, including the individual reader's fund of knowledge.

By its nature, a gradient is *relational* and *categorical.* Texts are grouped into categories along a continuum because they offer readers a similar level of support and challenge. The level is an approximation of its difficulty and within a level there is some variation. The challenges are not the same in every text in a level. One text may offer a challenge because of its technical language; another at the same level may be challenging because of its long sentences, archaic language or mature content. A given level is always seen in relation to the levels below and above it. As you move up the gradient, the texts are harder; as you move down, the texts are easier.

The gradient we use is illustrated in Figure 2–1, along with approximate corresponding grade levels. Grade levels are not the important factor when you are selecting books for students. You must start where they are in their development of reading abilities, and that may or may not be their grade level. The grade-level designations are useful, however, because students whose instructional levels are below their grade level need intensive daily instruction that moves them into increasingly challenging texts. The only way to bring the students to grade level is to begin the teaching where they are.

A gradient is not a precise sequence through which all students move. We do not recommend making students read all the books at one level before moving to the next. When students are reading books at a level with ease, fluency, and understanding, encountering very few problems, it's time to increase the text difficulty. You will also want to be sure that students have the opportunity to read the full range of genres at a given level. As the levels of difficulty increase, readers need to experience a variety of texts within each level. The point is not simply to "move up" levels but to increase their breadth of reading by applying their strategies to many different kinds of texts.

In our gradient, the upper grades have fewer levels within them than the early grades do. Most intermediate students reach a point at which they can decode texts at just about any level, no matter how difficult, although their reading sounds choppy and they may mispronounce quite a few words. Texts that they can read with ease, fluency, and deep understanding are another matter. Much more flexibility and a wider range of strategies across a greater variety of genres are required of advanced readers. Again, the point is not simply to move up the gradient, but to expand the students' breadth of experience with different types of texts and a range of content, authors, and formats. You will always want to consider the developmental appropriateness of the content as students approach levels beyond their present grade.

Also, a gradient is not a way to categorize students, whose background experiences and rate of progress will vary widely. The gradient is a large collection of titles that are categorized by level of difficulty. It is meant solely to support the effectiveness of the reading program and is a *teacher's* tool.

Values of a Gradient

Leveled books are *only a small part of the classroom collection,* and leveling books is not intended to limit students' reading. Nevertheless, the gradient serves some

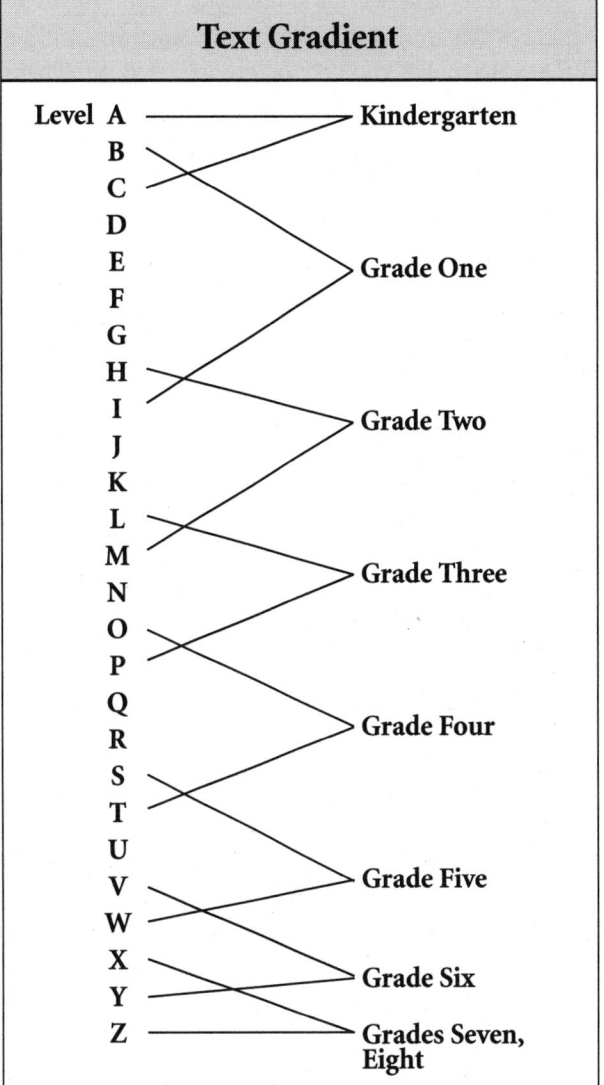

Figure 2–1. *Text Gradient*

important purposes in your instructional program (see Figure 2–2).

The gradient is a useful guide for selecting books for guided reading lessons, as well as for helping students make good choices in their independent reading and the reading they do at home, *but the levels should not be made obvious in the classroom.* As described in Chapter 1, books can be categorized by author, genre, topic, or series and placed in baskets or tubs to attract students' attention. Students will be attracted to books because the books are written by their favorite authors or because they like adventure stories, *not* because they want to read a "level T" book.

Your leveled collection should be in an unobtrusive area to which you alone have access, since you will be using it to make choices for guided reading. These books will not be among the books students peruse as they select them. For many of you, most of the books you use for guided reading will be in a school bookroom if you are fortunate to have a shared collection (see Chapter 12).

If some students consistently choose books that are too hard and find it difficult to make good selections, you'll want to guide them through the process. You can place a small collection of books at the right independent reading level in a basket that is not labeled and ask them to limit their selections to those books for a while. Then, talk with the students about what made these books "just right," so that they learn to monitor their own choices.

The gradient will also be a big help as you work with your grade-level colleagues and teachers at other grade levels. Having a common leveling system and gradient will help you understand student records as they are passed along (see Chapter 9). Also, your conversations about texts for each grade level will be more comprehensible, because you are working from the same basic definitions. Having a common language will help you as you teach the students and communicate with one another about them. Finally, the gradient will help you make wise expenditures when you do

have resources to spend. You can identify the gaps in your collection and fill in the levels that are most needed.

Relationship of the Text Gradient to the Reading Process

Each successive level of the gradient makes greater and more varied demands on the reading process. (In *Guiding Readers and Writers, Grades 3–6*, we discuss in detail the strategies for comprehending written texts.) By the time students enter the intermediate grades, most have developed a full and rich range of in-the-head strategies that operate simultaneously as they process continuous texts. These strategies include:

- Using a range of strategies for decoding and understanding the meaning of the words (*solving words*).
- Checking on their reading to be sure of the meaning and correcting themselves when needed (*monitoring and self-correcting*).
- Picking up the important information from print as the eyes move across it (*gathering*).
- Anticipating what will follow—at the word, phrase, sentence, and text level (*predicting*).
- Sustaining smooth, phrased reading that reflects rapid word solving while thinking about the meaning of the text (*maintaining fluency*).
- Varying reading style and rate according to purpose for reading and the type of text (*adjusting*).

These strategies are not employed or learned one at a time. Instead, readers apply them all to every text they read. The process is easier to orchestrate for simple texts, of course, and becomes much more demanding for complex texts. For example, it is easy to gather information in a straightforward and easy-to-remember text like *Henry and Mudge: The First Book* (Rylant 1996, Level J). It becomes much harder in books like *Stone Fox* (Gardiner 1980, Level P), because there are more difficult words and concepts and much more to remember while reading. While they are sustaining their reading of a text, readers are also required to go beyond it. They develop strategies for expanding meaning:

- Searching for, noticing, and making connections to their own personal experience, to their knowledge

---

Value of an Established Gradient of Text

- ❖ Provides guidance in selecting books for instruction in guided reading.

- ❖ Serves as a teacher's guide for helping students choose books for independent reading and home reading.

- ❖ Helps in documenting students' reading progress over time.

- ❖ Provides a basis for teachers to talk with one another about text difficulty and text selection.

- ❖ Helps in planning and evaluating the classroom collection and a school book collection.

Figure 2–2. Value of an Established Gradient of Text

of the world (content knowledge), and to other texts they have read (*connecting*).

■ Thinking about what the writer implies but does not tell explicitly (*inferring*).

■ Putting together and remembering the important information as an ongoing statement of what the text is all about (*summarizing*).

■ Revising their own background knowledge as new understanding is acquired (*synthesizing*).

■ Closely examining elements of the text to know more about the writer's craft and the construction of text (*analyzing*).

■ Evaluating and critiquing a text for quality or authenticity (*critiquing*).

All of these strategies for thinking beyond a text are employed at lower levels; even texts like the Henry and Mudge series require making inferences about what characters are thinking or feeling, picking up important details and using them to understand the problem and the characters, and even noticing some ways the writer helps you understand how characters feel. But, in general, more is required as you move up the levels. Concepts are more complex and less familiar to students; new ideas must be synthesized, more ideas must to be inferred. This ability to cope with text complexity is built over time and through experience.

Looking at Readers—Changes Over Time

Figure 2–3 summarizes the shifts we see in readers over time in several broad phases and coordinates these changes with the guided reading levels used in this book, with grade levels, and with the traditional basal reading levels found in commercially produced reading programs.

The chart follows readers from their entry into school through the end of elementary school, which is typically either grade five or six.

In the first years of school, children gradually learn what written language sounds like as they enjoy listening to stories. They learn the alphabetic principle (that there is a relationship between sounds and letters) and, through many early experiences with print, they learn how written language works. An important step for emergent readers is learning to match the print word by word and to hear the sounds in words and connect them with a few letters.

Early readers generally have word-by-word matching (one spoken word to one cluster of letters with white space on either side) under control and can read fluently, with appropriate phrasing, books from levels C through about G. They no longer need to point to words but control the process with their eyes. Early readers have learned to use several sources of information to check on their reading—for example, whether it makes sense, sounds right, or looks right in terms of the visual print information (letter-sound coordination). They also are building a core of frequently encountered words that they recognize automatically. Early readers are processing simple texts, mostly narratives, that require following a story line and recognizing story-telling characteristics. While the stories are not complex, they offer opportunities to make personal, world, and book-to-book connections.

Transitional readers are moving from mostly oral to primarily silent reading and have a large core of known words that they recognize rapidly and automatically. They have a broad range of word-solving skills and can handle multisyllable words by taking them apart. These word-solving strategies are used "on the run" while processing continuous texts. They are learning to use simple graphic illustrations in informational texts and extending their knowledge of texts to a wider range of genres.

Self-extending readers read silently most of the time, but are fluent and smooth in their oral reading of texts at levels N through S. They have a broad range of flexible word-solving strategies, although they are still learning more about how words work. They have developed interconnected systems that allow them to expand their reading abilities as they successfully process more difficult and varied texts. Levels N through S contain substantially longer and more complex texts than earlier levels. There is also a greater range of genre.

Advanced readers are in their final years of elementary school. Their word-solving abilities approach adult levels, although they will become more skilled by delving into the study of words (for example, word roots). Reading texts at levels T through X or Y, they are required to employ a full range of strategies and to sus-

Change in Reading Over Time			
Level	**Grade**	**Approximate Basal Level**	**Shifts in the Reading Process**
A	Kindergarten Grade One	Readiness	***Emergent Readers*** are just becoming aware of print. They enjoy listening to stories and begin to understand the differences in syntax and vocabulary that are likely to appear in written (versus oral) language. They read orally and are learning to match word by word and to read left to right. At first, they point with their fingers, but their eyes will start to take over the process. They use information from pictures and rely on meaning and language to interpret simple texts. They use word matching, spaces, and some visual information to check themselves while reading. They are learning to hear sounds in words and connect them with letters; they recognize a few frequently encountered words.
B	Kindergarten Grade One	PP1	
C	Kindergarten Grade One	PP1	***Early Readers*** read orally, mostly without finger pointing, and are beginning to read very softly or silently some of the time. They are familiar with most easy frequently encountered words, and quickly recognize them while reading. They know many letter-sound relationships, and use letter-sound information to solve words while reading. They can use this knowledge of words to check on themselves as readers. On easy texts they read fluently with phrasing, using the punctuation. They are beginning to use several sources of information (meaning, syntax, and visual aspects of print) in combination as they process longer pieces of text. They still rely on pictures as an important source of information, but they are beginning to process print with less picture support.
D	Grade One	PP2	
E	Grade One	PP3	
F	Grade One	Primer	
G	Grade One		
H	Grade One/Grade Two	Grade One	***Transitional Readers*** read silently most of the time; when reading aloud, they read with fluency and phrasing on appropriate levels of text. They have a large core of known words that they recognize automatically while reading continuous text. They use multiple sources of information (letter-sound relationships, word structure, syntax, and meaning) to check their reading and solve problems. They do not rely on illustrations but use them to enhance understanding, and they can draw information from graphic illustrations in informational texts. They have a range of flexible word-solving strategies, and are beginning to read in several different genres. They are beginning to expand their range in reading simple informational texts on topics that are accessible to them. They are also learning to sustain their reading over longer texts, including easy chapter books.
I	Grade One/Grade Two		
J	Grade Two	Grade Two	
K	Grade Two		
L	Grade Two/Grade Three		
M	Grade Two/Grade Three		

Figure 2–3.   Change in Reading Over Time

Change in Reading Over Time *(continued)*			
Level	Grade	Approximate Basal Level	Shifts in the Reading Process
N	Grade Three	Grade Three	***Self-Extending Readers*** read silently most of the time and are fluent and phrased in oral reading. They use all sources of information (word structure, syntax, and meaning) in a smoothly orchestrated way. They can sustain reading over long texts requiring several days or weeks. They enjoy illustrations and use them to enhance comprehension. They analyze words in flexible ways and make excellent attempts at new, multisyllable words, even technical ones. Self-extending readers are in a continuous process of building background knowledge, which they bring to their reading of texts. They have systems for learning more about the reading process, building higher-level skills as they encounter a wide variety of texts. They become absorbed in books and identify with characters; they connect texts with others they read.
O	Grade Three/Grade Four		
P	Grade Three/Grade Four		
Q	Grade Four	Grade Four	
R	Grade Four		
S	Grade Four/Grade Five		***Advanced Readers*** read silently; when asked to read aloud they exhibit fluency and phrasing. They effectively use their understanding of how words work; employ a wide range of word-solving strategies, including making analogies to known words and using word roots, base words, and affixes. They constantly acquire new vocabulary through reading and use reading as a tool for learning in the content areas. As they read a wide variety of texts, they constantly develop new strategies and knowledge. They consistently go beyond the text to form interpretations and apply understanding to other areas. They are able to sustain interest and understanding over long texts; they read for extended periods of time. They notice and comment on aspects of the writer's craft and read to explore their world, including philosophical, ethical, and social issues. They actively work to connect texts. They develop favorite topics, genres, and authors that form the basis of life-long reading preferences.
T	Grade Four/Grade Five		
U	Grade Five	Grade Five	
V	Grade Five/Grade Six		
W	Grade Five/Grade Six		
X	Grade Six	Grade Six	
Y	Grade Six/Grade Seven Grade Eight		
Z	Grade Seven/Grade Eight		Middle school and junior high school readers approach adult competency in processing texts, but they are still expanding their content knowledge and their ability to read more sophisticated and complex texts.

Figure 2–3. Change in Reading Over Time (continued)

tain interest and understanding when reading long books. They read for extended periods of time; through experience, they have increased their rate of reading as well as their ability to make quick connections, predictions, and inferences. They use reading to learn about themselves and their world as they explore important social problems and issues through both fiction and nonfiction. They take on very complex texts, such as Lloyd Alexander's works of high fantasy. At the same time, they increase their ability to read a wide variety of nonfiction, and are able to use reading as a tool for learning.

Analyzing the texts at each level of this gradient is a way of increasing your understanding of reading. One of the questions that helps us think about the reading process is to ask ourselves: *What does this text require of the reader?* Or, to put it another way, *To read this text with accuracy, fluency, and understanding, the reader must* _____. So another way a text gradient helps us as teachers is by providing a kind of road map of the reading process. Learning to read is not a linear process, with one discrete "skill" being learned at a time. It is a matter of developing complex, interrelated systems that can be applied to the reading of increasingly difficult texts. (See Fountas and Pinnell 2001.)

Creating a Gradient of Text

To create a leveled collection of books, you evaluate texts against the characteristics established for each level and you also think about the likely levels of reader knowledge. A quality literacy program requires thinking about what makes texts difficult in relation to your students and recommending texts for their use. A gradient of text makes it easier for you to select books for readers that meet their needs and allow them to use their strengths.

To create a gradient of text you need to pay attention to all of the factors that contribute to reading difficulty. It means classifying books along a continuum based on the combination of variables that support and confirm readers' strategic actions and offer the problem-solving opportunities that continue to expand the reading process.

Again, the gradient *is not a precise sequence* through which all students move as they progress in their reading development. It is a group of categories arranged in levels of difficulty from which you can select texts that are suitable for groups and individuals. The gradient is not a rigidly defined set of categories. We recognize that a student's background knowledge will vary widely according to the experiences that he or she has had at home, in the community, and in school.

As individuals, student readers cannot be categorized (for example, as a "level M reader"). They will be developing reading ability in many dimensions. As they gain reading experience, for example, they learn how texts are organized; they also develop content knowledge as part of their experiences and study. All of

this knowledge has an impact on the level of text a student can read, and it does so *differentially*. In other words, for an individual student, background experience will affect reading level. Any given student will probably feel comfortable reading a range of levels. This range is based on the reader's background knowledge, general understanding of vocabulary, experience in reading texts with different structures, experience in reading different genres, and interests.

Your expertise in understanding your students will also be a factor in helping students begin to take control of their own reading development. For example, we want students to learn how to select texts that

- They will enjoy.
- They can read with confidence and competence.
- Will increase their content and literary knowledge.
- Will expand the range of genres that they read and enjoy.
- Will help them understand themselves and their worlds.

The gradient is a classification system—nothing more. At the risk of presenting simplistic metaphors, we ask you to think about articles of clothing. In general, you probably have a size that you start with when shopping for clothes. As you start trying on garments, however, you may find that you need a smaller or larger size depending on the style, cut, fabric, and type of clothing. You can wear some more close fitting and you'll want some particular pieces to be loose fitting. In addition, you may have preferences based on color, personal image, or texture. Finally, particular kinds of clothing are worn on particular occasions. Even with all these variations, however, we still need to consider a basic "size range."

This size range is analogous to the gradient of text. Bottom line, no matter how interested students are in the topic, the text must be within a range that is accessible to them. No matter how engaging a plot or character might be, the reader must be able to access the information in the print. So when you consider text difficulty, be aware of the limitations and make cautious selections and test decisions against students' reading behaviors (as you sample oral reading), their conversation about texts, and their evidence of understanding in journal responses.

Fact and Fiction Texts Along the Gradient

We use this gradient to categorize both fiction and factual texts. These genres pose different challenges for students. Examining fiction is likely to require looking at features such as plot complexity, literary language and devices, multisyllable words, poetic vocabulary, character development, and sophistication of the problem or theme.

When examining nonfiction, you look at slightly different factors. Vocabulary will always be a concern, but here the difficulty may be related not just to the number of syllables in a word but to its technical meaning. Nonfiction texts often incorporate the language of a particular discipline to communicate information. Also, nonfiction is likely to be organized in sections or chapters, each focusing on a different topic (rather than a "story"). It may include graphic features that communicate some of the meaning and must be examined. Factual texts present particular difficulties to students because of the amount of "content" and the number of organizational features; that is why they are seldom appropriate for children in kindergarten and first grade, who are just beginning to build a reading process. Factual texts can be deceptive, so it is important to look closely at the particular features that challenge young readers. It is perfectly possible for the same reader to find a longer chapter book of fiction quite a bit easier than a short informational text, and that is true of adults as well.

In placing fiction and nonfiction along the gradient of difficulty, we considered a wide range of features for both genres. These features are described in depth in Chapter 3. However, if we are to use a common gradient to support our work in guided reading, levels must be consistent for both fiction and nonfiction. A factual text may *look* easier than a fiction text at the same level but nonetheless be of comparable difficulty.

Getting Started

You can create a gradient using the books that are available in your school. Here's the process we used to level books:

1. We gathered a selection of books we considered to be good examples of texts appropriate for grades 3, 4, 5, and 6. We also included some "short reads," such as articles or short stories.

2. Then we convened "leveling teams" composed of expert teachers of grades 2 through 6. The groups selected those books they thought were appropriate for including in the collection for guided reading.

3. Working together, we placed books in groups by difficulty and talked about the characteristics of the books, focusing on:
   - Vocabulary.
   - Sentence complexity.
   - Length.
   - Illustration support.
   - Text structure.
   - Suitability.
   - Content knowledge.

4. We selected three or four prototype texts for each level we had identified and created some formal descriptions for each group. We tried to include fiction and nonfiction among the prototypes and thought about what the texts require of the reader as well as how the texts support the reader.

5. Teams of teachers tested the prototypes with students at several grade levels.

6. We reconvened the teams and shared our observations of students' reading behaviors while reading and discussing the various texts. We

Figure 2–4. Teachers Leveling Books

found that we needed to make some adjustments in our prototypes.

7. We eliminated some texts and selected others, and then started comparing a larger group of texts against the prototypes, creating categories.

8. We tested the prototypes again, meanwhile adding to the texts in each category along the gradient.

9. Over the next several years, the leveling teams met periodically to reevaluate the prototypes and cluster texts within categories. The reexamination and adjusting of levels in an ongoing process (see the form in Appendix 3).

10. Within categories along the gradient, we sorted texts by genre and discussed the range of texts within each level to assure variety.

Prototypes and Benchmarks

A useful prototype is one that you have tested again and again and that has proved to be highly reliable and stable for the level. It is a book that will be appropriate for the large majority of students who are demonstrating similar behaviors at a certain point in time. It can serve as a benchmark against which other books can be compared, and it can also be helpful in assessing students' reading so that you can find other books for them.

Assessing students' reading levels requires sampling oral reading and also some conversation with the student about the text. Accuracy is part of the picture. The foundation of reading at any level or in any genre is being able to process the print with an acceptable level of accuracy; but accuracy seems to be a *contingent* factor, meaning that it is necessary *but not sufficient* for comprehension. We all know that sometimes students can say the words but don't understand what they read; certainly, however, they can't understand if they can't read the words.

There are a number of ways besides accuracy to assess whether students understand what they read. You may use the range of assessment procedures we describe in Fountas and Pinnell 2001. Day to day, however, you will want to gather evidence of understanding by:

- Observing how students talk with one another about the texts.
- Examining the kinds of comments and questions students share.
- Looking at what students write about their reading.
- Involving students in analysis and critique.
- Talking with students about their interests and responses.
- Observing phrasing and fluency in oral reading

As you gather information about the way students respond to texts, you will also be gaining insight into text difficulty.

The prototypes or benchmarks that you identify can be integrated into a more formal assessment system that will help you group students initially for guided reading. (See Fountas and Pinnell 2001, conference protocols.) First, select a 250-word passage from a benchmark text to use for assessment. Next, while the student reads the passage, note accuracy and other important aspects of reading behavior such as repeats and corrections. Then have a discussion or ask the student some questions that prompt literal recall as well as draw out inferences and predictions about what will happen next or what information one is likely to find in the text. Answers to those questions will provide important evidence about how well the student comprehended the text.

Assuring High Quality in the Leveled Text Collection

The leveled books your students read, like the other texts that support your literacy program, should be of high quality. The important work you do with students in guided reading depends on the suitability and variety of the titles available. In Figure 2–5, we suggest ten principles to keep in mind as you create your collection.

In addition, it is essential for students to enjoy their reading. Upper elementary students are unlikely to be motivated to read simply to "practice" reading. They need texts that not only are accessible to them but that pique their interest and give them something enjoyable and important to talk and think about afterward.

A Universal Gradient

As we have worked with classroom and school collections, it has become increasingly clear that no one publisher can supply the great variety of texts needed in the intermediate grades. Publishers offer many different kinds of books and some have created leveling systems. What we provide here could be described as a "universal gradient," one that allows you to select and level texts from a wide variety of publishers. We encourage you to get to know the characteristics in our system and then add in new books as you get to know them. Bringing your own thinking to categorizing texts has several benefits:

■ You will think deeply about the characteristics of texts.

■ You will become more skillful at analyzing texts for the supports and challenges they offer the readers in your classes.

■ In the process, you will find that you are also preparing to introduce texts, discuss them with children, and support them in comprehending texts.

Selecting high-quality texts and organizing them into a gradient of difficulty allows you to create your own instructional sequences. Since students in the upper elementary grades expand their reading strategies by meeting the demands of increasingly difficult texts, your selections are very important. There will be better and weaker books illustrating various text char-

acteristics. The important thing is to provide quality texts that support the development of literacy.

Remember that the task of finding good books is ongoing. The collection is always being revised; you add excellent books as you find them and remove books that are less effective. You will select a relatively limited number of books for guided reading. Those selections should be the ones with the strongest potential to achieve your goals. Books that do not fit into that category can be used for independent reading or reading at home.

Summary

The concept of a gradient of text is based on the way in which children build a reading process. This helpful "ladder" is a tool with many benefits; the most important is to provide appropriate texts for guided reading. In the process of creating a text gradient, you will find yourself delving into texts and noticing aspects that you haven't noticed before. This deep look at texts will help you talk with your students about texts and support their learning.

Suggestions for Professional Development

1. Work with colleagues to begin exploring texts that you plan to include in the leveled collection. You'll find that you bring a great deal of expertise to the process. (This beginning examination will ground your thinking as you work with the text leveling process in Chapter 3.)

2. Ask each member of your grade-level group to bring to a meeting five books that are just about right for most readers in that grade at your school, paying attention to variety in difficulty and genre. All books should have been read by the person who brings them.

3. Working as a whole group or in pairs, look at each text. Ask:
   Meaning
   ■ What information do readers need to bring to the text in order to read it with understanding? (Think about personal knowledge, world knowledge, and literary knowledge.)
   ■ Are there places in the text that are likely to lead

Ten Suggestions for Creating a High-Quality Leveled Collection

1. Purchase texts from a variety of publishers.

2. Select texts that do not have racial or cultural stereotypes.

3. Include texts by African-American, Asian, Latino, and Native American authors.

4. Select books by authors who are popular with students.

5. Include books on topics that are interesting to today's students.

6. Include a variety of fiction genres.

7. Include informational texts with a variety of organizational structures and on a variety of topics.

8. Select books that have high-quality illustrations and interesting and useful graphic features.

9. Include as many shorter texts as you can find—short stories and articles.

10. Select books in series that have the same characters and/or topics.

Figure 2–5. Ten Suggestions for Creating a High-Quality Leveled Collection

to confusion? If so, what strategies will readers need to resolve the confusion?

Language

■ Are there language structures in the text that students may never have heard or said before?

■ Are there idioms that may make understanding difficult?

■ Is there literary or technical language that will be challenging?

■ Are there vocabulary words that are challenging and essential to the meaning?

Organization

■ Are there any challenges in the way the text is organized?

■ Does the print layout assist readers or offer challenge?

■ Are there graphic features that readers will have to examine and get information from? What are the challenges in "reading" these graphics?

Words

■ What word-solving challenges does this text provide?

■ Does it contain words that students know but must understand in new ways (word connotations) in order to comprehend the text?

■ Are there multisyllable words that students will need to break apart and relate to other words or parts of words that they know?

4. Use these questions to prompt a good discussion of texts and identify the characteristics that you will need to know about in order to select and introduce texts effectively. Once you have had this discussion, try placing the texts along a continuum of difficulty. It may help to decide which would be best for most students at the beginning of the year, which in the middle of the year, and which toward the end of the year.

CHAPTER THREE

Understanding Text Characteristics: Supports and Challenges

The accessibility of texts has been a topic for discussion over many years of reading instruction. Many of us became frustrated with published reading programs because the materials were either too difficult for or inaccessible to many of our students. Most of the students' reading was done in literature anthologies and content area textbooks, and all students read the same texts.

Textbooks were (and most still are) a particular problem because of the background knowledge readers need, as well as the technical language and difficult vocabulary contained in them. In addition, textbooks need to cover a large amount of curriculum, so they are often written in broad strokes with few intriguing details. When publishers try to make textbooks easier, the "dumbing down" makes them dull and uninteresting. Materials are often seen as reading for "study" and learning; little attention is paid to the role texts play in building a reading process. Frequently it assumes that learning to read is accomplished in the primary grades and that intermediate students can figure out how to read the texts given them; so reading is simply assigned. We take the position that as the texts change, we will need to teach readers to process them. The texts at the intermediate level are not the same as those at the primary level.

Upper elementary students expand their reading powers by successfully processing texts that provide new opportunities to learn. Good readers have a "self-extending" system that allows them to learn from engaging with a variety of texts. That means text selection is extremely important in supporting students as they learn more about how to be good readers. *What they read matters.*

We do not mean to imply that developing reading skill is a spontaneous process that magically "happens" if students are reading the right texts. The other extremely important ingredient here is *teaching.*

Students are able to expand their power to process increasingly more complex texts because you help them anticipate before reading a text, introduce and demonstrate reading strategies, tell them about reading, support and prompt them as they engage in the process, and encourage them to extend their understanding of texts after reading.

Excellent teaching begins with matching books to readers, intentionally selecting books that will be accessible to the readers *with your help*. Not all of the texts you use in your classroom will be matched to readers. There will be textbooks and other materials that all students need to read to satisfy the demands of the curriculum, and you can find ways to make these materials accessible (books on tape, reading aloud to students, shared reading, for example). But every day, students should read two kinds of accessible texts: (1) texts that they can read independently for extended periods of time and (2) texts that offer challenge and can be read with teacher support, giving the individual the opportunity to learn to read better. The more we understand about texts and what makes them accessible to students, the better choices we can make in matching books to readers, and the more productive independent and guided reading will be.

Accessibility

A number of terms are used to describe the relationship between text difficulty and readers—*manageability, readability, accessibility.* Accessibility means that a given reader:

■ Can process the text well, using knowledge of what makes sense, sounds right, and looks right—simultaneously—in a smoothly operating system.

■ Reads most of the time at a good rate[1] with phrasing and intonation (that is, in oral reading, putting words together in groups so the reading sounds like language).

■ Knows or rapidly solves *most* of the words and reads with a high level of accuracy.

When these three characteristics (see Figure 3–1) are true relative to the reading of a text, the text is just about the right level of difficulty for the student to read independently.

What about a more challenging text for guided reading? Using your understanding of the three characteristics of accessible texts, you select a book that *requires* problem solving of various kinds—for example, there may be:

■ Plot subtleties
■ Layers of meaning
■ Difficult technical and/or multisyllable words
■ New literary structures
■ New genres
■ Challenging concepts
■ Symbolic language
■ New graphic features

With your introduction and teaching support, you "unlock" the text for students in a way that allows them to read it in a way that exhibits the three characteristics.

We are not seeking complete accuracy here. The three characteristics do not imply perfect performance. We expect growing readers to experience some challenges. They slow down to problem-solve and then speed up again, and that's the key. They solve problems while keeping the overall meaning of the text in mind. But we don't want them to experience tedious problem solving on just about every word or even every four or five words. If that were the case, comprehension would be severely hampered, and students would not learn the sophisticated strategies they need as upper elementary readers. The problem solving must take place against a backdrop of fluent, accurate reading.

---

[1] Oral and silent reading rates for instructional levels H through Y are defined in Fountas and Pinnell 2001, p. 492. Levels H–M—oral reading 75–100 words per minute, silent reading 75–100 words per minute; levels L–P—oral, 100–125, silent, 115–140; levels O–T—oral, 115–140, silent, 130–175; levels S–W—oral, 125–150, silent, 160–200; levels V–Y—oral, 135–170, silent, 185–225.

Characteristics of Reading That Indicate Accessible Text

1. Smooth processing.
2. Good rate, with phrasing and intonation.
3. Word recognition and rapid word solving.

Figure 3–1. Characteristics of Reading That Indicate Accessible Text

We like the idea of a *considerate* text (Armbruster 1984; Armbruster and Anderson 1981, 1985), which is one that assists readers by the author's clear organization of the information. To us, a considerate text means that the writer signals when something—time, setting, topic, perspective—is about to change. Organization of the text is made clear, often through key words like *first, next, most important,* or by headings and subheadings. The voices of characters are clear; dialogue is either marked or easy to attribute to the right speaker. Difficult or technical words are contextualized and sometimes defined within the text. If one feature of the text is challenging, other features are made easier. A text may be considerate and yet too hard for a given reader, but, in general, given an appropriate level, considerate texts are very helpful in working with students in grades 3–6. Considerate texts are excellent for guided reading because the "bones are showing"; that is, the organization is not too hard to discern. Students easily see some of these helpful features and learn more about them as they read, thus acquiring a foundation for reading texts that are less considerate. When texts are inconsiderate, it's up to us to expose the "bones" to support effective processing.

Accessibility has sometimes been called *readability,* a relational term that means, *How easy is it for this reader (or these readers, or readers at a certain grade level or age level) to read this book?* Another term that we like very much is *manageability,* which refers to the individual's ability to read the print, use the organizational features or structure, and construct meaning from a given text.

Researchers who study the readability or manageability of texts have identified a range of factors that seem to relate to the challenges that texts offer readers and have created tools, usually called *readability formulas,* by which to rate these factors. These formulas may be mathematical or may be checklists; generally, they focus on only a few of the many factors we have related to text difficulty.

Readability Formulas

There are many readability formulas, and two are discussed in detail here. Each provides some useful information. Ideally, perhaps, we should apply a variety of different techniques to any one text, thereby building up a fuller picture of the supports and challenges; however, there's usually not enough time for that.

Fry Readability Graph

One of the simplest and easiest-to-use formulas was developed by Edward Fry (1977). The formula analyzes sentence and word length. Choosing three 100-word passages from a text, you count the total number of sentences and the total number of syllables in each passage. Then you plot these numbers on Fry's graph (see Figure 3–2) and average the three scores to get an estimate of readability.

Cloze Procedure

A cloze procedure gives you another view of how accessible a text is to a reader. Type a 275-word passage from a text that students have not read. Skip the first sentence and then, at random, delete one of the first five words in the second sentence. Continue deleting every fifth word until you have marked out 50 words. Be sure the entire last sentence is complete. (You can vary the difficulty level by deleting every tenth word.) The result will look like the example in Figure 3–3. (The answers to this example are included at the end of this chapter.)

If you try completing this cloze procedure yourself, you'll see that you bring a great deal of knowledge to guessing the deleted words You depend heavily on the sentence context as well as meaning of the whole text and, perhaps, the language or writing style. How many words did you guess precisely, and how many times did you guess a word with the same meaning?

The cloze procedure has been criticized because it is a contrived task that deprives the reader of information; the reading process can break down, and you do not get a true picture of what the reader can do. (It does not tell you anything about the reader's ability to decode the missing words using visual patterns, letters,

and sounds, for example.) If you need to know just how readers are using context, though, it provides some useful information.

Limitations

Any formula or procedure provides only a very rough estimate of the readability of a text. Using a readability procedure to assess a text and match it to readers' level (by grade) will not assure comprehension. At best, it provides another piece of information to consider. General limitations of readability procedures include the following:

- Vocabulary difficulty will most likely be measured only one way—word length, defined by number of syllables. It makes sense that there is a relationship between the difficulty of a text and the number of multisyllable words; but there are many other factors related to vocabulary difficulty. For example, there are any number of difficult one-syllable words: think of *casque, eke, feign, hoist, mauve, orb, quirt, stoat, stob, svelte, thwart,* or *vie* for a start. Even a short word like *bow* has an array of meanings and two pronunciations. Sentence difficulty is not accurately measured by its length; often, short sentences require readers to make more inferences in order to construct meaning.
- The difficulty of reading material is directly related to the reader's background knowledge, which is not figured into the formula.
- There is no attention to content, graphic features, organization of ideas, genre, etc.

A number of researchers have concluded that readability formulas must be either replaced by or supplemented with qualitative information (Anderson and Armbruster 1984; Beck, McKeown, and Gromoll 1989).

Key Factors that Influence Readability

Some key factors that influence text difficulty are summarized in Figure 3–4 and discussed in more detail below.

Vocabulary

The words in the text reflect the difficulty of the topic and/or the sophistication of the writing style. It might seem that the simpler the words, the easier the text, but

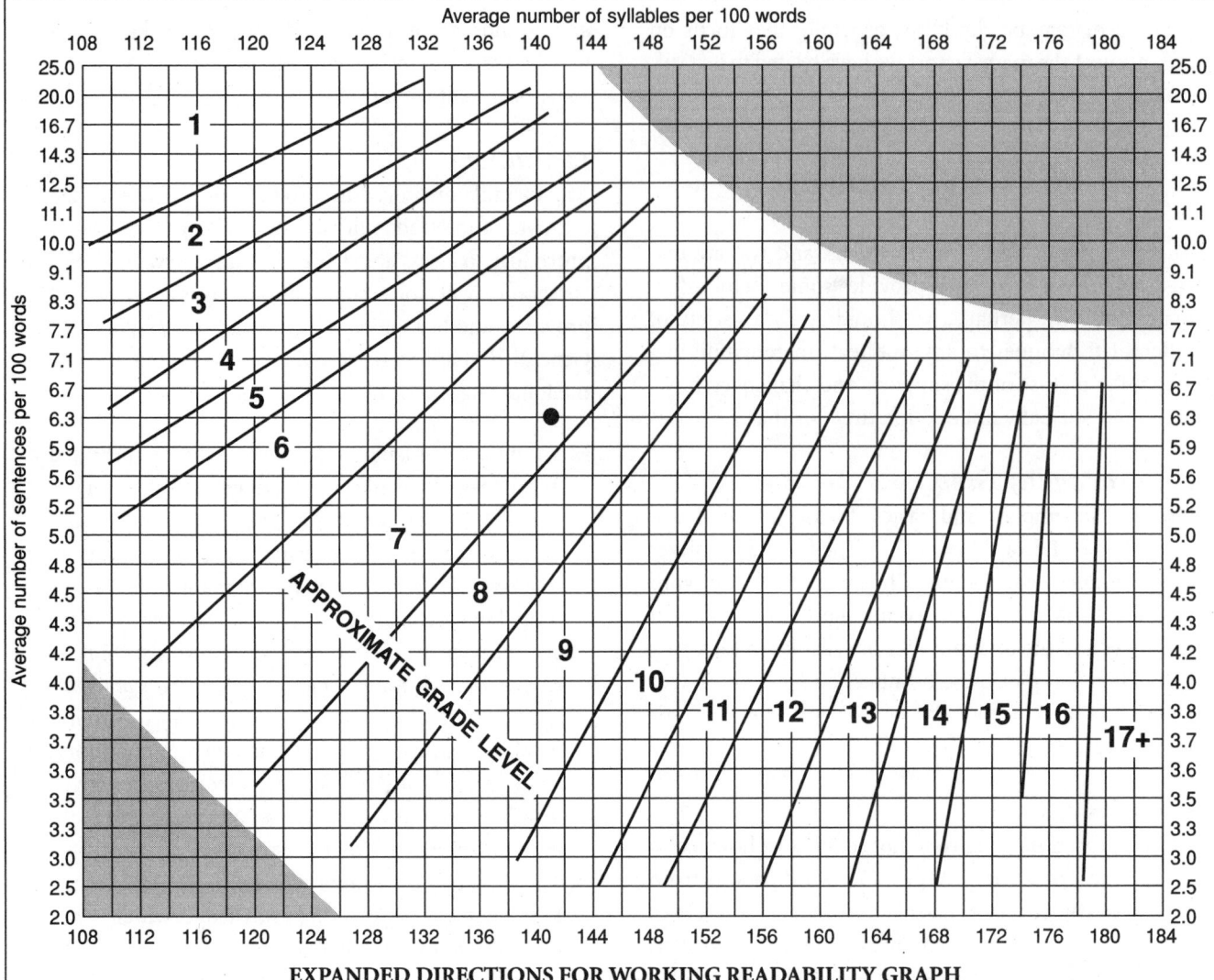

Average number of syllables per 100 words

Average number of sentences per 100 words

APPROXIMATE GRADE LEVEL

EXPANDED DIRECTIONS FOR WORKING READABILITY GRAPH

1. Randomly select three (3) sample passages and count out exactly 100 words each, beginning with the beginning of a sentence. Do count proper nouns, initializations, and numerals.

2. Count the number of sentences in the 100 words, estimating length of the fraction of the last sentence to the nearest one-tenth.

3. Count the total number of syllables in the 100-word passage. If you don't have a hand counter available, an easy way is simply to put a mark above every syllable over one in each word; then, when you get to the end of the passage, count the number of marks and add 100. Small calculators can also be used as counters by pushing numeral 1, then pushing the + sign for each word or syllable.

4. enter graph with *average* sentence length and *average* number of syllables; plot dot where the two lines intersect. Area where dot is plotted will give you the approximate grade level.

5. If a great deal of variability is found in syllable count or sentence count, putting more samples into the average is desirable.

6. A word is defined as a group of symbols with a space on either side; thus *1945* is one word.

7. A syllable is defined as a phonetic syllable. Generally, there are as many syllables as vowel sounds. For example, *stopped* is one syllable and *wanted* is two syllables. When counting syllables for numerals and initalizations, count one syllable for each symbol. For example, *1945* is four syllables.

Figure 3–2.   Fry Readability Graph

Example of a Cloze Assessment[2]

"All right!" Grandma said. "_____ else are we going _____ get these walnuts chopped _____?"

She gave Josh a _____ of walnuts and a _____ of wood for breaking _____ nuts into smaller pieces. _____ was a tradition: whenever _____ made stolen the youngest _____ always got to smash _____ the walnuts. Josh took _____ wood and started pounding _____ a mad-man, as if _____ wanted to pulverize each _____ right down to dust.

_____ we finished making the _____Grandma put it in _____ big bowl, covered it _____ a towel, and put _____ on the stove. It _____ take an hour for _____ dough to rise. Teddy, _____, and Cyn dragged Grandma _____ the living room and _____ her back onto the _____. Brad climbed onto her _____.

"Story! Story!" they yelled. "_____ us a story, Grandma."

"_____ right, all right," Grandma _____. "Cliff, Nate, you boys _____ over here. Don't tell _____ you're too old for _____ of your grandma's stories _____ I know you're not! _____ ever tell you about _____ first time I went _____ a vacation? You know _____did-n't get a vacation _____ I was forty-one years _____!"

How come?" I asked.

"_____ couldn't afford it when _____ was younger. We had _____spend every cent we _____ on rent and food."

"_____ you poor, Grandma?" Cyn _____.

"I don't know," she _____. She stopped and seemed _____ think about it. "Maybe _____ little. Being poor is _____ to be ashamed of. _____ had food, we had _____, we had beds to _____ in. We just didn't _____ anything left over for _____ and such. But on _____ forty-first birthday my brother _____ took me out to _____, to the desert.

[2] Fletcher 1995, 18.

Figure 3–3. Example of a Cloze Assessment

it's not quite that cut-and-dried. The level of word sophistication must be appropriate to the conceptual underpinnings of the text if what is said is to be coherent. For example, in a book about space or in a novel with a mysterious moonlit setting, the word *orb* could be replaced by *sphere* without changing the meaning, but replacing it with *ball* would alter the style and therefore the meaning as well. Merely simplifying words does not necessarily make a text easier to understand (Beck, McCaslin, and McKeown 1980).

Sentence Complexity

In general, although vocabulary has a more direct relationship to difficulty, texts with long complex sentences are harder than texts with simple sentences. Again, however, the situation is not cut-and-dried. Sentence length alone accounts for only a small part of the difficulty (Davidson, Wilson, and Herman 1985). Artificially short sentences, which are sometimes used in textbooks to bring down the readability level, sound choppy and may change the meaning or make it harder for readers to construct meaning. For example, take this passage, from Cushman's *The Midwife's Apprentice* (1995): "She had failed. Strange sensations tickled her throat, but she did not cry, for she did not know how, and a heavy weight sat in her chest, but she did not moan or wail, for she had never learned to give voice to what was inside her. She knew only to run away." The combination of the long sentence sandwiched between two short ones carries the feeling of emotion and the meaning of the text. But suppose Cushman had instead written: "She had failed. Her throat tickled. She did not cry. She did not know how. There was a heavy weight on her chest. She did not moan." The flow of the text simply isn't the same. What would readers learn or feel from reading such a chopped up text? When we are working with authentic texts, we need to look at sentence complexity within the whole.

Conversely, some writers use shorter sentences for

Key Factors That Influence Text Difficulty

❖ Vocabulary

❖ Sentence complexity

❖ Length

❖ Cohesiveness and coherence

❖ Text structure

❖ Content knowledge

❖ Suitability

Figure 3–4.   Key Factors That Influence Text Difficulty

effect and embed a great deal of complex meaning within them.

That Golz should be one of them too. That Golz should be in such obvious communication with the fascists. Golz that he had known for nearly twenty years. Golz who had captured the gold train that winter with Lucacz in Siberia. Golz who had fought against Kolchak, and in Poland. In the Caucasus. In China, and here since the first October. But he *had* been close to Tukachevsky. To Voroshilov, yes, too. But to Tukachevsky. And to who else? Here to Karkov of course. And to Lucacz. But all the Hungarians had been intriguers. He hated Gall. Golz hated Gall. Remember that. Make a note of that. Golz has always hated Gall. But he favors Putz. Remember that. And Duval is his chief of staff. See what stems from that. You've heard him say Copic's a fool. That is definitive. That exists. And now this dispatch from the fascist lines. Only by pruning out of these rotten branches can the tree remain healthy and grow. The rot must become apparent for it is destroyed. But Golz of all men. That Golz should be one of the traitors. He knew that you could trust no one. No one. Ever. Not your wife. Not your brother. Not your oldest comrade. No one. Ever.[3]

---

[3] Hemingway, Ernest. 1940. *For Whom the Bell Tolls*. New York: Scribner. p. 421.

Total words, including reference: 230
213 words in the passage
39 "sentences"
5.5 words per sentence

You may not agree with this great writer's use of punctuation; indeed, he breaks the rules for his own reasons. But in this paragraph from *For Whom the Bell Tolls*, (Hemingway 1940), it is obvious that comprehension demands are much higher than the 5.5 words per "sentence" would indicate.

Length

The length of the text adds to the demands on the reader. Many readers, even adults, find an extremely long text intimidating. Meaning and memory must be sustained over many days or even weeks. The reader must consistently return to the text without letting too much time go by. In general, the longer the text, the more complex the plot, the longer the time span, and the more likely characters are to develop in complex ways. As with other factors, however, length alone can't be used to judge difficulty; some short texts are packed with complex meaning and some longer ones simply recount one simple adventure after another. (For many of your upper elementary students, however, length will be a major consideration in choosing books.)

Cohesiveness and Coherence

Think about reading a text in which topics, events, or characters seem to jump out of nowhere or it's hard to tell how one idea or section relates to another. Most writers work hard to put in the "bridges," or connecting passages, that help the reader understand how parts fit within the whole. In fiction, writers reveal characters by what they do, how they look, what they think, or what others think about them, and with these revelations they help the readers make hypotheses. A coherent text supports meaning and carries the reader along. Irrelevant details or jumps from topic to topic make it harder to discern meaning.

Text Structure

A text's structure is the way information is organized and presented. A narrative structure, for example, typically opens with an event followed by a series of additional chronological events (although more complex texts may use flashbacks or flash-forwards). The events and the characters who move through them reveal an overall theme or themes. Expository texts can have a variety of organizational structures (cause and effect, temporal sequence, comparison/contrast, description, problem/solution), as described in Chapter 4 and Fountas and Pinnell 2001. The reader's comprehension is supported when the organization of the text is presented clearly and "called out" by words, titles, and headings. One of the difficulties in reading expository texts is that readers must internalize so many different organizational patterns (Calfee and Chambliss 1988).

Content Knowledge

Readers' background knowledge is strongly related to their ability to comprehend the text (Adams and Bruce 1982). What immediately comes to mind is vocabulary; however, the role of background knowledge goes far beyond words. Reading in various content areas provides the definitions a reader needs to understand the vocabulary, and is also likely to promote expertise in the various expository organizational structures. Readers use not only their experiential knowledge and their content knowledge but their *knowledge of text*. The extent to which a text requires readers to use background knowledge is a factor in judging its difficulty:

■ How are the demands of this text related to the typical funds of knowledge that students have at this age level (based on a typical curriculum)?
■ How are the demands of this text related to the funds of knowledge *these* students have?
■ How are the demands of this text related to the *range* of experiences these students have?

Addressing these questions helps you, first, determine the approximate difficulty level of a text and then be more precise when you select and introduce it to students.

You can also look for the way the writer of a text makes information available to the reader. For example, are unfamiliar concepts described and illustrated or does the writer expect the reader to know them? How well are the concepts explained? Are the examples interesting and understandable? An expository text that is friendly in its use of technical concepts is more available to students; a friendly narrative text helps

them understand nuances.

Suitability

A text may be the right level of difficulty for your students and at the same time be unsuitable because of the theme, the topic, or the writing style. For example, the topic might be too sophisticated or mature. Or students may not find the topic or theme interesting (Anderson, Shirey, Wilson, and Fielding 1986). On the other hand, if material is very interesting to students, they may overlook poor writing and/or may persevere in reading a text that is too difficult. The interesting material should be integral to the text, not a "gimmick" to attract students' attention. The quality of the writing also contributes to suitability. The text needs to "hang together" in a way that provides the needed information, creates interest, and keeps the reader moving.

Key Questions

The two central questions to consider in any discussion of readability are:

■ What does the text require of the reader?
■ What does the reader bring to the text?

Readability procedures and formulas address the first question in a very limited way (Ruddell 1997). Cloze procedures include the reader but do not account for their attitudes and the way readers construct meaning. A qualitative look at texts provides more information. For example, the readability checklist developed by Irwin and Davis (1980) focuses on two concepts:

■ *Understandability* refers to the way the writer has accounted for readers' background knowledge, the way concepts and ideas are developed, and the syntactic difficulty of sentences. Some texts offer more support to readers in terms of comprehension. To determine understandability, you would analyze the assumptions that the writer makes about the readers' prior knowledge, vocabulary, and experiences; you might also ask how links to that understanding are provided within the text. You would notice the degree to which definitions and examples are provided as well as how explicitly important concepts and relationships (cause and effect, for example) are stated.

■ *Learnability* refers to the way the text is organized to present ideas, engage the reader, and reinforce the readers' acquisition of knowledge. For example, there may be special features such as an index or chapter titles and headings that clearly show the reader how to recognize and find information. To determine learnability, you would analyze whether the text has a clear and simple organizational pattern, provides opportunities to encounter concepts several times (for example, in summaries or end-of-section questions), or appeals to students in its physical layout, illustrations, writing style, or concepts.

The Friendly Text Evaluation Scale (Singer 1992) was designed to be used in combination with readability formulas. The principle is similar to Irwin and Davis's readability checklist in that you are looking into the organization and structure of a text from the point of view of the reader, estimating what makes it "friendly" or "understandable." For example, to what extent is the reader acquainted with the purpose, sequence, and contents? Does one idea build logically on another? Are there signals to the reader as to what to expect (introductory paragraphs, for example)? A "friendly" text will define new terms in language that readers can understand and use with examples, analogies, and metaphors that help readers understand new ideas and become interested in them. Sometimes, authors explicitly highlight important information or make explicit connections between ideas.

Another consideration in the evaluation of text difficulty is how authors treat issues related to race relations and how they portray minority groups. Here, you need to think about whether the text respects personal and cultural differences and portrays problems and issues in a way that provides insights for all ethnic, linguistic, and racial groups. Does it present ethnic characters in positive ways or patronize them?

Evaluating texts for readability is a complex process, so the challenge of creating a gradient of leveled texts should come as no surprise. There is nothing more intricate than the human brain. Throw literacy into the mix, and we realize that teaching reading is much more complex than rocket science. Written language requires a vast range of cognitive and affective actions to access and comprehend.

The Internet

Chances are your students are searching the Internet for materials to support them in their content area studies. While this resource is unprecedented and wonderful, it nevertheless presents an additional challenge. What is readable and suitable in this context? You can apply the same criteria to assess the appropriateness of Web materials as you would apply to any other kind of text. In Figure 3–5 we list some questions that you may want to ask about texts, including Internet, novels, factual texts, articles, and others.

Readability: The Essential First Step in Reading Instruction

Whatever texts your students read, your ability to analyze them for a broad range of qualities is very important in your success as a teacher of reading. In a sense, it doesn't matter which techniques you use. The important thing is that you learn to "size up" a text's appropriateness and the benefits it offers your students.

Over the last years, we have observed teachers and students as they participate in guided and independent reading. We have analyzed numerous sessions in terms of how successful students were in:

■ Reading the specific text with ease, fluency, phrasing, and understanding.
■ Learning more about the reading process.

We have had the pleasure of working with highly skilled teachers who reflect continually on their teaching. Our conversations with them have centered on the nature of the texts students read, behaviors indicating successful processing, students' needs in terms of comprehending strategies, and teaching procedures. When we meet together to reflect on guided reading lessons and watch them over and over on videotape, one thing is crystal clear: *the teaching can be good only if the text is right.*

We have seen good teachers and competent students struggle if the text is too hard. The learning process breaks down; the atmosphere is tense. The teacher doesn't know what to attend to because there are so many problems. Concepts are not available no matter how much you discuss them; words are hard and often mispronounced (without understanding).

Questions to Ask About Texts

1. What concepts, background information, or vocabulary are needed to understand this text?

2. To what extent does the text provide readers with definitions and examples to help them understand concepts?

3. Are there a sufficient number of examples to help students understand concepts?

4. Are important relationships (for example, cause and effect) explicitly stated or do readers need to infer them?

5. Are concepts summarized or does the text require readers to select the important information and remember it?

6. Do paragraphs, chapters, and sections have clear summaries of main ideas?

7. What is the level of sentence complexity? Are there embedded clauses?

8. Is the organizational pattern simple, straightforward, and clear?

9. To what extent do the titles, headings, and subheadings help readers find information?

10. Is the writing style appealing and interesting?

11. Does the text include illustrations? How helpful are these illustrations?

12. Are graphic features (maps, charts, cutaways, graphs, etc.) helpful in terms of understanding information?

13. Does the text present positive images of a variety of ethnic and cultural groups?

14. To what extent does the text offer readers the opportunity to infer meaning?

15. To what extent does the text offer readers the opportunity to add to their own knowledge?

16. Are there opportunities to analyze the text's structure?

17. Is this a text that requires readers to be critical?

18. To what extent is the text interesting and appealing to these readers?

19. What are the strengths and weaknesses of this text in terms of helping these readers gain information and expand their reading abilities?

Figure 3–5. Questions to Ask About Texts

Students read slowly, word by word. Meaning is lost.

The "too easy" picture is not as difficult to contemplate; after all, the students are gaining experience as fluent readers. But if the text is too easy, you are not accomplishing your goal as a teacher. Students whiz through them; there's not much to discuss and no problems to untangle (and therefore no attendant learning). Students may be bored.

Either way, no matter how good a teacher you are, if the text is not right, the picture is negative. Of course, we know that matching texts to readers does not in itself equal good instruction. You can have an appropriate text and still miss many opportunities to help students take on new learning. All of us work continually on helping our students develop an effective reading process through text introductions, instructional interaction, and postreading discussion. But starting with the right text goes a long way. That is why readability (or manageability, if you prefer that term) is so important. Simply recognizing readability is an important step toward the complex analysis required to understand and work with the texts that upper elementary students read.

Summary

Research on the readability and manageability of texts shows that text characteristics should be considered when matching books to readers. We can measure the readability of texts in a number of ways, but no one formula or method will do the job precisely. We need to look at a wide range of factors and keep the readers in mind.

Suggestions for Professional Development

1. Explore readability with colleagues in your school. You can invite teachers from grades 3 and above to this meeting, but if you want to grasp the big picture, make it K–5 or K–6.
2. An important concept to keep coming back to in this meeting is that at each grade level, teachers are *reading aloud* to students texts they cannot read independently but are able to comprehend. This "lift" is critical to developing the ability to take on more difficult texts over time.
3. Collect three or four texts from every grade level. You can use the basal reading system if you have one, or you can have teachers select texts that students are likely to read and that they consider appropriate for "average" students at some point in the year.
4. Explore readability formulas:

■ Ask several teachers to perform a cloze procedure using one of the texts. It is not necessary to collect a great deal of data. You will generate a really interesting conversation from only three or four examples. If you have not already done so, have each participant take the sample cloze test in this chapter and then compare results with one another and with the "answers" (see below). What thinking processes did you engage in to predict the words?

■ Apply the Fry readability formula to at least one text at every grade level. Look at the general trends. Then look at the texts to determine the range of factors that seem to be related to difficulty.

■ Think about the texts in relation to the understandability and learnability factors listed on the Irwin and Davis readability checklist.

■ Finally, consider the texts in the light of Figure 3–5, Questions to Ask About Texts. Come up with some principles for examining texts for purchase.

Answers to Cloze Exercise, Figure 3–3					
How	the	the	me	I	clothes
to	like	Brad	one	to	sleep
up	he	into	because	had	have
pile	walnut	pushed	I	Were	vacations
block	When	couch	the	asked	my
the	dough	lap	on	said	Paul
that	a	Tell	I	to	Arizona
Grandma	with	All	until	a	
kid	it	said	old	nothing	
up	would	come	we	We	

Figure 3–6.   Answers to Cloze Exercize

CHAPTER FOUR

ANALYZING TEXT FEATURES TO DETERMINE LEVELS

Have you ever as an adult reread a book you'd read in junior high or high school? For example, perhaps you read *Middlemarch* (Eliot 1871, 1996)[1] in your high school senior English class. Your teacher may have attempted to increase your understanding through lecture or discussion, or presented her own interpretation of the book. But the nuances of this work of literature might be clearer after much more "life experience." You would recognize Dorothea's passionate commitment to intellectual ideas, unusual for a woman of her times. While your reading as a high school senior may have been excellent, the text probably was more accessible to you as an adult.

That's the essence of text difficulty. Readers apply everything they know, at a point in time, to understanding a text. Text accessibility is always related to the individual reader's particular background. There are levels of understanding. Not every reader will take away the same meaning. But if we can select texts that have good potential for reader understanding, and if we can support readers' processing, we will be able to enrich their reading experiences. The process starts with "leveling" texts so that we know the supports and challenges we have to work with.

When we seek to determine readability, manageability, or the level of texts, we are matching characteristics of the text with aspects of the reading process. We are exploring this essential and critical question: *What does this text* demand *of the reader?* Don't be intimidated or overwhelmed with the number of factors there are to examine. Your examination will heighten your awareness of a text's demands on the students you teach. Reading a text is complicated; so is looking at the level of difficulty. As teachers, it helps us to know that as we look at texts, we are really thinking about readers. What knowledge and strategies will they need

in order to be able to read this text with understanding? What are the opportunities to learn? Leveling books sets us up for thinking about our instruction.

Putting Knowledge of Text into Action

When we assign levels to books, we are looking at readability or accessibility across a broad range of text characteristics, as shown in Figure 4–1 (see also Chapter 3). The process requires reading the book and then analyzing it in several different ways that together represent the supports and challenges in the text. You can make your analyses more reliable by checking them with fellow teachers. You will find that you and your colleagues have excellent insight into the underlying difficulties of text. When you have read and discussed several books at a level, you will have a good sense of the composite of characteristics that make it more difficult or easier than the books at another level.

Genre
The origin of the word *genre* is the French word meaning *type.* Genre refers to a classification system for categories of fiction and nonfiction that have similar characteristics. (For more specific information about genres, refer to Chapter 23 of Fountas and Pinnell, *Guiding Readers and Writers, Grades 3–6.*)

FICTION
◼ *Traditional literature* includes stories that have been handed down orally through the ages. These stories have no known author; they include folk and fairy tales, myths, legends, and epics.
◼ *Fantasy* includes stories that have fantastic or unworldly elements; these stories are similar to traditional literature but have a known author. They are constructed so that the events, however fantas-

---

[1] Eliot, G. 1996. *Middlemarch.* New York: Barnes & Noble.

Factors Related to Text Difficulty

Factor/Definition	Features to Examine
Genre Means "type" or "kind" and refers to a classification system formed to provide a way of talking about the characteristics of texts.	❖ Each genre has characteristic features. ❖ Fiction genres: traditional literature, fantasy, science fiction, realistic fiction, historical fiction. ❖ Nonfiction genres: informational texts, biography, autobiography, memoir.
Text Structure Refers to the way information is organized and presented. Fiction texts and biography are generally meant to be read from beginning to end because they have a narrative structure. But with nonfiction texts, the reader may skip to sections of interest because they are usually topically organized and may have sections, headings, and side headings.	❖ Fiction: narration, development of plot; information given in heads; how characters are revealed; relevance of setting; use of literary devices such as flashbacks or changes in perspective; chapters that continue or chapters that stand alone. ❖ Nonfiction: enumeration, established sequence, temporal sequence; description, compare/contrast, cause/effect, problem/solution; combination of structures. Structures are signaled by words that indicate patterns; for example, *first, second; while, yet; because, since, thus; conclude, the evidence is; furthermore.*
Content Refers to the subject matter that readers are required to understand.	❖ Information on cover, and in chapter titles. ❖ Topics. ❖ Background knowledge required. ❖ Information in graphics, titles, heads.
Themes and Ideas Refers to the "big picture," the universality of the problem in the text and its relevance to peoples' lives.	❖ Sophistication of themes (from simple everyday problems to issues requiring maturity).
Language and Literary Features Refers to the writer's style and use of literary devices. Literary features are those elements typically used in literature to capture imagination, stir emotions, create empathy or suspense, and give readers a sense that characters and story are real.	❖ Perspective. ❖ Language structure and quality. ❖ Word choice. ❖ Literary devices. ❖ Figurative language. ❖ Dialogue—assigned (specifying character) or unassigned.
Vocabulary and Words Refers to the words and their accessibility to readers. Vocabulary generally refers to the meaning of words that readers may decode but not understand. Word solving refers to the decoding process.	❖ Multisyllable words. ❖ Complex layers of meaning (as in metaphor). ❖ Content/technical words. ❖ Words particular to written rather than oral language.
Sentence Complexity Refers to the syntactic patterns readers will encounter in the text; sentences may be simple (short, with one subject and predicate) or complex (longer, with embedded clauses).	❖ Length of sentences. ❖ Sentence style. ❖ Embedded clauses.

Figure 4–1. Factors Related to Text Difficulty

Factors Related to Text Difficulty *(continued)*	
Factor/ Definition	**Features to Examine**
Book and Print Features Refers to the physical aspects of the text—what readers cope with in terms of length, size, spacing, and layout. It also refers to the illustrations and their function, as well as the relationship between the text and illustrations. It may refer to graphics if they are included.	❖ Length of text, length of chapters. ❖ Illustrations—placement and relation to text. ❖ Punctuation. ❖ Print size, style, and spacing (between words and lines). ❖ Layout of print and illustrations, including format: columns, margins, white space, shading, sidebars, insets, bulleted and numbered lists. Also includes placement of phrases and line breaks, sentences that end on a page, or carry over to the next. ❖ Graphic features such as diagrams, tables, graphs, drawings, illustrations and maps with legends. ❖ Organizational features (such as indexes and glossaries).

Figure 4–1.   Factors Related to Text Difficulty (continued)

tic, seem believable within the world depicted. Sometimes fantasy is highly complex.

■ *Science fiction* is fantasy that incorporates technology or scientific information. Some stories seek to provide a glimpse of the future or some time in the distant past. Others open up completely imaginary worlds.

■ *Realistic fiction* includes stories that are true to life because they portray characters or events that could really exist in the here and now. Many stories reveal the human condition or probe social issues.

■ *Historical fiction* includes stories that are realistic but take place at some time in the past. Stories are concerned with universal human problems and sometimes help readers understand historical events or current times.

NONFICTION

■ A *biography* is the story of a real person's life. Biographies may be authentic, or they may be fictionalized to create greater interest for readers. The degree to which a biography is fictionalized alters its authenticity.

■ An *autobiography* is the story a person writes about his or her own life.

■ A *memoir* is autobiographical writing that focuses on a particular event that had great impact on an individual. A memoir may focus on another person.

■ *Information books* focus on a science or social sciences discipline or on recreation—history, geography, sociology, the physical sciences. The reader derives content knowledge from informational texts.

Text Structure

Text structure refers to the way information is organized and presented. A *narrative* is typically chronological, although flashbacks or flash-forwards may be used. Characters interact throughout a series of events related to an overall theme or themes. Lower-level texts have simple plots; plots become more complex as you move up the gradient of difficulty. Expository texts employ a variety of organizational structures: *cause and effect, temporal sequence, comparison/contrast, description, problem/solution*. These structures are often signaled by particular words, phrases, and headings. Structure aids coherence. Most writers work hard to show how parts fit within the whole, how one idea connects with another. A coherent text leads the reader to meaning.

Content, Themes, and Ideas

A text is easier when it is close to the students' own experience. That's one reason narrative texts are the easiest for students to use in beginning reading.

Informational texts are more difficult because they usually provide information about something that the reader doesn't know. When looking at texts, think about what kind of background experiences your students will bring to the reading.

In learning to read, familiar content supports children's learning about print. As students move through the grades, however, they learn to take more information from the print and match it to their own funds of knowledge. They know enough about the print to use it as a tool for learning. If the content is too far from students' own background knowledge, simply decoding the words will not make the text understandable.

Language and Literary Features

Clarity of language is important whatever the genre. The sophistication of the language as well as the literary features contributes to the readability of a text. Early texts are generally simple narratives with a beginning, a middle, and an end. Higher-level texts have literary devices such as flashbacks or stories within stories. They also include idiom, dialect, literary language and poetic devices such as metaphor, simile, and onomatopoeia. The key here is that metaphor should contribute to understanding rather than confuse the reader. Managing the literary features of texts is built through experience.

VOCABULARY AND WORDS

Students may not know what certain words mean. In this case they must use a range of strategies to solve the word. Texts that have large numbers of unfamiliar words pose greater challenges. Alternatively, students may understand the words but not be able to decode them, because they've never seen them written down and aren't yet able to take them apart and link them to a known word in their vocabulary. In this case, a combination of strong decoding skills and the ability to use context is very helpful.

SENTENCE COMPLEXITY

A sentence's complexity has to do with its syntax, the way words are put together to form phrases and clauses. Shorter sentences usually have a single subject and predicate. Longer sentences may have compound or complex subjects and predicates, with many embedded clauses.

Book and Print Features

Book and print features are the physical aspects of the text. The way a text is laid out—font size, margins, spacing between words and lines, placement of phrases and sentences—can support the reader or make a text harder. If the features of a text work together to support the reader in constructing meaning, the text is more accessible.

LENGTH

In general, the longer the text, the more demanding it is. Chapters can be long or short. However, see the caveats relative to length discussed in the Chapter 3.

PRINT

The size and clarity of the print contribute to ease in reading. Ample space between words and between lines helps make the text friendly to the reader because it is easier to search for and pick up information. Print features such as italics, boldface, or a larger type size are used to signal meaning.

ILLUSTRATIONS

In narrative texts, illustrations help the reader form images of the setting and characters. They enhance the mood of the story, prompt emotional responses, and help the reader comprehend the meaning in a deeper way. In informational texts, illustrations (photographs, drawings, diagrams, maps, cross-sections) help students understand the concepts and ideas being discussed. Illustrations that are clearly related to the information in the text and that are themselves easy to understand assist the reader. Graphic features that are clearly labeled and explained through legends and keys are easier for readers to process and understand.

LAYOUT

The placement of print in space is a factor in helping readers find information. How the text appears on the page can make the text more "reader friendly." For example, look at the page from *Henry and Mudge and the Best Day of All* (Rylant 1997) shown in Figure 4–2. Even though the sentences are quite long, the layout helps the reader process the print. All sentences start at the left-hand margin rather than being run together. In contrast, when a new sentence continues in the middle of the line, the layout is slightly harder. A sentence that carries over to a new page introduces even more difficulty.

ORGANIZATIONAL FEATURES

Paragraphs break up text into groups of ideas. Paragraphed text can be continuous and unbroken, or it can be organized into chapters, sections, or columns. For longer texts, the use of headings at logical breaks helps the reader gather and summarize meaning. The degree to which organizational aids are clearly laid out, meaningful, and available contributes to text manageability. The text may also have supports such as a glossary or index that allow the readers to access information quickly.

PUNCTUATION

Punctuation is used to signal the meaning being delivered by the words and phrases as well as the relationship between ideas. As readers encounter longer and more complex sentences, punctuation helps them identify the units of meaning. More difficult texts require more sophisticated uses of punctuation. Simpler texts contain periods, commas, question marks, quotation marks, and exclamation marks; as the gradient increases, readers encounter semicolons, dashes, ellipses, quotes within quotes, and the like.

Putting Knowledge of Text into Action

Every text demands that readers:

- Use strategies to recognize and solve words.
- Orchestrate different sources of information in comprehending the text.
- Use the punctuation and sentence structure to identify phrase units.
- Monitor their reading to be sure it makes sense, looks right, and sounds right—and correct themselves when necessary to gain meaning.
- Recognize important elements of narrative (setting, plot, characters, perspective) and use them to anticipate, analyze, and understand the text.
- Recognize important informational structures

Figure 4–2. *Page from* Henry and Mudge and the Best Day of All

(compare/contrast, description, cause/effect, temporal sequence, problem/solution) and use them to anticipate, analyze, and understand the text.

■ Sustain attention and memory over periods of time.
■ Activate and use background knowledge and make personal and text connections.
■ Revise their ideas as they take new ideas and information from the text.
■ Recognize elements of the writer's craft.
■ Think critically about the text, making judgments as to accuracy and quality.

The reading process is *not* a collection of discrete strategies that you use *one at a time.* You don't use some strategies on lower-level texts and others on higher-level texts. So, even though harder texts demand more of the reader, the requirements pertain to the depth and sophistication of strategies rather than to additional strategies. For example, in a simple, easy chapter book like *Henry and Mudge: The First Book* (Rylant 1990), readers are required to use background knowledge—relative to pets, family, dog collars—that most children have. It also requires readers to infer that Henry is lonely and afraid to walk to school alone, feelings most children understand. Nevertheless, the strategies required are the same as those required by highly sophisticated texts like *Number the Stars* (Lowry 1989), a story about the Holocaust.

Our goal in using a gradient of text is to provide a graduated "ladder" that leads to growth in the full range of strategies as students meet the demands of increasingly difficult and more complex texts.

Thinking About Texts in Terms of Teaching

As teachers we recognize that readers orchestrate the full range of strategies every time they read a high-quality text. Teachers' guides sometimes suggest that you can use a particular text to "teach inferencing" or to "teach visualizing." It is simply not true that a text requires a single strategy or is the "best" text for teaching certain concepts. Complex strategies cannot be taught in one (or even ten!) lessons. Readers must use them again and again as an integrated part of the reading process they bring to many different texts. Some strategies will need to be introduced explicitly; others the students will discover and apply for themselves. Further, just because a reader can demonstrate a strategy such as "inferring" does not necessarily mean he has gained the full meaning of a text or can draw inferences from other texts.

Our job as teachers is, while keeping the reading process in mind, to see the potential in each text and decide what to call to students' attention. We have identified twelve broad, interrelated categories of strategies for processing text and expanding meaning (see Chapter 2; also see Fountas and Pinnell 2001). We always keep these strategies in mind as we look at texts and what they demand of readers.

Text analysis reveals the supports and challenges offered in a text. We then think, *What do my students need to do in order to read this text with fluency, understanding, and—we should not forget—some enjoyment!* After all, we want students to read voluntarily, and that will not happen if the experience is painful or boring day after day.

Our introductions to texts are derived from our analysis of the text characteristics. In the introduction, we "unlock" the text by providing the support students need to use the twelve categories of "in-the-head" strategies in an orchestrated way. We may demonstrate our own thinking to help students understand what they will need to do or how they'll need to think as they read the text. We may touch on one or several aspects of the text; we may bring one or several strategies to conscious attention. The challenge here is simultaneously to:

■ Provide the information and support students need to read *this* text.
■ Enable students to improve their reading by using strategies successfully.

Text analysis is basic to meeting those challenges. Below are some examples (from easier to harder) that illustrate the process of text analysis, what we call "thinking through a text."

Realistic Fiction, Level J (see Figure 4–3)

Henry and Mudge: The First Book is a wonderful first experience in reading chapter books. The seven chapters, each averaging about eight pages, are tied together by the themes of home, family, and pets.

The story, which focuses on the young boy Henry and his large dog Mudge, is a simple third-person narrative with one episode per chapter; the text is organized chronologically. The content will be familiar to young students. Even if they do not have pets, most are familiar with some of the problems and issues related to having them. Henry and Mudge's everyday problems offer much opportunity for readers to empathize with the characters. For example, Henry is scared of walking to school alone. When he walks alone, he thinks about tornadoes, dogs that bite, bullies, and ghosts. He walks fast and never looks behind him. When Mudge is with him, however, he thinks about rain, rocks, vanilla ice cream, and good dreams. He likes walking to school!

The chapters are narrated alternately by Henry and Mudge, but the change is signaled by the appropriate name's being used in the chapter titles (Henry, Mudge, Henry, Mudge). The setting, which is not critical to understanding the story, is the home and neighborhood.

The language of this book is straightforward; it includes many easy frequently encountered words and no technical language. The writer has used very few words of more than two syllables. Most of the sentences are simple, and there are only a few embedded clauses. Dialogue is assigned to characters with words like *said, cried,* and *thought.* The font is clear, the print size large (a 14- or 16-point font). The layout supports young readers who are just beginning to read longer pages of print. As mentioned earlier, new sentences always start at the left margin and there is plenty of space between lines (see Figure 4–2). There is an illustration on every page and lots of white space. The pictures evoke feelings and add meaning to the story. There is some symbolism: on one page, the illustrator shows seven of Mudge's collars, each bigger than the one before.

In introducing this text, you would want readers to understand Henry and Mudge and their special relationship. The whole book is really about how Henry feels about Mudge and Mudge feels about Henry. Becoming aware of this strong relationship in the first few chapters helps students understand how Henry feels when Mudge gets lost later in the book. You might point out chapter titles and help students realize how titles sometimes help you think what the chapter might be about.

Traditional Literature, Level K (see Figure 4–4)

The Pancake is a traditional cumulative tale that will be familiar to many children as *The Gingerbread Boy.* The story is presented as one long continuous narrative with no chapter divisions. The plot unfolds chronologically. Episodes are highly predictable; events and language are repetitive.

The theme, or "moral," of the story could be "don't boast" or "don't be too cocky." Other possible themes include "people working together" or "watch out for tricky foxes." The same basic ideas are repeated page after page. Told in third-person narrative, the tale features "flat" characters (i.e., they do not have complex motives). Readers can empathize with the "seven hungry children," who are mentioned several times. The language of the text is rhythmic; the writer has repeated the same adjectives and verbs in pairs (for example, *swelled and rose, thick and tempting*). The language is representative of traditional tales:

> "Please, mother," they cried.
> "let us eat the pancake right away!
> We are so hungry."
> "Wait, my dear ones,"
> said the woman.
> "Before we eat,
> I must flip the pancake over
> and cook it on the other side."
> (p. 8)

At the same time, the long, complex sentences provide some challenge, and there are interesting adjectives that many children might not have read before, such as *splendid* and *tempting.* There are a few three-syllable words and several compound words, along with many frequently encountered words.

The text is forty-seven pages long, with between eleven and fourteen lines of text on each page. The layout is consistent, alternating full pages of print with pages showing an illustration and a half-page of print. Illustrations appear on every spread and are closely related to the text on that spread. The font is medium-size (14- or 16-point) and there are clear spaces between words and between lines. Dialogue is assigned, and a full range of punctuation is used except for semicolons and dashes. A challenge to young readers might be the longer "lists" of actions that are joined by and set off by commas.

Introducing *The Pancake,* you would certainly remind children of *The Gingerbread Man* if they are familiar with that story. You would want to highlight

Text Analysis, *Henry and Mudge: The First Book,* by Cynthia Rylant (Level J)

Genre	
Realistic Fiction	❖ A story about a boy and his pet that is fiction but could be real.
Text Structure	
Narrative	❖ One major event and a few episodes per chapter. ❖ Organized chronologically. ❖ Chapter titles signal change in perspective. ❖ Past tense; third-person narrative. ❖ Lead gives characters and setting.
Expository	N/A
Content, Themes, Ideas	
Content	❖ Familiar, everyday experiences—eating, sleeping, playing, school. ❖ Story about a boy and a dog. ❖ Dealing with everyday problems. ❖ Exploration of feelings such as loneliness, fear. ❖ Chapter titles support context. ❖ Chapters stand alone but are related by sequence and theme.
Themes	❖ Friendship, family relationships.
Ideas	❖ Straightforward communication of ideas. ❖ Most ideas do not require inference.
Language and Literary Features	
Perspective	❖ Chapters alternate perspective—first chapter is told from Henry's perspective, second from Mudge's, and so on.
Language Structure/Quality	❖ Mostly simple sentences, joined by *and*. ❖ Some embedded clauses. ❖ Dialogue is assigned to characters.
Literary Language/ Literary Devices	❖ Setting is home and neighborhood; not critical to understanding the story.
Vocabulary	❖ Generally simple, familiar words.
Words	❖ Only a few three-syllable words. ❖ Many easy frequently encountered words.
Book and Print Features	
Length	❖ 40 pages; average of 8 pages per chapter. ❖ Over 250 words; 117 words in first chapter.
Print	❖ Medium font (14- to 16-point). ❖ Clear, simple print; no italics, bold, or all capitals.
Layout	❖ Good space between words and between lines. ❖ Phrases. ❖ Sentences start on left margin. ❖ Pictures on every page. ❖ Lots of white space.
Punctuation	❖ Full range of punctuation except for semicolons and dashes. ❖ Dialogue clearly marked and separated by a phrase identifying the speaker.
Illustrations	❖ Pictures of characters extend the meaning and evoke feelings. ❖ Pictures of characters reveal personality, are appealing. ❖ Pictures have some simple symbolism (for example, Mudge's collection of collars from small to huge).

Figure 4–3.   Text Analysis, Henry and Mudge: The First Book, *by Cynthia Rylant (Level J)*

Text Analysis, *The Pancake,* by Anita Lobel (Level K)

Genre

Traditional Literature	❖ Folktale about a pancake who comes to life and rolls away from the other characters, only to be tricked and eaten by a fox. ❖ Version of *The Gingerbread Man*.

Text Structure

Narrative	❖ Traditional, cumulative tale. ❖ Episodes follow in sequence with repeated events. ❖ Straightforward revelation of plot in temporal sequence. ❖ One long continuous narrative; no chapter divisions. ❖ Third-person narrative; past tense.
Expository	N/A

Content, Themes, Ideas

Content	❖ Familiar story to many children.
Themes	❖ Traditional tale with some moral lessons—"Don't be too cocky!" or "People should work together."
Ideas	❖ Same ideas repeated page after page.

Language and Literary Features

Perspective	❖ Third-person narrator. ❖ Reader empathizes with the hungry children.
Language Structure/ Quality	❖ Long, complex sentences.
Literary Language/ Literary Devices	❖ Repeated use of the same adjectives and adverbs in pairs. ❖ Rhythmic language that moves the story along. ❖ Repetition of phrases. ❖ Characters are "flat," in that they do not change or develop (The Pancake is eaten rather than learning a lesson. The lesson is for the readers.) ❖ Little interpretation of characters' motives other than children being hungry. ❖ Personality of the Pancake dominates.
Vocabulary	❖ Interesting adjectives (*splendid, tempting, soggy, stupid*). ❖ Use of the unusual verb *shall*.
Words	❖ Words with letter clusters. ❖ Mostly one- and two-syllable words. ❖ Many easy frequently encountered words. ❖ A few three-syllable words and compound words (*mouth-watering, delicious, wonderful*).

Book and Print Features

Length	❖ 47 pages. ❖ About 11–14 lines on text pages and about 5–6 lines on picture pages.
Print	❖ Medium font (14- to 16-point). ❖ Clear spaces between words and between lines.
Layout	❖ Consistent layout of print—alternating full pages of text with half pages.
Punctuation	❖ Full range of punctuation except for semicolons and dashes. ❖ Long sentences with phrases separated by commas. ❖ Dialogue separated by phrase identifying speaker; standard punctuation.
Illustrations	❖ Show engaging characters. ❖ Closely follow text.

Figure 4–4. *Text Analysis,* The Pancake, *by Anita Lobel (Level K)*

some of the difficult words by using them in conversation; your conversation can also give children a feel for the language of the story. If they have heard folktales read aloud, they will have expectations for this kind of story. You may also want to draw attention to and/or demonstrate the way you read a long sentence, pausing at each comma to show what this mark of punctuation means.

Biography, Level Q (see Figure 4–5)

A Pocketful of Goobers: A Story About George Washington Carver (Mitchell 1986) is a well-written biography of the famous scientist who found over three hundred uses for peanuts. It is a third-person narrative, beginning with Carver's early life and continuing through his old age. While the text is clear and readable, readers need some background information (how Carver persisted in spite of the shadow of slavery and endemic racism, for example) in order to understand it. The author takes a few liberties in ascribing feelings and dialogue to Carver; but the circumstances she describes speak for themselves.

The theme of the biography is the subject's triumph over the odds against him (societal factors). There are some abstract ideas within the text that might require discussion. For example, Carver is told that he should learn all he can so that someday he can "give back" to his people.

Sentence structure is for the most part simple; a full range of punctuation is used. While most concepts are explained within the text, one section deals with Carver's scientific experiments; the language here includes more-technical words (*technician* and *substance,* for example). There are also some more-difficult words related to his profession (*university* and *dean,* for example).

The text is sixty-four pages long and has five chapters with between five and eight pages each. The font is 12 point and easy to read. There are many words in italics or all capitals for emphasis. Illustrations are soft black-and-white charcoal drawings; most are full-page. The text is made more interesting by the inclusion of an illustration every three or four pages. Chapters begin with a full half-page of white space. Two informational tools are provided: an author's note in the front and a list of more facts about Carver in the back.

In introducing the book, you will want to ask students what they already know and then enrich their knowledge. Establishing the setting is important, but it's not necessary to present a long lesson on slavery or Carver's time period; students will learn more as they read and discuss this text. Students will be interested in the significance of the title (*goobers* was an African word for *peanut*). Many adults have heard peanuts called "goober peas" but do not know that the word has African origins. You may also want to "unlock" some of the scientific words and help students with some strategies to recognize word parts.

Historical Fiction, Level S (see Figure 4–6)

A Witch of Fourth Street is a wonderful collection of nine interconnected short stories. Each story has its own plot and contributes to the overall plot of the collection. The settings are important, because this is historical fiction. Stories are presented as third-person narratives. Each is told from the point of view of one main character—a different one in every story. Some of these narrators are present in some of the other stories, however, and are revealed more fully as we discover how others see them.

The stories are full of complex ideas, presented both implicitly and explicitly. Understanding the text requires inference and analysis. For example, in one story a character dies, but the event is implied metaphorically rather than specifically stated:

> Until the breeze fell to a murmur of voices, and the great wings softly let him down; down to the very edge of Moscow, to the very street, to the very house, to the very room, to the very bed that was waiting for him. The curtains fell over him like warm blankets; the murmur of voices fell over him like the voices of his mother and father. And he slept and sighed *ah ah haha humm kremph,* but very gently, very, very gently. And the children of Second Avenue in New York city never saw Samuel Moscowitz from Moscow again. (p. 109/110)

There are multiple themes: the Holocaust and immigration figure strongly as the characters' stories are told. The text has complex sentences but the language is mostly straightforward. A challenge to the

Text Analysis, *A Pocketful of Goobers,* by Barbara Mitchell (Level Q)

Genre	
Biography	❖ Authentic biography of George Washington Carver, a botanist and chemist who was born to a slave family in southern United States and went on to make important scientific discoveries Covers his life from 1864 to 1943.
Text Structure	
Narrative	N/A
Expository	❖ Nonfiction text—biography. ❖ Presented in narrative form. ❖ Organized in straightforward temporal sequence.
Content, Themes, Ideas	
Content	❖ Background knowledge provided in the author's note (examples—goober is African word for *peanut*; information on slavery). ❖ Some background knowledge required to understand the significance of George's experiments.
Themes	❖ Persistence in overcoming society's wrongs. ❖ Value of education. ❖ Contributions of a brilliant man who was ignored and ridiculed because of race but kept on learning
Ideas	❖ Some abstract ideas (example: learning all he could and then "giving back" to his people).
Language and Literary Features	
Perspective	❖ Told in third-person narrative, past tense. ❖ George's feelings shown through action and some dialogue.
Language Structure/Quality	❖ Well-written biography. ❖ Most concepts elaborated to help the reader.
Literary Language/Literary Devices	❖ Most sentences have only one or two embedded clauses.
Vocabulary	❖ Requires background information (for example, Ku Klux Klan, university, dean, technician, and substance.
Words	❖ Most of the three- and four-syllable words are related to George's scientific experiments and his profession.
Book and Print Features	
Length	❖ 64 pages; 5 chapters—range from 5 to 8 pages each.
Print	❖ Easy-to-read font—approximately 12-point. ❖ Words in italics and all capitals for emphasis.
Layout	❖ Balance of illustrations and print. ❖ Paragraphing clear. ❖ Chapters begin with 1/2 page of white space.
Punctuation	❖ Full range of punctuation.
Illustrations	❖ Soft, black-and-white charcoal drawings. ❖ Mostly full-page drawings. ❖ Approximately one illustration every 3–4 pages.
Organizational Features	❖ Author's note in the front. ❖ List of more facts about the subject in the back.

Figure 4–5. Text Analysis, A Pocketful of Goobers, *by Barbara Mitchell (Level Q)*

Text Analysis, *The Witch of Fourth Street* (Level S)

Genre	
Historical Fiction Short Stories	❖ Stories of New York's East side, where many immigrants lived in the early 1900s.
Text Structure	
Narrative	❖ Short stories that intertwine. ❖ Well-developed story structure. ❖ Complex plot (overall theme and subplots). ❖ Setting is important to understanding the text.
Expository	N/A
Content, Themes, Ideas	
Content	❖ Unfamiliar content to most students. ❖ Requires background information (examples: Holocaust, immigration).
Themes	❖ Multiple and interrelated themes, both concrete and abstract (examples: immigration, stereotypes, discrimination, Holocaust, courage).
Ideas	❖ Complex ideas. ❖ Both implicit and explicit.
Language and Literary Features	
Perspective	❖ Third-person narrative. ❖ Each story told from point of view of a main character. ❖ Stories reveal more about each main character from another's point of view. ❖ Requires inference and analysis (example: when/whether one character dies).
Language Structure/ Quality	❖ Paragraphs. ❖ Complex sentences. ❖ Short stories.
Literary Language/Literary Devices	❖ Mostly straightforward language. ❖ Dialect (examples: *gee-up, give 'em up, neither, huh*). ❖ Onomatopoetic words (example: *clikety-clik*). ❖ Use of simile or metaphor (example: *She held her penny tightly in her fingers as if it were about to fly from a bird from its nest.*)
Vocabulary	❖ Words from language other than English (examples: *humn kremph, macushla, matzo*) ❖ Dialect. ❖ Many frequently encountered words. ❖ Vocabulary specific to the setting (examples: *highballing; goulash*).
Words	❖ Mostly one- or two-syllable words. ❖ Some multisyllable words that are easy to solve. ❖ Some words from language other than English.
Book and Print Features	
Length	❖ 110 pages; 9 stories, each about 15 pages. ❖ About 250 words per page.
Print	❖ Small, clear font (about 10-point). ❖ Clear spacing. ❖ Varied print style—use of italics and all capitals for emphasis.
Layout	❖ Paragraphs. ❖ Sentences carried over to the next page. ❖ One picture per story. ❖ On pages where stories begin—white space.

Figure 4–6. Text Analysis, The Witch of Fourth Street *by Myron Levoy (Level S)*

Text Analysis, *The Witch of Fourth Street* (Level S) *(continued)*	
Book and Print Features (continued)	
Punctuation	❖ Full range of punctuation—dashes, ellipses. ❖ Punctuation for embedded clauses in complex sentences.
Illustrations	❖ 9 illustrations. ❖ Black-and-white line drawings. ❖ Illustrations enhance interpretation of the text.

Figure 4–6.   *Text Analysis,* The Witch of Fourth Street *(Level S) (continued)*

reader is dealing with some dialect, as well as some words that are from languages other than English. There are also some onomatopoetic words, and the author uses metaphor frequently. Vocabulary specific to the setting (*bambino, hand organ, macushla, elevated train line, highballing, goulash*) may require some discussion either before or after reading the stories. Most of the words are one or two syllables; any multisyllable words are generally easy to solve.

The whole book is 110 pages; each story is about fifteen pages. The length and challenge of these stories is just about right for a single lesson; however, you will want students to read the entire text, because the interconnections among the stories offer the opportunity to build a more sophisticated understanding of text structure and enable readers to synthesize the whole meaning.

The print is presented in a clear font, but it is small (about 10-point). There is clear spacing and varied print style—italics and capital letters are used for emphasis, for example. Sentences are organized into paragraphs and carried over between pages. The text contains nine black-and-white line drawings, one per story, that enhance readers' knowledge of the setting and help them interpret the text. The pages on which a story begins have a half-page of white space above the title. The text contains the full range of punctuation for complex sentences, including dashes and ellipses.

Informational Text, Level U (see Figure 4–7)

Insects (Bird and Short 1999) is an informational text full of beautiful photographs, drawings, and charts.

The print and graphics present a great deal of information about insects—for example, the different kinds of insects, the parts of their bodies, what they eat. Information is presented in a straightforward way, with many details; it is organized into categories.

Readers are required to acquire and integrate information from both the print and the graphics, many of which require interpretation. Readers will also need to understand the way information is organized into categories and subcategories. Overall, *Insects* presents three layers of headings—section, main heading, and subheadings. Each heading signals that more details are being provided about the particular categories and subcategories. (A sample page layout is provided in Figure 4–8.)

The sentences in the text are generally simple, with few embedded clauses and simple punctuation, but the words are highly technical and related to the subject matter. There are many multisyllable words that will not be familiar to students and that they will find difficult to pronounce. It would be a good idea to show them how to look at these longer words and recognize some root words or word parts. Students will not need to be able to say aloud perfectly every single word in this text. You would not want readers to be blocked from reading and understanding the ideas in the text as they struggle to pronounce words like *stribulating, tracheae,* and *ovipositor.* After all, as adults, we read many words in texts even when we are unsure of the exact pronunciation. The goal is to help students see how these scientific words are connected to the subject matter. For example, *metamorphosis* may be understood by learning:

morph = form or shape
meta = change or alteration
osis = state or condition

A *metamorphosis,* therefore, is the state of changing in form.

An index, species life history, and punctuation guide are provided to help readers. These tools are complex

Text Analysis, *Insects,* by Bettina Bird and Joan Short (Level U)	
Genre	
Informational	❖ Informational text about insects, including those that undergo no change, those that partially change, and those that undergo a complete metamorphosis. Provides information about their bodies, their life histories, their behavior, and their ability to survive.
Text Structure	
Narrative	N/A
Expository	❖ Concrete information. ❖ Straightforward presentation of information. ❖ Information organized into categories with major ideas and subcategories ❖ Provides many details. ❖ Requires integration of information from text and graphics.
Content, Themes, Ideas	
Content	❖ Content unfamiliar to most upper elementary students. ❖ Highly technical subject matter.
Themes	N/A
Ideas	❖ Complex ideas supported with details and illustrations. ❖ Complex ideas supported with tools such as glossary.
Language and Literary Features	
Perspective	N/A
Language Structure/ Quality	❖ Generally simple sentences with few embedded clauses. ❖ Organized into paragraphs, sections, and chapters.
Literary Language/Literary Devices	N/A
Vocabulary	❖ Many technical words related to subject matter.
Words	❖ Many multisyllable words. ❖ Words require complex analysis. ❖ Many frequently encountered words.
Book and Print Features	
Length	❖ 45 pages of text and additional pages for the index, life histories, and pronunciation guide. ❖ 4 sections, each with 2–3 subsections and further sub-subsections.
Print	❖ Print in a variety of sizes related to main ideas and subcategories. ❖ Size of print is clue to categorically organized information.
Layout	❖ Every page has both print and illustrations. ❖ Attractive layout with clear headings and subheadings.
Punctuation	❖ Simple punctuation.
Illustrations	❖ Many diagrams, charts, and photographs that provide important information.

Figure 4–7.   Text Analysis, Insects, *by Bettina Bird and Joan Short (Level S)*

Mouth Parts

An insect's mouth is simply a hole in the lower part of the head. A flap called a *labrum*, or lip, is attached to the top of the mouth opening. Around the mouth opening are several mouth parts which vary in shape from species to species according to the way the insect feeds.

Insects that bite and chew their food (such as grasshoppers) have two pairs of jaws. The front pair (*mandibles*) often have sharp teeth and are used for biting, tearing and chewing. The second pair (*maxillae*) are behind the mandibles. The maxillae hold the food that is in the insect's mouth and push it down the insect's throat. Both pairs of jaws move in a sideways fashion.

Insects that live on fluids like nectar and plant sap have a long tube for sucking. The sucking tube is usually called a *proboscis*. The butterfly's proboscis coils up under the insect's head when it is not feeding.

Insects that pierce plants to suck sap (such as cicadas), or the skin of animals or humans to suck blood (such as mosquitoes), have sharp, needle-like spikes called *stylets* as part of the sucking tube. The stylets help to pierce the food source.

THE THORAX

The thorax is the part of an insect's body between the head and the abdomen. An insect's legs and wings are joined to segments of the thorax. Muscles that control the movements of the legs and wings are attached to the inner walls of these segments.

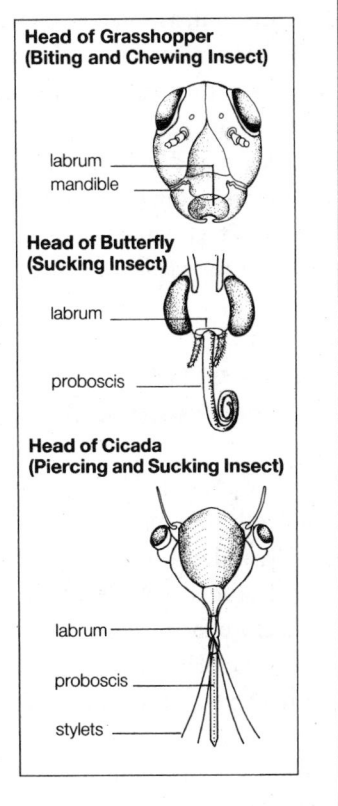

11

Figure 4–8.   Page from Insects

because of the subject matter. Presumably, students reading at this level will already be familiar with these tools rather than learning to use them for the first time; nevertheless, you may want to point them out and practice using them within the context of this text.

Insects is forty-eight pages long. It is divided into four sections, each with several subsections. The print size varies with the level or hierarchy of the idea; in other words, it is related to the nature of the information being presented. Print is also included in many of the graphics in the form of labels and legends. This text would not need to be read from beginning to end, but it bears a great deal of close examination, because you can find so much information of different kinds on different parts of each page. You may want to show students how they can generate different questions and then find places in the text that answer precisely what they want to know.

Every page has both print and illustrations. The layout is attractive and invites the reader to scan for information. You will want to point out how some information is provided in the graphics and print connected to them; this information is important and part of what you need to read to find out about insects.

Summary

The more complex texts are, the greater their demands on readers, and that's good: reading them offers a chance for learning. The trick is to guide students to texts they can read successfully with the help of your text introduction and teaching. In this way, you "up the ante," asking students to expand their reading powers by applying their processing strategies in new ways.

Whether we are guiding students' choices for independent reading (in school or at home) or introducing books in guided reading, detailed knowledge of the texts and their accessibility is an indispensable tool for us as teachers. At first, it may seem overwhelming to consider so many different text characteristics in making your judgments. But, as you continue to work with texts—analyzing them, talking about them, and observing students as they read them—you will develop a mental framework for detecting text factors that offer chances to learn and/or will cause confusion for students. Your understanding of the characteristics will help you level new texts and teach more effectively with texts you select for readers.

Suggestions for Professional Development

1. Work with your grade-level colleagues to analyze a few texts in depth. You might select one fiction text, one biography, and one informational text that you have used with students. Ask everyone to read these three books before the meeting.

2. In pairs, using the blank form in Figure 4–9, examine each of the texts. Write notes in the appropriate boxes.

3. Compare your analyses with those of others in the group. Then discuss each text, asking:
   - ■ What does this text demand of the reader in terms of comprehension? In terms of word solving?
   - ■ What aspects of the text will support the reader? What aspects will be a challenge?
   - ■ What can typical students in your school learn from reading this text?
   - ■ What would you want to "unlock" in a book introduction so that these typical students will have some background when they encounter the problem while reading independently? What will you want to leave for them to discover on their own?
   - ■ For which students in your classes would this text be "just right"? Identify one of these students by name and share his or her characteristics as a reader with your colleagues.

4. Make a combined list of the characteristics—what they know and can do, as well as what they need to know—of readers who would find this text just right (with support, they could read the text in a way that exhibits smooth processing at a good rate, with phrasing, intonation, word recognition, and rapid word solving).

When you complete these activities, you will have engaged in a thorough analysis of the three texts and will have done the kind of thinking that results in a good introduction and successful teaching in guided reading. Your notes are a good resource for you as you plan your introduction.

Text Analysis of: _____	
FACTOR	**FEATURES**
Genre	
Text Structure	
Narrative	
Expository	
Content, Themes, Ideas	
Content	
Themes	
Ideas	
Language and Literary Features	
Perspective	
Language Structure/ Quality	
Literary Language/ Literary Devices	
Vocabulary	
Words (Decoding)	
Book and Print Features	
Length	
Print	
Layout	
Punctuation	
Illustrations	

Figure 4–9. Text Analysis

CHAPTER FIVE

CREATING A HIGH-QUALITY LEVELED BOOK COLLECTION

For readers of all ages, two facts relative to guided reading consistently stand out:

- To expand the ability to read with ease, good problem solving, and understanding, readers must work on texts that are within their control but that include a few challenges.
- To teach skillfully in guided reading lessons, teachers must select texts that are within the readers' control, presenting only a few challenges in terms of word solving, concepts and ideas, and language.

At first glance, it may appear that these two points are the same, just stated in slightly different language. They do speak to the same issue, but one has to do with learning, the other with teaching. Appropriate text selection is so important that the point is worth making in both contexts.

Good readers have developed "working systems" that make it possible for them to learn more about the process of reading simply by engaging in it (Clay 2001). As we read, we meet challenges to word solving or understanding; we apply strategies with ease and fluency to solve problems and learn more from the process. If the text is too hard, the whole process breaks down, and comprehension is lost. The struggling reader is not performing effectively and cannot learn more; it is therefore of paramount importance for students to read texts effectively every day. Text selection is basic to that learning.

For most elementary students, reading itself is not a sufficient means by which to expand their abilities; they require teaching. In lessons and conferences, teachers make a difference in student learning by interacting in ways that support efficient processing of texts that offer appropriate supports and challenges. If the text is too easy, students do not have enough opportunities to learn; if it is too hard, no amount of good teaching will "work." Good text selection is a necessary but not sufficient factor in the success of a reading program.

Gradient Versus Grade Level

In considering *gradient* and *grade level*, we are thinking about two different but related hierarchies. *Grade level* refers to the traditional organizational strata for students in elementary schools. They enter a grade; spend nine-and-a-half months learning according to the established curriculum; and, given satisfactory performance, move on to the next higher grade. The term also refers to the *expected performance* or *standard of performance* (in this case performance in reading) for the grade level. We do have grade-level expectations; if a student is performing significantly below those levels, then extra instruction is required.

Gradient, on the other hand, is defined as a slope of increasing and decreasing steps along a continuum. In a text gradient the books are placed in categories that are more narrowly and specifically defined than *grade level*. The characteristics at a level, taken together, generally represent text difficulty as indicated by the supports and challenges to the reader. *In general*, if a child can read (with appropriate support) one or two books at a level, then most of the others will be accessible to him or her (again, with support). If the texts are quite easy for the reader, then the next level on the gradient may be appropriate.

The point of the gradient is to think about continuous progress along it. The idea is for the students to read books at the appropriate level and to be working always on expanding the variety of texts read within the level or moving to the next level. Grade level is somewhat incidental to this day-to-day process. *Good teaching begins where the readers are and takes them where they need to be.* Since readers in any grade have different levels of development, a variety of text levels will be required for effective teaching.

While it may seem paradoxical to lay the gradient alongside grade-level expectations, that is exactly what we need to do when we think of our teaching and the changes we expect in students over time. We select books for daily teaching against a background of expected grade-level performance and progress over time. This juxtaposition helps us know which students need extra help of what particular kind.

How the Gradient Supports Teaching and Learning

Organizing books and other texts along a gradient of difficulty provides essential support for teaching in several ways:

■ The leveled collection supports the selection of books for guided reading. In addition, knowing how the characteristics of a text relate to its difficulty helps you introduce books to students. The introduction makes the text more accessible to students, thus mediating the difficulty level for the group you are working with.

■ When you are helping children choose books for independent reading, the level of the books on the gradient will not be obvious. There will simply be good books, well displayed, from which all students choose. In minilessons, you will be teaching students how to examine texts to decide whether they are "easy," "just right," or "challenging." They will read a variety of texts, not just books at their "level." It's extremely helpful, however, if you have the level in mind as you help students make their selections. You will also want to give book talks that draw students' attention to good books in the range of levels needed by your group.

■ You will use the leveled collections to help students who are struggling in their reading make good choices for their independent reading in school and at home. Knowing levels will help you check whether students are looking within the appropriate range of books.

■ You may want to create some baskets of appropriate books for particular literature study groups. That does not mean you should limit students to the levels they can read. If you want them (or they choose) to discuss books that are too difficult for them to read independently, you can find another way to make the texts accessible (books on tape or buddy reading).

A good leveled collection is made up of texts you select and organize yourself. A great deal of learning takes place in the process. The gradient supports text selection and allows you to fit the program to the students rather than force them through a fixed sequence of texts or make them read materials that are too difficult.

The Leveled Collection

The leveled collection consists of books grouped along the gradient of difficulty. The books at each level are described by a cluster of characteristics; no text will have every characteristic listed for the level. To estimate the level of a text, you need to identify the characteristics that most closely represent that particular text. Studying your students' responses to the text over time, you will discover more about the text and can determine whether the level designation is reliable or needs to be adjusted.

Clarifications

The gradient is not rigidly defined. It is not a precise sequence through which all students move as they progress in their reading development. It is a group of categories arranged in levels of difficulty from which you can select texts that are suitable for groups and individuals.

An individual student cannot be categorized (for example, we can't say, "Tommy is a level M reader"). Students develop reading ability along many dimensions. Their background knowledge will vary widely according to the experiences they have had at home, in the community, and in school. As they gain reading experience, however, they learn how texts are organized; they also develop content knowledge as part of their experiences and study. Any given student feels comfortable reading a range of levels based on her general understanding of vocabulary, her experience in reading texts with different structures, her experience in reading different genres, and her interests.

The Gradient

We have organized texts from easier to harder in the order of the alphabet, from A to Z. Remember that the level designation is only an approximation of the difficulty; within each level, some books will be easier and some harder.

It is important to see the gradient as a continuum of progress for your readers. Your primary goal is to determine the level that is appropriate for students to read independently and in guided reading instruction.

Grade-Level Designations

We've included approximate grade-level ranges in relation to the gradient levels because knowing whether your students are reading within a range appropriate for their grade level is essential information. Responsible and competent teaching means knowing what student achievement is expected. If students fall below the standards associated with their grade level, they will require extra instruction or intervention to help them extend their reading abilities; they will need to begin that work on the level of text that is right for them.

Certainly, one would not want simply to teach at the grade level no matter the circumstances. Students will not learn if they are required to read material that is too difficult. That kind of daily frustration only makes matters worse. To expand their strategies, they need to read texts that are instructionally appropriate for them. Every day, every student deserves to read a text that he or she can understand.

If you have readers who are working well below grade level, you will want to look for texts at the lower levels but remember that age-appropriate content is important as well. Students in upper elementary grades do not want to read material for "babies." There are informational and fictional texts at every level that are content appropriate.

Value of Leveling

Different publishers have different leveling systems. We are always looking at one set of materials or another and wondering, *what is the set of characteristics used to determine the level?* We have tried to provide a system that will work for many different types of books from many different publishers, but any system you use must be made your own by learning more about the characteristics that define it. Bringing your own thinking to categorizing texts has several benefits:

■ You will think deeply about the characteristics of texts and what they demand of readers. These

demands, if they are within the reader's control, provide for learning.
■ You will become more skillful at analyzing texts.
■ When you think about texts, you will find that you are also preparing to introduce texts, discuss them with children, and support comprehension.

Selecting high-quality texts and organizing them into a gradient of difficulty allows you to create your own instructional sequences. You will understand the increasing demands of the text on your readers and will be able to teach them how to work with these demands.

Since students in the upper elementary grades expand their reading strategies by meeting the demands of increasingly difficult texts, your selections are very important. There will be better and weaker books illustrating each text characteristic. The important thing is to provide quality texts that support the development of literacy.

Variety in Format

The earlier levels of the text gradient, described in *Matching Books to Readers, Using Leveled Books in Guided Reading, K–3* introduce children to early print concepts in the beginning stages of reading. For more skilled readers (levels J and up), the leveled collection includes a wider range of text. Essentially four kinds of books are included, with varieties within each.

PICTURE BOOKS

Many traditional picture books have simple plots, characterizations, and vocabulary. If you select carefully, you can find topics and subjects that are interesting and amusing for students in grade 2 and early grade 3.

More complex picture books for older readers provide an opportunity to expand vocabulary, interpret stories, and analyze illustrations and their contributions to the expression of meaning. A picture book like this is, in essence, a short story—a piece of complex reading that can be completed in a single sitting and be the basis for discussion and analysis.

The reading levels for these more complex picture books range from about M or N all the way to adult. They have a wide range of themes that provoke much thought and discussion. These picture books for older readers are best when read aloud or used as the basis of a book club discussion. Many of them may be required as part of the curriculum or be part of your classroom library. If you use them for literature study, their placement on the gradient will give you an idea how accessible they are for readers.

EASY CHAPTER BOOKS

Many of the first chapter books are simple narratives organized into short chapters and sections. These beginning chapter books may be much easier than many of the more complex picture books students read. They contain many easy frequently encountered words and simple sentences. The themes and settings are close to students' own experiences. Characters are memorable and do not change much during the story. There are many "series" books in this category. These books are quite helpful in that readers are required to sustain reading over longer stretches of text and to remember information over several days.

CHAPTER BOOKS

A wide variety of longer, more complex chapter books are included in the gradient. Books range from about 100 pages to over 300 pages and have complex plots; there are often subplots. Characters develop in response to the events in the story. Readers are required to sustain reading over one to two weeks, and there is much opportunity for discussion at various points. The authors of these books use complex literary language, and themes are increasingly mature as the gradient rises.

SHORT STORY COLLECTIONS

We include numerous short story collections. They address different cultures and themes. Short stories are excellent texts for guided reading. You can choose some short stories to improve students' reading strategies and instruct them to select others in the same collections for their independent reading.

Variety in Genre

Our book lists include a variety of fiction and nonfiction. Lower-level narratives are mostly realistic fiction that focuses on themes close to the lives of children. Picture books are likely to include traditional tales, fantasy, and realistic stories. As you move up the gradient, there is more opportunity for students to experience other worlds vicariously. Settings may be distant in time or space, requiring readers to imagine other cultures and technologies.

Informational books present complex ideas and may use technical language that is more difficult for students. Biographies have a structure similar to narratives, but some of them incorporate the additional difficulty of understanding concepts related to historical times. In general, the informational books within any given level are shorter than the narrative texts. Students need to understand specific concepts related to the content and become familiar with the organizational structures typical of informational texts.

The Demands of Texts on Readers

Every text demands that the reader use a combination of strategies to solve words and construct meaning. *At every level of this gradient,* texts demand that readers:

- Recognize easy frequently encountered words quickly and automatically.
- Use multiple sources of information in an integrated way while reading for meaning.
- When reading orally, read at a good pace, with phrasing, slowing down to problem solve and speeding up again.
- Read silently when reading independently.
- Use a range of strategies to problem-solve new words, particularly multisyllable words.
- Correct errors that result in loss of meaning.
- Make inferences to understand what is implied but not stated.
- Work to understand characters.
- Recognize important elements of setting.
- Predict and analyze the plot.
- Sustain attention to meaning and interpretation over several days of reading.
- Bring background knowledge to bear in understanding concepts and topics.
- Predict events, outcomes, and problem resolutions while reading sections of text.
- Determine the perspective from which narrative texts are told.
- Understand the organizational structures used to present information.
- Revise interpretations as new information becomes available.
- Recognize relevant aspects of the writer's craft.
- Think critically about the concepts and ideas in the text.

This long list is only a sampling of what readers do during the act of processing text with understanding. Readers meet the demands of texts by simultaneously engaging in these strategies. Reading texts that are easy makes fewer demands on the processing system.

As a teacher you select books from a level on the gradient that is just challenging enough to require processing strategies such as those listed above, and your readers go into action. As they read more, they gain power, and texts at that particular level become easier, making fewer demands. Then you select books from a level that is just a bit more challenging, and the readers again use this complex constellation of strategies. Teachers use the gradient of text as a ladder to help readers learn how to apply their strategies to increasingly more demanding texts.

Balancing Readability and Theme

Because our gradient is based on a range of characteristics rather than a single dimension, you may find a wider range of easier-to-harder texts at the upper levels. There are good reasons to place books with mature themes and subtle messages at the higher levels even though the text may be easy to read. First, the ideas may be very demanding. Second, the circumstances may be hard to understand without a certain degree of life experience. In *The Midwife's Apprentice* (Cushman 1995), for example, a young girl who has been deserted is found by a midwife and eventually takes on the profession herself.

A High-Quality Collection of Genres at All Levels

You will want both your classroom collection and the school collection to be of high quality, supporting students' learning and adding to their reading enjoyment. It is important to include a wide variety of topics, themes, and genres so that you can find books that will interest students as well as expand their reading strategies. Some characteristics of a high-quality collection were described in Figure 2–5.

■ You will want to include both fiction and nonfiction, and we advise searching for as many shorter texts as you can find. Collections of short stories and articles are very useful for guided reading.

■ Purchase texts from a number of publishers. Buy single titles so you can consider each book separately. Sometimes buying in "sets" may seem economical, but you want to avoid acquiring a great number of books written to the same formula, some high-quality titles mixed with lower quality ones, or a number of books that neither you nor your students enjoy.

■ Select books by authors and topics that are popular with students, and be sure that your collection reflects the diversity of our multicultural society: include a variety of African-American, Asian, Latino, and Native American, as well as Caucasian authors.

■ Series books like the Matt Christopher or Amber Brown books are always appealing; once students have read one or two in guided reading, they may choose to read more for independent reading (in school or at home).

■ High-quality illustrations and interesting graphic features engage students' interest and have the additional value of helping them learn to search for information in many different sources.

Finally, look at the general quality of texts. Students deserve to read books that are put together with care using quality materials. They should have good bindings, professional layout, and striking illustrations.

Summary

The leveled book collection is vital to your guided reading lessons. This collection will include multiple copies of books at all levels appropriate for the students in your class. It is not necessary to have a lot of books at the extreme low and high levels for your group; you can borrow books from the school bookroom if you have one. You can organize your multiple copies of leveled books into a teacher's collection that is not accessible to students. In the photograph in Figure 5–1, notice the collection of multiple copies of books the teacher keeps on special shelves for use in guided reading lessons.

You will use these titles for your guided reading lessons, introducing particular students to particular books that will support their development as readers. This collection is also helpful in giving students limited choices for their independent reading. You might create a specially selected basket or box of books for a particular group of readers, choices you think will interest them and that are within the range of levels they can read with fluency and comprehension.

Suggestions for Professional Development

If possible, work in cross-grade-level groups to examine texts. Every teacher in the upper elementary grades needs a thorough knowledge of the characteristics and demands of texts in levels J through at least W. (Third-grade teachers, for example, will almost certainly have children reading at level J or even lower; at the same time, these teachers need to have a vision of where their students are going, of the demands of the texts they will be likely to read in fourth, fifth, and sixth grades.)

1. Prepare for the meeting by collecting several titles at each level, J through X or Y. (Tailor the specific levels to the interests of your group; however, be sure to go beyond the specific grade-level designations. You'll be using this collection of titles to explore texts in the next three chapters, so it is worth spending a little time on it.) As a resource, use classroom collections, your school's book collection, and the library. You may want to visit a local public library to get more titles. Many libraries now have substantial collections of series books, etc. Finally, you can take your group to visit a local children's bookstore to examine titles.

2. Place the books in piles or tubs by level and make them easily accessible to participants.

3. Spend some time examining the books and talking about them informally with one another. Ask everyone to sample books from at least three levels. Since most of the books will be from your school, chances are several teachers in the group will know them well. For unfamiliar books, you'll find that teachers can tell quite lot about a book from reading material on the front and back of the book, sampling one or two chapters, and looking at the illustrations.

4. Now do a few comparisons to help you think about the demands of texts on readers and how those demands shift over time. Depending on the interests of your group, select two texts at least two levels apart for comparison. For example, you compare:

- A level J book with a level L book.
- A level M book with a level O book.
- A level P book with a level R book.

5. In pairs, perhaps using the chart of text characteristics presented in Figure 4–9, discuss:
   - What do readers have to know and do to read text 1 (the lower-level book)?
   - What *different* demands does text 2 (the higher-level book) present to readers?

6. *Alternative A.* If you have time, choose still another book two levels higher than text 2. Ask again: Compared to text 2, what *different* demands does text 3 present to readers? This alternative will help the group begin to see the gradient and the leveled book collection as a long continuum.

7. *Alternative B.* If you have time, choose another text at the text 2 level, asking: Compared to text 2a, what *different* demands does text 2b present to readers? Repeat the process with still another book at that level. This alternative will help the group see the variation within a level that allows students to develop flexibility.

8. Bring participants back to a general discussion. Ask pairs to share some of their discoveries and provide examples from specific texts.

9. Ask everyone to continue to work with these gradient texts, looking deeper into the levels. Participants may want to take books home to examine in greater depth.

Figure 5–1.   Teacher's Leveled Classroom Collection

CHAPTER SIX

UNDERSTANDING LEVELS OF TEXT: J TO M

When we think about levels of texts, we are always exploring *combinations of characteristics*. Not every characteristic typical of a level applies to every text categorized at that level. A certain factor makes one text challenging; something else presents a challenge in a different text. Thinking about levels in this complex way may seem difficult, but it helps us in our teaching. We want students to experience different combinations of demands so that they expand their reading powers.

It is also true that some characteristics are important in differentiating texts at earlier levels, while others become more important later on. For example, greater print variety (italics, all capitals, boldface) or more-sophisticated punctuation (dashes, parentheses, ellipses) may provide challenges in texts for the levels that third or fourth graders read but are no longer a factor once students have become accustomed to them. Length is an important factor in general at most lower levels; however, as students grow more sophisticated, they will encounter difficulties in both long and very short texts. Factors such as technical vocabulary, idea sophistication, theme maturity, and sentence complexity are important in the assessment at all levels.

This chapter begins with descriptions of texts generally considered appropriate for students in grade 2. Elementary school is a time of transition. You may have students in grade 3, 4, or even grade 5, who are reading at this level, and you will need to select texts that are appropriate to their development of a reading process.

Level Descriptions

Our goal is to give you a good idea of the cluster of characteristics readers will encounter at each level. These descriptions cannot be exhaustive; rather, they are inventories that will help you understand the level and that you can use to categorize texts for yourself.

For each level, we discuss important characteristics that contribute to the difficulty of the text as well as those that support readers. Then we present several examples. We also discuss some of the important new demands that texts at this level make of readers. These are the important general parameters:

■ All books are identified by genre and content.
■ Relevant specialized background information is indicated.
■ Font size is indicated as easy-to-read (as large as or larger than that in Figure 6–5); medium (about the same as Figure 7–2, in Chapter 7); and small (smaller than Figures 8–1 and 8–2, in Chapter 8).
■ For each example, we indicate the number of pages and the approximate length of chapters; these factors affect the length of the text and the amount of time the reader is required to sustain reading.
■ When relevant, we indicate vocabulary demands, as well as the extent to which multisyllable and technical words are used.
■ When relevant, we comment on the language complexity and/or the literary language included in the text.
■ The text structure is referred to as *simple and straightforward* or *more complex.*

As we said, not every book at a level will have all the attributes listed here. A book may be difficult and short, or easy and long. It is also important to remember that the way a text is introduced will influence how difficult or easy it is for the reader to process. As a teacher you are constantly balancing the text level and the amount of support you provide to readers. You may decide to provide a high level of support as you move readers to a new level, or a lean introduction at a level the readers are now processing well.

These characteristics are meant to be heuristic in that they will help you think about texts and what they require of readers. The precise demands on your students will be individually determined but will be affected by:

■ The ongoing experiences with literature and content areas that students have in your school.
■ The way you introduce texts to students and converse with them as they read them.

Transitional Readers (Levels H Through M; Grades 2/3)

In Chapter 2 we described changes in the reading process over time. These broad descriptions do not represent discrete stages; rather, they give us a general road map of the development of a reading process. We have matched reader descriptions with approximate grade levels and gradient levels, but we have also indicated overlap. *We do not designate certain book levels for readers at any one grade level.* No matter where you teach, you will undoubtedly have a range of readers at every grade level.

This road map gives us a vision of development of reading across grades so that:

■ We can be concerned about and give extra help to students who are lagging behind. These are the students who will find it most difficult to profit from whole-class instruction and who will likely not do as much successful reading as the others.
■ We can guide advanced students to books that challenge them in a variety of ways. This may not mean simply moving up the gradient, because many of these students can "decode" just about anything. Instead, we want to pay attention to the topics, genres, and themes that interest them and are appropriate. We want to create more varied opportunities for them.

From level H through M, readers are making the transition to mostly silent reading. They have learned to process text smoothly, and many operations have become automatic. They can orchestrate several different kinds of information as they engage in reading continuous text; while they enjoy and take meaning from illustrations, they do not need to rely on them. They are just beginning to notice and interpret the graphic features of informational texts. Levels H through M are appropriate for most second graders, but many third- and even fourth-grade teachers have transitional readers in their classrooms.

If you are working with transitional readers in the intermediate grades, your goal will be to engage them daily in reading a large amount of continuous text and to increase their variety in reading, including learning much more about how informational texts are organized. When introducing new genres to these readers, you want to be sure that the material is within their ability to process successfully. By providing daily reading that is instructional, you can increase their ability to apply strategies to harder texts.

Level J

We have provided descriptions of Levels H and I in Fountas and Pinnell 1996, and in Fountas and Pinnell 2001. We begin here with Level J.

Characteristics

Level J includes a variety of short informational texts on familiar topics, as well as easy narratives. The longer narratives have short chapters that may or may not have titles. Characters are usually well presented but don't show a great deal of change or development, since plots are relatively simple and texts are not long. Only one or two characters are generally featured.

Most texts contain dialogue, which is usually assigned to the speaker by signal words like *said, cried,* and *answered.* Print is in a larger font, with clear spaces between words and lines. There are illustrations on most pages. Sentences usually return to the left margin to start. Informational texts focus on topics that are familiar to second graders.

Some books offer a large amount of print with easy words and language; others offer challenge in that they present new information or use literary language. Texts have many frequently encountered words, as well as some technical words and unfamiliar words. Technical words are explained within the text, and there are clear illustrations to help the reader.

Examples

MOUSE TALES (SEE FIGURE 6–1)

Fiction (animal fantasy—short tales about the same animal characters); sixty-four pages (seven chapters, about eight pages per chapter); easy-to-read font; assigned dialogue; sentences start at left margin; supportive illustrations on every page.

HENRY AND MUDGE IN PUDDLE TROUBLE

Fiction about a young boy and his large dog Mudge; forty-eight pages (three chapters, about sixteen pages per chapter); easy-to-read font; assigned dialogue; sen-tences start at the left margin; supportive illustrations on almost every page; familiar experiences; straightforward plot; mostly one- and two-syllable words; many frequently encountered words.

SEEDS (SEE FIGURE 6–2)

Informational text; twenty-four pages (no chapters, a short informational paragraph about a different aspect of seeds on each page); large font; assigned dialogue; glossary, Internet sites, index, word lists; easy-to-read font; mostly familiar material; clear illustrations; a few technical words; new meanings for familiar words; mostly one- and two-syllable words.

THE OLD MOUSE

There was an old mouse

who went for a walk every day.

The old mouse

did not like children.

When he saw them on the street

he would shout,

"Go away, horrid things!"

One day the old mouse

was taking his walk.

All at once, his suspenders broke,

and his pants fell down.

48

49

Figure 6–1. Mouse Tales, *Level J*

The wind moves seeds. Some seeds have soft hairs. These hairs catch the wind. The seeds float to new places where they can grow.

14

Photo: Pasque Flower Seed Head

15

Figure 6–2. Seeds, *Level J*

Level K

Characteristics

At level K, chapter books are still simple but are slightly longer, presenting more text to read (see Figures 6–3 and 6–4). Chapters are short; most pages have illustrations but they are less important to students' understanding of the meaning of the text. As with level J, stories have multiple episodes related to a single plot, but there will be more to remember. Texts feature only one or two characters, and there is little development. There is generally dialogue, sometimes unassigned (without identifying words like *said*).

In most level K texts, the layout is still very friendly to the reader in that sentences usually start at the left margin; the print is in a large, clear font, and there are clear spaces between words and between lines.

Illustrations include interesting artwork that enhances meaning. Some stories are based on concepts that are distant in space and time, and readers will be using the text as a way to expand their understanding of cultures beyond their experiences. Readers will encounter greater variety in writing styles. Informational texts are like Level J in that they use some technical language that is clearly explained within the text and include supportive illustrations. Topics tend to be concrete—animals, plants, and other phenomena that will be familiar to students. Generally, informational texts are shorter but difficult, because different concepts are presented on each page or in each section.

Examples

NATE THE GREAT AND THE TARDY TORTOISE (SEE FIGURE 6–3)

Realistic fiction/mystery; series book; forty-two pages (no chapter divisions); easy-to-read font; assigned dialogue; sentences start at left margin; straightforward plot; mostly one- and two-syllable words; familiar topics with a few technical words; colored illustrations on most pages; some pages all print; language typical of mysteries; character's thinking revealed through talk to self.

Frog and Toad Are Friends

Animal fantasy; sixty-four pages (five chapters, about eleven words per chapter); easy-to-read font with clear spaces; assigned dialogue; literary language; humor.

What Happens When You Recycle? (*See Figure 6–4.*)

Informational text; sixteen pages (seven chapters, two pages per chapter); large font; index; familiar topic; a few technical words; mostly one- and two-syllable words; supportive illustrations on every page; requires background awareness of environmental issues.

Level L

Characteristics

Chapter books at level L are longer and more complex. They have more sophisticated plots. Characters are likely to develop and change in response to the events in the story; one or two characters are featured. Vocabulary includes more multisyllable words that present challenges in terms of new labels for familiar concepts. These longer texts have many easy and harder frequently encountered words. There are illustrations on most pages, but there are some whole pages of print. A major change at level L is that the layout is more difficult. For most texts, sentences end in the middle of lines and continue from one line to the next. The font is generally smaller, and there is more print on the page.

Informational books present some new concepts that students can connect with their own background knowledge; the number of new concepts presented is limited, but as in level K, even shorter informational texts are difficult because a different concept is presented on each page or in each section. Simple biographies, told in temporal sequence, tell the stories of past times.

"I cannot look for it,"
I said.
"I will give you a clue,"
Claude said. "The sock matches
the one on my right foot."
"Good idea," I said.
Sludge and I walked away.
Claude yelled after us.

"If you find my sock,
and it doesn't look
as good as my right sock,
I don't want it.
I need a match."
I, Nate the Great,
needed some pancakes.
Sludge needed a bone.
We went home.

Figure 6–3. Nate the Great and the Tardy Tortoise, *Level K*

Too Much Garbage

The landfills are filling up too fast. We throw away too much. To help, we can recycle many things or use them again.

Look at how much less garbage there is when we recycle.

4

5

Figure 6–4. What Happens When You Recycle?, *Level K*

Examples

PINKY AND REX AND THE SPELLING BEE (SEE FIGURE 6–5)

Realistic fiction; series book; forty pages (six chapters, about six lines per chapter); large font; less space between lines than earlier levels; about 25 percent of the pages contain only print; assigned dialogue; sentences start in the middle of lines; everyday experiences; themes relate to friendship and problems at school; somewhat complex issues and feelings depicted.

HORRIBLE HARRY IN ROOM 2B

Realistic fiction; easy chapter book in a series; fifty-six pages (five chapters, about ten pages per chapter); medium font; about 40 percent of the pages contain only print; assigned dialogue; sentences start in the middle of lines; everyday experiences/school setting; mostly one- and two-syllable words; black-and-white illustrations on every other page.

LOOKING AT INSECTS (SEE FIGURE 6–6)

Informational text/science; twenty-one pages (nine sections of two pages each); glossary, index; large, easy-to-read font; colored illustrations, diagrams and photographs; question-answer format in each section, with answers at the back of the book; some technical vocabulary; mostly simple straightforward sentences, and many stand-alone phrases in answer section with picture support.

Level M

Characteristics

A change at level M is that texts have many whole pages of print without illustrations. Illustrations are usually black-and-white drawings or photographs and are scattered throughout the text; they extend the meaning and enhance enjoyment. Chapters are longer. Most texts have a great deal of text in smaller print with narrower word spacing. Vocabulary is greatly expanded, includ-

Sitting down next to Rex, Pinky said, "So what if you're not good at spelling? It doesn't matter."

"That's easy for you to say," said Rex. "You're not going to make a fool of yourself. I *hate* looking stupid. It's bad enough to make mistakes when you're all by yourself. But when you have to stand up in

4

front of the whole class… I just know everyone is going to laugh at me, Pinky. They'll laugh and they'll say, 'That Rex is *so* stupid.'"

"I won't laugh at you," Pinky told Rex. "And I won't think you're stupid, either."

"You're just saying that because you know you're smarter than I am."

"Maybe in some things I am," said Pinky. "But you're smarter in other things. Like games. And you know lots more about dinosaurs than I do. You even know how to spell all their names."

This made Rex feel a little better. "Maybe you're right," she said. "But I'll tell you one thing. If everybody laughs at me, I'm moving to the moon."

5

Figure 6–5. Pinky and Rex and the Spelling Bee, *Level L*

ing many multisyllable words and technical words.

Topics of informational texts are widely varied, from subjects that are familiar to students to new topics they are expected to study and learn. Sections of informational texts may provide different information but there is elaboration to help the reader. Most technical terms are explained and illustrated within the text. Real biographies, structured as simple narratives, require readers to think about historical concepts.

Examples

MATT CHRISTOPHER: MAN OUT AT FIRST [A PEACH STREET MUDDERS STORY] (SEE FIGURE 6–7)

Realistic fiction/sports story; series book; sixty pages (ten chapters, about five pages per chapter); no table of contents; medium font; ten black-and-white illustrations; simple narrative sequence; familiar experiences, one or two episodes in each chapter; descriptions of sports; fast moving; mostly one- and two-syllable words; some technical language; larger number of characters to remember and follow in action.

A PICTURE BOOK OF FREDERICK DOUGLASS

Informational text/biography; familiar subject to many children; twenty-nine pages (no chapter divisions; five to nine lines per page); medium font; color illustrations on every page; told as a narrative; little dialogue or fictionalization; chronological organization; requires some knowledge of historical events and circumstances (for example, slavery); list of dates and events plus author's note.

CAVES (SEE FIGURE 6–8)

Informational text; twenty-four pages (six chapters, two, three, or four pages per chapter); glossary and index; easy-to-read font; supportive illustrations, with legends,

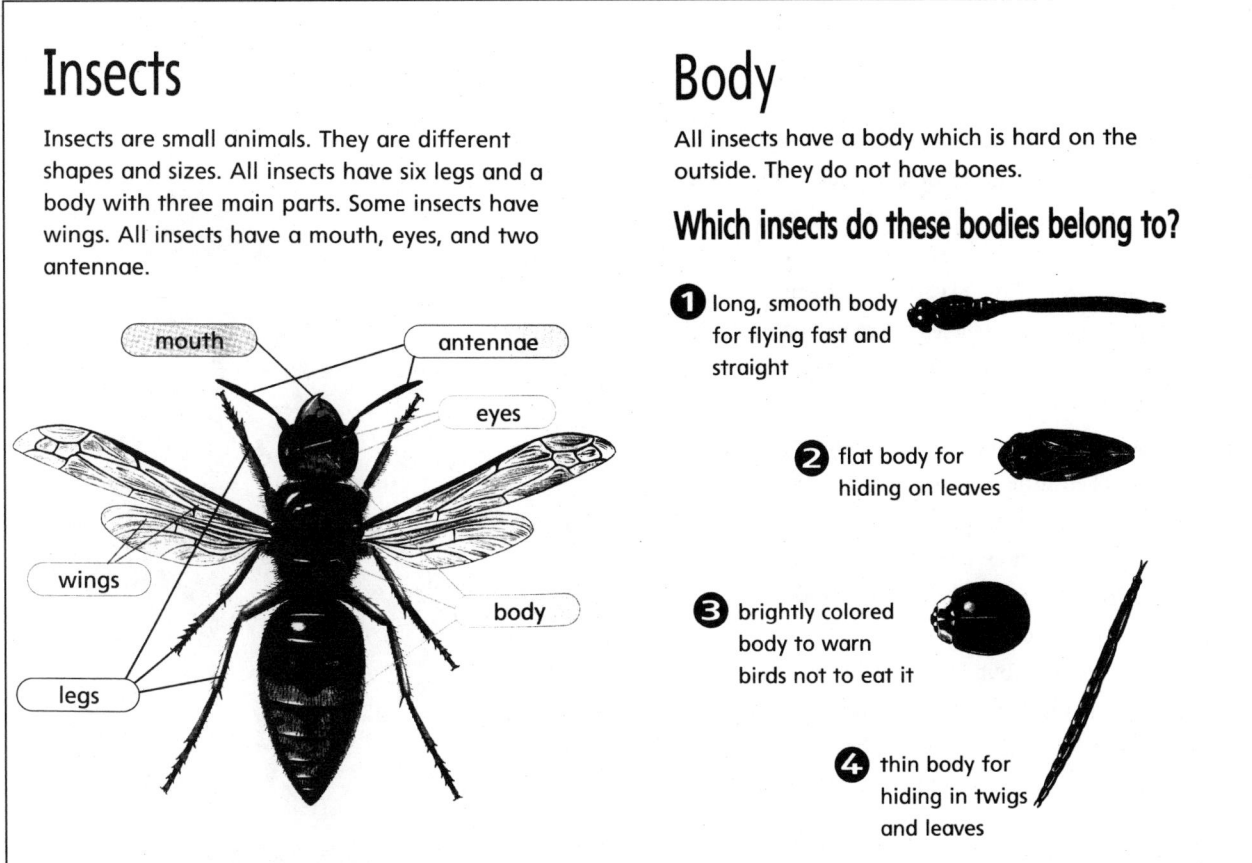

Insects

Insects are small animals. They are different shapes and sizes. All insects have six legs and a body with three main parts. Some insects have wings. All insects have a mouth, eyes, and two antennae.

mouth • antennae • eyes • wings • body • legs

Body

All insects have a body which is hard on the outside. They do not have bones.

Which insects do these bodies belong to?

1 long, smooth body for flying fast and straight

2 flat body for hiding on leaves

3 brightly colored body to warn birds not to eat it

4 thin body for hiding in twigs and leaves

Figure 6–6. Looking at Insects, *Level L*

on every page; cutaway diagram of cave formation; different information in each chapter; some unfamiliar concepts; technical words related to aspects of caves (for example, *stalactites*); quite a few multisyllable words.

Summary

Readers of texts at levels J through M are growing in their ability to process longer, more complex narrative texts over several days as opposed to the short, straightforward texts (which can often be read in twenty or thirty minutes) at lower levels. Literary elements such as characters, setting, and plot become more important to understanding the stories. Instead of stories with only one or two episodes, these longer texts, some with several chapters, show characters changing and developing through their experiences. Readers are increasingly required to think about how characters feel and their motivations for doing what they do. .

Books, especially at levels J and K, have many frequently encountered words; in general you will not see many three- and four-syllable words or many technical or specialized words. Layout may be very friendly, with sentences beginning on the left, a large, clear font, and plenty of space between lines; but it gradually becomes more sophisticated by level M. Just about all of the texts at these levels, however, are parsimonious about the amount of text on any one page; in many texts there are half-page illustrations on every page or every other page.

Most children reading at level J and up have been reading silently most of the time. This transformation usually begins soon after they no longer need the finger to guide their reading, which happens around level C or D. Children usually read orally through several more levels. Reading then becomes "whisper" reading, and you will find some children spontaneously switching to silent reading around levels G, H, or I. The switch is an important one. While there are reasons to read aloud (reading stories and books to children and

He turned his attention back to the game and saw Nick Chong and Alfie both strike out. A pop-up by Bus Mercer ended the Mudders' turn at bat. The score was tied, 3–3.

At a nod from Coach Parker, Turtleneck grabbed his glove and headed out to first base. He felt good as he warmed up with the rest of the infield.

Barry McGee caught a long fly ball for the first out. Then little Sammy McFall walked. Man on first, one out.

Frankie Bass hit a dribbler to Sparrow. Sparrow scooped it up and quickly tossed it to Bus covering second.

Sammy was out, but Frankie, a fast runner, had almost made it to first. Turtleneck lowered his glove and waited for the next batter.

Then, out of the corner of his eye, he caught a blur of motion.

A split second later, a fast-moving baseball smacked hard into Turtleneck's chest!

14

Figure 6–7. Matt Christopher: Man Out at First, *Level M*

adults, reading scripts of various kinds, reading poetry for the pleasure of the sound, and so on), reading is, in general, a silent activity. As children grow in fluent processing, they read very softly and begin to read parts without voicing the words.

Suggestions for Professional Development

Continue exploring leveled texts with colleagues in your school. Again, we suggest that you work in cross-grade-level groups. Use the collection of books at levels J through X that you gathered for your Chapter 5 professional development discussions. This time, focus on levels J, K, L, and M. If you need more titles at these levels, collect them. You will need at least three titles per level. Try to include one nonfiction book for each level.

1. Before the meeting, divide into four groups or pairs and assign a level to each. Distribute the books you have collected and ask the group members to read the three or four texts they have been given. (If you have a very small group, have the whole group do one level at a time.)

2. Have each group create a list: *What does this text call for readers to do?* If you completed the professional development suggestions at the end of Chapters 4

How Most Caves Form

Most solution caves are found where there is a thick layer of rock called limestone. This layer of limestone lies under the soil and plants. Over time, cracks open in the limestone.

Water seeps down through the soil and flows through the cracks. The water dissolves the limestone. After many thousands or millions of years, the water makes openings under the ground.

Figure 6–8. Caves, *Level M*

and 5, you have analyzed texts and also become familiar with the kinds of changes in text demands along the gradient. Now, simply brainstorm a list of demands, looking at the books you have read.

3. Make a grid on which to organize the text demands you list (see the example in Figure 6–9), and check whether the statement is characteristic of each of the books at the level. This grid will take a fair amount of time to produce—forty-five minutes to an hour.

4. Bring the entire group together and compare the grids. Ask:

- What variety is there *within* levels in what texts call on readers to do?
- What variety is there *across* levels in what texts call on readers to do?
- What significant changes do you notice from level J through level M? If you like, you can record these statements on a chart with two columns, one labeled *From* and the other labeled *To*.

5. Complete the discussion by asking the group to make some concluding statements about texts at levels J through M.

Comparison of Text Demands for Levels J, K, L, M

What does the text call for the reader to do?	1. Level____	2. Level____	3. Level____
1.			
2.			
3.			
4.			
5.			
6.			
7.			
8.			
9.			
10.			
Notes/Questions:			

Figure 6–9. Comparison of Text Demands for Levels J, K, L, M

CHAPTER SEVEN

UNDERSTANDING LEVELS OF
TEXT: N TO S

As readers build their processing systems by reading a variety of increasingly difficult texts, they expand their abilities to meet more complex demands. We call these readers *self-extending*, because they have developed a system for expanding their reading processes by encountering and solving the problems of complex and varied texts. In other words, they learn more about reading by reading every day; however, that does not mean that instruction is unnecessary. These readers need support, demonstration, and carefully selected texts for the system to work.

Children have been building this self-extending system since the early grades, and, by the time they begin reading their first chapter books, the foundation of the system is in place. There is much room in which to grow, however.

Successful reading of texts at levels N through S on the gradient, which are appropriate for most readers in grades 3 and 4, requires largely unconscious orchestration of information; readers concentrate primarily on the deeper meaning. Self-extending readers can sustain silent reading over longer periods of time as well as through longer texts. Their oral reading is fluent at these levels, and their phrasing identifies units of meaning. It is important to help readers maintain fluency as they move on to longer, more complex texts. Students are rapidly developing tastes as readers, and learning more about themselves and their world through reading. They are learning rapid and sophisticated ways of taking words apart, although they will benefit from further word study.

In grades 3 and 4, there is great change in how and what students read. The variety in students' reading increases dramatically. They are introduced to new genres as well as to topics, themes, and settings that are not within their personal experiences. The challenge for these readers will be to delve deeply into their reading, thinking about aspects of text such as character, plot, and theme. The texts at these levels are much richer than earlier stories and provide opportunity for discussion. These readers need to spend more time reading more books in order to increase their flexibility.

Level N

Characteristics

Level N includes longer texts organized in a variety of ways. Topics of informational texts and settings for narrative texts go well beyond readers' personal experience. Chapter books present memorable characters that are well developed and change in response to the events of the story. They also offer an opportunity to feel empathy for characters and to experience suspense. Writers use devices such as irony and whimsy to create interest. Characters are revealed through what they say, think, and do, as well as through what others say about them.

Informational texts require much more content knowledge. There are many technical words, but these are usually explained within the text. Biographies are longer and focus on subjects that are less well known to students. They are expected to learn about these subjects through reading.

Examples

SHOESHINE GIRL (SEE FIGURE 7–1)
Realistic fiction featuring problems related to growing up; eighty-four pages (eleven chapters, seven or eight pages per chapter); medium font; a few black-and-white drawings; straightforward narrative structure;

character development; requires readers to empathize with characters and predict motivations.

MY NAME IS MARIA ISABEL

Realistic fiction about an immigrant in a new school; fifty-seven pages (ten chapters, six or seven pages per chapter); medium font; a few black-and-white drawings; a few Spanish words; requires understanding traditions of a cultural group.

HELEN KELLER: COURAGE IN THE DARK (SEE FIGURE 7–2)

Biography told chronologically as a straightforward narrative; forty-seven pages (five chapters of various lengths); Braille alphabet included at end; illustrations on almost every page; large, easy-to-read font; sentence structure generally simple; two- and three-syllable words but few technical words.

Level O

Characteristics

A range of challenges are presented in chapter books at level O. Books have multiple characters who are revealed through what they say, think, and do or through what others say about them. Characters encounter everyday experiences; some must deal with serious problems such as war or death.

This level includes a wide variety of genres, including realistic fiction, historical fiction, biography, science fiction, humor, and traditional literature. Most chapter books have between fifty and two hundred pages. Texts have only a few illustrations, and they are usually black-and-white drawings or photographs.

Vocabulary is sophisticated and varied. There are many multisyllable words. Frequently encountered words, both easy and more difficult, are used; most

---

Rossi

"Well, it's a long trip. I'd have been scared. Are you having a good time in Palmville?"

"I just got here," said Sarah Ida.

"I think you'll like it. There's a lot to see. Come on down the street. I'll show you where I live."

They walked down to Rossi's house. It was old, like Aunt Claudia's. It was half covered with creepy-looking vines.

Sarah Ida met Rossi's mother. Mrs. Wigginhorn was pretty in the same way Rossi was. She had pale hair and a sweet smile.

She said, "I hope you'll enjoy your visit here."

Rossi showed Sarah Ida her room. "My daddy made this shelf for my library. These are all my books. Any time you want to borrow some—"

"I don't read much," said Sarah Ida. She was looking at something else. She was looking at a blue and white pig on the dresser. "What's this?" she asked.

"That's my bank," said Rossi.

14

Figure 7–1. Shoeshine Girl, *Level N*

Chapter 4

When Helen was fourteen, she attended the Wright-Humason School for the Deaf in New York City. The school helped her improve her speech and lip-reading skills. Using the hand alphabet and Braille, Helen also learned German and French.

But that wasn't enough for Helen. She had a new goal. Helen wanted to go to college. She wanted to study with students who could see and hear.

32

For three years, Helen worked very hard to prepare for the entrance exams. The tests were copied into Braille so that Helen could read them. She worried that she might not pass. Then one day, a letter with the good news arrived. Helen had been accepted to Radcliffe College!

33

Figure 7–2. Helen Keller: Courage in the Dark, *Level N*

words will be within readers' decoding control. Readers are expected to form new meanings for known words. Highly complex sentences require a full range of punctuation, which is important to accessing the meaning of the text.

Examples

BEEZUS AND RAMONA
Realistic fiction about family (sibling) relationships; series book; 159 pages (six chapters, twenty to thirty pages each); mostly one-, and two-syllable words; medium font; everyday experiences; many frequently encountered words and some three-syllable words; some black-and-white drawings; complex sentences with commas, dashes, embedded clauses.

MIEKO AND THE FIFTH TREASURE (SEE FIGURE 7–3)
Realistic fiction on the themes of war, pain, and perseverance; seventy-nine pages (eleven chapters, six or so pages each); small font; illustrated with calligraphy; assigned dialogue; complex sentences with commas,

dashes, embedded clauses; requires understanding traditions of a cultural group.

HAIRY LITTLE CRITTERS (SEE FIGURE 7–4)
Informational text (many small pieces of information organized around a single topic); thirty-one pages (eight sections, four or five pages per section); table of contents, index, and information about the author; font varies from large to smaller print under illustrations; some technical words (for example, *marsupials, rodents, crepuscular, spinifex*) with no help in pronunciation; photographs on every page; calls for synthesis of information.

Level P

Characteristics
Level P includes a wide variety of fiction and nonfiction. Informational texts and biographies present complex ideas on many different topics that may be unfamiliar. Technical language is evident. Fiction texts

"The war is over now," he said, putting his arms around her. "There are no more bombs."

But Mieko could not stop the sobs shaking her whole body.

"Shh—shh! You must stop crying," Grandpa whispered. "Your tears will not help those who were killed by the atom bomb. Their souls must swim across the River of Death to heaven. Every tear you shed drops into the river and makes it deeper."

Mieko shuddered, imagining what it would be like to struggle in that icy cold water. Gradually, she became quiet.

Grandpa straightened the bedclothes.

"Enough of dreary thoughts," he said. "Try to sleep like my rock in the garden."

As soon as he was gone Mieko went to the open window. She pushed up her bangs, letting the night air cool her damp forehead. With no moonlight Mieko could barely see Grandpa's rock. She was sorry for it, so awfully alone out there in the swallowing dark. It looked as alone as she felt.

16

T W O

おばあさん
の家

GRANDMA'S
HOME

Every morning Mieko put on the dress that Grandma had sewn out of an old summer cotton kimono. It had no buttons or belt so that Mieko could easily slip it over her head. Grandma had taken the long-sleeved blouses and baggy trousers that Mieko had brought and put them into the scrapbag.

"I don't understand why the government made

Figure 7–3. Mieko and the Fifth Treasure, *Level O*

include novels with longer chapters. Characters are concerned with issues related to growing up and family relationships and the problems of preadolescence.

In comparison to previous levels, in general, level P texts are longer, have more complex ideas and language, and use a more sophisticated vocabulary. They include more detailed descriptions of setting. More interpretation is required to understand themes at several levels. Many texts are long (over one hundred pages), requiring readers to sustain interest and attention over several days. At this level, length becomes less important than the structural complexity, theme sophistication, and necessary background experience.

Examples

FANTASTIC MR. FOX
Animal fantasy, in which animals are personified humorously; eighty-one pages (eighteen chapters, each three to five pages long); medium font; some black-and-white drawings; humorous language; assigned dialogue; words in italics for emphasis; full range of punctuation.

YANG THE YOUNGEST AND HIS TERRIBLE EAR
(SEE FIGURE 7–5)
Realistic fiction centered on familiar themes and concepts related to the relationships and expectations of family members and friends; 134 pages (eight chapters, seventeen or so pages per chapter); medium font; one whole-page or two half-page black-and-white illustrations per chapter; every title page illustrated with symbolic articles; first-person narrative; a great deal of dialogue; straightforward plot; characters learn and change; comparison of cultures; requires seeing things from different perspectives.

STONE FOX
Realistic action-packed fiction centered on themes of responsibility and selflessness (Wyoming setting is

Hairy Little Critters

Birds have feathers and reptiles have scales, but the clever little critters in this book have coats made from all kinds of hair. They belong to a group of animals called mammals, and they live in many different habitats (or homes) all over the world. Each critter has its own strategy for survival.

Figure 7–4. Hairy Little Critters, *Level O*

important to the story); eighty-one pages (ten chapters, eight or nine pages per chapter); one or two black-and-white drawings in each chapter; straightforward story; character development through meeting responsibilities; some unassignèd dialogue; writing style includes mixture of complex and very short sentences; poignant ending requiring interpretation.

MAPS AND CODES (SEE FIGURE 7–6)
Informational text on maps (purposes, types, how they are made; purpose of keys and legends and the meaning of "scale") and codes and signals (semaphore, Braille, how to make a secret code); includes a short story related to map making; thirty-one pages (four sections, each about eight pages); varied font sizes but easy to read; technical words related to subject matter; many illustrations, maps, diagrams, and directions (for example, how to read Braille); writing style conversational; a great deal of content; presents complex and elaborate meanings of the word "code."

Level Q

Description
A change at level Q is that most narrative texts will have very few illustrations. The cover illustrations contribute to readers' anticipation, but just about all understanding comes from print. Illustrations in informational books at this level carry a great deal of meaning and require interpretation.

Chapter books at level Q employ a complex sentence structure and more difficult vocabulary, with

4

Mr. Conner, Matthew's father, opened the door. "Hello, you must be . . . uh . . ." He turned to Matthew.

"This is Yingtao," said Matthew.

"Sorry," said Mr. Conner. "I have a hard time with Chinese names."

"That's okay," I told him. "I have a hard time with American names."

Mr. Conner looked startled. Maybe he wasn't expecting me to speak whole sentences.

"Your mom's getting some groceries," he said to Matthew. "Supper will be a little late."

"Come on, let's go to my room," Matthew said to me.

"Shouldn't we go to the store and help your mother carry the groceries home?" I asked.

54

"It's all right," said Matthew. "Mom's driving."

I was surprised. Since Matthew had told me that his father had lost his job and couldn't afford to pay for music lessons, I expected the Conner family to be really poor. "Your family can afford to drive a car?" I asked.

Now Matthew looked surprised. "Of course. Everybody drives."

"In China, only officials and executives of big companies have cars," I told him.

The Conners certainly didn't look poor. Their house was made of wood, painted in a nice light blue color, and it had a yard both in front and in back, with neatly cut lawns.

"Do you share your house with another family?" I asked.

Matthew shook his head. "Nope. We have it all to ourselves. Eric and I each have our own room."

I looked around in wonder at the spacious living room with its matching sofa and armchairs, and at the dining room, which had a table, matching dining chairs, and cupboards.

"I really like your house," I told Matthew.

Matthew looked pleased. "Dad bought this house cheap and fixed it up. Eric and I helped him."

55

Figure 7–5.   Yang the Youngest and His Terrible Ear, *Level P*

themes that will engage third or fourth graders. Themes require interpretation; characters are memorable and prompt empathy for and understanding of how they change. Children's literature selections offer sophisticated humor, complex plots, and interesting ideas that will be a good foundation for group discussion. In addition, illustrations and their relationships to the text can be analyzed. All texts contain difficult words, some from languages other than English, for readers to solve.

Thoughts and perspectives of characters are revealed in a variety of ways—through dialogue and from the viewpoint of other characters. Books are generally quite long, requiring the reader to sustain interest and meaning over many days. Some books have more mature themes, focusing on problems of society as they affect children.

Examples

DEAR MR. HENSHAW (SEE FIGURE 7–7)
Realistic fiction centering on family problems, growing up, and school issues; 134 pages (unique format—a series of letters and journal entries ranging from three sentences to ten pages); dialogue between characters recounted, and also presented in the form of letters; moves from simple language in beginning of book to complex sentences; no technical language; requires inferences as to characters' feelings and motivations; requires inferences as to what is happening to characters.

ANASTASIA KRUPNIK
Realistic fiction centering on friends and family relationships; 113 pages (11 chapters, most about 10 pages); straightforward narrative; a great deal of dialogue, much of

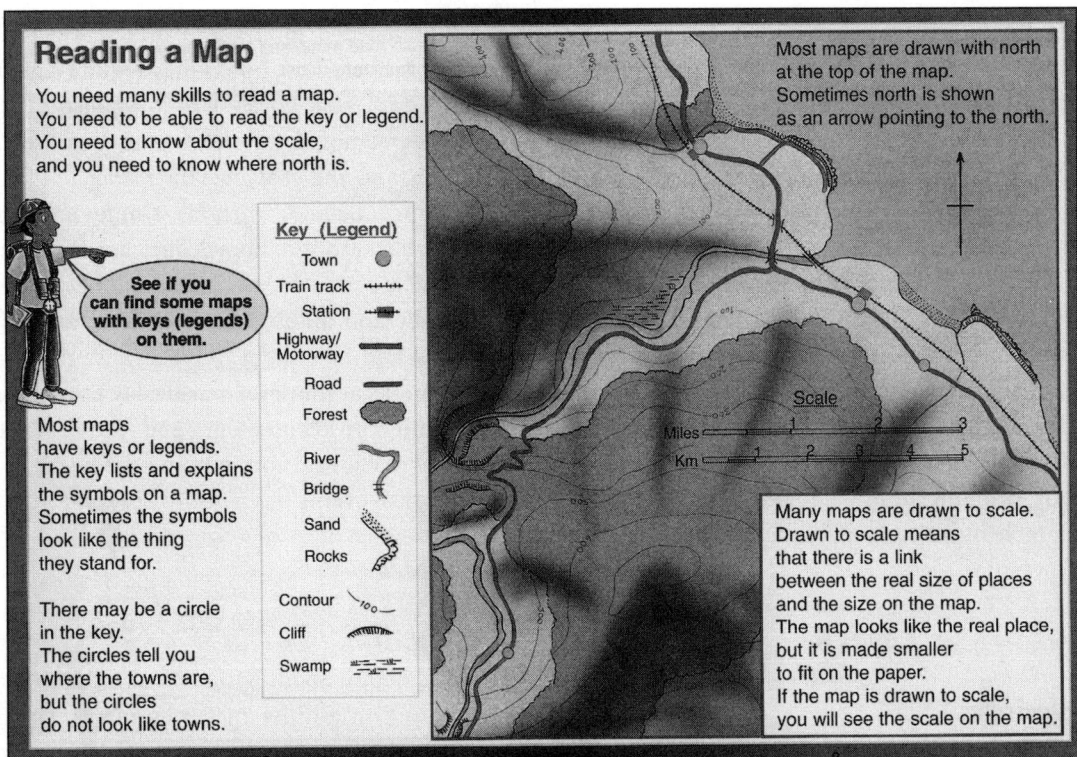

Figure 7–6. Maps and Codes, *Level P*

Today I wrote a fictitious name, or pseud. as they sometimes say, on my lunchbag. I printed Joe Kelly on it because that was the name of the boy in *Ways to Amuse a Dog* so I knew it was fictitious. I guess I fooled the thief because nobody stole the water chestnuts and chicken livers wrapped in bacon that Katy broiled just for me. They are good even when they are cold. I hope the thief drooled when he watched me eat them.

Monday, January 8
Dear Mr. Pretend Henshaw,

Dad phoned me from Hermiston, Oregon! I just looked in my book of road maps and saw where it is, up there by the Columbia River. He said he was waiting for a load of potatoes. I could hear a juke box and a bunch of men talking. I asked about Bandit, and he said Bandit was fine, a great listener on a long haul even though he doesn't have much to say. I asked Dad if I could ride with him sometime next

46

summer when school is out, and he said he'd see. (I *hate* answers like that.) Anyway, he said he was sending the support check and he was sorry he forgot and he hoped I liked the jacket.

I sure wish Dad lived with us again, but he said he would phone in about a week and to keep my nose clean. He had to go to make sure the potatoes were loaded so they wouldn't shift going around curves.

This has been a good day. My lunch was safe again.

Mr. Fridley is so funny. Lots of kids are having their teeth straightened so when they eat lunch, they take out their retainers and wrap them in paper napkins while they eat because nobody wants to look at a spitty retainer. Sometimes they forget and throw the napkin with the retainer into the garbage. Then they have to hunt through the cans of gooey garbage until they find their retainers because retainers cost a lot of money, and parents get mad if they get lost. Mr. Fridley always stands by the gar-

47

Figure 7–7. Dear Mr. Henshaw, *Level Q*

it unassigned; development of characters and their relationships; samples of Anastasia's handwritten lists from her private notebook included throughout.

AMAZING SPIDERS (SEE FIGURE 7–8)

Information book; thirty-one pages (eleven sections, two or three pages per section); many small pieces of information organized under phrases and all related to a big idea; page layout is like a "web," organizing different bits of information; interesting facts presented in conversational language; some entries require background knowledge (for example, that the *tarantella* dance relates to the *tarantula* spider); only a few technical words; pronunciation guide provided for technical words; table of contents and index.

Level R

Characteristics

Books in Level R, both fiction and nonfiction, represent a range of times in history. In general, these texts extend the skills needed for level Q over a wider variety of texts. Some very long books may require a great deal of sustained interest. Vocabulary is sophisticated, requiring understanding of the connotative shadings of meaning, and will challenge the reader.

Literary devices such as simile and metaphor require background knowledge, as do some of the technical aspects of texts. Informational books such as biography and autobiography extend readers' understanding and take them to places distant in time and space. Books at this level may deal with mature themes like family problems, war, and death. Readers are required to connect concepts and themes with political or historical events or environmental information.

Examples

FIG PUDDING (SEE FIGURE 7–9)

Realistic fiction about family relationships (each chapter focuses on a different family member); 136 pages (nine chapters, varying from four to thirty-five pages); variety of short and longer, more complex sentences;

Figure 7–8. Amazing Spiders, *Level Q*

some stretches of unassigned dialogue; medium font; literary language; description.

HER PIANO SANG
Informational text/biography told as a narrative; sixty-four pages (eight chapters, ranging from three to nine pages); afterword, list of works, bibliography, index; black-and-white illustrations; many words from music and other languages; complex and symbolic words in table of contents; theme of perseverance, talent.

SADAKO AND THE THOUSAND PAPER CRANES
Informational text/history; sixty-four pages (nine chapters, five to seven pages each); prologue and epilogue; black-and-white illustrations add to mood; theme of war and death; requires background knowledge about history and health; evokes empathy with character; requires understanding of cultural traditions; genre, topic, and sophistication of the writing places new demands on readers.

THE CHOCOLATE FLIER (SEE FIGURE 7–10)
Informational text/history/biography about the Berlin Airlift, told in straightforward narrative (biography section on Gail Halverson); forty-seven pages (three sections of varied lengths); unfamiliar topic for most students; table of contents, glossary, index, and information about the author; tables in each section; small font; authentic photographs from World War II on every page; legends under photographs; insets present "did you know" facts; technical or content-related words in boldface and presented in glossary.

Level S

Characteristics
Texts at level S present complex ideas and information that will be a good foundation for group discussions.

Under the Kitchen Table

3. Under the Kitchen Table

Grandma Annie liked to say that Teddy was born with "the heebie-jeebies in his veins and his brains." I couldn't agree more, and I should know because I've baby-sat him, plenty. Lots of times Dad and Mom went out shopping, they'd take the baby and put me "in charge" of the other kids. That wouldn't have been half bad if it hadn't been for Teddy. He could make any baby-sitter miserable because he never slowed down and he never stopped coming up with new ways of getting into trouble.

One time Mom asked me to baby-sit the other kids while she took Brad to the doctor's. All Teddy did was "feed" the fish by dumping Cheerios into their bowl. He took Cyn's jewelry and put it onto her stuffed animals. He tossed Mom and Dad's toothbrushes into the toilet. When Mom got back, Teddy got into trouble and I got into trouble, too, for not minding him better.

40

"You've got to keep a closer eye on Teddy," Mom told me.

What was I supposed to do: put him in a strait-jacket? Tie him up? There are laws against stuff like that.

Take how Teddy acted on New Year's Day when we were at Aunt Pat and Uncle Arthur's house for their big holiday feast.

The holiday feast was a combination dinner where each family brought one major dish, or dessert. Just thinking about it made my mouth water. Uncle Eddie always fixed spaghetti with a thick sausage and meatball sauce. Aunt Pat and Uncle Arthur had spent a dozen years in South Carolina. Uncle Arthur always made his famous she-crab bisque; Aunt Pat fixed fried chicken with sweet potato biscuits. Aunt Marilyn always baked these delicious little dough pockets, some stuffed with meat, others with spinach and onions and mint. Grandma Annie usually made a couple blueberry pies, plus a double batch of stollen.

We always made fig pudding. Or, I should say, Dad made it. He had a friend from college, a guy who grew prize-winning figs on his farm in California. Just before the holidays, a UPS truck pulled up in front of our house with a box of figs as it did every year. On Saturday, the day before the feast, Dad cooked.

As a cook, Dad was the exact opposite of Grandma. Grandma invited everyone into the kitchen. She handed out jobs; she put you to work. Dad called

41

Figure 7–9. Fig Pudding, *Level R*

Soviets Take Control

After leaving western Germany, all east-bound supplies had to pass through a hundred miles of Soviet-held territory to reach western Berlin. In June 1948, the Soviets blocked all ways into the city.

They stopped railroad transport. No more **barges** glided through the **canals**. The famous highway, the German Autobahn, was closed. The supply of electric power to the western sectors of Berlin was cut off. The **blockade** was complete.

Or was it? There was still one way into the city that was not closed.

> "
> *In June 1948, the Soviets blocked all ways into the city.*
> "

Berlin was filled with troops after the war.

Figure 7–10.   The Chocolate Flier, *Level R*

They reflect a wide variety of topics and cultures. At this level, words present many shadings of meaning that readers must construct from their interpretations of the text. Sentences and paragraphs are complex, requiring rapid and fluent reading with attention to meaning and automatic assimilation of punctuation.

Many works of historical fiction are included in this level of the gradient; students at this age tend to find historical events interesting. There are also many more biographies. Texts present settings that are far distant from students' own experiences. Literary selections offer opportunities for readers to make connections with previously read texts as well as with historical events. This category includes chapter books in many genres. Picture books present complex ideas and information that will be a good foundation for group discussions.

Examples

BRIDGE TO TERABITHIA (SEE FIGURE 7–11)
Realistic fiction about the mature themes of friendship

and death; 128 pages (thirteen chapters, most chapters eight to ten pages long); small font; requires in-depth understanding of characters; some long sequences of description and reflection.

THE STAR FISHER
Historical fiction centered around friendship, prejudice, and persecution; 150 pages (fourteen chapters, most around ten pages long); acknowledgments; small font; italics to indicate characters speaking in Chinese; some archaic words; many multisyllable words; long, complex sentences with full range of punctuation.

THE STORY OF HARRIET TUBMAN: CONDUCTOR OF THE UNDERGROUND RAILROAD (SEE FIGURE 7–12)
Informational book/biography; 108 pages (twelve chapters, each seven or eight pages long); medium font; narrative style; some events fictionalized; covers long period of history; timeline in back; requires background knowledge of history and social problems; black-and-white illustrations.

FIVE

The Giant Killers

Leslie liked to make up stories about the giants that threatened the peace of Terabithia, but they both knew that the real giant in their lives was Janice Avery. Of course, it wasn't only Jess and Leslie that she was after. She had two friends, Wilma Dean and Bobby Sue Henshaw, who were almost as big as she was, and the three of them would roam the playground, grabbing up hopscotch rocks, running through jump ropes, and laughing while second graders screamed. They would even stand outside the girls' room first thing every morning and make the little girls give them their milk money before they'd let them go to the bathroom.

May Belle, unfortunately, was a slow learner. Her daddy had brought her a package of Twinkies, and she was so proud that as soon as she got on the bus she forgot everything she knew and yelled to another first grader, "Guess what I got in my lunch today, Billy Jean?"

"What?"

The Giant Killers | 49

"Twinkies!" she shouted so loud you could have heard her in the back seat even if you were deaf in both ears. Out of the corner of his eye, Jess thought he saw Janice Avery perk up.

When they sat down, May Belle was still screeching about her dadgum Twinkies over the roar of the motor. "My daddy brung 'um to me from Washington!"

Jess threw another look at the back seat. "You better shut up about those dang Twinkies," he said in her ear.

"You just jealous 'cause Daddy didn't bring you none."

"OK." He shrugged across her head at Leslie to say *I warned her, didn't I?* and Leslie nodded back.

Neither of them was too surprised to see May Belle come screaming toward them at recess time.

"She stole my Twinkies!"

Jess sighed. "May Belle, didn't I tell you?"

"You gotta kill Janice Avery. Kill her! Kill her! Kill her!"

"*Shhh,*" Leslie said, stroking May Belle's head, but May Belle didn't want comfort, she wanted revenge.

"You gotta beat her up into a million pieces!"

He'd sooner tangle with Mrs. Godzilla herself. "Fighting ain't gonna get back nothing, May Belle. Them Twinkies is well on the way to padding Janice Avery's bottom by now."

Leslie snickered, but May Belle was not to be distracted. "You're just yeller, Jesse Aarons. If you wasn't yeller, you'd beat somebody up if they took your little sister's Twinkies." She broke into a fresh round of sobbing.

Jess stiffened. He avoided Leslie's eyes. Lord, there was no escape. He'd have to fight the female gorilla now.

"Look, May Belle," Leslie was saying. "If Jess picks a fight with Janice Avery, you know perfectly well what will happen."

May Belle wiped her nose on the back of her hand. "She'll beat him up."

Figure 7–11. Bridge to Terabithia, *Level S*

Summary

The exemplars we have highlighted at levels N, O, P, Q, R, and S represent a wide variety of writing styles, genres, and formats. At these levels, length, as a characteristic, becomes less important. Many more informational books are included at these levels, demanding that readers access and use much more background knowledge than at previous levels.

Suggestions for Professional Development

Continue exploring leveled texts with colleagues in your school. Again, we suggest that you work in cross-grade-level groups. Use the collection of books at levels J through X that you gathered for your Chapter 5 professional development discussions. This time focus on levels N, O, P, Q, R, and S. If you need more titles at these levels, collect them. You will need at least three

titles per level. Try to include one nonfiction book for each level.

1. Before the meeting, divide into six pairs and assign a level to each. Distribute the books you have collected and ask the members of each group to read the texts they have been given. (If you have a very small group, have the whole group do one level at a time and use only two titles at each level.)

2. Have each group create a list: *What does this text call for readers to do?* If you completed the professional development suggestions at the end of Chapters 4 and 5, you have analyzed texts and become familiar with the kinds of changes in text demands along the gradient. Now, simply brainstorm a list of demands, looking at the books you have read.

3. Make a grid on which to organize the text demands you list (see the example in Figure 7–13), and check whether the statement is characteristic of each of the books at the level. This grid will take a fair amount of time to produce—forty-five minutes to an hour.

2.

The First Years

LIKE ALL the other babies in the quarter, Harriet Ross cut her first teeth on a piece of pork rind. The rind was tied to a string, and the string hung around her neck.

She learned to walk on the hard-packed earth outside the cabin, getting up, falling down, getting up again— a small naked creature, who answered to the name of Minta or Minty.

When she finally mastered the skill of walking, she began playing with other small children. All of the little ones, too young to run errands, were placed under the care of a woman, so old she could no longer work. She was a fierce-looking old woman, head wrapped in a white bandanna which she called a head rag. She sat crouched over, on the doorstep of her cabin, sucking on an empty clay pipe.

Though she was very old, she could still switch a small child with vigor, using a tough young shoot from

12

THE FIRST YEARS

a black gum tree, to enforce obedience. She never let the children out of her sight, warning them of the creek where they might drown, cautioning them about the nearby woods where they might get lost, shooing them out of the cabins lest they burn themselves in the hot ashes in the fireplaces. The children were afraid of her. She was toothless and she mumbled when she talked. The skin on her face was creased by a thousand wrinkles.

When she was in good humor, she told them stories about what she called the Middle Passage. The mumbling old voice evoked the clank of chains, the horror of thirst, the black smell of death, below deck in the hold of a slave ship. The children were too young to understand the meaning of the stories and yet they were frightened, standing motionless, listening to her, and shivering even if the sun was hot.

The mothers of these children worked in the fields. A few of them, like Old Rit, worked in or around the Big House.

Because the mothers were not at home, a family rarely ate together, all at the same time. The grownups ate from the skillet or black iron pot in which the food was cooked. Some of them ate from tin plates, balanced on the knees, eating for the most part with their hands.

The children were fed in a haphazard fashion, a bit of corn bread here, a scrap of pork there; occasionally

13

Figure 7–12. The Story of Harriet Tubman: Conductor of the Underground Railroad, *Level S*

4. Bring the entire group together and compare the grids. Ask:
   ▪ What variety is there *within* levels in what texts call on readers to do?
   ▪ What variety is there *across* levels in what texts call on readers to do?
   ▪ What significant changes do you notice from level N through level S? If you like, you can record these statements on a chart with two columns, one labeled *From* and the other labeled *To.*

5. Complete the discussion by asking the group to make some concluding statements about texts at levels N through S.

Comparison of Text Demands for Levels N, O, P, Q, R, S			
What does the text call for the reader to do?	1. Level_____	2. Level_____	3. Level_____
1.			
2.			
3.			
4.			
5.			
6.			
7.			
8.			
9.			
10.			
Notes/Questions:			

Figure 7–13. Comparison of Text Demands for Levels N, O, P, Q, R, S

CHAPTER EIGHT

UNDERSTANDING LEVELS OF
TEXT: T TO Z

As self-extending readers encounter a larger variety of texts and apply their processing skills to longer and more difficult texts, they greatly expand their reading power. Most students in fifth and sixth grade fall into a category we call "advanced," in that they read quickly, paying attention to meaning almost all the time. They immediately and automatically recognize most of the words they read and rapidly apply a wide range of word-solving strategies. They are developing strategies for rapidly expanding their vocabularies.

These readers have the stamina to engage in large amounts of reading and to sustain the activity over days and weeks, quickly remembering what has been previously read. They can skim and scan for information or can lose themselves in books, identifying with the characters and experiencing unfolding events along with them. By now, they have read a large number of texts and are building networks of understanding that help them recognize and appreciate the writer's craft. They are developing an understanding of aspects of literature such as figurative language and symbolism. Our goal for these advanced readers is to further broaden their experience with texts.

They need to become even more sophisticated in their ability to read all kinds of informational texts, thereby expanding their knowledge of content-area topics, and to integrate information from a range of graphic features. They tend to need much more experience looking at how informational texts are organized and using tools such as indexes, charts, pronunciation guides, glossaries, and headings and subheadings.

Their reading of narrative encompasses all genres; many readers will take on the more difficult works of fantasy that require suspending disbelief, entering into other worlds, engaging the imagination, and interpreting actions. At the same time, they will be reading realistic fiction that grapples with serious social issues and provides the opportunity to understand perspectives very different from their own. These levels offer a way for students to explore their world through reading and to learn to analyze and criticize the texts they read.

Although this chapter explores exemplar texts at levels T through Z, we recognize that books at levels Y and Z are not appropriate for most elementary school students, even though they may be able to read them accurately. With fiction, the themes and topics may be uninteresting or too mature, or the writing styles and text structures so complex that they will not enjoy the reading. Even excellent texts may require more experience to truly understand them. Along the same lines, informational texts at Y and Z may require so much background knowledge or be so dense that elementary students may have difficulty in sustaining their attention and understanding the topics. Nevertheless these levels complete the spectrum of students' reading development, and you may have some students for whom these texts are appropriate.

Level T

Characteristics

Selections at level T include a variety of genres and text structures. Chapter books are long, with few illustrations, and they require the reader to recognize character development as well as symbolism. All selections contain many sophisticated, multisyllable words that readers will need to analyze in terms of both literal and connotative meaning.

The range of books at level T incorporates fantasy, historical fiction, informational books, biographies, and realistic fiction. Readers need to know more about political and historical events and about the problems of different cultural and racial groups. Themes include growing up, demonstrating courage, and experiencing hardship and prejudice.

Examples for Level T

SOUNDER

Historical fiction centering on themes of death and social issues; 116 pages (thirteen chapters, each about nine pages); small font; author's note; short sentences among long, complex sentences; symbols between sections of text to indicate passage of time or new episode; characters not named; symbolism; some representa- tion of southern dialect; requires background knowl- edge of historical events and issues.

THE WATSONS GO TO BIRMINGHAM (SEE FIGURE 8–1)

Historical fiction with the quality of a memoir on mature themes—prejudice, death, growing up through traumatic experience (moves from humor, everyday events, to tragedy); 210 pages (fifteen chapters, most twelve to sixteen pages); author's note; requires con- nection to background knowledge of historical events, civil rights struggle.

THE DOUBLE LIFE OF POCAHONTAS

Informational text/biography; eighty-five pages (five chap- ters of varying lengths); well-researched; map, bibliogra- phy, author's notes; no dialogue; not fictionalized; some

---

heat but he didn't have to tell us this, it seemed like the cold automatically made us want to get together and huddle up. My little sister, Joetta, sat in the middle and all you could see were her eyes because she had a scarf wrapped around her head. I was next to her, and on the outside was my mother.

Momma was the only one who wasn't born in Flint so the cold was coldest to her. All you could see were her eyes too, and they were shooting bad looks at Dad. She always blamed him for bringing her all the way from Alabama to Michigan, a state she called a giant icebox. Dad was bundled up on the other side of Joey, trying to look at anything but Momma. Next to Dad, sitting with a little space between them, was my older brother, Byron.

Byron had just turned thirteen so he was officially a teenage juvenile delinquent and didn't think it was "cool" to touch anybody or let anyone touch him, even if it meant he froze to death. Byron had tucked the blanket between him and Dad down into the cushion of the couch to make sure he couldn't be touched.

Dad turned on the TV to try to make us forget how cold we were but all that did was get him in trouble. There was a special news report on Channel 12 tell- ing about how bad the weather was and Dad groaned when the guy said, "If you think it's cold now, wait until tonight, the temperature is expected to drop into record-low territory, possibly reaching the negative twenties! In fact, we won't be seeing anything above zero for the next four to five days!" He was smiling

2

when he said this but none of the Watson family thought it was funny. We all looked over at Dad. He just shook his head and pulled the blanket over his eyes.

Then the guy on TV said, "Here's a little something we can use to brighten our spirits and give us some hope for the future: The temperature in Atlanta, Geor- gia, is forecast to reach . . ." Dad coughed real loud and jumped off the couch to turn the TV off but we all heard the weatherman say, ". . . the mid-seventies!" The guy might as well have tied Dad to a tree and said, "Ready, aim, fire!"

"Atlanta!" Momma said. "That's a hundred and fifty miles from home!"

"Wilona . . . ," Dad said.

"I knew it," Momma said. "I knew I should have listened to Moses Henderson!"

"Who?" I asked.

Dad said, "Oh Lord, not that sorry story. You've got to let me tell about what happened with him."

Momma said, "There's not a whole lot to tell, just a story about a young girl who made a bad choice. But if you do tell it, make sure you get all the facts right."

We all huddled as close as we could get because we knew Dad was going to try to make us forget about being cold by cutting up. Me and Joey started smiling right away, and Byron tried to look cool and bored.

"Kids," Dad said, "I almost wasn't your father. You guys came real close to having a clown for a daddy named Hambone Henderson. . . ."

"Daniel Watson, you stop right there. You're the one

3

Figure 8–1. The Watsons Go to Birmingham, *Level T*

Native American words and technical words; requires background information about the times and events; requires critical examination of previous knowledge.

FOLLOW THAT FIN! STUDYING DOLPHIN BEHAVIOR (SEE FIGURE 8–2)

Informational text/science; forty pages of text (four sections of varying lengths), eight more pages of support material (glossary, index, references, credentials of writer); varied fonts—regular and small; headings divide sections; illustrations on every page (photographs of animals, factual insets resembling scientists' observational notes, drawings, labels, graphs); some technical words (for example, *synchronous, compartment, juvenile*), mostly explained in the text; some help with pronunciation in text; generally simple sentences and conversational style that is similar to narrative; information connected by the writing style; sections cohesive in the meaning conveyed.

Level U

Characteristics

Informational texts at level U cover a wide range of topics and present specific technical information. As with

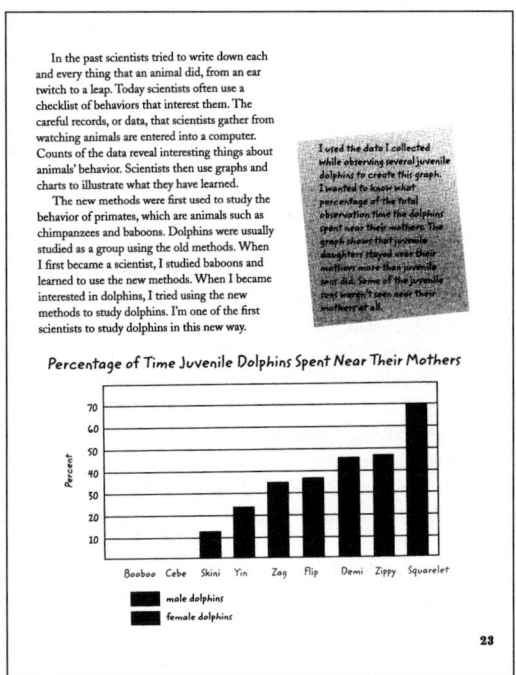

Figure 8–2. Follow That Fin!, *Level T*

earlier levels, illustrations require interpretation and connection to text. Narrative texts are complex; there are plots and subplots. Texts typically have several different themes and many characters. Characters, too, are complex, with multiple dimensions to their personalities. Writers use symbolism, and themes are more abstract. Creative formats are also used (for example, short stories connected by common characters).

Examples

TUCK EVERLASTING

Fantasy centered on themes of love, friendship, choices, death versus everlasting life; 139 pages (twenty-five chapters, each five or six pages long); magical events; symbolism; layers of meaning; complex and literary language; epilogue; understanding enhanced by literary experience with traditional literature.

THE VIEW FROM SATURDAY (SEE FIGURE 8–3)

Realistic fiction (series of twelve interconnected stories with recurring characters, each story told by a different character); 162 pages (story length varies); long, complex sentences with full range of punctuation; many words from languages other than English; intriguing questions and answers at the end.

INSECTS (SEE FIGURE 8–4)

Informational text; fifty-eight pages (four chapters of varying lengths); main headings and two levels of subheadings; photographs, labeled drawings, illustrations of life cycles; life history chart, pronunciation guide, index; medium font; large number of technical words; detailed information, with many unfamiliar concepts; descriptions of complex processes.

Level V

Characteristics

Biographies at this level go beyond simple narratives to provide a significant amount of historical information. Many biographies are not "fictionalized" for easier reading; they focus on harsh themes and difficult periods of history. Other longer biographies are told in narrative style but present complex themes.

4

Mrs. Olinski sat, waiting, until all the members of her class were seated. Then she introduced herself. "I am Mrs. Olinski. I am one of those people who gets to use all those good parking spaces at the mall." She turned toward the blackboard and wrote in big, block letters:

MRS. OLINSKI
PARAPLEGIC

As she wrote *paraplegic*, Mrs. Olinski spelled it out, "P-A-R-A-P-L-E-G-I-C. It means that I am paralyzed from the waist down."

Mrs. Olinski had thought about what she would say to this, her first sixth-grade class in ten years. She wrote it all down, revised, memorized, and rehearsed until she could deliver her lines with a light touch. Her voice held steady, but her hands did not, and the O of Olinski was the rough shape of an oil spill.

Then a student in the back—Hamilton Knapp—stood up. "Excuse me, Mrs. Olinski," he said, hesitating slightly, mispronouncing her name. "I can't see what you've written. Could you write a little higher on the blackboard, please?"

94

Mrs. Olinski replied, "Not at the moment," and managed an embarrassed smile. The rest of her prepared remarks flew out of her head. She thought she had thought of everything. But here she was with a problem about sight lines to the blackboard. Given time, she would figure it out, but she wished it had not come up on the very first hour of her very first day back.

After Hamilton Knapp sat down, she laughed nervously. "I was about to tell you that being a paraplegic does not mean that there is anything wrong with my hearing or my eyesight, but I guess we'll have to figure out what to do about the eyesight of those of you who will be seated in the back of the room."

Mrs. Olinski decided that she would write nothing more on the blackboard for the rest of the morning but would leave what she had already written right there so that she could check it out after lunch. She would return before the rest of the class, wheel herself to the back of the room while it was still empty, and check out the sight lines.

She took the roll, checking on the spelling and pronunciation of each child's name, and passed out general supplies and the books for the social studies she would be teaching. Finally, she assigned seats in alphabetical order, last names first.

The year of her accident, Mrs. Olinski had had two Jennifers in her class. This semester, Jennifer was out of fashion, and J-names for boys were in. She had J-names from Jared to Julian, including two Jasons. When she returned from lunch and saw CRIPPLE written on the blackboard, she knew more than the names had changed. Sixth graders had changed.

95

Figure 8–3. The View from Saturday, *Level U*

DRAGONFLY NAIAD

The dragonfly naiad's mask is an unusual device for catching prey. This special extra mouth part is like a folding arm with a pair of claw-like pincers at the end. As soon as something edible (such as a tiny fish or mosquito larva) comes within reach, the mask shoots out to catch the victim in its pincers. Then the mask brings the food back to the naiad's strong true jaws. When the mask is not in use it is folded under the naiad's head.

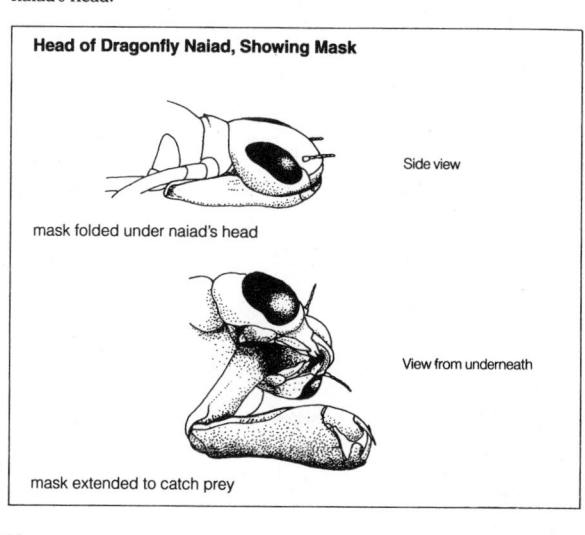

Head of Dragonfly Naiad, Showing Mask

Side view

mask folded under naiad's head

View from underneath

mask extended to catch prey

Opposite: Dragonfly naiad underwater on a plant stem. The mask is folded under the naiad's head

38

Figure 8–4. Insects, *Level U*

Fiction includes science fiction that presents sophisticated ideas and concepts. In many of the works of realistic or historical fiction, the writer is conveying a significant message beyond the specific. Texts require readers to think critically. Full appreciation of texts requires noticing aspects of the writer's craft. Most long texts have print in a small font; texts may be two hundred to three hundred pages but contain many more words than texts with larger print.

Examples

THE FIGHTING GROUND (SEE FIGURE 8–5)

Historical fiction on the themes of war, survival, and growing up; 157 pages (no chapters; takes place over a twenty-four-hour period, and time designations break up book into sections); some German words, with guide in the back; some unassigned dialogue; traumatic experience and change of attitude for hero; narrative structure, with several episodes each section.

A WRINKLE IN TIME

Fantasy/science fiction centering on themes of family relationships, technology, space and time, good and evil; 211 pages (twelve chapters, most twelve to fourteen pages); "family tree" connecting book to author's other books; scientific words and concepts; literary language; humor; information about author in back.

STEALING HOME: THE STORY OF JACKIE ROBINSON (SEE FIGURE 8–6)

Informational text/biography told in chronological order; 117 pages (ten chapters, most ten to twelve pages); medium font; long paragraphs; no dialogue; many facts, dates, and figures; black-and-white original photographs; themes of courage, prejudice; some fictionalization for easier reading and greater interest; requires some knowledge of sports, historical social issues.

3:16

In the immense silence all that Jonathan could hear was his own breath. It came at first in short, reaching gasps. As it slowed to normal, he felt a pain growing inside, a pain spreading through his body, pressing from within.

He began to cry. The cry came at first in pieces, as if the cry itself had been shattered and existed only in fragmentary, jagged bits. But bit by bit the cry grew whole, taking over until every part of him cried.

Deep, racking sobs came then, dry and hard. He felt a terrible loneliness. He did not know what he was or what would become of him. He did not know what to do, where to go. All he knew was pain.

3:30

Exhausted, Jonathan could cry no more. He rolled over onto his back and realized he was still holding the gun. Slowly, he let it go. But his fingers, as if frozen in memory, remained tightly cramped and

54

clawed, shaped like a shell over what they no longer held.

Lying on his back, Jonathan stared up at the overhanging trees, a laced and dark-green net. High above him the leaves constantly shifted, making a soft, hissing sound. He closed his eyes and shuddered.

3:35

Jonathan pushed himself to a sitting posture and looked about, wondering where he was. He tried to recall which direction he had come from, but could not. He pulled up his knees and, leaning forward, rested his chin on his arms. Tightly hugging himself, he rocked softly back and forth, sniffling.

His sleeve was torn. There was a smear of blood on his shoe. He touched the spot, finding it still sticky. He wondered whose blood it was.

"O God, O God, O God," he whispered. He had failed in all he had meant to do.

He was alive and wished that he was dead, but not being dead, he was scared that he might die.

55

Figure 8–5. The Fighting Ground, *Level V*

Level W

Characteristics

Texts at level W have themes that explore the human condition, with the same kinds of challenges mentioned at earlier levels. Fiction and nonfiction texts present characters who suffer hardship and learn from it. The writing is sophisticated, with complex sentences, literary language, and symbolism. Texts vary in length; print is generally small. Comprehending texts at this level requires awareness of social and political issues; through these texts, readers come to understand social problems at deeper levels.

Fantasy and science fiction introduce heroic characters, moral questions, and contests between good and evil. Informational texts may present complex graphic information and require a wide range of content knowledge. Readers must understand all the basic nonfiction organizational structures. Narrative biographies include many details and prompt readers to make inferences about what motivated the subject's achievements.

Examples

DRAGONWINGS

Historical fiction/adventure centering on themes of immigration, survival, prejudice, and poverty; 248 pages (twelve chapters, most about twenty pages long); no table of contents; medium font; afterword; language/tradition reflects Chinese culture; Chinese speech indicated by regular font, English speech indicated by italics; many multisyllabic words; complex, literary language; requires background knowledge of social issues and historical events; requires/expands understanding of diversity in language and culture.

DICEY'S SONG (SEE FIGURE 8–7)

Realistic fiction centering on surviving family problems, including child desertion; 211 pages (twelve chapters, each fourteen to sixteen pages); foreword; small font; complex characters who develop and change; description of characters' thoughts; requires inferences into feelings and motivations.

Jackie Robinson proudly wearing the uniform of the Brooklyn Dodgers

petitor I ever saw. It's been wonderful having you on the team." And Hooper meant every word.

Branch Rickey had done everything he could to make the move to the big leagues as smooth as possible for Jackie. The Royals and Dodgers played seven exhibition games that preseason. Rickey let Jackie know just how important he thought those games were. He wanted Jackie to go all out, hoping that the Dodgers would see just how good Robinson was. In the seven games he batted .625 and stole seven bases.

Rickey also worked behind the scenes. He met with Brooklyn's black leaders and told them that he was concerned about the reaction of the black community. He feared that black fans would be overenthusiastic. Rickey didn't want welcoming committees, parades, big signs, or anything else that would make Jackie's situation any more noticeable than it already was. Rickey also worried that black fans filling the ballparks and celebrating their new hero might cause white fans to stay away. Although some black leaders were insulted by what Rickey was saying, most agreed and a committee was formed. A slogan was adopted: "Don't spoil Jackie's chances."

The Robinsons were now a family of three. Jackie, Jr., had been born in November, 1947. Jackie and Rachel had enjoyed where they lived in Montreal but finding something nice in New York was a problem. They had to settle for a small

77

Figure 8–6. Stealing Home: The Story of Jackie Robinson, *Level V*

The Life and Words of Martin Luther King, Jr.

Informational text/biography including many quotes from King; ninety-six pages (fourteen chapters, most about six pages); small font; long paragraphs; not fictionalized; no dialogue; many original black-and-white photos; includes large amount of detail; deals with prejudice, civil rights struggle, tragedy.

Ocean Detectives: Solving the Mysteries of the Sea (SEE Figure 8–8)

Informational text/science; fifty-nine pages (six sections of varying lengths), five pages of support material (glossary, references, index, credentials of writer); small but varied fonts; legends under illustrations; many photographs, charts, diagrams, and drawings;

presents scientists by name along with reports of their research and their findings; cohesive and interrelated text, with some extra facts in insets; technical language (for example, *coho salmon, zooplankton, copepods*) and many names of animals; many complex sentences; clear, understandable style.

Level X

Characteristics

Books at level X include science fiction that incorporates technical knowledge as well as high fantasy depicting quests and the struggle between good and evil. Readers are required to go beyond the literal meaning

about Gram. There would be some surprises for everyone, Dicey guessed. She knew Gram had already been surprised: at Dicey's reaction when her sailboat—the one she had hoped over and dreamed over—sank into the shallow water by Gram's dock. Even James was surprised by how calm she stayed, maybe because he had seen Dicey's face as they hauled it down the quarter-mile path through the marsh, seen her strain and pull and check to be sure the wheels they'd removed from a wagon and fixed to the legs of the sawhorse cradle didn't fall off, seen how much it mattered to her.

Dicey had watched the water pouring in through the leaks where the boards had shrunk apart with all those years of drying out. She had watched—they had all stood and watched, as the little boat filled up with water and settled quietly down onto the sandy bottom of the Chesapeake Bay.

"I should have remembered," Gram had said. "I knew, if only I remembered."

"You can't sail in that," Sammy declared.

Dicey had stared down at the chipped paint on the gunwales of the boat, which still showed above the water. The boat was her lucky charm, her rabbit's foot, her horseshoe, her pot of gold, it was the prize she'd set for herself for leading them from nowhere to somewhere. OK, she said to herself, thinking about what needed to be done. They'd have to bail it out before they could get it out of the water. They'd have to take it back to the barn. She told James to find something to bail with. They'd have to slide the cradle back into the water, it would probably take all four children to do that.

"You don't rest a minute, do you," Gram had said. Dicey shook her head; she had already gotten used to her grandmother's way of asking questions without question marks. "But you'd do better to let it sit out here a day or so," Gram had advised. "Let the wood soak up water, to swell up again. I knew that once, but I forgot. I'm sorry, girl," she said.

Dicey hadn't answered, just looked at Gram where she stood on the dock with the wind blowing her curly gray hair around her face.

"Dicey doesn't mind, as long as she knows what to do about things," Maybeth told Gram.

"Is that right," Gram asked Dicey.

"I guess so," Dicey said.

"What do you do when there's nothing you *can* do," Gram said.

"I dunno, I do something else," Dicey said.

"That doesn't make sense," James pointed out. "That's illogical."

Gram looked around at all of them.

"Which one of your sons built this boat?" Dicey asked, but Gram had turned away to go back to the house and didn't answer.

Remembering that scene, Dicey reminded herself that they all had a lot of learning to do. The boat was back in the barn and she had to begin scraping off the old layers of paint. But not quite yet. Gram and James would be back soon, and they'd have lunch, and then Dicey wanted to go downtown to see about a job. She'd been thinking about what kind of job she could get, all those long first three days of school. There wasn't much else to think about in school. As far as she was concerned, about all school was good for was using up your days. Dicey hadn't talked to anyone, except to answer teachers' questions. That was OK with her, because she had important things to think about. Getting a job, to bring in some money was one. Tillermans always needed more money, because there were so many of them to feed. Dicey knew Gram worried about that. For that matter, Dicey worried about that too, and had worried all her life, because at thirteen, she was the oldest. That worry about food had been her single biggest worry all summer long, when they had traveled down here, after Momma disappeared. The other worries—about what James was thinking, because what James thought in his head told him what to do; about whether or not Maybeth was retarded as people claimed, or only shy, slow, and frightened, which was what Dicey thought; about why Sammy was so angry he hit out and didn't mind how much the person he fought with hurt him;—those worries, and worries about how

2   3

Figure 8–7. Dicey's Song, *Level W*

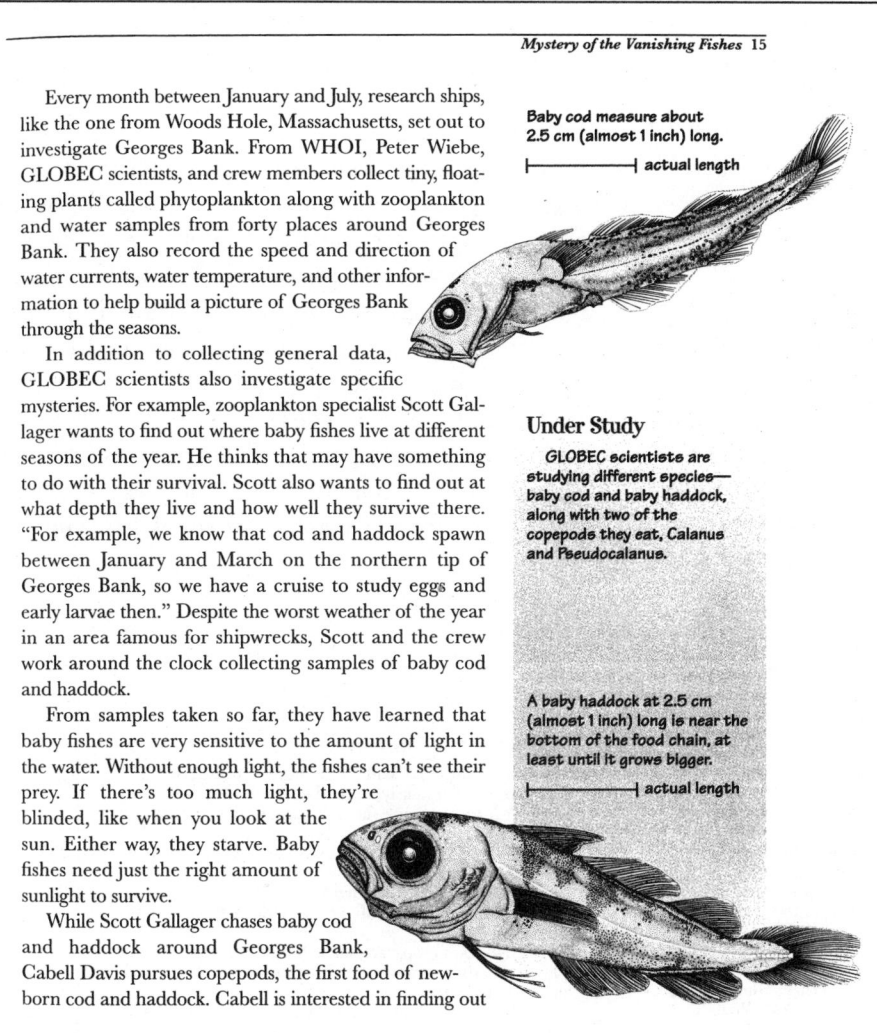

Every month between January and July, research ships, like the one from Woods Hole, Massachusetts, set out to investigate Georges Bank. From WHOI, Peter Wiebe, GLOBEC scientists, and crew members collect tiny, floating plants called phytoplankton along with zooplankton and water samples from forty places around Georges Bank. They also record the speed and direction of water currents, water temperature, and other information to help build a picture of Georges Bank through the seasons.

In addition to collecting general data, GLOBEC scientists also investigate specific mysteries. For example, zooplankton specialist Scott Gallager wants to find out where baby fishes live at different seasons of the year. He thinks that may have something to do with their survival. Scott also wants to find out at what depth they live and how well they survive there. "For example, we know that cod and haddock spawn between January and March on the northern tip of Georges Bank, so we have a cruise to study eggs and early larvae then." Despite the worst weather of the year in an area famous for shipwrecks, Scott and the crew work around the clock collecting samples of baby cod and haddock.

From samples taken so far, they have learned that baby fishes are very sensitive to the amount of light in the water. Without enough light, the fishes can't see their prey. If there's too much light, they're blinded, like when you look at the sun. Either way, they starve. Baby fishes need just the right amount of sunlight to survive.

While Scott Gallager chases baby cod and haddock around Georges Bank, Cabell Davis pursues copepods, the first food of newborn cod and haddock. Cabell is interested in finding out

Mystery of the Vanishing Fishes 15

Baby cod measure about 2.5 cm (almost 1 inch) long.

├───────────┤ actual length

Under Study

GLOBEC scientists are studying different species— baby cod and baby haddock, along with two of the copepods they eat, Calanus and Pseudocalanus.

A baby haddock at 2.5 cm (almost 1 inch) long is near the bottom of the food chain, at least until it grows bigger.

├───────────┤ actual length

Figure 8–8. Ocean Detectives: Solving the Mysteries of the Sea, *Level W*

of the text to construct implied meaning by a writer's use of symbolism. There is a continuing increase in the sophistication of vocabulary, language, and topic.

Examples

WHERE THE RED FERN GROWS (SEE FIGURE 8–9)
Realistic fiction about a boy and his dog centering on themes of family relationships, hunting, death; 261 pages (twenty chapters of varying lengths); story told in flashback; has the quality of a memoir; poetic language and description; shows setting that will be unfamiliar for most students; mystical quality; ideas implied rather

than told.

HARRIET BEECHER STOWE AND THE BEECHER PREACHERS (SEE FIGURE 8–10)
Informational text/biography; 131 pages (nine chapters, twelve to fourteen pages per chapter); family tree; afterword, author's notes, bibliography, index; well researched; no dialogue but slightly fictionalized for interest; many facts and historical characters; black-and-white portraits and photographs; many quotes from the subject; sophisticated and scholarly language.

Level Y

Characteristics
Books categorized as level Y present subtle themes and complex plots. As with earlier levels, they include a whole range of social problems as themes, but more explicit details (for example, about death or prejudice) are provided. Texts also include irony and satire, literary devices that require readers to think beyond the literal meaning of the text. Books at level Y include many more complex works of fantasy that depict hero figures and heroic journeys. Readers are required to discern underlying lessons and also to analyze texts for traditional elements.

Examples

THE GIVER (SEE FIGURE 8–11)
Fantasy/science fiction about a future world; 180 pages (twenty-three chapters, most six to eight pages); small

font; some words used in new ways, which reader must infer; requires reader to relate strange new society to present one; generic words like *dwelling* in relation to the new society require reader to infer what led to structuring the society; many layers of meaning; uncertain ending.

Anne Frank: The Diary of a Young Girl
(see Figure 8–12)

Informational text/diary (Anne's reflections presented chronologically in the order in which she wrote them); 283 pages (no chapters, entries vary in length); small font; sample of Anne's handwriting, diagram of room, and cover and frontispiece pictures; requires background knowledge of historical events and social issues; requires interpreting events from diary entries; no dialogue; fast-moving; short and long sentences; some fragments.

Level Z

Characteristics

Informational books deal with controversial social concepts and political issues and include detailed historical accounts of periods that are less well known generally. They also provide a great deal of technical information; readers learn new ways of finding technical information and encounter complex examples of the basic organizational structures for informational texts. Fiction texts explore a wide range of mature themes relative to the human condition. High fantasy presents heroic quests, symbolism, and complex characters. Some texts provide graphic details of hardship and violence.

---

158   WHERE THE RED FERN GROWS

"Yes, they followed me," I said. "They're outside."

"Well, call them in," he said. "I've got something for them."

I called to them. Little Ann came in the store, walking like she was scared. Old Dan came to the door and stopped. I tried to coax him in. It was no use. My dogs, never being allowed in the house, were scared to come in.

Grandpa walked over to a hoop of cheese and cut off two chunks about the size of my fist. He walked to the door, talking to Old Dan. "What's the matter, boy?" he said. "You scared to come in? Well, that shows you're a good dog."

He handed him a piece of the cheese. I heard it rattle in his throat as he gulped it down.

Grandpa came back and set Little Ann up on the counter. He chuckled as he broke the cheese up in small pieces and fed her.

"Yes, sir," he said, "I think we have the best darn coon hounds in these Ozark Mountains, and just as sure as shootin', we're going to win that gold cup."

Grandpa didn't have to say that. The way I was feeling, I already had the cup. All I had to do was go and get it.

Finished with his feeding of Little Ann, Grandpa said, "Now, let's see. The hunt starts on the twenty-third. That's about—well, let's see—this is the seventeenth." Counting on his fingers he finally figured it out. "That's six days from now," he said in a jubilant voice.

I nodded my head.

"We can leave here early on the morning of the twenty-second," he said, "and barring accidents, we should make the campground in plenty of time for the grand opening."

I asked how we were going.

"We'll go in my buggy," he said. "I'll load the tent and everything the night before."

I asked him what he wanted me to bring.

WHERE THE RED FERN GROWS   159

"Nothing," he said, "but these two little hounds, and you be here early; and I believe I'd let these dogs rest, 'cause we want them in tiptop shape when we get there."

I saw the thinking wrinkles bunch up on Grandpa's forehead.

"You reckon your daddy would like to go?" he asked. "As late in the fall as it is, I don't think he's too busy, is he?"

"No, our crops are all gathered," I said. "We've been clearing some of the bottom land, but that's almost done now."

"Well, ask him," he said. "Tell him I'd like to have him go."

"I'll ask him," I said, "but you know how Papa is. The farm comes first with him."

"I know," Grandpa said, "but you ask him anyway, and tell him what I said. Now it's getting late and you had better be heading for home."

I was almost to the door when Grandpa said, "Wait a minute."

He walked over behind the candy counter and shook out one of the quarter sacks. He filled it up to the brim, bounced it on the counter a few times, and dropped in a few more gumdrops.

With a twinkle in his eye, and a smile on his face, he handed it to me saying, "Save some for your sisters."

I was so choked up I couldn't say anything. I took it and flew out the door, calling to my dogs.

On my way home I didn't walk on the ground. I was way up in the clouds just skipping along. With a song, I told the sycamore trees and the popeyed gray squirrels how happy I was.

Little Ann sensed my happiness. She pranced along on the trail. With a doggish grin on her face, she begged for a piece of candy, which I so gladly gave.

Even Old Dan felt the pleasant atmosphere. His long red tail fanned the air. Once he raised his head and bawled. I stood still and listened to the droning

Figure 8–9. Where the Red Fern Grows, *Level X*

Isabella Beecher Hooker

CHAPTER FIVE

The argument in Washington was—as always, it seemed—between the North and the South. California wanted to come into the Union as a free state, but Southerners insisted that another free state would make the North even more powerful than it already was. And they'd had enough of the North trying to control them, acting self-righteous, flooding them with hateful antislavery propaganda. If California became a free state, some of the Southern states threatened to secede, to leave the Union. Three of the country's greatest political statesmen were leading the debate: John C. Calhoun for the South, Daniel Webster of Massachusetts for the North, and Henry Clay, senator from Kentucky—called the Great Compromiser, because twice before he had saved the Union when it seemed on the brink of breaking up. All three men were famous orators. All three were at the end of their careers and making their last passionate plea for what they believed.

Calhoun maintained that secession could be avoided only if the South had equal rights in new territories and if the North was legally restrained from meddling in the question of slavery. Henry Clay proposed various concessions to the South, but the one to which the North objected most strenuously was

in June, but Harriet went ahead. In the spring of 1850 she took three of her children with her (Hattie, fourteen years old; Fred, ten; and Georgiana, seven) and left the other two (Eliza, fourteen, and Henry, twelve) with Calvin. She wanted to make the trip and get settled in Maine before July, when another baby was due.

Although Harriet didn't realize it, her future was being decided at that very moment—not in Brunswick or in Cincinnati but in Washington, D.C., where something called the Fugitive Slave Law was being debated.

Figure 8–10. Harriet Beecher Stowe and the Beecher Preachers, *Level X*

Examples

THE HERO AND THE CROWN (*SEE FIGURE 8–13*)
Sophisticated fantasy; 246 pages (25 chapters, most nine to twelve pages each.) Extensive detail; long complex sentence structure; very challenging vocabulary; flashbacks and dream sequences; mature themes around a strong heroine who battles dragons, pain, and rejection.

WE SHALL NOT BE MOVED: THE WOMEN'S FACTORY STRIKE OF 1909 (*SEE FIGURE 8–14*)
Informational text/history; 165 pages (eleven chapters, most twelve to fourteen pages); epilogue, bibliography, index; describes New York setting at the time; requires understanding of social issues not usually familiar to students; no dialogue; not fictionalized; well researched; black-and-white photographs with legends; detailed accounts.

TO BE A SLAVE
Informational text/history (quotes or "stories" from former slaves organized into categories such as resistance to slavery and emancipation); 160 pages (seven chapters of varying lengths); epilogue, foreword, and prologue; many archaic words; author commentary in italics; dialect represented; requires readers to build meaning from short pieces of information; voice of storytellers evident.

Then all of the citizens had been ordered to go into the nearest building and stay there. IMMEDIATELY, the rasping voice through the speakers had said. LEAVE YOUR BICYCLES WHERE THEY ARE.

Instantly, obediently, Jonas had dropped his bike on its side on the path behind his family's dwelling. He had run indoors and stayed there, alone. His parents were both at work, and his little sister, Lily, was at the Childcare Center where she spent her after-school hours.

Looking through the front window, he had seen no people: none of the busy afternoon crew of Street Cleaners, Landscape Workers, and Food Delivery people who usually populated the community at that time of day. He saw only the abandoned bikes here and there on their sides; an upturned wheel on one was still revolving slowly.

He had been frightened then. The sense of his own community silent, waiting, had made his stomach churn. He had trembled.

But it had been nothing. Within minutes the speakers had crackled again, and the voice, reassuring now and less urgent, had explained that a Pilot-in-Training had misread his navigational instructions and made a wrong turn. Desperately the Pilot had been trying to make his way back before his error was noticed.

NEEDLESS TO SAY, HE WILL BE RELEASED, the voice had said, followed by silence. There was an ironic tone to that final message, as if the Speaker found it amusing; and Jonas had smiled a little, though he knew what a grim statement it had been. For a contributing citizen to be released from the community was a final decision, a terrible punishment, an overwhelming statement of failure.

2

Even the children were scolded if they used the term lightly at play, jeering at a teammate who missed a catch or stumbled in a race. Jonas had done it once, had shouted at his best friend, "That's it, Asher! You're released!" when Asher's clumsy error had lost a match for his team. He had been taken aside for a brief and serious talk by the coach, had hung his head with guilt and embarrassment, and apologized to Asher after the game.

Now, thinking about the feeling of fear as he pedaled home along the river path, he remembered that moment of palpable, stomach-sinking terror when the aircraft had streaked above. It was not what he was feeling now with December approaching. He searched for the right word to describe his own feeling.

Jonas was careful about language. Not like his friend, Asher, who talked too fast and mixed things up, scrambling words and phrases until they were barely recognizable and often very funny.

Jonas grinned, remembering the morning that Asher had dashed into the classroom, late as usual, arriving breathlessly in the middle of the chanting of the morning anthem. When the class took their seats at the conclusion of the patriotic hymn, Asher remained standing to make his public apology as was required.

"I apologize for inconveniencing my learning community." Asher ran through the standard apology phrase rapidly, still catching his breath. The Instructor and class waited patiently for his explanation. The students had all been grinning, because they had listened to Asher's explanations so many times before.

"I left home at the correct time but when I was riding

3

Figure 8–11. The Giver, *Level Y*

Summary

Books at the upper end of the continuum call for readers to use extensive background knowledge and varied strategies to process information presented in a variety of ways. Readers at these levels become truly advanced as their processing systems adjust to a broad range of genres.

These complex texts can be read at several levels of understanding. Upper elementary students may read and enjoy them and derive rich understanding, yet miss some of the more obscure and symbolic meaning. Many adult readers will enjoy, learn from, and even be challenged by books at these levels.

Suggestions for Professional Development

Continue exploring leveled texts with colleagues in your school. Again, we encourage working in cross-grade-level groups. Use the collection of books at levels J through X that you gathered for your Chapter 5 professional development discussions. This time, focus on levels T, U, V, W, and X, and add titles at levels Y and Z. You will need at least three titles per level. Try to include one nonfiction book for each level.

1. Before the meeting, divide your group into pairs and assign a level or levels to each pair. Distribute the books you have collected and ask the group members

254   ANNE FRANK

Friday, 30 June, 1944

Dear Kitty,

Bad weather, or *bad weather at a stretch to the thirtieth of June*.[1] Isn't that well said! Oh yes, I have a smattering of English already; just to show that I can, I'm reading *An Ideal Husband* with the aid of a dictionary. War going wonderfully! Bobroisk, Mogilef, and Orsa have fallen, lots of prisoners.

Everything's all right here and tempers are improving. The superoptimists are triumphing. Elli has changed her hair style, Miep has the week off. That's the latest news.

Yours, Anne

Thursday, 6 July, 1944

Dear Kitty,

It strikes fear to my heart when Peter talks of later being a criminal, or of gambling; although it's meant as a joke, of course, it gives me the feeling that he's afraid of his own weakness. Again and again I hear from both Margot and Peter: "Yes, if I was as strong and plucky as you are, if I always stuck to what I wanted, if I had such persistent energy, yes then . . . !"

I wonder if it's really a good quality not to let myself be influenced. Is it really good to follow almost entirely my own conscience?

Quite honestly, I can't imagine how anyone can say: "I'm weak," and then remain so. After all, if you know it, why not fight against it, why not try to train your character? The answer was: "Because it's so much easier not to!" This

[1] In English in the original.

THE DIARY OF A YOUNG GIRL   255

reply rather discouraged me. Easy? Does that mean that a lazy, deceitful life is an easy life? Oh no, that can't be true, it mustn't be true, people can so easily be tempted by slackness . . . and by money.

I thought for a long time about the best answer to give Peter, how to get him to believe in himself and, above all, to try and improve himself; I don't know whether my line of thought is right though, or not.

I've so often thought how lovely it would be to have someone's complete confidence, but now, now that I'm that far, I realize how difficult it is to think what the other person is thinking and then to find the *right* answer. More especially because the very ideas of "easy" and "money" are something entirely foreign and new to me. Peter's beginning to lean on me a bit and that mustn't happen under any circumstances. A type like Peter finds it difficult to stand on his own feet, but it's even harder to stand on your own feet as a conscious, living being. Because if you do, then it's twice as difficult to steer a right path through the sea of problems and still remain constant through it all. I'm just drifting around, have been searching for days, searching for a good argument against that terrible word "easy," something to settle it once and for all.

How can I make it clear to him that what appears easy and attractive will drag him down into the depths, depths where there is no comfort to be found, no friends and no beauty, depths from which it is almost impossible to raise oneself?

We all live, but we don't know the why or the wherefore. We all live with the object of being happy; our lives are all different and yet the same. We three have been brought up in good circles, we have the chance to learn, the possibility of attaining something, we have all reason to hope for much happiness, but . . . we must earn it for ourselves. And that is never easy. You must work and do good, not be lazy and gamble, if you wish to earn happi-

Figure 8–12.   Anne Frank: The Diary of a Young Girl, *Level Y*

to read the texts they have been given. (If you have a very small group, have the whole group do one level at a time and use only two titles at each level.)

2. Have each group create a list: *What does this text call for readers to do?* If you used the professional development suggestions at the end of Chapters 4 and 5, you have analyzed texts and also become familiar with the kinds of changes in text demands along the gradient. Now, simply brainstorm a list of demands, looking at the books you have read.

3. Make a grid on which to organize the text demands you list (see the example in Figure 8–15), and check whether the statement is characteristic of each of the books at the level. This grid will take a fair amount

of time to produce—forty-five minutes to an hour.

4. Bring the entire group together and compare the grids. Ask:
   - What variety is there *within* levels in what texts call on readers to do?
   - What variety is there *across* levels in what texts call on readers to do?
   - What significant changes do you notice from level T through level Z? If you like, you can record these statements on a chart with two columns, one labeled *From* and the other labeled *To*.

5. Complete the discussion by asking the group to make some concluding statements about texts at levels T through Z.

shadows of the trees lying across the horses' flanks and the men's faces.

Hornmar emerged round the looming bulk of the castle, leading Kethtaz, who tiptoed delicately, ears hard forward and tail high. Hornmar saw her and wordlessly brought Kethtaz to her, and gave his bridle into her hand. The first sola's equerry waited impassively, holding Dgeth. Hornmar turned away to mount his own horse, for he was riding with the army; but meanwhile he was giving the king's daughter the honor of holding the king's stirrup. This was not a small thing: holding the king's stirrup conferred luck upon the holder, and often in times past the queen had demanded the honor herself. But often too the king ordered one who was considered lucky—a victorious general, or a first son, or even a first sola—to hold his stirrup for him, especially when the king rode to war, or to a tricky diplomatic campaign that might suddenly turn to war.

No one said anything, but Aerin could feel a mental chill pass across the courtyard as some of the mounted men wondered if the witchwoman's daughter began their mission with a bad omen, and she wondered if Hornmar had done her a favor. If the army rode out expecting the worst, they were likely to find it.

Aerin held Kethtaz's reins grimly, but Kethtaz did not like grimness, and prodded her with his nose till she smiled involuntarily and petted him. She looked up when she heard the king's footsteps, and when she met her father's eyes she was glad she had yielded to Tor's request. Arlbeth kissed her forehead, and cupped her chin in his hands, and looked at her for a long moment; then he turned to Kethtaz, and Aerin grasped the stirrup and turned it for Arlbeth's foot.

At that moment there was a small commotion at the courtyard gate, and a man on a tired horse stepped onto the glassy stone. The horse stopped, swaying on wide-spaced legs, for it was too weary to walk trustingly on the smooth surface; and the man dismounted and dropped the reins, and ran to where the king stood. Arlbeth turned, his hand still on Aerin's shoulder, as the man came up to them.

110

"Majesty," he said.

Arlbeth inclined his head as if he were in his great hall and this man only the first of a long morning's suppliants. "Majesty," the man said again, as if he could not remember his message, or dared not give it. The man's gaze flicked to Aerin's face as she stood, her hand still holding the stirrup for mounting, and she was startled to see the gleam of hope in the man's eyes as he looked at her.

"The Black Dragon has come," he said at last. "Maur, who has not been seen for generations, the last of the great dragons, great as a mountain. Maur has awakened."

Sweat ran down the man's face, and his horse gave a gasping shuddering breath that meant its wind was broken, so hard had it been ridden. "I beg you for . . . help. My village even now may be no more. Other villages will soon follow." The man's voice rose in panic. "In a year—in a season Damar may all be black with the dragon's breath."

"This is mischief from across the Border," Tor said, and Arlbeth nodded. There was silence for a long, sad, grim moment, and when Arlbeth spoke again, his voice was heavy. "As Tor says, the Black Dragon's awakening is mischief, sent us, and sent us crucially at just this moment when we dare not heed it." The messenger's shoulders slumped, and he put his hands over his face.

Arlbeth went on, so quietly that none but Aerin and Tor and the man might hear. "We go now to meet a trouble that may be even deadlier than dragons, for it is human and Damarian and spurred by mischief. Damar may yet face the dragon; a Damar broken to bits would be nothing, even though the dragon lay dead." He turned to Kethtaz again, set his foot in the stirrup, and mounted. Aerin stepped back as Kethtaz pranced, for he cared nothing for dragons and much for bearing the king at the head of a procession.

"We shall return as soon as we may, and go to meet your Black Dragon. Rest, and take a fresh horse, and go back to your village. All those who wish it may come to our City and await us in its shelter." He raised his arm, and his company rustled like leaves, waiting the order to march; and one of the sofor led the messenger's wind-broken horse to one side, and the king's procession passed

111

Figure 8–13. The Hero and the Crown, *Level Z*

102   WE SHALL NOT BE MOVED

bered descriptions of Miss Morgan from the society pages in which she was said to be shy and docile, active in church work. She had been plump as a girl, almost stodgy-looking, with an indecisive mouth. Surely her father was infuriated by the change.

The woman who turned up at Clinton Hall was thirty-seven years old now, no longer plump, certainly far from indecisive. Tall, dark-haired, surrounded by the smoke of her Turkish cigarettes, she moved fast and spoke fast. Her voice was low and slightly hoarse, and everything she said had a directness. She was there to work, she told them. She craved work, was addicted to it. Perhaps she felt guilty for having been born to wealth. Perhaps she was rebelling against her all-powerful father, whose piercing eyes and heavy eyebrows she seemed to have inherited. Yet she said nothing about herself or her father; there was no personal talk at all, just calm and disciplined graciousness. She would start by joining the League's executive board as a provisional member, she would march on a picket line, and after that she would see for herself what needed doing.

Mrs. Belmont inspired awe, but Anne Morgan was almost approachable. She shook hands with everyone, spoke to everyone. And in mid-December she gave a luncheon at the Colony Club —

The certificate that formally created the International Ladies Garment Workers Union.

Figure 8–14. We Shall Not Be Moved: The Women's Factory Strike of 1909; *Level Z*

Comparison of Text Demands for Levels T, U, V, W, X, Y, Z

What does the text call for the reader to do?	1. Level____	2. Level____	3. Level____
1.			
2.			
3.			
4.			
5.			
6.			
7.			
8.			
9.			
10.			
Notes/Questions:			

Figure 8–15. Comparison of Text Demands for Levels T, U, V, W, X, Y, Z

CHAPTER NINE

LEVELED BOOKS FOR GUIDED AND INDEPENDENT READING

Matching books to readers is the foundation for helping students build and expand reading strategies in the upper elementary grades. Often in the past we have tried to match readers to books. We handed "grade level" books to students in a particular grade and demanded they "get through" them, a process that may have been possible but was often tedious and even painful for some. Or we assigned reading and assumed all students could accomplish it with understanding and fluency. Of course, our goal is to raise the reading levels of every student by keeping a close eye on standards; however, we also recognize how reading skills develop. Every day, students must read material that will allow them to use and expand the strategies they currently control. You don't get better by struggling through material you do not understand; you *do* get better by meeting challenges successfully.

There are many ways to think about matching books to readers, and all have value. For example, when selecting books for literature study, we pay careful attention to subject matter, writing style, and language use. We want books that appeal to students and expand their knowledge of a variety of texts. The content and literary quality of books is of primary importance, and the themes and concepts should be appropriate; however, we are not necessarily concerned with students' ability to process them independently. We may make these books available by reading them aloud or providing them on tape; the goal is for the students to comprehend the language and ideas and to discuss the books with others.

When selecting books for independent and guided reading, we also consider content, themes, and ideas, but we add another requirement. The book must be matched to the readers' current strengths. Successful independent reading means that the individual can process the text with ease, fluency, and understanding using his or her current strategies and skills. Successful performance in guided reading means that, *with teaching and support,* the student can read the text at the level with ease, fluency, and understanding, expanding his current strategies in the process. To match books to readers we need to analyze the supports and demands of texts carefully in relation to what we know about individual readers.

Using the Gradient to Match Books to Readers

A gradient of text is an invaluable tool in supporting reading instruction. In Chapter 2, we defined a gradient of text as a varied collection organized into approximate levels of difficulty. Texts that demand more in terms of concept, theme, vocabulary, length, and so on, are more difficult. When texts are placed along a continuum from easier to harder, we can cluster them into categories, or "levels." We level texts by analyzing a complex range of characteristics, and we test and retest the level designations as we use the texts with students, a process that results in a highly reliable gradient.

On our gradient, level A texts are the easiest. Look at the two pages from a level A book shown in Figure 9–1. The picture provides all the information needed for the reader to process the print. The text says "Dad is reading," and there is a full-page photo of a man reading. This level of text would not normally be used in the intermediate grades, but it illustrates the bottom of the continuum. Compare it with the level K texts in Chapter 6, the level N texts in Chapter 7, and the level Y and Z texts in Chapter 8, and you get an idea of how a reading process develops over time.

Within a level, there are a large number of titles and these texts are not identical; they vary widely and offer different kinds of challenges. One text may pose a particular kind of challenge; another will make different demands. Fiction and nonfiction texts, and all the genres within those categories, are included. By and large, however, most of the books categorized in a level are accessible to the reader who can successfully read one or two of them.

The Leveled Collection as a Dynamic Tool

You may start with a basic collection, perhaps using the lists in this book; but you can add titles to the collection by engaging in the leveling process yourself. Teachers constantly monitor students' reading to determine their interests and needs. A classroom teacher evaluating her leveled book collection asks:

- At which levels do I need more titles? (Consider the grade level, the specific reading levels of your students, and the progress students make during the year.)
- Do I need more variety in the titles within levels? (Consider genres, your students' reading background or lack of it, their interests, and particular students who may need to read more titles on a level in order to gain the "mileage" they need.)
- Are there some texts that should be removed from my collection? (Consider quality, appeal to students.)
- Which texts do I need multiple copies of for guided reading? (Consider quality, the supports and challenges in texts as matched to your learners, and the

opportunities for learning texts provide.)
- Which texts do I need one copy (or two or three copies) of in my classroom library for independent reading? (Consider quality, students' interests, and accessibility or manageability.)

The texts you use for independent and guided reading are not separate and discrete collections; they will overlap, but you need to decide how you will allocate these resources.

What the Gradient Is—And Is Not (See Figure 9–2)

The gradient is neither a precise sequence of texts that everyone must read nor a reading "program." Gradient levels are not intended to function as "labels" for individual readers. In fact, classroom collections are to be organized around topics, themes, genres, and authors rather than by levels (see Chapter 1). The text gradient is designed to be a flexible tool to help the teacher choose texts for reading instruction. While in general all students read books at most levels, it should be clear that:

- They are not expected to read *every* book on a level.
- There is no "order" to the books at any given level.
- Students making fast progress will skip levels.
- You can always move up or down the gradient as you see the need for easier or more challenging texts for your students.
- For independent reading, students do not choose from books organized into levels.

Dad is reading.

14

Figure 9–1. Dad, *Level A*

What the Text Gradient Is and Is Not	
The gradient is ...	**The gradient is not ...**
❖ A tool for matching books to readers	❖ A "reading program"
❖ A guide for making decisions	❖ A set of books that every student must read
❖ A flexible system is always considered in relation to readers' abilities and experience	❖ A rigid sequence that defines reading progress
❖ A support for teachers as they work with children	❖ A way of labeling readers

Figure 9–2. What the Text Gradient Is and Is Not

In other words, the gradient is a tool for the teacher, not the student. It helps the teacher select better texts to support improved reading achievement. While it can be used effectively to document progress, the gradient is not the sole definition of achievement in reading. Teachers look closely at oral reading behaviors as well as at how students talk and write about their reading in relation to the gradient. It is the combination of the range of observations about reading that inform and define an individual's continued progress.

The Gradient in Relation to Processing Text

When we discuss matching books to readers, we sometimes use terms like *easy, just right,* and *difficult* or *challenging.* The question is always whether the text is appropriate for individual readers, so these designations are relative and vary with the level of teacher support required.

An "easy" text is one that the reader can independently process with accuracy and fluency, with appropriate phrasing, and excellent understanding. Reading easy texts is effortless; word solving requires very little attention. As adults, most texts are easy for us, and we enjoy reading them for relaxation and escape. The same is true for your students; those who like to read will select a range of texts from easy to harder, depending on their purposes for reading. It is beneficial for your students to read easy texts once in a while, because they will build fluency and increase their enjoyment.

Reading a "difficult" text is quite different from reading an easy text. Here the reader is forced to attend very closely to the print and to employ a range of word-solving strategies. The reader may have to untangle sentence structure that is unfamiliar or difficult or

may reread to capture nuances of plot or follow the organizational patterns. If the concepts are quite challenging, the reader may have to seek additional information by consulting references or asking someone for help. If the text is too hard, the process begins to break down. The reading is slow, choppy, word by word. Readers become frustrated and cease to enjoy the process. Those who read difficult texts day after day embed ineffective strategies into the routine they habitually bring to reading. They *expect* reading to be slow and tedious. They *expect* not to understand most or all of what they read.

A "just right" text for a particular individual is one that provides a context for building a more effective reading process. The just-right text provides a small amount of challenge so that the readers will engage in some kind of problem solving while reading, thus expanding their ability. Selecting the right texts for readers depends not only on their current development but on the level of instructional support you plan to give them.

Using the Gradient to Support Guided Reading

A "just right" text for guided reading is one that readers can process successfully *with teacher support.* An "easy" text is one that students can read effortlessly. Easy texts would not normally be selected for guided reading except when you decide to work intensively on fluency and phrasing. A "difficult" text would not be selected for guided reading either, because students would not be able to use their strategies effectively *even with teacher support.*

By using the gradient, you can identify a collection of books that is within the range of the students in your class; within that range, there will be one or two levels of texts within each student's control that if he reads them with the support of your teaching, he will strengthen his processing strategies. From the collection of books at those levels, you select texts for each student that will offer learning opportunities.

It is essential for students to read successfully, and that can of course be achieved with easy books; but fueling reading power requires successful problem solving. Your students need to learn how to read a wide range of books with different organizational patterns, writing styles, topics, and themes. They need to practice successful processing in all the genres, and they need to apply strategies effectively to increasingly difficult levels of texts. When you guide the reading process, the child learns effective strategies that influence her success in independent reading.

The Guided Reading Lesson

Your support and teaching takes place in all the elements of the lesson. Let's look at how each guided reading lesson element supports the reader's development.

TEXT INTRODUCTION

The introduction is how you prepare readers for the way the text "works"—that is, you talk about how it is organized and provide important background information they will need in order to understand it. In the introduction, you may casually introduce vocabulary or unusual language structures. You might point out a few words or something unusual or new in the way the print is laid out. You leave work for readers to do but provide just enough support to enable them to take on a more difficult text than they can read on their own. Through the introduction, you mediate the difficulty of the text. For a very challenging text for a particular group of students, you may provide a very rich introduction; for one that is almost within a group's independent reading power, your introduction can be very brief and "lean."

An example of a supportive introduction is shown in Figure 9–3. (This level Q biography was discussed in Chapter 4 in connection with text characteristic analysis.)

In this introduction the teacher introduces the title, setting, and genre and also provides the background information students need to be aware of George Washington Carver's significance as a historical figure and the context in which he lived. She probes students' knowledge and adds to it; she also makes connections to what they have learned about how words work. As we found in Chapter 4, the book has quite a few technical words; this teacher knows that calling attention to word roots and endings will remind her students to use what they know to figure out these words. She also recognizes the connections students have been making to other texts of the same genre and invites them to raise questions and make comments. She encourages them to respond personally to the text as well as to make some inferences. Finally, she points out an important feature of the text—the note from the author—and asks them to read the first two chapters and write about what they've read. Students begin reading with a clear idea of what this text will be about, how it will be organized, the kinds of words they are likely to meet, and what they are expected to do.

READING THE TEXT

Most of the time, your students are processing the text silently while you confer with other readers or meet with another group. We suggest that they remain together at the table because they tend to stay more focused. As students read, you occasionally ask some of them to read aloud softly so you can observe their behavior. Sampling their reading like this gives you a good idea of how well you "matched" the text to the readers and how effective your introduction was in mediating the text for them. You may also talk briefly with students, providing extra support or prompting them to use effective strategies you've already taught them. If you have to do too much "telling," either the text was too hard or your introduction was too scanty.

AFTER READING THE TEXT

After reading, you discuss the meaning of the text with the students; you have the opportunity to clear up misconceptions and encourage students to think more deeply about their reading by providing evidence for their thinking. If students are reading longer chapter books over several days, this ongoing discussion serves as a support for their continued reading. You also teach

Introduction to *A Pocketful of Goobers:*
A Story about George Washington Carver

❖ **Introduces the title, setting, and genre.**

❖ **Establishes significance of subject.**

TEACHER: We are going to read a true story called *A Pocketful of Goobers*. It's about a very important man named George Washington Carver. George's story is important because it changed farming in this country. Here he is on the cover.

JANINE: He's on a farm and he's showing people something.

❖ **Probes student knowledge.**

TEACHER: Does anyone know what goobers are?

SEVERAL STUDENTS: No.

❖ **Provides information.**

❖ **Defines new vocabulary.**

TEACHER: Goobers are peanuts. Sometimes they're called goober peas. Peanuts look a little bit like peas, don't they? And they grow like peas in little pods. Look at the picture of page 38.

EVAN: It looks like peas.

TEACHER: Yes, they're goobers. Many of the slaves from Africa lived off peanuts and they called them by their African name: Goobers.

JANINE: That's the title, *Pocketful of Goobers*.

❖ **Probes students' knowledge.**

TEACHER: Yes, like in the title. George Washington Carver taught people how to farm better, especially how to grow peanuts. He found over 300 ways to use peanuts. Can you think of some?

CHILDREN: "peanut butter," peanuts, peanut candy.

❖ **Calls students' attention to word parts.**

❖ **Connects to word study.**

TEACHER: Well, George found that peanuts are very good for you. They have nutritional value. They have a lot of vitamins; they have carbohydrates.

Here's *nutrition*, and *nutritional*. Do you see the *-al* ending that we've studied before?

[Writes *nutrition* and *nutritional* on the white board.]

Children read.

❖ **Provides more information.**

❖ **Uses vocabulary in conversation.**

TEACHER: You can make a lot of things out of the peanut. It has peanut oil in it, and you can use that to cook, to make margarine, even makeup, or cosmetics. It even gives us something that is just like milk and is nutritious.

[writes *nutritious* on the white board.]

❖ **Calls students' attention to word parts.**

❖ **Connects to word study.**

TEACHER: There's the *-tious* ending. Before George's work in agriculture, some people ate peanuts but they really didn't have all those products made from peanuts. Since George found so many ways to use them, then people in the South part of the U.S., especially African American people, were able to grow peanuts as crop. So, they had a better life.

Figure 9–3. Introduction to A Pocketful of Goobers

Introduction to *A Pocketful of Goobers:*
A Story about George Washington Carver (continued)

❖ **Reminds students of genre name and characteristics.**

TEACHER: This book is about George's life. It's called a …

EVAN: Autobiography. No, biography.

TEACHER: Well, both of those are stories about people's lives, but there's one big difference. In an autobiography, the person writes the story about his or her own life. In a biography, somebody else writes the story about the person. Which one do you think this is?

ALL STUDENTS: It's a biography.

TEACHER: Yes, this is a biography because somebody else, Barbara Mitchell, wrote it about George Washington Carver.

ANDREW: I've read a biography about Abraham Lincoln before. It was good.

JANINE: I've read one on Helen Keller and Louisa May Alcott.

❖ **Recognizes connections students are making; provides summary of the text.**

TEACHER: That's great. I bet you learned a lot about those people. George was an African-American boy who was born to a slave woman. His mother was killed, but someone else raised George. He was very smart; he found a way to go to school and study agriculture. That's how he learned how to be a scientist and help people with their farming.

❖ **Pauses, conversationally, to invite student comment.**

EVAN: Didn't this happen a long time ago?

JANINE: It must have, because his mother was a slave, remember?

❖ **Responds to student questions, encouraging more.**

TEACHER: Yes. George was born just when slavery was ending, in the 1860's. That was almost a hundred and fifty years ago. He was born in Missouri.

KRISTEN: The South was where all the slaves were.

TEACHER: The South did have the most slaves, but there were slaves all over the country.

ANDREW: They ended it with the Civil War.

❖ **Elaborates information about the context.**

❖ **Probes for personal response.**

TEACHER: That's right Andrew. After the war, slavery was abolished, but many black people were still treated unfairly. When you read, you'll see that even though George wasn't a slave, he still wasn't always treated well, and he still didn't have all the rights that white people had. Do you think this made it hard for him to go to school and to get a good job?

EVAN: Yeah. He couldn't go to lots of schools.

KRISTEN: And I bet people always teased him and stuff and called him mean names.

TEACHER: That was hard, but he never gave up.

❖ **Prompts for inference.**

TEACHER: It was important for George Washington Carver to help people farm better.

JANINE: Because back then that's the way everybody got their food. There weren't all the grocery stores like we have.

EVAN: It was how people made their money, by selling their crops.

KRISTEN: Yeah, Like on Little House on the Prairie; when the crops died, they became poor.

Figure 9–3. Introduction to A Pocketful of Goobers *(continued)*

Introduction to *A Pocketful of Goobers:* *A Story about George Washington Carver* (continued)

❖ **Further defines the focus of the text.**

❖ **Draws attention to text feature.**

TEACHER: In this book you're going to learn more about George's childhood and school. There is an important note from the author at the beginning of the book that gives you some background information. Be sure to read that carefully.

❖ **Provides direction to readers.**

Read the first two chapters, up to page 25, and as you finish each chapter, write one or two sentences telling what you think was important about the way George lived his life. Stop after Chapter 2 so we can discuss what you've learned so far.

Figure 9–3.   Introduction to A Pocketful of Goobers *(continued)*

specific processing skills that will help students be more effective readers.

Using the Gradient to Support Assessment

Documenting Change

To document your students' reading development, you may use systematic assessments like those described in *Guiding Readers and Writers, Grades 3–6: Teaching Comprehension, Genre, and Content Literacy* (Fountas and Pinnell 2001), in which students read silently as well as orally and then answer questions and write about the text. This information will allow you to evaluate the student's accuracy, rate, fluency, and comprehension of the text at that level.

The gradient is also a way to document your students' reading progress over time. As they read books in guided reading lessons, you will note how successfully they process them. At regular intervals, you can record students' reading levels (see the example in Figure 9–4). These records can be passed along from year to year in the school or even to other schools in the district.

Look at the record of Catherine's reading progress shown in Figure 9–4. The titles and levels read are listed along the top. (A clear dot on the graph indicates reading above 90 percent accuracy; a filled-in dot means accuracy was below 90 percent.) Catherine began reading at level A in kindergarten and made

quick progress through the primary grades. As she read more sophisticated texts, Catherine also encountered greater variety and read for a longer time within each level. She was assessed reading a variety of fiction and nonfiction texts. In fourth grade, she read at level P for quite a while but then moved rapidly over the next several levels. She finished her elementary years reading at level W. Catherine's reading development was smooth, and each teacher was able to build on her previous success.

Using Benchmark Books

A benchmark book is a reliable exemplar selected for each level on the gradient that you can use to determine a reader's level and to measure progress over time. Chapters 6, 7, and 8 contain examples of prototype fiction and nonfiction for levels J through Z on the gradient.

To create a set of benchmark books, you need to identify some very reliable books at each level of the gradient. After you have used the gradient of text for a while, you will begin to notice that a particular text at a given level is almost always just right for students who are reading well at that level. That text is "stable" in that the results do not vary widely from reading to reading.

After identifying several stable fiction and nonfiction books at each level, try them out with a range of students (not necessarily matched to level). Sample their oral reading, have conversations with them, perhaps ask them to do a little writing about what they've read. Then look at the texts again, asking:

School Record of Book Reading Progress

Student's Name: *Catherine Peters*   **School:** *Brown*

Record book reading progress three or four times per year, as agreed upon with your school faculty. Note dates in bottom row. Put an open circle ○ at the child's instructional level on each date indicated. A filled in circle ● indicates student is having some difficulty at the level. Mark the level ○* if additional teaching is also being provided by specialists. Give the year and descriptions of additional reading services on back.

Teacher	Bishins				Ward				Glazer				Bousquet				Phillips				Melhado			
Book Level	K	K	K	K	1	1	1	1	2	2	2	2	3	3	3	3	4	4	4	4	5	5	5	5
Z (7-8)																								
Y																								
X																								
W (6+)																								O
V																						O	O	
U																								
T (5)																					O			
S																				O				
R																			O					
Q (4)																								
P																●	O	O						
O														O	O									
N (3)												O	O											
M											●													
L										O														
K																								
J (2)								O	O															
I																								
H							O																	
G																								
F						O																		
E																								
D				O	O																			
C (1)		O																						
B																								
A	O																							
Date	10/1	1/5	3/14	6/1	10/2	1/9	3/7	5/30	10/3	1/10	3/3	6/1	10/1	1/6	3/3	5/31	10/6	1/15	3/12	5/28	10/3	1/6	3/20	5/31

Figure 9–4.   Record of Book Reading Progress

Are the results consistent across different readers?

Are these books too difficult for students who are not yet reading at this level?

Are these books quite easy for students who are reading above this level?

Consider factors like accuracy, comprehension, and fluency as you work with the texts. Remember that successful reading means much more than simply reading the right words.

Over time, you will build up a collection of reliable texts that you can use to:

Assess and group students at the beginning of the year (and assess new students whenever they enter your classroom).

Help you make decisions about your reading group configurations.

Systematically document reading progress over time.

It's best to select the set of benchmark books in collaboration with the other teachers in your school or district. When everyone is involved, you are all more committed to using the gradient and better understand the supports and challenges in the texts.

Creating Conference Protocols

After you have selected some benchmark texts, you may want to create conference protocols to systematize your assessment further. A conference protocol is a standardized procedure that may be used with any text to assess what students can read without support (see Figure 9–5).

You first select a text and then provide a very brief introduction—one or two sentences delivered in a standard way. You then ask the student to read the text silently and write a response guided by a prompt. Afterward the student reads the response aloud and discusses it with you on the basis of questions you create. In the example in Figure 9–5, note that some of the questions require the student to go beyond the text (BT) and others ask the reader to provide information from the text (T). Finally you use a typed passage (100 to 200 words) from the silently read text and code the student's reading behaviors (substitutions, insertions, deletions, repeats, and long pauses) as he or she reads

the passage aloud. (A coding system is described on page 490 of *Guiding Readers and Writers, Grades 3–6*.) Also indicate the starting and ending time so that you can calculate the rate (words per minute) for the reading. (A general guide for rate of reading is provided on page 492 of *Guiding Readers and Writers, Grades 3–6*. You can also use the rubric for assessing fluency on page 491.)

Using the Gradient to Group Students

Assessment systems like those described above, in conjunction with your daily observations, provide valuable information for forming groups for guided reading at the start of the school year.

For one thing, you'll have identified the level of text each student can read with instructional support and can form groups based on these levels.

Your assessment may reveal other needs, however. For example, some students may:

Need help in reading the social studies or science textbook.

Be unfamiliar with the structure of a certain genre.

Need more help in summarizing and thinking about texts.

Need to learn how to skim and scan a text.

Need to learn to read more fluently.

Need to read with more expression.

Need to attend to characterization.

Need to recognize aspects of a writer's style.

In this case, you may want to pull together a temporary group of students needing work in the same area, select a text level that is accessible to them all, and focus on that aspect of processing.

Using the Gradient to Support Independent Reading

The terms *easy, just right,* and *challenging* are also used to describe students' independent reading within the reading workshop. *Easy* means the same thing in both guided and independent reading: the individual can read the text without effort and understands it easily. In

CONFERENCE PROTOCOL:
Level N (Non-Fiction)

Frogs by Michael Tyler

Text Introduction

This is a book about frogs. The three sections that you are going to read will tell you about the size, shape, and color of different kinds of frogs. You will also learn about the differences between frogs and toads.

Instructions

Silently read pages 5–15. Be sure to read all of the captions that go with the pictures. After you have finished, write a paragraph comparing frogs and toads. Use information from the book to help you do this. When we meet again, I will ask you to talk with me about what you wrote and to share your thinking about what you read. As we talk about this book, I may also have a few questions to ask you. [When the student returns, have her/him read the response aloud and discuss it. Prompt the child to share his/her thinking further.]

Discussion Questions [Answers]

[Accept reasonable answers that the student accurately supports with evidence from the text.]

T1. How are tree frogs' feet different from those of frogs that live on the ground?
[They have sticky disks on them to help them hold on to trees.]

T2. Tell two things you learned about frogs.
[Frogs have smooth skin, leap, need to live near a source of moisture, vary in size 5/8" – 12", and have eyes and nostrils on top of the head so they can see and breathe while under water, etc.]

BT3. Why is life harder for frogs that live in the desert?
[It is dry in the desert and frogs need moisture to live. They have to dig into the ground to stay moist.]

BT4. What is something that helps frogs to protect themselves in their environment?
[Their colors help them blend into their environment so they will be protected.]

T5. What are two different ways that frogs can swim?
[Frogs can kick with their strong back legs or use dog-paddle style.]

BT6. An animal leaps up next to you. It has smooth skin. It is green in color. Is it a frog or a toad? [It is a frog.]

Figure 9–5.   Conference Protocol: Level N (Nonfiction)

independent reading, *just right* refers to books with only a few challenges that students can read successfully *without teacher support*. The student evaluates the text herself, marking it *just right* on her reading list if the reading was successful and enjoyable and at the same time the text presented something to learn, either about content or about the reading process (see the example in Figure 9–6).

The term *challenging* as used by students to evaluate their independent reading does not mean the same as *difficult*. Students may select a text for independent reading that is just beyond their present reading level but be so motivated to read it that they persist. They do not struggle over every word but may have to reread some of the material, do some research, or ask for some help; nevertheless, the reading is successful. Of course not every text on a student's reading list should be labeled with a C, but an occasional bout with a challenging book is a good experience.

We do not recommend organizing students' independent reading around leveled texts; it's more important for your students to learn to use a range of criteria for selecting books for themselves. You don't want them to see themselves as limited to a level. Of course, they do have to consider the difficulty of a text. You'll want them to read *just right* books most of the time, *easy* books some of the time, and occasionally tackle a *challenging* text. You'll want them to vary the genre and range of authors.

Sam's reading list in his response journal (Figure 9–6) shows all the books he's read so far this year. He has designated each book as E (easy), JR (just right), or

Reading List

Select a book to read. Enter the title and author on your reading list. When you have completed it, write the genre, and the date. If you abandoned it, write an (A) and the date you abandoned it in the date column. Note whether the book was easy (E), just right (JR) or a challenging (C) book for you.

#	Title	Author	Genre	Date Completed	E JR, C
1	Arthur and the lost Diary	Marc Brown	F	9/19	E
2	On the Field with Derek Jeter	Matt Christopher	RF	9/21	JR
3	Jordans Lucky Day	Jenny Giles	RF	9/29	JR
4	Sideways Stories from wayside school	Louis Sachar	RF	10/3	C
5	Horable Harry and His Secret	Suzy Kline	RF	10/11	Jr
6	Song and Dance man	Karen Ackerman	RF	10/11	JR
7	Tar Beach	Faith Ringgold	RF	10/14	C
8	Unicorns Dont Give Sleigh Rides	Debbie Dadey + Marcia Thornton Jones	RF	1/5	JR
9	Dear Mr. Henshaw	Beverly Cleary	RF	1/6	C
10	Meet M and M	Pat Ross	RF	1/9	E
11	Third grade Pet	Judy Cox	RF	11/19	Jr
12	Spectacular Stone Soup	Patricia Reilly Giff	FR	12/3	E
13	Bill Gates	Charnan Simon	B	12/8	C

Figure 9–6.   Sam's Reading List

C (challenging). We want readers to be aware of the "matches" they are making for themselves, and these three levels provide enough discrimination for students to realize that they change as readers over time. Books that were challenging before may now seem easy, so this documentation system helps them realize their growth as readers. The list also helps you as a teacher monitor students' behavior so that you can guide their choices when necessary:

■ Are they consistently reading easy books rather than challenging themselves with just right books?
■ Are they consistently selecting books that are too hard? (In this case, they may be abandoning too many books.)

■ Are they reading a wide variety of genres?

Poor readers have a tendency either to make "safe" choices (always going for short and very easy books) *or* to choose books that are much too difficult just to pretend to be one of the group. These students lack confidence and do not really know themselves as readers. You'll want to guide them through a wide range of reading, including:

■ Shorter and longer texts.
■ Picture books, easy chapter books, short story collections, and longer chapter books.
■ Award-winning books.
■ Series books.
■ Different genres.
■ Different topics.
■ Different authors and illustrators.
■ Different cultures and books that show the diversity of Earth's people.

This variety will build breadth in their reading.

In the reading workshop, you will be providing minilessons on how to select books and how to tell if a book is just right. You want students to become skilled at selecting books for themselves. If they consistently choose books that are too hard, they may be making their way through them but not gaining full meaning.

In independent reading, the concept of *just right* is both similar to and different from the way we use it in guided reading. The term is similar in the two instructional settings in that the text is mostly under the students' control and offers challenges that can be met successfully. The difference is that in guided reading, successful processing is taking place with strong and skillful teacher support, so that the *just right* text is probably a little more difficult than the same student can read independently. For independent reading, the student must process the text alone. A *just right* text is one that the student can read smoothly with understanding.

In your collection of books for independent reading, you can pencil the level unobtrusively inside a book's front or back cover. This designation is a quick reference (for you alone) if you need to help readers make selections. Knowing the levels of text is helpful for you as a teacher in several ways:

- You can use your knowledge of levels to be sure that you build a classroom library that offers the appropriate range of books from which your students can choose.
- For struggling students, you can make a basket of books holding a varied collection at levels you know they can read and suggest that they choose from those texts.
- You can notice and compare the levels students are choosing to read for independent reading and the levels you are choosing for them in guided reading.
- You can guide readers toward easier or harder books, according to their needs.

Summary

The gradient of text *is a teacher's tool* rather than something you want your students to pay attention to as an important aspect of their reading development. They will be aware that texts vary in the demands they make on readers, and you will explicitly teach them how to select texts based on the amount of challenge as well as interest and other factors. The gradient supports your decisions relative to guided reading, assessment, grouping for instruction, and guiding students' independent reading. It is a "ladder" by which to recognize your students' progress; more important, it will help you match books to readers so that you can ensure that they make consistent reading progress.

Suggestions for Professional Development

After you have created a gradient of text and worked with it for a while, set up a meeting to create your own set of benchmark books. Work with colleagues at grades 3, 4, and 5, or involve teachers at every grade level in your school. These benchmarks will provide a picture of the path of progress.

1. Have each teacher bring several well-known texts to a discussion of why these texts might be good benchmarks.
2. Select five potential benchmarks at each level and identify passages of about 250 words to be used in benchmark assessment. Try to select passages for which comprehension depends on reading other parts of the text.
3. Have teachers at appropriate grade levels try these assessments with their students using an informal reading inventory or miscue analysis (see Chapter 28 in *Guiding Readers and Writers, Grades 3–6*). Have students read passages until the material becomes too hard.
4. Look at the results of your inventories. Ask:
   - Did the books clearly discriminate among readers, showing some books they could read and others beyond their ability?
   - What are the specific characteristics of texts that add to their level of difficulty?
   - What are the specific characteristics of the texts that support readers?
   - Did the selected passages of the text present any problems for readers? Do you need to select other passages?
   - Which texts were stable at each level in that students who can read other books at that level can also read these texts at 90 to 95 percent accuracy and with understanding?
5. Assemble again to discuss and revise the set of benchmark books.
6. Revise the set over time, trying out new benchmark texts.
7. Assemble packets of benchmark texts that can be used as assessment packets by everyone in the school.

CHAPTER TEN

THE CLASSROOM LIBRARY

A strong collection of books is the foundation for the good reading instruction that helps students become competent readers. In times past, most classroom libraries were filled with books that featured primarily European (Caucasian) characters and gave us a limited view of society. Now, many wonderful books are available featuring all cultures, and this diversity is reflected in the lists in this book. You will want to be sure that the fiction and nonfiction texts your students choose to read reflect a wide range of sociocultural and linguistic groups—Latino, Native American, African American, Asian—in a positive way. Also be sure to include books *written* by members of many diverse cultures.

You do not need a complete classroom collection before you implement the reading workshop. In fact, we recommend that you assemble a basic collection and then build it over time. Think of your classroom library just as you would any other collection of books, each one carefully selected because it meets a need and provides enjoyment and learning. You'll want to build your collection throughout your career as a teacher, always discarding those books that are uninteresting, worn out, or inappropriate for your students and acquiring others that meet their needs and capture their interests. (If you're concerned about the cost of assembling a library, Chapter 12 provides some specific suggestions for how to acquire books with little or no money.)

Organization of the Classroom Library

The purpose of the classroom library is to encourage and motivate students to read. It is most important that books be attractively displayed and accessible (see Figure 10–1). You can make your classroom collection inviting by:

- Displaying books in baskets or tubs so they are easy to see and look through (rather than tightly packed in a bookcase with spines out).
- Being sure books you have talked about or students have recommended are included.
- Organizing books in categories so they can be found easily.
- Including both short and long texts.
- Allowing students to suggest titles to add to the library.

Figure 10–1. The Classroom Library

■ Providing a way for students to recommend books to others.

■ Offering a range of texts from easy to difficult so that every student will find something "just right" to read.

The key to an efficient and interesting classroom library is organization. Figure 10–2 lists eight steps for organizing your library effectively.

Start by acquiring colorful plastic tubs or baskets, preferably all the same size (at least shoebox size or larger). These containers need to be large enough so that you can place books in them with the front cover facing out. Don't cram the books into them. There should be room to flip through the books, seeing each title quickly.

Compare browsing through books in this fashion with searching through books tightly packed in a bookcase in alphabetical order, spines facing out. In the latter case, instead of browsing, you laboriously take out one title after another and put it back. You bump up against other readers who are slipping out books and looking at them. It's hard to find the kind of books you like, because genres are mixed in willy-nilly. Inevitably, the shelves become untidy and the books are no longer in alphabetical order. Think too about your own browsing in a bookstore on a Saturday morning—the books are categorized by topic and genre so that you can find the kinds of books you want. You want your students to have a similar experience, perhaps with more support than adults need.

Identify a large shelf area where you can place many baskets at levels students can reach—three shelves, one at table height, one higher, and one lower, work well. (If you have empty space on top of the shelves, display attractive hardcover picture books that will engage readers.) Several students should be able to browse through the books simultaneously without disturbing other students or interfering with your small-group instruction.

Next, identify the categories of books you want to display and label the bins or baskets (see Figure 10–3). These categories will arise from your curriculum and your work with students. Some sample categories are:

■ Favorite authors (Judy Blume, Avi, Gary Paulsen, Madeleine L'Engle, Gary Soto, Mildred Taylor, Karen Hesse, Katherine Paterson).

■ Favorite illustrators or styles of illustration (Jerry Pinkney, Susan Jeffers, Ed Young, Jan Brett).

■ Genres that students already like and those they are learning about (traditional literature, fantasy, science fiction, realistic fiction, historical fiction, biography, autobiography, memoir, informational books).

■ Particular categories of books (survival stories, friendship stories, stories about strong women, sports stories, humorous books, books about families, books about social issues such as war or prejudice).

■ Informational books on particular topics (dinosaurs, insects, wolves, dolphins, ecology, space, the ocean, health and the human body, the earth, historical events or people, rocks, volcanoes).

Steps for Organizing the Classroom Library

1. Acquire colorful plastic baskets or tubs of a uniform size.

2. Identify a large section of shelving that is accessible to students.

3. Identify the categories of books you want to display and label the baskets accordingly with large, clear print.

4. Place selected books, in categories, in the baskets. The books should face out so that students can flip through them, getting a clear view of the front of each one.

5. Add baskets and categories as you need them.

6. Change categories as needed (when studying different authors, genres, or topics, for example).

7. Revise collections (take away titles and add new ones) in the baskets as students read them.

8. Acquire and add duplicate copies of the most popular titles.

Figure 10–2. Steps for Organizing the Classroom Library

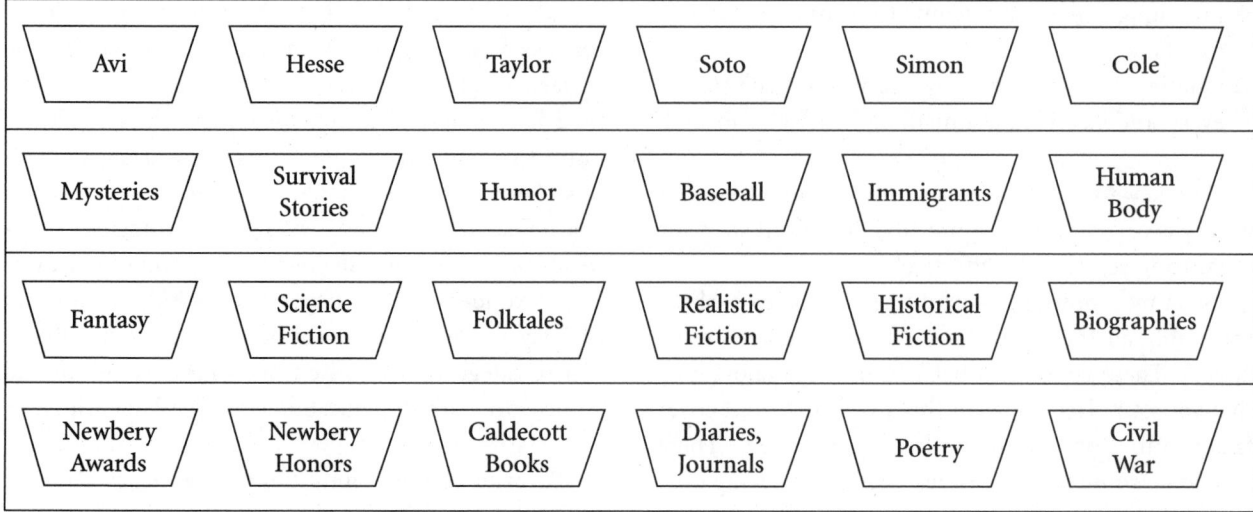

Avi	Hesse	Taylor	Soto	Simon	Cole
Mysteries	Survival Stories	Humor	Baseball	Immigrants	Human Body
Fantasy	Science Fiction	Folktales	Realistic Fiction	Historical Fiction	Biographies
Newbery Awards	Newbery Honors	Caldecott Books	Diaries, Journals	Poetry	Civil War

Figure 10–3. Section of a Classroom Library

■ Different versions of the same folktale or fairy tale (Cinderella, Sleeping Beauty, Beauty and the Beast).

■ Popular series (Cam Jansen, Henry and Mudge, Nate the Great, Arthur, the Boxcar Children, Polk Street School Kids, the Magic Treehouse, Narnia, Horrible Harry, Beezus and Ramona, Dear America).

Series books are especially attractive to many students. After you have introduced one or two books in a series (through book talks or in guided reading), you can put out a basket labeled for the series and point out that several more are available for choosing.

You can add baskets and categories as you acquire more books and/or as you introduce new areas of learning. Your social studies and science curriculum will undoubtedly lead to baskets of books on those topics. You can also change categories as needed. For example, students will move beyond a particular series or may have read all or most of the books by an author and will be ready for something new. Take away titles when they are not needed and add new ones. You'll also want to keep an eye on students' reading lists and their reading interests. Find a way to acquire and add duplicate copies of the most popular titles. In these ways, you can keep the library fresh and interesting.

How Many Books Do You Need?

The classroom collection should contain many different kinds of titles to meet students' interests, broaden their scope of reading, and enable them to read massive amounts of material, thus building "mileage" as readers. An excellent classroom library would contain between three to five hundred books. Unless you have extra resources, however, it will take several years to build a collection like that.

Also keep in mind that you will not put out all your books at once. Always keep "fresh" books coming into the library—not literally newly purchased, necessarily, but new to the students. By introducing "new" books with book talks, you can pique their interest anew. At any given time, there should be enough titles for all students to have good choices of books that interest them *and* that they can read successfully.

The charts in this section estimate number of books for starter, basic, and expanded libraries, broken out into a range of levels, for grades 3, 4, 5, and 6. We have included levels only to ensure that you will purchase or acquire a range of books. You may need to adjust these estimates and ranges if you have large numbers of students reading substantially lower or higher than grade level. The book list organized by level (Appendix 6) will be very helpful in selecting individual titles at levels appropriate for your students. To select titles in a variety of genres, refer to the list organized by genre (Appendix 6). You will also add many unleveled books to your library for students to choose for independent reading.

Getting Started

First, look at the books you already have in your classroom and those that might be available in the school.

The charts in this section assume you are starting from scratch, and that is not usually the case. If you subtract the books you already have from the numbers on the charts, you'll have a more accurate estimate of what you need. The charts also assume a class size of between twenty-five and thirty students. If you have fewer students, you may not need as many titles, but you will still want to have good variety.

Then, think about the resources you will need. Paperback books purchased from a supplier who offers school discounts will cost between $4.00 and $5.00 each on average. With that price in mind, we have listed an estimated cost for starter, basic, and expanded libraries. Since you probably already have some paperback books, your costs will be less than those we have listed. The suggestions for acquiring books in Chapter 12 will help reduce costs further, but first you need to know what you need.

Figures 10–4, 10–5, 10–6, and 10–7 are purchasing guides for starter, basic, and expanded classroom libraries for grades 3 through 6. The numbers on these chart indicate single titles, but you may want to acquire two or three copies of very popular books. A basic guideline for a starter library is to go for variety rather than multiple copies or many titles in a series. The largest number of titles suggested are at the levels associated with each grade level. Slightly smaller numbers are suggested at the levels just below and above the grade level. This plan allows for many books at levels generally considered appropriate for the grade level. The assumption is that you have the greatest number of students reading at that level. You will want to adjust these numbers if your class varies from this pattern.

Suggestions for Professional Development

Evaluate your classroom library to determine your needs and make an action plan. You may want to ask grade-level colleagues to work with you and make suggestions. Or you may want to work together as a faculty to improve all grade-level libraries.

1. Begin by taking an inventory of the books you currently possess. Organize and count them by category. Ask:

Single-Title Classroom Library, Grade 3			
Level	Starter	Basic	Expanded
I	10	20	30
J	10	20	30
K	10	20	30
L	15	30	45
M	15	30	45
N	20	40	60
O	20	40	60
P	20	40	60
Q	15	30	45
R	15	30	45
Total Number of Titles	**150 titles**	**300 titles**	**450 titles**
Estimated total cost*	**$600 to $750**	**$1,200 to $1,500**	**$1,800 to $2,250**
*Assumes starting with no books in the classroom			

Figure 10–4. Single-Title Classroom Library, Grade 3

Single-Title Classroom Library, Grade 4			
Level	Starter	Basic	Expanded
K	10	20	30
L	10	20	30
M	10	20	30
N	15	30	45
O	15	30	45
P	20	40	60
Q	20	40	60
R	20	40	60
S	15	30	45
T	15	30	45
Total number of titles	150 titles	300 titles	450 titles
Estimated total cost*	$600 to $750	$1,200 to $1,500	$1,800 to $2,250
*Assumes starting with no books in the classroom			

Figure 10–5.   Single-Title Classroom Library, Grade 4

Single-Title Classroom Library, Grade 5			
Level	Starter	Basic	Expanded
O	10	20	30
P	10	20	30
Q	10	20	30
R	15	30	45
S	15	30	45
T	20	40	60
U	20	40	60
V	20	40	60
W	15	30	45
X	15	30	45
Total number of titles	150 titles	300 titles	450 titles
Estimated total cost*	$600 to $750	$1,200 to $1,500	$1,800 to $2,250
*Assumes starting with no books in the classroom			

Figure 10–6.   Single-Title Classroom Library, Grade 5

Single-Title Classroom Library, Grade 6			
Level	Starter	Basic	Expanded
P	10	20	30
Q	10	20	30
R	10	20	30
S	15	30	45
T	15	30	45
U	15	30	45
V	20	40	60
W	20	40	60
X	20	40	60
Y	15	30	45
Total number of titles	**150 titles**	**300 titles**	**450 titles**
Estimated total cost*	**$600 to $750**	**$1,200 to $1,500**	**$1,800 to $2,250**
*Assumes starting with no books for guided reading.			

Figure 10–7. Single-Title Classroom Library, Grade 6

■ What genres are represented? Do I have enough variety?

■ How many of these titles are suitable for my students' reading levels?

■ How many of these titles are so interesting to my students that they want to read them?

■ Are my students' cultures, languages, and communities represented?

■ Are *all* kinds of diversity represented?

■ Does the library allow readers in my room to pursue an interest in a topic? An author? A type of book? Can they read in depth?

2. Share your findings with your colleagues and discuss next steps.

3. Next, look at the way books are displayed in the room. Use the list of steps and suggestions in this chapter to determine:

■ How accessible are books to students?

■ To what extent do the book displays invite readers?

4. Now, use the charts in this book to estimate how many books you need. Consider:

■ The levels at which you need to acquire more books and how many.

■ The categories or genres in which you have fewer books and would like to acquire more.

■ Authors, topics, and types of books that are popular with your students and represent purchases you would like to make.

5. Discuss your findings with colleagues and then make a "short list" of the numbers and types of books you want to acquire. Use the book lists organized by level and genre as a resource (see Appendixes 6 and 7).

CHAPTER ELEVEN

THE CLASSROOM COLLECTION FOR GUIDED READING

Having a collection of leveled books is essential for effective teaching in guided reading. Your goal is to help readers expand their strategies and apply them to increasingly challenging texts. For the experience to have positive instructional and emotional value, difficulty must increase consistently but gradually. Just think what it would be like to select books from shelves of hundreds with no guide as to the approximate level of challenge they provide. Therefore, you will need access to a good leveled book collection, with multiple copies of titles, to support your teaching in guided reading.

The leveled collection makes it possible to:

■ Quickly survey the choices available to you.
■ Narrow your choices to those students are most likely to be able to read successfully.
■ Keep books in order for efficient access.
■ Have a concrete and visible way to monitor students' reading progress.

The guidance in this chapter is directed to the individual teacher in a single classroom. As soon as you can, however, you'll want to begin sharing a book collection with other teachers at grades three through six. If many or most of the staff at a grade level or in several grades are using books for guided reading, you will want to create a school bookroom, as described in Chapter 12. The school bookroom is the most economical option and provides the greatest variety of texts to meet students' needs.

Organization of the Leveled Collection

The leveled collection is a tool for the teacher. Effective organization of these books can save valuable time during the instructional day as well as planning time.

Location

First, think about a good location for your leveled books. Students will not be choosing these books on their own, so find a location that is very convenient for you—perhaps a shelf close to your reading table or desk, so that as you think about students' reading and go over your records, you'll have easy access to the books.

You can set up a small rolling office cart, or rolling cart with two or three shelves. You can organize all the supplies you need for guided reading. The cart holds your clipboard with student records, a dry-erase whiteboard, markers, a Magnadoodle, a tray of magnetic letters, stick-on notes, writing pads, and multiple copies of the books you've selected for students to read next. If students are reading longer books, they will keep those in their own book boxes until they are finished, but you will still have one book for yourself on the cart. You can roll this cart over to your storage place when you are returning books and selecting new ones.

Storage and Retrieval

You can use plastic tubs or boxes similar to those recommended for your classroom library, or you may want to use shoe boxes or magazine boxes. You can also cut down large cereal boxes and cover them with colored paper. These boxes can be stored on bookshelves; it will help if you can see titles easily without pulling out each box. A complicated index isn't necessary; simply scan what's available when you're selecting books.

Multiple Copies

You will need multiple copies of each title, which should be kept together to increase efficiency and reduce wear and tear. For thin books, elastic bands work well. Another technique is to put multiple copies of individual titles in gallon-size resealable storage bags. Don't label the bags—the titles will be visible—and you'll be able to reuse them as needed.

Labeling and Arrangement

Label the boxes with the letter representing the level (see Figure 11–1). Also, place the level letter in an unobtrusive place on the book, perhaps in pencil inside the back cover, as a quick reference when you are returning books to your storage area.

The lists in the back of this book will help you organize your collection initially. If you have titles other than the thousands we have included here, get to know the levels well and then make your own decisions about the level of your books. Then try the books with readers; over time, you will confidently assign the appropriate level .

Arrange the boxes along the shelf in order of level. As you build the collection, you will identify the levels where you need the most books and you can add more storage units.

Within each box, arrange books alphabetically by title or author. You'll want a variety of titles at each level. If you have an adequate collection, no one student will read every book at the level, and you will also be using short stories and articles.

Figure 11–1.   Labeled Boxes Containing Multiple Copies of Each Title

Connections Between the Guided Reading Collection and the Classroom Library

There will be some overlap between your leveled collection and your classroom library because you would not want to reserve all the good books for guided reading. For the most part, however, students will not have read a text you choose for them because it will be at a slightly higher level than the books they can read independently. If, on occasion, a student says, "I read this," he will not have done so with same kind of teaching support you will provide and will learn more when he rereads it. Tell students that when you reread a book, you notice things you didn't notice the first time.

Getting Started

We suggest that you select titles for your guided reading collection first, before you create your classroom library for independent reading, and try to avoid having the same titles in both collections. A little overlap is not a serious problem, but you wouldn't want them to be essentially identical.

Carefully choose excellent titles at each level, paying attention to variety—you want fiction and nonfiction in a range of genres. You'll also want a number of short story collections, because short reads are good opportunities to develop students' processing strategies. They can then apply their learning to longer texts that they read independently.

Making the Most of Limited Resources

The single-classroom leveled collection isn't the most cost effective way to go. Many of the sets will be sitting unused because they either have already been read or won't be read until later in the year. Shared resources are always more economical. Even sharing between two or three classrooms greatly reduces the cost of a collection and increases its variety. For example, there's no need for both fifth-grade classrooms in your school to have eight copies of Avi's *Blue Heron*, a book that would take a group of fifth graders about a week to read. The multiple copies can move back and forth between the classrooms. Even if you place a single copy in the book rack for independent reading in each classroom, you have purchased ten copies instead of sixteen and saved approximately $30.00, which is enough to buy six copies of another title. Sharing a leveled collection takes a little more cooperation, but the payoff is great.

How Many Books Do You Need?

Discovering just how many books you need for guided reading is a matter of trial and error. The number relates to your class size, the reading levels of your students, and how many guided reading groups you have.

Suggested here are levels, titles, numbers of copies, and cost for a basic and expanded classroom collection. Remember that your first step is to inventory the books you already have. For example, you may already have three or four copies of a title. If you are building a collection with a colleague, you may be able to assemble five or six copies between you. You can then purchase a few more to make the basic collection.

We have suggested quantities of books by level, but you will want to adjust these recommendations based on your assessment of the students in your class. Also, things change over a period of years. In schools where teachers, kindergarten through the upper grades, have been delivering a dynamic literacy program for several years, the average *level* of reading shifts over time. The point of guided reading is not to "push" students beyond their interests or appropriate topics and themes; nevertheless, in schools that have used guided reading for a number of years, benchmark testing shows more students reading at or above grade level (Scharer, Williams, and Pinnell 2001). This increase is especially evident in schools where a large number of students are reading well below grade level when the language and literacy framework, which includes guided reading, is first implemented.

The bottom line: it's not economically feasible to have multiple copies of leveled books that are outside your grade's usual range of reading. You should borrow titles from teachers at other grades to meet the needs of your students who read substantially (more than one year) below grade level or who are very advanced. The reading groups created for these students will be smaller and you won't need as many copies.

Basic and Expanded Collections of Leveled Books for Grade 3

In third grade, the variety of student reading material greatly increases. Students will be reading chapter books and many kinds of informational books. You will want to include biographies and informational texts in your collection and provide explicit teaching on how they are organized. Fiction will expand to include historical fiction and some simple fantasy. Students will be building reading stamina by taking on longer chapter books.

Third grade is also a time when students will become very much aware of their own tastes and interests as readers. They will gravitate to realistic fiction, and it is good for them to read a wide range of it. They like series books such as the Kids of Polk Street School series and the Ramona series. With your encouragement and instructional support, they can explore a wider range of genres. Guided reading is the place where they can meet new fiction and nonfiction genres and learn to enjoy them. You'll also want to promote a great deal of independent reading along with your guided reading lessons.

In third grade, you will need to cover a span of at least eight levels, K through R, with the largest number of titles needed at levels N, O, and P. Figures 11–2 and 11–3 suggest levels, number of titles, and estimated cost for basic collections with six and eight copies of each title. An expanded collection concentrates on the same span of levels, with more titles per level. Number of books and estimated cost for an expanded collection with six copies and eight copies are shown in Figures 11–4 and 11–5.

Basic and Expanded Collections of Leveled Books for Grade 4

Like third graders, fourth graders will tend to select mostly realistic fiction, but instructional support in guided reading can help them continue to explore other genres as well. At this age the peer group is becoming much more important; for independent reading, they will enjoy trading books with friends and forming book clubs. The Ramona series continues to be popular, as well as series like Jenny Archer and the Boxcar Children. Students enjoy informational books and "blended" genres like the Magic School Bus series. They enjoy history from a personal point of view, as in the If You Lived in the Time Of series, as well as historical fiction, such as Jean Fritz's *The Cabin Faced West* or Mildred Taylor's *Mississippi Bridge*. Through guided reading, you can help them gain deeper understanding of themselves and others by reading about times, places, and people distant from themselves.

For a typical fourth-grade classroom, you will need

Basic Collection with Six Copies of Each Title, Grade 3			
Level	Number of Titles Each Level	Number of Books	Estimated Cost @ $5.00 Per Book
K	5	30	$150
L	5	30	$150
M	5	30	$150
N	8	48	$240
O	8	48	$240
P	8	48	$240
Q	5	30	$150
R	5	30	$150
	49	294	$1,560

Figure 11–2. Basic Collection with Six Copies of Each Title, Grade 3

Basic Collection with Eight Copies of Each Title, Grade 3			
Level	Number of Titles Each Level	Number of Books	Estimated Cost @ $5.00 Per Book
K	5	40	$200
L	5	40	$200
M	5	40	$200
N	8	64	$320
O	8	64	$320
P	8	64	$320
Q	5	40	$200
R	5	40	$200
	49	392	$1,960

Figure 11–3. Basic Collection with Eight Copies of Each Title, Grade 3

a span of eight levels, N through U; most students will be reading at levels Q, R, and S. Figures 11–6 and 11–7 present suggested levels, number of titles, and estimated cost for basic collections with six and eight copies of each title. Numbers of books and estimated costs for an expanded collection with six copies and eight copies are shown in Figures 11–8 and 11–9.

Basic and Expanded Collections of Leveled Books for Grade 5

Through reading, fifth graders explore important and serious social issues such as war, prejudice, and poverty (for example, Yoshiko Uchida's *Journey to Topaz* or Lois Lowry's *Number the Stars*). As they approach teenage years, they may challenge their parents' authority and

Expanded Collection with Six Copies of Each Title, Grade 3			
Level	Number of Titles Each Level	Number of Books	Estimated Cost @ $5.00 Per Book
K	5	30	$150
L	5	30	$150
M	10	60	$300
N	10	60	$300
O	10	60	$300
P	10	60	$300
Q	10	60	$300
R	5	30	$150
	65	390	$1,950

Figure 11–4.   *Expanded Collection with Six Copies of Each Title, Grade 3*

Expanded Collection with Eight Copies of Each Title, Grade 3			
Level	Number of Titles Each Level	Number of Books	Estimated Cost @ $5.00 Per Book
K	5	40	$200
L	5	40	$200
M	10	80	$400
N	10	80	$400
O	10	80	$400
P	10	80	$400
Q	10	80	$400
R	5	40	$200
	65	520	$2,600

Figure 11–5.   *Expanded Collection with Eight Copies of Each Title, Grade 3*

find books about growing up very appealing. They enjoy a wide range of biography as well as historical fiction, such as Katherine Paterson's *Lyddie*, and use it to learn about the past. Since students are expected to learn content by reading, you will want to be sure to include a range of informational books so that students can learn about their organizational features as well as using reference tools and interpreting graphic features.

For a typical fifth-grade classroom, you will need a span of eight levels, Q through X; most students will be reading at levels T, U, and V. Figures 11–10 and 11–11 present suggested levels, number of titles, and estimated cost for basic collections with six and eight copies of each title. Number of books and estimated cost for an expanded collection with six copies and eight copies are shown in Figures 11–12 and 11–13.

Basic Collection with Six Copies of Each Title, Grade 4			
Level	Number of Titles Each Level	Number of Books	Estimated Cost @ $5.00 Per Book
N	5	30	$150
O	5	30	$150
P	5	30	$150
Q	8	48	$240
R	8	48	$240
S	8	48	$240
T	5	30	$150
U	5	30	$150
	49	294	$1,470

Figure 11–6.   Basic Collection with Eight Copies of Each Title, Grade 4

Basic Collection with Eight Copies of Each Title, Grade 4			
Level	Number of Titles Each Level	Number of Books	Estimated Cost @ $5.00 Per Book
N	5	40	$200
O	5	40	$200
P	5	40	$200
Q	8	64	$320
R	8	64	$320
S	8	64	$320
T	5	40	$200
U	5	40	$200
	49	392	$1,960

Figure 11–7.   Basic Collection with Eight Copies of Each Title, Grade 4

Basic and Expanded Collections of Leveled Books for Grade 6

In sixth grade, students are poised to enter adolescence. Their bodies are changing, although there is wide variation in physical development. They are searching for identity and a sense of self, and use reading as a way to broaden understanding of life. Books like Karen Hesse's *Out of the Dust,* Cynthia Voigt's *Dicey's Song,* Cynthia Rylant's *Missing May,* and Mildred Taylor's *Roll of Thunder, Hear My Cry* capture their attention because they show early adolescents meeting and dealing with tragedy and hardship. Sixth graders also explore complex works of fantasy, often in series by authors such as Madeline L'Engle, Susan Cooper, and Ursula Le Guin.

Expanded Collection with Six Copies of Each Title, Grade 4			
Level	Number of Titles Each Level	Number of Books	Estimated Cost @ $5.00 Per Book
N	5	30	$150
O	5	30	$150
P	10	60	$300
Q	10	60	$300
R	10	60	$300
S	10	60	$300
T	10	60	$300
U	5	30	$150
	65	390	$1,950

Figure 11–8.   *Expanded Collection with Six Copies of Each Title, Grade 4*

Expanded Collection with Eight Copies of Each Title, Grade 4			
Level	Number of Titles Each Level	Number of Books	Estimated Cost @ $5.00 Per Book
N	5	40	$200
O	5	40	$200
P	10	80	$400
Q	10	80	$400
R	10	80	$400
S	10	80	$400
T	10	80	$400
U	5	40	$200
	65	520	$2,600

Figure 11–9.   *Expanded Collection with Eight Copies of Each Title, Grade 4*

Many students are ready to explore mature themes such as sexuality or abuse.

Figures 11–14 and 11–15 suggest levels, number of titles, and estimated cost for basic collections with six and eight copies of each title. Number of books and estimated cost for an expanded collection with six copies and eight copies are shown in Figures 11–16 and 11–17.

Final Thoughts

It may seem overwhelming to bring together the number and levels of the books you need, but the collection should be built over several years. In fact, we advise against purchasing the whole collection at once. For one thing, you must read and know the books yourself,

Basic Collection with Six Copies of Each Title, Grade 5			
Level	Number of Titles Each Level	Number of Books	Estimated Cost @ $5.00 Per Book
Q	5	30	$150
R	5	30	$150
S	5	30	$150
T	8	48	$240
U	8	48	$240
V	8	48	$240
W	5	30	$150
X	5	30	$150
	49	294	$1,470

Figure 11–10. Basic Collection with Six Copies of Each Title, Grade 5

Basic Collection with Eight Copies of Each Title, Grade 5			
Level	Number of Titles Each Level	Number of Books	Estimated Cost @ $5.00 Per Book
Q	5	40	$200
R	5	40	$200
S	5	40	$200
T	8	64	$320
U	8	64	$320
V	8	64	$320
W	5	40	$200
X	5	40	$200
	49	392	$1,960

Figure 11–11. Basic Collection with Eight Copies of Each Title, Grade 5

and while all teachers are familiar with some children's literature, reading and reflecting on such a large volume of books takes time.

Get to know the books slowly as you acquire them and explore them with students. You will discover those that appeal to students and offer a great deal to learn, and you can increase the number of copies you have of those texts. Also, you'll always want to add new books to the collection to keep your own teaching interesting and fresh. Adjust your collection as you think about the number of students in your classes, their present reading levels, and their predicted progress over the year.

The leveled collection is used primarily to support

Expanded Collection with Six Copies of Each Title, Grade 5			
Level	Number of Titles Each Level	Number of Books	Estimated Cost @ $5.00 Per Book
Q	5	30	$150
R	5	30	$150
S	10	60	$300
T	10	60	$300
U	10	60	$300
V	10	60	$300
W	10	60	$300
X	5	30	$150
	65	390	$1,950

Figure 11–12.   *Expanded Collection with Six Copies of Each Title, Grade 5*

Expanded Collection with Eight Copies of Each Title, Grade 5			
Level	Number of Titles Each Level	Number of Books	Estimated Cost @ $5.00 Per Book
Q	5	40	$200
R	5	40	$200
S	10	80	$400
T	10	80	$400
U	10	80	$400
V	10	80	$400
W	10	80	$400
X	5	40	$200
	65	520	$2,600

Figure 11–13.   *Expanded Collection with Eight Copies of Each Title, Grade 5*

guided reading, but remember that you can always draw from this resource to create a special basket of books for students who need more guidance in finding just-right books for their independent reading, at school or at home. In addition, students may have read good books in guided reading that they will explore more deeply in a literature discussion group.

Suggestions for Professional Development

1. Evaluate and organize your classroom collection so that you can get started. Begin by collecting in one place all of the books you have in the classroom that you think would be appropriate for guided reading.

Basic Collection with Six Copies of Each Title, Grade 6			
Level	Number of Titles Each Level	Number of Books	Estimated Cost @ $5.00 Per Book
R	5	30	$150
S	5	30	$150
T	5	30	$150
U	8	48	$240
V	8	48	$240
W	8	48	$240
X	5	30	$150
Y	5	30	$150
	49	**294**	**$1,470**

Figure 11–14. *Basic Collection with Six Copies of Each Title, Grade 6*

Basic Collection with Eight Copies of Each Title, Grade 6			
Level	Number of Titles Each Level	Number of Books	Estimated Cost @ $5.00 Per Book
R	5	40	$200
S	5	40	$200
T	5	40	$200
U	8	64	$320
V	8	64	$320
W	8	64	$320
X	5	40	$200
Y	5	40	$200
	49	**392**	**$1,960**

Figure 11–15. *Basic Collection with Eight Copies of Each Title, Grade 6*

2. Using the lists in this book and/or your own analysis (as guided by the prototypes in Chapters 5, 6, and 7), write the guided reading levels on the inside cover of each book or on a sticker on the front or back.

3. Organize the books in labeled boxes or baskets.

4. Locate a good place in your classroom for your collection. The books should be easily accessible to you but not to the students.

5. Consult the charts in this book and make some judgments about the levels you need most.

6. Now, look at your collection. The gaps will be obvious. Make a list of the levels where you need to add titles.

Expanded Collection with Six Copies of Each Title, Grade 6			
Level	Number of Titles Each Level	Number of Books	Estimated Cost @ $5.00 Per Book
Q	5	30	$150
R	5	30	$150
S	10	60	$300
T	10	60	$300
U	10	60	$300
V	10	60	$300
W	10	60	$300
X	5	30	$150
	65	390	$1,950

Figure 11–16. Expanded Collection with Six Copies of Each Title, Grade 6

Expanded Collection with Eight Copies of Each Title, Grade 6			
Level	Number of Titles Each Level	Number of Books	Estimated Cost @ $5.00 Per Book
R	5	40	$200
S	5	40	$200
T	10	80	$400
U	10	80	$400
V	10	80	$400
W	10	80	$400
X	10	80	$400
Y	5	40	$200
	65	520	$2,600

Figure 11–17. Expanded Collection with Eight Copies of Each Title, Grade 6

7. Look through the lists in this book and identify some titles you either have read at these levels or that others have recommended. Add specific titles to your list.

8. Keep this list handy so that you can add to it constantly. When you have the opportunity to order books, you will be ready! Also, you can use books clubs strategically to add quality to your collection.

CHAPTER TWELVE

THE SCHOOL BOOKROOM

A school bookroom is, of course, a room in which multiple copies of leveled books are arranged from levels A through Z. But it is much more than that. It is a place where you and your colleagues can share insights about the supports and challenges in texts, revise and enrich the text support for your guided reading instruction, discuss your common vision for reading progress and standards throughout the intermediate grades, and discuss books, authors, and readers.

The bookroom may serve teachers at one, several, or even all grade levels. Given the wide range of levels and materials needed within even one intermediate grade, it makes much more economical sense to share a good collection across the grades. If you can find a space in the school to house leveled books, and if you and your colleagues work together, you can create a rich resource for the guided reading program. The gradient of text, with many copies of a large number of titles, is also the foundation for talking about students' reading progress and for planning part of your system of assessment.

Getting Started

As with classroom libraries and classroom leveled collections, you will want to acquire a schoolwide collection gradually. First, gather together all the books for guided reading that you have in the current school bookroom and in classrooms. (Leave the books teachers and students need to support independent reading in classrooms.) You can also check the school library for multiple copies of books that would be useful for guided reading. It may be hard, at first, for teachers to take books *out* of their classroom—they've very likely been hard to come by—but a smoothly functioning school bookroom will benefit everyone.

Organize the books by level, noting:

■ The numbers of titles you have for each level.
■ The numbers of copies of each title.

Compare your current supply with the "starter" tables presented later in this chapter. Considering the range of reading levels of students in the intermediate grades, make some hard decisions about levels where more books are needed and direct any resources toward those purchases.

This starter set will be a learning tool for your first year of implementing guided reading. With careful planning, it can also enrich classroom independent reading. As you work with the books and meet regularly with your colleagues, you will be able to purchase additional materials strategically in subsequent years, making the most of limited resources and keeping fresh material coming into the program to excite students and teachers.

We have estimated the average cost of a paperback at $5.00, but you may be able to acquire them at up to a 20 percent discount. As you look at the numbers, you will see that it is worth a little trouble to find suppliers who will give you a discount. You are submitting large orders over time, so don't hesitate to ask for good prices. (Chapter 13 provides many suggestions for acquiring free books.)

Location

An important decision to make is where the school bookroom will be located. Space is always at a premium in elementary schools, and your first inclination will be to settle for a closet or some other place no one else wants. Nevertheless, we urge you to compete for the best possible space. You will need ample room for shelves so that your collection can grow.

The bookroom is often where teachers have their most interesting conversations. If you can, locate your books in a central area with good lighting and ventilation. Have some open space in the middle where you can place a table for browsing and reading, sorting and organizing books, and talking about books over lunch or during planning periods.

Books should be placed on shelves that are easily accessible so that teachers can pull out the boxes, look through them, and return them. If books are hard to take out and return, people in a hurry will leave them out of order. A neat, organized room will attract teachers to congregate there and will highlight the value of the collection.

In many schools, teachers have found a way to create a meeting room that combines many functions:

■ Meeting together for professional development.
■ Coming together to plan and talk.
■ Housing the leveled book collection, with procedures for using and returning books.
■ Displaying student work.
■ Showcasing a professional book collection.
■ Housing videotapes or other professional development support materials.

Such a room is highly valuable in creating a professional learning community in your school. Your materials are easily accessible in an attractive and inviting place.

An alternative is to house the leveled book collection in the school library—the shelves are already there—but you'll need a congenial relationship with the school librarian. Since students do not need to use the leveled book collection, it can be in a less accessible part of the library. An added benefit is that teachers monitoring their students on assigned trips to the library can examine and select books from the leveled book collection at the same time.

Organizing and Using the Bookroom

Place all books for each guided reading level in consecutive level order so that you will have an instant and concrete picture of reading progress over time. Getting to know these books well is a goal every staff member will achieve over time. You'll find that once you have used them for guided reading over a year or two, just a glance at the title or front cover will summon a mental map of the supports and challenges in the text and you will be able to consider this information in relation to the students you teach.

You may want to place all copies of a title in a labeled magazine box or covered cereal or shoe box. Label the box with title, genre, and level. If books are relatively thin, you may be able to put multiple copies of two titles in one box (see Figure 12–1). Place all boxes together by level so that when you look at the shelves, you can instantly find the levels you need (in the photo in Figure 12–2, notice how the books are arranged so as to be accessible to everyone).

You will also need to develop a way to use the bookroom cooperatively. It is terrific if an instructional assistant or parent volunteer can monitor the bookroom and keep it in order, but that's not always possible. If you don't have extra support, responsibility for overseeing the room can rotate each month. And even if you have help like this, you still want the staff to "own" the room and take care of it. Figure 12–3 shows the guidelines one group of teachers created.

A good system for keeping track of who has which set of books is to give each teacher

Figure 12–1. A Book Box

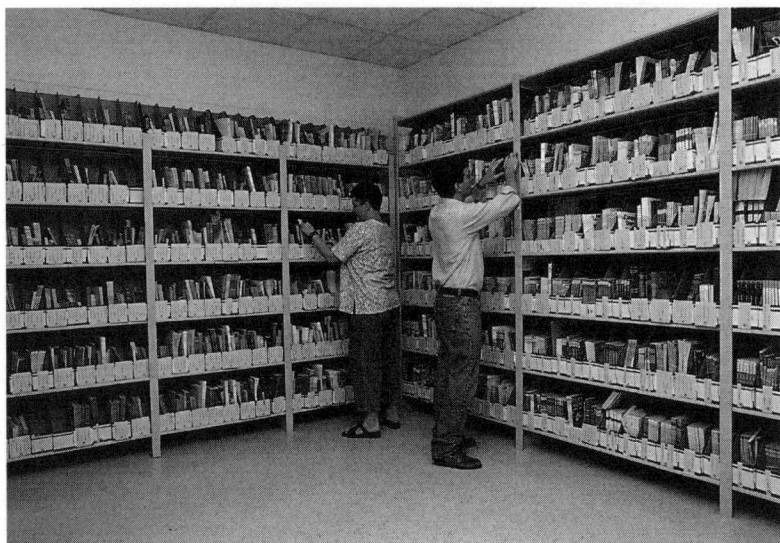

Figure 12–2. A School Bookroom

a tub of clothespins with his or her name on them. After taking a set of books to use with students in your classroom, you simply attach a clothespin to the box containing the books. You may also use checkout cards (drop a card with your name on it in the box when you take the books, for example) or write down in a notebook the title of the set you've taken. When you return the books, you retrieve the card or clothespin or mark through the entry in the notebook.

Bookrooms that degenerate into a shambles because no one is responsible for them will seriously undermine your guided reading program. Periodically, meet in the bookroom to evaluate how it's going. Take an inventory of books; replace those that are worn out; determine what levels need new acquisitions.

Estimated Costs of the School Bookroom Collection

Figures 12–4 through 12–9 suggest levels, number of books, and cost to support leveled reading in grades 3 through 6 for starter, basic, and expanded collections, first with eight copies of each title, then with twelve. These charts are based on two classes of 25 to 30 students at each grade level, for a total of 200 to 240 students. Adjust these estimates as necessary to reflect your particular situation.

A starter collection will help you get underway with guided reading; you can add to the collection as you go.

As outlined in Figure 12–4, a starter collection would include ten titles each for the most frequently used levels, with eight copies of each title. We have included some books on the lower levels, but if you have a good primary collection in your school, you may not need to purchase these. The total cost of the starter collection for a school with eight intermediate classrooms is approximately $6,000 (eight copies of each title) or $9,500 (twelve copies of each title [see Figure 12–5]). This starter set concentrates on variety, so you shouldn't purchase more than one or two titles in a series. Ask your students to look in the school library or their community library for other books in a series to read independently.

The basic collection allows for more titles. With the basic collection, students will be able to read a wider variety of genres as well as more series books. As shown in Figures 12–6 and 12–7, a basic collection for a school bookroom will cost approximately $11,000 (eight copies of each title) to $17,000 (twelve copies of each title). *These costs do not reflect possible discounts.*

The expanded collection shown in Figures 12–8 and 12–9 provides a rich variety of titles, allowing you to cover a range of genres and provide for students' extensive reading.

Remember that the books in these collections will be used over many years. The starter collection costs about $256 (25 students per class) or $213 (30 students per class) per current student. But since the students will be using the collection over a minimum of a four-year period, the costs are actually $64 to $53.25 per student. And even those figures are misleading. You will be using this collection over many years for different groups of students. Of course, there will be replacement costs for books that wear out or are lost. You'll also want to add new resources to the collection gradually. But if you assume just two cycles of students using the books over an eight-year period, the costs shrink to between $32.00 to $26.63 per student. We hope these figures will help you convince administrators to support your collection and also help you acquire outside funding (see Chapter 13).

Guidelines for Using a School Bookroom

1. When you check books out, please leave a clothespin or place an index card with your name in the box.

2. For K–2 teachers: Please keep the books for only two weeks and then return them so that others can use them.

3. For grades 3–5 teachers: Please keep the books for only three weeks. Be sure to return them so that others can use them.

4. Everyone is responsible for refiling the books returned.

5. Assigned teachers agree to check the room for order at the first of each month.

Here is our schedule:

September: Grade 5 teachers [names]

October: Grade 3 teachers [names]

November: Grade 4 teachers [names]

December: Grade 2 teachers [names]

January: Kindergarten and Grade 1 teachers [names]

February: Kindergarten and Grade 1 teachers [names]

March: Grades 4 and 5 teachers [names]

April: Grades 2 and 3 teachers [names]

May: Meeting of all staff to evaluate book room use and suggest new titles.

June: Final check and celebration lunch!

Figure 12–3. Guidelines for Using a School Bookroom

Advantages of the School Bookroom

Perhaps the first advantage generated by the school bookroom is the work you do with colleagues to create it. When all of you open your classroom doors and share and talk about books, you have richer conversations about your students. These commonly held and known texts help you create a common language that you can use to discuss your work and help one another learn. Here are some other advantages:

■ Books are always in use rather than sitting unused in individual classrooms.

■ You can work with the book collection over time to replace titles and constantly enrich it.

■ The collection does not need to be replaced in total.

■ The book collection is an integral part of ongoing assessment, about which everyone communicates.

■ The bookroom becomes a gathering place where a learning community is creating and fostered.

■ The book collection is a visible reference relative to reading progress and gives all staff a "big picture" of their goals and standards.

■ The book collection supports excellent teaching by creating a shared resource that is efficient, convenient, and effective.

The charts and descriptions presented in this chapter reflect bookrooms that will provide support for a massive amount of student reading. A student moving from third through sixth grade will read more than two hundred books of fiction and nonfiction in guided reading, independent reading, literature study, and reading at home. The elementary years are the time to build reading power and enjoyment. This foundation is essential not only for meeting the challenges of middle school (or junior high) and high school, but for becoming a lifelong reader.

Example of a Starter Book Collection for a School Bookroom, Grades 3–5, Eight Copies of Each Title			
Levels	Number of Titles Each Level	Number of Books	Estimated Average Cost @ $5.00 Per Book
I	5	40	$200
J	5	40	$200
K	10	80	$400
L	10	80	$400
M	10	80	$400
N	10	80	$400
O	10	80	$400
P	10	80	$400
Q	10	80	$400
R	10	80	$400
S	10	80	$400
T	10	80	$400
U	10	80	$400
V	10	80	$400
W	10	80	$400
X	5	40	$200
Total Grades 3–5	**145**	**1160**	**$5,800**
Additional titles for elementary schools where sixth grade is included:			
X	5	40	$200
Y	10	80	$400
Total Grade 6	**15**	**120**	**$600**
Total Grades 3–6	**160**	**1280**	**$6,400**

Figure 12–4. *Example of a Starter Book Collection for a School Bookroom, Grades 3–5, Eight Copies of Each Title*

Example of a Starter Book Collection for a School Bookroom, Grades 3–5, Twelve Copies of Each Title			
Levels	**Number of Titles Each Level**	**Number of Books**	**Estimated Average Cost @ $5.00 Per Book**
H	5	60	$300
I	5	60	$300
J	10	120	$600
K	10	120	$600
L	10	120	$600
M	10	120	$600
N	10	120	$600
O	10	120	$600
P	10	120	$600
Q	10	120	$600
R	10	120	$600
S	10	120	$600
T	10	120	$600
U	10	120	$600
V	10	120	$600
W	10	120	$600
X	5	60	$300
Total Grades 3–5	**155**	**1860**	**$9,300**
Additional titles for elementary schools where sixth grade is included:			
X	10	120	$600
Y	20	240	$1200
Total Grade 6	**30**	**360**	**$1800**
Total Grades 3–6	**185**	**2220**	**$11,100**

Figure 12–5.   Example of a Starter Book Collection for a School Bookroom, Grades 3–5, Twelve Copies of Each Title

Example of a Basic Book Collection for a School Bookroom, Grades 3–5, Eight Copies of Each Title			
Levels	**Number of Titles Each Level**	**Number of Books**	**Estimated Average Cost @ $5.00 Per Book**
H	5	40	$200
I	5	40	$200
J	10	80	$400
K	10	80	$400
L	20	160	$800
M	20	160	$800
N	20	160	$800
O	20	160	$800
P	20	160	$800
Q	20	160	$800
R	20	160	$800
S	20	160	$800
T	20	160	$800
U	20	160	$800
V	20	160	$800
W	10	80	$400
X	10	80	$400
Total Grades 3–5	**270**	**1260**	**$10,800**
Additional titles for elementary schools where sixth grade is included:			
W	10	80	$400
X	10	80	$400
Y	10	80	$400
Total Grade 6	**30**	**240**	**$1,200**
Total Grades 3–6	**300**	**2400**	**$12,000**

Figure 12–6.   *Example of a Basic Book Collection for a School Bookroom, Grades 3–5, Eight Copies of Each Title*

Example of a Basic Book Collection for a School Bookroom, Grades 3–5, Twelve Copies of Each Title			
Levels	Number of Titles Each Level	Number of Books	Estimated Average Cost @ $5.00 Per Book
H	5	60	$300
I	5	60	$300
J	10	120	$600
K	10	120	$600
L	20	240	$1,200
M	20	240	$1,200
N	20	240	$1,200
O	20	240	$1,200
P	20	240	$1,200
Q	20	240	$1,200
R	20	240	$1,200
S	20	240	$1,200
T	20	240	$1,200
U	20	240	$1,200
V	20	240	$1,200
W	10	120	$600
X	10	120	$600
Total Grades 3–5	**270**	**3240**	**$16,200**
Additional titles for elementary schools where sixth grade is included:			
W	10	120	$600
X	10	120	$600
Y	10	120	$600
Total Grade 6	30	360	$1,800
Total Grades 3–6	**300**	**3600**	**$18,000**

Figure 12–7. *Example of a Basic Book Collection for a School Bookroom, Grades 3–5, Twelve Copies of Each Title*

	Example of an Expanded Book Collection for a School Bookroom, Grades 3–5, Eight Copies of Each Title		
Levels	**Number of Titles Each Level**	**Number of Books**	**Estimated Average Cost @ $5.00 Per Book**
H	10	80	$400
I	10	80	$400
J	15	120	$600
K	15	120	$600
L	25	200	$1,000
M	25	200	$1,000
N	25	200	$1,000
O	25	200	$1,000
P	25	200	$1,000
Q	25	200	$1,000
R	25	200	$1,000
S	25	200	$1,000
T	25	200	$1,000
U	25	200	$1,000
V	25	200	$1,000
W	20	160	$800
X	20	160	$800
Total Grades 3–5	**365**	**2920**	**$14,600**
Additional titles for elementary schools where sixth grade is included:			
W	5	40	$200
X	5	40	$200
Y	25	200	$1,000
Total Grade 6	**35**	**280**	**$1,400**
Total Grades 3–6	**400**	**3200**	**$16,000**

Figure 12–8.   *Example of an Expanded Book Collection for a School Bookroom, Grades 3–5, Eight Copies of Each Title*

Example of an Expanded Book Collection for a School Book Room, Grades 3-5 with Twelve Copies of Each Title			
Levels	Number of Titles Each Level	Number of Books	Estimated Average Cost @ $5.00 Per Book
H	10	120	$600
I	10	120	$600
J	15	180	$900
K	15	180	$900
L	25	300	$1,500
M	25	300	$1,500
N	25	300	$1,500
O	25	300	$1,500
P	25	300	$1,500
Q	25	300	$1,500
R	25	300	$1,500
S	25	300	$1,500
T	25	300	$1,500
U	25	300	$1,500
V	25	300	$1,500
W	20	240	$1,200
X	20	240	$1,200
Total Grades 3-5	365	4380	$21,900
Additional titles for elementary schools where sixth grade is included:			
W	5	60	$300
X	5	60	$300
Y	25	300	$1,500
Total Grade 6	35	420	$2,100
Total Grades 3-6	400	4800	$24,000

Figure 12–9.   Example of an Expanded Book Collection for a School Bookroom, Grades 3–5 with Twelve Copies of Each Title

Suggestions for Professional Development

Work as a team to plan and organize your bookroom. Again, the school librarian can offer excellent advice. The book lists at the back of this book will be a resource, but remember you can also add books that do not appear on the lists. Begin by getting to know some books at each level.

1. Hold a meeting with colleagues to assess your current situation and make a plan.
   - Ask teachers to come with a list of all the books in their classrooms and the number of copies they could contribute to the shared collection. (They should bring with them a copy of any title of which they have more than one copy. They can write their name on the inside back cover just in case you decide later to break up the collection.)
   - Collect one copy of any books you already have in a shared book collection and bring these copies to the meeting.
   - Spend some time placing the books in leveled categories.
   - Then make a chart (similar to the charts in this chapter) of the number of titles and copies of each title at each level.
   - You may also want to assess the range of genres by counting fiction and nonfiction or simply entering an evaluative comment (for example, "good variety," or "only realistic fiction").

2. Now you are ready to begin your planning.
   - Decide what your goals are for the first year and the number of titles you need at each level.
   - Divide into teams to look for titles at each level.
   - Bring your findings back to another meeting and formulate a beginning book order.

3. After you have a minimal starter collection physically on hand, hold a meeting to organize the bookroom.
   - Decide on your location and how you will clear out other materials that are currently in the space.
   - Decide how you will store books and make a plan for acquiring magazine boxes, shoe boxes, or other containers.
   - Create a plan for getting help from volunteers if needed.
   - Create a timeline for setting up the bookroom.
   - Decide how books will be taken from and returned to the bookroom by teachers.

4. Schedule a regular series of short meetings (perhaps every two weeks during lunch) to monitor how well the bookroom is functioning.

CHAPTER THIRTEEN

How to Write Grant Proposals to Acquire More Books

When you begin a dynamic reading program, you will need and want more books. Your beginning inventory will give you an idea how many *more* books you need. That's definitely the place to start: you'll be ready when an administrator, the parents' association, or a local business asks you how you would spend available funds. Having very specific plans even for smaller amounts of money will build others' confidence in your ability to use resources wisely.

After you exhaust all your internal sources, you may decide to seek outside funding, perhaps by writing a proposal to receive a grant. There are three levels to this process: (1) a letter either seeking funds or opening a conversation about funding to support book acquisition; (2) *a concept paper,* a brief form of a proposal and often sufficient for the funding agency's purposes; and (3) a full proposal for a grant to support the purchase of books. Grant proposals may of course be far more encompassing than simply purchasing books; you may find that building your book collection is one very important component of a larger, long-term project for improving your literacy program.

Getting Started

A successful proposal is not produced just by sitting down and writing. All well-conceived, successful plans take a good bit of thinking and planning. It is good for teachers to work together because mutual effort adds to the creativity and is also persuasive to sponsors. Before you even begin, you will want to think about some basic essentials, some sources of funding.

Essential Elements

Almost all guides to proposal writing will tell you that there are two essential elements in seeking funds:

- You need a good idea.
- You need to relate your idea to a problem that it solves.

When you write a proposal for a good book collection, your "good idea" is to provide a large amount of high-quality reading material for the students in your school. Your short-term goal is to increase the amount and quality of reading your students do, and the long-term goal is to raise reading achievement. You may think your cause is so worthy that the reasons for funding are self-evident, but that is not the case. Funding agencies will want to know the specifics—what the problems are and how your idea will solve them. You need to make a logical argument. For example:

- A large number of students are reading below grade level and/or are uninterested in reading.
- There is evidence that increasing the amount of reading (or the variety/quality of reading) is one factor in increasing reading achievement.
- To increase reading (or the variety of reading), we need many books (or a variety of books) in classrooms.
- Currently, there are not enough books (or enough variety of books).
- Therefore, we need more books and we know which ones we need.

Requesting funding is like applying for a job; your proposal is a persuasive document assuring the sponsor that

- Your plan is well conceived.
- You have considered effectiveness and efficiency.
- The plan is cost-effective.

- The person or persons who will implement the plan are knowledgeable, qualified, and committed to the goals.
- This funding will make a measurable difference in students' achievement in literacy.
- You will be accountable for the outcomes of the program.

Following the Guidelines of the Sponsoring Agency

You should usually identify your potential sponsor before you begin writing your proposal, because funding agencies have different procedures, preferences, and requirements. Some agencies have a specific vision and mission, and all funds must be expended to serve that mission; agency personnel and board members do not want to waste their time reading thousands of proposals that may or may not fit that mission.

Sponsors who have definite agendas for giving away dollars will tell you exactly what they expect to see in a proposal. Government and state agencies will usually issue a "request for proposals" (RFP) that provides very specific guidelines. For others, the guidelines are less specific. Some require an initial letter and a series of interim approvals before you are permitted to submit a proposal. Often, a proposal that does not follow the RFP or guidelines will simply be discarded, and no one will read and consider it. All your hard work will have been wasted.

Some steps you can take toward making an effective proposal are:

1. Identify one or more potential funding agencies.
2. Contact the agency and ask for their guidelines, mission statement, and descriptions of projects previously funded. (All of this information will be available in an annual report.)
3. Read the guidelines and other documents very carefully.
4. Decide what step to take first—a letter of inquiry, a concept paper, or a proposal.
5. Outline your proposal, following the guidelines precisely.

In some cases, you may even want to use some of the specific language that you find in the RFP. There may be an "evaluation section" that lets you know how the proposals will be judged, and this is very valuable informa-

tion. For example, if an RFP, in a section called "Impact on Students," asks this:

> Describe the evidence to be used to assess impact on students for the proposed project. Specify measures and procedures for data collection and reporting.

You wouldn't want to say something vague like this:

> We will look at how students are progressing in reading.

Instead, respond appropriately and thoroughly, like this:

> Several forms of evidence will be gathered to document the impact on students of the proposed reading program.

- Students' oral reading performance on a specified set of benchmark texts will be gathered using a standardized procedure (see attached example[1])

  Performance will be rated for fluency, rate (words per minute), and accuracy. A rubric for measuring fluency is attached to this proposal. After the oral reading, students will be asked to respond to several questions designed to assess comprehension. Data will include level of text read successfully (that is, above 95 percent accuracy), rate of reading (words per minute), fluency rating, and number of comprehension questions answered successfully. Scores will be recorded at the beginning, middle, and end of the academic year.
- A standardized test, the [name of test], will be administered at the beginning of grade 2.
- Scores on the state proficiency test [name of test] will be administered and collected at the end of grade 4.
- Additionally, classroom teachers will be asked to rate students' performance on classroom reading tasks.
- Parents will be surveyed to gather evidence that students are reading more at home. The

---

[1] You would attach relevant documents. The benchmark testing example in Chapter 9 contains one such procedure, and you can also find help in the assessment chapter (Chapter 28) of *Guiding Readers and Writers Grades 3–6* (Fountas and Pinnell 2001).

survey is attached to this proposal.

■ Student scores will be collected each year to determine trends in achievement. Scores on standardized test scores will be compared over a three-year period to students' scores in schools that are similar in demographic characteristics but do not have the infusion of books.

A small project would not require such an elaborate documentation system; you could use any *one* of the kinds of data listed above. The key is to demonstrate that you will be evaluating your efforts in a responsible way. Be specific; tell the funding agency exactly what you are prepared to do and use the language that they suggest.

Here's another example. The directions in the RFP say:

The [Foundation or Government Agency] seeks proposals to fund projects designed to enhance the reading comprehension abilities of at-risk students. Proposals that show potential for helping students extend the meaning of fictional and expository texts are encouraged.

Your proposal could incorporate some of the language in the above two sentences—for example:

A key to higher achievement is engaging intermediate-level students in large amounts of reading of a wide variety of texts, both fiction and nonfiction. Our book collection, and the program we propose to implement, will provide specific instruction and a large amount of reading of a wide variety of texts. The book collection will be composed of many high-quality fiction and expository texts. Through specific and explicit instruction directed toward developing comprehension strategies, teachers will assist students in extending the meaning of these texts through writing and oral discussion. Since most of the students in our school are "at risk"—that is, their family incomes are below the poverty level—this instruction and opportunity to read fiction and expository texts is of critical importance.

You will not be submitting the proposal if your plan does not fit into the mission of the funding agency, but if it does, you want to make that clear. Those who read the proposal will be looking for precisely that information.

Sources of Funding

A critical decision in getting started is selecting a prospective sponsor. There are many different sources of funding, private and public, individual and corporate, and the funding source to which you apply has general implications for the form your request will take. Some ways to identify funding sources are:

■ Work through your network of friends and acquaintances, especially those outside education. Let them know you are hoping to obtain more books for the students in your school to read. If you have a good idea, people will keep you in mind when they hear about a source of funding to support your work. After all, you are not seeking these funds for yourself but to support your students.

■ Your public library will have lists and directories of philanthropic foundations. Look through the foundations' documents, and read their mission statements; look carefully at organizations that fund education.

■ Keep in touch with your state education agency so that you will be informed about any special allocations of funds that will fit your goals. State education agencies issue RFPs for such funding.

■ Check the *Federal Register,* a document published by the U.S. Office of Education that describes federal programs The *Federal Register* will be available in libraries as well as on government websites.

■ Surf the Internet for possible funding sources.

■ Become involved in partnerships with a local university where the teachers are interested in beginning new projects and have skills and resources to apply for funding. A good match is a university professor who wants to do research and a classroom teacher interested in improving instruction.

■ Join professional associations like the International Reading Association and the National Council of Teachers of English. Both national and state organizations often offer small grants for teachers.

GOVERNMENT SOURCES

Since literacy is a critical skill for productive citizenship, it is in the state and national interest to improve literacy education. Often, special funds to support literacy learning are allocated by the state and federal government and are distributed by state education agencies or the U.S. Department of Education. Dispersal of these funds must follow the legal guidelines specified in the related legislation. Usually, application for state and federal funding requires an elaborate proposal; it would be difficult for an individual classroom teacher to attempt such a project. Also, there are usually strict guidelines regarding the eligibility of individuals and organizations. For example, state agencies accept proposals from schools, but those applications usually must be approved at the district level before they are sent.

Grant opportunities at the national level are listed in the *Federal Register*. The RFP will specify who is eligible to apply for funds, the approximate amount to be provided, and guidelines for writing the proposal. Your district may have a grants office where you can obtain information about grant opportunities. It is a good idea to keep in constant touch with your grants office or the superintendent's office. Opportunities sometimes arise quickly and the deadlines are tight. Those in the know are ahead of the game.

It may seem daunting to apply for funds at this level; organizing and preparing an elaborate grant proposal takes a lot of effort. But good communication is the key. If your school is applying for "excellence" money, school reform money, or literacy improvement funds, you may be able to include resources for more books within the scope of a larger, more comprehensive effort. Check the guidelines to see whether and what amount of materials will be allowed as part of the funding effort.

PRIVATE FOUNDATIONS

There are many different kinds of foundations. Individuals or families may establish foundations for particular purposes. It will be important to read the background information about the foundation so that you understand how your work can fit within its mission.

Foundations usually prefer that you send a letter of inquiry or a "concept paper," which is a brief (usually two or three pages) description of your proposed project. Foundation staff members will usually read your letter or concept paper and may have it reviewed by outside consultants. Based on that preliminary examination, you may be invited to submit a more detailed proposal (structured according to foundation guidelines) and/or to meet with someone from the foundation.

An individual or group of individuals may establish a foundation to serve a particular community. In this case, the foundation seeks ongoing contributions from citizens and outlines a broad program of funding to support community improvement—health, environment, education, and so on. The foundation is usually governed by a board of community members. Its mission is to make the community a better place to live. A community foundation will have guidelines that tell you the categories of activity they seek to fund. If your proposal fits within a category, ask for the procedures for grant application.

Many large corporations also establish philanthropic branches. Sometimes the mission of the corporate foundation is related to the business; for example, a software company might fund technology in education or a publishing company's foundation might fund projects related to literacy. Alternately, the corporate foundation may wish to fund efforts within certain geographic areas (where their plants or offices are located, for example). A good way to start is to call the large companies in your area to find out if they have programs that fund educational efforts. If they do, ask for the guidelines.

It may help to know someone who is an officer or employee of the corporation. For example, one teacher had a good friend who worked for a large grocery chain. The African American employees of the chain were looking for a good cause. After communication and deliberation, they got together to provide funding over a period of years to support young African American children in a tutoring program.

SERVICE CLUB ORGANIZATIONS

Service clubs offer a way for community leaders to get together to improve life in the community. A few examples are:

- The Junior League.
- The Lions' Club.
- The Kiwanis Club.
- The Rotary Club.
- The Optimist Club (arm of the Optimist International Organization).
- Your school district may have its own versions of service organizations—Parent Teacher Associations, for example, or "booster" clubs, which are usually connected to sports but may be formed to support other activities such as music or literacy. These serv-

ice clubs may be tapped to supply books for in-class reading or for home and summer reading programs.

INDIVIDUALS

Often, individuals form their own giving programs and are known for generous contributions to initiatives that help children. If you know someone who is interested in literacy and makes a practice of donating to special projects, you can start with a courteous letter to the person or to an assistant to introduce your idea. If you have a mutual friend or acquaintance, ask for advice on how to approach the individual; you may even be able to arrange a meeting.

Achieving a "Fit" Between Sponsors and Your Project

To be successful in securing funding, you need to look at what you do from the perspective of the potential sponsor. The sponsor will be asking questions like this:

- Does this proposal fit within our mission?
- Is it worthwhile?
- Is there research to support it?
- Will it benefit the population we want to serve?
- Will the benefit be supplemental (rather than replacing what the school should do anyway)?
- Are the applicants qualified?
- Do they have a good plan?
- Will the dollars be efficiently used?
- How do they plan to show us that the dollars made a difference?

Frankly, it is hard for sponsors to do a good job giving away money. Funding agencies are besieged with requests, all serving different agendas. They need assurance that their dollars will make a difference rather than just support someone's pet project. Increasing the number, variety, and quality of the books that students read, within a program that provides good instruction from a skilled and committed teacher, is well worth funding.

The Personal Touch

There are formal actions involved in seeking funding, but funding agencies like a personal touch. You want to maintain a respectful but friendly relationship with your potential sponsors. Many individuals and companies prefer not to be contacted personally, so a letter will be the only way to present your case. When possible, though, try to manage a personal introduction to the decision makers for the funding agency or staff members who inform them.

Meet with the Sponsor

Ask for a meeting and put your best foot forward. Chances are, you will get no more than one hour to state your case. Prepare to make clear, concise descriptions of your problem and your plan to solve it. Some specific suggestions for a successful meeting are presented in Figure 13–1. In general, simply follow the rules of social courtesy. Be on time and well prepared. Leave at the designated time unless invited to remain.

You want to inform the funding agency of your work, but you also want to be sure that you listen and learn. Let your enthusiasm show, but going into long monologues or deluging the potential sponsor with stacks of paper will generally work against your cause. Have one or two very well prepared pieces of paper; emphasize research and your own staff's commitment; and be prepared to offer more details and/or reports if asked.

Be as specific as you can about what you are doing. Potential sponsors prefer simple reports of the results for individual students or identified groups of students rather than jargon. They are especially responsive to results from their own community or possibilities for students in the local region. Bringing the voices of your students and their parents into the conversation is very effective. Consider very brief vignettes or video segments (for example, a "before and after" portrait of a reader or writer). Bring a sample or two of the kinds of books you need to buy, photographs of classrooms richly supplied with books, one students' reading list for the year showing a great and varied amount of reading.

Invite the Sponsor to Visit Your School

If the potential sponsor is interested in your work, a representative might be persuaded to visit the school. Usually, these visits are brief, so you'll need to plan very carefully. You want the person to experience the essence of your program. Walking through several classrooms gives the impression of a large number of students highly engaged in reading. In addition, you may want to have the visitor observe part of a lesson or a conference. Have

---

Suggestions for Successful Meetings with Potential Sponsors

1. Be sure that your principal or appropriate administrators in your district are informed on an ongoing basis about your efforts to secure funds.

2. If you have a personal contact with the sponsoring agency, ask that person to introduce you and your proposed ideas and to "feel out" whether a meeting would be possible and/or appropriate. Your contact can attest to your sincerity, trustworthiness, and commitment.

3. Prepare and send any advance materials requested by the funding agency.

4. Work collaboratively with staff support people in the funding agency's office to schedule convenient times and places for the meeting.

5. Prepare carefully for the meeting by practicing what you want to say and asking others for feedback.

6. Funding agency representatives will usually prefer to meet with one person, two, or three rather than a large group.

7. Don't deluge the representative with paper but have one excellent, concise, and well-prepared page that clearly shows what you plan to do and why.

8. Try to bring your students' lives and voices into the conversation. Your potential sponsor needs to know that these dollars will make a difference for them and to have a vision of what that difference will be.

9. Listen carefully to the comments and questions of the funding agency representative. These statements offer you insight into the agency's vision and priorities.

10. Follow basic rules of conversation. Answer all questions clearly, specifically, honestly, and concisely. Don't hedge or gush. Avoid long monologues; pause to allow for comments or questions.

11. Be on time (a little early) for the meeting. Be prepared to leave graciously when time is up unless you are invited to stay longer.

12. Invite the agency representative to visit your school, see you working, and meet the students.

Figure 13–1. Suggestions for Successful Meetings with Potential Sponsors

the building administrator and key staff members available to answer questions, but keep the visit as informal as possible. You want to communicate that you are well prepared for the visit and are serious about what you want to do, but you don't want a visitor to think you are putting on a show. As much as possible, provide an authentic picture of what life is like in this building every day—what teachers and students are doing. As in any meeting, answer questions as clearly and honestly as you can. Make the visitor feel at home.

Developing a Letter Requesting Funds

Applying for funds often starts with a letter. For small local grants a letter may be all that is required. The letter in Figure 13–2 is an example of an introductory letter to a funding agency or individual. (The left-hand column identifies the goal of each part of the letter.) Notice that the letter specifically identifies the problem and proposes a clear solution. The request is supported by research; the contributions the school staff are prepared to make are documented; and, the qualifications of those who will lead the effort are presented. Funding agencies need to know that their funds will be well used.

Of course, you will want to modify and personalize this letter to accomplish your own purposes. Also, if you know the addressee very well, you may find the letter a bit too formal. In general, shorter is better, so you may want to eliminate one of the sections. When in doubt, write a very professional letter that presents a formal, supported request.

Developing a Concept Paper Proposing a Funded Project

A concept paper is a brief description of your proposed project. A concept paper for a small grant for money to support a book collection would be no more than three pages. Sometimes the concept paper is a preliminary proposal; if it is well received, you will be invited to submit a more detailed proposal. Occasionally, your project will be funded on the basis of the concept paper

Components of a Letter Seeking Support for a School Book Collection	
Component	**Example of a Statement**
Greeting	Be certain that you have the appropriate individual to address. Be sure that you have his/her accurate name and title and that you spell the name of the funding agency correctly.
Introduce yourself and your idea.	As the teachers and staff of Greensview Elementary School, we are committed to raising our students' achievement in reading. We are seeking sponsorship for a plan to dramatically increase the amount of reading students do at school and at home.
Recognize the funding agency or individual. [Mention any specific contributions made.]	In the past, you have made many important contributions to the education of students in our school. Your partnership has made a significant difference. We are especially appreciate of your sponsoring our subscription to *Time for Kids*.
Provide background information. [Discuss important features of your school. Establish general need if appropriate.]	At Greensview, we serve a population of 530 children, 312 of whom are in grades 3 to 5. Our school is located in an urban area where there are high levels of unemployment and poverty. Over 95% of our students are eligible for free and reduced price lunch. Many of our students are vulnerable to membership in neighborhood gangs, which can be prevented by success in school.
Identify the problem. [Be as specific as you can in documenting the problem.]	We are most concerned about our intermediate grade students. While we have made very good progress in starting Greensview children on the road to reading, the demands in grades 3, 4, and 5 are great. We want our students to become highly proficient readers who can use reading for a variety of purposes. Current reading levels of 57% of our intermediate staff are below recommended national standards.[1] The number of our fourth graders' meeting state standards on the proficiency test improved from 37 percent to 46 percent over the last two years, but we continue to dedicate ourselves to a 100 percent passing rate. Finally, a recent study showed that many of our students do not read voluntarily at home. This situation must change if our students are to succeed in school and later life.

Figure 13–2. Components of a Letter Seeking Support for a School Book Collection

---

[1]The recommended national standards from the Center on Education and the Economy are described in New Standards. *Performance Standards: Volume 1—Elementary School: English Language Arts, Mathematics, Science, Applied Learning.* 1998. National Center on Education and the Economy and the University of Pittsburgh. Printed in the United States of America by Harcourt Brace Educational Measurement.

Components of a Letter Seeking Support for a School Book Collection *(continued)*

Component	Example of a Statement
Propose your solution. [Make a clear summary statement of what you propose to do. Back it with evidence. Cite research in the text or in footnotes.]	This year we are implementing an intensive, research-based instructional program in reading and it is already making a difference. Research has shown that the amount of reading students do is related to increased achievement.[2] The approach combines explicit teaching in small groups and a large amount of independent reading. As teachers, we select books that students can read successfully and, through instruction, gradually increase the difficulty and variety. We want intermediate students to read many kinds of fiction and nonfiction and expand their skills. Our students are reading at least on chapter book per week. They are reading at school and at home every day, and we are running out of books!
Describe the solution. [Be concise in describing your plan of action. If the sponsor wants more a more detailed plan, you can provide it later.]	We propose to increase the number and variety of books available to students by building a school book collection to support guided reading (small group instruction), independent reading, and home reading. This collection is efficient and cost-effective because it is shared among teachers and students at grades 3, 4, and 5. The collection will ensure that every student has sufficient books to read massively and widely.
Establish your credibility. [Persuade the sponsor that you can do the job.]	All of the intermediate teachers on our staff have successfully completed an intensive training course to improve their instruction. They are highly knowledgeable about selecting books for instruction. We have made an inventory of our current collection and have a plan for acquiring precisely those volumes we need to support good instruction.
Establish your commitment and that of your colleagues. [Indicate specific "in kind" contributions the school community has made and is prepared to make.]	We have developed a plan of action to make the most of any resources we receive. Members of our staff have reserved and committed extra time in the summer to organize the collection. Parents have formed a volunteer group and are prepared to help us maintain the collection and assure efficient use. We have placed the highest priority on these books for students. We used available funds from the district, as well as a small grant from the state. We held a book fair that helped us to obtain some books. Teachers and parents have already contributed over 300 books. A local office supply store has agreed to donate 30 cardboard library book boxes to protect our books.

Figure 13–2. Components of a Letter Seeking Support for a School Book Collection (continued)

---

[2]Researchers found that children who scored in the 98th percentile read 65 books per year; children who scored in the 90th percentile read 21.2 books per year; children scored in the 20th percentile read .7 books per year; and children who scored in the 2nd percentile read 0 books per year (see Anderson, R.C., P.T. Wilson, L.G. Fielding. 1998. Growth in Reading and How Children Spend Their Time Outside of School. *Reading Research Quarterly*, 23: 285-303.

Components of a Letter Seeking Support for a School Book Collection (continued)

Component	Example of a Statement
Describe how you will tell whether your project is making a difference. [Assure the sponsor that you will document and report the outcomes of your program. Be sure that you include student achievement measures.]	We expect the implementation of our instructional program to have positive outcomes for students' reading achievement. We have designed a rigorous evaluation system that is consistent with national [or state] standards. We will document the number of students who meet grade level standards, as measured by passage reading and assessment of comprehension. We will also document and report the number of students who meet criteria on the state proficiency test in reading.
End with a summary statement about impact. [Be specific about the significance of the investment.]	This project, if funded, will make a difference in reading achievement for 312 students during the 2002-2003 school year. These children will read over 12,480 books during the year. But, the collection will be used for many years to come. It will never need replacing in entirety. Over 8 years, about 700 children will have read selected books from the collection at a cost of about [ ] per child.
End with willingness to provide more information.	We would be happy to show you the collection we have started as well as to have you visit our school and observe reading instruction. We hope that your [company, agency] priorities can include this positive contribution to our students' literacy learning.
Signature	Principal, School Leadership Team, Parent Volunteer Coordinator

Figure 13–2. Components of a Letter Seeking Support for a School Book Collection (continued)

alone, and all you will be expected to submit is a detailed budget. In any case, a concept paper is well worth developing because it forces you to put your ideas into concise form. The example of a concept paper presented in Figure 13–3 is less than fifteen hundred words.

In this example, the different components of the concept paper have identifying headings, but you wouldn't necessarily need them. Notice that the concept paper is roughly parallel to the letter of application but provides slightly more information. It begins with a statement of rationale and purpose. Be sure that you demonstrate that you know the demographic details describing students in your school.

If you have completed any informal studies that show need, you can refer to them here. Knowing the students adds to your credibility. Specific objectives let the funding agency know precisely what you plan to do, and the plan of action that follows demonstrates that you have thought through the process and are well pre-

pared. The time line provides the details of your schedule for carrying out your plan. Finally, a few sentences about evaluation show how you will document outcomes. A summary statement brings the application to a close but offers further details if there is interest.

Writing a Proposal

Effective proposals present your ideas in clear language. When in doubt, use plain language rather than educational jargon. Often, you will be communicating with persons outside the field of education. You may need to use "insider" words like *guided reading*, but be sure to define them in your text.

Another mistake proposal writers sometimes make is to use sweeping generalizations that are not supported by specific evidence. The more you can make *supported* rather than general statements, the more credibility your proposal will have. (Figure 13–4 contains some examples of supported statements.) Making supported statements is especially important when you are talking about the problems and issues in your school. You'll want to provide evidence that those problems exist and document their severity.

Proposals also tend to have specific guidelines as to the length of each section, the overall length, and the number of appendices allowed. Follow these guidelines precisely; your proposal could be disqualified if you do not follow them. More is not necessarily better when it comes to a proposal; too many words can get in the way of your message.

Components of a Proposal
Figure 13–5 lists the components of a full proposal for a grant to provide books for guided, independent, and home reading in grades 3 through 5.

- The first component, an abstract or summary, is very important. Indeed, the prospective sponsor may read nothing else! An example of an abstract is presented in Figure 13–6. This abstract is 150 words long and provides the important information about the proposal.
- Next, write an introduction and rationale. Your purpose here is to convince the potential sponsor of the importance of your idea.
- Provide a clear statement of purpose.
- Describe the students to be served by the project. Here, you can clearly establish the fact that your students need more books and that the funds can make a difference for a large number of them.
- Next, state the specific objectives of the proposal. There is sometimes confusion between goals and objectives. Goals are broader, overall statements, while objectives are more specific and can be measured.

Example of a Concept Paper

Introduction and Rationale
As a school staff, our primary goal is to raise achievement in reading for students in grades three, four, and five at Greensview School in Urban City. Reading is the most important skill our students will develop in elementary school. Our goal is to assure that every one of our students enters middle school with the high levels of proficiency in reading that is essential for later school success and a quality life. We are especially committed to our students' developing the ability to read with good comprehension and to use fiction and nonfiction texts as tools for learning. This goal is possible given the preparation we have undertaken and the commitment of our staff.

Purpose
Over the last year we have investigated research-based best practice in reading instruction and prepared our staff to implement a dynamic reading program that will massively increase time for teaching reading as well as students' independent reading. Our proposal provides for a 100 percent increase in the time for daily reading instruction and a 300 percent increase the amount of school and home reading students do. A high quality school book collection, with both fiction and nonfiction materials, is essential to support our program, which includes small group reading, independent individual reading, and home reading. In this proposal, we seek funds in the amount of $20,820, to support the acquisition of classroom books and a school book collection that will provide the rich text resources that our students need.

Population to be Served
At Greensview, we serve a population of 530 children, 312 of whom are in grades 3 to 5. Our school is located in an urban area where there are high levels of unemployment and poverty. Over 95percent of our students are eligible for free and reduced price lunch. Many of our students are vulnerable to membership in neighborhood gangs, which can be prevented by success in school. We are most concerned about our intermediate grade students. While we have made very good progress in starting Greensview children on the road to reading, the demands in grades 3, 4, and 5 are great. We want our students to become highly proficient readers who can use reading for a variety of purposes. Current reading levels of 57 percent are below recommended national standards.[1]

Figure 13–3. Example of a Concept Paper

Example of a Concept Paper *(continued)*

The number of our fourth graders meeting state standards on the proficiency test improved from 37 percent to 46 percent over the last two years, but we continue to dedicate ourselves to a 100 percent passing rate. Finally, a recent study showed that many of our students do not read voluntarily at home. This situation must change if our students are to succeed in school and later life.

Specific Objectives

We propose to dramatically increase[2] the number of third, fourth, and fifth grade students who meet national standards for reading achievement. We also seek to increase the number of fourth grade students who meet state criteria on the proficiency test in reading. Finally, our goal is to increase the amount of reading students do at school and at home to at least one chapter book per week.

Plan of Action

Four years ago, the primary teachers in our school undertook an extensive project to improve classroom instruction. They established small group guided reading as well as a systematic and intensive phonics and spelling program. Reading and writing in kindergarten were greatly increased. As a result, we find that our students coming into third grade are reading more and at higher levels of text. For example, using a systematic end-of-year assessment, we test our students using nationally recommended benchmarks for reading.[3] In Fall, 1998, only 25 percent of entering third graders were able to read Level M, the national recommended standard. Further, only 15 percent of those students performed successfully on assessment of comprehension of the same passages. In Fall, 2001, 47 percent of entering third graders were able to read Level M with high accuracy and satisfactory performance on comprehension.

We see this increase as evidence of a dramatic improvement in our program, and we expect scores to rise further as we improve our work in the primary grades. We must, however, provide for further progress in the intermediate grades, especially as the demands for performance rise sharply and much more sophisticated skills in reading and writing are required.

Research indicates that students who do not become highly proficient readers in the upper elementary years are unlikely to do so throughout their lives. In addition, these elementary years are the time when students build up a large volume of reading and develop important habits. Research has shown that the amount of reading students do makes a difference in achievement.[4]

Last year, intermediate teachers took steps to examine the literacy program and to expand their skills. A leadership team, including the principal and teachers in grades 3 to 5, participated in a year of training; in addition, a literacy facilitator has been employed and trained to work with the staff over the next two years. We will dedicate one hour of instructional time per day for reading. All grade 3, 4, and 5 teachers will participate in ongoing training and coaching to improve classroom instruction. Our approach combines explicit teaching in small groups and a large amount of independent reading. In classrooms where we have implemented this approach, our students are reading at least one chapter book per week. They are reading at school and at home every day, and we are running out of books!

As teachers, we select books that students can read successfully and, through instruction, gradually increase the difficulty and variety. We want intermediate students to read many kinds of fiction and nonfiction and expand their skills. Our teachers are highly knowledgeable about selecting books for instruction. We have already done a great deal of investigation to assure that we acquire a collection that will support acceleration of progress in reading. We have made an inventory of our current collection and have a plan for acquiring precisely those volumes we need to support good instruction.

We have developed a plan of action to make the most of any resources we receive. Members of our staff have reserved and committed extra time in the summer to organize the collection. Parents have formed a volunteer group and are prepared to help us maintain the collection and assure efficient use.

Figure 13–3. Example of a Concept Paper (continued)

Example of a Concept Paper *(continued)*

We have placed the highest priority on these books for students. We used available funds from the district, as well as a small grant from the state. We held a book fair that helped us to obtain some books. Teachers and parents have already contributed over 300 books. A local office supply store has agreed to donate 30 cardboard library book boxes to protect our books. Our staff has committed volunteer time in the summer to organize the collection.

Time Line

Given the plans that we have already put into action, we will be able to complete the organizational work to have the book collection ready for use in September, 2002. With the assistance of parent volunteers, the collection will be maintained and evaluated during the 2002-2003 academic year. During that time, grade 3, 4, and 5 teachers will participate in ongoing training and coaching (at least 40 hours). This training is sponsored through a local university-school partnership. In summer 2003, more books will be added to the collection, which will provide the full basic collection for teachers' use in 2003-2004.

Evaluation Plan

In Spring, 2002, 2003, and 2004, we will collect and report scores on a systematic benchmark assessment system that we use to determine the percentage of students who meet national standards for reading level. We will also collect and report the percentages of fourth graders who successfully meet criteria for the state proficiency test in reading. In addition, we will collect and compile data on students' weekly reading to determine the amount and kind of reading that they do. These data will be considered by the entire school staff at an evaluation meet each fall.

Summary Statement

In this concept paper, we have described a plan of action for expanding the reading skills of students in grades 3, 4, and 5 at Greensview, an urban school serving a high risk population. Our plan will put books into students' hands and engage them through motivation and intensive reading instruction. Our goals are to increase the number of students who meet standards for proficient reading as well as to increase the amount students read at school and at home. A basic school book collection, with over 3,000 books, varied by fiction and nonfiction, is essential to support our plans. This collection will serve over 400 students during the next three years, and will be an important component of our reading instruction for years to come. We will be happy to provide a more detailed proposal for this plan.

[1] The recommended national standards from the Center on Education and the Economy are described in New Standards. *Performance Standards: Volume 1 – Elementary School: English Language Arts, Mathematics, Science, Applied Learning.* 1997. National Center on Education and the Economy and the University of Pittsburgh. Printed in the United States of America by Harcourt Brace Educational Measurement.

[2] If possible, consult with the funding agency to determine whether a specific percentage (for example, to 85 percent) is required.

[3] New Standards.

[4] Researchers found that children who scored in the 98th percentile read 65 books per year; children who scored in the 90th percentile read 21.2 books per year; children who scored in the 20th percentile read .7 books per year; and children who scored in the 2nd percentile read 0 books per year (see Anderson, R.C., P.T. Wilson, L.G. Fielding. 1998. Growth in Reading and How Children Spend Their Time Outside of School. *Reading Research Quarterly,* 23: 285-303.

Figure 13–3. Example of a Concept Paper (continued)

Grounding Statements in Evidence

General Statements	Supported Statements
Students in grades 3, 4, and 5 need more help in reading.	Our yearly assessment revealed that 65 percent of our third grades, 57 percent of fourth graders, and 51 percent of fifth graders do not meet national standards for reading performance at the end of the year. We are concerned that 49 percent of fifth graders are going on to middle school lacking the necessary reading skills to succeed.
Students in our school are falling behind in reading.	In fall of this year, systematic assessment revealed that 35 percent of entering third graders are reading at least 10 points below grade level standards.
Students in our school are reluctant to read.	A survey of parents revealed that the average time our students spend reading at home is only 10 minutes. For 57 percent of students surveyed, the time is less than 3minutes! Our analysis of school reading program revealed that students read an average of only 10 books per year. Reading practice is critically important for upper elementary students. We propose to increase the number of books read by 300 percent.

Figure 13–4.   Grounding Statements in Evidence

Some examples of goals and their related objectives are presented in Figure 13–7.

◼ In the plan of action, present exactly what you plan to do. While you do not want to include unimportant details (such as the colors of boxes), you do need enough detail to convince the sponsor that you know what you are doing.

◼ Your evaluation plan should detail precisely what you will do to determine whether the program is working or not. Both the plan of action and the evaluation plan should be more detailed than you presented in your concept paper, but be sure to adhere to any stated length restrictions.

◼ Both plan of action and evaluation design should be reflected in the time line. A simple way to present a time line is to detail briefly the actions during each month of the time period proposed. (A sample time line is presented in Figure 13–8.)

◼ At the end of the proposal proper, present a statement of impact that summarizes the potential this proposal has for making a difference. Refer to student outcomes. Include specific numbers when possible.

◼ Develop a budget (an example is presented in Figure 13–9).

◼ Include appendixes that extend the proposal. One appendix might be a bibliography if you have supported your rationale with research. Another could contain the curriculum vitae or brief biographical

Components of a Proposal

❖ Abstract or Summary

❖ Introduction and Rationale

❖ Purpose

❖ Students to be Served

❖ Objectives

❖ Plan of Action

❖ Timeline

❖ Evaluation Plan

❖ Statement of Impact

❖ Personnel

❖ Budget

❖ Appendixes

❖ Letters of Endorsement

❖ Vita of Project Personnel

❖ Documentation of Achievements

Figure 13–5.   Components of a Proposal

Example of an Abstract

We propose to increase the reading opportunities and reading achievement for students in grades 3, 4, and 5 at Greensview Elementary School. In this proposal, we describe a plan of action for establishing an efficient, economical, high-quality book collection to support small group reading instruction and independent and home reading. Students will read appropriate fiction and nonfiction books daily and expand their skills as they read greater variety. Our goal is to provide high-quality instruction that will assure that students are highly proficient readers of fiction and nonfiction as they leave elementary school. The requested funds would provide over 3,000 books for instructional and home reading and influence the reading achievement of 700 children over the next 8 years. The effectiveness of the project will be evaluated through documentation of the number of books read and collection of scores on individual and standardized tests for all students involved.

Figure 13–6. Example of an Abstract

Sample Goals and Related Objectives

Goal 1. *To increase grade three, four, and five students' reading.*

❖ Objective 1. To increase the number of books read during small group reading instruction.

❖ Objective 2. To increase the number of books students read independently during the reading block of time.

❖ Objective 3. To increase the time and number of books that students read at home.

Goal 2. *To improve the effectiveness of reading instruction for students in grades three, four, and five.*

❖ Objective 1. To increase the time for small group reading instruction during the reading block of time.

❖ Objective 2. To provide appropriate materials to support effective small group reading instruction.

❖ Objective 3. To increase the number, quality, and variety of texts to support small group reading instruction.

Goal 3. *To raise reading achievement of upper elementary grade students at Greensview School.*

❖ Objective 1. To increase the number of students who meet established grade level standards for reading at the end of grade three, four, and five.

❖ Objective 2. To increase the number of fourth grade students who meet criteria for satisfactory performance on the state proficiency test.

Figure 13–7. Sample Goals and Related Objectives

sketches of project personnel; still another can provide letters of support from credible people who can testify to your efforts.

These components may vary from proposal to proposal. Sometimes you will be responding to a specific RFP, and in that case, you will follow those directions rather than these general guidelines.

Writing a complete proposal is a lengthy process.

The good news is that once you have prepared one of these proposals, you can draw from it to write others for different sponsors and use it as a source for verbiage for letters of application and/or concept papers. Figure 13–10 summarizes the steps in preparing a proposal. Obviously you need to begin well ahead of your deadline and revise and refine as you go. Establishing clear deadlines for each step of work will help you avoid as much last-minute stress as possible.

Sample Time Line for Establishing Classroom and School Book Collections		
Month	**Tasks**	**Personnel Responsible**
March	Complete long-range plans for staff training and reserve dates.	Principal Primary literacy team [1]
April	Make inventory of current collection. Complete lists of books to order. Contact publisher representatives and negotiate for best prices.	Primary literacy team
May	Make final selections and create orders. Involve total staff to provide input. Plan staff training.	Primary literacy team All staff Principal
June	Hold day of staff training to prepare for organizing and using the collection and to use instructional techniques.	Staff development coordinator All staff.
July	Unpack books, label, and organize them. Place books for classroom collections in classrooms. Create system for using the collection.	Primary literacy team Volunteers
August	Hold two days of staff training on instruction. Use books as part of training. Organize and label classroom collections. Train volunteers to assist in maintaining the book collection.	Staff development coordinator All staff Volunteers
September	Implement instructional program. Assess students' reading and form reading groups. Hold two meetings to discuss use of classroom collections and school book collection.	School staff development coordinator All staff
Monthly	Hold monthly meetings for further professional development. Mid-year—collect evaluation data on students.	School staff development coordinator Primary literacy team All staff
April	Assess classroom collections and school book collection. Evaluate levels; note needs for next year. Have appreciation lunch for volunteers.	Primary literacy team All staff Volunteers
May	Place new book orders. Collect final evaluation data on students.	Primary literacy team All staff
June	Analyze evaluation data. Prepare final report. Hold project evaluation meeting.	Primary literacy team All staff Principal

Figure 13–8. Sample Time Line for Establishing Classroom and School Book Collections

[1]The primary literacy team consists of one teacher from each grade level (K, 1, 2, 3), the principal, the school staff developer, and the Reading Recovery teacher and/or special education teacher.

		Funds Requested		
Sample Budget for a Proposal				
Item	Description	Year 1	Year 2	Total
1	Personnel			
a.	Project Director and Committee	Donated	Donated	-0-
b.	Clerical Support (Yr. 1 = 80 hours @ $16.00) (Yr. 2 = 40 hours @ $16.00)	$1,280	$ 640	$1,920
c.	Volunteer Support	Donated	Donated	-0-
	Total Personnel	**$1,280**	**$640**	**$1,920**
2.	Materials and Supplies			
a.	Boxes for Books (Yr. 1 = 200 @ $2.00) (Yr. 2 = 100 @ $2.00)	$400	$200	$600
b.	Supplies	$50	$25	$75
	Total for Materials and Supplies	**$450**	**$225**	**$675**
3.	**Books**			
a.	Single Titles for Independent Reading in Classrooms Grade 3 (Levels K-R) = 75 single titles x 3 classrooms= 225 books x $5.00 Grade 4 (Levels N-U) = 75 single titles x 3 classrooms = 225 books x $5.00 Grade 5 (Levels Q-X) = 100 single titles x 2 classrooms = 200 books x $5.00	$2,250 [450 books]	$1,000 [200 books]	$3,250 [650 books]
b.	Basic Collection for Grades 3 to 5* Additional 7 copies of 67 titles @ $5.00 = $2,345. Additional 203 titles, 12 copies each = $12,180	$7,265 [1,453 books]	$7,260 [1,452 books]	$14,525 [2,905 books]
	Total for Books	**$9,515**	**$8,260**	**$17,775**
4.	Other			
a.	Miscellaneous Expenses	$100	$100	$200
b.	Overhead	**Donated**	**Donated**	-0-
	Total Other	**$100**	**$100**	**$200**
	TOTAL REQUESTED	**$11,345**	**$9,225**	**$20,570**

Figure 13–9. Sample Budget for a Proposal

---

*One-half of the book collection is purchased each year so that selections may be tested and evaluated carefully.

Sample Budget for a Proposal *(continued)*

NOTES TO THE BUDGET:

1a. Our school's literacy coordinator, assisted by a voluntary committee of teachers, will provide leadership by acting as a steering committee to acquire and organize the collection for use. The committee members are: [NAMES]. The school librarian, [NAME] will assist in providing for a convenient space to house the collection. These individuals have made a commitment to the project and have reserved four days in the summer to work on the project.

1b. In Year 1, the equivalent of two weeks of clerical support is needed to unpack, organize, and label books and to establish the check-out system so that the collection can be efficiently used. In Year 2, the equivalent of one week of clerical support is needed to expand the collection and house new books.

1c. Parent volunteers have been secured to maintain the collection during the next two years. On a regular basis, parents will file any new books that are ordered, refile books that are used and check the order of the collection. Volunteer efforts will be coordinated by [NAME].

2a. To keep the collection in an orderly and attractive way, heavy cardboard "magazine" boxes will be used. These boxes may be purchased at discount from a school supplier. Boxes will hold an average of 10 books each and will be needed for the entire collection, including those titles in the current inventory.

2b. General supplies will be needed to label books and magazine boxes and to create the checkout system, for example, tape, a labeling system, markers, and library cards.

3a. With our current average class size of 28 students per class, our analysis indicates that each classroom needs a library of single titles of at least 100 books. This classroom library of single titles will be supplemented by the school library resources as well as by borrowing some single titles from the basic school collection (3b). Grade 3 and 4 classrooms already have an average of 25 books, but grade 5 classrooms are not at all well supplied. We propose supplying classrooms with 500 titles during Year 1 and 200 additional titles during Year 2.

3b. Our goal over the two-year period is to create a basic collection to be shared across grades three, four, and five classrooms. Currently, in addition to the single title classroom copies, we possess 67 titles with multiple copies from levels H to X that we consider suitable for the collection, but we do not have enough copies of some of these titles. We especially need titles at levels P through U to support readers in grades 4 and 5. We propose to add an average of 6 books per title to expand to sets of 12 copies each for the 67 titles. To expand the shared book collection, we propose to add 203 titles, with 6 copies of each in Year 1 and 6 more copies in Year 2. The total collection will house 3,240 books in all and will be used by 672 students over a nine year period. Free shipping costs will negotiated with book suppliers.

4a. It is anticipated that some funds will be needed for miscellaneous expenses (for example, providing refreshments for parent volunteers or making telephone calls to books suppliers). A small amount is included in the budget to support these expenses.

4b. Administrative or "overhead" costs of 8 percent are usually built into grant applications. These costs have been waived by the superintendent and board in order to maximize the use of funds to buy books for students.

Figure 13–9. Sample Budget for a Proposal (continued)

Summary

There are a number of ways to apply for funding to support your book collection, ranging from person-to-person contact with potential sponsors to writing a letter of application or concept paper to preparing a full proposal. While it is a great deal of work and effort to produce a proposal, the process sometimes brings colleagues together around important problems. Securing funding means that someone important recognizes the importance of your work, so it is a real boost for the success of your project. If you go about it the right way, you can deepen the vision you share with your colleagues and even have some fun doing it.

Suggestions for Professional Development

1. Prior to a staff meeting, identify one or two potential sponsors for building classroom collections and/or a school bookroom collection.
2. As a whole group, generate ideas.
3. Form teams to write a letter of inquiry, a concept paper, or a full proposal. If you have two sources,

Steps in Writing a Proposal for a Grant to Support Guided, Independent, and Home Reading

1. Prepare some clear statements about:
   - ❖ What you need.
   - ❖ Why you need it.
   - ❖ What problem it addresses.
   - ❖ How it will solve the problem.
   - ❖ Specific details such as number of books and levels.
2. Total costs and costs per student.
3. Identify local, state, and federal funding sources.
4. Select one funding source to begin.
5. Research and obtain guidelines if available.
6. Read the guidelines to determine the priorities of the funding agency. Seek advice from individuals if possible.
7. Using the guidelines and the specific statements you have prepared, generate ideas, design the proposal, and outline the budget.
8. Develop a work plan for writing the proposal; share jobs.
9. Perform any research needed to write the proposal (such as documentation of student performance in past years).
10. Write the first draft of the proposal.
11. Complete the budget.
12. Assemble attachments, if appropriate. Ask for letters of support well before your deadline.
13. Complete forms for the funding agency, if applicable.
14. Review and edit the draft, involving several outside people who can give feedback.
15. Prepare final copy, being sure that it is business-like, professional, and attractive.
16. Write a cover letter.
17. Submit proposal by the deadline.

Figure 13–10. Steps in Writing a Proposal for a Grant to Support Guided, Independent, and Home Readings

form two teams. (If you have only one source, form teams to prepare specific components.)

4. Have teams read the guidelines of the funding agency carefully and use the examples and suggestions in this chapter to prepare their document.
5. Have members of the staff not on the writing teams review the documents and make suggestions.
6. Revise the documents.
7. Ask outsiders to read your letters, papers, or proposals and provide suggestions. You might consider people from the business community or any person familiar with funded projects.
8. Finalize your letters, concept papers, or proposals and submit them to the potential funding agencies.
9. Celebrate together if any of your grants or applications is funded!

CHAPTER FOURTEEN

BOOK CLUBS, GIFTS, AND COST-EFFECTIVE PLANNING

Like any valuable collection, good book collections are gathered over time. Receiving a grant will give your book collection a big boost, and it is helpful in the beginning to acquire a critical mass of books, at least the starter collection described in Chapter 12. But sometimes those funds are hard to come by and require a lot of effort. Even if you have a starter or basic collection, you will still need to increase your number of books over time. Your classroom needs a rich collection of single titles, and you need access to multiple copies for guided reading and literature study. You'll need to make the most of the resources you have and explore creative ways to acquire books at little or no cost.

Using Internal Resources Strategically

As we've seen, the school bookroom is the most economical option for acquiring the multiple copies of titles needed for guided reading and literature study. For classroom libraries you will need single copies of a range of titles, but you may find that you can get better prices if a group of teachers coordinate their orders, putting them together to make a larger purchase.

Internal resources are likely to be combinations of:

■ Yearly textbook allocations.
■ Yearly materials budgets.
■ Donations of cash from the parents' association or a local business.
■ Special funds provided specifically for purchasing books.
■ Gifts of books.

Sometimes districts will purchase large quantities of books to support guided and independent reading; the deep discounts possible with large orders like this really help. Also, almost every school has some discretion in terms of its yearly budget for books and materials. While restrictions are usually attached to these funds, it is often possible to direct some portion of the money to buying books for the collection—after all, they are your textbooks for teaching reading. And these days, with literacy receiving national attention, state or local funding is often designated specifically for purchasing books. This funding is different from the resources described in the previous chapter because you do not have to write proposals to receive it. Local individuals and businesses may also make gifts of books. In general, never turn down any good books someone offers to give you, but do remember that not all books are appropriate for guided reading.

Becoming Involved in Purchasing

Unfortunately, large sums of money are often spent on books without much thought. Ordering books is a difficult and time-consuming job, and busy administrators have little time to spend doing so. You and your colleagues may want to volunteer to examine and order books. Your time will be well spent—you will not only have a better chance of acquiring quality resources for your students but also become more familiar with the texts and thus use them more effectively.

Try to purchase individual titles rather than "kits." Kits will no doubt include some high-quality books, and they may appear economical, but they will also include books that you won't wish to use or that will not interest your students. In addition, be cautious about the levels assigned to books by their publisher. Leveling books is an inexact science, a complex process in which many factors must be considered. A given publisher uses particular scales that are not necessarily the same as those of other publishers and that may not necessarily apply to your students. The gradient of text we have described here can guide your selection but it, too, is not the final authority. The best authority is you, based on your own analysis. You and your colleagues can best decide the specific books your students need.

Spending Resources Strategically

You may or may not be able to make suggestions on the way funds are spent, but it is wise to be prepared. In other words, know the books you want to order *before* the funds become available. You will be ready at a moment's notice to place your order!

Titles for a starter set should be identified by school personnel who know the students and their interests and needs—therefore we do not provide a "short list." You can easily make your own wish list, however. After you have made an inventory of the books you already have, take your list to a local bookstore that has a large collection of children's books. (If there are no large children's bookstores in your area, plan this visit in conjunction with an out-of-town trip to a conference or a social event.) Spend some time browsing through and even reading sections of these books and place check marks after titles you especially like. Often, the owner or manager will be happy to work with you and advise you, since they know you may become a very good customer.

You can also look up books on the Internet on bookseller websites; you'll be able to see a facsimile of the front cover of the book and read summary material and reviews by customers. Unfortunately, though, you cannot examine the books and think about them in relation to your own students. Another place you will find collections of books to examine is at bookseller displays set up at local state and national reading conferences. Some of these books are sold as kits, and it's important to examine each book individually, not buy a collection blindly. Booksellers will sometimes also bring collections of books to your school or a central office so that teachers can look at them. Don't neglect trade books—that is where you will find the greatest variety.

Whatever your strategy, this knowledge of the titles you need gives you power. Sometimes small sums of money must be spent very quickly, and administrators will be grateful for a "ready-to-go" order.

Money Saved Is Money Earned

Any money you save is money you can use to buy more books. When you purchase books, maximize your purchasing power—large orders receive bigger discounts and are more likely to include free or reduced shipping costs. Another way to save money is to reduce your photocopying costs. Think carefully before you duplicate those worksheets—ask your students to write in their response journal instead. If you and your colleagues promise your principal that you will decrease photocopying costs by at least 25 percent, you will have a surprising amount of money to spend on books. (A teacher recently told us how much students liked and took pride in writing in their journals and how much time she saved by no longer having to stand at the copy machine.) Also, if you can eliminate the need for one consumable workbook or unnecessary textbook, you will save more dollars.

Look for ways to conserve costs across the board:

- Produce larger book orders by placing them once a year or once every two years.
- Develop an action plan for making the best use of supplies.
- Involve students in conserving supplies.

Don't do without supplies you and your students need, but carefully evaluate all purchases. Sometimes "homemade" versions of expensive items can be just as effective. Eliminate expensive items that have no proven value and pour the resources into something that does have value—promoting students' engagement with text.

Acquiring Leveled Texts Without Spending Money

If you are just beginning to implement reading workshop and guided reading, it may seem nearly impossible to get enough books. And it is true that good collections are built over several years. There are ways, though, to get enough texts to begin even if you have limited resources.

Reshape and Reuse What You Already Have

All schools have books. Chances are, you have the thick anthologies typically used in basal reading systems.

These anthologies are full of articles and stories that may be excellent texts for guided reading. Here are some suggestions:

1. Gather anthologies used at several grade levels appropriate for your range of students.
2. Go through each anthology, identifying selections that have potential. Using the characteristics and prototypes provided in this book, identify a level for each selection.
3. Pencil in the level in the table of contents or make an "index" for the selections.
4. Use the selections exactly as you would leveled books. Each teacher will need only eight to twelve copies of the anthology.
5. Try the leveled selections over time and adjust them as you use them with students.

One enterprising group of teachers received permission from the administration to "razor blade" selections out of old anthologies that were no longer used. With simple bindings the articles and short stories became individual texts in their leveled book collections.

You may find treasures by visiting the book storage room in your school or your district's warehouse. Old children's magazines may be a source for good short stories and informational pieces as well, although you will want to be sure that the information is not dated. Consult your school librarian in every step of building a school book collection. Texts or funds may be available to make the link between library and leveled book collection.

Work with Public Libraries

Many public libraries allow teachers to check out large numbers of books for as many as twenty or thirty days. You can certainly get many good read-aloud selections from libraries and use public library books to supplement your individual titles, leaving your own funds free to acquire multiple titles. Very well resourced libraries may even let you check out multiple copies of books to supplement your guided reading program. Visit the public library in the same way you visit a bookstore—get to know what is there and find out what their regulations allow you to do.

Using a public library in this way does require some special organizational procedures in your classroom.

You can identify these books with a colorful sticky note and/or place them in a special basket or area and enlist your students' help in caring for them. On the classroom calendar, place a red ring around the date for returning or renewing books. Students who select public library books for individual reading will need to watch the calendar carefully and be sure the books are back in the classroom a day or two before they need to be returned.

Use Book Clubs

Book clubs are an excellent source for texts. Most book clubs give free books to the teacher when students order a certain number. Also, your students have the opportunity to purchase books at a reasonable cost. Owning a book you have selected yourself is strong motivation to increase home reading. Scholastic and Troll are the two most frequently used book clubs, and Figure 14–1 lists some of their features.

Book clubs will send students a colorful flier/order form at regular intervals. Since these books are popular trade books, you are likely to know some of them—especially the series books. Look at the book club flier yourself before handing it out so that you can plan some book talks (see Chapter 1) to get students interested in a variety of good books. Without taking over the process, you can guide students' selection through discussion.

Students can read the books they purchase for independent reading and then, if they choose, can lend them to their friends or to the classroom library or include them on the rack or shelf of student-recommended books. As students order books, you will be able to choose free books. Again, using your inventory and the lists in this book, order those books that meet your needs.

Hold Book Fairs at the School

A local bookseller will often be happy to hold a book fair at your school, bringing in a large number of books to sell at a discount. Typically, students at all grade levels participate. Advertise the book fair well in advance, giving parents an idea of the kinds of books that will be available and how much they will cost. Remind students the night before so that they remember to bring money if they are going to purchase a book. During the day of the fair, different groups of students are allowed

Book Clubs for Elementary Students		
Scholastic Book Clubs Call 1-800-SCHOLASTIC (1-800-724-6527) scholastic.com		Bonus points are accumulated. Use bonus points to order free books from the catalogs.
CLUB	**LEVEL**	**DESCRIPTION**
Lucky	2-3	Fiction and nonfiction titles. Picture books. Early chapter books. Junior novels.
Arrow	4-5-6	Award-winning titles. Fiction, nonfiction (biography, history, informational) Variety of themes.
Club de Lectura	Pre K-5	Spanish and bilingual books. Spanish cassettes. From picture books and beginning readers to chapter books. Translations and original literature in Spanish.
Troll Book Club Call 1-800-541-1097 1-888-99-TROLL (1-888-718-7655) Fax 1-888-71-TROLL (1-888-718-7655) Troll Book Clubs 2 Lethbridge Plaza Mahwah, NJ 07430 www.troll.com [call 800 number for password]		Use bonus points to order any selection in catalogs. Paperback selections at different grade levels. Selections range from picture books to longer chapter books. Select grade level: Pre-K-K, K-1, 2-3, 4-6

Figure 14–1.   Book Clubs for Elementary Students

to browse the books and make purchases.

If you can, visit the fair before your students do so that you have an idea of the books that will be sold. Sometimes, you can even give the bookseller a list of books you would like to see. As with the book clubs, you can give book talks before the fair. Often, the school gets deep discounts or free books in proportion to student purchases for sponsoring the fair. Again, students can elect to "lend" books to the class after reading them.

Work with Parents to Hold Fund-Raisers

Fund-raising events can generate resources to support book purchases. Remember that it only takes $250 to supply one level of a basic collection for a school bookroom. People who attend fund-raising events such as entertainment shows, bake sales, or fairs like to know that their dollars will be used for something as worthwhile as buying books for the students to read.

Make Donations, Loans, and Gifts Possible

There are many creative ways that individuals can contribute to a classroom or school book collection.

A "Lending" Program

One teacher invited parents to lend books to the class for a year (Figure 14–2 is the letter she sent home with her students). As the books came in, she made a list of the lenders and their addresses. She had students write a brief thank-you note to send home with the lenders' child. At the end of the year, lenders were contacted and asked whether they would like to have the books returned or to leave them in the classroom for next year's group. Many parents decided to donate the books permanently.

A "Birthday" Present for the Class

Sometimes schools establish a new student-birthday tradition by suggesting that parents or family members purchase a book for the school or classroom collection instead of bringing cupcakes or other refreshments. The student's name is written on the title page as an acknowledgment of the gift. You can even provide a master list of titles from which caregivers can choose.

"Adopt a School"

In many communities, local businesses "adopt" a particular school to sponsor and help. The company may send volunteers to the school to work with students or provide other kinds of administrative or custodial services, and these volunteers can be quite helpful in organizing and caring for the bookroom. Sometimes employees of a business may be interested in sponsoring one student's reading for a year. If you consider that the basic collection is used by many students over sev-

---

Example of a Letter Requesting the Loan of Books

Dear Parents,

This year, students in our class will be reading a great deal. They will read biographies, informational books, and a variety of novels. We need a large number of books in our classroom library so that everyone can find books that are interesting and that will help them learn.

We have already collected several hundred books but we need more because our class will read over 1,000 books this year!

Can you help us by lending us some books that your children have already read? We will treat these books with care and return them at the end of the year, unless you decide to leave them in the room for next year's students.

We are looking for paperback and hardback books that are in good condition and suitable for children age __ to __[1]. To lend us books, write your name and address on the inside back cover of each book and send it to school with your child. We will return it to you at the end of the school year if you write "please return" inside the back cover.

Students will be reading these books at school and at home. We will make every effort to take good care of the books, but sometimes there are unavoidable accidents, so please do not lend us any book that is precious or irreplaceable and you would be very upset to lose.

Thank you for your help. You will be providing valuable learning opportunities for the students in our class.

Sincerely,

Teacher and Grade 5 Students

Figure 14–2. *Example of a Letter Requesting the Loan of Books*

[1]Put in an age range that will not seem out of line to parents but will help you match the range of reading levels in your class.

eral years, the cost is quite reasonable—about $12,000, or $30 per child for a school with 100 children at each intermediate grade level; and, of course, the collection will be used over many years.

Contributions to the classroom collection or the school bookroom are concrete demonstrations of support. From businesspeople's point of view, it is a way to contribute to the community and have that contribution recognized. You can place a book plate inside the front cover acknowledging the gift. You can also have students write thank-you notes, mentioning a specific book as appropriate. Expressing appreciation and letting the business know how important the contribution is to students' learning builds a tremendous amount of goodwill in the community.

Summary

Just as you prioritize your time, you need to prioritize your resources. Deciding where to spend the money (even a small amount) you have at your discretion helps you realize what you think is important. Buying high-quality books for your classroom or school will positively affect your students' reading achievement, thereby giving them an essential tool for a successful future.

Suggestions for Professional Development

Take some further steps down the road to a good classroom or school book collection by creating that starter list or "wish list" for yourself at either the classroom or the school level (better still, do it for both). Knowing what you need is the first step to acquiring a high-quality book collection.

1. If you prepared an inventory at the end of Chapter 13, look at it again. If not, make an inventory of the books you currently have and the number of copies of each title. Notice the number of titles you have at each level.
2. Compare your current inventory with the recommendations for number of titles and copies of titles in Chapters 11 and 12.
3. If you are working on a classroom set, compare your inventory to the suggestions for your grade level for a basic and expanded set.
4. If you are working toward a school bookroom, decide whether your goal is a starter, basic, or expanded set and make comparisons with your inventory.
5. Set goals for:
   ◾ The number of copies you need of titles you already have.
   ◾ The number of additional titles you need at each level.
   ◾ The number of copies you need for the additional titles.
6. Browse through the lists in this book and visit some bookstores to identify titles would like to have. Then make your "short list."
7. Next, set some goals for the year and create an action plan. If you can add even one or two levels to your book collection or fifty single titles to a classroom collection, you will have accomplished a great deal during the year.
8. Think back over the suggestions in this chapter and consider:
   ◾ Ways to save money.
   ◾ Some texts you already have that can be reshaped and used to enhance the collection.
   ◾ Ways to acquire books without money.
9. Establish a time line for your action plan and assign responsibilities for accomplishing your goals.

APPENDIXES

Record of Book Reading Progress

Student's Name: _____   **School**: _____

Record book reading progress three or four times per year, as agreed upon with your school faculty. Note dates in bottom row. Put an open circle ◯ at the child's instructional level on each date indicated. A filled in circle ● indicates student is having some difficulty at the level. Mark the level ◯* if additional teaching is also being provided by specialists. Give the year and descriptions of additional reading services on back.

Teacher																								
Book Level	K	K	K	K	1	1	1	1	2	2	2	2	3	3	3	3	4	4	4	4	5	5	5	5
Z (7-8)																								
Y																								
X																								
W (6+)																								
V																								
U																								
T (5)																								
S																								
R																								
Q (4)																								
P																								
O																								
N (3)																								
M																								
L																								
K																								
J (2)																								
I																								
H																								
G																								
F																								
E																								
D																								
C (1)																								
B																								
A																								
Date																								

Trade Book Publishers

Aladinn
Albert Whitman & Co.
Alfred A. Knopf
Avon Books
Avon Camelot
Ballantine Books
Bantam Books
Bantam Doubleday Dell
Bantam Skylark
Barron's Educational
Beach Tree Books
Beech Tree
Candlewick Press
Clarion
Crabtree

Creative Arts Book Co.
Delacorte Press
Dell Publishing
Dell Yearling
Dial
Dutton
Farrar, Straus & Giroux
Follett
Franklin Watts
G.P. Putnam Sons
Greenwillow
Harcourt Brace
Harper & Row
HarperCollins
Harpertrophy

Hearst
Henry Holt & Co.
Holiday House
Houghton Mifflin
Hyperion
Ladybird Books
Language for Learning
Association
Little, Brown & Co.
Macmillan
Milkweed
Millbrook Press
Orchard Books
Paper Star
Penguin Group

Pleasant Company
Puffin Books
Random House
Scholastic
Seal Books
Secret Passage Press
Signet Classics
Tundra
Viking
W.H. Freeman & Co.
Warner Books
William Morrow Co.
Yearling

Book Publishers and Distributors

Some companies publish their own titles, while others distribute series books from a variety of sources. Ordering information on series books is available from the following sources. Trade Titles may be ordered form any paperback supplier, many of which offer a flat paperback discount to schools.

Benchmark Education
629 Fifth Avenue
Pelham, NY 10803
Phone 1-877-236-2465
Fax 1-914-738-5063
benchmarkeducation.com

Capstone Press
151 Good Counsel Drive
P.O. Box 669
Mankato, MN 56002-0669
Phone 1-800-747-4992
Fax 1-888-262-0705
www.capstone-press.com

Dominie Press, Inc.
1949 Kellogg Avenue
Carlsbad, CA 92008
Phone 1-800-232-4570
Fax 1-760-431-8777
www.dominie.com
info@dominie.com

Grolier Press
90 Sherman Turnpike
Danbury, CT 06816
Phone 1-800-621-1115
Fax 1-203-797-3197
http://publishing.grolier.com

Hampton Brown
P.O. Box 369
Marina, CA 93933
Phone 1-800-333-3510

Houghton Mifflin
1900 South Batavia
Geneva, Ill. 60134
Phone 1-800-733-2828
Fax 1-800-733-2098
www.eduplace.com

Kaeden Books
P.O. Box 16190
Rocky River, OH 44116
Phone 1-800-890-READ
Fax 1-440-356-5081

Modern Curriculum Press
4350 Equity Drive
P.O. Box 2649
Columbus, OH 43216
Phone 1-800-321-3106
Fax 1-800-393-3156
www.pearsonlearning.com

Mondo Publishing
980 Avenue of the Americas
New York, NY 10018
Phone 1-888-88MONDO
Fax 1-212-268-3560
www.mondopub.com

Richard C. Owen Publishers
P.O. Box 585
Katonah, NY 10536
Phone 1-800-336-5588
Fax 1-914-232-3977
www.rcowen.com

Rigby
P.O. Box 797
Crystal Lake, IL 60039-0797
Phone 1-800-822-8661
Fax –800-427-4429
www.rigby.com

Steck Vaughn
P.O. Box 690789
Orlando, FL 32819-0789
Phone 1-800-531-5015
Fax 1-800-699-9459
www.steck-vaughn.com

Scholastic Inc.
P.O. Box 7502
Jefferson City, MD 65102
Phone 1-800-724-6527
Fax 1-800-223-4011

Sundance
P.O. Box 1326
234 Taylor St.
Littleton, MA 01460
Phone 1-800-343-3204
Fax 1-800-456-2419

Troll Publications
100 Corporate Drive
Matwah, NJ 07430
Phone 1-800-526-5289
Fax 1-800-979-8765
www.troll.com

Wright Group/McGraw Hill
19201 120th Avenue NE
Bothell, WA 98011-9512
Phone 1-800-523-2371
Fax 1-800-543-7323
www.wrightgroup.com

Evaluation Response for Text Gradient

Directions: Since any text gradient is always in the process of construction as it is used with varying groups of children, we expect our list to change every year. We encourage you to try the levels with your students and to provide feedback based on your own experiences. Please suggest changes to existing book levels and suggest new books for the list. Please provide the information requested below.

Name: _____   Grade Level You Teach: _____

Telephone: (___) _____   E-mail address: _____

Address (street, city, state): _____

Book Evaluated:

Book Title: _____

Level: J   K   L   M   N   O   P   Q   R   S   T   U   V   W   X   Y   Z

Author: _____

Publisher: _____

This book is:

_____ A book listed on the gradient that I have evaluated with my class.
(Complete SECTION A and make comments in SECTION C.)

_____ A book listed on the gradient that I am recommending as a benchmark for a level.
(Complete SECTION A and make comments in SECTION C.)

_____ A new book that I suggest adding to the collection.
(Complete SECTION B and make comments in SECTION C.)

SECTION A: (for an evaluation of a book currently included in the list)

Is it appropriately placed on the level (explain)? _____
To what level should the book be moved?
J   K   L   M   N   O   P   Q   R   S   T   U   V   W   X   Y   Z

Are there points of difficulty that make it harder than it seems? _____

_____

Is the text supportive in ways that might not be noticeable when examining the superficial characteristics?

_____

SECTION B: (for the recommendation of a new book) Indicate recommended level:

How does this book support readers at this level? _____

_____

What challenges does it offer? _____

_____

SECTION C: Please place additional comments on the back or on another sheet.

Mail this form to:
Irene Fountas, Lesley University, 1815 Massachusetts Ave., Suite 378, Cambridge, Massachusetts 02140.
Fax: (617) 349-8490   E-mail: ifountas@mail.lesley.edu
Gay Su Pinnell, The Ohio State University, 200 Ramseyer Hall, 29 W. Woodruff Avenue, Columbus, Ohio 43210.
Fax: (614) 292-4260   E-mail: pinnell.1@osu.edu

HOW TO USE THE BOOK LIST

The following is a sampling of books from level J through Z, providing texts of various genres from approximately early grade two through grade six. The books include a variety of formats including picture books, short story collections, and chapter books, including fiction and nonfiction. A level is only an approximation and some levels will be adjusted over time as they are used with students. Please provide your feedback and suggestions for books to be leveled or adjusted on the form in Appendix 2.

A comprehensive list of 7500 books for grades kindergarten through three is provided in *Matching Books to Readers, K-3* (Fountas and Pinnell 1999).

Using the List

The list is sorted in three ways, by *alphabet,* by *level,* and by *genre,* with five columns on each page. Notice the three dark edged tabs placed alongside the book. These tabs make it possible to quickly turn to the section you want to use.

■ The first column indicates the *title* of the book. The book is placed alphabetically using the first word of the title—unless it is *a* or *the,* in which case the article follows the title.

■ The second column indicates the level of the book, J to Z.

■ The third column provides the type of book, or *genre.* Some books might fit more than one genre so only one genre is indicated. The following code is used to indicate the genre:

TL	Traditional Literature
RF	Realistic Fiction
HF	Historical Fiction
SF	Science Fiction
F	Fantasy
B	Biography (includes autobiography and memoir)
I	Information Book

■ The fourth column provides the name of the *author* or specific reading *series.*

■ The fifth column indicates the *publisher's or distributor's name.* Addresses and phone numbers for each distributor of reading series and collections are provided in Appendix 1. Trade books are available from a variety of general paperback distributors.

Book List
Organized by Title

Title	Level	Genre	Author/Series	Publisher/Distributor
13th Floor, The: A Ghost Story	U	F	Fleischman, Sid	Bantam Doubleday Dell
18th Emergency, The	R	RF	Byars, Betsy	Bantam Doubleday Dell
26 Fairmount Avenue	N	B	dePaola, Tomie	Putnam
40 Nights To Knowing the Sky	Z	I	Schaaf, Fred	Henry Holt & Co.
5 Novels	V	F	Pinkwater, Daniel	Farrar, Straus and Giroux
52 Days by Camel: My Sahara Adventure	T	I	Raskin, Lawrie	Annick Press
89th Kitten, The	O	RF	Nilsson, Eleanor	Scholastic
Abby	M	RF	Hanel, Wolfram	North-South Books
Abe Lincoln: Log Cabin To White House	Z	B	North, Sterling	Random House
Abe Lincoln's Hat	M	B	Brenner, Martha	Random House
Abel's Island	T	F	Steig, William	Farrar Straus and Giroux
Abigail Adams: Girl of Colonial Days	R	B	Wagoner, Jean Brown	Aladdin
About The B'nai Bagels	T	RF	Konigsburg, E. L.	Dell
Abracadabra	L	RF	Reading Unlimited	Celebration Press
Abracadabra Kid, The	X	B	Fleischman, Sid	Beech Tree Books
Abraham Lincoln	O	B	Early Biographies	Compass Point Books
Abraham Lincoln	Q	B	Gross, Ruth Belov	Scholastic
Abraham Lincoln	S	B	Parin d'Aulaire, Ingri & Edgar	Bantam Doubleday Dell
Abraham Lincoln	L	B	Pebble Books	Grolier, Capstone
Abraham Lincoln: President of a Divided Country	O	B	Greene, Carol	Children's Press
Abraham Lincoln: The Great Emancipator	R	B	Stevenson, Augusta	Aladdin
Abraham's Battle: A Novel of Gettysburg	T	HF	Banks, Sara Harrell	Atheneum Books
Absent Author, The	N	RF	Roy, Ron	Random House
Absolutely Normal Chaos	V	RF	Creech, Sharon	HarperTrophy
Absolutely True Story, The: How I Visited Yellowstone Park With the Terrible Rupes	R	RF	Roberts, Willo Davis	Aladdin
Accidental Angel (Secret Sisters)	P	RF	Byrd, Sandra	WaterBrook Press
Ace: The Very Important Pig	R	F	King-Smith, Dick	Knopf
Acid Rain	L	I	Wonder World	Wright Group/McGraw Hill
Across Five Aprils	Z	HF	Hunt, Irene	Follett
Across the Lines	W	HF	Reeder, Carolyn	Avon Camelot
Adam Joshua Capers: Halloween Monster	N	RF	Smith, Janice Lee	HarperTrophy
Adam Joshua Capers: Kid Next Door, The	N	RF	Smith, Janice Lee	HarperTrophy
Adam Joshua Capers: Monster in the Third	N	RF	Smith, Janice Lee	HarperTrophy
Adam Joshua Capers: Nelson in Love	N	RF	Smith, Janice Lee	HarperTrophy
Adam Joshua Capers: Show-and-Tell War, The	N	RF	Smith, Janice Lee	HarperTrophy
Adam Joshua Capers: Superkid!	N	RF	Smith, Janice Lee	HarperTrophy
Adam Joshua Capers: Turkey Trouble	N	RF	Smith, Janice Lee	HarperTrophy
Adam of the Road	W	HF	Gray, Elizabeth Janet	Scholastic
Addie's Bad Day	J	RF	Robins, Joan	HarperTrophy
Addie's Dakota Winter	T	RF	Lawlor, Laurie	Pocket Books
Addy Learns a Lesson: A School Story	Q	HF	The American Girls Collection	Pleasant Company
Addy Saves the Day: A Summer Story	Q	HF	The American Girls Collection	Pleasant Company
Addy's Surprise: A Christmas Story	Q	HF	The American Girls Collection	Pleasant Company
Adios, Anna	N	RF	Giff, Patricia Reilly	Bantam Doubleday Dell
Adventure In Alaska	O	I	Kramer, S.A.	Random House
Adventure of the Buried Treasure, The	L	RF	McArthur, Nancy	Scholastic
Adventures of Ali Baba Bernstein, The	O	RF	Hurwitz, Johanna	Scholastic
Adventures of George Washington, The	N	B	Davidson, Margaret	Scholastic
Adventures of Granny Gatman, The	L	RF	Meadows, Graham	Dominie Press
Adventures of Huckleberry Finn, The	Z	HF	Twain, Mark	Scholastic
Adventures of Ratman	M	F	Weiss, Ellen & Freidman, Mel	Random House
Adventures of Snail at School	J	F	Stadler, John	HarperTrophy
Adventures of Spider, The	R	TL	Arkhurst, Joyce C.	Scholastic
Adventures of the Shark Lady	Q	I	McGovern, Ann	Scholastic
Adventures of Tom Sawyer, The	Z	HF	Twain, Mark	Scholastic

Title	Level	Genre	Author/Series	Publisher/Distributor
Aesop & Company: With Scenes from His Legendary Life	O	TL	Bader, Barbara	Houghton Mifflin
African-American Scientists	O	B	St. John, Jetty	Capstone Press
African-Americans in the Old West	V	I	Cornerstones of Freedom	Children's Press
African-Americans in the Thirteen Colonies	V	I	Cornerstones of Freedom	Children's Press
After the Dancing Days	W	HF	Rostkowski, Margaret I.	HarperTrophy
After the Goat Man	R	RF	Byars, Betsy	Puffin
After the Rain	Z	RF	Mazer, Norma Fox	Avon Books
After the War	W	HF	Matas, Carol	Aladdin
Afternoon of the Elves	S	F	Lisle, Janet Taylor	Scholastic
Afternoon on the Amazon	M	F	Osborne, Mary Pope	Random House
Against the Odds	P	I	Layden, Joe	Scholastic
Against the Odds	R	I	Wildcats	Wright Group/McGraw Hill
Against the Rules	R	RF	Costello, Emily	Dell
Agnes the Sheep	R	F	Taylor, William	Bantam Doubleday Dell
Ah Liang's Gift	J	RF	Sunshine	Wright Group/McGraw Hill
Ah-choo!	J	RF	Samuels, Aurora	Sadlier-Oxford
Ahyoka and the Talking Leaves	S	HF	Roop, Peter and Connie	Beech Tree Books
Ajeemah and his Son	S	HF	Berry, James	HarperTrophy
Aladdin & the Magic Lamp	J	TL	Traditional Tales	Dominie
Alcatraz	V	I	Cornerstones of Freedom	Bantam Doubleday Dell
Aldo Ice Cream	O	RF	Hurwitz, Johanna	The Penguin Group
Aldo Peanut Butter	O	RF	Hurwitz, Johanna	The Penguin Group
Alexander and the Wind-Up Mouse	L	F	Lionni, Leo	Scholastic
Alexander Graham Bell	P	B	Linder, Greg	Capstone Press
Alexander Graham Bell	V	B	Petrie, A. Roy	Fitzhenry & Whiteside
Alexander Graham Bell: An Inventive Life	U	B	MacLeod, Elizabeth	Kids Can Press Ltd.
Alfred the Curious	O	RF	PM Emerald	Rigby
Ali Baba Bernstein, Lost and Found	O	RF	Hurwitz, Johanna	Avon
Alice in Rapture: Sort of	U	RF	Naylor, Phyllis Reynolds	Aladdin
Alice in Wonderland	V	F	Carroll, Lewis	Scholastic
Alice the Brave	U	RF	Naylor, Phyllis Reynolds	Aladdin
Alice's Diary, Living With Diabetes	S	I	Gibson, Marie	Pacific Learning
Alida's Song	Y	RF	Paulsen, Gary	Random House
Alien in the Classroom	N	F	Keene, Carolyn	Pocket Books
Aliens Ate My Homework	Q	F	Coville, Bruce	Pocket Books
Aliens Don't Wear Braces	M	F	Dadey, D. & Jones, M. T.	Scholastic
Aliens for Breakfast	M	F	Etra, J. & Spinner, S.	Random House
Aliens for Dinner	M	F	Spinner, Stephanie	Random House
Aliens for Lunch	M	F	Spinner, S. & Etra, J.	Random House
Alison Wendlebury	J	RF	Literacy 2000	Rigby
Alison's Puppy	K	RF	Bauer, Marion Dane	Hyperion
Alison's Wings	K	RF	Bauer, Marion Dane	Hyperion
All About Bats	J	I	Ready Readers	Modern Curriculum
All About Cats and Kittens	N	I	Neye, Emily	Grosset & Dunlap
All About Codes	Q	I	Riley, Gail Blasser	Steck-Vaughn
All About Deer	Q	I	Arnosky, Jim	Scholastic
All About Me!	J	RF	Pacific Literacy	Pacific Learning
All About Owls	Q	I	Arnosky, Jim	Scholastic
All About Plants	L	I	Home Connection Collection	Rigby
All About Sam	P	RF	Lowry, Lois	Bantam Doubleday Dell
All About Seeds	Q	I	Berger, Melvin	Scholastic
All About Stacy	L	RF	Giff, Patricia Reilly	Bantam Doubleday Dell
All About Things People Do	K	I	Rice, Melanie & Chris	Scholastic
All Alone in the Universe	S	RF	Perkins, Lynne Rae	Greenwillow Books
All But Alice	U	RF	Naylor, Phyllis Reynolds	Dell
All For the Better: A Story of El Barrio	R	RF	Mohr, Nicholasa	Steck Vaughn
All Is Well	R	HF	Litchman, Kristin Embry	Bantam Doubleday Dell
All Kinds of Animals	O	I	It's Science	Children's Press
All Kinds of Eyes	L	I	Discovery World	Rigby

Title	Level	Genre	Author/Series	Publisher/Distributor
All Kinds of Flowers	L	I	Turner, Teresa	Steck-Vaughn
All Kinds of Museums	N	I	Ramsey, Joe	Wright Group/McGraw Hill
All Pigs Are Beautiful	N	I	King-Smith, Dick	Candlewick Press
All-of-a-Kind Family	Q	RF	Taylor, Sydney	Bantam Doubleday Dell
All-Star Fever	M	RF	Christopher, Matt	Little, Brown & Co.
Allen Jay and the Underground Railroad	O	HF	Brill, Marlene Targ	Carolrhoda Books
Allie's Basketball Dream	J	RF	Barber, B. & Ligasan, D.	Scholastic
Alligator Alley	M	RF	Schultz, Irene	Wright Group/McGraw Hill
Alligator Tails and Crocodile Cakes	K	F	Moon, Nicola	Wright Group/McGraw Hill
Alligator, The	M	I	Crewe, Sabrina	Steck-Vaughn
Alligators & Crocodiles	U	I	The Untamed World	Steck-Vaughn
Almost Starring Skinnybones	O	RF	Park, Barbara	Random House
Alphabet, The	R	I	Literacy 2000	Rigby
Alroy's Very Nearly Clean Bedroom	N	RF	SupaDoopers	Sundance
Altogether, One at a Time	S	RF	Konigsburg, E.L.	Simon & Schuster
Alvin Ailey	P	B	Pinkney, Andrea Davis	Hyperion
Always My Dad	N	RF	Wyeth, Sharon Dennis	Alfred A. Knopf
Amalia and the Grasshopper	K	RF	Tello, J. & Krupinski, L.	Scholastic
Amanda Joins the Circus	R	F	Avi	Bantam Doubleday Dell
Amanda Pig and Her Big Brother Oliver	L	F	Van Leeuwen, Jean	Puffin Books
Amaze Us!	T	I	Wildcats	Wright Group/McGraw Hill
Amazing Animal Rescue Team, The	Q	I	Blankenhorn, Rebecca	Steck-Vaughn
Amazing Birds of the Rain Forest	M	I	Daniel, Claire	Steck-Vaughn
Amazing But True Sports Stories	Q	I	Hollander, Phyllis and Zander	Scholastic
Amazing Eggs	J	I	Discovery World	Rigby
Amazing Impossible Erie Canal, The	S	I	Harness, Cheryl	Simon & Schuster
Amazing Journeys	P	I	Literacy 2000	Rigby
Amazing Maze, The	J	RF	Foundations	Wright Group/McGraw Hill
Amazing Spiders	Q	I	Eyewitness Juniors	Alfred A. Knopf
Amazing Trains	L	I	Pair-It Books	Steck-Vaughn
Amber Brown Goes Fourth	N	RF	Danziger, Paula	Scholastic
Amber Brown is Feeling Blue	N	RF	Danziger, Paula	Scholastic
Amber Brown is Not a Crayon	N	RF	Danziger, Paula	Scholastic
Amber Brown Sees Red	N	RF	Danziger, Paula	Scholastic
Amber Brown Wants Extra Credit	N	RF	Danziger, Paula	Scholastic
Amber Cat, The	P	RF	McKay, Hilary	Simon & Schuster
Amber Spyglass, The	Z	F	Pullman, Phillip	Alfred A. Knopf
Amelia Bedelia	L	F	Parish, Peggy	HarperTrophy
Amelia Bedelia and the Baby	L	F	Parish, Peggy	Harper & Row
Amelia Bedelia and the Surprise Shower	L	F	Parish, Peggy	Harper & Row
Amelia Bedelia Goes Camping	L	F	Parish, Peggy	Avon Camelot
Amelia Bedelia Helps Out	L	F	Parish, Peggy	Avon Camelot
Amelia Bedelia's Family Album	L	F	Parish, Peggy	Avon Books
Amelia Earhart	Q	B	Lowe, David	Rigby
Amelia Earhart	P	B	Parlin, John	Bantam Doubleday Dell
Amelia Earhart	P	B	Rosenthal, M. & Freeman, D.	Capstone Press
Amelia Earhart: Challenging the Skies	S	B	Sloate, Susan	Fawcett Columbine
Amelia Earhart: Courage in the Sky	S	B	Kerby, Mona	Puffin Books
Amelia Earhart: Flying for Adventure	S	B	Wade, Mary Dodson	The Millbrook Press
Amelia Earhart: Young Aviator	R	B	Gormley, Beatrice	Aladdin
America Street: A Multicultural Anthology of Stories	R	RF	Mazer, Anne	Persea Books
America's Most Wanted Fifth-Graders	R	RF	Lawrence, Jan and Raskin, Linda	Scholastic
American Alligator, The	R	I	Potts, Steve	Capstone Press
American Bison, The	R	I	Potts, Steve	Capstone Press
American Dragons: Twenty-Five Asian American Voices	Z	RF	Yep, Laurence	HarperTrophy
American Eyes: New Asian-American Short Stories for Young Adults	Z	RF	Carlson, Lori M.	Ballantine Books
American Flag, The	N	I	A True Book	Children's Press

Title	Level	Genre	Author/Series	Publisher/Distributor
American Revolution, The	T	I	Bliven, Bruce Jr.	Random House
American Revolution, The	V	I	Carter, Alden R.	Franklin Watts
Amigo	O	F	Baylor, Byrd	Aladdin
Among the Hidden	Z	SF	Haddix, Margaret Peterson	Aladdin
Among the Volcanoes	Y	RF	Castaneda, Omar S.	Bantam Doubleday Dell
Amos and the Alien	R	F	Paulsen, Gary	Bantam Doubleday Dell
Amos Binder, Secret Agent	R	RF	Paulsen, Gary	Bantam Doubleday Dell
Amos Fortune: Free Man	V	HF	Yates, Elizabeth	Puffin Books
Amos Gets Famous	R	F	Paulsen, Gary	Bantam Doubleday Dell
Amos Gets Married	R	F	Paulsen, Gary	Bantam Doubleday Dell
Amos Goes Bananas	R	F	Paulsen, Gary	Bantam Doubleday Dell
Amos's Killer Concert Caper	R	F	Paulsen, Gary	Bantam Doubleday Dell
Amy's True Prize	Q	HF	The Little Women Journals	Avon
An Acceptable Time	X	F	L'Engle, Madeleine	Laurel-Leaf Books
An Ancient Heritage: The Arab-American Minority	Z	I	Ashabranner, Brent	Harper Collins
An Early Winter	T	RF	Bauer, Marion Dane	Houghton Mifflin
An Indian Winter	U	I	Freedman, Russell	Scholastic
An Island Far From Home	W	HF	Donahue, John	Carolrhonda Books
An Island Like You: Stories of the Barrio	Z	RF	Cofer, Judith Ortiz	The Penguin Group
Anastasia, Absolutely	Q	RF	Lowry, Lois	Bantam Doubleday Dell
Anastasia Again!	Q	RF	Lowry, Lois	Bantam Doubleday Dell
Anastasia, Ask Your Analyst	Q	RF	Lowry, Lois	Bantam Doubleday Dell
Anastasia At This Address	Q	RF	Lowry, Lois	Bantam Doubleday Dell
Anastasia At Your Service	Q	RF	Lowry, Lois	Bantam Doubleday Dell
Anastasia Has the Answers	Q	RF	Lowry, Lois	Bantam Doubleday Dell
Anastasia Krupnik	Q	RF	Lowry, Lois	Bantam Doubleday Dell
Anastasia On Her Own	Q	RF	Lowry, Lois	Bantam Doubleday Dell
Anastasia's Chosen Career	Q	RF	Lowry, Lois	Bantam Doubleday Dell
Ancient Greece	S	I	Journey Into Civilization	Chelsea House
Ancient Greeks	Q	I	Worldwise	Grolier
Ancient Romans	Q	I	Worldwise	Grolier
And Grandpa Sat on Friday	K	RF	Marshall, Val & Tester, Bronwyn	SRA/McGraw-Hill
And I Mean it Stanley	J	RF	Bonsall, Crosby	HarperCollins
And One For All	V	RF	Nelson, Theresa	Dell
And Still the Turtle Watched	Q	RF	MacGill-Callahan, Sheila	The Penguin Group
And Then What Happened Paul Revere?	R	B	Fritz, Jean	Bantam Doubleday Dell
Andrew Carnegie: Builder of Libraries	P	B	Community Builders	Children's Press
Androcles and the Lion	L	TL	PM Tales and Plays-Silver	Rigby
Andy and Tamika	N	RF	Adler, David A.	Harcourt Brace
Angel for Solomon Singer, An	O	RF	Rylant, Cynthia	Orchard Books
Angel Park Hoopstars: Nothing But Net	O	RF	Hughes, Dean	Alfred A. Knopf
Angel Park Hoopstars: Point Guard	O	RF	Hughes, Dean	Alfred A. Knopf
Angel Park Soccer Stars: Backup Goalie	O	RF	Hughes, Dean	Random House
Angel Park Soccer Stars: Defense!	O	RF	Hughes, Dean	Alfred A. Knopf
Angel Park Soccer Stars: Psyched!	O	RF	Hughes, Dean	Random House
Angel Park Soccer Stars: Total Soccer	O	RF	Hughes, Dean	Alfred A. Knopf
Angel Park Soccer Stars: Victory Goal	O	RF	Hughes, Dean	Alfred A. Knopf
Angel's Mother's Boyfriend	O	RF	Delton, Judy	Houghton Mifflin
Angels and Other Strangers	T	RF	Paterson, Katherine	HarperTrophy
Angels Don't Know Karate	M	F	Dadey, D. & Jones, M. T.	Scholastic
Angry Bull and Other Cases, The	O	RF	Simon, Seymour	Avon
Animal Adventures	N	HF	Little House	HarperTrophy
Animal Babies	R	I	Kalman, Bobbie	Crabtree
Animal Band, The	K	TL	PM Tales and Plays- Purple	Rigby
Animal Champions	O	I	Jones, Teri Crawford	Pearson Learning
Animal Dazzlers: The Role of Brilliant Colors in Nature	T	I	Collard, Susan B. III	Franklin Watts
Animal Farm	Z	F	Orwell, George	Harcourt Brace
Animal Friends	N	I	Literacy 2000	Rigby
Animal Homes	K	I	Pair-It Books	Steck-Vaughn

Title	Level	Genre	Author/Series	Publisher/Distributor
Animal Reports	L	I	Little Red Readers	Sundance
Animal Shelters	N	I	Book Shop	Mondo
Animal Stories by Young Writers	R	F	Rubel, William and Mandel, Gerry	Tricycle Press
Animal, the Vegetable, and John D Jones, The	R	RF	Byars, Betsy	Bantam Doubleday Dell
Animal Tracks	L	I	Dorros, Arthur	Scholastic
Animals and Their Teeth	K	I	Sunshine	Wright Group/McGraw Hill
Animals and Their Young	N	I	Kratky, Lada Josefa	Hampton-Brown
Animals at Work	M	I	Graham, Pamela	Rigby
Animals' Eyes and Ears	K	I	Early Connections	Benchmark Education
Animals in Danger	M	I	Pair-It Books	Steck-Vaughn
Animals on the Move	K	I	Planet Earth	Rigby
Animals Talk, Too	N	I	Literacy 2000	Rigby
Anna, Grandpa, and the Big Storm	N	RF	Stevens, Carla	The Penguin Group
Anna Is Still Here	V	HF	Vos, Ida	Puffin Books
Annabel the Actress Starring in Gorilla My Dreams	L	RF	Conford, Ellen	Simon & Schuster
Anne Frank	S	B	Epstein, Rachel	Franklin Watts
Anne Frank: Beyond the Diary	X	I	Van der Rol, R. & Verhoeven, R.	Puffin Books
Anne Frank: Life in Hiding	W	B	Hurwitz, Johanna	Avon
Anne Frank: The Diary of a Young Girl	Y	B	Frank, Anne	Bantam
Anne of Green Gables	V	RF	Montgomery, L. M.	Scholastic
Annie Bananie Moves To Barry Avenue	L	RF	Komaiko, Leah	Bantam Doubleday Dell
Annie John	Z	RF	Kincaid, Jamaica	Farrar, Straus and Giroux
Annie Oakley	R	I	Wilson, Ellen	Aladdin
Annie's Pet	J	RF	Bank Street	Bantam Doubleday Dell
Another Day, Another Challenge	L	RF	Literacy 2000	Rigby
Another Point of View	P	RF	Wildcats	Wright Group/McGraw Hill
Ant	O	I	Chinery, Michael	Troll
Ant Cities	O	I	Dorros, Arthur	HarperCollins
Ant City	J	RF	PM Turquoise	Rigby
Antarctic Penguins	N	I	PM Animal Facts: Silver	Rigby
Antarctic Seals	N	I	PM Animal Facts: Silver	Rigby
Anthony Burns: Defeat and Triumph of a Fugitive Slave	Y	B	Hamilton, Virginia	Alfred A. Knopf
Ants	N	I	Daronco, Mickey & Presti, Lori	Benchmark Education
Apache Indians, The	P	I	Lund, Bill	Capstone Press
Apple Tree, The	J	I	Sunshine	Wright Group/McGraw Hill
Appointment with Action	P	RF	Wildcats	Wright Group/McGraw Hill
Apprenticeship of Lucas Whitaker, The	U	HF	DeFelice, Cynthia	Avon
April Morning	X	HF	Fast, Howard	Bantam
Archaeologists Dig for Clues	P	I	Duke, Kate	HarperCollins
Arctic Investigations: Exploring the Frozen Ocean	T	I	Young, Karen Romano	Steck Vaughn
Arctic Life	M	I	Robinson, F.R.	Steck-Vaughn
Arctic Tundra	M	I	Forman, Michael H.	Children's Press
Are All The Giants Dead?	V	F	Norton, Mary	Harcourt Brace
Are We Hurting the Earth?	K	I	Early Connections	Benchmark Education
Are You There God? It's Me, Margaret.	T	RF	Blume, Judy	Bantam Doubleday Dell
Arguments	K	F	Read Alongs	Rigby
Ariel of the Sea	U	F	Calhoun, Dia	Winslow Press
Ark, The	O	HF	Geisert, Arthur	Houghton Mifflin
Arkadians, The	W	F	Alexander, Lloyd	Puffin Books
Arlington National Cemetery	V	I	Cornerstones of Freedom	Bantam Doubleday Dell
Armadillo, The	R	I	Potts, Steve	Capstone Press
Armies of Ants	M	I	Retan, Walter	Scholastic
Around the World in a Hundred Years: From Henry the Navigator to Magellan	V	I	Fritz, Jean	Putnam & Grosset
Around-the-World Lunch, The	K	RF	Canetti, Yanitzia	Steck-Vaughn
Art Around the World	M	I	Discovery World	Rigby
Art Around the World	J	I	Early Connections	Benchmark Education
Art Lesson, The	M	B	dePaola, Tomie	Putnam
Art Riddle Contest, The	Q	RF	Medearis, Angela Shelf	Steck-Vaughn

Title	Level	Genre	Author/Series	Publisher/Distributor
Arthur Accused!	M	F	Brown, Marc	Little, Brown & Co.
Arthur and the Big Blow-Up	M	F	Brown, Marc	Little, Brown & Co.
Arthur and the Cootie-Catcher	M	F	Brown, Marc	Little, Brown & Co.
Arthur and the Crunch Cereal Contest	M	F	Brown, Marc	Little, Brown & Co.
Arthur and the Lost Diary	M	F	Brown, Marc	Little, Brown & Co.
Arthur and the Popularity Test	M	F	Brown, Marc	Little, Brown & Co.
Arthur and the Scare-Your-Pants-Off Club	M	F	Brown, Marc	Little, Brown & Co.
Arthur and the TL Contest	M	F	Brown, Marc	Little, Brown & Co.
Arthur, For the Very First Time	R	RF	MacLachlan, Patricia	Bantam Doubleday Dell
Arthur Makes the Team	M	F	Brown, Marc	Little, Brown & Co.
Arthur Rocks with BINKY	M	F	Brown, Marc	Little, Brown & Co.
Arthur's Back to School Day	K	F	Hoban, Lillian	HarperTrophy
Arthur's Camp-Out	K	F	Hoban, Lillian	HarperTrophy
Arthur's Christmas Cookies	K	F	Hoban, Lillian	HarperTrophy
Arthur's Funny Money	K	F	Hoban, Lillian	HarperTrophy
Arthur's Great Big Valentine	K	F	Hoban, Lillian	HarperTrophy
Arthur's Honey Bear	K	F	Hoban, Lillian	Harper Collins
Arthur's Loose Tooth	K	F	Hoban, Lillian	Harper Collins
Arthur's Mystery Envelope	M	F	Brown, Marc	Little, Brown & Co.
Arthur's Pen Pal	K	F	Hoban, Lillian	Harper Collins
Arthur's Prize Reader	K	F	Hoban, Lillian	HarperTrophy
Artists and Their Art	Q	I	Medearis, Michael	Steck-Vaughn
Ashes for Gold	K	TL	Folk Tales	Mondo
Ask Einstein!	N	RF	Trussell-Cullen, Alan	Pacific Learning
Ask Mr. Bear	J	F	Flack, Marjorie	Macmillan
Asli's Story	S	I	Jansen, Adrienne	Pacific Learning
Assassination of Abraham Lincoln, The	V	B	Cornerstones of Freedom	Children's Press
Assassination of John F. Kennedy, The	V	B	Cornerstones of Freedom	Children's Press
Assassination of Martin Luther King Jr.	V	B	Cornerstones of Freedom	Children's Press
Asteroid, The	M	F	PM Gold	Rigby
Astronauts	M	I	Deedrick, Tami	Capstone Press
At Her Majesty's Request: An African Princess in Victorian England	X	HF	Myers, Walter Dean	Scholastic
At the Edge of the Sea	M	I	Sunshine	Wright Group/McGraw Hill
At the Water Hole	K	I	Foundations	Wright Group/McGraw Hill
Attaboy, Sam	P	RF	Lowry, Lois	Bantam Doubleday Dell
Attack and Defense	Q	I	Weldon Owen	Wright Group/McGraw Hill
Aunt Clara Brown: Official Pioneer	P	B	Lowery, Linda	Lerner Publishing Group
Aunt Eater Loves a Mystery	J	F	Cushman, Doug	HarperTrophy
Aunt Eater's Mystery Christmas	J	F	Cushman, Doug	HarperTrophy
Aunt Eater's Mystery Vacation	J	F	Cushman, Doug	HarperTrophy
Aunt Flossie's Hats (and Crab Cakes Later)	M	RF	Howard, Elizabeth	Scholastic
Australia	N	I	A True Book	Children's Press
Australia	O	I	Dahl, Michael	Capstone Press
Australia	Q	I	First Reports	Compass Point Books
Auto Mechanics	M	I	Boraas, Tracey	Capstone Press
Autumn	M	I	Pebble Books	Capstone Press
Autumn Street	V	HF	Lowry, Lois	Bantam Doubleday Dell
Avi	T	B	Markham, Lois	Learning Works, The
Avion My Uncle Flew, The	Y	RF	Fisher, Cyrus	The Penguin Group
Awake and Dreaming	S	F	Person, Kit	Puffin Books
Awfully Short for the Fourth Grade	Q	RF	Woodruff, Elvira	Bantam Doubleday Dell
Awumpalema	L	TL	Literacy 2000	Rigby
B-E-S-T Friends	L	RF	Giff, Patricia Reilly	Bantam Doubleday Dell
Baba Yaga	K	TL	Literacy 2000	Rigby
Babe Didrikson: Athlete of the Century	R	B	Knudson, R.R.	Bantam Doubleday Dell
Babe Ruth: One of Baseball's Greatest	R	I	Van Riper, Guernsey	Aladdin
Babe the Gallant Pig	R	F	King-Smith, Dick	Random House
Baby	T	RF	MacLachlan, Patricia	Language for Learning Assoc.
Baby Animal Zoo	O	I	Martin, Ann M.	Scholastic

Title	Level	Genre	Author/Series	Publisher/Distributor
Baby Grand, the Moon in July, and Me, The	P	RF	Barnes, Joyce Annette	The Penguin Group
Baby Island	P	RF	Brink, Carol R.	Simon & Schuster
Baby Sister for Frances, A	K	F	Hoban, Lillian	Scholastic
Baby Whale Rescue: The True Story of J.J.	P	I	Arnold, C. & Hewett, R.	Troll
Baby-Sitter Burglaries, The	S	RF	Keene, Carolyn	Pocket Books
Baby-Sitters Club: Abby and the Best Kid Ever	O	RF	Martin, Ann M.	Scholastic
Baby-Sitters Club: Abby the Bad Sport	O	RF	Martin, Ann M.	Scholastic
Baby-Sitters Club: Claudia and the Bad Joke	O	RF	Martin, Ann M.	Scholastic
Baby-Sitters Club: Claudia and the Little Liar	O	RF	Martin, Ann M.	Scholastic
Baby-Sitters Club: Claudia and the New Girl	O	RF	Martin, Ann M.	Scholastic
Baby-Sitters Club: Claudia and the Phantom Phone Calls	O	RF	Martin, Ann M.	Scholastic
Baby-Sitters Club: Dawn and Too Many Sitters	O	RF	Martin, Ann M.	Scholastic
Baby-Sitters Club: Dawn's Big Move	O	RF	Martin, Ann M.	Scholastic
Baby-Sitters Club: Dawn's Wicked Stepsister	O	RF	Martin, Ann M.	Scholastic
Baby-Sitters Club: Get Well Soon, Mallory	O	RF	Martin, Ann M.	Scholastic
Baby-Sitters Club: Ghost at Dawn's House, The	O	RF	Martin, Ann M.	Scholastic
Baby-Sitters Club: Good-bye Stacey, Good-bye	O	RF	Martin, Ann M.	Scholastic
Baby-Sitters Club: Hello, Mallory	O	RF	Martin, Ann M.	Scholastic
Baby-Sitters Club: Jessi and the Bad Baby-Sitter	O	RF	Martin, Ann M.	Scholastic
Baby-Sitters Club: Jessi and the Superbrat	O	RF	Martin, Ann M.	Scholastic
Baby-Sitters Club: Jessi Ramsey, Pet-sitter	O	RF	Martin, Ann M.	Scholastic
Baby-Sitters Club: Kristy and the Snobs	O	RF	Martin, Ann M.	Scholastic
Baby-Sitters Club: Kristy's Big Day	O	RF	Martin, Ann M.	Scholastic
Baby-Sitters Club: Kristy's Great Idea	O	RF	Martin, Ann M.	Scholastic
Baby-Sitters Club: Mary Anne and Camp BSC	O	RF	Martin, Ann M.	Scholastic
Baby-Sitters Club: Mary Anne Saves the Day	O	RF	Martin, Ann M.	Scholastic
Baby-Sitters Club Mystery: Beware, Dawn!	O	RF	Martin, Ann M.	Scholastic
Baby-Sitters Club Mystery: Claudia, Clue in the Photograph	O	RF	Martin, Ann M.	Scholastic
Baby-Sitters Club Mystery: Claudia, Mystery at the Museum	O	RF	Martin, Ann M.	Scholastic
Baby-Sitters Club Mystery: Claudia, Recipe for Danger	O	RF	Martin, Ann M.	Scholastic
Baby-Sitters Club Mystery: Dawn, Disappearing Dogs	O	RF	Martin, Ann M.	Scholastic
Baby-Sitters Club Mystery: Dawn, Halloween Mystery	O	RF	Martin, Ann M.	Scholastic
Baby-Sitters Club Mystery: Dawn, Surfer Ghost	O	RF	Martin, Ann M.	Scholastic
Baby-Sitters Club Mystery: Jessi, Jewel Thieves	O	RF	Martin, Ann M.	Scholastic
Baby-Sitters Club Mystery: Kristy, Haunted Mansion	O	RF	Martin, Ann M.	Scholastic
Baby-Sitters Club Mystery: Kristy, Missing Child	O	RF	Martin, Ann M.	Scholastic
Baby-Sitters Club Mystery: Kristy, Missing Fortune	O	RF	Martin, Ann M.	Scholastic
Baby-Sitters Club Mystery: Kristy, Vampires	O	RF	Martin, Ann M.	Scholastic
Baby-Sitters Club Mystery: Mallory, Ghost Cat	O	RF	Martin, Ann M.	Scholastic
Baby-Sitters Club Mystery: Mary Anne, y Library Myster	O	RF	Martin, Ann M.	Scholastic
Baby-Sitters Club Mystery: Mary Anne, Secret in the Attic	O	RF	Martin, Ann M.	Scholastic
Baby-Sitters Club Mystery: Mary Anne, Zoo Mystery	O	RF	Martin, Ann M.	Scholastic
Baby-Sitters Club Mystery: Mystery at Claudia's House	O	RF	Martin, Ann M.	Scholastic
Baby-Sitters Club Mystery: Stacey and the Mystery Money	O	RF	Martin, Ann M.	Scholastic
Baby-Sitters Club Mystery: Stacey, Haunted Masquerade	O	RF	Martin, Ann M.	Scholastic
Baby-Sitters Club Mystery: Stacey, Missing Ring	O	RF	Martin, Ann M.	Scholastic
Baby-Sitters Club Mystery: Stacey, Mystery at the Empty House	O	RF	Martin, Ann M.	Scholastic
Baby-Sitters Club Mystery: Stacy, Mystery at the Mall	O	RF	Martin, Ann M.	Scholastic
Baby-Sitters Club Special Edition, The: Readers Request	O	RF	Martin, Ann M.	Scholastic
Baby-Sitters Club: Welcome to the BSC, Abby	O	RF	Martin, Ann M.	Scholastic

Title	Level	Genre	Author/Series	Publisher/Distributor
Baby-Sitters Little Sister	O	RF	Martin, Ann M.	Scholastic
Baby-Sitters Little Sister: Karen's Big Sister	O	RF	Martin, Ann M.	Scholastic
Baby-Sitters Little Sister: Karen's Dinosaur	O	RF	Martin, Ann M.	Scholastic
Baby-Sitters Little Sister: Karen's Monsters	O	RF	Martin, Ann M.	Scholastic
Baby-Sitters Little Sister: Karen's Mystery Super Special	O	RF	Martin, Ann M.	Scholastic
Baby-Sitters Little Sister (Karen's Stepmother)	O	RF	Martin, Ann M.	Scholastic
Baby-Snatcher	Z	RF	Terris, Susan	Scholastic
Back Home	O	RF	Pinkney, Gloria Jean	The Penguin Group
Back To The Day Lincoln Was Shot!	S	I	Gormley, Beatrice	Scholastic
Back to the Dentist	M	RF	City Kids	Rigby
Back To The Titanic!	S	F	Gormley, Beatrice	Scholastic
Back Yard Angel	O	RF	Delton, Judy	Houghton Mifflin
Backward Bird Dog, The	R	F	Wallace, Bill	Bantam Doubleday Dell
Backyard Hunter: The Praying Mantis	P	I	Lavies, Bianca	The Penguin Group
Bad, Badder, Baddest	U	RF	Voigt, Cynthia	Scholastic
Bad Beginning, The	V	F	Snicket, Lemony	HarperTrophy
Bad Dad List, The	M	RF	Kenna, Anna	Pacific Learning
Bad Day for Ballet	N	RF	Keene, Carolyn	Pocket Books
Bad Day for Benjamin, A	L	RF	Reading Unlimited	Celebration Press
Bad Girls	U	RF	Voigt, Cynthia	Scholastic
Bad Spell for the Worst Witch, A	P	F	Murphy, Jill	Puffin Books
Bad-Luck Penny, The	L	F	O'Connor, Jane	Grosset & Dunlap
Badger in the Basement	Q	RF	Daniels, Lucy	Barron's Educational
Bagels for Kids	O	I	Pacific Literacy	Pacific Learning
Bakers	M	I	Deedrick, Tami	Capstone Press
Bald Bandit, The	N	RF	Roy, Ron	Random House
Bald Eagle Free Again!, The	P	I	Young Readers' Series	Barron's Educational Series
Bald Eagle, The	N	I	A True Book	Children's Press
Bald Eagle, The	R	I	Potts, Steve	Capstone Press
Bald Eagles	Q	I	Wilde, Buck	Rigby
Ballad of Robin Hood, The	P	HF	Literacy 2000	Rigby
Ballad of the Civil War, A	T	HF	Stolz, Mary	HarperTrophy
Balto and the Great Race	P	RF	Kimmel, Elizabeth Cody	Random House
Bandit Moon	V	HF	Fleischman, Sid	Dell Yearling
Banished, The	W	F	Levin, Betty	William Morrow
Bank Robbery and Jack and the Beanstalk, The	L	TL	New Way:Literature	Steck-Vaughn
Barefoot: Escape on the Underground Railroad	S	HF	Edwards, Pamela Duncan	HarperTrophy
Bargain For Frances, A	K	F	Hoban, Russell	HarperTrophy
Barn Party	K	F	O'Brien, Claire	Wright Group/McGraw Hill
Barney	P	RF	Literacy 2000	Rigby
Barney's Lovely Lunch	K	RF	Windmill Books	Rigby
Barrel in the Basement, The	R	F	Wallace, Barbara Brooks	Aladdin
Barrel of Gold, A	K	F	Story Box	Wright Group/McGraw Hill
Baseball Ballerina	J	RF	Cristaldi, Kathryn	Random House
Baseball Birthday Party, The	J	RF	Prager, Annabelle	Random House
Baseball Fever	O	RF	Hurwitz, Johanna	William Morrow
Baseball Flyhawk	M	RF	Christopher, Matt	Little, Brown & Co.
Baseball Heroes, The	M	RF	Schultz, Irene	Wright Group/McGraw Hill
Baseball in April and Other Stories	U	RF	Soto, Gary	Harcourt Brace
Baseball in the Barrios	P	I	Horenstein, Henry	Harcourt Brace
Baseball Megastars	O	I	Weber, Bruce	Scholastic
Baseball Pals	M	RF	Christopher, Matt	Little, Brown & Co.
Baseball Pitching Challenge and Other Cases, The	O	RF	Simon, Seymour	Avon
Baseball Saved Us	O	HF	Mochizuki, Ken	Scholastic
Baseball's Best: Five True Stories	O	B	Step into Reading	Random House
Baseball's Greatest Pitchers	P	B	Kramer, S. A.	Random House
Basket Counts, The	M	RF	Christopher, Matt	Little, Brown & Co.
Bat Bones and Spider Stew	K	RF	Poploff, Michelle	Bantam Doubleday Dell

Title	Level	Genre	Author/Series	Publisher/Distributor
Bat-Poet, The	S	F	Jarrell, Randall	HarperCollins
Bats	O	I	Gibbons, Gail	Holiday House
Bats	O	I	Holmes, Kevin J.	Capstone Press
Bats	P	I	Literacy 2000	Rigby
Bats	M	I	PM Animal Facts Gold	Rigby
Bats: The Amazing Upside-Downers	S	I	A First Book	Franklin Watts
Battle for Iwo Jima, The	W	I	Cornerstones of Freedom	Children's Press
Battle for the Castle, The	P	F	Winthrop, Elizabeth	Yearling
Battle of Chancellorsville, The	V	I	Cornerstones of Freedom	Children's Press
Battle of the Alamo, The	V	I	Cornerstones of Freedom	Children's Press
Battle of the Little Bighorn, The	V	I	Cornerstones of Freedom	Children's Press
Battle of Words, A	O	RF	Literacy 2000	Rigby
Be A Perfect Person In Just Three Days!	N	RF	Manes, Stephen	Dell
Be a Plant Scientist	L	I	Paul, Michele	Wright Group/McGraw Hill
Be Ready at Eight	K	F	Parish, Peggy	Simon & Schuster
Beacons of Light: Lighthouses	O	I	Gibbons, Gail	Scholastic
Beanbag	K	RF	Literacy 2000	Rigby
Beans on the Roof	L	RF	Byars, Betsy	Bantam Doubleday Dell
Bear and the Trolls, The	L	TL	PM Tales and Plays-Silver	Rigby
Bear at the Beach	K	F	Carmichael, Clay	North-South Books
Bear Called Paddington, A	T	F	Bond, Michael	Bantam Doubleday Dell
Bear Collection, The	N	I	PM Ruby	Rigby
Bear For Miguel, A	K	RF	Alphin, Elaine Marie	HarperTrophy
Bear Goes to Town	K	F	Browne, Anthony	Doubleday
Bear Shadow	J	F	Asch, Frank	Simon & Schuster
Bear That Heard Crying, The	P	HF	Kinsey-Warnock, N. & Kinsey, H.	The Penguin Group
Bear, The	M	I	Crewe, Sabrina	Steck-Vaughn
Bear's Bargain	J	F	Asch, Frank	Scholastic
Bear's Diet	L	RF	PM Gold	Rigby
Bears	O	I	Holmes, Kevin J.	Capstone Press
Bears' Christmas	M	F	Berenstain, Stan, & Jan	Random House
Bears' House, The	T	RF	Sachs, Marilyn	Puffin Books
Bears On Hemlock Mountain, The	M	RF	Dalgliesh, Alice	Aladdin Paperback
Bears' Picnic	M	F	Berenstain, Stan, & Jan	Random House
Bearstone	V	RF	Hobbs, Will	Hearst
Beast and the Halloween Horror	M	RF	Giff, Patricia Reilly	Bantam Doubleday Dell
Beast in Ms. Rooney's Room, The	M	RF	Giff, Patricia Reilly	Bantam Doubleday Dell
Beating the Drought	M	RF	Noonan, Diana	Pacific Learning
Beatles, The	N	B	Venezia, Mike	Children's Press
Beatrix Potter	O	B	Wallner, Alexandra	Holiday House
Beauregard the Cat	M	RF	Book Shop	Mondo
Beautiful Land: A Story of the Oklahoma Land Rush	S	I	Antle, Nancy	The Penguin Group
Beautiful Pig	J	F	Read Alongs	Rigby
Beauty	V	RF	Wallace, Bill	Holiday House
Beauty and the Beast	K	TL	PM Tales and Plays- Gold	Rigby
Beauty and the Beast	K	TL	Sunshine	Wright Group/McGraw Hill
Beaver Engineers	N	I	Reeder, Tracey	Wright Group/McGraw Hill
Beaver, The	M	I	Crewe, Sabrina	Steck-Vaughn
Beavers	N	I	Book Shop	Mondo
Beavers Beware!	K	I	Bank Street	Bantam Doubleday Dell
Bedtime at Aunt Carmen's	K	RF	Ready Readers	Pearson Learning
Bedtime for Frances	K	F	Hoban, Russell	Scholastic
Bedtime Story, A	K	RF	Book Shop	Mondo
Bee, The	M	I	Crewe, Sabrina	Steck-Vaughn
Beekeeper, The	M	I	Literacy 2000	Rigby
Bees	N	I	A True Book	Children's Press
Bees	O	I	Holmes, Kevin J.	Capstone Press
Beethoven Lives Upstairs	S	I	Nichol, Barbara	Orchard Books
Beetles, Lightly Toasted	Q	RF	Naylor, Phyllis Reynolds	Bantam Doubleday Dell

Title	Level	Genre	Author/Series	Publisher/Distributor
Beezus & Ramona	O	RF	Cleary, Beverly	Avon
Beginnings of Sports	R	I	PM Nonfiction -Ruby	Rigby
Behind Rebel Lines	T	HF	Reit, Seymour	Harcourt Brace
Behind The Bedroom Wall	V	HF	Williams, Laura E.	Milkweed Editions
Behind the Couch	N	F	Gerstein, Mordicai	Hyperion
Behind the Scenes	R	I	Literacy 2000	Rigby
Being Danny's Dog	U	RF	Naylor, Phyllis Reynolds	Aladdin
Bell, the Book, and the Spellbinder, The	S	F	Strickland, Brad	Puffin Books
Belle Prater's Boy	V	RF	White, Ruth	Bantam Doubleday Dell
Below the Green Pond	N	I	Read All About It	Steck-Vaughn
Ben and Me	S	HF	Lawson, Robert	Little, Brown & Co.
Ben Franklin of Old Philadelphia	U	B	Cousins, Margaret	Random House
Ben's Tune	N	RF	PM Ruby	Rigby
Benjamin Franklin	N	B	Biography	Benchmark Education
Benjamin Franklin	U	B	Kent, Deborah	Scholastic
Benjamin Franklin: A Man with Many Jobs	O	B	Greene, Carol	Children's Press
Benjamin Franklin: Young Printer	R	B	Stevenson, Augusta	Aladdin
Beowulf	U	TL	Literacy 2000	Rigby
Berenstain Bear Scouts and the Coughing Catfish	M	F	Berenstain, Stan & Jan	Scholastic
Berenstain Bear Scouts Ghost Versus Ghost	P	F	Berenstain, Stan, & Jan	Scholastic
Berenstain Bears and the Ghost of the Auto Graveyard, The	M	F	Berenstain, Stan & Jan	Random House
Berenstain Bears & the Missing Honey	M	F	Berenstain, Stan, & Jan	Random House
Berlioz The Bear	N	F	Brett, Jan	Scholastic
Bess's Log Cabin Quilt	P	HF	Love, D. Anne	Bantam Doubleday Dell
Best Bad Thing, The	U	RF	Uchida, Yoshiko	Aladdin
Best Birthday Present, The	K	RF	Literacy 2000	Rigby
Best Clown in Town, The	L	RF	Bradley, Tom	Dominie Press
Best Detective, The	N	RF	Keene, Carolyn	Pocket Books
Best Enemies	P	RF	Leverich, Kathleen	Beech Tree Books
Best Enemies Again	P	RF	Leverich, Kathleen	Alfred A. Knopf
Best Enemies Forever	P	RF	Leverich, Kathleen	William Morrow
Best Friends for Frances	K	F	Hoban, Russell	HarperTrophy
Best Little Monkeys in the World, The	J	F	Standiford, Natalie	Random House
Best Nest	J	F	Eastman, P.D.	Random House
Best Older Sister, The	L	RF	Choi, Sook Nyul	Bantam Doubleday Dell
Best Part, The	K	RF	PM Story Books -Silver	Rigby
Best School Year Ever, The	P	RF	Robinson, Barbara	HarperTrophy
Best Teacher in the World, The	K	RF	Chardiet, Bernice	Scholastic
Best Way to Play, The	K	I	Cosby, Bill	Scholastic
Best Wishes	O	B	Rylant, Cynthia	Richard C. Owen
Best Wishes for Eddie	M	RF	Nayer, Judy	Pearson Learning
Best Worst Day, The	L	RF	Graves, Bonnie	Hyperion
Best-Loved Doll, The	L	RF	Caudill, Rebecca	Henry Holt & Co.
Beth's Snow Dancer	Q	HF	The Little Women Journals	Avon
Betsy and Tacy Go Downtown	Q	HF	Lovelace, Maud Hart	HarperTrophy
Betsy and Tacy Go Over the Big Hill	Q	HF	Lovelace, Maud Hart	HarperTrophy
Betsy and the Boys	P	RF	Haywood, Carolyn	Harcourt Brace
Betsy Ross: Designer of Our Flag	R	B	Weil, Ann	Aladdin
Betsy-Tacy: 60th Anniversary Edition	Q	HF	Lovelace, Maud Hart	HarperTrophy
Better Brown Stories, The	T	F	Ahlberg, Allan	The Penguin Group
Better Than TV	J	RF	Miller, Sara Swan	Bantam Doubleday Dell
Between Earth and Sky: Legends of Native American Sacred Places	Z	TL	Bruchac, Joseph	Voyager Books
Between the Dragon and the Eagle	W	HF	Schneider, Mical	Carolrhoda Books
Beware!	N	RF	Cartwright, Pauline	Pacific Learning
Beyond Belief	Z	I	Steiger, Brad	Scholastic
Beyond Providence	X	RF	Schnur, Steven	Harcourt Brace
Beyond the Beyond	Q	I	Wildcats	Wright Group/McGraw Hill
Beyond the Burning Lands	U	F	Christopher, John	Aladdin

Title	Level	Genre	Author/Series	Publisher/Distributor
Beyond the Mango Tree	V	RF	Zemser, Amy Bronwen	HarperTrophy
Beyond the Myth: The Story of Joan of Arc	Z	B	Brooks, Polly Schoyer	Houghton Mifflin
Beyond the Western Sea, Book II: Lord Kirkle's Money	V	HF	Avi	Avon Camelot
BFG, The	U	F	Dahl, Roald	The Penguin Group
Bicycle Book, The	O	I	PM Nonfiction -Emerald	Rigby
Bicycle Man, The	P	RF	Say, Allen	Houghton Mifflin
Bicycle Rider	O	B	Scioscia, Mary	HarperTrophy
Big Al	L	F	Yoshi, Andrew C.	Scholastic
Big Balloon Festival, The	L	RF	PM Gold	Rigby
Big Balloon Race, The	K	RF	Coerr, Eleanor	HarperTrophy
Big Beet, The	L	F	Ready Readers	Pearson Learning
Big Boy	O	TL	Mollel, Tololwa M.	Houghton Mifflin
Big Chase, The	M	F	SupaDoopers	Sundance
Big Dipper and You, The	Q	I	Krupp, E.C.	Mulberry Books
Big Fish Little Fish	K	TL	Folk Tales	Wright Group/McGraw Hill
Big Fish, The	M	RF	Yukish, Joe	Kaeden Books
Big Green Caterpillar, The	J	RF	Literacy 2000	Rigby
Big Lie, The: A True Story	T	B	Leitner, Isabella	Scholastic
Big Mama and Grandma Ghana	J	RF	Shelf Medearis, A.	Scholastic
Big Max	J	F	Platt, Kin	HarperTrophy
Big Orange Spot, The	L	F	Pinkwater, Daniel Manus	Scholastic
Big Picture, The	R	I	Bennett, Mary	Pacific Learning
Big Prize, The	K	F	Adventures in Reading	Dominie
Big Race, The	L	RF	Pattrick, Steve	Rigby
Big Race, the	N	F	Pye, Trevor	Pacific Learning
Big Sneeze, The	K	F	Brown, Ruth	Lothrop
Big Storm, The	Q	I	Hiscock, Bruce	Aladdin
Big Toe Robbery, The	N	F	PM Ruby	Rigby
Big Wave, The	Q	RF	Buck, Pearl S.	Scholastic
Bigfoot Doesn't Square Dance	M	F	Dadey, D. & Jones, M. T.	Scholastic
Biggest Klutz in Fifth Grade, The	V	RF	Wallace, Bill	Simon & Schuster
Bighorn Sheep, The	R	I	Mattern, Joanne	Capstone Press
Bill	J	RF	Sunshine	Wright Group/McGraw Hill
Bill Clinton: Forty-Second President of the U.S.	O	B	Greene, Carol	Children's Press
Bill Cosby: The Changing Black Image	X	B	Rosenberg, Robert	Millbrook Press
Bill Gates: Helping People Use Computers	P	B	Community Builders	Children's Press
Bill of Rights, The	N	I	A True Book	Children's Press
Bill of Rights, The	V	I	Cornerstones of Freedom	Bantam Doubleday Dell
Billie the Hippo	N	I	Pacific Literacy	Pacific Learning
Billy Magee's New Car	J	RF	Foundations	Wright Group/McGraw Hill
Billy the Ghost and Me	L	F	Greer, Gery & Ruddick, Bob	HarperTrophy
Birchbark House, The	T	HF	Erdrich, Louise	Hyperion
Bird Behavior: Living Together	M	I	Sunshine	Wright Group/McGraw Hill
Bird in the Basket, The	M	RF	Beveridge, Barbara	Pacific Learning
Bird's-Eye View	J	RF	PM Turquoise	Rigby
Bird's-Eye View, A	K	I	People, Spaces & Places	Rand McNally
Birds and How They Grow	N	I	National Geographic Society	National Geographic Society
Birds At My Feeder	R	I	Kalman, Bobbie	Crabtree
Birds' Nests	J	I	Wonder World	Wright Group/McGraw Hill
Birds of a Feather	N	RF	Literacy 2000	Rigby
Birds of Prey	O	I	Woolley, M. & Pigdon, K.	Mondo
Birds of Prey: A Look at Daytime Raptors	U	I	Collard, Sneed B. III	Franklin Watts
Birds of the City	M	I	Sunshine	Wright Group/McGraw Hill
Birthday	N	RF	Steptoe, John	Henry Holt & Co.
Birthday Bike for Brimhall, A	K	RF	Delton, Judy	Bantam Doubleday Dell
Birthday Disaster	Q	RF	Literacy 2000	Rigby
Birthday for Frances, A	K	F	Hoban, Russell	Scholastic
Birthday Room, The	V	RF	Henkes, Kevin	William Morrow
Birthday Surprises: Ten Great Stories to Unwrap	R	RF	Hurwitz, Johanna	William Morrow

Title	Level	Genre	Author/Series	Publisher/Distributor
Bite of the Gold Bug, The: A Story of the Alaskan Gold Rush	S	I	DeClements, Barthe	The Penguin Group
Black Boy	Z	RF	Wright, Richard	HarperPerennial
Black Diamond: Story of the Negro Baseball Leagues	Q	I	McKissack, Patricia & Fred	Scholastic
Black Eagles, African Americans in Aviation	X	B	Haskins, Jim	Scholastic
Black Gold	R	RF	Henry, Marguerite	Aladdin
Black Hearts in Battersea	V	HF	Aiken, Joan	Houghton Mifflin
Black Heroes of the American Revolution	X	B	Davis, Burke	Harcourt Brace
Black Holes	N	I	A True Book	Children's Press
Black Pearl, The	W	RF	O'Dell, Scott	Bantam Doubleday Dell
Black Pioneers of Science and Invention	Y	B	Haber, Louis	Harcourt Brace
Black Stallion, The	T	RF	Farley, Walter	Language for Learning Assoc.
Black Star, Bright Dawn	V	RF	O'Dell, Scott	Ballantine Books
Black Velvet Mystery, The	N	RF	Keene, Carolyn	Pocket Books
Black-Eyed Susan	Q	HF	Armstrong, Jennifer	Alfred A. Knopf
Blackberries in the Dark	N	RF	Jukes, Mavis	Alfred A. Knopf
Blackboard Bear	J	F	Alexander, Martha	The Penguin Group
Blackwater Swamp	T	RF	Wallace, Bill	Language for Learning Assoc.
Blast Off!	N	I	Home Connection Collection	Rigby
Bless Me, Ultima	Z	RF	Anaya, Rudolfo	Warner Books
Blimps	N	I	A True Book	Children's Press
Blind Man and the Elephant, The	K	TL	Backstein, Karen	Scholastic
Blind Outlaw, The	P	RF	Rounds, Glen	Scholastic
Bloomability	V	RF	Creech, Sharon	Harper Collins
Blossom Promise, A	O	RF	Byars, Betsy	Bantam Doubleday Dell
Blossoms and the Green Phantom, The	O	RF	Byars, Betsy	Dell
Blossoms Meet the Vulture Lady, The	O	RF	Byars, Betsy	Bantam Doubleday Dell
Blubber	T	RF	Blume, Judy	Bantam Doubleday Dell
Blue Door, The	X	HF	Rinaldi, Ann	Scholastic
Blue Heron	W	RF	Avi	Avon
Blue Hill Meadows, The	M	RF	Rylant, Cynthia	Harcourt Brace
Blue Ice	T	RF	Salata, Estelle	Fitzhenry and Whiteside
Blue Ribbon Blues	M	RF	Spinelli, Jerry	Random House
Blue Sword, The	Y	F	McKinley, Robin	Puffin Books
Blue Whales	U	I	The Untamed World	Steck-Vaughn
Blue Willow	V	RF	Gates, Doris	Puffin Books
Blue-Eyed Daisy, A	W	RF	Rylant, Cynthia	Simon & Schuster
Blueberries for Sal	M	RF	McCloskey, Robert	Scholastic
Boats Afloat	M	I	Sunshine	Wright Group/McGraw Hill
Bobo's Magic Wishes	L	F	Little Readers	Houghton Mifflin
Body Numbers	K	I	Discovery World	Rigby
Bogeymen Don't Play Football	M	F	Dadey, D. & Jones, M. T.	Scholastic
Boggart and the Monster, The	U	F	Cooper, Susan	Aladdin
Boggart, The	U	F	Cooper, Susan	Simon & Schuster
Bonanza Girl	T	RF	Beatty, Patricia	Scholastic
Bone Dance	X	RF	Brooks, Martha	Random House
Bony-Legs	K	F	Cole, Joanna	Scholastic
Boodil My Dog	Q	RF	Lindenbaum, Pija	Henry Holt & Co.
Book About Planets and Stars, A	R	I	Reigot, Betty Polisar	Scholastic
Book About Your Skeleton, A	M	I	Gross, Ruth Belov	Scholastic
Book of Black Heroes from A to Z	P	B	Hudson, W. and Wesley, V. W.	Scholastic
Book of Monsters: Tales to Give You the Creeps	T	F	Coville, Bruce	Scholastic
Book of Spine Tinglers: Tales To Make You Shiver	T	F	Coville, Bruce	Scholastic
Book of Three, The	U	F	Alexander, Lloyd	Bantam Doubleday Dell
Booker T. Washington	O	B	First Biographies	Steck-Vaughn
Booker T. Washington	P	B	McLoone, Margo	Capstone Press
Bookworm Who Hatched, A	O	B	Aardema, Verna	Richard C. Owen
Boomtowns of the West	S	I	Kalman, Bobbie	Crabtree
Born To Trot	R	RF	Henry, Marguerite	Aladdin
Borning Room, The	Y	HF	Fleischman, Paul	Harper Collins

Title	Level	Genre	Author/Series	Publisher/Distributor
Borreguita and the Coyote	O	TL	Aardema, Verna	Scholastic
Borrowers, The	S	F	Norton, Mary	Harcourt Brace
Boston Tea Party: Rebellion in the Colonies	T	I	Adventures in Colonial America	Troll
Boston Tea Party, The	V	I	Cornerstones of Freedom	Children's Press
Boston Tea Party, The	S	I	We The People	Compass Point Books
Botticelli	P	B	Venezia, Mike	Children's Press
Boundless Grace	M	RF	Hoffman, Mary	Scholastic
Bowman's Store: A Journey to Myself	Z	B	Bruchac, Joseph	Lee & Low Books, Inc.
Boxcar Children: Amusement Park Mystery, The	O	RF	Warner, Gertrude Chandler	Albert Whitman & Co.
Boxcar Children: Animal Shelter Mystery, The	O	RF	Warner, Gertrude Chandler	Albert Whitman & Co.
Boxcar Children: Basketball Mystery, The	O	RF	Warner, Gertrude Chandler	Albert Whitman & Co.
Boxcar Children: Benny Uncovers a Mystery	O	RF	Warner, Gertrude Chandler	Albert Whitman & Co.
Boxcar Children: Bicycle Mystery	O	RF	Warner, Gertrude Chandler	Albert Whitman & Co.
Boxcar Children: Black Pearl Mystery, The	O	RF	Warner, Gertrude Chandler	Albert Whitman & Co.
Boxcar Children: Blue Bay Mystery	O	RF	Warner, Gertrude Chandler	Albert Whitman & Co.
Boxcar Children: Boxcar Children, The	O	RF	Warner, Gertrude Chandler	Albert Whitman & Co.
Boxcar Children: Bus Station Mystery	O	RF	Warner, Gertrude Chandler	Albert Whitman & Co.
Boxcar Children: Caboose Mystery	O	RF	Warner, Gertrude Chandler	Albert Whitman & Co.
Boxcar Children: Camp-Out Mystery, The	O	RF	Warner, Gertrude Chandler	Albert Whitman & Co.
Boxcar Children: Canoe Trip Mystery, The	O	RF	Warner, Gertrude Chandler	Albert Whitman & Co.
Boxcar Children: Castle Mystery, The	O	RF	Warner, Gertrude Chandler	Albert Whitman & Co.
Boxcar Children: Cereal Box Mystery, The	O	RF	Warner, Gertrude Chandler	Albert Whitman & Co.
Boxcar Children: Deserted Library Mystery, The	O	RF	Warner, Gertrude Chandler	Albert Whitman & Co.
Boxcar Children: Dinosaur Mystery, The	O	RF	Warner, Gertrude Chandler	Albert Whitman & Co.
Boxcar Children: Disappearing Friend Mystery, The	O	RF	Warner, Gertrude Chandler	Albert Whitman & Co.
Boxcar Children: Firehouse Mystery, The	O	RF	Warner, Gertrude Chandler	Albert Whitman & Co.
Boxcar Children: Ghost Ship Mystery, The	O	RF	Warner, Gertrude Chandler	Albert Whitman & Co.
Boxcar Children: Haunted Cabin Mystery, The	O	RF	Warner, Gertrude Chandler	Albert Whitman & Co.
Boxcar Children: Lighthouse Mystery, The	O	RF	Warner, Gertrude Chandler	Albert Whitman & Co.
Boxcar Children: Mike's Mystery	O	RF	Warner, Gertrude Chandler	Albert Whitman & Co.
Boxcar Children: Mountain Top Mystery	O	RF	Warner, Gertrude Chandler	Albert Whitman & Co.
Boxcar Children: Mystery at Snowflake Inn, The	O	RF	Warner, Gertrude Chandler	Albert Whitman & Co.
Boxcar Children: Mystery at the Alamo, The	O	RF	Warner, Gertrude Chandler	Albert Whitman & Co.
Boxcar Children: Mystery at the Dog Show, The	O	RF	Warner, Gertrude Chandler	Albert Whitman & Co.
Boxcar Children: Mystery at the Fair	O	RF	Warner, Gertrude Chandler	Albert Whitman & Co.
Boxcar Children: Mystery Behind the Wall	O	RF	Warner, Gertrude Chandler	Albert Whitman & Co.
Boxcar Children: Mystery Bookstore, The	O	RF	Warner, Gertrude Chandler	Albert Whitman & Co.
Boxcar Children: Mystery Cruise, The	O	RF	Warner, Gertrude Chandler	Albert Whitman & Co.
Boxcar Children: Mystery Girl, The	O	RF	Warner, Gertrude Chandler	Albert Whitman & Co.
Boxcar Children: Mystery Horse, The	O	RF	Warner, Gertrude Chandler	Albert Whitman & Co.
Boxcar Children: Mystery in San Francisco, The	O	RF	Warner, Gertrude Chandler	Albert Whitman & Co.
Boxcar Children: Mystery in the Cave, The	O	RF	Warner, Gertrude Chandler	Albert Whitman & Co.
Boxcar Children: Mystery in the Old Attic, The	O	RF	Warner, Gertrude Chandler	Albert Whitman & Co.
Boxcar Children: Mystery in the Sand	O	RF	Warner, Gertrude Chandler	Albert Whitman & Co.
Boxcar Children: Mystery in Washington, DC, The	O	RF	Warner, Gertrude Chandler	Albert Whitman & Co.
Boxcar Children: Mystery of the Hidden Beach	O	RF	Warner, Gertrude Chandler	Albert Whitman & Co.
Boxcar Children: Mystery of the Lost Mine, The	O	RF	Warner, Gertrude Chandler	Albert Whitman & Co.
Boxcar Children: Mystery of the Lost Village, The	O	RF	Warner, Gertrude Chandler	Albert Whitman & Co.
Boxcar Children: Mystery of the Missing Cat, The	O	RF	Warner, Gertrude Chandler	Albert Whitman & Co.
Boxcar Children: Mystery of the Mixed-Up Zoo, The	O	RF	Warner, Gertrude Chandler	Albert Whitman & Co.
Boxcar Children: Mystery of the Stolen Music, The	O	RF	Warner, Gertrude Chandler	Scholastic
Boxcar Children: Mystery on Stage, The	O	RF	Warner, Gertrude Chandler	Albert Whitman & Co.
Boxcar Children: Mystery on the Train, The	O	RF	Warner, Gertrude Chandler	Albert Whitman & Co.
Boxcar Children: Mystery Ranch	O	RF	Warner, Gertrude Chandler	Albert Whitman & Co.
Boxcar Children: Outer Space Mystery, The	O	RF	Warner, Gertrude Chandler	Albert Whitman & Co.
Boxcar Children: Pizza Mystery, The	O	RF	Warner, Gertrude Chandler	Albert Whitman & Co.
Boxcar Children Return, The	O	RF	Warner, Gertrude Chandler	Scholastic
Boxcar Children: Schoolhouse Mystery	O	RF	Warner, Gertrude Chandler	Albert Whitman & Co.
Boxcar Children: Snowbound Mystery	O	RF	Warner, Gertrude Chandler	Albert Whitman & Co.
Boxcar Children: Soccer Mystery, The	O	RF	Warner, Gertrude Chandler	Scholastic

Title	Level	Genre	Author/Series	Publisher/Distributor
Boxcar Children Special: The Mystery at Snowflake Inn	O	RF	Warner, Gertrude Chandler	Albert Whitman & Co.
Boxcar Children Special: The Mystery at the Ballpark	O	RF	Warner, Gertrude Chandler	Albert Whitman & Co.
Boxcar Children Special: The Mystery at the Fair	O	RF	Warner, Gertrude Chandler	Albert Whitman & Co.
Boxcar Children Special: The Pilgrim Village Mystery	O	RF	Warner, Gertrude Chandler	Albert Whitman & Co.
Boxcar Children: Surprise Island	O	RF	Warner, Gertrude Chandler	Scholastic
Boxcar Children: Woodshed Mystery, The	O	RF	Warner, Gertrude Chandler	Albert Whitman & Co.
Boxcar Children: Yellow House Mystery, The	O	RF	Warner, Gertrude Chandler	Albert Whitman & Co.
Boy	T	B	Dahl, Roald	Puffin Books
Boy and His Donkey, A	K	F	Literacy 2000	Rigby
Boy Called Slow, A	S	B	Bruchac, Joseph	Putnam & Grosset
Boy in the Doghouse, A	N	RF	Duffey, Betsy	Simon & Schuster
Boy Named Boomer, A	K	B	Esiason, Boomer	Scholastic
Boy Who Ate Dog Biscuits, The	N	RF	Sachs, Betsy	Random House
Boy Who Cried Bigfoot, The	N	F	The Zack Files	Grossett&Dunlap
Boy Who Cried Wolf, The	K	TL	Aesop's Fables	Dominie
Boy Who Cried Wolf, The	L	TL	Literacy 2000	Rigby
Boy Who Cried Wolf, The	J	TL	Littledale, Freya	Scholastic
Boy Who Cried Wolf, The	K	TL	PM Tales and Plays- Purple	Rigby
Boy Who Lost His Face, The	R	RF	Sachar, Louis	Alfred A. Knopf
Boy Who Owned the School, The	U	RF	Paulsen, Gary	Bantam Doubleday Dell
Boy Who Reversed Himself, The	Y	SF	Sleator, William	Puffin Books
Boy Who Stretched to the Sky, The	M	F	Book Bank	Wright Group/McGraw Hill
Boy Who Turned Into a T.V. Set, The	L	F	Manes, Stephen	Avon Camelot
Boy Who Went to the North Wind, The	L	TL	Literacy 2000	Rigby
Boy's Will, A	S	HF	Haugaard, Erik Christian	Houghton Mifflin
Boys Against Girls	S	RF	Naylor, Phyllis Reynolds	Bantam Doubleday Dell
Boys Start the War and the Girls Get Even, The	S	RF	Naylor, Phyllis Reynolds	Bantam Doubleday Dell
Boys Will Be	X	RF	Brooks, Bruce	Hyperion
Bozo the Clone	N	SF	The Zack Files	Grosset & Dunlap
Bracelet, The	R	HF	Uchida, Yoshiko	Philomel Books
Brachiosaurus in the River	L	F	Wesley & The Dinosaurs	Wright Group/McGraw Hill
Brad and Butter Play Ball!	N	RF	Hughes, Dean	William Morrow
Brady	V	HF	Fritz, Jean	Puffin Books
Brain	V	I	You And Your Body	Troll
Brain-in-a-Box	M	F	Matthews, Steve	Sundance
Brainstorm!: The Stories of Twenty American Kid Inventors	P	B	Tucker, Tom	Farrar, Straus and Giroux
Brand New Butterfly, A	L	I	Literacy 2000	Rigby
Brave As	P	RF	Marriott, Janice	Pacific Learning
Brave Little Tailor, The	J	TL	PM Tales and Plays Turquoise	Rigby
Brave Maddie Egg	M	RF	Standiford, Natalie	Random House
Bravest Dog Ever, The: The True Story of Balto	L	I	Standiford, Natalie	Random House
Bravo Amelia Bedelia!	L	F	Parish, Herman	Avon
Brazil	N	I	A True Book	Children's Press
Brazil	O	I	Dahl, Michael	Capstone Press
Brazil	Q	I	First Reports	Compass Point Books
Bread and Jam for Frances	K	F	Hoban, Russell	Scholastic
Break with Charity, A: A Story About the Salem Witch Trials	X	I	Rinaldi, Ann	Harcourt Brace
Breath of the Dragon	P	RF	Giles, Gail	Bantam Doubleday Dell
Breathing	L	I	Book Shop	Mondo
Bremen-Town Musicians, The	K	TL	Gross, Ruth	Scholastic
Brendan the Navigator: A History Mystery about the Discovery of America	R	I	Fritz, Jean	The Penguin Group
Brian's Brilliant Career	P	RF	Literacy 2000	Rigby
Brian's Song	Z	I	Blinn, William	Bantam Doubleday Dell
Brian's Winter	R	RF	Paulsen, Gary	Bantam Doubleday Dell
Bridge to Terabithia	S	RF	Paterson, Katherine	HarperTrophy
Bridges	N	I	Wildcats	Wright Group/McGraw Hill
Bridging the Gap	Q	I	Miller, Steve	Pacific Learning

Title	Level	Genre	Author/Series	Publisher/Distributor
Bright Ideas	Q	I	Weldon Owen	Wright Group/McGraw Hill
Bright Paddles	P	HF	Downi, Mary Alice	Fitzhenry and Whiteside
Bright Shadow	T	F	Avi	Aladdin
Brighty of the Grand Canyon	R	RF	Henry, Marguerite	Aladdin
Brigid Beware	L	RF	Leverich, Kathleen	Random House
Brigid Bewitched	L	RF	Leverich, Kathleen	Random House
Brigid the Bad	L	RF	Leverich, Kathleen	Random House
Bringing the Rain to Kapiti Plain	J	TL	Aardema, Verna	Scholastic
Bringing the Sea Back Home	L	F	Literacy 2000	Rigby
Brith The Terrible	M	F	Literacy 2000	Rigby
Broccoli Tapes, The	S	RF	Slepian, Jan	Scholastic
Broken Blade, The	T	HF	Durbin, William	Yearling
Broken Bridge, The	Z	RF	Pullman, Philip	Alfred A. Knopf
Broken Window and Other Cases, The	O	RF	Simon, Seymour	Avon
Bronze Bow, The	U	HF	Speare, Elizabeth George	Houghton Mifflin
Brookfield Days	N	HF	Little House	HarperTrophy
Brother To Shadows	Z	SF	Norton, Andre	Avon
Brown Bears	K	I	PM Animal Facts: Turquoise	Rigby
Brown Sunshine of Sawdust Valley	O	RF	Henry, Marguerite	Aladdin
Bryce Canyon National Park	N	I	A True Book	Children's Press
Bubbling Crocodile	K	F	Pacific Literacy	Pacific Learning
Buck Stops Here, The	T	I	Provensen, Alice	Harcourt Brace
Bud, Not Buddy	T	RF	Curtis, Christopher Paul	Random House
Buddy: The First Seeing Eye Dog	M	I	Moore, Eva	Scholastic
Buffalo Before Breakfast	M	F	Osborne, Mary Pope	Random House
Buffalo Bill and the Pony Express	K	B	Coerr, Eleanor	HarperTrophy
Buffalo Gal	U	RF	Wallace, Bill	Simon & Schuster
Buffalo, The	M	I	Crewe, Sabrina	Steck-Vaughn
Buffalo Woman	N	TL	Goble, Paul	Aladdin
Bug Off!	L	F	Dussling, Jennifer	Grosset & Dunlap
Bugs	O	I	Parker, N. W. & Wright, J. R.	Mulberry Books
Bugs and Other Insects	N	I	Kalman, Bobbie	Crabtree
Build, Build, Build	M	I	Sunshine	Wright Group/McGraw Hill
Build It Strong!	M	I	First Science	Children's Press
Building a Dream: Mary Bethune's School	R	B	Kelso, Richard	Steck-Vaughn
Building Homes, Building Hope	O	I	Bovez, Marcie	Wright Group/McGraw Hill
Building the Capital City	V	I	Cornerstones of Freedom	Bantam Doubleday Dell
Bull Harris and the Purple Ooze	M	RF	SupaDoopers	Sundance
Bull in a China Shop, A	K	F	Literacy 2000	Rigby
Bull Run	Y	HF	Fleischman, Paul	HarperCollins
Bully for you Teddy Roosevelt!	X	B	Fritz, Jean	Penguin Putnam Books
Bully of Barkham Street	R	RF	Stolz, Mary	Harper Trophy
Bumps in the Night	K	F	Allard, Harry	Bantam Doubleday Dell
Bungee 70528	O	RF	Belcher, Angie	Pacific Learning
Bunnicula	Q	F	Howe, James	Avon
Bunnicula Strikes Again!	Q	F	Howe, James	Simon & Schuster
Bunnies in the Bathroom	Q	RF	Baglio, Ben M.	Scholastic
Bunny Runs Away	K	F	Chardiet, B. & Maccarone, G.	Scholastic
Buried Eye, The	M	F	Schultz, Irene	Wright Group/McGraw Hill
Burning Questions of Bingo Brown	T	RF	Byars, Betsy	Language for Learning Assoc.
Bush Bunyip, The	J	F	Book Shop	Mondo
Buster Baxter, Cat Saver	M	F	Brown, Marc	Little, Brown & Co.
Buster Makes the Grade	M	F	Brown, Marc	Little, Brown & Co.
Buster's Dino Dilemma	M	F	Brown, Marc	Little, Brown & Co.
Busy Guy, A	K	RF	Rookie Readers	Children's Press
Busybody Nora	N	RF	Hurwitz, Johanna	The Penguin Group
But I'll Be Back Again	V	B	Rylant, Cynthia	Beech Tree Books
Butterflies	O	I	Holmes, Kevin J.	Capstone Press
Butterflies and Moths	N	I	Kalman, Bobbie	Crabtree
Butterflies of the Sea	L	I	Swartz, Stanley L.	Dominie Press

Title	Level	Genre	Author/Series	Publisher/Distributor
Butterfly Farm Burglar, The	M	RF	Schultz, Irene	Wright Group/McGraw Hill
Butterfly, The	M	I	Crewe, Sabrina	Steck-Vaughn
Butterfly's Life, A	K	I	Burke, Melissa Blackwell	Steck-Vaughn
Button Soup	K	RF	Bank Street	Bantam Doubleday Dell
Buttons for General Washington	M	HF	Roop, Peter & Connie	Carolrhoda Books
Buzby	J	F	Hoban, Julia	HarperTrophy
By Lakes and Rivers	N	I	Animal Trackers	Crabtree
By the Great Horn Spoon!	V	HF	Fleischman, Sid	Little, Brown & Co.
By the Seashore	N	I	Animal Trackers	Crabtree
By the Shores of Silver Lake	Q	HF	Wilder, Laura Ingalls	HarperTrophy
Bye, Bye, Bali Kai	U	RF	Luger, Harriett	Harcourt Brace
Cabbage Princess, The	K	TL	Literacy 2000	Rigby
Cabin Faced West, The	R	HF	Fritz, Jean	Bantam Doubleday Dell
Cabin in the Hills, The	J	RF	PM Turquoise	Rigby
Caddie Woodlawn	R	HF	Brink, Carol Ryrie	Bantam Doubleday Dell
Cage, The	Z	B	Sender, Ruth Minsky	Simon & Schuster
Cake, The	M	RF	Read Alongs	Rigby
Calamity Kate	Q	RF	Deary, Terry	HarperTrophy
Caleb's Choice	S	HF	Wisler, Clifton G.	The Penguin Group
Calico Bush	V	HF	Field, Rachel	Simon & Schuster
Calico Captive	S	HF	Speare, Elizabeth George	Yearling
California	Q	I	Geography Department	Capstone Press
California	T	I	Sea To Shining Sea	Children's Press
California Gold Rush, The	V	I	Cornerstones of Freedom	Children's Press
California Gold Rush, The	T	I	McNeer, May	Random House
California Gold Rush, The	S	I	We The People	Compass Point Books
Call It Courage	X	RF	Sperry, Armstrong	Aladdin
Call Me Francis Tucket	V	HF	Paulsen, Gary	Yearling
Call Me Ruth	R	RF	Sachs, Marilyn	Beech Tree Books
Call of the Wild	Y	RF	London, Jack	Signet Classics
Cam Jansen and the Chocolate Fudge Mystery	L	RF	Adler, David A.	Puffin Books
Cam Jansen and the Ghostly Mystery	L	RF	Adler, David A.	Puffin Books
Cam Jansen and the Mystery at the Haunted House	L	RF	Adler, David A.	Puffin Books
Cam Jansen and the Mystery at the Monkey House	L	RF	Adler, David A.	Puffin Books
Cam Jansen and the Mystery of Flight 54	L	RF	Adler, David A.	Puffin Books
Cam Jansen and the Mystery of the Babe Ruth Baseball	L	RF	Adler, David A.	Puffin Books
Cam Jansen and the Mystery of the Carnival Prize	L	RF	Adler, David A.	Puffin Books
Cam Jansen and the Mystery of the Circus Clown	L	RF	Adler, David A.	Puffin Books
Cam Jansen and the Mystery of the Dinosaur Bones	L	RF	Adler, David A.	Puffin Books
Cam Jansen and the Mystery of the Gold Coins	L	RF	Adler, David A.	Puffin Books
Cam Jansen and the Mystery of the Monkey House	L	RF	Adler, David A.	Puffin Books
Cam Jansen and the Mystery of the Monster Movie	L	RF	Adler, David A.	Puffin Books
Cam Jansen and the Mystery of the Stolen Corn Popper	L	RF	Adler, David A.	Puffin Books
Cam Jansen and the Mystery of the Stolen Diamonds	L	RF	Adler, David A.	Puffin Books
Cam Jansen and the Mystery of the Television Dog	L	RF	Adler, David A.	Puffin Books
Cam Jansen and the Mystery of the U.F.O.	L	RF	Adler, David A.	Puffin Books
Cam Jansen and the Scary Snake Mystery	L	RF	Adler, David A.	Puffin Books
Camel Called Bump-Along, A	K	F	Evangeline Nicholas Collection	Wright Group/McGraw Hill
Camouflage	J	I	Sunshine	Wright Group/McGraw Hill
Camp Big Paw	J	RF	Cushman, Doug	HarperTrophy
Camp Knock Knock	K	RF	Duffey, Betsy	Bantam Doubleday Dell
Camp Knock Knock Mystery, The	K	RF	Duffey, Betsy	Bantam Doubleday Dell
Camping with Claudine	K	RF	Literacy 2000	Rigby
Can Do, Jenny Archer	M	RF	Conford, Ellen	Random House
Can I Have a Dinosaur?	L	RF	Literacy 2000	Rigby
Can You Imagine?	O	B	McKissack, Patricia	Richard C. Owen
Can't You Make Them Behave, King George?	R	I	Fritz, Jean	Putnam & Grossett
Canada	O	I	Dahl, Michael	Capstone Press
Canada	Q	I	First Reports	Compass Point Books
Canada Celebrates Multiculturalism	T	I	Kalman, Bobbie	Crabtree

Title	Level	Genre	Author/Series	Publisher/Distributor
Canada Geese Quilt, The	P	RF	Kinsey-Warnock, Natalie	Bantam Doubleday Dell
Canada: The Culture	T	I	Kalman, Bobbie	Crabtree
Canada: The Land	T	I	Kalman, Bobbie	Crabtree
Canada: The People	T	I	Kalman, Bobbie	Crabtree
Canary Caper, The	N	RF	Roy, Ron	Random House
Candlelight Service	O	RF	Literacy 2000	Rigby
Candy Corn Contest, The	L	RF	Giff, Patricia Reilly	Bantam Doubleday Dell
Cannonball Chris	L	RF	Marzollo, J.	Random House
Canoe Diary	O	I	Bishop, Nic	Pacific Learning
Canyons	V	F	Paulsen, Gary	Laurel-Leaf Books
Capitol, The	V	I	Cornerstones of Freedom	Bantam Doubleday Dell
Caps for Sale	K	F	Slobodkina, Esphyr	Harper & Row
Captain Bumble	K	F	Story Box	Wright Group/McGraw Hill
Captain Felonius	L	F	Literacy 2000	Rigby
Captain Grey	U	HF	Avi	HarperTrophy
Car Trouble	L	RF	PM Gold	Rigby
Caribou Journey, A	Q	I	Miller, Debbie S.	Little, Brown & Co.
Caribou (Reindeer)	N	I	PM Animal Facts: Silver	Rigby
Carlita Ropes the Twister	L	F	Pair-It Books	Steck-Vaughn
Carole: The Inside Story	R	RF	Bryant, Bonnie	Skylark Books
Carolina Crow Girl	T	F	Hobbs, Valerie	Puffin Books
Carpenters	L	I	Community Workers	Compass Point Books
Carrots Don't Talk!	J	F	Ready Readers	Pearson Learning
Carry on, Mr. Bowditch	Y	B	Latham, Jean Lee	Houghton Mifflin
Cartoonist, The	S	RF	Byars, Betsy	Puffin Books
Case for Jenny Archer, A	M	RF	Conford, Ellen	Random House
Case of Capital Intrigue, The	S	RF	Keene, Carolyn	Pocket Books
Case of Hermie the Missing Hamster, The	N	RF	Preller, James	Scholastic
Case of the Captured Queen	S	RF	Keene, Carolyn	Pocket Books
Case of the Cat's Meow, The	K	RF	Bonsall, Crosby	HarperTrophy
Case of the Christmas Snowman, The	N	RF	Preller, James	Scholastic
Case of the Cool-Itch Kid, The	L	RF	Giff, Patricia Reilly	Bantam Doubleday Dell
Case of the Dangerous Solution, The	S	RF	Keene, Carolyn	Pocket Books
Case of the Dirty Bird, The	O	RF	Paulsen, Gary	Bantam Doubleday Dell
Case of the Disappearing Bones	N	RF	SupaDoopers	Sundance
Case of the Double Cross, The	K	RF	Bonsall, Crosby	HarperTrophy
Case of the Dumb Bells, The	K	RF	Bonsall, Crosby	HarperTrophy
Case of the Elevator Duck, The	M	RF	Berends, Polly Berrien	Random House
Case of the Floating Crime, The	S	RF	Keene, Carolyn	Pocket Books
Case of the Hungry Stranger, The	M	RF	Bonsall, Crosby	HarperTrophy
Case of the Invisible Cat, The	Q	RF	Parker, A.E.	Scholastic
Case of the Lion Dance	U	RF	Yep, Laurence	HarperTrophy
Case of the Measled Cowboy, The	P	F	Erickson, John R.	Puffin Books
Case of the Midnight Rustler, The	P	F	Erickson, John R.	Puffin Books
Case of the Missing Cat, The	P	F	Erickson, John R.	Puffin Books
Case of the Nervous Newsboy, The	N	RF	Hildick, E.W.	Sundance
Case of the Sabotaged School Play, The	R	RF	Singer, Marilyn	Bantam Doubleday Dell
Case of the Scaredy Cats, The	K	RF	Bonsall, Crosby	HarperTrophy
Case of the Secret Valentine, The	N	RF	Preller, James	Scholastic
Case of the Spooky Sleepover, The	N	RF	Preller, James	Scholastic
Case of the Stolen Baseball Cards, The	N	RF	Preller, James	Scholastic
Case of the Twin Teddy Bears, The	S	RF	Keene, Carolyn	Pocket Books
Case of the Two Masked Robbers, The	K	F	Hoban, Lillian	HarperTrophy
Casey's Case	Q	RF	Literacy 2000	Rigby
Casey's Code	Q	RF	Riley, Gail Blasser	Steck-Vaughn
Cass Becomes a Star	L	B	Literacy 2000	Rigby
Cassidy's Magic	S	F	Literacy 2000	Rigby
Cassie Binegar	T	RF	MacLachlan, Patricia	HarperTrophy
Castle in the Attic, The	R	F	Winthrop, Elizabeth	Bantam Doubleday Dell
Castle of Llyr, The	W	F	Alexander, Lloyd	Dell

Title	Level	Genre	Author/Series	Publisher/Distributor
Cat!	S	I	Kroll, Virginia L.	Dawn
Cat and Rat	M	TL	Young, Ed	Henry Holt & Co.
Cat Ate My Gymsuit, The	U	RF	Danziger, Paula	Putnam & Grosset
Cat Burglar of Pethaven Drive, The	N	F	Literacy 2000	Rigby
Cat Called Tim, A	L	RF	New Way: Literature	Steck-Vaughn
Cat Concert	J	F	Literacy 2000	Rigby
Cat Crazy	O	RF	Baglio, Ben M.	Scholastic
Cat in the Hat	J	F	Seuss, Dr.	Random House
Cat Running	U	RF	Snyder, Zilpha Keatley	Bantam Doubleday Dell
Cat Talk	N	I	Long, Don	Pacific Learning
Cat Walk	R	F	Stolz, Mary	Bantam Doubleday Dell
Cat Who Went To Heaven, The	S	F	Coatsworth, Elizabeth	Aladdin
Cat Who Wore a Pot on Her Head, The	N	F	Slepian, Jan & Seidler, Ann	Scholastic
Cat's Meow, The	Q	F	Soto, Gary	Scholastic
Catch Me If You Can!: The Roadrunner	M	I	Chukran, Bobbi A.	Wright Group/McGraw Hill
Catch That Pass!	M	RF	Christopher, Matt	Little, Brown & Co.
Catcher With a Glass Arm	M	RF	Christopher, Matt	Little, Brown & Co.
Catcher's Mask, The	M	RF	Christopher, Matt	Little, Brown & Co.
Catching the Sun	M	TL	Paul, Michele	Wright Group/McGraw Hill
Caterpillars	M	I	Book Shop	Mondo
Caterpillars	P	I	Mini Pets	Steck-Vaughn
Catherine, Called Birdy	U	HF	Cushman, Karen	Clarion
Cats	J	I	PM Animal Facts: Orange	Rigby
Cats' Burglar, The	K	F	Parish, Peggy	Hearst
Cats, Cats, Cats	Q	I	Literacy 2000	Rigby
Cats of the Night	K	RF	Book Bank	Wright Group/McGraw Hill
Cattle	L	I	PM Animal Facts: Purple	Rigby
Catwings	N	F	Le Guin, Ursula K.	Scholastic
Catwings Return	N	F	Le Guin, Ursula K.	Scholastic
Caught by the Sea	N	RF	Keating, Rosemary	Pacific Learning
Caught in a Flash	P	I	Bishop, Nic	Pacific Learning
Caves	M	I	Discovery World	Rigby
Caves	R	I	The Wonders of our World	Crabtree
Caves	R	I	Wood, Jenny	Scholastic
Caves and Caverns	O	I	Gibbons, Gail	Harcourt Brace
Cay, The	V	HF	Taylor, Theodore	Avon
CD and the Giant Cat	V	SF	Odgers, Darrel and Sally	Rigby
Ceiling of Stars, A	U	RF	Creel, Ann Howard	Pleasant Company
Celery Stalks at Midnight, The	R	F	Howe, James	Atheneum
Cells	J	I	Wonder World	Wright Group/McGraw Hill
Center Court Sting	M	RF	Christopher, Matt	Little, Brown & Co.
Centerburg Tales: More Adventures of Homer Price	Q	RF	McCloskey, Robert	Puffin Books
Centerfield Ballhawk	M	RF	Christopher, Matt	Little, Brown & Co.
Cesar Chavez	N	B	Biography	Benchmark Education
Cesar Chavez	P	B	Davis, Lucile	Capstone Press
Cesar Chavez	Y	B	Rodriguez, Consuelo	Chelsea House
Chair For My Mother, A	M	RF	Williams, Vera B.	Scholastic
Chalk Box Kid, The	N	RF	Bulla, Clyde Robert	Random House
Challenge at Second Base	M	RF	Christopher, Matt	Little, Brown & Co.
Chancy and the Grand Rascal	R	F	Fleischman, Sid	Beech Tree
Chang's Paper Pony	L	RF	Coerr, Eleanor	HarperTrophy
Change for Zoe, A	K	RF	Home Connection Collection	Rigby
Change The Locks	S	RF	French, Simon	Scholastic
Changes for Addy	Q	HF	The American Girls Collection	Pleasant Company
Changes For Addy: A Winter Story	Q	HF	The American Girls Collection	Pleasant Company
Changes For Felicity: A Winter Story	Q	HF	The American Girls Collection	Pleasant Company
Changes For Josefina: A Winter Story	Q	HF	The American Girls Collection	Pleasant Company
Changes For Kirsten: A Winter Story	Q	HF	The American Girls Collection	Pleasant Company
Changes For Molly: A Winter Story	Q	HF	The American Girls Collection	Pleasant Company
Changes For Samantha: A Winter Story	Q	HF	The American Girls Collection	Pleasant Company

Title	Level	Genre	Author/Series	Publisher/Distributor
Changing Times	Q	RF	Treasured Horses Collection	Scholastic
Charles Lindbergh	O	B	Early Biographies	Compass Point Books
Charley Skedaddle	U	HF	Beatty, Patricia	Troll
Charlie	L	F	Literacy 2000	Rigby
Charlie and the Chocolate Factory	R	F	Dahl, Roald	Bantam Doubleday Dell
Charlie and the Great Glass Elevator	R	F	Dahl, Roald	Bantam Doubleday Dell
Charlie Is a Chicken	P	RF	Smith, Jane Denitz	HarperTrophy
Charlie Malarkey and the Singing Moose	R	F	Kennedy, William & Brendan	Puffin Books
Charlie Needs a Cloak	J	RF	dePaola, Tomie	Prentice-Hall
Charlotte's Web	R	F	White, E. B.	HarperTrophy
Chasing Redbird	V	RF	Creech, Sharon	Harper Collins
Chasing Tornadoes	P	I	Gold, Becky	Pearson Learning
Cheerful King, The	K	F	Little Books	Sadlier-Oxford
Chefs	L	I	Community Workers	Compass Point Books
Cherokee Indians, The	P	I	Lund, Bill	Capstone Press
Cherries and Cherry Pits	M	RF	Williams, Vera B.	Houghton Mifflin
Chester Cricket's New Home	S	F	Selden, George	Bantam Doubleday Dell
Chester Cricket's Pigeon Ride	S	F	Selden, George	Bantam Doubleday Dell
Chester the Wizard	M	F	Reading Unlimited	Celebration Press
Cheyenne, The	N	I	A New True Book	Children's Press
Chicago Winds	K	I	Evangeline Nicholas Collection	Wright Group/McGraw Hill
Chick Challenge	O	RF	Baglio, Ben M.	Scholastic
Chicken in the Middle of the Road	J	RF	Book Shop	Mondo
Chicken Little	L	TL	Traditional Tales & More	Rigby
Chicken Soup with Rice	M	F	Sendak, Maurice	Harper Collins
Chicken Sunday	N	RF	Polacco, Patricia	Scholastic
Chickens	L	I	PM Animal Facts: Purple	Rigby
Chickens Have Chicks	M	I	Animals and Their Young	Compass Point Books
Chief Joseph of the Nez Percé	P	B	McAuliffe, Bill	Capstone Press
Child in Prison Camp, A	X	HF	Takashima, Shizuye	Tundra Books
Child of the Owl	W	RF	Yep, Laurence	HarperTrophy
Child of the Wolves	U	RF	Hall, Elizabeth	Bantam Doubleday Dell
Child's Day, A	T	I	Historic Communities	Crabtree
Child's Portrait of Shakespeare, A	Q	B	Burdett, Lois	Firefly Books
Children Around the World	M	I	People, Spaces & Places	Rand McNally
Children as Young Scientists	K	I	Early Connections	Benchmark Education
Children of Christmas: Stories for the Season	R	RF	Rylant, Cynthia	Orchard Books
Children of Clay: A Family of Pueblo Potters	S	I	Swentzell, Rina	Lerner Publications
Children of Green Knowe, The	T	F	Boston, L.M.	Harcourt Brace
Children of Sierra Leone, The	J	I	Books For Young Learners	Richard C. Owen
Children of the Dust Bowl	Y	I	Stanley, Jerry	Crown Publishers
Children of the Earth and Sky	P	I	Krensky, Stephen	Scholastic
Children of the Fire	P	HF	Robinet, Harriette	Aladdin
Children of the Longhouse	S	HF	Bruchac, Joseph	The Penguin Group
Children of the River	X	RF	Crew, Linda	Bantam Doubleday Dell
Children of the Wild West	X	I	Freedman, Russell	Clarion Books
Children's Clothing of the 1800's	S	I	Historic Communities	Crabtree
Childtimes: A Three-Generation Memoir	X	B	Greenfield, E. & Little, L. J.	HarperTrophy
China	N	I	A True Book	Children's Press
China	O	I	Dahl, Michael	Capstone Press
China	Q	I	First Reports	Compass Point Books
China: The Culture	T	I	Kalman, Bobbie	Crabtree
China: The Land	T	I	Kalman, Bobbie	Crabtree
China: The People	T	I	Kalman, Bobbie	Crabtree
China's Bravest Girl: The Legend of Hua Mu Lan	O	TL	Chin, Charlie	Children's Press
Chipmunk at Hollow Tree Lane	K	F	Sherrow, Victoria	Scholastic
Chisholm Trail, The	V	I	Cornerstones of Freedom	Bantam Doubleday Dell
Chocolate!	P	I	Velarde, Linda	Rigby
Chocolate	N	I	What's For Lunch?	Children's Press
Chocolate by Hershey: A Story about Milton S. Hershey	R	B	Burford, Betty	Carolrhoda Books

Title	Level	Genre	Author/Series	Publisher/Distributor
Chocolate Fever	O	F	Smith, Robert	Bantam Doubleday Dell
Chocolate Flier, The	R	I	Beames, Margaret	Rigby
Chocolate Touch, The	N	F	Catling, Patrick Skene	Bantam Doubleday Dell
Chocolate-Chip Muffins	J	RF	Sunshine	Wright Group/McGraw Hill
Chocolate-Covered Contest, The	S	RF	Keene, Carolyn	Pocket Books
Choosing Up Sides	V	RF	Ritter, John H.	Puffin Books
Christa McAuliffe: Teacher in Space	W	B	Naden, Corinne J. & Blue, Rose	Millbrook
Christina's Ghost	R	F	Wright, Betty Ren	Bantam Doubleday Dell
Christmas in the Big Woods	J	HF	Wilder, Laura Ingalls	Harper Collins
Christmas Spurs, The	R	RF	Wallace, Bill	Bantam Doubleday Dell
Christmas: Why We Celebrate It the Way We Do	P	I	Hintz, Martin & Kate	Capstone Press
Christopher Columbus: A Great Explorer	O	B	Greene, Carol	Children's Press
Chug the Tractor	K	F	PM Story Books	Rigby
Cinderella	K	TL	Once Upon a Time	Wright Group/McGraw Hill
Cinderella	K	TL	PM Tales and Plays- Gold	Rigby
Circle of Gold	R	RF	Boyd, Candy Dawson	Bantam Doubleday Dell
Circle of Quiet, A	Z	B	L'Engle, Madeleine	Harper Collins
Circle Unbroken, A	V	HF	Hotze, Sollace	Houghton Mifflin
Circulatory System, The	N	I	A True Book	Children's Press
Circus Mystery, The	M	RF	Schultz, Irene	Wright Group/McGraw Hill
Cities Around the World	M	I	Pair-It Books	Steck-Vaughn
Cities of Splendor: The Facts and the Fables	R	TL	Landscapes of Legend	Children's Press
Cities: The Building of America	Q	I	Thompson, Gare	Children's Press
Cities: Then and Now	O	I	People, Spaces & Places	Rand McNally
City Green	M	RF	DiSalvo-Ryan, DyAnne	Scholastic
City Mouse-Country Mouse	J	TL	Aesop	Scholastic
City of Gold & Lead, The	V	F	Christopher, John	Aladdin
City Through the Ages	U	I	Steele, Philip	Troll Associates
Civil Rights Marches	V	I	Cornerstones of Freedom	Children's Press
Civil War on Sunday	M	F	Osborner, Mary Pope	Random House
Clara and the Bookwagon	K	RF	Levinson, Nancy Smiler	HarperTrophy
Clara Barton: Founder of the American Red Cross	R	B	Stevenson, Augusta	Aladdin
Clarence the Crocodile	L	F	New Way: Literature	Steck-Vaughn
Class Clown	O	RF	Hurwitz, Johanna	Scholastic
Class Play, The	J	RF	Little Readers	Houghton Mifflin
Class President	O	RF	Hurwitz, Johanna	Scholastic
Class Trip to the Cave of Doom	Q	F	McMullan, K.H.	Grosset & Dunlap
Claudine's Concert	L	RF	Literacy 2000	Rigby
Clay Marble, The	V	RF	Ho, Minfong	Farrar, Straus and Giroux
Cleopatra	X	B	Green, Robert	Franklin Watts
Cleopatra	T	B	Stanley, Diane & Vennema, Peter	Mulberry Books
Clever Mr. Brown	K	F	Story Box	Wright Group/McGraw Hill
Clifford, the Big Red Dog	K	F	Bridwell, Norman	Scholastic
Clifford, the Small Red Puppy	K	F	Bridwell, Norman	Scholastic
Cloak of the Wind	O	HF	Voyages in…	Wright Group/McGraw Hill
Clocks and More Clocks	J	RF	Hutchins, Pat	Scholastic
Clockwork	Z	F	Pullman, Philip	Scholastic
Close Call, A	M	RF	Kenna, Anna	Pacific Learning
Close to Home: A Story of the Polio Epidemic	R	I	Weaver, Lydia	Bantam Doubleday Dell
Clothes	O	I	Wonder World	Wright Group/McGraw Hill
Clothes & Crafts in Ancient Egypt	T	I	Balkwill, Richard	Dillon Press
Clothes & Crafts in Ancient Greece	T	I	Steele, Philip	Dillon Press
Clothes & Crafts in Aztec Times	T	I	Dawson,Imogen	Dillon Press
Clothes & Crafts in Roman Times	T	I	Steele, Philip	Dillon Press
Clothes & Crafts in the Middle Ages	T	I	Dawson, Imogen	Dillon Press
Clothes & Crafts in Victorian Times	T	I	Steele, Philip	Dillon Press
Cloud Book, The	N	I	dePaola, Tomie	Scholastic
Cloud Catcher	P	F	Jernigan, E. Wesley	Rigby
Clouds	J	I	Early Connections	Benchmark Education
Clouds	N	I	Literacy 2000	Rigby

Title	Level	Genre	Author/Series	Publisher/Distributor
Clouds of Terror	L	HF	Welsh, Catherine A.	Carolrhoda Books
Clouds, Rain and Fog	K	I	Sunshine	Wright Group/McGraw Hill
Cloudy With a Chance of Meatballs	M	F	Barrett, Judi	Atheneum Books
Clubhouse, The	K	RF	PM Gold	Rigby
Clue at the Zoo, The	L	RF	Giff, Patricia Reilly	Bantam Doubleday Dell
Clue in the Castle, The	M	RF	Schultz, Irene	Wright Group/McGraw Hill
Clue in the Glue, The	N	RF	Keene, Carolyn	Pocket Books
Clue Jr.: The Case of the Chocolate Fingerprints	O	RF	Hinter, Parker C.	Scholastic
Clue of the Gold Doubloons, The	S	RF	Keene, Carolyn	Pocket Books
Clues in the Woods	M	RF	Parrish, Peggy	Bantam
Clyde Tombaugh and the Search for Planet X	N	B	Wetterer, Margaret K.	Carolrhoda Books
Coach Amos	R	RF	Paulsen, Gary	Bantam Doubleday Dell
Coast to Coast	N	I	People, Spaces & Places	Rand McNally
Cobwebs, Elephants, and Stars	M	F	Sunshine	Wright Group/McGraw Hill
Cold As Ice	T	RF	Keene, Carolyn	Pocket Books
Cold Shoulder Road	V	RF	Aiken, Joan	Bantam Doubleday Dell
Colin Powell: Straight to the Top	S	B	Blue, Rose & Naden, Corinne J.	The Millbrook Press
Colonial Crafts	T	I	Historic Communities	Crabtree
Colonial Life	T	I	Historic Communities	Crabtree
Colonial Times from A to Z	T	I	Kalman, Bobbie	Crabtree
Colonial Town, A: Williamsburg	T	I	Historic Communities	Crabtree
Color Wizard, The	J	F	Bank Street	Bantam Doubleday Dell
Colorado	T	I	Sea To Shining Sea	Children's Press
Colors of Australia	P	I	Colors of the World	Carolrhoda Books
Colors of Germany	P	I	Colors of the World	Carolrhoda Books
Colors of Ghana	P	I	Colors of the World	Carolrhoda Books
Colors of India	P	I	Colors of the World	Carolrhoda Books
Colors of Kenya	P	I	Colors of the World	Carolrhoda Books
Colors of Mexico	P	I	Colors of the World	Carolrhoda Books
Comanche Indians, The	P	I	Lund, Bill	Capstone Press
Come Back, Amelia Bedelia	L	F	Parish, Peggy	Harper & Row
Come Morning	V	HF	Guccione, Leslil Davis	Lerner Publications
Come Sing, Jimmy Jo	V	RF	Patterson, Katherine	The Penguin Group
Comeback Challenge, The	M	RF	Christopher, Matt	Little, Brown & Co.
Comeback Dog, The	O	RF	Thomas, Jane Resh	Bantam Doubleday Dell
Comets	U	I	A First Book	Franklin Watts
Comets and Meteor Showers	N	I	A True Book	Children's Press
Commander Toad and the Big Black Hole	K	F	Yolen, Jane	Putnam & Grosset
Commander Toad and the Dis-Asteroid	K	F	Yolen, Jane	Putnam & Grosset
Commander Toad and the Intergalactic Spy	K	F	Yolen, Jane	Putnam & Grosset
Commander Toad and the Planet of the Grapes	K	F	Yolen, Jane	Putnam & Grosset
Commander Toad and the Space Pirates	K	F	Yolen, Jane	Putnam & Grosset
Commander Toad And The Voyage Home	K	F	Yolen, Jane	Putnam & Grosset
Communication	N	I	Literacy 2000	Rigby
Computer Nut, The	R	SF	Byars, Betsy	Bantam Doubleday Dell
Computers Are for Everyone	K	I	Sunshine	Wright Group/McGraw Hill
Concert Night	K	RF	Literacy 2000	Rigby
Congress	N	I	A True Book	Children's Press
Connecticut	T	I	Sea To Shining Sea	Children's Press
Connie's Dance	M	RF	Windmill Books	Rigby
Constellations	N	I	A True Book	Children's Press
Constitution, The	N	I	A True Book	Children's Press
Constitution, The	V	I	Cornerstones of Freedom	Children's Press
Construction Workers	M	I	Deedrick, Tami	Capstone Press
Contemporary Age, The	R	I	Journey Through History	Barron's Educational Series
Contender, The	Z	RF	Lipsythe, Robert	HarperTrophy
Conversation Club, The	L	F	Stanley, Diane	Aladdin
Cookcamp, The	S	RF	Paulsen, Gary	Bantam Doubleday Dell
Cooped Up	K	RF	Pacific Literacy	Pacific Learning
Copper Lady, The	M	HF	Ross, Alice & Kent	Carolrhoda Books

Title	Level	Genre	Author/Series	Publisher/Distributor
Coral	J	I	Marine Life For Yng. Readers	Dominie
Coral Reef	P	I	Habitats	Children's Press
Coral Reefs	Q	I	First Reports	Compass Point Books
Corduroy	K	F	Freeman, Don	Scholastic
Corey's Christmas Wish	M	RF	Pony Tails	Skylark
Corn: An American Indian Gift	M	I	Pair-It Books	Steck-Vaughn
Corn Is Maize: The Gift of the Indians	O	I	Aliki	Steck-Vaughn
Coronado's Golden Quest	R	F	Weisberg, Barbara	Steck-Vaughn
Corvettes	T	I	Gronvall, Kal	Capstone Press
Costume Party, The	J	RF	City Kids	Rigby
Cottle Street	N	RF	Pulford, Elizabeth	Rigby
Cotton Plant to Cotton Shirt	L	I	Schaefer, Lola M.	Benchmark Education
Could It Be?	J	RF	Bank Street	Bantam Doubleday Dell
Count Karlstein	Y	F	Pullman, Philip	Alfred A. Knopf
Count Your Money with the Polk Street School	M	RF	Giff, Patricia Reilly	Bantam Doubleday Dell
Counterfeit Tackle, The	M	RF	Christopher, Matt	Little, Brown & Co.
Countess Veronica	Q	RF	Robinson, Nancy K.	Scholastic
Counting Insects	K	I	Early Connections	Benchmark Education
Country Fair	J	HF	Wilder, Laura Ingalls	Harper Collins
Courage of Sarah Noble, The	O	HF	Dalgliesh, Alice	Aladdin
Cousins	T	RF	Hamilton, Virginia	Language for Learning Assoc.
Cousins in the Castle	U	F	Wallace, Barbara Brooks	Aladdin
Cow	O	I	Older, Jules	Charlesbridge
Cowboy Trade, The	S	I	Rounds, Glen	Holiday House
Cowboys	T	I	Sandler, Martin W.	HarperTrophy
Cowboys of the Wild West	X	I	Freedman, Russell	Clarion Books
Cowpokes and Desperadoes	O	RF	Paulsen, Gary	Bantam Doubleday Dell
Cows Have Calves	M	I	Animals and Their Young	Compass Point Books
Coyote in Trouble	L	TL	Beveridge, Barbara	Pacific Learning
Coyote Not-So-Clever	N	TL	Beveridge, Barbara	Pacific Learning
Coyote, The	R	I	Mattern, Joanne	Capstone Press
Crabs	M	I	Wonder World	Wright Group/McGraw Hill
Crabs, Shrimp, & Lobsters	M	I	Marine Life For Yng. Readers	Dominie
Cracker Jackson	T	RF	Byars, Betsy	Puffin Books
CrackerJack Halfback	M	RF	Christopher, Matt	Little, Brown & Co.
Crafty Jackal	L	TL	Folk Tales	Wright Group/McGraw Hill
Crane Wife, The	M	F	Pair-It Books	Steck-Vaughn
Cranes	N	I	Cole, Sally	Wright Group/McGraw Hill
Crash	U	RF	Spinelli, Jerry	Alfred A. Knopf
Crazy Fish	T	RF	Mazer, Norma Fox	Avon
Creature from Beneath the Ice and Other Cases, The	O	RF	Simon, Seymour	Avon
Creature of Cassidy's Creek, The	N	RF	PM Emerald	Rigby
Creatures in the Dark	N	I	Literacy 2000	Rigby
Creatures of the Reef	S	I	Belcher, Angie	Pacific Learning
Creep Show	L	F	Dussling, Jennifer	Grosset & Dunlap
Creepy Creatures	Q	I	Weldon Owen	Wright Group/McGraw Hill
Cricket Boy and Other Stories, The	L	TL	New Way: Literature	Steck-Vaughn
Cricket in Times Square, The	S	F	Selden, George	Bantam Doubleday Dell
Crime At the Chat Café	S	RF	Keene, Carolyn	Pocket Books
Crime for Christmas, A	S	RF	Keene, Carolyn	Pocket Books
Crime in the Queen's Court	S	RF	Keene, Carolyn	Pocket Books
Crinkum Crankum	M	F	Pacific Literacy	Pacific Learning
Crispus Attucks: Black Leader of Colonial Patriots	R	I	Millender, Dharathula H.	Aladdin
Crocodile in the Library, A	L	F	Pacific Literacy	Pacific Learning
Crocodile's Christmas Jandals, The	L	F	Pacific Literacy	Pacific Learning
Crocodilians	U	I	Short, Joan & Bird, Bettina	Mondo
Crocodilians: Reminders of Age of Dinosaurs	S	I	A First Book	Franklin Watts
Crosby Crocodile's Disguise	K	F	LIteracy 2000	Rigby
Crowded Dock and Other Cases, The	O	RF	Simon, Seymour	Avon

Title	Level	Genre	Author/Series	Publisher/Distributor
Crowfoot	U	B	Hacker, Carlotta	Fitzhenry & Whiteside
Cry of the Crow, The	S	RF	George, Jean Craighead	HarperTrophy
Crying Rocks and Other Cases, The	O	RF	Simon, Seymour	Avon
Crystal Unicorn, The	N	RF	PM Emerald	Rigby
Cub in the Cupboard	Q	RF	Baglio, Ben M.	Scholastic
Cuba	O	I	Mara, William P.	Capstone Press
Cubby's Gum	J	F	Ready Readers	Pearson Learning
Cuckoo Child, The	Q	F	King-Smith, Dick	Hyperion
Culpepper's Canyon	O	RF	Paulsen, Gary	Bantam Doubleday Dell
Cunning Creatures	K	I	Home Connection Collection	Rigby
Cupids Don't Flip Hamburgers	M	F	Dadey, D. & Jones, M. T.	Scholastic
Curious George Rides a Bike	J	F	Rey, Margaret	Scholastic
Curse of Being Pharaoh, The	P	RF	Marriott, Janice	Pacific Learning
Curse of the Cobweb Queen, The	L	F	Hayes, Geoffrey	Random House
Curse of the Squirrel, The	N	F	Yep, Laurence	Random House
Cut From the Same Cloth: American Women of Myth Legend, and Tall Tale	T	TL	San Souci, Robert D.	Puffin Books
Cyberspace	S	SF	Wildcats	Wright Group/McGraw Hill
Cybil War, The	S	RF	Byars, Betsy	Scholastic
Cyclops Doesn't Roller-Skate	M	F	Dadey, D. & Jones, M. T.	Scholastic
Da Vinci	P	B	Venezia, Mike	Children's Press
Dabble Duck	K	RF	Ellis, Anne Leo	HarperTrophy
Dad's Surprise	J	RF	Foundations	Wright Group/McGraw Hill
Daddy Saved the Day	K	RF	Medearis, Angela Shelf	Rigby
Daily Life in a Plains Indian Village: 1868	T	I	Terry, Michael Bad Hand	Clarion
Dame Shirley and the Gold Rush	R	B	Rawls, Jim	Steck-Vaughn
Dan the Dunce	J	TL	Tales from Hans Andersen	Wright Group/McGraw Hill
Dance at Grandpa's	J	HF	Wilder, Laura Ingalls	Harper Collins
Dance with Rosie	N	RF	Giff, Patricia Reilly	The Penguin Group
Dancing Carl	U	RF	Paulsen, Gary	Aladdin
Dancing with Jacques	P	HF	Voyages in…	Wright Group/McGraw Hill
Dancing with Manatees	N	I	McNulty, Faith	Scholastic
Danger Guys	N	RF	Abbott, Tony	HarperTrophy
Danger Guys Blast Off	N	RF	Abbott, Tony	HarperTrophy
Danger Guys on Ice	N	RF	Abbott, Tony	HarperTrophy
Danger In Quicksand Swamp	W	RF	Wallace, Bill	Simon & Schuster
Danger on Midnight River	O	RF	Paulsen, Gary	Bantam Doubleday Dell
Danger on Panther Peak	R	RF	Wallace, Bill	Pocket Books
Danger on Parade	T	RF	Keene, Carolyn	Pocket Books
Dangerous Animals	R	I	Weldon Owen	Wright Group/McGraw Hill
Dangerous Comet and Other Cases, The	O	RF	Simon, Seymour	Avon
Dangerous Wishes	U	F	Sleator, William	The Penguin Group
Daniel Boone: Man of the Forests	O	B	Greene, Carol	Children's Press
Daniel's Dog	K	RF	Bogart, Jo Allen	Scholastic
Daniel's Duck	K	RF	Bulla, Clyde Robert	HarperTrophy
Danny and the Dinosaur	J	F	Hoff, Syd	Scholastic
Danny, Champion of the World	T	RF	Dahl, Roald	Language for Learning Assoc.
Danny's Big Jump	L	RF	Reeder, Tracey	Wright Group/McGraw Hill
Danny's Desert Rats	X	RF	Naylor, Phyllis Reynolds	Aladdin
Darcy and Gran Don't Like Babies	K	RF	Cutler, Jane	Scholastic
Daring Rescue of Marlon the Swimming Pig, The	P	F	Saunders, S.	Random House
Dark and Full of Secrets	N	RF	Carrick, Carol	Houghton Mifflin
Dark Is Rising, The	X	F	Cooper, Susan	Macmillan
Dark Side of the Creek, The	M	RF	Harlow, Joan Hiatt	Wright Group/McGraw Hill
Dark Stairs	V	RF	Byars, Betsy	Puffin Books
Dark-Thirty: Southern Tales of the Supernatural	R	F	McKissack, Patricia C.	Alfred A. Knopf
Daughter of the Mountains	V	HF	Rankin, Louise	The Penguin Group
Davin	R	F	Gordon, Dan & Gordon, Zaki	Bantam Doubleday Dell
Dawn of Fear	X	HF	Cooper, Susan	Simon & Schuster

Title	Level	Genre	Author/Series	Publisher/Distributor
Day at the Races, A	M	RF	Michaels, Eric	Pearson Learning
Day for J.J. and Me, A	M	RF	Evangeline Nicholas Collection	Wright Group/McGraw Hill
Day I Lost My Bus Pass, The	J	RF	City Kids	Rigby
Day in Space, A	L	SF	Lord, Suzanne. & Epstein, Jolie	Scholastic
Day in Town, A	K	RF	Story Box	Wright Group/McGraw Hill
Day It Rained Forever, The: A Story of the Johnstown Flood	S	I	Gross, Virginia T.	The Penguin Group
Day Jimmy's Boa Ate the Wash, The	K	F	Noble, Trinka, H.	Scholastic
Day Martin Luther King, Jr., Was Shot, The	Y	B	Haskins, Jim	Scholastic
Day No Pigs Would Die, A	Z	HF	Peck, Sylvia	Random House
Day of Ahmed's Secret, A	M	RF	Heide, F. P. & Gilliland, J. H.	Scholastic
Day of Pleasure, A: Stories of a Boy Growing Up in Warsaw	W	B	Singer, Isaac Bashevis	Farrar, Straus, Giroux
Day of the Blizzard	Q	I	Moskin, Marietta	Scholastic
Day of the Dragon King	M	F	Osborne, Mary Pope	Random House
Day of the Rain, The	L	F	Cowley, Joy	Dominie
Day of the Snow, The	L	F	Cowley, Joy	Dominie
Day of the Wind, The	L	F	Cowley, Joy	Dominie
Day the Fifth Grade Disappeared, The	Q	F	Fields, Terri	Scholastic
Day the Sky Turned Green, The	M	F	Reeves, Barbara	Pearson Learning
Day with Wilbur Robinson, A	N	RF	Joyce, William	HarperTrophy
Days of Courage: The Little Rock Story	R	I	Kelso, Richard	Steck-Vaughn
Days With Frog and Toad	K	F	Lobel, Arnold	HarperTrophy
Dayton and the Happy Tree	M	RF	Sunshine	Wright Group/McGraw Hill
Dead Letter	S	RF	Byars, Betsy	Puffin Books
Deadbolts and Dinkles	N	RF	Tapp, Kathy Kennedy	Mondo
Deadly Dungeon, The	N	RF	Roy, Ron	Random House
Dear Diary	P	RF	Literacy 2000	Rigby
Dear Future	Q	RF	Literacy 2000	Rigby
Dear Grandma	M	I	Storyteller Nonfiction	Wright Group/McGraw Hill
Dear Levi: Letters from the Overland Trail	T	HF	Woodruff, Elvira	Alfred A. Knopf
Dear Mr. Henshaw	Q	RF	Cleary, Beverly	HarperCollins
Death's Door	V	RF	Byars, Betsy	Puffin Books
December Secrets	L	RF	Giff, Patricia Reilly	Bantam Doubleday Dell
Declaration of Independence, The	N	I	A True Book	Children's Press
Declaration of Independence, The	V	I	Cornerstones of Freedom	Children's Press
Dede and the Dinosaur	K	F	Cumpiano, Ina	Hampton-Brown
DeDe Takes Charge!	O	RF	Hurwitz, Johanna	Morrow
Deer in the Wood, The	J	HF	Wilder, Laura Ingalls	Harper Collins
Defenders, The	T	B	McGovern, Ann	Language for Learning Assoc.
Definitely Cool	X	RF	Wilkinson, Brenda	Scholastic
Delaware	T	I	Sea to Shining Sea	Children's Press
Dentists	M	I	Ready, Dee	Capstone Press
Deputy Dan and the Bank Robbers	L	RF	Rosenbloom, Joseph	Random House
Deputy Dan Gets His Man	L	RF	Rosembloom, Joseph	Random House
Desert Birds	N	I	A New True Book	Children's Press
Desert Giant: The World of the Saguaro Cactus	L	I	Bash, Barbara	Scholastic
Desert Machine, The	K	I	Sunshine	Wright Group/McGraw Hill
Desert Run, The	P	I	Bonallack, John	Pacific Learning
Desert Treasure	M	RF	Pair-It Books	Steck-Vaughn
Deserts	N	I	A True Book	Children's Press
Deserts	Q	I	First Reports	Compass Point Books
Deserts	O	I	Gibbons, Gail	Holiday House
Deserts	N	I	Habitats of the World	Dominie Press
Deserts	R	I	The Wonders of our World	Crabtree
Destination Disaster	P	RF	Beale, Fleur	Rigby
Detective Dinosaur	J	F	Skofield, James	HarperTrophy
Detective Stories	Z	RF	Pullman, Philip	Kingfisher
Devil's Arithmetic, The	X	F	Yolen, Jane	Puffin Books
Devil's Bridge	R	RF	DeFelice, Cynthia	Avon

Title	Level	Genre	Author/Series	Publisher/Distributor
Devil's Highway, The	T	HF	Applegate, Stan	Peachtree
DeWitt and Lila Wallace: Charity for All	P	B	Community Builders	Children's Press
Diamond Champs, The	M	RF	Christopher, Matt	Little, Brown & Co.
Diamond of Doom, The	M	RF	Schultz, Irene	Wright Group/McGraw Hill
Diary of a Honeybee	L	I	Literacy 2000	Rigby
Diary of a Pioneer Boy	Q	HF	Massie, Elizabeth	Steck-Vaughn
Diary of Anne Frank, The	Y	B	Frank, Anne	Pocket Books
Dicey's Song	W	RF	Voigt, Cynthia	Ballantine Books
Dick Whittington	L	TL	PM Tales and Plays-Silver	Rigby
Did You Carry The Flag Today, Charley?	N	RF	Caudill, Rebecca	Bantam Doubleday Dell
Did You Hear Wind Sing Your Name?	N	TL	Book Shop	Mondo
Diego Rivera	O	B	First Biographies	Steck-Vaughn
Diego Rivera	P	B	Venezia, Mike	Children's Press
Diego Rivera: An Artist's Life	L	B	Pair-It Books	Steck-Vaughn
Different Beat, A	U	RF	Boyd, Candy Dawson	The Penguin Group
Different Dragons	O	RF	Little, Jean	The Penguin Group
Difficult Day, The	J	RF	Read Alongs	Rigby
Digestive System, The	N	I	A True Book	Children's Press
Digging Dinosaurs	P	I	Nayer, Judy	Pearson Learning
Digging Up Tyrannosaurus Rex	P	I	Horner, John & Don Lessem	Crown Publishers
Dingoes at Dinnertime	M	F	Osborne, Mary Pope	Random House
Dinosaur Babies	L	I	Penner, Lucille Recht	Random House
Dinosaur Connection, The	O	I	Wilde, Buck	Rigby
Dinosaur Days	L	I	Milton, Joyce	Random House
Dinosaur Days	K	RF	Ready Readers	Pearson Learning
Dinosaur Detective	O	I	Wildcats	Wright Group/McGraw Hill
Dinosaur Girl	N	RF	Devereux, Susan	Rigby
Dinosaur Hunters	L	I	McMullan, Kate	Random House
Dinosaur on the Motorway	K	F	Wesley and the Dinosaurs	Wright Group/McGraw Hill
Dinosaur Time	K	I	Parish, Peggy	HarperTrophy
Dinosaurs	K	I	Book Shop	Mondo
Dinosaurs Before Dark	M	F	Osborne, Mary Pope	Random House
Dipplidocus in the Garden, A	K	F	Wesley and the Dinosaurs	Wright Group/McGraw Hill
Dirt Bike Racer	M	RF	Christopher, Matt	Little, Brown & Co.
Dirt Bike Runaway	M	RF	Christopher, Matt	Little, Brown & Co.
Dirty Beasts	O	F	Dahl, Roald	The Penguin Group
Dirty Socks Don't Win Games	R	RF	Marney, Dean	Scholastic
Disability Rights Movement, The	W	I	Cornerstones of Freedom	Children's Press
Disappearing Acts	S	RF	Byars, Betsy	Puffin Books
Disappearing Bike Shop, The	Q	SF	Woodruff, Elvira	Bantam Doubleday Dell
Disappearing Cookies and Other Cases, The	O	RF	Simon, Seymour	Avon
Disappearing Ice Cream and Other Cases, The	O	RF	Simon, Seymour	Avon
Disappearing Snowball and Other Cases, The	O	RF	Simon, Seymour	Avon
Discovering Dinosaurs	M	F	Little Books	Sadlier-Oxford
Discovering Jupiter: The Amazing Collision in Space	T	I	Berger, Melvin	Scholastic
Discovering the Past	S	I	Literacy 2000	Rigby
Discovering the Titanic	O	I	Trumbore, Cindy	Pearson Learning
Distant Stars and Other Cases, The	O	RF	Simon, Seymour	Avon
Ditching School	J	RF	City Kids	Rigby
Dive to the Deep Ocean: Voyages of Exploration and Discovery	W	I	Kovacs, Deborah	Steck-Vaughn
Divers' Dream	P	I	Pacific Literacy	Pacific Learning
Do The Funky Pickle	U	RF	Spinelli, Jerry	Scholastic
Do You Know Me?	Q	RF	Farmer, Nancy	The Penguin Group
Do You Like Cats?	K	I	Bank Street	Bantam Doubleday Dell
Doctor's Office, The	K	I	Pebble Books	Grolier, Capstone
Doctors	L	I	Community Workers	Compass Point Books
Doctors	M	I	Ready, Dee	Capstone Press
Does Third Grade Last Forever?	O	RF	Schanback, Mindy	Troll
Dog Called Kitty, A	R	RF	Wallace, Bill	Pocket Books

Title	Level	Genre	Author/Series	Publisher/Distributor
Dog I Share, The	N	RF	Marriott, Janice	Pacific Learning
Dog in The Freezer, The	W	F	Mazer, Harry	Simon & Schuster
Dog on Barkham Street, A	R	RF	Stolz, Mary	Harper Trophy
Dog that Pitched a No-Hitter, The	L	F	Christopher, Matt	Little Brown & Co.
Dog that Stole Football Plays, The	M	F	Christopher, Matt	Little, Brown & Co.
Dog that Stole Home, The	L	F	Christopher, Matt	Little, Brown & Co.
Dog Years	R	RF	Warner, Sally	Alfred A. Knopf
Dog's Best Friend, A	M	RF	Pair-It Books	Steck-Vaughn
Dog-Gone Hollywood	L	F	Sharmat, Marjorie Weinman	Random House
Doggy Dare	O	RF	Baglio, Ben M.	Scholastic
Dogs	J	I	PM Animal Facts: Orange	Rigby
Dogs at Work	J	I	Little Readers	Houghton Mifflin
Dogs Don't Tell Jokes	O	RF	Sachar, Louis	Alfred A. Knopf
Dogsong	V	RF	Paulsen, Gary	Simon & Schuster
Dogstar	J	F	Literacy 2000	Rigby
Doing the Dishes	L	RF	City Kids	Rigby
Doll's House, The	R	RF	Godden, Rumer	The Penguin Group
Dollhouse Murders, The	S	RF	Wright, Betty Ren	Scholastic
Dolphin	L	I	Morris, Robert A.	HarperTrophy
Dolphin Adventure	P	RF	Grover, Wayne	Beech Tree Books
Dolphin on the Wall, The	K	RF	PM Story Books -Silver	Rigby
Dolphin, The	P	I	Animal Close-Ups	Charlesbridge
Dolphin Treasure	P	RF	Grover, Wayne	Beech Tree Books
Dolphin's First Day: The Story of a Bottlenose Dolphin	N	I	Zoehfeld, Kathleen Weidnetz	Scholastic
Dolphins!	L	I	Bokoske, S. & Davidson, M.	Random House
Dolphins	O	I	Holmes, Kevin J.	Capstone Press
Dolphins	N	I	Kalman, Bobbie	Crabtree
Dolphins	J	I	Wonder World	Wright Group/McGraw Hill
Dolphins at Daybreak	M	F	Osborne, Mary Pope	Random House
Dolphins, The	L	RF	PM Gold	Rigby
Dom's Handplant	L	RF	Literacy 2000	Rigby
Dominic	R	F	Steig, William	Farrar, Straus and Giroux
Don't Be My Valentine: A Classroom Mystery	J	RF	Lexau, Joan M.	HarperTrophy
Don't Call Me Beanhead!	N	RF	Wojciechowski, Susan	Candlewick Press
Don't Eat Too Much Turkey	J	RF	Cohen, Miriam	Bantam Doubleday Dell
Don't Forget the Bacon	M	RF	Hutchins, Pat	Puffin Books
Don't Split the Pole: Tales of Down-Home Folk Wisdom	S	RF	Tate, Eleanora E.	Bantam Doubleday Dell
Don't Worry	J	RF	Literacy 2000	Rigby
Donald's Garden	K	RF	Reading Unlimited	Celebration Press
Donavan's Word Jar	N	RF	DeGross, Monalisa	HarperCollins
Donkey	M	F	Literacy 2000	Rigby
Donkey's Tale, The	J	TL	Bank Street	Bantam Doubleday Dell
Donna O'Neeshuck Was Chased By Some Cows	L	RF	Grossman, Bill	HarperTrophy
Door in the Wall, The	U	HF	De Angeli, Marguerite	Bantam Doubleday Dell
Doorbell Rang, The	J	RF	Hutchins, Pat	Greenwillow
Double Danger	P	F	Hager, Mandy	Pacific Learning
Double Life of Pocahontas, The	T	B	Fritz, Jean	Language for Learning Assoc.
Double Play at Short	M	RF	Christopher, Matt	Little, Brown & Co.
Double Switch	M	RF	Noonan, Diana	Pacific Learning
Double Trouble	M	TL	Literacy 2000	Rigby
Douglas Fir	O	I	Davis, Wendy	Children's Press
Dove Is a Beau	T	F	Yolen, Jane	Harcourt Brace
Down on the Ice	P	I	Alchin, Rupert	Pacific Learning
Down to a Sunless Sea: The Strange World of Hydrothermal Vents	W	I	Madin, Kate	Steck-Vaughn
Dr. Jekyll, Orthodontist	N	RF	The Zack Files	Grosset & Dunlap
Dr. MacTavish's Creature	N	RF	PM Emerald	Rigby
Dr. Quinn Medicine Woman	T	B	McKenna, Colleen O'Shaughnessy	Language for Learning Assoc.
Dr. Seuss and His Stories	N	B	Coglon, Kari	Wright Group/McGraw Hill

Title	Level	Genre	Author/Series	Publisher/Distributor
Dracula Doesn't Drink Lemonade	M	F	Dadey, D. & Jones, M. T.	Scholastic
Dragon Bones	O	F	Hindman, Paul	Random House
Dragon Breath	L	F	O'Connor, Jane	Grosset & Dunlap
Dragon Cauldron	W	F	Yep, Laurence	Harper Collins
Dragon Chronicles, The: Dragon's Milk	V	F	Fletcher, Susan	Aladdin
Dragon Feet	K	F	Books For Young Learners	Pacific Learning
Dragon Fire	P	F	Cowley, Joy	Pacific Learning
Dragon for Sale	Q	F	MacDonald, Marianne	Troll
Dragon in the Family, A	Q	F	Koller, Jackie French	Pocket Books
Dragon in the Ghetto Caper, The	R	RF	Konigsburg, E.L.	Aladdin
Dragon King's Palace, The	T	TL	Literacy 2000	Rigby
Dragon of the Lost Sea	W	F	Yep, Laurence	Harper Collins
Dragon Parade: A Chinese New Year Story	O	I	Chin, Steven A.	Steck-Vaughn
Dragon Prince, The: A Chinese Beauty and the Beast Tale	P	TL	Yep, Laurence	HarperCollins
Dragon Quest	Q	F	Koller, Jackie French	Pocket Books
Dragon Slayer	P	F	Cowley, Joy	Pacific Learning
Dragon Steel	W	F	Yep, Laurence	Harper Collins
Dragon Trouble	Q	F	Koller, Jackie French	Pocket Books
Dragon War	W	F	Yep, Laurence	Harper Collins
Dragon Who Had the Measles, The	J	F	Literacy 2000	Rigby
Dragon's Birthday, The	K	F	Literacy 2000	Rigby
Dragon's Blood	X	F	Yolen, Jane	Harcourt Brace
Dragon's Gate	W	HF	Yep, Laurence	Harper Collins
Dragon's Scales, The	J	F	Albee, Sarah	Random House
Dragonling, The	Q	F	Koller, Jackie French	Pocket Books
Dragons and Kings	Q	F	Koller, Jackie French	Pocket Books
Dragons Don't Cook Pizza	M	F	Dadey, D. & Jones, M. T.	Scholastic
Dragons Galore	N	F	Wildcats	Wright Group/McGraw Hill
Dragons of Blueland, The	L	F	Gannett, R.	Random House
Dragons of Krad	Q	F	Koller, Jackie French	Pocket Books
Dragonsong	V	F	McCaffrey, Anne	Bantam Doubleday Dell
Dragonwings	W	HF	Yep, Lawrence	HarperTrophy
Dreadful Future of Blossom Culp, The	U	SF	Peck, Richard	Bantam Doubleday Dell
Dream Boat	M	RF	Nagelkerke, Bill	Rigby
Dream Catchers	M	RF	Storyteller-Night Crickets	Wright Group/McGraw Hill
Dream Come True, A	O	B	Hurwitz, Johanna	Richard C. Owen
Dream Eater, The	N	F	Garrison, Christian	Aladdin
Dred Scott Decision, The	X	I	Cornerstones of Freedom	Children's Press
Drew and the Homeboy Question	U	RF	Armstrong, Robb	HarperTrophy
Drinking Gourd, The	M	HF	Monjo, F. N.	HarperTrophy
Drought Marker, The	M	F	Literacy 2000	Rigby
Drummer Hoff	J	TL	Emberly, Barbara	Prentice-Hall
Drylongso	V	RF	Hamilton, Virginia	Harcourt Brace
Duck in the Gun, The	M	F	Literacy 2000	Rigby
Duckling Diary	O	RF	Baglio, Ben M.	Scholastic
Ducks Crossing	M	RF	Wilson, Trevor	Pacific Learning
Dunc and Amos and the Red Tattoos	R	RF	Paulsen, Gary	Bantam Doubleday Dell
Dunc and Amos Go to the Dogs	R	RF	Paulsen, Gary	Bantam Doubleday Dell
Dunc and Amos Hit the Big Top	R	RF	Paulsen, Gary	Bantam Doubleday Dell
Dunc and Amos Meet the Slasher	R	RF	Paulsen, Gary	Bantam Doubleday Dell
Dunc and the Flaming Ghost	R	F	Paulsen, Gary	Bantam Doubleday Dell
Dunc and the Greased Sticks of Doom	R	RF	Paulsen, Gary	Bantam Doubleday Dell
Dunc and the Haunted Castle	R	RF	Paulsen, Gary	Bantam Doubleday Dell
Dunc and the Scam Artists	R	RF	Paulsen, Gary	Bantam Doubleday Dell
Dunc Breaks the Record	R	RF	Paulsen, Gary	Bantam Doubleday Dell
Dunc Gets Tweaked	R	RF	Paulsen, Gary	Bantam Doubleday Dell
Dunc's Doll	R	RF	Paulsen, Gary	Bantam Doubleday Dell
Dunc's Dump	R	RF	Paulsen, Gary	Bantam Doubleday Dell
Dunc's Halloween	R	RF	Paulsen, Gary	Bantam Doubleday Dell

Title	Level	Genre	Author/Series	Publisher/Distributor
Dunc's Undercover Christmas	R	RF	Paulsen, Gary	Bantam Doubleday Dell
Dunkin' Dazza's Daring Dribble	O	RF	SupaDoopers	Sundance
Dunkin' Dazza's Soaring Slammer	O	RF	SupaDoopers	Sundance
Dustland	V	F	Hamilton, Virginia	Scholastic
Dynamic Duos	P	F	Moore, David	Scholastic
E is for Elisa	N	RF	Hurwitz, Johanna	Puffin Books
Eagle Song	S	RF	Bruchac, Joseph	Puffin
Ear, the Eye, and the Arm, The	Y	SF	Farmer, Nancy	Puffin Books
Early Bird's Alarm Clock, The	J	F	Daniel, Claire	Steck-Vaughn
Earth	N	I	A True Book	Children's Press
Earth to Matthew	U	RF	Danziger, Paula	PaperStar
Earthborn	Z	F	Card, Orson Scott	Tor
Earthfall	Z	F	Card, Orson Scott	Tor
Earthquake!: A Story of Old San Francisco	S	I	Kudlinski, Kathleen V.	The Penguin Group
Earthquake in the Third Grade	N	RF	Myers, Laurie	Clarion
Earthquake!: San Francisco, 1906	R	I	Wilson, Kate	Steck-Vaughn
Earthquake Terror	X	RF	Kehret, Peg	Puffin Books
Earthquakes	N	I	A True Book	Children's Press
Earthquakes	O	I	Branley, Franklyn M.	HarperCollins
Earthquakes	T	I	Simon, Seymour	Mulberry Books
Earthquakes	R	I	The Wonders of our World	Crabtree
Earthquakes	R	I	Weldon Owen	Wright Group/McGraw Hill
Earthworms	O	I	Holmes, Kevin J.	Capstone Press
East of the Sun & West of the Moon	P	TL	Mayer, Mercer	Aladdin
Easter Bunny that Ate My Sister, The	Q	F	Marney, Dean	Scholastic
Easter Island: Giant Stone Statues Tell of a Rich and Tragic Past	W	I	Arnold, Caroline	Houghton Mifflin
Eat!	M	RF	Kroll, Steven	Hyperion
Echohawk	X	HF	Durrant, Lynda	Bantam Doubleday Dell
Eclipses: Nature's Blackouts	T	I	Aronson, Billy	Franklin Watts
Ed and Me	L	RF	McPhail, David	Harcourt Brace
Eddie and the Fire Engine	P	RF	Haywood, Carolyn	Beech Tree Books
Edgar Badger's Balloon Day	K	F	Kulling, Monica	Mondo
Edgar Badger's Butterfly Day	K	F	Kulling, Monica	Mondo
Edgar Badger's Fishing Day	K	F	Kulling, Monica	Mondo
Edgar Badger's Fix-it Day	K	F	Kulling, Monica	Mondo
Edward's Night Light	M	RF	Reading Corners	Dominie
Edwin and Emily	K	RF	Williams, Suzanne	Hyperion
Eenie, Meanie, Murphy, NO!	S	RF	McKenna, Colleen O'Shaunessy	Scholastic
Eeny, Meeny, Miney Mole	M	F	Yolen, Jane	Harcourt Brace
Effie	K	F	Allinson, Beverly	Scholastic
Egg To Chick	J	I	Selsam, Millicent E.	HarperTrophy
Eggs and Baby Birds	M	I	Sunshine	Wright Group/McGraw Hill
Eggs, Eggs, Eggs	J	I	Wonder World	Wright Group/McGraw Hill
Eggs, Larvae and Flies	K	I	Sunshine	Wright Group/McGraw Hill
Egypt Game, The	U	RF	Snyder, Zilpha Keatley	Bantam Doubleday Dell
Egypt: The Culture	U	I	Kalman, Bobbie	Crabtree
Egypt: The Land	U	I	Kalman, Bobbie	Crabtree
Egypt: The People	U	I	Kalman, Bobbie	Crabtree
Egytian Town	U	I	Steedman, Scott	Franklin Watts
Einstein-Champion of the World	N	RF	Trussell-Cullen, Alan	Pacific Learning
EL Bronx Remembered	Z	RF	Mohr, Nicholasa	Harper Trophy
El Chino	P	B	Say, Allen	Houghton Mifflin
El Greco	R	B	Venezia, Mike	Children's Press
Elaine	J	B	Stepping Stones	Nelson/Michaels
Elaine and the Flying Frog	M	RF	Chang, Heidi	Scholastic
Elbert's Bad Word	M	RF	Wood, Audrey	Harcourt Brace
Eleanor	S	B	Cooney, Barbara	Puffin Books
Eleanor Roosevelt	P	B	Davis, Lucile	Capstone Press
Eleanor Roosevelt, A Life of Discovery	W	B	Freedman, Russell	Clarion Books

Title	Level	Genre	Author/Series	Publisher/Distributor
Eleanor Roosevelt: Fighter for Social Justice	O	B	Childhood of Famous Americans	Aladdin
Eleanor Roosevelt: First Lady of the World	R	B	Faber, Doris	The Penguin Group
Electric Spark and Other Cases, The	O	RF	Simon, Seymour	Avon
Electricity	O	I	Winkelman, Barbara Gaines	Wright Group/McGraw Hill
Electrifying Cows and Other Cases, The	O	RF	Simon, Seymour	Avon
Elephant and the Bad Baby, The	J	F	Hayes, S.	Sundance
Elephant in the House, An	J	F	Read Alongs	Rigby
Elephants	N	I	Meadows, Graham & Vial, Claire	Dominie Press
Elephants	K	I	PM Animal Facts: Turquoise	Rigby
Elephants	U	I	The Untamed World	Steck-Vaughn
Eleven Kids, One Summer	O	RF	Martin, Ann M.	Scholastic
Elisa in the Middle	N	RF	Hurwitz, Johanna	The Penguin Group
Eliza the Hypnotizer	M	RF	Granger, Michele	Scholastic
Elizabeth Blackwell: First Woman Doctor	O	B	Greene, Carol	Children's Press
Elizabeth Blackwell: Girl Doctor	O	B	Henry, Joanne Landers	Simon & Schuster
Elizabeth Cady Stanton	P	B	Davis, Lucile	Capstone Press
Elizabeth the First: Queen of England	O	B	Greene, Carol	Children's Press
Elizabite: Adventures of a Carnivorous Plant	K	F	Rey, H.A.	Houghton Mifflin
Ella Enchanted	U	F	Carson Levine, Gail	HarperTrophy
Ellen Tebbits	P	RF	Cleary, Beverly	Dell Publishing
Ellie	Z	RF	Borntrager, Mary Christner	Herald Press
Ellie Brader Hates Mr. G.	R	RF	Johnston, Janet	Pocket Books
Ellis Island	N	I	A True Book	Children's Press
Ellis Island	V	I	Cornerstones of Freedom	Children's Press
Elmer and the Dragon	M	F	Gannett, Ruth	Random House
Elves and the Shoemaker, The	K	TL	New Way Orange	Steck-Vaughn
Elves and the Shoemaker, The	J	TL	PM Tales and Plays Turquoise	Rigby
Elves Don't Wear Hard Hats	M	F	Dadey, D. & Jones, M. T.	Scholastic
Elvis the Turnip…and Me	N	F	The Zack Files	Gosset & Dunlap
Emancipation Proclamation, The	V	I	Cornerstones of Freedom	Children's Press
Emergency Vehicles	K	I	PM Plus	Rigby
Emilio and the River	M	RF	Sunshine	Wright Group/McGraw Hill
Emily and Alice	L	RF	Champion, Joyce	Harcourt Brace
Emily Arrow Promises to Do Better This Year	M	RF	Giff, Patricia Reilly	Bantam Doubleday Dell
Emily at School	L	RF	Williams, Suzanne	Hyperion
Emily Dickinson: American Poet	O	B	Greene, Carol	Children's Press
Emily Eyefinger	M	F	Ball, Duncan	Aladdin
Emily's Runaway Imagination	P	F	Cleary, Beverly	Avon Camelot
Emma	L	RF	Kesselman, Wendy	HarperTrophy
Emma, the Birthday Clown	M	RF	Sunshine	Wright Group/McGraw Hill
Emperor and the Nightingale, The	L	TL	Literacy 2000	Rigby
Emperor's New Clothes, The	J	TL	Tales from Hans Andersen	Wright Group/McGraw Hill
Empty Envelope, The	N	RF	Roy, Ron	Random House
Enchanted Horse, The	R	F	Nabb, Magdalen	Hyperion
Encyclopedia Brown Boy Detective	P	RF	Sobol, Donald J.	Bantam Doubleday Dell
Encyclopedia Brown Carries On	P	RF	Sobol, Donald J.	Bantam Doubleday Dell
Encyclopedia Brown: Case of Pablo's Nose	P	RF	Sobol, Donald J.	Scholastic
Encyclopedia Brown: Case of the Dead Eagles	P	RF	Sobol, Donald J.	Bantam Doubleday Dell
Encyclopedia Brown: Case of the Disgusting Sneakers	P	RF	Sobol, Donald J.	Bantam Doubleday Dell
Encyclopedia Brown: Case of the Midnight Visitor	P	RF	Sobol, Donald J.	Bantam Doubleday Dell
Encyclopedia Brown: Case of the Mysterious Handprints	P	RF	Sobol, Donald J.	Bantam Doubleday Dell
Encyclopedia Brown: Case of the Secret Pitch	P	RF	Sobol, Donald J.	Bantam Doubleday Dell
Encyclopedia Brown: Case of the Sleeping Dog	P	RF	Sobol, Donald J.	Scholastic
Encyclopedia Brown: Case of the Slippery Salamander	P	RF	Sobol, Donald J.	Scholastic
Encyclopedia Brown: Case of the Treasure Hunt	P	RF	Sobol, Donald J.	Bantam Doubleday Dell
Encyclopedia Brown: Case of the Two Spies	P	RF	Sobol, Donald J.	Bantam Doubleday Dell
Encyclopedia Brown Finds the Clues	P	RF	Sobol, Donald J.	Bantam Doubleday Dell
Encyclopedia Brown Gets His Man	P	RF	Sobol, Donald J.	Bantam Doubleday Dell
Encyclopedia Brown Keeps the Peace	P	RF	Sobol, Donald J.	Bantam Doubleday Dell
Encyclopedia Brown Lends a Hand	P	RF	Sobol, Donald J.	Bantam Doubleday Dell

Title	Level	Genre	Author/Series	Publisher/Distributor
Encyclopedia Brown Saves the Day	P	RF	Sobol, Donald J.	Bantam Doubleday Dell
Encyclopedia Brown Sets the Pace	P	RF	Sobol, Donald J.	Bantam Doubleday Dell
Encyclopedia Brown Shows the Way	P	RF	Sobol, Donald J.	Bantam Doubleday Dell
Encyclopedia Brown Solves Them All	P	RF	Sobol, Donald J.	Bantam Doubleday Dell
Encyclopedia Brown Takes the Cake	P	RF	Sobol, Donald J.	Bantam Doubleday Dell
Encyclopedia Brown Takes the Case	P	RF	Sobol, Donald J.	Bantam
Encyclopedia Brown Tracks Them Down	P	RF	Sobol, Donald J.	Bantam Doubleday Dell
Encyclopedia Brown's Book of Strange But True Crimes	P	RF	Sobol, Donald J. & Rose Sobol	Scholastic
Encyclopedia of Tiny Creatures	J	I	Discovery World	Rigby
Endangered Animals	N	I	A New True Book	Children's Press
Endangered Desert Animals	R	I	Taylor, Dave	Crabtree
Endangered Forest Animals	R	I	Taylor, Dave	Crabtree
Endangered Grassland Animals	R	I	Taylor, Dave	Crabtree
Endangered Island Animals	R	I	Taylor, Dave	Crabtree
Endangered Mountain Animals	R	I	Taylor, Dave	Crabtree
Endangered Ocean Animals	R	I	Taylor, Dave	Crabtree
Endangered Savannah Animals	R	I	Taylor, Dave	Crabtree
Endangered Wetland Animals	R	I	Taylor, Dave	Crabtree
Endurance, Shackleton's Antarctic Expedition	S	I	Marriott, Janice	Pacific Learning
Enormous Crocodile, The	N	F	Dahl, Roald	The Penguin Group
Enormous Egg, The	R	F	Butterworth, Oliver	Little, Brown & Co.
Er-Lang and the Suns: A Tale from China	M	TL	Folk Tales	Mondo
Erosion	M	I	Schaefer, Lola M.	Benchmark Education
Errol the Peril	Q	F	Literacy 2000	Rigby
Eruption	R	I	Wildcats	Wright Group/McGraw Hill
Escape!	N	SF	Cartwright, Pauline	Pacific Learning
Escape From Slavery: Five Journeys to Freedom	Q	B	Rappaport, Doreen	HarperTrophy
ESP TV	R	SF	Rodgers, Mary	HarperTrophy
Eureka! It's an Airplane	S	I	Bendick, Jeanne	Scholastic
Eureka!: Stories of Everyday Inventions	P	I	Literacy 2000	Rigby
Eva	Z	F	Dickenson, Eva	Laurel-Leaf Books
Everglades	T	I	George, Jean Craighead	HarperTrophy
Every Body Tells a Story	R	I	Weldon Owen	Wright Group/McGraw Hill
Every Living Thing	R	RF	Rylant, Cynthia	Aladdin
Everybody Cooks Rice	M	I	Dooley, Norah	Scholastic
Everybody Eats Bread	J	I	Literacy 2000	Rigby
Everyday Forces	M	I	Discovery World	Rigby
Everyone Else's Parents Said Yes	U	RF	Danziger, Paula	PaperStar
Everyone Knows About Cars	L	I	Book Shop	Mondo
Everything Changes	L	I	Discovery World	Rigby
Everywhere	R	RF	Brooks, Bruce	Scholastic
Evil Queen Tut and the Great Ant Pyramids	N	F	The Zack Files	Grossett&Dunlap
Exotic Tropical Fish	L	I	Swartz, Stanley L.	Dominie Press
Experiment with Movement	Q	I	Murphy, Bryan	Scholastic
Experiment with Water	Q	I	Murphy, Bryan	Scholastic
Explorers: Searching for Adventure	M	I	Pair-It Books	Steck-Vaughn
Explorers: Women in Profile	T	B	Hacker, Carolotta	Crabtree
Exploring an Ocean Tide Pool	W	I	Bendick, Jeanne	Henry Holt & Co.
Exploring Freshwater Habitats	P	I	Snowball, Diane	Mondo
Exploring Land Habitats	P	I	Phinney, Margaret Yatsevitch	Mondo
Exploring Saltwater Habitats	P	I	Smith, Sue	Mondo
Exploring Space	R	I	Weldon Owen	Wright Group/McGraw Hill
Exploring the Titanic	Q	I	Ballard, Robert D.	Scholastic
Exploring Tree Habitats	P	I	Seifert, Patti	Mondo
Exploring with Lewis and Clark	O	I	People, Spaces & Places	Rand McNally
Expressway Jewels	M	RF	Evangeline Nicholas Collection	Wright Group/McGraw Hill
Extraordinary American Indians	W	B	Avery, Susan & Skinner, Linda	Children's Press
Extraordinary Black Americans: From Colonial to Contemporary Times	W	B	Altman, Susan	Children's Press

Title	Level	Genre	Author/Series	Publisher/Distributor
Extraordinary Jewish Americans	W	B	Brooks, Philip	Children's Press
Extraordinary Life, An: The Story of a Monarch Butterfly	V	I	Pringle, Laurence	Orchard Books
Extraordinary People with Disabilities	W	B	Kent, D. & Quinlan, K. A.	Children's Press
Extraordinary Women in Politics	W	B	Gulatta, Charles	Children's Press
Extraordinary Women Journalists	W	B	Price-Groff, Claire	Children's Press
Extraordinary Women of Medicine	W	B	Stille, Darlene R.	Children's Press
Extraordinary Women of the American West	W	B	Alter, Judy	Children's Press
Extraordinary Women Scientists	W	B	Stille, Darlene R.	Children's Press
Extraordinary Young People	W	B	Brill, Marlene Targ	Children's Press
Extreme Lives	N	I	Wildcats	Wright Group/McGraw Hill
Extreme Sports	R	I	PM Nonfiction -Ruby	Rigby
Extreme Sports	P	I	Wildcats	Wright Group/McGraw Hill
Eye in the Sky	P	F	Marriott, Janice	Pacific Learning
Eye Spy	P	I	Wildcats	Wright Group/McGraw Hill
Eyes of the Amaryllis, The	V	RF	Babbitt, Natalie	Farrar, Straus and Giroux
Fables	N	TL	Lobel, Arnold	Harper Collins
Fables by Aesop	K	TL	Reading Unlimited	Celebration Press
Fabulous Animal Families	K	I	Home Connection Collection	Rigby
Fabulous Freckles	K	RF	Literacy 2000	Rigby
Fabulous Spotted Egg, The	T	TL	Literacy 2000	Rigby
Face to Face	W	RF	Bauer, Marion Dane	Bantam Doubleday Dell
Face-Off	O	RF	Christopher, Matt	Little, Brown & Co.
Facing the Flood	Q	RF	Kleinhenz, Sydnie Meltzer	Steck-Vaughn
Facing West: A Story of the Oregon Trail	S	I	Kudlinski, Kathleen V.	The Penguin Group
Factory Through the Ages	U	I	Steele, Philip	Troll Associates
Facts and Fictions of Minna Pratt, The	U	RF	MacLachlan, Patricia	HarperTrophy
Facts and Fun About the Presidents	S	I	Sullivan, George	Scholastic
Fair Day	J	RF	City Kids	Rigby
Fair Swap, A	K	TL	PM Story Books -Silver	Rigby
Falcon, The	N	RF	PM Emerald	Rigby
Falcon's Feathers, The	N	RF	Roy, Ron	Random House
Families	J	I	Storyteller-Night Crickets	Wright Group/McGraw Hill
Families Are Different	K	RF	Pellegrini, Nina	Scholastic
Families of the Deep Blue Sea	P	I	Mallory, Kenneth	Charlesbridge Publishing
Family Dinner	Q	RF	Cutler, Jane	Farrar, Straus and Giroux
Family Tree	S	RF	Ayres, Katherine	Bantam Doubleday Dell
Family Under the Bridge, The	R	RF	Savage Carlson, Natalie	Scholastic
Famous Animals	Q	I	Literacy Tree	Rigby
Famous Children	O	I	Literacy 2000	Rigby
Fancy Feet	L	RF	Giff, Patricia Reilly	Bantam Doubleday Dell
Fangs and Me	N	RF	Gilmore, Rachna	Fitzhenry and Whiteside
Fantastic Animal Features	Q	I	Parker, Heather	Steck-Vaughn
Fantastic Mr. Fox	P	F	Dahl, Roald	The Penguin Group
Fantastic Water Pot and Other Cases, The	O	RF	Simon, Seymour	Avon
Far-Out Frisbee and Other Cases, The	O	RF	Simon, Seymour	Avon
Farewell to Manzanar	Z	B	Houston, J.W. & Houston, J.D.	Houghton Mifflin
Farm Life Long Ago	L	I	Pair-It Books	Steck-Vaughn
Farm Through the Ages	U	I	Steele, Philip	Troll
Farmer and His Two Lazy Sons, The	J	TL	Aesop's Fables	Dominie
Farmer Boy	Q	HF	Wilder, Laura Ingalls	HarperTrophy
Farmer Boy Birthday, A	J	HF	Wilder, Laura Ingalls	Harper Collins
Farmer Boy Days	M	HF	Wilder, Laura Ingalls	HarperTrophy
Farmer in the Soup, The	K	TL	Littledale, Freya	Scholastic
Farmer Joe's Hot Day	J	F	Richards/Zimmerman	Scholastic
Farmers	M	I	Ready, Dee	Capstone Press
Farthest Shore, The	Z	F	Le Guin, Ursula	Bamtam
Fast and Funny	J	RF	Story Box	Wright Group/McGraw Hill
Fast Sam, Cool Clyde, and Stuff	Y	RF	Myers, Walter Dean	Puffin Books
Fastest Ketchup in the Cafeteria and Other Cases, The	O	RF	Simon, Seymour	Avon

Title	Level	Genre	Author/Series	Publisher/Distributor
Father Water, Mother Woods	V	RF	Paulsen, Gary	Bantam Doubleday Dell
Father's Arcane Daughter	V	RF	Konigsburg, E. L.	Aladdin
Favorite Greek Myths	Y	TL	Pope, Mary Osborne	Scholastic
Fearless Explorer and Other Cases, The	O	RF	Simon, Seymour	Avon
Feathers and Flight	Q	I	Weldon Owen	Wright Group/McGraw Hill
Feathery Fables	P	TL	Krueger, Carol	Rigby
Felicia the Critic	P	RF	Conford, Ellen	Little, Brown & Co.
Felicity Learns a Lesson	Q	HF	The American Girls Collection	Pleasant Company
Felicity Saves the Day	Q	HF	The American Girls Collection	Pleasant Company
Felicity's Surprise	Q	HF	The American Girls Collection	Pleasant Company
Felita	P	RF	Mohr, Nicholasa	Dell
Ferret In The Bedroom, Lizards In The Fridge	T	RF	Wallace, Bill	Language for learning Assoc.
Festival Fun	N	I	Wildcats	Wright Group/McGraw Hill
Fibers Made by People	M	I	Sunshine	Wright Group/McGraw Hill
Fiesta!	M	I	Festivals and Holidays	Children's Press
Fifth Grade: Here Comes Trouble	S	RF	McKenna, Colleen O'Shaughnessy	Scholastic
Fig Pudding	R	RF	Fletcher, Ralph	Clarion Books
Fig Pudding	S	RF	McKenna, Colleen	Scholastic
Fight in the Schoolyard, The	K	RF	City Kids	Rigby
Fight on the Hill, The	J	F	Read Alongs	Rigby
Fighting Ground, The	V	HF	Avi	HarperTrophy
Fighting Tackle	M	RF	Christopher, Matt	Little, Brown & Co.
Figure in the Shadows, The	S	F	Bellairs, John	The Penguin Group
Fiji Flood, The	M	F	Schultz, Irene	Wright Group/McGraw Hill
Final Freedom, The	V	RF	Wallace, Bill	Pocket Books
Find A Stranger, Say Goodbye	X	RF	Lowry, Lois	Dell
Finding Buck McHenry	S	RF	Slote, Alfred	Scholastic
Finding Providence: The Story of Roger Williams	P	B	Avi	HarperTrophy
Finding the Titanic	Q	I	Ballard, Robert D.	Scholastic
Finding Your Way	R	I	Bonallack, John	Pacific Learning
Fine Lines	O	B	Heller, Ruth	Richard C. Owen
Fire and Wind	L	TL	PM Story Books -Silver	Rigby
Fire at the Triangle Factory	P	HF	Littlefield, Holly	Carolrhoda Books
Fire Cat, The	J	F	Averill, Esther	HarperTrophy
Fire Fighters	L	I	Community Workers	Compass Point Books
Fire Fighters	M	I	Ready, Dee	Capstone Press
Fire! Fire!	O	I	Wildcats	Wright Group/McGraw Hill
Fire in the Hills	Y	RF	Myers, Anna	Puffin Books
Fire in the Sky	R	HF	Ransom, Candice F.	Carolrhoda Books
Fire in the Wind	U	RF	Levin, Betty	Beech Tree
Fire Station, The	J	I	Pebble Books	Grolier, Capstone
Fire! The Beginnings of the Labor Movement	R	HF	Goldin, Barbara Diamond	Puffin Books
Fire-Bird, The	U	TL	Literacy 2000	Rigby
Fireflies in the Night	M	I	Hawes, Judy	HarperTrophy
Firefly Named Torchy, A	L	F	Waber, Bernard	Houghton Mifflin
Firelight Secrets	O	RF	PM Ruby	Rigby
Firetalking	O	B	Polacco, Patricia	Richard C. Owen
First Americans, The	O	I	People, Spaces & Places	Rand McNally
First Apple	N	RF	Russell, Ching Yueng	The Penguin Group
First Book About Africa: An Introduction for Young Readers	Q	I	Ellis, Veronica Freeman	Just Us Books
First Flight	K	B	Shea, George	HarperTrophy
First Four Years, The	R	HF	Wilder, Laura Ingalls	HarperTrophy
First Grade Takes a Test	J	RF	Cohen, Miriam	Bantam Doubleday Dell
First Hot-Air Balloons, The	M	I	Moore, Philip	Wright Group/McGraw Hill
First Ladies	U	B	Cornerstones of Freedom	Children's Press
First Ladies of the White House	U	B	Skarmeas, Nancy	Ideals Publications Inc.
First Ladies: Women Who Called the White House Home	U	B	Gormley, Beatrice	Scholastic
First On The Moon	Y	I	Hehner, Barbara	Hyperion/Madison Press

Title	Level	Genre	Author/Series	Publisher/Distributor
Fish	L	I	Marine Life For Yng. Readers	Dominie
Fish Face	M	RF	Giff, Patricia Reilly	Bantam Doubleday Dell
Fish for Sale	K	RF	SupaDoopers	Sundance
Fish that Hide	L	I	Swartz, Stanley L.	Dominie Press
Fishy, Flashy Fourth, The	M	RF	Schultz, Irene	Wright Group/McGraw Hill
Five Brave Explorers	Q	B	Hudson, Wade	Scholastic
Five Brilliant Scientists	Q	B	Steward, Susan McKinney	Scholastic
Five Funny Frights	K	RF	Bauer, Judith	Scholastic
Five Notable Inventors	Q	B	Hudson, Wade	Scholastic
Five True Dog Stories	M	I	Davidson, Margaret	Scholastic
Five True Horse Stories	M	I	Davidson, Margaret	Scholastic
Five-Dog Night, The	P	RF	Christelow, Eileen	Clarion Books
Flag For Our Country, A	N	I	Spencer, Eve	Steck-Vaughn
Flags	R	I	Pattrick, Steve	Rigby
Flaming Arrows	T	HF	Steele, William O.	Harcourt Brace
Flamingos	N	I	Cole, Sally	Wright Group/McGraw Hill
Flat Stanley	M	F	Brown, Jeff	HarperTrophy
Flea Story, A	L	F	Lionni, Leo	Scholastic
Fledgling, The	U	F	Langton, Jane	Scholastic
Flicking the Switch	O	I	Pacific Literacy	Pacific Learning
Flies	N	I	A True Book	Children's Press
Flight of the Union, The	L	B	White, Tekla	Carolrhoda Books
Flight: The Journey of Charles Lindbergh	R	I	Burleigh, Robert	Putnam & Grosset
Floating and Sinking	J	I	Book Shop	Mondo
Floods	N	I	A True Book	Children's Press
Flora, a Friend for the Animals	J	RF	Sunshine	Wright Group/McGraw Hill
Florence Kelley	P	B	Saller, Carol	Carolrhoda Books
Florence Nightingale	P	B	Davis, Lucile	Capstone Press
Florida	Q	I	Geography Department	Capstone Press
Flossie and the Fox	O	F	McKissack, Patricia	Scholastic
Flour	K	I	Wonder World	Wright Group/McGraw Hill
Flower Girls # 1: Violet	L	RF	Leverich, Kathleen	HarperTrophy
Flower Girls # 2: Daisy	L	RF	Leverich, Kathleen	HarperTrophy
Flower Girls # 3: Heather	L	RF	Leverich, Kathleen	HarperTrophy
Flower Girls # 4: Rose	L	RF	Leverich, Kathleen	HarperTrophy
Flower of Sheba, The	L	TL	Orgel, Doris & Schecter, Ellen	Bantam Doubleday Dell
Flowers	L	I	Pebble Books	Grolier, Capstone
Flowers For Algernon	Z	RF	Keyes, Daniel	Harcourt Brace
Flowers for Mrs. Falepau	M	RF	Book Bank	Wright Group/McGraw Hill
Flows & Quakes and Spinning Winds	K	I	Home Connection Collection	Rigby
Flunking of Joshua T. Bates, The	Q	RF	Shreve, Susan	Alfred A. Knopf
Fly Homer Fly	N	F	Peet, Bill	Houghton Mifflin
Fly Trap	L	F	Anastasio, Dina	Grosset & Dunlap
Flying Ace: The Story of Amelia Earhart	P	B	Eyewitness Readers	DK Publishing
Flying Fingers	K	RF	Literacy 2000	Rigby
Flying Flea, Callie, and Me, The	S	F	Wallace, Carol & Bill	Pocket Books
Flying Free: America's First Black Aviators	T	B	Hart, Philip S.	Lerner Publications
Flying Solo	R	RF	Fletcher, Ralph	Bantam Doubleday Dell
Flying Trunk,The	M	TL	Tales from Hans Andersen	Wright Group/McGraw Hill
Flying With the Eagle, Racing the Great Bear Stories from Native North America	U	TL	Bruchac, Joseph	Troll Medallion
Flying-Saucer People and Other Cases, The	O	RF	Simon, Seymour	Avon
Follow That Fin!: Studying Dolphin Behavior	T	I	Samuels, Amy	Steck-Vaughn
Follow That Fish	K	F	Bank Street	Bantam Doubleday Dell
Food and Festivals: Israel	O	I	Randall, Ronne	Steck-Vaughn
Food and Festivals: Italy	O	I	Pirotta, Saviour	Steck-Vaughn
Food & Feasts Between the Two World Wars	T	I	Steele, Philip	Dillon Press
Food & Feasts In Ancient Egypt	T	I	Balkwill, Richard	Dillon Press
Food & Feasts In Ancient Greece	T	I	Steele, Philip	Dillon Press

Title	Level	Genre	Author/Series	Publisher/Distributor
Food & Feasts In Ancient Rome	T	I	Steele, Philip	Dillon Press
Food & Feasts In the Middle Ages	T	I	Dawson, Imogen	Dillon Press
Food & Feasts In Tudor Times	T	I	Balkwill, Richard	Dillon Press
Food & Feasts With the Aztecs	T	I	Dawson, Imogen	Dillon Press
Food & Feasts With the Vikings	T	I	Martell, Hazel	Dillon Press
Food Journey, The	K	I	Home Connection Collection	Rigby
Foolish Gretel	O	TL	Armstrong, Jennifer	Random House
Football Friends	L	RF	Marzollo, J., D. & D.	Scholastic
Football Fugitive	M	RF	Christopher, Matt	Little, Brown & Co.
For The Life of Laetitia	Y	RF	Hodge, Merle	Farrar Straus Giroux
For the Love of Pooch	N	RF	Literacy 2000	Rigby
For the Love of Turtles	N	RF	Palacios, Argentina	Rigby
Forest Community, A	Q	I	Massie, Elizabeth	Steck-Vaughn
Forest Mammals	R	I	Kalman, Bobbie	Crabtree
Forest's Life, A: From Meadow to Mature Woodland	T	I	A First Book	Franklin Watts
Forests	N	I	Habitats of the World	Dominie
Forests	R	I	The Wonders of Our World	Crabtree
Forests, Grasslands, Deserts	M	I	People, Spaces & Places	Rand McNally
Forever Amber Brown	N	RF	Danziger, Paula	Scholastic
Forever Friends	X	RF	Boyd, Candy Dawson	Puffin Books
Forged By Fire	Z	RF	Draper, Sharon M.	Aladdin
Forgetful Fran	P	RF	Key, Alexander	Scholastic
Forgotten Door, The	T	SF	Key, Alexander	Language for Learning Assoc.
Forgotten Heroes, The: The Story of the Buffalo Soldiers	X	I	Cox, Clinton	Scholastic
Forgotten Hiding Place, The	M	RF	Schultz, Irene	Wright Group/McGraw Hill
Forgotten Princess, The	L	TL	Literacy 2000	Rigby
Fort Life	T	I	Historic Communities	Crabtree
Fort Sumter	V	I	Cornerstones of Freedom	Children's Press
Fortune Branches Out, A	R	RF	Mahy, Margaret	Bantam Doubleday Dell
Fortune's Friend: Tales of Rivalry and Riches	Q	TL	Literacy 2000	Rigby
Fortune-Tellers, The	O	TL	Alexander, Lloyd	Puffin Books
Forty-Three Cats	K	RF	Sunshine	Wright Group/McGraw Hill
Fossils Alive!	Q	I	Daniel, Claire	Steck-Vaughn
Fossils: Pictures from the Past	Q	I	Daniel, Claire	Steck-Vaughn
Foster's War	V	HF	Reeder, Carolyn	Scholastic
Foul Play on the Sidelines	R	RF	Costello, Emily	Dell
Fountains of Life: The Story of Deep-Sea Vents	S	I	A First Book	Franklin Watts
Four A's, The	Q	RF	Wildcats	Wright Group/McGraw Hill
Four Friends and Other Stories, The	L	TL	New Way: Literature	Steck-Vaughn
Four on the Shore	K	F	Marshall, Edward	Puffin Books
Fourth Grade Celebrity	Q	RF	Giff, Patricia Reilly	Bantam Doubleday Dell
Fourth Grade Is a Jinx	P	RF	McKenna, Colleen	Scholastic
Fourth Grade Wizards, The	Q	RF	DeClements, Barthe	The Penguin Group
Fourth-Graders Don't Believe In Witches	P	F	Fields, Terri	Scholastic
Fox All Week	J	F	Marshall, Edward	Puffin Books
Fox and His Friends	J	F	Marshall, Edward	Puffin Books
Fox and the Crow, The	J	TL	Aesop's Fables	Dominie
Fox and The Crow, The	K	TL	Ready Readers	Pearson Learning
Fox and the Little Red Hen	L	TL	Traditional Tales & More	Rigby
Fox at School	J	F	Marshall, Edward	Puffin Books
Fox Be Nimble	J	F	Marshall, James	Puffin Books
Fox In Love	J	F	Marshall, Edward	Puffin Books
Fox in the Frost	Q	RF	Baglio, Ben M.	Scholastic
Fox on Stage	J	F	Marshall, James	Puffin Books
Fox on the Job	J	F	Marshall, James	Puffin Books
Fox on Wheels	J	F	Marshall, Edward	Puffin Books
Fox Outfoxed	J	F	Marshall, James	Puffin Books
Fox Steals Home, The	M	RF	Christopher, Matt	Little, Brown & Co.
Foxes	M	I	PM Animal Facts: Gold	Rigby

Title	Level	Genre	Author/Series	Publisher/Distributor
Fraidy Cats	J	F	Krensky, Stephen	Scholastic
France	O	I	Dahl, Michael	Capstone Press
Frances Hodgson Burnett: Beyond the Secret Garden	U	B	Carpenter, A. S. & Shirley, Jean	Lerner Publications
Francisco Goya	R	B	Venezia, Mike	Children's Press
Frank The Fish Gets His Wish	J	F	Appleton-Smith, Laura	Flyleaf Publishing
Frankenstein Doesn't Plant Petunias	M	F	Dadey, D. & Jones, M. T.	Scholastic
Frankenstein Doesn't Slam Hockey Pucks	M	F	Dadey, D. & Jones, M. T.	Scholastic
Franklin Delano Roosevelt	V	B	Freedman, Russell	Clarion
Franklin Goes To School	K	F	Bourgeois, P. & Clark, B.	Scholastic
Franklin Plays the Game	K	F	Bourgeois, P. & Clark, B.	Scholastic
Freaky Friday	R	F	Rodgers, Mary	HarperTrophy
Freckle Juice	M	RF	Blume, Judy	Bantam Doubleday Dell
Freddy's Train Ride	K	RF	Pair-It Books	Steck-Vaughn
Frederick Douglass	P	B	McLoone, Margo	Capstone Press
Frederick Douglass: Fights For Freedom	M	B	Davidson, Margaret	Language for Learning Assoc.
Frederick Douglass: The Last Days of Slavery	R	B	Miller, William	Lee & Low Books
Free Fall	Q	I	Basalaj, Kathy	Pacific Learning
Freedom Crossing	R	HF	Clark, Margaret Goff	Scholastic
Freedom Songs	T	HF	Moore, Yvette	Language for Learning Assoc.
Freeze, Goldilocks!	M	F	Pacific Literacy	Pacific Learning
Freshwater Giants: Hippopatamus, River Dolphins and Manatees	S	I	Perry, Phyllis J.	Franklin Watts
Freshwater Habitats	N	I	Habitats of the World	Dominie Press
Freshwater Pond, A	T	I	Small Worlds	Crabtree
Frida Kahlo	R	B	Venezia, Mike	Children's Press
Frida María: A Story of the Old Southwest	M	RF	Lattimore, Deborah Nourse	Harcourt Brace
Friends are Forever	K	F	Literacy 2000	Rigby
Friends, The	Z	RF	Guy, Rosa	Bantam Doubleday Dell
Friends, The	T	RF	Yumoto, Kazumi	Yearling
Friendship and the Gold Cadillac, The	S	HF	Taylor, Mildred	Bantam Doubleday Dell
Friendship Pact, The	Q	RF	Pfeffer, Susan Beth	Scholastic
Friendship, The	S	HF	Taylor, Mildred	Puffin Books
Frightful's Mountain	U	RF	George, Jean	Puffin Books
Frindle	R	RF	Clements, Andrew	Aladdin
Frog and Toad All Year	K	F	Little Readers	Houghton Mifflin
Frog and Toad Are Friends	K	F	Lobel, Arnold	Harper & Row
Frog and Toad Together	K	F	Lobel, Arnold	Harper Collins
Frog Prince, The	K	TL	Tarcov, Edith H.	Scholastic
Frog Princess, The	K	TL	Literacy 2000	Rigby
Frog, The	M	I	Crewe, Sabrina	Steck-Vaughn
Frog Who Thought He Was A Horse, The	L	F	Literacy 2000	Rigby
Frog Who Would Be King, The	N	TL	Walker, Kate	Mondo
Froggy Learns to Swim	J	F	London, Jonathan	Scholastic
Frogs	N	I	Book Shop	Mondo
Frogs	K	I	Wonder World	Wright Group/McGraw Hill
Frogs and Toads	P	I	Crabapples	Crabtree
Frogs of Betts, The	N	RF	SupaDoopers	Sundance
From Cotton Plant to Cotton Shirt	N	I	Schaefer, Lola M.	Benchmark Education
From Cow to Milk Carton	M	I	Miles, Annie	Wright Group/McGraw Hill
From Here to There: Transportation Timelines	P	I	Discovery World	Rigby
From Paper Airplanes to Outer Space	O	B	Simon, Seymour	Richard C. Owen
From Rocks to Sand: The Story of a Beach	J	I	Wonder World	Wright Group/McGraw Hill
From the Mixed-up Files of Mrs. Basil E. Frankweiler	S	RF	Konigsburg, E.L.	Bantam Doubleday Dell
From the Notebooks of Melanin Sun	Z	RF	Woodson, Jacqueline	Scholastic
Frost in the Night, A: A Girlhood on the Eve of the Third Reich	X	B	Baer, Edith	Sunburst
Frown, The	K	RF	Read Alongs	Rigby
Frozen Man	T	I	Getz, David	Henry Holt & Co.
Fudge	O	RF	Graeber, Charlotte Towner	Simon & Schuster
Fudge-a-Mania	Q	RF	Blume, Judy	Bantam Doubleday Dell

Title	Level	Genre	Author/Series	Publisher/Distributor
Full House Stephanie	Q	RF	Herman, Gail	Pocket Books
Fun with Fingerprints	M	I	Sokoloff, Myka-Lynne	Wright Group/McGraw Hill
Funny Bananas: The Mystery in the Museum	N	RF	McHargue, Georgess	Dell Publishing
Funny Bones	J	F	Ahlberg, A & J	Viking
Funny Old Man and the Funny Old Woman, The	M	F	Book Shop	Mondo
Fur, Feathers, and Flippers: How Animals Live Where They Do	T	I	Lauber, Patricia	Scholastic
Future-Telling Lady and Other Stories, The	S	RF	Berry, James	HarperTrophy
Fuzz and the Glass Eye	M	RF	Pulford, Elizabeth	Rigby
Gadget War, The	N	RF	Duffey, Betsy	The Penguin Group
Gail Devers: A Runner's Dream	L	B	Pair-It Books	Steck-Vaughn
Gail & Me	L	RF	Literacy 2000	Rigby
Galaxies	N	I	A True Book	Children's Press
Galaxies	T	I	Simon, Seymour	Mulberry Books
Gallo and Zorro	J	F	Literacy 2000	Rigby
Game for Jamie, A	M	RF	Sunshine	Wright Group/McGraw Hill
Games from Long Ago	T	I	Historic Communities	Crabtree
Garbage Collectors	M	I	Deedrick, Tami	Capstone Press
Garden of Eden Motel, The	W	RF	Hamilton, Morse	William Morrow
Garfield and the Beast in the Basement	Q	F	Davis, Jim	Troll
Garfield and the Mysterious Mummy	Q	F	Davis, Jim	Troll
Gargoyles Don't Drive School Buses	M	F	Dadey, D. & Jones, M. T.	Scholastic
Gasp!	L	F	Book Shop	Mondo
Gaston the Giant	K	F	New Way Orange	Steck-Vaughn
Gathering: A Northwoods Counting Book	Q	I	Bowen, Betsy	Houghton Mifflin
Gathering Blue	X	F	Lowry, Lois	Houghton Mifflin
Gathering of Days, A: A New England Girl's Journal, 1830-32	U	HF	Blos, Joan	Aladdin
Gathering of Flowers, A	Z	RF	Thomas, Joyce Carol	HarperTrophy
Gathering, The	V	F	Hamilton, Virginia	Harcourt Brace
General Butterfingers	O	RF	Gardiner, John Reynolds	Puffin Books
Genghis Khan: A Dog Star is Born	L	RF	Sharmat, Marjorie Weinman	Random House
Genies Don't Ride Bicycles	M	F	Dadey, D. & Jones, M. T.	Scholastic
Gentle Annie: The True Story of a Civil War Nurse	R	I	Shura, Mary Frances	Scholastic
Gentlehands	Z	RF	Kerr, M. E.	Harper Trophy
Gentleman Outlaw and Me - Eli, The: A Story of the Old West	T	HF	Hahn, Mary Downing	Avon Camelot
George and Martha	L	F	Marshall, James	Houghton Mifflin
George Handel	R	B	Venezia, Mike	Children's Press
George the Drummer Boy	K	HF	Benchley, Nathaniel	HarperTrophy
George Washington	O	B	Early Biographies	Compass Point Books
George Washington	L	B	Pebble Books	Grolier, Capstone
George Washington: A Picture Book Biography	R	B	Giblin, James Cross	Scholastic
George Washington Carver	N	B	Biography	Benchmark Education
George Washington Carver	P	B	McLoone, Margo	Capstone Press
George Washington Carver: Scientist and Teacher	O	B	Greene, Carol	Children's Press
George Washington: The Man Who Would Not Be King	U	B	Krensky, Stephen	Scholastic
George Washington: Young Leader	O	B	Childhood of Famous Americans	Aladdin
George Washington: Young Leader	R	B	Santrey, Laurence	Troll
George Washington's Breakfast	P	B	Fritz, Jean	Putnam & Grosset
George Washington's Mother	M	B	Fritz, Jean	Scholastic
George Washington's Socks	T	B	Woodruff, Elvira	Language for Learning Assoc.
George's Marvelous Medicine	P	F	Dahl, Roald	The Penguin Group
Georgia	Q	I	Geography Department	Capstone Press
Georgia	U	I	LaDoux, Rita C.	Lerner Publications
Georgia	T	I	Sea to Shining Sea	Children's Press
Georgia O'Keeffe	M	B	Lowery, Linda	Carolrhoda Books
Georgia O'Keeffe	R	B	Venezia, Mike	Children's Press
Gerbil Genius	O	RF	Baglio, Ben M.	Scholastic

Title	Level	Genre	Author/Series	Publisher/Distributor
Gerbilitis	P	RF	Spinner, S. & Weiss, E.	HarperTrophy
Germany	O	I	Dahl, Michael	Capstone Press
Gertie's Green Thumb	O	F	Dexter, Catherine	Dell Publishing
Get A Grip, Pip!	P	RF	Literacy 2000	Rigby
Get on Board: The Story of the Underground Railroad	V	I	Haskins, Jim	Scholastic
Get On Out of Here, Philip Hall	Y	RF	Greene, Bette	Puffin Books
Get-Up Machine, The	J	F	Sunshine	Wright Group/McGraw Hill
Getting Cold! Getting Hot!	K	RF	Sunshine	Wright Group/McGraw Hill
Getting Lincoln's Goat	V	RF	Goldman, E. M.	Bantam Doubleday Dell
Getting Rid of Katherine	Q	RF	Wright, Betty Ren	Troll
Getting To Know Sharks	K	I	Little Books	Sadlier-Oxford
Gettysburg Address, The	V	I	Cornerstones of Freedom	Children's Press
Gettysburg Address, The	T	I	Lincoln, Abraham	Houghton Mifflin
Geysers: When Earth Roars	U	I	A First Book	Franklin Watts
Ghana	O	I	Davis, Lucile	Capstone Press
Ghost Belonged to Me, The	V	F	Peck, Richard	The Penguin Group
Ghost Cadet	T	SF	Alphin, Elaine Marie	Language for Learning Assoc.
Ghost Come Calling, The	Q	F	Wright, Betty	Scholastic
Ghost Dog	M	F	Allen, Eleanor	Scholastic
Ghost Fox, The	P	F	Yep, Laurence	Scholastic
Ghost in Tent 19, The	M	F	O'Connor, J. & J.	Random House
Ghost in the Tokaido Inn, The	U	F	Hoobler, Dorothy & Thomas	The Penguin Group
Ghost Named Wanda, A	N	F	The Zack Files	Grosset & Dunlap
Ghost of Popcorn Hill, The	N	F	Wright, Betty Ren	Scholastic
Ghost On Saturday Night, The	Q	F	Fleischman, Sid	Beech Tree Books
Ghost Pony, The	O	RF	Betancourt, Jeanne	Scholastic
Ghost School	M	F	Clifford, Eth	Scholastic
Ghost Town at Sundown	M	F	Osborne, Mary Pope	Random House
Ghost Town Treasure	M	RF	Bulla, Clyde Robert	The Penguin Group
Ghost Twins: Mystery at Kickingbird Lake	P	F	Regan, Dian Curtis	Scholastic
Ghostmobile, The	S	F	Tapp, Kathy Kennedy	Scholastic
Ghosts Beneath Our Feet	R	F	Wright, Betty Ren	Scholastic
Ghosts Don't Eat Potato Chips	M	F	Dadey, D. & Jones, M. T.	Scholastic
Ghosts!: Ghostly Tales from Folklore	J	TL	Schwartz, Alvin	HarperTrophy
Ghouls Don't Scoop Ice Cream	M	F	Dadey, D. & Jones, M. T.	Scholastic
Giant in the Forest, A	J	F	Reading Unlimited	Celebration Press
Giant Jack's Boots	M	F	Book Bank	Wright Group/McGraw Hill
Giant Jam Sandwich, The	K	F	Vernon Lord, John	Houghton Mifflin
Giant Pandas	U	I	The Untamed World	Steck-Vaughn
Giant's Cake	M	F	Learning Media	Mondo
Giants Don't Go Snowboarding	M	F	Dadey, D. & Jones, M. T.	Scholastic
Giants, Monsters & Mythical Beasts	O	I	Literacy 2000	Rigby
Gib Rides Home	V	RF	Snyder, Zilpha Keatley	Bantam Doubleday Dell
Gift for Mama, A	N	RF	Hautzig, Esther	The Penguin Group
Gift of the Girl Who Couldn't Hear, The	U	RF	Shreve, Susan	Beech Tree Books
Gift of the Pirate Queen, The	S	RF	Giff, Patricia Reilly	Yearling
Gift to Share, A	K	RF	Pair-It Books	Steck-Vaughn
Gift-Giver, The	S	RF	Hansen, Joyce	Houghton Mifflin
Gifts to Make	K	I	Pair-It Books	Steck-Vaughn
Gigantic Ants and Other Cases, The	O	RF	Simon, Seymour	Avon
Ginger Brown: The Nobody Boy	L	RF	Wyeth, Sharon Dennis	Random House
Ginger Brown: Too Many Houses	L	RF	Wyeth, Sharon Dennis	Random House
Ginger Pye	U	RF	Estes, Eleanor	Scholastic
Ginger's War	N	HF	Daniel, Lea	Wright Group/McGraw Hill
Gingerbread Boy, The	L	TL	Galdone, Paul	Clarion
Gingerbread Man, The	J	TL	Traditional Tales & More	Rigby
Giraffe and the Pelly and Me, The	P	F	Dahl, Roald	The Penguin Group
Giraffe, The	P	I	Animal Close-Ups	Charlesbridge Publishing
Giraffes	P	I	Crabapples	Crabtree
Giraffes	N	I	Meadows, Graham & Vial, Claire	Dominie Press

Title	Level	Genre	Author/Series	Publisher/Distributor
Giraffes	O	I	Reeder, Tracey	Wright Group/McGraw Hill
Girl Called Al, A	P	RF	Greene, Constance C.	Puffin Books
Girl Called Boy, A	U	F	Hurmence, Belinda	Clarion
Girl From Yamhill, A	W	B	Cleary, Beverly	Bantam Doubleday Dell
Girl in the Golden Bower, The	Q	TL	Yolen, Jane	Little, Brown, & Co.
Girl In the Window, The	U	RF	Yeo, Wilma	Scholastic
Girl Named Disaster, A	X	RF	Farmer, Nancy	The Penguin Group
Girl Who Chased Away Sorrow, The: The Diary of Sarah Nita, a Navajo Girl	T	HF	Turner, Ann	Scholastic
Girl Who Climbed to the Moon, The	L	F	Sunshine	Wright Group/McGraw Hill
Girl Who Knew it All, The	Q	RF	Giff, Patricia Reilly	Bantam Doubleday Dell
Girl Who Loved the Wind, The	Q	TL	Yolen, Jane	HarperTrophy
Girl Who Married the Moon, The: Tales from Native North America	U	TL	Bruchac, Joseph & Ross, Gayle	Troll Medallion
Girl Who Owned a City, The	X	F	Nelson, O.T.	Laurel-Leaf Books
Girl With the Silver Eyes, The	U	F	Roberts, Willo Davis	Scholastic
Girl-Son, The	R	HF	Neuberger, Anne E.	Carolrhoda Books
Girls to the Rescue, Book #3	Q	RF	Lansky, Bruce	Meadowbrook Press
Girls to the Rescue, Book #4	Q	RF	Lansky, Bruce	Meadowbrook Press
Girls to the Rescue, Book #6	Q	RF	Lansky, Bruce	Meadowbrook Press
Giver, The	Y	F	Lowry, Lois	Bantam Doubleday Dell
Glaciers	T	I	Gallant, Roy A.	Franklin Watts
Gladys and Max Love Bob	M	RF	Book Bank	Wright Group/McGraw Hill
Glass Slipper for Rosie, A	N	RF	Giff, Patricia Reilly	The Penguin Group
Glenda	P	F	Udry, Janice	HarperTrophy
Glenda Glinka: Witch-At-Large	P	F	Udry, Janice May	HarperTrophy
Glorious Days, Dreadful Days: The Battle of Bunker Hill	R	I	Kirby, Philippa	Steck-Vaughn
Glorious Flight, The: Across the Channel with Louis Blériot	O	B	Provensen, Alice & Martin	Puffin Books
Glory Field, The	X	HF	Myers, Walter Dean	Scholastic
Glory Girl, The	S	RF	Byars, Betsy	The Penguin Group
Gluepots	K	RF	Book Bank	Wright Group/McGraw Hill
Go and Hush the Baby	K	RF	Byars, Betsy	Viking
Go Annie, Go!	K	RF	Pacific Literacy	Pacific Learning
Go Free or Die: A Story About Harriet Tubman	R	B	Ferris, Jeri	Carolrhoda Books
Go-cart Day	K	RF	City Kids	Rigby
Go-cart Team, The	O	I	PM Nonfiction -Emerald	Rigby
Goat in the Garden	Q	RF	Baglio, Ben M.	Scholastic
Goat Monster and Other Stories, The	L	F	New Way: Literature	Steck-Vaughn
Goats	L	I	PM Animal Facts: Purple	Rigby
Goblins Don't Play Video Games	M	RF	Dadey, D. & Jones, M. T.	Scholastic
Godzilla Ate My Homework	O	F	Jones, Marcia	Scholastic
Going for Gold!	P	B	Eyewitness Readers	DK Publishing
Going Home	T	RF	Mohr, Nicholasa	The Penguin Group
Going Lobstering	O	I	Pallotta, Jerry & Bolster, Rob	Charlesbridge Publishing
Going Places	K	I	Early Connections	Benchmark Education
Going Solo	T	B	Dahl, Roald	Puffin Books
Going Swimming	J	RF	City Kids	Rigby
Going to the Bank	J	I	Foundations	Wright Group/McGraw Hill
Going to the City	J	I	People, Spaces & Places	Rand McNally
Going to the Hairdresser	J	I	Foundations	Wright Group/McGraw Hill
Going to Town	J	HF	Wilder, Laura Ingalls	Harper Collins
Going West	O	HF	Van Leeuwen, Jean	The Penguin Group
Going West	J	HF	Wilder, Laura Ingalls	HarperCollins
Gold Cadillac, The	S	HF	Taylor, Mildred D.	Puffin Books
Gold Dust Kids, The	N	HF	Dionetti, Michelle	Wright Group/McGraw Hill
Gold Dust Letters, The	S	RF	Lisle, Janet Taylor	Avon Camelot
Gold Fever!	N	HF	Step into Reading	Random House
Golden Compass, The	Z	F	Pullman, Philip	Ballantine Books

Title	Level	Genre	Author/Series	Publisher/Distributor
Golden Goose, The	M	TL	Literacy 2000	Rigby
Golden Goose, The	L	TL	Sunshine	Wright Group/McGraw Hill
Golden Sword of Dragonwalk	Q	F	Stine, R. L.	Scholastic
Goldfish	J	I	PM Animal Facts: Orange	Rigby
Goldfish Charlie and the Case of the Missing Planet	R	SF	Mazer, Anne	Troll
Goldilocks and the Three Bears	K	TL	New Way: Literature	Steck-Vaughn
Goldilocks and the Three Bears	K	TL	Once Upon a Time	Wright Group/McGraw Hill
Goldilocks and The Three Bears	J	TL	PM Tales and Plays Turquoise	Rigby
Goliath and the Burglar	L	RF	Dicks, Terrance	Barron's Educational Series
Goliath and the Buried Treasure	L	RF	Dicks, Terrance	Barron's Educational Series
Goliath and the Cub Scouts	L	RF	Dicks, Terrance	Barron's Educational Series
Goliath at the Dog Show	L	RF	Dicks, Terrance	Barron's Educational Series
Goliath at the Seaside	L	RF	Dicks, Terrance	Barron's Educational Series
Goliath Goes to Summer School	L	RF	Dicks, Terrance	Barron's Educational Series
Goliath on Vacation	L	RF	Dicks, Terrance	Barron's Educational Series
Goliath's Birthday	L	RF	Dicks, Terrance	Barron's Educational Series
Goliath's Christmas	L	RF	Dicks, Terrance	Barron's Educational Series
Goliath's Easter Parade	L	RF	Dicks, Terrance	Barron's Educational Series
Golly Sisters Go West, The	K	RF	Byars, Betsy	HarperTrophy
Golly Sisters Ride Again, The	K	RF	Byars, Betsy	HarperTrophy
Gone from Home	W	RF	Johnson, Angela	Alfred A. Knopf
Gone-Away Lake	V	RF	Enright, Elizabeth	Harcourt Inc.
Good As New	L	RF	Douglass, Barbara	Scholastic
Good Dog, Bonita	N	RF	Giff, Patricia Reilly	Bantam Doubleday Dell
Good Driving, Amelia Bedelia	L	F	Parish, Peggy	Harper & Row
Good Grief. . . Third Grade	O	RF	McKenna, Colleen	Scholastic
Good Master, The	S	RF	Seredy, Kate	Scholastic
Good Morning Mrs. Martin	K	F	Book Bank	Wright Group/McGraw Hill
Good Night, Mr. Tom	Z	HF	Magorian, Michelle	HarperTrophy
Good Work, Amelia Bedelia	L	F	Parish, Peggy	Avon Camelot
Good-Bye, Billy Radish	V	HF	Skurzynski, Gloria	Aladdin
Good-Bye Marianne	T	B	Watts, Irene N.	Tundra Books
Good-Bye My Wishing Star	S	RF	Grove, Vicki	Scholastic
Good-for-Nothing Dog, The	M	RF	Schultz, Irene	Wright Group/McGraw Hill
Goodbye, Chicken Little	Q	RF	Byars, Betsy	HarperTrophy
Goodbye, Vietnam	V	RF	Whelan, Gloria	Alfred A. Knopf
Goody Hall	V	RF	Babbitt, Natalie	Farrar, Straus and Giroux
Gooey Chewy Contest, The	L	F	Goldsmith, Howard	Mondo
Goose on the Loose	Q	RF	Baglio, Ben M.	Scholastic
Goose's Gold, The	N	RF	Roy, Ron	Random House
Gooseberry Park	P	F	Rylant, Cynthia	Scholastic
Goosebumps: It Came From Beneath the Sink	T	F	Stine, R. L.	Language for Learning Assoc.
Gorganzola Zombies in the Park	O	F	Levy, Elizabeth	HarperTrophy
Gorillas	T	I	Burgel, Paul H. & Hartwig, M.	Carolrhoda Books
Gorillas	U	I	The Untamed World	Steck-Vaughn
Gorillas: Gentle Giants on the Forest	L	I	Milton, Joyce	Random House
Grab Hands and Run	V	RF	Temple, Frances	HarperTrophy
Grace	U	HF	Walsh, Jill Paton	Farrar, Straus and Giroux
Grace the Pirate	O	F	Lasky, Kathryn	Hyperion
Grace's Letter to Lincoln	P	HF	Roop, Peter and Connie	Hyperion
Grain of Rice, A	P	TL	Pittman, Helena Clare	Bantam Doubleday Dell
Grams, Her Boyfriend, My Family, and Me	U	RF	Derby, Pat	Sunburst
Grand Canyon Journey, A: Tracing Time in Stone	W	I	A First Book	Franklin Watts
Grand Escape, The	S	F	Naylor, Phyllis Reynolds	Bantam Doubleday Dell
Grand Mothers: Poems, Reminiscences, and Short Stories About Keepers of Our Traditions	Y	B	Giovanni, Nikki	Henry Holt & Co.
Grand Trees of America: Our State and Champion Trees	T	I	Jorgenson, Lisa	Roberts Rinehart
Grandad's Dinosaur	K	F	Girling, Brough	Wright Group/McGraw Hill
Grandad's Mask	K	RF	PM Turquoise	Rigby
Grandma Mix-Up, The	K	RF	McCully, Emily Arnold	HarperTrophy

Title	Level	Genre	Author/Series	Publisher/Distributor
Grandma Moses	N	B	Biography	Benchmark Education
Grandma Moses: Painter of Rural America	T	B	O'Neal, Zibby	The Penguin Group
Grandma's Heart	K	I	Wonder World	Wright Group/McGraw Hill
Grandma's Pictures of The Past	J	RF	Home Connection Collection	Rigby
Grandmas At Bat	K	RF	McCully, Emily Arnold	HarperTrophy
Grandmas at the Lake	K	RF	McCully, Emily Arnold	HarperTrophy
Grandpa at the Beach	K	RF	Lewis, Rob	Mondo
Grandpa Comes To Stay	K	RF	Lewis, Rob	Mondo
Grandpa's Birthday	J	RF	Literacy 2000	Rigby
Grandpa's Face	Q	RF	Greenfield, Eloise	Putnam & Grosset
Grandpa's Mountain	T	RF	Reeder, Carolyn	Avon Camelot
Granny and the Desperadoes	J	RF	Parish, Peggy	Simon & Schuster
Grant Wood	R	B	Venezia, Mike	Children's Press
Grasshopper and the Ants	K	TL	Sunshine	Wright Group/McGraw Hill
Grasshopper on the Road	K	F	Lobel, Arnold	HarperTrophy
Grasslands	N	I	A True Book	Children's Press
Grasslands	Q	I	First Reports	Compass Point Books
Gratefully Yours	T	HF	Buchanan, Jane	Puffin Books
Graven Images: Three Stories by Paul Fleischman	U	F	Fleischman, Paul	HarperTrophy
Gravity: Simple Experiments for Young Scientists	T	I	White, Larry	Millbrook Press
Gray Heroes Elder Tales from Around the World	Z	TL	Yolen, Jane	Penguin Books
Great African Americans in Business	T	B	Rediger, Pat	Crabtree
Great African Americans in Civil Rights	T	B	Rediger, Pat	Crabtree
Great African Americans in Entertainment	T	B	Rediger, Pat	Crabtree
Great African Americans in Film	T	B	Parker, Janice	Crabtree
Great African Americans in Government	T	B	Dudley, Karen	Crabtree
Great African Americans in History	T	B	Hacker, Carlotta	Crabtree
Great African Americans in Jazz	T	B	Hacker, Carlotta	Crabtree
Great African Americans in Literature	T	B	Rediger, Pat	Crabtree
Great African Americans in Music	T	B	Rediger, Pat	Crabtree
Great African Americans in Sports	T	B	Rediger, Pat	Crabtree
Great African Americans in the Arts	T	B	Hacker, Carlotta	Crabtree
Great African Americans in the Olympics	T	B	Hunter, Shaun	Crabtree
Great Apes, The	S	I	A First Book	Franklin Watts
Great Brain at the Academy, The	T	RF	Fitzgerald, John D.	Yearling
Great Brain Does It Again, The	T	RF	Fitzgerald, John D.	Yearling
Great Brain Reforms, The	T	RF	Fitzgerald, John D.	Yearling
Great Brain, The	T	RF	Fitzgerald, John D.	Language for Learning Assoc.
Great Chicago Fire, 1871, The	Z	HF	Massie, Elizabeth	Pocket Books
Great Day for Up	J	F	Seuss, Dr.	Random House
Great Depression, The	X	I	Cornerstones of Freedom	Children's Press
Great Dimpole Oak, The	S	RF	Lisle, Janet Taylor	Puffin Books
Great Dinosaur Hunt, The	M	F	Schultz, Irene	Wright Group/McGraw Hill
Great Escapes of World War II	Z	I	Sullivan, George	Scholastic
Great Expectations	S	HF	Bullseye Step Into Classics	Random House
Great Genghis Khan Look-Alike Contest, The	L	RF	Sharmat, Marjorie Weinman	Random House
Great Ghosts	L	F	Cohen, Daniel	Scholastic
Great Gilly Hopkins, The	S	RF	Paterson, Katherine	Hearst
Great Grumbler and the Wonder Tree, The	K	F	Mahy, Margaret	Pacific Learning Publishers
Great Houdini, The: World Famous Magician and Escape Artist	M	B	Kulling, Monica	Random House
Great Ice Battle, The	M	F	Abbott, Tony	Scholastic
Great Interactive Dream Machine, The	Y	SF	Peck, Richard	Puffin Books
Great Kapok Tree, The	R	I	Cherry, Lynne	Scholastic
Great Little Madison, The	X	B	Fritz, Jean	G.P. Putnam's Sons
Great Migration, The	R	I	Lawrence, Jacob	HarperCollins
Great Quarterback Switch, The	M	RF	Christopher, Matt	Little, Brown & Co.
Great Riddle Mystery, The	M	RF	MacClean, James R.	Pearson Learning
Great Snake Escape, The	J	F	Coxe, Molly	HarperTrophy
Great Sporting Events	R	I	PM Nonfiction -Ruby	Rigby

Title	Level	Genre	Author/Series	Publisher/Distributor
Great Wall of China, The	Q	I	Fisher, Leonard Everett	Aladdin
Great Wheel, The	U	RF	Lawson, Robert	Scholastic
Great White Sharks	U	I	The Untamed World	Steck-Vaughn
Great-Grandpa's In The Litter Box	N	F	The Zack Files	Grosset & Dunlap
Greatest Binnie in the World, The	M	RF	Sunshine	Wright Group/McGraw Hill
Greatest of All, The: A Japanese Folktale	L	TL	Kimmel, Eric A.	Holiday House
Greece: The Culture	U	I	Kalman, Bobbie	Crabtree
Greece: The Land	U	I	Kalman, Bobbie	Crabtree
Greece: The People	U	I	Kalman, Bobbie	Crabtree
Greedy Cat and the Birthday Cake	M	F	Cowley, Joy	Pacific Learning
Greedy Goat, The	L	TL	Book Shop	Mondo
Greek and Roman Eras, The	R	I	Journey Through History	Barron's Educational Series
Greeks, The	M	I	Footsteps in Time	Children's Press
Green Book, The	V	F	Walsh, Jill Paton	Farrar, Straus and Giroux
Green Eggs and Ham	J	F	Seuss, Dr.	Random House
Green Thumbs	Q	I	Literacy 2000	Rigby
Green Thumbs, Everyone	N	RF	Giff, Patricia Reilly	Bantam Doubleday Dell
Green with Red Spots Horrible	N	RF	SupaDoopers	Sundance
Greenwitch	X	F	Cooper, Susan	Scholastic
Greg's Microscope	K	I	Selsam, Millicent E.	HarperTrophy
Gregory, the Terrible Eater	L	F	Sharmat, Marjorie Weinman	Scholastic
Gremlins Don't Chew Bubble Gum	M	F	Dadey, D. & Jones, M. T.	Scholastic
Grey King, The	X	F	Cooper, Susan	Simon & Schuster
Gristmill, The	T	I	Historic Communities	Crabtree
Grizzly Bear, The	R	I	Potts, Steve	Capstone Press
Grizzly Bears	N	I	Woolley, M. & Pigdon, K.	Mondo
Grizzly Mistake and Other Cases, The	O	RF	Simon, Seymour	Avon
Growin'	R	RF	Grimes, Nikki	Puffin Books
Growing Ideas	O	B	Van Leeuwen, Jean	Richard C. Owen
Growing Up	P	I	It's Science	Children's Press
Growing Up in Coal Country	X	I	Bartoletti, Susan Campbell	Houghton Mifflin
Growing Up Stories	T	RF	Byars, Betsy	Kingfisher
Guardian of the Dark	W	F	Spencer, Bev	Scholastic
Guatemala	O	I	Dahl, Michael	Capstone Press
Guess Who?	L	I	Home Connection Collection	Rigby
Guests	T	HF	Dorris, Michael	Hyperion
Guide Dog, The	K	I	Foundations	Wright Group/McGraw Hill
Guinea Pig Gang	O	RF	Baglio, Ben M.	Scholastic
Guinea Pigs	S	I	Hansen, Elvig	Carolrhoda Books
Guinea Pigs	J	I	PM Animal Facts: Orange	Rigby
Gulf	X	F	Westfall, Robert	Scholastic
Gulliver's Stories	Q	F	Dolch, E. W. and Marguerite P.	Scholastic
Gung Hay Fat Choy	N	I	Behrens, June	Children's Press
Gus and Grandpa	J	RF	Mills, Claudia	Sunburst
Gwen Torrence	P	B	Stewart, Mark	Children's Press
Gypsy Game, The	U	RF	Snyder, Zilpha Keatly	Yearling
Ha-Ha Party, The	J	RF	Sunshine	Wright Group/McGraw Hill
Habibi	V	B	Nye, Naomi Shihab	Simon & Schuster
Hailstorm, The	J	RF	PM Turquoise	Rigby
Hair Party, The	J	RF	Literacy 2000	Rigby
Hairy Little Critters	O	I	Wilde, Buck	Rigby
Half for You, Half for Me	K	TL	Literacy 2000	Rigby
Halloween Horror and Other Cases, The	O	RF	Simon, Seymour	Avon
Halloween: Why We Celebrate It the Way We Do	P	I	Hintz, Martin & Kate	Capstone Press
Hamster Hotel	O	RF	Baglio, Ben M.	Scholastic
Hamster in a Handbasket	Q	RF	Baglio, Ben M.	Scholastic
Hand, Hand, Fingers, Thumb	J	F	Perkins, Al	Random House
Hand Tools	M	I	Wonder World	Wright Group/McGraw Hill
Handful of Time, A	U	F	Pearson, Kit	Puffin Books
Hang a Left at Venus	N	F	The Zack Files	Grossett&Dunlap

Title	Level	Genre	Author/Series	Publisher/Distributor
Hang in there, Oscar Martin!	N	RF	Noonan, Diana	Pacific Learning
Hanged Man, The	Z	RF	Block, Francesca Lia	Harper Collins
Hannah	N	RF	Whelan, Gloria	Random House
Hannah and the Angels	Q	F	Lowery, Linda	Random House
Hannah of Fairfield	Q	HF	Pioneer Daughters	Puffin Books
Hannah's Fancy Notions: A Story of Industrial New England	R	HF	Ross, Pat	The Penguin Group
Hannah's Helping Hands	Q	HF	Van Leeuwen, Jean	Puffin Books
Hannah's Winter of Hope	Q	HF	Van Leeuwen, Jean	Puffin Books
Hannibal	T	B	Green, Robert	Franklin Watts
Hansel and Gretel	K	TL	Enrichment	Wright Group/McGraw Hill
Hanukkah	N	I	Festivals and Holidays	Children's Press
Happily Ever After	O	F	Quindlen, Anna	The Penguin Group
Happy Accidents!	Q	I	Trussell-Cullen, Alan	Rigby
Happy Birthday, Addy!	Q	HF	The American Girls Collection	Pleasant Company
Happy Birthday, Anna, Sorpresa!	N	RF	Giff, Patricia Reilly	Bantam Doubleday Dell
Happy Birthday, Dear Duck	K	F	Bunting, Eve	Clarion
Happy Birthday, Felicity!	Q	HF	The American Girls Collection	Pleasant Company
Happy Birthday, Josefina!	Q	HF	The American Girls Collection	Pleasant Company
Happy Birthday, Kirsten!	Q	HF	The American Girls Collection	Pleasant Company
Happy Birthday, Martin Luther King	L	B	Marzollo, Jean	Scholastic
Happy Birthday, Molly!	Q	HF	The American Girls Collection	Pleasant Company
Happy Birthday, Moon	L	F	Asch, Frank	Simon & Schuster
Happy Birthday, Samantha!	Q	HF	The American Girls Collection	Pleasant Company
Happy Valentine's Day, Miss Hildy!	K	RF	Grambling, Lois	Random House
Hard Drive to Short	M	RF	Christopher, Matt	Little, Brown & Co.
Hare and the Tortoise, The	P	TL	Aesop's Fables	Dominie
Hare and the Tortoise, The	K	TL	Literacy 2000	Rigby
Hare and the Tortoise, The	K	TL	PM Tales and Plays- Purple	Rigby
Harold and the Purple Crayon	K	F	Johnson, Crockett	Harper & Row
Harriet Beecher Stowe and the Beecher Preachers	X	B	Fritz, Jean	The Penguin Group
Harriet the Spy	T	RF	Fitzhugh, Louise	Harper Collins
Harriet Tubman	P	B	McLoone, Margo	Capstone Press
Harriet's Hare	O	F	King-Smith, Dick	Alfred A. Knopf
Harris and Me	V	RF	Paulsen, Gary	Bantam Doubleday Dell
Harry and Chicken	S	F	Sheldon, Dyan	Candlewick Press
Harry and the Lady Next Door	J	F	Zion, Gene	HarperTrophy
Harry and Willy and Carrothead	L	RF	Caseley, Judith	Scholastic
Harry Cat's Pet Puppy	R	F	Selden, George	Bantam Doubleday Dell
Harry Hates Shopping!	K	F	Armitage, Ronda and David	Scholastic
Harry Houdini: Master of Magic	R	B	Kraske, Robert	Scholastic
Harry Houdini: Young Magician	O	B	Childhood of Famous Americans	Aladdin
Harry Houdini-Wonderdog!	N	RF	Taylor, William	Pacific Learning
Harry On Vacation	S	SF	Sheldon, Dyan	Candlewick Press
Harry Potter and the Chamber of Secrets	V	F	Rowling, J. K.	Scholastic
Harry Potter and the Goblet of Fire	V	F	Rowling, J. K.	Scholastic
Harry Potter and the Prisoner of Azkaban	V	F	Rowling, J.K.	Scholastic
Harry Potter and the Sorcerer's Stone	V	F	Rowling, J. K.	Scholastic
Harry the Explorer	S	F	Sheldon, Dyan	Candlewick Press
Harry's Mad	P	F	King-Smith, Dick	Alfred A. Knopf
Hat Came Back, The	K	RF	Literacy 2000	Rigby
Hatchet	R	RF	Paulsen, Gary	Aladdin
Hau Kola Hello Friend	O	B	Goble, Paul	Richard C. Owen
Haunted	Q	F	Herman, Emily	Wright Group/McGraw Hill
Haunted Bike, The	L	F	Herman, Gail	Grosset & Dunlap
Haunted Halloween, The	M	F	Schultz, Irene	Wright Group/McGraw Hill
Haunting of Grade Three, The	O	RF	Maccarone, Grace	Scholastic
Have You Seen a Javelina?	K	F	Literacy 2000	Rigby
Have You Seen Birds?	K	I	Oppenheim, J. & Reid, B.	Scholastic
Have You Seen Hyacinth Macaw?	R	RF	Giff, Patricia Reilly	Dell

Title	Level	Genre	Author/Series	Publisher/Distributor
Having a Haircut	J	RF	City Kids	Rigby
Hawaii	T	I	Sea to Shining Sea	Children's Press
Hawaiian Magic	R	I	Morris, Rod	Pacific Learning
Haymeadow, The	T	RF	Paulsen, Gary	Dell
He Bear, She Bear	J	F	Berenstain, Stan, & Jan	Random House
He Who Listens	K	RF	Literacy 2000	Rigby
Head For the Hills!	O	I	Walker, Paul Robert	Random House
Head Full of Notions, A: A Story about Robert Fulton	S	B	Russell Bowen, Andy	Carolrhoda Books
Headless Horseman, The	L	TL	Standiford, Natalie	Random House
Heart's Blood	X	F	Yolen, Jane	Harcourt Brace
Heat Is On, The	U	I	Tanaka, Shelley	Firefly Books
Heather at the Barre	Q	RF	Sinykin, Sheri Cooper	Magic Attic
Heather, Belle of the Ball	Q	RF	Sinykin, Sheri Cooper	Magic Attic
Heather Goes to Hollywood	Q	RF	Sinykin, Sheri Cooper	Magic Attic
Heather Takes the Reins	Q	RF	Sinykin, Sheri Cooper	Magic Attic
Heather's Book	K	RF	Ready Readers	Pearson Learning
Heavy Weight and Other Cases, The	O	RF	Simon, Seymour	Avon
Hedgehog Bakes a Cake	J	F	Bank Street	Bantam Doubleday Dell
Hedgehog in the Hall	Q	RF	Daniels, Lucy	Barron's Educational
Helen Keller	N	B	Davidson, Margaret	Scholastic
Helen Keller: A Light For The Blind	R	B	Kudlinski, Kathleen V.	The Penguin Group
Helen Keller: Courage in the Dark	N	B	Hurwitz, Johanna	Random House
Helen Keller: Crusader for the Blind and Deaf	P	B	Graff, Stewart & Polly Anne	Bantam Doubleday Dell
Helen Keller: From Tragedy to Triumph	O	B	Childhood of Famous Americans	Aladdin
Helen Keller's Teacher	N	B	Davidson, Margaret	Scholastic
Helicopters	N	I	A True Book	Children's Press
Hello, Mrs. Piggle-Wiggle	O	F	MacDonald, Betty	HarperTrophy
Hello, My Name Is Scrambled Eggs	R	RF	Gilson, Jamie	Pocket Books
Help! I'm a Prisoner in the Library	Q	RF	Clifford, Eth	Scholastic
Help! I'm Trapped in an Alien's Body	Q	F	Strasser, Todd	Scholastic
Help! I'm Trapped in My Lunch Lady's Body	Q	F	Strasser, Todd	Scholastic
Help! I'm Trapped in My Teacher's Body	Q	F	Strasser, Todd	Scholastic
Help! I'm Trapped in Obedience School	Q	F	Strasser, Todd	Scholastic
Help! I'm Trapped in Obedience School Again	Q	F	Strasser, Todd	Scholastic
Help! I'm Trapped in Santa's Body	Q	F	Strasser, Todd	Scholastic
Help! I'm Trapped in the First Day of School	Q	F	Strasser, Todd	Scholastic
Help! I'm Trapped in the First Day of Summer Camp	Q	F	Strasser, Todd	Scholastic
Help! I'm Trapped in the President's Body	Q	F	Strasser, Todd	Scholastic
Helpful Change, A	L	RF	Behr, Alexandra	Hampton-Brown
Helpful Harry and Other Stories	L	RF	New Way: Literature	Steck-Vaughn
Helping the Hoiho	S	I	Literacy 2000	Rigby
Henri de Toulouse-Lautrec	R	B	Venezia, Mike	Children's Press
Henri Matisse	R	B	Venezia, Mike	Children's Press
Henri Rousseau	T	B	Rabott, Ernest	HarperTrophy
Henry	T	RF	Bawden, Nina	Bantam Doubleday Dell
Henry and Beezus	O	RF	Cleary, Beverly	Avon
Henry and Mudge and Annie's Good Move	J	RF	Rylant, Cynthia	Aladdin
Henry and Mudge and the Bedtime Thumps	J	RF	Rylant, Cynthia	Aladdin
Henry and Mudge and the Best Day of All	J	RF	Rylant, Cynthia	Aladdin
Henry and Mudge and the Careful Cousin	J	RF	Rylant, Cynthia	Aladdin
Henry and Mudge and the Forever Sea	J	RF	Rylant, Cynthia	Aladdin
Henry and Mudge and the Happy Cat	J	RF	Rylant, Cynthia	Aladdin
Henry and Mudge and the Long Weekend	J	RF	Rylant, Cynthia	Aladdin
Henry and Mudge and the Sneaky Crackers	J	RF	Rylant, Cynthia	Aladdin
Henry and Mudge and the Snowman Plan	J	RF	Rylant, Cynthia	Aladdin
Henry and Mudge and the Starry Night	J	RF	Rylant, Cynthia	Aladdin
Henry and Mudge and the Wild Wind	J	RF	Rylant, Cynthia	Aladdin
Henry and Mudge Get the Cold Shivers	J	RF	Rylant, Cynthia	Aladdin
Henry and Mudge in Puddle Trouble	J	RF	Rylant, Cynthia	Aladdin
Henry and Mudge in the Family Trees	J	RF	Rylant, Cynthia	Aladdin

Title	Level	Genre	Author/Series	Publisher/Distributor
Henry and Mudge in the Green Time	J	RF	Rylant, Cynthia	Aladdin
Henry and Mudge in the Sparkle Days	J	RF	Rylant, Cynthia	Aladdin
Henry and Mudge Take the Big Test	J	RF	Rylant, Cynthia	Aladdin
Henry and Mudge: The First Book	J	RF	Rylant, Cynthia	Aladdin
Henry and Mudge Under the Yellow Moon	J	RF	Rylant, Cynthia	Aladdin
Henry and Ribsy	O	RF	Cleary, Beverly	Hearst
Henry and the Clubhouse	O	RF	Cleary, Beverly	Avon
Henry and the Paper Route	O	RF	Cleary, Beverly	Hearst
Henry Ford: Young Man with Ideas	O	B	Childhood of Famous Americans	Aladdin
Henry Huggins	O	RF	Cleary, Beverly	Avon
Henry Reed, Inc.	X	F	Robertson, Keith	Puffin Books
Henry's Choice	M	RF	Reading Unlimited	Celebration Press
Her Piano Sang: A Story About Clara Schumann	R	B	Allman, Barbara	Carolrhoda Books
Her Seven Brothers	O	TL	Goble, Paul	Aladdin
Herbie Jones	N	RF	Kline, Suzy	The Penguin Group
Herbie Jones and Hamburger Head	N	RF	Kline, Suzy	The Penguin Group
Herbie Jones and the Birthday Showdown	N	RF	Kline, Suzy	The Penguin Group
Herbie Jones and the Class Gift	N	RF	Kline, Suzy	The Penguin Group
Herbie Jones and the Dark Attic	N	RF	Kline, Suzy	Puffin Books
Herbie Jones and the Monster Ball	N	RF	Kline, Suzy	The Penguin Group
Hercules and Other Greek Legends	T	TL	Wildcats	Wright Group/McGraw Hill
Hercules Doesn't Pull Teeth	M	F	Dadey, D. & Jones, M. T.	Scholastic
Here Comes McBroom	O	F	Fleischman, Sid	Beech Tree Books
Here Comes the Strike Out	K	RF	Kessler, Leonard	Harper Trophy
Here's to You, Rachel Robinson	T	RF	Blume, Judy	Bantam Doubleday Dell
Herman the Helper	J	F	Kraus, Robert	Simon & Schuster
Hero and the Crown, The	Z	F	McKinley, Robin	Puffin Books
Heroes	N	I	Wildcats	Wright Group/McGraw Hill
Heroes & Idealists	U	B	Real Lives	Troll
Hey, Al	N	F	Yorinks, Arthur	Farrar, Straus and Giroux
Hey, New Kid!	N	RF	Duffey, Betsy	The Penguin Group
Hey World, Here I Am!	S	RF	Little, Jean	HarperTrophy
Hidden Hand, The	M	RF	Schultz, Irene	Wright Group/McGraw Hill
Hidden World	R	I	Weldon Owen	Wright Group/McGraw Hill
Hide to Survive	L	I	Home Connection Collection	Rigby
Hiding Places	J	RF	Storyteller-Night Crickets	Wright Group/McGraw Hill
High Flying	R	I	Weldon Owen	Wright Group/McGraw Hill
Hilary & the Lions	M	F	Desaix, Frank	Farrar, Straus and Giroux
Hill of Fire	L	RF	Lewis, T.P.	Harper Collins
Hillary Rodham Clinton: A New Kind of First Lady	S	B	Guernsey, JoAnn Bren	Lerner Publications
Hippopotamus Ate the Teacher, A	J	F	Thaler, Mike	Avon
Hippos	K	I	PM Animal Facts: Turquoise	Rigby
Hiroshima	S	HF	Yep, Laurence	Scholastic
History of Machines, The	O	I	McKinnon, Judith	Rigby
Hit-Away Kid, The	M	RF	Christopher, Matt	Little, Brown & Co.
Hitty: Her First Hundred Years	U	F	Field, Rachel	Aladdin
Ho, Ho, Benjamin, Feliz Navidad	N	RF	Giff, Patricia Reilly	Bantam Doubleday Dell
Hobbit, The	Z	F	Tolkien, J.R.R	Ballantine Books
Hobby: The Young Merlin Trilogy	V	F	Yolen, Jane	Scholastic
Hocus Pocus	M	I	Wildcats	Wright Group/McGraw Hill
Holes	V	RF	Sachar, Louis	Random House
Holly & Mac	N	RF	SupaDoopers	Sundance
Home: A Journey Through America	R	I	Locker, Thomas	Voyageur Books
Home Crafts	T	I	Historic Communities	Crabtree
Home for Diggory, A	K	RF	Pacific Literacy	Pacific Learning
Home for the Howl-idays	S	F	Regan, Dian Curtis	Scholastic
Home in the Sky	K	RF	Baker, Jeannie	Scholastic
Home Sweet Home, Goodbye	R	RF	Stowe, Cynthia	Scholastic
Homecoming	X	RF	Voigt, Cynthia	Ballantine Books
Homer Price	Q	RF	McCloskey, Robert	Puffin Books

Title	Level	Genre	Author/Series	Publisher/Distributor
Homes Are for Living	M	I	Cumpiano, Ina	Hampton-Brown
Homesick, My Own Story	X	B	Fritz, Jean	Penguin Books
Honey Bees	M	I	Kahkonen, Sharon	Steck-Vaughn
Honey Tree, The	L	F	Literacy 2000	Rigby
Honorable Prison, The	W	HF	Becerra de Jenkins, Lyll	The Penguin Group
Hoops	X	RF	Myers, Walter Dean	Bantam Doubleday Dell
Hoopstars: Go to the Hoop!	M	RF	Hughes, Dean	Random House
Hooray for the Golly Sisters!	K	RF	Byars, Betsy	HarperTrophy
Hop on Pop	J	F	Seuss, Dr.	Random House
Hop to it, Minty!	O	RF	PM Ruby	Rigby
Hope Was Here	W	RF	Bauer, Joan	G.P. Putnam's Sons
Horrakapotchkin	M	F	Pacific Literacy	Pacific Learning
Horrible Harry and the Ant Invasion	L	RF	Kline, Suzy	Scholastic
Horrible Harry and the Christmas Surprise	L	RF	Kline, Susy	Scholastic
Horrible Harry and the Drop of Doom	L	RF	Kline, Suzy	Puffin Books
Horrible Harry and the Dungeon	L	RF	Kline, Suzy	The Penguin Group
Horrible Harry and the Green Slime	L	RF	Kline, Suzy	The Penguin Group
Horrible Harry and the Kickball Wedding	L	RF	Kline, Susy	The Penguin Group
Horrible Harry in Room 2B	L	RF	Kline, Suzy	The Penguin Group
Horrible Harry, Moves up to Third Grade	L	RF	Kline, Suzy	Puffin Books
Horrible Harry's Secret	L	RF	Kline, Suzy	The Penguin Group
Horrors of the Haunted Museum	Q	RF	Stine, R. L.	Scholastic
Horse and His Boy, The	T	F	Lewis, C. S.	Collier Books
Horse in Harry's Room, The	J	F	Hoff, Syd	Harper Collins
Horse, of Course, The	Q	I	Elliot-Reep, Tracey	Rigby
Horse Power	O	I	Pacific Literacy	Pacific Learning
Horses	N	I	A New True Book	Children's Press
Horses	P	I	Crabapples	Crabtree
Horses	L	I	PM Animal Facts: Purple	Rigby
Horses Have Foals	M	I	Animals and Their Young	Compass Point Books
Hospitals	L	I	Book Shop	Mondo
Hot Air Balloons	L	I	Pair-It Books	Steck-Vaughn
Hot and Cold Summer, The	O	RF	Hurwitz, Johanna	Scholastic
Hot and Cold Weather	K	I	Sunshine	Wright Group/McGraw Hill
Hot Fudge Hero	L	RF	Brisson, Pat	Henry Holt & Co.
Houdini's Last Trick	O	B	Hass, E.A.	Random House
Hour of the Olympics	M	F	Osborne, Mary Pope	Random House
House Gobbaleen, The	P	F	Alexander, Lloyd	The Penguin Group
House in the Snow, The	S	RF	Engh, M.J.	Scholastic
House of Dies Drear	V	HF	Hamilton, Virginia	Aladdin
House of Mirrors, The	M	F	Weaver, Betty-May	Wright Group/McGraw Hill
House of Stairs	Z	F	Sleator, William	Puffin Books
House of the Horrible Ghosts	M	F	Hayes, Geoffrey	Random House
House of Wings, The	R	RF	Byars, Betsy	The Penguin Group
House on Mango Street, The	W	B	Cisneros, Sandra	Alfred A. Knopf
House on Walenska Street, The	N	RF	Herman, Charlotte	The Penguin Group
House that Jack Built, The	J	TL	Peppe, Rodney	Delacorte
House That Jack's Friends Built, The	J	RF	Pair-It Books	Steck-Vaughn
House that Stood on Booker Hill, The	J	RF	Ready Readers	Pearson Learning
House Through the Ages	U	I	Steele, Philip	Troll Associates
House with a Clock in its Walls, The	S	F	Bellairs, John	The Penguin Group
Houses	M	I	Wonder World	Wright Group/McGraw Hill
How a Book is Made	N	I	Aliki	Harper & Row
How a Volcano is Formed	M	I	Wonder World	Wright Group/McGraw Hill
How Animals Move	L	I	Discovery World	Rigby
How Bullfrog Found His Sound	M	F	Michaels, Eric	Pearson Learning
How Did This City Grow?	M	I	Schaefer, Lola M.	Benchmark Education
How Do Plants Get Food?	L	I	Goldish, Meish	Steck-Vaughn
How Does It Breathe?	K	I	Home Connection Collection	Rigby
How Does It Grow?	L	I	Home Connection Collection	Rigby

Title	Level	Genre	Author/Series	Publisher/Distributor
How Fire Came to Earth	K	TL	Literacy 2000	Rigby
How Flamingos Came to Have Red Legs: A South American Folk Tale	M	TL	Jensen, Ned	Wright Group/McGraw Hill
How Flexible Are You?	M	I	Marks, Ashley	Wright Group/McGraw Hill
How Goods Are Moved	K	I	People, Spaces & Places	Rand McNally
How Grandmother Spider Got the Sun	J	TL	Little Readers	Houghton Mifflin
How I Fixed the Year 1000 Problem	N	F	The Zack Files	Grossett&Dunlap
How I Met Archie	M	RF	Kenna, Anna	Pacific Learning
How I Met Einstein, a Character Comes to Life	S	I	Trussell-Cullen, Alan	Pacific Learning
How I Went from Bad to Verse	N	F	The Zack Files	Grossett&Dunlap
How Is a Crayon Made?	P	I	Charles, Oz	Scholastic
How Kittens Grow	L	I	Selsam, Millicent E.	Scholastic
How Much Does This Hold?	K	RF	Coulton, Mia	Kaeden Books
How Much Is That Guinea Pig in the Window?	L	RF	Rocklin, Joanne	Scholastic
How My Family Lives in America	O	I	Kuklin, Susan	Aladdin
How Spiders Got Eight Legs	L	F	Pair-It Books	Steck-Vaughn
How the Giraffe Became a Giraffe	M	TL	Sunshine	Wright Group/McGraw Hill
How the Rattlesnake Got Its Rattle	L	TL	Pair-It Books	Steck-Vaughn
How the Tortoise Got His Shell and Other Stories	K	TL	New Way: Literature	Steck-Vaughn
How the Water Got to the Plains	L	TL	Home Connection Collection	Rigby
How Things Work	R	I	Weldon Owen	Wright Group/McGraw Hill
How To Be Cool in the Third Grade	N	RF	Duffey, Betsy	The Penguin Group
How To Choose a Pet	L	I	Discovery World	Rigby
How To Cook Scones	J	I	Book Shop	Mondo
How To Eat Fried Worms	R	RF	Rockwell, Thomas	Bantam Doubleday Dell
How To Grow Crystals	P	I	Book Shop	Mondo
How To Make a Kite	M	I	Reeder, Paul	Wright Group/McGraw Hill
How To Make Salsa	J	I	Book Shop	Mondo
How To Speak Dolphin in Three Easy Lessons	N	F	The Zack Files	Grosset & Dunlap
How Turtle Raced Beaver	J	TL	Literacy 2000	Rigby
How's the Weather?	N	I	Berger, Melvin and Gilda	Ideals Children's Books
Howard Carter: Searching for King Tut	S	B	Ford, Barbara	W. H. Freeman & Co.
Howie Merton and the Magic Dust	M	F	Reeves, Faye Couch	Random House
Howliday Inn	P	F	Howe, James	Atheneum Books
Howling at the Hauntly's	M	RF	Dadey, Debbie & Jones, Marcia	Scholastic
Howling Dog and Other Cases, The	O	RF	Simon, Seymour	Avon
Hubble Space Telescope, The	N	I	A True Book	Children's Press
Huberta the Hiking Hippo	L	RF	Literacy 2000	Rigby
Hue Boy	M	RF	Mitchell, Rita Phillips	The Penguin Group
Hugo Hogget: Story Based on an Ecuadoran Legend	K	TL	Cumpiano, Ina	Hampton-Brown
Human Body, The	Q	I	Weldon Owen	Wright Group/McGraw Hill
Humpback Whale, The	S	I	Frahm, Randy	Capstone Press
Hundred Dresses, The	O	RF	Estes, Eleanor	Scholastic
Hundred Penny Box, The	P	RF	Mathis, Sharon Bell	Puffin Books
Hungry, Hungry Sharks	L	I	Cole, Joanna	Random House
Hunt for Pirate Gold, The	M	F	Schultz, Irene	Wright Group/McGraw Hill
Hunting the Horned Lizard	R	I	Bishop, Nic	Pacific Learning
Hurdles and Jumps	M	I	Reeder, Tracey	Wright Group/McGraw Hill
Hurray For Ali Baba Bernstein	O	RF	Hurwitz, Johanna	Scholastic
Hurricane Machine and Other Cases, The	O	RF	Simon, Seymour	Avon
Hurricanes!	P	I	Hopping, Jean	Scholastic
Hurricanes & Tornadoes	R	I	The Wonders of our World	Crabtree
Hushtown: A Peaceful Community	Q	RF	Massie, Elizabeth	Steck-Vaughn
Hyenas	O	I	Holmes, Kevin J.	Capstone Press
Hypnotized Frog and Other Cases, The	O	RF	Simon, Seymour	Avon
I Am a Gypsy Pot	K	F	Evangeline Nicholas Collection	Wright Group/McGraw Hill
I Am A Star: Child of the Holocaust	W	I	Auerbacher, Inge	The Penguin Group
I Am Regina	U	HF	Keehn, Sally	Bantam Doubleday Dell
I Am Rosa Parks	O	B	Parks, Rosa	Dial Books
I Am the Cheese	Z	RF	Cormier, Robert	Laurel-Leaf Books

Title	Level	Genre	Author/Series	Publisher/Distributor
I Am the Ice Worm	S	F	Easley, Mary Ann	Yearling
I, Amber Brown	N	RF	Danziger, Paula	Scholastic
I Can Read with My Eyes Shut	J	F	Seuss, Dr.	Random House
I Can't Said the Ant	M	F	Cameron, Polly	Scholastic
I Don't Believe It!	L	RF	Tuer, Judy	Rigby
I Dream	K	RF	Sunshine	Wright Group/McGraw Hill
I Get the Creeps	K	RF	Reading Corners	Dominie
I Hate Camping	M	RF	Petersen, P. J.	The Penguin Group
I Hate Company	M	RF	Petersen, P.J.	The Penguin Group
I Hate English	L	RF	Levine, Ellen	Scholastic
I Hate My Best Friend	L	RF	Rosner, Ruth	Hyperion
I Have a Dream	Q	B	Davidson, Margaret	Scholastic
I Have Lived a Thousand Years	Y	B	Bitton-Jackson, Livia	Simon & Schuster
I Know a Lady	L	RF	Zolotow, Charlotte	The Penguin Group
I Like Shopping	M	RF	Sunshine	Wright Group/McGraw Hill
I Love Guinea Pigs	O	I	King-Smith, Dick	Candlewick Press
I Love the Beach	M	B	Literacy 2000	Rigby
I Love to Sneeze	J	F	Bank Street	Bantam Doubleday Dell
I. M. Pei	M	B	Biography	Benchmark Education
I Play Soccer	J	RF	City Kids	Rigby
I Rode a Horse of Milk White Jade	V	HF	Wilson, Diane Lee	HarperTrophy
I Saw You in the Bathtub	J	TL	Schwartz, Alvin	HarperTrophy
I Was a Sixth Grade Alien	S	F	Coville, Bruce	Pocket Books
I Was a Third Grade Science Project	N	RF	Auch, Mary Jane	Yearling
I Was So Mad	J	RF	Mayer, Mercer	Donovan
I Went to the Dentist	K	RF	City Kids	Rigby
I Went to the Movies	J	RF	City Kids	Rigby
I Wonder Why Snakes Shed Their Skins and Other Questions About Reptiles	O	I	O'Neill, Amanda	Scholastic
I'm No One Else But Me	M	RF	Book Bank	Wright Group/McGraw Hill
I'm Out of My Body...Please Leave a Message	N	F	The Zack Files	Grosset & Dunlap
I'm So Hungry and Other Plays	M	F	Learning Media	Pacific Learning
Ibis: A True Whale Story	K	I	Himmelman, John	Scholastic
Ice Dove and Other Stories, The	M	RF	deAnda, Diane	Arte Publico
Ice Magic	M	RF	Christopher, Matt	Little, Brown & Co.
Ice Mummy: The Discovery of a 5,000-Year-Old Man	P	I	Dubowski, Mark & Cathy East	Random House
Iceberg Hermit, The	X	RF	Roth, Arthur	Scholastic
Icy Question and Other Cases, The	O	RF	Simon, Seymour	Avon
Iditarod: Dogsled Race Across Alaska	Q	I	Fuerst, Jeffery B.	Wright Group/McGraw Hill
If I Forget, You Remember	V	RF	Williams, Carol Lynch	Bantam Doubleday Dell
If You Give A Moose A Muffin	K	F	Numeroff, Laura Joffe	Harper Collins
If You Give A Mouse A Cookie	K	F	Numeroff, Laura Joffe	Harper Collins
If You Grew Up with Abraham Lincoln	Q	I	McGovern, Ann	Scholastic
If You Grew Up with George Washington	Q	I	Gross, Ruth Belov	Scholastic
If You Lived 100 Years Ago	Q	I	McGovern, Ann	Scholastic
If You Lived at the Time of Martin Luther King	Q	I	Levine, Ellen	Scholastic
If You Lived at the Time of the American Revolution	Q	I	Moore, Kay	Scholastic
If You Lived at the Time of the Civil War	Q	I	Moore, Kay	Scholastic
If You Lived at the Time of the Great San Francisco Earthquake	Q	I	Levine, Ellen	Scholastic
If You Lived in Colonial Times	Q	I	McGovern, Ann	Scholastic
If you Lived in the Alaska Territory	Q	I	Levinson, Nancy Smiler	Scholastic
If You Lived with the Cherokee	Q	I	Roop, Peter & Connie	Scholastic
If You Lived with the Hopi	Q	I	Kamma, Anne	Scholastic
If You Lived with the Iroquois	Q	I	Levine, Ellen	Scholastic
If You Lived with the Sioux Indians	Q	I	McGovern, Ann	Scholastic
If You Sailed on the Mayflower in 1620	Q	I	McGovern, Ann	Scholastic
If You Traveled on the Underground Railroad	Q	I	Levine, Ellen	Scholastic
If You Traveled West in a Covered Wagon	Q	I	Levine, Ellen	Scholastic

Title	Level	Genre	Author/Series	Publisher/Distributor
If You Were There in 1492: Everyday Life in the Time of Columbus	U	I	Brenner, Barbara	Aladdin
If You Were There When They Signed the Constitution	Q	I	Levy, Elizabeth	Scholastic
If Your Name was Changed at Ellis Island	Q	I	Levine, Ellen	Scholastic
Iggie's House	R	RF	Blume, Judy	Bantam Doubleday Dell
Illinois	Q	I	Geography Department	Capstone Press
Imagine That	J	F	Story Box	Wright Group/McGraw Hill
Imagine This, James Robert	P	F	Weber, Rebecca	Rigby
Immigrants	T	I	Sandler, Martin W.	HarperTrophy
Immigrants: Coming to America	R	I	Thompson, Gare	Children's Press
Impossible Bend and Other Cases, The	O	RF	Simon, Seymour	Avon
In a Dark, Dark Room	J	TL	Schwartz, Alvin	HarperTrophy
In a Faraway Forest	K	F	Kratky, Lada Josefa	Hampton-Brown
In a New Land	L	HF	Sunshine	Wright Group/McGraw Hill
In a Pickle	M	RF	SupaDoopers	Sundance
In Aunt Lucy's Kitchen	M	RF	Rylant, Cynthia	Aladdin
In Danger	M	I	Home Connection Collection	Rigby
In Hiding, Animals Under Cover	L	I	Burke, Melissa Blackwell	Steck-Vaughn
In Search of the Grand Canyon	W	I	Fraser, Mary Ann	Henry Holt & Co.
In Search of the Great Bears	S	I	Literacy 2000	Rigby
In Short: A Collection of Brief Creative Nonfiction	Z	I	Kitchen, J. & Jones, M. P.	W. W. Norton
In the Clouds	M	RF	Literacy 2000	Rigby
In the Dinosaur's Paw	M	RF	Giff, Patricia Reilly	Bantam Doubleday Dell
In the Fast Lane	R	I	Literacy 2000	Rigby
In the Land of the Polar Bear	J	RF	Robinson, F.R.	Steck-Vaughn
In the News	Q	I	Wildcats	Wright Group/McGraw Hill
In the Path of Lewis & Clark: Traveling the Missouri	V	I	Lourie, Peter	Silver Burdett Press
In the Rain Forest	Q	I	Wildcats	Wright Group/McGraw Hill
In the Year of the Boar and Jackie Robinson	S	HF	Lord, Bette Bao	HarperTrophy
In-Between Days, The	P	RF	Bunting, Eve	HarperTrophy
Incident at Hawk's Hill	V	F	Eckert, Allen W.	Little, Brown & Co.
Incredible Creatures	P	I	Weldon Owen	Wright Group/McGraw Hill
Incredible Journey,The	V	F	Burnford, Sheila	Bantam Doubleday Dell
Incredible Places	P	I	Wildcats	Wright Group/McGraw Hill
Incredible Shrinking Kid, The	P	F	Abbott, Tony	Scholastic
Incredible Shrinking Machine and Other Cases, The	O	RF	Simon, Seymour	Avon
India	O	I	Dahl, Michael	Capstone Press
Indian in the Cupboard, The	R	F	Banks, Lynne Reid	Avon
Indian School, The	P	RF	Whelan, Gloria	HarperTrophy
Indian-Head Pennies and Other Cases, The	O	RF	Simon, Seymour	Avon
Inn Keepers Apprentice	Z	B	Say, Allen	The Penguin Group
Insects	U	I	Bird, Bettina & Short, Joan	Mondo
Insects	J	I	MacLulich, Carolyn	Scholastic
Insects All Around	K	I	Early Connections	Benchmark Education
Insects & Spiders	U	I	World Book Looks at Science	World Book
Insects & Spiders	R	I	Worldwise	Franklin Watts
Inside a Rain Forest	M	I	Pair-It Books	Steck-Vaughn
Instead of Three Wishes: Magical Short Stories	Y	F	Turner, Megan Whalen	The Penguin Group
Interrupting The Big Sleep	P	RF	Marriott, Janice	Pacific Learning
Into Space	J	I	Momentum Literacy Program	Troll
Inventors	T	I	Sandler, Martin W.	HarperTrophy
Inventors: Making Things Better	M	I	Pair-It Books	Steck-Vaughn
Invincible Louisa	Z	B	Meigs, Cornelia	Scholastic
Invisible Dog, The	M	F	King-Smith, Dick	Alfred A. Knopf
Invisible in the Third Grade	M	RF	Cuyler, Margery	Scholastic
Invisible Spy, The	J	F	Foundations	Wright Group/McGraw Hill
Invisible Stanley	O	F	Brown, Jeff	HarperTrophy
Iowa	T	I	Sea to Shining Sea	Children's Press
Iron Giant, The	O	SF	Hughes, Ted	Alfred A. Knopf
Iron Ring, The	W	F	Alexander, Lloyd	Puffin Books

Title	Level	Genre	Author/Series	Publisher/Distributor
Ironman	Z	RF	Crutcher, Chris	Laurel-Leaf Books
Iroquois Indians, The	P	I	Lund, Bill	Capstone Press
Irrational Season, The	Z	B	L'Engle, Madeleine	Harper Collins
Is it a Fish?	K	I	Sunshine	Wright Group/McGraw Hill
Is There Life in Outer Space	O	I	Branley, Franklyn M.	HarperCollins
Isabella: A Wish for Miguel	Q	HF	Childhood Journeys	Aladdin
Ishi's: Tale of Lizard	P	TL	Hinton, L. & Roth, S. L.	Farrar Straus Giroux
Island Baby	M	RF	Keller, Holly	Scholastic
Island Keeper	T	RF	Mazer, Harry	Language for Learning Assoc.
Island of the Blue Dolphins	V	HF	O'Dell, Scott	Bantam Doubleday Dell
Island of the Skog, The	M	F	Kellogg, Steven	Dial Books
Island on Bird Street, The	X	HF	Orlev, Uri	Houghton Mifflin
Island, The	R	RF	Paulsen, Gary	Bantam Doubleday Dell
Islander, The	T	F	Rylant, Cynthia	Random House
Isn't It Cool?	R	I	Yurkovic, Diana Short	Rigby
Israel	O	I	Thoennes, Kristin	Capstone Press
It Came From Ohio!: My Life as a Writer	R	B	Stine, R.L.	Scholastic
It Came Through the Wall	O	F	Healey, Tim	Mondo
It Takes A Village	L	RF	Cowen-Fletcher, J.	Scholastic
It Was On Fire When I Lay Down On It	Z	B	Fulghum, Robert	Ballantine Books
It Wasn't My Fault	L	RF	Lester, Helen	Houghton Mifflin
It'll Be All Right on the Night!	Q	I	Quinn, Pat	Pacific Learning
It's a Fiesta, Benjamin	N	RF	Giff, Patricia Reilly	Bantam Doubleday Dell
It's About Time	M	I	Storyteller Nonfiction	Wright Group/McGraw Hill
It's All in Your Mind, James Robert	P	F	Literacy 2000	Rigby
It's Halloween	K	RF	Prelutsky, Jack	Scholastic
It's Just a Trick	O	RF	Literacy 2000	Rigby
It's New, It's Improved, It's Terrible!	Q	RF	Manes, Stephen	Bantam Skylark
It's Not Easy Being George	S	RF	Smith, Janice Lee	HarperTrophy
It's Not the End of the World	T	RF	Blume, Judy	Dell
It's the Fashion	S	I	Literacy 2000	Rigby
Italy	O	I	Thoennes, Kristin	Capstone Press
Izzy, Willy-Nilly	X	RF	Voigt, Cynthia	Aladdin
J.T.	Q	RF	Wagner, Jane	Bantam Doubleday Dell
Jack and the Beanstalk	K	TL	Weisner, David	Scholastic
Jack and the Magic Harp	K	TL	PM Tales and Plays- Gold	Rigby
Jack's New Power: Stories From a Caribbean Year	W	RF	Gantos, Jack	Sunburst
Jackaroo	Y	RF	Voigt, Cynthia	Scholastic
Jackie Robinson	O	B	Early Biographies	Compass Point Books
Jackie Robinson and the Breaking of the Color Barrier	S	B	Shorto, Russell	Millbrook Press
Jackie Robinson and the Story of All-Black Baseball	N	I	O'Connor, Jim	Random House
Jackie Robinson: Baseball's First Black Major Leaguer	O	B	Greene, Carol	Children's Press
Jackie Robinson Breaks the Color Line	V	B	Cornerstones of Freedom	Children's Press
Jacob Have I Loved	U	RF	Paterson, Katherine	HarperTrophy
Jacob Two-Two and the Dinosaur	P	F	Richler, Mordecai	Tundra Books
Jacob Two-Two Meets the Hooded Fang	P	F	Richler, Mordecai	Seal Books
Jacob's Rescue: A Holocaust Story	Y	HF	Drucker, M. & Halperin, M.	Bantam Doubleday Dell
Jacques Cousteau	L	B	Biography	Benchmark Education
Jaguars	U	I	Green, Michael	Capstone Press
Jake and the Copycats	J	RF	Rocklin, Joanne	Bantam Doubleday Dell
Jamaica and Brianna	K	RF	Little Readers	Houghton Mifflin
Jamaica's Find	K	RF	Havill, Juanita	Scholastic
Jamberry	J	F	Degen, Bruce	Harper & Row
James and the Giant Peach	Q	F	Dahl, Roald	The Penguin Group
Jamestown Colony, The	V	I	Cornerstones of Freedom	Children's Press
Jamestown Colony, The	S	I	We The People	Compass Point Books
Jamestown: New World Adventure	T	I	Adventures in Colonial America	Troll
Jane Addams	P	B	Community Builders	Children's Press
Jane Goodall and the Wild Chimpanzees	L	B	Birnbaum, Bette	Steck-Vaughn
Jane's Mansion	N	I	Literacy 2000	Rigby

Title	Level	Genre	Author/Series	Publisher/Distributor
Japan	N	I	A True Book	Children's Press
Jar of Dreams, A	R	RF	Uchida, Yoshiko	Aladdin
Jason and the Aliens Down the Street	O	F	Greer, Greg & Ruddick, Bob	HarperTrophy
Jason Kidd Story, The	P	RF	Moore, David	Scholastic
Jason's Gold	T	HF	Hobbs, Will	William Morrow
Jazmin's Notebook	Z	RF	Grimes, Nikki	The Penguin Group
Jazz Kid, The	Y	RF	Lincoln Collier, James	The Penguin Group
Jazz, Pizzazz, and the Silver Threads	P	RF	Quattlebaum, Mary	Bantam Doubleday Dell
Jean Craighead George	S	B	Cary, Alice	Learning Works, The
Jelly Beans	M	I	Stadler, Charlotte	Benchmark Education Co.
Jenius The Amazing Guinea Pig	N	F	King-Smith, Dick	Hyperion
Jennifer, Hecate, Macbeth, William McKinley, and Me, Elizabeth	R	RF	Konigsburg, E. L.	Yearling
Jennifer, Too	L	RF	Havill, Juanita	Hyperion
Jenny and the Cornstalk	L	TL	Pair-It Books	Steck-Vaughn
Jenny Archer, Author	M	RF	Conford, Ellen	Little, Brown & Co.
Jenny Archer to the Rescue	M	RF	Conford, Ellen	Little, Brown & Co.
Jericho	T	RF	Hickman, Janet	Hearst
Jericho's Journey	U	RF	Wisler, G. Clifton	Penguin Group
Jerry on the Line	R	RF	Seabrooke, Brenda	Puffin Books
Jesse	Y	RF	Soto, Gary	Scholastic
Jesse Jackson	P	B	Simon, Charnan	Children's Press
Jesse Owens: Olympic Hero	P	B	Sabin, Francene	Troll
Jigsaw Jones Mystery: The Case of the Christmas Snowman	M	RF	Ruller, James	Scholastic
Jillian Jiggs	J	RF	Gilman, Phoebe	Scholastic
Jim Ugly	Q	RF	Fleischman, Sid	Bantam Doubleday Dell
Jim's Dog Muffins	K	RF	Cohen, Miriam	Bantam Doubleday Dell
Jimmy Lee Did It	J	RF	Cummings, Pat	Lothrop
Jingo Django	V	RF	Fleischman, Sid	Bantam Doubleday Dell
Jip His Story	V	HF	Paterson, Katherine	The Penguin Group
JJ Rabbit and the Monster	K	F	Moon, Nicola	Wright Group/McGraw Hill
Jo Jo Winnie Again	O	RF	Sachs, Marilyn	Dutton
Jo's Troubled Heart	Q	HF	The Little Women Journals	Avon
Job for Giant Jim, A	J	RF	Sunshine	Wright Group/McGraw Hill
Job for Jenny Archer, A	M	RF	Conford, Ellen	Random House
Joe and Betsy the Dinosaur	K	F	Hoban, Lillian	HarperTrophy
Joe Cocker Spaniel	N	RF	SupaDoopers	Sundance
Joey Pigza Swallowed the Key	T	RF	Gantos, Jack	HarperTrophy
Joey's Head	L	F	Cretan, G.	Simon & Schuster
Johann Sebastian Bach: Great Man of Music	O	B	Greene, Carol	Children's Press
John A Macdonald	W	B	Waite, Peter B.	Fitzhenry & Whiteside
John F. Kennedy	V	B	World Leaders: Past and Present	Chelsea House
John F. Kennedy: America's Youngest President	O	B	Childhood of Famous Americans	Aladdin
John James Audubon	M	B	Biography	Benchmark Education
John James Audubon: Wildlife Artist	V	B	A First Book	Franklin Watts
Johnny Appleseed	K	TL	Moore, Eva	Scholastic
Johnny Lion's Book	J	F	Hurd, Edith Thacher	Harper Collins
Johnny Long Legs	M	RF	Christopher, Matt	Little, Brown & Co.
Jokes and Riddles	O	I	Literacy 2000	Rigby
Jonathan Buys a Present	J	RF	PM Story Books-Turquoise	Rigby
Jordan and the Northside Reps	K	RF	PM Story Books -Silver	Rigby
Jordan's Lucky Day	K	RF	PM Story Books-Turquoise	Rigby
Josefina Learns a Lesson	Q	HF	The American Girls Collection	Pleasant Company
Josefina Saves the Day	Q	HF	The American Girls Collection	Pleasant Company
Josefina Story Quilt	L	F	Coerr, Eleanor	HarperTrophy
Josefina's Surprise	Q	HF	The American Girls Collection	Pleasant Company
Joseph: 1861-A Rumble of War	V	HF	Pryor, Bonnie	Avon
Josephine's Imagination	L	RF	Dobrin, Arnold	Scholastic
Joshua T. Bates	Q	RF	Shreve, Susan	Alfred A. Knopf

Title	Level	Genre	Author/Series	Publisher/Distributor
Joshua T. Bates in Trouble Again	Q	RF	Shreve, Susan	Alfred A. Knopf
Joshua T. Bates Takes Charge	Q	RF	Shreve, Susan	Alfred A. Knopf
Journal, The: Dear Future II	Q	SF	Literacy 2000	Rigby
Journey	S	RF	MacLachlan, Patricia	Yearling
Journey Home	V	RF	Uchida, Yoshika	Aladdin
Journey Home, The	S	RF	Holland, Isabelle	Scholastic
Journey Into Terror	U	RF	Wallace, Bill	Simon & Schuster
Journey Outside	V	F	Steele, Mary Q.	The Penguin Group
Journey to America	U	HF	Levitin, Sonia	Simon & Schuster
Journey to an 800 Number	V	RF	Konigsburg, E. L.	Aladdin
Journey to Jo'burg	S	HF	Naidoo, Beverly	HarperTrophy
Journey to Nowhere	T	HF	Auch, Mary Jane	Bantam Doubleday Dell
Journey to the Center of the Earth, A	X	SF	Verne, Jules	Harper Collins
Journey to the New World	S	HF	Brocker, Susan	Rigby
Journey to Topaz	U	HF	Uchida, Yoshiko	Creative Arts Book Co.
Judy Moody	L	RF	McDonald, Megan	Candlewick Press
Julian, Dream Doctor	N	RF	Cameron, Ann	Random House
Julian, Secret Agent	N	RF	Cameron, Ann	Random House
Julian's Glorious Summer	N	RF	Cameron, Ann	Random House
Julie	U	RF	George, Jean Craighead	Harper Trophy
Julie of the Wolves	U	RF	George, Jean Craighead	Harper Collins
Julie's Mornings	K	F	Ready Readers	Pearson Learning
Julie's Wolf Pack	U	RF	George, Jean Craighead	HarperTrophy
Jump Ship to Freedom	U	HF	Collier, James and Christopher	Bantam Doubleday Dell
Jump!: The Adventures of Brer Rabbit	T	TL	Harris, Joel Chandler	Harcourt Brace
Jump the Broom	L	RF	Books For Young Learners	Pacific Learning
Jumping Into Nothing	M	RF	Willner-Pardo, Gina	Houghton Mifflin
Junebug	Q	RF	Mead, Alice	Bantam Doubleday Dell
Jungle Book, The	U	F	Kipling, Rudyard	Scholastic
Junie B. Jones and a Little Monkey Business	M	RF	Park, Barbara	Random House
Junie B. Jones and Her Big Fat Mouth	M	RF	Park, Barbara	Random House
Junie B. Jones and Some Sneaky Peeky Spying	M	RF	Park, Barbara	Random House
Junie B. Jones and that Meanie Jim's Birthday	M	RF	Park, Barbara	Random House
Junie B. Jones and the Mushy Gushy Valentine	M	RF	Park, Barbara	Random House
Junie B. Jones and the Stupid Smelly Bus	M	RF	Park, Barbara	Random House
Junie B. Jones and the Yucky Blucky Fruitcake	M	RF	Park, Barbara	Random House
Junie B. Jones Has a Monster Under Her Bed	M	RF	Park, Barbara	Random House
Junie B. Jones Has a Peep in Her Pocket	M	RF	Park, Barbara	Random House
Junie B. Jones Is a Beauty Shop Guy	M	RF	Park, Barbara	Random House
Junie B. Jones Is a Party Animal	M	RF	Park, Barbara	Random House
Junie B. Jones is (almost) a Flower Girl	M	RF	Park, Barbara	Random House
Junie B. Jones Is Not a Crook	M	RF	Park, Barbara	Random House
Junie B. Jones Loves Handsome Warren	M	RF	Park, Barbara	Random House
Junie B. Jones Smells Something Fishy	M	RF	Park, Barbara	Random House
Junior Gymnasts: Katie's Big Move	M	RF	Slater, Teddy	Scholastic
Junkpile Robot, The	L	F	Ready Readers	Pearson Learning
Junkyard Dog, The	N	RF	PM Emerald	Rigby
Jupiter	N	I	A True Book	Children's Press
Just a Few Words, Mr. Lincoln	N	I	Fritz, Jean	Putnam
Just As Long As We're Together	T	RF	Blume, Judy	Bantam Doubleday Dell
Just Call Me Stupid	R	RF	Birdseye, Tom	Puffin Books
Just for Fun	J	F	Literacy 2000	Rigby
Just Hanging Around	J	I	Storyteller-Night Crickets	Wright Group/McGraw Hill
Just Juice	Q	RF	Hesse, Karen	Scholastic
Just Like Me	J	F	Story Box	Wright Group/McGraw Hill
Just Plain Cat	O	RF	Robinson, Nancy K.	Scholastic
Just Tell Me When We're Dead!	O	RF	Clifford, Eth	Scholastic
Just Us Women	J	RF	Caines, Jeannette	Scholastic
Justin and the Best Biscuits in the World	P	RF	Pitts, Walter & Mildred	Alfred A. Knopf
Justin Morgan Had a Horse	R	HF	Henry, Marguerite	Scholastic
Kangaroo, The	M	I	Crewe, Sabrina	Steck-Vaughn

Title	Level	Genre	Author/Series	Publisher/Distributor
Kangaroos	N	I	A New True Book	Children's Press
Kangaroos	K	I	PM Animal Facts: Turquoise	Rigby
Katarina	X	HF	Winter, Kathryn	Scholastic
Kate Shelley and the Midnight Express	M	B	Wetterer, Margaret	Carolrhoda Books
Katherine Paterson	S	B	Cary, Alice	Learning Works, The
Katy and the Big Snow	L	F	Burton, Virginia L.	Scholastic
Kayaking	Q	I	Lund, Bill	Capstone Press
Keelboat Annie	N	TL	Johnson, Janet P.	Troll
Keep Ms. Sugarman in the Fourth Grade	M	RF	Levy, Elizabeth	HarperTrophy
Keep Out, Our Dog Buries What it Can't Eat	P	RF	Beale, Fleur	Pacific Learning
Keep Smiling Through	V	RF	Rinaldi, Ann	Harcourt Brace
Keep the Lights Burning Abbie	K	HF	Roop, Peter & Connie	Scholastic
Keep Your Eye On Amanda!	R	F	Avi	Avon
Keeping Days, The	Z	HF	Johnston, Norma	Puffin Books
Keeping Room, The	V	HF	Myers, Anna	Puffin Books
Keeping Score	J	I	Early Connections	Benchmark Education
Keeping Tadpoles	N	I	Discovery World	Rigby
Keeping Warm! Keeping Cool!	K	I	Sunshine	Wright Group/McGraw Hill
Keisha Leads the Way: Magic Attic Club	Q	RF	Reed, Teresa	Magic Attic
Keisha the Fairy Snow Queen: Magic Attic Club	Q	RF	Reed, Teresa	Magic Attic
Keisha to the Rescue: Magic Attic Club	Q	RF	Reed, Teresa	Magic Attic
Keisha's Maze Mystery (Magic Attic)	Q	RF	Benson, Lauren	Magic Attic
Ken Griffey Jr. & Ken Griffey Sr.	T	B	Star Families	Crestwood House
Kenny and the Little Kickers	J	F	Mareollo, Claudio	Scholastic
Kenya	O	I	Dahl, Michael	Capstone Press
Kerri Strug: Heart of Gold	L	B	Strug, K. & Brown, G.	Scholastic
Kerry	K	RF	PM Story Books -Silver	Rigby
Kerry's Double	K	RF	PM Story Books -Silver	Rigby
Ketchup Deal, The	P	F	Marriott, Janice	Pacific Learning
Key to the Playhouse, The	O	RF	York, Carol	Scholastic
Key to the Treasure	N	RF	Parish, Peggy	Bantam Doubleday Dell
Kick, Pass, and Run	J	RF	Kessler, Leonard	HarperTrophy
Kid Heroes of the Environment	Q	I	Dee, Catherine	Scholastic
Kid in the Red Jacket, The	O	RF	Park, Barbara	Random House
Kid Power	P	RF	Pfeffer, Susan Beth	Scholastic
Kid Who Only Hit Homers, The	M	RF	Christopher, Matt	Little, Brown & Co.
Kid Who Ran For President, The	T	RF	Gutman, Dan	Language for Learning Assoc.
Kids at Work: Lewis Hine and the Crusade Against Child Labor	T	B	Freedman, Russell	Clarion
Kids Can Cook	M	I	Literacy 2000	Rigby
Kids in Ms. Colman's Class: Author Day	M	RF	Martin, Ann M.	Scholastic
Kids in the Circus	L	I	Robinson, Fay	Wright Group/McGraw Hill
Killer Bees	S	I	Blau, Melinda	Steck-Vaughn
Kilmer's Pet Monster	L	RF	Dadey, D. & Jones, M. T.	Scholastic
Kind of Thief, A	U	RF	Alcock, Vivien	Bantam Doubleday Dell
Kind Prince and Rupert, The	L	F	New Way: Literature	Steck-Vaughn
King Arthur	M	F	Brown, Marc	Little, Brown & Co.
King Beast's Birthday	L	F	Literacy 2000	Rigby
King Emmett the Second	R	RF	Stolz, Mary	Bantam Doubleday Dell
King Max	Q	F	King-Smith, Dick	Troll
King Midas and the Golden Touch	K	TL	PM Gold	Rigby
King Midas & the Golden Touch	J	TL	Traditional Tales	Dominie
King of Shadows	Z	F	Cooper, Susan	Margaret K. McElderry Books
King of the Wind	R	HF	Henry, Marguerite	Aladdin
King, the Mice and the Cheese	K	F	Gurney, Nancy	Random House
King's Dream and Sammy's New Yellow Sweater, The	L	TL	New Way: Literature	Steck-Vaughn
King's Equal, The	O	TL	Paterson, Katherine	HarperTrophy
King's Race and Other Stories, The	L	F	New Way: Literature	Steck-Vaughn
Kirsten Learns a Lesson	Q	HF	The American Girls Collection	Pleasant Company

Title	Level	Genre	Author/Series	Publisher/Distributor
Kirsten Saves the Day	Q	HF	The American Girls Collection	Pleasant Company
Kirsten's Surprise	Q	HF	The American Girls Collection	Pleasant Company
Kiss the Dust	W	RF	Laird, Elizabeth	The Penguin Group
Kit's Castle	L	RF	Powling, Chris	Wright Group/McGraw Hill
Kitchen, The	T	I	Historic Communities	Crabtree
Kites	N	I	Literacy 2000	Rigby
Kites	O	I	PM Nonfiction -Emerald	Rigby
Kitten Crowd	O	RF	Baglio, Ben M.	Scholastic
Kitten in the Cold	Q	RF	Baglio, Ben M.	Scholastic
Kitten That Won First Prize, The	Q	RF	Baglio, Ben M.	Scholastic
Kittens in the Kitchen	Q	RF	Daniels, Lucy	Barron's Educational
Klondike Gold Rush, The	S	I	A First Book	Franklin Watts
Knee Knock Rise	S	F	Babbitt, Natalie	Farrar, Straus and Giroux
Knife, The	N	RF	Cartwright, Pauline	Pacific Learning
Knight at Dawn, The	M	F	Osborne, Mary Pope	Random House
Knightly News	P	RF	Kenna, Anna	Pacific Learning
Knights & Armor	Q	I	Worldwise	Grolier
Knights Don't Teach Piano	M	F	Dadey, D. & Jones, M. T.	Scholastic
Knit, Knit, Knit, Knit	J	F	Literacy 2000	Rigby
Knitwits	Q	RF	Taylor, William	Scholastic
Knock! Knock!	K	RF	Carter, Jackie	Scholastic
Knot in the Grain (and Other Stories)	X	F	McKinley, Robin	Harper Trophy
Knots in My Yo-yo String: The Autobiography of a Kid	U	B	Spinelli, Jerry	Alfred A. Knopf
Knots on a Counting Rope	P	RF	Martin Jr., B. & Archambault, J.	Henry Holt & Co.
Know-Nothing Birthday, A	K	RF	Spirn, Michele Sobel	HarperTrophy
Know-Nothings, The	K	RF	Spirn, Michele Sobel	HarperTrophy
Koala Is Not a Bear, A	P	I	Crabapples	Crabtree
Koalas	N	I	A New True Book	Children's Press
Koi's Python	P	RF	Moore, Miriam	Hyperion
Korky Paul: Biography of an Illustrator	M	B	Heapy, Teresa	Rigby
Koya DeLaney and the Good Girl Blues	P	RF	Greenfield, Eloise	Scholastic
Kristy and the Walking Disaster	O	RF	Martin, Ann M.	Scholastic
Kwanzaa	O	I	Chocolate, Deborah M. Newton	Children's Press
Kwanzaa	K	I	Visions	Wright Group/McGraw Hill
La Causa: The Migrant Farmworkers' Story	U	I	deRuiz, Dana Catharine	Steck-Vaughn
Lad Who Went to the North Wind, The	J	F	Book Shop	Mondo
Lady Bird Johnson	Q	B	Simon, Charnan	Children's Press
Lady with the Hat, The	Z	HF	Orlev, Uri	The Penguin Group
Ladybug, The	O	I	Crewe, Sabrina	Steck-Vaughn
Ladybug, The	O	I	Garland, Peter	Rigby
Lamb in the Laundry	Q	RF	Baglio, Ben M.	Scholastic
Lamb Lessons	O	RF	Baglio, Ben M.	Scholastic
Lamborghinis	U	I	Green, Michael	Capstone Press
Lamp from the Warlock's Tomb, The	S	F	Bellairs, John	Puffin Books
Lampfish of Twill, The	U	F	Lisle, Janet Taylor	Scholastic
Land I Lost, The	P	I	Nhuong, Huynh Quang	HarperTrophy
Land of the Dragons	P	I	Morris, Rod	Pacific Learning
Land of the Great Big "No!"	L	RF	Trussell-Cullen, Alan	Dominie Press
Landry News, The	R	RF	Clements, Andrew	Simon & Schuster
Landslides, Slumps, & Creep	U	I	A First Book	Franklin Watts
Langston Hughes: An Illustrated Edition	X	B	Meltzer, Milton	Millbrook Press
Langston Hughes: Young Black Poet	O	B	Childhood of Famous Americans	Aladdin
Last Chance for Magic	P	F	Chew, Ruth	Scholastic
Last Look	P	RF	Bulla, Clyde Robert	Puffin Books
Last One In Is a Rotten Egg	J	RF	Kessler, Leonard	HarperTrophy
Last Puppy, The	K	F	Asch, Frank	Simon & Schuster
Later, Gator	R	RF	Yep, Laurence	Hyperion
Laughter Is the Best Medicine	P	I	Literacy Tree	Rigby
Laura and Mr. Edwards	M	HF	Wilder, Laura Ingalls	HarperTrophy
Laura and Nellie	M	HF	Wilder, Laura Ingalls	HarperTrophy

Title	Level	Genre	Author/Series	Publisher/Distributor
Laura Ingalls Wilder	O	B	Allen, Thomas B.	Putnam
Laura Ingalls Wilder	K	B	Biography	Benchmark Education
Laura Ingalls Wilder	P	B	Blair, Gwenda & Allen, Thomas	Lerner Publishing Group
Laura Ingalls Wilder: A Biography	R	B	Anderson, William	HarperTrophy
Laura Ingalls Wilder: An Author's Story	N	B	Glasscock, Sarah	Steck-Vaughn
Laura Ingalls Wilder: Author of the Little House Books	O	B	Greene, Carol	Children's Press
Laura Ingalls Wilder: Growing Up in the Little House	P	B	Giff, Patricia Reilly	Puffin Books
Laura Ingalls Wilder, Pioneer Girl	R	B	Stine, Megan	Bantam Doubleday Dell
Laura's Ma	M	HF	Wilder, Laura Ingalls	HarperTrophy
Laura's Pa	M	HF	Wilder, Laura Ingalls	HarperTrophy
Lavender	O	RF	Hesse, Karen	Henry Holt & Co.
Lazy Bones Jones	P	F	Welch, Sheila Kelly	Pacific Learning
Lazy Jackal, The	M	F	Sunshine	Wright Group/McGraw Hill
Lazy Lions, Lucky Lambs	M	RF	Giff, Patricia Reilly	Bantam Doubleday Dell
Leaders of the People	U	B	Real Lives	Troll
Leaders: People Who Make a Difference	R	I	You Are There	Children's Press
Leaping Lizards	M	I	Stadler, Charlotte	Benchmark Education Co.
Leaves	K	I	Pebble Books	Grolier, Capstone
Leaving Home	Z	RF	Keillor, Garrison	The Penguin Group
Leaving Home: 15 Distinguished Authors Explore Personal Journeys	Z	RF	Rochman, H. & McCampbell, D.	HarperTrophy
Left Behind	L	RF	Carrick, Carol	Clarion Books
Leftovers, The: Catch Flies!	N	RF	Howard, Tristan	Scholastic
Leftovers, The: Fast Break	N	RF	Howard, Tristan	Scholastic
Leftovers, The: Get Jammed	N	RF	Howard, Tristan	Scholastic
Leftovers, The: Reach Their Goal	N	RF	Howard, Tristan	Scholastic
Leftovers, The: Strike Out!	N	RF	Howard, Tristan	Scholastic
Legend of the Bluebonnet, The	O	TL	dePaola, Tomie	Scholastic
Legend of the Hummingbird, The	K	TL	Folk Tales	Mondo
Legend of the Red Bird, The	K	TL	Sunshine	Wright Group/McGraw Hill
Legendary Places	N	I	Wildcats	Wright Group/McGraw Hill
Legends	S	TL	Goodman, R., R. Pierce, Betty Jane Wagner	Houghton Mifflin
Lemonade Trick, The	Q	RF	Corbett, Scott	Scholastic
Lend a Hand	K	F	Kratky, Lada	Hampton-Brown
Lentil	M	RF	McCloskey, Robert	Scholastic
Leon's Story	T	B	Tillage, Leon Walter	Farrar, Straus and Giroux
Leonard Bernstein	R	B	Venezia, Mike	Children's Press
Leontyne Price: Opera Superstar	N	B	Williams, Sylvia B.	Children's Press
Leprechauns Don't Play Basketball	M	F	Dadey, D. & Jones, M. T.	Scholastic
Let the Circle Be Unbroken	X	HF	Taylor, Mildred D.	The Penguin Group
Let's Be Enemies	J	RF	Sendak, Maurice	Harper & Row
Let's Build a Playground	O	I	Myers, Edward	Pearson Learning
Let's Get Moving	M	I	Literacy 2000	Rigby
Let's Go, Philadelphia!	M	RF	Giff, Patricia Reilly	Bantam Doubleday Dell
Letter Carriers	L	I	Community Workers	Compass Point Books
Letter from Fish Bay, A	N	B	Cowley, Joy	Pacific Learning
Letter From Phoenix Farm, A	O	B	Yolen, Jane	Richard C. Owen
Letter, the Witch, and the Ring, The	S	F	Bellairs, John	The Penguin Group
Letter to Mrs. Roosevelt, A	R	HF	DeYoung, C. Coco	Delacorte Press
Letters From a Slave Girl: The Story of Harriet Jacobs	X	HF	Lyons, Mary E.	Simon & Schuster
Letters from Camp A Mystery	V	RF	Klise, Kate	Harper Trophy
Letters from Rifka	S	HF	Hesse, Karen	Puffin Books
Letters from the Sea	S	I	Voyages in Time	Wright Group/McGraw Hill
Letters to Julia	W	RF	Holmes, Barbara Ware	HarperTrophy
Letting Swift River Go	M	HF	Yolen, Jane	Little, Brown & Co.
Lewis and Clark	V	B	Cornerstones of Freedom	Children's Press
Lewis and Clark Expedition, The	S	I	We The People	Compass Point Books
Lewis & Clark: Explorers of the American West	S	I	Kroll, Steven	Holiday House

Title	Level	Genre	Author/Series	Publisher/Distributor
Lexington and Concord	V	I	Cornerstones of Freedom	Children's Press
Liar, Liar, Pants on Fire	O	RF	Korman, Gordon	Scholastic
Liberty Bell, The	V	I	Cornerstones of Freedom	Children's Press
Librarians	M	I	Ready, Dee	Capstone Press
Library Card, The	R	RF	Spinelli, Jerry	Scholastic
Library of Congress, The	V	I	Cornerstones of Freedom	Children's Press
Life and Death of Martin Luther King, Jr.,The	Y	B	Haskins, James	Beech Tree
Life and Words of Martin Luther King, Jr., The	W	B	Peck, Ira	Scholastic
Life in the City	J	I	Early Connections	Benchmark Education
Life in the Desert	M	I	Pair-It Books	Steck-Vaughn
Life in the Oceans: Animals, People, Plants	T	I	Baker, Lucy	Scholastic
Life in the Rainforests: Animals, People, Plants	T	I	Baker, Lucy	Scholastic
Life of a Miner	T	I	Life in the Old West	Crabtree
Life on a Plantation	T	I	Historic Communities	Crabtree
Light	J	I	Momentum Literacy Program	Troll
Light at Tern Rock, The	N	RF	Sauer, Julia L.	Scholastic
Light in the Storm, A	T	HF	Hesse, Karen	Scholastic
Lighthouse Mermaid, The	M	F	Karr, Kathleen	Hyperion
Lightning	T	I	Kramer, Stephen	Carolrhoda Books
Lightning	L	I	Pebble Books	Grolier, Capstone
Lightweight Rocket and Other Cases, The	O	RF	Simon, Seymour	Avon
Like Jake and Me	O	RF	Jukes, Mavis	Alfred A. Knopf
Lilacs, Lotuses, and Ladybugs	L	RF	Evangeline Nicholas Collection	Wright Group/McGraw Hill
Lili the Brave	N	RF	Armstrong, Jennifer	Random House
Lily and Miss Liberty	N	HF	Stephens, Carla	Scholastic
Lily's Crossing	S	HF	Giff, Patricia Reilly	Delacourte Press
Limestone Caves	N	I	A First Book	Franklin Watts
Limestone Caves	N	I	Davis, Gary	Children's Press
Lincoln: A Photobiography	V	B	Freedman, Russell	Clarion
Lincoln Memorial, The	V	I	Cornerstones of Freedom	Children's Press
Lincoln-Douglas Debates, The	W	I	Cornerstones of Freedom	Children's Press
Lion and the Mouse, The	M	TL	Aesop's Fables	Dominie
Lion and the Mouse, The	J	TL	Little Books	Sadlier-Oxford
Lion and the Mouse, The	K	TL	Pair-It Books	Steck-Vaughn
Lion and the Mouse, The	J	TL	Sunshine	Wright Group/McGraw Hill
Lion Dancer: Ernie Wan's Chinese New Year	N	B	Waters, K. & Slovenz-Low, M.	Scholastic
Lion in the Night, The	J	F	Momentum Literacy Program	Troll
Lion Tamer's Daughter, The- And Other Stories	Z	F	Dickinson, Peter	Laurel-Leaf Books
Lion, the Witch and the Wardrobe, The	T	F	Lewis, C. S.	HarperTrophy
Lion to Guard Us, A	P	HF	Bulla, Clyde Robert	HarperTrophy
Lionel and Amelia	L	F	Book Shop	Mondo
Lionel and His Friends	K	RF	Krensky, Stephen	Puffin Books
Lionel and Louise	K	RF	Krensky, Stephen	Puffin Books
Lionel at Large	K	RF	Krensky, Stephen	Puffin Books
Lionel In The Fall	K	RF	Krensky, Stephen	Puffin Books
Lionel In The Spring	K	RF	Krensky, Stephen	Puffin Books
Lionel In The Summer	K	RF	Krensky, Stephen	Puffin Books
Lionel In The Winter	K	RF	Krensky, Stephen	Puffin Books
Lions	O	I	Holmes, Kevin J.	Capstone Press
Lions	N	I	Meadows, Graham & Vial, Claire	Dominie Press
Lions	L	I	Pair-It Books	Steck-Vaughn
Lions and Tigers	K	I	PM Animal Facts: Turquoise	Rigby
Lions at Lunchtime	M	F	Osborne, Mary Pope	Random House
Lisa's Diary	L	RF	Pritchett, Jan	Rigby
Listen Children: An Anthology of Black Literature	U	RF	Strickland, Dorothy S.	Bantam Doubleday Dell
Listening in Bed	M	RF	Book Bank	Wright Group/McGraw Hill
Listening to Crickets: A Story about Rachel Carson	R	HF	Ransom, Candice F.	Carolrhoda Books
Little Adventure, A	J	RF	PM Story Books -Silver	Rigby
Little Bear	J	F	Minarik, E.H.	Harper Collins
Little Bear's Friend	J	F	Minarik, E.H.	HarperTrophy

Title	Level	Genre	Author/Series	Publisher/Distributor
Little Bear's Visit	J	F	Minarik, E.H.	HarperTrophy
Little Black, A Pony	J	RF	Farley, Walter	Random House
Little Blue and Little Yellow	J	F	Lionni, Leo	Scholastic
Little Brown Jay, The: A Tale from India	K	TL	Claire, Elizabeth	Mondo
Little Caribou	N	I	Fox-Davies, Sarah	Candlewick Press
Little Cats	P	I	Crabapples	Crabtree
Little Chief	K	F	Hoff, Syd	Harper Collins
Little Clearing in the Woods	Q	HF	Wilkes, Maria D.	HarperTrophy
Little Dinosaur Escapes	J	F	PM Turquoise	Rigby
Little Farm in the Ozarks	R	HF	MacBride, Roger Lea	HarperTrophy
Little Firefighter, The	M	RF	Sunshine	Wright Group/McGraw Hill
Little Fireman	J	RF	Brown, Margaret Wise	Harper Collins
Little Gorilla	J	F	Bornstein, Ruth	Clarion
Little Hawk's New Name	M	HF	Bolognese, Don	Scholastic
Little House Birthday, A	J	HF	Wilder, Laura Ingalls	Harper Collins
Little House by Boston Bay	Q	HF	Wiley, Melissa	HarperTrophy
Little House Farm Days	M	HF	Wilder, Laura Ingalls	HarperTrophy
Little House Friends	M	HF	Wilder, Laura Ingalls	HarperTrophy
Little House in Brookfield	Q	HF	Wilkes, Maria D.	HarperTrophy
Little House in the Big Woods	Q	HF	Wilder, Laura Ingalls	HarperTrophy
Little House in the Highlands	Q	HF	Wiley, Melissa	HarperTrophy
Little House on Rocky Ridge	R	HF	MacBride, Roger Lea	HarperTrophy
Little House on the Prairie	Q	HF	Wilder, Laura Ingalls	HarperTrophy
Little Icicle	O	RF	Szymanski, Lois	Avon Camelot
Little Knight, The	K	F	Reading Unlimited	Celebration Press
Little Leaf's Journey and the Lost Tooth, The	K	F	New Way Ornage	Steck-Vaughn
Little Lefty	M	RF	Christopher, Matt	Little, Brown & Co.
Little, Little Man, The	M	F	Book Bank	Wright Group/McGraw Hill
Little Miss Stoneybrook and Dawn	O	RF	Martin, Ann M.	Scholastic
Little Old Lady Who Danced on the Moon, The	M	RF	Sunshine	Wright Group/McGraw Hill
Little Pear	O	HF	Lattimore, Eleanor F.	Harcourt Brace
Little Pear and His Friends	O	HF	Lattimore, Eleanor F.	Harcourt Brace
Little Penguin's Tale	L	F	Wood, Audrey	Scholastic
Little Polar Bear and the Brave Little Hare	K	F	de Beer, Hans	North-South Books
Little Prairie House, A	J	HF	Wilder, Laura Ingalls	Harper Collins
Little Princess, A	L	RF	All Aboard Reading	Grosset & Dunlap
Little Red Riding Hood	K	TL	Enrichment	Wright Group/McGraw Hill
Little Red Riding Hood	J	TL	PM Tales and Plays Turquoise	Rigby
Little Runner of the Longhouse	K	HF	Baker, Betty	HarperTrophy
Little Sea Pony, The	N	F	Cresswell, Helen	HarperTrophy
Little Shopping, A	M	RF	Rylant, Cynthia	Aladdin
Little Soup's Birthday	K	RF	Peck, Robert Newton	Bantam Doubleday Dell
Little Spider, The	K	F	Literacy 2000	Rigby
Little Swan	M	RF	Geras, Adele	Random House
Little Tin Soldier, The	M	TL	Tales from Hans Andersen	Wright Group/McGraw Hill
Little Town at the Crossroads	Q	HF	Wilkes, Maria D.	HarperTrophy
Little Town in the Ozarks	R	HF	MacBride, Roger Lea	HarperTrophy
Little Town on the Prairie	Q	HF	Wilder, Laura Ingalls	HarperTrophy
Little Vampire and the Midnight Bear	L	F	Kwitz, M. D.	Puffin Books
Little Walrus Rising	K	F	Young, Carol	Scholastic
Little Whale, The	M	F	Sunshine	Wright Group/McGraw Hill
Little Witch Goes to School	K	F	Hautzig, Deborah	Random House
Little Witch's Big Night	K	F	Hautzig, Deborah	Random House
Little Women	M	HF	Bullseye	Random House
Littles and the Great Halloween Scare, The	M	F	Peterson, John	Scholastic
Littles and the Lost Children, The	M	F	Peterson, John	Scholastic
Littles and the Terrible Tiny Kid, The	M	F	Peterson, John	Scholastic
Littles and the Trash Tinies, The	M	F	Peterson, John	Scholastic
Littles Give a Party, The	M	F	Peterson, John	Scholastic
Littles Go Exploring, The	M	F	Peterson, John	Scholastic

Title	Level	Genre	Author/Series	Publisher/Distributor
Littles Go to School, The	M	F	Peterson, John	Scholastic
Littles Have a Wedding, The	M	F	Peterson, John	Scholastic
Littles Take a Trip, The	M	F	Peterson, John	Scholastic
Littles, The	M	F	Peterson, John	Scholastic
Littles to the Rescue, The	M	F	Peterson, John	Scholastic
Living in Space	O	I	Nayer, Judy	Pearson Learning
Living in the Sky	K	RF	Sunshine	Wright Group/McGraw Hill
Living Rain Forest, The	S	I	Bishop, Nic	Pacific Learning
Living Up The Street	Y	RF	Soto, Gary	Bantam Doubleday Dell
Lizard Music	T	F	Pinkwater, D. Manus	Bantam Doubleday Dell
Lizard's Grandmother	J	F	Sunshine	Wright Group/McGraw Hill
Lizards	L	I	Wonder World	Wright Group/McGraw Hill
Lizards and Salamanders	M	I	Reading Unlimited	Celebration Press
Lizzie's Lizard	L	I	Storyteller Nonfiction	Wright Group/McGraw Hill
Llama in the Family, A	O	RF	Hurwitz, Johanna	Scholastic
Llama Pajamas	N	RF	Clymer, Susan	Scholastic
Local News	W	RF	Soto, Gary	Scholastic
Locked in the Library!	M	F	Brown, Marc	Little, Brown & Co.
Log Cabin in the Woods	R	HF	Henry, Joanne Landers	Scholastic
Lois Lowry	T	B	Markham, Lois	Learning Works, Inc.
Lon Po Po: A Red-Riding Hood Story from China	S	TL	Young, Ed	Scholastic
Lonely Dragon, The	J	F	Momentum Literacy Program	Troll
Lonely Giant, The	K	F	Literacy 2000	Rigby
Long Ago and Far Away	T	I	Wildcats	Wright Group/McGraw Hill
Long Grass of Tumbledown Road	M	F	Read Alongs	Rigby
Long, Long Ago	M	I	Literacy 2000	Rigby
Long Shot for Paul	M	RF	Christopher, Matt	Little, Brown & Co.
Long Way from Chicago, A	V	HF	Peck, Richard	Puffin Books
Long Way to a New Land, A	L	HF	Sandin, Joan	HarperTrophy
Long Way to Go, A	R	I	O'Neal, Zibby	The Penguin Group
Long Way Westward, The	L	HF	Sandin, Joan	HarperTrophy
Long Winter, The	Q	HF	Ingalls Wilder, Laura	HarperTrophy
Long-Lost Friends, The	M	RF	Schultz, Irene	Wright Group/McGraw Hill
Look at Dogs, A	M	I	Pair-It Books	Steck-Vaughn
Look at Minerals, A: From Galena to Gold	S	I	A First Book	Franklin Watts
Look at Rocks, A: From Coal to Kimerlite	S	I	A First Book	Franklin Watts
Look at Snakes, A	M	I	Pair-It Books	Steck-Vaughn
Look at Spiders, A	M	I	Pair-It-Books	Steck-Vaughn
Look at the Moon	N	I	Book Shop	Mondo
Look Inside	J	I	Storyteller Nonfiction	Wright Group/McGraw Hill
Look Out For Your Tail	J	F	Literacy 2000	Rigby
Look Out, Washington D.C.!	O	RF	Giff, Patricia Reilly	Bantam Doubleday Dell
Look What Came from China	O	I	Harvey, Miles	Franklin Watts
Look What Came from Egypt	O	I	Harvey, Miles	Franklin Watts
Look What Came from France	O	I	Harvey, Miles	Franklin Watts
Look What Came from Italy	O	I	Harvey, Miles	Franklin Watts
Look What Came from Mexico	O	I	Harvey, Miles	Franklin Watts
Look What Came from Russia	O	I	Harvey, Miles	Franklin Watts
Look What Came from the United States	O	I	Davis, Kevin	Franklin Watts
Look What I Made!	M	I	Literacy 2000	Rigby
Look Who's Playing First Base	M	RF	Christopher, Matt	Little, Brown & Co.
Looking at Animals in Cold Places	O	I	Butterfield, Moira	Steck-Vaughn
Looking at Animals in Hot Places	O	I	Butterfield, Moira	Steck-Vaughn
Looking at Animals in the Ocean	O	I	Butterfield, Moira	Steck-Vaughn
Looking at Insects	L	I	Discovery World	Rigby
Looking Back, A Book of Memories	X	B	Lowry, Lois	Delacorte Press
Looking for Dad	M	RF	SupaDoopers	Sundance
Looking For Patterns	J	I	Early Connections	Benchmark Education
Looking for Shapes	K	I	Early Connections	Benchmark Education

Title	Level	Genre	Author/Series	Publisher/Distributor
Looking for the Queen	O	I	Frederick, Shirley	Hampton-Brown
Looking into Space	L	I	Early Connections	Benchmark Education
Loose Bolts	O	SF	Neufeld, David	Wright Group/McGraw Hill
Loose Laces	L	RF	Reading Unlimited	Celebration Press
Lord of the Rings, The	Z	F	Tolkien, J. R. R.	Houghton Mifflin
Lost!	L	F	Mitchell, Julie	Rigby
Lost and Found Game, The	M	RF	Nayer, Judy	Pearson Learning
Lost at the White House: A 1909 Easter Story	L	HF	Griest, Lisa	Carolrhoda Books
Lost Children, The	M	TL	Goble, Paul	Aladdin
Lost Continent and Other Cases, The	O	RF	Simon, Seymour	Avon
Lost Flower Children, The	Q	RF	Lisle, Janet Taylor	Philomel Books
Lost Garden, The	W	B	Yep, Laurence	Beech Tree Books
Lost Hikers and Other Cases, The	O	RF	Simon, Seymour	Avon
Lost in Cyberspace	Y	SF	Peck, Richard	Puffin Books
Lost in Space	M	SF	Pacific Literacy	Pacific Learning
Lost in the Forest	K	RF	Robinson, Fay	Wright Group/McGraw Hill
Lost on a Mountain in Maine	R	RF	Fendler, Donn	Peter Smith Publications
Lost Sandals, The	N	RF	Bennett, Jean	Pacific Learning
Lost Star: The Story of Amelia Earhart	T	B	Lauber, Patricia	Language for Learning Assoc.
Lost Tooth, The	J	I	New Way Orange	Steck-Vaughn
Lotus Seed, The	P	HF	Garland, Sherry	Harcourt Brace
Lou Gehrig: One of Baseball's Greatest	O	B	Childhood of Famous Americans	Aladdin
Louis Armstrong	Z	B	Brown, Sandford	Franklin Watts
Louis Braille: Boy Who Invented Books for the Blind	N	B	Davidson, Margaret	Scholastic
Louis Pasteur	N	B	Biography	Benchmark Education
Louis Riell	W	B	Neering, Rosemary	Fitzhenry & Whiteside
Louisa May Alcott: Young Novelist	O	B	Childhood of Famous Americans	Aladdin
Louisiana Purchase, The	V	I	Cornerstones of Freedom	Children's Press
Love, from the Fifth-Grade Celebrity	Q	RF	Giff, Patricia Reilly	Bantam Doubleday Dell
Love from Your Friend, Hannah	Y	HF	Skolsky, Mindy Warshaw	Harper Trophy
Love Me, Love My Broccoli	S	RF	Peters, Julie Anne	Avon Camelot
Love You, Soldier	R	HF	Hest, Amy	Puffin Books
Lucky Baseball Bat, The	M	RF	Christopher, Matt	Little, Brown & Co.
Lucky Feather, The	L	F	Literacy 2000	Rigby
Lucky Last Luke	M	RF	Clark, Margaret	Sundance
Lucky Stars	L	RF	Adler, David A.	Random House
Lucky Stone, The	P	RF	Clifton, Lucille	Bantam Doubleday Dell
Lucy Meets a Dragon	L	F	Literacy 2000	Rigby
Luis Rodriguez	S	B	Schwartz, Michael	Steck-Vaughn
Luis W. Alvarez	R	B	Hispanic Stories	Steck-Vaughn
Luke's Bully	N	RF	Winthrop, Elizabeth	Puffin Books
Luke's Go-cart	L	RF	PM Gold	Rigby
Lulu Goes to Witch School	K	F	O'Connor, Jane	HarperTrophy
Lunch at the Joy House Café	K	RF	Blackaby, Susan	Hampton-Brown
Lunchbox Mystery, The	N	RF	Lohans, Alison	Scholastic
Luther Burbank	O	B	Faber, Doris	Garrard Publishing Co.
Lyddie	U	HF	Paterson, Katherine	The Penguin Group
M.C. Higgins the Great	X	RF	Hamilton, Virginia	Macmillan
M & M and The Bad News Babies	K	RF	Ross, Pat	The Penguin Group
M & M and the Big Bag	K	RF	Ross, Pat	The Penguin Group
M & M and the Halloween Monster	K	RF	Ross, Pat	The Penguin Group.
M & M and the Haunted House Game	K	RF	Ross, Pat	The Penguin Group
M & M and the Mummy Mess	K	RF	Ross, Pat	The Penguin Group
M & M and the Santa Secrets	K	RF	Ross, Pat	The Penguin Group
M & M and the Super Child Afternoon	K	RF	Ross, Pat	The Penguin Group
Ma and Pa Dracula	O	F	Martin, Ann M.	Scholastic
Machines in the Home	N	I	Morrison, Rob	Rigby
Mad Scientist, The	M	F	Schultz, Irene	Wright Group/McGraw Hill
Mad Scientist's Secret, The	P	SF	Miller, Marvin	Scholastic
Madeline	K	F	Bemelmans, Ludwig	Scholastic

Title	Level	Genre	Author/Series	Publisher/Distributor
Madeline's Rescue	K	F	Bemelmans, Ludwig	Scholastic
Magic All Around	L	F	Literacy 2000	Rigby
Magic Box, The	K	F	Brenner, Barbara	Bantam Doubleday Dell
Magic Finger, The	N	F	Dahl, Roald	The Penguin Group
Magic Fish, The	L	TL	Littledale, Freya	Scholastic
Magic Money	L	RF	Adler, David A.	Random House
Magic Moscow, The	P	RF	Pinkwater, Daniel	Aladdin
Magic Porridge Pot, The	L	TL	Sunshine	Wright Group/McGraw Hill
Magic Ride, The	M	F	Book Bank	Wright Group/McGraw Hill
Magic School Bus	P	F	Cole, Joanna & Degen, Bruce	Scholastic
Magic School Bus and the Electric Field Trip, The	P	F	Cole, Joanna & Degen, Bruce	Scholastic
Magic School Bus Answers Questions	P	F	Cole, Joanna & Degen, Bruce	Scholastic
Magic School Bus At the Waterworks	P	F	Cole, Joanna & Degen, Bruce	Scholastic
Magic School Bus Blows Its Top	P	F	Cole, Joanna & Degen, Bruce	Scholastic
Magic School Bus Briefcase	P	F	Cole, Joanna & Degen, Bruce	Scholastic
Magic School Bus Butterfly and the Bog Beast	P	F	Cole, Joanna & Degen, Bruce	Scholastic
Magic School Bus Explores the Senses	P	F	Cole, Joanna & Degen, Bruce	Scholastic
Magic School Bus Explores the World of Animals	P	F	Cole, Joanna & Degen, Bruce	Scholastic
Magic School Bus Gets a Bright Idea	P	F	Cole, Joanna & Degen, Bruce	Scholastic
Magic School Bus Gets All Dried Up	P	F	Cole, Joanna & Degen, Bruce	Scholastic
Magic School Bus Gets Ants in Its Pants	P	F	Cole, Joanna & Degen, Bruce	Scholastic
Magic School Bus Gets Baked in a Cake	P	F	Cole, Joanna & Degen, Bruce	Scholastic
Magic School Bus Gets Cold Feet	P	F	Cole, Joanna & Degen, Bruce	Scholastic
Magic School Bus Gets Eaten	P	F	Cole, Joanna & Degen, Bruce	Scholastic
Magic School Bus Gets Programmed	P	F	Cole, Joanna & Degen, Bruce	Scholastic
Magic School Bus Goes Upstream	P	F	Cole, Joanna & Degen, Bruce	Scholastic
Magic School Bus Going Batty	P	F	Cole, Joanna & Degen, Bruce	Scholastic
Magic School Bus Hops Home	P	F	Cole, Joanna & Degen, Bruce	Scholastic
Magic School Bus in a Pickle	P	F	Cole, Joanna & Degen, Bruce	Scholastic
Magic School Bus in the Arctic	P	F	Cole, Joanna & Degen, Bruce	Scholastic
Magic School Bus in the Haunted Museum	P	F	Cole, Joanna & Degen, Bruce	Scholastic
Magic School Bus in the Rain Forest	P	F	Cole, Joanna & Degen, Bruce	Scholastic
Magic School Bus Inside a Beehive	P	F	Cole, Joanna & Degen, Bruce	Scholastic
Magic School Bus Inside a Hurricane	P	F	Cole, Joanna & Degen, Bruce	Scholastic
Magic School Bus Inside Ralphie	P	F	Cole, Joanna & Degen, Bruce	Scholastic
Magic School Bus Inside the Earth	P	F	Cole, Joanna & Degen, Bruce	Scholastic
Magic School Bus Inside the Human Body	P	F	Cole, Joanna & Degen, Bruce	Scholastic
Magic School Bus Kicks Up a Storm	P	F	Cole, Joanna & Degen, Bruce	Scholastic
Magic School Bus Liz Sorts It Out	P	F	Cole, Joanna & Degen, Bruce	Scholastic
Magic School Bus Lost in the Solar System	P	F	Cole, Joanna & Degen, Bruce	Scholastic
Magic School Bus Makes a Rainbow	P	F	Cole, Joanna & Degen, Bruce	Scholastic
Magic School Bus Meets the Rot Squad	P	TL	Cole, Joanna & Degen, Bruce	Scholastic
Magic School Bus on the Ocean Floor	P	F	Cole, Joanna & Degen, Bruce	Scholastic
Magic School Bus Out of This World	P	F	Cole, Joanna & Degen, Bruce	Scholastic
Magic School Bus Plants Seeds	P	F	Cole, Joanna & Degen, Bruce	Scholastic
Magic School Bus Plays Ball	P	F	Cole, Joanna & Degen, Bruce	Scholastic
Magic School Bus Science Explorations	P	F	Cole, Joanna & Degen, Bruce	Scholastic
Magic School Bus Search for the Missing Bones	P	F	Cole, Joanna & Degen, Bruce	Scholastic
Magic School Bus Sees Stars	P	F	Cole, Joanna & Degen, Bruce	Scholastic
Magic School Bus Shows and Tells	P	F	Cole, Joanna & Degen, Bruce	Scholastic
Magic School Bus Space Explorers	P	F	Cole, Joanna & Degen, Bruce	Scholastic
Magic School Bus Spins a Web	P	F	Cole, Joanna & Degen, Bruce	Scholastic
Magic School Bus Takes a Dive	P	F	Cole, Joanna & Degen, Bruce	Scholastic
Magic School Bus Taking Flight	P	F	Cole, Joanna & Degen, Bruce	Scholastic
Magic School Bus The Truth About Bats	P	F	Cole, Joanna & Degen, Bruce	Scholastic
Magic School Bus The Wild Whale Watch	P	F	Cole, Joanna & Degen, Bruce	Scholastic
Magic School Bus Twister Trouble	P	F	Cole, Joanna & Degen, Bruce	Scholastic
Magic School Bus Ups and Downs	P	F	Cole, Joanna & Degen, Bruce	Scholastic
Magic School Bus Visits the Planets	P	F	Cole, Joanna & Degen, Bruce	Scholastic
Magic School Bus Wet All Over	P	F	Cole, Joanna & Degen, Bruce	Scholastic

Title	Level	Genre	Author/Series	Publisher/Distributor
Magic Squad and the Dog of Great Potential, The	P	RF	Quattlebaum, Mary	Bantam Doubleday Dell
Magic Store, The	J	RF	Sunshine	Wright Group/McGraw Hill
Magical Adventures of Pretty Pearl, The	W	F	Hamilton, Virginia	HarperTrophy
Magician's Nephew, The	T	F	Lewis, C. S.	HarperTrophy
Magnet Book, The	T	I	Levine, Shar & Johnstone, Leslie	Sterling
Mail Carriers	M	I	Ready, Dee	Capstone Press
Mailman Mario & His Boris-Busters	L	RF	Parker, John	Dominie Press
Maisie's Race	L	RF	Mawter, Jeni	Wright Group/McGraw Hill
Make a Bottle Orchestra	J	I	Sunshine	Wright Group/McGraw Hill
Make a Cloud, Measure the Wind	M	I	Reimer, Luther	Wright Group/McGraw Hill
Make a Guitar	J	I	Sunshine	Wright Group/McGraw Hill
Make a Shake and a Bakeless Cake	L	I	Cole, Sally	Wright Group/McGraw Hill
Make A Wish, Molly	O	RF	Cohen, Barbara	Bantam Doubleday Dell
Make Like a Tree and Leave	U	RF	Danziger, Paula	PaperStar
Make Masks for a Play	J	I	Sunshine	Wright Group/McGraw Hill
Make Prints and Patterns	K	I	Sunshine	Wright Group/McGraw Hill
Make Room For Elisa	N	RF	Hurwitz, Johanna	The Penguin Group
Make Way For Ducklings	L	RF	McCloskey, Robert	Puffin Books
Make Way for Sam Houston	X	B	Fritz, Jean	Putnam & Grosset
Making Friends	J	RF	Foundations	Wright Group/McGraw Hill
Making Friends on Beacon Street	M	RF	Literacy 2000	Rigby
Making Lily Laugh!	M	RF	Dreyer, Ellen	Pearson Learning
Making Pop-ups	O	I	Brian, Janeen	Mondo
Mall Mystery, The	M	F	Schultz, Irene	Wright Group/McGraw Hill
Mama, Let's Dance	W	RF	Hermes, Patricia	Scholastic
Mammals	N	I	Simply Science	Compass Point Books
Mammals of the Sea	Q	I	Weldon Owen	Wright Group/McGraw Hill
Man From The Sky	S	RF	Avi	BeechTree
Man Out at First	M	RF	Christopher, Matt	Little Brown & Co.
Man Who Kept His Heart in a Bucket, The	S	TL	Levitin, Sonia	The Penguin Group
Man Who Paints Nature, The	O	B	Locker, Thomas	Richard C. Owen
Man Who Tricked a Ghost, The	N	TL	Yep, Laurence	Troll Medallion
Man Who Was Poe, The	T	B	Avi	Avon
Manatee, The	V	I	Silverstein, A. and Nunn, L.	The Millbrook Press
Manatee Winter	K	RF	Zoehfeld, Kathleen Weidnetz	Scholastic
Manatees and Dugongs	M	I	Cole, Sally	Wright Group/McGraw Hill
Maniac Magee	V	RF	Spinelli, Jerry	Scholastic
Manly Ferry Pigeon, The	K	RF	Sunshine	Wright Group/McGraw Hill
Mansion in the Mist, The	S	F	Bellairs, John	Puffin Books
Manual of House Monsters, A	O	F	Marijanovic, Stanislav	Mondo
Many Happy Returns: A Review of Recycling	R	I	Literacy 2000	Rigby
Many Waters	V	F	L'Engle, Madeleine	Bantam Doubleday Dell
Map Mysteries	M	I	Gard, Stephen	Rigby
Maps and Codes	P	I	Wildcats	Wright Group/McGraw Hill
Maps and Our World	Q	I	Weldon Owen	Wright Group/McGraw Hill
Marcella	L	RF	Literacy 2000	Rigby
Marching to Freedom: The Story of Martin Luther King, Jr	P	B	Milton, Joyce	Bantam Doubleday Dell
Mare for Young Wolf, A	L	HF	Shefelman, Janice	Random House
Margaret Bourke-White	O	B	Welch, Catherine	Carolrhoda Books
Margaret Bourke-White: A Photographer's Life	P	B	Keller, Emily	Lerner Publications
Margaret Wise Brown	O	B	Greene, Carol	Children's Press
Maria: A Christmas Story	R	RF	Taylor, Theodore	Avon Camelot
Maria Tallchief	R	B	Native American Stories	Steck-Vaughn
Marian Anderson: Singer	V	B	American Women of Achievement	Chelsea House
Marie Curie	O	B	Early Biographies	Compass Point Books
Marie: Summer in the Country	Q	HF	Girlhood Journeys	Aladdin
Mariel of Redwall	Z	F	Jacques, Brian	Avon Books
Marigold and Grandma On The Town	J	F	Calmenson, Stephanie	HarperTrophy
Mario Mixwell	M	B	Reimer, Luther	Wright Group/McGraw Hill

Title	Level	Genre	Author/Series	Publisher/Distributor
Mario's Mayan Journey	P	F	Book Shop	Mondo
Mark Twain	W	B	Cox, Clinton	Scholastic
Mark Twain: Young Writer	O	B	Childhood of Famous Americans	Aladdin
Market Day for Mrs. Wordy	K	RF	Sunshine	Wright Group/McGraw Hill
Marlfox: A Novel of Redwall	Z	F	Jacques, Brian	Ace Books
Marrying Malcolm Murgatroyd	T	RF	Farrell, Mame	Sunburst
Martha Washington: America's First First Lady	O	B	Childhood of Famous Americans	Aladdin
Martial Arts	R	I	Malane, Donna	Pacific Learning
Martians Don't Take Temperatures	M	F	Dadey, D. & Jones, M. T.	Scholastic
Martin and the Teacher's Pets	K	RF	Chardiet, B. & Maccarone, G.	Scholastic
Martin and the Tooth Fairy	K	RF	Chardiet, B. & Maccarone, G.	Scholastic
Martin Luther King	T	B	Bray, Rosemary L.	William Morrow
Martin Luther King Day	R	I	Lowery, Linda	Scholastic
Martin Luther King, Jr.	L	B	Pebble Books	Grolier, Capstone
Martin Luther King, Jr., A Man Who Changed Things	O	B	Greene, Carol	Children's Press
Martin Luther King, Jr. and the March Toward Freedom	R	B	Hakim, Rita	The Millbrook Press
Martin Luther King, Jr.: Young Man with a Dream	O	B	Childhood of Famous Americans	Aladdin
Martin's Mice	P	F	King-Smith, Dick	Knopf
Martin's Mighty Hit	M	RF	Windmill Books	Rigby
Marvelous Treasure, The	M	RF	Sunshine	Wright Group/McGraw Hill
Marvin and the Mean Words	M	RF	Kline, Suzy	PaperStar
Marvin Redpost: A Flying Birthday Cake?	M	RF	Sachar, Louis	Random House
Marvin Redpost: Alone in His Teacher's House	M	RF	Sachar, Louis	Random House
Marvin Redpost (Class President)	M	RF	Sachar, Louis	Random House
Marvin Redpost: Is He a Girl?	M	RF	Sachar, Louis	Random House
Marvin Redpost: Kidnapped at Birth?	M	RF	Sachar, Louis	Random House
Marvin Redpost, Super Fast, Out of Control!	M	RF	Sachar, Louis	Random House
Marvin Redpost: Why Pick on Me?	M	RF	Sachar, Louis	Random House
Mary by Myself	Q	F	Smith, Jane Denitz	HarperTrophy
Mary Marony and the Chocolate Surprise	M	RF	Kline, Suzy	Bantam Doubleday Dell
Mary Marony and the Snake	M	RF	Kline, Suzy	Bantam Doubleday Dell
Mary Marony Hides Out	M	RF	Kline, Suzy	Bantam Doubleday Dell
Mary Marony, Mummy Girl	M	RF	Kline, Suzy	Bantam Doubleday Dell
Mary McLeod Bethune	U	B	Cornerstones of Freedom	Children's Press
Mary McLeod Bethune	O	B	Greenfield, Eloise	HarperTrophy
Mary McLeod Bethune-Voice of Black Hope	S	B	Meltzer. Milton	Puffin Books
Mary on Horseback	Q	RF	Wells, Rosemary	Puffin Books
Mary Todd Lincoln: Girl of the Bluegrass	O	B	Childhood of Famous Americans	Aladdin
Masks	M	I	Literacy 2000	Rigby
Master Puppeteer, The	X	HF	Paterson, Katherine	Harper Collins
Matchbox, The	S	HF	Literacy 2000	Rigby
Matchlock Gun, The	P	HF	Edmonds, Walter D.	Putnam & Grosset
Materials and Their Uses	L	I	Discovery World	Rigby
Math Wiz, The	N	RF	Duffey, Betsy	The Penguin Group
Mathew Brady: Civil War Photographer	T	B	A First Book	Franklin Watts
Matilda	S	F	Dahl, Roald	The Penguin Group
Matter of Conscience, A: The Trial of Anne Hutchinson	U	I	Nichols, Joan Kane	Steck-Vaughn
Matthew and Tilly	L	RF	Jones, Rebecca C.	The Penguin Group
Matthew Henson	L	B	Biography	Benchmark Education
Matthew Henson: Arctic Explorer	O	B	Podojil, Catherine	Wright Group/McGraw Hill
Matthew Likes to Read	J	RF	Pacific Literacy	Pacific Learning
Matthew's Tantrum	J	RF	Literacy 2000	Rigby
Mattimeo: A Tale from Redwall	Z	F	Jacques, Brian	Avon
Maura's Angel	X	F	Banks, Lynne Reid	Avon
Max	J	RF	Isadora, Rachel	Macmillan
Max and Me and the Time Machine	T	SF	Greer, Gery and Ruddick, Bob	Harper Trophy
Max Malone and the Great Cereal Rip-off	N	RF	Herman, Charlotte	Henry Holt & Co.
Max Malone Makes a Million	N	RF	Herman, Charlotte	Henry Holt & Co.

Title	Level	Genre	Author/Series	Publisher/Distributor
Max Malone, Superstar	N	RF	Herman, Charlotte	Scholastic
Max the Man Mountain	Q	RF	McFarlane, Peter	Harper Collins
Maxie, Rosie, and Earl-Partners in Grime	O	RF	Park, Barbara	Random House
May Chinn: The Best Medicine	U	B	Butts, Ellen & Schwartz, Joyce	W. H. Freeman and Co.
Maya Angelou: Greeting the Morning	W	B	King, Sarah E.	The Millbrook Press
Maya Angelou: Journey of the Heart	X	B	Pettit, Jayne	Puffin Books
Maya, The	N	I	A New True Book	Children's Press
Maya, The	S	I	Journey Into Civilization	Chelsea House
Maze, The	V	RF	Hobbs, Will	Morrow Junior Books
McBroom's Wonderful One-Acre Farm	O	RF	Fleischman, Sid	Beech Tree Books
Me and My Little Brain	T	RF	Fitzgerald, John D.	Dell
Me, Mop, and the Moondance Kid	S	RF	Myers, Walter Dean	Bantam Doubleday Dell
Me Too	K	RF	Mayer, Mercer	Donovan
Meanest Thing to Say, The	K	RF	Cosby, Bill	Scholastic
Measure Up!	K	I	Early Connections	Benchmark Education
Measuring the Weather	R	I	Gaynor, Bill	Pacific Learning
Measuring Tools	M	I	Daronco, Mickey & Presti, Lori	Benchmark Education
Meat Eaters, Plant Eaters	K	I	Planet Earth	Rigby
Medal for Molly, A	N	RF	PM Emerald	Rigby
Medal for Nickie, A	M	RF	Sunshine	Wright Group/McGraw Hill
Medieval Feast, A	Q	I	Aliki	Harper Collins
Medieval Town	Q	I	Worldwise	Grolier
Meerkats	O	I	Weaver, Robyn	Capstone Press
Meet Abraham Lincoln	O	B	Cary, Barbara	Step-Up Books
Meet Addy	Q	HF	The American Girls Collection	Pleasant Company
Meet Benjamin Franklin	O	B	Scarf, Maggi	Step-Up Books
Meet Calliope Day	R	F	Haddad, Charles	Random House
Meet Felicity	Q	HF	The American Girls Collection	Pleasant Company
Meet George Washington	O	B	Heilbroner, Joan	Random House
Meet Hillary Rodham Clinton	Q	B	Spain, Valerie	Random House
Meet John F. Kennedy	Q	B	White, Nancy Bean	Random House
Meet Josefina	Q	HF	The American Girls Collection	Pleasant Company
Meet Kirsten	Q	HF	The American Girls Collection	Pleasant Company
Meet M & M	K	RF	Ross, Pat	The Penguin Group
Meet Martin Luther King, Jr.	R	B	de Kay, James T.	Random House
Meet Molly	Q	HF	The American Girls Collection	Pleasant Company
Meet Samantha	Q	HF	The American Girls Collection	Pleasant Company
Meet the Austins	W	RF	L'Engle, Madeleine	Laurel-Leaf Books
Meet the Lincoln Lions Band	L	RF	Giff, Patricia Reilly	Bantam Doubleday Dell
Meet the Molesons	L	F	Bos, Burny	North-South Books
Meet the Octopus	K	I	Book Shop	Mondo
Meet the Villarreals	M	B	Kratky, Lada Josefa	Hampton-Brown
Meet Thomas Jefferson	O	B	Barrett, Marvin	Step-Up Books
Meg and Mog	J	F	Nicoll, Helen	Viking
Meg Mackintosh and The Case of the Curious Whale Watch	O	RF	Landon, Lucinda	Secret Passage Press
Meg Mackintosh and The Case of the Missing Babe Ruth Baseball	O	RF	Landon, Lucinda	Secret Passage Press
Meg Mackintosh and The Mystery at Camp Creepy	O	RF	Landon, Lucinda	Secret Passage Press
Meg Mackintosh and The Mystery at the Medieval Castle	O	RF	Landon, Lucinda	Secret Passage Press
Meg Mackintosh and The Mystery at the Soccer Match	O	RF	Landon, Lucinda	Secret Passage Press
Meg Mackintosh and The Mystery in the Locked Library	O	RF	Landon, Lucinda	Secret Passage Press
Meg's Dearest Wish	Q	HF	The Little Women Journals	Avon
Megan in Ancient Greece	Q	HF	Korman, Susan	Magic Attic
Megan's Balancing Act	Q	RF	Korman, Susan	Magic Attic
Megan's Island	R	RF	Roberts, Willo Davis	Aladdin
Mei Fuh: Memories From China	P	B	Schaeffer, Edith	Houghton Mifflin

Title	Level	Genre	Author/Series	Publisher/Distributor
Melting Snow Sculptures and Other Cases, The	O	RF	Simon, Seymour	Avon
Memorial Day	K	I	Frost, Helen	Capstone Press
Memories of Anne Frank	X	B	Gold, Alison Leslie	Scholastic
Mercury	N	I	A True Book	Children's Press
Merlin and the Dragons	U	TL	Yolen, Jane	The Penguin Group
Merlin: The Young Merlin Trilogy	V	F	Yolen, Jane	Scholastic
Mermaid Island	L	F	Frith, Margaret	Grosset & Dunlap
Mermaids Don't Run Track	M	F	Dadey, D. & Jones, M. T.	Scholastic
Message, The	R	F	Applegate, K.A.	Scholastic
Messy Bessey's Closet	K	RF	Rookie Readers	Children's Press
Messy Bessey's School Desk	J	RF	Rookie Readers	Children's Press
Meteorite!: The Last Days of the Dinosaurs	W	I	Norris, Richard	Steck-Vaughn
Meteors: The Truth Behind Shooting Stars	T	I	Aronson, Billy	Franklin Watts
Mexico	O	I	Dahl, Michael	Capstone Press
Mice	O	I	Holmes, Kevin J.	Capstone Press
Mice	J	I	PM Animal Facts: Orange	Rigby
Michael Jordan	Q	B	Lovitt, Chip	Scholastic
Michigan	Q	I	One nation	Capstone Press
Middle Ages, The	R	I	Journey Through History	Barron's Educational Series
Middle Moffat, The	T	RF	Estes, Eleanor	Language for Learning Assoc.
Midnight Fox, The	R	RF	Byars, Betsy	Scholastic
Midnight Horse, The	V	F	Fleischman, Sid	Bantam Doubleday Dell
Midnight Magic	U	F	Avi	Scholastic
Midnight on the Moon	M	F	Osborne, Mary Pope	Random House
Midwife's Apprentice, The	X	HF	Cushman, Karen	HarperTrophy
Mieko and the Fifth Treasure	O	HF	Coerr, Eleanor	Bantam Doubleday Dell
Mighty Mammals	Q	I	Weldon Owen	Wright Group/McGraw Hill
Mighty, The	V	RF	Philbrick, Rodman	Scholastic
Mike Swan, Sink or Swim	J	RF	Heiligman, Deborah	Bantam Doubleday Dell
Mile High, A	K	F	Book Bank	Wright Group/McGraw Hill
Milkshake Man, The	L	F	Cole, Sally	Wright Group/McGraw Hill
Miller Who Tried to Please Everyone, The	Q	TL	Aesop's Fables	Dominie
Milo's Great Invention	M	RF	Pair-It Books	Steck-Vaughn
Milton Hershey: Chocolate King Town Builder	P	B	Simon, Charnan	Children's Press
Milton the Early Riser	J	F	Kraus, Robert	Aladdin
Min-Yo and the Moon Dragon	N	TL	Hillman, Elizabeth	Harcourt Brace
Mina's Spring of Colors	P	RF	Gilmore, Rachna	Fitzhenry & Whiteside
Minerva's Dream	M	F	Pair-It Books	Steck-Vaughn
Mini Mammals	R	I	Weldon Owen	Wright Group/McGraw Hill
Minnie and Moo Go to Paris	J	F	Cazet, Denys	DK Publishing, Inc.
Miracle at the Plate	M	RF	Christopher, Matt	Little, Brown & Co.
Miracle Worker, The	Z	B	Gibson, William	Bantam Doubleday Dell
Miracles on Maple Hill	R	RF	Sorensen, Virginia	Scholastic
Miranda and the Movies	U	HF	Kendall, Jane	Harcourt Brace
Mirandy and Brother Wind	R	F	McKissack, Patricia	Alfred A. Knopf
Mischief	M	RF	Pacific Literacy	Pacific Learning
Misfortune Cookie, The	N	F	The Zack Files	Grosset & Dunlap
Misha Disappears	K	RF	Literacy 2000	Rigby
Mishmash	N	RF	Cone, Molly	Pocket Books
Miss Geneva's Lantern	P	RF	Book Shop	Mondo
Miss McKenzie Had a Farm	J	F	Pair-It Books	Steck-Vaughn
Miss Mouse Gets Married	K	TL	Folk Tales	Wright Group/McGraw Hill
Miss Nelson Has a Field Day	L	RF	Allard, Harry	Scholastic
Miss Nelson is Missing	L	RF	Allard, Harry	Houghton Mifflin
Miss Rumphius	M	RF	Cooney, Barbara	The Penguin Group
Missing Fossil Mystery, The	L	RF	Herman, Emily	Hyperion
Missing May	W	RF	Rylant, Cynthia	Bantam Doubleday Dell
Missing Osprey Nest, The	N	RF	Herman, Emily	Wright Group/McGraw Hill
Missing Pet, The	K	RF	Pair-It Books	Steck-Vaughn

Title	Level	Genre	Author/Series	Publisher/Distributor
Missing Tooth, The	J	RF	Cole, Joanna	Random House
Missing Will, The	M	RF	Schultz, Irene	Wright Group/McGraw Hill
Mississippi Bridge	S	HF	Taylor, Mildred	Bantam Doubleday Dell
Misty of Chincoteague	R	RF	Henry, Marguerite	Aladdin
Misty's Twilight	R	RF	Henry, Marguerite	Aladdin
Mitch and Amy	O	RF	Cleary, Beverly	Harper Collins
Mitchell Is Moving	J	F	Sharmat, Marjorie Weinman	Simon & Schuster
Mitten, The	M	TL	Brett, Jan	Scholastic
Mix, Make and Munch	J	I	Home Connection Collection	Rigby
Mixed-up Max	Q	F	King-Smith, Dick	Troll
Moana's Island	M	RF	Sunshine	Wright Group/McGraw Hill
Moccasin Trail	W	RF	McGraw, Eloise	Scholastic
Modern Times	R	I	Journey Through History	Barron's Educational Series
Mog at the Zoo	L	F	Nicoll, Helen	The Penguin Group
Mog's Mumps	L	F	Nicoll, Helen	The Penguin Group
Moki	Q	HF	Penny, Grace Jackson	Penguin Group
Mollie Whuppie	K	TL	New Way Orange	Steck-Vaughn
Molly Learns a Lesson	Q	HF	The American Girls Collection	Pleasant Company
Molly Pitcher: Young Patriot	O	B	Childhood of Famous Americans	Aladdin
Molly Saves the Day	Q	HF	The American Girls Collection	Pleasant Company
Molly the Brave and Me	K	RF	O'Connor, Jane	Random House
Molly's Pilgrim	M	RF	Cohen, Barbara	Bantam Doubleday Dell
Molly's Surprise	Q	HF	The American Girls Collection	Pleasant Company
Mom, You're Fired!	O	RF	Robinson, Nancy K.	Scholastic
Mom's Getting Married	K	RF	Sunshine	Wright Group/McGraw Hill
Momotaro	M	F	Sunshine	Wright Group/McGraw Hill
Monet	R	B	Venezia, Mike	Children's Press
Money Boot, The	N	RF	Russell, Ginny	Fitzhenry and Whiteside
Money Riddles That Count	K	I	Fetty, Margaret	Steck-Vaughn
Mongols, The	S	I	Journey Into Civilization	Chelsea House
Monkey Island	V	RF	Fox, Paula	Orchard Books
Monkeys and Apes	K	I	PM Animal Facts: Turquoise	Rigby
Monster for Hire	M	F	Wilson, Trevor	Mondo
Monster from the Sea, The	K	TL	Bank Street	Bantam Doubleday Dell
Monster Manners	J	F	Cole, Joanna	Scholastic
Monster Movie	K	F	Cole, Joanna	Scholastic
Monster of Mirror Mountain, The	K	F	Literacy 2000	Rigby
Monster of the Year	S	F	Coville, Bruce	Pocket Books
Monster Rabbit Runs Amuck!	M	RF	Giff, Patricia Reilly	Bantam Doubleday Dell
Monster Under The Bed, The	K	F	Ready Readers	Pearson Learning
Monster's Ring, The	R	F	Coville, Bruce	Pocket Books
Monsters Don't Scuba Dive	M	F	Dadey, D. & Jones, M. T.	Scholastic
Monsters Next Door, The	L	RF	Dadey, D. & Jones, M. T.	Scholastic
Monsters of the Deep	L	I	Swartz, Stanley L.	Dominie Press
Monticello	V	I	Cornerstones of Freedom	Children's Press
Moon and the Mirror, The	M	TL	Literacy 2000	Rigby
Moon Boy	J	F	Bank Street	Bantam Doubleday Dell
Moon Bridge, The	W	HF	Savin, Marcia	Scholastic
Moon Over Tennessee: A Boy's Civil War Journal	W	B	Crist-Evans, Craig	Houghton Mifflin
Moon Stories	J	F	Ready Readers	Pearson Learning
Moon, The	U	I	A First Book	Franklin Watts
Moon, The	Q	I	Eye on the Universe	Crabtree
Moon, The	N	I	Literacy 2000	Rigby
Moonhorse	M	F	Osborne, Mary Pope	Alfred A. Knopf
Moonlight on the River	R	RF	Kovacs, Deborah	The Penguin Group
Moonwalk: The First Trip to the Moon	O	I	Donnelly, Judy	Random House
Moose, The	R	I	Hemstock, Annie	Capstone Press
More Adventures of the Great Brain	T	RF	Fitzgerald, John D.	Yearling
More Monsters in School	N	RF	Godfrey, M.	Fitzhenry and Whiteside
More Perfect Union: The Story of Our Constitution	S	I	Maestro, Betsy & Giulio	William Morrow

Title	Level	Genre	Author/Series	Publisher/Distributor
More Stories from Grandma's Attic	O	RF	Richardson, Arleta	Chariot Victor Publishing
More Stories Huey Tells	N	RF	Cameron, Ann	Alfred A. Knopf
More Stories Julian Tells	N	RF	Cameron, Ann	Random House
More Tales of Amanda Pig	L	F	Van Leeuwen, Jean	The Penguin Group
More Tales of Oliver Pig	L	F	Van Leeuwen, Jean	The Penguin Group
Morgan's Zoo	Q	F	Howe, James	Aladdin
Morning Girl	S	HF	Dorris, Michael	Hyperion
Morning Star	J	F	Literacy 2000	Rigby
Morris and Boris at the Circus	J	F	Wiseman, B.	HarperTrophy
Morris Goes to School	J	F	Wiseman, B.	HarperTrophy
Mossflower	Z	F	Jacques, Brian	Ace Books
Most Beautiful Place in the World, The	O	RF	Cameron, Ann	Alfred A. Knopf
Most Wonderful Doll in the World, The	O	RF	McGinley, Phyllis	Scholastic
Mostly Michael	Q	RF	Smith, Robert Kimmel	Bantam Doubleday Dell
Mother Hippopotamus Gets Wet	J	F	Foundations	Wright Group/McGraw Hill
Mother Hippopotamus Goes Canoeing	L	F	Foundations	Wright Group/McGraw Hill
Mother Sea Turtle	K	I	Foundations	Wright Group/McGraw Hill
Mother's Helpers	K	RF	Ready Readers	Pearson Learning
Mount Vernon	V	I	Cornerstones of Freedom	Children's Press
Mountain Bike Challenge, The	Q	I	Morgan, Patrick	Pacific Learning
Mountain Bike Mania	O	RF	Belcher, Angie	Rigby
Mountain Gorillas	O	I	Wonder World	Wright Group/McGraw Hill
Mountain Lion, The	O	I	Crewe, Sabrina	Steck-Vaughn
Mountain Man and the President, The	Q	B	First Reports	Compass Point Books
Mountains	S	I	Weitzman, David	Steck-Vaughn
Mountains of Quilt, The	N	F	Willard, Nancy	Harcourt Brace
Mouse and the Elephant, The	J	TL	Little Readers	Houghton Mifflin
Mouse and the Motorcycle, The	O	F	Cleary, Beverly	Avon Camelot
Mouse Called Wolf, A	O	F	King-Smith, Dick	Alfred A. Knopf
Mouse Magic	O	RF	Baglio, Ben M.	Scholastic
Mouse of Amherst, The	Q	F	Spires, Elizabeth	Farrar, Straus and Giroux
Mouse Rap, The	W	RF	Myers, Walter Dean	HarperTrophy
Mouse Soup	J	F	Lobel, Arnold	Harper Collins
Mouse Tales	J	F	Lobel, Arnold	Harper Collins
Mouse Who Wanted to Marry, The	J	F	Bank Street	Bantam Doubleday Dell
Moves Make the Man, The	Z	RF	Brooks, Bruce	Harper Trophy
Moving Mama to Town	X	RF	Young, Ronder Thomas	Bantam Doubleday Dell
Mr. Ape	O	F	King-Smith, Dick	Alfred A. Knopf
Mr. Beep	M	F	Read Alongs	Rigby
Mr. Bumbleticker Goes Shopping	J	RF	Foundations	Wright Group/McGraw Hill
Mr. Bumbleticker Goes to the Zoo	L	RF	Foundations	Wright Group/McGraw Hill
Mr. Gumpy's Motor Car	L	RF	Burningham, John	Harper Collins
Mr. Gumpy's Outing	L	RF	Burningham, John	Holt, Henry & Co.
Mr. Lincoln's Drummer	W	HF	Wisler, G. Clifton	The Penguin Group
Mr. Mysterious & Company	R	F	Fleischman, Sid	Beech Tree
Mr. Popper's Penguins	Q	F	Atwater, Richard and Florence	Dell
Mr. Potter's Pet	N	F	King-Smith, Dick	Hyperion
Mr. President: A Book of U.S. Presidents	S	B	Sullivan, George	Scholastic
Mr. Putter and Tabby Bake the Cake	J	RF	Rylant, Cynthia	Harcourt Brace
Mr. Putter and Tabby Fly the Plane	J	RF	Rylant, Cynthia	Harcourt Brace
Mr. Putter and Tabby Pick the Pears	J	RF	Rylant, Cynthia	Harcourt Brace
Mr. Putter and Tabby Pour the Tea	J	RF	Rylant, Cynthia	Harcourt Brace
Mr. Putter and Tabby Walk the Dog	J	RF	Rylant, Cynthia	Harcourt Brace
Mr. Putter & Tabby Row the Boat	J	RF	Rylant, Cynthia	Harcourt Brace
Mr. Putter & Tabby Take the Train	J	RF	Rylant, Cynthia	Harcourt Inc.
Mr. Putter & Tabby Toot the Horn	J	RF	Rylant, Cynthia	Harcourt Brace
Mr. Revere and I	U	F	Lawson, Robert	Little, Brown & Co.
Mr. Sun and Mr. Sea	L	F	Sunshine	Wright Group/McGraw Hill
Mr. Tucket	U	HF	Paulsen, Gary	Bantam Doubleday Dell
Mrs. Always Goes Shopping	M	RF	Sunshine	Wright Group/McGraw Hill

Title	Level	Genre	Author/Series	Publisher/Distributor
Mrs. Barnett's Birthday	J	RF	Sunshine	Wright Group/McGraw Hill
Mrs. Bubble's Baby	M	F	Pacific Literacy	Pacific Learning
Mrs. Frisby and the Rats of NIMH	V	F	O'Brien, Robert C.	Aladdin
Mrs. Huggins and Her Hen Hannah	K	F	Dabcovich, Lydia	Dutton
Mrs. Jeepers' Batty Vacation	L	RF	Dadey, D. & Jones, M. T.	Scholastic
Mrs. Jeepers in Outer Space	M	RF	Dadey, D. & Jones, M. T.	Scholastic
Mrs. Piggle-Wiggle	O	F	MacDonald, Betty	Scholastic
Mrs. Piggle-Wiggle's Farm	O	F	MacDonald, Betty	Scholastic
Mrs. Piggle-Wiggle's Magic	O	F	MacDonald, Betty	Scholastic
Mrs. Sheep's Garden	K	F	Kratky, Lada	Hampton-Brown
Much Ado About Aldo	O	RF	Hurwitz, Johanna	The Penguin Group
Mud Pony, The	M	TL	Reading Rainbow	Scholastic
Mud Pony, The	L	TL	Sunshine	Wright Group/McGraw Hill
Mufaro's Beautiful Daughters: An African Tale	N	TL	Steptoe, John	Scholastic
Muffy's Secret Admirer	M	RF	Brown, Marc	Little, Brown & Co.
Muggie Maggie	O	RF	Cleary, Beverly	Avon Camelot
Mummies	M	I	All Aboard Reading	Grosset & Dunlap
Mummies and Their Mysteries	T	I	Wilcox, Charlotte	Carolrhoda Books
Mummies Don't Coach Softball	M	F	Dadey, D. & Jones, M. T.	Scholastic
Mummies in the Morning	M	F	Osborne, Mary Pope	Random House
Mummies Made in Egypt	R	I	Aliki	Harper Collins
Mummy's Curse, The	O	F	SupaDoopers	Sundance
Mummy's Gold, The	L	F	McMullan, Kate	Grosset & Dunlap
Muscles: Our Muscular System	T	I	Simon, Seymour	HarperTrophy
Music of Dolphins, The	V	RF	Hesse, Karen	Scholastic
Mustangs	U	I	Gillespie, Lorrine	Capstone Press
Mutt and the Lifeguards	M	RF	Sunshine	Wright Group/McGraw Hill
My Body	M	I	Schaefer, Lola M.	Benchmark Education
My Brother, Ant	J	RF	Byars, Betsy	Viking
My Brother is a Superhero	X	RF	Sheldon, Dyan	Candlewick Press
My Brother is a Visitor From Another Planet	R	F	Sheldon, Dyan	Candlewick Press
My Brother Louis Measures Worms and Other Louis Stories	T	RF	Robinson, Barbara	HarperTrophy
My Brother, My Sister, and I	V	HF	Watkins, Yoko Kawashima	Aladdin
My Brother Sam is Dead	Y	HF	Collier, James and Christopher	Scholastic
My Brother, the Spy	N	RF	SupaDoopers	Sundance
My Daniel	T	HF	Conrad, Pam	Harper Trophy
My Dream of Martin Luther King	R	I	Ringgold, Faith	Crown
My Family & the Wasps	N	F	Parker, John	Dominie Press
My Father	J	RF	Mayer, Laura	Scholastic
My Father The Mad Professor	P	F	Odgers, Sally	Rigby
My Father's Dragon	N	F	Gannett, Ruth Stiles	Random House
My First Book of Biographies: Great Men and Women Every Child Should Know	P	B	Marzollo, Jean	Scholastic
My Friend the Monster	N	F	Bulla, Clyde Robert	Harper & Row
My Great-Aunt Arizona	N	RF	Houston, Gloria	HarperCollins
My Hiroshima	T	HF	Morimoto, Junko	The Penguin Group
My Life as a Fifth-Grade Comedian	T	RF	Levy, Elizabeth	Harper Trophy
My Life in Dog Years	S	B	Paulsen, Gary	Bantam Doubleday Dell
My Mother Got Married (And Other Disasters)	O	RF	Park, Barbara	Random House
My Mysterious World	O	B	Mahy, Margaret	Richard C. Owen
My Name is Maria Isabel	N	RF	Ada, Alma Flor	Aladdin
My Name is Not Angelica	V	HF	O'Dell, Scott	Bantam Doubleday Dell
My Name is Yun Jim	N	RF	Murphy, Catherine	Wright Group/McGraw Hill
My New Mom	K	RF	Sunshine	Wright Group/McGraw Hill
My Own Two Feet	W	B	Cleary, Beverly	Avon
My Prairie Summer	M	RF	Pair-It Books	Steck-Vaughn
My Scrapbook	K	I	Storyteller Nonfiction	Wright Group/McGraw Hill
My Side of the Mountain	U	RF	George, Jean Craighead	The Penguin Group
My Sister Annie	S	RF	Dodds, Bill	Boyds Mills Press

Title	Level	Genre	Author/Series	Publisher/Distributor
My Sister the Witch	R	RF	Conford, Ellen	Troll
My Sister's Getting Married	K	RF	Foundations	Wright Group/McGraw Hill
My Sloppy Tiger Goes to School	J	F	Sunshine	Wright Group/McGraw Hill
My Son, the Time Traveler	N	F	The Zack Files	Grosset & Dunlap
My Teacher Flunked the Planet	S	F	Coville, Bruce	Pocket Books
My Teacher Fried My Brains	S	F	Coville, Bruce	Pocket Books
My Teacher Glows in the Dark	S	F	Coville, Bruce	Pocket Books
My Teacher Is an Alien	S	F	Coville, Bruce	Pocket Books
My Teacher Turns into a Tyrannosaurus	O	F	SupaDoopers	Sundance
My Treasure Garden	J	RF	Book Bank	Wright Group/McGraw Hill
My Two Families	K	RF	PM Story Books -Silver	Rigby
My Wartime Summers	V	HF	Cutler, Jane	Harper Collins
My Weird Mother	M	RF	SupaDoopers	Sundance
My Wonderful Aunt, Story Five	M	F	Sunshine	Wright Group/McGraw Hill
My Wonderful Aunt, Story Four	M	F	Sunshine	Wright Group/McGraw Hill
My Wonderful Aunt, Story One	M	F	Sunshine	Wright Group/McGraw Hill
My Wonderful Aunt, Story Six	M	F	Sunshine	Wright Group/McGraw Hill
My Wonderful Aunt, Story Three	M	F	Sunshine	Wright Group/McGraw Hill
My Wonderful Aunt, Story Two	M	F	Sunshine	Wright Group/McGraw Hill
My Writing Day	O	B	Adler, David A.	Richard C. Owen
Mysterious Green Swimmer and Other Cases, The	O	RF	Simon, Seymour	Avon
Mysterious I.O.U., The	M	RF	Schultz, Irene	Wright Group/McGraw Hill
Mysterious Ocean Highway: Benjamin Franklin and the Gulf Stream	T	B	Heiligman, Deborah	Steck-Vaughn
Mysterious Tracks and Other Cases, The	O	RF	Simon, Seymour	Avon
Mystery in the Night Woods	M	F	Peterson, John	Scholastic
Mystery of Moody Manor, The	M	F	Dionetti, Michelle	Wright Group/McGraw Hill
Mystery of Pony Hollow, The	N	F	Hall, Lynn	Random House
Mystery of the Blue Ring, The	L	RF	Giff, Patricia Reilly	Bantam Doubleday Dell
Mystery of the Cupboard	R	F	Banks, Lynne Reid	Avon Camelot
Mystery of the Dark Old House, The	M	F	Schultz, Irene	Wright Group/McGraw Hill
Mystery of the Fire in the Sky	Q	RF	Mystery Solvers	Troll
Mystery of the Missing Dog, The	J	F	Levy, Elizabeth	Scholastic
Mystery of the Missing Dog, The	M	RF	Schultz, Irene	Wright Group/McGraw Hill
Mystery of the Missing Leopard, The	Q	F	Leonhardt, Alice	Steck-Vaughn
Mystery of the Missing Malamute, The	M	RF	Kleinhenz, Sydnie Meltzer	Wright Group/McGraw Hill
Mystery of the Phantom Pony, The	N	RF	Stepping Stone	Random House
Mystery of the Pirate Ghost, The	L	F	Hayes, Geoffrey	Random House
Mystery of the Stolen Bike, The	M	F	Brown, Marc	Little, Brown & Co.
Mystery of the Talking Tail, The	M	F	SupaDoopers	Sundance
Mystery of the Three Keys, The	M	RF	Schultz, Irene	Wright Group/McGraw Hill
Mystery of the Tooth Gremlin	L	RF	Graves, Bonnie	Hyperion
Mystery on October Road	O	RF	Herzig, A.C. & Mali, Jane	Scholastic
Mystery Seeds	L	RF	Reading Unlimited	Celebration Press
Mystery Stories	R	RF	Higgins, James	Houghton Mifflin
Myth or Mystery?	Q	F	Weber, Rebecca	Rigby
Mythical Beasts	T	F	Wildcats	Wright Group/McGraw Hill
Mythmakers	T	I	Wildcats	Wright Group/McGraw Hill
Myths	S	TL	Goodman, Ronald, Robert Pierce, Betty Jane Wagner	Houghton Mifflin
Nadia Comaneci	M	B	Cole, Sally	Wright Group/McGraw Hill
Nana's in the Plum Tree	M	RF	Pacific Literacy	Pacific Learning
Nana's Kitchen	J	RF	Walton, Darwin McBeth	Steck-Vaughn
Nannies for Hire	M	RF	Hest, Amy	William Morrow
Nasty, Stinky Sneakers	R	RF	Bunting, Eve	HarperTrophy
Natchez Under the Hill	T	HF	Applegate, Stan	Peachtree
Nate the Great	K	RF	Sharmat, Marjorie Weinman	Bantam Doubleday Dell
Nate the Great and Me	K	RF	Sharmat, Marjorie Weinman	Random House
Nate the Great and the Boring Beach Bag	K	RF	Sharmat, Marjorie Weinman	Bantam Doubleday Dell
Nate the Great and the Crunchy Christmas	K	RF	Sharmat, Marjorie Weinman	Bantam Doubleday Dell

Title	Level	Genre	Author/Series	Publisher/Distributor
Nate the Great and the Fishy Prize	K	RF	Sharmat, Marjorie Weinman	Bantam Doubleday Dell
Nate the Great and the Halloween Hunt	K	RF	Sharmat, Marjorie Weinman	Bantam Doubleday Dell
Nate the Great and the Lost List	K	RF	Sharmat, Marjorie Weinman	Bantam Doubleday Dell
Nate the Great and the Missing Key	K	RF	Sharmat, Marjorie Weinman	Bantam Doubleday Dell
Nate the Great and the Mushy Valentine	K	RF	Sharmat, Marjorie Weinman	Bantam Doubleday Dell
Nate the Great and the Musical Note	K	RF	Sharmat, Marjorie Weinman	Bantam Doubleday Dell
Nate the Great and the Phony Clue	K	RF	Sharmat, Marjorie Weinman	Bantam Doubleday Dell
Nate the Great and the Pillowcase	K	RF	Sharmat, Marjorie Weinman	Bantam Doubleday Dell
Nate the Great and the Snowy Trail	K	RF	Sharmat, Marjorie Weinman	Bantam Doubleday Dell
Nate the Great and the Sticky Case	K	RF	Sharmat, Marjorie Weinman	Bantam Doubleday Dell
Nate the Great and the Stolen Base	K	RF	Sharmat, Marjorie Weinman	Bantam Doubleday Dell
Nate the Great and the Tardy Tortoise	K	RF	Sharmat, Marjorie Weinman	Bantam Doubleday Dell
Nate the Great Goes Down in the Dumps	K	RF	Sharmat, Marjorie Weinman	Bantam Doubleday Dell
Nate the Great Goes Undercover	K	RF	Sharmat, Marjorie Weinman	Bantam Doubleday Dell
Nate the Great Saves the King of Sweden	K	RF	Sharmat, Marjorie Weinman	Bantam Doubleday Dell
Nate the Great Stalks Stupidweed	K	RF	Sharmat, Marjorie Weinman	Bantam Doubleday Dell
Nathan and Nicholas Alexander	K	F	Delacre, Lulu	Scholastic
National Anthem, The	N	I	A True Book	Children's Press
Native American Stories	Q	TL	Bruchac, Joseph	Fulcrum Publishing
Native Americans	P	I	Weldon Owen	Wright Group/McGraw Hill
Nature! Wild and Wonderful	O	B	Pringle, Laurence	Richard C. Owen
Nature's Celebration	M	I	Literacy 2000	Rigby
Nature's Power	Q	I	Hummer, Patricia K.	Steck-Vaughn
Neighbor From Outer Space, The	N	F	George, Maureen	Scholastic
Neil Armstrong: Young Flyer	O	B	Childhood of Famous Americans	Aladdin
Nellie McClung	W	B	Benham, Mary Lile	Fitzhenry & Whiteside
Nelson is Kidnapped	K	RF	PM Story Books -Silver	Rigby
Nelson Mandela	Q	B	First Biographies	Steck-Vaughn
Nelson Mandela: Freedom for South Africa	R	B	Dell, Pamela	Children's Press
Nelson Mandela "No Easy Walk To Freedom"	X	B	Denenberg, Barry	Scholastic
Nelson Mandela: South Africa's Silent Voice of Protest	X	B	Hargrove, Jim	Children's Press
Nelson the Baby Elephant	J	F	PM Turquoise	Rigby
Neptune	N	I	A True Book	Children's Press
Nervous System, The	N	I	A True Book	Children's Press
Nesting Place, The	K	HF	PM Turquoise	Rigby
Netherlands, The	O	I	Dahl, Michael	Capstone Press
Never Bored on Boards	O	I	Literacy 2000	Rigby
Never Cry Wolf	Z	B	Mowat, Farley	Bantam Doubleday Dell
Never Hit a Ghost with a Baseball Bat	O	RF	Clifford, Eth	Scholastic
Never Hitch a Ride With a Martian!	N	SF	Clark, Tony	Pacific Learning
Never Say Quit	T	RF	Wallace, Bill	Pocket Books
Never Trust a Cat Who Wears Earrings	N	F	The Zack Files	Grosset & Dunlap
Never Turn Back: Father Serra's Mission	S	B	Rawls, Jim	Steck-Vaughn
New Bike, The	J	RF	Sunshine	Wright Group/McGraw Hill
New Friends in a New Land: A Thanksgiving Story	N	I	Stamper, Judith Bauer	Steck-Vaughn
New Jersey	Q	I	Kummer, Patricia K.	Capstone Press
New Kid in Town	N	RF	Kroll, Stephen	Avon Camelot
New Kids In Town	Y	B	Bode, Janet	Scholastic
New Kind of Magic, The	P	F	Szymanski, Lois	Avon Camelot
New Land: A First Year on the Praire, The	M	I	Reynolds, Marilynn	Orca Book Publishers
New Light for the Lodge, A	L	F	Smith, Ben	Wright Group/McGraw Hill
New Mexico	S	I	Thompson, Kathleen	Steck-Vaughn
New School, The	J	RF	City Kids	Rigby
New Year's Around the World	O	I	Trumbore, Cindy	Pearson Learning
New York	Q	I	Geography Department	Capstone Press
New York	S	I	Thompson, Kathleen	Steck-Vaughn
New York City	T	I	Kent, Deborah	Childrens Press
Newbery Halloween, A: A Dozen Scary Stories by Newbery Award-Winning Authors	W	F	Greenberg, M.H. & Waugh, C.G.	Delacorte

Title	Level	Genre	Author/Series	Publisher/Distributor
Newborn Animals	J	I	Momentum Literacy Program	Troll
Newf	N	TL	Killilea, Marie	Putnam & Grosset
News Flash!	R	I	Hill, Sharon	Pacific Learning
Newspaper Kids, The	Q	RF	Phillips, Juanita	Harper Collins
Newt	J	F	Novak, Matt	HarperTrophy
Next Spring an Oriole	N	HF	Whelan, Gloria	Random House
Next Stop, New York City!	O	RF	Giff, Patricia Reilly	Bantam Doubleday Dell
Next Time I Will	K	RF	Bank Street	Bantam Doubleday Dell
Nez Perce Tribe, The	O	I	Lassieur, Allison	Capstone Press
Nibble, Nibble, Jenny Archer	M	RF	Conford, Ellen	Little, Brown & Co.
Nice New Neighbors	K	RF	Brandenberg, Franz	Scholastic
Nicketty-Nacketty Noo-Noo-Noo	K	F	Cowley, Joy	Mondo
Nigeria	O	I	Thoennes, Kristin	Capstone Press
Night Birds on Nantucket	V	HF	Aiken, Joan	Houghton Mifflin
Night Crossing, The	O	HF	Ackerman, Karen	Alfred A. Knopf
Night Flyers, The	W	RF	Jones, Elizabeth McDavid	Pleasant Company
Night Journey, The	T	HF	Lasky, Kathryn	Puffin Books
Night Journeys	U	HF	Avi	Avon Books
Night Lights, A Cruise Around the Solar System	R	I	Hill, David	Pacific Learning
Night Music	P	HF	Voyages in…	Wright Group/McGraw Hill
Night of the Chupacabras	Y	RF	Lee, Marie G.	Avon Camelot
Night of the Ninjas	M	F	Osborne, Mary Pope	Random House
Night of the Twisters	U	RF	Ruckman, Ivy	HarperTrophy
Night Owls, The	M	I	Wonder World	Wright Group/McGraw Hill
Night Queen's Blue Velvet Dress, The	Q	F	Pair-It Books	Steck-Vaughn
Night Swimmers, The	S	RF	Byars, Betsy	Dell
Night Terrors, Stories of Shadow and Substance	Z	F	Duncan, Lois	Aladdin
Night the Heads Came, The	Y	SF	Sleator, William	Puffin Books
Night the White Deer Died, The	Z	HF	Paulsen, Gary	Dell
Night Without Stars, A	S	RF	Howe, James	Aladdin
Nightingale, The	J	TL	Tales from Hans Andersen	Wright Group/McGraw Hill
Nightjohn	W	HF	Paulsen, Gary	Bantam Doubleday Dell
Nightmare	M	RF	Pulford, Elizabeth	Rigby
Nightmare Mountain	X	RF	Kehret, Peg	Puffin Books
Nighty-Nightmare	R	F	Howe, James	Avon Camelot
Nine Lives of Adventure Cat, The	L	F	Clymer, Susan	Scholastic
Nine Man Tree	Z	RF	Peck, Robert Newton	Random House
Nine True Dolphin Stories	M	I	Davidson, Margaret	Scholastic
Ninjas Don't Bake Pumpkin Pies	M	RF	Dadey, D. & Jones, M. T.	Scholastic
Nissa's Place	Y	RF	LaFaye, A.	Simon & Schuster
No Arm in Left Field	M	RF	Christopher, Matt	Little, Brown & Co.
No Copycats Allowed!	L	RF	Graves, Bonnie	Hyperion
No Dinner for Sally	J	RF	Literacy 2000	Rigby
No Dogs Allowed	O	RF	Cutler, Jane	Farrar, Straus and Giroux
No Fighting, No Biting!	K	RF	Minarik, Else Holmelund	HarperTrophy
No Flying in the House	P	F	Brock, Betty	Harper Collins
No Jumping On The Bed!	L	F	Arnold, Tedd	Scholastic
No Laughing Matter (Ragged Island Mysteries)	Q	RF	Bensen, Rosie	Wright Group/McGraw Hill
No More Magic	R	SF	Avi	Alfred A. Knopf
No More Monsters for Me!	J	F	Parish, Peggy	HarperTrophy
No One is Going to Nashville	O	RF	Jukes, Mavis	Alfred A. Knopf
No Pretty Pictures: A Child of War	Z	B	Lobel, Anita	Greenwillow Books
No Promises in the Wind	Z	HF	Hunt, Irene	Berkley Books
No Room For a Dog	N	RF	Nichols, Joan Kane	Hearst
No Tooth, No Quarter!	K	F	Buller, Jon	Random House
No Trouble at All!	M	RF	Powell, Joyce	Rigby
No Way, Winky Blue!	N	F	Jane, Pamela	Mondo
Nobel Prize Winners	T	B	Hacker, Carlotta	Crabtree
Nobody's Family Is Going to Change	U	RF	Fitzhugh, Louise	Farrar, Straus and Giroux

Title	Level	Genre	Author/Series	Publisher/Distributor
Noonday Friends, The	R	RF	Stolz, Mary	Scholastic
Norma Jean, Jumping Bean	J	RF	Cole, Joanna	Random House
Norman Newman and the Werewolf of Walnut Street	Q	F	Conford, Ellen	Troll
Norman Rockwell	T	B	Cohen, Joel H.	Grolier Publishing
North America	Q	I	Petersen, David	Grolier Publishing
North Carolina	T	I	Fradin, Dennis Brindell	Childrens Press
North Carolina	S	I	Portrait of America	Steck-Vaughn
North Star To Freedom	U	I	Gorrell, Gena K.	Random House
Nose for Trouble, A	P	RF	Wilson, Nancy Hope	Avon
Not Guilty	X	B	Sullivan, George	Scholastic
Not Now! Said the Cow	J	F	Bank Street	Bantam Doubleday Dell
Not That I Care	V	RF	Vail, Rachel	Scholastic
Not Too Young and Other Stories	L	TL	New Way: Literature	Steck-Vaughn
Not What It Seems	P	RF	Wildcats	Wright Group/McGraw Hill
Not-Just-Anybody Family, The	O	RF	Byars, Betsy	Dell
Not-So-Dead Fish and Other Cases, The	O	RF	Simon, Seymour	Avon
Not-So-Perfect Rosie	N	RF	Giff, Patricia Reilly	The Penguin Group
Nothing But The Truth	U	RF	Avi	Hearst
Nothing But Trouble, Trouble, Trouble	Q	RF	Hermes, Patricia	Scholastic
Nothing to Be Scared About	K	RF	Sunshine	Wright Group/McGraw Hill
Nothing's Fair in Fifth Grade	R	RF	DeClements, Barthe	Scholastic
Novio Boy	X	TL	Soto, Gary	Harcourt Brace
Now Is Your Time! The African-American Struggle	Y	I	Myers, Walter Dean	Harper Collins
Now Listen, Stanley	K	F	Literacy 2000	Rigby
Now You See Me...Now You Don't	N	F	The Zack Files	Grosset & Dunlap
Number One	J	SF	Pacific Literacy	Pacific Learning
Number the Stars	U	HF	Lowry, Lois	Bantam Doubleday Dell
Nurses	M	I	Ready, Dee	Capstone Press
Obadiah the Bold	N	RF	Turkle, Brinton	The Penguin Group
Obee & Mungedeech	T	RF	Martin, Trude	Aladdin
Obstacles in Our Way	L	RF	McAlister, Margaret	Rigby
Ocean Animals	J	I	Early Connections	Benchmark Education
Ocean Detectives: Solving Mysteries of the Sea	W	I	Cerullo, Mary	Steck-Vaughn
Ocean Life	Q	I	Weldon Owen	Wright Group/McGraw Hill
Ocean Life: Tide Pool Creatures	Q	I	Leonhardt, Alice	Steck-Vaughn
Ocean Tide Pool	P	I	L'Hommedieu, Arthur John	Grolier
Oceans	Q	I	First Reports	Compass Point Books
Oceans	Q	I	The Wonders of our World	Crabtree
Octopuses and Squids	O	I	Wonder World	Wright Group/McGraw Hill
Octopuses, Squid, & Cuttlefish	L	I	Marine Life For Yng. Readers	Dominie
Oddballs	X	B	Sleator, William	Puffin Books
Odder Than Ever	Z	F	Coville, Bruce	Harcourt Inc.
Oddly Enough	Z	F	Coville, Bruce	Pocket Books
Odds on Oliver	P	RF	Greene, Carol	Puffin Books
Of Mice and Men	Z	RF	Steinbeck, John	The Penguin Group
Of Nightingales That Weep	U	HF	Paterson, Katherine	Harper Collins
Off and Running	S	RF	Soto, Gary	Dell
Off the Map, The Journals of Lewis and Clark	U	I	Roop, Peter and Connie	Walker and Company
Off To Sea: An Inside Look at a Research Cruise	T	I	Kovacs, Deborah	Steck-Vaughn
Off To Squintum's/The Four Musicians	N	TL	Collins, Gillian	Mondo
Oh Boy, Boston!	O	RF	Giff, Patricia Reilly	Bantam Doubleday Dell
Oh, Brother	P	RF	Wilson, Johnnice M.	Scholastic
Oh, Columbus!	K	F	Literacy 2000	Rigby
Ohio	Q	I	Geography Department	Capstone Press
Ohio	S	I	Thompson, Kathleen	Steck-Vaughn
Ojibwa Indians, The	P	I	Lund, Bill	Capstone Press
Ola Shakes It Up	T	RF	Hyppolite, Joanne	Random House
Old Bones	M	RF	Sunshine	Wright Group/McGraw Hill
Old Devil Wind	J	F	Martin, Bill Jr.	Harcourt Brace
Old Enough for Magic	L	F	Pickett, A.	HarperTrophy

Title	Level	Genre	Author/Series	Publisher/Distributor
Old Friends	M	RF	Literacy 2000	Rigby
Old Key, The	T	TL	Literacy 2000	Rigby
Old Man and the Bear, The	M	RF	Hanel, Wolfram	North-South Books
Old Meadow, The	S	F	Selden, George	Farrar, Straus and Giroux
Old Recipe Book, The	L	F	Smith, Ben	Wright Group/McGraw Hill
Old Red Rocking Chair, The	M	RF	Root, Phyllis	Scholastic
Old Tom and the Rogue	M	HF	Wilson, Trevor	Dominie Press
Old Woman and Her Pig, The: An Old English Tale	K	TL	Litzinger, Rosanne	Harcourt Brace
Old Woman Who Lived in a Vinegar Bottle	M	TL	Douglas, Ann	Mondo
Old Yeller	V	RF	Gipson, Fred	Scholastic
Oliver and Amanda's Halloween	L	F	Van Leeuwen, Jean	Puffin Books
Olympics and the Mini Olympics, The	N	I	Mack, Rachel	Wright Group/McGraw Hill
On and Off the Road	M	I	Wildcats	Wright Group/McGraw Hill
On Board The Titanic	T	I	Tanaka, Shelley	Hyperion/Madison Press
On Fortune's Wheel	Z	F	Voigt, Cynthia	Aladdin
On Friday the Giant	K	F	The Giant	Wright Group/McGraw Hill
On Guard	R	RF	Napoli, Donna Jo	Puffin Books
On Monday the Giant	K	F	The Giant	Wright Group/McGraw Hill
On My Honor	S	RF	Bauer, Marion Dane	Bantam Doubleday Dell
On Site	S	I	Pollock, John	Mondo
On Sunday the Giant	K	F	The Giant	Wright Group/McGraw Hill
On the Banks of Plum Creek	Q	HF	Wilder, Laura Ingalls	Harper Collins
On the Banks of the Bayou	Q	HF	MacBride, Roger Lea	Harper Collins
On The Far Side Of The Mountain	V	RF	George, Jean Craighead	Puffin Books
On the Open Plains	J	I	Momentum Literacy Program	Troll
On the Right Track	N	I	Gard, Stephen	Rigby
On the Way Home	S	HF	Wilder, Laura Ingalls	Harper Collins
On the Way to the Moon	O	F	Gold, Becky	Pearson Learning
On Thursday the Giant	K	F	The Giant	Wright Group/McGraw Hill
On Top of Concord Hill	Q	HF	Wilkes, Maria D.	HarperCollins
On Tuesday the Giant	K	F	The Giant	Wright Group/McGraw Hill
On Wednesday the Giant	K	F	The Giant	Wright Group/McGraw Hill
On With the Show!	M	I	Pair-It Books	Steck-Vaughn
On-Line Spaceman and Other Cases, The	O	RF	Simon, Seymour	Avon
Once I Was a Plum Tree	Q	RF	Hurwitz, Johanna	Beech Tree Books
Once on this Island	S	HF	Whelan, Gloria	HarperTrophy
Once upon a Rhyme	M	F	Pacific Literacy	Pacific Learning
Once Upon a Time	O	B	Bunting, Eve	Richard C. Owen
Once Upon a Time in Junior High	U	RF	Norment, Lisa	Scholastic
Once When I Was Shipwrecked	L	F	Literacy 2000	Rigby
One Bad Thing About Father, The	M	RF	Monjo, F.N.	HarperTrophy
One Bird	Y	RF	Mori, Kyoko	Ballantine Books
One Day in the Alpine Tundra	P	I	George, Jean Craighead	Harper Collins
One Day in the Desert	P	I	George, Jean Craighead	Harper Collins
One Day in the Tropical Rain Forest	P	I	George, Jean Craighead	HarperTrophy
One Day in the Woods	P	I	George, Jean Craighead	HarperTrophy
One Drop of Water and a Million More	K	I	Book Bank	Wright Group/McGraw Hill
One- Eyed Jake	M	F	Hutchins, Pat	Morrow
One Fat Summer	Y	RF	Lipsyte, Robert	Harper Collins
One Giant Leap	S	I	Fraser, Mary Ann	Henry Holt & Co.
One Hundredth Thing about Caroline, The	R	RF	Lowry, Lois	Bantam Doubleday Dell
One in the Middle Is the Green Kangaroo, The	M	RF	Blume, Judy	Bantam Doubleday Dell
One Man Show	O	B	Asch, Frank	Richard C. Owen
One More River	V	HF	Banks, Lynne Reid	Avon Camelot
One More River to Cross	X	B	Haskins, Jim	Scholastic
One Potato, Tu	T	RF	Pearson, Gayle	Scholastic
One Thing I'm Good At	R	RF	Williams, Karen Lynn	William Morrow
One Who Came Back, The	X	RF	Mazzio, Joann	Houghton Mifflin
One-Eyed Cat	S	RF	Fox, Paula	Bantam Doubleday Dell
Onion John	U	HF	Krumgold, Joseph	Harper & Row

Title	Level	Genre	Author/Series	Publisher/Distributor
Onion Sundaes	L	RF	Adler, David A.	Random House
Onion Tears	Q	RF	Kidd, Diana	William Morrow
Only Earth and Sky Last Forever	Y	HF	Benchley, Nathaniel	Harper Collins
Oogly Gum Chasing Game, The	K	F	Literacy 2000	Rigby
Oprah Winfrey, A Voice for the People	U	B	Brooks, Philip	Grolier Publishing
Orca Song	K	RF	Armour	Scholastic
Ordinary Genius, The Story of Albert Einstein	U	B	McPherson, Stephanie S.	The Lerner Group
Ordinary Miracles	Y	RF	Tolan, Stephanie S.	Morrow
Oregon Trail, The	V	I	Cornerstones of Freedom	Children's Press
Original Adventures of Hank the Cowdog, The	Q	F	Erickson, John R.	Gulf
Orphan of Ellis Island, The	S	HF	Woodruff, Elvira	Scholastic
Orphan Train Adventures: Caught in the Act	W	HF	Nixon, Joan Lowery	Bantam Doubleday Dell
Orphan Train Adventures: Circle of Love	W	HF	Nixon, Joan Lowery	Bantam Doubleday Dell
Orphan Train Adventures: Dangerous Promise, A	W	HF	Nixon, Joan Lowery	Dell
Orphan Train Adventures: Family Apart, A	W	HF	Nixon, Joan Lowery	Dell
Orphan Train Adventures: In the Face of Danger	W	HF	Nixon, Joan Lowery	Dell
Orphan Train Adventures: Keeping Secrets	W	HF	Nixon, Joan Lowery	Dell
Orphan Train Adventures: Place to Belong, A	W	HF	Nixon, Joan Lowery	Dell
Orphan Train Children: Aggie's Home	Q	HF	Nixon, Joan Lowery	Yearling
Oscar Otter	J	F	Benchley, Nathaniel	HarperTrophy
Oscar & Tatiana	N	RF	Literacy 2000	Rigby
Osceola: Patriot and Warrior	T	B	Jumper, Moses & Sonder, Ben	Steck-Vaughn
Others See Us	Z	F	Sleator, William	Puffin Books
Otherwise Known As Sheila the Great	R	RF	Blume, Judy	Bantam Doubleday Dell
Otis Spofford	O	RF	Cleary, Beverly	Avon
Ouch!	L	RF	Noonan, Diana	Dominie Press
Our American Flag	O	I	McCloskey, Susan	Wright Group/McGraw Hill
Our Baby	J	RF	Foundations	Wright Group/McGraw Hill
Our Book of Maps	N	I	Discovery World	Rigby
Our Busy Bodies	K	I	Home Connection Collection	Rigby
Our Changing Earth	R	I	Belcher, Angie	Pacific Learning
Our Endangered Planet (Oceans)	W	I	Hoff, M. and Rodgers, M.	Lerner Publications
Our Government	M	I	People, Spaces & Places	Rand McNally
Our Money	J	I	Early Connections	Benchmark Education
Our New Principal	K	RF	City Kids	Rigby
Our Old Friend, Bear	J	RF	PM Story Books -Silver	Rigby
Our Only May Amelia	R	HF	Holm, Jennifer	Harper Collins
Our Planet	R	I	Worldwise	Grolier
Our World of Wonders	Q	I	Canetti, Yanitzia	Steck-Vaughn
Out and About	Q	I	Weldon Owen	Wright Group/McGraw Hill
Out of Darkness: The Story of Louis Braille	S	B	Freedman, Russell	Houghton Mifflin
Out of the Dust	X	HF	Hesse, Karen	Scholastic
Outcast of Redwall, The	Z	F	Jacques, Brian	Ace Books
Outrageously Alice	U	RF	Naylor, Phyllis Reynolds	Aladdin
Outside and Inside Bats	Q	I	Markle, Sandra	Simon & Schuster
Outside and Inside Kangaroos	Q	I	Markle, Sandra	Atheneum
Outside and Inside Sharks	Q	I	Markle, Sandra	Simon & Schuster
Outside and Inside Snakes	Q	I	Markle, Sandra	Simon & Schuster
Outside and Inside Spiders	Q	I	Markle, Sandra	Simon & Schuster
Outside Dog, The	K	RF	Pomerantz, Charlotte	HarperTrophy
Outsiders, The	Z	RF	Hinton, S.E.	The Penguin Group
Over Sea, Under Stone	X	F	Cooper, Susan	Simon & Schuster
Overcoming Challenges: The Life of Charles F Bolden, Jr	Q	B	Walton, Darwin McBeth	Steck-Vaughn
Owl and the Pussy Cat	L	TL	Lear, Edward	Scholastic
Owl At Home	J	F	Lobel, Arnold	Harper Collins
Owl in the Office	Q	RF	Baglio, Ben M.	Scholastic
Owl Moon	O	B	Yolen, Jane	Scholastic
Owls	O	I	Holmes, Kevin J.	Capstone Press
Owls	R	I	Kalman, Bobbie	Crabtree

Title	Level	Genre	Author/Series	Publisher/Distributor
Owls	M	I	PM Animal Facts: Gold	Rigby
Owls in the Family	P	F	Mowat, Farley	Bantam Doubleday Dell
Owls in the Garden	L	RF	PM Gold	Rigby
Ox-Cart Man	K	HF	Hall, Donald	Scholastic
P.S. Longer Letter Later	U	RF	Danziger, P. & Martin, A.	Scholastic
P.W. Cracker Sees the World	Q	F	Yoshizawa, Linda	Steck-Vaughn
Pablo Picasso	P	B	Lowery, Linda	Lerner Publishing Group
Pack 109	J	RF	Thaler, Mike	Scholastic
Pagemaster, The	P	F	Horowitz, Jordan	Scholastic
Paint Brush Kid, The	M	RF	Bulla, Clyde Robert	Random House
Painting Lesson, The	K	F	Pacific Literacy	Pacific Learning
Pajama Party	M	RF	Hest, Amy	William Morrow
Panama Canal, The	W	I	Cornerstones of Freedom	Children's Press
Pancake, The	K	TL	Lobel, Anita	Bantam Doubleday Dell
Pandas in the Mountains	M	F	PM Gold	Rigby
Papagayo the Mischief Maker	N	TL	McDermott, Gerald	Harcourt Brace
Paper Birds, The	K	RF	Foundations	Wright Group/McGraw Hill
Paper Route, The	K	RF	New Way Green	Steck-Vaughn
Parachutes	J	RF	Storyteller-Moon Rising	Wright Group/McGraw Hill
Parakeet Girl, The	J	RF	Sadler, Marilyn	Random House
Parakeets	J	I	PM Animal Facts: Orange	Rigby
Parents' Night Fright	K	RF	Levy, Elizabeth	Scholastic
Park's Quest	U	RF	Paterson, Katherine	Puffin Books
Part of the Sky, A	Z	HF	Peck, Robert Newton	Random House
Partners	L	I	Home Connection Collection	Rigby
Party Games	J	RF	Foundations	Wright Group/McGraw Hill
Paru Has a Bath	J	RF	Pacific Literacy	Pacific Learning
Passager: The Young Merlin Trilogy	V	F	Yolen, Jane	Scholastic
Patches	M	RF	Szymanski, Lois	Avon Camelot
Patrick and the Leprechaun	L	F	PM Gold	Rigby
Patrick Doyle is Full of Blarney	O	HF	Armstrong, Jennifer	Random House
Paul Cezanne	Q	B	Venezia, Mike	Childrens Press
Paul Gauguin	Q	B	Venezia, Mike	Childrens Press
Paul Harvey's The Rest Of The Story	Z	I	Harvey Jr., Paul	Bantam Books
Paul Klee	Q	B	Venezia, Mike	Childrens Press
Paul Revere	V	B	Cornerstones of Freedom	Childrens Press
Pawnee Nation, The	O	I	Walters, Anna Lee	Capstone Press
Peanut	Q	I	Selsam, Millicent	William Morrow
Peanut Butter Gang, The	K	F	Siracusa, Catherine	Hyperion
Pearl, The	Z	RF	Steinbeck, John	Penguin Books
Pedro's Journal	Q	HF	Conrad, Pam	Bantam Doubleday Dell
Pee Wee Scouts: A Big Box of Memories,	L	RF	Delton, Judy	Bantam Doubleday Dell
Pee Wee Scouts: Bad, Bad Bunnies	L	RF	Delton, Judy	Bantam, Doubleday, Dell
Pee Wee Scouts: Blue Skies, French Fries	L	RF	Delton, Judy	Bantam Doubleday Dell
Pee Wee Scouts: Cookies and Crutches	L	RF	Delton, Judy	Bantam Doubleday Dell
Pee Wee Scouts: Fishy Wishes	L	RF	Delton, Judy	Bantam Doubleday Dell
Pee Wee Scouts: Greedy Groundhogs	L	RF	Delton, Judy	Bantam Doubleday Dell
Pee Wee Scouts: Grumpy Pumpkins	L	RF	Delton, Judy	Bantam Doubleday Dell
Pee Wee Scouts: Halloween Helpers	L	RF	Delton, Judy	Bantam Doubleday Dell
Pee Wee Scouts: Lights, Action, Land-Ho!	L	RF	Delton, Judy	Bantam Doubleday Dell
Pee Wee Scouts: Lucky Dog Days	L	RF	Delton, Judy	Bantam Doubleday Dell
Pee Wee Scouts: Moans and Groans and Dinosaur Bones	L	RF	Delton, Judy	Bantam Doubleday Dell
Pee Wee Scouts: Molly for Mayor	L	RF	Delton, Judy	Bantam Doubleday Dell
Pee Wee Scouts on First	L	RF	Delton, Judy	Bantam Doubleday Dell
Pee Wee Scouts on Parade	L	RF	Delton, Judy	Bantam Doubleday Dell
Pee Wee Scouts on Skis	L	RF	Delton, Judy	Bantam Doubleday Dell
Pee Wee Scouts: Peanut-Butter Pilgrims	L	RF	Delton, Judy	Bantam Doubleday Dell
Pee Wee Scouts: Pedal Power	L	RF	Delton, Judy	Bantam Doubleday Dell

Title	Level	Genre	Author/Series	Publisher/Distributor
Pee Wee Scouts: Piles of Pets	L	RF	Delton, Judy	Bantam Doubleday Dell
Pee Wee Scouts: Rosy Noses, Freezing Toes	L	RF	Delton, Judy	Bantam Doubleday Dell
Pee Wee Scouts: Sky Babies	L	RF	Delton, Judy	Bantam Doubleday Dell
Pee Wee Scouts: Sonny's Secret	L	RF	Delton, Judy	Bantam Doubleday Dell
Pee Wee Scouts: Spring Sprouts	L	RF	Delton, Judy	Bantam Doubleday Dell
Pee Wee Scouts: Teeny Weeny Zucchinis	L	RF	Delton, Judy	Bantam Doubleday Dell
Pee Wee Scouts: The Pee Wee Jubilee	L	RF	Delton, Judy	Bantam Doubleday Dell
Pee Wee Scouts: The Pooped Troop	L	RF	Delton, Judy	Bantam Doubleday Dell
Pee Wee Scouts: Trash Bash	L	RF	Delton, Judy	Bantam Doubleday Dell
Pee Wee Scouts: Tricks and Treats	L	RF	Delton, Judy	Bantam Doubleday Dell
Penguin, The	O	I	Crewe, Sabrina	Steck-Vaughn
Penguins	O	I	Holmes, Kevin J.	Capstone Press
Penguins of the Galápagos	P	I	Young Readers' Series	Barron's Educational Series
Pennsylvania	Q	I	Geography Department	Capstone Press
Penny Changes the Day, A	J	RF	Fetty, Margaret	Steck-Vaughn
People Are Living Things	K	I	Home Connection Collection	Rigby
People at Work	J	I	Momentum Literacy Program	Troll
People Could Fly, American Black Folktales	W	TL	Hamilton, Virginia	Alfred A. Knopf
People from the Past	R	I	Weldon Owen	Wright Group/McGraw Hill
Perfect Pony, A	O	RF	Szymanski, Lois	Avon Camelot
Perfect the Pig	L	F	Jeschke, Susan	Scholastic
Peril in the Bessledorf Parachute Factory	U	RF	Naylor, Phyllis Reynolds	Atheneum Books
Perilous Road, The	U	HF	Steele, William	Scholastic
Peru	O	I	Thoennes, Kristin	Capstone Press
Pet for You, A	K	I	Pair-It Books	Steck-Vaughn
Pet Parade	O	RF	Giff, Patricia Reilly	Bantam Doubleday Dell
Pet Sitters Plus Five	L	RF	Springstubb, Tricia	Scholastic
Pet Vet	N	I	Pacific Literacy	Pacific Learning
Pete's Story	L	F	Literacy 2000	Rigby
Peter and the North Wind	L	TL	Littledale, Freya	Scholastic
Peter Tchaikovsky	Q	B	Venezia, Mike	Childrens Press
Peter the Pumpkin-Eater	M	RF	Scott, Janine	Rigby
Pets	J	F	Pacific Literacy	Pacific Learning
Pets Need People	M	I	Literacy 2000	Rigby
Phan's Diary	N	RF	PM Ruby	Rigby
Phantom Tollbooth, The	W	F	Juster, Norton	Bantam Doubleday Dell
Phantoms Don't Drive Sports Cars	M	F	Dadey, D. & Jones, M. T.	Scholastic
Pheasant and Kingfisher	L	TL	Book Shop	Mondo
Philip Hall Likes Me. I Reckon Maybe.	Y	RF	Greene, Bette	Puffin Books
Philippines, The	O	I	Davis, Lucile	Capstone Press
Phoebe The Spy	R	HF	Berry Griffin, Judith	Scholastic
Phoenix Rising	W	RF	Hesse, Karen	Penguin Group
Photographic Memory	O	RF	PM Ruby	Rigby
Photos, Photos	N	I	Wildcats	Wright Group/McGraw Hill
Picasso	Q	B	Venezia, Mike	Childrens Press
Picked for the Team	L	RF	PM Gold	Rigby
Picking Apples and Pumpkins	L	I	Hutchings, A. & R.	Scholastic
Picking Up Papers	K	RF	City Kids	Rigby
Pickle Puss	L	RF	Giff, Patricia Reilly	Bantam Doubleday Dell
Picture Book of Abraham Lincoln, A	M	B	Adler, David A.	Holiday House
Picture Book of Amelia Earhart, A	M	B	Adler, David A.	Holiday House
Picture Book of Anne Frank, A	M	B	Adler, David A.	Holiday House
Picture Book of Benjamin Franklin, A	M	B	Adler, David A.	Holiday House
Picture Book of Christopher Columbus, A	M	B	Adler, David A.	Holiday House
Picture Book of Davy Crockett, A	M	TL	Adler, David A.	Holiday House
Picture Book of Eleanor Roosevelt, A	M	B	Adler, David A.	Holiday House
Picture Book of Florence Nightingale, A	M	B	Adler, David A.	Holiday House
Picture Book of Frederick Douglass, A	M	B	Adler, David A.	Holiday House
Picture Book of George Washington, A	M	B	Adler, David A.	Holiday House
Picture Book of George Washington Carver, A	M	B	Adler, David A.	Holiday House

Title	Level	Genre	Author/Series	Publisher/Distributor
Picture Book of Harriet Tubman, A	M	B	Adler, David A.	Holiday House
Picture Book of Helen Keller, A	M	B	Adler, David A.	Holiday House
Picture Book of Jackie Robinson, A	M	B	Adler, David A.	Holiday House
Picture Book of Jesse Owens, A	N	B	Adler, David A.	Holiday House
Picture Book of John F. Kennedy, A	N	B	Adler, David A.	Holiday House
Picture Book of Louis Braille, A	M	B	Adler, David A.	Holiday House
Picture Book of Martin Luther King, Jr., A	M	B	Adler, David A.	Holiday House
Picture Book of Patrick Henry, A	M	B	Adler, David A.	Holiday House
Picture Book of Paul Revere, A	M	B	Adler, David A.	Holiday House
Picture Book of Robert E. Lee, A	N	B	Adler, David A.	Holiday House
Picture Book of Rosa Parks, A	M	B	Adler, David A.	Holiday House
Picture Book of Sacagawea, A	M	B	Adler, David A.	Holiday House
Picture Book of Simon Bolivar, A	Q	B	Adler, David A.	Bantam Doubleday Dell
Picture Book of Sitting Bull, A	M	B	Adler, David A.	Holiday House
Picture Book of Sojourner Truth, A	M	B	Adler, David A.	Holiday House
Picture Book of Thomas Alva Edison, A	M	B	Adler, David A.	Holiday House
Picture Book of Thomas Jefferson, A	M	B	Adler, David A.	Holiday House
Picture Book of Thurgood Marshall, A	M	B	Adler, David A.	Holiday House
Picture of Freedom, A	T	HF	McKissack, Patricia C.	Scholastic
Pie Magic	N	F	Cornell, Laura	Beech Tree Books
Pied Piper of Hamelin, The	K	TL	Hautzig, Deborah	Random House
Pied Piper, The	M	TL	Sunshine	Wright Group/McGraw Hill
Pierre	K	RF	Sendak, Maurice	Scholastic
Pierre August Renoir	Q	B	Venezia, Mike	Childrens Press
Piggle	K	F	Bonsall, Crosby	Harper Collins
Piglet in a Playpen	Q	RF	Baglio, Ben M.	Scholastic
Pigman & Me, The	Z	B	Zindel, Paul	Dell
Pigman's Legacy, The	Z	RF	Zindel, Paul	Harper & Row
Pignocchio	L	F	Pair-It Books	Steck-Vaughn
Pigs	L	I	PM Animal Facts: Purple	Rigby
Pigs Have Piglets	M	I	Animals and Their Young	Compass Point Books
Pigs Might Fly	R	F	King-Smith, Dick	Scholastic
Pike River Phantom, The	R	F	Wright, Betty	Scholastic
Pile in Pete's Room, The	K	RF	Sunshine	Wright Group/McGraw Hill
Pilgrims of Plimouth, The	T	I	Sewall, Marcia	Simon & Schuster
Pilgrims, The	V	I	Cornerstones of Freedom	Children's Press
Pinballs, The	S	RF	Byars, Betsy	HarperTrophy
Pine Hollow: Changing Leads	W	RF	Bryant, Bonnie	Bantam Doubleday Dell
Pine Hollow: Conformation Faults	W	RF	Bryant, Bonnie	Bantam Doubleday Dell
Pine Hollow: Reining In	W	RF	Bryant, Bonnie	Bantam Doubleday Dell
Pine Hollow: The Long Ride	W	RF	Bryant, Bonnie	Bantam Doubleday Dell
Pine Hollow: The Trail Home	W	RF	Bryant, Bonnie	Bantam Doubleday Dell
Pinky and Rex	L	RF	Howe, James	Simon & Schuster
Pinky and Rex and the Bully	L	RF	Howe, James	Simon & Schuster
Pinky and Rex and the Double-Dad Weekend	L	RF	Howe, James	Simon & Schuster
Pinky and Rex and the Mean Old Witch	L	RF	Howe, James	Simon & Schuster
Pinky and Rex and the New Baby	L	RF	Howe, James	Simon & Schuster
Pinky and Rex and the New Neighbors	L	RF	Howe, James	Simon & Schuster
Pinky and Rex and the Perfect Pumpkin	L	RF	Howe, James	Simon & Schuster
Pinky and Rex and the School Play	L	RF	Howe, James	Simon & Schuster
Pinky and Rex and the Spelling Bee	L	RF	Howe, James	Simon & Schuster
Pinky and Rex Get Married	L	RF	Howe, James	Simon & Schuster
Pinky and Rex Go to Camp	L	RF	Howe, James	Aladdin
Pioneer Bear	L	F	Sandin, Joan	Random House
Pioneer Cat	N	HF	Hooks, William H.	Random House
Pioneer Girl, The Story of Laura Ingalls Wilder	R	B	Anderson, William	Harper Collins
Pioneer Way, The	Q	I	Kummer, Patricia K.	Steck-Vaughn
Pioneers	T	I	Sandler, Martin W.	HarperTrophy
Pippi Goes on Board	O	F	Lindgren, Astrid	Puffin Books
Pippi in the South Seas	O	F	Lindgren, Astrid	Puffin Books

Title	Level	Genre	Author/Series	Publisher/Distributor
Pippi Longstocking	O	F	Lindgren, Astrid	The Penguin Group
Pirate Pie	M	F	Vaughan, Marcia	Pacific Learning
Pirate's Promise	N	RF	Bulla, Clyde Robert	HarperTrophy
Pirates Don't Wear Pink Sunglasses	M	F	Dadey, D. & Jones, M. T.	Scholastic
Pirates Past Noon	M	F	Osborne, Mary Pope	Scholastic
Pitching Trouble	N	RF	Kroll, Stephen	Avon Camelot
Pizza for Everyone	K	I	Pair-It Books	Steck-Vaughn
Place Called Heartbreak, A: A Story of Vietnam	U	I	Myers, Walter Dean	Steck-Vaughn
Place in the Sun, A	U	HF	Rubalcaba, Jill	Puffin Books
Place to Call Home, A	Y	RF	Koller, Jackie French	Aladdin
Place To Hide, A	X	B	Petit, Jayne	Scholastic
Plain Girl	Q	RF	Sorensen, Virginia	Harcourt Brace
Planet Boring	P	F	Cook, Nathan	Pacific Learning
Planet of Junior Brown, The	Z	RF	Hamilton, Virginia	Aladdin
Planets, The	Q	I	Weldon Owen	Wright Group/McGraw Hill
Planets, The	J	I	Wonder World	Wright Group/McGraw Hill
Planning a Birthday Party	N	I	Book Shop	Mondo
Plant Kingdom, The	Q	I	Weldon Owen	Wright Group/McGraw Hill
Plant That Ate Dirty Socks Goes Up in Space	S	F	McArthur, Nancy	Avon Camelot
Platypus	P	I	Short, J., Green, J., and Bird, B.	Mondo
Play Ball!	R	I	Weldon Owen	Wright Group/McGraw Hill
Play Ball, Amelia Bedelia	L	F	Parish, Peggy	Harper & Row
Playing Favorites	N	RF	Kroll, Steven	Avon Camelot
Playing with Words	O	B	Howe, James	Richard C. Owen
Please Don't Be Mine, Julie Valentine!	R	RF	Strasser, Todd	Scholastic
Pleasing the Ghost	V	F	Creech, Sharon	Harper Collins
Plumbers	M	I	Boraas, Tracey	Capstone Press
Pluto	N	I	A First Book	Franklin Watts
Pluto	N	I	A True Book	Children's Press
Plymouth Colony, The	S	I	We The People	Compass Point Books
Pocket for Corduroy, A	K	F	Freeman, Don	Scholastic
Pocket Full of Acorns, A	L	RF	Beames, Michael	Dominie Press
Pocket Full of Seeds, A	V	HF	Sachs, Marilyn	Scholastic
Pocketful of Goobers: Story of George Washington Carver	Q	B	Mitchell, Barbara	Carolrhoda Books
Polar Bear, The	S	I	Hemstock, Annie	Capstone Press
Polar Bears	N	I	PM Animal Facts: Silver	Rigby
Polar Bears	K	I	Wonder World	Wright Group/McGraw Hill
Polar Bears Past Bedtime	M	F	Osborne, Mary Pope	Random House
Polar Regions	N	I	Habitats of the World	Dominie Press
Police Officers	L	I	Community Workers	Compass Point Books
Police Officers	M	I	Ready, Dee	Capstone Press
Pompeii...Buried Alive!	N	I	Kunhardt, Edith	Random House
Ponies at the Point	Q	RF	Baglio, Ben M.	Scholastic
Pony Express, The	V	I	Cornerstones of Freedom	Children's Press
Pony For Jeremiah, A	R	HF	Miller, Robert H.	Silver Burdett Press
Pony Named Shawney, A	P	RF	Small, Mary	Mondo
Pony on the Porch	Q	RF	Baglio, Ben M.	Scholastic
Pony Pals: A Pony for Keeps	O	RF	Betancourt, Jeanne	Scholastic
Pony Pals: A Pony in Trouble	O	RF	Betancourt, Jeanne	Scholastic
Pony Pals: Detective Pony	O	RF	Betancourt, Jeanne	Scholastic
Pony Pals: Don't Hurt My Pony	O	RF	Betancourt, Jeanne	Scholastic
Pony Pals: Give Me Back My Pony	O	RF	Betancourt, Jeanne	Scholastic
Pony Pals: Good-bye Pony	O	RF	Betancourt, Jeanne	Scholastic
Pony Pals: I Want a Pony	O	RF	Betancourt, Jeanne	Scholastic
Pony Pals: Keep Out, Pony!	O	RF	Betancourt, Jeanne	Scholastic
Pony Pals: Pony to the Rescue	O	RF	Betancourt, Jeanne	Scholastic
Pony Pals, Pony-Sitters	O	RF	Betancourt, Jeanne	Scholastic
Pony Pals: Runaway Pony	O	RF	Betancourt, Jeanne	Scholastic
Pony Pals: The Blind Pony	O	RF	Betancourt, Jeanne	Scholastic

Title	Level	Genre	Author/Series	Publisher/Distributor
Pony Pals: The Girl Who Hated Ponies	O	RF	Betancourt, Jeanne	Scholastic
Pony Pals: The Lonely Pony	O	RF	Betancourt, Jeanne	Scholastic
Pony Pals: Too Many Ponies	O	RF	Betancourt, Jeanne	Scholastic
Pony Parade	O	RF	Baglio, Ben M.	Scholastic
Pony Tails: Jasmine and the Jumping Pony	P	RF	Bryant, Bonnie	Bantam Doubleday Dell
Pony Tails: Jasmine's Christmas Ride	P	RF	Bryant, Bonnie	Bantam Doubleday Dell
Pony Tails: May Takes the Lead	P	RF	Bryant, Bonnie	Bantam Doubleday Dell
Pony Trouble	L	RF	Gasque, Dale Blackwell	Hyperion
Pookie and Joe	K	F	Literacy 2000	Rigby
Pool of Fire, The	V	F	Christopher, John	Aladdin
Poopsie Pomerantz Pick Up Your Feet	P	RF	Giff, Patricia Reilly	Dell
Poor Girl, Rich Girl	T	RF	Wilson, Johnniece Marshall	Language for Learning Assoc.
Popcorn Book, The	N	I	dePaola, Tomie	Holiday House
Popcorn Book, The	K	I	Reading Unlimited	Celebration Press
Popcorn Shop, The	J	RF	Low, Alice	Scholastic
Poppleton	J	F	Rylant, Cynthia	Scholastic
Poppleton and Friends	J	F	Rylant, Cynthia	Blue Sky Press
Poppleton Everyday	J	F	Rylant, Cynthia	Scholastic
Poppleton Forever	J	F	Rylant, Cynthia	Scholastic
Poppleton Has Fun	J	F	Rylant, Cynthia	Scholastic
Poppleton In Fall	J	F	Rylant, Cynthia	Scholastic
Poppleton in Spring	J	F	Rylant, Cynthia	Scholastic
Poppy	S	F	Avi	Avon
Poppy and Rye	S	F	Avi	Avon
Porcupine's Pajama Party	J	F	Harshman, Terry Webb	HarperTrophy
Postcard Pest, The	M	RF	Giff, Patricia Reilly	Bantam Doubleday Dell
Postcards From France	N	I	Arnold, Helen	Steck-Vaughn
Postcards From Kenya	N	I	Arnold, Helen	Steck-Vaughn
Postcards From South Africa	N	I	Dawson, Zoe	Steck-Vaughn
Postcards From Vietnam	N	I	Allard, Denise	Steck-Vaughn
Postman Pete	J	RF	Book Shop	Mondo
Pot of Stone Soup, A	L	TL	Ready Readers	Pearson Learning
Potato	N	RF	Peirce, Robin	Wright Group/McGraw Hill
Potter in Fiji, A	N	I	Wonder World	Wright Group/McGraw Hill
Powder Puff Puzzle, The	L	RF	Giff, Patricia Reilly	Bantam Doubleday Dell
Power Machines	N	I	Robbins, Ken	Henry Holt & Company
Power of Nature, The	K	I	Early Connections	Benchmark Education
Power of Water, The	L	I	Home Connection Collection	Rigby
Powerhouse, Inside a Nuclear Power Plant	Z	I	Wilcox, Charlotte	Carolrhoda Books
Powers of Congress, The	W	I	Cornerstones of Freedom	Children's Press
Powwow Summer: A Family Celebrates the Circle of Life	S	I	Rendon, Marcie R.	Carolrhoda Books
Prairie Songs	Q	HF	Conrad, Pam	HarperTrophy
Preacher's Boy	T	RF	Paterson, Katherine	Houghton Mifflin
Prehistoric Record Breakers	N	I	Discovery World	Rigby
Prehistory to Egypt	R	I	Journey Through History	Barron's Educational Series
Present From Aunt Skidoo, The	M	RF	Literacy 2000	Rigby
Presidency, The	N	I	A True Book	Children's Press
Presidential Elections	W	I	Cornerstones of Freedom	Children's Press
Presidents' Day	K	I	Frost, Helen	Capstone Press
Pretty Good Magic	J	RF	Dubowski, C. E. & Dubowski, M.	Random House
Pride of Puerto Rico: The Life of Roberto Clemente	W	B	Walker, Paul Robert	Harcourt Brace
Pride of the Rockets	N	RF	Kroll, Stephen	Avon Camelot
Prince Amos	R	RF	Paulsen, Gary	Bantam Doubleday Dell
Prince William	Q	B	Rand, Gloria	Henry Holt & Company
Princess and the Castle, The	J	F	Leonhardt, Alice	Steck-Vaughn
Princess and the Peas, The	K	TL	Enrichment	Wright Group/McGraw Hill
Princess and the Wise Woman, The	K	TL	Ready Readers	Pearson Learning
Princess Euphorbia	N	RF	SupaDoopers	Sundance
Princess Josie's Pets	L	RF	Macdonald, Maryann	Hyperion

Title	Level	Genre	Author/Series	Publisher/Distributor
Princess Rosa's Winter	K	F	Hindley, Judy	Wright Group/McGraw Hill
Princess Who Loved to Cook, The	M	F	Cartwright, Pauline	Dominie Press
Princess Who Wanted the Moon, The	M	F	Lane, Sheila and Marion Kemp	Wood Lock Educational
Priscilla and the Dinosaurs	L	RF	Sunshine	Wright Group/McGraw Hill
Private Notebook of Katie Roberts, Age 11, The	P	RF	Hest, Amy	Candlewick Press
Prize for Purry, A	K	RF	Literacy 2000	Rigby
Project Apollo	N	I	A True Book	Children's Press
Project Gemini	N	I	A True Book	Children's Press
Project Mercury	N	I	A True Book	Children's Press
Promise Me the Moon	V	RF	Barnes, Joyce Annette Barnes	The Penguin Group
Proof of Magic	N	F	Dionetti, Michelle	Wright Group/McGraw Hill
Proud Taste For Scarlet And Miniver	W	F	Konigsburg, E. L.	Dell
Prudence	N	I	Raatma, Lucia	Capstone Press
Pterodactyl at the Airport	K	F	Wesley & the Dinosaurs	Wright Group/McGraw Hill
Pueblo Indians, The	P	I	Ross, Pamela	Capstone Press
Pumpkin House, The	J	F	Literacy 2000	Rigby
Pumpkins	M	I	Ray, Mary Lyn	Harcourt Brace
Puppets	P	I	Trussell-Cullen, Alan	Rigby
Puppies, Dogs, and Blue Northers	S	I	Paulsen, Gary	Delacorte Press
Puppies in the Pantry	Q	RF	Baglio, Ben M.	Scholastic
Puppy Love	N	RF	Duffey, Betsy	Puffin Books
Puppy Puzzle	O	RF	Baglio, Ben M.	Scholastic
Puppy Who Wanted a Boy, The	L	F	Thayer, Jane	Scholastic
Purple Climbing Days	M	RF	Giff, Patricia Reilly	Bantam Doubleday Dell
Purple Walrus and Other Perfect Pets	O	RF	Wildcats	Wright Group/McGraw Hill
Pushcart War, The	Y	F	Merrill, Jean	Bantam Doubleday Dell
Puss-in-Boots	K	TL	PM Tales and Plays- Purple	Rigby
Qillak	M	RF	Jensen, Ned	Wright Group/McGraw Hill
Quackers, the Troublesome Duck	M	F	Ellen, Leslie	Pearson Learning
Quake!	T	RF	Cottonwood, Joe	Language for Learning Assoc.
Queen Eleanor: Independent Spirit in the Medieval World	X	B	Brooks, Polly Schoyer	Houghton Mifflin
Queen of the Pool	N	RF	PM Emerald	Rigby
Queen's Parrot, The: A Play	J	TL	Literacy 2000	Rigby
Questions and Answers About Forest Animals	P	I	Chinery, Michael	Kingfisher
Questions and Answers About Freshwater Animals	P	I	Chinery, Michael	Kingfisher
Quilt Story, The	L	HF	Johnston, T. & de Paola, T.	Scholastic
Quilt with a Difference, A	N	I	Pacific Literacy	Pacific Learning
R is for Radish!	J	F	Coxe, Molly	Random House
Rabbit Catches the Sun	M	F	Sunshine	Wright Group/McGraw Hill
Rabbit Race	O	RF	Baglio, Ben M.	Scholastic
Rabbit Stew	L	F	Literacy 2000	Rigby
Rabbit's Birthday Kite	J	F	Bank Street	Bantam Doubleday Dell
Rabbits	N	I	Literacy 2000	Rigby
Rabbits Have Bunnies	M	I	Animals and Their Young	Compass Point Books
Rabble Starkey	T	RF	Lowry, Lois	Bantam Doubleday Dell
Raccoons	M	I	PM Animal Facts: Gold	Rigby
Race to Green End, The	J	F	PM Turquoise	Rigby
Rachel to the Rescue	O	RF	SupaDoopers	Sundance
Ragweed	U	F	Avi	Avon
Rain	K	I	Pebble Books	Grolier, Capstone
Rain Forest	R	I	Worldwise	Grolier
Rain Forest Adventure	L	F	Pair-It Books	Steck-Vaughn
Rain Forest, The	Q	I	Fusselman, Fred	Rigby
Rain Forest Tree, A	Q	I	Kite, Lorien	Crabtree
Rain Ghost, The	X	F	Kilworth, Garry	Scholastic
Rain or Shine	Q	I	Weldon Owen	Wright Group/McGraw Hill
Rain, Snow, and Hail	J	I	Discovery World	Rigby
Rainbow People, The	V	F	Yep, Lawrence	HarperTrophy
Rainbow Solution, The	N	RF	Literacy 2000	Rigby

Title	Level	Genre	Author/Series	Publisher/Distributor
Rainbow Wings	M	F	Nevinski, Margaret	Wright Group/McGraw Hill
Rainbows All Around	M	RF	Hardin, Suzanne	Pacific Learning
Rainbows of the Sea	L	I	Thomas, Meredith	Mondo
Rairarubia	S	F	Adams, W. Royce	Lost Coast Press
Ralph S. Mouse	O	F	Cleary, Beverly	Harper Trophy
Ramona and Her Father	O	RF	Cleary, Beverly	Avon
Ramona and Her Mother	O	RF	Cleary, Beverly	Avon
Ramona Forever	O	RF	Cleary, Beverly	Hearst
Ramona Quimby, Age 8	O	RF	Cleary, Beverly	Hearst
Ramona the Brave	O	RF	Cleary, Beverly	Hearst
Ramona the Pest	O	RF	Cleary, Beverly	Avon
Raptors: Hunters in the Sky	R	I	Rauzon, Mark J.	Wright Group/McGraw Hill
Rapunzel	L	TL	Literacy 2000	Rigby
Rascal	V	HF	North, Sterling	Scholastic
Rat's Tale, A	T	F	Seidler, Tor	HarperTrophy
Rats!	O	RF	Cutler, Jane	Farrar, Straus and Giroux
Rats on the Range and Other Stories	O	F	Marshall, James	The Penguin Group
Rats on the Roof and Other Stories	O	F	Marshall, James	The Penguin Group
Raven's Gift	L	F	Books For Young Learners	Richard C. Owen
Ready, Set, Go!	K	RF	Pacific Literacy	Pacific Learning
Real Thief, The	U	F	Steig, William	Farrar, Straus and Giroux
Red and Blue Mittens	M	RF	Reading Unlimited	Celebration Press
Red Cap	W	HF	Wisler, G. Clifton	The Penguin Group
Red Dog	U	RF	Wallace, Bill	Simon & Schuster
Red Egg and Ginger	K	RF	SooHoo, Suzanne & Patrick	Rigby
Red Means Good Fortune: A Story of San Francisco's Chinatown	S	I	Goldin, Barbara Diamond	The Penguin Group
Red Ribbon Rosie	M	RF	Marzollo, Jean	Random House
Red Scarf Girl: Memoir of the Cultural Revolution	Z	B	Jiang, Ji Li	HarperTrophy
Red-Tailed Hawk, The	L	RF	Books For Young Learners	Richard C. Owen
Reduce, Reuse, and Recycle	K	I	Early Connections	Benchmark Education
Refugees, The	P	RF	Marriott, Janice	Pacific Learning
Relationships of Living Things	R	I	Atwater, Mary & Baptiste et al	Macmillan/McGraw-Hill
Remarkable Journey of Prince Jen, The	V	F	Alexander, Lloyd	Bantam Doubleday Dell
Remember Not To Forget: A Memory of the Holocaust	V	I	Finkelstein, Norman H.	William & Morrow
Remember the Ladies: The First Women's Rights Convention	U	I	Johnston, Norma	Scholastic
Remembering the Big Quake	R	I	Trussell-Cullen, Alan	Pacific Learning
Rent a Third Grader	O	RF	Hiller, B.B.	Scholastic
Report To the Principal's Office	U	RF	Spinelli, Jerry	Scholastic
Reptiles and Amphibians	R	I	Weldon Owen	Wright Group/McGraw Hill
Rescue!	J	RF	Sunshine	Wright Group/McGraw Hill
Rescue	O	RF	Wildcats	Wright Group/McGraw Hill
Rescue, The	L	RF	Pacific Learning	Pacific Learning
Rescuers, The	S	F	Sharp, Margery	Dell Publishing
Rescuing Nelson	J	F	PM Turquoise	Rigby
Respect the Winds	M	TL	Reeder, Paul	Wright Group/McGraw Hill
Return of Rinaldo, the Sly Fox	M	TL	Scheffler, Ursel	North-South Books
Return of the Great Brain, The	T	RF	Fitzgerald, John D.	Dell
Return of the Home Run Kid	N	RF	Christopher, Matt	Scholastic
Return of the Third-Grade Ghosthunters, The	M	RF	Maccarone, Grace	Scholastic
Return to Howliday Inn	P	F	Howe, James	Avon Camelot
Revenge of the Mummy	P	RF	Parker, A.E.	Scholastic
Revolutionary Poet: A Story About Phillis Wheatley	Q	B	Weidt, Maryann N.	Carolrhoda Books
Revolutionary War on Wednesday	M	F	Osborne, Mary Pope	Random House
Rhinos	O	I	Holmes, Kevin J.	Capstone Press
Rhythm and Shoes	N	I	Pacific Literacy	Pacific Learning
Ribsy	O	RF	Cleary, Beverly	Hearst
Riches from Nature	K	I	Early Connections	Benchmark Education

Title	Level	Genre	Author/Series	Publisher/Distributor
Riddle of The Red Purse, The	L	RF	Giff, Patricia Reilly	Bantam Doubleday Dell
Riddle of the Rosetta Stone, The	V	I	Giblin, James Cross	HarperTrophy
Riddles of the Universe	S	I	Bonallack, John	Pacific Learning
Riding Freedom	P	HF	Ryan, Pam Munoz	Scholastic
Riding to Craggy Rock	J	RF	PM Turquoise	Rigby
Rifle, The	T	HF	Paulsen, Gary	Dell
Right or Wrong?	O	RF	Wildcats	Wright Group/McGraw Hill
Right Place for Jupiter, The	K	RF	PM Story Books -Silver	Rigby
Righteous Revenge of Artemis Bonner, The	U	RF	Myers, Walter Dean	HarperTrophy
Rinaldo the Sly Fox	M	TL	Scheffler, Ursel	North-South Books
Ring of Endless Light, A	W	F	L'Engle, Madeleine	Dell
Rip-Roaring Russell	M	RF	Hurwitz, Johanna	The Penguin Group
Ripeka's Carving	J	RF	Literacy 2000	Rigby
Riptide	O	RF	Weller, Frances Ward	Putnam & Grosset
Rising Stars of the NBA	P	B	Layden, Joe	Scholastic
River Apart, A	U	HF	Sutherland, Robert	Fitzhenry and Whiteside
River Rapids Ride, The	L	RF	Sunshine	Wright Group/McGraw Hill
River Rats	O	RF	Belcher, Angie	Pacific Learning
River Runners	M	RF	Belcher, Angie	Rigby
River, The	R	RF	Paulsen, Gary	Dell
River Through the Ages	U	I	Steele, Philip	Troll Associates
Road Goes By, A	J	I	Momentum Literacy Program	Troll
Road Through the Ages	U	I	Steele, Philip	Troll Associates
Road to Memphis, The	X	HF	Taylor, Mildred D.	The Penguin Group
Road to Seneca Falls, The	R	B	Swain, Gwenyth	Carolrhoda Books
Roald Dahl's Revolting Rhymes	P	F	Dahl, Roald	Puffin Books
Robber Pig and the Ginger Bear	M	F	Read Alongs	Rigby
Robber Pig and the Green Eggs	M	F	Read Alongs	Rigby
Robber, The	M	RF	Sunshine	Wright Group/McGraw Hill
Robert Goddard	K	B	Schaefer, Lola M.	Capstone Press
Robin Hood and the Silver Trophy	L	TL	PM Tales and Plays-Silver	Rigby
Robinson Crusoe	P	TL	Dolch, E. W. and Marguerite P.	Scholastic
Rock Climbing	Q	I	Lund, Bill	Capstone Press
Rock Climbing	N	I	Ramsey, Joe	Wright Group/McGraw Hill
Rocks & Minerals	R	I	The Wonders of our World	Crabtree
Rodney, the Surfing Duck	N	F	SupaDoopers	Sundance
Roll of Thunder, Hear My Cry	W	HF	Taylor, Mildred D.	The Penguin Group
Roller Skates!	J	RF	Calmenson, Stephanie	Scholastic
Rollerama	N	RF	SupaDoopers	Sundance
Rollo and Tweedy and the Ghost at Dougal Castle	K	F	Allen, Laura Jean	HarperTrophy
Rooster's Gift, The	M	F	Conrad, Pam	HarperCollins
Root Cellar, The	V	HF	Lunn, Janet	The Penguin Group
Rosa and Fredo	M	F	SupaDoopers	Sundance
Rosa Parks	P	B	Greenfield, Eloise	HarperTrophy
Rosa Parks: My Story	U	B	Parks, Rosa	Scholastic
Rosa's Tonsils	K	RF	Foundations	Wright Group/McGraw Hill
Roses for Renee	J	RF	Evangeline Nicholas Collection	Wright Group/McGraw Hill
Rosie the Riveter	Z	I	Colman, Penny	Crown Publishers, Inc.
Rosie's Big City Ballet	N	RF	Giff, Patricia Reilly	The Penguin Group
Rosie's Nutcracker Dreams	N	RF	Giff, Patricia Reilly	The Penguin Group
Rosie's Story	L	RF	Book Shop	Mondo
Rotating Rollerblades and Other Cases, The	O	RF	Simon, Seymour	Avon
Rough Riders, The	W	B	Cornerstones of Freedom	Children's Press
Rough-Faced Girl, The	S	TL	Martin, R. & Shannon, D.	Scholastic
Round and Round: The Story of Wheels	N	I	McAlister, Margaret	Rigby
Row, Row, Row Your Boat	J	RF	Bank Street	Bantam Doubleday Dell
Royal Baby-Sitters, The	J	RF	Sunshine	Wright Group/McGraw Hill
Royal Drum, The	L	TL	Book Shop	Mondo
Ruby and the Smoke, The	Y	F	Pullman, Phillip	Laurel-Leaf Books
Ruby the Copycat	K	RF	Rathman, Peggy	Scholastic

Title	Level	Genre	Author/Series	Publisher/Distributor
Rules	J	I	Early Connections	Benchmark Education
Rumpelstiltskin	J	TL	Book Shop	Mondo
Rumpelstiltskin	M	TL	Once Upon a Time	Wright Group/McGraw Hill
Rumpelstiltskin	K	TL	PM Tales and Plays- Gold	Rigby
Rumpelstiltskin	J	TL	Traditional Tales	Dominie
Rumpelstiltskin	N	TL	Zelinsky, Paul O.	Scholastic
Runaway Ralph	O	F	Cleary, Beverly	Hearst
Runaway to Freedom: A Story of the Underground Railway	T	I	Smucker, Barbara	Harper Trophy
Rupert and the Griffin	Q	F	Hillman, Robert	Rigby
Russell and Elisa	M	RF	Hurwitz, Johanna	The Penguin Group
Russell Rides Again	M	RF	Hurwitz, Johanna	The Penguin Group
Russell Sprouts	M	RF	Hurwitz, Johanna	The Penguin Group
Russia	O	I	Thoennes, Kristin	Capstone Press
Ryan's Dog Ringo	P	RF	Gibson, Marie	Rigby
Sable	O	RF	Hesse, Karen	Henry Holt & Co.
Sacajawea	N	B	Biography	Benchmark Education
Sacajawea	Y	B	Bruchac, Joseph	Harcourt
Sadako and the Thousand Paper Cranes	R	HF	Coerr, Eleanor	Bantam Doubleday Dell
Sadie and the Snowman	L	RF	Morgan, Allen	Scholastic
Safe Return	Q	RF	Dexter, Catherine	Candlewick Press
Salamandastron	Z	F	Jacques, Brian	Ace Books
Salem Days: Life in a Colonial Seaport	T	I	Adventures in Colonial America	Troll
Salty Dog	L	RF	Rand, Gloria	Henry Holt & Co.
Sam and Kim	O	I	Pacific Literacy	Pacific Learning
Sam and the Firefly	J	F	Eastman, P.D.	Random House
Sam King and Little Bull	L	RF	Wilson, Trevor	Dominie Press
Sam the Minuteman	J	HF	Benchley, Nathaniel	HarperTrophy
Sam Who Never Forgets	K	F	Rice, Eve	Morrow
Sam's Big Clean-up	K	RF	Windmill Books	Rigby
Sam's Glasses	M	RF	Literacy 2000	Rigby
Sam's Solution	K	RF	Literacy 2000	Rigby
Samantha Saves the Day	Q	RF	The American Girls Collection	Pleasant Company
Samantha's Surprise	Q	RF	The American Girls Collection	Pleasant Company
Samuel's Choice	S	HF	Berleth, Richard	Scholastic
Samurai's Daughter, The	Q	TL	San Souci, Robert D.	The Penguin Group
San Domingo	R	I	Henry, Marguerite	Scholastic
Sand On The Move: The Story of Dunes	U	I	A First Book	Franklin Watts
Sandwich Hero, The	K	RF	Literacy 2000	Rigby
Sandy's Suitcase	K	RF	Edwards, Elsy	SRA/McGraw-Hill
Santa Claus Doesn't Mop Floors	M	F	Dadey, D. & Jones, M. T.	Scholastic
Santa Fe Trail, The	V	I	Cornerstones of Freedom	Children's Press
Santa Fe Trail, The	S	I	We The People	Compass Point Books
Sara Crewe	O	HF	Burnett, Frances Hodgson	Scholastic
Sarah Bishop	X	HF	O'Dell, Scott	Scholastic
Sarah Morton Daniel's Day: Day in the Life of, A	Q	B	Waters, Kate	Scholastic
Sarah, Plain and Tall	R	HF	MacLachlan, Patricia	HarperTrophy
Sarny: A Life Remembered	W	HF	Paulsen, Gary	Delacorte Press
Saturn	N	I	A First Book	Franklin Watts
Saturn	N	I	A True Book	Children's Press
Saturnalia	W	RF	Fleischman, Paul	Harper Collins
Save the Everglades	R	I	Stamper, Judith Bauer	Steck-Vaughn
Save the Manatee	N	I	Friesinger, Alison	Random House
Save the River!	M	SF	Pair-It Books	Steck-Vaughn
Save the Sea Turtles!	M	I	Leonhardt, Alice	Steck-Vaughn
Saving the Park	N	RF	Wilson, Sarah	Pacific Learning
Saving The Yellow Eye	P	I	Darby, John	Pacific Learning
Say "Cheese"	L	RF	Giff, Patricia Reilly	Bantam Doubleday Dell
Say Hola, Sarah	N	RF	Giff, Patricia Reilly	Bantam Doubleday Dell
Scaly Things	Q	I	Weldon Owen	Wright Group/McGraw Hill

Title	Level	Genre	Author/Series	Publisher/Distributor
Scared Stiff	V	F	Malcolm, Jahnna N.	Scholastic
Scaredy Dog	K	RF	Thomas, Jane Resh	Hyperion
Scary Day, The	N	RF	Bennett, Jean	Pacific Learning
Scary Spiders!	J	RF	Sunshine	Wright Group/McGraw Hill
Schernoff Discoveries, The	T	RF	Paulsen, Gary	Dell
School Bus Drivers	M	I	Ready, Dee	Capstone Press
School Mouse, The	P	F	King-Smith, Dick	Hyperion
School Mural, The	L	RF	Pair-It Books	Steck-Vaughn
School Principals	M	I	Boraas, Tracey	Capstone Press
School Vacation	J	RF	City Kids	Rigby
School's Out	N	RF	Hurwitz, Johanna	Scholastic
Schoolyard Mystery, The	L	RF	Levy, Elizabeth	Scholastic
Science Fair Surprise, The	Q	RF	Burke, Melissa Blackwell	Steck-Vaughn
Science-Just Add Salt	L	I	Markle, Sandra	Scholastic
Scorpions	Z	RF	Myers, Walter Dean	HarperTrophy
Scrappers No Easy Out	Q	RF	Hughes, Dean	Aladdin
Scrappers No Fear	Q	RF	Hughes, Dean	Aladdin
Scruffy	K	RF	Parish, Peggy	HarperTrophy
Sea Monsters Don't Ride Motorcycles	M	RF	Dadey, D. & Jones, M. T.	Scholastic
Sea Otter Rescue: The Aftermath of an Oil Spill	W	I	Smith, Roland	Scholastic
Sea Otters	L	I	Storyteller Nonfiction	Wright Group/McGraw Hill
Sea Star	R	RF	Henry, Marguerite	Aladdin
Sea Turtles	K	I	Marine Life For Yng. Readers	Dominie
Sea Wall, The	K	I	Foundations	Wright Group/McGraw Hill
Seabirds	S	I	A First Book	Franklin Watts
Seals and Sea Lions	N	I	Cole, Sally	Wright Group/McGraw Hill
Search for Delicious, The	U	F	Babbitt, Natalie	Farrar, Straus and Giroux
Search for the Lost Cave, The	M	F	Schultz, Irene	Wright Group/McGraw Hill
Searching for Sea Lions	P	I	Westerskov, Kim	Pacific Learning
Seashells	K	I	Marine Life For Yng. Readers	Dominie
Seasons	N	I	A True Book	Children's Press
Seasons	N	I	Simply Science	Compass Point Books
Seat Belt Song, The	K	RF	PM Turquoise	Rigby
Seawall	O	RF	PM Ruby	Rigby
Seaward	X	F	Cooper, Susan	Simon & Schuster
Second Chance	N	RF	Kroll, Stephen	Avon Camelot
Second Grade-Friends Again!	M	RF	Cohen, Miriam	Scholastic
Second Mrs. Giaconda, The	T	HF	Konigsburg, E. L.	Language for Learning Assoc.
Second Story Sally	N	RF	SupaDoopers	Sundance
Second-Grade Friends	M	RF	Cohen, Miriam	Scholastic
Second-Grade Star	N	RF	Alberts, Nancy	Scholastic
Secondhand Star	L	RF	Macdonald, Maryann	Hyperion
Secret at the Polk Street School, The	M	RF	Giff, Patricia Reilly	Bantam Doubleday Dell
Secret Garden, The	U	RF	Burnett, Frances H.	Scholastic
Secret Hideaway, The	K	RF	PM Gold	Rigby
Secret Land of the Past	N	F	Schlein, Miriam	Scholastic
Secret of Bunratty Castle, The	Q	F	Vaughan, Marcia	Rigby
Secret of Foghorn Island, The	L	F	Step into Reading	Random House
Secret of Kiribu Tapu Lagoon, The	S	I	Literacy 2000	Rigby
Secret of NIMH, The	V	F	O'Brien, Robert C.	Scholastic
Secret of the Monster Book, The	M	F	Schultz, Irene	Wright Group/McGraw Hill
Secret of the Old Oak Trunk, The	M	F	Schultz, Irene	Wright Group/McGraw Hill
Secret of the Seal, The	P	RF	Davis, Deborah	Alfred A. Knopf
Secret of the Silver Shoes, The	Q	F	Massie, Elizabeth	Steck-Vaughn
Secret of the Song, The	M	F	Schultz, Irene	Wright Group/McGraw Hill
Secret Secret Passage, The	P	RF	Parker, A. E.	Scholastic
Secret Silver Lining, A (Ragged Island Mysteries)	Q	RF	Bensen, Rosie	Wright Group/McGraw Hill
Secret Soldier, The: The Story of Deborah Sampson	O	B	McGovern, Ann	Scholastic
Secret, The	N	RF	PM Emerald	Rigby
Secret Valley, The	O	HF	Bulla, Clyde Robert	Scholastic

Title	Level	Genre	Author/Series	Publisher/Distributor
Secrets of the Desert	Q	I	Literacy 2000	Rigby
Secrets of the Rain Forest	O	I	Myers, Edward	Pearson Learning
See You in Second Grade	J	RF	Cohen, Miriam	Bantam Doubleday Dell
See You Tomorrow, Charles	J	RF	Cohen, Miriam	Bantam Doubleday Dell
Seed is a Promise, A	O	I	Merrill, Claire	Scholastic
Seedfolks	W	RF	Fleishman, Paul	HarperTrophy
Seeds	J	I	Pebble Books	Grolier, Capstone
Seeing the Circle	O	B	Bruchac, Joseph	Richard C. Owen
Seeing the School Doctor	K	RF	City Kids	Rigby
Seekers of Truth	U	B	Real Lives	Troll
Sees Behind Trees	T	HF	Dorris, Michael	Language for Learning Assoc.
Selchie's Seed, The	W	F	Levey Oppenheim, Shulamith	Harcourt Brace
Selena Who Speaks in Silence	J	RF	Evangeline Nicholas Collection	Wright Group/McGraw Hill
Self-Discipline	N	I	Raatma, Lucia	Capstone Press
Selfish Giant, The	L	F	Literacy 2000	Rigby
Selu and Kana Ti	K	TL	Folk Tales	Mondo
Seminole Indians, The	P	I	Lund, Bill	Capstone Press
Serpent's Children, The	W	HF	Yep, Laurence	HarperTrophy
Seven Foolish Fishermen	K	TL	PM Tales and Plays- Gold	Rigby
Seven Kisses in a Row	O	RF	MacLachlan, Patricia	Harper Collins
Seven Stones of Sligo	O	TL	PM Ruby	Rigby
Seven Treasure Hunts, The	M	RF	Byars, Betsy	HarperTrophy
Seventh Grade Weirdo	S	RF	Wardlaw, Lee	Scholastic
Seventh Tower, The: The Fall	W	F	Nix, Garth	Scholastic
Shades of Gray	W	HF	Reeder, Carolyn	Avon Camelot
Shadow of a Bull	U	RF	Wojciechowska, Maia	Simon & Schuster
Shadow of the Wolf	N	I	Whelan, Gloria	Random House
Shadow Over Second	M	RF	Christopher, Matt	Little, Brown & Co.
Shady Deal, The: Tales of Cleverness and Cunning	Q	TL	Parkes, Brenda & Stott-Thornton, Janet	Rigby
Shaggy Sheep, The	J	RF	Kratky, Lada Josefa	Hampton-Brown
Shapes of Water, The, Stories About Patterns and Shapes	N	I	Shannan, Gillian and others	Pacific Learning
Shark in School	N	RF	Giff, Patricia Reilly	Bantam Doubleday Dell
Shark Lady: The Adventures of Eugenie Clark	O	B	McGovern, Ann	Scholastic
Sharks	T	I	Simon, Seymour	Harper Trophy
Sharks	L	I	Wonder World	Wright Group/McGraw Hill
Sharks and Rays	L	I	Marine Life For Yng. Readers	Dominie Press
Sharks and Rays	Q	I	Weldon Owen	Wright Group/McGraw Hill
Sheeba	L	F	Noonan, Diana	Dominie Press
Sheep	L	I	PM Animal Facts: Purple	Rigby
Sheep Have Lambs	M	I	Animals and Their Young	Compass Point Books
Sheepdog in the Snow	Q	RF	Baglio, Ben M.	Scholastic
Sheila Rae, the Brave	K	F	Henkes, Kevin	Scholastic
Shh! We're Writing the Constitution	T	I	Fritz, Jean	G.P. Putnam's Sons
Shiloh	R	RF	Naylor, Phyllis Reynolds	Bantam Doubleday Dell
Shingo's Grandfather	K	RF	Sunshine	Wright Group/McGraw Hill
Shining Blue Planet and Other Cases, The	O	RF	Simon, Seymour	Avon
Ship in a Bottle, The	M	RF	Herman, Emily	Wright Group/McGraw Hill
Ships	L	I	Wonder World	Wright Group/McGraw Hill
Ships at Sea	K	I	PM Plus	Rigby
Shipwreck Saturday	K	RF	Cosby, Bill	Scholastic
Shoebag	P	F	James, Mary	Scholastic
Shoes for Everyone: A Story About Jan Matzeliger	R	B	Mitchell, Barbara	Carolrhoda Books
Shoes Through the Ages	Q	I	Brill, Marlene Targ	Steck-Vaughn
Shoeshine Girl	N	RF	Bulla, Clyde Robert	HarperTrophy
Shooting Star, The	M	RF	PM Gold	Rigby
Shooting Stars	R	RF	Costello, Emily	Dell
Shopping with a Crocodile	L	F	Pacific Literacy	Pacific Learning
Shortest Kid in the World	K	RF	Bliss, Corinne Demas	Random House
Shortstop from Tokyo	M	RF	Christopher, Matt	Little, Brown & Co.

Title	Level	Genre	Author/Series	Publisher/Distributor
Shorty	M	RF	Literacy 2000	Rigby
Show and Tell	K	RF	City Kids	Rigby
Show Me a Snake Hole	L	RF	Frederick, Shirley	Hampton-Brown
Show Time at the Polk Street School	M	RF	Giff, Patricia Reilly	Bantam Doubleday Dell
Show-and-Tell	J	RF	Foundations	Wright Group/McGraw Hill
Sidetrack Sam	K	RF	Literacy 2000	Rigby
Sidewalk Story	N	RF	Mathis, Sharon Bell	The Penguin Group
Sideways Arithmetic from Wayside School	S	I	Sachar, Louis	Scholastic
Sideways Stories from Wayside School	P	F	Sachar, Louis	Hearst
Sierra	Q	I	Siebert, Diane	HarperCollins
Sign of the Beaver	T	HF	Speare, Elizabeth George	Bantam Doubleday Dell
Sign of the Chrysanthemum, The	U	RF	Paterson, Katherine	HarperTrophy
Silent Hero, The	O	I	Shea, George	Random House
Silent to the Bone	V	RF	Konigsburg, E. L.	Atheneum
Silent World, A	L	RF	Literacy 2000	Rigby
Silk Route, The	U	HF	Major, John S.	HarperCollins
Silkworms	N	I	Blackburn, Rachel	Wright Group/McGraw Hill
Silly Tilly's Valentine	K	F	Hoban, Lillian	HarperTrophy
Silly Willy	M	RF	Book Shop	Mondo
Silly Willy and Silly Billy	J	F	Foundations	Wright Group/McGraw Hill
Silver	N	RF	Whelan, Gloria	Random House
Silver and Prince	L	RF	PM Story Books -Silver	Rigby
Silverwing: How One Small Bat Became a Noble Hero	U	F	Oppel, Kenneth	Simon & Schuster
Simon and the Aliens	N	SF	SupaDoopers	Sundance
Simon's Big Challenge	Q	RF	Day, Mark	Steck-Vaughn
Sing Down the Moon	T	HF	O'Dell, Scott	Language for Learning Assoc.
Sing for Your Father, Su Phan	W	HF	Pevsner, Stella and Tang, Fay	Bantam Doubleday Dell
Sing to the Moon	K	F	Story Box	Wright Group/McGraw Hill
Singing Drum, The	T	TL	Literacy 2000	Rigby
Sioux Indians, The	P	I	Lund, Bill	Capstone Press
Sister	W	RF	Greenfield, Eloise	Harper Collins
Sister Sister Homegirl on the Range	S	RF	Quin-Harkin, Janet	Pocket Books
Six Foolish Fishermen	L	TL	Elkin,Benjamin	Children's Press
Six Things to Make	L	I	Book Shop	Mondo
Six Voyages of Pleasant Fieldmouse, The	R	F	Wahl, Jan	Tom Doherty
Sixteen Short Stories by Outstanding Writers	Z	RF	Gallo, Donald R.	Dell
Sixth Grade Can Really Kill You	S	RF	DeClements, Barthe	Scholastic
Sixth Grade Secrets	S	RF	Sachar, Louis	Scholastic
Sixth-Grade Sleepover	R	RF	Bunting, Eve	Scholastic
Skateboard Tough	M	RF	Christopher, Matt	Little, Brown & Co.
Skateboarding	O	I	PM Nonfiction -Emerald	Rigby
Skates of Uncle Richard, The	P	RF	Fenner, Carol	Random House
Skateway to Freedom	V	HF	Alma, Ann	Orca Book Publishers
Skating at Rainbow Lake	J	RF	PM Story Books -Silver	Rigby
Skeleton On The Bus, The	J	F	Literacy 2000	Rigby
Skeletons Don't Play Tubas	M	F	Dadey, D. & Jones, M. T.	Scholastic
Skinny-Bones	O	RF	Park, Barbara	Random House
Skirt, The	N	RF	Soto, Gary	Bantam Doubleday Dell
Skunks	M	I	PM Animal Facts: Gold	Rigby
Sky Dogs	U	RF	Yolen, Jane	Harcourt Brace
Sky High	L	F	Pair-It Books	Steck-Vaughn
Sky Rider	O	RF	Belcher, Angie	Pacific Learning
Sky Watch	Q	I	Weldon Owen	Wright Group/McGraw Hill
Sky's the Limit, The	P	I	Christiansen, Tony	Pacific Learning
Sky's the Limit, The	Q	RF	Wildcats	Wright Group/McGraw Hill
SkyFire	J	F	Asch, Frank	Scholastic
Skylark	R	HF	MacLachlan, Patricia	HarperTrophy
Slam!	W	RF	Myers, Walter Dean	Scholastic
Slam Dunk Saturday	M	RF	Marzollo, Jean	Random House
Sleepers, Wake	T	SF	Jacobs, Paul Samuel	Language for Learning Assoc.

Title	Level	Genre	Author/Series	Publisher/Distributor
Sleeping Beauty	K	TL	Enrichment	Wright Group/McGraw Hill
Sleeping Beauty, The	L	TL	PM Tales and Plays-Silver	Rigby
Slim Shorty and the Mules	L	RF	Reading Unlimited	Celebration Press
Slither McCreep and His Brother, Joe	K	RF	Johnston, Tony	Harcourt Brace
Slugs and Snails	N	I	Book Shop	Mondo
Slugs and Snails	P	I	Mini Pets	Steck-Vaughn
Slump, The	N	RF	Kroll, Stephen	Avon Camelot
Sly Fox and Little Red Hen	K	TL	PM Tales and Plays- Purple	Rigby
Small Wolf	J	HF	Benchley, Nathaniel	HarperTrophy
Smallest Cow in the World, The	K	RF	Paterson, Katherine	HarperTrophy
Smallest Tree, The	K	F	Literacy 2000	Rigby
Smartest Bear and His Brother Oliver, The	N	F	Bach, Alice	Bantam Doubleday Dell
Smartest Man in Ireland, The	S	F	Hunter, Mollie	Harcourt Brace
Smasher	O	RF	King-Smith, Dick	Random House
Smile, The	K	RF	Read Alongs	Rigby
Smokey the Dragon	M	F	Bennett, Jean	Dominie Press
Smoky the Cow Horse	S	RF	James, Will	Scholastic
Snaggle Doodles	M	RF	Giff, Patricia Reilly	Bantam Doubleday Dell
Snails	O	I	Holmes, Kevin J.	Capstone Press
Snake!	M	RF	Sunshine	Wright Group/McGraw Hill
Snake, The	O	I	Crewe, Sabrina	Steck-Vaughn
Snakes	K	I	Foundations	Wright Group/McGraw Hill
Snakes!	L	I	Recht Penner, Lucille	Random House
Snakes	J	I	Sunshine	Wright Group/McGraw Hill
Snakes	Q	I	Weldon Owen	Wright Group/McGraw Hill
Snakes	L	I	Wonder World	Wright Group/McGraw Hill
Sneakers	K	I	Sunshine	Wright Group/McGraw Hill
Snot Stew	P	F	Wallace, Bill	Pocket Books
Snow Bright and the Seven Sumos	M	F	SupaDoopers	Sundance
Snow Bright and the Tooth Magician	M	F	SupaDoopers	Sundance
Snow Daughter, The	L	TL	Sunshine	Wright Group/McGraw Hill
Snow Goes To Town	L	F	Literacy 2000	Rigby
Snow Treasure	R	HF	McSwigan, Marie	Scholastic
Snow Walker, The	L	HF	Wetterer, M. K. and Charles M.	Carolrhoda Books
Snow White and the Seven Dwarfs	K	TL	PM Tales and Plays- Gold	Rigby
Snowball War, The	K	RF	Chardiet, Bernice	Scholastic
Snowboarding Diary	O	I	PM Nonfiction -Emerald	Rigby
Snowshoe Thompson	K	HF	Smiler Levinson, N.	HarperTrophy
So Far From the Bamboo Grove	V	HF	Watkins, Yoko Kawashima	William Morrow
Soap Soup and Other Verses	K	TL	Kuskin, Karla	HarperTrophy
Soccer Cousins	K	RF	Marzollo, Jean	Scholastic
Soccer Mania!	M	RF	Tamar, Erika	Random House
Soccer Sam	M	RF	Marzollo, Jean	Random House
Soccer Stars, Best Friend Face-off	R	RF	Costello, Emily	Dell
Sock Gobbler and Other Stories, The	M	F	Learning Media	Pacific Learning
Socks	O	RF	Cleary, Beverly	Avon
Sod Houses on the Great Plains	N	I	Rounds, Glen	Holiday House
Soil	N	I	Simply Science	Compass Point Books
Sojourner Truth	P	B	McLoone, Margo	Capstone Press
Sojourner Truth: Ain't I a Woman?	V	B	McKissack, F. and P.	Scholastic
Solar System, The	N	I	A True Book	Children's Press
Soldier Boy	T	HF	Burks, Brian	Harcourt Brace
Soldier's Heart	V	HF	Paulsen, Gary	Random House
Solids, Liquids, Gases	N	I	Simply Science	Compass Point Books
Solitary Blue, A	W	RF	Voigt, Cynthia	Scholastic
Solo Flyer	L	RF	PM Gold	Rigby
Solo Girl	M	RF	Pinkey, Andrea Davis	Hyperion
Some Dog!	O	RF	PM Ruby	Rigby
Some Friend	R	RF	Warner, Sally	Alfred A. Knopf
Some Machines are Enormous	J	I	Book Shop	Mondo

Title	Level	Genre	Author/Series	Publisher/Distributor
Some of the Kinder Planets	U	SF	Wynne-Jones, Tim	The Penguin Group
Someday a Tree	P	RF	Bunting, Eve	Clarion
Someday Cyril	N	RF	Gershator, Phillis	Mondo
Somehow Tenderness Survives: Stories of Southern Africa	X	B	Rochman, Hazel	HarperTrophy
Someone is Following Pip Ramsey	N	RF	Roy, Ron	Random House
Someone to Count On	T	RF	Hermes, Patricia	Language for Learning Assoc.
Something Everyone Needs	J	RF	Ready Readers	Pearson Learning
Something Noise, The	J	RF	Windmill Books	Rigby
Something Queer at the Ball Park	N	RF	Levy, Elizabeth	Bantam Doubleday Dell
Something Queer at the Haunted School	N	RF	Levy, Elizabeth	Bantam Doubleday Dell
Something Queer at the Lemonade Stand	N	RF	Levy, Elizabeth	Bantam Doubleday Dell
Something Queer at the Library	N	RF	Levy, Elizabeth	Bantam Doubleday Dell
Something Queer at the Scary Movie	N	RF	Levy, Elizabeth	Hyperion
Something Queer in Outer Space	N	RF	Levy, Elizabeth	Hyperion
Something Queer in the Cafeteria	N	RF	Levy, Elizabeth	Hyperion
Something Queer in the Wild West	N	RF	Levy, Elizabeth	Hyperion
Something Queer Is Going On	N	RF	Levy, Elizabeth	Bantam Doubleday Dell
Something Queer on Vacation	N	RF	Levy, Elizabeth	Bantam Doubleday Dell
Something Soft for Danny Bear	M	F	Literacy 2000	Rigby
Something Upstairs	T	RF	Avi	Language for Learning Assoc.
Something Very Sorry	R	RF	Bohlmeijer, Arno	Putnam & Grosset
Somewhere	J	TL	Book Shop	Mondo
Song Lee and the Hamster Hunt	L	RF	Kline, Suzy	The Penguin Group
Song Lee and the Leech Man	L	RF	Kline, Suzy	The Penguin Group
Song Lee In Room 2B	L	RF	Kline, Suzy	The Penguin Group
Song of the Giraffe	O	RF	Jacobs, Shannon K.	Little, Brown & Co.
Song of the Mantis, The	S	I	Literacy 2000	Rigby
Song of the Trees	S	HF	Taylor, Mildred	Bantam Doubleday Dell
Sons of Liberty	Y	RF	Griffin, Adele	Hyperion
Sophie Hits Six	M	F	King-Smith, Dick	Candlewick Press
Sophie in the Saddle	M	F	King-Smith, Dick	Candlewick Press
Sophie Is Seven	M	F	King-Smith, Dick	Candlewick Press
Sophie's Lucky	M	F	King-Smith, Dick	Candlewick Press
Sophie's Snail	M	F	King-Smith, Dick	Candlewick Press
Sophie's Tom	M	F	King-Smith, Dick	Candlewick Press
SOS Titanic	V	HF	Bunting, Eve	Harcourt Brace
Sound, Heat & Light: Energy at Work	L	I	Berger, Melvin	Scholastic
Sounder	T	RF	Armstrong, William	Scholastic
Sounds	J	I	Early Connections	Benchmark Education
Soup	Q	RF	Peck, Robert Newton	Bantam Doubleday Dell
South Korea	O	I	Davis, Lucile	Capstone Press
Souvenirs	K	RF	Literacy 2000	Rigby
Space	R	I	Worldwise	Grolier
Space Dog and Roy	L	F	Standiford, Natalie	Random House
Space Dog and the Pet Show	L	F	Standiford, Natalie	Random House
Space Dog in Trouble	L	F	Standiford, Natalie	Random House
Space Dog the Hero	L	F	Standiford, Natalie	Random House
Space Junk	O	RF	Wildcats	Wright Group/McGraw Hill
Space Quest	O	I	Discovery World	Rigby
Space Race	J	F	Sunshine	Wright Group/McGraw Hill
Space Rock	L	F	Buller, Jon	Random House
Space Station Plot and Other Cases, The	O	RF	Simon, Seymour	Avon
Space Stations	N	I	A True Book	Children's Press
Space Stations	O	I	Ryan, Cheryl	Wright Group/McGraw Hill
Spanish Omelette	L	RF	PM Story Books -Silver	Rigby
Spanish-American War, The	W	I	Cornerstones of Freedom	Children's Press
Special Effects	M	I	Wildcats	Wright Group/McGraw Hill
Special Gifts	M	RF	Rylant, Cynthia	Aladdin
Special Present, The	L	RF	Cole, Sally	Wright Group/McGraw Hill

Title	Level	Genre	Author/Series	Publisher/Distributor
Special Ride, The	K	RF	PM Gold	Rigby
Spectacular Stone Soup	L	RF	Giff, Patricia Reilly	Yearling
Speeding Sleigh and Other Cases, The	O	RF	Simon, Seymour	Avon
Speedy Pasta and Other Cases, The	O	RF	Simon, Seymour	Avon
Speedy Snake and Other Cases, The	O	RF	Simon, Seymour	Avon
Speedy Soapbox Car and Other Cases, The	O	RF	Simon, Seymour	Avon
Spell Casters, Phoebe's Fortune	R	F	Warriner, Holly	Aladdin
Spencer School Sleepover, The	M	RF	Floyd, Lucy	Wright Group/McGraw Hill
Spider Boy	R	RF	Fletcher, Ralph	Bantam Doubleday Dell
Spider Kane and the Mystery at Jumbo Nightcrawler's	O	F	Osborne, Mary Pope	Random House
Spider Kane and the Mystery Under the May-Apple	O	F	Osborne, Mary Pope	Random House
Spider Man	M	I	Literacy 2000	Rigby
Spider Relatives	Q	I	Literacy 2000	Rigby
Spider, The	O	I	Crewe, Sabrina	Steck-Vaughn
Spider's Web, A	L	I	Wonder World	Wright Group/McGraw Hill
Spiders	M	I	Book Shop	Mondo
Spiders	O	I	Holmes, Kevin J.	Capstone Press
Spiders	P	I	Mini Pets	Steck-Vaughn
Spies on the Devil's Belt	W	HF	Haynes, Betsy	Scholastic
Spirit of Hope	N	F	Book Shop	Mondo
Spirit of St. Louis, The	V	I	Cornerstones of Freedom	Children's Press
Spirit Quest	S	RF	Sharpe, Susan	Scholastic
Splatter	N	RF	Marriott, Janice	Pacific Learning
Spoiled Rotten	L	RF	DeClements, Barthe	Hyperion
Spooky Tail of Prewitt Peacock, The	M	F	Peet, Bill	Houghton Mifflin
Sports Bloopers	P	I	Hollander, Phyllis & Zander	Scholastic
Sports for All	Q	I	Weldon Owen	Wright Group/McGraw Hill
Sports Heroes	R	I	PM Nonfiction -Ruby	Rigby
Sports Mysteries: Case of the Basketball Video	P	RF	Edwards, T. J.	Scholastic
Sports Mysteries: Case Of The Missing Pitcher	P	RF	Edwards, T. J.	Scholastic
Sports on Wheels	R	I	PM Nonfiction -Ruby	Rigby
Sports Technology	R	I	PM Nonfiction -Ruby	Rigby
Spot's First Christmas	J	RF	Hill, Eric	Putnam
Spray-Paint Mystery, The	O	RF	Medearis, Angela Shelf	Scholastic
Spreading the Word	Q	I	Wildcats	Wright Group/McGraw Hill
Spring Fever!	T	F	Lerangis, Peter	Language for Learning Assoc.
Spy Down the Street, The	M	F	Schultz, Irene	Wright Group/McGraw Hill
Spy in the Attic, The	M	RF	Scheffler, Ursel	North-South Books
Spy on Third Base, The	M	RF	Christopher, Matt	Little, Brown & Co.
Squanto and the First Thanksgiving	L	HF	Celsi, Teresa	Steck-Vaughn
Squanto: Friend of the Pilgrims	O	B	Bulla, Clyde Robert	Scholastic
Squirrels	N	I	Storyteller Nonfiction	Wright Group/McGraw Hill
Squirrels in the School	Q	RF	Baglio, Ben M.	Scholastic
Stacey and the Haunted Masquerade	O	RF	Martin, Ann M.	Scholastic
Stacey and the Missing Ring	O	RF	Martin, Ann M.	Scholastic
Stacey and the Mystery at the Mall	O	RF	Martin, Ann M.	Scholastic
Stacey and the Mystery Money	O	RF	Martin, Ann M.	Scholastic
Stacy Says Good-Bye	L	RF	Giff, Patricia Reilly	Bantam Doubleday Dell
Stage Fright	N	RF	Martin, Ann	Scholastic
Stan the Hot Dog Man	K	RF	Kessler, E.& L.	HarperTrophy
Standing in the Light	T	RF	Osborne, Mary Pope	Scholastic
Standing Tall: The Stories of Ten Hispanic Americans	S	B	Palacios, Argentina	Scholastic
Stanley and the Magic Lamp	P	F	Brown, Jeff	HarperTrophy
Star	M	RF	Simon, Jo Ann	Random House
Star Fisher, The	S	RF	Yep, Lawrence	Scholastic
Star Thief	P	RF	Bilbrough, Norman	Pacific Learning
Starfish & Urchins	K	I	Marine Life For Yng. Readers	Dominie
Starfishers to the Rescue	M	SF	Dreyer, Ellen	Pearson Learning
Starring First Grade	J	RF	Cohen, Miriam	Bantam Doubleday Dell
Starring Rosie	N	RF	Giff, Patricia Reilly	The Penguin Group

Title	Level	Genre	Author/Series	Publisher/Distributor
Stars	N	I	A True Book	Children's Press
Statue of Liberty, The	N	I	A True Book	Children's Press
Statue of Liberty, The	J	I	Penner, Lucille	Random House
Stay Away from Simon!	O	RF	Carrick, Carol	Clarion
Stay! Keeper's Story	U	F	Lowry, Lois	Random House
Staying Healthy: Eating Right	O	I	McGinty, Alice B.	Franklin Watts
Staying Nine	O	RF	Conrad, Pam	HarperTrophy
Steal Away…to Freedom	Z	RF	Armstrong, Jennifer	Scholastic
Stealing Freedom	U	HF	Carbone, Lisa	Random House
Stealing Home: The Story of Jackie Robinson	V	B	Denenberg, Barry	Scholastic
Stems	K	I	Pebble Books	Grolier, Capstone
Sterkarm Handshake, The	Z	F	Price, Susan	Scholastic
Sticks and Stones, Bobbie Bones	P	RF	Roberts, Brenda C.	Scholastic
Stone Fox	P	RF	Gardiner, John Reynolds	Harper Trophy
Stone Soup	J	TL	McGovern, Ann	Scholastic
Stone Soup	J	TL	PM Tales and Plays Turquoise	Rigby
Stone Works	K	I	Wonder World	Wright Group/McGraw Hill
Stories From the Days of Christopher Columbus	U	HF	Young, R.A & J. Dockery	August House
Stories Huey Tells, The	N	RF	Cameron, Ann	Alfred A. Knopf
Stories in Stone: The World of Animal Fossils	U	I	A First Book	Franklin Watts
Stories Julian Tells, The	N	RF	Cameron, Ann	Alfred A. Knopf
Stories of the North	Y	RF	London, Jack	Scholastic
Storm at Coldwater Creek	M	HF	Blackaby, Susan	Wright Group/McGraw Hill
Storm Book, The	P	I	Zolotow, Charlotte	Harper Collins
Storm in the Night	N	RF	Stolz, Mary	Harper Collins
Storms!	L	I	Pair-It Books	Steck-Vaughn
Stormy, Misty's Foal	R	RF	Henry, Marguerite	Aladdin
Story, a Story, A: An African Tale	M	TL	Haley, Gail E.	Aladdin
Story of a Book, The	L	I	Reeder, Paul	Wright Group/McGraw Hill
Story of Alexander Graham Bell, Inventor of the Telephone	O	B	Davidson, Margaret	Scholastic
Story of Benjamin Franklin, Amazing American	O	B	Davidson, Margaret	Scholastic
Story of Big Bess Call, The	M	TL	Bovetz, Marcie	Wright Group/McGraw Hill
Story of Doña Chila, The	P	B	Moore, Eva	Scholastic
Story of George Washington Carver, The	Q	B	Moore, Eva	Bantam Doubleday Dell
Story of Geronimo, The	T	B	Cornerstones of Freedom	Children's Press
Story of Harriet Tubman: Freedom, The	U	B	Sterling, Dorothy	Bantam Doubleday Dell
Story of Harriet Tubman, The: Conductor of the Underground Railroad	S	B	McMullan, Kate	Scholastic
Story of Hungbu and Nolbu, The	K	TL	Book Shop	Mondo
Story of Jackie Robinson, Bravest Man in Baseball	O	B	Davidson, Margaret	Scholastic
Story of Jeans, The	M	I	Discovery World	Rigby
Story of Laura Ingalls Wilder, Pioneer Girl, The	Q	B	Stine, Megan	Bantam Doubleday Dell
Story of Muhammad Ali: Heavyweight Champion of the World, The	S	B	Denenberg, Barry	Dell Publishing
Story of Ruby Bridges, The	O	B	Coles, Robert	Scholastic
Story of Small Fry, The	P	I	Vaughan, Marcia	Rigby
Story of the Mayflower Compact, The	T	I	Cornerstones of Freedom	Children's Press
Story of The Persian Gulf War, The	W	I	Cornerstones of Freedom	Children's Press
Story of The Sinking of the Battleship Maine, The	W	I	Cornerstones of Freedom	Children's Press
Story of The Surrender at Yorktown, The	V	I	Cornerstones of Freedom	Children's Press
Story of the White House, The	S	I	Waters, Kate	Scholastic
Story of The Women's Movement, The	V	I	Cornerstones of Freedom	Children's Press
Story of Thomas Alva Edison, Inventor, The	R	B	Davidson, Margaret	Scholastic
Story of Walt Disney, Maker of Magical Worlds, The	O	B	Selden, Bernice	Bantam Doubleday Dell
Story of William Tell, The	M	TL	PM Story Books -Silver	Rigby
Story of You, The	M	I	Sunshine	Wright Group/McGraw Hill
Story Teller's Story, A	O	B	Martin, Rafe	Richard C. Owen
Storytellers	L	I	Storyteller Nonfiction	Wright Group/McGraw Hill
Stowaway	W	HF	Hesse, Karen	Simon & Schuster

Title	Level	Genre	Author/Series	Publisher/Distributor
Straight Line Wonder, The	J	F	Book Shop	Mondo
Strange Clues and Other Cases, The	O	RF	Simon, Seymour	Avon
Strange Creatures	N	SF	Cartwright, Pauline	Pacific Learning
Strange Museum and Other Cases, The	O	RF	Simon, Seymour	Avon
Strange Shoe, The	L	TL	PM Tales and Plays-Silver	Rigby
Stranger at the Window	U	RF	Alcock, Vivien	Houghton Mifflin
Stranger Came Ashore, A	U	F	Hunter, Mollie	HarperTrophy
Strawberry Hill	Y	RF	LaFaye, A.	Simon & Schuster
Stray, The	R	RF	King-Smith, Dick	Alfred A. Knopf
Streak, The	N	RF	Kroll, Stephen	Avon Camelot
Street Action	O	I	Wildcats	Wright Group/McGraw Hill
Street Musicians	J	RF	Sunshine	Wright Group/McGraw Hill
Strider	R	RF	Cleary, Beverly	Harper Collins
Strike	O	I	Pacific Literacy	Pacific Learning
Strike Me Down with a Stringbean	L	F	Read Alongs	Rigby
String Food	K	I	Home Connection Collection	Rigby
String Performers	J	I	Home Connection Collection	Rigby
Striped Ice Cream	N	RF	Lexau, Joan M.	Scholastic
Stuart Little	R	F	White, E.B.	HarperTrophy
Stumpy's Secret	P	RF	Hager, Mandy	Pacific Learning
Sub, The	P	RF	Peterson, P.J.	Puffin Books
Subtle Knife, The	Z	F	Pullman, Philip	Ballantine Books
Sugar Cakes Cyril	M	RF	Gershator, Phillis	Mondo
Sugar Snow	J	HF	Wilder, Laura Ingalls	Harper Collins
Sugaring Season (Making Maple Syrup)	S	I	Burns, Diane	Carolrhoda Books
Sugaring Time	S	I	Lasky, Kathryn	Macmillan
Suki and the Case of the Lost Bunnies	K	RF	Ready Readers	Pearson Learning
Sulky Simon	J	RF	Windmill Books	Rigby
Summer Camp	J	RF	City Kids	Rigby
Summer I Shrank My Grandmother, The	Q	F	Woodruff, Elvira	Bantam Doubleday Dell
Summer in the South, A	Q	F	Marshall, James	Houghton Mifflin
Summer Life, A	Z	RF	Soto, Gary	Bantam Doubleday Dell
Summer of My German Soldier	Z	HF	Greene, Bette	Dell Publishing
Summer of the Great-Grandmother, The	Z	B	L'Engle, Madeleine	Harper Collins
Summer of the Swans, The	U	RF	Byars, Betsy	The Penguin Group
Summer Reading is Killing Me!	N	F	Scieszka, Jon	Puffin Books
Summer Sands	M	RF	Evangeline Nicholas Collection	Wright Group/McGraw Hill
Summer Switch	R	F	Rodgers, Mary	HarperTrophy
Summer to Die, A	T	RF	Lowry, Lois	Dell
Summer Wheels	O	B	Bunting, Eve	Harcourt Brace
Summertime in the Big Woods	J	HF	Wilder, Laura Ingalls	Harper Collins
Sun	O	I	Vogt, Gregory L.	Capstone Press
Sun & Spoon	R	RF	Henkes, Kevin	The Penguin Group
Sun, The	N	I	Literacy 2000	Rigby
Sun, The	J	I	Wonder World	Wright Group/McGraw Hill
Sun, the Wind, & Tashira, The	J	TL	Folk Tales	Mondo
Sunburn	J	RF	City Kids	Rigby
Sunflower That Went Flop, The	K	F	Story Box	Wright Group/McGraw Hill
Sunny-Side Up	M	RF	Giff, Patricia Reilly	Bantam Doubleday Dell
Sunset of the Sabertooth	M	F	Osborne, Mary Pope	Random House
Sunshine	L	I	Pebble Books	Grolier, Capstone
Super Amos	R	RF	Paulsen, Gary	Bantam Doubleday Dell
Super Supermarket Plan, The	J	RF	Home Connection Collection	Rigby
Super-tuned!	N	RF	PM Emerald	Rigby
Supercharged Infield	M	RF	Christopher, Matt	Little, Brown & Co.
Superfudge	Q	RF	Blume, Judy	Bantam Doubleday Dell
Supermarket Chase, The	L	RF	Sunshine	Wright Group/McGraw Hill
Supermarket, The	K	I	Pebble Books	Grolier, Capstone
Supernova	N	RF	PM Ruby	Rigby
Supreme Court, The	N	I	A True Book	Children's Press

Title	Level	Genre	Author/Series	Publisher/Distributor
Suprising Myself	O	B	Fritz, Jean	Richard C. Owen
Surf's Up	P	RF	Wildcats	Wright Group/McGraw Hill
Surprise Dinner, The	L	RF	PM Gold	Rigby
Surprise Party	K	I	Hutchins, Pat	Macmillan
Surprise Party, The	J	RF	Proger, Annabelle	Random House
Surprising Swimmers: Nature's Most R Amazing Animals		I	Fredericks, Anthony D.	NorthWord Press
Survival!: Fire	R	HF	Duey, K. & Bale, K. A.	Aladdin
Survival of Fish, The	M	I	Science	Wright Group/McGraw Hill
Survive!	Q	RF	Wildcats	Wright Group/McGraw Hill
Susan B. Anthony	P	B	Davis, Lucile	Capstone Press
Susan B. Anthony: Champion of Women's Rights	R	B	Monsell, Helen Albee	Simon & Schuster
Susanna of the Alamo	T	B	Jakes, John	Language for Learning Assoc.
Swamp of the Hideous Zombies	M	F	Hayes, Geoffrey	Random House
Sweet Clara and the Freedom Quilt	S	HF	Hopkinson, Deborah	Scholastic
Sweet Memories Still	Q	RF	Kinsey-Warnock, Natalie	Bantam Doubleday Dell
Swiftly Tilting Planet, A	V	F	L'Engle, Madeleine	Bantam Doubleday Dell
Switcharound	R	RF	Lowry, Lois	Random House
Sword in the Stone, The	J	TL	Maccarone, Grace	Scholastic
Sydney-Where Biscuits Go Surfing	R	RF	Coy, Michael	Scholastic
Take A Look	N	I	Wildcats	Wright Group/McGraw Hill
Take Care of Our Earth	M	I	Pair-It Books	Steck-Vaughn
Taken by the Wind	M	RF	Wahman, Joe	Wright Group/McGraw Hill
Taking Care of Terrific	S	RF	Lowry, Lois	Dell
Taking Care of Yoki	R	RF	Campbell, Barbara	HarperTrophy
Taking Sides	S	RF	Soto, Gary	Harcourt Brace
Tale of Peter Rabbit, The	L	TL	Potter, Beatrix	Scholastic
Tale of the Golden Goose, The	L	TL	Behr, Alexandra	Hampton-Brown
Tale of Veruschka Babuschka, The	M	TL	Literacy 2000	Rigby
Talent Contest, The	K	RF	PM Story Books -Silver	Rigby
Tales from the Homeplace: Adventures of a Texas Farm Girl	S	RF	Burandt, H. and Dale, S.	Bantam Doubleday Dell
Tales from the Underground Railroad	S	HF	Connell, Kate	Steck-Vaughn
Tales of a Fourth Grade Nothing	Q	RF	Blume, Judy	Bantam Doubleday Dell
Tales of Amanda Pig	L	F	Van Leeuwen, Jean	Puffin Books
Tales of Olga da Polga, The	P	F	Bond, Michael	Houghton Mifflin
Talk About a Family	O	RF	Greenfield, Eloise	HarperTrophy
Talking Earth, The	U	RF	George, Jean Craighead	HarperTrophy
Talking to Faith Ringgold	S	B	Ringgold, F.,Freeman, L.&Roucher,N.	Crown Publishers, Inc.
Tall Tale and Other Cases, The	O	RF	Simon, Seymour	Avon
Tall Tales	O	RF	PM Emerald	Rigby
Tamika and the Wisdom Rings	O	RF	Yarbrough, Camille	Random House
Tangerine	U	RF	Bloor, Edward	Scholastic
Tar Beach	P	HF	Ringgold, Faith	Crown
Tarantula in My Purse, The	U	B	George, Jean Craighead	Harper Collins
Tasmanian Devils	R	I	Morris, Rod	Pacific Learning
Tasmanian Devils	M	I	PM Animal Facts: Gold	Rigby
Taste of Blackberries, A	P	RF	Buchanan Smith, Doris	Scholastic
Taste of Salt: The Story of Modern Haiti	W	I	Temple, Frances	HarperTrophy
Tea	K	I	Wonder World	Wright Group/McGraw Hill
Teach Us, Amelia Bedelia	L	F	Parish, Peggy	Scholastic
Teacher's Pet	L	F	Dicks, Terrance	Scholastic
Teacher's Pet	O	RF	Hurwitz, Johanna	Scholastic
Teachers	M	I	Deedrick, Tami	Capstone Press
Tears of a Tiger	Z	RF	Draper, Sharon M.	Simon & Schuster
Tecumseh	V	B	Cornerstones of Freedom	Children's Press
Teddy Bears Cure a Cold	K	F	Gretz, Susanna	Scholastic
Teeny Tiny Woman, The	J	TL	Seuling, Barbara	Scholastic
Teeth	K	I	Sunshine	Wright Group/McGraw Hill
Tell Me a Story	O	B	London, Jonathan	Richard C. Owen

Title	Level	Genre	Author/Series	Publisher/Distributor
Tell Me No Lies	M	RF	Dionetti, Michelle	Wright Group/McGraw Hill
Telling Stories Through Art	N	I	Reimer, Luther	Wright Group/McGraw Hill
Ten Apples Up on Top	J	F	LaSieg, Theo	Random House
Ten O'Clock Club, The	N	F	Beach York, Carol	Scholastic
Ten True Animal Rescues	O	I	Betancourt, Jeanne	Scholastic
Tenement Writer, The: An Immigrant's Story	T	I	Sonder, Ben	Steck-Vaughn
Tent, The	V	RF	Paulsen, Gary	Bantam Doubleday Dell
Terrible Fright, A	K	TL	Story Box	Wright Group/McGraw Hill
Terrible Test Mark and Other Cases, The	O	RF	Simon, Seymour	Avon
Terrible Tiger and Sleeping Beauty	L	TL	New Way: Literature	Steck-Vaughn
Terror In the Towers	O	B	Kerson, Adrian	Random House
Tess and Paddy	J	RF	Sunshine	Wright Group/McGraw Hill
Texas	Q	I	Geography Department	Capstone Press
Thailand	O	I	Thoennes, Kristin	Capstone Press
Thank You, Amelia Bedelia	L	F	Little Readers	Houghton Mifflin
Thank You, Jackie Robinson	P	B	Cohen, Barbara	Scholastic
Thanksgiving: Why We Celebrate It the Way We Do	P	I	Hintz, Martin & Kate	Capstone Press
That Fat Hat	K	F	Barkan, Joanne	Scholastic
That Wild Berries Should Grow	U	HF	Whelan, Gloria	William B. Eerdmans
That's a Laugh: Four Funny Fables	M	TL	Literacy 2000	Rigby
That's Really Weird!	K	F	Read Alongs	Rigby
Theft in Time, A: Timedetectors II	V	HF	Odgers, Darrel & Sally	Rigby
Then Again, Maybe I Won't	T	RF	Blume, Judy	Language for Learning Assoc.
Then and Now	J	I	Discovery World	Rigby
There Is a Carrot in My Ear and Other Noodle Tales	J	F	Schwartz, Alvin	HarperTrophy
There's A Boy In The Girls' Bathroom	Q	RF	Sachar, Louis	Alfred A. Knopf
There's a Frog in My Sleeping Bag	R	RF	Clymer, Susan	Scholastic
There's a Hamster in My Lunchbox	R	RF	Clymer, Susan	Scholastic
There's a Hippopotamus Under My Bed	J	RF	Thaler, Mike	Avon
There's a Rainbow in the River	L	RF	Home Connection Collection	Rigby
There's a Ship Outside My Window	O	RF	PM Ruby	Rigby
There's a Tarantula in My Homework	R	RF	Clymer, Susan	Scholastic
There's an Alligator Under My Bed	J	RF	Mayer, Mercer	The Penguin Group
There's an Owl in the Shower	Q	RF	George, Jean Craighead	Harper Collins
There's No Place Like Home	R	I	Hill, David	Pacific Learning
There's Something in My Attic	J	RF	Mayer, Mercer	The Penguin Group
These Lands Are Ours: Tecumseh's Fight For the Old Northwest	T	B	Connell, Kate	Steck-Vaughn
These Old Rags	M	RF	Evangeline Nicholas Collection	Wright Group/McGraw Hill
They Led The Way: 14 American Women	O	B	Johnston, Johanna	Scholastic
They Shall Be Heard: Susan B. Anthony Elizabeth Cady Stanton	T	B	Connell, Kate	Steck-Vaughn
They Survived Mount St. Helens!	O	I	Stine, Megan	Random House
Thief in the Village, A	V	RF	Berry, James	Puffin Books
Thief of Hearts	V	RF	Yep, Laurence	Harper Collins
Things Change	M	I	Bourne, Phyllis Montenegro	Hampton-Brown
Things Don't Change Much	L	RF	Rushby, Pamela	Rigby
Things With Wings	J	I	Storyteller Nonfiction	Wright Group/McGraw Hill
Think Like a Scientist	Q	I	Burke, Melissa Blackwell	Steck-Vaughn
Thinking About Ants	L	I	Book Shop	Mondo
Third Grade Bullies	N	RF	Levy, Elizabeth	Hyperion
Third Grade Stars	P	RF	Ransom, Candice	Troll
Thirteen	R	RF	Ransom, Candice	Scholastic
This Can't Be Happening at Macdonald Hall	S	RF	Korman, Gordon	Scholastic
This Is My House	L	I	Dorros, Arthur	Scholastic
This Place is Dry	R	I	Cobb, Vicki	Walker and Co.
This Place is Wet	R	I	Cobb, Vicki	Walker and Co.
Thomas Alva Edison: Great Inventor	Q	B	Levinson, Nancy Smiler	Scholastic
Thomas Edison	P	B	Linder, Greg	Capstone Press
Thomas Jefferson: Author, Inventor, President	N	B	Rookie Biographies	Children's Press

Title	Level	Genre	Author/Series	Publisher/Distributor
Thomas Jefferson: Man with a Vision	U	B	Crisman, Ruth	Scholastic
Those Amazingly Useful Ears	O	I	Frederick, Shirley	Hampton-Brown
Thoughts, Pictures, and Words	O	B	Kuskin, Karla	Richard C. Owen
Three Bears, The	K	TL	Galdone, Paul	Clarion
Three Billy Goats Gruff, The	K	TL	Asbjornsen, P. C. & Moe, J. E.	Harcourt Brace
Three Billy Goats Gruff, The	K	TL	Stevens, Janet	Harcourt Brace
Three Blind Mice Mystery, The	L	F	Krensky, Stephen	Bantam Doubleday Dell
Three By the Sea	K	RF	Marshall, Edward	Puffin Books
Three Days on a River in a Red Canoe	K	I	Williams, Vera B.	Scholastic
Three Ducks Went Wandering	K	RF	Roy, Ron	Clarion
Three Investigators, The Mystery of the Fiery Eye	Y	RF	Arthur, Robert	Random House
Three Little Pigs	L	TL	Galdone, Paul	Houghton Mifflin
Three Little Pigs	L	TL	Once Upon a Time	Wright Group/McGraw Hill
Three Little Pigs, The	L	TL	Marshall, James	Scholastic
Three Sillies, The	L	F	Literacy 2000	Rigby
Three Smart Pals	L	RF	Rocklin, Joanne	Scholastic
Three Stories You Can Read to Your Cat	K	F	Miller, Sara Swan	Houghton Mifflin
Three Stories You Can Read to Your Dog	K	F	Miller, Sara Swan	Houghton Mifflin
Three Wishes, The	L	TL	Book Shop	Mondo
Three Wishes, The	O	TL	Literacy 2000	Rigby
Three Wishes, The	K	TL	Sunshine	Wright Group/McGraw Hill
Through Grandpa's Eyes	P	RF	MacLachlan, Patricia	HarperTrophy
Through the Eyes of Your Ancestors: A Step-by-Step Guide to Uncovering Your Family's History	V	I	Taylor, Maureen	Houghton Mifflin
Through the Garden Door	M	F	Reeves, Barbara	Pearson Learning
Through the Medicine Cabinet	N	F	The Zack Files	Grosset & Dunlap
Throw-Away Pets	N	RF	Duffey, Betsy	Puffin Books
Throwing Shadows	T	RF	Konigsburg, E. L.	Language for Learning Assoc.
Thumbelina	K	TL	Tales from Hans Andersen	Wright Group/McGraw Hill
Thunder At Gettysburg	S	I	Gauch, Patricia Lee	Bantam Doubleday Dell
Thunder Rolling in the Mountains	U	HF	O'Dell, Scott & Hall, Elizabeth	Bantam Doubleday Dell
Thunder Valley	T	RF	Paulsen, Gary	Bantam Doubleday Dell
Thunderstorms	N	I	A True Book	Children's Press
Thurgood Marshall: First Black Supreme Court Justice	N	B	Rookie Biographies	Children's Press
Tickle-Bugs, The	J	F	Literacy 2000	Rigby
Ties That Bind, Ties That Break	X	HF	Namioka, Lensey	Delacorte Press
Tiger Eyes	W	RF	Blume, Judy	Bantam Doubleday Dell
Tiger Woods: An American Master	R	B	Edwards, Nicholas	Scholastic
Tigers at Twilight	M	F	Osborne, Mary Pope	Random House
Tight End	M	RF	Christopher, Matt	Little, Brown & Co.
Till's Christmas	R	RF	Thacker, Nola	Scholastic
Tiltawhirl John	U	RF	Paulsen, Gary	The Penguin Group
Timber Box, The	M	TL	Enrichment	Wright Group/McGraw Hill
Time Apart, A	T	RF	Stanley, Diane	William Morrow
Time Benders	T	SF	Paulsen, Gary	Bantam Doubleday Dell
Time Capsule, The	M	SF	Book Bank	Wright Group/McGraw Hill
Time for Andrew	S	F	Hahn, Mary	Avon Camelot
Time Machine and Other Cases, The	O	RF	Simon, Seymour	Avon
Time of Angels, A	W	F	Hesse, Karen	Hyperion
Time Warp Trio: 2095	P	SF	Scieszka, Jon	The Penguin Group
Time Warp Trio: Good, the Bad, and the Goofy, The	P	SF	Scieszka, Jon	The Penguin Group
Time Warp Trio: The Knights of the Kitchen Table	P	F	Scieszka, Jon	The Penguin Group
Time Warp Trio: The Not-So-Jolly Roger	P	F	Scieszka, Jon	The Penguin Group
Time Warp Trio: Tut Tut	P	F	Scieszka, Jon	The Penguin Group
Time Warp Trio: Your Mother Was a Neanderthal	P	F	Scieszka, Jon	The Penguin Group
Timedetectors	V	SF	Literacy 2000	Rigby
Timedetectors	N	SF	SupaDoopers	Sundance
Timothy Whuffenpuffen-Whippersnapper	S	F	Literacy 2000	Rigby
Timothy's Five-City Tour	M	F	Pair-It Books	Steck-Vaughn
Tin Lizzy	M	RF	Windmill Books	Rigby

Title	Level	Genre	Author/Series	Publisher/Distributor
Titanic Crossing	R	HF	Williams, Barbara	Scholastic
Titanic Sinks!, The	T	I	Conklin, Thomas	Random House
Titanic, The	V	I	Cornerstones of Freedom	Children's Press
Titanic, The: Lost. . .and Found	N	I	Donnelly, Judy	Random House
To Be a Slave	Z	I	Lester, Julius	Dial Books
To Fly with the Swallows: A Story of Old California	S	I	deRuiz, Dana Catharine	Steck-Vaughn
To JJ From CC	P	RF	Literacy 2000	Rigby
To Kill a Mockingbird	Z	HF	Lee, Harper	Warner Books
To the Moon and Beyond	S	I	Lott, Linda	Wright Group/McGraw Hill
To the Top!: Climbing the World's Highest Mountain	N	B	Kramer, S. A.	Random House
Toad for Tuesday, A	O	F	Erickson, Russell E.	Beech Tree Books
Toby and the Accident	J	RF	PM Turquoise	Rigby
Today I Got Yelled At	J	RF	City Kids	Rigby
Toilet Paper Tigers, The	Q	RF	Korman, Gordon	Bantam Doubleday Dell
Toliver's Secret	T	HF	Brady, Esther Wood	Alfred A. Knopf
Tom, Babette, & Simon	T	F	Avi	Avon
Tom Edison's Bright Idea	N	B	Keller, Jack	Steck-Vaughn
Tom Sawyer	J	B	Hall, Richard	Rigby
Tom, the Dragon	M	F	New Way Orange	Steck-Vaughn
Tom the TV Cat	J	F	Heilbroner, Joan	Random House
Tom's Midnight Garden	V	F	Pierce, Philippa	HarperTrophy
Tomato Picking Day	L	I	Pipher, Tom	Wright Group/McGraw Hill
Tomatoes	M	I	Cole, Sally	Wright Group/McGraw Hill
Tomorrow's Wizard	R	F	MacLachlan, Patricia	Scholastic
Tongue Twister Prize, The	J	RF	Little Books	Sadlier-Oxford
Tongues: Are for Tasting, Licking, Tricking	L	I	Literacy 2000	Rigby
Tonight on the Titanic	M	F	Osborne, Mary Pope	Random House
Toning The Sweep	Y	RF	Johnson, Angela	Scholastic
Too Busy for Pets!	K	RF	Sunshine	Wright Group/McGraw Hill
Too Hot to Handle	M	RF	Christopher, Matt	Little, Brown & Co.
Too Many Babas	K	TL	Croll, Carolyn	HarperTrophy
Too Many Babas	K	TL	Little Readers	Houghton Mifflin
Too Many Mice	J	F	Bank Street	Bantam Doubleday Dell
Too Many Rabbits	J	RF	Parish, Peggy	Bantam Doubleday Dell
Too Many Steps	J	RF	Foundations	Wright Group/McGraw Hill
Too Many Tamales	M	RF	Soto, Gary	Putnam & Grosset
Too Much Magic	R	F	Sterman, Betsy & Samuel	HarperTrophy
Too Much Noise	J	TL	McGovern, Ann	Scholastic
Too Much Talk and Other Stories	J	RF	New Way: Literature	Steck-Vaughn
Too Much Trouble for Grandpa	J	RF	Sokoloff, Myka-Lynne	Sadlier-Oxford
Too Small Jill	J	RF	Little Books	Sadlier-Oxford
Too Soon to Say Goodbye	S	RF	Kent, Deborah	Scholastic
Tools and Gadgets	T	I	Historic Communities	Crabtree
Tooter Pepperday	L	RF	Spinelli, Jerry	Random House
Toothpaste Millionaire, The	T	RF	Merrill, Jean	Houghton Mifflin
Top Cat	O	I	Byars, Betsy	The Penguin Group
Torn Thread	W	HF	Isaacs, Anne	Scholastic
Tornado	O	I	Byars, Betsy	HarperTrophy
Tornadoes!	N	I	Hopping, Lorraine Jean	Scholastic
Totara Tree, The	M	RF	Book Bank	Wright Group/McGraw Hill
Touch of Gold and Other Stories, The	M	TL	Lane, Sheila, Marion Kemp	Wood Lock Educational
Touchdown for Tommy	M	RF	Christopher, Matt	Little, Brown & Co.
Tournament Trouble	R	RF	Costello, Emily	Dell
Town Mouse and Country Mouse	K	TL	PM Tales and Plays- Purple	Rigby
Tracker	T	RF	Paulsen, Gary	Scholastic
Tractor Trailers	N	I	Schaefer, Lola M.	Capstone Press
Train Time	L	I	Baehr, Lisa	Hampton-Brown
Trains on the Rails	K	I	PM Plus	Rigby
Traitor: The Case of Benedict Arnold	X	B	Fritz, Jean	Putnam & Grosset
Transcontinental Railroad, The	V	I	Cornerstones of Freedom	Children's Press

Title	Level	Genre	Author/Series	Publisher/Distributor
Transforming Trash	S	I	Quinn, Pat	Pacific Learning
Trapped!	O	RF	SupaDoopers	Sundance
Trapped By a Teacher	Q	RF	Duke, Mary Ann	Rigby
Trash Can Band, The	J	RF	Little Books	Sadlier-Oxford
Travelers and Traders	Q	I	Weldon Owen	Wright Group/McGraw Hill
Travels with Rainie Marie	S	B	Martin, Patricia	Hyperion
Treasure Hunting	M	RF	Literacy 2000	Rigby
Treasure Island	Z	HF	Stevenson, Robert Lewis	Scholastic
Treasure of Alpheus Winterborn, The	S	F	Bellairs, John	The Penguin Group
Treasure of El Patrón, The	T	RF	Paulsen, Gary	Bantam Doubleday Dell
Treasure of the Lost Lagoon, The	K	F	Hayes, Geoffrey	Random House
Treasure on Fraser Street, The	K	RF	Rushby, Pamela	Rigby
Treasures in the Dust	U	HF	Porter, Tracey	HarperTrophy
Treasury of Pirate Stories, A	S	F	Bradman, Tony	Kingfisher
Tree by Leaf	V	F	Voigt, Cynthia	Simon & Schuster
Trees	K	I	Early Connections	Benchmark Education
Trees	J	I	Literacy 2000	Rigby
Trees and Leaves	S	I	Nature Club	Troll
Trees and Plants in the Rain Forest	O	I	Pirotta, Saviour	Steck-Vaughn
Trees Belong To Everyone	L	I	Literacy 2000	Rigby
Triathlon	Q	I	Lund, Bill	Capstone Press
Triceratops on the Farm	L	F	Wesley & the Dinosaurs	Wright Group/McGraw Hill
Trickster Ghost, The	O	F	Showell, E.	Scholastic
Tricksters	M	RF	SupaDoopers	Sundance
Triffic the Extraordinary Pig	R	F	King-Smith, Dick	Bantam Doubleday Dell
Trip Around the Gulf of Mexico, A	M	I	People, Spaces & Places	Rand McNally
Trip to Freedom	M	B	Nguyen, Andrea Quynhgiao	Rigby
Triplet Trouble and the Bicycle Race	L	RF	Dadey, D. & Jones, M. T.	Scholastic
Triplet Trouble and the Class Trip	L	RF	Dadey, D. & Jones, M. T.	Scholastic
Triplet Trouble and the Cookie Contest	L	RF	Dadey, D. & Jones, M. T.	Scholastic
Triplet Trouble and the Field Day Disaster	L	RF	Dadey, D. & Jones, M. T.	Scholastic
Triplet Trouble and the Pizza Party	L	RF	Dadey, D. & Jones, M. T.	Scholastic
Triplet Trouble and the Red Heart Race	L	RF	Dadey, D. & Jones, M. T.	Scholastic
Triplet Trouble and the Runaway Reindeer	L	RF	Dadey, D. & Jones, M. T.	Scholastic
Triplet Trouble and the Talent Show	L	RF	Dadey, D. & Jones, M. T.	Scholastic
Triplet Trouble and the Talent Show Mess	L	RF	Dadey, D. & Jones, M. T.	Scholastic
Trog	M	F	Sunshine	Wright Group/McGraw Hill
Trojan Horse, The	N	I	Literacy 2000	Rigby
Trojan Horse, The: How the Greeks Won the War	N	HF	Little, Emily	Random House
Trolls Don't Ride Roller Coasters	M	F	Dadey, D. & Jones, M. T.	Scholastic
Tropical Rainforests	N	I	Habitats of the World	Dominie Press
Trouble Dolls	P	F	Buffett, Jimmy & Savannah Jane	Harcourt Brace
Trouble River	S	HF	Byars, Betsy	Scholastic
Trouble with Buster, The	N	RF	Lorimer, Janet	Scholastic
Trouble with Herbert, The	L	F	Eyles, Heather	Mondo
Trouble with Oatmeal, The	O	RF	PM Emerald	Rigby
Trouble with Parents, The	N	RF	SupaDoopers	Sundance
Trouble with Patrick, The	O	RF	Whitaker, Alan	Rigby
Trouble with Tuck, The	R	RF	Taylor, Theodore	Avon
Troublemaker	M	RF	SupaDoopers	Sundance
Troubling a Star	V	F	L'Engle, Madeleine	Dell
Trout Summer	T	RF	Conly, Jane Leslie	Scholastic
Trucker	P	RF	Beale, Fleur	Pacific Learning
Trucks on the Road	K	I	PM Plus	Rigby
True Confessions	S	RF	Tashjian, Janet	Scholastic
True Confessions of Charlotte Doyle, The	V	HF	Avi	Avon
True Crimes and How They Were Solved	Z	I	Larsen, Anita	Scholastic
True Stories about Abraham Lincoln	O	B	Gross, Ruth Belov	Scholastic
True Story of Balto, The	L	I	Standiford, Natalie	Random House
True Story of the Three Little Pigs, The	Q	TL	Scieszka, Jon	Scholastic

Title	Level	Genre	Author/Series	Publisher/Distributor
True-Life Treasure Hunts	N	I	Donnelly, Judy	Random House
Trumpet of the Swan, The	R	F	White, E. B.	Scholastic
Truth About the Moon, The	M	TL	Bess, Clayton	Houghton Mifflin
Tubes in My Ears: My Trip to the Hospital	K	I	Book Shop	Mondo
Tuck Everlasting	U	F	Babbitt, Natalie	Farrar, Straus and Giroux
Tucket's Gold	U	HF	Paulsen, Gary	Bantam
Tucket's Ride	U	HF	Paulsen, Gary	Bantam Doubleday Dell
Tummy Ache	J	RF	Sunshine	Wright Group/McGraw Hill
Tundra	Q	I	First Reports	Compass Point Books
Turkey That Ate My Father, The	Q	F	Marney, Dean	Scholastic
Turkey Trouble	M	RF	Giff, Patricia Reilly	Bantam Doubleday Dell
Turkeys' Side of It, The	N	RF	Smith, Janice Lee	HarperTrophy
Turn Homeward, Hannalee	T	HF	Beatty, Patricia	William Morrow
Turtle Flies South	K	F	Literacy 2000	Rigby
Turtles	S	I	A First Book	Franklin Watts
Tut's Mummy: Lost and Found	P	I	Donnelly, Judy	Random House
Tutankhamen's Gift	R	I	Sabuda, Robert	Simon & Schuster
TV Kid, The	R	RF	Byars, Betsy	Puffin Books
TV Reporters	M	I	Boraas, Tracey	Capstone Press
TV Time-Out	M	RF	Blackaby, Susan	Wright Group/McGraw Hill
Twelve Dancing Princesses	M	I	Enrichment	Wright Group/McGraw Hill
Twenty-One Balloons, The	V	SF	DuBois, William	Scholastic
Twiddle Twins' Haunted House, The	L	F	Goldsmith, Howard	Mondo
Twiddle Twins' Music Box Mystery, The	L	F	Goldsmith, Howard	Mondo
Twiddle Twins' Single Footprint Mystery, The	L	F	Goldsmith, Howard	Mondo
Twilight In Grace Falls	W	RF	Honeycutt, Natalie	Avon
Twinkie Squad, The	S	RF	Korman, Gordon	Scholastic
Twisters and Other Wind Storms	P	I	Wildcats	Wright Group/McGraw Hill
Twisting Up a Storm	R	I	Duksta, Cheryl	Pacific Learning
Twits, The	P	F	Dahl, Roald	The Penguin Group
Two Foolish Cats	K	F	Literacy 2000	Rigby
Two Hungry Hippos	M	I	Adams, Alison	Benchmark Education Co.
Two Plus One Goes A.P.E.	L	RF	Springstubb, Tricia	Scholastic
Two Runaways, The	M	RF	Schultz, Irene	Wright Group/McGraw Hill
Two Silly Trolls	J	F	Jewell, Nancy	HarperTrophy
Two Tickets to Freedom: The True Story of Ellen and William Craft	S	HF	Freedman, Florence	Scholastic
Two-Part Invention	Z	B	L'Engle, Madeleine	Harper Collins
Tyler Toad and Thunder	M	F	Crowe, Robert	Dutton
Tyrannosaurus the Terrible	L	F	Wesley & the Dinosaurs	Wright Group/McGraw Hill
Ugly Duckling, The	J	TL	PM Tales and Plays Turquoise	Rigby
Ugly Mug	P	RF	Joseph, Vivienne	Pacific Learning
Ultimate Field Trip 1: Adventures in the Amazon Rain Forest	S	I	Goodman, Susan E.	Simon & Schuster
Umbrellas	M	I	Sunshine	Wright Group/McGraw Hill
Unbelievable!	K	SF	Shulman, Lisa	Hampton-Brown
Uncle Elephant	J	F	Lobel, Arnold	Harper Collins
Under My Nose	O	B	Ehlert, Lois	Richard C. Owen
Under the Blood-Red Sun	W	HF	Salisbury, Graham	Bantam Doubleday Dell
Under the City	K	RF	Sunshine	Wright Group/McGraw Hill
Under the Ground	P	I	Literacy 2000	Rigby
Under the Ground	Q	I	Wildcats	Wright Group/McGraw Hill
Undercover Tailback	O	RF	Christopher, Matt	Scholastic
Underground Railroad, The	V	I	Bial, Raymond	Houghton Mifflin
Underground Railroad, The	V	I	Cornerstones of Freedom	Children's Press
Underwater Animals	Q	I	Weldon Owen	Wright Group/McGraw Hill
Undying Glory: The Story of the Massachusetts 54th Regiment	U	HF	Cox, Clinton	Scholastic
Unexpected Treasure	N	RF	Dionetti, Michelle	Wright Group/McGraw Hill
Unicorns Don't Give Sleigh Rides	M	F	Dadey, D. & Jones, M. T.	Scholastic

Title	Level	Genre	Author/Series	Publisher/Distributor
United States Holocaust Memorial Museum, The	W	I	Cornerstones of Freedom	Children's Press
Universal Solvent and Other Cases, The	O	RF	Simon, Seymour	Avon
Universe, The	Q	I	Pair-It-Books	Steck-Vaughn
Unusual Spiders	N	I	Jensen, Ned	Wright Group/McGraw Hill
Up and Away	Q	I	Weldon Owen	Wright Group/McGraw Hill
Up and Away!: Taking a Flight	N	RF	Book Shop	Mondo
Up High in the Mountains	N	RF	Wildcats	Wright Group/McGraw Hill
Up in the Air	P	I	Wildcats	Wright Group/McGraw Hill
Ups and Downs of Carl Davis III, The	T	RF	Guy, Rosa	Language for Learning Assoc.
Upside-Down Reader, The	L	F	Gruber, Wolfram	North-South Books
Uranus	N	I	A True Book	Children's Press
Uranus	O	I	Vogt, Gregory L.	Capstone Press
US and Uncle Fraud	S	RF	Lowry, Lois	Houghton Mifflin
Usborne Book of Inventors, The	W	I	Reid, Struan and Fara, Patricia	Scholastic
Using Nature's Gifts	K	I	People, Spaces & Places	Rand McNally
Using the Library	L	I	Wonder World	Wright Group/McGraw Hill
Vacation Journal, A	M	B	Discovery World	Rigby
Vacation Under the Volcano	M	F	Osborne, Mary Pope	Random House
Vagabond Crabs	J	I	Literacy 2000	Rigby
Valentine Star, The	M	RF	Giff, Patricia Reilly	Bantam Doubleday Dell
Vampire Trouble	L	F	Dadey, D. & Jones, M. T.	Scholastic
Vampire Who Came For Christmas, The	Q	F	Curtis Regan, Dian	Bantam Doubleday Dell
Vampires Don't Wear Polka Dots	M	F	Dadey, D. & Jones, M. T.	Scholastic
Van Gogh Cafe, The	S	RF	Rylant, Cynthia	Harcourt Brace
Vehicles for Fun and Sports	K	I	PM Plus	Rigby
Vehicles in the Air	K	I	PM Plus	Rigby
Velveteen Rabbit, The	Q	F	Williams, Margery	Hearst
Venus	N	I	A True Book	Children's Press
Venus	Q	I	Vogt, Gregory L.	The Millbrook Press
Very Special Kwanzaa, A	O	I	Chocolate, Debbi	Scholastic
Very Strange Dollhouse, A	L	F	Dussling, Jennifer	Grosset & Dunlap
Veterinarians	L	I	Ready, Dee	Capstone Press
Vicar of Nibbleswick, The	O	RF	Dahl, Roald	Puffin Books
Vicky the High Jumper	K	I	Literacy 2000	Rigby
Vietnam	O	I	Dahl, Michael	Capstone Press
Vietnam Women's Memorial, The	W	I	Cornerstones of Freedom	Children's Press
View from Saturday, The	U	F	Konigsburg, E. L.	Atheneum Books
Viking Ships at Sunrise	M	F	Osborne, Mary Pope	Random House
Vikings, The	S	I	Journey Into Civilization	Chelsea House
Virtual Fred	O	SF	Courtney, Vincent	Random House
Volcano Goddess Will See You Now, The	N	F	The Zack Files	Grosset & Dunlap
Volcanoes	N	I	A True Book	Children's Press
Volcanoes	Q	I	Weldon Owen	Wright Group/McGraw Hill
Volcanoes	Q	I	Worldwise	Grolier
Volcanoes and Earthquakes	T	I	Lauber, Patricia	Language for Learning Assoc.
Voyage of the Frog, The	S	RF	Paulsen, Gary	Bantam Doubleday Dell
Voyage, The	M	F	Pair-It Books	Steck-Vaughn
Vulpes The Red Fox	T	F	George, Jean Craighead	Puffin Books
Wacky Jacks	L	RF	Adler, David A.	Random House
Wacky Wheels	N	I	Pacific Literacy	Pacific Learning
Wagon Wheels	K	HF	Brenner, Barbara	HarperTrophy
Wainscott Weasel, The	T	F	Seidler, Tor	Harper Collins
Wait Till Helen Comes	U	F	Downing Hahn, Mary	Houghton Mifflin
Waiting for the Rain	J	RF	Foundations	Wright Group/McGraw Hill
Wake Me in Spring	J	F	Preller, James	Scholastic
Wake Up, Emily, It's Mother's Day	M	RF	Giff, Patricia Reilly	Yearling
Walk in My World, A	Y	RF	Mazer, Anne	Persea Books
Walk Through a Rainforest, A: Life in the Ituri Forest of Zaire	V	RF	Creech, Sharon	Harper Collins
Walk Two Moons	V	RF	Creech, Sharon	Harper Collins

Title	Level	Genre	Author/Series	Publisher/Distributor
Walk With Grandpa, A	L	RF	Read Alongs	Rigby
Walkathon, The	K	RF	PM Story Books -Silver	Rigby
Walking	M	I	Literacy 2000	Rigby
Walking For Freedom: The Montgomery Bus Boycott	R	I	Kelso, Richard	Steck-Vaughn
Walking the Road to Freedom:A Story About Sojourner Truth	Q	B	Ferris, Jeri	Dell
Wall of Names, A: The Story of the Vietnam Veterans Memorial	O	HF	Donnelly, Judy	Random House
Wall, The	P	HF	Bunting, Eve	Clarion
Walter the Warlock	M	F	Hautzig, Deborah	Random House
Walter's Worries	L	F	Pacific Literacy	Pacific Learning
Wanderer, The	V	RF	Creech, Sharon	HarperCollins
Wanted Dead or Alive: The True Story of Harriet Tubman	P	B	McGovern, Ann	Scholastic
Wanted…Mud Blossom	P	RF	Byars, Betsy	Dell
War Comes to Willy Freeman	U	HF	Collier, J. L., &Collier, C.	Dell Publishing
War Dog Heroes: True Stories of Dog Courage in Wartime	S	I	Sanderson, Jeannette	Scholastic
War of 1812, The	S	I	A First Book	Franklin Watts
War Shirt, The	K	RF	Spang, Bently	Rigby
War With Grandpa, The	S	RF	Kimmel Smith, Robert	Bantam Doubleday Dell
Warthogs	O	I	Holmes, Kevin J.	Capstone Press
Warton and the King of the Skies	O	F	Erickson, Russell E.	Houghton Mifflin
Waste of Space, A	M	RF	SupaDoopers	Sundance
Watch Out, Man-Eating Snake	L	RF	Giff, Patricia Reilly	Bantam Doubleday Dell
Watcher, The	Z	RF	Howe, James	Simon & Schuster
Watchers: I.D.	V	SF	Lerangis, Peter	Scholastic
Watchers: Island	V	SF	Lerangis, Peter	Scholastic
Watchers: Lab 6	V	SF	Lerangis, Peter	Scholastic
Watchers: Last Stop	V	SF	Lerangis, Peter	Scholastic
Watchers: Rewind	V	SF	Lerangis, Peter	Scholastic
Watchers: War	V	SF	Lerangis, Peter	Scholastic
Watching Every Drop	M	I	Home Connection Collection	Rigby
Watching Josh	M	RF	Eaton, Deborah	Wright Group/McGraw Hill
Watching the Whales	L	RF	Foundations	Wright Group/McGraw Hill
Water	J	I	Momentum Literacy Program	Troll
Water	N	I	Simply Science	Compass Point Books
Water Buffalo Days	P	B	Nhuong, Huynh Quang	HarperTrophy
Water for the World	M	I	Home Connection Collection	Rigby
Water Goes Up! Water Goes Down!	K	I	Early Connections	Benchmark Education
Waterhole	K	I	Planet Earth	Rigby
Watership Down	Y	F	Adams, Richard	Avon
Watsons Go to Birmingham-1963, The	T	HF	Curtis, Christopher Paul	Bantam Doubleday Dell
Waves: The Changing Surface of the Sea	J	I	Wonder World	Wright Group/McGraw Hill
Wax Museum	L	I	Cook, Donald	Grosset & Dunlap
Way West, The: Journal of a Pioneer Woman	R	B	Knight, Amelia Stewart	Simon & Schuster
Wayside School Gets a Little Stranger	P	F	Sachar, Louis	Avon Camelot
Wayside School is Falling Down	P	F	Sachar, Louis	Avon
We Are All Alike	M	I	Schaefer, Lola M.	Benchmark Education
We Remember the Holocaust	Y	I	Adler, David A.	Henry Holt
We Scream for Ice Cream	K	RF	Chardiet, B. & Maccarone, G.	Scholastic
We Shall Not Be Moved	Z	I	Dash, Joan	Scholastic
We Use Numbers	J	I	Early Connections	Benchmark Education
We Want Jobs!: A Story of the Great Depression	R	I	Norrell, Robert J.	Steck-Vaughn
We're Off to Thunder Mountain	L	RF	Book Shop	Mondo
Weather	N	I	Literacy 2000	Rigby
Weather	N	I	Simply Science	Compass Point Books
Weather Watch	N	I	Wonders!	Hampton-Brown
Weather Watching	Q	I	Weldon Owen	Wright Group/McGraw Hill
Weather Words and What They Mean	R	I	Gibbons, Gail	Scholastic

Title	Level	Genre	Author/Series	Publisher/Distributor
Weaving Contest, The	O	TL	Literacy 2000	Rigby
Wedding Day Disaster	M	RF	SupaDoopers	Sundance
Week of the Jellyhoppers, The	R	F	Literacy 2000	Rigby
Weight Lifting	Q	I	Lund, Bill	Capstone Press
Weird Walkers	R	I	Fredericks, Anthony D.	NorthWord Press
Well I Never	K	F	Story Box	Wright Group/McGraw Hill
Well, The	T	HF	Taylor, Mildred D.	Puffin Books
Werewolf Chronicles, The	T	F	Philbrick, R. & Harnett, L.	Scholastic
Werewolves Don't Go To Summer Camp	M	F	Dadey, D. & Jones, M. T.	Scholastic
West Side Kids: Don't Call Me Slob-o	R	RF	Orgel, Doris	Hyperion
West Side Kids: The Big Idea	R	RF	Schecter, Ellen	Hyperion
West Side Kids: The Pet Sitters	R	RF	Schecter, Ellen	Hyperion
West Virginia: Facts and Symbols	O	I	Feeney, Kathy	Capstone Press
Westing Game, The	V	RF	Raskin, Ellen	The Penguin Group
Wet Day at School, A	J	RF	Sunshine	Wright Group/McGraw Hill
Wetlands	Q	I	First Reports	Compass Point Books
Whale Is Not A Fish, A: And Other Animal Mix-ups	P	I	Berger, Melvin	Scholastic
Whale Tales	N	I	Westerskov, Kim	Pacific Learning
Whale, The	O	I	Crewe, Sabrina	Steck-Vaughn
Whales	N	I	Book Shop	Mondo
Whales	O	I	Holmes, Kevin J.	Capstone Press
Whales	N	I	PM Animal Facts: Silver	Rigby
Whales	M	I	Wonder World	Wright Group/McGraw Hill
Whales' Song, The	N	I	Sheldon, Dyan	The Penguin Group
Whales-The Gentle Giants	L	I	Milton, Joyce	Random House
What a Day!	K	RF	Miranda, Anne	Hampton-Brown
What a Great Idea!	L	RF	Shelton, Flip	Rigby
What Am I Made Of?	N	I	Bennett, David	Scholastic
What Are My Chances?	J	I	Early Connections	Benchmark Education
What Are You Figuring Now?	P	B	Ferris, Jeri	Scholastic
What Can It Be?	N	I	Schaefer, Lola M.	Benchmark Education
What Can You Do with an Elephant House?	R	I	Gaynor, Miriam and Goodwin, A.	Pacific Learning
What Changes Our Earth?	K	I	People, Places & Spaces	Rand McNally
What Do Fish Have To Do With Anything?	W	RF	Avi	Candlewick Press
What Do You Hear When Cows Sing?	J	F	Maestro, Marco & Giulio	HarperTrophy
What Do You Think?	O	I	Wildcats	Wright Group/McGraw Hill
What Happens When You Recycle?	K	I	Discovery World	Rigby
What Hearts	S	RF	Brooks, Bruce	Language for Learning Assoc.
What in the World is the World Wide Web?	S	I	Quinn, Pat	Pacific Learning
What Is a Fly?	M	I	Sunshine	Wright Group/McGraw Hill
What Is a Park?	J	I	People, Places & Spaces	Rand McNally
What is a Reptile?	M	I	Now I Know	Troll
What Is Matter?	L	I	Schaefer, Lola M.	Benchmark Education
What Jamie Saw	T	RF	Coman, Carolyn	The Penguin Group
What Joy Found	L	RF	Ready Readers	Pearson Learning
What Kind of Babysitter Is This?	L	RF	Johnson, Dolores	Scholastic
What Made Teddalik Laugh	M	TL	Folk Tales	Wright Group/McGraw Hill
What Makes a Bird a Bird?	O	I	Garelick, May	Mondo
What Next, Baby Bear?	L	F	Murphy, Jill	Dial
What Shall I Do?	M	RF	Sunshine	Wright Group/McGraw Hill
What Were Castles For?	R	I	Usborne Starting Point History	EDC Publishing
What Would You Do?	J	RF	Sunshine	Wright Group/McGraw Hill
What's Cooking?	Q	I	Cartwright, Pauline	Pacific Learning
What's Cooking, Jenny Archer?	M	RF	Conford, Ellen	Little Brown & Co.
What's for Dinner, Dad?	K	RF	Sunshine	Wright Group/McGraw Hill
What's Inside?	K	I	Wonder World	Wright Group/McGraw Hill
What's It Like to Be a Fish?	L	I	Little Readers	Houghton Mifflin
What's Living at Your Place?	Q	I	Chapman, Bruce	Pacific Learning
What's Missing?	K	I	Book Bank	Wright Group/McGraw Hill
What's the Big Idea, Ben Franklin?	O	B	Fritz, Jean	Scholastic

Title	Level	Genre	Author/Series	Publisher/Distributor
What's the Matter, Kelly Beans?	N	RF	Enderle, Judith R. & Tessler, S. G.	Candlewick Press
What's the Matter with Herbie Jones?	N	RF	Kline, Suzy	The Penguin Group
What's Underneath?	K	I	Discovery World	Rigby
When I Broke the Office Window	L	RF	City Kids	Rigby
When I Forgot	N	RF	Marriott, Janice	Pacific Learning
When I Get Bigger	K	RF	Mayer, Mercer	Donovan
When I Was Young and Wild Bill's Secret Wish	P	RF	Miggs, W.B.	Pacific Learning
When Justice Failed: The Fred Korematsu Story	U	B	Chin, Steven A.	Steck-Vaughn
When My Dad Came to School	M	RF	City Kids	Rigby
When Plague Strikes	X	I	Giblin, James Cross	Harper Collins
When the Circus Came to Town	R	RF	Horvath, Polly	Sunburst
When the Giants Came to Town	L	F	Leonard, Marcia	Scholastic
When the King Rides By	J	F	Book Shop	Mondo
When the Tripods Came	V	F	Christopher, John	Aladdin
When The Truck Got Stuck!	M	RF	Cowley, Joy	Pacific Learning
When the Volcano Erupted	J	F	PM Turquoise	Rigby
When the Water Closes Over My Head	R	RF	Napoli, Donna	Puffin Books
When Tony Got Lost at the Zoo	L	RF	City Kids	Rigby
When Will We Be Sisters?	K	RF	Kroll, Virginia	Scholastic
Where Are the Bears?	K	F	Winters, Kay	Bantam Doubleday Dell
Where Did the Maya Go?	P	F	Carroll, Cynthia	Rigby
Where Do You Live?	N	I	People, Places & Spaces	Rand McNally
Where Do You Think You're Going, Christopher Columbus?	S	B	Fritz, Jean	Putnam & Grosset
Where Does the Wind Go?	M	I	Book Shop	Mondo
Where in the World is the Perfect Family?	P	RF	Hest, Amy	The Penguin Group
Where Jeans Come From	K	I	Ready Readers	Pearson Learning
Where People Live	J	RF	Early Connections	Benchmark Education
Where the Lilies Bloom	Y	RF	Cleavers, Vera and Bill	HarperTrophy
Where the Red Fern Grows	X	RF	Rawls, Wilson	Bantam Doubleday Dell
Where the Wild Things Are	J	F	Sendak, Maurice	Harper & Row
Where to Look for a Dinosaur	O	F	Most, Bernard	Harcourt Brace
Where Was Patrick Henry on the 29th of May?	R	B	Fritz, Jean	Scholastic
Where's Tony?	J	RF	City Kids	Rigby
Which Way, Jack?	O	F	Yurkovic, Diana Short	Rigby
Which Witch?	S	F	Ibbotson, Eva	Puffin Books
Whipping Boy, The	R	F	Fleischman, Sid	Troll
White Bird	N	RF	Bulla, Clyde Robert	Random House
White Elephants and Yellow Jackets	O	I	Webb, Derek	Rigby
White Fang	Y	RF	London, Jack	Scholastic
White Horse, The	K	F	Literacy 2000	Rigby
White House, The	V	I	Cornerstones of Freedom	Children's Press
White Mountain, The	V	F	Christopher, John	Aladdin
White-Tailed Deer, The	R	I	Zwaschka, Michael	Capstone Press
Who Is Carrie?	W	HF	Collier, J. L. and Collier, C.	Bantam Doubleday Dell
Who Killed Mr. Boddy?	P	RF	Parker, A. E.	Scholastic
Who Looks After Me?	M	I	Literacy 2000	Rigby
Who Makes the Rules?	M	I	Schafer, Lola M.	Benchmark Education
Who Pushed Humpty?	K	TL	Literacy 2000	Rigby
Who Put That Hair in My Toothbrush?	U	RF	Spinelli, Jerry	Little, Brown
Who Really Killed Cock Robin?	U	RF	George, Jean Craighead	HarperTrophy
Who Sank the Boat?	K	F	Allen Pamela	Coward
Who Shot the President?: The Death of John F. Kennedy	P	I	Donnelly, Judy	Random House
Who Stole the Wizard of Oz?	P	RF	Avi	Alfred A. Knopf
Who Were the First People?	R	I	Usborne Starting Point History	EDC Publishing
Who Were the Romans?	R	I	Usborne Starting Point History	EDC Publishing
Who Were the Vikings?	R	I	Usborne Starting Point History	EDC Publishing
Who's a Pest?	J	F	Bonsall, Crosby	HarperTrophy
Who's Afraid of the Big, Bad Bully?	K	RF	Slater, Teddy	Scholastic
Who's in Love with Arthur?	M	F	Brown, Marc	Little, Brown & Co.

Title	Level	Genre	Author/Series	Publisher/Distributor
Who's That Stepping on Plymouth Rock?	R	I	Fritz, Jean	Putnam & Grosset
Whoops! It Works!	O	I	Lopez, Orlando	Pearson Learning
Whose Side Are You On?	K	TL	Cisco, Cheyenne	Sadlier-Oxford
Whose Side Are You On?	Q	RF	Moore, Emily	Bantam Doubleday Dell
Why Coyote Howls at Night	K	TL	Little Books	Sadlier-Oxford
Why Coyote Howls at Night	Q	TL	Moore, Emily	Farrar, Straus and Giroux
Why Crocodiles Live in Rivers	M	F	Sunshine	Wright Group/McGraw Hill
Why Don't You Get a Horse, Sam Adams?	R	B	Fritz, Jean	G.P. Putnam's Sons
Why People Move	K	I	People, Places & Spaces	Rand McNally
Why Rabbits Have Long Ears	L	TL	Literacy 2000	Rigby
Why the Bear's Tail is Short	J	F	Sunshine	Wright Group/McGraw Hill
Why the Kangaroo Hops	K	I	Sunshine	Wright Group/McGraw Hill
Why the Leopard Has Spots	L	I	Pair-It Books	Steck-Vaughn
Why the Ocean Is Salty	Q	I	Leonhardt, Alice	Steck-Vaughn
Why The Sea Is Salty	L	TL	Literacy 2000	Rigby
Wilamina and the Weather Conditions	M	F	Reimer, Luther	Wright Group/McGraw Hill
Wild and Wooly Mammoths	P	I	Aliki	HarperCollins
Wild Babies	O	I	Simon, Seymour	Harper Collins
Wild Bird and Other Stories of Adventure	O	RF	Belcher, Angie	Pacific Learning
Wild Cats	Q	I	Leonhardt, Alice	Steck-Vaughn
Wild Culpepper Cruise, The	O	RF	Paulsen, Gary	Bantam Doubleday Dell
Wild Horses	R	I	Wilde, Buck	Rigby
Wild Swans, The	L	TL	Tales from Hans Andersen	Wright Group/McGraw Hill
Wild, Wild Wolves	M	I	Milton, Joyce	Random House
Wild Willie and King Kyle Detectives	N	F	Joosse, Barbara M.	Bantam Doubleday Dell
Wild, Wooly Child, The	J	F	Read Alongs	Rigby
Wilde Street Club and Molly, The	M	RF	Sunshine	Wright Group/McGraw Hill
Wilde Street Club and the Duck Man, The	M	RF	Sunshine	Wright Group/McGraw Hill
Wildfires	N	I	A True Book	Children's Press
Wilfrid Laurier	W	B	Spigelman, Martin	Fitzhenry & Whiteside
Will Rogers	O	B	Schott, Jane A.	Carolrhoda Books
William Problem, The	S	RF	Baker, Barbara	Puffin Books
William's Wheelchair Race	K	RF	Sunshine	Wright Group/McGraw Hill
Williamsburg	V	I	Cornerstones of Freedom	Children's Press
Williwaw!	V	RF	Bodoff, Tom	Knopf
Wilma Mankiller	P	B	Lowery, Linda	Carolrhoda Books
Wind and Storms	K	I	Sunshine	Wright Group/McGraw Hill
Wind and the Sun and Other Stories, The	J	F	New Way Orange	Steck-Vaughn
Wind Blew, The	J	RF	Hutchins, Pat	Puffin Books
Wind in the Door, A	V	F	L'Engle, Madeleine	Bantam Doubleday Dell
Wind Power	J	I	Pacific Literacy	Pacific Learning
Window, The	V	RF	Ingold, Jeanette	Harcourt Brace
Winged Cat, The: A Tale of Ancient Egypt	U	TL	Lattimore, Deborah Nourse	HarperCollins
Wingman	O	F	Pinkwater, Daniel	Bantam Skylark
Wingman on Ice	M	RF	Christopher, Matt	Little, Brown & Co.
Wings	Q	F	Brittain, Bill	HarperTrophy
Wings	W	TL	Yolen, Jane & Nolan, Dennis	Harcourt Brace
Winklepoo the Wicked	M	F	Sunshine	Wright Group/McGraw Hill
Winter Days in the Big Woods	J	HF	Wilder, Laura Ingalls	Harper Collins
Winter on the Farm	J	HF	Wilder, Laura Ingalls	Harper Collins
Winter Room, The	U	RF	Paulsen, Gary	Bantam Doubleday Dell
Winter Survival	O	I	Wilde, Buck	Rigby
Winter Woollies	K	I	Storyteller Nonfiction	Wright Group/McGraw Hill
Winterdance: The Fine Madness of Running the Iditarod	W	B	Paulsen, Gary	Harcourt Brace
Wish Fish, The	P	TL	Krueger, Carol	Rigby
Wish Giver, The	T	F	Brittain, Bill	HarperTrophy
Wish on a Unicorn	T	RF	Hesse, Karen	The Penguin Group
Witch Hunt: It Happened in Salem Village	Q	I	Krensky, Stephen	Random House
Witch of Blackbird Pond, The	W	HF	Speare, Elizabeth George	Bantam Doubleday Dell

Title	Level	Genre	Author/Series	Publisher/Distributor
Witch of Fourth Street, The	S	HF	Levoy, Myron	Language for Learning Assoc.
Witch's Cat	P	F	Chew, Ruth	Scholastic
Witchcraft of Salem Village, The	U	I	Jackson, Shirley	Random House
Witches Don't Do Backflips	M	F	Dadey, D. & Jones, M. T.	Scholastic
Witches of Worm, The	V	F	Snyder, Zilpha K.	Random House
Witches, The	R	F	Dahl, Roald	The Penguin Group
Wizard and Wart at Sea	J	F	Smith, Janice Lee	HarperTrophy
Wizard of Earthsea, A	Z	F	LeGuin, Ursula K.	Bantam Doubleday Dell
Wizard of Oz, The	U	F	Baum, L. Frank	Scholastic
Wizards Don't Need Computers	M	F	Dadey, D. & Jones, M. T.	Scholastic
Wolf, The	S	I	Dahl, Michael	Capstone Press
Wolf's First Deer	M	RF	Book Bank	Wright Group/McGraw Hill
Wolfman Sam	O	RF	Levy, Elizabeth	HarperTrophy
Wolfmen Don't Hula Dance	M	RF	Dadey, D. & Jones, M. T.	Scholastic
Wolves	Q	I	Literacy 2000	Rigby
Wolves	N	I	PM Animal Facts: Silver	Rigby
Wolves of Willoughby Chase, The	V	HF	Aiken, Joan	Bantam Doubleday Dell
Woman Hollering Creek	Z	RF	Cisneros, Sandra	Random House
Woman Who Flummoxed the Fairies, The	O	TL	Forest, Heather	Harcourt Brace
Women Inventors	O	B	Blashfield, Jean	Capstone Press
Women of Valor	U	B	Real Lives	Troll
Women Who Shaped the West	V	B	Cornerstones of Freedom	Children's Press
Women's Voting Rights	V	I	Cornerstones of Freedom	Children's Press
Wonder Kid Meets the Evil Lunch Snatcher	M	RF	Duncan, Lois	Little, Brown & Co.
Wonderful Alexander and the Catwings	N	F	Schindler, S.D.	Scholastic
Wonderful Eyes	M	I	Science	Wright Group/McGraw Hill
Woodlanders Begin, The	M	F	Schultz, Irene	Wright Group/McGraw Hill
Woods, Irons, and Greens	R	I	Wildcats	Wright Group/McGraw Hill
Woodsong	T	B	Paulsen, Gary	Dell
Wordful Child, A	O	B	Lyon, George Ella	Richard C. Owen
Words	M	I	Pacific Literacy	Pacific Learning
Words	U	RF	Paulsen, Gary	The Penguin Group
Words of Stone	V	RF	Henkes, Kevin	The Penguin Group
Working Cotton	N	RF	Williams, Sherley Anne	Harcourt Brace
Working on Water	L	I	Home Connection Collection	Rigby
World of Dogs, The	Q	I	Pair-It-Books	Steck-Vaughn
World of Imagination, A	R	I	Literacy 2000	Rigby
World's Best Dog-Walker, The	Q	RF	Zollman, Pam	Steck-Vaughn
World's Greatest Toe Show, The	M	RF	Lamb, Nancy & Singer, Muff	Troll
Worms	P	I	Mini Pets	Steck-Vaughn
Worst Show-and-Tell Ever, The	J	SF	Walsh, Rita	Troll
Worst Witch at Sea, The	P	F	Murphy, Jill	Candlewick Press
Worst Witch Strikes Again, The	P	F	Murphy, Jill	Candlewick Press
Worst Witch, The	P	F	Murphy, Jill	Puffin Books
Wreck Trek	S	I	Belcher, Angie	Pacific Learning
Wright Brothers at Kitty Hawk, The	K	B	Schaefer, Lola M.	Capstone Press
Wright Brothers, The	M	B	Biography	Benchmark Education
Wright Brothers, The	Y	B	Freedman, Russell	Holiday House
Wright Brothers, The	U	B	Sobol, Donald J.	Scholastic
Wringer	U	RF	Spinelli, Jerry	HarperTrophy
Wrinkle in Time, A	V	F	L'Engle, Madeleine	Bantom Doubleday Dell
Write Up a Storm with the Polk Street School	M	RF	Giff, Patricia Reilly	Bantam Doubleday Dell
Writer of the Plains: A Story about Willa Cather	Q	B	Streissguth, Tom	Carolrhoda Books
Writer's Work, A	N	I	Wonder World	Wright Group/McGraw Hill
Writing Bug, The	O	B	Hopkins, Lee Bennett	Richard C. Owen
Wrong Way Around Magic	N	F	Chew, Ruth	Scholastic
Wrong-Way Rabbit, The	J	F	Slater, Teddy	Scholastic
Wyoming: Facts and Symbols	O	I	Dubois, Muriel L.	Capstone Press
Yang the Eldest and His Odd Jobs	P	RF	Namioka, Lensey	Bantam Doubleday Dell
Yang the Second and Her Secret Admirer	P	RF	Namioka, Lensey	Bantam Doubleday Dell

Title	Level	Genre	Author/Series	Publisher/Distributor
Yang the Third & Her Impossible Family	P	RF	Namiaka, Lensey	Bantam Doubleday Dell
Yang the Youngest and His Terrible Ear	P	RF	Namioka, Lensey	Bantam Doubleday Dell
Year Mom Won the Pennant, The	M	RF	Christopher, Matt	Little, Brown & Co.
Year of Impossible Goodbyes	W	HF	Choi, Sook Nyui	Yearling
Year of the Sawdust Man, The	Y	RF	LaFaye, A.	Simon & Schuster
Yearling, The	X	RF	Rawlings, Marjorie Kinnan	Simon & Schuster
Yellow Overalls	L	F	Literacy 2000	Rigby
Yikes! Grandma's a Teenager	N	F	The Zack Files	Grossett&Dunlap
Yo-Yo's	O	I	PM Nonfiction -Emerald	Rigby
Yolonda's Genius	V	RF	Fenner, Carol	Aladdin
Yonder	M	RF	Johnston, Tony	The Penguin Group
You Are Much Too Small	J	F	Bank Street	Bantam Doubleday Dell
You Be The Detective	Q	RF	Miller, Marvin	Scholastic
You Be The Detective II	Q	RF	Miller, Marvin	Scholastic
You Be The Jury	Q	I	Miller, Marvin	Scholastic
You Be The Jury: Courtroom V	Q	I	Miller, Marvin	Bantam Doubleday Dell
You Can Always Tell Cathy from Caitlin	K	RF	Sunshine	Wright Group/McGraw Hill
You Can Canoe!: A Book of Sporting Activities	O	I	Yurkovic, Diana Short	Rigby
You Can Cook	M	I	Woo, Lornette	Steck-Vaughn
You Can't Catch Me	J	F	Oppenheim, Joanne	Houghton Mifflin
You Can't Eat Your Chicken Pox, Amber Brown	N	RF	Danziger, Paula	Scholastic
You Shouldn't Have to Say Good-bye	T	RF	Hermes, Patricia	Scholastic
You Want Women to Vote, Lizzie Stanton?	W	B	Fritz, Jean	The Penguin Group
You're My Nikki	M	RF	Eisenberg, Phyllis Rose	The Penguin Group
You're Out	N	RF	Kroll, Stephen	Avon Camelot
Young Arthur Ashe: Brave Champion	L	B	First Start Biography	Troll
Young Cam Jansen and the Ice Skate Mystery	J	RF	Adler, David A.	Puffin Books
Young Cam Jansen and the Lost Tooth	J	RF	Adler, David A.	Puffin Books
Young Cam Jansen and the Missing Cookie	J	RF	Adler, David A.	Puffin Books
Young Clara Barton: Battlefield Nurse	L	B	First Start Biography	Troll
Young Geographers	O	I	People, Spaces & Places	Rand McNally
Young Jackie Robinson: Baseball Hero	L	B	First Start Biography	Troll
Young Joan	X	HF	Dana, Barbara	HarperTrophy
Young Land Lords, The	X	RF	Myers, Walter Dean	The Penguin Group
Young Mozart	O	B	Isadora, Rachel	The Penguin Group
Young Rosa Parks: Civil Rights Heroine	L	B	First Start Biography	Troll
Young Thurgood Marshall: Fighter for Equality	L	B	First Start Biography	Troll
Young Wolf's First Hunt	M	RF	Shefelman, Janice	Random House
Your Move, J.P.!	R	RF	Lowry, Lois	Random House
Your Teeth	J	I	Pebble Books	Grolier, Capstone
Yuck!	K	F	Little Readers	Houghton Mifflin
Zack's Alligator	K	F	Mozelle, Shirley	HarperTrophy
Zack's Alligator Goes to School	K	F	Mozelle, Shirley	HarperTrophy
Zap! I'm a Mind Reader	N	SF	The Zack Files	Grosset & Dunlap
Zebras	O	I	Holmes, Kevin J.	Capstone Press
Zebras	N	I	Meadows, Graham & Vial, Claire	Dominie Press
Zeely	R	RF	Hamilton, Virginia	Macmillan
Zero's Slider	M	RF	Christopher, Matt	Little, Brown & Co.
Zeros and Ones	S	I	Wildcats	Wright Group/McGraw Hill
Zlata's Diary	X	B	Filipovic, Zlata	Puffin Books
Zoe at the Fancy Dress Ball	J	RF	Literacy 2000	Rigby
Zombies Don't Play Soccer	M	F	Dadey, D. & Jones, M. T.	Scholastic
Zomo the Rabbit: A Trickster Tale from West Africa	M	TL	McDermott, Gerald	Harcourt Brace
Zoo Keepers	M	I	Deedrick, Tami	Capstone Press
Zooman Sam	P	RF	Lowry, Lois	Houghton Mifflin

Book List
Organized by Level

Title	Level	Genre	Author/Series	Publisher/Distributor
Addie's Bad Day	J	RF	Robins, Joan	HarperTrophy
Adventures of Snail at School	J	F	Stadler, John	HarperTrophy
Ah Liang's Gift	J	RF	Sunshine	Wright Group/McGraw Hill
Ah-choo!	J	RF	Samuels, Aurora	Sadlier-Oxford
Aladdin & the Magic Lamp	J	TL	Traditional Tales	Dominie
Alison Wendlebury	J	RF	Literacy 2000	Rigby
All About Bats	J	I	Ready Readers	Modern Curriculum
All About Me!	J	RF	Pacific Literacy	Pacific Learning
Allie's Basketball Dream	J	RF	Barber, B. & Ligasan, D.	Scholastic
Amazing Eggs	J	I	Discovery World	Rigby
Amazing Maze, The	J	RF	Foundations	Wright Group/McGraw Hill
And I Mean it Stanley	J	RF	Bonsall, Crosby	HarperCollins
Annie's Pet	J	RF	Bank Street	Bantam Doubleday Dell
Ant City	J	RF	PM Turquoise	Rigby
Apple Tree, The	J	I	Sunshine	Wright Group/McGraw Hill
Art Around the World	J	I	Early Connections	Benchmark Education
Ask Mr. Bear	J	F	Flack, Marjorie	Macmillan
Aunt Eater Loves a Mystery	J	F	Cushman, Doug	HarperTrophy
Aunt Eater's Mystery Christmas	J	F	Cushman, Doug	HarperTrophy
Aunt Eater's Mystery Vacation	J	F	Cushman, Doug	HarperTrophy
Baseball Ballerina	J	RF	Cristaldi, Kathryn	Random House
Baseball Birthday Party, The	J	RF	Prager, Annabelle	Random House
Bear Shadow	J	F	Asch, Frank	Simon & Schuster
Bear's Bargain	J	F	Asch, Frank	Scholastic
Beautiful Pig	J	F	Read Alongs	Rigby
Best Little Monkeys in the World, The	J	F	Standiford, Natalie	Random House
Best Nest	J	F	Eastman, P.D.	Random House
Better Than TV	J	RF	Miller, Sara Swan	Bantam Doubleday Dell
Big Green Caterpillar, The	J	RF	Literacy 2000	Rigby
Big Mama and Grandma Ghana	J	RF	Shelf Medearis, A.	Scholastic
Big Max	J	F	Platt, Kin	HarperTrophy
Bill	J	RF	Sunshine	Wright Group/McGraw Hill
Billy Magee's New Car	J	RF	Foundations	Wright Group/McGraw Hill
Bird's-Eye View	J	RF	PM Turquoise	Rigby
Birds' Nests	J	I	Wonder World	Wright Group/McGraw Hill
Blackboard Bear	J	F	Alexander, Martha	The Penguin Group
Boy Who Cried Wolf, The	J	TL	Littledale, Freya	Scholastic
Brave Little Tailor, The	J	TL	PM Tales and Plays Turquoise	Rigby
Bringing the Rain to Kapiti Plain	J	TL	Aardema, Verna	Scholastic
Bush Bunyip, The	J	F	Book Shop	Mondo
Buzby	J	F	Hoban, Julia	HarperTrophy
Cabin in the Hills, The	J	RF	PM Turquoise	Rigby
Camouflage	J	I	Sunshine	Wright Group/McGraw Hill
Camp Big Paw	J	RF	Cushman, Doug	HarperTrophy
Carrots Don't Talk!	J	F	Ready Readers	Pearson Learning
Cat Concert	J	F	Literacy 2000	Rigby
Cat in the Hat	J	F	Seuss, Dr.	Random House
Cats	J	I	PM Animal Facts: Orange	Rigby
Cells	J	I	Wonder World	Wright Group/McGraw Hill
Charlie Needs a Cloak	J	RF	dePaola, Tomie	Prentice-Hall
Chicken in the Middle of the Road	J	RF	Book Shop	Mondo
Children of Sierra Leone, The	J	I	Books For Young Learners	Richard C. Owen
Chocolate-Chip Muffins	J	RF	Sunshine	Wright Group/McGraw Hill
Christmas in the Big Woods	J	HF	Wilder, Laura Ingalls	Harper Collins
City Mouse-Country Mouse	J	TL	Aesop	Scholastic
Class Play, The	J	RF	Little Readers	Houghton Mifflin

Title	Level	Genre	Author/Series	Publisher/Distributor
Clocks and More Clocks	J	RF	Hutchins, Pat	Scholastic
Clouds	J	I	Early Connections	Benchmark Education
Color Wizard, The	J	F	Bank Street	Bantam Doubleday Dell
Coral	J	I	Marine Life For Yng. Readers	Dominie
Costume Party, The	J	RF	City Kids	Rigby
Could It Be?	J	RF	Bank Street	Bantam Doubleday Dell
Country Fair	J	HF	Wilder, Laura Ingalls	Harper Collins
Cubby's Gum	J	F	Ready Readers	Pearson Learning
Curious George Rides a Bike	J	F	Rey, Margaret	Scholastic
Dad's Surprise	J	RF	Foundations	Wright Group/McGraw Hill
Dan the Dunce	J	TL	Tales from Hans Andersen	Wright Group/McGraw Hill
Dance at Grandpa's	J	HF	Wilder, Laura Ingalls	Harper Collins
Danny and the Dinosaur	J	F	Hoff, Syd	Scholastic
Day I Lost My Bus Pass, The	J	RF	City Kids	Rigby
Deer in the Wood, The	J	HF	Wilder, Laura Ingalls	Harper Collins
Detective Dinosaur	J	F	Skofield, James	HarperTrophy
Difficult Day, The	J	RF	Read Alongs	Rigby
Ditching School	J	RF	City Kids	Rigby
Dogs	J	I	PM Animal Facts: Orange	Rigby
Dogs at Work	J	I	Little Readers	Houghton Mifflin
Dogstar	J	F	Literacy 2000	Rigby
Dolphins	J	I	Wonder World	Wright Group/McGraw Hill
Don't Be My Valentine: A Classroom Mystery	J	RF	Lexau, Joan M.	HarperTrophy
Don't Eat Too Much Turkey	J	RF	Cohen, Miriam	Bantam Doubleday Dell
Don't Worry	J	RF	Literacy 2000	Rigby
Donkey's Tale, The	J	TL	Bank Street	Bantam Doubleday Dell
Doorbell Rang, The	J	RF	Hutchins, Pat	Greenwillow
Dragon Who Had the Measles,The	J	F	Literacy 2000	Rigby
Dragon's Scales, The	J	F	Albee, Sarah	Random House
Drummer Hoff	J	TL	Emberly, Barbara	Prentice-Hall
Early Bird's Alarm Clock, The	J	F	Daniel, Claire	Steck-Vaughn
Egg To Chick	J	I	Selsam, Millicent E.	HarperTrophy
Eggs, Eggs, Eggs	J	I	Wonder World	Wright Group/McGraw Hill
Elaine	J	B	Stepping Stones	Nelson/Michaels
Elephant and the Bad Baby, The	J	F	Hayes, S.	Sundance
Elephant in the House, An	J	F	Read Alongs	Rigby
Elves and the Shoemaker, The	J	TL	PM Tales and Plays Turquoise	Rigby
Emperor's New Clothes, The	J	TL	Tales from Hans Andersen	Wright Group/McGraw Hill
Encyclopedia of Tiny Creatures	J	I	Discovery World	Rigby
Everybody Eats Bread	J	I	Literacy 2000	Rigby
Fair Day	J	RF	City Kids	Rigby
Families	J	I	Storyteller-Night Crickets	Wright Group/McGraw Hill
Farmer and His Two Lazy Sons, The	J	TL	Aesop's Fables	Dominie
Farmer Boy Birthday, A	J	HF	Wilder, Laura Ingalls	Harper Collins
Farmer Joe's Hot Day	J	F	Richards/Zimmerman	Scholastic
Fast and Funny	J	RF	Story Box	Wright Group/McGraw Hill
Fight on the Hill, The	J	F	Read Alongs	Rigby
Fire Cat, The	J	F	Averill, Esther	HarperTrophy
Fire Station, The	J	I	Pebble Books	Grolier, Capstone
First Grade Takes a Test	J	RF	Cohen, Miriam	Bantam Doubleday Dell
Floating and Sinking	J	I	Book Shop	Mondo
Flora, a Friend for the Animals	J	RF	Sunshine	Wright Group/McGraw Hill
Fox All Week	J	F	Marshall, Edward	Puffin Books
Fox and His Friends	J	F	Marshall, Edward	Puffin Books
Fox and the Crow, The	J	TL	Aesop's Fables	Dominie
Fox at School	J	F	Marshall, Edward	Puffin Books
Fox Be Nimble	J	F	Marshall, James	Puffin Books
Fox In Love	J	F	Marshall, Edward	Puffin Books
Fox on Stage	J	F	Marshall, James	Puffin Books
Fox on the Job	J	F	Marshall, James	Puffin Books

Title	Level	Genre	Author/Series	Publisher/Distributor
Fox on Wheels	J	F	Marshall, Edward	Puffin Books
Fox Outfoxed	J	F	Marshall, James	Puffin Books
Fraidy Cats	J	F	Krensky, Stephen	Scholastic
Frank The Fish Gets His Wish	J	F	Appleton-Smith, Laura	Flyleaf Publishing
Froggy Learns to Swim	J	F	London, Jonathan	Scholastic
From Rocks to Sand: The Story of a Beach	J	I	Wonder World	Wright Group/McGraw Hill
Funny Bones	J	F	Ahlberg, A & J	Viking
Gallo and Zorro	J	F	Literacy 2000	Rigby
Get-Up Machine, The	J	F	Sunshine	Wright Group/McGraw Hill
Ghosts!: Ghostly Tales from Folklore	J	TL	Schwartz, Alvin	HarperTrophy
Giant in the Forest, A	J	F	Reading Unlimited	Celebration Press
Gingerbread Man, The	J	TL	Traditional Tales & More	Rigby
Going Swimming	J	RF	City Kids	Rigby
Going to the Bank	J	I	Foundations	Wright Group/McGraw Hill
Going to the City	J	I	People, Spaces & Places	Rand McNally
Going to the Hairdresser	J	I	Foundations	Wright Group/McGraw Hill
Going to Town	J	HF	Wilder, Laura Ingalls	Harper Collins
Going West	J	HF	Wilder, Laura Ingalls	HarperCollins
Goldfish	J	I	PM Animal Facts: Orange	Rigby
Goldilocks and The Three Bears	J	TL	PM Tales and Plays Turquoise	Rigby
Grandma's Pictures of The Past	J	RF	Home Connection Collection	Rigby
Grandpa's Birthday	J	RF	Literacy 2000	Rigby
Granny and the Desperadoes	J	RF	Parish, Peggy	Simon & Schuster
Great Day for Up	J	F	Seuss, Dr.	Random House
Great Snake Escape, The	J	F	Coxe, Molly	HarperTrophy
Green Eggs and Ham	J	F	Seuss, Dr.	Random House
Guinea Pigs	J	I	PM Animal Facts: Orange	Rigby
Gus and Grandpa	J	RF	Mills, Claudia	Sunburst
Ha-Ha Party, The	J	RF	Sunshine	Wright Group/McGraw Hill
Hailstorm, The	J	RF	PM Turquoise	Rigby
Hair Party, The	J	RF	Literacy 2000	Rigby
Hand, Hand, Fingers, Thumb	J	F	Perkins, Al	Random House
Harry and the Lady Next Door	J	F	Zion, Gene	HarperTrophy
Having a Haircut	J	RF	City Kids	Rigby
He Bear, She Bear	J	F	Berenstain, Stan, & Jan	Random House
Hedgehog Bakes a Cake	J	F	Bank Street	Bantam Doubleday Dell
Henry and Mudge and Annie's Good Move	J	RF	Rylant, Cynthia	Aladdin
Henry and Mudge and the Bedtime Thumps	J	RF	Rylant, Cynthia	Aladdin
Henry and Mudge and the Best Day of All	J	RF	Rylant, Cynthia	Aladdin
Henry and Mudge and the Careful Cousin	J	RF	Rylant, Cynthia	Aladdin
Henry and Mudge and the Forever Sea	J	RF	Rylant, Cynthia	Aladdin
Henry and Mudge and the Happy Cat	J	RF	Rylant, Cynthia	Aladdin
Henry and Mudge and the Long Weekend	J	RF	Rylant, Cynthia	Aladdin
Henry and Mudge and the Sneaky Crackers	J	RF	Rylant, Cynthia	Aladdin
Henry and Mudge and the Snowman Plan	J	RF	Rylant, Cynthia	Aladdin
Henry and Mudge and the Starry Night	J	RF	Rylant, Cynthia	Aladdin
Henry and Mudge and the Wild Wind	J	RF	Rylant, Cynthia	Aladdin
Henry and Mudge Get the Cold Shivers	J	RF	Rylant, Cynthia	Aladdin
Henry and Mudge in Puddle Trouble	J	RF	Rylant, Cynthia	Aladdin
Henry and Mudge in the Family Trees	J	RF	Rylant, Cynthia	Aladdin
Henry and Mudge in the Green Time	J	RF	Rylant, Cynthia	Aladdin
Henry and Mudge in the Sparkle Days	J	RF	Rylant, Cynthia	Aladdin
Henry and Mudge Take the Big Test	J	RF	Rylant, Cynthia	Aladdin
Henry and Mudge: The First Book	J	RF	Rylant, Cynthia	Aladdin
Henry and Mudge Under the Yellow Moon	J	RF	Rylant, Cynthia	Aladdin
Herman the Helper	J	F	Kraus, Robert	Simon & Schuster
Hiding Places	J	RF	Storyteller-Night Crickets	Wright Group/McGraw Hill
Hippopotamus Ate the Teacher, A	J	F	Thaler, Mike	Avon
Hop on Pop	J	F	Seuss, Dr.	Random House

Title	Level	Genre	Author/Series	Publisher/Distributor
Horse in Harry's Room, The	J	F	Hoff, Syd	Harper Collins
House that Jack Built, The	J	TL	Peppe, Rodney	Delacorte
House That Jack's Friends Built, The	J	RF	Pair-It Books	Steck-Vaughn
House that Stood on Booker Hill, The	J	RF	Ready Readers	Pearson Learning
How Grandmother Spider Got the Sun	J	TL	Little Readers	Houghton Mifflin
How To Cook Scones	J	I	Book Shop	Mondo
How To Make Salsa	J	I	Book Shop	Mondo
How Turtle Raced Beaver	J	TL	Literacy 2000	Rigby
I Can Read with My Eyes Shut	J	F	Seuss, Dr.	Random House
I Love to Sneeze	J	F	Bank Street	Bantam Doubleday Dell
I Play Soccer	J	RF	City Kids	Rigby
I Saw You in the Bathtub	J	TL	Schwartz, Alvin	HarperTrophy
I Was So Mad	J	RF	Mayer, Mercer	Donovan
I Went to the Movies	J	RF	City Kids	Rigby
Imagine That	J	F	Story Box	Wright Group/McGraw Hill
In a Dark, Dark Room	J	TL	Schwartz, Alvin	HarperTrophy
In the Land of the Polar Bear	J	RF	Robinson, F.R.	Steck-Vaughn
Insects	J	I	MacLulich, Carolyn	Scholastic
Into Space	J	I	Momentum Literacy Program	Troll
Invisible Spy, The	J	F	Foundations	Wright Group/McGraw Hill
Jake and the Copycats	J	RF	Rocklin, Joanne	Bantam Doubleday Dell
Jamberry	J	F	Degen, Bruce	Harper & Row
Jillian Jiggs	J	RF	Gilman, Phoebe	Scholastic
Jimmy Lee Did It	J	RF	Cummings, Pat	Lothrop
Job for Giant Jim, A	J	RF	Sunshine	Wright Group/McGraw Hill
Johnny Lion's Book	J	F	Hurd, Edith Thacher	Harper Collins
Jonathan Buys a Present	J	RF	PM Story Books-Turquoise	Rigby
Just for Fun	J	F	Literacy 2000	Rigby
Just Hanging Around	J	I	Storyteller-Night Crickets	Wright Group/McGraw Hill
Just Like Me	J	F	Story Box	Wright Group/McGraw Hill
Just Us Women	J	RF	Caines, Jeannette	Scholastic
Keeping Score	J	I	Early Connections	Benchmark Education
Kenny and the Little Kickers	J	F	Mareollo, Claudio	Scholastic
Kick, Pass, and Run	J	RF	Kessler, Leonard	HarperTrophy
King Midas & the Golden Touch	J	TL	Traditional Tales	Dominie
Knit, Knit, Knit, Knit	J	F	Literacy 2000	Rigby
Lad Who Went to the North Wind, The	J	F	Book Shop	Mondo
Last One In Is a Rotten Egg	J	RF	Kessler, Leonard	HarperTrophy
Let's Be Enemies	J	RF	Sendak, Maurice	Harper & Row
Life in the City	J	I	Early Connections	Benchmark Education
Light	J	I	Momentum Literacy Program	Troll
Lion and the Mouse, The	J	TL	Little Books	Sadlier-Oxford
Lion and the Mouse, The	J	TL	Sunshine	Wright Group/McGraw Hill
Lion in the Night, The	J	F	Momentum Literacy Program	Troll
Little Adventure, A	J	RF	PM Story Books -Silver	Rigby
Little Bear	J	F	Minarik, E.H.	Harper Collins
Little Bear's Friend	J	F	Minarik, E.H.	HarperTrophy
Little Bear's Visit	J	F	Minarik, E.H.	HarperTrophy
Little Black, A Pony	J	RF	Farley, Walter	Random House
Little Blue and Little Yellow	J	F	Lionni, Leo	Scholastic
Little Dinosaur Escapes	J	F	PM Turquoise	Rigby
Little Fireman	J	RF	Brown, Margaret Wise	Harper Collins
Little Gorilla	J	F	Bornstein, Ruth	Clarion
Little House Birthday, A	J	HF	Wilder, Laura Ingalls	Harper Collins
Little Prairie House, A	J	HF	Wilder, Laura Ingalls	Harper Collins
Little Red Riding Hood	J	TL	PM Tales and Plays Turquoise	Rigby
Lizard's Grandmother	J	F	Sunshine	Wright Group/McGraw Hill
Lonely Dragon, The	J	F	Momentum Literacy Program	Troll
Look Inside	J	I	Storyteller Nonfiction	Wright Group/McGraw Hill
Look Out For Your Tail	J	F	Literacy 2000	Rigby

Title	Level	Genre	Author/Series	Publisher/Distributor
Looking For Patterns	J	I	Early Connections	Benchmark Education
Lost Tooth, The	J	I	New Way Orange	Steck-Vaughn
Magic Store, The	J	RF	Sunshine	Wright Group/McGraw Hill
Make a Bottle Orchestra	J	I	Sunshine	Wright Group/McGraw Hill
Make a Guitar	J	I	Sunshine	Wright Group/McGraw Hill
Make Masks for a Play	J	I	Sunshine	Wright Group/McGraw Hill
Making Friends	J	RF	Foundations	Wright Group/McGraw Hill
Marigold and Grandma On The Town	J	F	Calmenson, Stephanie	HarperTrophy
Matthew Likes to Read	J	RF	Pacific Literacy	Pacific Learning
Matthew's Tantrum	J	RF	Literacy 2000	Rigby
Max	J	RF	Isadora, Rachel	Macmillan
Meg and Mog	J	F	Nicoll, Helen	Viking
Messy Bessey's School Desk	J	RF	Rookie Readers	Children's Press
Mice	J	I	PM Animal Facts: Orange	Rigby
Mike Swan, Sink or Swim	J	RF	Heiligman, Deborah	Bantam Doubleday Dell
Milton the Early Riser	J	F	Kraus, Robert	Aladdin
Minnie and Moo Go to Paris	J	F	Cazet, Denys	DK Publishing, Inc.
Miss McKenzie Had a Farm	J	F	Pair-It Books	Steck-Vaughn
Missing Tooth, The	J	RF	Cole, Joanna	Random House
Mitchell Is Moving	J	F	Sharmat, Marjorie Weinman	Simon & Schuster
Mix, Make and Munch	J	I	Home Connection Collection	Rigby
Monster Manners	J	F	Cole, Joanna	Scholastic
Moon Boy	J	F	Bank Street	Bantam Doubleday Dell
Moon Stories	J	F	Ready Readers	Pearson Learning
Morning Star	J	F	Literacy 2000	Rigby
Morris and Boris at the Circus	J	F	Wiseman, B.	HarperTrophy
Morris Goes to School	J	F	Wiseman, B.	HarperTrophy
Mother Hippopotamus Gets Wet	J	F	Foundations	Wright Group/McGraw Hill
Mouse and the Elephant, The	J	TL	Little Readers	Houghton Mifflin
Mouse Soup	J	F	Lobel, Arnold	Harper Collins
Mouse Tales	J	F	Lobel, Arnold	Harper Collins
Mouse Who Wanted to Marry, The	J	F	Bank Street	Bantam Doubleday Dell
Mr. Bumbleticker Goes Shopping	J	RF	Foundations	Wright Group/McGraw Hill
Mr. Putter and Tabby Bake the Cake	J	RF	Rylant, Cynthia	Harcourt Brace
Mr. Putter and Tabby Fly the Plane	J	RF	Rylant, Cynthia	Harcourt Brace
Mr. Putter and Tabby Pick the Pears	J	RF	Rylant, Cynthia	Harcourt Brace
Mr. Putter and Tabby Pour the Tea	J	RF	Rylant, Cynthia	Harcourt Brace
Mr. Putter and Tabby Walk the Dog	J	RF	Rylant, Cynthia	Harcourt Brace
Mr. Putter & Tabby Row the Boat	J	RF	Rylant, Cynthia	Harcourt Brace
Mr. Putter & Tabby Take the Train	J	RF	Rylant, Cynthia	Harcourt Inc.
Mr. Putter & Tabby Toot the Horn	J	RF	Rylant, Cynthia	Harcourt Brace
Mrs. Barnett's Birthday	J	RF	Sunshine	Wright Group/McGraw Hill
My Brother, Ant	J	RF	Byars, Betsy	Viking
My Father	J	RF	Mayer, Laura	Scholastic
My Sloppy Tiger Goes to School	J	F	Sunshine	Wright Group/McGraw Hill
My Treasure Garden	J	RF	Book Bank	Wright Group/McGraw Hill
Mystery of the Missing Dog, The	J	F	Levy, Elizabeth	Scholastic
Nana's Kitchen	J	RF	Walton, Darwin McBeth	Steck-Vaughn
Nelson the Baby Elephant	J	F	PM Turquoise	Rigby
New Bike, The	J	RF	Sunshine	Wright Group/McGraw Hill
New School, The	J	RF	City Kids	Rigby
Newborn Animals	J	I	Momentum Literacy Program	Troll
Newt	J	F	Novak, Matt	HarperTrophy
Nightingale, The	J	TL	Tales from Hans Andersen	Wright Group/McGraw Hill
No Dinner for Sally	J	RF	Literacy 2000	Rigby
No More Monsters for Me!	J	F	Parish, Peggy	HarperTrophy
Norma Jean, Jumping Bean	J	RF	Cole, Joanna	Random House
Not Now! Said the Cow	J	F	Bank Street	Bantam Doubleday Dell
Number One	J	SF	Pacific Literacy	Pacific Learning
Ocean Animals	J	I	Early Connections	Benchmark Education

Title	Level	Genre	Author/Series	Publisher/Distributor
Old Devil Wind	J	F	Martin, Bill Jr.	Harcourt Brace
On the Open Plains	J	I	Momentum Literacy Program	Troll
Oscar Otter	J	F	Benchley, Nathaniel	HarperTrophy
Our Baby	J	RF	Foundations	Wright Group/McGraw Hill
Our Money	J	I	Early Connections	Benchmark Education
Our Old Friend, Bear	J	RF	PM Story Books -Silver	Rigby
Owl At Home	J	F	Lobel, Arnold	Harper Collins
Pack 109	J	RF	Thaler, Mike	Scholastic
Parachutes	J	RF	Storyteller-Moon Rising	Wright Group/McGraw Hill
Parakeet Girl, The	J	RF	Sadler, Marilyn	Random House
Parakeets	J	I	PM Animal Facts: Orange	Rigby
Party Games	J	RF	Foundations	Wright Group/McGraw Hill
Paru Has a Bath	J	RF	Pacific Literacy	Pacific Learning
Penny Changes the Day, A	J	RF	Fetty, Margaret	Steck-Vaughn
People at Work	J	I	Momentum Literacy Program	Troll
Pets	J	F	Pacific Literacy	Pacific Learning
Planets, The	J	I	Wonder World	Wright Group/McGraw Hill
Popcorn Shop, The	J	RF	Low, Alice	Scholastic
Poppleton	J	F	Rylant, Cynthia	Scholastic
Poppleton and Friends	J	F	Rylant, Cynthia	Blue Sky Press
Poppleton Everyday	J	F	Rylant, Cynthia	Scholastic
Poppleton Forever	J	F	Rylant, Cynthia	Scholastic
Poppleton Has Fun	J	F	Rylant, Cynthia	Scholastic
Poppleton In Fall	J	F	Rylant, Cynthia	Scholastic
Poppleton in Spring	J	F	Rylant, Cynthia	Scholastic
Porcupine's Pajama Party	J	F	Harshman, Terry Webb	HarperTrophy
Postman Pete	J	RF	Book Shop	Mondo
Pretty Good Magic	J	RF	Dubowski, C. E. & Dubowski, M.	Random House
Princess and the Castle, The	J	F	Leonhardt, Alice	Steck-Vaughn
Pumpkin House, The	J	F	Literacy 2000	Rigby
Queen's Parrot, The: A Play	J	TL	Literacy 2000	Rigby
R is for Radish!	J	F	Coxe, Molly	Random House
Rabbit's Birthday Kite	J	F	Bank Street	Bantam Doubleday Dell
Race to Green End, The	J	F	PM Turquoise	Rigby
Rain, Snow, and Hail	J	I	Discovery World	Rigby
Rescue!	J	RF	Sunshine	Wright Group/McGraw Hill
Rescuing Nelson	J	F	PM Turquoise	Rigby
Riding to Craggy Rock	J	RF	PM Turquoise	Rigby
Ripeka's Carving	J	RF	Literacy 2000	Rigby
Road Goes By, A	J	I	Momentum Literacy Program	Troll
Roller Skates!	J	RF	Calmenson, Stephanie	Scholastic
Roses for Renee	J	RF	Evangeline Nicholas Collection	Wright Group/McGraw Hill
Row, Row, Row Your Boat	J	RF	Bank Street	Bantam Doubleday Dell
Royal Baby-Sitters, The	J	RF	Sunshine	Wright Group/McGraw Hill
Rules	J	I	Early Connections	Benchmark Education
Rumpelstiltskin	J	TL	Book Shop	Mondo
Rumpelstiltskin	J	TL	Traditional Tales	Dominie
Sam and the Firefly	J	F	Eastman, P.D.	Random House
Sam the Minuteman	J	HF	Benchley, Nathaniel	HarperTrophy
Scary Spiders!	J	RF	Sunshine	Wright Group/McGraw Hill
School Vacation	J	RF	City Kids	Rigby
See You in Second Grade	J	RF	Cohen, Miriam	Bantam Doubleday Dell
See You Tomorrow, Charles	J	RF	Cohen, Miriam	Bantam Doubleday Dell
Seeds	J	I	Pebble Books	Grolier, Capstone
Selena Who Speaks in Silence	J	RF	Evangeline Nicholas Collection	Wright Group/McGraw Hill
Shaggy Sheep, The	J	RF	Kratky, Lada Josefa	Hampton-Brown
Show-and-Tell	J	RF	Foundations	Wright Group/McGraw Hill
Silly Willy and Silly Billy	J	F	Foundations	Wright Group/McGraw Hill
Skating at Rainbow Lake	J	RF	PM Story Books -Silver	Rigby
Skeleton On The Bus, The	J	F	Literacy 2000	Rigby

Title	Level	Genre	Author/Series	Publisher/Distributor
SkyFire	J	F	Asch, Frank	Scholastic
Small Wolf	J	HF	Benchley, Nathaniel	HarperTrophy
Snakes	J	I	Sunshine	Wright Group/McGraw Hill
Some Machines are Enormous	J	I	Book Shop	Mondo
Something Everyone Needs	J	RF	Ready Readers	Pearson Learning
Something Noise, The	J	RF	Windmill Books	Rigby
Somewhere	J	TL	Book Shop	Mondo
Sounds	J	I	Early Connections	Benchmark Education
Space Race	J	F	Sunshine	Wright Group/McGraw Hill
Spot's First Christmas	J	RF	Hill, Eric	Putnam
Starring First Grade	J	RF	Cohen, Miriam	Bantam Doubleday Dell
Statue of Liberty, The	J	I	Penner, Lucille	Random House
Stone Soup	J	TL	McGovern, Ann	Scholastic
Stone Soup	J	TL	PM Tales and Plays Turquoise	Rigby
Straight Line Wonder, The	J	F	Book Shop	Mondo
Street Musicians	J	RF	Sunshine	Wright Group/McGraw Hill
String Performers	J	I	Home Connection Collection	Rigby
Sugar Snow	J	HF	Wilder, Laura Ingalls	Harper Collins
Sulky Simon	J	RF	Windmill Books	Rigby
Summer Camp	J	RF	City Kids	Rigby
Summertime in the Big Woods	J	HF	Wilder, Laura Ingalls	Harper Collins
Sun, The	J	I	Wonder World	Wright Group/McGraw Hill
Sun, the Wind, & Tashira, The	J	TL	Folk Tales	Mondo
Sunburn	J	RF	City Kids	Rigby
Super Supermarket Plan, The	J	RF	Home Connection Collection	Rigby
Surprise Party, The	J	RF	Proger, Annabelle	Random House
Sword in the Stone, The	J	TL	Maccarone, Grace	Scholastic
Teeny Tiny Woman, The	J	TL	Seuling, Barbara	Scholastic
Ten Apples Up on Top	J	F	LaSieg, Theo	Random House
Tess and Paddy	J	RF	Sunshine	Wright Group/McGraw Hill
Then and Now	J	I	Discovery World	Rigby
There Is a Carrot in My Ear and Other Noodle Tales	J	F	Schwartz, Alvin	HarperTrophy
There's a Hippopotamus Under My Bed	J	RF	Thaler, Mike	Avon
There's an Alligator Under My Bed	J	RF	Mayer, Mercer	The Penguin Group
There's Something in My Attic	J	RF	Mayer, Mercer	The Penguin Group
Things With Wings	J	I	Storyteller Nonfiction	Wright Group/McGraw Hill
Tickle-Bugs, The	J	F	Literacy 2000	Rigby
Toby and the Accident	J	RF	PM Turquoise	Rigby
Today I Got Yelled At	J	RF	City Kids	Rigby
Tom Sawyer	J	B	Hall, Richard	Rigby
Tom the TV Cat	J	F	Heilbroner, Joan	Random House
Tongue Twister Prize, The	J	RF	Little Books	Sadlier-Oxford
Too Many Mice	J	F	Bank Street	Bantam Doubleday Dell
Too Many Rabbits	J	RF	Parish, Peggy	Bantam Doubleday Dell
Too Many Steps	J	RF	Foundations	Wright Group/McGraw Hill
Too Much Noise	J	TL	McGovern, Ann	Scholastic
Too Much Talk and Other Stories	J	RF	New Way: Literature	Steck-Vaughn
Too Much Trouble for Grandpa	J	RF	Sokoloff, Myka-Lynne	Sadlier-Oxford
Too Small Jill	J	RF	Little Books	Sadlier-Oxford
Trash Can Band, The	J	RF	Little Books	Sadlier-Oxford
Trees	J	I	Literacy 2000	Rigby
Tummy Ache	J	RF	Sunshine	Wright Group/McGraw Hill
Two Silly Trolls	J	F	Jewell, Nancy	HarperTrophy
Ugly Duckling, The	J	TL	PM Tales and Plays Turquoise	Rigby
Uncle Elephant	J	F	Lobel, Arnold	Harper Collins
Vagabond Crabs	J	I	Literacy 2000	Rigby
Waiting for the Rain	J	RF	Foundations	Wright Group/McGraw Hill
Wake Me in Spring	J	F	Preller, James	Scholastic
Water	J	I	Momentum Literacy Program	Troll
Waves: The Changing Surface of the Sea	J	I	Wonder World	Wright Group/McGraw Hill

Title	Level	Genre	Author/Series	Publisher/Distributor
We Use Numbers	J	I	Early Connections	Benchmark Education
Wet Day at School, A	J	RF	Sunshine	Wright Group/McGraw Hill
What Are My Chances?	J	I	Early Connections	Benchmark Education
What Do You Hear When Cows Sing?	J	F	Maestro, Marco & Giulio	HarperTrophy
What Is a Park?	J	I	People, Places & Spaces	Rand McNally
What Would You Do?	J	RF	Sunshine	Wright Group/McGraw Hill
When the King Rides By	J	F	Book Shop	Mondo
When the Volcano Erupted	J	F	PM Turquoise	Rigby
Where People Live	J	RF	Early Connections	Benchmark Education
Where the Wild Things Are	J	F	Sendak, Maurice	Harper & Row
Where's Tony?	J	RF	City Kids	Rigby
Who's a Pest?	J	F	Bonsall, Crosby	HarperTrophy
Why the Bear's Tail is Short	J	F	Sunshine	Wright Group/McGraw Hill
Wild, Wooly Child, The	J	F	Read Alongs	Rigby
Wind and the Sun and Other Stories, The	J	F	New Way Orange	Steck-Vaughn
Wind Blew, The	J	RF	Hutchins, Pat	Puffin Books
Wind Power	J	I	Pacific Literacy	Pacific Learning
Winter Days in the Big Woods	J	HF	Wilder, Laura Ingalls	Harper Collins
Winter on the Farm	J	HF	Wilder, Laura Ingalls	Harper Collins
Wizard and Wart at Sea	J	F	Smith, Janice Lee	HarperTrophy
Worst Show-and-Tell Ever, The	J	SF	Walsh, Rita	Troll
Wrong-Way Rabbit, The	J	F	Slater, Teddy	Scholastic
You Are Much Too Small	J	F	Bank Street	Bantam Doubleday Dell
You Can't Catch Me	J	F	Oppenheim, Joanne	Houghton Mifflin
Young Cam Jansen and the Ice Skate Mystery	J	RF	Adler, David A.	Puffin Books
Young Cam Jansen and the Lost Tooth	J	RF	Adler, David A.	Puffin Books
Young Cam Jansen and the Missing Cookie	J	RF	Adler, David A.	Puffin Books
Your Teeth	J	I	Pebble Books	Grolier, Capstone
Zoe at the Fancy Dress Ball	J	RF	Literacy 2000	Rigby
Alison's Puppy	K	RF	Bauer, Marion Dane	Hyperion
Alison's Wings	K	RF	Bauer, Marion Dane	Hyperion
All About Things People Do	K	I	Rice, Melanie & Chris	Scholastic
Alligator Tails and Crocodile Cakes	K	F	Moon, Nicola	Wright Group/McGraw Hill
Amalia and the Grasshopper	K	RF	Tello, J. & Krupinski, L.	Scholastic
And Grandpa Sat on Friday	K	RF	Marshall, Val & Tester, Bronwyn	SRA/McGraw-Hill
Animal Band, The	K	TL	PM Tales and Plays- Purple	Rigby
Animal Homes	K	I	Pair-It Books	Steck-Vaughn
Animals and Their Teeth	K	I	Sunshine	Wright Group/McGraw Hill
Animals' Eyes and Ears	K	I	Early Connections	Benchmark Education
Animals on the Move	K	I	Planet Earth	Rigby
Are We Hurting the Earth?	K	I	Early Connections	Benchmark Education
Arguments	K	F	Read Alongs	Rigby
Around-the-World Lunch, The	K	RF	Canetti, Yanitzia	Steck-Vaughn
Arthur's Back to School Day	K	F	Hoban, Lillian	HarperTrophy
Arthur's Camp-Out	K	F	Hoban, Lillian	HarperTrophy
Arthur's Christmas Cookies	K	F	Hoban, Lillian	HarperTrophy
Arthur's Funny Money	K	F	Hoban, Lillian	HarperTrophy
Arthur's Great Big Valentine	K	F	Hoban, Lillian	HarperTrophy
Arthur's Honey Bear	K	F	Hoban, Lillian	Harper Collins
Arthur's Loose Tooth	K	F	Hoban, Lillian	Harper Collins
Arthur's Pen Pal	K	F	Hoban, Lillian	Harper Collins
Arthur's Prize Reader	K	F	Hoban, Lillian	HarperTrophy
Ashes for Gold	K	TL	Folk Tales	Mondo
At the Water Hole	K	I	Foundations	Wright Group/McGraw Hill
Baba Yaga	K	TL	Literacy 2000	Rigby
Baby Sister for Frances, A	K	F	Hoban, Lillian	Scholastic
Bargain For Frances, A	K	F	Hoban, Russell	HarperTrophy
Barn Party	K	F	O'Brien, Claire	Wright Group/McGraw Hill
Barney's Lovely Lunch	K	RF	Windmill Books	Rigby

Title	Level	Genre	Author/Series	Publisher/Distributor
Barrel of Gold, A	K	F	Story Box	Wright Group/McGraw Hill
Bat Bones and Spider Stew	K	RF	Poploff, Michelle	Bantam Doubleday Dell
Be Ready at Eight	K	F	Parish, Peggy	Simon & Schuster
Beanbag	K	RF	Literacy 2000	Rigby
Bear at the Beach	K	F	Carmichael, Clay	North-South Books
Bear For Miguel, A	K	RF	Alphin, Elaine Marie	HarperTrophy
Bear Goes to Town	K	F	Browne, Anthony	Doubleday
Beauty and the Beast	K	TL	PM Tales and Plays- Gold	Rigby
Beauty and the Beast	K	TL	Sunshine	Wright Group/McGraw Hill
Beavers Beware!	K	I	Bank Street	Bantam Doubleday Dell
Bedtime at Aunt Carmen's	K	RF	Ready Readers	Pearson Learning
Bedtime for Frances	K	F	Hoban, Russell	Scholastic
Bedtime Story, A	K	RF	Book Shop	Mondo
Best Birthday Present, The	K	RF	Literacy 2000	Rigby
Best Friends for Frances	K	F	Hoban, Russell	HarperTrophy
Best Part, The	K	RF	PM Story Books -Silver	Rigby
Best Teacher in the World, The	K	RF	Chardiet, Bernice	Scholastic
Best Way to Play, The	K	I	Cosby, Bill	Scholastic
Big Balloon Race, The	K	RF	Coerr, Eleanor	HarperTrophy
Big Fish Little Fish	K	TL	Folk Tales	Wright Group/McGraw Hill
Big Prize, The	K	F	Adventures in Reading	Dominie
Big Sneeze, The	K	F	Brown, Ruth	Lothrop
Bird's-Eye View, A	K	I	People, Spaces & Places	Rand McNally
Birthday Bike for Brimhall, A	K	RF	Delton, Judy	Bantam Doubleday Dell
Birthday for Frances, A	K	F	Hoban, Russell	Scholastic
Blind Man and the Elephant, The	K	TL	Backstein, Karen	Scholastic
Body Numbers	K	I	Discovery World	Rigby
Bony-Legs	K	F	Cole, Joanna	Scholastic
Boy and His Donkey, A	K	F	Literacy 2000	Rigby
Boy Named Boomer, A	K	B	Esiason, Boomer	Scholastic
Boy Who Cried Wolf, The	K	TL	Aesop's Fables	Dominie
Boy Who Cried Wolf, The	K	TL	PM Tales and Plays- Purple	Rigby
Bread and Jam for Frances	K	F	Hoban, Russell	Scholastic
Bremen-Town Musicians, The	K	TL	Gross, Ruth	Scholastic
Brown Bears	K	I	PM Animal Facts: Turquoise	Rigby
Bubbling Crocodile	K	F	Pacific Literacy	Pacific Learning
Buffalo Bill and the Pony Express	K	B	Coerr, Eleanor	HarperTrophy
Bull in a China Shop, A	K	F	Literacy 2000	Rigby
Bumps in the Night	K	F	Allard, Harry	Bantam Doubleday Dell
Bunny Runs Away	K	F	Chardiet, B. & Maccarone, G.	Scholastic
Busy Guy, A	K	RF	Rookie Readers	Children's Press
Butterfly's Life, A	K	I	Burke, Melissa Blackwell	Steck-Vaughn
Button Soup	K	RF	Bank Street	Bantam Doubleday Dell
Cabbage Princess, The	K	TL	Literacy 2000	Rigby
Camel Called Bump-Along, A	K	F	Evangeline Nicholas Collection	Wright Group/McGraw Hill
Camp Knock Knock	K	RF	Duffey, Betsy	Bantam Doubleday Dell
Camp Knock Knock Mystery, The	K	RF	Duffey, Betsy	Bantam Doubleday Dell
Camping with Claudine	K	RF	Literacy 2000	Rigby
Caps for Sale	K	F	Slobodkina, Esphyr	Harper & Row
Captain Bumble	K	F	Story Box	Wright Group/McGraw Hill
Case of the Cat's Meow, The	K	RF	Bonsall, Crosby	HarperTrophy
Case of the Double Cross, The	K	RF	Bonsall, Crosby	HarperTrophy
Case of the Dumb Bells, The	K	RF	Bonsall, Crosby	HarperTrophy
Case of the Scaredy Cats, The	K	RF	Bonsall, Crosby	HarperTrophy
Case of the Two Masked Robbers, The	K	F	Hoban, Lillian	HarperTrophy
Cats' Burglar, The	K	F	Parish, Peggy	Hearst
Cats of the Night	K	RF	Book Bank	Wright Group/McGraw Hill
Change for Zoe, A	K	RF	Home Connection Collection	Rigby
Cheerful King, The	K	F	Little Books	Sadlier-Oxford

Title	Level	Genre	Author/Series	Publisher/Distributor
Chicago Winds	K	I	Evangeline Nicholas Collection	Wright Group/McGraw Hill
Children as Young Scientists	K	I	Early Connections	Benchmark Education
Chipmunk at Hollow Tree Lane	K	F	Sherrow, Victoria	Scholastic
Chug the Tractor	K	F	PM Story Books	Rigby
Cinderella	K	TL	Once Upon a Time	Wright Group/McGraw Hill
Cinderella	K	TL	PM Tales and Plays- Gold	Rigby
Clara and the Bookwagon	K	RF	Levinson, Nancy Smiler	HarperTrophy
Clever Mr. Brown	K	F	Story Box	Wright Group/McGraw Hill
Clifford, the Big Red Dog	K	F	Bridwell, Norman	Scholastic
Clifford, the Small Red Puppy	K	F	Bridwell, Norman	Scholastic
Clouds, Rain and Fog	K	I	Sunshine	Wright Group/McGraw Hill
Clubhouse, The	K	RF	PM Gold	Rigby
Commander Toad and the Big Black Hole	K	F	Yolen, Jane	Putnam & Grosset
Commander Toad and the Dis-Asteroid	K	F	Yolen, Jane	Putnam & Grosset
Commander Toad and the Intergalactic Spy	K	F	Yolen, Jane	Putnam & Grosset
Commander Toad and the Planet of the Grapes	K	F	Yolen, Jane	Putnam & Grosset
Commander Toad and the Space Pirates	K	F	Yolen, Jane	Putnam & Grosset
Commander Toad And The Voyage Home	K	F	Yolen, Jane	Putnam & Grosset
Computers Are for Everyone	K	I	Sunshine	Wright Group/McGraw Hill
Concert Night	K	RF	Literacy 2000	Rigby
Cooped Up	K	RF	Pacific Literacy	Pacific Learning
Corduroy	K	F	Freeman, Don	Scholastic
Counting Insects	K	I	Early Connections	Benchmark Education
Crosby Crocodile's Disguise	K	F	LIteracy 2000	Rigby
Cunning Creatures	K	I	Home Connection Collection	Rigby
Dabble Duck	K	RF	Ellis, Anne Leo	HarperTrophy
Daddy Saved the Day	K	RF	Medearis, Angela Shelf	Rigby
Daniel's Dog	K	RF	Bogart, Jo Allen	Scholastic
Daniel's Duck	K	RF	Bulla, Clyde Robert	HarperTrophy
Darcy and Gran Don't Like Babies	K	RF	Cutler, Jane	Scholastic
Day in Town, A	K	RF	Story Box	Wright Group/McGraw Hill
Day Jimmy's Boa Ate the Wash, The	K	F	Noble, Trinka, H.	Scholastic
Days With Frog and Toad	K	F	Lobel, Arnold	HarperTrophy
Dede and the Dinosaur	K	F	Cumpiano, Ina	Hampton-Brown
Desert Machine, The	K	I	Sunshine	Wright Group/McGraw Hill
Dinosaur Days	K	RF	Ready Readers	Pearson Learning
Dinosaur on the Motorway	K	F	Wesley and the Dinosaurs	Wright Group/McGraw Hill
Dinosaur Time	K	I	Parish, Peggy	HarperTrophy
Dinosaurs	K	I	Book Shop	Mondo
Dipplidocus in the Garden, A	K	F	Wesley and the Dinosaurs	Wright Group/McGraw Hill
Do You Like Cats?	K	I	Bank Street	Bantam Doubleday Dell
Doctor's Office, The	K	I	Pebble Books	Grolier, Capstone
Dolphin on the Wall, The	K	RF	PM Story Books -Silver	Rigby
Donald's Garden	K	RF	Reading Unlimited	Celebration Press
Dragon Feet	K	F	Books For Young Learners	Pacific Learning
Dragon's Birthday, The	K	F	Literacy 2000	Rigby
Edgar Badger's Balloon Day	K	F	Kulling, Monica	Mondo
Edgar Badger's Butterfly Day	K	F	Kulling, Monica	Mondo
Edgar Badger's Fishing Day	K	F	Kulling, Monica	Mondo
Edgar Badger's Fix-it Day	K	F	Kulling, Monica	Mondo
Edwin and Emily	K	RF	Williams, Suzanne	Hyperion
Effie	K	F	Allinson, Beverly	Scholastic
Eggs, Larvae and Flies	K	I	Sunshine	Wright Group/McGraw Hill
Elephants	K	I	PM Animal Facts: Turquoise	Rigby
Elizabite: Adventures of a Carnivorous Plant	K	F	Rey, H.A.	Houghton Mifflin
Elves and the Shoemaker,The	K	TL	New Way Orange	Steck-Vaughn
Emergency Vehicles	K	I	PM Plus	Rigby
Fables by Aesop	K	TL	Reading Unlimited	Celebration Press
Fabulous Animal Families	K	I	Home Connection Collection	Rigby
Fabulous Freckles	K	RF	Literacy 2000	Rigby

Title	Level	Genre	Author/Series	Publisher/Distributor
Fair Swap, A	K	TL	PM Story Books -Silver	Rigby
Families Are Different	K	RF	Pellegrini, Nina	Scholastic
Farmer in the Soup, The	K	TL	Littledale, Freya	Scholastic
Fight in the Schoolyard, The	K	RF	City Kids	Rigby
First Flight	K	B	Shea, George	HarperTrophy
Fish for Sale	K	RF	SupaDoopers	Sundance
Five Funny Frights	K	RF	Bauer, Judith	Scholastic
Flour	K	I	Wonder World	Wright Group/McGraw Hill
Flows & Quakes and Spinning Winds	K	I	Home Connection Collection	Rigby
Flying Fingers	K	RF	Literacy 2000	Rigby
Follow That Fish	K	F	Bank Street	Bantam Doubleday Dell
Food Journey, The	K	I	Home Connection Collection	Rigby
Forty-Three Cats	K	RF	Sunshine	Wright Group/McGraw Hill
Four on the Shore	K	F	Marshall, Edward	Puffin Books
Fox and The Crow, The	K	TL	Ready Readers	Pearson Learning
Franklin Goes To School	K	F	Bourgeois, P. & Clark, B.	Scholastic
Franklin Plays the Game	K	F	Bourgeois, P. & Clark, B.	Scholastic
Freddy's Train Ride	K	RF	Pair-It Books	Steck-Vaughn
Friends are Forever	K	F	Literacy 2000	Rigby
Frog and Toad All Year	K	F	Little Readers	Houghton Mifflin
Frog and Toad Are Friends	K	F	Lobel, Arnold	Harper & Row
Frog and Toad Together	K	F	Lobel, Arnold	Harper Collins
Frog Prince, The	K	TL	Tarcov, Edith H.	Scholastic
Frog Princess, The	K	TL	Literacy 2000	Rigby
Frogs	K	I	Wonder World	Wright Group/McGraw Hill
Frown, The	K	RF	Read Alongs	Rigby
Gaston the Giant	K	F	New Way Orange	Steck-Vaughn
George the Drummer Boy	K	HF	Benchley, Nathaniel	HarperTrophy
Getting Cold! Getting Hot!	K	RF	Sunshine	Wright Group/McGraw Hill
Getting To Know Sharks	K	I	Little Books	Sadlier-Oxford
Giant Jam Sandwich, The	K	F	Vernon Lord, John	Houghton Mifflin
Gift to Share, A	K	RF	Pair-It Books	Steck-Vaughn
Gifts to Make	K	I	Pair-It Books	Steck-Vaughn
Gluepots	K	RF	Book Bank	Wright Group/McGraw Hill
Go and Hush the Baby	K	RF	Byars, Betsy	Viking
Go Annie, Go!	K	RF	Pacific Literacy	Pacific Learning
Go-cart Day	K	RF	City Kids	Rigby
Going Places	K	I	Early Connections	Benchmark Education
Goldilocks and the Three Bears	K	TL	New Way: Literature	Steck-Vaughn
Goldilocks and the Three Bears	K	TL	Once Upon a Time	Wright Group/McGraw Hill
Golly Sisters Go West, The	K	RF	Byars, Betsy	HarperTrophy
Golly Sisters Ride Again, The	K	RF	Byars, Betsy	HarperTrophy
Good Morning Mrs. Martin	K	F	Book Bank	Wright Group/McGraw Hill
Grandad's Dinosaur	K	F	Girling, Brough	Wright Group/McGraw Hill
Grandad's Mask	K	RF	PM Turquoise	Rigby
Grandma Mix-Up, The	K	RF	McCully, Emily Arnold	HarperTrophy
Grandma's Heart	K	I	Wonder World	Wright Group/McGraw Hill
Grandmas At Bat	K	RF	McCully, Emily Arnold	HarperTrophy
Grandmas at the Lake	K	RF	McCully, Emily Arnold	HarperTrophy
Grandpa at the Beach	K	RF	Lewis, Rob	Mondo
Grandpa Comes To Stay	K	RF	Lewis, Rob	Mondo
Grasshopper and the Ants	K	TL	Sunshine	Wright Group/McGraw Hill
Grasshopper on the Road	K	F	Lobel, Arnold	HarperTrophy
Great Grumbler and the Wonder Tree, The	K	F	Mahy, Margaret	Pacific Learning Publishers
Greg's Microscope	K	I	Selsam, Millicent E.	HarperTrophy
Guide Dog, The	K	I	Foundations	Wright Group/McGraw Hill
Half for You, Half for Me	K	TL	Literacy 2000	Rigby
Hansel and Gretel	K	TL	Enrichment	Wright Group/McGraw Hill
Happy Birthday, Dear Duck	K	F	Bunting, Eve	Clarion
Happy Valentine's Day, Miss Hildy!	K	RF	Grambling, Lois	Random House

Title	Level	Genre	Author/Series	Publisher/Distributor
Hare and the Tortoise, The	K	TL	Literacy 2000	Rigby
Hare and the Tortoise, The	K	TL	PM Tales and Plays- Purple	Rigby
Harold and the Purple Crayon	K	F	Johnson, Crockett	Harper & Row
Harry Hates Shopping!	K	F	Armitage, Ronda and David	Scholastic
Hat Came Back, The	K	RF	Literacy 2000	Rigby
Have You Seen a Javelina?	K	F	Literacy 2000	Rigby
Have You Seen Birds?	K	I	Oppenheim, J. & Reid, B.	Scholastic
He Who Listens	K	RF	Literacy 2000	Rigby
Heather's Book	K	RF	Ready Readers	Pearson Learning
Here Comes the Strike Out	K	RF	Kessler, Leonard	Harper Trophy
Hippos	K	I	PM Animal Facts: Turquoise	Rigby
Home for Diggory, A	K	RF	Pacific Literacy	Pacific Learning
Home in the Sky	K	RF	Baker, Jeannie	Scholastic
Hooray for the Golly Sisters!	K	RF	Byars, Betsy	HarperTrophy
Hot and Cold Weather	K	I	Sunshine	Wright Group/McGraw Hill
How Does It Breathe?	K	I	Home Connection Collection	Rigby
How Fire Came to Earth	K	TL	Literacy 2000	Rigby
How Goods Are Moved	K	I	People, Spaces & Places	Rand McNally
How Much Does This Hold?	K	RF	Coulton, Mia	Kaeden Books
How the Tortoise Got His Shell and Other Stories	K	TL	New Way: Literature	Steck-Vaughn
Hugo Hogget: Story Based on an Ecuadoran Legend	K	TL	Cumpiano, Ina	Hampton-Brown
I Am a Gypsy Pot	K	F	Evangeline Nicholas Collection	Wright Group/McGraw Hill
I Dream	K	RF	Sunshine	Wright Group/McGraw Hill
I Get the Creeps	K	RF	Reading Corners	Dominie
I Went to the Dentist	K	RF	City Kids	Rigby
Ibis: A True Whale Story	K	I	Himmelman, John	Scholastic
If You Give A Moose A Muffin	K	F	Numeroff, Laura Joffe	Harper Collins
If You Give A Mouse A Cookie	K	F	Numeroff, Laura Joffe	Harper Collins
In a Faraway Forest	K	F	Kratky, Lada Josefa	Hampton-Brown
Insects All Around	K	I	Early Connections	Benchmark Education
Is it a Fish?	K	I	Sunshine	Wright Group/McGraw Hill
It's Halloween	K	RF	Prelutsky, Jack	Scholastic
Jack and the Beanstalk	K	TL	Weisner, David	Scholastic
Jack and the Magic Harp	K	TL	PM Tales and Plays- Gold	Rigby
Jamaica and Brianna	K	RF	Little Readers	Houghton Mifflin
Jamaica's Find	K	RF	Havill, Juanita	Scholastic
Jim's Dog Muffins	K	RF	Cohen, Miriam	Bantam Doubleday Dell
JJ Rabbit and the Monster	K	F	Moon, Nicola	Wright Group/McGraw Hill
Joe and Betsy the Dinosaur	K	F	Hoban, Lillian	HarperTrophy
Johnny Appleseed	K	TL	Moore, Eva	Scholastic
Jordan and the Northside Reps	K	RF	PM Story Books -Silver	Rigby
Jordan's Lucky Day	K	RF	PM Story Books-Turquoise	Rigby
Julie's Mornings	K	F	Ready Readers	Pearson Learning
Kangaroos	K	I	PM Animal Facts: Turquoise	Rigby
Keep the Lights Burning Abbie	K	HF	Roop, Peter & Connie	Scholastic
Keeping Warm! Keeping Cool!	K	I	Sunshine	Wright Group/McGraw Hill
Kerry	K	RF	PM Story Books -Silver	Rigby
Kerry's Double	K	RF	PM Story Books -Silver	Rigby
King Midas and the Golden Touch	K	TL	PM Gold	Rigby
King, the Mice and the Cheese	K	F	Gurney, Nancy	Random House
Knock! Knock!	K	RF	Carter, Jackie	Scholastic
Know-Nothing Birthday, A	K	RF	Spirn, Michele Sobel	HarperTrophy
Know-Nothings, The	K	RF	Spirn, Michele Sobel	HarperTrophy
Kwanzaa	K	I	Visions	Wright Group/McGraw Hill
Last Puppy, The	K	F	Asch, Frank	Simon & Schuster
Laura Ingalls Wilder	K	B	Biography	Benchmark Education
Leaves	K	I	Pebble Books	Grolier, Capstone
Legend of the Hummingbird, The	K	TL	Folk Tales	Mondo
Legend of the Red Bird, The	K	TL	Sunshine	Wright Group/McGraw Hill
Lend a Hand	K	F	Kratky, Lada	Hampton-Brown

Title	Level	Genre	Author/Series	Publisher/Distributor
Lion and the Mouse, The	K	TL	Pair-It Books	Steck-Vaughn
Lionel and His Friends	K	RF	Krensky, Stephen	Puffin Books
Lionel and Louise	K	RF	Krensky, Stephen	Puffin Books
Lionel at Large	K	RF	Krensky, Stephen	Puffin Books
Lionel In The Fall	K	RF	Krensky, Stephen	Puffin Books
Lionel In The Spring	K	RF	Krensky, Stephen	Puffin Books
Lionel In The Summer	K	RF	Krensky, Stephen	Puffin Books
Lionel In The Winter	K	RF	Krensky, Stephen	Puffin Books
Lions and Tigers	K	I	PM Animal Facts: Turquoise	Rigby
Little Brown Jay, The: A Tale from India	K	TL	Claire, Elizabeth	Mondo
Little Chief	K	F	Hoff, Syd	Harper Collins
Little Knight, The	K	F	Reading Unlimited	Celebration Press
Little Leaf's Journey and the Lost Tooth, The	K	F	New Way Ornage	Steck-Vaughn
Little Polar Bear and the Brave Little Hare	K	F	de Beer, Hans	North-South Books
Little Red Riding Hood	K	TL	Enrichment	Wright Group/McGraw Hill
Little Runner of the Longhouse	K	HF	Baker, Betty	HarperTrophy
Little Soup's Birthday	K	RF	Peck, Robert Newton	Bantam Doubleday Dell
Little Spider, The	K	F	Literacy 2000	Rigby
Little Walrus Rising	K	F	Young, Carol	Scholastic
Little Witch Goes to School	K	F	Hautzig, Deborah	Random House
Little Witch's Big Night	K	F	Hautzig, Deborah	Random House
Living in the Sky	K	RF	Sunshine	Wright Group/McGraw Hill
Lonely Giant, The	K	F	Literacy 2000	Rigby
Looking for Shapes	K	I	Early Connections	Benchmark Education
Lost in the Forest	K	RF	Robinson, Fay	Wright Group/McGraw Hill
Lulu Goes to Witch School	K	F	O'Connor, Jane	HarperTrophy
Lunch at the Joy House Café	K	RF	Blackaby, Susan	Hampton-Brown
M & M and The Bad News Babies	K	RF	Ross, Pat	The Penguin Group
M & M and the Big Bag	K	RF	Ross, Pat	The Penguin Group
M & M and the Halloween Monster	K	RF	Ross, Pat	The Penguin Group.
M & M and the Haunted House Game	K	RF	Ross, Pat	The Penguin Group
M & M and the Mummy Mess	K	RF	Ross, Pat	The Penguin Group
M & M and the Santa Secrets	K	RF	Ross, Pat	The Penguin Group
M & M and the Super Child Afternoon	K	RF	Ross, Pat	The Penguin Group
Madeline	K	F	Bemelmans, Ludwig	Scholastic
Madeline's Rescue	K	F	Bemelmans, Ludwig	Scholastic
Magic Box, The	K	F	Brenner, Barbara	Bantam Doubleday Dell
Make Prints and Patterns	K	I	Sunshine	Wright Group/McGraw Hill
Manatee Winter	K	RF	Zoehfeld, Kathleen Weidnetz	Scholastic
Manly Ferry Pigeon, The	K	RF	Sunshine	Wright Group/McGraw Hill
Market Day for Mrs. Wordy	K	RF	Sunshine	Wright Group/McGraw Hill
Martin and the Teacher's Pets	K	RF	Chardiet, B. & Maccarone, G.	Scholastic
Martin and the Tooth Fairy	K	RF	Chardiet, B. & Maccarone, G.	Scholastic
Me Too	K	RF	Mayer, Mercer	Donovan
Meanest Thing to Say, The	K	RF	Cosby, Bill	Scholastic
Measure Up!	K	I	Early Connections	Benchmark Education
Meat Eaters, Plant Eaters	K	I	Planet Earth	Rigby
Meet M & M	K	RF	Ross, Pat	The Penguin Group
Meet the Octopus	K	I	Book Shop	Mondo
Memorial Day	K	I	Frost, Helen	Capstone Press
Messy Bessey's Closet	K	RF	Rookie Readers	Children's Press
Mile High, A	K	F	Book Bank	Wright Group/McGraw Hill
Misha Disappears	K	RF	Literacy 2000	Rigby
Miss Mouse Gets Married	K	TL	Folk Tales	Wright Group/McGraw Hill
Missing Pet, The	K	RF	Pair-It Books	Steck-Vaughn
Mollie Whuppie	K	TL	New Way Orange	Steck-Vaughn
Molly the Brave and Me	K	RF	O'Connor, Jane	Random House
Mom's Getting Married	K	RF	Sunshine	Wright Group/McGraw Hill
Money Riddles That Count	K	I	Fetty, Margaret	Steck-Vaughn
Monkeys and Apes	K	I	PM Animal Facts: Turquoise	Rigby

Title	Level	Genre	Author/Series	Publisher/Distributor
Monster from the Sea, The	K	TL	Bank Street	Bantam Doubleday Dell
Monster Movie	K	F	Cole, Joanna	Scholastic
Monster of Mirror Mountain, The	K	F	Literacy 2000	Rigby
Monster Under The Bed, The	K	F	Ready Readers	Pearson Learning
Mother Sea Turtle	K	I	Foundations	Wright Group/McGraw Hill
Mother's Helpers	K	RF	Ready Readers	Pearson Learning
Mrs. Huggins and Her Hen Hannah	K	F	Dabcovich, Lydia	Dutton
Mrs. Sheep's Garden	K	F	Kratky, Lada	Hampton-Brown
My New Mom	K	RF	Sunshine	Wright Group/McGraw Hill
My Scrapbook	K	I	Storyteller Nonfiction	Wright Group/McGraw Hill
My Sister's Getting Married	K	RF	Foundations	Wright Group/McGraw Hill
My Two Families	K	RF	PM Story Books -Silver	Rigby
Nate the Great	K	RF	Sharmat, Marjorie Weinman	Bantam Doubleday Dell
Nate the Great and Me	K	RF	Sharmat, Marjorie Weinman	Random House
Nate the Great and the Boring Beach Bag	K	RF	Sharmat, Marjorie Weinman	Bantam Doubleday Dell
Nate the Great and the Crunchy Christmas	K	RF	Sharmat, Marjorie Weinman	Bantam Doubleday Dell
Nate the Great and the Fishy Prize	K	RF	Sharmat, Marjorie Weinman	Bantam Doubleday Dell
Nate the Great and the Halloween Hunt	K	RF	Sharmat, Marjorie Weinman	Bantam Doubleday Dell
Nate the Great and the Lost List	K	RF	Sharmat, Marjorie Weinman	Bantam Doubleday Dell
Nate the Great and the Missing Key	K	RF	Sharmat, Marjorie Weinman	Bantam Doubleday Dell
Nate the Great and the Mushy Valentine	K	RF	Sharmat, Marjorie Weinman	Bantam Doubleday Dell
Nate the Great and the Musical Note	K	RF	Sharmat, Marjorie Weinman	Bantam Doubleday Dell
Nate the Great and the Phony Clue	K	RF	Sharmat, Marjorie Weinman	Bantam Doubleday Dell
Nate the Great and the Pillowcase	K	RF	Sharmat, Marjorie Weinman	Bantam Doubleday Dell
Nate the Great and the Snowy Trail	K	RF	Sharmat, Marjorie Weinman	Bantam Doubleday Dell
Nate the Great and the Sticky Case	K	RF	Sharmat, Marjorie Weinman	Bantam Doubleday Dell
Nate the Great and the Stolen Base	K	RF	Sharmat, Marjorie Weinman	Bantam Doubleday Dell
Nate the Great and the Tardy Tortoise	K	RF	Sharmat, Marjorie Weinman	Bantam Doubleday Dell
Nate the Great Goes Down in the Dumps	K	RF	Sharmat, Marjorie Weinman	Bantam Doubleday Dell
Nate the Great Goes Undercover	K	RF	Sharmat, Marjorie Weinman	Bantam Doubleday Dell
Nate the Great Saves the King of Sweden	K	RF	Sharmat, Marjorie Weinman	Bantam Doubleday Dell
Nate the Great Stalks Stupidweed	K	RF	Sharmat, Marjorie Weinman	Bantam Doubleday Dell
Nathan and Nicholas Alexander	K	F	Delacre, Lulu	Scholastic
Nelson is Kidnapped	K	RF	PM Story Books -Silver	Rigby
Nesting Place, The	K	HF	PM Turquoise	Rigby
Next Time I Will	K	RF	Bank Street	Bantam Doubleday Dell
Nice New Neighbors	K	RF	Brandenberg, Franz	Scholastic
Nicketty-Nacketty Noo-Noo-Noo	K	F	Cowley, Joy	Mondo
No Fighting, No Biting!	K	RF	Minarik, Else Holmelund	HarperTrophy
No Tooth, No Quarter!	K	F	Buller, Jon	Random House
Nothing to Be Scared About	K	RF	Sunshine	Wright Group/McGraw Hill
Now Listen, Stanley	K	F	Literacy 2000	Rigby
Oh, Columbus!	K	F	Literacy 2000	Rigby
Old Woman and Her Pig, The: An Old English Tale	K	TL	Litzinger, Rosanne	Harcourt Brace
On Friday the Giant	K	F	The Giant	Wright Group/McGraw Hill
On Monday the Giant	K	F	The Giant	Wright Group/McGraw Hill
On Sunday the Giant	K	F	The Giant	Wright Group/McGraw Hill
On Thursday the Giant	K	F	The Giant	Wright Group/McGraw Hill
On Tuesday the Giant	K	F	The Giant	Wright Group/McGraw Hill
On Wednesday the Giant	K	F	The Giant	Wright Group/McGraw Hill
One Drop of Water and a Million More	K	I	Book Bank	Wright Group/McGraw Hill
Oogly Gum Chasing Game, The	K	F	Literacy 2000	Rigby
Orca Song	K	RF	Armour	Scholastic
Our Busy Bodies	K	I	Home Connection Collection	Rigby
Our New Principal	K	RF	City Kids	Rigby
Outside Dog, The	K	RF	Pomerantz, Charlotte	HarperTrophy
Ox-Cart Man	K	HF	Hall, Donald	Scholastic
Painting Lesson, The	K	F	Pacific Literacy	Pacific Learning
Pancake, The	K	TL	Lobel, Anita	Bantam Doubleday Dell
Paper Birds, The	K	RF	Foundations	Wright Group/McGraw Hill

Title	Level	Genre	Author/Series	Publisher/Distributor
Paper Route, The	K	RF	New Way Green	Steck-Vaughn
Parents' Night Fright	K	RF	Levy, Elizabeth	Scholastic
Peanut Butter Gang, The	K	F	Siracusa, Catherine	Hyperion
People Are Living Things	K	I	Home Connection Collection	Rigby
Pet for You, A	K	I	Pair-It Books	Steck-Vaughn
Picking Up Papers	K	RF	City Kids	Rigby
Pied Piper of Hamelin, The	K	TL	Hautzig, Deborah	Random House
Pierre	K	RF	Sendak, Maurice	Scholastic
Piggle	K	F	Bonsall, Crosby	Harper Collins
Pile in Pete's Room, The	K	RF	Sunshine	Wright Group/McGraw Hill
Pizza for Everyone	K	I	Pair-It Books	Steck-Vaughn
Pocket for Corduroy, A	K	F	Freeman, Don	Scholastic
Polar Bears	K	I	Wonder World	Wright Group/McGraw Hill
Pookie and Joe	K	F	Literacy 2000	Rigby
Popcorn Book, The	K	I	Reading Unlimited	Celebration Press
Power of Nature, The	K	I	Early Connections	Benchmark Education
Presidents' Day	K	I	Frost, Helen	Capstone Press
Princess and the Peas, The	K	TL	Enrichment	Wright Group/McGraw Hill
Princess and the Wise Woman, The	K	TL	Ready Readers	Pearson Learning
Princess Rosa's Winter	K	F	Hindley, Judy	Wright Group/McGraw Hill
Prize for Purry, A	K	RF	Literacy 2000	Rigby
Pterodactyl at the Airport	K	F	Wesley & the Dinosaurs	Wright Group/McGraw Hill
Puss-in-Boots	K	TL	PM Tales and Plays- Purple	Rigby
Rain	K	I	Pebble Books	Grolier, Capstone
Ready, Set, Go!	K	RF	Pacific Literacy	Pacific Learning
Red Egg and Ginger	K	RF	SooHoo, Suzanne & Patrick	Rigby
Reduce, Reuse, and Recycle	K	I	Early Connections	Benchmark Education
Riches from Nature	K	I	Early Connections	Benchmark Education
Right Place for Jupiter, The	K	RF	PM Story Books -Silver	Rigby
Robert Goddard	K	B	Schaefer, Lola M.	Capstone Press
Rollo and Tweedy and the Ghost at Dougal Castle	K	F	Allen, Laura Jean	HarperTrophy
Rosa's Tonsils	K	RF	Foundations	Wright Group/McGraw Hill
Ruby the Copycat	K	RF	Rathman, Peggy	Scholastic
Rumpelstiltskin	K	TL	PM Tales and Plays- Gold	Rigby
Sam Who Never Forgets	K	F	Rice, Eve	Morrow
Sam's Big Clean-up	K	RF	Windmill Books	Rigby
Sam's Solution	K	RF	Literacy 2000	Rigby
Sandwich Hero, The	K	RF	Literacy 2000	Rigby
Sandy's Suitcase	K	RF	Edwards, Elsy	SRA/McGraw-Hill
Scaredy Dog	K	RF	Thomas, Jane Resh	Hyperion
Scruffy	K	RF	Parish, Peggy	HarperTrophy
Sea Turtles	K	I	Marine Life For Yng. Readers	Dominie
Sea Wall, The	K	I	Foundations	Wright Group/McGraw Hill
Seashells	K	I	Marine Life For Yng. Readers	Dominie
Seat Belt Song, The	K	RF	PM Turquoise	Rigby
Secret Hideaway, The	K	RF	PM Gold	Rigby
Seeing the School Doctor	K	RF	City Kids	Rigby
Selu and Kana Ti	K	TL	Folk Tales	Mondo
Seven Foolish Fishermen	K	TL	PM Tales and Plays- Gold	Rigby
Sheila Rae, the Brave	K	F	Henkes, Kevin	Scholastic
Shingo's Grandfather	K	RF	Sunshine	Wright Group/McGraw Hill
Ships at Sea	K	I	PM Plus	Rigby
Shipwreck Saturday	K	RF	Cosby, Bill	Scholastic
Shortest Kid in the World	K	RF	Bliss, Corinne Demas	Random House
Show and Tell	K	RF	City Kids	Rigby
Sidetrack Sam	K	RF	Literacy 2000	Rigby
Silly Tilly's Valentine	K	F	Hoban, Lillian	HarperTrophy
Sing to the Moon	K	F	Story Box	Wright Group/McGraw Hill
Sleeping Beauty	K	TL	Enrichment	Wright Group/McGraw Hill
Slither McCreep and His Brother, Joe	K	RF	Johnston, Tony	Harcourt Brace

Title	Level	Genre	Author/Series	Publisher/Distributor
Sly Fox and Little Red Hen	K	TL	PM Tales and Plays- Purple	Rigby
Smallest Cow in the World, The	K	RF	Paterson, Katherine	HarperTrophy
Smallest Tree, The	K	F	Literacy 2000	Rigby
Smile, The	K	RF	Read Alongs	Rigby
Snakes	K	I	Foundations	Wright Group/McGraw Hill
Sneakers	K	I	Sunshine	Wright Group/McGraw Hill
Snow White and the Seven Dwarfs	K	TL	PM Tales and Plays- Gold	Rigby
Snowball War, The	K	RF	Chardiet, Bernice	Scholastic
Snowshoe Thompson	K	HF	Smiler Levinson, N.	HarperTrophy
Soap Soup and Other Verses	K	TL	Kuskin, Karla	HarperTrophy
Soccer Cousins	K	RF	Marzollo, Jean	Scholastic
Souvenirs	K	RF	Literacy 2000	Rigby
Special Ride, The	K	RF	PM Gold	Rigby
Stan the Hot Dog Man	K	RF	Kessler, E.& L.	HarperTrophy
Starfish & Urchins	K	I	Marine Life For Yng. Readers	Dominie
Stems	K	I	Pebble Books	Grolier, Capstone
Stone Works	K	I	Wonder World	Wright Group/McGraw Hill
Story of Hungbu and Nolbu, The	K	TL	Book Shop	Mondo
String Food	K	I	Home Connection Collection	Rigby
Suki and the Case of the Lost Bunnies	K	RF	Ready Readers	Pearson Learning
Sunflower That Went Flop, The	K	F	Story Box	Wright Group/McGraw Hill
Supermarket, The	K	I	Pebble Books	Grolier, Capstone
Surprise Party	K	I	Hutchins, Pat	Macmillan
Talent Contest, The	K	RF	PM Story Books -Silver	Rigby
Tea	K	I	Wonder World	Wright Group/McGraw Hill
Teddy Bears Cure a Cold	K	F	Gretz, Susanna	Scholastic
Teeth	K	I	Sunshine	Wright Group/McGraw Hill
Terrible Fright, A	K	TL	Story Box	Wright Group/McGraw Hill
That Fat Hat	K	F	Barkan, Joanne	Scholastic
That's Really Weird!	K	F	Read Alongs	Rigby
Three Bears, The	K	TL	Galdone, Paul	Clarion
Three Billy Goats Gruff, The	K	TL	Asbjornsen, P. C. & Moe, J. E.	Harcourt Brace
Three Billy Goats Gruff, The	K	TL	Stevens, Janet	Harcourt Brace
Three By the Sea	K	RF	Marshall, Edward	Puffin Books
Three Days on a River in a Red Canoe	K	I	Williams, Vera B.	Scholastic
Three Ducks Went Wandering	K	RF	Roy, Ron	Clarion
Three Stories You Can Read to Your Cat	K	F	Miller, Sara Swan	Houghton Mifflin
Three Stories You Can Read to Your Dog	K	F	Miller, Sara Swan	Houghton Mifflin
Three Wishes, The	K	TL	Sunshine	Wright Group/McGraw Hill
Thumbelina	K	TL	Tales from Hans Andersen	Wright Group/McGraw Hill
Too Busy for Pets!	K	RF	Sunshine	Wright Group/McGraw Hill
Too Many Babas	K	TL	Croll, Carolyn	HarperTrophy
Too Many Babas	K	TL	Little Readers	Houghton Mifflin
Town Mouse and Country Mouse	K	TL	PM Tales and Plays- Purple	Rigby
Trains on the Rails	K	I	PM Plus	Rigby
Treasure of the Lost Lagoon, The	K	F	Hayes, Geoffrey	Random House
Treasure on Fraser Street, The	K	RF	Rushby, Pamela	Rigby
Trees	K	I	Early Connections	Benchmark Education
Trucks on the Road	K	I	PM Plus	Rigby
Tubes in My Ears: My Trip to the Hospital	K	I	Book Shop	Mondo
Turtle Flies South	K	F	Literacy 2000	Rigby
Two Foolish Cats	K	F	Literacy 2000	Rigby
Unbelievable!	K	SF	Shulman, Lisa	Hampton-Brown
Under the City	K	RF	Sunshine	Wright Group/McGraw Hill
Using Nature's Gifts	K	I	People, Spaces & Places	Rand McNally
Vehicles for Fun and Sports	K	I	PM Plus	Rigby
Vehicles in the Air	K	I	PM Plus	Rigby
Vicky the High Jumper	K	I	Literacy 2000	Rigby
Wagon Wheels	K	HF	Brenner, Barbara	HarperTrophy
Walkathon, The	K	RF	PM Story Books -Silver	Rigby

Title	Level	Genre	Author/Series	Publisher/Distributor
War Shirt, The	K	RF	Spang, Bently	Rigby
Water Goes Up! Water Goes Down!	K	I	Early Connections	Benchmark Education
Waterhole	K	I	Planet Earth	Rigby
We Scream for Ice Cream	K	RF	Chardiet, B. & Maccarone, G.	Scholastic
Well I Never	K	F	Story Box	Wright Group/McGraw Hill
What a Day!	K	RF	Miranda, Anne	Hampton-Brown
What Changes Our Earth?	K	I	People, Places & Spaces	Rand McNally
What Happens When You Recycle?	K	I	Discovery World	Rigby
What's for Dinner, Dad?	K	RF	Sunshine	Wright Group/McGraw Hill
What's Inside?	K	I	Wonder World	Wright Group/McGraw Hill
What's Missing?	K	I	Book Bank	Wright Group/McGraw Hill
What's Underneath?	K	I	Discovery World	Rigby
When I Get Bigger	K	RF	Mayer, Mercer	Donovan
When Will We Be Sisters?	K	RF	Kroll, Virginia	Scholastic
Where Are the Bears?	K	F	Winters, Kay	Bantam Doubleday Dell
Where Jeans Come From	K	I	Ready Readers	Pearson Learning
White Horse, The	K	F	Literacy 2000	Rigby
Who Pushed Humpty?	K	TL	Literacy 2000	Rigby
Who Sank the Boat?	K	F	Allen Pamela	Coward
Who's Afraid of the Big, Bad Bully?	K	RF	Slater, Teddy	Scholastic
Whose Side Are You On?	K	TL	Cisco, Cheyenne	Sadlier-Oxford
Why Coyote Howls at Night	K	TL	Little Books	Sadlier-Oxford
Why People Move	K	I	People, Places & Spaces	Rand McNally
Why the Kangaroo Hops	K	I	Sunshine	Wright Group/McGraw Hill
William's Wheelchair Race	K	RF	Sunshine	Wright Group/McGraw Hill
Wind and Storms	K	I	Sunshine	Wright Group/McGraw Hill
Winter Woollies	K	I	Storyteller Nonfiction	Wright Group/McGraw Hill
Wright Brothers at Kitty Hawk, The	K	B	Schaefer, Lola M.	Capstone Press
You Can Always Tell Cathy from Caitlin	K	RF	Sunshine	Wright Group/McGraw Hill
Yuck!	K	F	Little Readers	Houghton Mifflin
Zack's Alligator	K	F	Mozelle, Shirley	HarperTrophy
Zack's Alligator Goes to School	K	F	Mozelle, Shirley	HarperTrophy
Abracadabra	L	RF	Reading Unlimited	Celebration Press
Abraham Lincoln	L	B	Pebble Books	Grolier, Capstone
Acid Rain	L	I	Wonder World	Wright Group/McGraw Hill
Adventure of the Buried Treasure, The	L	RF	McArthur, Nancy	Scholastic
Adventures of Granny Gatman, The	L	RF	Meadows, Graham	Dominie Press
Alexander and the Wind-Up Mouse	L	F	Lionni, Leo	Scholastic
All About Plants	L	I	Home Connection Collection	Rigby
All About Stacy	L	RF	Giff, Patricia Reilly	Bantam Doubleday Dell
All Kinds of Eyes	L	I	Discovery World	Rigby
All Kinds of Flowers	L	I	Turner, Teresa	Steck-Vaughn
Amanda Pig and Her Big Brother Oliver	L	F	Van Leeuwen, Jean	Puffin Books
Amazing Trains	L	I	Pair-It Books	Steck-Vaughn
Amelia Bedelia	L	F	Parish, Peggy	HarperTrophy
Amelia Bedelia and the Baby	L	F	Parish, Peggy	Harper & Row
Amelia Bedelia and the Surprise Shower	L	F	Parish, Peggy	Harper & Row
Amelia Bedelia Goes Camping	L	F	Parish, Peggy	Avon Camelot
Amelia Bedelia Helps Out	L	F	Parish, Peggy	Avon Camelot
Amelia Bedelia's Family Album	L	F	Parish, Peggy	Avon Books
Androcles and the Lion	L	TL	PM Tales and Plays-Silver	Rigby
Animal Reports	L	I	Little Red Readers	Sundance
Animal Tracks	L	I	Dorros, Arthur	Scholastic
Annabel the Actress Starring in Gorilla My Dreams	L	RF	Conford, Ellen	Simon & Schuster
Annie Bananie Moves To Barry Avenue	L	RF	Komaiko, Leah	Bantam Doubleday Dell
Another Day, Another Challenge	L	RF	Literacy 2000	Rigby
Awumpalema	L	TL	Literacy 2000	Rigby
B-E-S-T Friends	L	RF	Giff, Patricia Reilly	Bantam Doubleday Dell
Bad Day for Benjamin, A	L	RF	Reading Unlimited	Celebration Press
Bad-Luck Penny, The	L	F	O'Connor, Jane	Grosset & Dunlap

Title	Level	Genre	Author/Series	Publisher/Distributor
Bank Robbery and Jack and the Beanstalk, The	L	TL	New Way:Literature	Steck-Vaughn
Be a Plant Scientist	L	I	Paul, Michele	Wright Group/McGraw Hill
Beans on the Roof	L	RF	Byars, Betsy	Bantam Doubleday Dell
Bear and the Trolls, The	L	TL	PM Tales and Plays-Silver	Rigby
Bear's Diet	L	RF	PM Gold	Rigby
Best Clown in Town, The	L	RF	Bradley, Tom	Dominie Press
Best Older Sister, The	L	RF	Choi, Sook Nyul	Bantam Doubleday Dell
Best Worst Day, The	L	RF	Graves, Bonnie	Hyperion
Best-Loved Doll, The	L	RF	Caudill, Rebecca	Henry Holt & Co.
Big Al	L	F	Yoshi, Andrew C.	Scholastic
Big Balloon Festival, The	L	RF	PM Gold	Rigby
Big Beet, The	L	F	Ready Readers	Pearson Learning
Big Orange Spot, The	L	F	Pinkwater, Daniel Manus	Scholastic
Big Race, The	L	RF	Pattrick, Steve	Rigby
Billy the Ghost and Me	L	F	Greer, Gery & Ruddick, Bob	HarperTrophy
Bobo's Magic Wishes	L	F	Little Readers	Houghton Mifflin
Boy Who Cried Wolf, The	L	TL	Literacy 2000	Rigby
Boy Who Turned Into a T.V. Set, The	L	F	Manes, Stephen	Avon Camelot
Boy Who Went to the North Wind, The	L	TL	Literacy 2000	Rigby
Brachiosaurus in the River	L	F	Wesley & The Dinosaurs	Wright Group/McGraw Hill
Brand New Butterfly, A	L	I	Literacy 2000	Rigby
Bravest Dog Ever, The: The True Story of Balto	L	I	Standiford, Natalie	Random House
Bravo Amelia Bedelia!	L	F	Parish, Herman	Avon
Breathing	L	I	Book Shop	Mondo
Brigid Beware	L	RF	Leverich, Kathleen	Random House
Brigid Bewitched	L	RF	Leverich, Kathleen	Random House
Brigid the Bad	L	RF	Leverich, Kathleen	Random House
Bringing the Sea Back Home	L	F	Literacy 2000	Rigby
Bug Off!	L	F	Dussling, Jennifer	Grosset & Dunlap
Butterflies of the Sea	L	I	Swartz, Stanley L.	Dominie Press
Cam Jansen and the Chocolate Fudge Mystery	L	RF	Adler, David A.	Puffin Books
Cam Jansen and the Ghostly Mystery	L	RF	Adler, David A.	Puffin Books
Cam Jansen and the Mystery at the Haunted House	L	RF	Adler, David A.	Puffin Books
Cam Jansen and the Mystery at the Monkey House	L	RF	Adler, David A.	Puffin Books
Cam Jansen and the Mystery of Flight 54	L	RF	Adler, David A.	Puffin Books
Cam Jansen and the Mystery of the Babe Ruth Baseball	L	RF	Adler, David A.	Puffin Books
Cam Jansen and the Mystery of the Carnival Prize	L	RF	Adler, David A.	Puffin Books
Cam Jansen and the Mystery of the Circus Clown	L	RF	Adler, David A.	Puffin Books
Cam Jansen and the Mystery of the Dinosaur Bones	L	RF	Adler, David A.	Puffin Books
Cam Jansen and the Mystery of the Gold Coins	L	RF	Adler, David A.	Puffin Books
Cam Jansen and the Mystery of the Monkey House	L	RF	Adler, David A.	Puffin Books
Cam Jansen and the Mystery of the Monster Movie	L	RF	Adler, David A.	Puffin Books
Cam Jansen and the Mystery of the Stolen Corn Popper	L	RF	Adler, David A.	Puffin Books
Cam Jansen and the Mystery of the Stolen Diamonds	L	RF	Adler, David A.	Puffin Books
Cam Jansen and the Mystery of the Television Dog	L	RF	Adler, David A.	Puffin Books
Cam Jansen and the Mystery of the U.F.O.	L	RF	Adler, David A.	Puffin Books
Cam Jansen and the Scary Snake Mystery	L	RF	Adler, David A.	Puffin Books
Can I Have a Dinosaur?	L	RF	Literacy 2000	Rigby
Candy Corn Contest, The	L	RF	Giff, Patricia Reilly	Bantam Doubleday Dell
Cannonball Chris	L	RF	Marzollo, J.	Random House
Captain Felonius	L	F	Literacy 2000	Rigby
Car Trouble	L	RF	PM Gold	Rigby
Carlita Ropes the Twister	L	F	Pair-It Books	Steck-Vaughn
Carpenters	L	I	Community Workers	Compass Point Books
Case of the Cool-Itch Kid, The	L	RF	Giff, Patricia Reilly	Bantam Doubleday Dell
Cass Becomes a Star	L	B	Literacy 2000	Rigby
Cat Called Tim, A	L	RF	New Way: Literature	Steck-Vaughn
Cattle	L	I	PM Animal Facts: Purple	Rigby
Chang's Paper Pony	L	RF	Coerr, Eleanor	HarperTrophy
Charlie	L	F	Literacy 2000	Rigby

Title	Level	Genre	Author/Series	Publisher/Distributor
Chefs	L	I	Community Workers	Compass Point Books
Chicken Little	L	TL	Traditional Tales & More	Rigby
Chickens	L	I	PM Animal Facts: Purple	Rigby
Clarence the Crocodile	L	F	New Way: Literature	Steck-Vaughn
Claudine's Concert	L	RF	Literacy 2000	Rigby
Clouds of Terror	L	HF	Welsh, Catherine A.	Carolrhoda Books
Clue at the Zoo, The	L	RF	Giff, Patricia Reilly	Bantam Doubleday Dell
Come Back, Amelia Bedelia	L	F	Parish, Peggy	Harper & Row
Conversation Club, The	L	F	Stanley, Diane	Aladdin
Cotton Plant to Cotton Shirt	L	I	Schaefer, Lola M.	Benchmark Education
Coyote in Trouble	L	TL	Beveridge, Barbara	Pacific Learning
Crafty Jackal	L	TL	Folk Tales	Wright Group/McGraw Hill
Creep Show	L	F	Dussling, Jennifer	Grosset & Dunlap
Cricket Boy and Other Stories, The	L	TL	New Way: Literature	Steck-Vaughn
Crocodile in the Library, A	L	F	Pacific Literacy	Pacific Learning
Crocodile's Christmas Jandals, The	L	F	Pacific Literacy	Pacific Learning
Curse of the Cobweb Queen, The	L	F	Hayes, Geoffrey	Random House
Danny's Big Jump	L	RF	Reeder, Tracey	Wright Group/McGraw Hill
Day in Space, A	L	SF	Lord, Suzanne. & Epstein, Jolie	Scholastic
Day of the Rain, The	L	F	Cowley, Joy	Dominie
Day of the Snow, The	L	F	Cowley, Joy	Dominie
Day of the Wind, The	L	F	Cowley, Joy	Dominie
December Secrets	L	RF	Giff, Patricia Reilly	Bantam Doubleday Dell
Deputy Dan and the Bank Robbers	L	RF	Rosenbloom, Joseph	Random House
Deputy Dan Gets His Man	L	RF	Rosembloom, Joseph	Random House
Desert Giant: The World of the Saguaro Cactus	L	I	Bash, Barbara	Scholastic
Diary of a Honeybee	L	I	Literacy 2000	Rigby
Dick Whittington	L	TL	PM Tales and Plays-Silver	Rigby
Diego Rivera: An Artist's Life	L	B	Pair-It Books	Steck-Vaughn
Dinosaur Babies	L	I	Penner, Lucille Recht	Random House
Dinosaur Days	L	I	Milton, Joyce	Random House
Dinosaur Hunters	L	I	McMullan, Kate	Random House
Doctors	L	I	Community Workers	Compass Point Books
Dog that Pitched a No-Hitter, The	L	F	Christopher, Matt	Little Brown & Co.
Dog that Stole Home, The	L	F	Christopher, Matt	Little, Brown & Co.
Dog-Gone Hollywood	L	F	Sharmat, Marjorie Weinman	Random House
Doing the Dishes	L	RF	City Kids	Rigby
Dolphin	L	I	Morris, Robert A.	HarperTrophy
Dolphins!	L	I	Bokoske, S. & Davidson, M.	Random House
Dolphins, The	L	RF	PM Gold	Rigby
Dom's Handplant	L	RF	Literacy 2000	Rigby
Donna O'Neeshuck Was Chased By Some Cows	L	RF	Grossman, Bill	HarperTrophy
Dragon Breath	L	F	O'Connor, Jane	Grosset & Dunlap
Dragons of Blueland, The	L	F	Gannett, R.	Random House
Ed and Me	L	RF	McPhail, David	Harcourt Brace
Emily and Alice	L	RF	Champion, Joyce	Harcourt Brace
Emily at School	L	RF	Williams, Suzanne	Hyperion
Emma	L	RF	Kesselman, Wendy	HarperTrophy
Emperor and the Nightingale, The	L	TL	Literacy 2000	Rigby
Everyone Knows About Cars	L	I	Book Shop	Mondo
Everything Changes	L	I	Discovery World	Rigby
Exotic Tropical Fish	L	I	Swartz, Stanley L.	Dominie Press
Fancy Feet	L	RF	Giff, Patricia Reilly	Bantam Doubleday Dell
Farm Life Long Ago	L	I	Pair-It Books	Steck-Vaughn
Fire and Wind	L	TL	PM Story Books -Silver	Rigby
Fire Fighters	L	I	Community Workers	Compass Point Books
Firefly Named Torchy, A	L	F	Waber, Bernard	Houghton Mifflin
Fish	L	I	Marine Life For Yng. Readers	Dominie
Fish that Hide	L	I	Swartz, Stanley L.	Dominie Press
Flea Story, A	L	F	Lionni, Leo	Scholastic

Title	Level	Genre	Author/Series	Publisher/Distributor
Flight of the Union, The	L	B	White, Tekla	Carolrhoda Books
Flower Girls # 1: Violet	L	RF	Leverich, Kathleen	HarperTrophy
Flower Girls # 2: Daisy	L	RF	Leverich, Kathleen	HarperTrophy
Flower Girls # 3: Heather	L	RF	Leverich, Kathleen	HarperTrophy
Flower Girls # 4: Rose	L	RF	Leverich, Kathleen	HarperTrophy
Flower of Sheba, The	L	TL	Orgel, Doris & Schecter, Ellen	Bantam Doubleday Dell
Flowers	L	I	Pebble Books	Grolier, Capstone
Fly Trap	L	F	Anastasio, Dina	Grosset & Dunlap
Football Friends	L	RF	Marzollo, J., D. & D.	Scholastic
Forgotten Princess, The	L	TL	Literacy 2000	Rigby
Four Friends and Other Stories, The	L	TL	New Way: Literature	Steck-Vaughn
Fox and the Little Red Hen	L	TL	Traditional Tales & More	Rigby
Frog Who Thought He Was A Horse, The	L	F	Literacy 2000	Rigby
Gail Devers: A Runner's Dream	L	B	Pair-It Books	Steck-Vaughn
Gail & Me	L	RF	Literacy 2000	Rigby
Gasp!	L	F	Book Shop	Mondo
Genghis Khan: A Dog Star is Born	L	RF	Sharmat, Marjorie Weinman	Random House
George and Martha	L	F	Marshall, James	Houghton Mifflin
George Washington	L	B	Pebble Books	Grolier, Capstone
Ginger Brown: The Nobody Boy	L	RF	Wyeth, Sharon Dennis	Random House
Ginger Brown: Too Many Houses	L	RF	Wyeth, Sharon Dennis	Random House
Gingerbread Boy, The	L	TL	Galdone, Paul	Clarion
Girl Who Climbed to the Moon, The	L	F	Sunshine	Wright Group/McGraw Hill
Goat Monster and Other Stories, The	L	F	New Way: Literature	Steck-Vaughn
Goats	L	I	PM Animal Facts: Purple	Rigby
Golden Goose, The	L	TL	Sunshine	Wright Group/McGraw Hill
Goliath and the Burglar	L	RF	Dicks, Terrance	Barron's Educational Series
Goliath and the Buried Treasure	L	RF	Dicks, Terrance	Barron's Educational Series
Goliath and the Cub Scouts	L	RF	Dicks, Terrance	Barron's Educational Series
Goliath at the Dog Show	L	RF	Dicks, Terrance	Barron's Educational Series
Goliath at the Seaside	L	RF	Dicks, Terrance	Barron's Educational Series
Goliath Goes to Summer School	L	RF	Dicks, Terrance	Barron's Educational Series
Goliath on Vacation	L	RF	Dicks, Terrance	Barron's Educational Series
Goliath's Birthday	L	RF	Dicks, Terrance	Barron's Educational Series
Goliath's Christmas	L	RF	Dicks, Terrance	Barron's Educational Series
Goliath's Easter Parade	L	RF	Dicks, Terrance	Barron's Educational Series
Good As New	L	RF	Douglass, Barbara	Scholastic
Good Driving, Amelia Bedelia	L	F	Parish, Peggy	Harper & Row
Good Work, Amelia Bedelia	L	F	Parish, Peggy	Avon Camelot
Gooey Chewy Contest, The	L	F	Goldsmith, Howard	Mondo
Gorillas: Gentle Giants on the Forest	L	I	Milton, Joyce	Random House
Great Genghis Khan Look-Alike Contest, The	L	RF	Sharmat, Marjorie Weinman	Random House
Great Ghosts	L	F	Cohen, Daniel	Scholastic
Greatest of All, The: A Japanese Folktale	L	TL	Kimmel, Eric A.	Holiday House
Greedy Goat, The	L	TL	Book Shop	Mondo
Gregory, the Terrible Eater	L	F	Sharmat, Marjorie Weinman	Scholastic
Guess Who?	L	I	Home Connection Collection	Rigby
Happy Birthday, Martin Luther King	L	B	Marzollo, Jean	Scholastic
Happy Birthday, Moon	L	F	Asch, Frank	Simon & Schuster
Harry and Willy and Carrothead	L	RF	Caseley, Judith	Scholastic
Haunted Bike, The	L	F	Herman, Gail	Grosset & Dunlap
Headless Horseman, The	L	TL	Standiford, Natalie	Random House
Helpful Change, A	L	RF	Behr, Alexandra	Hampton-Brown
Helpful Harry and Other Stories	L	RF	New Way: Literature	Steck-Vaughn
Hide to Survive	L	I	Home Connection Collection	Rigby
Hill of Fire	L	RF	Lewis, T.P.	Harper Collins
Honey Tree, The	L	F	Literacy 2000	Rigby
Horrible Harry and the Ant Invasion	L	RF	Kline, Suzy	Scholastic
Horrible Harry and the Christmas Surprise	L	RF	Kline, Susy	Scholastic
Horrible Harry and the Drop of Doom	L	RF	Kline, Suzy	Puffin Books

Title	Level	Genre	Author/Series	Publisher/Distributor
Horrible Harry and the Dungeon	L	RF	Kline, Suzy	The Penguin Group
Horrible Harry and the Green Slime	L	RF	Kline, Suzy	The Penguin Group
Horrible Harry and the Kickball Wedding	L	RF	Kline, Susy	The Penguin Group
Horrible Harry in Room 2B	L	RF	Kline, Suzy	The Penguin Group
Horrible Harry, Moves up to Third Grade	L	RF	Kline, Suzy	Puffin Books
Horrible Harry's Secret	L	RF	Kline, Suzy	The Penguin Group
Horses	L	I	PM Animal Facts: Purple	Rigby
Hospitals	L	I	Book Shop	Mondo
Hot Air Balloons	L	I	Pair-It Books	Steck-Vaughn
Hot Fudge Hero	L	RF	Brisson, Pat	Henry Holt & Co.
How Animals Move	L	I	Discovery World	Rigby
How Do Plants Get Food?	L	I	Goldish, Meish	Steck-Vaughn
How Does It Grow?	L	I	Home Connection Collection	Rigby
How Kittens Grow	L	I	Selsam, Millicent E.	Scholastic
How Much Is That Guinea Pig in the Window?	L	RF	Rocklin, Joanne	Scholastic
How Spiders Got Eight Legs	L	F	Pair-It Books	Steck-Vaughn
How the Rattlesnake Got Its Rattle	L	TL	Pair-It Books	Steck-Vaughn
How the Water Got to the Plains	L	TL	Home Connection Collection	Rigby
How To Choose a Pet	L	I	Discovery World	Rigby
Huberta the Hiking Hippo	L	RF	Literacy 2000	Rigby
Hungry, Hungry Sharks	L	I	Cole, Joanna	Random House
I Don't Believe It!	L	RF	Tuer, Judy	Rigby
I Hate English	L	RF	Levine, Ellen	Scholastic
I Hate My Best Friend	L	RF	Rosner, Ruth	Hyperion
I Know a Lady	L	RF	Zolotow, Charlotte	The Penguin Group
In a New Land	L	HF	Sunshine	Wright Group/McGraw Hill
In Hiding, Animals Under Cover	L	I	Burke, Melissa Blackwell	Steck-Vaughn
It Takes A Village	L	RF	Cowen-Fletcher, J.	Scholastic
It Wasn't My Fault	L	RF	Lester, Helen	Houghton Mifflin
Jacques Cousteau	L	B	Biography	Benchmark Education
Jane Goodall and the Wild Chimpanzees	L	B	Birnbaum, Bette	Steck-Vaughn
Jennifer, Too	L	RF	Havill, Juanita	Hyperion
Jenny and the Cornstalk	L	TL	Pair-It Books	Steck-Vaughn
Joey's Head	L	F	Cretan, G.	Simon & Schuster
Josefina Story Quilt	L	F	Coerr, Eleanor	HarperTrophy
Josephine's Imagination	L	RF	Dobrin, Arnold	Scholastic
Judy Moody	L	RF	McDonald, Megan	Candlewick Press
Jump the Broom	L	RF	Books For Young Learners	Pacific Learning
Junkpile Robot, The	L	F	Ready Readers	Pearson Learning
Katy and the Big Snow	L	F	Burton, Virginia L.	Scholastic
Kerri Strug: Heart of Gold	L	B	Strug, K. & Brown, G.	Scholastic
Kids in the Circus	L	I	Robinson, Fay	Wright Group/McGraw Hill
Kilmer's Pet Monster	L	RF	Dadey, D. & Jones, M. T.	Scholastic
Kind Prince and Rupert, The	L	F	New Way: Literature	Steck-Vaughn
King Beast's Birthday	L	F	Literacy 2000	Rigby
King's Dream and Sammy's New Yellow Sweater, The	L	TL	New Way: Literature	Steck-Vaughn
King's Race and Other Stories, The	L	F	New Way: Literature	Steck-Vaughn
Kit's Castle	L	RF	Powling, Chris	Wright Group/McGraw Hill
Land of the Great Big "No!"	L	RF	Trussell-Cullen, Alan	Dominie Press
Left Behind	L	RF	Carrick, Carol	Clarion Books
Letter Carriers	L	I	Community Workers	Compass Point Books
Lightning	L	I	Pebble Books	Grolier, Capstone
Lilacs, Lotuses, and Ladybugs	L	RF	Evangeline Nicholas Collection	Wright Group/McGraw Hill
Lionel and Amelia	L	F	Book Shop	Mondo
Lions	L	I	Pair-It Books	Steck-Vaughn
Lisa's Diary	L	RF	Pritchett, Jan	Rigby
Little Penguin's Tale	L	F	Wood, Audrey	Scholastic
Little Princess, A	L	RF	All Aboard Reading	Grosset & Dunlap
Little Vampire and the Midnight Bear	L	F	Kwitz, M. D.	Puffin Books
Lizards	L	I	Wonder World	Wright Group/McGraw Hill

Title	Level	Genre	Author/Series	Publisher/Distributor
Lizzie's Lizard	L	I	Storyteller Nonfiction	Wright Group/McGraw Hill
Long Way to a New Land, A	L	HF	Sandin, Joan	HarperTrophy
Long Way Westward, The	L	HF	Sandin, Joan	HarperTrophy
Looking at Insects	L	I	Discovery World	Rigby
Looking into Space	L	I	Early Connections	Benchmark Education
Loose Laces	L	RF	Reading Unlimited	Celebration Press
Lost!	L	F	Mitchell, Julie	Rigby
Lost at the White House: A 1909 Easter Story	L	HF	Griest, Lisa	Carolrhoda Books
Lucky Feather, The	L	F	Literacy 2000	Rigby
Lucky Stars	L	RF	Adler, David A.	Random House
Lucy Meets a Dragon	L	F	Literacy 2000	Rigby
Luke's Go-cart	L	RF	PM Gold	Rigby
Magic All Around	L	F	Literacy 2000	Rigby
Magic Fish, The	L	TL	Littledale, Freya	Scholastic
Magic Money	L	RF	Adler, David A.	Random House
Magic Porridge Pot, The	L	TL	Sunshine	Wright Group/McGraw Hill
Mailman Mario & His Boris-Busters	L	RF	Parker, John	Dominie Press
Maisie's Race	L	RF	Mawter, Jeni	Wright Group/McGraw Hill
Make a Shake and a Bakeless Cake	L	I	Cole, Sally	Wright Group/McGraw Hill
Make Way For Ducklings	L	RF	McCloskey, Robert	Puffin Books
Marcella	L	RF	Literacy 2000	Rigby
Mare for Young Wolf, A	L	HF	Shefelman, Janice	Random House
Martin Luther King, Jr.	L	B	Pebble Books	Grolier, Capstone
Materials and Their Uses	L	I	Discovery World	Rigby
Matthew and Tilly	L	RF	Jones, Rebecca C.	The Penguin Group
Matthew Henson	L	B	Biography	Benchmark Education
Meet the Lincoln Lions Band	L	RF	Giff, Patricia Reilly	Bantam Doubleday Dell
Meet the Molesons	L	F	Bos, Burny	North-South Books
Mermaid Island	L	F	Frith, Margaret	Grosset & Dunlap
Milkshake Man, The	L	F	Cole, Sally	Wright Group/McGraw Hill
Miss Nelson Has a Field Day	L	RF	Allard, Harry	Scholastic
Miss Nelson is Missing	L	RF	Allard, Harry	Houghton Mifflin
Missing Fossil Mystery, The	L	RF	Herman, Emily	Hyperion
Mog at the Zoo	L	F	Nicoll, Helen	The Penguin Group
Mog's Mumps	L	F	Nicoll, Helen	The Penguin Group
Monsters Next Door, The	L	RF	Dadey, D. & Jones, M. T.	Scholastic
Monsters of the Deep	L	I	Swartz, Stanley L.	Dominie Press
More Tales of Amanda Pig	L	F	Van Leeuwen, Jean	The Penguin Group
More Tales of Oliver Pig	L	F	Van Leeuwen, Jean	The Penguin Group
Mother Hippopotamus Goes Canoeing	L	F	Foundations	Wright Group/McGraw Hill
Mr. Bumbleticker Goes to the Zoo	L	RF	Foundations	Wright Group/McGraw Hill
Mr. Gumpy's Motor Car	L	RF	Burningham, John	Harper Collins
Mr. Gumpy's Outing	L	RF	Burningham, John	Holt, Henry & Co.
Mr. Sun and Mr. Sea	L	F	Sunshine	Wright Group/McGraw Hill
Mrs. Jeepers' Batty Vacation	L	RF	Dadey, D. & Jones, M. T.	Scholastic
Mud Pony, The	L	TL	Sunshine	Wright Group/McGraw Hill
Mummy's Gold, The	L	F	McMullan, Kate	Grosset & Dunlap
Mystery of the Blue Ring, The	L	RF	Giff, Patricia Reilly	Bantam Doubleday Dell
Mystery of the Pirate Ghost, The	L	F	Hayes, Geoffrey	Random House
Mystery of the Tooth Gremlin	L	RF	Graves, Bonnie	Hyperion
Mystery Seeds	L	RF	Reading Unlimited	Celebration Press
New Light for the Lodge, A	L	F	Smith, Ben	Wright Group/McGraw Hill
Nine Lives of Adventure Cat, The	L	F	Clymer, Susan	Scholastic
No Copycats Allowed!	L	RF	Graves, Bonnie	Hyperion
No Jumping On The Bed!	L	F	Arnold, Tedd	Scholastic
Not Too Young and Other Stories	L	TL	New Way: Literature	Steck-Vaughn
Obstacles in Our Way	L	RF	McAlister, Margaret	Rigby
Octopuses, Squid, & Cuttlefish	L	I	Marine Life For Yng. Readers	Dominie
Old Enough for Magic	L	F	Pickett, A.	HarperTrophy

Title	Level	Genre	Author/Series	Publisher/Distributor
Old Recipe Book, The	L	F	Smith, Ben	Wright Group/McGraw Hill
Oliver and Amanda's Halloween	L	F	Van Leeuwen, Jean	Puffin Books
Once When I Was Shipwrecked	L	F	Literacy 2000	Rigby
Onion Sundaes	L	RF	Adler, David A.	Random House
Ouch!	L	RF	Noonan, Diana	Dominie Press
Owl and the Pussy Cat	L	TL	Lear, Edward	Scholastic
Owls in the Garden	L	RF	PM Gold	Rigby
Partners	L	I	Home Connection Collection	Rigby
Patrick and the Leprechaun	L	F	PM Gold	Rigby
Pee Wee Scouts: A Big Box of Memories,	L	RF	Delton, Judy	Bantam Doubleday Dell
Pee Wee Scouts: Bad, Bad Bunnies	L	RF	Delton, Judy	Bantam, Doubleday, Dell
Pee Wee Scouts: Blue Skies, French Fries	L	RF	Delton, Judy	Bantam Doubleday Dell
Pee Wee Scouts: Cookies and Crutches	L	RF	Delton, Judy	Bantam Doubleday Dell
Pee Wee Scouts: Fishy Wishes	L	RF	Delton, Judy	Bantam Doubleday Dell
Pee Wee Scouts: Greedy Groundhogs	L	RF	Delton, Judy	Bantam Doubleday Dell
Pee Wee Scouts: Grumpy Pumpkins	L	RF	Delton, Judy	Bantam Doubleday Dell
Pee Wee Scouts: Halloween Helpers	L	RF	Delton, Judy	Bantam Doubleday Dell
Pee Wee Scouts: Lights, Action, Land-Ho!	L	RF	Delton, Judy	Bantam Doubleday Dell
Pee Wee Scouts: Lucky Dog Days	L	RF	Delton, Judy	Bantam Doubleday Dell
Pee Wee Scouts: Moans and Groans and Dinosaur Bones	L	RF	Delton, Judy	Bantam Doubleday Dell
Pee Wee Scouts: Molly for Mayor	L	RF	Delton, Judy	Bantam Doubleday Dell
Pee Wee Scouts on First	L	RF	Delton, Judy	Bantam Doubleday Dell
Pee Wee Scouts on Parade	L	RF	Delton, Judy	Bantam Doubleday Dell
Pee Wee Scouts on Skis	L	RF	Delton, Judy	Bantam Doubleday Dell
Pee Wee Scouts: Peanut-Butter Pilgrims	L	RF	Delton, Judy	Bantam Doubleday Dell
Pee Wee Scouts: Pedal Power	L	RF	Delton, Judy	Bantam Doubleday Dell
Pee Wee Scouts: Piles of Pets	L	RF	Delton, Judy	Bantam Doubleday Dell
Pee Wee Scouts: Rosy Noses, Freezing Toes	L	RF	Delton, Judy	Bantam Doubleday Dell
Pee Wee Scouts: Sky Babies	L	RF	Delton, Judy	Bantam Doubleday Dell
Pee Wee Scouts: Sonny's Secret	L	RF	Delton, Judy	Bantam Doubleday Dell
Pee Wee Scouts: Spring Sprouts	L	RF	Delton, Judy	Bantam Doubleday Dell
Pee Wee Scouts: Teeny Weeny Zucchinis	L	RF	Delton, Judy	Bantam Doubleday Dell
Pee Wee Scouts: The Pee Wee Jubilee	L	RF	Delton, Judy	Bantam Doubleday Dell
Pee Wee Scouts: The Pooped Troop	L	RF	Delton, Judy	Bantam Doubleday Dell
Pee Wee Scouts: Trash Bash	L	RF	Delton, Judy	Bantam Doubleday Dell
Pee Wee Scouts: Tricks and Treats	L	RF	Delton, Judy	Bantam Doubleday Dell
Perfect the Pig	L	F	Jeschke, Susan	Scholastic
Pet Sitters Plus Five	L	RF	Springstubb, Tricia	Scholastic
Pete's Story	L	F	Literacy 2000	Rigby
Peter and the North Wind	L	TL	Littledale, Freya	Scholastic
Pheasant and Kingfisher	L	TL	Book Shop	Mondo
Picked for the Team	L	RF	PM Gold	Rigby
Picking Apples and Pumpkins	L	I	Hutchings, A. & R.	Scholastic
Pickle Puss	L	RF	Giff, Patricia Reilly	Bantam Doubleday Dell
Pignocchio	L	F	Pair-It Books	Steck-Vaughn
Pigs	L	I	PM Animal Facts: Purple	Rigby
Pinky and Rex	L	RF	Howe, James	Simon & Schuster
Pinky and Rex and the Bully	L	RF	Howe, James	Simon & Schuster
Pinky and Rex and the Double-Dad Weekend	L	RF	Howe, James	Simon & Schuster
Pinky and Rex and the Mean Old Witch	L	RF	Howe, James	Simon & Schuster
Pinky and Rex and the New Baby	L	RF	Howe, James	Simon & Schuster
Pinky and Rex and the New Neighbors	L	RF	Howe, James	Simon & Schuster
Pinky and Rex and the Perfect Pumpkin	L	RF	Howe, James	Simon & Schuster
Pinky and Rex and the School Play	L	RF	Howe, James	Simon & Schuster
Pinky and Rex and the Spelling Bee	L	RF	Howe, James	Simon & Schuster
Pinky and Rex Get Married	L	RF	Howe, James	Simon & Schuster
Pinky and Rex Go to Camp	L	RF	Howe, James	Aladdin
Pioneer Bear	L	F	Sandin, Joan	Random House

Title	Level	Genre	Author/Series	Publisher/Distributor
Play Ball, Amelia Bedelia	L	F	Parish, Peggy	Harper & Row
Pocket Full of Acorns, A	L	RF	Beames, Michael	Dominie Press
Police Officers	L	I	Community Workers	Compass Point Books
Pony Trouble	L	RF	Gasque, Dale Blackwell	Hyperion
Pot of Stone Soup, A	L	TL	Ready Readers	Pearson Learning
Powder Puff Puzzle, The	L	RF	Giff, Patricia Reilly	Bantam Doubleday Dell
Power of Water, The	L	I	Home Connection Collection	Rigby
Princess Josie's Pets	L	RF	Macdonald, Maryann	Hyperion
Priscilla and the Dinosaurs	L	RF	Sunshine	Wright Group/McGraw Hill
Puppy Who Wanted a Boy, The	L	F	Thayer, Jane	Scholastic
Quilt Story, The	L	HF	Johnston, T. & de Paola, T.	Scholastic
Rabbit Stew	L	F	Literacy 2000	Rigby
Rain Forest Adventure	L	F	Pair-It Books	Steck-Vaughn
Rainbows of the Sea	L	I	Thomas, Meredith	Mondo
Rapunzel	L	TL	Literacy 2000	Rigby
Raven's Gift	L	F	Books For Young Learners	Richard C. Owen
Red-Tailed Hawk, The	L	RF	Books For Young Learners	Richard C. Owen
Rescue, The	L	RF	Pacific Learning	Pacific Learning
Riddle of The Red Purse, The	L	RF	Giff, Patricia Reilly	Bantam Doubleday Dell
River Rapids Ride, The	L	RF	Sunshine	Wright Group/McGraw Hill
Robin Hood and the Silver Trophy	L	TL	PM Tales and Plays-Silver	Rigby
Rosie's Story	L	RF	Book Shop	Mondo
Royal Drum, The	L	TL	Book Shop	Mondo
Sadie and the Snowman	L	RF	Morgan, Allen	Scholastic
Salty Dog	L	RF	Rand, Gloria	Henry Holt & Co.
Sam King and Little Bull	L	RF	Wilson, Trevor	Dominie Press
Say "Cheese"	L	RF	Giff, Patricia Reilly	Bantam Doubleday Dell
School Mural, The	L	RF	Pair-It Books	Steck-Vaughn
Schoolyard Mystery, The	L	RF	Levy, Elizabeth	Scholastic
Science-Just Add Salt	L	I	Markle, Sandra	Scholastic
Sea Otters	L	I	Storyteller Nonfiction	Wright Group/McGraw Hill
Secondhand Star	L	RF	Macdonald, Maryann	Hyperion
Secret of Foghorn Island, The	L	F	Step into Reading	Random House
Selfish Giant, The	L	F	Literacy 2000	Rigby
Sharks	L	I	Wonder World	Wright Group/McGraw Hill
Sharks and Rays	L	I	Marine Life For Yng. Readers	Dominie Press
Sheeba	L	F	Noonan, Diana	Dominie Press
Sheep	L	I	PM Animal Facts: Purple	Rigby
Ships	L	I	Wonder World	Wright Group/McGraw Hill
Shopping with a Crocodile	L	F	Pacific Literacy	Pacific Learning
Show Me a Snake Hole	L	RF	Frederick, Shirley	Hampton-Brown
Silent World, A	L	RF	Literacy 2000	Rigby
Silver and Prince	L	RF	PM Story Books -Silver	Rigby
Six Foolish Fishermen	L	TL	Elkin,Benjamin	Children's Press
Six Things to Make	L	I	Book Shop	Mondo
Sky High	L	F	Pair-It Books	Steck-Vaughn
Sleeping Beauty, The	L	TL	PM Tales and Plays-Silver	Rigby
Slim Shorty and the Mules	L	RF	Reading Unlimited	Celebration Press
Snakes!	L	I	Recht Penner, Lucille	Random House
Snakes	L	I	Wonder World	Wright Group/McGraw Hill
Snow Daughter, The	L	TL	Sunshine	Wright Group/McGraw Hill
Snow Goes To Town	L	F	Literacy 2000	Rigby
Snow Walker, The	L	HF	Wetterer, M. K. and Charles M.	Carolrhoda Books
Solo Flyer	L	RF	PM Gold	Rigby
Song Lee and the Hamster Hunt	L	RF	Kline, Suzy	The Penguin Group
Song Lee and the Leech Man	L	RF	Kline, Suzy	The Penguin Group
Song Lee In Room 2B	L	RF	Kline, Suzy	The Penguin Group
Sound, Heat & Light: Energy at Work	L	I	Berger, Melvin	Scholastic
Space Dog and Roy	L	F	Standiford, Natalie	Random House
Space Dog and the Pet Show	L	F	Standiford, Natalie	Random House

Title	Level	Genre	Author/Series	Publisher/Distributor
Space Dog in Trouble	L	F	Standiford, Natalie	Random House
Space Dog the Hero	L	F	Standiford, Natalie	Random House
Space Rock	L	F	Buller, Jon	Random House
Spanish Omelette	L	RF	PM Story Books -Silver	Rigby
Special Present, The	L	RF	Cole, Sally	Wright Group/McGraw Hill
Spectacular Stone Soup	L	RF	Giff, Patricia Reilly	Yearling
Spider's Web, A	L	I	Wonder World	Wright Group/McGraw Hill
Spoiled Rotten	L	RF	DeClements, Barthe	Hyperion
Squanto and the First Thanksgiving	L	HF	Celsi, Teresa	Steck-Vaughn
Stacy Says Good-Bye	L	RF	Giff, Patricia Reilly	Bantam Doubleday Dell
Storms!	L	I	Pair-It Books	Steck-Vaughn
Story of a Book, The	L	I	Reeder, Paul	Wright Group/McGraw Hill
Storytellers	L	I	Storyteller Nonfiction	Wright Group/McGraw Hill
Strange Shoe, The	L	TL	PM Tales and Plays-Silver	Rigby
Strike Me Down with a Stringbean	L	F	Read Alongs	Rigby
Sunshine	L	I	Pebble Books	Grolier, Capstone
Supermarket Chase, The	L	RF	Sunshine	Wright Group/McGraw Hill
Surprise Dinner, The	L	RF	PM Gold	Rigby
Tale of Peter Rabbit, The	L	TL	Potter, Beatrix	Scholastic
Tale of the Golden Goose, The	L	TL	Behr, Alexandra	Hampton-Brown
Tales of Amanda Pig	L	F	Van Leeuwen, Jean	Puffin Books
Teach Us, Amelia Bedelia	L	F	Parish, Peggy	Scholastic
Teacher's Pet	L	F	Dicks, Terrance	Scholastic
Terrible Tiger and Sleeping Beauty	L	TL	New Way: Literature	Steck-Vaughn
Thank You, Amelia Bedelia	L	F	Little Readers	Houghton Mifflin
There's a Rainbow in the River	L	RF	Home Connection Collection	Rigby
Things Don't Change Much	L	RF	Rushby, Pamela	Rigby
Thinking About Ants	L	I	Book Shop	Mondo
This Is My House	L	I	Dorros, Arthur	Scholastic
Three Blind Mice Mystery, The	L	F	Krensky, Stephen	Bantam Doubleday Dell
Three Little Pigs	L	TL	Galdone, Paul	Houghton Mifflin
Three Little Pigs	L	TL	Once Upon a Time	Wright Group/McGraw Hill
Three Little Pigs, The	L	TL	Marshall, James	Scholastic
Three Sillies, The	L	F	Literacy 2000	Rigby
Three Smart Pals	L	RF	Rocklin, Joanne	Scholastic
Three Wishes, The	L	TL	Book Shop	Mondo
Tomato Picking Day	L	I	Pipher, Tom	Wright Group/McGraw Hill
Tongues: Are for Tasting, Licking, Tricking	L	I	Literacy 2000	Rigby
Tooter Pepperday	L	RF	Spinelli, Jerry	Random House
Train Time	L	I	Baehr, Lisa	Hampton-Brown
Trees Belong To Everyone	L	I	Literacy 2000	Rigby
Triceratops on the Farm	L	F	Wesley & the Dinosaurs	Wright Group/McGraw Hill
Triplet Trouble and the Bicycle Race	L	RF	Dadey, D. & Jones, M. T.	Scholastic
Triplet Trouble and the Class Trip	L	RF	Dadey, D. & Jones, M. T.	Scholastic
Triplet Trouble and the Cookie Contest	L	RF	Dadey, D. & Jones, M. T.	Scholastic
Triplet Trouble and the Field Day Disaster	L	RF	Dadey, D. & Jones, M. T.	Scholastic
Triplet Trouble and the Pizza Party	L	RF	Dadey, D. & Jones, M. T.	Scholastic
Triplet Trouble and the Red Heart Race	L	RF	Dadey, D. & Jones, M. T.	Scholastic
Triplet Trouble and the Runaway Reindeer	L	RF	Dadey, D. & Jones, M. T.	Scholastic
Triplet Trouble and the Talent Show	L	RF	Dadey, D. & Jones, M. T.	Scholastic
Triplet Trouble and the Talent Show Mess	L	RF	Dadey, D. & Jones, M. T.	Scholastic
Trouble with Herbert, The	L	F	Eyles, Heather	Mondo
True Story of Balto, The	L	I	Standiford, Natalie	Random House
Twiddle Twins' Haunted House, The	L	F	Goldsmith, Howard	Mondo
Twiddle Twins' Music Box Mystery, The	L	F	Goldsmith, Howard	Mondo
Twiddle Twins' Single Footprint Mystery, The	L	F	Goldsmith, Howard	Mondo
Two Plus One Goes A.P.E.	L	RF	Springstubb, Tricia	Scholastic
Tyrannosaurus the Terrible	L	F	Wesley & the Dinosaurs	Wright Group/McGraw Hill
Upside-Down Reader, The	L	F	Gruber, Wolfram	North-South Books
Using the Library	L	I	Wonder World	Wright Group/McGraw Hill

Title	Level	Genre	Author/Series	Publisher/Distributor
Vampire Trouble	L	F	Dadey, D. & Jones, M. T.	Scholastic
Very Strange Dollhouse, A	L	F	Dussling, Jennifer	Grosset & Dunlap
Veterinarians	L	I	Ready, Dee	Capstone Press
Wacky Jacks	L	RF	Adler, David A.	Random House
Walk With Grandpa, A	L	RF	Read Alongs	Rigby
Walter's Worries	L	F	Pacific Literacy	Pacific Learning
Watch Out, Man-Eating Snake	L	RF	Giff, Patricia Reilly	Bantam Doubleday Dell
Watching the Whales	L	RF	Foundations	Wright Group/McGraw Hill
Wax Museum	L	I	Cook, Donald	Grosset & Dunlap
We're Off to Thunder Mountain	L	RF	Book Shop	Mondo
Whales-The Gentle Giants	L	I	Milton, Joyce	Random House
What a Great Idea!	L	RF	Shelton, Flip	Rigby
What Is Matter?	L	I	Schaefer, Lola M.	Benchmark Education
What Joy Found	L	RF	Ready Readers	Pearson Learning
What Kind of Babysitter Is This?	L	RF	Johnson, Dolores	Scholastic
What Next, Baby Bear?	L	F	Murphy, Jill	Dial
What's It Like to Be a Fish?	L	I	Little Readers	Houghton Mifflin
When I Broke the Office Window	L	RF	City Kids	Rigby
When the Giants Came to Town	L	F	Leonard, Marcia	Scholastic
When Tony Got Lost at the Zoo	L	RF	City Kids	Rigby
Why Rabbits Have Long Ears	L	TL	Literacy 2000	Rigby
Why the Leopard Has Spots	L	I	Pair-It Books	Steck-Vaughn
Why The Sea Is Salty	L	TL	Literacy 2000	Rigby
Wild Swans, The	L	TL	Tales from Hans Andersen	Wright Group/McGraw Hill
Working on Water	L	I	Home Connection Collection	Rigby
Yellow Overalls	L	F	Literacy 2000	Rigby
Young Arthur Ashe: Brave Champion	L	B	First Start Biography	Troll
Young Clara Barton: Battlefield Nurse	L	B	First Start Biography	Troll
Young Jackie Robinson: Baseball Hero	L	B	First Start Biography	Troll
Young Rosa Parks: Civil Rights Heroine	L	B	First Start Biography	Troll
Young Thurgood Marshall: Fighter for Equality	L	B	First Start Biography	Troll
Abby	M	RF	Hanel, Wolfram	North-South Books
Abe Lincoln's Hat	M	B	Brenner, Martha	Random House
Adventures of Ratman	M	F	Weiss, Ellen & Freidman, Mel	Random House
Afternoon on the Amazon	M	F	Osborne, Mary Pope	Random House
Aliens Don't Wear Braces	M	F	Dadey, D. & Jones, M. T.	Scholastic
Aliens for Breakfast	M	F	Etra, J. & Spinner, S.	Random House
Aliens for Dinner	M	F	Spinner, Stephanie	Random House
Aliens for Lunch	M	F	Spinner, S. & Etra, J.	Random House
All-Star Fever	M	RF	Christopher, Matt	Little, Brown & Co.
Alligator Alley	M	RF	Schultz, Irene	Wright Group/McGraw Hill
Alligator, The	M	I	Crewe, Sabrina	Steck-Vaughn
Amazing Birds of the Rain Forest	M	I	Daniel, Claire	Steck-Vaughn
Angels Don't Know Karate	M	F	Dadey, D. & Jones, M. T.	Scholastic
Animals at Work	M	I	Graham, Pamela	Rigby
Animals in Danger	M	I	Pair-It Books	Steck-Vaughn
Arctic Life	M	I	Robinson, F.R.	Steck-Vaughn
Arctic Tundra	M	I	Forman, Michael H.	Children's Press
Armies of Ants	M	I	Retan, Walter	Scholastic
Art Around the World	M	I	Discovery World	Rigby
Art Lesson, The	M	B	dePaola, Tomie	Putnam
Arthur Accused!	M	F	Brown, Marc	Little, Brown & Co.
Arthur and the Big Blow-Up	M	F	Brown, Marc	Little, Brown & Co.
Arthur and the Cootie-Catcher	M	F	Brown, Marc	Little, Brown & Co.
Arthur and the Crunch Cereal Contest	M	F	Brown, Marc	Little, Brown & Co.
Arthur and the Lost Diary	M	F	Brown, Marc	Little, Brown & Co.
Arthur and the Popularity Test	M	F	Brown, Marc	Little, Brown & Co.
Arthur and the Scare-Your-Pants-Off Club	M	F	Brown, Marc	Little, Brown & Co.
Arthur and the TL Contest	M	F	Brown, Marc	Little, Brown & Co.
Arthur Makes the Team	M	F	Brown, Marc	Little, Brown & Co.

Title	Level	Genre	Author/Series	Publisher/Distributor
Arthur Rocks with BINKY	M	F	Brown, Marc	Little, Brown & Co.
Arthur's Mystery Envelope	M	F	Brown, Marc	Little, Brown & Co.
Asteroid, The	M	F	PM Gold	Rigby
Astronauts	M	I	Deedrick, Tami	Capstone Press
At the Edge of the Sea	M	I	Sunshine	Wright Group/McGraw Hill
Aunt Flossie's Hats (and Crab Cakes Later)	M	RF	Howard, Elizabeth	Scholastic
Auto Mechanics	M	I	Boraas, Tracey	Capstone Press
Autumn	M	I	Pebble Books	Capstone Press
Back to the Dentist	M	RF	City Kids	Rigby
Bad Dad List, The	M	RF	Kenna, Anna	Pacific Learning
Bakers	M	I	Deedrick, Tami	Capstone Press
Baseball Flyhawk	M	RF	Christopher, Matt	Little, Brown & Co.
Baseball Heroes, The	M	RF	Schultz, Irene	Wright Group/McGraw Hill
Baseball Pals	M	RF	Christopher, Matt	Little, Brown & Co.
Basket Counts, The	M	RF	Christopher, Matt	Little, Brown & Co.
Bats	M	I	PM Animal Facts Gold	Rigby
Bear, The	M	I	Crewe, Sabrina	Steck-Vaughn
Bears' Christmas	M	F	Berenstain, Stan, & Jan	Random House
Bears On Hemlock Mountain, The	M	RF	Dalgliesh, Alice	Aladdin Paperback
Bears' Picnic	M	F	Berenstain, Stan, & Jan	Random House
Beast and the Halloween Horror	M	RF	Giff, Patricia Reilly	Bantam Doubleday Dell
Beast in Ms. Rooney's Room, The	M	RF	Giff, Patricia Reilly	Bantam Doubleday Dell
Beating the Drought	M	RF	Noonan, Diana	Pacific Learning
Beauregard the Cat	M	RF	Book Shop	Mondo
Beaver, The	M	I	Crewe, Sabrina	Steck-Vaughn
Bee, The	M	I	Crewe, Sabrina	Steck-Vaughn
Beekeeper, The	M	I	Literacy 2000	Rigby
Berenstain Bear Scouts and the Coughing Catfish	M	F	Berenstain, Stan & Jan	Scholastic
Berenstain Bears and the Ghost of the Auto Graveyard, The	M	F	Berenstain, Stan & Jan	Random House
Berenstain Bears & the Missing Honey	M.	F	Berenstain, Stan, & Jan	Random House
Best Wishes for Eddie	M	RF	Nayer, Judy	Pearson Learning
Big Chase, The	M	F	SupaDoopers	Sundance
Big Fish, The	M	RF	Yukish, Joe	Kaeden Books
Bigfoot Doesn't Square Dance	M	F	Dadey, D. & Jones, M. T.	Scholastic
Bird Behavior: Living Together	M	I	Sunshine	Wright Group/McGraw Hill
Bird in the Basket, The	M	RF	Beveridge, Barbara	Pacific Learning
Birds of the City	M	I	Sunshine	Wright Group/McGraw Hill
Blue Hill Meadows, The	M	RF	Rylant, Cynthia	Harcourt Brace
Blue Ribbon Blues	M	RF	Spinelli, Jerry	Random House
Blueberries for Sal	M	RF	McCloskey, Robert	Scholastic
Boats Afloat	M	I	Sunshine	Wright Group/McGraw Hill
Bogeymen Don't Play Football	M	F	Dadey, D. & Jones, M. T.	Scholastic
Book About Your Skeleton, A	M	I	Gross, Ruth Belov	Scholastic
Boundless Grace	M	RF	Hoffman, Mary	Scholastic
Boy Who Stretched to the Sky, The	M	F	Book Bank	Wright Group/McGraw Hill
Brain-in-a-Box	M	F	Matthews, Steve	Sundance
Brave Maddie Egg	M	RF	Standiford, Natalie	Random House
Brith The Terrible	M	F	Literacy 2000	Rigby
Buddy: The First Seeing Eye Dog	M	I	Moore, Eva	Scholastic
Buffalo Before Breakfast	M	F	Osborne, Mary Pope	Random House
Buffalo, The	M	I	Crewe, Sabrina	Steck-Vaughn
Build, Build, Build	M	I	Sunshine	Wright Group/McGraw Hill
Build It Strong!	M	I	First Science	Children's Press
Bull Harris and the Purple Ooze	M	RF	SupaDoopers	Sundance
Buried Eye, The	M	F	Schultz, Irene	Wright Group/McGraw Hill
Buster Baxter, Cat Saver	M	F	Brown, Marc	Little, Brown & Co.
Buster Makes the Grade	M	F	Brown, Marc	Little, Brown & Co.
Buster's Dino Dilemma	M	F	Brown, Marc	Little, Brown & Co.
Butterfly Farm Burglar, The	M	RF	Schultz, Irene	Wright Group/McGraw Hill

Title	Level	Genre	Author/Series	Publisher/Distributor
Butterfly, The	M	I	Crewe, Sabrina	Steck-Vaughn
Buttons for General Washington	M	HF	Roop, Peter & Connie	Carolrhoda Books
Cake, The	M	RF	Read Alongs	Rigby
Can Do, Jenny Archer	M	RF	Conford, Ellen	Random House
Case for Jenny Archer, A	M	RF	Conford, Ellen	Random House
Case of the Elevator Duck, The	M	RF	Berends, Polly Berrien	Random House
Case of the Hungry Stranger, The	M	RF	Bonsall, Crosby	HarperTrophy
Cat and Rat	M	TL	Young, Ed	Henry Holt & Co.
Catch Me If You Can!: The Roadrunner	M	I	Chukran, Bobbi A.	Wright Group/McGraw Hill
Catch That Pass!	M	RF	Christopher, Matt	Little, Brown & Co.
Catcher With a Glass Arm	M	RF	Christopher, Matt	Little, Brown & Co.
Catcher's Mask, The	M	RF	Christopher, Matt	Little, Brown & Co.
Catching the Sun	M	TL	Paul, Michele	Wright Group/McGraw Hill
Caterpillars	M	I	Book Shop	Mondo
Caves	M	I	Discovery World	Rigby
Center Court Sting	M	RF	Christopher, Matt	Little, Brown & Co.
Centerfield Ballhawk	M	RF	Christopher, Matt	Little, Brown & Co.
Chair For My Mother, A	M	RF	Williams, Vera B.	Scholastic
Challenge at Second Base	M	RF	Christopher, Matt	Little, Brown & Co.
Cherries and Cherry Pits	M	RF	Williams, Vera B.	Houghton Mifflin
Chester the Wizard	M	F	Reading Unlimited	Celebration Press
Chicken Soup with Rice	M	F	Sendak, Maurice	Harper Collins
Chickens Have Chicks	M	I	Animals and Their Young	Compass Point Books
Children Around the World	M	I	People, Spaces & Places	Rand McNally
Circus Mystery, The	M	RF	Schultz, Irene	Wright Group/McGraw Hill
Cities Around the World	M	I	Pair-It Books	Steck-Vaughn
City Green	M	RF	DiSalvo-Ryan, DyAnne	Scholastic
Civil War on Sunday	M	F	Osborner, Mary Pope	Random House
Close Call, A	M	RF	Kenna, Anna	Pacific Learning
Cloudy With a Chance of Meatballs	M	F	Barrett, Judi	Atheneum Books
Clue in the Castle, The	M	RF	Schultz, Irene	Wright Group/McGraw Hill
Clues in the Woods	M	RF	Parrish, Peggy	Bantam
Cobwebs, Elephants, and Stars	M	F	Sunshine	Wright Group/McGraw Hill
Comeback Challenge, The	M	RF	Christopher, Matt	Little, Brown & Co.
Connie's Dance	M	RF	Windmill Books	Rigby
Construction Workers	M	I	Deedrick, Tami	Capstone Press
Copper Lady, The	M	HF	Ross, Alice & Kent	Carolrhoda Books
Corey's Christmas Wish	M	RF	Pony Tails	Skylark
Corn: An American Indian Gift	M	I	Pair-It Books	Steck-Vaughn
Count Your Money with the Polk Street School	M	RF	Giff, Patricia Reilly	Bantam Doubleday Dell
Counterfeit Tackle, The	M	RF	Christopher, Matt	Little, Brown & Co.
Cows Have Calves	M	I	Animals and Their Young	Compass Point Books
Crabs	M	I	Wonder World	Wright Group/McGraw Hill
Crabs, Shrimp, & Lobsters	M	I	Marine Life For Yng. Readers	Dominie
CrackerJack Halfback	M	RF	Christopher, Matt	Little, Brown & Co.
Crane Wife, The	M	F	Pair-It Books	Steck-Vaughn
Crinkum Crankum	M	F	Pacific Literacy	Pacific Learning
Cupids Don't Flip Hamburgers	M	F	Dadey, D. & Jones, M. T.	Scholastic
Cyclops Doesn't Roller-Skate	M	F	Dadey, D. & Jones, M. T.	Scholastic
Dark Side of the Creek, The	M	RF	Harlow, Joan Hiatt	Wright Group/McGraw Hill
Day at the Races, A	M	RF	Michaels, Eric	Pearson Learning
Day for J.J. and Me, A	M	RF	Evangeline Nicholas Collection	Wright Group/McGraw Hill
Day of Ahmed's Secret, A	M	RF	Heide, F. P. & Gilliland, J. H.	Scholastic
Day of the Dragon King	M	F	Osborne, Mary Pope	Random House
Day the Sky Turned Green, The	M	F	Reeves, Barbara	Pearson Learning
Dayton and the Happy Tree	M	RF	Sunshine	Wright Group/McGraw Hill
Dear Grandma	M	I	Storyteller Nonfiction	Wright Group/McGraw Hill
Dentists	M	I	Ready, Dee	Capstone Press
Desert Treasure	M	RF	Pair-It Books	Steck-Vaughn
Diamond Champs, The	M	RF	Christopher, Matt	Little, Brown & Co.

Title	Level	Genre	Author/Series	Publisher/Distributor
Diamond of Doom, The	M	RF	Schultz, Irene	Wright Group/McGraw Hill
Dingoes at Dinnertime	M	F	Osborne, Mary Pope	Random House
Dinosaurs Before Dark	M	F	Osborne, Mary Pope	Random House
Dirt Bike Racer	M	RF	Christopher, Matt	Little, Brown & Co.
Dirt Bike Runaway	M	RF	Christopher, Matt	Little, Brown & Co.
Discovering Dinosaurs	M	F	Little Books	Sadlier-Oxford
Doctors	M	I	Ready, Dee	Capstone Press
Dog that Stole Football Plays, The	M	F	Christopher, Matt	Little, Brown & Co.
Dog's Best Friend, A	M	RF	Pair-It Books	Steck-Vaughn
Dolphins at Daybreak	M	F	Osborne, Mary Pope	Random House
Don't Forget the Bacon	M	RF	Hutchins, Pat	Puffin Books
Donkey	M	F	Literacy 2000	Rigby
Double Play at Short	M	RF	Christopher, Matt	Little, Brown & Co.
Double Switch	M	RF	Noonan, Diana	Pacific Learning
Double Trouble	M	TL	Literacy 2000	Rigby
Dracula Doesn't Drink Lemonade	M	F	Dadey, D. & Jones, M. T.	Scholastic
Dragons Don't Cook Pizza	M	F	Dadey, D. & Jones, M. T.	Scholastic
Dream Boat	M	RF	Nagelkerke, Bill	Rigby
Dream Catchers	M	RF	Storyteller-Night Crickets	Wright Group/McGraw Hill
Drinking Gourd, The	M	HF	Monjo, F. N.	HarperTrophy
Drought Marker, The	M	F	Literacy 2000	Rigby
Duck in the Gun, The	M	F	Literacy 2000	Rigby
Ducks Crossing	M	RF	Wilson, Trevor	Pacific Learning
Eat!	M	RF	Kroll, Steven	Hyperion
Edward's Night Light	M	RF	Reading Corners	Dominie
Eeny, Meeny, Miney Mole	M	F	Yolen, Jane	Harcourt Brace
Eggs and Baby Birds	M	I	Sunshine	Wright Group/McGraw Hill
Elaine and the Flying Frog	M	RF	Chang, Heidi	Scholastic
Elbert's Bad Word	M	RF	Wood, Audrey	Harcourt Brace
Eliza the Hypnotizer	M	RF	Granger, Michele	Scholastic
Elmer and the Dragon	M	F	Gannett, Ruth	Random House
Elves Don't Wear Hard Hats	M	F	Dadey, D. & Jones, M. T.	Scholastic
Emilio and the River	M	RF	Sunshine	Wright Group/McGraw Hill
Emily Arrow Promises to Do Better This Year	M	RF	Giff, Patricia Reilly	Bantam Doubleday Dell
Emily Eyefinger	M	F	Ball, Duncan	Aladdin
Emma, the Birthday Clown	M	RF	Sunshine	Wright Group/McGraw Hill
Er-Lang and the Suns: A Tale from China	M	TL	Folk Tales	Mondo
Erosion	M	I	Schaefer, Lola M.	Benchmark Education
Everybody Cooks Rice	M	I	Dooley, Norah	Scholastic
Everyday Forces	M	I	Discovery World	Rigby
Explorers: Searching for Adventure	M	I	Pair-It Books	Steck-Vaughn
Expressway Jewels	M	RF	Evangeline Nicholas Collection	Wright Group/McGraw Hill
Farmer Boy Days	M	HF	Wilder, Laura Ingalls	HarperTrophy
Farmers	M	I	Ready, Dee	Capstone Press
Fibers Made by People	M	I	Sunshine	Wright Group/McGraw Hill
Fiesta!	M	I	Festivals and Holidays	Children's Press
Fighting Tackle	M	RF	Christopher, Matt	Little, Brown & Co.
Fiji Flood, The	M	F	Schultz, Irene	Wright Group/McGraw Hill
Fire Fighters	M	I	Ready, Dee	Capstone Press
Fireflies in the Night	M	I	Hawes, Judy	HarperTrophy
First Hot-Air Balloons, The	M	I	Moore, Philip	Wright Group/McGraw Hill
Fish Face	M	RF	Giff, Patricia Reilly	Bantam Doubleday Dell
Fishy, Flashy Fourth, The	M	RF	Schultz, Irene	Wright Group/McGraw Hill
Five True Dog Stories	M	I	Davidson, Margaret	Scholastic
Five True Horse Stories	M	I	Davidson, Margaret	Scholastic
Flat Stanley	M	F	Brown, Jeff	HarperTrophy
Flowers for Mrs. Falepau	M	RF	Book Bank	Wright Group/McGraw Hill
Flying Trunk, The	M	TL	Tales from Hans Andersen	Wright Group/McGraw Hill
Football Fugitive	M	RF	Christopher, Matt	Little, Brown & Co.
Forests, Grasslands, Deserts	M	I	People, Spaces & Places	Rand McNally

Title	Level	Genre	Author/Series	Publisher/Distributor
Forgotten Hiding Place, The	M	RF	Schultz, Irene	Wright Group/McGraw Hill
Fox Steals Home, The	M	RF	Christopher, Matt	Little, Brown & Co.
Foxes	M	I	PM Animal Facts: Gold	Rigby
Frankenstein Doesn't Plant Petunias	M	F	Dadey, D. & Jones, M. T.	Scholastic
Frankenstein Doesn't Slam Hockey Pucks	M	F	Dadey, D. & Jones, M. T.	Scholastic
Freckle Juice	M	RF	Blume, Judy	Bantam Doubleday Dell
Frederick Douglass: Fights For Freedom	M	B	Davidson, Margaret	Language for Learning Assoc.
Freeze, Goldilocks!	M	F	Pacific Literacy	Pacific Learning
Frida María: A Story of the Old Southwest	M	RF	Lattimore, Deborah Nourse	Harcourt Brace
Frog, The	M	I	Crewe, Sabrina	Steck-Vaughn
From Cow to Milk Carton	M	I	Miles, Annie	Wright Group/McGraw Hill
Fun with Fingerprints	M	I	Sokoloff, Myka-Lynne	Wright Group/McGraw Hill
Funny Old Man and the Funny Old Woman, The	M	F	Book Shop	Mondo
Fuzz and the Glass Eye	M	RF	Pulford, Elizabeth	Rigby
Game for Jamie, A	M	RF	Sunshine	Wright Group/McGraw Hill
Garbage Collectors	M	I	Deedrick, Tami	Capstone Press
Gargoyles Don't Drive School Buses	M	F	Dadey, D. & Jones, M. T.	Scholastic
Genies Don't Ride Bicycles	M	F	Dadey, D. & Jones, M. T.	Scholastic
George Washington's Mother	M	B	Fritz, Jean	Scholastic
Georgia O'Keeffe	M	B	Lowery, Linda	Carolrhoda Books
Ghost Dog	M	F	Allen, Eleanor	Scholastic
Ghost in Tent 19, The	M	F	O'Connor, J. & J.	Random House
Ghost School	M	F	Clifford, Eth	Scholastic
Ghost Town at Sundown	M	F	Osborne, Mary Pope	Random House
Ghost Town Treasure	M	RF	Bulla, Clyde Robert	The Penguin Group
Ghosts Don't Eat Potato Chips	M	F	Dadey, D. & Jones, M. T.	Scholastic
Ghouls Don't Scoop Ice Cream	M	F	Dadey, D. & Jones, M. T.	Scholastic
Giant Jack's Boots	M	F	Book Bank	Wright Group/McGraw Hill
Giant's Cake	M	F	Learning Media	Mondo
Giants Don't Go Snowboarding	M	F	Dadey, D. & Jones, M. T.	Scholastic
Gladys and Max Love Bob	M	RF	Book Bank	Wright Group/McGraw Hill
Goblins Don't Play Video Games	M	RF	Dadey, D. & Jones, M. T.	Scholastic
Golden Goose, The	M	TL	Literacy 2000	Rigby
Good-for-Nothing Dog, The	M	RF	Schultz, Irene	Wright Group/McGraw Hill
Great Dinosaur Hunt, The	M	F	Schultz, Irene	Wright Group/McGraw Hill
Great Houdini, The: World Famous Magician and Escape Artist	M	B	Kulling, Monica	Random House
Great Ice Battle, The	M	F	Abbott, Tony	Scholastic
Great Quarterback Switch, The	M	RF	Christopher, Matt	Little, Brown & Co.
Great Riddle Mystery, The	M	RF	MacClean, James R.	Pearson Learning
Greatest Binnie in the World, The	M	RF	Sunshine	Wright Group/McGraw Hill
Greedy Cat and the Birthday Cake	M	F	Cowley, Joy	Pacific Learning
Greeks, The	M	I	Footsteps in Time	Children's Press
Gremlins Don't Chew Bubble Gum	M	F	Dadey, D. & Jones, M. T.	Scholastic
Hand Tools	M	I	Wonder World	Wright Group/McGraw Hill
Hard Drive to Short	M	RF	Christopher, Matt	Little, Brown & Co.
Haunted Halloween, The	M	F	Schultz, Irene	Wright Group/McGraw Hill
Henry's Choice	M	RF	Reading Unlimited	Celebration Press
Hercules Doesn't Pull Teeth	M	F	Dadey, D. & Jones, M. T.	Scholastic
Hidden Hand, The	M	RF	Schultz, Irene	Wright Group/McGraw Hill
Hilary & the Lions	M	F	Desaix, Frank	Farrar, Straus and Giroux
Hit-Away Kid, The	M	RF	Christopher, Matt	Little, Brown & Co.
Hocus Pocus	M	I	Wildcats	Wright Group/McGraw Hill
Homes Are for Living	M	I	Cumpiano, Ina	Hampton-Brown
Honey Bees	M	I	Kahkonen, Sharon	Steck-Vaughn
Hoopstars: Go to the Hoop!	M	RF	Hughes, Dean	Random House
Horrakapotchkin	M	F	Pacific Literacy	Pacific Learning
Horses Have Foals	M	I	Animals and Their Young	Compass Point Books
Hour of the Olympics	M	F	Osborne, Mary Pope	Random House
House of Mirrors, The	M	F	Weaver, Betty-May	Wright Group/McGraw Hill

Title	Level	Genre	Author/Series	Publisher/Distributor
House of the Horrible Ghosts	M	F	Hayes, Geoffrey	Random House
Houses	M	I	Wonder World	Wright Group/McGraw Hill
How a Volcano is Formed	M	I	Wonder World	Wright Group/McGraw Hill
How Bullfrog Found His Sound	M	F	Michaels, Eric	Pearson Learning
How Did This City Grow?	M	I	Schaefer, Lola M.	Benchmark Education
How Flamingos Came to Have Red Legs: A South American Folk Tale	M	TL	Jensen, Ned	Wright Group/McGraw Hill
How Flexible Are You?	M	I	Marks, Ashley	Wright Group/McGraw Hill
How I Met Archie	M	RF	Kenna, Anna	Pacific Learning
How the Giraffe Became a Giraffe	M	TL	Sunshine	Wright Group/McGraw Hill
How To Make a Kite	M	I	Reeder, Paul	Wright Group/McGraw Hill
Howie Merton and the Magic Dust	M	F	Reeves, Faye Couch	Random House
Howling at the Hauntly's	M	RF	Dadey, Debbie & Jones, Marcia	Scholastic
Hue Boy	M	RF	Mitchell, Rita Phillips	The Penguin Group
Hunt for Pirate Gold, The	M	F	Schultz, Irene	Wright Group/McGraw Hill
Hurdles and Jumps	M	I	Reeder, Tracey	Wright Group/McGraw Hill
I Can't Said the Ant	M	F	Cameron, Polly	Scholastic
I Hate Camping	M	RF	Petersen, P. J.	The Penguin Group
I Hate Company	M	RF	Petersen, P.J.	The Penguin Group
I Like Shopping	M	RF	Sunshine	Wright Group/McGraw Hill
I Love the Beach	M	B	Literacy 2000	Rigby
I. M. Pei	M	B	Biography	Benchmark Education
I'm No One Else But Me	M	RF	Book Bank	Wright Group/McGraw Hill
I'm So Hungry and Other Plays	M	F	Learning Media	Pacific Learning
Ice Dove and Other Stories, The	M	RF	deAnda, Diane	Arte Publico
Ice Magic	M	RF	Christopher, Matt	Little, Brown & Co.
In a Pickle	M	RF	SupaDoopers	Sundance
In Aunt Lucy's Kitchen	M	RF	Rylant, Cynthia	Aladdin
In Danger	M	I	Home Connection Collection	Rigby
In the Clouds	M	RF	Literacy 2000	Rigby
In the Dinosaur's Paw	M	RF	Giff, Patricia Reilly	Bantam Doubleday Dell
Inside a Rain Forest	M	I	Pair-It Books	Steck-Vaughn
Inventors: Making Things Better	M	I	Pair-It Books	Steck-Vaughn
Invisible Dog, The	M	F	King-Smith, Dick	Alfred A. Knopf
Invisible in the Third Grade	M	RF	Cuyler, Margery	Scholastic
Island Baby	M	RF	Keller, Holly	Scholastic
Island of the Skog, The	M	F	Kellogg, Steven	Dial Books
It's About Time	M	I	Storyteller Nonfiction	Wright Group/McGraw Hill
Jelly Beans	M	I	Stadler, Charlotte	Benchmark Education Co.
Jenny Archer, Author	M	RF	Conford, Ellen	Little, Brown & Co.
Jenny Archer to the Rescue	M	RF	Conford, Ellen	Little, Brown & Co.
Jigsaw Jones Mystery: The Case of the Christmas Snowman	M	RF	Ruller, James	Scholastic
Job for Jenny Archer, A	M	RF	Conford, Ellen	Random House
John James Audubon	M	B	Biography	Benchmark Education
Johnny Long Legs	M	RF	Christopher, Matt	Little, Brown & Co.
Jumping Into Nothing	M	RF	Willner-Pardo, Gina	Houghton Mifflin
Junie B. Jones and a Little Monkey Business	M	RF	Park, Barbara	Random House
Junie B. Jones and Her Big Fat Mouth	M	RF	Park, Barbara	Random House
Junie B. Jones and Some Sneaky Peeky Spying	M	RF	Park, Barbara	Random House
Junie B. Jones and that Meanie Jim's Birthday	M	RF	Park, Barbara	Random House
Junie B. Jones and the Mushy Gushy Valentine	M	RF	Park, Barbara	Random House
Junie B. Jones and the Stupid Smelly Bus	M	RF	Park, Barbara	Random House
Junie B. Jones and the Yucky Blucky Fruitcake	M	RF	Park, Barbara	Random House
Junie B. Jones Has a Monster Under Her Bed	M	RF	Park, Barbara	Random House
Junie B. Jones Has a Peep in Her Pocket	M	RF	Park, Barbara	Random House
Junie B. Jones Is a Beauty Shop Guy	M	RF	Park, Barbara	Random House
Junie B. Jones Is a Party Animal	M	RF	Park, Barbara	Random House
Junie B. Jones is (almost) a Flower Girl	M	RF	Park, Barbara	Random House
Junie B. Jones Is Not a Crook	M	RF	Park, Barbara	Random House

Title	Level	Genre	Author/Series	Publisher/Distributor
Junie B. Jones Loves Handsome Warren	M	RF	Park, Barbara	Random House
Junie B. Jones Smells Something Fishy	M	RF	Park, Barbara	Random House
Junior Gymnasts: Katie's Big Move	M	RF	Slater, Teddy	Scholastic
Kangaroo, The	M	I	Crewe, Sabrina	Steck-Vaughn
Kate Shelley and the Midnight Express	M	B	Wetterer, Margaret	Carolrhoda Books
Keep Ms. Sugarman in the Fourth Grade	M	RF	Levy, Elizabeth	HarperTrophy
Kid Who Only Hit Homers, The	M	RF	Christopher, Matt	Little, Brown & Co.
Kids Can Cook	M	I	Literacy 2000	Rigby
Kids in Ms. Colman's Class: Author Day	M	RF	Martin, Ann M.	Scholastic
King Arthur	M	F	Brown, Marc	Little, Brown & Co.
Knight at Dawn, The	M	F	Osborne, Mary Pope	Random House
Knights Don't Teach Piano	M	F	Dadey, D. & Jones, M. T.	Scholastic
Korky Paul: Biography of an Illustrator	M	B	Heapy, Teresa	Rigby
Laura and Mr. Edwards	M	HF	Wilder, Laura Ingalls	HarperTrophy
Laura and Nellie	M	HF	Wilder, Laura Ingalls	HarperTrophy
Laura's Ma	M	HF	Wilder, Laura Ingalls	HarperTrophy
Laura's Pa	M	HF	Wilder, Laura Ingalls	HarperTrophy
Lazy Jackal, The	M	F	Sunshine	Wright Group/McGraw Hill
Lazy Lions, Lucky Lambs	M	RF	Giff, Patricia Reilly	Bantam Doubleday Dell
Leaping Lizards	M	I	Stadler, Charlotte	Benchmark Education Co.
Lentil	M	RF	McCloskey, Robert	Scholastic
Leprechauns Don't Play Basketball	M	F	Dadey, D. & Jones, M. T.	Scholastic
Let's Get Moving	M	I	Literacy 2000	Rigby
Let's Go, Philadelphia!	M	RF	Giff, Patricia Reilly	Bantam Doubleday Dell
Letting Swift River Go	M	HF	Yolen, Jane	Little, Brown & Co.
Librarians	M	I	Ready, Dee	Capstone Press
Life in the Desert	M	I	Pair-It Books	Steck-Vaughn
Lighthouse Mermaid, The	M	F	Karr, Kathleen	Hyperion
Lion and the Mouse, The	M	TL	Aesop's Fables	Dominie
Lions at Lunchtime	M	F	Osborne, Mary Pope	Random House
Listening in Bed	M	RF	Book Bank	Wright Group/McGraw Hill
Little Firefighter, The	M	RF	Sunshine	Wright Group/McGraw Hill
Little Hawk's New Name	M	HF	Bolognese, Don	Scholastic
Little House Farm Days	M	HF	Wilder, Laura Ingalls	HarperTrophy
Little House Friends	M	HF	Wilder, Laura Ingalls	HarperTrophy
Little Lefty	M	RF	Christopher, Matt	Little, Brown & Co.
Little, Little Man, The	M	F	Book Bank	Wright Group/McGraw Hill
Little Old Lady Who Danced on the Moon, The	M	RF	Sunshine	Wright Group/McGraw Hill
Little Shopping, A	M	RF	Rylant, Cynthia	Aladdin
Little Swan	M	RF	Geras, Adele	Random House
Little Tin Soldier, The	M	TL	Tales from Hans Andersen	Wright Group/McGraw Hill
Little Whale, The	M	F	Sunshine	Wright Group/McGraw Hill
Little Women	M	HF	Bullseye	Random House
Littles and the Great Halloween Scare, The	M	F	Peterson, John	Scholastic
Littles and the Lost Children, The	M	F	Peterson, John	Scholastic
Littles and the Terrible Tiny Kid, The	M	F	Peterson, John	Scholastic
Littles and the Trash Tinies, The	M	F	Peterson, John	Scholastic
Littles Give a Party, The	M	F	Peterson, John	Scholastic
Littles Go Exploring, The	M	F	Peterson, John	Scholastic
Littles Go to School, The	M	F	Peterson, John	Scholastic
Littles Have a Wedding, The	M	F	Peterson, John	Scholastic
Littles Take a Trip, The	M	F	Peterson, John	Scholastic
Littles, The	M	F	Peterson, John	Scholastic
Littles to the Rescue, The	M	F	Peterson, John	Scholastic
Lizards and Salamanders	M	I	Reading Unlimited	Celebration Press
Locked in the Library!	M	F	Brown, Marc	Little, Brown & Co.
Long Grass of Tumbledown Road	M	F	Read Alongs	Rigby
Long, Long Ago	M	I	Literacy 2000	Rigby
Long Shot for Paul	M	RF	Christopher, Matt	Little, Brown & Co.
Long-Lost Friends, The	M	RF	Schultz, Irene	Wright Group/McGraw Hill

Title	Level	Genre	Author/Series	Publisher/Distributor
Look at Dogs, A	M	I	Pair-It Books	Steck-Vaughn
Look at Snakes, A	M	I	Pair-It Books	Steck-Vaughn
Look at Spiders, A	M	I	Pair-It-Books	Steck-Vaughn
Look What I Made!	M	I	Literacy 2000	Rigby
Look Who's Playing First Base	M	RF	Christopher, Matt	Little, Brown & Co.
Looking for Dad	M	RF	SupaDoopers	Sundance
Lost and Found Game, The	M	RF	Nayer, Judy	Pearson Learning
Lost Children, The	M	TL	Goble, Paul	Aladdin
Lost in Space	M	SF	Pacific Literacy	Pacific Learning
Lucky Baseball Bat, The	M	RF	Christopher, Matt	Little, Brown & Co.
Lucky Last Luke	M	RF	Clark, Margaret	Sundance
Mad Scientist, The	M	F	Schultz, Irene	Wright Group/McGraw Hill
Magic Ride, The	M	F	Book Bank	Wright Group/McGraw Hill
Mail Carriers	M	I	Ready, Dee	Capstone Press
Make a Cloud, Measure the Wind	M	I	Reimer, Luther	Wright Group/McGraw Hill
Making Friends on Beacon Street	M	RF	Literacy 2000	Rigby
Making Lily Laugh!	M	RF	Dreyer, Ellen	Pearson Learning
Mall Mystery, The	M	F	Schultz, Irene	Wright Group/McGraw Hill
Man Out at First	M	RF	Christopher, Matt	Little Brown & Co.
Manatees and Dugongs	M	I	Cole, Sally	Wright Group/McGraw Hill
Map Mysteries	M	I	Gard, Stephen	Rigby
Mario Mixwell	M	B	Reimer, Luther	Wright Group/McGraw Hill
Martians Don't Take Temperatures	M	F	Dadey, D. & Jones, M. T.	Scholastic
Martin's Mighty Hit	M	RF	Windmill Books	Rigby
Marvelous Treasure, The	M	RF	Sunshine	Wright Group/McGraw Hill
Marvin and the Mean Words	M	RF	Kline, Suzy	PaperStar
Marvin Redpost: A Flying Birthday Cake?	M	RF	Sachar, Louis	Random House
Marvin Redpost: Alone in His Teacher's House	M	RF	Sachar, Louis	Random House
Marvin Redpost (Class President)	M	RF	Sachar, Louis	Random House
Marvin Redpost: Is He a Girl?	M	RF	Sachar, Louis	Random House
Marvin Redpost: Kidnapped at Birth?	M	RF	Sachar, Louis	Random House
Marvin Redpost, Super Fast, Out of Control!	M	RF	Sachar, Louis	Random House
Marvin Redpost: Why Pick on Me?	M	RF	Sachar, Louis	Random House
Mary Marony and the Chocolate Surprise	M	RF	Kline, Suzy	Bantam Doubleday Dell
Mary Marony and the Snake	M	RF	Kline, Suzy	Bantam Doubleday Dell
Mary Marony Hides Out	M	RF	Kline, Suzy	Bantam Doubleday Dell
Mary Marony, Mummy Girl	M	RF	Kline, Suzy	Bantam Doubleday Dell
Masks	M	I	Literacy 2000	Rigby
Measuring Tools	M	I	Daronco, Mickey & Presti, Lori	Benchmark Education
Medal for Nickie, A	M	RF	Sunshine	Wright Group/McGraw Hill
Meet the Villarreals	M	B	Kratky, Lada Josefa	Hampton-Brown
Mermaids Don't Run Track	M	F	Dadey, D. & Jones, M. T.	Scholastic
Midnight on the Moon	M	F	Osborne, Mary Pope	Random House
Milo's Great Invention	M	RF	Pair-It Books	Steck-Vaughn
Minerva's Dream	M	F	Pair-It Books	Steck-Vaughn
Miracle at the Plate	M	RF	Christopher, Matt	Little, Brown & Co.
Mischief	M	RF	Pacific Literacy	Pacific Learning
Miss Rumphius	M	RF	Cooney, Barbara	The Penguin Group
Missing Will, The	M	RF	Schultz, Irene	Wright Group/McGraw Hill
Mitten, The	M	TL	Brett, Jan	Scholastic
Moana's Island	M	RF	Sunshine	Wright Group/McGraw Hill
Molly's Pilgrim	M	RF	Cohen, Barbara	Bantam Doubleday Dell
Momotaro	M	F	Sunshine	Wright Group/McGraw Hill
Monster for Hire	M	F	Wilson, Trevor	Mondo
Monster Rabbit Runs Amuck!	M	RF	Giff, Patricia Reilly	Bantam Doubleday Dell
Monsters Don't Scuba Dive	M	F	Dadey, D. & Jones, M. T.	Scholastic
Moon and the Mirror, The	M	TL	Literacy 2000	Rigby
Moonhorse	M	F	Osborne, Mary Pope	Alfred A. Knopf
Mr. Beep	M	F	Read Alongs	Rigby

Title	Level	Genre	Author/Series	Publisher/Distributor
Mrs. Always Goes Shopping	M	RF	Sunshine	Wright Group/McGraw Hill
Mrs. Bubble's Baby	M	F	Pacific Literacy	Pacific Learning
Mrs. Jeepers in Outer Space	M	RF	Dadey, D. & Jones, M. T.	Scholastic
Mud Pony, The	M	TL	Reading Rainbow	Scholastic
Muffy's Secret Admirer	M	RF	Brown, Marc	Little, Brown & Co.
Mummies	M	I	All Aboard Reading	Grosset & Dunlap
Mummies Don't Coach Softball	M	F	Dadey, D. & Jones, M. T.	Scholastic
Mummies in the Morning	M	F	Osborne, Mary Pope	Random House
Mutt and the Lifeguards	M	RF	Sunshine	Wright Group/McGraw Hill
My Body	M	I	Schaefer, Lola M.	Benchmark Education
My Prairie Summer	M	RF	Pair-It Books	Steck-Vaughn
My Weird Mother	M	RF	SupaDoopers	Sundance
My Wonderful Aunt, Story Five	M	F	Sunshine	Wright Group/McGraw Hill
My Wonderful Aunt, Story Four	M	F	Sunshine	Wright Group/McGraw Hill
My Wonderful Aunt, Story One	M	F	Sunshine	Wright Group/McGraw Hill
My Wonderful Aunt, Story Six	M	F	Sunshine	Wright Group/McGraw Hill
My Wonderful Aunt, Story Three	M	F	Sunshine	Wright Group/McGraw Hill
My Wonderful Aunt, Story Two	M	F	Sunshine	Wright Group/McGraw Hill
Mysterious I.O.U., The	M	RF	Schultz, Irene	Wright Group/McGraw Hill
Mystery in the Night Woods	M	F	Peterson, John	Scholastic
Mystery of Moody Manor, The	M	F	Dionetti, Michelle	Wright Group/McGraw Hill
Mystery of the Dark Old House, The	M	F	Schultz, Irene	Wright Group/McGraw Hill
Mystery of the Missing Dog, The	M	RF	Schultz, Irene	Wright Group/McGraw Hill
Mystery of the Missing Malamute, The	M	RF	Kleinhenz, Sydnie Meltzer	Wright Group/McGraw Hill
Mystery of the Stolen Bike, The	M	F	Brown, Marc	Little, Brown & Co.
Mystery of the Talking Tail, The	M	F	SupaDoopers	Sundance
Mystery of the Three Keys, The	M	RF	Schultz, Irene	Wright Group/McGraw Hill
Nadia Comaneci	M	B	Cole, Sally	Wright Group/McGraw Hill
Nana's in the Plum Tree	M	RF	Pacific Literacy	Pacific Learning
Nannies for Hire	M	RF	Hest, Amy	William Morrow
Nature's Celebration	M	I	Literacy 2000	Rigby
New Land: A First Year on the Praire, The	M	I	Reynolds, Marilynn	Orca Book Publishers
Nibble, Nibble, Jenny Archer	M	RF	Conford, Ellen	Little, Brown & Co.
Night of the Ninjas	M	F	Osborne, Mary Pope	Random House
Night Owls, The	M	I	Wonder World	Wright Group/McGraw Hill
Nightmare	M	RF	Pulford, Elizabeth	Rigby
Nine True Dolphin Stories	M	I	Davidson, Margaret	Scholastic
Ninjas Don't Bake Pumpkin Pies	M	RF	Dadey, D. & Jones, M. T.	Scholastic
No Arm in Left Field	M	RF	Christopher, Matt	Little, Brown & Co.
No Trouble at All!	M	RF	Powell, Joyce	Rigby
Nurses	M	I	Ready, Dee	Capstone Press
Old Bones	M	RF	Sunshine	Wright Group/McGraw Hill
Old Friends	M	RF	Literacy 2000	Rigby
Old Man and the Bear, The	M	RF	Hanel, Wolfram	North-South Books
Old Red Rocking Chair, The	M	RF	Root, Phyllis	Scholastic
Old Tom and the Rogue	M	HF	Wilson, Trevor	Dominie Press
Old Woman Who Lived in a Vinegar Bottle	M	TL	Douglas, Ann	Mondo
On and Off the Road	M	I	Wildcats	Wright Group/McGraw Hill
On With the Show!	M	I	Pair-It Books	Steck-Vaughn
Once upon a Rhyme	M	F	Pacific Literacy	Pacific Learning
One Bad Thing About Father, The	M	RF	Monjo, F.N.	HarperTrophy
One- Eyed Jake	M	F	Hutchins, Pat	Morrow
One in the Middle Is the Green Kangaroo, The	M	RF	Blume, Judy	Bantam Doubleday Dell
Our Government	M	I	People, Spaces & Places	Rand McNally
Owls	M	I	PM Animal Facts: Gold	Rigby
Paint Brush Kid, The	M	RF	Bulla, Clyde Robert	Random House
Pajama Party	M	RF	Hest, Amy	William Morrow
Pandas in the Mountains	M	F	PM Gold	Rigby
Patches	M	RF	Szymanski, Lois	Avon Camelot
Peter the Pumpkin-Eater	M	RF	Scott, Janine	Rigby

Title	Level	Genre	Author/Series	Publisher/Distributor
Pets Need People	M	I	Literacy 2000	Rigby
Phantoms Don't Drive Sports Cars	M	F	Dadey, D. & Jones, M. T.	Scholastic
Picture Book of Abraham Lincoln, A	M	B	Adler, David A.	Holiday House
Picture Book of Amelia Earhart, A	M	B	Adler, David A.	Holiday House
Picture Book of Anne Frank, A	M	B	Adler, David A.	Holiday House
Picture Book of Benjamin Franklin, A	M	B	Adler, David A.	Holiday House
Picture Book of Christopher Columbus, A	M	B	Adler, David A.	Holiday House
Picture Book of Davy Crockett, A	M	B	Adler, David A.	Holiday House
Picture Book of Eleanor Roosevelt, A	M	B	Adler, David A.	Holiday House
Picture Book of Florence Nightingale, A	M	B	Adler, David A.	Holiday House
Picture Book of Frederick Douglass, A	M	B	Adler, David A.	Holiday House
Picture Book of George Washington, A	M	B	Adler, David A.	Holiday House
Picture Book of George Washington Carver, A	M	B	Adler, David A.	Holiday House
Picture Book of Harriet Tubman, A	M	B	Adler, David A.	Holiday House
Picture Book of Helen Keller, A	M	B	Adler, David A.	Holiday House
Picture Book of Jackie Robinson, A	M	B	Adler, David A.	Holiday House
Picture Book of Louis Braille, A	M	B	Adler, David A.	Holiday House
Picture Book of Martin Luther King, Jr., A	M	B	Adler, David A.	Holiday House
Picture Book of Patrick Henry, A	M	B	Adler, David A.	Holiday House
Picture Book of Paul Revere, A	M	B	Adler, David A.	Holiday House
Picture Book of Rosa Parks, A	M	B	Adler, David A.	Holiday House
Picture Book of Sacagawea, A	M	B	Adler, David A.	Holiday House
Picture Book of Sitting Bull, A	M	B	Adler, David A.	Holiday House
Picture Book of Sojourner Truth, A	M	B	Adler, David A.	Holiday House
Picture Book of Thomas Alva Edison, A	M	B	Adler, David A.	Holiday House
Picture Book of Thomas Jefferson, A	M	B	Adler, David A.	Holiday House
Picture Book of Thurgood Marshall, A	M	B	Adler, David A.	Holiday House
Pied Piper, The	M	TL	Sunshine	Wright Group/McGraw Hill
Pigs Have Piglets	M	I	Animals and Their Young	Compass Point Books
Pirate Pie	M	F	Vaughan, Marcia	Pacific Learning
Pirates Don't Wear Pink Sunglasses	M	F	Dadey, D. & Jones, M. T.	Scholastic
Pirates Past Noon	M	F	Osborne, Mary Pope	Scholastic
Plumbers	M	I	Boraas, Tracey	Capstone Press
Polar Bears Past Bedtime	M	F	Osborne, Mary Pope	Random House
Police Officers	M	I	Ready, Dee	Capstone Press
Postcard Pest, The	M	RF	Giff, Patricia Reilly	Bantam Doubleday Dell
Present From Aunt Skidoo, The	M	RF	Literacy 2000	Rigby
Princess Who Loved to Cook, The	M	F	Cartwright, Pauline	Dominie Press
Princess Who Wanted the Moon, The	M	F	Lane, Sheila and Marion Kemp	Wood Lock Educational
Pumpkins	M	I	Ray, Mary Lyn	Harcourt Brace
Purple Climbing Days	M	RF	Giff, Patricia Reilly	Bantam Doubleday Dell
Qillak	M	RF	Jensen, Ned	Wright Group/McGraw Hill
Quackers, the Troublesome Duck	M	F	Ellen, Leslie	Pearson Learning
Rabbit Catches the Sun	M	F	Sunshine	Wright Group/McGraw Hill
Rabbits Have Bunnies	M	I	Animals and Their Young	Compass Point Books
Raccoons	M	I	PM Animal Facts: Gold	Rigby
Rainbow Wings	M	F	Nevinski, Margaret	Wright Group/McGraw Hill
Rainbows All Around	M	RF	Hardin, Suzanne	Pacific Learning
Red and Blue Mittens	M	RF	Reading Unlimited	Celebration Press
Red Ribbon Rosie	M	RF	Marzollo, Jean	Random House
Respect the Winds	M	TL	Reeder, Paul	Wright Group/McGraw Hill
Return of Rinaldo, the Sly Fox	M	TL	Scheffler, Ursel	North-South Books
Return of the Third-Grade Ghosthunters, The	M	RF	Maccarone, Grace	Scholastic
Revolutionary War on Wednesday	M	F	Osborne, Mary Pope	Random House
Rinaldo the Sly Fox	M	TL	Scheffler, Ursel	North-South Books
Rip-Roaring Russell	M	RF	Hurwitz, Johanna	The Penguin Group
River Runners	M	RF	Belcher, Angie	Rigby
Robber Pig and the Ginger Bear	M	F	Read Alongs	Rigby
Robber Pig and the Green Eggs	M	F	Read Alongs	Rigby
Robber, The	M	RF	Sunshine	Wright Group/McGraw Hill

Title	Level	Genre	Author/Series	Publisher/Distributor
Rooster's Gift, The	M	F	Conrad, Pam	HarperCollins
Rosa and Fredo	M	F	SupaDoopers	Sundance
Rumpelstiltskin	M	TL	Once Upon a Time	Wright Group/McGraw Hill
Russell and Elisa	M	RF	Hurwitz, Johanna	The Penguin Group
Russell Rides Again	M	RF	Hurwitz, Johanna	The Penguin Group
Russell Sprouts	M	RF	Hurwitz, Johanna	The Penguin Group
Sam's Glasses	M	RF	Literacy 2000	Rigby
Santa Claus Doesn't Mop Floors	M	F	Dadey, D. & Jones, M. T.	Scholastic
Save the River!	M	SF	Pair-It Books	Steck-Vaughn
Save the Sea Turtles!	M	I	Leonhardt, Alice	Steck-Vaughn
School Bus Drivers	M	I	Ready, Dee	Capstone Press
School Principals	M	I	Boraas, Tracey	Capstone Press
Sea Monsters Don't Ride Motorcycles	M	RF	Dadey, D. & Jones, M. T.	Scholastic
Search for the Lost Cave, The	M	F	Schultz, Irene	Wright Group/McGraw Hill
Second Grade-Friends Again!	M	RF	Cohen, Miriam	Scholastic
Second-Grade Friends	M	RF	Cohen, Miriam	Scholastic
Secret at the Polk Street School, The	M	RF	Giff, Patricia Reilly	Bantam Doubleday Dell
Secret of the Monster Book, The	M	F	Schultz, Irene	Wright Group/McGraw Hill
Secret of the Old Oak Trunk, The	M	F	Schultz, Irene	Wright Group/McGraw Hill
Secret of the Song, The	M	F	Schultz, Irene	Wright Group/McGraw Hill
Seven Treasure Hunts, The	M	RF	Byars, Betsy	HarperTrophy
Shadow Over Second	M	RF	Christopher, Matt	Little, Brown & Co.
Sheep Have Lambs	M	I	Animals and Their Young	Compass Point Books
Ship in a Bottle, The	M	RF	Herman, Emily	Wright Group/McGraw Hill
Shooting Star, The	M	RF	PM Gold	Rigby
Shortstop from Tokyo	M	RF	Christopher, Matt	Little, Brown & Co.
Shorty	M	RF	Literacy 2000	Rigby
Show Time at the Polk Street School	M	RF	Giff, Patricia Reilly	Bantam Doubleday Dell
Silly Willy	M	RF	Book Shop	Mondo
Skateboard Tough	M	RF	Christopher, Matt	Little, Brown & Co.
Skeletons Don't Play Tubas	M	F	Dadey, D. & Jones, M. T.	Scholastic
Skunks	M	I	PM Animal Facts: Gold	Rigby
Slam Dunk Saturday	M	RF	Marzollo, Jean	Random House
Smokey the Dragon	M	F	Bennett, Jean	Dominie Press
Snaggle Doodles	M	RF	Giff, Patricia Reilly	Bantam Doubleday Dell
Snake!	M	RF	Sunshine	Wright Group/McGraw Hill
Snow Bright and the Seven Sumos	M	F	SupaDoopers	Sundance
Snow Bright and the Tooth Magician	M	F	SupaDoopers	Sundance
Soccer Mania!	M	RF	Tamar, Erika	Random House
Soccer Sam	M	RF	Marzollo, Jean	Random House
Sock Gobbler and Other Stories, The	M	F	Learning Media	Pacific Learning
Solo Girl	M	RF	Pinkey, Andrea Davis	Hyperion
Something Soft for Danny Bear	M	F	Literacy 2000	Rigby
Sophie Hits Six	M	F	King-Smith, Dick	Candlewick Press
Sophie in the Saddle	M	F	King-Smith, Dick	Candlewick Press
Sophie Is Seven	M	F	King-Smith, Dick	Candlewick Press
Sophie's Lucky	M	F	King-Smith, Dick	Candlewick Press
Sophie's Snail	M	F	King-Smith, Dick	Candlewick Press
Sophie's Tom	M	F	King-Smith, Dick	Candlewick Press
Special Effects	M	I	Wildcats	Wright Group/McGraw Hill
Special Gifts	M	RF	Rylant, Cynthia	Aladdin
Spencer School Sleepover, The	M	RF	Floyd, Lucy	Wright Group/McGraw Hill
Spider Man	M	I	Literacy 2000	Rigby
Spiders	M	I	Book Shop	Mondo
Spooky Tail of Prewitt Peacock, The	M	F	Peet, Bill	Houghton Mifflin
Spy Down the Street, The	M	F	Schultz, Irene	Wright Group/McGraw Hill
Spy in the Attic, The	M	RF	Scheffler, Ursel	North-South Books
Spy on Third Base, The	M	RF	Christopher, Matt	Little, Brown & Co.
Star	M	RF	Simon, Jo Ann	Random House
Starfishers to the Rescue	M	SF	Dreyer, Ellen	Pearson Learning

Title	Level	Genre	Author/Series	Publisher/Distributor
Storm at Coldwater Creek	M	HF	Blackaby, Susan	Wright Group/McGraw Hill
Story, a Story, A: An African Tale	M	TL	Haley, Gail E.	Aladdin
Story of Big Bess Call, The	M	TL	Bovetz, Marcie	Wright Group/McGraw Hill
Story of Jeans, The	M	I	Discovery World	Rigby
Story of William Tell, The	M	TL	PM Story Books -Silver	Rigby
Story of You, The	M	I	Sunshine	Wright Group/McGraw Hill
Sugar Cakes Cyril	M	RF	Gershator, Phillis	Mondo
Summer Sands	M	RF	Evangeline Nicholas Collection	Wright Group/McGraw Hill
Sunny-Side Up	M	RF	Giff, Patricia Reilly	Bantam Doubleday Dell
Sunset of the Sabertooth	M	F	Osborne, Mary Pope	Random House
Supercharged Infield	M	RF	Christopher, Matt	Little, Brown & Co.
Survival of Fish, The	M	I	Science	Wright Group/McGraw Hill
Swamp of the Hideous Zombies	M	F	Hayes, Geoffrey	Random House
Take Care of Our Earth	M	I	Pair-It Books	Steck-Vaughn
Taken by the Wind	M	RF	Wahman, Joe	Wright Group/McGraw Hill
Tale of Veruschka Babuschka, The	M	TL	Literacy 2000	Rigby
Tasmanian Devils	M	I	PM Animal Facts: Gold	Rigby
Teachers	M	I	Deedrick, Tami	Capstone Press
Tell Me No Lies	M	RF	Dionetti, Michelle	Wright Group/McGraw Hill
That's a Laugh: Four Funny Fables	M	TL	Literacy 2000	Rigby
These Old Rags	M	RF	Evangeline Nicholas Collection	Wright Group/McGraw Hill
Things Change	M	I	Bourne, Phyllis Montenegro	Hampton-Brown
Through the Garden Door	M	F	Reeves, Barbara	Pearson Learning
Tigers at Twilight	M	F	Osborne, Mary Pope	Random House
Tight End	M	RF	Christopher, Matt	Little, Brown & Co.
Timber Box, The	M	TL	Enrichment	Wright Group/McGraw Hill
Time Capsule, The	M	SF	Book Bank	Wright Group/McGraw Hill
Timothy's Five-City Tour	M	F	Pair-It Books	Steck-Vaughn
Tin Lizzy	M	RF	Windmill Books	Rigby
Tom, the Dragon	M	F	New Way Orange	Steck-Vaughn
Tomatoes	M	I	Cole, Sally	Wright Group/McGraw Hill
Tonight on the Titanic	M	F	Osborne, Mary Pope	Random House
Too Hot to Handle	M	RF	Christopher, Matt	Little, Brown & Co.
Too Many Tamales	M	RF	Soto, Gary	Putnam & Grosset
Totara Tree, The	M	RF	Book Bank	Wright Group/McGraw Hill
Touch of Gold and Other Stories, The	M	TL	Lane, Sheila, Marion Kemp	Wood Lock Educational
Touchdown for Tommy	M	RF	Christopher, Matt	Little, Brown & Co.
Treasure Hunting	M	RF	Literacy 2000	Rigby
Tricksters	M	RF	SupaDoopers	Sundance
Trip Around the Gulf of Mexico, A	M	I	People, Spaces & Places	Rand McNally
Trip to Freedom	M	B	Nguyen, Andrea Quynhgiao	Rigby
Trog	M	F	Sunshine	Wright Group/McGraw Hill
Trolls Don't Ride Roller Coasters	M	F	Dadey, D. & Jones, M. T.	Scholastic
Troublemaker	M	RF	SupaDoopers	Sundance
Truth About the Moon, The	M	TL	Bess, Clayton	Houghton Mifflin
Turkey Trouble	M	RF	Giff, Patricia Reilly	Bantam Doubleday Dell
TV Reporters	M	I	Boraas, Tracey	Capstone Press
TV Time-Out	M	RF	Blackaby, Susan	Wright Group/McGraw Hill
Twelve Dancing Princesses	M	I	Enrichment	Wright Group/McGraw Hill
Two Hungry Hippos	M	I	Adams, Alison	Benchmark Education Co.
Two Runaways, The	M	RF	Schultz, Irene	Wright Group/McGraw Hill
Tyler Toad and Thunder	M	F	Crowe, Robert	Dutton
Umbrellas	M	I	Sunshine	Wright Group/McGraw Hill
Unicorns Don't Give Sleigh Rides	M	F	Dadey, D. & Jones, M. T.	Scholastic
Vacation Journal, A	M	B	Discovery World	Rigby
Vacation Under the Volcano	M	F	Osborne, Mary Pope	Random House
Valentine Star, The	M	RF	Giff, Patricia Reilly	Bantam Doubleday Dell
Vampires Don't Wear Polka Dots	M	F	Dadey, D. & Jones, M. T.	Scholastic
Viking Ships at Sunrise	M	F	Osborne, Mary Pope	Random House
Voyage, The	M	F	Pair-It Books	Steck-Vaughn

Title	Level	Genre	Author/Series	Publisher/Distributor
Wake Up, Emily, It's Mother's Day	M	RF	Giff, Patricia Reilly	Yearling
Walking	M	I	Literacy 2000	Rigby
Walter the Warlock	M	F	Hautzig, Deborah	Random House
Waste of Space, A	M	RF	SupaDoopers	Sundance
Watching Every Drop	M	I	Home Connection Collection	Rigby
Watching Josh	M	RF	Eaton, Deborah	Wright Group/McGraw Hill
Water for the World	M	I	Home Connection Collection	Rigby
We Are All Alike	M	I	Schaefer, Lola M.	Benchmark Education
Wedding Day Disaster	M	RF	SupaDoopers	Sundance
Werewolves Don't Go To Summer Camp	M	F	Dadey, D. & Jones, M. T.	Scholastic
Whales	M	I	Wonder World	Wright Group/McGraw Hill
What Is a Fly?	M	I	Sunshine	Wright Group/McGraw Hill
What is a Reptile?	M	I	Now I Know	Troll
What Made Teddalik Laugh	M	TL	Folk Tales	Wright Group/McGraw Hill
What Shall I Do?	M	RF	Sunshine	Wright Group/McGraw Hill
What's Cooking, Jenny Archer?	M	RF	Conford, Ellen	Little Brown & Co.
When My Dad Came to School	M	RF	City Kids	Rigby
When The Truck Got Stuck!	M	RF	Cowley, Joy	Pacific Learning
Where Does the Wind Go?	M	I	Book Shop	Mondo
Who Looks After Me?	M	I	Literacy 2000	Rigby
Who Makes the Rules?	M	I	Schafer, Lola M.	Benchmark Education
Who's in Love with Arthur?	M	F	Brown, Marc	Little, Brown & Co.
Why Crocodiles Live in Rivers	M	F	Sunshine	Wright Group/McGraw Hill
Wilamina and the Weather Conditions	M	F	Reimer, Luther	Wright Group/McGraw Hill
Wild, Wild Wolves	M	I	Milton, Joyce	Random House
Wilde Street Club and Molly, The	M	RF	Sunshine	Wright Group/McGraw Hill
Wilde Street Club and the Duck Man, The	M	RF	Sunshine	Wright Group/McGraw Hill
Wingman on Ice	M	RF	Christopher, Matt	Little, Brown & Co.
Winklepoo the Wicked	M	F	Sunshine	Wright Group/McGraw Hill
Witches Don't Do Backflips	M	F	Dadey, D. & Jones, M. T.	Scholastic
Wizards Don't Need Computers	M	F	Dadey, D. & Jones, M. T.	Scholastic
Wolf's First Deer	M	RF	Book Bank	Wright Group/McGraw Hill
Wolfmen Don't Hula Dance	M	RF	Dadey, D. & Jones, M. T.	Scholastic
Wonder Kid Meets the Evil Lunch Snatcher	M	RF	Duncan, Lois	Little, Brown & Co.
Wonderful Eyes	M	I	Science	Wright Group/McGraw Hill
Woodlanders Begin, The	M	F	Schultz, Irene	Wright Group/McGraw Hill
Words	M	I	Pacific Literacy	Pacific Learning
World's Greatest Toe Show, The	M	RF	Lamb, Nancy & Singer, Muff	Troll
Wright Brothers, The	M	B	Biography	Benchmark Education
Write Up a Storm with the Polk Street School	M	RF	Giff, Patricia Reilly	Bantam Doubleday Dell
Year Mom Won the Pennant, The	M	RF	Christopher, Matt	Little, Brown & Co.
Yonder	M	RF	Johnston, Tony	The Penguin Group
You Can Cook	M	I	Woo, Lornette	Steck-Vaughn
You're My Nikki	M	RF	Eisenberg, Phyllis Rose	The Penguin Group
Young Wolf's First Hunt	M	RF	Shefelman, Janice	Random House
Zero's Slider	M	RF	Christopher, Matt	Little, Brown & Co.
Zombies Don't Play Soccer	M	F	Dadey, D. & Jones, M. T.	Scholastic
Zomo the Rabbit: A Trickster Tale from West Africa	M	TL	McDermott, Gerald	Harcourt Brace
Zoo Keepers	M	I	Deedrick, Tami	Capstone Press
26 Fairmount Avenue	N	B	dePaola, Tomie	Putnam
Absent Author, The	N	RF	Roy, Ron	Random House
Adam Joshua Capers: Halloween Monster	N	RF	Smith, Janice Lee	HarperTrophy
Adam Joshua Capers: Kid Next Door, The	N	RF	Smith, Janice Lee	HarperTrophy
Adam Joshua Capers: Monster in the Third	N	RF	Smith, Janice Lee	HarperTrophy
Adam Joshua Capers: Nelson in Love	N	RF	Smith, Janice Lee	HarperTrophy
Adam Joshua Capers: Show-and-Tell War, The	N	RF	Smith, Janice Lee	HarperTrophy
Adam Joshua Capers: Superkid!	N	RF	Smith, Janice Lee	HarperTrophy
Adam Joshua Capers: Turkey Trouble	N	RF	Smith, Janice Lee	HarperTrophy
Adios, Anna	N	RF	Giff, Patricia Reilly	Bantam Doubleday Dell
Adventures of George Washington, The	N	B	Davidson, Margaret	Scholastic

Title	Level	Genre	Author/Series	Publisher/Distributor
Alien in the Classroom	N	F	Keene, Carolyn	Pocket Books
All About Cats and Kittens	N	I	Neye, Emily	Grosset & Dunlap
All Kinds of Museums	N	I	Ramsey, Joe	Wright Group/McGraw Hill
All Pigs Are Beautiful	N	I	King-Smith, Dick	Candlewick Press
Alroy's Very Nearly Clean Bedroom	N	RF	SupaDoopers	Sundance
Always My Dad	N	RF	Wyeth, Sharon Dennis	Alfred A. Knopf
Amber Brown Goes Fourth	N	RF	Danziger, Paula	Scholastic
Amber Brown is Feeling Blue	N	RF	Danziger, Paula	Scholastic
Amber Brown is Not a Crayon	N	RF	Danziger, Paula	Scholastic
Amber Brown Sees Red	N	RF	Danziger, Paula	Scholastic
Amber Brown Wants Extra Credit	N	RF	Danziger, Paula	Scholastic
American Flag, The	N	I	A True Book	Children's Press
Andy and Tamika	N	RF	Adler, David A.	Harcourt Brace
Animal Adventures	N	HF	Little House	HarperTrophy
Animal Friends	N	I	Literacy 2000	Rigby
Animal Shelters	N	I	Book Shop	Mondo
Animals and Their Young	N	I	Kratky, Lada Josefa	Hampton-Brown
Animals Talk, Too	N	I	Literacy 2000	Rigby
Anna, Grandpa, and the Big Storm	N	RF	Stevens, Carla	The Penguin Group
Antarctic Penguins	N	I	PM Animal Facts: Silver	Rigby
Antarctic Seals	N	I	PM Animal Facts: Silver	Rigby
Ants	N	I	Daronco, Mickey & Presti, Lori	Benchmark Education
Ask Einstein!	N	RF	Trussell-Cullen, Alan	Pacific Learning
Australia	N	I	A True Book	Children's Press
Bad Day for Ballet	N	RF	Keene, Carolyn	Pocket Books
Bald Bandit, The	N	RF	Roy, Ron	Random House
Bald Eagle, The	N	I	A True Book	Children's Press
Be A Perfect Person In Just Three Days!	N	RF	Manes, Stephen	Dell
Bear Collection, The	N	I	PM Ruby	Rigby
Beatles, The	N	B	Venezia, Mike	Children's Press
Beaver Engineers	N	I	Reeder, Tracey	Wright Group/McGraw Hill
Beavers	N	I	Book Shop	Mondo
Bees	N	I	A True Book	Children's Press
Behind the Couch	N	F	Gerstein, Mordicai	Hyperion
Below the Green Pond	N	I	Read All About It	Steck-Vaughn
Ben's Tune	N	RF	PM Ruby	Rigby
Benjamin Franklin	N	B	Biography	Benchmark Education
Berlioz The Bear	N	F	Brett, Jan	Scholastic
Best Detective, The	N	RF	Keene, Carolyn	Pocket Books
Beware!	N	RF	Cartwright, Pauline	Pacific Learning
Big Race, the	N	F	Pye, Trevor	Pacific Learning
Big Toe Robbery, The	N	F	PM Ruby	Rigby
Bill of Rights, The	N	I	A True Book	Children's Press
Billie the Hippo	N	I	Pacific Literacy	Pacific Learning
Birds and How They Grow	N	I	National Geographic Society	National Geographic Society
Birds of a Feather	N	RF	Literacy 2000	Rigby
Birthday	N	RF	Steptoe, John	Henry Holt & Co.
Black Holes	N	I	A True Book	Children's Press
Black Velvet Mystery, The	N	RF	Keene, Carolyn	Pocket Books
Blackberries in the Dark	N	RF	Jukes, Mavis	Alfred A. Knopf
Blast Off!	N	I	Home Connection Collection	Rigby
Blimps	N	I	A True Book	Children's Press
Boy in the Doghouse, A	N	RF	Duffey, Betsy	Simon & Schuster
Boy Who Ate Dog Biscuits, The	N	RF	Sachs, Betsy	Random House
Boy Who Cried Bigfoot, The	N	F	The Zack Files	Grossett&Dunlap
Bozo the Clone	N	SF	The Zack Files	Grosset & Dunlap
Brad and Butter Play Ball!	N	RF	Hughes, Dean	William Morrow
Brazil	N	I	A True Book	Children's Press
Bridges	N	I	Wildcats	Wright Group/McGraw Hill
Brookfield Days	N	HF	Little House	HarperTrophy

Title	Level	Genre	Author/Series	Publisher/Distributor
Bryce Canyon National Park	N	I	A True Book	Children's Press
Buffalo Woman	N	TL	Goble, Paul	Aladdin
Bugs and Other Insects	N	I	Kalman, Bobbie	Crabtree
Busybody Nora	N	RF	Hurwitz, Johanna	The Penguin Group
Butterflies and Moths	N	I	Kalman, Bobbie	Crabtree
By Lakes and Rivers	N	I	Animal Trackers	Crabtree
By the Seashore	N	I	Animal Trackers	Crabtree
Canary Caper, The	N	RF	Roy, Ron	Random House
Caribou (Reindeer)	N	I	PM Animal Facts: Silver	Rigby
Case of Hermie the Missing Hamster, The	N	RF	Preller, James	Scholastic
Case of the Christmas Snowman, The	N	RF	Preller, James	Scholastic
Case of the Disappearing Bones	N	RF	SupaDoopers	Sundance
Case of the Nervous Newsboy, The	N	RF	Hildick, E.W.	Sundance
Case of the Secret Valentine, The	N	RF	Preller, James	Scholastic
Case of the Spooky Sleepover, The	N	RF	Preller, James	Scholastic
Case of the Stolen Baseball Cards, The	N	RF	Preller, James	Scholastic
Cat Burglar of Pethaven Drive, The	N	F	Literacy 2000	Rigby
Cat Talk	N	I	Long, Don	Pacific Learning
Cat Who Wore a Pot on Her Head, The	N	F	Slepian, Jan & Seidler, Ann	Scholastic
Catwings	N	F	Le Guin, Ursula K.	Scholastic
Catwings Return	N	F	Le Guin, Ursula K.	Scholastic
Caught by the Sea	N	RF	Keating, Rosemary	Pacific Learning
Cesar Chavez	N	B	Biography	Benchmark Education
Chalk Box Kid, The	N	RF	Bulla, Clyde Robert	Random House
Cheyenne, The	N	I	A New True Book	Children's Press
Chicken Sunday	N	RF	Polacco, Patricia	Scholastic
China	N	I	A True Book	Children's Press
Chocolate	N	I	What's For Lunch?	Children's Press
Chocolate Touch, The	N	F	Catling, Patrick Skene	Bantam Doubleday Dell
Circulatory System, The	N	I	A True Book	Children's Press
Cloud Book, The	N	I	dePaola, Tomie	Scholastic
Clouds	N	I	Literacy 2000	Rigby
Clue in the Glue, The	N	RF	Keene, Carolyn	Pocket Books
Clyde Tombaugh and the Search for Planet X	N	B	Wetterer, Margaret K.	Carolrhoda Books
Coast to Coast	N	I	People, Spaces & Places	Rand McNally
Comets and Meteor Showers	N	I	A True Book	Children's Press
Communication	N	I	Literacy 2000	Rigby
Congress	N	I	A True Book	Children's Press
Constellations	N	I	A True Book	Children's Press
Constitution, The	N	I	A True Book	Children's Press
Cottle Street	N	RF	Pulford, Elizabeth	Rigby
Coyote Not-So-Clever	N	TL	Beveridge, Barbara	Pacific Learning
Cranes	N	I	Cole, Sally	Wright Group/McGraw Hill
Creature of Cassidy's Creek, The	N	RF	PM Emerald	Rigby
Creatures in the Dark	N	I	Literacy 2000	Rigby
Crystal Unicorn, The	N	RF	PM Emerald	Rigby
Curse of the Squirrel, The	N	F	Yep, Laurence	Random House
Dance with Rosie	N	RF	Giff, Patricia Reilly	The Penguin Group
Dancing with Manatees	N	I	McNulty, Faith	Scholastic
Danger Guys	N	RF	Abbott, Tony	HarperTrophy
Danger Guys Blast Off	N	RF	Abbott, Tony	HarperTrophy
Danger Guys on Ice	N	RF	Abbott, Tony	HarperTrophy
Dark and Full of Secrets	N	RF	Carrick, Carol	Houghton Mifflin
Day with Wilbur Robinson, A	N	RF	Joyce, William	HarperTrophy
Deadbolts and Dinkles	N	RF	Tapp, Kathy Kennedy	Mondo
Deadly Dungeon, The	N	RF	Roy, Ron	Random House
Declaration of Independence, The	N	I	A True Book	Children's Press
Desert Birds	N	I	A New True Book	Children's Press
Deserts	N	I	A True Book	Children's Press
Deserts	N	I	Habitats of the World	Dominie Press

Title	Level	Genre	Author/Series	Publisher/Distributor
Did You Carry The Flag Today, Charley?	N	RF	Caudill, Rebecca	Bantam Doubleday Dell
Did You Hear Wind Sing Your Name?	N	TL	Book Shop	Mondo
Digestive System, The	N	I	A True Book	Children's Press
Dinosaur Girl	N	RF	Devereux, Susan	Rigby
Dog I Share, The	N	RF	Marriott, Janice	Pacific Learning
Dolphin's First Day: The Story of a Bottlenose Dolphin	N	I	Zoehfeld, Kathleen Weidnetz	Scholastic
Dolphins	N	I	Kalman, Bobbie	Crabtree
Don't Call Me Beanhead!	N	RF	Wojciechowski, Susan	Candlewick Press
Donavan's Word Jar	N	RF	DeGross, Monalisa	HarperCollins
Dr. Jekyll, Orthodontist	N	RF	The Zack Files	Grosset & Dunlap
Dr. MacTavish's Creature	N	RF	PM Emerald	Rigby
Dr. Seuss and His Stories	N	B	Coglon, Kari	Wright Group/McGraw Hill
Dragons Galore	N	F	Wildcats	Wright Group/McGraw Hill
Dream Eater, The	N	F	Garrison, Christian	Aladdin
E is for Elisa	N	RF	Hurwitz, Johanna	Puffin Books
Earth	N	I	A True Book	Children's Press
Earthquake in the Third Grade	N	RF	Myers, Laurie	Clarion
Earthquakes	N	I	A True Book	Children's Press
Einstein-Champion of the World	N	RF	Trussell-Cullen, Alan	Pacific Learning
Elephants	N	I	Meadows, Graham & Vial, Claire	Dominie Press
Elisa in the Middle	N	RF	Hurwitz, Johanna	The Penguin Group
Ellis Island	N	I	A True Book	Children's Press
Elvis the Turnip…and Me	N	F	The Zack Files	Gosset & Dunlap
Empty Envelope, The	N	RF	Roy, Ron	Random House
Endangered Animals	N	I	A New True Book	Children's Press
Enormous Crocodile, The	N	F	Dahl, Roald	The Penguin Group
Escape!	N	SF	Cartwright, Pauline	Pacific Learning
Evil Queen Tut and the Great Ant Pyramids	N	F	The Zack Files	Grossett&Dunlap
Extreme Lives	N	I	Wildcats	Wright Group/McGraw Hill
Fables	N	TL	Lobel, Arnold	Harper Collins
Falcon, The	N	RF	PM Emerald	Rigby
Falcon's Feathers, The	N	RF	Roy, Ron	Random House
Fangs and Me	N	RF	Gilmore, Rachna	Fitzhenry and Whiteside
Festival Fun	N	I	Wildcats	Wright Group/McGraw Hill
First Apple	N	RF	Russell, Ching Yueng	The Penguin Group
Flag For Our Country, A	N	I	Spencer, Eve	Steck-Vaughn
Flamingos	N	I	Cole, Sally	Wright Group/McGraw Hill
Flies	N	I	A True Book	Children's Press
Floods	N	I	A True Book	Children's Press
Fly Homer Fly	N	F	Peet, Bill	Houghton Mifflin
For the Love of Pooch	N	RF	Literacy 2000	Rigby
For the Love of Turtles	N	RF	Palacios, Argentina	Rigby
Forests	N	I	Habitats of the World	Dominie
Forever Amber Brown	N	RF	Danziger, Paula	Scholastic
Freshwater Habitats	N	I	Habitats of the World	Dominie Press
Frog Who Would Be King, The	N	TL	Walker, Kate	Mondo
Frogs	N	I	Book Shop	Mondo
Frogs of Betts, The	N	RF	SupaDoopers	Sundance
From Cotton Plant to Cotton Shirt	N	I	Schaefer, Lola M.	Benchmark Education
Funny Bananas: The Mystery in the Museum	N	RF	McHargue, Georgess	Dell Publishing
Gadget War, The	N	RF	Duffey, Betsy	The Penguin Group
Galaxies	N	I	A True Book	Children's Press
George Washington Carver	N	B	Biography	Benchmark Education
Ghost Named Wanda, A	N	F	The Zack Files	Grosset & Dunlap
Ghost of Popcorn Hill, The	N	F	Wright, Betty Ren	Scholastic
Gift for Mama, A	N	RF	Hautzig, Esther	The Penguin Group
Ginger's War	N	HF	Daniel, Lea	Wright Group/McGraw Hill
Giraffes	N	I	Meadows, Graham & Vial, Claire	Dominie Press
Glass Slipper for Rosie, A	N	RF	Giff, Patricia Reilly	The Penguin Group
Gold Dust Kids, The	N	HF	Dionetti, Michelle	Wright Group/McGraw Hill

Title	Level	Genre	Author/Series	Publisher/Distributor
Gold Fever!	N	HF	Step into Reading	Random House
Good Dog, Bonita	N	RF	Giff, Patricia Reilly	Bantam Doubleday Dell
Goose's Gold, The	N	RF	Roy, Ron	Random House
Grandma Moses	N	B	Biography	Benchmark Education
Grasslands	N	I	A True Book	Children's Press
Great-Grandpa's In The Litter Box	N	F	The Zack Files	Grosset & Dunlap
Green Thumbs, Everyone	N	RF	Giff, Patricia Reilly	Bantam Doubleday Dell
Green with Red Spots Horrible	N	RF	SupaDoopers	Sundance
Grizzly Bears	N	I	Woolley, M. & Pigdon, K.	Mondo
Gung Hay Fat Choy	N	I	Behrens, June	Children's Press
Hang a Left at Venus	N	F	The Zack Files	Grossett&Dunlap
Hang in there, Oscar Martin!	N	RF	Noonan, Diana	Pacific Learning
Hannah	N	RF	Whelan, Gloria	Random House
Hanukkah	N	I	Festivals and Holidays	Children's Press
Happy Birthday, Anna, Sorpresa!	N	RF	Giff, Patricia Reilly	Bantam Doubleday Dell
Harry Houdini-Wonderdog!	N	RF	Taylor, William	Pacific Learning
Helen Keller	N	B	Davidson, Margaret	Scholastic
Helen Keller: Courage in the Dark	N	B	Hurwitz, Johanna	Random House
Helen Keller's Teacher	N	B	Davidson, Margaret	Scholastic
Helicopters	N	I	A True Book	Children's Press
Herbie Jones	N	RF	Kline, Suzy	The Penguin Group
Herbie Jones and Hamburger Head	N	RF	Kline, Suzy	The Penguin Group
Herbie Jones and the Birthday Showdown	N	RF	Kline, Suzy	The Penguin Group
Herbie Jones and the Class Gift	N	RF	Kline, Suzy	The Penguin Group
Herbie Jones and the Dark Attic	N	RF	Kline, Suzy	Puffin Books
Herbie Jones and the Monster Ball	N	RF	Kline, Suzy	The Penguin Group
Heroes	N	I	Wildcats	Wright Group/McGraw Hill
Hey, Al	N	F	Yorinks, Arthur	Farrar, Straus and Giroux
Hey, New Kid!	N	RF	Duffey, Betsy	The Penguin Group
Ho, Ho, Benjamin, Feliz Navidad	N	RF	Giff, Patricia Reilly	Bantam Doubleday Dell
Holly & Mac	N	RF	SupaDoopers	Sundance
Horses	N	I	A New True Book	Children's Press
House on Walenska Street, The	N	RF	Herman, Charlotte	The Penguin Group
How a Book is Made	N	I	Aliki	Harper & Row
How I Fixed the Year 1000 Problem	N	F	The Zack Files	Grossett&Dunlap
How I Went from Bad to Verse	N	F	The Zack Files	Grossett&Dunlap
How To Be Cool in the Third Grade	N	RF	Duffey, Betsy	The Penguin Group
How To Speak Dolphin in Three Easy Lessons	N	F	The Zack Files	Grosset & Dunlap
How's the Weather?	N	I	Berger, Melvin and Gilda	Ideals Children's Books
Hubble Space Telescope, The	N	I	A True Book	Children's Press
I, Amber Brown	N	RF	Danziger, Paula	Scholastic
I Was a Third Grade Science Project	N	RF	Auch, Mary Jane	Yearling
I'm Out of My Body...Please Leave a Message	N	F	The Zack Files	Grosset & Dunlap
It's a Fiesta, Benjamin	N	RF	Giff, Patricia Reilly	Bantam Doubleday Dell
Jackie Robinson and the Story of All-Black Baseball	N	I	O'Connor, Jim	Random House
Jane's Mansion	N	I	Literacy 2000	Rigby
Japan	N	I	A True Book	Children's Press
Jenius The Amazing Guinea Pig	N	F	King-Smith, Dick	Hyperion
Joe Cocker Spaniel	N	RF	SupaDoopers	Sundance
Julian, Dream Doctor	N	RF	Cameron, Ann	Random House
Julian, Secret Agent	N	RF	Cameron, Ann	Random House
Julian's Glorious Summer	N	RF	Cameron, Ann	Random House
Junkyard Dog, The	N	RF	PM Emerald	Rigby
Jupiter	N	I	A True Book	Children's Press
Just a Few Words, Mr. Lincoln	N	I	Fritz, Jean	Putnam
Kangaroos	N	I	A New True Book	Children's Press
Keelboat Annie	N	TL	Johnson, Janet P.	Troll
Keeping Tadpoles	N	I	Discovery World	Rigby
Key to the Treasure	N	RF	Parish, Peggy	Bantam Doubleday Dell
Kites	N	I	Literacy 2000	Rigby

Title	Level	Genre	Author/Series	Publisher/Distributor
Knife, The	N	RF	Cartwright, Pauline	Pacific Learning
Koalas	N	I	A New True Book	Children's Press
Laura Ingalls Wilder: An Author's Story	N	B	Glasscock, Sarah	Steck-Vaughn
Leftovers, The: Catch Flies!	N	RF	Howard, Tristan	Scholastic
Leftovers, The: Fast Break	N	RF	Howard, Tristan	Scholastic
Leftovers, The: Get Jammed	N	RF	Howard, Tristan	Scholastic
Leftovers, The: Reach Their Goal	N	RF	Howard, Tristan	Scholastic
Leftovers, The: Strike Out!	N	RF	Howard, Tristan	Scholastic
Legendary Places	N	I	Wildcats	Wright Group/McGraw Hill
Leontyne Price: Opera Superstar	N	B	Williams, Sylvia B.	Children's Press
Letter from Fish Bay, A	N	B	Cowley, Joy	Pacific Learning
Light at Tern Rock, The	N	RF	Sauer, Julia L.	Scholastic
Lili the Brave	N	RF	Armstrong, Jennifer	Random House
Lily and Miss Liberty	N	HF	Stephens, Carla	Scholastic
Limestone Caves	N	I	A First Book	Franklin Watts
Limestone Caves	N	I	Davis, Gary	Children's Press
Lion Dancer: Ernie Wan's Chinese New Year	N	B	Waters, K. & Slovenz-Low, M.	Scholastic
Lions	N	I	Meadows, Graham & Vial, Claire	Dominie Press
Little Caribou	N	I	Fox-Davies, Sarah	Candlewick Press
Little Sea Pony, The	N	F	Cresswell, Helen	HarperTrophy
Llama Pajamas	N	RF	Clymer, Susan	Scholastic
Look at the Moon	N	I	Book Shop	Mondo
Lost Sandals, The	N	RF	Bennett, Jean	Pacific Learning
Louis Braille: Boy Who Invented Books for the Blind	N	B	Davidson, Margaret	Scholastic
Louis Pasteur	N	B	Biography	Benchmark Education
Luke's Bully	N	RF	Winthrop, Elizabeth	Puffin Books
Lunchbox Mystery, The	N	RF	Lohans, Alison	Scholastic
Machines in the Home	N	I	Morrison, Rob	Rigby
Magic Finger, The	N	F	Dahl, Roald	The Penguin Group
Make Room For Elisa	N	RF	Hurwitz, Johanna	The Penguin Group
Mammals	N	I	Simply Science	Compass Point Books
Man Who Tricked a Ghost, The	N	TL	Yep, Laurence	Troll Medallion
Math Wiz, The	N	RF	Duffey, Betsy	The Penguin Group
Max Malone and the Great Cereal Rip-off	N	RF	Herman, Charlotte	Henry Holt & Co.
Max Malone Makes a Million	N	RF	Herman, Charlotte	Henry Holt & Co.
Max Malone, Superstar	N	RF	Herman, Charlotte	Scholastic
Maya, The	N	I	A New True Book	Children's Press
Medal for Molly, A	N	RF	PM Emerald	Rigby
Mercury	N	I	A True Book	Children's Press
Min-Yo and the Moon Dragon	N	TL	Hillman, Elizabeth	Harcourt Brace
Misfortune Cookie, The	N	F	The Zack Files	Grosset & Dunlap
Mishmash	N	RF	Cone, Molly	Pocket Books
Missing Osprey Nest, The	N	RF	Herman, Emily	Wright Group/McGraw Hill
Money Boot, The	N	RF	Russell, Ginny	Fitzhenry and Whiteside
Moon, The	N	I	Literacy 2000	Rigby
More Monsters in School	N	RF	Godfrey, M.	Fitzhenry and Whiteside
More Stories Huey Tells	N	RF	Cameron, Ann	Alfred A. Knopf
More Stories Julian Tells	N	RF	Cameron, Ann	Random House
Mountains of Quilt, The	N	F	Willard, Nancy	Harcourt Brace
Mr. Potter's Pet	N	F	King-Smith, Dick	Hyperion
Mufaro's Beautiful Daughters: An African Tale	N	TL	Steptoe, John	Scholastic
My Brother, the Spy	N	RF	SupaDoopers	Sundance
My Family & the Wasps	N	F	Parker, John	Dominie Press
My Father's Dragon	N	F	Gannett, Ruth Stiles	Random House
My Friend the Monster	N	F	Bulla, Clyde Robert	Harper & Row
My Great-Aunt Arizona	N	RF	Houston, Gloria	HarperCollins
My Name is Maria Isabel	N	RF	Ada, Alma Flor	Aladdin
My Name is Yun Jim	N	RF	Murphy, Catherine	Wright Group/McGraw Hill
My Son, the Time Traveler	N	F	The Zack Files	Grosset & Dunlap
Mystery of Pony Hollow, The	N	F	Hall, Lynn	Random House

Title	Level	Genre	Author/Series	Publisher/Distributor
Mystery of the Phantom Pony, The	N	RF	Stepping Stone	Random House
National Anthem, The	N	I	A True Book	Children's Press
Neighbor From Outer Space, The	N	F	George, Maureen	Scholastic
Neptune	N	I	A True Book	Children's Press
Nervous System, The	N	I	A True Book	Children's Press
Never Hitch a Ride With a Martian!	N	SF	Clark, Tony	Pacific Learning
Never Trust a Cat Who Wears Earrings	N	F	The Zack Files	Grosset & Dunlap
New Friends in a New Land: A Thanksgiving Story	N	I	Stamper, Judith Bauer	Steck-Vaughn
New Kid in Town	N	RF	Kroll, Stephen	Avon Camelot
Newf	N	TL	Killilea, Marie	Putnam & Grosset
Next Spring an Oriole	N	HF	Whelan, Gloria	Random House
No Room For a Dog	N	RF	Nichols, Joan Kane	Hearst
No Way, Winky Blue!	N	F	Jane, Pamela	Mondo
Not-So-Perfect Rosie	N	RF	Giff, Patricia Reilly	The Penguin Group
Now You See Me...Now You Don't	N	F	The Zack Files	Grosset & Dunlap
Obadiah the Bold	N	RF	Turkle, Brinton	The Penguin Group
Off To Squintum's/The Four Musicians	N	TL	Collins, Gillian	Mondo
Olympics and the Mini Olympics, The	N	I	Mack, Rachel	Wright Group/McGraw Hill
On the Right Track	N	I	Gard, Stephen	Rigby
Oscar & Tatiana	N	RF	Literacy 2000	Rigby
Our Book of Maps	N	I	Discovery World	Rigby
Papagayo the Mischief Maker	N	TL	McDermott, Gerald	Harcourt Brace
Pet Vet	N	I	Pacific Literacy	Pacific Learning
Phan's Diary	N	RF	PM Ruby	Rigby
Photos, Photos	N	I	Wildcats	Wright Group/McGraw Hill
Picture Book of Jesse Owens, A	N	B	Adler, David A.	Holiday House
Picture Book of John F. Kennedy, A	N	B	Adler, David A.	Holiday House
Picture Book of Robert E. Lee, A	N	B	Adler, David A.	Holiday House
Pie Magic	N	F	Cornell, Laura	Beech Tree Books
Pioneer Cat	N	HF	Hooks, William H.	Random House
Pirate's Promise	N	RF	Bulla, Clyde Robert	HarperTrophy
Pitching Trouble	N	RF	Kroll, Stephen	Avon Camelot
Planning a Birthday Party	N	I	Book Shop	Mondo
Playing Favorites	N	RF	Kroll, Steven	Avon Camelot
Pluto	N	I	A First Book	Franklin Watts
Pluto	N	I	A True Book	Children's Press
Polar Bears	N	I	PM Animal Facts: Silver	Rigby
Polar Regions	N	I	Habitats of the World	Dominie Press
Pompeii...Buried Alive!	N	I	Kunhardt, Edith	Random House
Popcorn Book, The	N	I	dePaola, Tomie	Holiday House
Postcards From France	N	I	Arnold, Helen	Steck-Vaughn
Postcards From Kenya	N	I	Arnold, Helen	Steck-Vaughn
Postcards From South Africa	N	I	Dawson, Zoe	Steck-Vaughn
Postcards From Vietnam	N	I	Allard, Denise	Steck-Vaughn
Potato	N	RF	Peirce, Robin	Wright Group/McGraw Hill
Potter in Fiji, A	N	I	Wonder World	Wright Group/McGraw Hill
Power Machines	N	I	Robbins, Ken	Henry Holt & Company
Prehistoric Record Breakers	N	I	Discovery World	Rigby
Presidency, The	N	I	A True Book	Children's Press
Pride of the Rockets	N	RF	Kroll, Stephen	Avon Camelot
Princess Euphorbia	N	RF	SupaDoopers	Sundance
Project Apollo	N	I	A True Book	Children's Press
Project Gemini	N	I	A True Book	Children's Press
Project Mercury	N	I	A True Book	Children's Press
Proof of Magic	N	F	Dionetti, Michelle	Wright Group/McGraw Hill
Prudence	N	I	Raatma, Lucia	Capstone Press
Puppy Love	N	RF	Duffey, Betsy	Puffin Books
Queen of the Pool	N	RF	PM Emerald	Rigby
Quilt with a Difference, A	N	I	Pacific Literacy	Pacific Learning
Rabbits	N	I	Literacy 2000	Rigby

Title	Level	Genre	Author/Series	Publisher/Distributor
Rainbow Solution, The	N	RF	Literacy 2000	Rigby
Return of the Home Run Kid	N	RF	Christopher, Matt	Scholastic
Rhythm and Shoes	N	I	Pacific Literacy	Pacific Learning
Rock Climbing	N	I	Ramsey, Joe	Wright Group/McGraw Hill
Rodney, the Surfing Duck	N	F	SupaDoopers	Sundance
Rollerama	N	RF	SupaDoopers	Sundance
Rosie's Big City Ballet	N	RF	Giff, Patricia Reilly	The Penguin Group
Rosie's Nutcracker Dreams	N	RF	Giff, Patricia Reilly	The Penguin Group
Round and Round: The Story of Wheels	N	I	McAlister, Margaret	Rigby
Rumpelstiltskin	N	TL	Zelinsky, Paul O.	Scholastic
Sacajawea	N	B	Biography	Benchmark Education
Saturn	N	I	A First Book	Franklin Watts
Saturn	N	I	A True Book	Children's Press
Save the Manatee	N	I	Friesinger, Alison	Random House
Saving the Park	N	RF	Wilson, Sarah	Pacific Learning
Say Hola, Sarah	N	RF	Giff, Patricia Reilly	Bantam Doubleday Dell
Scary Day, The	N	RF	Bennett, Jean	Pacific Learning
School's Out	N	RF	Hurwitz, Johanna	Scholastic
Seals and Sea Lions	N	I	Cole, Sally	Wright Group/McGraw Hill
Seasons	N	I	A True Book	Children's Press
Seasons	N	I	Simply Science	Compass Point Books
Second Chance	N	RF	Kroll, Stephen	Avon Camelot
Second Story Sally	N	RF	SupaDoopers	Sundance
Second-Grade Star	N	RF	Alberts, Nancy	Scholastic
Secret Land of the Past	N	F	Schlein, Miriam	Scholastic
Secret, The	N	RF	PM Emerald	Rigby
Self-Discipline	N	I	Raatma, Lucia	Capstone Press
Shadow of the Wolf	N	I	Whelan, Gloria	Random House
Shapes of Water, The, Stories About Patterns and Shapes	N	I	Shannan, Gillian and others	Pacific Learning
Shark in School	N	RF	Giff, Patricia Reilly	Bantam Doubleday Dell
Shoeshine Girl	N	RF	Bulla, Clyde Robert	HarperTrophy
Sidewalk Story	N	RF	Mathis, Sharon Bell	The Penguin Group
Silkworms	N	I	Blackburn, Rachel	Wright Group/McGraw Hill
Silver	N	RF	Whelan, Gloria	Random House
Simon and the Aliens	N	SF	SupaDoopers	Sundance
Skirt, The	N	RF	Soto, Gary	Bantam Doubleday Dell
Slugs and Snails	N	I	Book Shop	Mondo
Slump, The	N	RF	Kroll, Stephen	Avon Camelot
Smartest Bear and His Brother Oliver, The	N	F	Bach, Alice	Bantam Doubleday Dell
Sod Houses on the Great Plains	N	I	Rounds, Glen	Holiday House
Soil	N	I	Simply Science	Compass Point Books
Solar System, The	N	I	A True Book	Children's Press
Solids, Liquids, Gases	N	I	Simply Science	Compass Point Books
Someday Cyril	N	RF	Gershator, Phillis	Mondo
Someone is Following Pip Ramsey	N	RF	Roy, Ron	Random House
Something Queer at the Ball Park	N	RF	Levy, Elizabeth	Bantam Doubleday Dell
Something Queer at the Haunted School	N	RF	Levy, Elizabeth	Bantam Doubleday Dell
Something Queer at the Lemonade Stand	N	RF	Levy, Elizabeth	Bantam Doubleday Dell
Something Queer at the Library	N	RF	Levy, Elizabeth	Bantam Doubleday Dell
Something Queer at the Scary Movie	N	RF	Levy, Elizabeth	Hyperion
Something Queer in Outer Space	N	RF	Levy, Elizabeth	Hyperion
Something Queer in the Cafeteria	N	RF	Levy, Elizabeth	Hyperion
Something Queer in the Wild West	N	RF	Levy, Elizabeth	Hyperion
Something Queer Is Going On	N	RF	Levy, Elizabeth	Bantam Doubleday Dell
Something Queer on Vacation	N	RF	Levy, Elizabeth	Bantam Doubleday Dell
Space Stations	N	I	A True Book	Children's Press
Spirit of Hope	N	F	Book Shop	Mondo
Splatter	N	RF	Marriott, Janice	Pacific Learning
Squirrels	N	I	Storyteller Nonfiction	Wright Group/McGraw Hill

Title	Level	Genre	Author/Series	Publisher/Distributor
Stage Fright	N	RF	Martin, Ann	Scholastic
Starring Rosie	N	RF	Giff, Patricia Reilly	The Penguin Group
Stars	N	I	A True Book	Children's Press
Statue of Liberty, The	N	I	A True Book	Children's Press
Stories Huey Tells, The	N	RF	Cameron, Ann	Alfred A. Knopf
Stories Julian Tells, The	N	RF	Cameron, Ann	Alfred A. Knopf
Storm in the Night	N	RF	Stolz, Mary	Harper Collins
Strange Creatures	N	SF	Cartwright, Pauline	Pacific Learning
Streak, The	N	RF	Kroll, Stephen	Avon Camelot
Striped Ice Cream	N	RF	Lexau, Joan M.	Scholastic
Summer Reading is Killing Me!	N	F	Scieszka, Jon	Puffin Books
Sun, The	N	I	Literacy 2000	Rigby
Super-tuned!	N	RF	PM Emerald	Rigby
Supernova	N	RF	PM Ruby	Rigby
Supreme Court, The	N	I	A True Book	Children's Press
Take A Look	N	I	Wildcats	Wright Group/McGraw Hill
Telling Stories Through Art	N	I	Reimer, Luther	Wright Group/McGraw Hill
Ten O'Clock Club, The	N	F	Beach York, Carol	Scholastic
Third Grade Bullies	N	RF	Levy, Elizabeth	Hyperion
Thomas Jefferson: Author, Inventor, President	N	B	Rookie Biographies	Children's Press
Through the Medicine Cabinet	N	F	The Zack Files	Grosset & Dunlap
Throw-Away Pets	N	RF	Duffey, Betsy	Puffin Books
Thunderstorms	N	I	A True Book	Children's Press
Thurgood Marshall: First Black Supreme Court Justice	N	B	Rookie Biographies	Children's Press
Timedetectors	N	SF	SupaDoopers	Sundance
Titanic, The: Lost. . .and Found	N	I	Donnelly, Judy	Random House
To the Top!: Climbing the World's Highest Mountain	N	B	Kramer, S. A.	Random House
Tom Edison's Bright Idea	N	B	Keller, Jack	Steck-Vaughn
Tornadoes!	N	I	Hopping, Lorraine Jean	Scholastic
Tractor Trailers	N	I	Schaefer, Lola M.	Capstone Press
Trojan Horse, The	N	I	Literacy 2000	Rigby
Trojan Horse, The: How the Greeks Won the War	N	HF	Little, Emily	Random House
Tropical Rainforests	N	I	Habitats of the World	Dominie Press
Trouble with Buster, The	N	RF	Lorimer, Janet	Scholastic
Trouble with Parents, The	N	RF	SupaDoopers	Sundance
True-Life Treasure Hunts	N	I	Donnelly, Judy	Random House
Turkeys' Side of It, The	N	RF	Smith, Janice Lee	HarperTrophy
Unexpected Treasure	N	RF	Dionetti, Michelle	Wright Group/McGraw Hill
Unusual Spiders	N	I	Jensen, Ned	Wright Group/McGraw Hill
Up and Away!: Taking a Flight	N	RF	Book Shop	Mondo
Up High in the Mountains	N	RF	Wildcats	Wright Group/McGraw Hill
Uranus	N	I	A True Book	Children's Press
Venus	N	I	A True Book	Children's Press
Volcano Goddess Will See You Now, The	N	F	The Zack Files	Grosset & Dunlap
Volcanoes	N	I	A True Book	Children's Press
Wacky Wheels	N	I	Pacific Literacy	Pacific Learning
Water	N	I	Simply Science	Compass Point Books
Weather	N	I	Literacy 2000	Rigby
Weather	N	I	Simply Science	Compass Point Books
Weather Watch	N	I	Wonders!	Hampton-Brown
Whale Tales	N	I	Westerskov, Kim	Pacific Learning
Whales	N	I	Book Shop	Mondo
Whales	N	I	PM Animal Facts: Silver	Rigby
Whales' Song, The	N	I	Sheldon, Dyan	The Penguin Group
What Am I Made Of?	N	I	Bennett, David	Scholastic
What Can It Be?	N	I	Schaefer, Lola M.	Benchmark Education
What's the Matter, Kelly Beans?	N	RF	Enderle, Judith R. & Tessler, S. G.	Candlewick Press
What's the Matter with Herbie Jones?	N	RF	Kline, Suzy	The Penguin Group
When I Forgot	N	RF	Marriott, Janice	Pacific Learning
Where Do You Live?	N	I	People, Places & Spaces	Rand McNally

Title	Level	Genre	Author/Series	Publisher/Distributor
White Bird	N	RF	Bulla, Clyde Robert	Random House
Wild Willie and King Kyle Detectives	N	F	Joosse, Barbara M.	Bantam Doubleday Dell
Wildfires	N	I	A True Book	Children's Press
Wolves	N	I	PM Animal Facts: Silver	Rigby
Wonderful Alexander and the Catwings	N	F	Schindler, S.D.	Scholastic
Working Cotton	N	RF	Williams, Sherley Anne	Harcourt Brace
Writer's Work, A	N	I	Wonder World	Wright Group/McGraw Hill
Wrong Way Around Magic	N	F	Chew, Ruth	Scholastic
Yikes! Grandma's a Teenager	N	F	The Zack Files	Grossett&Dunlap
You Can't Eat Your Chicken Pox, Amber Brown	N	RF	Danziger, Paula	Scholastic
You're Out	N	RF	Kroll, Stephen	Avon Camelot
Zap! I'm a Mind Reader	N	SF	The Zack Files	Grosset & Dunlap
Zebras	N	I	Meadows, Graham & Vial, Claire	Dominie Press
89th Kitten, The	O	RF	Nilsson, Eleanor	Scholastic
Abraham Lincoln	O	B	Early Biographies	Compass Point Books
Abraham Lincoln: President of a Divided Country	O	B	Greene, Carol	Children's Press
Adventure In Alaska	O	I	Kramer, S.A.	Random House
Adventures of Ali Baba Bernstein, The	O	RF	Hurwitz, Johanna	Scholastic
Aesop & Company: With Scenes from His Legendary Life	O	TL	Bader, Barbara	Houghton Mifflin
African-American Scientists	O	B	St. John, Jetty	Capstone Press
Aldo Ice Cream	O	RF	Hurwitz, Johanna	The Penguin Group
Aldo Peanut Butter	O	RF	Hurwitz, Johanna	The Penguin Group
Alfred the Curious	O	RF	PM Emerald	Rigby
Ali Baba Bernstein, Lost and Found	O	RF	Hurwitz, Johanna	Avon
All Kinds of Animals	O	I	It's Science	Children's Press
Allen Jay and the Underground Railroad	O	HF	Brill, Marlene Targ	Carolrhoda Books
Almost Starring Skinnybones	O	RF	Park, Barbara	Random House
Amigo	O	F	Baylor, Byrd	Aladdin
Angel for Solomon Singer, An	O	RF	Rylant, Cynthia	Orchard Books
Angel Park Hoopstars: Nothing But Net	O	RF	Hughes, Dean	Alfred A. Knopf
Angel Park Hoopstars: Point Guard	O	RF	Hughes, Dean	Alfred A. Knopf
Angel Park Soccer Stars: Backup Goalie	O	RF	Hughes, Dean	Random House
Angel Park Soccer Stars: Defense!	O	RF	Hughes, Dean	Alfred A. Knopf
Angel Park Soccer Stars: Psyched!	O	RF	Hughes, Dean	Random House
Angel Park Soccer Stars: Total Soccer	O	RF	Hughes, Dean	Alfred A. Knopf
Angel Park Soccer Stars: Victory Goal	O	RF	Hughes, Dean	Alfred A. Knopf
Angel's Mother's Boyfriend	O	RF	Delton, Judy	Houghton Mifflin
Angry Bull and Other Cases, The	O	RF	Simon, Seymour	Avon
Animal Champions	O	I	Jones, Teri Crawford	Pearson Learning
Ant	O	I	Chinery, Michael	Troll
Ant Cities	O	I	Dorros, Arthur	HarperCollins
Ark, The	O	HF	Geisert, Arthur	Houghton Mifflin
Australia	O	I	Dahl, Michael	Capstone Press
Baby Animal Zoo	O	I	Martin, Ann M.	Scholastic
Baby-Sitters Club: Abby and the Best Kid Ever	O	RF	Martin, Ann M.	Scholastic
Baby-Sitters Club: Abby the Bad Sport	O	RF	Martin, Ann M.	Scholastic
Baby-Sitters Club: Claudia and the Bad Joke	O	RF	Martin, Ann M.	Scholastic
Baby-Sitters Club: Claudia and the Little Liar	O	RF	Martin, Ann M.	Scholastic
Baby-Sitters Club: Claudia and the New Girl	O	RF	Martin, Ann M.	Scholastic
Baby-Sitters Club: Claudia and the Phantom Phone Calls	O	RF	Martin, Ann M.	Scholastic
Baby-Sitters Club: Dawn and Too Many Sitters	O	RF	Martin, Ann M.	Scholastic
Baby-Sitters Club: Dawn's Big Move	O	RF	Martin, Ann M.	Scholastic
Baby-Sitters Club: Dawn's Wicked Stepsister	O	RF	Martin, Ann M.	Scholastic
Baby-Sitters Club: Get Well Soon, Mallory	O	RF	Martin, Ann M.	Scholastic
Baby-Sitters Club: Ghost at Dawn's House, The	O	RF	Martin, Ann M.	Scholastic
Baby-Sitters Club: Good-bye Stacey, Good-bye	O	RF	Martin, Ann M.	Scholastic
Baby-Sitters Club: Hello, Mallory	O	RF	Martin, Ann M.	Scholastic

Title	Level	Genre	Author/Series	Publisher/Distributor
Baby-Sitters Club: Jessi and the Bad Baby-Sitter	O	RF	Martin, Ann M.	Scholastic
Baby-Sitters Club: Jessi and the Superbrat	O	RF	Martin, Ann M.	Scholastic
Baby-Sitters Club: Jessi Ramsey, Pet-sitter	O	RF	Martin, Ann M.	Scholastic
Baby-Sitters Club: Kristy and the Snobs	O	RF	Martin, Ann M.	Scholastic
Baby-Sitters Club: Kristy's Big Day	O	RF	Martin, Ann M.	Scholastic
Baby-Sitters Club: Kristy's Great Idea	O	RF	Martin, Ann M.	Scholastic
Baby-Sitters Club: Mary Anne and Camp BSC	O	RF	Martin, Ann M.	Scholastic
Baby-Sitters Club: Mary Anne Saves the Day	O	RF	Martin, Ann M.	Scholastic
Baby-Sitters Club Mystery: Beware, Dawn!	O	RF	Martin, Ann M.	Scholastic
Baby-Sitters Club Mystery: Claudia, Clue in the Photograph	O	RF	Martin, Ann M.	Scholastic
Baby-Sitters Club Mystery: Claudia, Mystery at the Museum	O	RF	Martin, Ann M.	Scholastic
Baby-Sitters Club Mystery: Claudia, Recipe for Danger	O	RF	Martin, Ann M.	Scholastic
Baby-Sitters Club Mystery: Dawn, Disappearing Dogs	O	RF	Martin, Ann M.	Scholastic
Baby-Sitters Club Mystery: Dawn, Halloween Mystery	O	RF	Martin, Ann M.	Scholastic
Baby-Sitters Club Mystery: Dawn, Surfer Ghost	O	RF	Martin, Ann M.	Scholastic
Baby-Sitters Club Mystery: Jessi, Jewel Thieves	O	RF	Martin, Ann M.	Scholastic
Baby-Sitters Club Mystery: Kristy, Haunted Mansion	O	RF	Martin, Ann M.	Scholastic
Baby-Sitters Club Mystery: Kristy, Missing Child	O	RF	Martin, Ann M.	Scholastic
Baby-Sitters Club Mystery: Kristy, Missing Fortune	O	RF	Martin, Ann M.	Scholastic
Baby-Sitters Club Mystery: Kristy, Vampires	O	RF	Martin, Ann M.	Scholastic
Baby-Sitters Club Mystery: Mallory, Ghost Cat	O	RF	Martin, Ann M.	Scholastic
Baby-Sitters Club Mystery: Mary Anne, Library Mystery	O	RF	Martin, Ann M.	Scholastic
Baby-Sitters Club Mystery: Mary Anne, Secret in the Attic	O	RF	Martin, Ann M.	Scholastic
Baby-Sitters Club Mystery: Mary Anne, Zoo Mystery	O	RF	Martin, Ann M.	Scholastic
Baby-Sitters Club Mystery: Mystery at Claudia's House	O	RF	Martin, Ann M.	Scholastic
Baby-Sitters Club Mystery: Stacey and the Mystery Money	O	RF	Martin, Ann M.	Scholastic
Baby-Sitters Club Mystery: Stacey, Haunted Masquerade	O	RF	Martin, Ann M.	Scholastic
Baby-Sitters Club Mystery: Stacey, Missing Ring	O	RF	Martin, Ann M.	Scholastic
Baby-Sitters Club Mystery: Stacey, Mystery at the Empty House	O	RF	Martin, Ann M.	Scholastic
Baby-Sitters Club Mystery: Stacy, Mystery at the Mall	O	RF	Martin, Ann M.	Scholastic
Baby-Sitters Club Special Edition, The: Readers Request	O	RF	Martin, Ann M.	Scholastic
Baby-Sitters Club: Welcome to the BSC, Abby	O	RF	Martin, Ann M.	Scholastic
Baby-Sitters Little Sister	O	RF	Martin, Ann M.	Scholastic
Baby-Sitters Little Sister: Karen's Big Sister	O	RF	Martin, Ann M.	Scholastic
Baby-Sitters Little Sister: Karen's Dinosaur	O	RF	Martin, Ann M.	Scholastic
Baby-Sitters Little Sister: Karen's Monsters	O	RF	Martin, Ann M.	Scholastic
Baby-Sitters Little Sister: Karen's Mystery Super Special	O	RF	Martin, Ann M.	Scholastic
Baby-Sitters Little Sister (Karen's Stepmother)	O	RF	Martin, Ann M.	Scholastic
Back Home	O	RF	Pinkney, Gloria Jean	The Penguin Group
Back Yard Angel	O	RF	Delton, Judy	Houghton Mifflin
Bagels for Kids	O	I	Pacific Literacy	Pacific Learning
Baseball Fever	O	RF	Hurwitz, Johanna	William Morrow
Baseball Megastars	O	I	Weber, Bruce	Scholastic
Baseball Pitching Challenge and Other Cases, The	O	RF	Simon, Seymour	Avon
Baseball Saved Us	O	HF	Mochizuki, Ken	Scholastic
Baseball's Best: Five True Stories	O	B	Step into Reading	Random House
Bats	O	I	Gibbons, Gail	Holiday House
Bats	O	I	Holmes, Kevin J.	Capstone Press
Battle of Words, A	O	RF	Literacy 2000	Rigby
Beacons of Light: Lighthouses	O	I	Gibbons, Gail	Scholastic
Bears	O	I	Holmes, Kevin J.	Capstone Press

Title	Level	Genre	Author/Series	Publisher/Distributor
Beatrix Potter	O	B	Wallner, Alexandra	Holiday House
Bees	O	I	Holmes, Kevin J.	Capstone Press
Beezus & Ramona	O	RF	Cleary, Beverly	Avon
Benjamin Franklin: A Man with Many Jobs	O	B	Greene, Carol	Children's Press
Best Wishes	O	B	Rylant, Cynthia	Richard C. Owen
Bicycle Book, The	O	I	PM Nonfiction -Emerald	Rigby
Bicycle Rider	O	B	Scioscia, Mary	HarperTrophy
Big Boy	O	TL	Mollel, Tololwa M.	Houghton Mifflin
Bill Clinton: Forty-Second President of the U.S.	O	B	Greene, Carol	Children's Press
Birds of Prey	O	I	Woolley, M. & Pigdon, K.	Mondo
Blossom Promise, A	O	RF	Byars, Betsy	Bantam Doubleday Dell
Blossoms and the Green Phantom, The	O	RF	Byars, Betsy	Dell
Blossoms Meet the Vulture Lady, The	O	RF	Byars, Betsy	Bantam Doubleday Dell
Booker T. Washington	O	B	First Biographies	Steck-Vaughn
Bookworm Who Hatched, A	O	B	Aardema, Verna	Richard C. Owen
Borreguita and the Coyote	O	TL	Aardema, Verna	Scholastic
Boxcar Children: Amusement Park Mystery, The	O	RF	Warner, Gertrude Chandler	Albert Whitman & Co.
Boxcar Children: Animal Shelter Mystery, The	O	RF	Warner, Gertrude Chandler	Albert Whitman & Co.
Boxcar Children: Basketball Mystery, The	O	RF	Warner, Gertrude Chandler	Albert Whitman & Co.
Boxcar Children: Benny Uncovers a Mystery	O	RF	Warner, Gertrude Chandler	Albert Whitman & Co.
Boxcar Children: Bicycle Mystery	O	RF	Warner, Gertrude Chandler	Albert Whitman & Co.
Boxcar Children: Black Pearl Mystery, The	O	RF	Warner, Gertrude Chandler	Albert Whitman & Co.
Boxcar Children: Blue Bay Mystery	O	RF	Warner, Gertrude Chandler	Albert Whitman & Co.
Boxcar Children: Boxcar Children, The	O	RF	Warner, Gertrude Chandler	Albert Whitman & Co.
Boxcar Children: Bus Station Mystery	O	RF	Warner, Gertrude Chandler	Albert Whitman & Co.
Boxcar Children: Caboose Mystery	O	RF	Warner, Gertrude Chandler	Albert Whitman & Co.
Boxcar Children: Camp-Out Mystery, The	O	RF	Warner, Gertrude Chandler	Albert Whitman & Co.
Boxcar Children: Canoe Trip Mystery, The	O	RF	Warner, Gertrude Chandler	Albert Whitman & Co.
Boxcar Children: Castle Mystery, The	O	RF	Warner, Gertrude Chandler	Albert Whitman & Co.
Boxcar Children: Cereal Box Mystery, The	O	RF	Warner, Gertrude Chandler	Albert Whitman & Co.
Boxcar Children: Deserted Library Mystery, The	O	RF	Warner, Gertrude Chandler	Albert Whitman & Co.
Boxcar Children: Dinosaur Mystery, The	O	RF	Warner, Gertrude Chandler	Albert Whitman & Co.
Boxcar Children: Disappearing Friend Mystery, The	O	RF	Warner, Gertrude Chandler	Albert Whitman & Co.
Boxcar Children: Firehouse Mystery, The	O	RF	Warner, Gertrude Chandler	Albert Whitman & Co.
Boxcar Children: Ghost Ship Mystery, The	O	RF	Warner, Gertrude Chandler	Albert Whitman & Co.
Boxcar Children: Haunted Cabin Mystery, The	O	RF	Warner, Gertrude Chandler	Albert Whitman & Co.
Boxcar Children: Lighthouse Mystery, The	O	RF	Warner, Gertrude Chandler	Albert Whitman & Co.
Boxcar Children: Mike's Mystery	O	RF	Warner, Gertrude Chandler	Albert Whitman & Co.
Boxcar Children: Mountain Top Mystery	O	RF	Warner, Gertrude Chandler	Albert Whitman & Co.
Boxcar Children: Mystery at Snowflake Inn, The	O	RF	Warner, Gertrude Chandler	Albert Whitman & Co.
Boxcar Children: Mystery at the Alamo, The	O	RF	Warner, Gertrude Chandler	Albert Whitman & Co.
Boxcar Children: Mystery at the Dog Show, The	O	RF	Warner, Gertrude Chandler	Albert Whitman & Co.
Boxcar Children: Mystery at the Fair	O	RF	Warner, Gertrude Chandler	Rigby
Boxcar Children: Mystery Behind the Wall	O	RF	Warner, Gertrude Chandler	HarperTrophy
Boxcar Children: Mystery Bookstore, The	O	RF	Warner, Gertrude Chandler	Albert Whitman & Co.
Boxcar Children: Mystery Cruise, The	O	RF	Warner, Gertrude Chandler	Albert Whitman & Co.
Boxcar Children: Mystery Girl, The	O	RF	Warner, Gertrude Chandler	Albert Whitman & Co.
Boxcar Children: Mystery Horse, The	O	RF	Warner, Gertrude Chandler	Albert Whitman & Co.
Boxcar Children: Mystery in San Francisco, The	O	RF	Warner, Gertrude Chandler	Albert Whitman & Co.
Boxcar Children: Mystery in the Cave, The	O	RF	Warner, Gertrude Chandler	Albert Whitman & Co.
Boxcar Children: Mystery in the Old Attic, The	O	RF	Warner, Gertrude Chandler	Albert Whitman & Co.
Boxcar Children: Mystery in the Sand	O	RF	Warner, Gertrude Chandler	Albert Whitman & Co.
Boxcar Children: Mystery in Washington, DC, The	O	RF	Warner, Gertrude Chandler	Albert Whitman & Co.
Boxcar Children: Mystery of the Hidden Beach	O	RF	Warner, Gertrude Chandler	Albert Whitman & Co.
Boxcar Children: Mystery of the Lost Mine, The	O	RF	Warner, Gertrude Chandler	Albert Whitman & Co.
Boxcar Children: Mystery of the Lost Village, The	O	RF	Warner, Gertrude Chandler	Albert Whitman & Co.
Boxcar Children: Mystery of the Missing Cat, The	O	RF	Warner, Gertrude Chandler	Albert Whitman & Co.
Boxcar Children: Mystery of the Mixed-Up Zoo, The	O	RF	Warner, Gertrude Chandler	Albert Whitman & Co.
Boxcar Children: Mystery of the Stolen Music, The	O	RF	Warner, Gertrude Chandler	Scholastic
Boxcar Children: Mystery on Stage, The	O	RF	Warner, Gertrude Chandler	Albert Whitman & Co.

Title	Level	Genre	Author/Series	Publisher/Distributor
Boxcar Children: Mystery on the Train, The	O	RF	Warner, Gertrude Chandler	Albert Whitman & Co.
Boxcar Children: Mystery Ranch	O	RF	Warner, Gertrude Chandler	Albert Whitman & Co.
Boxcar Children: Outer Space Mystery, The	O	RF	Warner, Gertrude Chandler	Albert Whitman & Co.
Boxcar Children: Pizza Mystery, The	O	RF	Warner, Gertrude Chandler	Albert Whitman & Co.
Boxcar Children Return, The	O	RF	Warner, Gertrude Chandler	Scholastic
Boxcar Children: Schoolhouse Mystery	O	RF	Warner, Gertrude Chandler	Albert Whitman & Co.
Boxcar Children: Snowbound Mystery	O	RF	Warner, Gertrude Chandler	Albert Whitman & Co.
Boxcar Children: Soccer Mystery, The	O	RF	Warner, Gertrude Chandler	Scholastic
Boxcar Children Special: The Mystery at Snowflake Inn	O	RF	Warner, Gertrude Chandler	Albert Whitman & Co.
Boxcar Children Special: The Mystery at the Ballpark	O	RF	Warner, Gertrude Chandler	Albert Whitman & Co.
Boxcar Children Special: The Mystery at the Fair	O	RF	Warner, Gertrude Chandler	Albert Whitman & Co.
Boxcar Children Special: The Pilgrim Village Mystery	O	RF	Warner, Gertrude Chandler	Albert Whitman & Co.
Boxcar Children: Surprise Island	O	RF	Warner, Gertrude Chandler	Scholastic
Boxcar Children: Woodshed Mystery, The	O	RF	Warner, Gertrude Chandler	Albert Whitman & Co.
Boxcar Children: Yellow House Mystery, The	O	RF	Warner, Gertrude Chandler	Albert Whitman & Co.
Brazil	O	I	Dahl, Michael	Capstone Press
Broken Window and Other Cases, The	O	RF	Simon, Seymour	Avon
Brown Sunshine of Sawdust Valley	O	RF	Henry, Marguerite	Aladdin
Bugs	O	I	Parker, N. W. & Wright, J. R.	Mulberry Books
Building Homes, Building Hope	O	I	Bovez, Marcie	Wright Group/McGraw Hill
Bungee 70528	O	RF	Belcher, Angie	Pacific Learning
Butterflies	O	I	Holmes, Kevin J.	Capstone Press
Can You Imagine?	O	B	McKissack, Patricia	Richard C. Owen
Canada	O	I	Dahl, Michael	Capstone Press
Candlelight Service	O	RF	Literacy 2000	Rigby
Canoe Diary	O	I	Bishop, Nic	Pacific Learning
Case of the Dirty Bird, The	O	RF	Paulsen, Gary	Bantam Doubleday Dell
Cat Crazy	O	RF	Baglio, Ben M.	Scholastic
Cat's Meow, The	O	F	Soto, Gary	Scholastic
Caves and Caverns	O	I	Gibbons, Gail	Harcourt Brace
Charles Lindbergh	O	B	Early Biographies	Compass Point Books
Chick Challenge	O	RF	Baglio, Ben M.	Scholastic
China	O	I	Dahl, Michael	Capstone Press
China's Bravest Girl: The Legend of Hua Mu Lan	O	TL	Chin, Charlie	Children's Press
Chocolate Fever	O	F	Smith, Robert	Bantam Doubleday Dell
Christopher Columbus: A Great Explorer	O	B	Greene, Carol	Children's Press
Cities: Then and Now	O	I	People, Spaces & Places	Rand McNally
Class Clown	O	RF	Hurwitz, Johanna	Scholastic
Class President	O	RF	Hurwitz, Johanna	Scholastic
Cloak of the Wind	O	HF	Voyages in...	Wright Group/McGraw Hill
Clothes	O	I	Wonder World	Wright Group/McGraw Hill
Clue Jr.: The Case of the Chocolate Fingerprints	O	RF	Hinter, Parker C.	Scholastic
Comeback Dog, The	O	RF	Thomas, Jane Resh	Bantam Doubleday Dell
Corn Is Maize: The Gift of the Indians	O	I	Aliki	Steck-Vaughn
Courage of Sarah Noble, The	O	HF	Dalgliesh, Alice	Aladdin
Cow	O	I	Older, Jules	Charlesbridge
Cowpokes and Desperadoes	O	RF	Paulsen, Gary	Bantam Doubleday Dell
Creature from Beneath the Ice and Other Cases, The	O	RF	Simon, Seymour	Avon
Crowded Dock and Other Cases, The	O	RF	Simon, Seymour	Avon
Crying Rocks and Other Cases, The	O	RF	Simon, Seymour	Avon
Cuba	O	I	Mara, William P.	Capstone Press
Culpepper's Canyon	O	RF	Paulsen, Gary	Bantam Doubleday Dell
Danger on Midnight River	O	RF	Paulsen, Gary	Bantam Doubleday Dell
Dangerous Comet and Other Cases, The	O	RF	Simon, Seymour	Avon
Daniel Boone: Man of the Forests	O	B	Greene, Carol	Children's Press
DeDe Takes Charge!	O	RF	Hurwitz, Johanna	Morrow
Deserts	O	I	Gibbons, Gail	Holiday House
Diego Rivera	O	B	First Biographies	Steck-Vaughn
Different Dragons	O	RF	Little, Jean	The Penguin Group
Dinosaur Connection, The	O	I	Wilde, Buck	Rigby

Title	Level	Genre	Author/Series	Publisher/Distributor
Dinosaur Detective	O	I	Wildcats	Wright Group/McGraw Hill
Dirty Beasts	O	F	Dahl, Roald	The Penguin Group
Disappearing Cookies and Other Cases, The	O	RF	Simon, Seymour	Avon
Disappearing Ice Cream and Other Cases, The	O	RF	Simon, Seymour	Avon
Disappearing Snowball and Other Cases, The	O	RF	Simon, Seymour	Avon
Discovering the Titanic	O	I	Trumbore, Cindy	Pearson Learning
Distant Stars and Other Cases, The	O	RF	Simon, Seymour	Avon
Does Third Grade Last Forever?	O	RF	Schanback, Mindy	Troll
Doggy Dare	O	RF	Baglio, Ben M.	Scholastic
Dogs Don't Tell Jokes	O	RF	Sachar, Louis	Alfred A. Knopf
Dolphins	O	I	Holmes, Kevin J.	Capstone Press
Douglas Fir	O	I	Davis, Wendy	Children's Press
Dragon Bones	O	F	Hindman, Paul	Random House
Dragon Parade: A Chinese New Year Story	O	I	Chin, Steven A.	Steck-Vaughn
Dream Come True, A	O	B	Hurwitz, Johanna	Richard C. Owen
Duckling Diary	O	RF	Baglio, Ben M.	Scholastic
Dunkin' Dazza's Daring Dribble	O	RF	SupaDoopers	Sundance
Dunkin' Dazza's Soaring Slammer	O	RF	SupaDoopers	Sundance
Earthquakes	O	I	Branley, Franklyn M.	HarperCollins
Earthworms	O	I	Holmes, Kevin J.	Capstone Press
Eleanor Roosevelt: Fighter for Social Justice	O	B	Childhood of Famous Americans	Aladdin
Electric Spark and Other Cases, The	O	RF	Simon, Seymour	Avon
Electricity	O	I	Winkelman, Barbara Gaines	Wright Group/McGraw Hill
Electrifying Cows and Other Cases, The	O	RF	Simon, Seymour	Avon
Eleven Kids, One Summer	O	RF	Martin, Ann M.	Scholastic
Elizabeth Blackwell: First Woman Doctor	O	B	Greene, Carol	Children's Press
Elizabeth Blackwell: Girl Doctor	O	B	Henry, Joanne Landers	Simon & Schuster
Elizabeth the First: Queen of England	O	B	Greene, Carol	Children's Press
Emily Dickinson: American Poet	O	B	Greene, Carol	Children's Press
Exploring with Lewis and Clark	O	I	People, Spaces & Places	Rand McNally
Face-Off	O	RF	Christopher, Matt	Little, Brown & Co.
Famous Children	O	I	Literacy 2000	Rigby
Fantastic Water Pot and Other Cases, The	O	RF	Simon, Seymour	Avon
Far-Out Frisbee and Other Cases, The	O	RF	Simon, Seymour	Avon
Fastest Ketchup in the Cafeteria and Other Cases, The	O	RF	Simon, Seymour	Avon
Fearless Explorer and Other Cases, The	O	RF	Simon, Seymour	Avon
Fine Lines	O	B	Heller, Ruth	Richard C. Owen
Fire! Fire!	O	I	Wildcats	Wright Group/McGraw Hill
Firelight Secrets	O	RF	PM Ruby	Rigby
Firetalking	O	B	Polacco, Patricia	Richard C. Owen
First Americans, The	O	I	People, Spaces & Places	Rand McNally
Flicking the Switch	O	I	Pacific Literacy	Pacific Learning
Flossie and the Fox	O	F	McKissack, Patricia	Scholastic
Flying-Saucer People and Other Cases, The	O	RF	Simon, Seymour	Avon
Food and Festivals: Israel	O	I	Randall, Ronne	Steck-Vaughn
Food and Festivals: Italy	O	I	Pirotta, Saviour	Steck-Vaughn
Foolish Gretel	O	TL	Armstrong, Jennifer	Random House
Fortune-Tellers, The	O	TL	Alexander, Lloyd	Puffin Books
France	O	I	Dahl, Michael	Capstone Press
From Paper Airplanes to Outer Space	O	B	Simon, Seymour	Richard C. Owen
Fudge	O	RF	Graeber, Charlotte Towner	Simon & Schuster
General Butterfingers	O	RF	Gardiner, John Reynolds	Puffin Books
George Washington	O	B	Early Biographies	Compass Point Books
George Washington Carver: Scientist and Teacher	O	B	Greene, Carol	Children's Press
George Washington: Young Leader	O	B	Childhood of Famous Americans	Aladdin
Gerbil Genius	O	RF	Baglio, Ben M.	Scholastic
Germany	O	I	Dahl, Michael	Capstone Press
Gertie's Green Thumb	O	F	Dexter, Catherine	Dell Publishing
Ghana	O	I	Davis, Lucile	Capstone Press
Ghost Pony, The	O	RF	Betancourt, Jeanne	Scholastic

Title	Level	Genre	Author/Series	Publisher/Distributor
Giants, Monsters & Mythical Beasts	O	I	Literacy 2000	Rigby
Gigantic Ants and Other Cases, The	O	RF	Simon, Seymour	Avon
Giraffes	O	I	Reeder, Tracey	Wright Group/McGraw Hill
Glorious Flight, The: Across the Channel with Louis Blériot	O	B	Provensen, Alice & Martin	Puffin Books
Go-cart Team, The	O	I	PM Nonfiction -Emerald	Rigby
Godzilla Ate My Homework	O	F	Jones, Marcia	Scholastic
Going Lobstering	O	I	Pallotta, Jerry & Bolster, Rob	Charlesbridge Publishing
Going West	O	HF	Van Leeuwen, Jean	The Penguin Group
Good Grief. . . Third Grade	O	RF	McKenna, Colleen	Scholastic
Gorganzola Zombies in the Park	O	F	Levy, Elizabeth	HarperTrophy
Grace the Pirate	O	F	Lasky, Kathryn	Hyperion
Grizzly Mistake and Other Cases, The	O	RF	Simon, Seymour	Avon
Growing Ideas	O	B	Van Leeuwen, Jean	Richard C. Owen
Guatemala	O	I	Dahl, Michael	Capstone Press
Guinea Pig Gang	O	RF	Baglio, Ben M.	Scholastic
Hairy Little Critters	O	I	Wilde, Buck	Rigby
Halloween Horror and Other Cases, The	O	RF	Simon, Seymour	Avon
Hamster Hotel	O	RF	Baglio, Ben M.	Scholastic
Happily Ever After	O	F	Quindlen, Anna	The Penguin Group
Harriet's Hare	O	F	King-Smith, Dick	Alfred A. Knopf
Harry Houdini: Young Magician	O	B	Childhood of Famous Americans	Aladdin
Hau Kola Hello Friend	O	B	Goble, Paul	Richard C. Owen
Haunting of Grade Three, The	O	RF	Maccarone, Grace	Scholastic
Head For the Hills!	O	I	Walker, Paul Robert	Random House
Heavy Weight and Other Cases, The	O	RF	Simon, Seymour	Avon
Helen Keller: From Tragedy to Triumph	O	B	Childhood of Famous Americans	Aladdin
Hello, Mrs. Piggle-Wiggle	O	F	MacDonald, Betty	HarperTrophy
Henry and Beezus	O	RF	Cleary, Beverly	Avon
Henry and Ribsy	O	RF	Cleary, Beverly	Hearst
Henry and the Clubhouse	O	RF	Cleary, Beverly	Avon
Henry and the Paper Route	O	RF	Cleary, Beverly	Hearst
Henry Ford: Young Man with Ideas	O	B	Childhood of Famous Americans	Aladdin
Henry Huggins	O	RF	Cleary, Beverly	Avon
Her Seven Brothers	O	TL	Goble, Paul	Aladdin
Here Comes McBroom	O	F	Fleischman, Sid	Beech Tree Books
History of Machines, The	O	I	McKinnon, Judith	Rigby
Hop to it, Minty!	O	RF	PM Ruby	Rigby
Horse Power	O	I	Pacific Literacy	Pacific Learning
Hot and Cold Summer, The	O	RF	Hurwitz, Johanna	Scholastic
Houdini's Last Trick	O	B	Hass, E.A.	Random House
How My Family Lives in America	O	I	Kuklin, Susan	Aladdin
Howling Dog and Other Cases, The	O	RF	Simon, Seymour	Avon
Hundred Dresses, The	O	RF	Estes, Eleanor	Scholastic
Hurray For Ali Baba Bernstein	O	RF	Hurwitz, Johanna	Scholastic
Hurricane Machine and Other Cases, The	O	RF	Simon, Seymour	Avon
Hyenas	O	I	Holmes, Kevin J.	Capstone Press
Hypnotized Frog and Other Cases, The	O	RF	Simon, Seymour	Avon
I Am Rosa Parks	O	B	Parks, Rosa	Dial Books
I Love Guinea Pigs	O	I	King-Smith, Dick	Candlewick Press
I Wonder Why Snakes Shed Their Skins and Other Questions About Reptiles	O	I	O'Neill, Amanda	Scholastic
Icy Question and Other Cases, The	O	RF	Simon, Seymour	Avon
Impossible Bend and Other Cases, The	O	RF	Simon, Seymour	Avon
Incredible Shrinking Machine and Other Cases, The	O	RF	Simon, Seymour	Avon
India	O	I	Dahl, Michael	Capstone Press
Indian-Head Pennies and Other Cases, The	O	RF	Simon, Seymour	Avon
Invisible Stanley	O	F	Brown, Jeff	HarperTrophy
Iron Giant, The	O	SF	Hughes, Ted	Alfred A. Knopf

Title	Level	Genre	Author/Series	Publisher/Distributor
Is There Life in Outer Space	O	I	Branley, Franklyn M.	HarperCollins
Israel	O	I	Thoennes, Kristin	Capstone Press
It Came Through the Wall	O	F	Healey, Tim	Mondo
It's Just a Trick	O	RF	Literacy 2000	Rigby
Italy	O	I	Thoennes, Kristin	Capstone Press
Jackie Robinson	O	B	Early Biographies	Compass Point Books
Jackie Robinson: Baseball's First Black Major Leaguer	O	B	Greene, Carol	Children's Press
Jason and the Aliens Down the Street	O	F	Greer, Greg & Ruddick, Bob	HarperTrophy
Jo Jo Winnie Again	O	RF	Sachs, Marilyn	Dutton
Johann Sebastian Bach: Great Man of Music	O	B	Greene, Carol	Children's Press
John F. Kennedy: America's Youngest President	O	B	Childhood of Famous Americans	Aladdin
Jokes and Riddles	O	I	Literacy 2000	Rigby
Just Plain Cat	O	RF	Robinson, Nancy K.	Scholastic
Just Tell Me When We're Dead!	O	RF	Clifford, Eth	Scholastic
Kenya	O	I	Dahl, Michael	Capstone Press
Key to the Playhouse, The	O	RF	York, Carol	Scholastic
Kid in the Red Jacket, The	O	RF	Park, Barbara	Random House
King's Equal, The	O	TL	Paterson, Katherine	HarperTrophy
Kites	O	I	PM Nonfiction -Emerald	Rigby
Kitten Crowd	O	RF	Baglio, Ben M.	Scholastic
Kristy and the Walking Disaster	O	RF	Martin, Ann M.	Scholastic
Kwanzaa	O	I	Chocolate, Deborah M. Newton	Children's Press
Ladybug, The	O	I	Crewe, Sabrina	Steck-Vaughn
Ladybug, The	O	I	Garland, Peter	Rigby
Lamb Lessons	O	RF	Baglio, Ben M.	Scholastic
Langston Hughes: Young Black Poet	O	B	Childhood of Famous Americans	Aladdin
Laura Ingalls Wilder	O	B	Allen, Thomas B.	Putnam
Laura Ingalls Wilder: Author of the Little House Books	O	B	Greene, Carol	Children's Press
Lavender	O	RF	Hesse, Karen	Henry Holt & Co.
Legend of the Bluebonnet, The	O	TL	dePaola, Tomie	Scholastic
Let's Build a Playground	O	I	Myers, Edward	Pearson Learning
Letter From Phoenix Farm, A	O	B	Yolen, Jane	Richard C. Owen
Liar, Liar, Pants on Fire	O	RF	Korman, Gordon	Scholastic
Lightweight Rocket and Other Cases, The	O	RF	Simon, Seymour	Avon
Like Jake and Me	O	RF	Jukes, Mavis	Alfred A. Knopf
Lions	O	I	Holmes, Kevin J.	Capstone Press
Little Icicle	O	RF	Szymanski, Lois	Avon Camelot
Little Miss Stoneybrook and Dawn	O	RF	Martin, Ann M.	Scholastic
Little Pear	O	HF	Lattimore, Eleanor F.	Harcourt Brace
Little Pear and His Friends	O	HF	Lattimore, Eleanor F.	Harcourt Brace
Living in Space	O	I	Nayer, Judy	Pearson Learning
Llama in the Family, A	O	RF	Hurwitz, Johanna	Scholastic
Look Out, Washington D.C.!	O	RF	Giff, Patricia Reilly	Bantam Doubleday Dell
Look What Came from China	O	I	Harvey, Miles	Franklin Watts
Look What Came from Egypt	O	I	Harvey, Miles	Franklin Watts
Look What Came from France	O	I	Harvey, Miles	Franklin Watts
Look What Came from Italy	O	I	Harvey, Miles	Franklin Watts
Look What Came from Mexico	O	I	Harvey, Miles	Franklin Watts
Look What Came from Russia	O	I	Harvey, Miles	Franklin Watts
Look What Came from the United States	O	I	Davis, Kevin	Franklin Watts
Looking at Animals in Cold Places	O	I	Butterfield, Moira	Steck-Vaughn
Looking at Animals in Hot Places	O	I	Butterfield, Moira	Steck-Vaughn
Looking at Animals in the Ocean	O	I	Butterfield, Moira	Steck-Vaughn
Looking for the Queen	O	I	Frederick, Shirley	Hampton-Brown
Loose Bolts	O	SF	Neufeld, David	Wright Group/McGraw Hill
Lost Continent and Other Cases, The	O	RF	Simon, Seymour	Avon
Lost Hikers and Other Cases, The	O	RF	Simon, Seymour	Avon
Lou Gehrig: One of Baseball's Greatest	O	B	Childhood of Famous Americans	Aladdin
Louisa May Alcott: Young Novelist	O	B	Childhood of Famous Americans	Aladdin
Luther Burbank	O	B	Faber, Doris	Garrard Publishing Co.

Title	Level	Genre	Author/Series	Publisher/Distributor
Ma and Pa Dracula	O	F	Martin, Ann M.	Scholastic
Make A Wish, Molly	O	RF	Cohen, Barbara	Bantam Doubleday Dell
Making Pop-ups	O	I	Brian, Janeen	Mondo
Man Who Paints Nature, The	O	B	Locker, Thomas	Richard C. Owen
Manual of House Monsters, A	O	F	Marijanovic, Stanislav	Mondo
Margaret Bourke-White	O	B	Welch, Catherine	Carolrhoda Books
Margaret Wise Brown	O	B	Greene, Carol	Children's Press
Marie Curie	O	B	Early Biographies	Compass Point Books
Mark Twain: Young Writer	O	B	Childhood of Famous Americans	Aladdin
Martha Washington: America's First First Lady	O	B	Childhood of Famous Americans	Aladdin
Martin Luther King, Jr., A Man Who Changed Things	O	B	Greene, Carol	Children's Press
Martin Luther King, Jr.: Young Man with a Dream	O	B	Childhood of Famous Americans	Aladdin
Mary McLeod Bethune	O	B	Greenfield, Eloise	HarperTrophy
Mary Todd Lincoln: Girl of the Bluegrass	O	B	Childhood of Famous Americans	Aladdin
Matthew Henson: Arctic Explorer	O	B	Podojil, Catherine	Wright Group/McGraw Hill
Maxie, Rosie, and Earl-Partners in Grime	O	RF	Park, Barbara	Random House
McBroom's Wonderful One-Acre Farm	O	RF	Fleischman, Sid	Beech Tree Books
Meerkats	O	I	Weaver, Robyn	Capstone Press
Meet Abraham Lincoln	O	B	Cary, Barbara	Step-Up Books
Meet Benjamin Franklin	O	B	Scarf, Maggi	Step-Up Books
Meet George Washington	O	B	Heilbroner, Joan	Random House
Meet Thomas Jefferson	O	B	Barrett, Marvin	Step-Up Books
Meg Mackintosh and The Case of the Curious Whale Watch	O	RF	Landon, Lucinda	Secret Passage Press
Meg Mackintosh and The Case of the Missing Babe Ruth Baseball	O	RF	Landon, Lucinda	Secret Passage Press
Meg Mackintosh and The Mystery at Camp Creepy	O	RF	Landon, Lucinda	Secret Passage Press
Meg Mackintosh and The Mystery at the Medieval Castle	O	RF	Landon, Lucinda	Secret Passage Press
Meg Mackintosh and The Mystery at the Soccer Match	O	RF	Landon, Lucinda	Secret Passage Press
Meg Mackintosh and The Mystery in the Locked Library	O	RF	Landon, Lucinda	Secret Passage Press
Melting Snow Sculptures and Other Cases, The	O	RF	Simon, Seymour	Avon
Mexico	O	I	Dahl, Michael	Capstone Press
Mice	O	I	Holmes, Kevin J.	Capstone Press
Mieko and the Fifth Treasure	O	HF	Coerr, Eleanor	Bantam Doubleday Dell
Mitch and Amy	O	RF	Cleary, Beverly	Harper Collins
Molly Pitcher: Young Patriot	O	B	Childhood of Famous Americans	Aladdin
Mom, You're Fired!	O	RF	Robinson, Nancy K.	Scholastic
Moonwalk: The First Trip to the Moon	O	I	Donnelly, Judy	Random House
More Stories from Grandma's Attic	O	RF	Richardson, Arleta	Chariot Victor Publishing
Most Beautiful Place in the World, The	O	RF	Cameron, Ann	Alfred A. Knopf
Most Wonderful Doll in the World, The	O	RF	McGinley, Phyllis	Scholastic
Mountain Bike Mania	O	RF	Belcher, Angie	Rigby
Mountain Gorillas	O	I	Wonder World	Wright Group/McGraw Hill
Mountain Lion, The	O	I	Crewe, Sabrina	Steck-Vaughn
Mouse and the Motorcycle, The	O	F	Cleary, Beverly	Avon Camelot
Mouse Called Wolf, A	O	F	King-Smith, Dick	Alfred A. Knopf
Mouse Magic	O	RF	Baglio, Ben M.	Scholastic
Mr. Ape	O	F	King-Smith, Dick	Alfred A. Knopf
Mrs. Piggle-Wiggle	O	F	MacDonald, Betty	Scholastic
Mrs. Piggle-Wiggle's Farm	O	F	MacDonald, Betty	Scholastic
Mrs. Piggle-Wiggle's Magic	O	F	MacDonald, Betty	Scholastic
Much Ado About Aldo	O	RF	Hurwitz, Johanna	The Penguin Group
Muggie Maggie	O	RF	Cleary, Beverly	Avon Camelot
Mummy's Curse, The	O	F	SupaDoopers	Sundance
My Mother Got Married (And Other Disasters)	O	RF	Park, Barbara	Random House
My Mysterious World	O	B	Mahy, Margaret	Richard C. Owen
My Teacher Turns into a Tyrannosaurus	O	F	SupaDoopers	Sundance
My Writing Day	O	B	Adler, David A.	Richard C. Owen

Title	Level	Genre	Author/Series	Publisher/Distributor
Mysterious Green Swimmer and Other Cases, The	O	RF	Simon, Seymour	Avon
Mysterious Tracks and Other Cases, The	O	RF	Simon, Seymour	Avon
Mystery on October Road	O	RF	Herzig, A.C. & Mali, Jane	Scholastic
Nature! Wild and Wonderful	O	B	Pringle, Laurence	Richard C. Owen
Neil Armstrong: Young Flyer	O	B	Childhood of Famous Americans	Aladdin
Netherlands, The	O	I	Dahl, Michael	Capstone Press
Never Bored on Boards	O	I	Literacy 2000	Rigby
Never Hit a Ghost with a Baseball Bat	O	RF	Clifford, Eth	Scholastic
New Year's Around the World	O	I	Trumbore, Cindy	Pearson Learning
Next Stop, New York City!	O	RF	Giff, Patricia Reilly	Bantam Doubleday Dell
Nez Perce Tribe, The	O	I	Lassieur, Allison	Capstone Press
Nigeria	O	I	Thoennes, Kristin	Capstone Press
Night Crossing, The	O	HF	Ackerman, Karen	Alfred A. Knopf
No Dogs Allowed	O	RF	Cutler, Jane	Farrar, Straus and Giroux
No One is Going to Nashville	O	RF	Jukes, Mavis	Alfred A. Knopf
Not-Just-Anybody Family, The	O	RF	Byars, Betsy	Dell
Not-So-Dead Fish and Other Cases, The	O	RF	Simon, Seymour	Avon
Octopuses and Squids	O	I	Wonder World	Wright Group/McGraw Hill
Oh Boy, Boston!	O	RF	Giff, Patricia Reilly	Bantam Doubleday Dell
On the Way to the Moon	O	F	Gold, Becky	Pearson Learning
On-Line Spaceman and Other Cases, The	O	RF	Simon, Seymour	Avon
Once Upon a Time	O	B	Bunting, Eve	Richard C. Owen
One Man Show	O	B	Asch, Frank	Richard C. Owen
Otis Spofford	O	RF	Cleary, Beverly	Avon
Our American Flag	O	I	McCloskey, Susan	Wright Group/McGraw Hill
Owl Moon	O	B	Yolen, Jane	Scholastic
Owls	O	I	Holmes, Kevin J.	Capstone Press
Patrick Doyle is Full of Blarney	O	HF	Armstrong, Jennifer	Random House
Pawnee Nation, The	O	I	Walters, Anna Lee	Capstone Press
Penguin, The	O	I	Crewe, Sabrina	Steck-Vaughn
Penguins	O	I	Holmes, Kevin J.	Capstone Press
Perfect Pony, A	O	RF	Szymanski, Lois	Avon Camelot
Peru	O	I	Thoennes, Kristin	Capstone Press
Pet Parade	O	RF	Giff, Patricia Reilly	Bantam Doubleday Dell
Philippines, The	O	I	Davis, Lucile	Capstone Press
Photographic Memory	O	RF	PM Ruby	Rigby
Pippi Goes on Board	O	F	Lindgren, Astrid	Puffin Books
Pippi in the South Seas	O	F	Lindgren, Astrid	Puffin Books
Pippi Longstocking	O	F	Lindgren, Astrid	The Penguin Group
Playing with Words	O	B	Howe, James	Richard C. Owen
Pony Pals: A Pony for Keeps	O	RF	Betancourt, Jeanne	Scholastic
Pony Pals: A Pony in Trouble	O	RF	Betancourt, Jeanne	Scholastic
Pony Pals: Detective Pony	O	RF	Betancourt, Jeanne	Scholastic
Pony Pals: Don't Hurt My Pony	O	RF	Betancourt, Jeanne	Scholastic
Pony Pals: Give Me Back My Pony	O	RF	Betancourt, Jeanne	Scholastic
Pony Pals: Good-bye Pony	O	RF	Betancourt, Jeanne	Scholastic
Pony Pals: I Want a Pony	O	RF	Betancourt, Jeanne	Scholastic
Pony Pals: Keep Out, Pony!	O	RF	Betancourt, Jeanne	Scholastic
Pony Pals: Pony to the Rescue	O	RF	Betancourt, Jeanne	Scholastic
Pony Pals, Pony-Sitters	O	RF	Betancourt, Jeanne	Scholastic
Pony Pals: Runaway Pony	O	RF	Betancourt, Jeanne	Scholastic
Pony Pals: The Blind Pony	O	RF	Betancourt, Jeanne	Scholastic
Pony Pals: The Girl Who Hated Ponies	O	RF	Betancourt, Jeanne	Scholastic
Pony Pals: The Lonely Pony	O	RF	Betancourt, Jeanne	Scholastic
Pony Pals: Too Many Ponies	O	RF	Betancourt, Jeanne	Scholastic
Pony Parade	O	RF	Baglio, Ben M.	Scholastic
Puppy Puzzle	O	RF	Baglio, Ben M.	Scholastic
Purple Walrus and Other Perfect Pets	O	RF	Wildcats	Wright Group/McGraw Hill
Rabbit Race	O	RF	Baglio, Ben M.	Scholastic
Rachel to the Rescue	O	RF	SupaDoopers	Sundance

Title	Level	Genre	Author/Series	Publisher/Distributor
Ralph S. Mouse	O	F	Cleary, Beverly	Harper Trophy
Ramona and Her Father	O	RF	Cleary, Beverly	Avon
Ramona and Her Mother	O	RF	Cleary, Beverly	Avon
Ramona Forever	O	RF	Cleary, Beverly	Hearst
Ramona Quimby, Age 8	O	RF	Cleary, Beverly	Hearst
Ramona the Brave	O	RF	Cleary, Beverly	Hearst
Ramona the Pest	O	RF	Cleary, Beverly	Avon
Rats!	O	RF	Cutler, Jane	Farrar, Straus and Giroux
Rats on the Range and Other Stories	O	F	Marshall, James	The Penguin Group
Rats on the Roof and Other Stories	O	F	Marshall, James	The Penguin Group
Rent a Third Grader	O	RF	Hiller, B.B.	Scholastic
Rescue	O	RF	Wildcats	Wright Group/McGraw Hill
Rhinos	O	I	Holmes, Kevin J.	Capstone Press
Ribsy	O	RF	Cleary, Beverly	Hearst
Right or Wrong?	O	RF	Wildcats	Wright Group/McGraw Hill
Riptide	O	RF	Weller, Frances Ward	Putnam & Grosset
River Rats	O	RF	Belcher, Angie	Pacific Learning
Rotating Rollerblades and Other Cases, The	O	RF	Simon, Seymour	Avon
Runaway Ralph	O	F	Cleary, Beverly	Hearst
Russia	O	I	Thoennes, Kristin	Capstone Press
Sable	O	RF	Hesse, Karen	Henry Holt & Co.
Sam and Kim	O	I	Pacific Literacy	Pacific Learning
Sara Crewe	O	HF	Burnett, Frances Hodgson	Scholastic
Seawall	O	RF	PM Ruby	Rigby
Secret Soldier, The: The Story of Deborah Sampson	O	B	McGovern, Ann	Scholastic
Secret Valley, The	O	HF	Bulla, Clyde Robert	Scholastic
Secrets of the Rain Forest	O	I	Myers, Edward	Pearson Learning
Seed is a Promise, A	O	I	Merrill, Claire	Scholastic
Seeing the Circle	O	B	Bruchac, Joseph	Richard C. Owen
Seven Kisses in a Row	O	RF	MacLachlan, Patricia	Harper Collins
Seven Stones of Sligo	O	TL	PM Ruby	Rigby
Shark Lady: The Adventures of Eugenie Clark	O	B	McGovern, Ann	Scholastic
Shining Blue Planet and Other Cases, The	O	RF	Simon, Seymour	Avon
Silent Hero, The	O	I	Shea, George	Random House
Skateboarding	O	I	PM Nonfiction -Emerald	Rigby
Skinny-Bones	O	RF	Park, Barbara	Random House
Sky Rider	O	RF	Belcher, Angie	Pacific Learning
Smasher	O	RF	King-Smith, Dick	Random House
Snails	O	I	Holmes, Kevin J.	Capstone Press
Snake, The	O	I	Crewe, Sabrina	Steck-Vaughn
Snowboarding Diary	O	I	PM Nonfiction -Emerald	Rigby
Socks	O	RF	Cleary, Beverly	Avon
Some Dog!	O	RF	PM Ruby	Rigby
Song of the Giraffe	O	RF	Jacobs, Shannon K.	Little, Brown & Co.
South Korea	O	I	Davis, Lucile	Capstone Press
Space Junk	O	RF	Wildcats	Wright Group/McGraw Hill
Space Quest	O	I	Discovery World	Rigby
Space Station Plot and Other Cases, The	O	RF	Simon, Seymour	Avon
Space Stations	O	I	Ryan, Cheryl	Wright Group/McGraw Hill
Speeding Sleigh and Other Cases, The	O	RF	Simon, Seymour	Avon
Speedy Pasta and Other Cases, The	O	RF	Simon, Seymour	Avon
Speedy Snake and Other Cases, The	O	RF	Simon, Seymour	Avon
Speedy Soapbox Car and Other Cases, The	O	RF	Simon, Seymour	Avon
Spider Kane and the Mystery at Jumbo Nightcrawler's	O	F	Osborne, Mary Pope	Random House
Spider Kane and the Mystery Under the May-Apple	O	F	Osborne, Mary Pope	Random House
Spider, The	O	I	Crewe, Sabrina	Steck-Vaughn
Spiders	O	I	Holmes, Kevin J.	Capstone Press
Spray-Paint Mystery, The	O	RF	Medearis, Angela Shelf	Scholastic
Squanto: Friend of the Pilgrims	O	B	Bulla, Clyde Robert	Scholastic
Stacey and the Haunted Masquerade	O	RF	Martin, Ann M.	Scholastic

Title	Level	Genre	Author/Series	Publisher/Distributor
Stacey and the Missing Ring	O	RF	Martin, Ann M.	Scholastic
Stacey and the Mystery at the Mall	O	RF	Martin, Ann M.	Scholastic
Stacey and the Mystery Money	O	RF	Martin, Ann M.	Scholastic
Stay Away from Simon!	O	RF	Carrick, Carol	Clarion
Staying Healthy: Eating Right	O	I	McGinty, Alice B.	Franklin Watts
Staying Nine	O	RF	Conrad, Pam	HarperTrophy
Story of Alexander Graham Bell, Inventor of the Telephone	O	B	Davidson, Margaret	Scholastic
Story of Benjamin Franklin, Amazing American	O	B	Davidson, Margaret	Scholastic
Story of Jackie Robinson, Bravest Man in Baseball	O	B	Davidson, Margaret	Scholastic
Story of Ruby Bridges, The	O	B	Coles, Robert	Scholastic
Story of Walt Disney, Maker of Magical Worlds, The	O	B	Selden, Bernice	Bantam Doubleday Dell
Story Teller's Story, A	O	B	Martin, Rafe	Richard C. Owen
Strange Clues and Other Cases, The	O	RF	Simon, Seymour	Avon
Strange Museum and Other Cases, The	O	RF	Simon, Seymour	Avon
Street Action	O	I	Wildcats	Wright Group/McGraw Hill
Strike	O	I	Pacific Literacy	Pacific Learning
Summer Wheels	O	B	Bunting, Eve	Harcourt Brace
Sun	O	I	Vogt, Gregory L.	Capstone Press
Suprising Myself	O	B	Fritz, Jean	Richard C. Owen
Talk About a Family	O	RF	Greenfield, Eloise	HarperTrophy
Tall Tale and Other Cases, The	O	RF	Simon, Seymour	Avon
Tall Tales	O	RF	PM Emerald	Rigby
Tamika and the Wisdom Rings	O	RF	Yarbrough, Camille	Random House
Teacher's Pet	O	RF	Hurwitz, Johanna	Scholastic
Tell Me a Story	O	B	London, Jonathan	Richard C. Owen
Ten True Animal Rescues	O	I	Betancourt, Jeanne	Scholastic
Terrible Test Mark and Other Cases, The	O	RF	Simon, Seymour	Avon
Terror In the Towers	O	B	Kerson, Adrian	Random House
Thailand	O	I	Thoennes, Kristin	Capstone Press
There's a Ship Outside My Window	O	RF	PM Ruby	Rigby
They Led The Way: 14 American Women	O	B	Johnston, Johanna	Scholastic
They Survived Mount St. Helens!	O	I	Stine, Megan	Random House
Those Amazingly Useful Ears	O	I	Frederick, Shirley	Hampton-Brown
Thoughts, Pictures, and Words	O	B	Kuskin, Karla	Richard C. Owen
Three Wishes, The	O	TL	Literacy 2000	Rigby
Time Machine and Other Cases, The	O	RF	Simon, Seymour	Avon
Toad for Tuesday, A	O	F	Erickson, Russell E.	Beech Tree Books
Top Cat	O	I	Byars, Betsy	The Penguin Group
Tornado	O	I	Byars, Betsy	HarperTrophy
Trapped!	O	RF	SupaDoopers	Sundance
Trees and Plants in the Rain Forest	O	I	Pirotta, Saviour	Steck-Vaughn
Trickster Ghost, The	O	F	Showell, E.	Scholastic
Trouble with Oatmeal, The	O	RF	PM Emerald	Rigby
Trouble with Patrick, The	O	RF	Whitaker, Alan	Rigby
True Stories about Abraham Lincoln	O	B	Gross, Ruth Belov	Scholastic
Under My Nose	O	B	Ehlert, Lois	Richard C. Owen
Undercover Tailback	O	RF	Christopher, Matt	Scholastic
Universal Solvent and Other Cases, The	O	RF	Simon, Seymour	Avon
Uranus	O	I	Vogt, Gregory L.	Capstone Press
Very Special Kwanzaa, A	O	I	Chocolate, Debbi	Scholastic
Vicar of Nibbleswick, The	O	RF	Dahl, Roald	Puffin Books
Vietnam	O	I	Dahl, Michael	Capstone Press
Virtual Fred	O	SF	Courtney, Vincent	Random House
Wall of Names, A: The Story of the Vietnam Veterans Memorial	O	HF	Donnelly, Judy	Random House
Warthogs	O	I	Holmes, Kevin J.	Capstone Press
Warton and the King of the Skies	O	F	Erickson, Russell E.	Houghton Mifflin
Weaving Contest, The	O	TL	Literacy 2000	Rigby

Title	Level	Genre	Author/Series	Publisher/Distributor
West Virginia: Facts and Symbols	O	I	Feeney, Kathy	Capstone Press
Whale, The	O	I	Crewe, Sabrina	Steck-Vaughn
Whales	O	I	Holmes, Kevin J.	Capstone Press
What Do You Think?	O	I	Wildcats	Wright Group/McGraw Hill
What Makes a Bird a Bird?	O	I	Garelick, May	Mondo
What's the Big Idea, Ben Franklin?	O	B	Fritz, Jean	Scholastic
Where to Look for a Dinosaur	O	F	Most, Bernard	Harcourt Brace
Which Way, Jack?	O	F	Yurkovic, Diana Short	Rigby
White Elephants and Yellow Jackets	O	I	Webb, Derek	Rigby
Whoops! It Works!	O	I	Lopez, Orlando	Pearson Learning
Wild Babies	O	I	Simon, Seymour	Harper Collins
Wild Bird and Other Stories of Adventure	O	RF	Belcher, Angie	Pacific Learning
Wild Culpepper Cruise, The	O	RF	Paulsen, Gary	Bantam Doubleday Dell
Will Rogers	O	B	Schott, Jane A.	Carolrhoda Books
Wingman	O	F	Pinkwater, Daniel	Bantam Skylark
Winter Survival	O	I	Wilde, Buck	Rigby
Wolfman Sam	O	RF	Levy, Elizabeth	HarperTrophy
Woman Who Flummoxed the Fairies, The	O	TL	Forest, Heather	Harcourt Brace
Women Inventors	O	B	Blashfield, Jean	Capstone Press
Wordful Child, A	O	B	Lyon, George Ella	Richard C. Owen
Writing Bug, The	O	B	Hopkins, Lee Bennett	Richard C. Owen
Wyoming: Facts and Symbols	O	I	Dubois, Muriel L.	Capstone Press
Yo-Yo's	O	I	PM Nonfiction -Emerald	Rigby
You Can Canoe!: A Book of Sporting Activities	O	I	Yurkovic, Diana Short	Rigby
Young Geographers	O	I	People, Spaces & Places	Rand McNally
Young Mozart	O	B	Isadora, Rachel	The Penguin Group
Zebras	O	I	Holmes, Kevin J.	Capstone Press
Accidental Angel (Secret Sisters)	P	RF	Byrd, Sandra	WaterBrook Press
Against the Odds	P	I	Layden, Joe	Scholastic
Alexander Graham Bell	P	B	Linder, Greg	Capstone Press
All About Sam	P	RF	Lowry, Lois	Bantam Doubleday Dell
Alvin Ailey	P	B	Pinkney, Andrea Davis	Hyperion
Amazing Journeys	P	I	Literacy 2000	Rigby
Amber Cat, The	P	RF	McKay, Hilary	Simon & Schuster
Amelia Earhart	P	B	Parlin, John	Bantam Doubleday Dell
Amelia Earhart	P	B	Rosenthal, M. & Freeman, D.	Capstone Press
Andrew Carnegie: Builder of Libraries	P	B	Community Builders	Children's Press
Another Point of View	P	RF	Wildcats	Wright Group/McGraw Hill
Apache Indians, The	P	I	Lund, Bill	Capstone Press
Appointment with Action	P	RF	Wildcats	Wright Group/McGraw Hill
Archaeologists Dig for Clues	P	I	Duke, Kate	HarperCollins
Attaboy, Sam	P	RF	Lowry, Lois	Bantam Doubleday Dell
Aunt Clara Brown: Official Pioneer	P	B	Lowery, Linda	Lerner Publishing Group
Baby Grand, the Moon in July, and Me, The	P	RF	Barnes, Joyce Annette	The Penguin Group
Baby Island	P	RF	Brink, Carol R.	Simon & Schuster
Baby Whale Rescue: The True Story of J.J.	P	I	Arnold, C. & Hewett, R.	Troll
Backyard Hunter: The Praying Mantis	P	I	Lavies, Bianca	The Penguin Group
Bad Spell for the Worst Witch, A	P	F	Murphy, Jill	Puffin Books
Bald Eagle Free Again!, The	P	I	Young Readers' Series	Barron's Educational Series
Ballad of Robin Hood, The	P	HF	Literacy 2000	Rigby
Balto and the Great Race	P	RF	Kimmel, Elizabeth Cody	Random House
Barney	P	RF	Literacy 2000	Rigby
Baseball in the Barrios	P	I	Horenstein, Henry	Harcourt Brace
Baseball's Greatest Pitchers	P	B	Kramer, S. A.	Random House
Bats	P	I	Literacy 2000	Rigby
Battle for the Castle, The	P	F	Winthrop, Elizabeth	Yearling
Bear That Heard Crying, The	P	HF	Kinsey-Warnock, N. & Kinsey, H.	The Penguin Group
Berenstain Bear Scouts Ghost Versus Ghost	P	F	Berenstain, Stan, & Jan	Scholastic
Bess's Log Cabin Quilt	P	HF	Love, D. Anne	Bantam Doubleday Dell
Best Enemies	P	RF	Leverich, Kathleen	Beech Tree Books

Title	Level	Genre	Author/Series	Publisher/Distributor
Best Enemies Again	P	RF	Leverich, Kathleen	Alfred A. Knopf
Best Enemies Forever	P	RF	Leverich, Kathleen	William Morrow
Best School Year Ever, The	P	RF	Robinson, Barbara	HarperTrophy
Betsy and the Boys	P	RF	Haywood, Carolyn	Harcourt Brace
Bicycle Man, The	P	RF	Say, Allen	Houghton Mifflin
Bill Gates: Helping People Use Computers	P	B	Community Builders	Children's Press
Blind Outlaw, The	P	RF	Rounds, Glen	Scholastic
Book of Black Heroes from A to Z	P	B	Hudson, W. and Wesley, V. W.	Scholastic
Booker T. Washington	P	B	McLoone, Margo	Capstone Press
Botticelli	P	B	Venezia, Mike	Children's Press
Brainstorm!: The Stories of Twenty American Kid Inventors	P	B	Tucker, Tom	Farrar, Straus and Giroux
Brave As	P	RF	Marriott, Janice	Pacific Learning
Breath of the Dragon	P	RF	Giles, Gail	Bantam Doubleday Dell
Brian's Brilliant Career	P	RF	Literacy 2000	Rigby
Bright Paddles	P	HF	Downi, Mary Alice	Fitzhenry and Whiteside
Canada Geese Quilt, The	P	RF	Kinsey-Warnock, Natalie	Bantam Doubleday Dell
Case of the Measled Cowboy, The	P	F	Erickson, John R.	Puffin Books
Case of the Midnight Rustler, The	P	F	Erickson, John R.	Puffin Books
Case of the Missing Cat, The	P	F	Erickson, John R.	Puffin Books
Caterpillars	P	I	Mini Pets	Steck-Vaughn
Caught in a Flash	P	I	Bishop, Nic	Pacific Learning
Cesar Chavez	P	B	Davis, Lucile	Capstone Press
Charlie Is a Chicken	P	RF	Smith, Jane Denitz	HarperTrophy
Chasing Tornadoes	P	I	Gold, Becky	Pearson Learning
Cherokee Indians, The	P	I	Lund, Bill	Capstone Press
Chief Joseph of the Nez Percé	P	B	McAuliffe, Bill	Capstone Press
Children of the Earth and Sky	P	I	Krensky, Stephen	Scholastic
Children of the Fire	P	HF	Robinet, Harriette	Aladdin
Chocolate!	P	I	Velarde, Linda	Rigby
Christmas: Why We Celebrate It the Way We Do	P	I	Hintz, Martin & Kate	Capstone Press
Cloud Catcher	P	F	Jernigan, E. Wesley	Rigby
Colors of Australia	P	I	Colors of the World	Carolrhoda Books
Colors of Germany	P	I	Colors of the World	Carolrhoda Books
Colors of Ghana	P	I	Colors of the World	Carolrhoda Books
Colors of India	P	I	Colors of the World	Carolrhoda Books
Colors of Kenya	P	I	Colors of the World	Carolrhoda Books
Colors of Mexico	P	I	Colors of the World	Carolrhoda Books
Comanche Indians, The	P	I	Lund, Bill	Capstone Press
Coral Reef	P	I	Habitats	Children's Press
Curse of Being Pharaoh, The	P	RF	Marriott, Janice	Pacific Learning
Da Vinci	P	B	Venezia, Mike	Children's Press
Dancing with Jacques	P	HF	Voyages in…	Wright Group/McGraw Hill
Daring Rescue of Marlon the Swimming Pig, The	P	F	Saunders, S.	Random House
Dear Diary	P	RF	Literacy 2000	Rigby
Desert Run, The	P	I	Bonallack, John	Pacific Learning
Destination Disaster	P	RF	Beale, Fleur	Rigby
DeWitt and Lila Wallace: Charity for All	P	B	Community Builders	Children's Press
Diego Rivera	P	B	Venezia, Mike	Children's Press
Digging Dinosaurs	P	I	Nayer, Judy	Pearson Learning
Digging Up Tyrannosaurus Rex	P	I	Horner, John & Don Lessem	Crown Publishers
Divers' Dream	P	I	Pacific Literacy	Pacific Learning
Dolphin Adventure	P	RF	Grover, Wayne	Beech Tree Books
Dolphin, The	P	I	Animal Close-Ups	Charlesbridge
Dolphin Treasure	P	RF	Grover, Wayne	Beech Tree Books
Double Danger	P	F	Hager, Mandy	Pacific Learning
Down on the Ice	P	I	Alchin, Rupert	Pacific Learning
Dragon Fire	P	F	Cowley, Joy	Pacific Learning
Dragon Prince, The: A Chinese Beauty and the Beast Tale	P	TL	Yep, Laurence	HarperCollins

Title	Level	Genre	Author/Series	Publisher/Distributor
Dragon Slayer	P	F	Cowley, Joy	Pacific Learning
Dynamic Duos	P	F	Moore, David	Scholastic
East of the Sun & West of the Moon	P	TL	Mayer, Mercer	Aladdin
Eddie and the Fire Engine	P	RF	Haywood, Carolyn	Beech Tree Books
El Chino	P	B	Say, Allen	Houghton Mifflin
Eleanor Roosevelt	P	B	Davis, Lucile	Capstone Press
Elizabeth Cady Stanton	P	B	Davis, Lucile	Capstone Press
Ellen Tebbits	P	RF	Cleary, Beverly	Dell Publishing
Emily's Runaway Imagination	P	F	Cleary, Beverly	Avon Camelot
Encyclopedia Brown Boy Detective	P	RF	Sobol, Donald J.	Bantam Doubleday Dell
Encyclopedia Brown Carries On	P	RF	Sobol, Donald J.	Bantam Doubleday Dell
Encyclopedia Brown: Case of Pablo's Nose	P	RF	Sobol, Donald J.	Scholastic
Encyclopedia Brown: Case of the Dead Eagles	P	RF	Sobol, Donald J.	Bantam Doubleday Dell
Encyclopedia Brown: Case of the Disgusting Sneakers	P	RF	Sobol, Donald J.	Bantam Doubleday Dell
Encyclopedia Brown: Case of the Midnight Visitor	P	RF	Sobol, Donald J.	Bantam Doubleday Dell
Encyclopedia Brown: Case of the Mysterious Handprints	P	RF	Sobol, Donald J.	Bantam Doubleday Dell
Encyclopedia Brown: Case of the Secret Pitch	P	RF	Sobol, Donald J.	Bantam Doubleday Dell
Encyclopedia Brown: Case of the Sleeping Dog	P	RF	Sobol, Donald J.	Scholastic
Encyclopedia Brown: Case of the Slippery Salamander	P	RF	Sobol, Donald J.	Scholastic
Encyclopedia Brown: Case of the Treasure Hunt	P	RF	Sobol, Donald J.	Bantam Doubleday Dell
Encyclopedia Brown: Case of the Two Spies	P	RF	Sobol, Donald J.	Bantam Doubleday Dell
Encyclopedia Brown Finds the Clues	P	RF	Sobol, Donald J.	Bantam Doubleday Dell
Encyclopedia Brown Gets His Man	P	RF	Sobol, Donald J.	Bantam Doubleday Dell
Encyclopedia Brown Keeps the Peace	P	RF	Sobol, Donald J.	Bantam Doubleday Dell
Encyclopedia Brown Lends a Hand	P	RF	Sobol, Donald J.	Bantam Doubleday Dell
Encyclopedia Brown Saves the Day	P	RF	Sobol, Donald J.	Bantam Doubleday Dell
Encyclopedia Brown Sets the Pace	P	RF	Sobol, Donald J.	Bantam Doubleday Dell
Encyclopedia Brown Shows the Way	P	RF	Sobol, Donald J.	Bantam Doubleday Dell
Encyclopedia Brown Solves Them All	P	RF	Sobol, Donald J.	Bantam Doubleday Dell
Encyclopedia Brown Takes the Cake	P	RF	Sobol, Donald J.	Bantam Doubleday Dell
Encyclopedia Brown Takes the Case	P	RF	Sobol, Donald J.	Bantam
Encyclopedia Brown Tracks Them Down	P	RF	Sobol, Donald J.	Bantam Doubleday Dell
Encyclopedia Brown's Book of Strange But True Crimes	P	RF	Sobol, Donald J. & Rose Sobol	Scholastic
Eureka!: Stories of Everyday Inventions	P	I	Literacy 2000	Rigby
Exploring Freshwater Habitats	P	I	Snowball, Diane	Mondo
Exploring Land Habitats	P	I	Phinney, Margaret Yatsevitch	Mondo
Exploring Saltwater Habitats	P	I	Smith, Sue	Mondo
Exploring Tree Habitats	P	I	Seifert, Patti	Mondo
Extreme Sports	P	I	Wildcats	Wright Group/McGraw Hill
Eye in the Sky	P	F	Marriott, Janice	Pacific Learning
Eye Spy	P	I	Wildcats	Wright Group/McGraw Hill
Families of the Deep Blue Sea	P	I	Mallory, Kenneth	Charlesbridge Publishing
Fantastic Mr. Fox	P	F	Dahl, Roald	The Penguin Group
Feathery Fables	P	TL	Krueger, Carol	Rigby
Felicia the Critic	P	RF	Conford, Ellen	Little, Brown & Co.
Felita	P	RF	Mohr, Nicholasa	Dell
Finding Providence: The Story of Roger Williams	P	B	Avi	HarperTrophy
Fire at the Triangle Factory	P	HF	Littlefield, Holly	Carolrhoda Books
Five-Dog Night, The	P	RF	Christelow, Eileen	Clarion Books
Florence Kelley	P	B	Saller, Carol	Carolrhoda Books
Florence Nightingale	P	B	Davis, Lucile	Capstone Press
Flying Ace: The Story of Amelia Earhart	P	B	Eyewitness Readers	DK Publishing
Forgetful Fran	P	RF	Key, Alexander	Scholastic
Fourth Grade Is a Jinx	P	RF	McKenna, Colleen	Scholastic
Fourth-Graders Don't Believe In Witches	P	F	Fields, Terri	Scholastic
Frederick Douglass	P	B	McLoone, Margo	Capstone Press
Frogs and Toads	P	I	Crabapples	Crabtree
From Here to There: Transportation Timelines	P	I	Discovery World	Rigby

Title	Level	Genre	Author/Series	Publisher/Distributor
George Washington Carver	P	B	McLoone, Margo	Capstone Press
George Washington's Breakfast	P	B	Fritz, Jean	Putnam & Grosset
George's Marvelous Medicine	P	F	Dahl, Roald	The Penguin Group
Gerbilitis	P	RF	Spinner, S. & Weiss, E.	HarperTrophy
Get A Grip, Pip!	P	RF	Literacy 2000	Rigby
Ghost Fox, The	P	F	Yep, Laurence	Scholastic
Ghost Twins: Mystery at Kickingbird Lake	P	F	Regan, Dian Curtis	Scholastic
Giraffe and the Pelly and Me, The	P	F	Dahl, Roald	The Penguin Group
Giraffe, The	P	I	Animal Close-Ups	Charlesbridge Publishing
Giraffes	P	I	Crabapples	Crabtree
Girl Called Al, A	P	RF	Greene, Constance C.	Puffin Books
Glenda	P	F	Udry, Janice	HarperTrophy
Glenda Glinka: Witch-At-Large	P	F	Udry, Janice May	HarperTrophy
Going for Gold!	P	B	Eyewitness Readers	DK Publishing
Gooseberry Park	P	F	Rylant, Cynthia	Scholastic
Grace's Letter to Lincoln	P	HF	Roop, Peter and Connie	Hyperion
Grain of Rice, A	P	TL	Pittman, Helena Clare	Bantam Doubleday Dell
Growing Up	P	I	It's Science	Children's Press
Gwen Torrence	P	B	Stewart, Mark	Children's Press
Halloween: Why We Celebrate It the Way We Do	P	I	Hintz, Martin & Kate	Capstone Press
Hare and the Tortoise, The	P	TL	Aesop's Fables	Dominie
Harriet Tubman	P	B	McLoone, Margo	Capstone Press
Harry's Mad	P	F	King-Smith, Dick	Alfred A. Knopf
Helen Keller: Crusader for the Blind and Deaf	P	B	Graff, Stewart & Polly Anne	Bantam Doubleday Dell
Horses	P	I	Crabapples	Crabtree
House Gobbaleen, The	P	F	Alexander, Lloyd	The Penguin Group
How Is a Crayon Made?	P	I	Charles, Oz	Scholastic
How To Grow Crystals	P	I	Book Shop	Mondo
Howliday Inn	P	F	Howe, James	Atheneum Books
Hundred Penny Box, The	P	RF	Mathis, Sharon Bell	Puffin Books
Hurricanes!	P	I	Hopping, Jean	Scholastic
Ice Mummy: The Discovery of a 5,000-Year-Old Man	P	I	Dubowski, Mark & Cathy East	Random House
Imagine This, James Robert	P	F	Weber, Rebecca	Rigby
In-Between Days, The	P	RF	Bunting, Eve	HarperTrophy
Incredible Creatures	P	I	Weldon Owen	Wright Group/McGraw Hill
Incredible Places	P	I	Wildcats	Wright Group/McGraw Hill
Incredible Shrinking Kid, The	P	F	Abbott, Tony	Scholastic
Indian School, The	P	RF	Whelan, Gloria	HarperTrophy
Interrupting The Big Sleep	P	RF	Marriott, Janice	Pacific Learning
Iroquois Indians, The	P	I	Lund, Bill	Capstone Press
Ishi's: Tale of Lizard	P	TL	Hinton, L. & Roth, S. L.	Farrar Straus Giroux
It's All in Your Mind, James Robert	P	F	Literacy 2000	Rigby
Jacob Two-Two and the Dinosaur	P	F	Richler, Mordecai	Tundra Books
Jacob Two-Two Meets the Hooded Fang	P	F	Richler, Mordecai	Seal Books
Jane Addams	P	B	Community Builders	Children's Press
Jason Kidd Story, The	P	RF	Moore, David	Scholastic
Jazz, Pizzazz, and the Silver Threads	P	RF	Quattlebaum, Mary	Bantam Doubleday Dell
Jesse Jackson	P	B	Simon, Charnan	Children's Press
Jesse Owens: Olympic Hero	P	B	Sabin, Francene	Troll
Justin and the Best Biscuits in the World	P	RF	Pitts, Walter & Mildred	Alfred A. Knopf
Keep Out, Our Dog Buries What it Can't Eat	P	RF	Beale, Fleur	Pacific Learning
Ketchup Deal, The	P	F	Marriott, Janice	Pacific Learning
Kid Power	P	RF	Pfeffer, Susan Beth	Scholastic
Knightly News	P	RF	Kenna, Anna	Pacific Learning
Knots on a Counting Rope	P	RF	Martin Jr., B. & Archambault, J.	Henry Holt & Co.
Koala Is Not a Bear, A	P	I	Crabapples	Crabtree
Koi's Python	P	RF	Moore, Miriam	Hyperion
Koya DeLaney and the Good Girl Blues	P	RF	Greenfield, Eloise	Scholastic
Land I Lost, The	P	I	Nhuong, Huynh Quang	HarperTrophy
Land of the Dragons	P	I	Morris, Rod	Pacific Learning

Title	Level	Genre	Author/Series	Publisher/Distributor
Last Chance for Magic	P	F	Chew, Ruth	Scholastic
Last Look	P	RF	Bulla, Clyde Robert	Puffin Books
Laughter Is the Best Medicine	P	I	Literacy Tree	Rigby
Laura Ingalls Wilder	P	B	Blair, Gwenda & Allen, Thomas	Lerner Publishing Group
Laura Ingalls Wilder: Growing Up in the Little House	P	B	Giff, Patricia Reilly	Puffin Books
Lazy Bones Jones	P	F	Welch, Sheila Kelly	Pacific Learning
Lion to Guard Us, A	P	HF	Bulla, Clyde Robert	HarperTrophy
Little Cats	P	I	Crabapples	Crabtree
Lotus Seed, The	P	HF	Garland, Sherry	Harcourt Brace
Lucky Stone, The	P	RF	Clifton, Lucille	Bantam Doubleday Dell
Mad Scientist's Secret, The	P	SF	Miller, Marvin	Scholastic
Magic Moscow, The	P	RF	Pinkwater, Daniel	Aladdin
Magic School Bus	P	F	Cole, Joanna & Degen, Bruce	Scholastic
Magic School Bus and the Electric Field Trip, The	P	F	Cole, Joanna & Degen, Bruce	Scholastic
Magic School Bus Answers Questions	P	F	Cole, Joanna & Degen, Bruce	Scholastic
Magic School Bus At the Waterworks	P	F	Cole, Joanna & Degen, Bruce	Scholastic
Magic School Bus Blows Its Top	P	F	Cole, Joanna & Degen, Bruce	Scholastic
Magic School Bus Briefcase	P	F	Cole, Joanna & Degen, Bruce	Scholastic
Magic School Bus Butterfly and the Bog Beast	P	F	Cole, Joanna & Degen, Bruce	Scholastic
Magic School Bus Explores the Senses	P	F	Cole, Joanna & Degen, Bruce	Scholastic
Magic School Bus Explores the World of Animals	P	F	Cole, Joanna & Degen, Bruce	Scholastic
Magic School Bus Gets a Bright Idea	P	F	Cole, Joanna & Degen, Bruce	Scholastic
Magic School Bus Gets All Dried Up	P	F	Cole, Joanna & Degen, Bruce	Scholastic
Magic School Bus Gets Ants in Its Pants	P	F	Cole, Joanna & Degen, Bruce	Scholastic
Magic School Bus Gets Baked in a Cake	P	F	Cole, Joanna & Degen, Bruce	Scholastic
Magic School Bus Gets Cold Feet	P	F	Cole, Joanna & Degen, Bruce	Scholastic
Magic School Bus Gets Eaten	P	F	Cole, Joanna & Degen, Bruce	Scholastic
Magic School Bus Gets Programmed	P	F	Cole, Joanna & Degen, Bruce	Scholastic
Magic School Bus Goes Upstream	P	F	Cole, Joanna & Degen, Bruce	Scholastic
Magic School Bus Going Batty	P	F	Cole, Joanna & Degen, Bruce	Scholastic
Magic School Bus Hops Home	P	F	Cole, Joanna & Degen, Bruce	Scholastic
Magic School Bus in a Pickle	P	F	Cole, Joanna & Degen, Bruce	Scholastic
Magic School Bus in the Arctic	P	F	Cole, Joanna & Degen, Bruce	Scholastic
Magic School Bus in the Haunted Museum	P	F	Cole, Joanna & Degen, Bruce	Scholastic
Magic School Bus in the Rain Forest	P	F	Cole, Joanna & Degen, Bruce	Scholastic
Magic School Bus Inside a Beehive	P	F	Cole, Joanna & Degen, Bruce	Scholastic
Magic School Bus Inside a Hurricane	P	F	Cole, Joanna & Degen, Bruce	Scholastic
Magic School Bus Inside Ralphie	P	F	Cole, Joanna & Degen, Bruce	Scholastic
Magic School Bus Inside the Earth	P	F	Cole, Joanna & Degen, Bruce	Scholastic
Magic School Bus Inside the Human Body	P	F	Cole, Joanna & Degen, Bruce	Scholastic
Magic School Bus Kicks Up a Storm	P	F	Cole, Joanna & Degen, Bruce	Scholastic
Magic School Bus Liz Sorts It Out	P	F	Cole, Joanna & Degen, Bruce	Scholastic
Magic School Bus Lost in the Solar System	P	F	Cole, Joanna & Degen, Bruce	Scholastic
Magic School Bus Makes a Rainbow	P	F	Cole, Joanna & Degen, Bruce	Scholastic
Magic School Bus Meets the Rot Squad	P	F	Cole, Joanna & Degen, Bruce	Scholastic
Magic School Bus on the Ocean Floor	P	F	Cole, Joanna & Degen, Bruce	Scholastic
Magic School Bus Out of This World	P	F	Cole, Joanna & Degen, Bruce	Scholastic
Magic School Bus Plants Seeds	P	F	Cole, Joanna & Degen, Bruce	Scholastic
Magic School Bus Plays Ball	P	F	Cole, Joanna & Degen, Bruce	Scholastic
Magic School Bus Science Explorations	P	F	Cole, Joanna & Degen, Bruce	Scholastic
Magic School Bus Search for the Missing Bones	P	F	Cole, Joanna & Degen, Bruce	Scholastic
Magic School Bus Sees Stars	P	F	Cole, Joanna & Degen, Bruce	Scholastic
Magic School Bus Shows and Tells	P	F	Cole, Joanna & Degen, Bruce	Scholastic
Magic School Bus Space Explorers	P	F	Cole, Joanna & Degen, Bruce	Scholastic
Magic School Bus Spins a Web	P	F	Cole, Joanna & Degen, Bruce	Scholastic
Magic School Bus Takes a Dive	P	F	Cole, Joanna & Degen, Bruce	Scholastic
Magic School Bus Taking Flight	P	F	Cole, Joanna & Degen, Bruce	Scholastic
Magic School Bus The Truth About Bats	P	F	Cole, Joanna & Degen, Bruce	Scholastic
Magic School Bus The Wild Whale Watch	P	F	Cole, Joanna & Degen, Bruce	Scholastic
Magic School Bus Twister Trouble	P	F	Cole, Joanna & Degen, Bruce	Scholastic

Title	Level	Genre	Author/Series	Publisher/Distributor
Magic School Bus Ups and Downs	P	F	Cole, Joanna & Degen, Bruce	Scholastic
Magic School Bus Visits the Planets	P	F	Cole, Joanna & Degen, Bruce	Scholastic
Magic School Bus Wet All Over	P	F	Cole, Joanna & Degen, Bruce	Scholastic
Magic Squad and the Dog of Great Potential, The	P	RF	Quattlebaum, Mary	Bantam Doubleday Dell
Maps and Codes	P	I	Wildcats	Wright Group/McGraw Hill
Marching to Freedom: The Story of Martin Luther King, Jr	P	B	Milton, Joyce	Bantam Doubleday Dell
Margaret Bourke-White: A Photographer's Life	P	B	Keller, Emily	Lerner Publications
Mario's Mayan Journey	P	F	Book Shop	Mondo
Martin's Mice	P	F	King-Smith, Dick	Knopf
Matchlock Gun, The	P	HF	Edmonds, Walter D.	Putnam & Grosset
Mei Fuh: Memories From China	P	B	Schaeffer, Edith	Houghton Mifflin
Milton Hershey: Chocolate King Town Builder	P	B	Simon, Charnan	Children's Press
Mina's Spring of Colors	P	RF	Gilmore, Rachna	Fitzhenry & Whiteside
Miss Geneva's Lantern	P	RF	Book Shop	Mondo
My Father The Mad Professor	P	F	Odgers, Sally	Rigby
My First Book of Biographies: Great Men and Women Every Child Should Know	P	B	Marzollo, Jean	Scholastic
Native Americans	P	I	Weldon Owen	Wright Group/McGraw Hill
New Kind of Magic, The	P	F	Szymanski, Lois	Avon Camelot
Night Music	P	HF	Voyages in…	Wright Group/McGraw Hill
No Flying in the House	P	F	Brock, Betty	Harper Collins
Nose for Trouble, A	P	RF	Wilson, Nancy Hope	Avon
Not What It Seems	P	RF	Wildcats	Wright Group/McGraw Hill
Ocean Tide Pool	P	I	L'Hommedieu, Arthur John	Grolier
Odds on Oliver	P	RF	Greene, Carol	Puffin Books
Oh, Brother	P	RF	Wilson, Johnnice M.	Scholastic
Ojibwa Indians, The	P	I	Lund, Bill	Capstone Press
One Day in the Alpine Tundra	P	I	George, Jean Craighead	Harper Collins
One Day in the Desert	P	I	George, Jean Craighead	Harper Collins
One Day in the Tropical Rain Forest	P	I	George, Jean Craighead	HarperTrophy
One Day in the Woods	P	I	George, Jean Craighead	HarperTrophy
Owls in the Family	P	F	Mowat, Farley	Bantam Doubleday Dell
Pablo Picasso	P	B	Lowery, Linda	Lerner Publishing Group
Pagemaster, The	P	F	Horowitz, Jordan	Scholastic
Penguins of the Galápagos	P	I	Young Readers' Series	Barron's Educational Series
Planet Boring	P	F	Cook, Nathan	Pacific Learning
Platypus	P	I	Short, J., Green, J., and Bird, B.	Mondo
Pony Named Shawney, A	P	RF	Small, Mary	Mondo
Pony Tails: Jasmine and the Jumping Pony	P	RF	Bryant, Bonnie	Bantam Doubleday Dell
Pony Tails: Jasmine's Christmas Ride	P	RF	Bryant, Bonnie	Bantam Doubleday Dell
Pony Tails: May Takes the Lead	P	RF	Bryant, Bonnie	Bantam Doubleday Dell
Poopsie Pomerantz Pick Up Your Feet	P	RF	Giff, Patricia Reilly	Dell
Private Notebook of Katie Roberts, Age 11, The	P	RF	Hest, Amy	Candlewick Press
Pueblo Indians, The	P	I	Ross, Pamela	Capstone Press
Puppets	P	I	Trussell-Cullen, Alan	Rigby
Questions and Answers About Forest Animals	P	I	Chinery, Michael	Kingfisher
Questions and Answers About Freshwater Animals	P	I	Chinery, Michael	Kingfisher
Refugees, The	P	RF	Marriott, Janice	Pacific Learning
Return to Howliday Inn	P	F	Howe, James	Avon Camelot
Revenge of the Mummy	P	RF	Parker, A.E.	Scholastic
Riding Freedom	P	HF	Ryan, Pam Munoz	Scholastic
Rising Stars of the NBA	P	B	Layden, Joe	Scholastic
Roald Dahl's Revolting Rhymes	P	F	Dahl, Roald	Puffin Books
Robinson Crusoe	P	TL	Dolch, E. W. and Marguerite P.	Scholastic
Rosa Parks	P	B	Greenfield, Eloise	HarperTrophy
Ryan's Dog Ringo	P	RF	Gibson, Marie	Rigby
Saving The Yellow Eye	P	I	Darby, John	Pacific Learning
School Mouse, The	P	F	King-Smith, Dick	Hyperion

Title	Level	Genre	Author/Series	Publisher/Distributor
Searching for Sea Lions	P	I	Westerskov, Kim	Pacific Learning
Secret of the Seal, The	P	RF	Davis, Deborah	Alfred A. Knopf
Secret Secret Passage, The	P	RF	Parker, A. E.	Scholastic
Seminole Indians, The	P	I	Lund, Bill	Capstone Press
Shoebag	P	F	James, Mary	Scholastic
Sideways Stories from Wayside School	P	F	Sachar, Louis	Hearst
Sioux Indians, The	P	I	Lund, Bill	Capstone Press
Skates of Uncle Richard, The	P	RF	Fenner, Carol	Random House
Sky's the Limit, The	P	I	Christiansen, Tony	Pacific Learning
Slugs and Snails	P	I	Mini Pets	Steck-Vaughn
Snot Stew	P	F	Wallace, Bill	Pocket Books
Sojourner Truth	P	B	McLoone, Margo	Capstone Press
Someday a Tree	P	RF	Bunting, Eve	Clarion
Spiders	P	I	Mini Pets	Steck-Vaughn
Sports Bloopers	P	I	Hollander, Phyllis & Zander	Scholastic
Sports Mysteries: Case of the Basketball Video	P	RF	Edwards, T. J.	Scholastic
Sports Mysteries: Case Of The Missing Pitcher	P	RF	Edwards, T. J.	Scholastic
Stanley and the Magic Lamp	P	F	Brown, Jeff	HarperTrophy
Star Thief	P	RF	Bilbrough, Norman	Pacific Learning
Sticks and Stones, Bobbie Bones	P	RF	Roberts, Brenda C.	Scholastic
Stone Fox	P	RF	Gardiner, John Reynolds	Harper Trophy
Storm Book, The	P	I	Zolotow, Charlotte	Harper Collins
Story of Doña Chila, The	P	B	Moore, Eva	Scholastic
Story of Small Fry, The	P	I	Vaughan, Marcia	Rigby
Stumpy's Secret	P	RF	Hager, Mandy	Pacific Learning
Sub, The	P	RF	Peterson, P.J.	Puffin Books
Surf's Up	P	RF	Wildcats	Wright Group/McGraw Hill
Susan B. Anthony	P	B	Davis, Lucile	Capstone Press
Tales of Olga da Polga, The	P	F	Bond, Michael	Houghton Mifflin
Tar Beach	P	HF	Ringgold, Faith	Crown
Taste of Blackberries, A	P	RF	Buchanan Smith, Doris	Scholastic
Thank You, Jackie Robinson	P	B	Cohen, Barbara	Scholastic
Thanksgiving: Why We Celebrate It the Way We Do	P	I	Hintz, Martin & Kate	Capstone Press
Third Grade Stars	P	RF	Ransom, Candice	Troll
Thomas Edison	P	B	Linder, Greg	Capstone Press
Through Grandpa's Eyes	P	RF	MacLachlan, Patricia	HarperTrophy
Time Warp Trio: 2095	P	SF	Scieszka, Jon	The Penguin Group
Time Warp Trio: Good, the Bad, and the Goofy, The	P	SF	Scieszka, Jon	The Penguin Group
Time Warp Trio: The Knights of the Kitchen Table	P	F	Scieszka, Jon	The Penguin Group
Time Warp Trio: The Not-So-Jolly Roger	P	F	Scieszka, Jon	The Penguin Group
Time Warp Trio: Tut Tut	P	F	Scieszka, Jon	The Penguin Group
Time Warp Trio: Your Mother Was a Neanderthal	P	F	Scieszka, Jon	The Penguin Group
To JJ From CC	P	RF	Literacy 2000	Rigby
Trouble Dolls	P	F	Buffett, Jimmy & Savannah Jane	Harcourt Brace
Trucker	P	RF	Beale, Fleur	Pacific Learning
Tut's Mummy: Lost and Found	P	I	Donnelly, Judy	Random House
Twisters and Other Wind Storms	P	I	Wildcats	Wright Group/McGraw Hill
Twits, The	P	F	Dahl, Roald	The Penguin Group
Ugly Mug	P	RF	Joseph, Vivienne	Pacific Learning
Under the Ground	P	I	Literacy 2000	Rigby
Up in the Air	P	I	Wildcats	Wright Group/McGraw Hill
Wall, The	P	HF	Bunting, Eve	Clarion
Wanted Dead or Alive: The True Story of Harriet Tubman	P	B	McGovern, Ann	Scholastic
Wanted…Mud Blossom	P	RF	Byars, Betsy	Dell
Water Buffalo Days	P	B	Nhuong, Huynh Quang	HarperTrophy
Wayside School Gets a Little Stranger	P	F	Sachar, Louis	Avon Camelot
Wayside School is Falling Down	P	F	Sachar, Louis	Avon
Whale Is Not A Fish, A: And Other Animal Mix-ups	P	I	Berger, Melvin	Scholastic
What Are You Figuring Now?	P	B	Ferris, Jeri	Scholastic

Title	Level	Genre	Author/Series	Publisher/Distributor
When I Was Young and Wild Bill's Secret Wish	P	RF	Miggs, W.B.	Pacific Learning
Where Did the Maya Go?	P	F	Carroll, Cynthia	Rigby
Where in the World is the Perfect Family?	P	RF	Hest, Amy	The Penguin Group
Who Killed Mr. Boddy?	P	RF	Parker, A. E.	Scholastic
Who Shot the President?: The Death of John F. Kennedy	P	I	Donnelly, Judy	Random House
Who Stole the Wizard of Oz?	P	RF	Avi	Alfred A. Knopf
Wild and Wooly Mammoths	P	I	Aliki	HarperCollins
Wilma Mankiller	P	B	Lowery, Linda	Carolrhoda Books
Wish Fish, The	P	TL	Krueger, Carol	Rigby
Witch's Cat	P	F	Chew, Ruth	Scholastic
Worms	P	I	Mini Pets	Steck-Vaughn
Worst Witch at Sea, The	P	F	Murphy, Jill	Candlewick Press
Worst Witch Strikes Again, The	P	F	Murphy, Jill	Candlewick Press
Worst Witch, The	P	F	Murphy, Jill	Puffin Books
Yang the Eldest and His Odd Jobs	P	RF	Namioka, Lensey	Bantam Doubleday Dell
Yang the Second and Her Secret Admirer	P	RF	Namioka, Lensey	Bantam Doubleday Dell
Yang the Third & Her Impossible Family	P	RF	Namiaka, Lensey	Bantam Doubleday Dell
Yang the Youngest and His Terrible Ear	P	RF	Namioka, Lensey	Bantam Doubleday Dell
Zooman Sam	P	RF	Lowry, Lois	Houghton Mifflin
Abraham Lincoln	Q	B	Gross, Ruth Belov	Scholastic
Addy Learns a Lesson: A School Story	Q	HF	The American Girls Collection	Pleasant Company
Addy Saves the Day: A Summer Story	Q	HF	The American Girls Collection	Pleasant Company
Addy's Surprise: A Christmas Story	Q	HF	The American Girls Collection	Pleasant Company
Adventures of the Shark Lady	Q	I	McGovern, Ann	Scholastic
Aliens Ate My Homework	Q	F	Coville, Bruce	Pocket Books
All About Codes	Q	I	Riley, Gail Blasser	Steck-Vaughn
All About Deer	Q	I	Arnosky, Jim	Scholastic
All About Owls	Q	I	Arnosky, Jim	Scholastic
All About Seeds	Q	I	Berger, Melvin	Scholastic
All-of-a-Kind Family	Q	RF	Taylor, Sydney	Bantam Doubleday Dell
Amazing Animal Rescue Team, The	Q	I	Blankenhorn, Rebecca	Steck-Vaughn
Amazing But True Sports Stories	Q	I	Hollander, Phyllis and Zander	Scholastic
Amazing Spiders	Q	I	Eyewitness Juniors	Alfred A. Knopf
Amelia Earhart	Q	B	Lowe, David	Rigby
Amy's True Prize	Q	HF	The Little Women Journals	Avon
Anastasia, Absolutely	Q	RF	Lowry, Lois	Bantam Doubleday Dell
Anastasia Again!	Q	RF	Lowry, Lois	Bantam Doubleday Dell
Anastasia, Ask Your Analyst	Q	RF	Lowry, Lois	Bantam Doubleday Dell
Anastasia At This Address	Q	RF	Lowry, Lois	Bantam Doubleday Dell
Anastasia At Your Service	Q	RF	Lowry, Lois	Bantam Doubleday Dell
Anastasia Has the Answers	Q	RF	Lowry, Lois	Bantam Doubleday Dell
Anastasia Krupnik	Q	RF	Lowry, Lois	Bantam Doubleday Dell
Anastasia On Her Own	Q	RF	Lowry, Lois	Bantam Doubleday Dell
Anastasia's Chosen Career	Q	RF	Lowry, Lois	Bantam Doubleday Dell
Ancient Greeks	Q	I	Worldwise	Grolier
Ancient Romans	Q	I	Worldwise	Grolier
And Still the Turtle Watched	Q	RF	MacGill-Callahan, Sheila	The Penguin Group
Art Riddle Contest, The	Q	RF	Medearis, Angela Shelf	Steck-Vaughn
Artists and Their Art	Q	I	Medearis, Michael	Steck-Vaughn
Attack and Defense	Q	I	Weldon Owen	Wright Group/McGraw Hill
Australia	Q	I	First Reports	Compass Point Books
Awfully Short for the Fourth Grade	Q	RF	Woodruff, Elvira	Bantam Doubleday Dell
Badger in the Basement	Q	RF	Daniels, Lucy	Barron's Educational
Bald Eagles	Q	I	Wilde, Buck	Rigby
Beetles, Lightly Toasted	Q	RF	Naylor, Phyllis Reynolds	Bantam Doubleday Dell
Beth's Snow Dancer	Q	HF	The Little Women Journals	Avon
Betsy and Tacy Go Downtown	Q	HF	Lovelace, Maud Hart	HarperTrophy
Betsy and Tacy Go Over the Big Hill	Q	HF	Lovelace, Maud Hart	HarperTrophy
Betsy-Tacy: 60th Anniversary Edition	Q	HF	Lovelace, Maud Hart	HarperTrophy

Title	Level	Genre	Author/Series	Publisher/Distributor
Beyond the Beyond	Q	I	Wildcats	Wright Group/McGraw Hill
Big Dipper and You, The	Q	I	Krupp, E.C.	Mulberry Books
Big Storm, The	Q	I	Hiscock, Bruce	Aladdin
Big Wave, The	Q	RF	Buck, Pearl S.	Scholastic
Birthday Disaster	Q	RF	Literacy 2000	Rigby
Black Diamond: Story of the Negro Baseball Leagues	Q	I	McKissack, Patricia & Fred	Scholastic
Black-Eyed Susan	Q	HF	Armstrong, Jennifer	Alfred A. Knopf
Boodil My Dog	Q	RF	Lindenbaum, Pija	Henry Holt & Co.
Brazil	Q	I	First Reports	Compass Point Books
Bridging the Gap	Q	I	Miller, Steve	Pacific Learning
Bright Ideas	Q	I	Weldon Owen	Wright Group/McGraw Hill
Bunnicula	Q	F	Howe, James	Avon
Bunnicula Strikes Again!	Q	F	Howe, James	Simon & Schuster
Bunnies in the Bathroom	Q	RF	Baglio, Ben M.	Scholastic
By the Shores of Silver Lake	Q	HF	Wilder, Laura Ingalls	HarperTrophy
Calamity Kate	Q	RF	Deary, Terry	HarperTrophy
California	Q	I	Geography Department	Capstone Press
Canada	Q	I	First Reports	Compass Point Books
Caribou Journey, A	Q	I	Miller, Debbie S.	Little, Brown & Co.
Case of the Invisible Cat, The	Q	RF	Parker, A.E.	Scholastic
Casey's Case	Q	RF	Literacy 2000	Rigby
Casey's Code	Q	RF	Riley, Gail Blasser	Steck-Vaughn
Cats, Cats, Cats	Q	I	Literacy 2000	Rigby
Centerburg Tales: More Adventures of Homer Price	Q	RF	McCloskey, Robert	Puffin Books
Changes for Addy	Q	HF	The American Girls Collection	Pleasant Company
Changes For Addy: A Winter Story	Q	HF	The American Girls Collection	Pleasant Company
Changes For Felicity: A Winter Story	Q	HF	The American Girls Collection	Pleasant Company
Changes For Josefina: A Winter Story	Q	HF	The American Girls Collection	Pleasant Company
Changes For Kirsten: A Winter Story	Q	HF	The American Girls Collection	Pleasant Company
Changes For Molly: A Winter Story	Q	HF	The American Girls Collection	Pleasant Company
Changes For Samantha: A Winter Story	Q	HF	The American Girls Collection	Pleasant Company
Changing Times	Q	RF	Treasured Horses Collection	Scholastic
Child's Portrait of Shakespeare, A	Q	B	Burdett, Lois	Firefly Books
China	Q	I	First Reports	Compass Point Books
Cities: The Building of America	Q	I	Thompson, Gare	Children's Press
Class Trip to the Cave of Doom	Q	F	McMullan, K.H.	Grosset & Dunlap
Coral Reefs	Q	I	First Reports	Compass Point Books
Countess Veronica	Q	RF	Robinson, Nancy K.	Scholastic
Creepy Creatures	Q	I	Weldon Owen	Wright Group/McGraw Hill
Cub in the Cupboard	Q	RF	Baglio, Ben M.	Scholastic
Cuckoo Child, The	Q	F	King-Smith, Dick	Hyperion
Day of the Blizzard	Q	I	Moskin, Marietta	Scholastic
Day the Fifth Grade Disappeared, The	Q	F	Fields, Terri	Scholastic
Dear Future	Q	RF	Literacy 2000	Rigby
Dear Mr. Henshaw	Q	RF	Cleary, Beverly	HarperCollins
Deserts	Q	I	First Reports	Compass Point Books
Diary of a Pioneer Boy	Q	HF	Massie, Elizabeth	Steck-Vaughn
Disappearing Bike Shop, The	Q	SF	Woodruff, Elvira	Bantam Doubleday Dell
Do You Know Me?	Q	RF	Farmer, Nancy	The Penguin Group
Dragon for Sale	Q	F	MacDonald, Marianne	Troll
Dragon in the Family, A	Q	F	Koller, Jackie French	Pocket Books
Dragon Quest	Q	F	Koller, Jackie French	Pocket Books
Dragon Trouble	Q	F	Koller, Jackie French	Pocket Books
Dragonling, The	Q	F	Koller, Jackie French	Pocket Books
Dragons and Kings	Q	F	Koller, Jackie French	Pocket Books
Dragons of Krad	Q	F	Koller, Jackie French	Pocket Books
Easter Bunny that Ate My Sister, The	Q	F	Marney, Dean	Scholastic
Errol the Peril	Q	F	Literacy 2000	Rigby
Escape From Slavery: Five Journeys to Freedom	Q	B	Rappaport, Doreen	HarperTrophy
Experiment with Movement	Q	I	Murphy, Bryan	Scholastic

Title	Level	Genre	Author/Series	Publisher/Distributor
Experiment with Water	Q	I	Murphy, Bryan	Scholastic
Exploring the Titanic	Q	I	Ballard, Robert D.	Scholastic
Facing the Flood	Q	RF	Kleinhenz, Sydnie Meltzer	Steck-Vaughn
Family Dinner	Q	RF	Cutler, Jane	Farrar, Straus and Giroux
Famous Animals	Q	I	Literacy Tree	Rigby
Fantastic Animal Features	Q	I	Parker, Heather	Steck-Vaughn
Farmer Boy	Q	HF	Wilder, Laura Ingalls	HarperTrophy
Feathers and Flight	Q	I	Weldon Owen	Wright Group/McGraw Hill
Felicity Learns a Lesson	Q	HF	The American Girls Collection	Pleasant Company
Felicity Saves the Day	Q	HF	The American Girls Collection	Pleasant Company
Felicity's Surprise	Q	HF	The American Girls Collection	Pleasant Company
Finding the Titanic	Q	I	Ballard, Robert D.	Scholastic
First Book About Africa: An Introduction for Young Readers	Q	I	Ellis, Veronica Freeman	Just Us Books
Five Brave Explorers	Q	B	Hudson, Wade	Scholastic
Five Brilliant Scientists	Q	B	Steward, Susan McKinney	Scholastic
Five Notable Inventors	Q	B	Hudson, Wade	Scholastic
Florida	Q	I	Geography Department	Capstone Press
Flunking of Joshua T. Bates, The	Q	RF	Shreve, Susan	Alfred A. Knopf
Forest Community, A	Q	I	Massie, Elizabeth	Steck-Vaughn
Fortune's Friend: Tales of Rivalry and Riches	Q	TL	Literacy 2000	Rigby
Fossils Alive!	Q	I	Daniel, Claire	Steck-Vaughn
Fossils: Pictures from the Past	Q	I	Daniel, Claire	Steck-Vaughn
Four A's, The	Q	RF	Wildcats	Wright Group/McGraw Hill
Fourth Grade Celebrity	Q	RF	Giff, Patricia Reilly	Bantam Doubleday Dell
Fourth Grade Wizards, The	Q	RF	DeClements, Barthe	The Penguin Group
Fox in the Frost	Q	RF	Baglio, Ben M.	Scholastic
Free Fall	Q	I	Basalaj, Kathy	Pacific Learning
Friendship Pact, The	Q	RF	Pfeffer, Susan Beth	Scholastic
Fudge-a-Mania	Q	RF	Blume, Judy	Bantam Doubleday Dell
Full House Stephanie	Q	RF	Herman, Gail	Pocket Books
Garfield and the Beast in the Basement	Q	F	Davis, Jim	Troll
Garfield and the Mysterious Mummy	Q	F	Davis, Jim	Troll
Gathering: A Northwoods Counting Book	Q	I	Bowen, Betsy	Houghton Mifflin
Georgia	Q	I	Geography Department	Capstone Press
Getting Rid of Katherine	Q	RF	Wright, Betty Ren	Troll
Ghost Come Calling, The	Q	F	Wright, Betty	Scholastic
Ghost On Saturday Night, The	Q	F	Fleischman, Sid	Beech Tree Books
Girl in the Golden Bower, The	Q	TL	Yolen, Jane	Little, Brown, & Co.
Girl Who Knew it All, The	Q	RF	Giff, Patricia Reilly	Bantam Doubleday Dell
Girl Who Loved the Wind, The	Q	TL	Yolen, Jane	HarperTrophy
Girls to the Rescue, Book #3	Q	RF	Lansky, Bruce	Meadowbrook Press
Girls to the Rescue, Book #4	Q	RF	Lansky, Bruce	Meadowbrook Press
Girls to the Rescue, Book #6	Q	RF	Lansky, Bruce	Meadowbrook Press
Goat in the Garden	Q	RF	Baglio, Ben M.	Scholastic
Golden Sword of Dragonwalk	Q	F	Stine, R. L.	Scholastic
Goodbye, Chicken Little	Q	RF	Byars, Betsy	HarperTrophy
Goose on the Loose	Q	RF	Baglio, Ben M.	Scholastic
Grandpa's Face	Q	RF	Greenfield, Eloise	Putnam & Grosset
Grasslands	Q	I	First Reports	Compass Point Books
Great Wall of China, The	Q	I	Fisher, Leonard Everett	Aladdin
Green Thumbs	Q	I	Literacy 2000	Rigby
Gulliver's Stories	Q	F	Dolch, E. W. and Marguerite P.	Scholastic
Hamster in a Handbasket	Q	RF	Baglio, Ben M.	Scholastic
Hannah and the Angels	Q	F	Lowery, Linda	Random House
Hannah of Fairfield	Q	HF	Pioneer Daughters	Puffin Books
Hannah's Helping Hands	Q	HF	Van Leeuwen, Jean	Puffin Books
Hannah's Winter of Hope	Q	HF	Van Leeuwen, Jean	Puffin Books
Happy Accidents!	Q	I	Trussell-Cullen, Alan	Rigby
Happy Birthday, Addy!	Q	HF	The American Girls Collection	Pleasant Company

Title	Level	Genre	Author/Series	Publisher/Distributor
Happy Birthday, Felicity!	Q	HF	The American Girls Collection	Pleasant Company
Happy Birthday, Josefina!	Q	HF	The American Girls Collection	Pleasant Company
Happy Birthday, Kirsten!	Q	HF	The American Girls Collection	Pleasant Company
Happy Birthday, Molly!	Q	HF	The American Girls Collection	Pleasant Company
Happy Birthday, Samantha!	Q	HF	The American Girls Collection	Pleasant Company
Haunted	Q	F	Herman, Emily	Wright Group/McGraw Hill
Heather at the Barre	Q	RF	Sinykin, Sheri Cooper	Magic Attic
Heather, Belle of the Ball	Q	RF	Sinykin, Sheri Cooper	Magic Attic
Heather Goes to Hollywood	Q	RF	Sinykin, Sheri Cooper	Magic Attic
Heather Takes the Reins	Q	RF	Sinykin, Sheri Cooper	Magic Attic
Hedgehog in the Hall	Q	RF	Daniels, Lucy	Barron's Educational
Help! I'm a Prisoner in the Library	Q	RF	Clifford, Eth	Scholastic
Help! I'm Trapped in an Alien's Body	Q	F	Strasser, Todd	Scholastic
Help! I'm Trapped in My Lunch Lady's Body	Q	F	Strasser, Todd	Scholastic
Help! I'm Trapped in My Teacher's Body	Q	F	Strasser, Todd	Scholastic
Help! I'm Trapped in Obedience School	Q	F	Strasser, Todd	Scholastic
Help! I'm Trapped in Obedience School Again	Q	F	Strasser, Todd	Scholastic
Help! I'm Trapped in Santa's Body	Q	F	Strasser, Todd	Scholastic
Help! I'm Trapped in the First Day of School	Q	F	Strasser, Todd	Scholastic
Help! I'm Trapped in the First Day of Summer Camp	Q	F	Strasser, Todd	Scholastic
Help! I'm Trapped in the President's Body	Q	F	Strasser, Todd	Scholastic
Homer Price	Q	RF	McCloskey, Robert	Puffin Books
Horrors of the Haunted Museum	Q	RF	Stine, R. L.	Scholastic
Horse, of Course, The	Q	I	Elliot-Reep, Tracey	Rigby
Human Body, The	Q	I	Weldon Owen	Wright Group/McGraw Hill
Hushtown: A Peaceful Community	Q	RF	Massie, Elizabeth	Steck-Vaughn
I Have a Dream	Q	B	Davidson, Margaret	Scholastic
Iditarod: Dogsled Race Across Alaska	Q	I	Fuerst, Jeffery B.	Wright Group/McGraw Hill
If You Grew Up with Abraham Lincoln	Q	I	McGovern, Ann	Scholastic
If You Grew Up with George Washington	Q	I	Gross, Ruth Belov	Scholastic
If You Lived 100 Years Ago	Q	I	McGovern, Ann	Scholastic
If You Lived at the Time of Martin Luther King	Q	I	Levine, Ellen	Scholastic
If You Lived at the Time of the American Revolution	Q	I	Moore, Kay	Scholastic
If You Lived at the Time of the Civil War	Q	I	Moore, Kay	Scholastic
If You Lived at the Time of the Great San Francisco Earthquake	Q	I	Levine, Ellen	Scholastic
If You Lived in Colonial Times	Q	I	McGovern, Ann	Scholastic
If you Lived in the Alaska Territory	Q	I	Levinson, Nancy Smiler	Scholastic
If You Lived with the Cherokee	Q	I	Roop, Peter & Connie	Scholastic
If You Lived with the Hopi	Q	I	Kamma, Anne	Scholastic
If You Lived with the Iroquois	Q	I	Levine, Ellen	Scholastic
If You Lived with the Sioux Indians	Q	I	McGovern, Ann	Scholastic
If You Sailed on the Mayflower in 1620	Q	I	McGovern, Ann	Scholastic
If You Traveled on the Underground Railroad	Q	I	Levine, Ellen	Scholastic
If You Traveled West in a Covered Wagon	Q	I	Levine, Ellen	Scholastic
If You Were There When They Signed the Constitution	Q	I	Levy, Elizabeth	Scholastic
If Your Name was Changed at Ellis Island	Q	I	Levine, Ellen	Scholastic
Illinois	Q	I	Geography Department	Capstone Press
In the News	Q	I	Wildcats	Wright Group/McGraw Hill
In the Rain Forest	Q	I	Wildcats	Wright Group/McGraw Hill
Isabella: A Wish for Miguel	Q	HF	Childhood Journeys	Aladdin
It'll Be All Right on the Night!	Q	I	Quinn, Pat	Pacific Learning
It's New, It's Improved, It's Terrible!	Q	RF	Manes, Stephen	Bantam Skylark
J.T.	Q	RF	Wagner, Jane	Bantam Doubleday Dell
James and the Giant Peach	Q	F	Dahl, Roald	The Penguin Group
Jim Ugly	Q	RF	Fleischman, Sid	Bantam Doubleday Dell
Jo's Troubled Heart	Q	HF	The Little Women Journals	Avon
Josefina Learns a Lesson	Q	HF	The American Girls Collection	Pleasant Company
Josefina Saves the Day	Q	HF	The American Girls Collection	Pleasant Company

Title	Level	Genre	Author/Series	Publisher/Distributor
Josefina's Surprise	Q	HF	The American Girls Collection	Pleasant Company
Joshua T. Bates	Q	RF	Shreve, Susan	Alfred A. Knopf
Joshua T. Bates in Trouble Again	Q	RF	Shreve, Susan	Alfred A. Knopf
Joshua T. Bates Takes Charge	Q	RF	Shreve, Susan	Alfred A. Knopf
Journal, The: Dear Future II	Q	SF	Literacy 2000	Rigby
Junebug	Q	RF	Mead, Alice	Bantam Doubleday Dell
Just Juice	Q	RF	Hesse, Karen	Scholastic
Kayaking	Q	I	Lund, Bill	Capstone Press
Keisha Leads the Way: Magic Attic Club	Q	RF	Reed, Teresa	Magic Attic
Keisha the Fairy Snow Queen: Magic Attic Club	Q	RF	Reed, Teresa	Magic Attic
Keisha to the Rescue: Magic Attic Club	Q	RF	Reed, Teresa	Magic Attic
Keisha's Maze Mystery (Magic Attic)	Q	RF	Benson, Lauren	Magic Attic
Kid Heroes of the Environment	Q	I	Dee, Catherine	Scholastic
King Max	Q	F	King-Smith, Dick	Troll
Kirsten Learns a Lesson	Q	HF	The American Girls Collection	Pleasant Company
Kirsten Saves the Day	Q	HF	The American Girls Collection	Pleasant Company
Kirsten's Surprise	Q	HF	The American Girls Collection	Pleasant Company
Kitten in the Cold	Q	RF	Baglio, Ben M.	Scholastic
Kitten That Won First Prize, The	Q	RF	Baglio, Ben M.	Scholastic
Kittens in the Kitchen	Q	RF	Daniels, Lucy	Barron's Educational
Knights & Armor	Q	I	Worldwise	Grolier
Knitwits	Q	RF	Taylor, William	Scholastic
Lady Bird Johnson	Q	B	Simon, Charnan	Children's Press
Lamb in the Laundry	Q	RF	Baglio, Ben M.	Scholastic
Lemonade Trick, The	Q	RF	Corbett, Scott	Scholastic
Little Clearing in the Woods	Q	HF	Wilkes, Maria D.	HarperTrophy
Little House by Boston Bay	Q	HF	Wiley, Melissa	HarperTrophy
Little House in Brookfield	Q	HF	Wilkes, Maria D.	HarperTrophy
Little House in the Big Woods	Q	HF	Wilder, Laura Ingalls	HarperTrophy
Little House in the Highlands	Q	HF	Wiley, Melissa	HarperTrophy
Little House on the Prairie	Q	HF	Wilder, Laura Ingalls	HarperTrophy
Little Town at the Crossroads	Q	HF	Wilkes, Maria D.	HarperTrophy
Little Town on the Prairie	Q	HF	Wilder, Laura Ingalls	HarperTrophy
Long Winter, The	Q	HF	Ingalls Wilder, Laura	HarperTrophy
Lost Flower Children, The	Q	RF	Lisle, Janet Taylor	Philomel Books
Love, from the Fifth-Grade Celebrity	Q	RF	Giff, Patricia Reilly	Bantam Doubleday Dell
Mammals of the Sea	Q	I	Weldon Owen	Wright Group/McGraw Hill
Maps and Our World	Q	I	Weldon Owen	Wright Group/McGraw Hill
Marie: Summer in the Country	Q	HF	Girlhood Journeys	Aladdin
Mary by Myself	Q	F	Smith, Jane Denitz	HarperTrophy
Mary on Horseback	Q	RF	Wells, Rosemary	Puffin Books
Max the Man Mountain	Q	RF	McFarlane, Peter	Harper Collins
Medieval Feast, A	Q	I	Aliki	Harper Collins
Medieval Town	Q	I	Worldwise	Grolier
Meet Addy	Q	HF	The American Girls Collection	Pleasant Company
Meet Felicity	Q	HF	The American Girls Collection	Pleasant Company
Meet Hillary Rodham Clinton	Q	B	Spain, Valerie	Random House
Meet John F. Kennedy	Q	B	White, Nancy Bean	Random House
Meet Josefina	Q	HF	The American Girls Collection	Pleasant Company
Meet Kirsten	Q	HF	The American Girls Collection	Pleasant Company
Meet Molly	Q	HF	The American Girls Collection	Pleasant Company
Meet Samantha	Q	HF	The American Girls Collection	Pleasant Company
Meg's Dearest Wish	Q	HF	The Little Women Journals	Avon
Megan in Ancient Greece	Q	HF	Korman, Susan	Magic Attic
Megan's Balancing Act	Q	RF	Korman, Susan	Magic Attic
Michael Jordan	Q	B	Lovitt, Chip	Scholastic
Michigan	Q	I	One nation	Capstone Press
Mighty Mammals	Q	I	Weldon Owen	Wright Group/McGraw Hill
Miller Who Tried to Please Everyone, The	Q	TL	Aesop's Fables	Dominie

Title	Level	Genre	Author/Series	Publisher/Distributor
Mixed-up Max	Q	F	King-Smith, Dick	Troll
Moki	Q	HF	Penny, Grace Jackson	Penguin Group
Molly Learns a Lesson	Q	HF	The American Girls Collection	Pleasant Company
Molly Saves the Day	Q	HF	The American Girls Collection	Pleasant Company
Molly's Surprise	Q	HF	The American Girls Collection	Pleasant Company
Moon, The	Q	I	Eye on the Universe	Crabtree
Morgan's Zoo	Q	F	Howe, James	Aladdin
Mostly Michael	Q	RF	Smith, Robert Kimmel	Bantam Doubleday Dell
Mountain Bike Challenge, The	Q	I	Morgan, Patrick	Pacific Learning
Mountain Man and the President, The	Q	B	First Reports	Compass Point Books
Mouse of Amherst, The	Q	F	Spires, Elizabeth	Farrar, Straus and Giroux
Mr. Popper's Penguins	Q	F	Atwater, Richard and Florence	Dell
Mystery of the Fire in the Sky	Q	RF	Mystery Solvers	Troll
Mystery of the Missing Leopard, The	Q	F	Leonhardt, Alice	Steck-Vaughn
Myth or Mystery?	Q	F	Weber, Rebecca	Rigby
Native American Stories	Q	TL	Bruchac, Joseph	Fulcrum Publishing
Nature's Power	Q	I	Hummer, Patricia K.	Steck-Vaughn
Nelson Mandela	Q	B	First Biographies	Steck-Vaughn
New Jersey	Q	I	Kummer, Patricia K.	Capstone Press
New York	Q	I	Geography Department	Capstone Press
Newspaper Kids, The	Q	RF	Phillips, Juanita	Harper Collins
Night Queen's Blue Velvet Dress, The	Q	F	Pair-It Books	Steck-Vaughn
No Laughing Matter (Ragged Island Mysteries)	Q	RF	Bensen, Rosie	Wright Group/McGraw Hill
Norman Newman and the Werewolf of Walnut Street	Q	F	Conford, Ellen	Troll
North America	Q	I	Petersen, David	Grolier Publishing
Nothing But Trouble, Trouble, Trouble	Q	RF	Hermes, Patricia	Scholastic
Ocean Life	Q	I	Weldon Owen	Wright Group/McGraw Hill
Ocean Life: Tide Pool Creatures	Q	I	Leonhardt, Alice	Steck-Vaughn
Oceans	Q	I	First Reports	Compass Point Books
Oceans	Q	I	The Wonders of our World	Crabtree
Ohio	Q	I	Geography Department	Capstone Press
On the Banks of Plum Creek	Q	HF	Wilder, Laura Ingalls	Harper Collins
On the Banks of the Bayou	Q	HF	MacBride, Roger Lea	Harper Collins
On Top of Concord Hill	Q	HF	Wilkes, Maria D.	HarperCollins
Once I Was a Plum Tree	Q	RF	Hurwitz, Johanna	Beech Tree Books
Onion Tears	Q	RF	Kidd, Diana	William Morrow
Original Adventures of Hank the Cowdog, The	Q	F	Erickson, John R.	Gulf
Orphan Train Children: Aggie's Home	Q	HF	Nixon, Joan Lowery	Yearling
Our World of Wonders	Q	I	Canetti, Yanitzia	Steck-Vaughn
Out and About	Q	I	Weldon Owen	Wright Group/McGraw Hill
Outside and Inside Bats	Q	I	Markle, Sandra	Simon & Schuster
Outside and Inside Kangaroos	Q	I	Markle, Sandra	Atheneum
Outside and Inside Sharks	Q	I	Markle, Sandra	Simon & Schuster
Outside and Inside Snakes	Q	I	Markle, Sandra	Simon & Schuster
Outside and Inside Spiders	Q	I	Markle, Sandra	Simon & Schuster
Overcoming Challenges: The Life of Charles F Bolden, Jr	Q	B	Walton, Darwin McBeth	Steck-Vaughn
Owl in the Office	Q	RF	Baglio, Ben M.	Scholastic
P.W. Cracker Sees the World	Q	F	Yoshizawa, Linda	Steck-Vaughn
Paul Cezanne	Q	B	Venezia, Mike	Childrens Press
Paul Gauguin	Q	B	Venezia, Mike	Childrens Press
Paul Klee	Q	B	Venezia, Mike	Childrens Press
Peanut	Q	I	Selsam, Millicent	William Morrow
Pedro's Journal	Q	HF	Conrad, Pam	Bantam Doubleday Dell
Pennsylvania	Q	I	Geography Department	Capstone Press
Peter Tchaikovsky	Q	B	Venezia, Mike	Childrens Press
Picasso	Q	B	Venezia, Mike	Childrens Press
Picture Book of Simon Bolivar, A	Q	B	Adler, David A.	Bantam Doubleday Dell
Pierre August Renoir	Q	B	Venezia, Mike	Childrens Press
Piglet in a Playpen	Q	RF	Baglio, Ben M.	Scholastic

Title	Level	Genre	Author/Series	Publisher/Distributor
Pioneer Way, The	Q	I	Kummer, Patricia K.	Steck-Vaughn
Plain Girl	Q	RF	Sorensen, Virginia	Harcourt Brace
Planets, The	Q	I	Weldon Owen	Wright Group/McGraw Hill
Plant Kingdom, The	Q	I	Weldon Owen	Wright Group/McGraw Hill
Pocketful of Goobers: Story of George Washington Carver	Q	B	Mitchell, Barbara	Carolrhoda Books
Ponies at the Point	Q	RF	Baglio, Ben M.	Scholastic
Pony on the Porch	Q	RF	Baglio, Ben M.	Scholastic
Prairie Songs	Q	HF	Conrad, Pam	HarperTrophy
Prince William	Q	B	Rand, Gloria	Henry Holt & Company
Puppies in the Pantry	Q	RF	Baglio, Ben M.	Scholastic
Rain Forest, The	Q	I	Fusselman, Fred	Rigby
Rain Forest Tree, A	Q	I	Kite, Lorien	Crabtree
Rain or Shine	Q	I	Weldon Owen	Wright Group/McGraw Hill
Revolutionary Poet: A Story About Phillis Wheatley	Q	B	Weidt, Maryann N.	Carolrhoda Books
Rock Climbing	Q	I	Lund, Bill	Capstone Press
Rupert and the Griffin	Q	F	Hillman, Robert	Rigby
Safe Return	Q	RF	Dexter, Catherine	Candlewick Press
Samantha Saves the Day	Q	RF	The American Girls Collection	Pleasant Company
Samantha's Surprise	Q	RF	The American Girls Collection	Pleasant Company
Samurai's Daughter, The	Q	TL	San Souci, Robert D.	The Penguin Group
Sarah Morton Daniel's Day: Day in the Life of, A	Q	B	Waters, Kate	Scholastic
Scaly Things	Q	I	Weldon Owen	Wright Group/McGraw Hill
Science Fair Surprise, The	Q	RF	Burke, Melissa Blackwell	Steck-Vaughn
Scrappers No Easy Out	Q	RF	Hughes, Dean	Aladdin
Scrappers No Fear	Q	RF	Hughes, Dean	Aladdin
Secret of Bunratty Castle, The	Q	F	Vaughan, Marcia	Rigby
Secret of the Silver Shoes, The	Q	F	Massie, Elizabeth	Steck-Vaughn
Secret Silver Lining, A (Ragged Island Mysteries)	Q	RF	Bensen, Rosie	Wright Group/McGraw Hill
Secrets of the Desert	Q	I	Literacy 2000	Rigby
Shady Deal, The: Tales of Cleverness and Cunning	Q	TL	Parkes, Brenda & Stott-Thornton, Janet	Rigby
Sharks and Rays	Q	I	Weldon Owen	Wright Group/McGraw Hill
Sheepdog in the Snow	Q	RF	Baglio, Ben M.	Scholastic
Shoes Through the Ages	Q	I	Brill, Marlene Targ	Steck-Vaughn
Sierra	Q	I	Siebert, Diane	HarperCollins
Simon's Big Challenge	Q	RF	Day, Mark	Steck-Vaughn
Sky Watch	Q	I	Weldon Owen	Wright Group/McGraw Hill
Sky's the Limit, The	Q	RF	Wildcats	Wright Group/McGraw Hill
Snakes	Q	I	Weldon Owen	Wright Group/McGraw Hill
Soup	Q	RF	Peck, Robert Newton	Bantam Doubleday Dell
Spider Relatives	Q	I	Literacy 2000	Rigby
Sports for All	Q	I	Weldon Owen	Wright Group/McGraw Hill
Spreading the Word	Q	I	Wildcats	Wright Group/McGraw Hill
Squirrels in the School	Q	RF	Baglio, Ben M.	Scholastic
Story of George Washington Carver, The	Q	B	Moore, Eva	Bantam Doubleday Dell
Story of Laura Ingalls Wilder, Pioneer Girl, The	Q	B	Stine, Megan	Bantam Doubleday Dell
Summer I Shrank My Grandmother, The	Q	F	Woodruff, Elvira	Bantam Doubleday Dell
Summer in the South, A	Q	F	Marshall, James	Houghton Mifflin
Superfudge	Q	RF	Blume, Judy	Bantam Doubleday Dell
Survive!	Q	RF	Wildcats	Wright Group/McGraw Hill
Sweet Memories Still	Q	RF	Kinsey-Warnock, Natalie	Bantam Doubleday Dell
Tales of a Fourth Grade Nothing	Q	RF	Blume, Judy	Bantam Doubleday Dell
Texas	Q	I	Geography Department	Capstone Press
There's A Boy In The Girls' Bathroom	Q	RF	Sachar, Louis	Alfred A. Knopf
There's an Owl in the Shower	Q	RF	George, Jean Craighead	Harper Collins
Think Like a Scientist	Q	I	Burke, Melissa Blackwell	Steck-Vaughn
Thomas Alva Edison: Great Inventor	Q	B	Levinson, Nancy Smiler	Scholastic
Toilet Paper Tigers, The	Q	RF	Korman, Gordon	Bantam Doubleday Dell
Trapped By a Teacher	Q	RF	Duke, Mary Ann	Rigby

Title	Level	Genre	Author/Series	Publisher/Distributor
Travelers and Traders	Q	I	Weldon Owen	Wright Group/McGraw Hill
Triathlon	Q	I	Lund, Bill	Capstone Press
True Story of the Three Little Pigs, The	Q	TL	Scieszka, Jon	Scholastic
Tundra	Q	I	First Reports	Compass Point Books
Turkey That Ate My Father, The	Q	F	Marney, Dean	Scholastic
Under the Ground	Q	I	Wildcats	Wright Group/McGraw Hill
Underwater Animals	Q	I	Weldon Owen	Wright Group/McGraw Hill
Universe, The	Q	I	Pair-It-Books	Steck-Vaughn
Up and Away	Q	I	Weldon Owen	Wright Group/McGraw Hill
Vampire Who Came For Christmas, The	Q	F	Curtis Regan, Dian	Bantam Doubleday Dell
Velveteen Rabbit, The	Q	F	Williams, Margery	Hearst
Venus	Q	I	Vogt, Gregory L.	The Millbrook Press
Volcanoes	Q	I	Weldon Owen	Wright Group/McGraw Hill
Volcanoes	Q	I	Worldwise	Grolier
Walking the Road to Freedom:A Story About Sojourner Truth	Q	B	Ferris, Jeri	Dell
Weather Watching	Q	I	Weldon Owen	Wright Group/McGraw Hill
Weight Lifting	Q	I	Lund, Bill	Capstone Press
Wetlands	Q	I	First Reports	Compass Point Books
What's Cooking?	Q	I	Cartwright, Pauline	Pacific Learning
What's Living at Your Place?	Q	I	Chapman, Bruce	Pacific Learning
Whose Side Are You On?	Q	RF	Moore, Emily	Bantam Doubleday Dell
Why Coyote Howls at Night	Q	TL	Moore, Emily	Farrar, Straus and Giroux
Why the Ocean Is Salty	Q	I	Leonhardt, Alice	Steck-Vaughn
Wild Cats	Q	I	Leonhardt, Alice	Steck-Vaughn
Wings	Q	F	Brittain, Bill	HarperTrophy
Witch Hunt: It Happened in Salem Village	Q	I	Krensky, Stephen	Random House
Wolves	Q	I	Literacy 2000	Rigby
World of Dogs, The	Q	I	Pair-It-Books	Steck-Vaughn
World's Best Dog-Walker, The	Q	RF	Zollman, Pam	Steck-Vaughn
Writer of the Plains: A Story about Willa Cather	Q	B	Streissguth, Tom	Carolrhoda Books
You Be The Detective	Q	RF	Miller, Marvin	Scholastic
You Be The Detective II	Q	RF	Miller, Marvin	Scholastic
You Be The Jury	Q	I	Miller, Marvin	Scholastic
You Be The Jury: Courtroom V	Q	I	Miller, Marvin	Bantam Doubleday Dell
18th Emergency, The	R	RF	Byars, Betsy	Bantam Doubleday Dell
Abigail Adams: Girl of Colonial Days	R	B	Wagoner, Jean Brown	Aladdin
Abraham Lincoln: The Great Emancipator	R	B	Stevenson, Augusta	Aladdin
Absolutely True Story, The: How I Visited Yellowstone Park With the Terrible Rupes	R	RF	Roberts, Willo Davis	Aladdin
Ace: The Very Important Pig	R	F	King-Smith, Dick	Knopf
Adventures of Spider, The	R	TL	Arkhurst, Joyce C.	Scholastic
After the Goat Man	R	RF	Byars, Betsy	Puffin
Against the Odds	R	I	Wildcats	Wright Group/McGraw Hill
Against the Rules	R	RF	Costello, Emily	Dell
Agnes the Sheep	R	F	Taylor, William	Bantam Doubleday Dell
All For the Better: A Story of El Barrio	R	RF	Mohr, Nicholasa	Steck Vaughn
All Is Well	R	HF	Litchman, Kristin Embry	Bantam Doubleday Dell
Alphabet, The	R	I	Literacy 2000	Rigby
Amanda Joins the Circus	R	F	Avi	Bantam Doubleday Dell
Amelia Earhart: Young Aviator	R	B	Gormley, Beatrice	Aladdin
America Street: A Multicultural Anthology of Stories	R	RF	Mazer, Anne	Persea Books
America's Most Wanted Fifth-Graders	R	RF	Lawrence, Jan and Raskin, Linda	Scholastic
American Alligator, The	R	I	Potts, Steve	Capstone Press
American Bison, The	R	I	Potts, Steve	Capstone Press
Amos and the Alien	R	F	Paulsen, Gary	Bantam Doubleday Dell
Amos Binder, Secret Agent	R	RF	Paulsen, Gary	Bantam Doubleday Dell
Amos Gets Famous	R	F	Paulsen, Gary	Bantam Doubleday Dell
Amos Gets Married	R	F	Paulsen, Gary	Bantam Doubleday Dell
Amos Goes Bananas	R	F	Paulsen, Gary	Bantam Doubleday Dell

Title	Level	Genre	Author/Series	Publisher/Distributor
Amos's Killer Concert Caper	R	F	Paulsen, Gary	Bantam Doubleday Dell
And Then What Happened Paul Revere?	R	B	Fritz, Jean	Bantam Doubleday Dell
Animal Babies	R	I	Kalman, Bobbie	Crabtree
Animal Stories by Young Writers	R	F	Rubel, William and Mandel, Gerry	Tricycle Press
Animal, the Vegetable, and John D Jones, The	R	RF	Byars, Betsy	Bantam Doubleday Dell
Annie Oakley	R	I	Wilson, Ellen	Aladdin
Armadillo, The	R	I	Potts, Steve	Capstone Press
Arthur, For the Very First Time	R	RF	MacLachlan, Patricia	Bantam Doubleday Dell
Babe Didrikson: Athlete of the Century	R	B	Knudson, R.R.	Bantam Doubleday Dell
Babe Ruth: One of Baseball's Greatest	R	I	Van Riper, Guernsey	Aladdin
Babe the Gallant Pig	R	F	King-Smith, Dick	Random House
Backward Bird Dog, The	R	F	Wallace, Bill	Bantam Doubleday Dell
Bald Eagle, The	R	I	Potts, Steve	Capstone Press
Barrel in the Basement, The	R	F	Wallace, Barbara Brooks	Aladdin
Beginnings of Sports	R	I	PM Nonfiction -Ruby	Rigby
Behind the Scenes	R	I	Literacy 2000	Rigby
Benjamin Franklin: Young Printer	R	B	Stevenson, Augusta	Aladdin
Betsy Ross: Designer of Our Flag	R	B	Weil, Ann	Aladdin
Big Picture, The	R	I	Bennett, Mary	Pacific Learning
Bighorn Sheep, The	R	I	Mattern, Joanne	Capstone Press
Birds At My Feeder	R	I	Kalman, Bobbie	Crabtree
Birthday Surprises: Ten Great Stories to Unwrap	R	RF	Hurwitz, Johanna	William Morrow
Black Gold	R	RF	Henry, Marguerite	Aladdin
Book About Planets and Stars, A	R	I	Reigot, Betty Polisar	Scholastic
Born To Trot	R	RF	Henry, Marguerite	Aladdin
Boy Who Lost His Face, The	R	RF	Sachar, Louis	Alfred A. Knopf
Bracelet, The	R	HF	Uchida, Yoshiko	Philomel Books
Brendan the Navigator: A History Mystery about the Discovery of America	R	I	Fritz, Jean	The Penguin Group
Brian's Winter	R	RF	Paulsen, Gary	Bantam Doubleday Dell
Brighty of the Grand Canyon	R	RF	Henry, Marguerite	Aladdin
Building a Dream: Mary Bethune's School	R	B	Kelso, Richard	Steck-Vaughn
Bully of Barkham Street	R	RF	Stolz, Mary	Harper Trophy
Cabin Faced West, The	R	HF	Fritz, Jean	Bantam Doubleday Dell
Caddie Woodlawn	R	HF	Brink, Carol Ryrie	Bantam Doubleday Dell
Call Me Ruth	R	RF	Sachs, Marilyn	Beech Tree Books
Can't You Make Them Behave, King George?	R	I	Fritz, Jean	Putnam & Grossett
Carole: The Inside Story	R	RF	Bryant, Bonnie	Skylark Books
Case of the Sabotaged School Play, The	R	RF	Singer, Marilyn	Bantam Doubleday Dell
Castle in the Attic, The	R	F	Winthrop, Elizabeth	Bantam Doubleday Dell
Cat Walk	R	F	Stolz, Mary	Bantam Doubleday Dell
Caves	R	I	The Wonders of our World	Crabtree
Caves	R	I	Wood, Jenny	Scholastic
Celery Stalks at Midnight, The	R	F	Howe, James	Atheneum
Chancy and the Grand Rascal	R	F	Fleischman, Sid	Beech Tree
Charlie and the Chocolate Factory	R	F	Dahl, Roald	Bantam Doubleday Dell
Charlie and the Great Glass Elevator	R	F	Dahl, Roald	Bantam Doubleday Dell
Charlie Malarkey and the Singing Moose	R	F	Kennedy, William & Brendan	Puffin Books
Charlotte's Web	R	F	White, E. B.	HarperTrophy
Children of Christmas: Stories for the Season	R	RF	Rylant, Cynthia	Orchard Books
Chocolate by Hershey: A Story about Milton S. Hershey	R	B	Burford, Betty	Carolrhoda Books
Chocolate Flier, The	R	I	Beames, Margaret	Rigby
Christina's Ghost	R	F	Wright, Betty Ren	Bantam Doubleday Dell
Christmas Spurs, The	R	RF	Wallace, Bill	Bantam Doubleday Dell
Circle of Gold	R	RF	Boyd, Candy Dawson	Bantam Doubleday Dell
Cities of Splendor: The Facts and the Fables	R	TL	Landscapes of Legend	Children's Press
Clara Barton: Founder of the American Red Cross	R	B	Stevenson, Augusta	Aladdin
Close to Home: A Story of the Polio Epidemic	R	I	Weaver, Lydia	Bantam Doubleday Dell

Title	Level	Genre	Author/Series	Publisher/Distributor
Coach Amos	R	RF	Paulsen, Gary	Bantam Doubleday Dell
Computer Nut, The	R	SF	Byars, Betsy	Bantam Doubleday Dell
Contemporary Age, The	R	I	Journey Through History	Barron's Educational Series
Coronado's Golden Quest	R	F	Weisberg, Barbara	Steck-Vaughn
Coyote, The	R	I	Mattern, Joanne	Capstone Press
Crispus Attucks: Black Leader of Colonial Patriots	R	I	Millender, Dharathula H.	Aladdin
Dame Shirley and the Gold Rush	R	B	Rawls, Jim	Steck-Vaughn
Danger on Panther Peak	R	RF	Wallace, Bill	Pocket Books
Dangerous Animals	R	I	Weldon Owen	Wright Group/McGraw Hill
Dark-Thirty: Southern Tales of the Supernatural	R	F	McKissack, Patricia C.	Alfred A. Knopf
Davin	R	F	Gordon, Dan & Gordon, Zaki	Bantam Doubleday Dell
Days of Courage: The Little Rock Story	R	I	Kelso, Richard	Steck-Vaughn
Deserts	R	I	The Wonders of our World	Crabtree
Devil's Bridge	R	RF	DeFelice, Cynthia	Avon
Dirty Socks Don't Win Games	R	RF	Marney, Dean	Scholastic
Dog Called Kitty, A	R	RF	Wallace, Bill	Pocket Books
Dog on Barkham Street, A	R	RF	Stolz, Mary	Harper Trophy
Dog Years	R	RF	Warner, Sally	Alfred A. Knopf
Doll's House, The	R	RF	Godden, Rumer	The Penguin Group
Dominic	R	F	Steig, William	Farrar, Straus and Giroux
Dragon in the Ghetto Caper, The	R	RF	Konigsburg, E.L.	Aladdin
Dunc and Amos and the Red Tattoos	R	RF	Paulsen, Gary	Bantam Doubleday Dell
Dunc and Amos Go to the Dogs	R	RF	Paulsen, Gary	Bantam Doubleday Dell
Dunc and Amos Hit the Big Top	R	RF	Paulsen, Gary	Bantam Doubleday Dell
Dunc and Amos Meet the Slasher	R	RF	Paulsen, Gary	Bantam Doubleday Dell
Dunc and the Flaming Ghost	R	F	Paulsen, Gary	Bantam Doubleday Dell
Dunc and the Greased Sticks of Doom	R	RF	Paulsen, Gary	Bantam Doubleday Dell
Dunc and the Haunted Castle	R	RF	Paulsen, Gary	Bantam Doubleday Dell
Dunc and the Scam Artists	R	RF	Paulsen, Gary	Bantam Doubleday Dell
Dunc Breaks the Record	R	RF	Paulsen, Gary	Bantam Doubleday Dell
Dunc Gets Tweaked	R	RF	Paulsen, Gary	Bantam Doubleday Dell
Dunc's Doll	R	RF	Paulsen, Gary	Bantam Doubleday Dell
Dunc's Dump	R	RF	Paulsen, Gary	Bantam Doubleday Dell
Dunc's Halloween	R	RF	Paulsen, Gary	Bantam Doubleday Dell
Dunc's Undercover Christmas	R	RF	Paulsen, Gary	Bantam Doubleday Dell
Earthquake!: San Francisco, 1906	R	I	Wilson, Kate	Steck-Vaughn
Earthquakes	R	I	The Wonders of our World	Crabtree
Earthquakes	R	I	Weldon Owen	Wright Group/McGraw Hill
El Greco	R	B	Venezia, Mike	Children's Press
Eleanor Roosevelt: First Lady of the World	R	B	Faber, Doris	The Penguin Group
Ellie Brader Hates Mr. G.	R	RF	Johnston, Janet	Pocket Books
Enchanted Horse, The	R	F	Nabb, Magdalen	Hyperion
Endangered Desert Animals	R	I	Taylor, Dave	Crabtree
Endangered Forest Animals	R	I	Taylor, Dave	Crabtree
Endangered Grassland Animals	R	I	Taylor, Dave	Crabtree
Endangered Island Animals	R	I	Taylor, Dave	Crabtree
Endangered Mountain Animals	R	I	Taylor, Dave	Crabtree
Endangered Ocean Animals	R	I	Taylor, Dave	Crabtree
Endangered Savannah Animals	R	I	Taylor, Dave	Crabtree
Endangered Wetland Animals	R	I	Taylor, Dave	Crabtree
Enormous Egg, The	R	F	Butterworth, Oliver	Little, Brown & Co.
Eruption	R	I	Wildcats	Wright Group/McGraw Hill
ESP TV	R	SF	Rodgers, Mary	HarperTrophy
Every Body Tells a Story	R	I	Weldon Owen	Wright Group/McGraw Hill
Every Living Thing	R	RF	Rylant, Cynthia	Aladdin
Everywhere	R	RF	Brooks, Bruce	Scholastic
Exploring Space	R	I	Weldon Owen	Wright Group/McGraw Hill
Extreme Sports	R	I	PM Nonfiction -Ruby	Rigby
Family Under the Bridge, The	R	RF	Savage Carlson, Natalie	Scholastic
Fig Pudding	R	RF	Fletcher, Ralph	Clarion Books

Title	Level	Genre	Author/Series	Publisher/Distributor
Finding Your Way	R	I	Bonallack, John	Pacific Learning
Fire in the Sky	R	HF	Ransom, Candice F.	Carolrhoda Books
Fire! The Beginnings of the Labor Movement	R	HF	Goldin, Barbara Diamond	Puffin Books
First Four Years, The	R	HF	Wilder, Laura Ingalls	HarperTrophy
Flags	R	I	Pattrick, Steve	Rigby
Flight: The Journey of Charles Lindbergh	R	I	Burleigh, Robert	Putnam & Grosset
Flying Solo	R	RF	Fletcher, Ralph	Bantam Doubleday Dell
Forest Mammals	R	I	Kalman, Bobbie	Crabtree
Forests	R	I	The Wonders of Our World	Crabtree
Fortune Branches Out, A	R	RF	Mahy, Margaret	Bantam Doubleday Dell
Foul Play on the Sidelines	R	RF	Costello, Emily	Dell
Francisco Goya	R	B	Venezia, Mike	Children's Press
Freaky Friday	R	F	Rodgers, Mary	HarperTrophy
Frederick Douglass: The Last Days of Slavery	R	B	Miller, William	Lee & Low Books
Freedom Crossing	R	HF	Clark, Margaret Goff	Scholastic
Frida Kahlo	R	B	Venezia, Mike	Children's Press
Frindle	R	RF	Clements, Andrew	Aladdin
Gentle Annie: The True Story of a Civil War Nurse	R	I	Shura, Mary Frances	Scholastic
George Handel	R	B	Venezia, Mike	Children's Press
George Washington: A Picture Book Biography	R	B	Giblin, James Cross	Scholastic
George Washington: Young Leader	R	B	Santrey, Laurence	Troll
Georgia O'Keeffe	R	B	Venezia, Mike	Children's Press
Ghosts Beneath Our Feet	R	F	Wright, Betty Ren	Scholastic
Girl-Son, The	R	HF	Neuberger, Anne E.	Carolrhoda Books
Glorious Days, Dreadful Days: The Battle of Bunker Hill	R	I	Kirby, Philippa	Steck-Vaughn
Go Free or Die: A Story About Harriet Tubman	R	B	Ferris, Jeri	Carolrhoda Books
Goldfish Charlie and the Case of the Missing Planet	R	SF	Mazer, Anne	Troll
Grant Wood	R	B	Venezia, Mike	Children's Press
Great Kapok Tree, The	R	I	Cherry, Lynne	Scholastic
Great Migration, The	R	I	Lawrence, Jacob	HarperCollins
Great Sporting Events	R	I	PM Nonfiction -Ruby	Rigby
Greek and Roman Eras, The	R	I	Journey Through History	Barron's Educational Series
Grizzly Bear, The	R	I	Potts, Steve	Capstone Press
Growin'	R	RF	Grimes, Nikki	Puffin Books
Hannah's Fancy Notions: A Story of Industrial New England	R	HF	Ross, Pat	The Penguin Group
Harry Cat's Pet Puppy	R	F	Selden, George	Bantam Doubleday Dell
Harry Houdini: Master of Magic	R	B	Kraske, Robert	Scholastic
Hatchet	R	RF	Paulsen, Gary	Aladdin
Have You Seen Hyacinth Macaw?	R	RF	Giff, Patricia Reilly	Dell
Hawaiian Magic	R	I	Morris, Rod	Pacific Learning
Helen Keller: A Light For The Blind	R	B	Kudlinski, Kathleen V.	The Penguin Group
Hello, My Name Is Scrambled Eggs	R	RF	Gilson, Jamie	Pocket Books
Henri de Toulouse-Lautrec	R	B	Venezia, Mike	Children's Press
Henri Matisse	R	B	Venezia, Mike	Children's Press
Her Piano Sang: A Story About Clara Schumann	R	B	Allman, Barbara	Carolrhoda Books
Hidden World	R	I	Weldon Owen	Wright Group/McGraw Hill
High Flying	R	I	Weldon Owen	Wright Group/McGraw Hill
Home: A Journey Through America	R	I	Locker, Thomas	Voyageur Books
Home Sweet Home, Goodbye	R	RF	Stowe, Cynthia	Scholastic
House of Wings, The	R	RF	Byars, Betsy	The Penguin Group
How Things Work	R	I	Weldon Owen	Wright Group/McGraw Hill
How To Eat Fried Worms	R	RF	Rockwell, Thomas	Bantam Doubleday Dell
Hunting the Horned Lizard	R	I	Bishop, Nic	Pacific Learning
Hurricanes & Tornadoes	R	I	The Wonders of our World	Crabtree
Iggie's House	R	RF	Blume, Judy	Bantam Doubleday Dell
Immigrants: Coming to America	R	I	Thompson, Gare	Children's Press
In the Fast Lane	R	I	Literacy 2000	Rigby
Indian in the Cupboard, The	R	F	Banks, Lynne Reid	Avon

Title	Level	Genre	Author/Series	Publisher/Distributor
Insects & Spiders	R	I	Worldwise	Franklin Watts
Island, The	R	RF	Paulsen, Gary	Bantam Doubleday Dell
Isn't It Cool?	R	I	Yurkovic, Diana Short	Rigby
It Came From Ohio!: My Life as a Writer	R	B	Stine, R.L.	Scholastic
Jar of Dreams, A	R	RF	Uchida, Yoshiko	Aladdin
Jennifer, Hecate, Macbeth, William McKinley, and Me, Elizabeth	R	RF	Konigsburg, E. L.	Yearling
Jerry on the Line	R	RF	Seabrooke, Brenda	Puffin Books
Just Call Me Stupid	R	RF	Birdseye, Tom	Puffin Books
Justin Morgan Had a Horse	R	HF	Henry, Marguerite	Scholastic
Keep Your Eye On Amanda!	R	F	Avi	Avon
King Emmett the Second	R	RF	Stolz, Mary	Bantam Doubleday Dell
King of the Wind	R	HF	Henry, Marguerite	Aladdin
Landry News, The	R	RF	Clements, Andrew	Simon & Schuster
Later, Gator	R	RF	Yep, Laurence	Hyperion
Laura Ingalls Wilder: A Biography	R	B	Anderson, William	HarperTrophy
Laura Ingalls Wilder, Pioneer Girl	R	B	Stine, Megan	Bantam Doubleday Dell
Leaders: People Who Make a Difference	R	I	You Are There	Children's Press
Leonard Bernstein	R	B	Venezia, Mike	Children's Press
Letter to Mrs. Roosevelt, A	R	HF	DeYoung, C. Coco	Delacorte Press
Library Card, The	R	RF	Spinelli, Jerry	Scholastic
Listening to Crickets: A Story about Rachel Carson	R	HF	Ransom, Candice F.	Carolrhoda Books
Little Farm in the Ozarks	R	HF	MacBride, Roger Lea	HarperTrophy
Little House on Rocky Ridge	R	HF	MacBride, Roger Lea	HarperTrophy
Little Town in the Ozarks	R	HF	MacBride, Roger Lea	HarperTrophy
Log Cabin in the Woods	R	HF	Henry, Joanne Landers	Scholastic
Long Way to Go, A	R	I	O'Neal, Zibby	The Penguin Group
Lost on a Mountain in Maine	R	RF	Fendler, Donn	Peter Smith Publications
Love You, Soldier	R	HF	Hest, Amy	Puffin Books
Luis W. Alvarez	R	B	Hispanic Stories	Steck-Vaughn
Many Happy Returns: A Review of Recycling	R	I	Literacy 2000	Rigby
Maria: A Christmas Story	R	RF	Taylor, Theodore	Avon Camelot
Maria Tallchief	R	B	Native American Stories	Steck-Vaughn
Martial Arts	R	I	Malane, Donna	Pacific Learning
Martin Luther King Day	R	I	Lowery, Linda	Scholastic
Martin Luther King, Jr. and the March Toward Freedom	R	B	Hakim, Rita	The Millbrook Press
Measuring the Weather	R	I	Gaynor, Bill	Pacific Learning
Meet Calliope Day	R	F	Haddad, Charles	Random House
Meet Martin Luther King, Jr.	R	B	de Kay, James T.	Random House
Megan's Island	R	RF	Roberts, Willo Davis	Aladdin
Message, The	R	F	Applegate, K.A.	Scholastic
Middle Ages, The	R	I	Journey Through History	Barron's Educational Series
Midnight Fox, The	R	RF	Byars, Betsy	Scholastic
Mini Mammals	R	I	Weldon Owen	Wright Group/McGraw Hill
Miracles on Maple Hill	R	RF	Sorensen, Virginia	Scholastic
Mirandy and Brother Wind	R	F	McKissack, Patricia	Alfred A. Knopf
Misty of Chincoteague	R	RF	Henry, Marguerite	Aladdin
Misty's Twilight	R	RF	Henry, Marguerite	Aladdin
Modern Times	R	I	Journey Through History	Barron's Educational Series
Monet	R	B	Venezia, Mike	Children's Press
Monster's Ring, The	R	F	Coville, Bruce	Pocket Books
Moonlight on the River	R	RF	Kovacs, Deborah	The Penguin Group
Moose, The	R	I	Hemstock, Annie	Capstone Press
Mr. Mysterious & Company	R	F	Fleischman, Sid	Beech Tree
Mummies Made in Egypt	R	I	Aliki	Harper Collins
My Brother is a Visitor From Another Planet	R	F	Sheldon, Dyan	Candlewick Press
My Dream of Martin Luther King	R	I	Ringgold, Faith	Crown
My Sister the Witch	R	RF	Conford, Ellen	Troll
Mystery of the Cupboard	R	F	Banks, Lynne Reid	Avon Camelot

Title	Level	Genre	Author/Series	Publisher/Distributor
Mystery Stories	R	RF	Higgins, James	Houghton Mifflin
Nasty, Stinky Sneakers	R	RF	Bunting, Eve	HarperTrophy
Nelson Mandela: Freedom for South Africa	R	B	Dell, Pamela	Children's Press
News Flash!	R	I	Hill, Sharon	Pacific Learning
Night Lights, A Cruise Around the Solar System	R	I	Hill, David	Pacific Learning
Nighty-Nightmare	R	F	Howe, James	Avon Camelot
No More Magic	R	SF	Avi	Alfred A. Knopf
Noonday Friends, The	R	RF	Stolz, Mary	Scholastic
Nothing's Fair in Fifth Grade	R	RF	DeClements, Barthe	Scholastic
On Guard	R	RF	Napoli, Donna Jo	Puffin Books
One Hundredth Thing about Caroline, The	R	RF	Lowry, Lois	Bantam Doubleday Dell
One Thing I'm Good At	R	RF	Williams, Karen Lynn	William Morrow
Otherwise Known As Sheila the Great	R	RF	Blume, Judy	Bantam Doubleday Dell
Our Changing Earth	R	I	Belcher, Angie	Pacific Learning
Our Only May Amelia	R	HF	Holm, Jennifer	Harper Collins
Our Planet	R	I	Worldwise	Grolier
Owls	R	I	Kalman, Bobbie	Crabtree
People from the Past	R	I	Weldon Owen	Wright Group/McGraw Hill
Phoebe The Spy	R	HF	Berry Griffin, Judith	Scholastic
Pigs Might Fly	R	F	King-Smith, Dick	Scholastic
Pike River Phantom, The	R	F	Wright, Betty	Scholastic
Pioneer Girl, The Story of Laura Ingalls Wilder	R	B	Anderson, William	Harper Collins
Play Ball!	R	I	Weldon Owen	Wright Group/McGraw Hill
Please Don't Be Mine, Julie Valentine!	R	RF	Strasser, Todd	Scholastic
Pony For Jeremiah, A	R	HF	Miller, Robert H.	Silver Burdett Press
Prehistory to Egypt	R	I	Journey Through History	Barron's Educational Series
Prince Amos	R	RF	Paulsen, Gary	Bantam Doubleday Dell
Rain Forest	R	I	Worldwise	Grolier
Raptors: Hunters in the Sky	R	I	Rauzon, Mark J.	Wright Group/McGraw Hill
Relationships of Living Things	R	I	Atwater, Mary & Baptiste et al	Macmillan/McGraw-Hill
Remembering the Big Quake	R	I	Trussell-Cullen, Alan	Pacific Learning
Reptiles and Amphibians	R	I	Weldon Owen	Wright Group/McGraw Hill
River, The	R	RF	Paulsen, Gary	Dell
Road to Seneca Falls, The	R	B	Swain, Gwenyth	Carolrhoda Books
Rocks & Minerals	R	I	The Wonders of our World	Crabtree
Sadako and the Thousand Paper Cranes	R	HF	Coerr, Eleanor	Bantam Doubleday Dell
San Domingo	R	I	Henry, Marguerite	Scholastic
Sarah, Plain and Tall	R	HF	MacLachlan, Patricia	HarperTrophy
Save the Everglades	R	I	Stamper, Judith Bauer	Steck-Vaughn
Sea Star	R	RF	Henry, Marguerite	Aladdin
Shiloh	R	RF	Naylor, Phyllis Reynolds	Bantam Doubleday Dell
Shoes for Everyone: A Story About Jan Matzeliger	R	B	Mitchell, Barbara	Carolrhoda Books
Shooting Stars	R	RF	Costello, Emily	Dell
Six Voyages of Pleasant Fieldmouse, The	R	F	Wahl, Jan	Tom Doherty
Sixth-Grade Sleepover	R	RF	Bunting, Eve	Scholastic
Skylark	R	HF	MacLachlan, Patricia	HarperTrophy
Snow Treasure	R	HF	McSwigan, Marie	Scholastic
Soccer Stars, Best Friend Face-off	R	RF	Costello, Emily	Dell
Some Friend	R	RF	Warner, Sally	Alfred A. Knopf
Something Very Sorry	R	RF	Bohlmeijer, Arno	Putnam & Grosset
Space	R	I	Worldwise	Grolier
Spell Casters, Phoebe's Fortune	R	F	Warriner, Holly	Aladdin
Spider Boy	R	RF	Fletcher, Ralph	Bantam Doubleday Dell
Sports Heroes	R	I	PM Nonfiction -Ruby	Rigby
Sports on Wheels	R	I	PM Nonfiction -Ruby	Rigby
Sports Technology	R	I	PM Nonfiction -Ruby	Rigby
Stormy, Misty's Foal	R	RF	Henry, Marguerite	Aladdin
Story of Thomas Alva Edison, Inventor, The	R	B	Davidson, Margaret	Scholastic
Stray, The	R	RF	King-Smith, Dick	Alfred A. Knopf
Strider	R	RF	Cleary, Beverly	Harper Collins

Title	Level	Genre	Author/Series	Publisher/Distributor
Stuart Little	R	F	White, E.B.	HarperTrophy
Summer Switch	R	F	Rodgers, Mary	HarperTrophy
Sun & Spoon	R	RF	Henkes, Kevin	The Penguin Group
Super Amos	R	RF	Paulsen, Gary	Bantam Doubleday Dell
Surprising Swimmers: Nature's Most Amazing Animals	R	I	Fredericks, Anthony D.	NorthWord Press
Survival!: Fire	R	HF	Duey, K. & Bale, K. A.	Aladdin
Susan B. Anthony: Champion of Women's Rights	R	B	Monsell, Helen Albee	Simon & Schuster
Switcharound	R	RF	Lowry, Lois	Random House
Sydney-Where Biscuits Go Surfing	R	RF	Coy, Michael	Scholastic
Taking Care of Yoki	R	RF	Campbell, Barbara	HarperTrophy
Tasmanian Devils	R	I	Morris, Rod	Pacific Learning
There's a Frog in My Sleeping Bag	R	RF	Clymer, Susan	Scholastic
There's a Hamster in My Lunchbox	R	RF	Clymer, Susan	Scholastic
There's a Tarantula in My Homework	R	RF	Clymer, Susan	Scholastic
There's No Place Like Home	R	I	Hill, David	Pacific Learning
Thirteen	R	RF	Ransom, Candice	Scholastic
This Place is Dry	R	I	Cobb, Vicki	Walker and Co.
This Place is Wet	R	I	Cobb, Vicki	Walker and Co.
Tiger Woods: An American Master	R	B	Edwards, Nicholas	Scholastic
Till's Christmas	R	RF	Thacker, Nola	Scholastic
Titanic Crossing	R	HF	Williams, Barbara	Scholastic
Tomorrow's Wizard	R	F	MacLachlan, Patricia	Scholastic
Too Much Magic	R	F	Sterman, Betsy & Samuel	HarperTrophy
Tournament Trouble	R	RF	Costello, Emily	Dell
Triffic the Extraordinary Pig	R	F	King-Smith, Dick	Bantam Doubleday Dell
Trouble with Tuck, The	R	RF	Taylor, Theodore	Avon
Trumpet of the Swan, The	R	F	White, E. B.	Scholastic
Tutankhamen's Gift	R	I	Sabuda, Robert	Simon & Schuster
TV Kid, The	R	RF	Byars, Betsy	Puffin Books
Twisting Up a Storm	R	I	Duksta, Cheryl	Pacific Learning
Walking For Freedom: The Montgomery Bus Boycott	R	I	Kelso, Richard	Steck-Vaughn
Way West, The: Journal of a Pioneer Woman	R	B	Knight, Amelia Stewart	Simon & Schuster
We Want Jobs!: A Story of the Great Depression	R	I	Norrell, Robert J.	Steck-Vaughn
Weather Words and What They Mean	R	I	Gibbons, Gail	Scholastic
Week of the Jellyhoppers, The	R	F	Literacy 2000	Rigby
Weird Walkers	R	I	Fredericks, Anthony D.	NorthWord Press
West Side Kids: Don't Call Me Slob-o	R	RF	Orgel, Doris	Hyperion
West Side Kids: The Big Idea	R	RF	Schecter, Ellen	Hyperion
West Side Kids: The Pet Sitters	R	RF	Schecter, Ellen	Hyperion
What Can You Do with an Elephant House?	R	I	Gaynor, Miriam and Goodwin, A.	Pacific Learning
What Were Castles For?	R	I	Usborne Starting Point History	EDC Publishing
When the Circus Came to Town	R	RF	Horvath, Polly	Sunburst
When the Water Closes Over My Head	R	RF	Napoli, Donna	Puffin Books
Where Was Patrick Henry on the 29th of May?	R	B	Fritz, Jean	Scholastic
Whipping Boy, The	R	F	Fleischman, Sid	Troll
White-Tailed Deer, The	R	I	Zwaschka, Michael	Capstone Press
Who Were the First People?	R	I	Usborne Starting Point History	EDC Publishing
Who Were the Romans?	R	I	Usborne Starting Point History	EDC Publishing
Who Were the Vikings?	R	I	Usborne Starting Point History	EDC Publishing
Who's That Stepping on Plymouth Rock?	R	I	Fritz, Jean	Putnam & Grosset
Why Don't You Get a Horse, Sam Adams?	R	B	Fritz, Jean	G.P. Putnam's Sons
Wild Horses	R	I	Wilde, Buck	Rigby
Witches, The	R	F	Dahl, Roald	The Penguin Group
Woods, Irons, and Greens	R	I	Wildcats	Wright Group/McGraw Hill
World of Imagination, A	R	I	Literacy 2000	Rigby
Your Move, J.P.!	R	RF	Lowry, Lois	Random House
Zeely	R	RF	Hamilton, Virginia	Macmillan
Abraham Lincoln	S	B	Parin d'Aulaire, Ingri & Edgar	Bantam Doubleday Dell
Afternoon of the Elves	S	F	Lisle, Janet Taylor	Scholastic

Title	Level	Genre	Author/Series	Publisher/Distributor
Ahyoka and the Talking Leaves	S	HF	Roop, Peter and Connie	Beech Tree Books
Ajeemah and his Son	S	HF	Berry, James	HarperTrophy
Alice's Diary, Living With Diabetes	S	I	Gibson, Marie	Pacific Learning
All Alone in the Universe	S	RF	Perkins, Lynne Rae	Greenwillow Books
Altogether, One at a Time	S	RF	Konigsburg, E.L.	Simon & Schuster
Amazing Impossible Erie Canal, The	S	I	Harness, Cheryl	Simon & Schuster
Amelia Earhart: Challenging the Skies	S	B	Sloate, Susan	Fawcett Columbine
Amelia Earhart: Courage in the Sky	S	B	Kerby, Mona	Puffin Books
Amelia Earhart: Flying for Adventure	S	B	Wade, Mary Dodson	The Millbrook Press
Ancient Greece	S	I	Journey Into Civilization	Chelsea House
Anne Frank	S	B	Epstein, Rachel	Franklin Watts
Asli's Story	S	I	Jansen, Adrienne	Pacific Learning
Awake and Dreaming	S	F	Person, Kit	Puffin Books
Baby-Sitter Burglaries, The	S	RF	Keene, Carolyn	Pocket Books
Back To The Day Lincoln Was Shot!	S	I	Gormley, Beatrice	Scholastic
Back To The Titanic!	S	F	Gormley, Beatrice	Scholastic
Barefoot: Escape on the Underground Railroad	S	HF	Edwards, Pamela Duncan	HarperTrophy
Bat-Poet, The	S	F	Jarrell, Randall	HarperCollins
Bats: The Amazing Upside-Downers	S	I	A First Book	Franklin Watts
Beautiful Land: A Story of the Oklahoma Land Rush	S	I	Antle, Nancy	The Penguin Group
Beethoven Lives Upstairs	S	I	Nichol, Barbara	Orchard Books
Bell, the Book, and the Spellbinder, The	S	F	Strickland, Brad	Puffin Books
Ben and Me	S	HF	Lawson, Robert	Little, Brown & Co.
Bite of the Gold Bug, The: A Story of the Alaskan Gold Rush	S	I	DeClements, Barthe	The Penguin Group
Boomtowns of the West	S	I	Kalman, Bobbie	Crabtree
Borrowers, The	S	F	Norton, Mary	Harcourt Brace
Boston Tea Party, The	S	I	We The People	Compass Point Books
Boy Called Slow, A	S	B	Bruchac, Joseph	Putnam & Grosset
Boy's Will, A	S	HF	Haugaard, Erik Christian	Houghton Mifflin
Boys Against Girls	S	RF	Naylor, Phyllis Reynolds	Bantam Doubleday Dell
Boys Start the War and the Girls Get Even, The	S	RF	Naylor, Phyllis Reynolds	Bantam Doubleday Dell
Bridge to Terabithia	S	RF	Paterson, Katherine	HarperTrophy
Broccoli Tapes, The	S	RF	Slepian, Jan	Scholastic
Caleb's Choice	S	HF	Wisler, Clifton G.	The Penguin Group
Calico Captive	S	HF	Speare, Elizabeth George	Yearling
California Gold Rush, The	S	I	We The People	Compass Point Books
Cartoonist, The	S	RF	Byars, Betsy	Puffin Books
Case of Capital Intrigue, The	S	RF	Keene, Carolyn	Pocket Books
Case of the Captured Queen	S	RF	Keene, Carolyn	Pocket Books
Case of the Dangerous Solution, The	S	RF	Keene, Carolyn	Pocket Books
Case of the Floating Crime, The	S	RF	Keene, Carolyn	Pocket Books
Case of the Twin Teddy Bears, The	S	RF	Keene, Carolyn	Pocket Books
Cassidy's Magic	S	F	Literacy 2000	Rigby
Cat!	S	I	Kroll, Virginia L.	Dawn
Cat Who Went To Heaven, The	S	F	Coatsworth, Elizabeth	Aladdin
Change The Locks	S	RF	French, Simon	Scholastic
Chester Cricket's New Home	S	F	Selden, George	Bantam Doubleday Dell
Chester Cricket's Pigeon Ride	S	F	Selden, George	Bantam Doubleday Dell
Children of Clay: A Family of Pueblo Potters	S	I	Swentzell, Rina	Lerner Publications
Children of the Longhouse	S	HF	Bruchac, Joseph	The Penguin Group
Children's Clothing of the 1800's	S	I	Historic Communities	Crabtree
Chocolate-Covered Contest, The	S	RF	Keene, Carolyn	Pocket Books
Clue of the Gold Doubloons, The	S	RF	Keene, Carolyn	Pocket Books
Colin Powell: Straight to the Top	S	B	Blue, Rose & Naden, Corinne J.	The Millbrook Press
Cookcamp, The	S	RF	Paulsen, Gary	Bantam Doubleday Dell
Cowboy Trade, The	S	I	Rounds, Glen	Holiday House
Creatures of the Reef	S	I	Belcher, Angie	Pacific Learning
Cricket in Times Square, The	S	F	Selden, George	Bantam Doubleday Dell
Crime At the Chat Café	S	RF	Keene, Carolyn	Pocket Books

Title	Level	Genre	Author/Series	Publisher/Distributor
Crime for Christmas, A	S	RF	Keene, Carolyn	Pocket Books
Crime in the Queen's Court	S	RF	Keene, Carolyn	Pocket Books
Crocodilians: Reminders of Age of Dinosaurs	S	I	A First Book	Franklin Watts
Cry of the Crow, The	S	RF	George, Jean Craighead	HarperTrophy
Cyberspace	S	SF	Wildcats	Wright Group/McGraw Hill
Cybil War, The	S	RF	Byars, Betsy	Scholastic
Day It Rained Forever, The: A Story of the Johnstown Flood	S	I	Gross, Virginia T.	The Penguin Group
Dead Letter	S	RF	Byars, Betsy	Puffin Books
Disappearing Acts	S	RF	Byars, Betsy	Puffin Books
Discovering the Past	S	I	Literacy 2000	Rigby
Dollhouse Murders, The	S	RF	Wright, Betty Ren	Scholastic
Don't Split the Pole: Tales of Down-Home Folk Wisdom	S	RF	Tate, Eleanora E.	Bantam Doubleday Dell
Eagle Song	S	RF	Bruchac, Joseph	Puffin
Earthquake!: A Story of Old San Francisco	S	I	Kudlinski, Kathleen V.	The Penguin Group
Eenie, Meanie, Murphy, NO!	S	RF	McKenna, Colleen O'Shaughnessy	Scholastic
Eleanor	S	B	Cooney, Barbara	Puffin Books
Endurance, Shackleton's Antarctic Expedition	S	I	Marriott, Janice	Pacific Learning
Eureka! It's an Airplane	S	I	Bendick, Jeanne	Scholastic
Facing West: A Story of the Oregon Trail	S	I	Kudlinski, Kathleen V.	The Penguin Group
Facts and Fun About the Presidents	S	I	Sullivan, George	Scholastic
Family Tree	S	RF	Ayres, Katherine	Bantam Doubleday Dell
Fifth Grade: Here Comes Trouble	S	RF	McKenna, Colleen O'Shaughnessy	Scholastic
Fig Pudding	S	RF	McKenna, Colleen	Scholastic
Figure in the Shadows, The	S	F	Bellairs, John	The Penguin Group
Finding Buck McHenry	S	RF	Slote, Alfred	Scholastic
Flying Flea, Callie, and Me, The	S	F	Wallace, Carol & Bill	Pocket Books
Fountains of Life: The Story of Deep-Sea Vents	S	I	A First Book	Franklin Watts
Freshwater Giants: Hippopatamus, River Dolphins and Manatees	S	I	Perry, Phyllis J.	Franklin Watts
Friendship and the Gold Cadillac, The	S	HF	Taylor, Mildred	Bantam Doubleday Dell
Friendship, The	S	HF	Taylor, Mildred	Puffin Books
From the Mixed-up Files of Mrs. Basil E. Frankweiler	S	RF	Konigsburg, E.L.	Bantam Doubleday Dell
Future-Telling Lady and Other Stories, The	S	RF	Berry, James	HarperTrophy
Ghostmobile, The	S	F	Tapp, Kathy Kennedy	Scholastic
Gift of the Pirate Queen, The	S	RF	Giff, Patricia Reilly	Yearling
Gift-Giver, The	S	RF	Hansen, Joyce	Houghton Mifflin
Glory Girl, The	S	RF	Byars, Betsy	The Penguin Group
Gold Cadillac, The	S	HF	Taylor, Mildred D.	Puffin Books
Gold Dust Letters, The	S	RF	Lisle, Janet Taylor	Avon Camelot
Good Master, The	S	RF	Seredy, Kate	Scholastic
Good-Bye My Wishing Star	S	RF	Grove, Vicki	Scholastic
Grand Escape, The	S	F	Naylor, Phyllis Reynolds	Bantam Doubleday Dell
Great Apes, The	S	I	A First Book	Franklin Watts
Great Dimpole Oak, The	S	RF	Lisle, Janet Taylor	Puffin Books
Great Expectations	S	HF	Bullseye Step Into Classics	Random House
Great Gilly Hopkins, The	S	RF	Paterson, Katherine	Hearst
Guinea Pigs	S	I	Hansen, Elvig	Carolrhoda Books
Harry and Chicken	S	F	Sheldon, Dyan	Candlewick Press
Harry On Vacation	S	SF	Sheldon, Dyan	Candlewick Press
Harry the Explorer	S	F	Sheldon, Dyan	Candlewick Press
Head Full of Notions, A: A Story about Robert Fulton	S	B	Russell Bowen, Andy	Carolrhoda Books
Helping the Hoiho	S	I	Literacy 2000	Rigby
Hey World, Here I Am!	S	RF	Little, Jean	HarperTrophy
Hillary Rodham Clinton: A New Kind of First Lady	S	B	Guernsey, JoAnn Bren	Lerner Publications
Hiroshima	S	HF	Yep, Laurence	Scholastic
Home for the Howl-idays	S	F	Regan, Dian Curtis	Scholastic
House in the Snow, The	S	RF	Engh, M.J.	Scholastic
House with a Clock in its Walls, The	S	F	Bellairs, John	The Penguin Group

Title	Level	Genre	Author/Series	Publisher/Distributor
How I Met Einstein, a Character Comes to Life	S	I	Trussell-Cullen, Alan	Pacific Learning
Howard Carter: Searching for King Tut	S	B	Ford, Barbara	W. H. Freeman & Co.
Humpback Whale, The	S	I	Frahm, Randy	Capstone Press
I Am the Ice Worm	S	F	Easley, Mary Ann	Yearling
I Was a Sixth Grade Alien	S	F	Coville, Bruce	Pocket Books
In Search of the Great Bears	S	I	Literacy 2000	Rigby
In the Year of the Boar and Jackie Robinson	S	HF	Lord, Bette Bao	HarperTrophy
It's Not Easy Being George	S	RF	Smith, Janice Lee	HarperTrophy
It's the Fashion	S	I	Literacy 2000	Rigby
Jackie Robinson and the Breaking of the Color Barrier	S	B	Shorto, Russell	Millbrook Press
Jamestown Colony, The	S	I	We The People	Compass Point Books
Jean Craighead George	S	B	Cary, Alice	Learning Works, The
Journey	S	RF	MacLachlan, Patricia	Yearling
Journey Home, The	S	RF	Holland, Isabelle	Scholastic
Journey to Jo'burg	S	HF	Naidoo, Beverly	HarperTrophy
Journey to the New World	S	HF	Brocker, Susan	Rigby
Katherine Paterson	S	B	Cary, Alice	Learning Works, The
Killer Bees	S	I	Blau, Melinda	Steck-Vaughn
Klondike Gold Rush, The	S	I	A First Book	Franklin Watts
Knee Knock Rise	S	F	Babbitt, Natalie	Farrar, Straus and Giroux
Lamp from the Warlock's Tomb, The	S	F	Bellairs, John	Puffin Books
Legends	S	TL	Goodman, R., R. Pierce, Betty Jane Wagner	Houghton Mifflin
Letter, the Witch, and the Ring, The	S	F	Bellairs, John	The Penguin Group
Letters from Rifka	S	HF	Hesse, Karen	Puffin Books
Letters from the Sea	S	I	Voyages in Time	Wright Group/McGraw Hill
Lewis and Clark Expedition, The	S	I	We The People	Compass Point Books
Lewis & Clark: Explorers of the American West	S	I	Kroll, Steven	Holiday House
Lily's Crossing	S	HF	Giff, Patricia Reilly	Delacourte Press
Living Rain Forest, The	S	I	Bishop, Nic	Pacific Learning
Lon Po Po: A Red-Riding Hood Story from China	S	TL	Young, Ed	Scholastic
Look at Minerals, A: From Galena to Gold	S	I	A First Book	Franklin Watts
Look at Rocks, A: From Coal to Kimerlite	S	I	A First Book	Franklin Watts
Love Me, Love My Broccoli	S	RF	Peters, Julie Anne	Avon Camelot
Luis Rodriguez	S	B	Schwartz, Michael	Steck-Vaughn
Man From The Sky	S	RF	Avi	BeechTree
Man Who Kept His Heart in a Bucket, The	S	TL	Levitin, Sonia	The Penguin Group
Mansion in the Mist, The	S	F	Bellairs, John	Puffin Books
Mary McLeod Bethune-Voice of Black Hope	S	B	Meltzer. Milton	Puffin Books
Matchbox, The	S	HF	Literacy 2000	Rigby
Matilda	S	F	Dahl, Roald	The Penguin Group
Maya, The	S	I	Journey Into Civilization	Chelsea House
Me, Mop, and the Moondance Kid	S	RF	Myers, Walter Dean	Bantam Doubleday Dell
Mississippi Bridge	S	HF	Taylor, Mildred	Bantam Doubleday Dell
Mongols, The	S	I	Journey Into Civilization	Chelsea House
Monster of the Year	S	F	Coville, Bruce	Pocket Books
More Perfect Union: The Story of Our Constitution	S	I	Maestro, Betsy & Giulio	William Morrow
Morning Girl	S	HF	Dorris, Michael	Hyperion
Mountains	S	I	Weitzman, David	Steck-Vaughn
Mr. President: A Book of U.S. Presidents	S	B	Sullivan, George	Scholastic
My Life in Dog Years	S	B	Paulsen, Gary	Bantam Doubleday Dell
My Sister Annie	S	RF	Dodds, Bill	Boyds Mills Press
My Teacher Flunked the Planet	S	F	Coville, Bruce	Pocket Books
My Teacher Fried My Brains	S	F	Coville, Bruce	Pocket Books
My Teacher Glows in the Dark	S	F	Coville, Bruce	Pocket Books
My Teacher Is an Alien	S	F	Coville, Bruce	Pocket Books
Myths	S	TL	Goodman, Ronald, Robert Pierce, Betty Jane Wagner	Houghton Mifflin
Never Turn Back: Father Serra's Mission	S	B	Rawls, Jim	Steck-Vaughn
New Mexico	S	I	Thompson, Kathleen	Steck-Vaughn

Title	Level	Genre	Author/Series	Publisher/Distributor
New York	S	I	Thompson, Kathleen	Steck-Vaughn
Night Swimmers, The	S	RF	Byars, Betsy	Dell
Night Without Stars, A	S	RF	Howe, James	Aladdin
North Carolina	S	I	Portrait of America	Steck-Vaughn
Off and Running	S	RF	Soto, Gary	Dell
Ohio	S	I	Thompson, Kathleen	Steck-Vaughn
Old Meadow, The	S	F	Selden, George	Farrar, Straus and Giroux
On My Honor	S	RF	Bauer, Marion Dane	Bantam Doubleday Dell
On Site	S	I	Pollock, John	Mondo
On the Way Home	S	HF	Wilder, Laura Ingalls	Harper Collins
Once on this Island	S	HF	Whelan, Gloria	HarperTrophy
One Giant Leap	S	I	Fraser, Mary Ann	Henry Holt & Co.
One-Eyed Cat	S	RF	Fox, Paula	Bantam Doubleday Dell
Orphan of Ellis Island, The	S	HF	Woodruff, Elvira	Scholastic
Out of Darkness: The Story of Louis Braille	S	B	Freedman, Russell	Houghton Mifflin
Pinballs, The	S	RF	Byars, Betsy	HarperTrophy
Plant That Ate Dirty Socks Goes Up in Space	S	F	McArthur, Nancy	Avon Camelot
Plymouth Colony, The	S	I	We The People	Compass Point Books
Polar Bear, The	S	I	Hemstock, Annie	Capstone Press
Poppy	S	F	Avi	Avon
Poppy and Rye	S	F	Avi	Avon
Powwow Summer: A Family Celebrates the Circle of Life	S	I	Rendon, Marcie R.	Carolrhoda Books
Puppies, Dogs, and Blue Northers	S	I	Paulsen, Gary	Delacorte Press
Rairarubia	S	F	Adams, W. Royce	Lost Coast Press
Red Means Good Fortune: A Story of San Francisco's Chinatown	S	I	Goldin, Barbara Diamond	The Penguin Group
Rescuers, The	S	F	Sharp, Margery	Dell Publishing
Riddles of the Universe	S	I	Bonallack, John	Pacific Learning
Rough-Faced Girl, The	S	TL	Martin, R. & Shannon, D.	Scholastic
Samuel's Choice	S	HF	Berleth, Richard	Scholastic
Santa Fe Trail, The	S	I	We The People	Compass Point Books
Seabirds	S	I	A First Book	Franklin Watts
Secret of Kiribu Tapu Lagoon, The	S	I	Literacy 2000	Rigby
Seventh Grade Weirdo	S	RF	Wardlaw, Lee	Scholastic
Sideways Arithmetic from Wayside School	S	I	Sachar, Louis	Scholastic
Sister Sister Homegirl on the Range	S	RF	Quin-Harkin, Janet	Pocket Books
Sixth Grade Can Really Kill You	S	RF	DeClements, Barthe	Scholastic
Sixth Grade Secrets	S	RF	Sachar, Louis	Scholastic
Smartest Man in Ireland, The	S	F	Hunter, Mollie	Harcourt Brace
Smoky the Cow Horse	S	RF	James, Will	Scholastic
Song of the Mantis, The	S	I	Literacy 2000	Rigby
Song of the Trees	S	HF	Taylor, Mildred	Bantam Doubleday Dell
Spirit Quest	S	RF	Sharpe, Susan	Scholastic
Standing Tall: The Stories of Ten Hispanic Americans	S	B	Palacios, Argentina	Scholastic
Star Fisher, The	S	RF	Yep, Lawrence	Scholastic
Story of Harriet Tubman, The: Conductor of the Underground Railroad	S	B	McMullan, Kate	Scholastic
Story of Muhammad Ali: Heavyweight Champion of the World, The	S	B	Denenberg, Barry	Dell Publishing
Story of the White House, The	S	I	Waters, Kate	Scholastic
Sugaring Season (Making Maple Syrup)	S	I	Burns, Diane	Carolrhoda Books
Sugaring Time	S	I	Lasky, Kathryn	Macmillan
Sweet Clara and the Freedom Quilt	S	HF	Hopkinson, Deborah	Scholastic
Taking Care of Terrific	S	RF	Lowry, Lois	Dell
Taking Sides	S	RF	Soto, Gary	Harcourt Brace
Tales from the Homeplace: Adventures of a Texas Farm Girl	S	RF	Burandt, H. and Dale, S.	Bantam Doubleday Dell
Tales from the Underground Railroad	S	HF	Connell, Kate	Steck-Vaughn

Title	Level	Genre	Author/Series	Publisher/Distributor
Talking to Faith Ringgold	S	B	Ringgold, F., Freeman, L.& Roucher, N.	Crown Publishers, Inc.
This Can't Be Happening at Macdonald Hall	S	RF	Korman, Gordon	Scholastic
Thunder At Gettysburg	S	I	Gauch, Patricia Lee	Bantam Doubleday Dell
Time for Andrew	S	F	Hahn, Mary	Avon Camelot
Timothy Whuffenpuffen-Whippersnapper	S	F	Literacy 2000	Rigby
To Fly with the Swallows: A Story of Old California	S	I	deRuiz, Dana Catharine	Steck-Vaughn
To the Moon and Beyond	S	I	Lott, Linda	Wright Group/McGraw Hill
Too Soon to Say Goodbye	S	RF	Kent, Deborah	Scholastic
Transforming Trash	S	I	Quinn, Pat	Pacific Learning
Travels with Rainie Marie	S	B	Martin, Patricia	Hyperion
Treasure of Alpheus Winterborn, The	S	F	Bellairs, John	The Penguin Group
Treasury of Pirate Stories, A	S	F	Bradman, Tony	Kingfisher
Trees and Leaves	S	I	Nature Club	Troll
Trouble River	S	HF	Byars, Betsy	Scholastic
True Confessions	S	RF	Tashjian, Janet	Scholastic
Turtles	S	I	A First Book	Franklin Watts
Twinkie Squad, The	S	RF	Korman, Gordon	Scholastic
Two Tickets to Freedom: The True Story of Ellen and William Craft	S	HF	Freedman, Florence	Scholastic
Ultimate Field Trip 1: Adventures in the Amazon Rain Forest	S	I	Goodman, Susan E.	Simon & Schuster
US and Uncle Fraud	S	RF	Lowry, Lois	Houghton Mifflin
Van Gogh Cafe, The	S	RF	Rylant, Cynthia	Harcourt Brace
Vikings, The	S	I	Journey Into Civilization	Chelsea House
Voyage of the Frog, The	S	RF	Paulsen, Gary	Bantam Doubleday Dell
War Dog Heroes: True Stories of Dog Courage in Wartime	S	I	Sanderson, Jeannette	Scholastic
War of 1812, The	S	I	A First Book	Franklin Watts
War With Grandpa, The	S	RF	Kimmel Smith, Robert	Bantam Doubleday Dell
What Hearts	S	RF	Brooks, Bruce	Language for Learning Assoc.
What in the World is the World Wide Web?	S	I	Quinn, Pat	Pacific Learning
Where Do You Think You're Going, Christopher Columbus?	S	B	Fritz, Jean	Putnam & Grosset
Which Witch?	S	F	Ibbotson, Eva	Puffin Books
William Problem, The	S	RF	Baker, Barbara	Puffin Books
Witch of Fourth Street, The	S	HF	Levoy, Myron	Language for Learning Assoc.
Wolf, The	S	I	Dahl, Michael	Capstone Press
Wreck Trek	S	I	Belcher, Angie	Pacific Learning
Zeros and Ones	S	I	Wildcats	Wright Group/McGraw Hill
52 Days by Camel: My Sahara Adventure	T	I	Raskin, Lawrie	Annick Press
Abel's Island	T	F	Steig, William	Farrar Straus and Giroux
About The B'nai Bagels	T	RF	Konigsburg, E. L.	Dell
Abraham's Battle: A Novel of Gettysburg	T	HF	Banks, Sara Harrell	Atheneum Books
Addie's Dakota Winter	T	RF	Lawlor, Laurie	Pocket Books
Amaze Us!	T	I	Wildcats	Wright Group/McGraw Hill
American Revolution, The	T	I	Bliven, Bruce Jr.	Random House
An Early Winter	T	RF	Bauer, Marion Dane	Houghton Mifflin
Angels and Other Strangers	T	RF	Paterson, Katherine	HarperTrophy
Animal Dazzlers: The Role of Brilliant Colors in Nature	T	I	Collard, Susan B. III	Franklin Watts
Arctic Investigations: Exploring the Frozen Ocean	T	I	Young, Karen Romano	Steck Vaughn
Are You There God? It's Me, Margaret.	T	RF	Blume, Judy	Bantam Doubleday Dell
Avi	T	B	Markham, Lois	Learning Works, The
Baby	T	RF	MacLachlan, Patricia	Language for Learning Assoc.
Ballad of the Civil War, A	T	HF	Stolz, Mary	HarperTrophy
Bear Called Paddington, A	T	F	Bond, Michael	Bantam Doubleday Dell
Bears' House, The	T	RF	Sachs, Marilyn	Puffin Books
Behind Rebel Lines	T	HF	Reit, Seymour	Harcourt Brace
Better Brown Stories, The	T	F	Ahlberg, Allan	The Penguin Group

Title	Level	Genre	Author/Series	Publisher/Distributor
Big Lie, The: A True Story	T	B	Leitner, Isabella	Scholastic
Birchbark House, The	T	HF	Erdrich, Louise	Hyperion
Black Stallion, The	T	RF	Farley, Walter	Language for Learning Assoc.
Blackwater Swamp	T	RF	Wallace, Bill	Language for Learning Assoc.
Blubber	T	RF	Blume, Judy	Bantam Doubleday Dell
Blue Ice	T	RF	Salata, Estelle	Fitzhenry and Whiteside
Bonanza Girl	T	RF	Beatty, Patricia	Scholastic
Book of Monsters: Tales to Give You the Creeps	T	F	Coville, Bruce	Scholastic
Book of Spine Tinglers: Tales To Make You Shiver	T	F	Coville, Bruce	Scholastic
Boston Tea Party: Rebellion in the Colonies	T	I	Adventures in Colonial America	Troll
Boy	T	B	Dahl, Roald	Puffin Books
Bright Shadow	T	F	Avi	Aladdin
Broken Blade, The	T	HF	Durbin, William	Yearling
Buck Stops Here, The	T	I	Provensen, Alice	Harcourt Brace
Bud, Not Buddy	T	RF	Curtis, Christopher Paul	Random House
Burning Questions of Bingo Brown	T	RF	Byars, Betsy	Language for Learning Assoc.
California	T	I	Sea To Shining Sea	Children's Press
California Gold Rush, The	T	I	McNeer, May	Random House
Canada Celebrates Multiculturalism	T	I	Kalman, Bobbie	Crabtree
Canada: The Culture	T	I	Kalman, Bobbie	Crabtree
Canada: The Land	T	I	Kalman, Bobbie	Crabtree
Canada: The People	T	I	Kalman, Bobbie	Crabtree
Carolina Crow Girl	T	F	Hobbs, Valerie	Puffin Books
Cassie Binegar	T	RF	MacLachlan, Patricia	HarperTrophy
Child's Day, A	T	I	Historic Communities	Crabtree
Children of Green Knowe, The	T	F	Boston, L.M.	Harcourt Brace
China: The Culture	T	I	Kalman, Bobbie	Crabtree
China: The Land	T	I	Kalman, Bobbie	Crabtree
China: The People	T	I	Kalman, Bobbie	Crabtree
Cleopatra	T	B	Stanley, Diane & Vennema, Peter	Mulberry Books
Clothes & Crafts in Ancient Egypt	T	I	Balkwill, Richard	Dillon Press
Clothes & Crafts in Ancient Greece	T	I	Steele, Philip	Dillon Press
Clothes & Crafts in Aztec Times	T	I	Dawson, Imogen	Dillon Press
Clothes & Crafts in Roman Times	T	I	Steele, Philip	Dillon Press
Clothes & Crafts in the Middle Ages	T	I	Dawson, Imogen	Dillon Press
Clothes & Crafts in Victorian Times	T	I	Steele, Philip	Dillon Press
Cold As Ice	T	RF	Keene, Carolyn	Pocket Books
Colonial Crafts	T	I	Historic Communities	Crabtree
Colonial Life	T	I	Historic Communities	Crabtree
Colonial Times from A to Z	T	I	Kalman, Bobbie	Crabtree
Colonial Town, A: Williamsburg	T	I	Historic Communities	Crabtree
Colorado	T	I	Sea To Shining Sea	Children's Press
Connecticut	T	I	Sea To Shining Sea	Children's Press
Corvettes	T	I	Gronvall, Kal	Capstone Press
Cousins	T	RF	Hamilton, Virginia	Language for Learning Assoc.
Cowboys	T	I	Sandler, Martin W.	HarperTrophy
Cracker Jackson	T	RF	Byars, Betsy	Puffin Books
Crazy Fish	T	RF	Mazer, Norma Fox	Avon
Cut From the Same Cloth: American Women of Myth Legend, and Tall Tale	T	TL	San Souci, Robert D.	Puffin Books
Daily Life in a Plains Indian Village: 1868	T	I	Terry, Michael Bad Hand	Clarion
Danger on Parade	T	RF	Keene, Carolyn	Pocket Books
Danny, Champion of the World	T	RF	Dahl, Roald	Language for Learning Assoc.
Dear Levi: Letters from the Overland Trail	T	HF	Woodruff, Elvira	Alfred A. Knopf
Defenders, The	T	B	McGovern, Ann	Language for Learning Assoc.
Delaware	T	I	Sea to Shining Sea	Children's Press
Devil's Highway, The	T	HF	Applegate, Stan	Peachtree
Discovering Jupiter: The Amazing Collision in Space	T	I	Berger, Melvin	Scholastic
Double Life of Pocahontas, The	T	B	Fritz, Jean	Language for Learning Assoc.
Dove Is a Beau	T	F	Yolen, Jane	Harcourt Brace

Title	Level	Genre	Author/Series	Publisher/Distributor
Dr. Quinn Medicine Woman	T	B	McKenna, Colleen O'Shaughnessy	Language for Learning Assoc.
Dragon King's Palace, The	T	TL	Literacy 2000	Rigby
Earthquakes	T	I	Simon, Seymour	Mulberry Books
Eclipses: Nature's Blackouts	T	I	Aronson, Billy	Franklin Watts
Everglades	T	I	George, Jean Craighead	HarperTrophy
Explorers: Women in Profile	T	B	Hacker, Carolotta	Crabtree
Fabulous Spotted Egg, The	T	TL	Literacy 2000	Rigby
Ferret In The Bedroom, Lizards In The Fridge	T	RF	Wallace, Bill	Language for learning Assoc.
Flaming Arrows	T	HF	Steele, William O.	Harcourt Brace
Flying Free: America's First Black Aviators	T	B	Hart, Philip S.	Lerner Publications
Follow That Fin!: Studying Dolphin Behavior	T	I	Samuels, Amy	Steck-Vaughn
Food & Feasts Between the Two World Wars	T	I	Steele, Philip	Dillon Press
Food & Feasts In Ancient Egypt	T	I	Balkwill, Richard	Dillon Press
Food & Feasts In Ancient Greece	T	I	Steele, Philip	Dillon Press
Food & Feasts In Ancient Rome	T	I	Steele, Philip	Dillon Press
Food & Feasts In the Middle Ages	T	I	Dawson, Imogen	Dillon Press
Food & Feasts In Tudor Times	T	I	Balkwill, Richard	Dillon Press
Food & Feasts With the Aztecs	T	I	Dawson, Imogen	Dillon Press
Food & Feasts With the Vikings	T	I	Martell, Hazel	Dillon Press
Forest's Life, A: From Meadow to Mature Woodland	T	I	A First Book	Franklin Watts
Forgotten Door, The	T	SF	Key, Alexander	Language for Learning Assoc.
Fort Life	T	I	Historic Communities	Crabtree
Freedom Songs	T	HF	Moore, Yvette	Language for Learning Assoc.
Freshwater Pond, A	T	I	Small Worlds	Crabtree
Friends, The	T	RF	Yumoto, Kazumi	Yearling
Frozen Man	T	I	Getz, David	Henry Holt & Co.
Fur, Feathers, and Flippers: How Animals Live Where They Do	T	I	Lauber, Patricia	Scholastic
Galaxies	T	I	Simon, Seymour	Mulberry Books
Games from Long Ago	T	I	Historic Communities	Crabtree
Gentleman Outlaw and Me - Eli, The: A Story of the Old West	T	HF	Hahn, Mary Downing	Avon Camelot
George Washington's Socks	T	B	Woodruff, Elvira	Language for Learning Assoc.
Georgia	T	I	Sea to Shining Sea	Children's Press
Gettysburg Address, The	T	I	Lincoln, Abraham	Houghton Mifflin
Ghost Cadet	T	SF	Alphin, Elaine Marie	Language for Learning Assoc.
Girl Who Chased Away Sorrow, The: The Diary of Sarah Nita, a Navajo Girl	T	HF	Turner, Ann	Scholastic
Glaciers	T	I	Gallant, Roy A.	Franklin Watts
Going Home	T	RF	Mohr, Nicholasa	The Penguin Group
Going Solo	T	B	Dahl, Roald	Puffin Books
Good-Bye Marianne	T	B	Watts, Irene N.	Tundra Books
Goosebumps: It Came From Beneath the Sink	T	F	Stine, R. L.	Language for Learning Assoc.
Gorillas	T	I	Burgel, Paul H. & Hartwig, M.	Carolrhoda Books
Grand Trees of America: Our State and Champion Trees	T	I	Jorgenson, Lisa	Roberts Rinehart
Grandma Moses: Painter of Rural America	T	B	O'Neal, Zibby	The Penguin Group
Grandpa's Mountain	T	RF	Reeder, Carolyn	Avon Camelot
Gratefully Yours	T	HF	Buchanan, Jane	Puffin Books
Gravity: Simple Experiments for Young Scientists	T	I	White, Larry	Millbrook Press
Great African Americans in Business	T	B	Rediger, Pat	Crabtree
Great African Americans in Civil Rights	T	B	Rediger, Pat	Crabtree
Great African Americans in Entertainment	T	B	Rediger, Pat	Crabtree
Great African Americans in Film	T	B	Parker, Janice	Crabtree
Great African Americans in Government	T	B	Dudley, Karen	Crabtree
Great African Americans in History	T	B	Hacker, Carlotta	Crabtree
Great African Americans in Jazz	T	B	Hacker, Carlotta	Crabtree
Great African Americans in Literature	T	B	Rediger, Pat	Crabtree
Great African Americans in Music	T	B	Rediger, Pat	Crabtree
Great African Americans in Sports	T	B	Rediger, Pat	Crabtree
Great African Americans in the Arts	T	B	Hacker, Carlotta	Crabtree

Title	Level	Genre	Author/Series	Publisher/Distributor
Great African Americans in the Olympics	T	B	Hunter, Shaun	Crabtree
Great Brain at the Academy, The	T	RF	Fitzgerald, John D.	Yearling
Great Brain Does It Again, The	T	RF	Fitzgerald, John D.	Yearling
Great Brain Reforms, The	T	RF	Fitzgerald, John D.	Yearling
Great Brain, The	T	RF	Fitzgerald, John D.	Language for Learning Assoc.
Gristmill, The	T	I	Historic Communities	Crabtree
Growing Up Stories	T	RF	Byars, Betsy	Kingfisher
Guests	T	HF	Dorris, Michael	Hyperion
Hannibal	T	B	Green, Robert	Franklin Watts
Harriet the Spy	T	RF	Fitzhugh, Louise	Harper Collins
Hawaii	T	I	Sea to Shining Sea	Children's Press
Haymeadow, The	T	RF	Paulsen, Gary	Dell
Henri Rousseau	T	B	Rabott, Ernest	HarperTrophy
Henry	T	RF	Bawden, Nina	Bantam Doubleday Dell
Hercules and Other Greek Legends	T	TL	Wildcats	Wright Group/McGraw Hill
Here's to You, Rachel Robinson	T	RF	Blume, Judy	Bantam Doubleday Dell
Home Crafts	T	I	Historic Communities	Crabtree
Horse and His Boy, The	T	F	Lewis, C. S.	Collier Books
Immigrants	T	I	Sandler, Martin W.	HarperTrophy
Inventors	T	I	Sandler, Martin W.	HarperTrophy
Iowa	T	I	Sea to Shining Sea	Children's Press
Island Keeper	T	RF	Mazer, Harry	Language for Learning Assoc.
Islander, The	T	F	Rylant, Cynthia	Random House
It's Not the End of the World	T	RF	Blume, Judy	Dell
Jamestown: New World Adventure	T	I	Adventures in Colonial America	Troll
Jason's Gold	T	HF	Hobbs, Will	William Morrow
Jericho	T	RF	Hickman, Janet	Hearst
Joey Pigza Swallowed the Key	T	RF	Gantos, Jack	HarperTrophy
Journey to Nowhere	T	HF	Auch, Mary Jane	Bantam Doubleday Dell
Jump!: The Adventures of Brer Rabbit	T	TL	Harris, Joel Chandler	Harcourt Brace
Just As Long As We're Together	T	RF	Blume, Judy	Bantam Doubleday Dell
Ken Griffey Jr. & Ken Griffey Sr.	T	B	Star Families	Crestwood House
Kid Who Ran For President, The	T	RF	Gutman, Dan	Language for Learning Assoc.
Kids at Work: Lewis Hine and the Crusade Against Child Labor	T	B	Freedman, Russell	Clarion
Kitchen, The	T	I	Historic Communities	Crabtree
Leon's Story	T	B	Tillage, Leon Walter	Farrar, Straus and Giroux
Life in the Oceans: Animals, People, Plants	T	I	Baker, Lucy	Scholastic
Life in the Rainforests: Animals, People, Plants	T	I	Baker, Lucy	Scholastic
Life of a Miner	T	I	Life in the Old West	Crabtree
Life on a Plantation	T	I	Historic Communities	Crabtree
Light in the Storm, A	T	HF	Hesse, Karen	Scholastic
Lightning	T	I	Kramer, Stephen	Carolrhoda Books
Lion, the Witch and the Wardrobe, The	T	F	Lewis, C. S.	HarperTrophy
Lizard Music	T	F	Pinkwater, D. Manus	Bantam Doubleday Dell
Lois Lowry	T	B	Markham, Lois	Learning Works, Inc.
Long Ago and Far Away	T	I	Wildcats	Wright Group/McGraw Hill
Lost Star: The Story of Amelia Earhart	T	B	Lauber, Patricia	Language for Learning Assoc.
Magician's Nephew, The	T	F	Lewis, C. S.	HarperTrophy
Magnet Book, The	T	I	Levine, Shar & Johnstone, Leslie	Sterling
Man Who Was Poe, The	T	B	Avi	Avon
Marrying Malcolm Murgatroyd	T	RF	Farrell, Mame	Sunburst
Martin Luther King	T	B	Bray, Rosemary L.	William Morrow
Mathew Brady: Civil War Photographer	T	B	A First Book	Franklin Watts
Max and Me and the Time Machine	T	SF	Greer, Gery and Ruddick, Bob	Harper Trophy
Me and My Little Brain	T	RF	Fitzgerald, John D.	Dell
Meteors: The Truth Behind Shooting Stars	T	I	Aronson, Billy	Franklin Watts
Middle Moffat, The	T	RF	Estes, Eleanor	Language for Learning Assoc.
More Adventures of the Great Brain	T	RF	Fitzgerald, John D.	Yearling
Mummies and Their Mysteries	T	I	Wilcox, Charlotte	Carolrhoda Books

Title	Level	Genre	Author/Series	Publisher/Distributor
Muscles: Our Muscular System	T	I	Simon, Seymour	HarperTrophy
My Brother Louis Measures Worms and Other Louis Stories	T	RF	Robinson, Barbara	HarperTrophy
My Daniel	T	HF	Conrad, Pam	Harper Trophy
My Hiroshima	T	HF	Morimoto, Junko	The Penguin Group
My Life as a Fifth-Grade Comedian	T	RF	Levy, Elizabeth	Harper Trophy
Mysterious Ocean Highway: Benjamin Franklin and the Gulf Stream	T	B.	Heiligman, Deborah	Steck-Vaughn
Mythical Beasts	T	F	Wildcats	Wright Group/McGraw Hill
Mythmakers	T	I	Wildcats	Wright Group/McGraw Hill
Natchez Under the Hill	T	HF	Applegate, Stan	Peachtree
Never Say Quit	T	RF	Wallace, Bill	Pocket Books
New York City	T	I	Kent, Deborah	Childrens Press
Night Journey, The	T	HF	Lasky, Kathryn	Puffin Books
Nobel Prize Winners	T	B	Hacker, Carlotta	Crabtree
Norman Rockwell	T	B	Cohen, Joel H.	Grolier Publishing
North Carolina	T	I	Fradin, Dennis Brindell	Childrens Press
Obee & Mungedeech	T	RF	Martin, Trude	Aladdin
Off To Sea: An Inside Look at a Research Cruise	T	I	Kovacs, Deborah	Steck-Vaughn
Ola Shakes It Up	T	RF	Hyppolite, Joanne	Random House
Old Key, The	T	TL	Literacy 2000	Rigby
On Board The Titanic	T	I	Tanaka, Shelley	Hyperion/Madison Press
One Potato, Tu	T	RF	Pearson, Gayle	Scholastic
Osceola: Patriot and Warrior	T	B	Jumper, Moses & Sonder, Ben	Steck-Vaughn
Picture of Freedom, A	T	HF	McKissack, Patricia C.	Scholastic
Pilgrims of Plimouth, The	T	I	Sewall, Marcia	Simon & Schuster
Pioneers	T	I	Sandler, Martin W.	HarperTrophy
Poor Girl, Rich Girl	T	RF	Wilson, Johnniece Marshall	Language for Learning Assoc.
Preacher's Boy	T	RF	Paterson, Katherine	Houghton Mifflin
Quake!	T	RF	Cottonwood, Joe	Language for Learning Assoc.
Rabble Starkey	T	RF	Lowry, Lois	Bantam Doubleday Dell
Rat's Tale, A	T	F	Seidler, Tor	HarperTrophy
Return of the Great Brain, The	T	RF	Fitzgerald, John D.	Dell
Rifle, The	T	HF	Paulsen, Gary	Dell
Runaway to Freedom: A Story of the Underground Railway	T	I	Smucker, Barbara	Harper Trophy
Salem Days: Life in a Colonial Seaport	T	I	Adventures in Colonial America	Troll
Schernoff Discoveries, The	T	RF	Paulsen, Gary	Dell
Second Mrs. Giaconda, The	T	HF	Konigsburg, E. L.	Language for Learning Assoc.
Sees Behind Trees	T	HF	Dorris, Michael	Language for Learning Assoc.
Sharks	T	I	Simon, Seymour	Harper Trophy
Shh! We're Writing the Constitution	T	I	Fritz, Jean	G.P. Putnam's Sons
Sign of the Beaver	T	HF	Speare, Elizabeth George	Bantam Doubleday Dell
Sing Down the Moon	T	HF	O'Dell, Scott	Language for Learning Assoc.
Singing Drum, The	T	TL	Literacy 2000	Rigby
Sleepers, Wake	T	SF	Jacobs, Paul Samuel	Language for Learning Assoc.
Soldier Boy	T	HF	Burks, Brian	Harcourt Brace
Someone to Count On	T	RF	Hermes, Patricia	Language for Learning Assoc.
Something Upstairs	T	RF	Avi	Language for Learning Assoc.
Sounder	T	RF	Armstrong, William	Scholastic
Spring Fever!	T	F	Lerangis, Peter	Language for Learning Assoc.
Standing in the Light	T	RF	Osborne, Mary Pope	Scholastic
Story of Geronimo, The	T	B	Cornerstones of Freedom	Children's Press
Story of the Mayflower Compact, The	T	I	Cornerstones of Freedom	Children's Press
Summer to Die, A	T	RF	Lowry, Lois	Dell
Susanna of the Alamo	T	B	Jakes, John	Language for Learning Assoc.
Tenement Writer, The: An Immigrant's Story	T	I	Sonder, Ben	Steck-Vaughn
Then Again, Maybe I Won't	T	RF	Blume, Judy	Language for Learning Assoc.
These Lands Are Ours: Tecumseh's Fight For the Old Northwest	T	B	Connell, Kate	Steck-Vaughn

Title	Level	Genre	Author/Series	Publisher/Distributor
They Shall Be Heard: Susan B. Anthony Elizabeth Cady Stanton	T	B	Connell, Kate	Steck-Vaughn
Throwing Shadows	T	RF	Konigsburg, E. L.	Language for Learning Assoc.
Thunder Valley	T	RF	Paulsen, Gary	Bantam Doubleday Dell
Time Apart, A	T	RF	Stanley, Diane	William Morrow
Time Benders	T	SF	Paulsen, Gary	Bantam Doubleday Dell
Titanic Sinks!, The	T	I	Conklin, Thomas	Random House
Toliver's Secret	T	HF	Brady, Esther Wood	Alfred A. Knopf
Tom, Babette, & Simon	T	F	Avi	Avon
Tools and Gadgets	T	I	Historic Communities	Crabtree
Toothpaste Millionaire, The	T	RF	Merrill, Jean	Houghton Mifflin
Tracker	T	RF	Paulsen, Gary	Scholastic
Treasure of El Patrón, The	T	RF	Paulsen, Gary	Bantam Doubleday Dell
Trout Summer	T	RF	Conly, Jane Leslie	Scholastic
Turn Homeward, Hannalee	T	HF	Beatty, Patricia	William Morrow
Ups and Downs of Carl Davis III, The	T	RF	Guy, Rosa	Language for Learning Assoc.
Volcanoes and Earthquakes	T	I	Lauber, Patricia	Language for Learning Assoc.
Vulpes The Red Fox	T	F	George, Jean Craighead	Puffin Books
Wainscott Weasel, The	T	F	Seidler, Tor	Harper Collins
Watsons Go to Birmingham-1963, The	T	HF	Curtis, Christopher Paul	Bantam Doubleday Dell
Well, The	T	HF	Taylor, Mildred D.	Puffin Books
Werewolf Chronicles, The	T	F	Philbrick, R. & Harnett, L.	Scholastic
What Jamie Saw	T	RF	Coman, Carolyn	The Penguin Group
Wish Giver, The	T	F	Brittain, Bill	HarperTrophy
Wish on a Unicorn	T	RF	Hesse, Karen	The Penguin Group
Woodsong	T	B	Paulsen, Gary	Dell
You Shouldn't Have to Say Good-bye	T	RF	Hermes, Patricia	Scholastic
13th Floor, The: A Ghost Story	U	F	Fleischman, Sid	Bantam Doubleday Dell
Alexander Graham Bell: An Inventive Life	U	B	MacLeod, Elizabeth	Kids Can Press Ltd.
Alice in Rapture: Sort of	U	RF	Naylor, Phyllis Reynolds	Aladdin
Alice the Brave	U	RF	Naylor, Phyllis Reynolds	Aladdin
All But Alice	U	RF	Naylor, Phyllis Reynolds	Dell
Alligators & Crocodiles	U	I	The Untamed World	Steck-Vaughn
An Indian Winter	U	I	Freedman, Russell	Scholastic
Apprenticeship of Lucas Whitaker, The	U	HF	DeFelice, Cynthia	Avon
Ariel of the Sea	U	F	Calhoun, Dia	Winslow Press
Bad, Badder, Baddest	U	RF	Voigt, Cynthia	Scholastic
Bad Girls	U	RF	Voigt, Cynthia	Scholastic
Baseball in April and Other Stories	U	RF	Soto, Gary	Harcourt Brace
Being Danny's Dog	U	RF	Naylor, Phyllis Reynolds	Aladdin
Ben Franklin of Old Philadelphia	U	B	Cousins, Margaret	Random House
Benjamin Franklin	U	B	Kent, Deborah	Scholastic
Beowulf	U	TL	Literacy 2000	Rigby
Best Bad Thing, The	U	RF	Uchida, Yoshiko	Aladdin
Beyond the Burning Lands	U	F	Christopher, John	Aladdin
BFG, The	U	F	Dahl, Roald	The Penguin Group
Birds of Prey: A Look at Daytime Raptors	U	I	Collard, Sneed B. III	Franklin Watts
Blue Whales	U	I	The Untamed World	Steck-Vaughn
Boggart and the Monster, The	U	F	Cooper, Susan	Aladdin
Boggart, The	U	F	Cooper, Susan	Simon & Schuster
Book of Three, The	U	F	Alexander, Lloyd	Bantam Doubleday Dell
Boy Who Owned the School, The	U	RF	Paulsen, Gary	Bantam Doubleday Dell
Bronze Bow, The	U	HF	Speare, Elizabeth George	Houghton Mifflin
Buffalo Gal	U	RF	Wallace, Bill	Simon & Schuster
Bye, Bye, Bali Kai	U	RF	Luger, Harriett	Harcourt Brace
Captain Grey	U	HF	Avi	HarperTrophy
Case of the Lion Dance	U	RF	Yep, Laurence	HarperTrophy
Cat Ate My Gymsuit, The	U	RF	Danziger, Paula	Putnam & Grosset
Cat Running	U	RF	Snyder, Zilpha Keatley	Bantam Doubleday Dell
Catherine, Called Birdy	U	HF	Cushman, Karen	Clarion

Title	Level	Genre	Author/Series	Publisher/Distributor
Ceiling of Stars, A	U	RF	Creel, Ann Howard	Pleasant Company
Charley Skedaddle	U	HF	Beatty, Patricia	Troll
Child of the Wolves	U	RF	Hall, Elizabeth	Bantam Doubleday Dell
City Through the Ages	U	I	Steele, Philip	Troll Associates
Comets	U	I	A First Book	Franklin Watts
Cousins in the Castle	U	F	Wallace, Barbara Brooks	Aladdin
Crash	U	RF	Spinelli, Jerry	Alfred A. Knopf
Crocodilians	U	I	Short, Joan & Bird, Bettina	Mondo
Crowfoot	U	B	Hacker, Carlotta	Fitzhenry & Whiteside
Dancing Carl	U	RF	Paulsen, Gary	Aladdin
Dangerous Wishes	U	F	Sleator, William	The Penguin Group
Different Beat, A	U	RF	Boyd, Candy Dawson	The Penguin Group
Do The Funky Pickle	U	RF	Spinelli, Jerry	Scholastic
Door in the Wall, The	U	HF	De Angeli, Marguerite	Bantam Doubleday Dell
Dreadful Future of Blossom Culp, The	U	SF	Peck, Richard	Bantam Doubleday Dell
Drew and the Homeboy Question	U	RF	Armstrong, Robb	HarperTrophy
Earth to Matthew	U	RF	Danziger, Paula	PaperStar
Egypt Game, The	U	RF	Snyder, Zilpha Keatley	Bantam Doubleday Dell
Egypt: The Culture	U	I	Kalman, Bobbie	Crabtree
Egypt: The Land	U	I	Kalman, Bobbie	Crabtree
Egypt: The People	U	I	Kalman, Bobbie	Crabtree
Egytian Town	U	I	Steedman, Scott	Franklin Watts
Elephants	U	I	The Untamed World	Steck-Vaughn
Ella Enchanted	U	F	Carson Levine, Gail	HarperTrophy
Everyone Else's Parents Said Yes	U	RF	Danziger, Paula	PaperStar
Factory Through the Ages	U	I	Steele, Philip	Troll Associates
Facts and Fictions of Minna Pratt, The	U	RF	MacLachlan, Patricia	HarperTrophy
Farm Through the Ages	U	I	Steele, Philip	Troll
Fire in the Wind	U	RF	Levin, Betty	Beech Tree
Fire-Bird, The	U	TL	Literacy 2000	Rigby
First Ladies	U	B	Cornerstones of Freedom	Children's Press
First Ladies of the White House	U	B	Skarmeas, Nancy	Ideals Publications Inc.
First Ladies: Women Who Called the White House Home	U	B	Gormley, Beatrice	Scholastic
Fledgling, The	U	F	Langton, Jane	Scholastic
Flying With the Eagle, Racing the Great Bear Stories from Native North America	U	TL	Bruchac, Joseph	Troll Medallion
Frances Hodgson Burnett: Beyond the Secret Garden	U	B	Carpenter, A. S. & Shirley, Jean	Lerner Publications
Frightful's Mountain	U	RF	George, Jean	Puffin Books
Gathering of Days, A: A New England Girl's Journal, 1830-32	U	HF	Blos, Joan	Aladdin
George Washington: The Man Who Would Not Be King	U	B	Krensky, Stephen	Scholastic
Georgia	U	I	LaDoux, Rita C.	Lerner Publications
Geysers: When Earth Roars	U	I	A First Book	Franklin Watts
Ghost in the Tokaido Inn, The	U	F	Hoobler, Dorothy & Thomas	The Penguin Group
Giant Pandas	U	I	The Untamed World	Steck-Vaughn
Gift of the Girl Who Couldn't Hear, The	U	RF	Shreve, Susan	Beech Tree Books
Ginger Pye	U	RF	Estes, Eleanor	Scholastic
Girl Called Boy, A	U	F	Hurmence, Belinda	Clarion
Girl In the Window, The	U	RF	Yeo, Wilma	Scholastic
Girl Who Married the Moon, The: Tales from Native North America	U	TL	Bruchac, Joseph & Ross, Gayle	Troll Medallion
Girl With the Silver Eyes, The	U	F	Roberts, Willo Davis	Scholastic
Gorillas	U	I	The Untamed World	Steck-Vaughn
Grace	U	HF	Walsh, Jill Paton	Farrar, Straus and Giroux
Grams, Her Boyfriend, My Family, and Me	U	RF	Derby, Pat	Sunburst
Graven Images: Three Stories by Paul Fleischman	U	F	Fleischman, Paul	HarperTrophy
Great Wheel, The	U	RF	Lawson, Robert	Scholastic
Great White Sharks	U	I	The Untamed World	Steck-Vaughn

Title	Level	Genre	Author/Series	Publisher/Distributor
Greece: The Culture	U	I	Kalman, Bobbie	Crabtree
Greece: The Land	U	I	Kalman, Bobbie	Crabtree
Greece: The People	U	I	Kalman, Bobbie	Crabtree
Gypsy Game, The	U	RF	Snyder, Zilpha Keatly	Yearling
Handful of Time, A	U	F	Pearson, Kit	Puffin Books
Heat Is On, The	U	I	Tanaka, Shelley	Firefly Books
Heroes & Idealists	U	B	Real Lives	Troll
Hitty: Her First Hundred Years	U	F	Field, Rachel	Aladdin
House Through the Ages	U	I	Steele, Philip	Troll Associates
I Am Regina	U	HF	Keehn, Sally	Bantam Doubleday Dell
If You Were There in 1492: Everyday Life in the Time of Columbus	U	I	Brenner, Barbara	Aladdin
Insects	U	I	Bird, Bettina & Short, Joan	Mondo
Insects & Spiders	U	I	World Book Looks at Science	World Book
Jacob Have I Loved	U	RF	Paterson, Katherine	HarperTrophy
Jaguars	U	I	Green, Michael	Capstone Press
Jericho's Journey	U	RF	Wisler, G. Clifton	Penguin Group
Journey Into Terror	U	RF	Wallace, Bill	Simon & Schuster
Journey to America	U	HF	Levitin, Sonia	Simon & Schuster
Journey to Topaz	U	HF	Uchida, Yoshiko	Creative Arts Book Co.
Julie	U	RF	George, Jean Craighead	Harper Trophy
Julie of the Wolves	U	RF	George, Jean Craighead	Harper Collins
Julie's Wolf Pack	U	RF	George, Jean Craighead	HarperTrophy
Jump Ship to Freedom	U	HF	Collier, James and Christopher	Bantam Doubleday Dell
Jungle Book, The	U	F	Kipling, Rudyard	Scholastic
Kind of Thief, A	U	RF	Alcock, Vivien	Bantam Doubleday Dell
Knots in My Yo-yo String: The Autobiography of a Kid	U	B	Spinelli, Jerry	Alfred A. Knopf
La Causa: The Migrant Farmworkers' Story	U	I	deRuiz, Dana Catharine	Steck-Vaughn
Lamborghinis	U	I	Green, Michael	Capstone Press
Lampfish of Twill, The	U	F	Lisle, Janet Taylor	Scholastic
Landslides, Slumps, & Creep	U	I	A First Book	Franklin Watts
Leaders of the People	U	B	Real Lives	Troll
Listen Children: An Anthology of Black Literature	U	RF	Strickland, Dorothy S.	Bantam Doubleday Dell
Lyddie	U	HF	Paterson, Katherine	The Penguin Group
Make Like a Tree and Leave	U	RF	Danziger, Paula	PaperStar
Mary McLeod Bethune	U	B	Cornerstones of Freedom	Children's Press
Matter of Conscience, A: The Trial of Anne Hutchinson	U	I	Nichols, Joan Kane	Steck-Vaughn
May Chinn: The Best Medicine	U	B	Butts, Ellen & Schwartz, Joyce	W. H. Freeman and Co.
Merlin and the Dragons	U	TL	Yolen, Jane	The Penguin Group
Midnight Magic	U	F	Avi	Scholastic
Miranda and the Movies	U	HF	Kendall, Jane	Harcourt Brace
Moon, The	U	I	A First Book	Franklin Watts
Mr. Revere and I	U	F	Lawson, Robert	Little, Brown & Co.
Mr. Tucket	U	HF	Paulsen, Gary	Bantam Doubleday Dell
Mustangs	U	I	Gillespie, Lorrine	Capstone Press
My Side of the Mountain	U	RF	George, Jean Craighead	The Penguin Group
Night Journeys	U	HF	Avi	Avon Books
Night of the Twisters	U	RF	Ruckman, Ivy	HarperTrophy
Nobody's Family Is Going to Change	U	RF	Fitzhugh, Louise	Farrar, Straus and Giroux
North Star To Freedom	U	I	Gorrell, Gena K.	Random House
Nothing But The Truth	U	RF	Avi	Hearst
Number the Stars	U	HF	Lowry, Lois	Bantam Doubleday Dell
Of Nightingales That Weep	U	HF	Paterson, Katherine	Harper Collins
Off the Map, The Journals of Lewis and Clark	U	I	Roop, Peter and Connie	Walker and Company
Once Upon a Time in Junior High	U	RF	Norment, Lisa	Scholastic
Onion John	U	HF	Krumgold, Joseph	Harper & Row
Oprah Winfrey, A Voice for the People	U	B	Brooks, Philip	Grolier Publishing
Ordinary Genius, The Story of Albert Einstein	U	B	McPherson, Stephanie S.	The Lerner Group
Outrageously Alice	U	RF	Naylor, Phyllis Reynolds	Aladdin
P.S. Longer Letter Later	U	RF	Danziger, P. & Martin, A.	Scholastic

Title	Level	Genre	Author/Series	Publisher/Distributor
Park's Quest	U	RF	Paterson, Katherine	Puffin Books
Peril in the Bessledorf Parachute Factory	U	RF	Naylor, Phyllis Reynolds	Atheneum Books
Perilous Road, The	U	HF	Steele, William	Scholastic
Place Called Heartbreak, A: A Story of Vietnam	U	I	Myers, Walter Dean	Steck-Vaughn
Place in the Sun, A	U	HF	Rubalcaba, Jill	Puffin Books
Ragweed	U	F	Avi	Avon
Real Thief, The	U	F	Steig, William	Farrar, Straus and Giroux
Red Dog	U	RF	Wallace, Bill	Simon & Schuster
Remember the Ladies: The First Women's Rights Convention	U	I	Johnston, Norma	Scholastic
Report To the Principal's Office	U	RF	Spinelli, Jerry	Scholastic
Righteous Revenge of Artemis Bonner, The	U	RF	Myers, Walter Dean	HarperTrophy
River Apart, A	U	HF	Sutherland, Robert	Fitzhenry and Whiteside
River Through the Ages	U	I	Steele, Philip	Troll Associates
Road Through the Ages	U	I	Steele, Philip	Troll Associates
Rosa Parks: My Story	U	B	Parks, Rosa	Scholastic
Sand On The Move: The Story of Dunes	U	I	A First Book	Franklin Watts
Search for Delicious, The	U	F	Babbitt, Natalie	Farrar, Straus and Giroux
Secret Garden, The	U	RF	Burnett, Frances H.	Scholastic
Seekers of Truth	U	B	Real Lives	Troll
Shadow of a Bull	U	RF	Wojciechowska, Maia	Simon & Schuster
Sign of the Chrysanthemum, The	U	RF	Paterson, Katherine	HarperTrophy
Silk Route, The	U	HF	Major, John S.	HarperCollins
Silverwing: How One Small Bat Became a Noble Hero	U	F	Oppel, Kenneth	Simon & Schuster
Sky Dogs	U	RF	Yolen, Jane	Harcourt Brace
Some of the Kinder Planets	U	SF	Wynne-Jones, Tim	The Penguin Group
Stay! Keeper's Story	U	F	Lowry, Lois	Random House
Stealing Freedom	U	HF	Carbone, Lisa	Random House
Stories From the Days of Christopher Columbus	U	HF	Young, R.A & J. Dockery	August House
Stories in Stone: The World of Animal Fossils	U	I	A First Book	Franklin Watts
Story of Harriet Tubman: Freedom, The	U	B	Sterling, Dorothy	Bantam Doubleday Dell
Stranger at the Window	U	RF	Alcock, Vivien	Houghton Mifflin
Stranger Came Ashore, A	U	F	Hunter, Mollie	HarperTrophy
Summer of the Swans, The	U	RF	Byars, Betsy	The Penguin Group
Talking Earth, The	U	RF	George, Jean Craighead	HarperTrophy
Tangerine	U	RF	Bloor, Edward	Scholastic
Tarantula in My Purse, The	U	B	George, Jean Craighead	Harper Collins
That Wild Berries Should Grow	U	HF	Whelan, Gloria	William B. Eerdmans
Thomas Jefferson: Man with a Vision	U	B	Crisman, Ruth	Scholastic
Thunder Rolling in the Mountains	U	HF	O'Dell, Scott & Hall, Elizabeth	Bantam Doubleday Dell
Tiltawhirl John	U	RF	Paulsen, Gary	The Penguin Group
Treasures in the Dust	U	HF	Porter, Tracey	HarperTrophy
Tuck Everlasting	U	F	Babbitt, Natalie	Farrar, Straus and Giroux
Tucket's Gold	U	HF	Paulsen, Gary	Bantam
Tucket's Ride	U	HF	Paulsen, Gary	Bantam Doubleday Dell
Undying Glory: The Story of the Massachusetts 54th Regiment	U	HF	Cox, Clinton	Scholastic
View from Saturday, The	U	F	Konigsburg, E. L.	Atheneum Books
Wait Till Helen Comes	U	F	Downing Hahn, Mary	Houghton Mifflin
War Comes to Willy Freeman	U	HF	Collier, J. L., &Collier, C.	Dell Publishing
When Justice Failed: The Fred Korematsu Story	U	B	Chin, Steven A.	Steck-Vaughn
Who Put That Hair in My Toothbrush?	U	RF	Spinelli, Jerry	Little, Brown
Who Really Killed Cock Robin?	U	RF	George, Jean Craighead	HarperTrophy
Winged Cat, The: A Tale of Ancient Egypt	U	TL	Lattimore, Deborah Nourse	HarperCollins
Winter Room, The	U	RF	Paulsen, Gary	Bantam Doubleday Dell
Witchcraft of Salem Village, The	U	I	Jackson, Shirley	Random House
Wizard of Oz, The	U	F	Baum, L. Frank	Scholastic
Women of Valor	U	B	Real Lives	Troll
Words	U	RF	Paulsen, Gary	The Penguin Group
Wright Brothers, The	U	B	Sobol, Donald J.	Scholastic

Title	Level	Genre	Author/Series	Publisher/Distributor
Wringer	U	RF	Spinelli, Jerry	HarperTrophy
5 Novels	V	F	Pinkwater, Daniel	Farrar, Straus and Giroux
Absolutely Normal Chaos	V	RF	Creech, Sharon	HarperTrophy
African-Americans in the Old West	V	I	Cornerstones of Freedom	Children's Press
African-Americans in the Thirteen Colonies	V	I	Cornerstones of Freedom	Children's Press
Alcatraz	V	I	Cornerstones of Freedom	Bantam Doubleday Dell
Alexander Graham Bell	V	B	Petrie, A. Roy	Fitzhenry & Whiteside
Alice in Wonderland	V	F	Carroll, Lewis	Scholastic
American Revolution, The	V	I	Carter, Alden R.	Franklin Watts
Amos Fortune: Free Man	V	HF	Yates, Elizabeth	Puffin Books
And One For All	V	RF	Nelson, Theresa	Dell
Anna Is Still Here	V	HF	Vos, Ida	Puffin Books
Anne of Green Gables	V	RF	Montgomery, L. M.	Scholastic
Are All The Giants Dead?	V	F	Norton, Mary	Harcourt Brace
Arlington National Cemetery	V	I	Cornerstones of Freedom	Bantam Doubleday Dell
Around the World in a Hundred Years: From Henry the Navigator to Magellan	V	I	Fritz, Jean	Putnam & Grosset
Assassination of Abraham Lincoln, The	V	B	Cornerstones of Freedom	Children's Press
Assassination of John F. Kennedy, The	V	B	Cornerstones of Freedom	Children's Press
Assassination of Martin Luther King Jr.	V	B	Cornerstones of Freedom	Children's Press
Autumn Street	V	HF	Lowry, Lois	Bantam Doubleday Dell
Bad Beginning, The	V	F	Snicket, Lemony	HarperTrophy
Bandit Moon	V	HF	Fleischman, Sid	Dell Yearling
Battle of Chancellorsville, The	V	I	Cornerstones of Freedom	Children's Press
Battle of the Alamo, The	V	I	Cornerstones of Freedom	Children's Press
Battle of the Little Bighorn, The	V	I	Cornerstones of Freedom	Children's Press
Bearstone	V	RF	Hobbs, Will	Hearst
Beauty	V	RF	Wallace, Bill	Holiday House
Behind The Bedroom Wall	V	HF	Williams, Laura E.	Milkweed Editions
Belle Prater's Boy	V	RF	White, Ruth	Bantam Doubleday Dell
Beyond the Mango Tree	V	RF	Zemser, Amy Bronwen	HarperTrophy
Beyond the Western Sea, Book II: Lord Kirkle's Money	V	HF	Avi	Avon Camelot
Biggest Klutz in Fifth Grade, The	V	RF	Wallace, Bill	Simon & Schuster
Bill of Rights, The	V	I	Cornerstones of Freedom	Bantam Doubleday Dell
Birthday Room, The	V	RF	Henkes, Kevin	William Morrow
Black Hearts in Battersea	V	HF	Aiken, Joan	Houghton Mifflin
Black Star, Bright Dawn	V	RF	O'Dell, Scott	Ballantine Books
Bloomability	V	RF	Creech, Sharon	Harper Collins
Blue Willow	V·	RF	Gates, Doris	Puffin Books
Boston Tea Party, The	V	I	Cornerstones of Freedom	Children's Press
Brady	V	HF	Fritz, Jean	Puffin Books
Brain	V	I	You And Your Body	Troll
Building the Capital City	V	I	Cornerstones of Freedom	Bantam Doubleday Dell
But I'll Be Back Again	V	B	Rylant, Cynthia	Beech Tree Books
By the Great Horn Spoon!	V	HF	Fleischman, Sid	Little, Brown & Co.
Calico Bush	V	HF	Field, Rachel	Simon & Schuster
California Gold Rush, The	V	I	Cornerstones of Freedom	Children's Press
Call Me Francis Tucket	V	HF	Paulsen, Gary	Yearling
Canyons	V	F	Paulsen, Gary	Laurel-Leaf Books
Capitol, The	V	I	Cornerstones of Freedom	Bantam Doubleday Dell
Cay, The	V	HF	Taylor, Theodore	Avon
CD and the Giant Cat	V	SF	Odgers, Darrel and Sally	Rigby
Chasing Redbird	V	RF	Creech, Sharon	Harper Collins
Chisholm Trail, The	V	I	Cornerstones of Freedom	Bantam Doubleday Dell
Choosing Up Sides	V	RF	Ritter, John H.	Puffin Books
Circle Unbroken, A	V	HF	Hotze, Sollace	Houghton Mifflin
City of Gold & Lead, The	V	F	Christopher, John	Aladdin
Civil Rights Marches	V	I	Cornerstones of Freedom	Children's Press
Clay Marble, The	V	RF	Ho, Minfong	Farrar, Straus and Giroux
Cold Shoulder Road	V	RF	Aiken, Joan	Bantam Doubleday Dell

Title	Level	Genre	Author/Series	Publisher/Distributor
Come Morning	V	HF	Guccione, Leslil Davis	Lerner Publications
Come Sing, Jimmy Jo	V	RF	Patterson, Katherine	The Penguin Group
Constitution, The	V	I	Cornerstones of Freedom	Children's Press
Dark Stairs	V	RF	Byars, Betsy	Puffin Books
Daughter of the Mountains	V	HF	Rankin, Louise	The Penguin Group
Death's Door	V	RF	Byars, Betsy	Puffin Books
Declaration of Independence, The	V	I	Cornerstones of Freedom	Children's Press
Dogsong	V	RF	Paulsen, Gary	Simon & Schuster
Dragon Chronicles, The: Dragon's Milk	V	F	Fletcher, Susan	Aladdin
Dragonsong	V	F	McCaffrey, Anne	Bantam Doubleday Dell
Drylongso	V	RF	Hamilton, Virginia	Harcourt Brace
Dustland	V	F	Hamilton, Virginia	Scholastic
Ellis Island	V	I	Cornerstones of Freedom	Children's Press
Emancipation Proclamation, The	V	I	Cornerstones of Freedom	Children's Press
Extraordinary Life, An: The Story of a Monarch Butterfly	V	I	Pringle, Laurence	Orchard Books
Eyes of the Amaryllis, The	V	RF	Babbitt, Natalie	Farrar, Straus and Giroux
Father Water, Mother Woods	V	RF	Paulsen, Gary	Bantam Doubleday Dell
Father's Arcane Daughter	V	RF	Konigsburg, E. L.	Aladdin
Fighting Ground, The	V	HF	Avi	HarperTrophy
Final Freedom, The	V	RF	Wallace, Bill	Pocket Books
Fort Sumter	V	I	Cornerstones of Freedom	Children's Press
Foster's War	V	HF	Reeder, Carolyn	Scholastic
Franklin Delano Roosevelt	V	B	Freedman, Russell	Clarion
Gathering, The	V	F	Hamilton, Virginia	Harcourt Brace
Get on Board: The Story of the Underground Railroad	V	I	Haskins, Jim	Scholastic
Getting Lincoln's Goat	V	RF	Goldman, E. M.	Bantam Doubleday Dell
Gettysburg Address, The	V	I	Cornerstones of Freedom	Children's Press
Ghost Belonged to Me, The	V	F	Peck, Richard	The Penguin Group
Gib Rides Home	V	RF	Snyder, Zilpha Keatley	Bantam Doubleday Dell
Gone-Away Lake	V	RF	Enright, Elizabeth	Harcourt Inc.
Good-Bye, Billy Radish	V	HF	Skurzynski, Gloria	Aladdin
Goodbye, Vietnam	V	RF	Whelan, Gloria	Alfred A. Knopf
Goody Hall	V	RF	Babbitt, Natalie	Farrar, Straus and Giroux
Grab Hands and Run	V	RF	Temple, Frances	HarperTrophy
Green Book, The	V	F	Walsh, Jill Paton	Farrar, Straus and Giroux
Habibi	V	B	Nye, Naomi Shihab	Simon & Schuster
Harris and Me	V	RF	Paulsen, Gary	Bantam Doubleday Dell
Harry Potter and the Chamber of Secrets	V	F	Rowling, J. K.	Scholastic
Harry Potter and the Goblet of Fire	V	F	Rowling, J. K.	Scholastic
Harry Potter and the Prisoner of Azkaban	V	F	Rowling, J.K.	Scholastic
Harry Potter and the Sorcerer's Stone	V	F	Rowling, J. K.	Scholastic
Hobby: The Young Merlin Trilogy	V	F	Yolen, Jane	Scholastic
Holes	V	RF	Sachar, Louis	Random House
House of Dies Drear	V	HF	Hamilton, Virginia	Aladdin
I Rode a Horse of Milk White Jade	V	HF	Wilson, Diane Lee	HarperTrophy
If I Forget, You Remember	V	RF	Williams, Carol Lynch	Bantam Doubleday Dell
In the Path of Lewis & Clark: Traveling the Missouri	V	I	Lourie, Peter	Silver Burdett Press
Incident at Hawk's Hill	V	F	Eckert, Allen W.	Little, Brown & Co.
Incredible Journey, The	V	F	Burnford, Sheila	Bantam Doubleday Dell
Island of the Blue Dolphins	V	HF	O'Dell, Scott	Bantam Doubleday Dell
Jackie Robinson Breaks the Color Line	V	B	Cornerstones of Freedom	Children's Press
Jamestown Colony, The	V	I	Cornerstones of Freedom	Children's Press
Jingo Django	V	RF	Fleischman, Sid	Bantam Doubleday Dell
Jip His Story	V	HF	Paterson, Katherine	The Penguin Group
John F. Kennedy	V	B	World Leaders: Past and Present	Chelsea House
John James Audubon: Wildlife Artist	V	B	A First Book	Franklin Watts
Joseph: 1861-A Rumble of War	V	HF	Pryor, Bonnie	Avon
Journey Home	V	RF	Uchida, Yoshika	Aladdin
Journey Outside	V	F	Steele, Mary Q.	The Penguin Group

Title	Level	Genre	Author/Series	Publisher/Distributor
Journey to an 800 Number	V	RF	Konigsburg, E. L.	Aladdin
Keep Smiling Through	V	RF	Rinaldi, Ann	Harcourt Brace
Keeping Room, The	V	HF	Myers, Anna	Puffin Books
Letters from Camp A Mystery	V	RF	Klise, Kate	Harper Trophy
Lewis and Clark	V	B	Cornerstones of Freedom	Children's Press
Lexington and Concord	V	I	Cornerstones of Freedom	Children's Press
Liberty Bell, The	V	I	Cornerstones of Freedom	Children's Press
Library of Congress, The	V	I	Cornerstones of Freedom	Children's Press
Lincoln: A Photobiography	V	B	Freedman, Russell	Clarion
Lincoln Memorial, The	V	I	Cornerstones of Freedom	Children's Press
Long Way from Chicago, A	V	HF	Peck, Richard	Puffin Books
Louisiana Purchase, The	V	I	Cornerstones of Freedom	Children's Press
Manatee, The	V	I	Silverstein, A. and Nunn, L.	The Millbrook Press
Maniac Magee	V	RF	Spinelli, Jerry	Scholastic
Many Waters	V	F	L'Engle, Madeleine	Bantam Doubleday Dell
Marian Anderson: Singer	V	B	American Women of Achievement	Chelsea House
Maze, The	V	RF	Hobbs, Will	Morrow Junior Books
Merlin: The Young Merlin Trilogy	V	F	Yolen, Jane	Scholastic
Midnight Horse, The	V	F	Fleischman, Sid	Bantam Doubleday Dell
Mighty, The	V	RF	Philbrick, Rodman	Scholastic
Monkey Island	V	RF	Fox, Paula	Orchard Books
Monticello	V	I	Cornerstones of Freedom	Children's Press
Mount Vernon	V	I	Cornerstones of Freedom	Children's Press
Mrs. Frisby and the Rats of NIMH	V	F	O'Brien, Robert C.	Aladdin
Music of Dolphins, The	V	RF	Hesse, Karen	Scholastic
My Brother, My Sister, and I	V	HF	Watkins, Yoko Kawashima	Aladdin
My Name is Not Angelica	V	HF	O'Dell, Scott	Bantam Doubleday Dell
My Wartime Summers	V	HF	Cutler, Jane	Harper Collins
Night Birds on Nantucket	V	HF	Aiken, Joan	Houghton Mifflin
Not That I Care	V	RF	Vail, Rachel	Scholastic
Old Yeller	V	RF	Gipson, Fred	Scholastic
On The Far Side Of The Mountain	V	RF	George, Jean Craighead	Puffin Books
One More River	V	HF	Banks, Lynne Reid	Avon Camelot
Oregon Trail, The	V	I	Cornerstones of Freedom	Children's Press
Passager: The Young Merlin Trilogy	V	F	Yolen, Jane	Scholastic
Paul Revere	V	B	Cornerstones of Freedom	Childrens Press
Pilgrims, The	V	I	Cornerstones of Freedom	Children's Press
Pleasing the Ghost	V	F	Creech, Sharon	Harper Collins
Pocket Full of Seeds, A	V	HF	Sachs, Marilyn	Scholastic
Pony Express, The	V	I	Cornerstones of Freedom	Children's Press
Pool of Fire, The	V	F	Christopher, John	Aladdin
Promise Me the Moon	V	RF	Barnes, Joyce Annette Barnes	The Penguin Group
Rainbow People, The	V	F	Yep, Lawrence	HarperTrophy
Rascal	V	HF	North, Sterling	Scholastic
Remarkable Journey of Prince Jen, The	V	F	Alexander, Lloyd	Bantam Doubleday Dell
Remember Not To Forget: A Memory of the Holocaust	V	I	Finkelstein, Norman H.	William & Morrow
Riddle of the Rosetta Stone, The	V	I	Giblin, James Cross	HarperTrophy
Root Cellar, The	V	HF	Lunn, Janet	The Penguin Group
Santa Fe Trail, The	V	I	Cornerstones of Freedom	Children's Press
Scared Stiff	V	F	Malcolm, Jahnna N.	Scholastic
Secret of NIMH, The	V	F	O'Brien, Robert C.	Scholastic
Silent to the Bone	V	RF	Konigsburg, E. L.	Atheneum
Skateway to Freedom	V	HF	Alma, Ann	Orca Book Publishers
So Far From the Bamboo Grove	V	HF	Watkins, Yoko Kawashima	William Morrow
Sojourner Truth: Ain't I a Woman?	V	B	McKissack, F. and P.	Scholastic
Soldier's Heart	V	HF	Paulsen, Gary	Random House
SOS Titanic	V	HF	Bunting, Eve	Harcourt Brace
Spirit of St. Louis, The	V	I	Cornerstones of Freedom	Children's Press
Stealing Home: The Story of Jackie Robinson	V	B	Denenberg, Barry	Scholastic
Story of The Surrender at Yorktown, The	V	I	Cornerstones of Freedom	Children's Press

Title	Level	Genre	Author/Series	Publisher/Distributor
Story of The Women's Movement, The	V	I	Cornerstones of Freedom	Children's Press
Swiftly Tilting Planet, A	V	F	L'Engle, Madeleine	Bantam Doubleday Dell
Tecumseh	V	B	Cornerstones of Freedom	Children's Press
Tent, The	V	RF	Paulsen, Gary	Bantam Doubleday Dell
Theft in Time, A: Timedetectors II	V	HF	Odgers, Darrel & Sally	Rigby
Thief in the Village, A	V	RF	Berry, James	Puffin Books
Thief of Hearts	V	RF	Yep, Laurence	Harper Collins
Through the Eyes of Your Ancestors: A Step-by-Step Guide to Uncovering Your Family's History	V	I	Taylor, Maureen	Houghton Mifflin
Timedetectors	V	SF	Literacy 2000	Rigby
Titanic, The	V	I	Cornerstones of Freedom	Children's Press
Tom's Midnight Garden	V	F	Pierce, Philippa	HarperTrophy
Transcontinental Railroad, The	V	I	Cornerstones of Freedom	Children's Press
Tree by Leaf	V	F	Voigt, Cynthia	Simon & Schuster
Troubling a Star	V	F	L'Engle, Madeleine	Dell
True Confessions of Charlotte Doyle, The	V	HF	Avi	Avon
Twenty-One Balloons, The	V	SF	DuBois, William	Scholastic
Underground Railroad, The	V	I	Bial, Raymond	Houghton Mifflin
Underground Railroad, The	V	I	Cornerstones of Freedom	Children's Press
Walk Through a Rainforest, A: Life in the Ituri Forest of Zaire	V	RF	Creech, Sharon	Harper Collins
Walk Two Moons	V	RF	Creech, Sharon	Harper Collins
Wanderer, The	V	RF	Creech, Sharon	HarperCollins
Watchers: I.D.	V	SF	Lerangis, Peter	Scholastic
Watchers: Island	V	SF	Lerangis, Peter	Scholastic
Watchers: Lab 6	V	SF	Lerangis, Peter	Scholastic
Watchers: Last Stop	V	SF	Lerangis, Peter	Scholastic
Watchers: Rewind	V	SF	Lerangis, Peter	Scholastic
Watchers: War	V	SF	Lerangis, Peter	Scholastic
Westing Game, The	V	RF	Raskin, Ellen	The Penguin Group
When the Tripods Came	V	F	Christopher, John	Aladdin
White House, The	V	I	Cornerstones of Freedom	Children's Press
White Mountain, The	V	F	Christopher, John	Aladdin
Williamsburg	V	I	Cornerstones of Freedom	Children's Press
Williwaw!	V	RF	Bodoff, Tom	Knopf
Wind in the Door, A	V	F	L'Engle, Madeleine	Bantam Doubleday Dell
Window, The	V	RF	Ingold, Jeanette	Harcourt Brace
Witches of Worm, The	V	F	Snyder, Zilpha K.	Random House
Wolves of Willoughby Chase, The	V	HF	Aiken, Joan	Bantam Doubleday Dell
Women Who Shaped the West	V	B	Cornerstones of Freedom	Children's Press
Women's Voting Rights	V	I	Cornerstones of Freedom	Children's Press
Words of Stone	V	RF	Henkes, Kevin	The Penguin Group
Wrinkle in Time, A	V	F	L'Engle, Madeleine	Bantom Doubleday Dell
Yolonda's Genius	V	RF	Fenner, Carol	Aladdin
Across the Lines	W	HF	Reeder, Carolyn	Avon Camelot
Adam of the Road	W	HF	Gray, Elizabeth Janet	Scholastic
After the Dancing Days	W	HF	Rostkowski, Margaret I.	HarperTrophy
After the War	W	HF	Matas, Carol	Aladdin
An Island Far From Home	W	HF	Donahue, John	Carolrhonda Books
Anne Frank: Life in Hiding	W	B	Hurwitz, Johanna	Avon
Arkadians, The	W	F	Alexander, Lloyd	Puffin Books
Banished, The	W	F	Levin, Betty	William Morrow
Battle for Iwo Jima, The	W	I	Cornerstones of Freedom	Children's Press
Between the Dragon and the Eagle	W	HF	Schneider, Mical	Carolrhoda Books
Black Pearl, The	W	RF	O'Dell, Scott	Bantam Doubleday Dell
Blue Heron	W	RF	Avi	Avon
Blue-Eyed Daisy, A	W	RF	Rylant, Cynthia	Simon & Schuster
Castle of Llyr, The	W	F	Alexander, Lloyd	Dell
Child of the Owl	W	RF	Yep, Laurence	HarperTrophy
Christa McAuliffe: Teacher in Space	W	B	Naden, Corinne J. & Blue, Rose	Millbrook

Title	Level	Genre	Author/Series	Publisher/Distributor
Danger In Quicksand Swamp	W	RF	Wallace, Bill	Simon & Schuster
Day of Pleasure, A: Stories of a Boy Growing Up in Warsaw	W	B	Singer, Isaac Bashevis	Farrar, Straus, Giroux
Dicey's Song	W	RF	Voigt, Cynthia	Ballantine Books
Disability Rights Movement, The	W	I	Cornerstones of Freedom	Children's Press
Dive to the Deep Ocean: Voyages of Exploration and Discovery	W	I	Kovacs, Deborah	Steck-Vaughn
Dog in The Freezer, The	W	F	Mazer, Harry	Simon & Schuster
Down to a Sunless Sea: The Strange World of Hydrothermal Vents	W	I	Madin, Kate	Steck-Vaughn
Dragon Cauldron	W	F	Yep, Laurence	Harper Collins
Dragon of the Lost Sea	W	F	Yep, Laurence	Harper Collins
Dragon Steel	W	F	Yep, Laurence	Harper Collins
Dragon War	W	F	Yep, Laurence	Harper Collins
Dragon's Gate	W	HF	Yep, Laurence	Harper Collins
Dragonwings	W	HF	Yep, Lawrence	HarperTrophy
Easter Island: Giant Stone Statues Tell of a Rich and Tragic Past	W	I	Arnold, Caroline	Houghton Mifflin
Eleanor Roosevelt, A Life of Discovery	W	B	Freedman, Russell	Clarion Books
Exploring an Ocean Tide Pool	W	I	Bendick, Jeanne	Henry Holt & Co.
Extraordinary American Indians	W	B	Avery, Susan & Skinner, Linda	Children's Press
Extraordinary Black Americans: From Colonial to Contemporary Times	W	B	Altman, Susan	Children's Press
Extraordinary Jewish Americans	W	B	Brooks, Philip	Children's Press
Extraordinary People with Disabilities	W	B	Kent, D. & Quinlan, K. A.	Children's Press
Extraordinary Women in Politics	W	B	Gulatta, Charles	Children's Press
Extraordinary Women Journalists	W	B	Price-Groff, Claire	Children's Press
Extraordinary Women of Medicine	W	B	Stille, Darlene R.	Children's Press
Extraordinary Women of the American West	W	B	Alter, Judy	Children's Press
Extraordinary Women Scientists	W	B	Stille, Darlene R.	Children's Press
Extraordinary Young People	W	B	Brill, Marlene Targ	Children's Press
Face to Face	W	RF	Bauer, Marion Dane	Bantam Doubleday Dell
Garden of Eden Motel, The	W	RF	Hamilton, Morse	William Morrow
Girl From Yamhill, A	W	B	Cleary, Beverly	Bantam Doubleday Dell
Gone from Home	W	RF	Johnson, Angela	Alfred A. Knopf
Grand Canyon Journey, A: Tracing Time in Stone	W	I	A First Book	Franklin Watts
Guardian of the Dark	W	F	Spencer, Bev	Scholastic
Honorable Prison, The	W	HF	Becerra de Jenkins, Lyll	The Penguin Group
Hope Was Here	W	RF	Bauer, Joan	G.P. Putnam's Sons
House on Mango Street, The	W	B	Cisneros, Sandra	Alfred A. Knopf
I Am A Star: Child of the Holocaust	W	I	Auerbacher, Inge	The Penguin Group
In Search of the Grand Canyon	W	I	Fraser, Mary Ann	Henry Holt & Co.
Iron Ring, The	W	F	Alexander, Lloyd	Puffin Books
Jack's New Power: Stories From a Caribbean Year	W	RF	Gantos, Jack	Sunburst
John A Macdonald	W	B	Waite, Peter B.	Fitzhenry & Whiteside
Kiss the Dust	W	RF	Laird, Elizabeth	The Penguin Group
Letters to Julia	W	RF	Holmes, Barbara Ware	HarperTrophy
Life and Words of Martin Luther King, Jr., The	W	B	Peck, Ira	Scholastic
Lincoln-Douglas Debates, The	W	I	Cornerstones of Freedom	Children's Press
Local News	W	RF	Soto, Gary	Scholastic
Lost Garden, The	W	B	Yep, Laurence	Beech Tree Books
Louis Riell	W	B	Neering, Rosemary	Fitzhenry & Whiteside
Magical Adventures of Pretty Pearl, The	W	F	Hamilton, Virginia	HarperTrophy
Mama, Let's Dance	W	RF	Hermes, Patricia	Scholastic
Mark Twain	W	B	Cox, Clinton	Scholastic
Maya Angelou: Greeting the Morning	W	B	King, Sarah E.	The Millbrook Press
Meet the Austins	W	RF	L'Engle, Madeleine	Laurel-Leaf Books
Meteorite!: The Last Days of the Dinosaurs	W	I	Norris, Richard	Steck-Vaughn
Missing May	W	RF	Rylant, Cynthia	Bantam Doubleday Dell
Moccasin Trail	W	RF	McGraw, Eloise	Scholastic

Title	Level	Genre	Author/Series	Publisher/Distributor
Moon Bridge, The	W	HF	Savin, Marcia	Scholastic
Moon Over Tennessee: A Boy's Civil War Journal	W	B	Crist-Evans, Craig	Houghton Mifflin
Mouse Rap, The	W	RF	Myers, Walter Dean	HarperTrophy
Mr. Lincoln's Drummer	W	HF	Wisler, G. Clifton	The Penguin Group
My Own Two Feet	W	B	Cleary, Beverly	Avon
Nellie McClung	W	B	Benham, Mary Lile	Fitzhenry & Whiteside
Newbery Halloween, A: A Dozen Scary Stories by Newbery Award-Winning Authors	W	F	Greenberg, M.H. & Waugh, C.G.	Delacorte
Night Flyers, The	W	RF	Jones, Elizabeth McDavid	Pleasant Company
Nightjohn	W	HF	Paulsen, Gary	Bantam Doubleday Dell
Ocean Detectives: Solving Mysteries of the Sea	W	I	Cerullo, Mary	Steck-Vaughn
Orphan Train Adventures: Caught in the Act	W	HF	Nixon, Joan Lowery	Bantam Doubleday Dell
Orphan Train Adventures: Circle of Love	W	HF	Nixon, Joan Lowery	Bantam Doubleday Dell
Orphan Train Adventures: Dangerous Promise, A	W	HF	Nixon, Joan Lowery	Dell
Orphan Train Adventures: Family Apart, A	W	HF	Nixon, Joan Lowery	Dell
Orphan Train Adventures: In the Face of Danger	W	HF	Nixon, Joan Lowery	Dell
Orphan Train Adventures: Keeping Secrets	W	HF	Nixon, Joan Lowery	Dell
Orphan Train Adventures: Place to Belong, A	W	HF	Nixon, Joan Lowery	Dell
Our Endangered Planet (Oceans)	W	I	Hoff, M. and Rodgers, M.	Lerner Publications
Panama Canal, The	W	I	Cornerstones of Freedom	Children's Press
People Could Fly, American Black Folktales	W	TL	Hamilton, Virginia	Alfred A. Knopf
Phantom Tollbooth, The	W	F	Juster, Norton	Bantam Doubleday Dell
Phoenix Rising	W	RF	Hesse, Karen	Penguin Group
Pine Hollow: Changing Leads	W	RF	Bryant, Bonnie	Bantam Doubleday Dell
Pine Hollow: Conformation Faults	W	RF	Bryant, Bonnie	Bantam Doubleday Dell
Pine Hollow: Reining In	W	RF	Bryant, Bonnie	Bantam Doubleday Dell
Pine Hollow: The Long Ride	W	RF	Bryant, Bonnie	Bantam Doubleday Dell
Pine Hollow: The Trail Home	W	RF	Bryant, Bonnie	Bantam Doubleday Dell
Powers of Congress, The	W	I	Cornerstones of Freedom	Children's Press
Presidential Elections	W	I	Cornerstones of Freedom	Children's Press
Pride of Puerto Rico: The Life of Roberto Clemente	W	B	Walker, Paul Robert	Harcourt Brace
Proud Taste For Scarlet And Miniver	W	F	Konigsburg, E. L.	Dell
Red Cap	W	HF	Wisler, G. Clifton	The Penguin Group
Ring of Endless Light, A	W	F	L'Engle, Madeleine	Dell
Roll of Thunder, Hear My Cry	W	HF	Taylor, Mildred D.	The Penguin Group
Rough Riders, The	W	B	Cornerstones of Freedom	Children's Press
Sarny: A Life Remembered	W	HF	Paulsen, Gary	Delacorte Press
Saturnalia	W	RF	Fleischman, Paul	Harper Collins
Sea Otter Rescue: The Aftermath of an Oil Spill	W	I	Smith, Roland	Scholastic
Seedfolks	W	RF	Fleishman, Paul	HarperTrophy
Selchie's Seed, The	W	F	Levey Oppenheim, Shulamith	Harcourt Brace
Serpent's Children, The	W	HF	Yep, Laurence	HarperTrophy
Seventh Tower, The: The Fall	W	F	Nix, Garth	Scholastic
Shades of Gray	W	HF	Reeder, Carolyn	Avon Camelot
Sing for Your Father, Su Phan	W	HF	Pevsner, Stella and Tang, Fay	Bantam Doubleday Dell
Sister	W	RF	Greenfield, Eloise	Harper Collins
Slam!	W	RF	Myers, Walter Dean	Scholastic
Solitary Blue, A	W	RF	Voigt, Cynthia	Scholastic
Spanish-American War, The	W	I	Cornerstones of Freedom	Children's Press
Spies on the Devil's Belt	W	HF	Haynes, Betsy	Scholastic
Story of The Persian Gulf War, The	W	I	Cornerstones of Freedom	Children's Press
Story of The Sinking of the Battleship Maine, The	W	I	Cornerstones of Freedom	Children's Press
Stowaway	W	HF	Hesse, Karen	Simon & Schuster
Taste of Salt: The Story of Modern Haiti	W	I	Temple, Frances	HarperTrophy
Tiger Eyes	W	RF	Blume, Judy	Bantam Doubleday Dell
Time of Angels, A	W	F	Hesse, Karen	Hyperion
Torn Thread	W	HF	Isaacs, Anne	Scholastic
Twilight In Grace Falls	W	RF	Honeycutt, Natalie	Avon
Under the Blood-Red Sun	W	HF	Salisbury, Graham	Bantam Doubleday Dell
United States Holocaust Memorial Museum, The	W	I	Cornerstones of Freedom	Children's Press

Title	Level	Genre	Author/Series	Publisher/Distributor
Usborne Book of Inventors, The	W	I	Reid, Struan and Fara, Patricia	Scholastic
Vietnam Women's Memorial, The	W	I	Cornerstones of Freedom	Children's Press
What Do Fish Have To Do With Anything?	W	RF	Avi	Candlewick Press
Who Is Carrie?	W	HF	Collier, J. L. and Collier, C.	Bantam Doubleday Dell
Wilfrid Laurier	W	B	Spigelman, Martin	Fitzhenry & Whiteside
Wings	W	TL	Yolen, Jane & Nolan, Dennis	Harcourt Brace
Winterdance: The Fine Madness of Running the Iditarod	W	B	Paulsen, Gary	Harcourt Brace
Witch of Blackbird Pond, The	W	HF	Speare, Elizabeth George	Bantam Doubleday Dell
Year of Impossible Goodbyes	W	HF	Choi, Sook Nyui	Yearling
You Want Women to Vote, Lizzie Stanton?	W	B	Fritz, Jean	The Penguin Group
Abracadabra Kid, The	X	B	Fleischman, Sid	Beech Tree Books
An Acceptable Time	X	F	L'Engle, Madeleine	Laurel-Leaf Books
Anne Frank: Beyond the Diary	X	I	Van der Rol, R. & Verhoeven, R.	Puffin Books
April Morning	X	HF	Fast, Howard	Bantam
At Her Majesty's Request: An African Princess in Victorian England	X	HF	Myers, Walter Dean	Scholastic
Beyond Providence	X	RF	Schnur, Steven	Harcourt Brace
Bill Cosby: The Changing Black Image	X	B	Rosenberg, Robert	Millbrook Press
Black Eagles, African Americans in Aviation	X	B	Haskins, Jim	Scholastic
Black Heroes of the American Revolution	X	B	Davis, Burke	Harcourt Brace
Blue Door, The	X	HF	Rinaldi, Ann	Scholastic
Bone Dance	X	RF	Brooks, Martha	Random House
Boys Will Be	X	RF	Brooks, Bruce	Hyperion
Break with Charity, A: A Story About the Salem Witch Trials	X	I	Rinaldi, Ann	Harcourt Brace
Bully for you Teddy Roosevelt!	X	B	Fritz, Jean	Penguin Putnam Books
Call It Courage	X	RF	Sperry, Armstrong	Aladdin
Child in Prison Camp, A	X	HF	Takashima, Shizuye	Tundra Books
Children of the River	X	RF	Crew, Linda	Bantam Doubleday Dell
Children of the Wild West	X	I	Freedman, Russell	Clarion Books
Childtimes: A Three-Generation Memoir	X	B	Greenfield, E. & Little, L. J.	HarperTrophy
Cleopatra	X	B	Green, Robert	Franklin Watts
Cowboys of the Wild West	X	I	Freedman, Russell	Clarion Books
Danny's Desert Rats	X	RF	Naylor, Phyllis Reynolds	Aladdin
Dark Is Rising, The	X	F	Cooper, Susan	Macmillan
Dawn of Fear	X	HF	Cooper, Susan	Simon & Schuster
Definitely Cool	X	RF	Wilkinson, Brenda	Scholastic
Devil's Arithmetic, The	X	F	Yolen, Jane	Puffin Books
Dragon's Blood	X	F	Yolen, Jane	Harcourt Brace
Dred Scott Decision, The	X	I	Cornerstones of Freedom	Children's Press
Earthquake Terror	X	RF	Kehret, Peg	Puffin Books
Echohawk	X	HF	Durrant, Lynda	Bantam Doubleday Dell
Find A Stranger, Say Goodbye	X	RF	Lowry, Lois	Dell
Forever Friends	X	RF	Boyd, Candy Dawson	Puffin Books
Forgotten Heroes, The: The Story of the Buffalo Soldiers	X	I	Cox, Clinton	Scholastic
Frost in the Night, A: A Girlhood on the Eve of the Third Reich	X	B	Baer, Edith	Sunburst
Gathering Blue	X	F	Lowry, Lois	Houghton Mifflin
Girl Named Disaster, A	X	RF	Farmer, Nancy	The Penguin Group
Girl Who Owned a City, The	X	F	Nelson, O.T.	Laurel-Leaf Books
Glory Field, The	X	HF	Myers, Walter Dean	Scholastic
Great Depression, The	X	I	Cornerstones of Freedom	Children's Press
Great Little Madison, The	X	B	Fritz, Jean	G.P. Putnam's Sons
Greenwitch	X	F	Cooper, Susan	Scholastic
Grey King, The	X	F	Cooper, Susan	Simon & Schuster
Growing Up in Coal Country	X	I	Bartoletti, Susan Campbell	Houghton Mifflin
Gulf	X	F	Westfall, Robert	Scholastic
Harriet Beecher Stowe and the Beecher Preachers	X	B	Fritz, Jean	The Penguin Group

Title	Level	Genre	Author/Series	Publisher/Distributor
Heart's Blood	X	F	Yolen, Jane	Harcourt Brace
Henry Reed, Inc.	X	F	Robertson, Keith	Puffin Books
Homecoming	X	RF	Voigt, Cynthia	Ballantine Books
Homesick, My Own Story	X	B	Fritz, Jean	Penguin Books
Hoops	X	RF	Myers, Walter Dean	Bantam Doubleday Dell
Iceberg Hermit, The	X	RF	Roth, Arthur	Scholastic
Island on Bird Street, The	X	HF	Orlev, Uri	Houghton Mifflin
Izzy, Willy-Nilly	X	RF	Voigt, Cynthia	Aladdin
Journey to the Center of the Earth, A	X	SF	Verne, Jules	Harper Collins
Katarina	X	HF	Winter, Kathryn	Scholastic
Knot in the Grain (and Other Stories)	X	F	McKinley, Robin	Harper Trophy
Langston Hughes: An Illustrated Edition	X	B	Meltzer, Milton	Millbrook Press
Let the Circle Be Unbroken	X	HF	Taylor, Mildred D.	The Penguin Group
Letters From a Slave Girl: The Story of Harriet Jacobs	X	HF	Lyons, Mary E.	Simon & Schuster
Looking Back, A Book of Memories	X	B	Lowry, Lois	Delacorte Press
M.C. Higgins the Great	X	RF	Hamilton, Virginia	Macmillan
Make Way for Sam Houston	X	B	Fritz, Jean	Putnam & Grosset
Master Puppeteer, The	X	HF	Paterson, Katherine	Harper Collins
Maura's Angel	X	F	Banks, Lynne Reid	Avon
Maya Angelou: Journey of the Heart	X	B	Pettit, Jayne	Puffin Books
Memories of Anne Frank	X	B	Gold, Alison Leslie	Scholastic
Midwife's Apprentice, The	X	HF	Cushman, Karen	HarperTrophy
Moving Mama to Town	X	RF	Young, Ronder Thomas	Bantam Doubleday Dell
My Brother is a Superhero	X	RF	Sheldon, Dyan	Candlewick Press
Nelson Mandela "No Easy Walk To Freedom"	X	B	Denenberg, Barry	Scholastic
Nelson Mandela: South Africa's Silent Voice of Protest	X	B	Hargrove, Jim	Children's Press
Nightmare Mountain	X	RF	Kehret, Peg	Puffin Books
Not Guilty	X	B	Sullivan, George	Scholastic
Novio Boy	X	TL	Soto, Gary	Harcourt Brace
Oddballs	X	B	Sleator, William	Puffin Books
One More River to Cross	X	B	Haskins, Jim	Scholastic
One Who Came Back, The	X	RF	Mazzio, Joann	Houghton Mifflin
Out of the Dust	X	HF	Hesse, Karen	Scholastic
Over Sea, Under Stone	X	F	Cooper, Susan	Simon & Schuster
Place To Hide, A	X	B	Petit, Jayne	Scholastic
Queen Eleanor: Independent Spirit in the Medieval World	X	B	Brooks, Polly Schoyer	Houghton Mifflin
Rain Ghost, The	X	F	Kilworth, Garry	Scholastic
Road to Memphis, The	X	HF	Taylor, Mildred D.	The Penguin Group
Sarah Bishop	X	HF	O'Dell, Scott	Scholastic
Seaward	X	F	Cooper, Susan	Simon & Schuster
Somehow Tenderness Survives: Stories of Southern Africa	X	B	Rochman, Hazel	HarperTrophy
Ties That Bind, Ties That Break	X	HF	Namioka, Lensey	Delacorte Press
Traitor: The Case of Benedict Arnold	X	B	Fritz, Jean	Putnam & Grosset
When Plague Strikes	X	I	Giblin, James Cross	Harper Collins
Where the Red Fern Grows	X	RF	Rawls, Wilson	Bantam Doubleday Dell
Yearling, The	X	RF	Rawlings, Marjorie Kinnan	Simon & Schuster
Young Joan	X	HF	Dana, Barbara	HarperTrophy
Young Land Lords, The	X	RF	Myers, Walter Dean	The Penguin Group
Zlata's Diary	X	B	Filipovic, Zlata	Puffin Books
Alida's Song	Y	RF	Paulsen, Gary	Random House
Among the Volcanoes	Y	RF	Castaneda, Omar S.	Bantam Doubleday Dell
Anne Frank: The Diary of a Young Girl	Y	B	Frank, Anne	Bantam
Anthony Burns: Defeat and Triumph of a Fugitive Slave	Y	B	Hamilton, Virginia	Alfred A. Knopf
Avion My Uncle Flew, The	Y	RF	Fisher, Cyrus	The Penguin Group
Black Pioneers of Science and Invention	Y	B	Haber, Louis	Harcourt Brace
Blue Sword, The	Y	F	McKinley, Robin	Puffin Books

Title	Level	Genre	Author/Series	Publisher/Distributor
Borning Room, The	Y	HF	Fleischman, Paul	Harper Collins
Boy Who Reversed Himself, The	Y	SF	Sleator, William	Puffin Books
Bull Run	Y	HF	Fleischman, Paul	HarperCollins
Call of the Wild	Y	RF	London, Jack	Signet Classics
Carry on, Mr. Bowditch	Y	B	Latham, Jean Lee	Houghton Mifflin
Cesar Chavez	Y	B	Rodriguez, Consuelo	Chelsea House
Children of the Dust Bowl	Y	I	Stanley, Jerry	Crown Publishers
Count Karlstein	Y	F	Pullman, Philip	Alfred A. Knopf
Day Martin Luther King, Jr., Was Shot, The	Y	B	Haskins, Jim	Scholastic
Diary of Anne Frank, The	Y	B	Frank, Anne	Pocket Books
Ear, the Eye, and the Arm, The	Y	SF	Farmer, Nancy	Puffin Books
Fast Sam, Cool Clyde, and Stuff	Y	RF	Myers, Walter Dean	Puffin Books
Favorite Greek Myths	Y	TL	Pope, Mary Osborne	Scholastic
Fire in the Hills	Y	RF	Myers, Anna	Puffin Books
First On The Moon	Y	I	Hehner, Barbara	Hyperion/Madison Press
For The Life of Laetitia	Y	RF	Hodge, Merle	Farrar Straus Giroux
Get On Out of Here, Philip Hall	Y	RF	Greene, Bette	Puffin Books
Giver, The	Y	F	Lowry, Lois	Bantam Doubleday Dell
Grand Mothers: Poems, Reminiscences, and Short Stories About Keepers of Our Traditions	Y	B	Giovanni, Nikki	Henry Holt & Co.
Great Interactive Dream Machine, The	Y	SF	Peck, Richard	Puffin Books
I Have Lived a Thousand Years	Y	B	Bitton-Jackson, Livia	Simon & Schuster
Instead of Three Wishes: Magical Short Stories	Y	F	Turner, Megan Whalen	The Penguin Group
Jackaroo	Y	RF	Voigt, Cynthia	Scholastic
Jacob's Rescue: A Holocaust Story	Y	HF	Drucker, M. & Halperin, M.	Bantam Doubleday Dell
Jazz Kid, The	Y	RF	Lincoln Collier, James	The Penguin Group
Jesse	Y	RF	Soto, Gary	Scholastic
Life and Death of Martin Luther King, Jr.,The	Y	B	Haskins, James	Beech Tree
Living Up The Street	Y	RF	Soto, Gary	Bantam Doubleday Dell
Lost in Cyberspace	Y	SF	Peck, Richard	Puffin Books
Love from Your Friend, Hannah	Y	HF	Skolsky, Mindy Warshaw	Harper Trophy
My Brother Sam is Dead	Y	HF	Collier, James and Christopher	Scholastic
New Kids In Town	Y	B	Bode, Janet	Scholastic
Night of the Chupacabras	Y	RF	Lee, Marie G.	Avon Camelot
Night the Heads Came, The	Y	SF	Sleator, William	Puffin Books
Nissa's Place	Y	RF	LaFaye, A.	Simon & Schuster
Now Is Your Time! The African-American Struggle	Y	I	Myers, Walter Dean	Harper Collins
One Bird	Y	RF	Mori, Kyoko	Ballantine Books
One Fat Summer	Y	RF	Lipsyte, Robert	Harper Collins
Only Earth and Sky Last Forever	Y	HF	Benchley, Nathaniel	Harper Collins
Ordinary Miracles	Y	RF	Tolan, Stephanie S.	Morrow
Philip Hall Likes Me. I Reckon Maybe.	Y	RF	Greene, Bette	Puffin Books
Place to Call Home, A	Y	RF	Koller, Jackie French	Aladdin
Pushcart War, The	Y	F	Merrill, Jean	Bantam Doubleday Dell
Ruby and the Smoke, The	Y	F	Pullman, Phillip	Laurel-Leaf Books
Sacajawea	Y	B	Bruchac, Joseph	Harcourt
Sons of Liberty	Y	RF	Griffin, Adele	Hyperion
Stories of the North	Y	RF	London, Jack	Scholastic
Strawberry Hill	Y	RF	LaFaye, A.	Simon & Schuster
Three Investigators, The Mystery of the Fiery Eye	Y	RF	Arthur, Robert	Random House
Toning The Sweep	Y	RF	Johnson, Angela	Scholastic
Walk in My World, A	Y	RF	Mazer, Anne	Persea Books
Watership Down	Y	F	Adams, Richard	Avon
We Remember the Holocaust	Y	I	Adler, David A.	Henry Holt
Where the Lilies Bloom	Y	RF	Cleavers, Vera and Bill	HarperTrophy
White Fang	Y	RF	London, Jack	Scholastic
Wright Brothers, The	Y	B	Freedman, Russell	Holiday House
Year of the Sawdust Man, The	Y	RF	LaFaye, A.	Simon & Schuster
40 Nights To Knowing the Sky	Z	I	Schaaf, Fred	Henry Holt & Co.
Abe Lincoln: Log Cabin To White House	Z	B	North, Sterling	Random House

Title	Level	Genre	Author/Series	Publisher/Distributor
Across Five Aprils	Z	HF	Hunt, Irene	Follett
Adventures of Huckleberry Finn, The	Z	HF	Twain, Mark	Scholastic
Adventures of Tom Sawyer, The	Z	HF	Twain, Mark	Scholastic
After the Rain	Z	RF	Mazer, Norma Fox	Avon Books
Amber Spyglass, The	Z	F	Pullman, Phillip	Alfred A. Knopf
American Dragons: Twenty-Five Asian American Voices	Z	RF	Yep, Laurence	HarperTrophy
American Eyes: New Asian-American Short Stories for Young Adults	Z	RF	Carlson, Lori M.	Ballantine Books
Among the Hidden	Z	SF	Haddix, Margaret Peterson	Aladdin
An Ancient Heritage: The Arab-American Minority	Z	I	Ashabranner, Brent	Harper Collins
An Island Like You: Stories of the Barrio	Z	RF	Cofer, Judith Ortiz	The Penguin Group
Animal Farm	Z	F	Orwell, George	Harcourt Brace
Annie John	Z	RF	Kincaid, Jamaica	Farrar, Straus and Giroux
Baby-Snatcher	Z	RF	Terris, Susan	Scholastic
Between Earth and Sky: Legends of Native American Sacred Places	Z	TL	Bruchac, Joseph	Voyager Books
Beyond Belief	Z	I	Steiger, Brad	Scholastic
Beyond the Myth: The Story of Joan of Arc	Z	B	Brooks, Polly Schoyer	Houghton Mifflin
Black Boy	Z	RF	Wright, Richard	HarperPerennial
Bless Me, Ultima	Z	RF	Anaya, Rudolfo	Warner Books
Bowman's Store: A Journey to Myself	Z	B	Bruchac, Joseph	Lee & Low Books, Inc.
Brian's Song	Z	I	Blinn, William	Bantam Doubleday Dell
Broken Bridge, The	Z	RF	Pullman, Philip	Alfred A. Knopf
Brother To Shadows	Z	SF	Norton, Andre	Avon
Cage, The	Z	B	Sender, Ruth Minsky	Simon & Schuster
Circle of Quiet, A	Z	B	L'Engle, Madeleine	Harper Collins
Clockwork	Z	F	Pullman, Philip	Scholastic
Contender, The	Z	RF	Lipsythe, Robert	HarperTrophy
Day No Pigs Would Die, A	Z	HF	Peck, Sylvia	Random House
Detective Stories	Z	RF	Pullman, Philip	Kingfisher
Earthborn	Z	F	Card, Orson Scott	Tor
Earthfall	Z	F	Card, Orson Scott	Tor
EL Bronx Remembered	Z	RF	Mohr, Nicholasa	Harper Trophy
Ellie	Z	RF	Borntrager, Mary Christner	Herald Press
Eva	Z	F	Dickenson, Eva	Laurel-Leaf Books
Farewell to Manzanar	Z	B	Houston, J.W. & Houston, J.D.	Houghton Mifflin
Farthest Shore, The	Z	F	Le Guin, Ursula	Bamtam
Flowers For Algernon	Z	RF	Keyes, Daniel	Harcourt Brace
Forged By Fire	Z	RF	Draper, Sharon M.	Aladdin
Friends, The	Z	RF	Guy, Rosa	Bantam Doubleday Dell
From the Notebooks of Melanin Sun	Z	RF	Woodson, Jacqueline	Scholastic
Gathering of Flowers, A	Z	RF	Thomas, Joyce Carol	HarperTrophy
Gentlehands	Z	RF	Kerr, M. E.	Harper Trophy
Golden Compass, The	Z	F	Pullman, Philip	Ballantine Books
Good Night, Mr. Tom	Z	HF	Magorian, Michelle	HarperTrophy
Gray Heroes Elder Tales from Around the World	Z	TL	Yolen, Jane	Penguin Books
Great Chicago Fire, 1871, The	Z	HF	Massie, Elizabeth	Pocket Books
Great Escapes of World War II	Z	I	Sullivan, George	Scholastic
Hanged Man, The	Z	RF	Block, Francesca Lia	Harper Collins
Hero and the Crown, The	Z	F	McKinley, Robin	Puffin Books
Hobbit, The	Z	F	Tolkien, J.R.R	Ballantine Books
House of Stairs	Z	F	Sleator, William	Puffin Books
I Am the Cheese	Z	RF	Cormier, Robert	Laurel-Leaf Books
In Short: A Collection of Brief Creative Nonfiction	Z	I	Kitchen, J. & Jones, M. P.	W. W. Norton
Inn Keepers Apprentice	Z	B	Say, Allen	The Penguin Group
Invincible Louisa	Z	B	Meigs, Cornelia	Scholastic
Ironman	Z	RF	Crutcher, Chris	Laurel-Leaf Books
Irrational Season, The	Z	B	L'Engle, Madeleine	Harper Collins
It Was On Fire When I Lay Down On It	Z	B	Fulghum, Robert	Ballantine Books
Jazmin's Notebook	Z	RF	Grimes, Nikki	The Penguin Group

Title	Level	Genre	Author/Series	Publisher/Distributor
Keeping Days, The	Z	HF	Johnston, Norma	Puffin Books
King of Shadows	Z	F	Cooper, Susan	Margaret K. McElderry Books
Lady with the Hat, The	Z	HF	Orlev, Uri	The Penguin Group
Leaving Home	Z	RF	Keillor, Garrison	The Penguin Group
Leaving Home: 15 Distinguished Authors Explore Personal Journeys	Z	RF	Rochman, H. & McCampbell, D.	HarperTrophy
Lion Tamer's Daughter, The- And Other Stories	Z	F	Dickinson, Peter	Laurel-Leaf Books
Lord of the Rings, The	Z	F	Tolkien, J. R. R.	Houghton Mifflin
Louis Armstrong	Z	B	Brown, Sandford	Franklin Watts
Mariel of Redwall	Z	F	Jacques, Brian	Avon Books
Marlfox: A Novel of Redwall	Z	F	Jacques, Brian	Ace Books
Mattimeo: A Tale from Redwall	Z	F	Jacques, Brian	Avon
Miracle Worker, The	Z	B	Gibson, William	Bantam Doubleday Dell
Mossflower	Z	F	Jacques, Brian	Ace Books
Moves Make the Man, The	Z	RF	Brooks, Bruce	Harper Trophy
Never Cry Wolf	Z	B	Mowat, Farley	Bantam Doubleday Dell
Night Terrors, Stories of Shadow and Substance	Z	F	Duncan, Lois	Aladdin
Night the White Deer Died, The	Z	HF	Paulsen, Gary	Dell
Nine Man Tree	Z	RF	Peck, Robert Newton	Random House
No Pretty Pictures: A Child of War	Z	B	Lobel, Anita	Greenwillow Books
No Promises in the Wind	Z	HF	Hunt, Irene	Berkley Books
Odder Than Ever	Z	F	Coville, Bruce	Harcourt Inc.
Oddly Enough	Z	F	Coville, Bruce	Pocket Books
Of Mice and Men	Z	RF	Steinbeck, John	The Penguin Group
On Fortune's Wheel	Z	F	Voigt, Cynthia	Aladdin
Others See Us	Z	F	Sleator, William	Puffin Books
Outcast of Redwall, The	Z	F	Jacques, Brian	Ace Books
Outsiders, The	Z	RF	Hinton, S.E.	The Penguin Group
Part of the Sky, A	Z	HF	Peck, Robert Newton	Random House
Paul Harvey's The Rest Of The Story	Z	I	Harvey Jr., Paul	Bantam Books
Pearl, The	Z	RF	Steinbeck, John	Penguin Books
Pigman & Me, The	Z	B	Zindel, Paul	Dell
Pigman's Legacy, The	Z	RF	Zindel, Paul	Harper & Row
Planet of Junior Brown, The	Z	RF	Hamilton, Virginia	Aladdin
Powerhouse, Inside a Nuclear Power Plant	Z	I	Wilcox, Charlotte	Carolrhoda Books
Red Scarf Girl: Memoir of the Cultural Revolution	Z	B	Jiang, Ji Li	HarperTrophy
Rosie the Riveter	Z	I	Colman, Penny	Crown Publishers, Inc.
Salamandastron	Z	F	Jacques, Brian	Ace Books
Scorpions	Z	RF	Myers, Walter Dean	HarperTrophy
Sixteen Short Stories by Outstanding Writers	Z	RF	Gallo, Donald R.	Dell
Steal Away…to Freedom	Z	RF	Armstrong, Jennifer	Scholastic
Sterkarm Handshake, The	Z	F	Price, Susan	Scholastic
Subtle Knife, The	Z	F	Pullman, Philip	Ballantine Books
Summer Life, A	Z	RF	Soto, Gary	Bantam Doubleday Dell
Summer of My German Soldier	Z	HF	Greene, Bette	Dell Publishing
Summer of the Great-Grandmother, The	Z	B	L'Engle, Madeleine	Harper Collins
Tears of a Tiger	Z	RF	Draper, Sharon M.	Simon & Schuster
To Be a Slave	Z	I	Lester, Julius	Dial Books
To Kill a Mockingbird	Z	HF	Lee, Harper	Warner Books
Treasure Island	Z	HF	Stevenson, Robert Lewis	Scholastic
True Crimes and How They Were Solved	Z	I	Larsen, Anita	Scholastic
Two-Part Invention	Z	B	L'Engle, Madeleine	Harper Collins
Watcher, The	Z	RF	Howe, James	Simon & Schuster
We Shall Not Be Moved	Z	I	Dash, Joan	Scholastic
Wizard of Earthsea, A	Z	F	LeGuin, Ursula K.	Bantam Doubleday Dell
Woman Hollering Creek	Z	RF	Cisneros, Sandra	Random House

Book List
Organized by Genre

Title	Level	Genre	Author/Series	Publisher/Distributor
26 Fairmount Avenue	N	B	dePaola, Tomie	Putnam
Abe Lincoln: Log Cabin To White House	Z	B	North, Sterling	Random House
Abe Lincoln's Hat	M	B	Brenner, Martha	Random House
Abigail Adams: Girl of Colonial Days	R	B	Wagoner, Jean Brown	Aladdin
Abracadabra Kid, The	X	B	Fleischman, Sid	Beech Tree Books
Abraham Lincoln	O	B	Early Biographies	Compass Point Books
Abraham Lincoln	Q	B	Gross, Ruth Belov	Scholastic
Abraham Lincoln	S	B	Parin d'Aulaire, Ingri & Edgar	Bantam Doubleday Dell
Abraham Lincoln	L	B	Pebble Books	Grolier, Capstone
Abraham Lincoln: President of a Divided Country	O	B	Greene, Carol	Children's Press
Abraham Lincoln: The Great Emancipator	R	B	Stevenson, Augusta	Aladdin
Adventures of George Washington, The	N	B	Davidson, Margaret	Scholastic
African-American Scientists	O	B	St. John, Jetty	Capstone Press
Alexander Graham Bell	P	B	Linder, Greg	Capstone Press
Alexander Graham Bell	V	B	Petrie, A. Roy	Fitzhenry & Whiteside
Alexander Graham Bell: An Inventive Life	U	B	MacLeod, Elizabeth	Kids Can Press Ltd.
Alvin Ailey	P	B	Pinkney, Andrea Davis	Hyperion
Amelia Earhart	Q	B	Lowe, David	Rigby
Amelia Earhart	P	B	Parlin, John	Bantam Doubleday Dell
Amelia Earhart	P	B	Rosenthal, M. & Freeman, D.	Capstone Press
Amelia Earhart: Challenging the Skies	S	B	Sloate, Susan	Fawcett Columbine
Amelia Earhart: Courage in the Sky	S	B	Kerby, Mona	Puffin Books
Amelia Earhart: Flying for Adventure	S	B	Wade, Mary Dodson	The Millbrook Press
Amelia Earhart: Young Aviator	R	B	Gormley, Beatrice	Aladdin
And Then What Happened Paul Revere?	R	B	Fritz, Jean	Bantam Doubleday Dell
Andrew Carnegie: Builder of Libraries	P	B	Community Builders	Children's Press
Anne Frank	S	B	Epstein, Rachel	Franklin Watts
Anne Frank: Life in Hiding	W	B	Hurwitz, Johanna	Avon
Anne Frank: The Diary of a Young Girl	Y	B	Frank, Anne	Bantam
Anthony Burns: Defeat and Triumph of a Fugitive Slave	Y	B	Hamilton, Virginia	Alfred A. Knopf
Art Lesson, The	M	B	dePaola, Tomie	Putnam
Assassination of Abraham Lincoln, The	V	B	Cornerstones of Freedom	Children's Press
Assassination of John F. Kennedy, The	V	B	Cornerstones of Freedom	Children's Press
Assassination of Martin Luther King Jr.	V	B	Cornerstones of Freedom	Children's Press
Aunt Clara Brown: Official Pioneer	P	B	Lowery, Linda	Lerner Publishing Group
Avi	T	B	Markham, Lois	Learning Works, The
Babe Didrikson: Athlete of the Century	R	B	Knudson, R.R.	Bantam Doubleday Dell
Baseball's Best: Five True Stories	O	B	Step into Reading	Random House
Baseball's Greatest Pitchers	P	B	Kramer, S. A.	Random House
Beatles, The	N	B	Venezia, Mike	Children's Press
Beatrix Potter	O	B	Wallner, Alexandra	Holiday House
Ben Franklin of Old Philadelphia	U	B	Cousins, Margaret	Random House
Benjamin Franklin	N	B	Biography	Benchmark Education
Benjamin Franklin	U	B	Kent, Deborah	Scholastic
Benjamin Franklin: A Man with Many Jobs	O	B	Greene, Carol	Children's Press
Benjamin Franklin: Young Printer	R	B	Stevenson, Augusta	Aladdin
Best Wishes	O	B	Rylant, Cynthia	Richard C. Owen
Betsy Ross: Designer of Our Flag	R	B	Weil, Ann	Aladdin
Beyond the Myth: The Story of Joan of Arc	Z	B	Brooks, Polly Schoyer	Houghton Mifflin
Bicycle Rider	O	B	Scioscia, Mary	HarperTrophy
Big Lie, The: A True Story	T	B	Leitner, Isabella	Scholastic
Bill Clinton: Forty-Second President of the U.S.	O	B	Greene, Carol	Children's Press
Bill Cosby: The Changing Black Image	X	B	Rosenberg, Robert	Millbrook Press
Bill Gates: Helping People Use Computers	P	B	Community Builders	Children's Press
Black Eagles, African Americans in Aviation	X	B	Haskins, Jim	Scholastic
Black Heroes of the American Revolution	X	B	Davis, Burke	Harcourt Brace

Title	Level	Genre	Author/Series	Publisher/Distributor
Black Pioneers of Science and Invention	Y	B	Haber, Louis	Harcourt Brace
Book of Black Heroes from A to Z	P	B	Hudson, W. and Wesley, V. W.	Scholastic
Booker T. Washington	O	B	First Biographies	Steck-Vaughn
Booker T. Washington	P	B	McLoone, Margo	Capstone Press
Bookworm Who Hatched, A	O	B	Aardema, Verna	Richard C. Owen
Botticelli	P	B	Venezia, Mike	Children's Press
Bowman's Store: A Journey to Myself	Z	B	Bruchac, Joseph	Lee & Low Books, Inc.
Boy	T	B	Dahl, Roald	Puffin Books
Boy Called Slow, A	S	B	Bruchac, Joseph	Putnam & Grosset
Boy Named Boomer, A	K	B	Esiason, Boomer	Scholastic
Brainstorm!: The Stories of Twenty American Kid Inventors	P	B	Tucker, Tom	Farrar, Straus and Giroux
Buffalo Bill and the Pony Express	K	B	Coerr, Eleanor	HarperTrophy
Building a Dream: Mary Bethune's School	R	B	Kelso, Richard	Steck-Vaughn
Bully for you Teddy Roosevelt!	X	B	Fritz, Jean	Penguin Putnam Books
But I'll Be Back Again	V	B	Rylant, Cynthia	Beech Tree Books
Cage, The	Z	B	Sender, Ruth Minsky	Simon & Schuster
Can You Imagine?	O	B	McKissack, Patricia	Richard C. Owen
Carry on, Mr. Bowditch	Y	B	Latham, Jean Lee	Houghton Mifflin
Cass Becomes a Star	L	B	Literacy 2000	Rigby
Cesar Chavez	N	B	Biography	Benchmark Education
Cesar Chavez	P	B	Davis, Lucile	Capstone Press
Cesar Chavez	Y	B	Rodriguez, Consuelo	Chelsea House
Charles Lindbergh	O	B	Early Biographies	Compass Point Books
Chief Joseph of the Nez Percé	P	B	McAuliffe, Bill	Capstone Press
Child's Portrait of Shakespeare, A	Q	B	Burdett, Lois	Firefly Books
Childtimes: A Three-Generation Memoir	X	B	Greenfield, E. & Little, L. J.	HarperTrophy
Chocolate by Hershey: A Story about Milton S. Hershey	R	B	Burford, Betty	Carolrhoda Books
Christa McAuliffe: Teacher in Space	W	B	Naden, Corinne J. & Blue, Rose	Millbrook
Christopher Columbus: A Great Explorer	O	B	Greene, Carol	Children's Press
Circle of Quiet, A	Z	B	L'Engle, Madeleine	Harper Collins
Clara Barton: Founder of the American Red Cross	R	B	Stevenson, Augusta	Aladdin
Cleopatra	X	B	Green, Robert	Franklin Watts
Cleopatra	T	B	Stanley, Diane & Vennema, Peter	Mulberry Books
Clyde Tombaugh and the Search for Planet X	N	B	Wetterer, Margaret K.	Carolrhoda Books
Colin Powell: Straight to the Top	S	B	Blue, Rose & Naden, Corinne J.	The Millbrook Press
Crowfoot	U	B	Hacker, Carlotta	Fitzhenry & Whiteside
Da Vinci	P	B	Venezia, Mike	Children's Press
Dame Shirley and the Gold Rush	R	B	Rawls, Jim	Steck-Vaughn
Daniel Boone: Man of the Forests	O	B	Greene, Carol	Children's Press
Day Martin Luther King, Jr., Was Shot, The	Y	B	Haskins, Jim	Scholastic
Day of Pleasure, A: Stories of a Boy Growing Up in Warsaw	W	B	Singer, Isaac Bashevis	Farrar, Straus, Giroux
Defenders, The	T	B	McGovern, Ann	Language for Learning Assoc.
DeWitt and Lila Wallace: Charity for All	P	B	Community Builders	Children's Press
Diary of Anne Frank, The	Y	B	Frank, Anne	Pocket Books
Diego Rivera	O	B	First Biographies	Steck-Vaughn
Diego Rivera	P	B	Venezia, Mike	Children's Press
Diego Rivera: An Artist's Life	L	B	Pair-It Books	Steck-Vaughn
Double Life of Pocahontas, The	T	B	Fritz, Jean	Language for Learning Assoc.
Dr. Quinn Medicine Woman	T	B	McKenna, Colleen O'Shaughnessy	Language for Learning Assoc.
Dr. Seuss and His Stories	N	B	Coglon, Kari	Wright Group/McGraw Hill
Dream Come True, A	O	B	Hurwitz, Johanna	Richard C. Owen
El Chino	P	B	Say, Allen	Houghton Mifflin
El Greco	R	B	Venezia, Mike	Children's Press
Elaine	J	B	Stepping Stones	Nelson/Michaels
Eleanor	S	B	Cooney, Barbara	Puffin Books
Eleanor Roosevelt	P	B	Davis, Lucile	Capstone Press
Eleanor Roosevelt, A Life of Discovery	W	B	Freedman, Russell	Clarion Books

Title	Level	Genre	Author/Series	Publisher/Distributor
Eleanor Roosevelt: Fighter for Social Justice	O	B	Childhood of Famous Americans	Aladdin
Eleanor Roosevelt: First Lady of the World	R	B	Faber, Doris	The Penguin Group
Elizabeth Blackwell: First Woman Doctor	O	B	Greene, Carol	Children's Press
Elizabeth Blackwell: Girl Doctor	O	B	Henry, Joanne Landers	Simon & Schuster
Elizabeth Cady Stanton	P	B	Davis, Lucile	Capstone Press
Elizabeth the First: Queen of England	O	B	Greene, Carol	Children's Press
Emily Dickinson: American Poet	O	B	Greene, Carol	Children's Press
Escape From Slavery: Five Journeys to Freedom	Q	B	Rappaport, Doreen	HarperTrophy
Explorers: Women in Profile	T	B	Hacker, Carolotta	Crabtree
Extraordinary American Indians	W	B	Avery, Susan & Skinner, Linda	Children's Press
Extraordinary Black Americans: From Colonial to Contemporary Times	W	B	Altman, Susan	Children's Press
Extraordinary Jewish Americans	W	B	Brooks, Philip	Children's Press
Extraordinary People with Disabilities	W	B	Kent, D. & Quinlan, K. A.	Children's Press
Extraordinary Women in Politics	W	B	Gulatta, Charles	Children's Press
Extraordinary Women Journalists	W	B	Price-Groff, Claire	Children's Press
Extraordinary Women of Medicine	W	B	Stille, Darlene R.	Children's Press
Extraordinary Women of the American West	W	B	Alter, Judy	Children's Press
Extraordinary Women Scientists	W	B	Stille, Darlene R.	Children's Press
Extraordinary Young People	W	B	Brill, Marlene Targ	Children's Press
Farewell to Manzanar	Z	B	Houston, J.W. & Houston, J.D.	Houghton Mifflin
Finding Providence: The Story of Roger Williams	P	B	Avi	HarperTrophy
Fine Lines	O	B	Heller, Ruth	Richard C. Owen
Firetalking	O	B	Polacco, Patricia	Richard C. Owen
First Flight	K	B	Shea, George	HarperTrophy
First Ladies	U	B	Cornerstones of Freedom	Children's Press
First Ladies of the White House	U	B	Skarmeas, Nancy	Ideals Publications Inc.
First Ladies: Women Who Called the White House Home	U	B	Gormley, Beatrice	Scholastic
Five Brave Explorers	Q	B	Hudson, Wade	Scholastic
Five Brilliant Scientists	Q	B	Steward, Susan McKinney	Scholastic
Five Notable Inventors	Q	B	Hudson, Wade	Scholastic
Flight of the Union, The	L	B	White, Tekla	Carolrhoda Books
Florence Kelley	P	B	Saller, Carol	Carolrhoda Books
Florence Nightingale	P	B	Davis, Lucile	Capstone Press
Flying Ace: The Story of Amelia Earhart	P	B	Eyewitness Readers	DK Publishing
Flying Free: America's First Black Aviators	T	B	Hart, Philip S.	Lerner Publications
Frances Hodgson Burnett: Beyond the Secret Garden	U	B	Carpenter, A. S. & Shirley, Jean	Lerner Publications
Francisco Goya	R	B	Venezia, Mike	Children's Press
Franklin Delano Roosevelt	V	B	Freedman, Russell	Clarion
Frederick Douglass	P	B	McLoone, Margo	Capstone Press
Frederick Douglass: Fights For Freedom	M	B	Davidson, Margaret	Language for Learning Assoc.
Frederick Douglass: The Last Days of Slavery	R	B	Miller, William	Lee & Low Books
Frida Kahlo	R	B	Venezia, Mike	Children's Press
From Paper Airplanes to Outer Space	O	B	Simon, Seymour	Richard C. Owen
Frost in the Night, A: A Girlhood on the Eve of the Third Reich	X	B	Baer, Edith	Sunburst
Gail Devers: A Runner's Dream	L	B	Pair-It Books	Steck-Vaughn
George Handel	R	B	Venezia, Mike	Children's Press
George Washington	O	B	Early Biographies	Compass Point Books
George Washington	L	B	Pebble Books	Grolier, Capstone
George Washington: A Picture Book Biography	R	B	Giblin, James Cross	Scholastic
George Washington Carver	N	B	Biography	Benchmark Education
George Washington Carver	P	B	McLoone, Margo	Capstone Press
George Washington Carver: Scientist and Teacher	O	B	Greene, Carol	Children's Press
George Washington: The Man Who Would Not Be King	U	B	Krensky, Stephen	Scholastic
George Washington: Young Leader	O	B	Childhood of Famous Americans	Aladdin
George Washington: Young Leader	R	B	Santrey, Laurence	Troll
George Washington's Breakfast	P	B	Fritz, Jean	Putnam & Grosset

Title	Level	Genre	Author/Series	Publisher/Distributor
George Washington's Mother	M	B	Fritz, Jean	Scholastic
George Washington's Socks	T	B	Woodruff, Elvira	Language for Learning Assoc.
Georgia O'Keeffe	M	B	Lowery, Linda	Carolrhoda Books
Georgia O'Keeffe	R	B	Venezia, Mike	Children's Press
Girl From Yamhill, A	W	B	Cleary, Beverly	Bantam Doubleday Dell
Glorious Flight, The: Across the Channel with Louis Blériot	O	B	Provensen, Alice & Martin	Puffin Books
Go Free or Die: A Story About Harriet Tubman	R	B	Ferris, Jeri	Carolrhoda Books
Going for Gold!	P	B	Eyewitness Readers	DK Publishing
Going Solo	T	B	Dahl, Roald	Puffin Books
Good-Bye Marianne	T	B	Watts, Irene N.	Tundra Books
Grand Mothers: Poems, Reminiscences, and Short Stories About Keepers of Our Traditions	Y	B	Giovanni, Nikki	Henry Holt & Co.
Grandma Moses	N	B	Biography	Benchmark Education
Grandma Moses: Painter of Rural America	T	B	O'Neal, Zibby	The Penguin Group
Grant Wood	R	B	Venezia, Mike	Children's Press
Great African Americans in Business	T	B	Rediger, Pat	Crabtree
Great African Americans in Civil Rights	T	B	Rediger, Pat	Crabtree
Great African Americans in Entertainment	T	B	Rediger, Pat	Crabtree
Great African Americans in Film	T	B	Parker, Janice	Crabtree
Great African Americans in Government	T	B	Dudley, Karen	Crabtree
Great African Americans in History	T	B	Hacker, Carlotta	Crabtree
Great African Americans in Jazz	T	B	Hacker, Carlotta	Crabtree
Great African Americans in Literature	T	B	Rediger, Pat	Crabtree
Great African Americans in Music	T	B	Rediger, Pat	Crabtree
Great African Americans in Sports	T	B	Rediger, Pat	Crabtree
Great African Americans in the Arts	T	B	Hacker, Carlotta	Crabtree
Great African Americans in the Olympics	T	B	Hunter, Shaun	Crabtree
Great Houdini, The: World Famous Magician and Escape Artist	M	B	Kulling, Monica	Random House
Great Little Madison, The	X	B	Fritz, Jean	G.P. Putnam's Sons
Growing Ideas	O	B	Van Leeuwen, Jean	Richard C. Owen
Gwen Torrence	P	B	Stewart, Mark	Children's Press
Habibi	V	B	Nye, Naomi Shihab	Simon & Schuster
Hannibal	T	B	Green, Robert	Franklin Watts
Happy Birthday, Martin Luther King	L	B	Marzollo, Jean	Scholastic
Harriet Beecher Stowe and the Beecher Preachers	X	B	Fritz, Jean	The Penguin Group
Harriet Tubman	P	B	McLoone, Margo	Capstone Press
Harry Houdini: Master of Magic	R	B	Kraske, Robert	Scholastic
Harry Houdini: Young Magician	O	B	Childhood of Famous Americans	Aladdin
Hau Kola Hello Friend	O	B	Goble, Paul	Richard C. Owen
Head Full of Notions, A: A Story about Robert Fulton	S	B	Russell Bowen, Andy	Carolrhoda Books
Helen Keller	N	B	Davidson, Margaret	Scholastic
Helen Keller: A Light For The Blind	R	B	Kudlinski, Kathleen V.	The Penguin Group
Helen Keller: Courage in the Dark	N	B	Hurwitz, Johanna	Random House
Helen Keller: Crusader for the Blind and Deaf	P	B	Graff, Stewart & Polly Anne	Bantam Doubleday Dell
Helen Keller: From Tragedy to Triumph	O	B	Childhood of Famous Americans	Aladdin
Helen Keller's Teacher	N	B	Davidson, Margaret	Scholastic
Henri de Toulouse-Lautrec	R	B	Venezia, Mike	Children's Press
Henri Matisse	R	B	Venezia, Mike	Children's Press
Henri Rousseau	T	B	Rabott, Ernest	HarperTrophy
Henry Ford: Young Man with Ideas	O	B	Childhood of Famous Americans	Aladdin
Her Piano Sang: A Story About Clara Schumann	R	B	Allman, Barbara	Carolrhoda Books
Heroes & Idealists	U	B	Real Lives	Troll
Hillary Rodham Clinton: A New Kind of First Lady	S	B	Guernsey, JoAnn Bren	Lerner Publications
Homesick, My Own Story	X	B	Fritz, Jean	Penguin Books
Houdini's Last Trick	O	B	Hass, E.A.	Random House
House on Mango Street, The	W	B	Cisneros, Sandra	Alfred A. Knopf
Howard Carter: Searching for King Tut	S	B	Ford, Barbara	W. H. Freeman & Co.
I Am Rosa Parks	O	B	Parks, Rosa	Dial Books

Title	Level	Genre	Author/Series	Publisher/Distributor
I Have a Dream	Q	B	Davidson, Margaret	Scholastic
I Have Lived a Thousand Years	Y	B	Bitton-Jackson, Livia	Simon & Schuster
I Love the Beach	M	B	Literacy 2000	Rigby
I. M. Pei	M	B	Biography	Benchmark Education
Inn Keepers Apprentice	Z	B	Say, Allen	The Penguin Group
Invincible Louisa	Z	B	Meigs, Cornelia	Scholastic
Irrational Season, The	Z	B	L'Engle, Madeleine	Harper Collins
It Came From Ohio!: My Life as a Writer	R	B	Stine, R.L.	Scholastic
It Was On Fire When I Lay Down On It	Z	B	Fulghum, Robert	Ballantine Books
Jackie Robinson	O	B	Early Biographies	Compass Point Books
Jackie Robinson and the Breaking of the Color Barrier	S	B	Shorto, Russell	Millbrook Press
Jackie Robinson: Baseball's First Black Major Leaguer	O	B	Greene, Carol	Children's Press
Jackie Robinson Breaks the Color Line	V	B	Cornerstones of Freedom	Children's Press
Jacques Cousteau	L	B	Biography	Benchmark Education
Jane Addams	P	B	Community Builders	Children's Press
Jane Goodall and the Wild Chimpanzees	L	B	Birnbaum, Bette	Steck-Vaughn
Jean Craighead George	S	B	Cary, Alice	Learning Works, The
Jesse Jackson	P	B	Simon, Charnan	Children's Press
Jesse Owens: Olympic Hero	P	B	Sabin, Francene	Troll
Johann Sebastian Bach: Great Man of Music	O	B	Greene, Carol	Children's Press
John A Macdonald	W	B	Waite, Peter B.	Fitzhenry & Whiteside
John F. Kennedy	V	B	World Leaders: Past and Present	Chelsea House
John F. Kennedy: America's Youngest President	O	B	Childhood of Famous Americans	Aladdin
John James Audubon	M	B	Biography	Benchmark Education
John James Audubon: Wildlife Artist	V	B	A First Book	Franklin Watts
Kate Shelley and the Midnight Express	M	B	Wetterer, Margaret	Carolrhoda Books
Katherine Paterson	S	B	Cary, Alice	Learning Works, The
Ken Griffey Jr. & Ken Griffey Sr.	T	B	Star Families	Crestwood House
Kerri Strug: Heart of Gold	L	B	Strug, K. & Brown, G.	Scholastic
Kids at Work: Lewis Hine and the Crusade Against Child Labor	T	B	Freedman, Russell	Clarion
Knots in My Yo-yo String: The Autobiography of a Kid	U	B	Spinelli, Jerry	Alfred A. Knopf
Korky Paul: Biography of an Illustrator	M	B	Heapy, Teresa	Rigby
Lady Bird Johnson	Q	B	Simon, Charnan	Children's Press
Langston Hughes: An Illustrated Edition	X	B	Meltzer, Milton	Millbrook Press
Langston Hughes: Young Black Poet	O	B	Childhood of Famous Americans	Aladdin
Laura Ingalls Wilder	O	B	Allen, Thomas B.	Putnam
Laura Ingalls Wilder	K	B	Biography	Benchmark Education
Laura Ingalls Wilder	P	B	Blair, Gwenda & Allen, Thomas	Lerner Publishing Group
Laura Ingalls Wilder: A Biography	R	B	Anderson, William	HarperTrophy
Laura Ingalls Wilder: An Author's Story	N	B	Glasscock, Sarah	Steck-Vaughn
Laura Ingalls Wilder: Author of the Little House Books	O	B	Greene, Carol	Children's Press
Laura Ingalls Wilder: Growing Up in the Little House	P	B	Giff, Patricia Reilly	Puffin Books
Laura Ingalls Wilder, Pioneer Girl	R	B	Stine, Megan	Bantam Doubleday Dell
Leaders of the People	U	B	Real Lives	Troll
Leon's Story	T	B	Tillage, Leon Walter	Farrar, Straus and Giroux
Leonard Bernstein	R	B	Venezia, Mike	Children's Press
Leontyne Price: Opera Superstar	N	B	Williams, Sylvia B.	Children's Press
Letter from Fish Bay, A	N	B	Cowley, Joy	Pacific Learning
Letter From Phoenix Farm, A	O	B	Yolen, Jane	Richard C. Owen
Lewis and Clark	V	B	Cornerstones of Freedom	Children's Press
Life and Death of Martin Luther King, Jr.,The	Y	B	Haskins, James	Beech Tree
Life and Words of Martin Luther King, Jr., The	W	B	Peck, Ira	Scholastic
Lincoln: A Photobiography	V	B	Freedman, Russell	Clarion
Lion Dancer: Ernie Wan's Chinese New Year	N	B	Waters, K. & Slovenz-Low, M.	Scholastic
Lois Lowry	T	B	Markham, Lois	Learning Works, Inc.
Looking Back, A Book of Memories	X	B	Lowry, Lois	Delacorte Press
Lost Garden, The	W	B	Yep, Laurence	Beech Tree Books
Lost Star: The Story of Amelia Earhart	T	B	Lauber, Patricia	Language for Learning Assoc.
Lou Gehrig: One of Baseball's Greatest	O	B	Childhood of Famous Americans	Aladdin

Title	Level	Genre	Author/Series	Publisher/Distributor
Louis Armstrong	Z	B	Brown, Sandford	Franklin Watts
Louis Braille: Boy Who Invented Books for the Blind	N	B	Davidson, Margaret	Scholastic
Louis Pasteur	N	B	Biography	Benchmark Education
Louis Riell	W	B	Neering, Rosemary	Fitzhenry & Whiteside
Louisa May Alcott: Young Novelist	O	B	Childhood of Famous Americans	Aladdin
Luis Rodriguez	S	B	Schwartz, Michael	Steck-Vaughn
Luis W. Alvarez	R	B	Hispanic Stories	Steck-Vaughn
Luther Burbank	O	B	Faber, Doris	Garrard Publishing Co.
Make Way for Sam Houston	X	B	Fritz, Jean	Putnam & Grosset
Man Who Paints Nature, The	O	B	Locker, Thomas	Richard C. Owen
Man Who Was Poe, The	T	B	Avi	Avon
Marching to Freedom: The Story of Martin Luther King, Jr	P	B	Milton, Joyce	Bantam Doubleday Dell
Margaret Bourke-White	O	B	Welch, Catherine	Carolrhoda Books
Margaret Bourke-White: A Photographer's Life	P	B	Keller, Emily	Lerner Publications
Margaret Wise Brown	O	B	Greene, Carol	Children's Press
Maria Tallchief	R	B	Native American Stories	Steck-Vaughn
Marian Anderson: Singer	V	B	American Women of Achievement	Chelsea House
Marie Curie	O	B	Early Biographies	Compass Point Books
Mario Mixwell	M	B	Reimer, Luther	Wright Group/McGraw Hill
Mark Twain	W	B	Cox, Clinton	Scholastic
Mark Twain: Young Writer	O	B	Childhood of Famous Americans	Aladdin
Martha Washington: America's First First Lady	O	B	Childhood of Famous Americans	Aladdin
Martin Luther King	T	B	Bray, Rosemary L.	William Morrow
Martin Luther King, Jr.	L	B	Pebble Books	Grolier, Capstone
Martin Luther King, Jr., A Man Who Changed Things	O	B	Greene, Carol	Children's Press
Martin Luther King, Jr. and the March Toward Freedom	R	B	Hakim, Rita	The Millbrook Press
Martin Luther King, Jr.: Young Man with a Dream	O	B	Childhood of Famous Americans	Aladdin
Mary McLeod Bethune	U	B	Cornerstones of Freedom	Children's Press
Mary McLeod Bethune	O	B	Greenfield, Eloise	HarperTrophy
Mary McLeod Bethune-Voice of Black Hope	S	B	Meltzer. Milton	Puffin Books
Mary Todd Lincoln: Girl of the Bluegrass	O	B	Childhood of Famous Americans	Aladdin
Mathew Brady: Civil War Photographer	T	B	A First Book	Franklin Watts
Matthew Henson	L	B	Biography	Benchmark Education
Matthew Henson: Arctic Explorer	O	B	Podojil, Catherine	Wright Group/McGraw Hill
May Chinn: The Best Medicine	U	B	Butts, Ellen & Schwartz, Joyce	W. H. Freeman and Co.
Maya Angelou: Greeting the Morning	W	B	King, Sarah E.	The Millbrook Press
Maya Angelou: Journey of the Heart	X	B	Pettit, Jayne	Puffin Books
Meet Abraham Lincoln	O	B	Cary, Barbara	Step-Up Books
Meet Benjamin Franklin	O	B	Scarf, Maggi	Step-Up Books
Meet George Washington	O	B	Heilbroner, Joan	Random House
Meet Hillary Rodham Clinton	Q	B	Spain, Valerie	Random House
Meet John F. Kennedy	Q	B	White, Nancy Bean	Random House
Meet Martin Luther King, Jr.	R	B	de Kay, James T.	Random House
Meet the Villarreals	M	B	Kratky, Lada Josefa	Hampton-Brown
Meet Thomas Jefferson	O	B	Barrett, Marvin	Step-Up Books
Mei Fuh: Memories From China	P	B	Schaeffer, Edith	Houghton Mifflin
Memories of Anne Frank	X	B	Gold, Alison Leslie	Scholastic
Michael Jordan	Q	B	Lovitt, Chip	Scholastic
Milton Hershey: Chocolate King Town Builder	P	B	Simon, Charnan	Children's Press
Miracle Worker, The	Z	B	Gibson, William	Bantam Doubleday Dell
Molly Pitcher: Young Patriot	O	B	Childhood of Famous Americans	Aladdin
Monet	R	B	Venezia, Mike	Children's Press
Moon Over Tennessee: A Boy's Civil War Journal	W	B	Crist-Evans, Craig	Houghton Mifflin
Mountain Man and the President, The	Q	B	First Reports	Compass Point Books
Mr. President: A Book of U.S. Presidents	S	B	Sullivan, George	Scholastic
My First Book of Biographies: Great Men and Women Every Child Should Know	P	B	Marzollo, Jean	Scholastic
My Life in Dog Years	S	B	Paulsen, Gary	Bantam Doubleday Dell

Title	Level	Genre	Author/Series	Publisher/Distributor
My Mysterious World	O	B	Mahy, Margaret	Richard C. Owen
My Own Two Feet	W	B	Cleary, Beverly	Avon
My Writing Day	O	B	Adler, David A.	Richard C. Owen
Mysterious Ocean Highway: Benjamin Franklin and the Gulf Stream	T	B	Heiligman, Deborah	Steck-Vaughn
Nadia Comaneci	M	B	Cole, Sally	Wright Group/McGraw Hill
Nature! Wild and Wonderful	O	B	Pringle, Laurence	Richard C. Owen
Neil Armstrong: Young Flyer	O	B	Childhood of Famous Americans	Aladdin
Nellie McClung	W	B	Benham, Mary Lile	Fitzhenry & Whiteside
Nelson Mandela	Q	B	First Biographies	Steck-Vaughn
Nelson Mandela: Freedom for South Africa	R	B	Dell, Pamela	Children's Press
Nelson Mandela "No Easy Walk To Freedom"	X	B	Denenberg, Barry	Scholastic
Nelson Mandela: South Africa's Silent Voice of Protest	X	B	Hargrove, Jim	Children's Press
Never Cry Wolf	Z	B	Mowat, Farley	Bantam Doubleday Dell
Never Turn Back: Father Serra's Mission	S	B	Rawls, Jim	Steck-Vaughn
New Kids In Town	Y	B	Bode, Janet	Scholastic
No Pretty Pictures: A Child of War	Z	B	Lobel, Anita	Greenwillow Books
Nobel Prize Winners	T	B	Hacker, Carlotta	Crabtree
Norman Rockwell	T	B	Cohen, Joel H.	Grolier Publishing
Not Guilty	X	B	Sullivan, George	Scholastic
Oddballs	X	B	Sleator, William	Puffin Books
Once Upon a Time	O	B	Bunting, Eve	Richard C. Owen
One Man Show	O	B	Asch, Frank	Richard C. Owen
One More River to Cross	X	B	Haskins, Jim	Scholastic
Oprah Winfrey, A Voice for the People	U	B	Brooks, Philip	Grolier Publishing
Ordinary Genius, The Story of Albert Einstein	U	B	McPherson, Stephanie S.	The Lerner Group
Osceola: Patriot and Warrior	T	B	Jumper, Moses & Sonder, Ben	Steck-Vaughn
Out of Darkness: The Story of Louis Braille	S	B	Freedman, Russell	Houghton Mifflin
Overcoming Challenges: The Life of Charles F Bolden, Jr	Q	B	Walton, Darwin McBeth	Steck-Vaughn
Owl Moon	O	B	Yolen, Jane	Scholastic
Pablo Picasso	P	B	Lowery, Linda	Lerner Publishing Group
Paul Cezanne	Q	B	Venezia, Mike	Childrens Press
Paul Gauguin	Q	B	Venezia, Mike	Childrens Press
Paul Klee	Q	B	Venezia, Mike	Childrens Press
Paul Revere	V	B	Cornerstones of Freedom	Childrens Press
Peter Tchaikovsky	Q	B	Venezia, Mike	Childrens Press
Picasso	Q	B	Venezia, Mike	Childrens Press
Picture Book of Abraham Lincoln, A	M	B	Adler, David A.	Holiday House
Picture Book of Amelia Earhart, A	M	B	Adler, David A.	Holiday House
Picture Book of Anne Frank, A	M	B	Adler, David A.	Holiday House
Picture Book of Benjamin Franklin, A	M	B	Adler, David A.	Holiday House
Picture Book of Christopher Columbus, A	M	B	Adler, David A.	Holiday House
Picture Book of Davy Crockett, A	M	B	Adler, David A.	Holiday House
Picture Book of Eleanor Roosevelt, A	M	B	Adler, David A.	Holiday House
Picture Book of Florence Nightingale, A	M	B	Adler, David A.	Holiday House
Picture Book of Frederick Douglass, A	M	B	Adler, David A.	Holiday House
Picture Book of George Washington, A	M	B	Adler, David A.	Holiday House
Picture Book of George Washington Carver, A	M	B	Adler, David A.	Holiday House
Picture Book of Harriet Tubman, A	M	B	Adler, David A.	Holiday House
Picture Book of Helen Keller, A	M	B	Adler, David A.	Holiday House
Picture Book of Jackie Robinson, A	M	B	Adler, David A.	Holiday House
Picture Book of Jesse Owens, A	N	B	Adler, David A.	Holiday House
Picture Book of John F. Kennedy, A	N	B	Adler, David A.	Holiday House
Picture Book of Louis Braille, A	M	B	Adler, David A.	Holiday House
Picture Book of Martin Luther King, Jr., A	M	B	Adler, David A.	Holiday House
Picture Book of Patrick Henry, A	M	B	Adler, David A.	Holiday House
Picture Book of Paul Revere, A	M	B	Adler, David A.	Holiday House
Picture Book of Robert E. Lee, A	N	B	Adler, David A.	Holiday House
Picture Book of Rosa Parks, A	M	B	Adler, David A.	Holiday House

Title	Level	Genre	Author/Series	Publisher/Distributor
Picture Book of Sacagawea, A	M	B	Adler, David A.	Holiday House
Picture Book of Simon Bolivar, A	Q	B	Adler, David A.	Bantam Doubleday Dell
Picture Book of Sitting Bull, A	M	B	Adler, David A.	Holiday House
Picture Book of Sojourner Truth, A	M	B	Adler, David A.	Holiday House
Picture Book of Thomas Alva Edison, A	M	B	Adler, David A.	Holiday House
Picture Book of Thomas Jefferson, A	M	B	Adler, David A.	Holiday House
Picture Book of Thurgood Marshall, A	M	B	Adler, David A.	Holiday House
Pierre August Renoir	Q	B	Venezia, Mike	Childrens Press
Pigman & Me, The	Z	B	Zindel, Paul	Dell
Pioneer Girl, The Story of Laura Ingalls Wilder	R	B	Anderson, William	Harper Collins
Place To Hide, A	X	B	Petit, Jayne	Scholastic
Playing with Words	O	B	Howe, James	Richard C. Owen
Pocketful of Goobers: Story of George Washington Carver	Q	B	Mitchell, Barbara	Carolrhoda Books
Pride of Puerto Rico: The Life of Roberto Clemente	W	B	Walker, Paul Robert	Harcourt Brace
Prince William	Q	B	Rand, Gloria	Henry Holt & Company
Queen Eleanor: Independent Spirit in the Medieval World	X	B	Brooks, Polly Schoyer	Houghton Mifflin
Red Scarf Girl: Memoir of the Cultural Revolution	Z	B	Jiang, Ji Li	HarperTrophy
Revolutionary Poet: A Story About Phillis Wheatley	Q	B	Weidt, Maryann N.	Carolrhoda Books
Rising Stars of the NBA	P	B	Layden, Joe	Scholastic
Road to Seneca Falls, The	R	B	Swain, Gwenyth	Carolrhoda Books
Robert Goddard	K	B	Schaefer, Lola M.	Capstone Press
Rosa Parks	P	B	Greenfield, Eloise	HarperTrophy
Rosa Parks: My Story	U	B	Parks, Rosa	Scholastic
Rough Riders, The	W	B	Cornerstones of Freedom	Children's Press
Sacajawea	N	B	Biography	Benchmark Education
Sacajawea	Y	B	Bruchac, Joseph	Harcourt
Sarah Morton Daniel's Day: Day in the Life of, A	Q	B	Waters, Kate	Scholastic
Secret Soldier, The: The Story of Deborah Sampson	O	B	McGovern, Ann	Scholastic
Seeing the Circle	O	B	Bruchac, Joseph	Richard C. Owen
Seekers of Truth	U	B	Real Lives	Troll
Shark Lady: The Adventures of Eugenie Clark	O	B	McGovern, Ann	Scholastic
Shoes for Everyone: A Story About Jan Matzeliger	R	B	Mitchell, Barbara	Carolrhoda Books
Sojourner Truth	P	B	McLoone, Margo	Capstone Press
Sojourner Truth: Ain't I a Woman?	V	B	McKissack, F. and P.	Scholastic
Somehow Tenderness Survives: Stories of Southern Africa	X	B	Rochman, Hazel	HarperTrophy
Squanto: Friend of the Pilgrims	O	B	Bulla, Clyde Robert	Scholastic
Standing Tall: The Stories of Ten Hispanic Americans	S	B	Palacios, Argentina	Scholastic
Stealing Home: The Story of Jackie Robinson	V	B	Denenberg, Barry	Scholastic
Story of Alexander Graham Bell, Inventor of the Telephone	O	B	Davidson, Margaret	Scholastic
Story of Benjamin Franklin, Amazing American	O	B	Davidson, Margaret	Scholastic
Story of Doña Chila, The	P	B	Moore, Eva	Scholastic
Story of George Washington Carver, The	Q	B	Moore, Eva	Bantam Doubleday Dell
Story of Geronimo, The	T	B	Cornerstones of Freedom	Children's Press
Story of Harriet Tubman: Freedom, The	U	B	Sterling, Dorothy	Bantam Doubleday Dell
Story of Harriet Tubman, The: Conductor of the Underground Railroad	S	B	McMullan, Kate	Scholastic
Story of Jackie Robinson, Bravest Man in Baseball	O	B	Davidson, Margaret	Scholastic
Story of Laura Ingalls Wilder, Pioneer Girl, The	Q	B	Stine, Megan	Bantam Doubleday Dell
Story of Muhammad Ali: Heavyweight Champion of the World, The	S	B	Denenberg, Barry	Dell Publishing
Story of Ruby Bridges, The	O	B	Coles, Robert	Scholastic
Story of Thomas Alva Edison, Inventor, The	R	B	Davidson, Margaret	Scholastic
Story of Walt Disney, Maker of Magical Worlds, The	O	B	Selden, Bernice	Bantam Doubleday Dell
Story Teller's Story, A	O	B	Martin, Rafe	Richard C. Owen
Summer of the Great-Grandmother, The	Z	B	L'Engle, Madeleine	Harper Collins

Title	Level	Genre	Author/Series	Publisher/Distributor
Summer Wheels	O	B	Bunting, Eve	Harcourt Brace
Suprising Myself	O	B	Fritz, Jean	Richard C. Owen
Susan B. Anthony	P	B	Davis, Lucile	Capstone Press
Susan B. Anthony: Champion of Women's Rights	R	B	Monsell, Helen Albee	Simon & Schuster
Susanna of the Alamo	T	B	Jakes, John	Language for Learning Assoc.
Talking to Faith Ringgold	S	B	Ringgold, F.,Freeman, L.&Roucher,N.	Crown Publishers, Inc.
Tarantula in My Purse, The	U	B	George, Jean Craighead	Harper Collins
Tecumseh	V	B	Cornerstones of Freedom	Children's Press
Tell Me a Story	O	B	London, Jonathan	Richard C. Owen
Terror In the Towers	O	B	Kerson, Adrian	Random House
Thank You, Jackie Robinson	P	B	Cohen, Barbara	Scholastic
These Lands Are Ours: Tecumseh's Fight For the Old Northwest	T	B	Connell, Kate	Steck-Vaughn
They Led The Way: 14 American Women	O	B	Johnston, Johanna	Scholastic
They Shall Be Heard: Susan B. Anthony Elizabeth Cady Stanton	T	B	Connell, Kate	Steck-Vaughn
Thomas Alva Edison: Great Inventor	Q	B	Levinson, Nancy Smiler	Scholastic
Thomas Edison	P	B	Linder, Greg	Capstone Press
Thomas Jefferson: Author, Inventor, President	N	B	Rookie Biographies	Children's Press
Thomas Jefferson: Man with a Vision	U	B	Crisman, Ruth	Scholastic
Thoughts, Pictures, and Words	O	B	Kuskin, Karla	Richard C. Owen
Thurgood Marshall: First Black Supreme Court Justice	N	B	Rookie Biographies	Children's Press
Tiger Woods: An American Master	R	B	Edwards, Nicholas	Scholastic
To the Top!: Climbing the World's Highest Mountain	N	B	Kramer, S. A.	Random House
Tom Edison's Bright Idea	N	B	Keller, Jack	Steck-Vaughn
Tom Sawyer	J	B	Hall, Richard	Rigby
Traitor: The Case of Benedict Arnold	X	B	Fritz, Jean	Putnam & Grosset
Travels with Rainie Marie	S	B	Martin, Patricia	Hyperion
Trip to Freedom	M	B	Nguyen, Andrea Quynhgiao	Rigby
True Stories about Abraham Lincoln	O	B	Gross, Ruth Belov	Scholastic
Two-Part Invention	Z	B	L'Engle, Madeleine	Harper Collins
Under My Nose	O	B	Ehlert, Lois	Richard C. Owen
Vacation Journal, A	M	B	Discovery World	Rigby
Walking the Road to Freedom:A Story About Sojourner Truth	Q	B	Ferris, Jeri	Dell
Wanted Dead or Alive: The True Story of Harriet Tubman	P	B	McGovern, Ann	Scholastic
Water Buffalo Days	P	B	Nhuong, Huynh Quang	HarperTrophy
Way West, The: Journal of a Pioneer Woman	R	B	Knight, Amelia Stewart	Simon & Schuster
What Are You Figuring Now?	P	B	Ferris, Jeri	Scholastic
What's the Big Idea, Ben Franklin?	O	B	Fritz, Jean	Scholastic
When Justice Failed: The Fred Korematsu Story	U	B	Chin, Steven A.	Steck-Vaughn
Where Do You Think You're Going, Christopher Columbus?	S	B	Fritz, Jean	Putnam & Grosset
Where Was Patrick Henry on the 29th of May?	R	B	Fritz, Jean	Scholastic
Why Don't You Get a Horse, Sam Adams?	R	B	Fritz, Jean	G.P. Putnam's Sons
Wilfrid Laurier	W	B	Spigelman, Martin	Fitzhenry & Whiteside
Will Rogers	O	B	Schott, Jane A.	Carolrhoda Books
Wilma Mankiller	P	B	Lowery, Linda	Carolrhoda Books
Winterdance: The Fine Madness of Running the Iditarod	W	B	Paulsen, Gary	Harcourt Brace
Women Inventors	O	B	Blashfield, Jean	Capstone Press
Women of Valor	U	B	Real Lives	Troll
Women Who Shaped the West	V	B	Cornerstones of Freedom	Children's Press
Woodsong	T	B	Paulsen, Gary	Dell
Wordful Child, A	O	B	Lyon, George Ella	Richard C. Owen
Wright Brothers at Kitty Hawk, The	K	B	Schaefer, Lola M.	Capstone Press
Wright Brothers, The	M	B	Biography	Benchmark Education
Wright Brothers, The	Y	B	Freedman, Russell	Holiday House

Title	Level	Genre	Author/Series	Publisher/Distributor
Wright Brothers, The	U	B	Sobol, Donald J.	Scholastic
Writer of the Plains: A Story about Willa Cather	Q	B	Streissguth, Tom	Carolrhoda Books
Writing Bug, The	O	B	Hopkins, Lee Bennett	Richard C. Owen
You Want Women to Vote, Lizzie Stanton?	W	B	Fritz, Jean	The Penguin Group
Young Arthur Ashe: Brave Champion	L	B	First Start Biography	Troll
Young Clara Barton: Battlefield Nurse	L	B	First Start Biography	Troll
Young Jackie Robinson: Baseball Hero	L	B	First Start Biography	Troll
Young Mozart	O	B	Isadora, Rachel	The Penguin Group
Young Rosa Parks: Civil Rights Heroine	L	B	First Start Biography	Troll
Young Thurgood Marshall: Fighter for Equality	L	B	First Start Biography	Troll
Zlata's Diary	X	B	Filipovic, Zlata	Puffin Books
13th Floor, The: A Ghost Story	U	F	Fleischman, Sid	Bantam Doubleday Dell
5 Novels	V	F	Pinkwater, Daniel	Farrar, Straus and Giroux
Abel's Island	T	F	Steig, William	Farrar Straus and Giroux
Ace: The Very Important Pig	R	F	King-Smith, Dick	Knopf
Adventures of Ratman	M	F	Weiss, Ellen & Freidman, Mel	Random House
Adventures of Snail at School	J	F	Stadler, John	HarperTrophy
Afternoon of the Elves	S	F	Lisle, Janet Taylor	Scholastic
Afternoon on the Amazon	M	F	Osborne, Mary Pope	Random House
Agnes the Sheep	R	F	Taylor, William	Bantam Doubleday Dell
Alexander and the Wind-Up Mouse	L	F	Lionni, Leo	Scholastic
Alice in Wonderland	V	F	Carroll, Lewis	Scholastic
Alien in the Classroom	N	F	Keene, Carolyn	Pocket Books
Aliens Ate My Homework	Q	F	Coville, Bruce	Pocket Books
Aliens Don't Wear Braces	M	F	Dadey, D. & Jones, M. T.	Scholastic
Aliens for Breakfast	M	F	Etra, J. & Spinner, S.	Random House
Aliens for Dinner	M	F	Spinner, Stephanie	Random House
Aliens for Lunch	M	F	Spinner, S. & Etra, J.	Random House
Alligator Tails and Crocodile Cakes	K	F	Moon, Nicola	Wright Group/McGraw Hill
Amanda Joins the Circus	R	F	Avi	Bantam Doubleday Dell
Amanda Pig and Her Big Brother Oliver	L	F	Van Leeuwen, Jean	Puffin Books
Amber Spyglass, The	Z	F	Pullman, Phillip	Alfred A. Knopf
Amelia Bedelia	L	F	Parish, Peggy	HarperTrophy
Amelia Bedelia and the Baby	L	F	Parish, Peggy	Harper & Row
Amelia Bedelia and the Surprise Shower	L	F	Parish, Peggy	Harper & Row
Amelia Bedelia Goes Camping	L	F	Parish, Peggy	Avon Camelot
Amelia Bedelia Helps Out	L	F	Parish, Peggy	Avon Camelot
Amelia Bedelia's Family Album	L	F	Parish, Peggy	Avon Books
Amigo	O	F	Baylor, Byrd	Aladdin
Amos and the Alien	R	F	Paulsen, Gary	Bantam Doubleday Dell
Amos Gets Famous	R	F	Paulsen, Gary	Bantam Doubleday Dell
Amos Gets Married	R	F	Paulsen, Gary	Bantam Doubleday Dell
Amos Goes Bananas	R	F	Paulsen, Gary	Bantam Doubleday Dell
Amos's Killer Concert Caper	R	F	Paulsen, Gary	Bantam Doubleday Dell
An Acceptable Time	X	F	L'Engle, Madeleine	Laurel-Leaf Books
Angels Don't Know Karate	M	F	Dadey, D. & Jones, M. T.	Scholastic
Animal Farm	Z	F	Orwell, George	Harcourt Brace
Animal Stories by Young Writers	R	F	Rubel, William and Mandel, Gerry	Tricycle Press
Are All The Giants Dead?	V	F	Norton, Mary	Harcourt Brace
Arguments	K	F	Read Alongs	Rigby
Ariel of the Sea	U	F	Calhoun, Dia	Winslow Press
Arkadians, The	W	F	Alexander, Lloyd	Puffin Books
Arthur Accused!	M	F	Brown, Marc	Little, Brown & Co.
Arthur and the Big Blow-Up	M	F	Brown, Marc	Little, Brown & Co.
Arthur and the Cootie-Catcher	M	F	Brown, Marc	Little, Brown & Co.
Arthur and the Crunch Cereal Contest	M	F	Brown, Marc	Little, Brown & Co.
Arthur and the Lost Diary	M	F	Brown, Marc	Little, Brown & Co.
Arthur and the Popularity Test	M	F	Brown, Marc	Little, Brown & Co.
Arthur and the Scare-Your-Pants-Off Club	M	F	Brown, Marc	Little, Brown & Co.
Arthur and the TL Contest	M	F	Brown, Marc	Little, Brown & Co.

Title	Level	Genre	Author/Series	Publisher/Distributor
Arthur Makes the Team	M	F	Brown, Marc	Little, Brown & Co.
Arthur Rocks with BINKY	M	F	Brown, Marc	Little, Brown & Co.
Arthur's Back to School Day	K	F	Hoban, Lillian	HarperTrophy
Arthur's Camp-Out	K	F	Hoban, Lillian	HarperTrophy
Arthur's Christmas Cookies	K	F	Hoban, Lillian	HarperTrophy
Arthur's Funny Money	K	F	Hoban, Lillian	HarperTrophy
Arthur's Great Big Valentine	K	F	Hoban, Lillian	HarperTrophy
Arthur's Honey Bear	K	F	Hoban, Lillian	Harper Collins
Arthur's Loose Tooth	K	F	Hoban, Lillian	Harper Collins
Arthur's Mystery Envelope	M	F	Brown, Marc	Little, Brown & Co.
Arthur's Pen Pal	K	F	Hoban, Lillian	Harper Collins
Arthur's Prize Reader	K	F	Hoban, Lillian	HarperTrophy
Ask Mr. Bear	J	F	Flack, Marjorie	Macmillan
Asteroid, The	M	F	PM Gold	Rigby
Aunt Eater Loves a Mystery	J	F	Cushman, Doug	HarperTrophy
Aunt Eater's Mystery Christmas	J	F	Cushman, Doug	HarperTrophy
Aunt Eater's Mystery Vacation	J	F	Cushman, Doug	HarperTrophy
Awake and Dreaming	S	F	Person, Kit	Puffin Books
Babe the Gallant Pig	R	F	King-Smith, Dick	Random House
Baby Sister for Frances, A	K	F	Hoban, Lillian	Scholastic
Back To The Titanic!	S	F	Gormley, Beatrice	Scholastic
Backward Bird Dog, The	R	F	Wallace, Bill	Bantam Doubleday Dell
Bad Beginning, The	V	F	Snicket, Lemony	HarperTrophy
Bad Spell for the Worst Witch, A	P	F	Murphy, Jill	Puffin Books
Bad-Luck Penny, The	L	F	O'Connor, Jane	Grosset & Dunlap
Banished, The	W	F	Levin, Betty	William Morrow
Bargain For Frances, A	K	F	Hoban, Russell	HarperTrophy
Barn Party	K	F	O'Brien, Claire	Wright Group/McGraw Hill
Barrel in the Basement, The	R	F	Wallace, Barbara Brooks	Aladdin
Barrel of Gold, A	K	F	Story Box	Wright Group/McGraw Hill
Bat-Poet, The	S	F	Jarrell, Randall	HarperCollins
Battle for the Castle, The	P	F	Winthrop, Elizabeth	Yearling
Be Ready at Eight	K	F	Parish, Peggy	Simon & Schuster
Bear at the Beach	K	F	Carmichael, Clay	North-South Books
Bear Called Paddington, A	T	F	Bond, Michael	Bantam Doubleday Dell
Bear Goes to Town	K	F	Browne, Anthony	Doubleday
Bear Shadow	J	F	Asch, Frank	Simon & Schuster
Bear's Bargain	J	F	Asch, Frank	Scholastic
Bears' Christmas	M	F	Berenstain, Stan, & Jan	Random House
Bears' Picnic	M	F	Berenstain, Stan, & Jan	Random House
Beautiful Pig	J	F	Read Alongs	Rigby
Bedtime for Frances	K	F	Hoban, Russell	Scholastic
Behind the Couch	N	F	Gerstein, Mordicai	Hyperion
Bell, the Book, and the Spellbinder, The	S	F	Strickland, Brad	Puffin Books
Berenstain Bear Scouts and the Coughing Catfish	M	F	Berenstain, Stan & Jan	Scholastic
Berenstain Bear Scouts Ghost Versus Ghost	P	F	Berenstain, Stan, & Jan	Scholastic
Berenstain Bears and the Ghost of the Auto Graveyard, The	M	F	Berenstain, Stan & Jan	Random House
Berenstain Bears & the Missing Honey	M	F	Berenstain, Stan, & Jan	Random House
Berlioz The Bear	N	F	Brett, Jan	Scholastic
Best Friends for Frances	K	F	Hoban, Russell	HarperTrophy
Best Little Monkeys in the World, The	J	F	Standiford, Natalie	Random House
Best Nest	J	F	Eastman, P.D.	Random House
Better Brown Stories, The	T	F	Ahlberg, Allan	The Penguin Group
Beyond the Burning Lands	U	F	Christopher, John	Aladdin
BFG, The	U	F	Dahl, Roald	The Penguin Group
Big Al	L	F	Yoshi, Andrew C.	Scholastic
Big Beet, The	L	F	Ready Readers	Pearson Learning
Big Chase, The	M	F	SupaDoopers	Sundance
Big Max	J	F	Platt, Kin	HarperTrophy

Title	Level	Genre	Author/Series	Publisher/Distributor
Big Orange Spot, The	L	F	Pinkwater, Daniel Manus	Scholastic
Big Prize, The	K	F	Adventures in Reading	Dominie
Big Race, the	N	F	Pye, Trevor	Pacific Learning
Big Sneeze, The	K	F	Brown, Ruth	Lothrop
Big Toe Robbery, The	N	F	PM Ruby	Rigby
Bigfoot Doesn't Square Dance	M	F	Dadey, D. & Jones, M. T.	Scholastic
Billy the Ghost and Me	L	F	Greer, Gery & Ruddick, Bob	HarperTrophy
Birthday for Frances, A	K	F	Hoban, Russell	Scholastic
Blackboard Bear	J	F	Alexander, Martha	The Penguin Group
Blue Sword, The	Y	F	McKinley, Robin	Puffin Books
Bobo's Magic Wishes	L	F	Little Readers	Houghton Mifflin
Bogeymen Don't Play Football	M	F	Dadey, D. & Jones, M. T.	Scholastic
Boggart and the Monster, The	U	F	Cooper, Susan	Aladdin
Boggart, The	U	F	Cooper, Susan	Simon & Schuster
Bony-Legs	K	F	Cole, Joanna	Scholastic
Book of Monsters: Tales to Give You the Creeps	T	F	Coville, Bruce	Scholastic
Book of Spine Tinglers: Tales To Make You Shiver	T	F	Coville, Bruce	Scholastic
Book of Three, The	U	F	Alexander, Lloyd	Bantam Doubleday Dell
Borrowers, The	S	F	Norton, Mary	Harcourt Brace
Boy and His Donkey, A	K	F	Literacy 2000	Rigby
Boy Who Cried Bigfoot, The	N	F	The Zack Files	Grossett&Dunlap
Boy Who Stretched to the Sky, The	M	F	Book Bank	Wright Group/McGraw Hill
Boy Who Turned Into a T.V. Set, The	L	F	Manes, Stephen	Avon Camelot
Brachiosaurus in the River	L	F	Wesley & The Dinosaurs	Wright Group/McGraw Hill
Brain-in-a-Box	M	F	Matthews, Steve	Sundance
Bravo Amelia Bedelia!	L	F	Parish, Herman	Avon
Bread and Jam for Frances	K	F	Hoban, Russell	Scholastic
Bright Shadow	T	F	Avi	Aladdin
Bringing the Sea Back Home	L	F	Literacy 2000	Rigby
Brith The Terrible	M	F	Literacy 2000	Rigby
Bubbling Crocodile	K	F	Pacific Literacy	Pacific Learning
Buffalo Before Breakfast	M	F	Osborne, Mary Pope	Random House
Bug Off!	L	F	Dussling, Jennifer	Grosset & Dunlap
Bull in a China Shop, A	K	F	Literacy 2000	Rigby
Bumps in the Night	K	F	Allard, Harry	Bantam Doubleday Dell
Bunnicula	Q	F	Howe, James	Avon
Bunnicula Strikes Again!	Q	F	Howe, James	Simon & Schuster
Bunny Runs Away	K	F	Chardiet, B. & Maccarone, G.	Scholastic
Buried Eye, The	M	F	Schultz, Irene	Wright Group/McGraw Hill
Bush Bunyip, The	J	F	Book Shop	Mondo
Buster Baxter, Cat Saver	M	F	Brown, Marc	Little, Brown & Co.
Buster Makes the Grade	M	F	Brown, Marc	Little, Brown & Co.
Buster's Dino Dilemma	M	F	Brown, Marc	Little, Brown & Co.
Buzby	J	F	Hoban, Julia	HarperTrophy
Camel Called Bump-Along, A	K	F	Evangeline Nicholas Collection	Wright Group/McGraw Hill
Canyons	V	F	Paulsen, Gary	Laurel-Leaf Books
Caps for Sale	K	F	Slobodkina, Esphyr	Harper & Row
Captain Bumble	K	F	Story Box	Wright Group/McGraw Hill
Captain Felonius	L	F	Literacy 2000	Rigby
Carlita Ropes the Twister	L	F	Pair-It Books	Steck-Vaughn
Carolina Crow Girl	T	F	Hobbs, Valerie	Puffin Books
Carrots Don't Talk!	J	F	Ready Readers	Pearson Learning
Case of the Measled Cowboy, The	P	F	Erickson, John R.	Puffin Books
Case of the Midnight Rustler, The	P	F	Erickson, John R.	Puffin Books
Case of the Missing Cat, The	P	F	Erickson, John R.	Puffin Books
Case of the Two Masked Robbers, The	K	F	Hoban, Lillian	HarperTrophy
Cassidy's Magic	S	F	Literacy 2000	Rigby
Castle in the Attic, The	R	F	Winthrop, Elizabeth	Bantam Doubleday Dell
Castle of Llyr, The	W	F	Alexander, Lloyd	Dell
Cat Burglar of Pethaven Drive, The	N	F	Literacy 2000	Rigby

Title	Level	Genre	Author/Series	Publisher/Distributor
Cat Concert	J	F	Literacy 2000	Rigby
Cat in the Hat	J	F	Seuss, Dr.	Random House
Cat Walk	R	F	Stolz, Mary	Bantam Doubleday Dell
Cat Who Went To Heaven, The	S	F	Coatsworth, Elizabeth	Aladdin
Cat Who Wore a Pot on Her Head, The	N	F	Slepian, Jan & Seidler, Ann	Scholastic
Cat's Meow, The	O	F	Soto, Gary	Scholastic
Cats' Burglar, The	K	F	Parish, Peggy	Hearst
Catwings	N	F	Le Guin, Ursula K.	Scholastic
Catwings Return	N	F	Le Guin, Ursula K.	Scholastic
Celery Stalks at Midnight, The	R	F	Howe, James	Atheneum
Chancy and the Grand Rascal	R	F	Fleischman, Sid	Beech Tree
Charlie	L	F	Literacy 2000	Rigby
Charlie and the Chocolate Factory	R	F	Dahl, Roald	Bantam Doubleday Dell
Charlie and the Great Glass Elevator	R	F	Dahl, Roald	Bantam Doubleday Dell
Charlie Malarkey and the Singing Moose	R	F	Kennedy, William & Brendan	Puffin Books
Charlotte's Web	R	F	White, E. B.	HarperTrophy
Cheerful King, The	K	F	Little Books	Sadlier-Oxford
Chester Cricket's New Home	S	F	Selden, George	Bantam Doubleday Dell
Chester Cricket's Pigeon Ride	S	F	Selden, George	Bantam Doubleday Dell
Chester the Wizard	M	F	Reading Unlimited	Celebration Press
Chicken Soup with Rice	M	F	Sendak, Maurice	Harper Collins
Children of Green Knowe, The	T	F	Boston, L.M.	Harcourt Brace
Chipmunk at Hollow Tree Lane	K	F	Sherrow, Victoria	Scholastic
Chocolate Fever	O	F	Smith, Robert	Bantam Doubleday Dell
Chocolate Touch, The	N	F	Catling, Patrick Skene	Bantam Doubleday Dell
Christina's Ghost	R	F	Wright, Betty Ren	Bantam Doubleday Dell
Chug the Tractor	K	F	PM Story Books	Rigby
City of Gold & Lead, The	V	F	Christopher, John	Aladdin
Civil War on Sunday	M	F	Osborner, Mary Pope	Random House
Clarence the Crocodile	L	F	New Way: Literature	Steck-Vaughn
Class Trip to the Cave of Doom	Q	F	McMullan, K.H.	Grosset & Dunlap
Clever Mr. Brown	K	F	Story Box	Wright Group/McGraw Hill
Clifford, the Big Red Dog	K	F	Bridwell, Norman	Scholastic
Clifford, the Small Red Puppy	K	F	Bridwell, Norman	Scholastic
Clockwork	Z	F	Pullman, Philip	Scholastic
Cloud Catcher	P	F	Jernigan, E. Wesley	Rigby
Cloudy With a Chance of Meatballs	M	F	Barrett, Judi	Atheneum Books
Cobwebs, Elephants, and Stars	M	F	Sunshine	Wright Group/McGraw Hill
Color Wizard, The	J	F	Bank Street	Bantam Doubleday Dell
Come Back, Amelia Bedelia	L	F	Parish, Peggy	Harper & Row
Commander Toad and the Big Black Hole	K	F	Yolen, Jane	Putnam & Grosset
Commander Toad and the Dis-Asteroid	K	F	Yolen, Jane	Putnam & Grosset
Commander Toad and the Intergalactic Spy	K	F	Yolen, Jane	Putnam & Grosset
Commander Toad and the Planet of the Grapes	K	F	Yolen, Jane	Putnam & Grosset
Commander Toad and the Space Pirates	K	F	Yolen, Jane	Putnam & Grosset
Commander Toad And The Voyage Home	K	F	Yolen, Jane	Putnam & Grosset
Conversation Club, The	L	F	Stanley, Diane	Aladdin
Corduroy	K	F	Freeman, Don	Scholastic
Coronado's Golden Quest	R	F	Weisberg, Barbara	Steck-Vaughn
Count Karlstein	Y	F	Pullman, Philip	Alfred A. Knopf
Cousins in the Castle	U	F	Wallace, Barbara Brooks	Aladdin
Crane Wife, The	M	F	Pair-It Books	Steck-Vaughn
Creep Show	L	F	Dussling, Jennifer	Grosset & Dunlap
Cricket in Times Square, The	S	F	Selden, George	Bantam Doubleday Dell
Crinkum Crankum	M	F	Pacific Literacy	Pacific Learning
Crocodile in the Library, A	L	F	Pacific Literacy	Pacific Learning
Crocodile's Christmas Jandals, The	L	F	Pacific Literacy	Pacific Learning
Crosby Crocodile's Disguise	K	F	LIteracy 2000	Rigby
Cubby's Gum	J	F	Ready Readers	Pearson Learning
Cuckoo Child, The	Q	F	King-Smith, Dick	Hyperion

Title	Level	Genre	Author/Series	Publisher/Distributor
Cupids Don't Flip Hamburgers	M	F	Dadey, D. & Jones, M. T.	Scholastic
Curious George Rides a Bike	J	F	Rey, Margaret	Scholastic
Curse of the Cobweb Queen, The	L	F	Hayes, Geoffrey	Random House
Curse of the Squirrel, The	N	F	Yep, Laurence	Random House
Cyclops Doesn't Roller-Skate	M	F	Dadey, D. & Jones, M. T.	Scholastic
Dangerous Wishes	U	F	Sleator, William	The Penguin Group
Danny and the Dinosaur	J	F	Hoff, Syd	Scholastic
Daring Rescue of Marlon the Swimming Pig, The	P	F	Saunders, S.	Random House
Dark Is Rising, The	X	F	Cooper, Susan	Macmillan
Dark-Thirty: Southern Tales of the Supernatural	R	F	McKissack, Patricia C.	Alfred A. Knopf
Davin	R	F	Gordon, Dan & Gordon, Zaki	Bantam Doubleday Dell
Day Jimmy's Boa Ate the Wash, The	K	F	Noble, Trinka, H.	Scholastic
Day of the Dragon King	M	F	Osborne, Mary Pope	Random House
Day of the Rain, The	L	F	Cowley, Joy	Dominie
Day of the Snow, The	L	F	Cowley, Joy	Dominie
Day of the Wind, The	L	F	Cowley, Joy	Dominie
Day the Fifth Grade Disappeared, The	Q	F	Fields, Terri	Scholastic
Day the Sky Turned Green, The	M	F	Reeves, Barbara	Pearson Learning
Days With Frog and Toad	K	F	Lobel, Arnold	HarperTrophy
Dede and the Dinosaur	K	F	Cumpiano, Ina	Hampton-Brown
Detective Dinosaur	J	F	Skofield, James	HarperTrophy
Devil's Arithmetic, The	X	F	Yolen, Jane	Puffin Books
Dingoes at Dinnertime	M	F	Osborne, Mary Pope	Random House
Dinosaur on the Motorway	K	F	Wesley and the Dinosaurs	Wright Group/McGraw Hill
Dinosaurs Before Dark	M	F	Osborne, Mary Pope	Random House
Dipplidocus in the Garden, A	K	F	Wesley and the Dinosaurs	Wright Group/McGraw Hill
Dirty Beasts	O	F	Dahl, Roald	The Penguin Group
Discovering Dinosaurs	M	F	Little Books	Sadlier-Oxford
Dog in The Freezer, The	W	F	Mazer, Harry	Simon & Schuster
Dog that Pitched a No-Hitter, The	L	F	Christopher, Matt	Little Brown & Co.
Dog that Stole Football Plays, The	M	F	Christopher, Matt	Little, Brown & Co.
Dog that Stole Home, The	L	F	Christopher, Matt	Little, Brown & Co.
Dog-Gone Hollywood	L	F	Sharmat, Marjorie Weinman	Random House
Dogstar	J	F	Literacy 2000	Rigby
Dolphins at Daybreak	M	F	Osborne, Mary Pope	Random House
Dominic	R	F	Steig, William	Farrar, Straus and Giroux
Donkey	M	F	Literacy 2000	Rigby
Double Danger	P	F	Hager, Mandy	Pacific Learning
Dove Is a Beau	T	F	Yolen, Jane	Harcourt Brace
Dracula Doesn't Drink Lemonade	M	F	Dadey, D. & Jones, M. T.	Scholastic
Dragon Bones	O	F	Hindman, Paul	Random House
Dragon Breath	L	F	O'Connor, Jane	Grosset & Dunlap
Dragon Cauldron	W	F	Yep, Laurence	Harper Collins
Dragon Chronicles, The: Dragon's Milk	V	F	Fletcher, Susan	Aladdin
Dragon Feet	K	F	Books For Young Learners	Pacific Learning
Dragon Fire	P	F	Cowley, Joy	Pacific Learning
Dragon for Sale	Q	F	MacDonald, Marianne	Troll
Dragon in the Family, A	Q	F	Koller, Jackie French	Pocket Books
Dragon of the Lost Sea	W	F	Yep, Laurence	Harper Collins
Dragon Quest	Q	F	Koller, Jackie French	Pocket Books
Dragon Slayer	P	F	Cowley, Joy	Pacific Learning
Dragon Steel	W	F	Yep, Laurence	Harper Collins
Dragon Trouble	Q	F	Koller, Jackie French	Pocket Books
Dragon War	W	F	Yep, Laurence	Harper Collins
Dragon Who Had the Measles,The	J	F	Literacy 2000	Rigby
Dragon's Birthday, The	K	F	Literacy 2000	Rigby
Dragon's Blood	X	F	Yolen, Jane	Harcourt Brace
Dragon's Scales, The	J	F	Albee, Sarah	Random House
Dragonling, The	Q	F	Koller, Jackie French	Pocket Books
Dragons and Kings	Q	F	Koller, Jackie French	Pocket Books

Title	Level	Genre	Author/Series	Publisher/Distributor
Dragons Don't Cook Pizza	M	F	Dadey, D. & Jones, M. T.	Scholastic
Dragons Galore	N	F	Wildcats	Wright Group/McGraw Hill
Dragons of Blueland, The	L	F	Gannett, R.	Random House
Dragons of Krad	Q	F	Koller, Jackie French	Pocket Books
Dragonsong	V	F	McCaffrey, Anne	Bantam Doubleday Dell
Dream Eater, The	N	F	Garrison, Christian	Aladdin
Drought Marker, The	M	F	Literacy 2000	Rigby
Duck in the Gun, The	M	F	Literacy 2000	Rigby
Dunc and the Flaming Ghost	R	F	Paulsen, Gary	Bantam Doubleday Dell
Dustland	V	F	Hamilton, Virginia	Scholastic
Dynamic Duos	P	F	Moore, David	Scholastic
Early Bird's Alarm Clock, The	J	F	Daniel, Claire	Steck-Vaughn
Earthborn	Z	F	Card, Orson Scott	Tor
Earthfall	Z	F	Card, Orson Scott	Tor
Easter Bunny that Ate My Sister, The	Q	F	Marney, Dean	Scholastic
Edgar Badger's Balloon Day	K	F	Kulling, Monica	Mondo
Edgar Badger's Butterfly Day	K	F	Kulling, Monica	Mondo
Edgar Badger's Fishing Day	K	F	Kulling, Monica	Mondo
Edgar Badger's Fix-it Day	K	F	Kulling, Monica	Mondo
Eeny, Meeny, Miney Mole	M	F	Yolen, Jane	Harcourt Brace
Effie	K	F	Allinson, Beverly	Scholastic
Elephant and the Bad Baby, The	J	F	Hayes, S.	Sundance
Elephant in the House, An	J	F	Read Alongs	Rigby
Elizabite: Adventures of a Carnivorous Plant	K	F	Rey, H.A.	Houghton Mifflin
Ella Enchanted	U	F	Carson Levine, Gail	HarperTrophy
Elmer and the Dragon	M	F	Gannett, Ruth	Random House
Elves Don't Wear Hard Hats	M	F	Dadey, D. & Jones, M. T.	Scholastic
Elvis the Turnip…and Me	N	F	The Zack Files	Gosset & Dunlap
Emily Eyefinger	M	F	Ball, Duncan	Aladdin
Emily's Runaway Imagination	P	F	Cleary, Beverly	Avon Camelot
Enchanted Horse, The	R	F	Nabb, Magdalen	Hyperion
Enormous Crocodile, The	N	F	Dahl, Roald	The Penguin Group
Enormous Egg, The	R	F	Butterworth, Oliver	Little, Brown & Co.
Errol the Peril	Q	F	Literacy 2000	Rigby
Eva	Z	F	Dickenson, Eva	Laurel-Leaf Books
Evil Queen Tut and the Great Ant Pyramids	N	F	The Zack Files	Grossett&Dunlap
Eye in the Sky	P	F	Marriott, Janice	Pacific Learning
Fantastic Mr. Fox	P	F	Dahl, Roald	The Penguin Group
Farmer Joe's Hot Day	J	F	Richards/Zimmerman	Scholastic
Farthest Shore, The	Z	F	Le Guin, Ursula	Bamtam
Fight on the Hill, The	J	F	Read Alongs	Rigby
Figure in the Shadows, The	S	F	Bellairs, John	The Penguin Group
Fiji Flood, The	M	F	Schultz, Irene	Wright Group/McGraw Hill
Fire Cat, The	J	F	Averill, Esther	HarperTrophy
Firefly Named Torchy, A	L	F	Waber, Bernard	Houghton Mifflin
Flat Stanley	M	F	Brown, Jeff	HarperTrophy
Flea Story, A	L	F	Lionni, Leo	Scholastic
Fledgling, The	U	F	Langton, Jane	Scholastic
Flossie and the Fox	O	F	McKissack, Patricia	Scholastic
Fly Homer Fly	N	F	Peet, Bill	Houghton Mifflin
Fly Trap	L	F	Anastasio, Dina	Grosset & Dunlap
Flying Flea, Callie, and Me, The	S	F	Wallace, Carol & Bill	Pocket Books
Follow That Fish	K	F	Bank Street	Bantam Doubleday Dell
Four on the Shore	K	F	Marshall, Edward	Puffin Books
Fourth-Graders Don't Believe In Witches	P	F	Fields, Terri	Scholastic
Fox All Week	J	F	Marshall, Edward	Puffin Books
Fox and His Friends	J	F	Marshall, Edward	Puffin Books
Fox at School	J	F	Marshall, Edward	Puffin Books
Fox Be Nimble	J	F	Marshall, James	Puffin Books
Fox In Love	J	F	Marshall, Edward	Puffin Books

Title	Level	Genre	Author/Series	Publisher/Distributor
Fox on Stage	J	F	Marshall, James	Puffin Books
Fox on the Job	J	F	Marshall, James	Puffin Books
Fox on Wheels	J	F	Marshall, Edward	Puffin Books
Fox Outfoxed	J	F	Marshall, James	Puffin Books
Fraidy Cats	J	F	Krensky, Stephen	Scholastic
Frank The Fish Gets His Wish	J	F	Appleton-Smith, Laura	Flyleaf Publishing
Frankenstein Doesn't Plant Petunias	M	F	Dadey, D. & Jones, M. T.	Scholastic
Frankenstein Doesn't Slam Hockey Pucks	M	F	Dadey, D. & Jones, M. T.	Scholastic
Franklin Goes To School	K	F	Bourgeois, P. & Clark, B.	Scholastic
Franklin Plays the Game	K	F	Bourgeois, P. & Clark, B.	Scholastic
Freaky Friday	R	F	Rodgers, Mary	HarperTrophy
Freeze, Goldilocks!	M	F	Pacific Literacy	Pacific Learning
Friends are Forever	K	F	Literacy 2000	Rigby
Frog and Toad All Year	K	F	Little Readers	Houghton Mifflin
Frog and Toad Are Friends	K	F	Lobel, Arnold	Harper & Row
Frog and Toad Together	K	F	Lobel, Arnold	Harper Collins
Frog Who Thought He Was A Horse, The	L	F	Literacy 2000	Rigby
Froggy Learns to Swim	J	F	London, Jonathan	Scholastic
Funny Bones	J	F	Ahlberg, A & J	Viking
Funny Old Man and the Funny Old Woman, The	M	F	Book Shop	Mondo
Gallo and Zorro	J	F	Literacy 2000	Rigby
Garfield and the Beast in the Basement	Q	F	Davis, Jim	Troll
Garfield and the Mysterious Mummy	Q	F	Davis, Jim	Troll
Gargoyles Don't Drive School Buses	M	F	Dadey, D. & Jones, M. T.	Scholastic
Gasp!	L	F	Book Shop	Mondo
Gaston the Giant	K	F	New Way Orange	Steck-Vaughn
Gathering Blue	X	F	Lowry, Lois	Houghton Mifflin
Gathering, The	V	F	Hamilton, Virginia	Harcourt Brace
Genies Don't Ride Bicycles	M	F	Dadey, D. & Jones, M. T.	Scholastic
George and Martha	L	F	Marshall, James	Houghton Mifflin
George's Marvelous Medicine	P	F	Dahl, Roald	The Penguin Group
Gertie's Green Thumb	O	F	Dexter, Catherine	Dell Publishing
Get-Up Machine, The	J	F	Sunshine	Wright Group/McGraw Hill
Ghost Belonged to Me, The	V	F	Peck, Richard	The Penguin Group
Ghost Come Calling, The	Q	F	Wright, Betty	Scholastic
Ghost Dog	M	F	Allen, Eleanor	Scholastic
Ghost Fox, The	P	F	Yep, Laurence	Scholastic
Ghost in Tent 19, The	M	F	O'Connor, J. & J.	Random House
Ghost in the Tokaido Inn, The	U	F	Hoobler, Dorothy & Thomas	The Penguin Group
Ghost Named Wanda, A	N	F	The Zack Files	Grosset & Dunlap
Ghost of Popcorn Hill, The	N	F	Wright, Betty Ren	Scholastic
Ghost On Saturday Night, The	Q	F	Fleischman, Sid	Beech Tree Books
Ghost School	M	F	Clifford, Eth	Scholastic
Ghost Town at Sundown	M	F	Osborne, Mary Pope	Random House
Ghost Twins: Mystery at Kickingbird Lake	P	F	Regan, Dian Curtis	Scholastic
Ghostmobile, The	S	F	Tapp, Kathy Kennedy	Scholastic
Ghosts Beneath Our Feet	R	F	Wright, Betty Ren	Scholastic
Ghosts Don't Eat Potato Chips	M	F	Dadey, D. & Jones, M. T.	Scholastic
Ghouls Don't Scoop Ice Cream	M	F	Dadey, D. & Jones, M. T.	Scholastic
Giant in the Forest, A	J	F	Reading Unlimited	Celebration Press
Giant Jack's Boots	M	F	Book Bank	Wright Group/McGraw Hill
Giant Jam Sandwich, The	K	F	Vernon Lord, John	Houghton Mifflin
Giant's Cake	M	F	Learning Media	Mondo
Giants Don't Go Snowboarding	M	F	Dadey, D. & Jones, M. T.	Scholastic
Giraffe and the Pelly and Me, The	P	F	Dahl, Roald	The Penguin Group
Girl Called Boy, A	U	F	Hurmence, Belinda	Clarion
Girl Who Climbed to the Moon, The	L	F	Sunshine	Wright Group/McGraw Hill
Girl Who Owned a City, The	X	F	Nelson, O.T.	Laurel-Leaf Books
Girl With the Silver Eyes, The	U	F	Roberts, Willo Davis	Scholastic
Giver, The	Y	F	Lowry, Lois	Bantam Doubleday Dell

Title	Level	Genre	Author/Series	Publisher/Distributor
Glenda	P	F	Udry, Janice	HarperTrophy
Glenda Glinka: Witch-At-Large	P	F	Udry, Janice May	HarperTrophy
Goat Monster and Other Stories, The	L	F	New Way: Literature	Steck-Vaughn
Godzilla Ate My Homework	O	F	Jones, Marcia	Scholastic
Golden Compass, The	Z	F	Pullman, Philip	Ballantine Books
Golden Sword of Dragonwalk	Q	F	Stine, R. L.	Scholastic
Good Driving, Amelia Bedelia	L	F	Parish, Peggy	Harper & Row
Good Morning Mrs. Martin	K	F	Book Bank	Wright Group/McGraw Hill
Good Work, Amelia Bedelia	L	F	Parish, Peggy	Avon Camelot
Gooey Chewy Contest, The	L	F	Goldsmith, Howard	Mondo
Gooseberry Park	P	F	Rylant, Cynthia	Scholastic
Goosebumps: It Came From Beneath the Sink	T	F	Stine, R. L.	Language for Learning Assoc.
Gorganzola Zombies in the Park	O	F	Levy, Elizabeth	HarperTrophy
Grace the Pirate	O	F	Lasky, Kathryn	Hyperion
Grand Escape, The	S	F	Naylor, Phyllis Reynolds	Bantam Doubleday Dell
Grandad's Dinosaur	K	F	Girling, Brough	Wright Group/McGraw Hill
Grasshopper on the Road	K	F	Lobel, Arnold	HarperTrophy
Graven Images: Three Stories by Paul Fleischman	U	F	Fleischman, Paul	HarperTrophy
Great Day for Up	J	F	Seuss, Dr.	Random House
Great Dinosaur Hunt, The	M	F	Schultz, Irene	Wright Group/McGraw Hill
Great Ghosts	L	F	Cohen, Daniel	Scholastic
Great Grumbler and the Wonder Tree, The	K	F	Mahy, Margaret	Pacific Learning Publishers
Great Ice Battle, The	M	F	Abbott, Tony	Scholastic
Great Snake Escape, The	J	F	Coxe, Molly	HarperTrophy
Great-Grandpa's In The Litter Box	N	F	The Zack Files	Grosset & Dunlap
Greedy Cat and the Birthday Cake	M	F	Cowley, Joy	Pacific Learning
Green Book, The	V	F	Walsh, Jill Paton	Farrar, Straus and Giroux
Green Eggs and Ham	J	F	Seuss, Dr.	Random House
Greenwitch	X	F	Cooper, Susan	Scholastic
Gregory, the Terrible Eater	L	F	Sharmat, Marjorie Weinman	Scholastic
Gremlins Don't Chew Bubble Gum	M	F	Dadey, D. & Jones, M. T.	Scholastic
Grey King, The	X	F	Cooper, Susan	Simon & Schuster
Guardian of the Dark	W	F	Spencer, Bev	Scholastic
Gulf	X	F	Westfall, Robert	Scholastic
Gulliver's Stories	Q	F	Dolch, E. W. and Marguerite P.	Scholastic
Hand, Hand, Fingers, Thumb	J	F	Perkins, Al	Random House
Handful of Time, A	U	F	Pearson, Kit	Puffin Books
Hang a Left at Venus	N	F	The Zack Files	Grossett&Dunlap
Hannah and the Angels	Q	F	Lowery, Linda	Random House
Happily Ever After	O	F	Quindlen, Anna	The Penguin Group
Happy Birthday, Dear Duck	K	F	Bunting, Eve	Clarion
Happy Birthday, Moon	L	F	Asch, Frank	Simon & Schuster
Harold and the Purple Crayon	K	F	Johnson, Crockett	Harper & Row
Harriet's Hare	O	F	King-Smith, Dick	Alfred A. Knopf
Harry and Chicken	S	F	Sheldon, Dyan	Candlewick Press
Harry and the Lady Next Door	J	F	Zion, Gene	HarperTrophy
Harry Cat's Pet Puppy	R	F	Selden, George	Bantam Doubleday Dell
Harry Hates Shopping!	K	F	Armitage, Ronda and David	Scholastic
Harry Potter and the Chamber of Secrets	V	F	Rowling, J. K.	Scholastic
Harry Potter and the Goblet of Fire	V	F	Rowling, J. K.	Scholastic
Harry Potter and the Prisoner of Azkaban	V	F	Rowling, J.K.	Scholastic
Harry Potter and the Sorcerer's Stone	V	F	Rowling, J. K.	Scholastic
Harry the Explorer	S	F	Sheldon, Dyan	Candlewick Press
Harry's Mad	P	F	King-Smith, Dick	Alfred A. Knopf
Haunted	Q	F	Herman, Emily	Wright Group/McGraw Hill
Haunted Bike, The	L	F	Herman, Gail	Grosset & Dunlap
Haunted Halloween, The	M	F	Schultz, Irene	Wright Group/McGraw Hill
Have You Seen a Javelina?	K	F	Literacy 2000	Rigby
He Bear, She Bear	J	F	Berenstain, Stan, & Jan	Random House
Heart's Blood	X	F	Yolen, Jane	Harcourt Brace

Title	Level	Genre	Author/Series	Publisher/Distributor
Hedgehog Bakes a Cake	J	F	Bank Street	Bantam Doubleday Dell
Hello, Mrs. Piggle-Wiggle	O	F	MacDonald, Betty	HarperTrophy
Help! I'm Trapped in an Alien's Body	Q	F	Strasser, Todd	Scholastic
Help! I'm Trapped in My Lunch Lady's Body	Q	F	Strasser, Todd	Scholastic
Help! I'm Trapped in My Teacher's Body	Q	F	Strasser, Todd	Scholastic
Help! I'm Trapped in Obedience School	Q	F	Strasser, Todd	Scholastic
Help! I'm Trapped in Obedience School Again	Q	F	Strasser, Todd	Scholastic
Help! I'm Trapped in Santa's Body	Q	F	Strasser, Todd	Scholastic
Help! I'm Trapped in the First Day of School	Q	F	Strasser, Todd	Scholastic
Help! I'm Trapped in the First Day of Summer Camp	Q	F	Strasser, Todd	Scholastic
Help! I'm Trapped in the President's Body	Q	F	Strasser, Todd	Scholastic
Henry Reed, Inc.	X	F	Robertson, Keith	Puffin Books
Hercules Doesn't Pull Teeth	M	F	Dadey, D. & Jones, M. T.	Scholastic
Here Comes McBroom	O	F	Fleischman, Sid	Beech Tree Books
Herman the Helper	J	F	Kraus, Robert	Simon & Schuster
Hero and the Crown, The	Z	F	McKinley, Robin	Puffin Books
Hey, Al	N	F	Yorinks, Arthur	Farrar, Straus and Giroux
Hilary & the Lions	M	F	Desaix, Frank	Farrar, Straus and Giroux
Hippopotamus Ate the Teacher, A	J	F	Thaler, Mike	Avon
Hitty: Her First Hundred Years	U	F	Field, Rachel	Aladdin
Hobbit, The	Z	F	Tolkien, J.R.R	Ballantine Books
Hobby: The Young Merlin Trilogy	V	F	Yolen, Jane	Scholastic
Home for the Howl-idays	S	F	Regan, Dian Curtis	Scholastic
Honey Tree, The	L	F	Literacy 2000	Rigby
Hop on Pop	J	F	Seuss, Dr.	Random House
Horrakapotchkin	M	F	Pacific Literacy	Pacific Learning
Horse and His Boy, The	T	F	Lewis, C. S.	Collier Books
Horse in Harry's Room, The	J	F	Hoff, Syd	Harper Collins
Hour of the Olympics	M	F	Osborne, Mary Pope	Random House
House Gobbaleen, The	P	F	Alexander, Lloyd	The Penguin Group
House of Mirrors, The	M	F	Weaver, Betty-May	Wright Group/McGraw Hill
House of Stairs	Z	F	Sleator, William	Puffin Books
House of the Horrible Ghosts	M	F	Hayes, Geoffrey	Random House
House with a Clock in its Walls, The	S	F	Bellairs, John	The Penguin Group
How Bullfrog Found His Sound	M	F	Michaels, Eric	Pearson Learning
How I Fixed the Year 1000 Problem	N	F	The Zack Files	Grossett&Dunlap
How I Went from Bad to Verse	N	F	The Zack Files	Grossett&Dunlap
How Spiders Got Eight Legs	L	F	Pair-It Books	Steck-Vaughn
How To Speak Dolphin in Three Easy Lessons	N	F	The Zack Files	Grosset & Dunlap
Howie Merton and the Magic Dust	M	F	Reeves, Faye Couch	Random House
Howliday Inn	P	F	Howe, James	Atheneum Books
Hunt for Pirate Gold, The	M	F	Schultz, Irene	Wright Group/McGraw Hill
I Am a Gypsy Pot	K	F	Evangeline Nicholas Collection	Wright Group/McGraw Hill
I Am the Ice Worm	S	F	Easley, Mary Ann	Yearling
I Can Read with My Eyes Shut	J	F	Seuss, Dr.	Random House
I Can't Said the Ant	M	F	Cameron, Polly	Scholastic
I Love to Sneeze	J	F	Bank Street	Bantam Doubleday Dell
I Was a Sixth Grade Alien	S	F	Coville, Bruce	Pocket Books
I'm Out of My Body...Please Leave a Message	N	F	The Zack Files	Grosset & Dunlap
I'm So Hungry and Other Plays	M	F	Learning Media	Pacific Learning
If You Give A Moose A Muffin	K	F	Numeroff, Laura Joffe	Harper Collins
If You Give A Mouse A Cookie	K	F	Numeroff, Laura Joffe	Harper Collins
Imagine That	J	F	Story Box	Wright Group/McGraw Hill
Imagine This, James Robert	P	F	Weber, Rebecca	Rigby
In a Faraway Forest	K	F	Kratky, Lada Josefa	Hampton-Brown
Incident at Hawk's Hill	V	F	Eckert, Allen W.	Little, Brown & Co.
Incredible Journey,The	V	F	Burnford, Sheila	Bantam Doubleday Dell
Incredible Shrinking Kid, The	P	F	Abbott, Tony	Scholastic
Indian in the Cupboard, The	R	F	Banks, Lynne Reid	Avon
Instead of Three Wishes: Magical Short Stories	Y	F	Turner, Megan Whalen	The Penguin Group

Title	Level	Genre	Author/Series	Publisher/Distributor
Invisible Dog, The	M	F	King-Smith, Dick	Alfred A. Knopf
Invisible Spy, The	J	F	Foundations	Wright Group/McGraw Hill
Invisible Stanley	O	F	Brown, Jeff	HarperTrophy
Iron Ring, The	W	F	Alexander, Lloyd	Puffin Books
Island of the Skog, The	M	F	Kellogg, Steven	Dial Books
Islander, The	T	F	Rylant, Cynthia	Random House
It Came Through the Wall	O	F	Healey, Tim	Mondo
It's All in Your Mind, James Robert	P	F	Literacy 2000	Rigby
Jacob Two-Two and the Dinosaur	P	F	Richler, Mordecai	Tundra Books
Jacob Two-Two Meets the Hooded Fang	P	F	Richler, Mordecai	Seal Books
Jamberry	J	F	Degen, Bruce	Harper & Row
James and the Giant Peach	Q	F	Dahl, Roald	The Penguin Group
Jason and the Aliens Down the Street	O	F	Greer, Greg & Ruddick, Bob	HarperTrophy
Jenius The Amazing Guinea Pig	N	F	King-Smith, Dick	Hyperion
JJ Rabbit and the Monster	K	F	Moon, Nicola	Wright Group/McGraw Hill
Joe and Betsy the Dinosaur	K	F	Hoban, Lillian	HarperTrophy
Joey's Head	L	F	Cretan, G.	Simon & Schuster
Johnny Lion's Book	J	F	Hurd, Edith Thacher	Harper Collins
Josefina Story Quilt	L	F	Coerr, Eleanor	HarperTrophy
Journey Outside	V	F	Steele, Mary Q.	The Penguin Group
Julie's Mornings	K	F	Ready Readers	Pearson Learning
Jungle Book, The	U	F	Kipling, Rudyard	Scholastic
Junkpile Robot, The	L	F	Ready Readers	Pearson Learning
Just for Fun	J	F	Literacy 2000	Rigby
Just Like Me	J	F	Story Box	Wright Group/McGraw Hill
Katy and the Big Snow	L	F	Burton, Virginia L.	Scholastic
Keep Your Eye On Amanda!	R	F	Avi	Avon
Kenny and the Little Kickers	J	F	Mareollo, Claudio	Scholastic
Ketchup Deal, The	P	F	Marriott, Janice	Pacific Learning
Kind Prince and Rupert, The	L	F	New Way: Literature	Steck-Vaughn
King Arthur	M	F	Brown, Marc	Little, Brown & Co.
King Beast's Birthday	L	F	Literacy 2000	Rigby
King Max	Q	F	King-Smith, Dick	Troll
King of Shadows	Z	F	Cooper, Susan	Margaret K. McElderry Books
King, the Mice and the Cheese	K	F	Gurney, Nancy	Random House
King's Race and Other Stories, The	L	F	New Way: Literature	Steck-Vaughn
Knee Knock Rise	S	F	Babbitt, Natalie	Farrar, Straus and Giroux
Knight at Dawn, The	M	F	Osborne, Mary Pope	Random House
Knights Don't Teach Piano	M	F	Dadey, D. & Jones, M. T.	Scholastic
Knit, Knit, Knit, Knit	J	F	Literacy 2000	Rigby
Knot in the Grain (and Other Stories)	X	F	McKinley, Robin	Harper Trophy
Lad Who Went to the North Wind, The	J	F	Book Shop	Mondo
Lamp from the Warlock's Tomb, The	S	F	Bellairs, John	Puffin Books
Lampfish of Twill, The	U	F	Lisle, Janet Taylor	Scholastic
Last Chance for Magic	P	F	Chew, Ruth	Scholastic
Last Puppy, The	K	F	Asch, Frank	Simon & Schuster
Lazy Bones Jones	P	F	Welch, Sheila Kelly	Pacific Learning
Lazy Jackal, The	M	F	Sunshine	Wright Group/McGraw Hill
Lend a Hand	K	F	Kratky, Lada	Hampton-Brown
Leprechauns Don't Play Basketball	M	F	Dadey, D. & Jones, M. T.	Scholastic
Letter, the Witch, and the Ring, The	S	F	Bellairs, John	The Penguin Group
Lighthouse Mermaid, The	M	F	Karr, Kathleen	Hyperion
Lion in the Night, The	J	F	Momentum Literacy Program	Troll
Lion Tamer's Daughter, The- And Other Stories	Z	F	Dickinson, Peter	Laurel-Leaf Books
Lion, the Witch and the Wardrobe, The	T	F	Lewis, C. S.	HarperTrophy
Lionel and Amelia	L	F	Book Shop	Mondo
Lions at Lunchtime	M	F	Osborne, Mary Pope	Random House
Little Bear	J	F	Minarik, E.H.	Harper Collins
Little Bear's Friend	J	F	Minarik, E.H.	HarperTrophy

Title	Level	Genre	Author/Series	Publisher/Distributor
Little Bear's Visit	J	F	Minarik, E.H.	HarperTrophy
Little Blue and Little Yellow	J	F	Lionni, Leo	Scholastic
Little Chief	K	F	Hoff, Syd	Harper Collins
Little Dinosaur Escapes	J	F	PM Turquoise	Rigby
Little Gorilla	J	F	Bornstein, Ruth	Clarion
Little Knight, The	K	F	Reading Unlimited	Celebration Press
Little Leaf's Journey and the Lost Tooth, The	K	F	New Way Ornage	Steck-Vaughn
Little, Little Man, The	M	F	Book Bank	Wright Group/McGraw Hill
Little Penguin's Tale	L	F	Wood, Audrey	Scholastic
Little Polar Bear and the Brave Little Hare	K	F	de Beer, Hans	North-South Books
Little Sea Pony, The	N	F	Cresswell, Helen	HarperTrophy
Little Spider, The	K	F	Literacy 2000	Rigby
Little Vampire and the Midnight Bear	L	F	Kwitz, M. D.	Puffin Books
Little Walrus Rising	K	F	Young, Carol	Scholastic
Little Whale, The	M	F	Sunshine	Wright Group/McGraw Hill
Little Witch Goes to School	K	F	Hautzig, Deborah	Random House
Little Witch's Big Night	K	F	Hautzig, Deborah	Random House
Littles and the Great Halloween Scare, The	M	F	Peterson, John	Scholastic
Littles and the Lost Children, The	M	F	Peterson, John	Scholastic
Littles and the Terrible Tiny Kid, The	M	F	Peterson, John	Scholastic
Littles and the Trash Tinies, The	M	F	Peterson, John	Scholastic
Littles Give a Party, The	M	F	Peterson, John	Scholastic
Littles Go Exploring, The	M	F	Peterson, John	Scholastic
Littles Go to School, The	M	F	Peterson, John	Scholastic
Littles Have a Wedding, The	M	F	Peterson, John	Scholastic
Littles Take a Trip, The	M	F	Peterson, John	Scholastic
Littles, The	M	F	Peterson, John	Scholastic
Littles to the Rescue, The	M	F	Peterson, John	Scholastic
Lizard Music	T	F	Pinkwater, D. Manus	Bantam Doubleday Dell
Lizard's Grandmother	J	F	Sunshine	Wright Group/McGraw Hill
Locked in the Library!	M	F	Brown, Marc	Little, Brown & Co.
Lonely Dragon,'The	J	F	Momentum Literacy Program	Troll
Lonely Giant, The	K	F	Literacy 2000	Rigby
Long Grass of Tumbledown Road	M	F	Read Alongs	Rigby
Look Out For Your Tail	J	F	Literacy 2000	Rigby
Lord of the Rings, The	Z	F	Tolkien, J. R. R.	Houghton Mifflin
Lost!	L	F	Mitchell, Julie	Rigby
Lucky Feather, The	L	F	Literacy 2000	Rigby
Lucy Meets a Dragon	L	F	Literacy 2000	Rigby
Lulu Goes to Witch School	K	F	O'Connor, Jane	HarperTrophy
Ma and Pa Dracula	O	F	Martin, Ann M.	Scholastic
Mad Scientist, The	M	F	Schultz, Irene	Wright Group/McGraw Hill
Madeline	K	F	Bemelmans, Ludwig	Scholastic
Madeline's Rescue	K	F	Bemelmans, Ludwig	Scholastic
Magic All Around	L	F	Literacy 2000	Rigby
Magic Box, The	K	F	Brenner, Barbara	Bantam Doubleday Dell
Magic Finger, The	N	F	Dahl, Roald	The Penguin Group
Magic Ride, The	M	F	Book Bank	Wright Group/McGraw Hill
Magic School Bus	P	F	Cole, Joanna & Degen, Bruce	Scholastic
Magic School Bus and the Electric Field Trip, The	P	F	Cole, Joanna & Degen, Bruce	Scholastic
Magic School Bus Answers Questions	P	F	Cole, Joanna & Degen, Bruce	Scholastic
Magic School Bus At the Waterworks	P	F	Cole, Joanna & Degen, Bruce	Scholastic
Magic School Bus Blows Its Top	P	F	Cole, Joanna & Degen, Bruce	Scholastic
Magic School Bus Briefcase	P	F	Cole, Joanna & Degen, Bruce	Scholastic
Magic School Bus Butterfly and the Bog Beast	P	F	Cole, Joanna & Degen, Bruce	Scholastic
Magic School Bus Explores the Senses	P	F	Cole, Joanna & Degen, Bruce	Scholastic
Magic School Bus Explores the World of Animals	P	F	Cole, Joanna & Degen, Bruce	Scholastic
Magic School Bus Gets a Bright Idea	P	F	Cole, Joanna & Degen, Bruce	Scholastic
Magic School Bus Gets All Dried Up	P	F	Cole, Joanna & Degen, Bruce	Scholastic
Magic School Bus Gets Ants in Its Pants	P	F	Cole, Joanna & Degen, Bruce	Scholastic

Title	Level	Genre	Author/Series	Publisher/Distributor
Magic School Bus Gets Baked in a Cake	P	F	Cole, Joanna & Degen, Bruce	Scholastic
Magic School Bus Gets Cold Feet	P	F	Cole, Joanna & Degen, Bruce	Scholastic
Magic School Bus Gets Eaten	P	F	Cole, Joanna & Degen, Bruce	Scholastic
Magic School Bus Gets Programmed	P	F	Cole, Joanna & Degen, Bruce	Scholastic
Magic School Bus Goes Upstream	P	F	Cole, Joanna & Degen, Bruce	Scholastic
Magic School Bus Going Batty	P	F	Cole, Joanna & Degen, Bruce	Scholastic
Magic School Bus Hops Home	P	F	Cole, Joanna & Degen, Bruce	Scholastic
Magic School Bus in a Pickle	P	F	Cole, Joanna & Degen, Bruce	Scholastic
Magic School Bus in the Arctic	P	F	Cole, Joanna & Degen, Bruce	Scholastic
Magic School Bus in the Haunted Museum	P	F	Cole, Joanna & Degen, Bruce	Scholastic
Magic School Bus in the Rain Forest	P	F	Cole, Joanna & Degen, Bruce	Scholastic
Magic School Bus Inside a Beehive	P	F	Cole, Joanna & Degen, Bruce	Scholastic
Magic School Bus Inside a Hurricane	P	F	Cole, Joanna & Degen, Bruce	Scholastic
Magic School Bus Inside Ralphie	P	F	Cole, Joanna & Degen, Bruce	Scholastic
Magic School Bus Inside the Earth	P	F	Cole, Joanna & Degen, Bruce	Scholastic
Magic School Bus Inside the Human Body	P	F	Cole, Joanna & Degen, Bruce	Scholastic
Magic School Bus Kicks Up a Storm	P	F	Cole, Joanna & Degen, Bruce	Scholastic
Magic School Bus Liz Sorts It Out	P	F	Cole, Joanna & Degen, Bruce	Scholastic
Magic School Bus Lost in the Solar System	P	F	Cole, Joanna & Degen, Bruce	Scholastic
Magic School Bus Makes a Rainbow	P	F	Cole, Joanna & Degen, Bruce	Scholastic
Magic School Bus Meets the Rot Squad	P	F	Cole, Joanna & Degen, Bruce	Scholastic
Magic School Bus on the Ocean Floor	P	F	Cole, Joanna & Degen, Bruce	Scholastic
Magic School Bus Out of This World	P	F	Cole, Joanna & Degen, Bruce	Scholastic
Magic School Bus Plants Seeds	P	F	Cole, Joanna & Degen, Bruce	Scholastic
Magic School Bus Plays Ball	P	F	Cole, Joanna & Degen, Bruce	Scholastic
Magic School Bus Science Explorations	P	F	Cole, Joanna & Degen, Bruce	Scholastic
Magic School Bus Search for the Missing Bones	P	F	Cole, Joanna & Degen, Bruce	Scholastic
Magic School Bus Sees Stars	P	F	Cole, Joanna & Degen, Bruce	Scholastic
Magic School Bus Shows and Tells	P	F	Cole, Joanna & Degen, Bruce	Scholastic
Magic School Bus Space Explorers	P	F	Cole, Joanna & Degen, Bruce	Scholastic
Magic School Bus Spins a Web	P	F	Cole, Joanna & Degen, Bruce	Scholastic
Magic School Bus Takes a Dive	P	F	Cole, Joanna & Degen, Bruce	Scholastic
Magic School Bus Taking Flight	P	F	Cole, Joanna & Degen, Bruce	Scholastic
Magic School Bus The Truth About Bats	P	F	Cole, Joanna & Degen, Bruce	Scholastic
Magic School Bus The Wild Whale Watch	P	F	Cole, Joanna & Degen, Bruce	Scholastic
Magic School Bus Twister Trouble	P	F	Cole, Joanna & Degen, Bruce	Scholastic
Magic School Bus Ups and Downs	P	F	Cole, Joanna & Degen, Bruce	Scholastic
Magic School Bus Visits the Planets	P	F	Cole, Joanna & Degen, Bruce	Scholastic
Magic School Bus Wet All Over	P	F	Cole, Joanna & Degen, Bruce	Scholastic
Magical Adventures of Pretty Pearl, The	W	F	Hamilton, Virginia	HarperTrophy
Magician's Nephew, The	T	F	Lewis, C. S.	HarperTrophy
Mall Mystery, The	M	F	Schultz, Irene	Wright Group/McGraw Hill
Mansion in the Mist, The	S	F	Bellairs, John	Puffin Books
Manual of House Monsters, A	O	F	Marijanovic, Stanislav	Mondo
Many Waters	V	F	L'Engle, Madeleine	Bantam Doubleday Dell
Mariel of Redwall	Z	F	Jacques, Brian	Avon Books
Marigold and Grandma On The Town	J	F	Calmenson, Stephanie	HarperTrophy
Mario's Mayan Journey	P	F	Book Shop	Mondo
Marlfox: A Novel of Redwall	Z	F	Jacques, Brian	Ace Books
Martians Don't Take Temperatures	M	F	Dadey, D. & Jones, M. T.	Scholastic
Martin's Mice	P	F	King-Smith, Dick	Knopf
Mary by Myself	Q	F	Smith, Jane Denitz	HarperTrophy
Matilda	S	F	Dahl, Roald	The Penguin Group
Mattimeo: A Tale from Redwall	Z	F	Jacques, Brian	Avon
Maura's Angel	X	F	Banks, Lynne Reid	Avon
Meet Calliope Day	R	F	Haddad, Charles	Random House
Meet the Molesons	L	F	Bos, Burny	North-South Books
Meg and Mog	J	F	Nicoll, Helen	Viking
Merlin: The Young Merlin Trilogy	V	F	Yolen, Jane	Scholastic
Mermaid Island	L	F	Frith, Margaret	Grosset & Dunlap

Title	Level	Genre	Author/Series	Publisher/Distributor
Mermaids Don't Run Track	M	F	Dadey, D. & Jones, M. T.	Scholastic
Message, The	R	F	Applegate, K.A.	Scholastic
Midnight Horse, The	V	F	Fleischman, Sid	Bantam Doubleday Dell
Midnight Magic	U	F	Avi	Scholastic
Midnight on the Moon	M	F	Osborne, Mary Pope	Random House
Mile High, A	K	F	Book Bank	Wright Group/McGraw Hill
Milkshake Man, The	L	F	Cole, Sally	Wright Group/McGraw Hill
Milton the Early Riser	J	F	Kraus, Robert	Aladdin
Minerva's Dream	M	F	Pair-It Books	Steck-Vaughn
Minnie and Moo Go to Paris	J	F	Cazet, Denys	DK Publishing, Inc.
Mirandy and Brother Wind	R	F	McKissack, Patricia	Alfred A. Knopf
Misfortune Cookie, The	N	F	The Zack Files	Grosset & Dunlap
Miss McKenzie Had a Farm	J	F	Pair-It Books	Steck-Vaughn
Mitchell Is Moving	J	F	Sharmat, Marjorie Weinman	Simon & Schuster
Mixed-up Max	Q	F	King-Smith, Dick	Troll
Mog at the Zoo	L	F	Nicoll, Helen	The Penguin Group
Mog's Mumps	L	F	Nicoll, Helen	The Penguin Group
Momotaro	M	F	Sunshine	Wright Group/McGraw Hill
Monster for Hire	M	F	Wilson, Trevor	Mondo
Monster Manners	J	F	Cole, Joanna	Scholastic
Monster Movie	K	F	Cole, Joanna	Scholastic
Monster of Mirror Mountain, The	K	F	Literacy 2000	Rigby
Monster of the Year	S	F	Coville, Bruce	Pocket Books
Monster Under The Bed, The	K	F	Ready Readers	Pearson Learning
Monster's Ring, The	R	F	Coville, Bruce	Pocket Books
Monsters Don't Scuba Dive	M	F	Dadey, D. & Jones, M. T.	Scholastic
Moon Boy	J	F	Bank Street	Bantam Doubleday Dell
Moon Stories	J	F	Ready Readers	Pearson Learning
Moonhorse	M	F	Osborne, Mary Pope	Alfred A. Knopf
More Tales of Amanda Pig	L	F	Van Leeuwen, Jean	The Penguin Group
More Tales of Oliver Pig	L	F	Van Leeuwen, Jean	The Penguin Group
Morgan's Zoo	Q	F	Howe, James	Aladdin
Morning Star	J	F	Literacy 2000	Rigby
Morris and Boris at the Circus	J	F	Wiseman, B.	HarperTrophy
Morris Goes to School	J	F	Wiseman, B.	HarperTrophy
Mossflower	Z	F	Jacques, Brian	Ace Books
Mother Hippopotamus Gets Wet	J	F	Foundations	Wright Group/McGraw Hill
Mother Hippopotamus Goes Canoeing	L	F	Foundations	Wright Group/McGraw Hill
Mountains of Quilt, The	N	F	Willard, Nancy	Harcourt Brace
Mouse and the Motorcycle, The	O	F	Cleary, Beverly	Avon Camelot
Mouse Called Wolf, A	O	F	King-Smith, Dick	Alfred A. Knopf
Mouse of Amherst, The	Q	F	Spires, Elizabeth	Farrar, Straus and Giroux
Mouse Soup	J	F	Lobel, Arnold	Harper Collins
Mouse Tales	J	F	Lobel, Arnold	Harper Collins
Mouse Who Wanted to Marry, The	J	F	Bank Street	Bantam Doubleday Dell
Mr. Ape	O	F	King-Smith, Dick	Alfred A. Knopf
Mr. Beep	M	F	Read Alongs	Rigby
Mr. Mysterious & Company	R	F	Fleischman, Sid	Beech Tree
Mr. Popper's Penguins	Q	F	Atwater, Richard and Florence	Dell
Mr. Potter's Pet	N	F	King-Smith, Dick	Hyperion
Mr. Revere and I	U	F	Lawson, Robert	Little, Brown & Co.
Mr. Sun and Mr. Sea	L	F	Sunshine	Wright Group/McGraw Hill
Mrs. Bubble's Baby	M	F	Pacific Literacy	Pacific Learning
Mrs. Frisby and the Rats of NIMH	V	F	O'Brien, Robert C.	Aladdin
Mrs. Huggins and Her Hen Hannah	K	F	Dabcovich, Lydia	Dutton
Mrs. Piggle-Wiggle	O	F	MacDonald, Betty	Scholastic
Mrs. Piggle-Wiggle's Farm	O	F	MacDonald, Betty	Scholastic
Mrs. Piggle-Wiggle's Magic	O	F	MacDonald, Betty	Scholastic
Mrs. Sheep's Garden	K	F	Kratky, Lada	Hampton-Brown

Title	Level	Genre	Author/Series	Publisher/Distributor
Mummies Don't Coach Softball	M	F	Dadey, D. & Jones, M. T.	Scholastic
Mummies in the Morning	M	F	Osborne, Mary Pope	Random House
Mummy's Curse, The	O	F	SupaDoopers	Sundance
Mummy's Gold, The	L	F	McMullan, Kate	Grosset & Dunlap
My Brother is a Visitor From Another Planet	R	F	Sheldon, Dyan	Candlewick Press
My Family & the Wasps	N	F	Parker, John	Dominie Press
My Father The Mad Professor	P	F	Odgers, Sally	Rigby
My Father's Dragon	N	F	Gannett, Ruth Stiles	Random House
My Friend the Monster	N	F	Bulla, Clyde Robert	Harper & Row
My Sloppy Tiger Goes to School	J	F	Sunshine	Wright Group/McGraw Hill
My Son, the Time Traveler	N	F	The Zack Files	Grosset & Dunlap
My Teacher Flunked the Planet	S	F	Coville, Bruce	Pocket Books
My Teacher Fried My Brains	S	F	Coville, Bruce	Pocket Books
My Teacher Glows in the Dark	S	F	Coville, Bruce	Pocket Books
My Teacher Is an Alien	S	F	Coville, Bruce	Pocket Books
My Teacher Turns into a Tyrannosaurus	O	F	SupaDoopers	Sundance
My Wonderful Aunt, Story Five	M	F	Sunshine	Wright Group/McGraw Hill
My Wonderful Aunt, Story Four	M	F	Sunshine	Wright Group/McGraw Hill
My Wonderful Aunt, Story One	M	F	Sunshine	Wright Group/McGraw Hill
My Wonderful Aunt, Story Six	M	F	Sunshine	Wright Group/McGraw Hill
My Wonderful Aunt, Story Three	M	F	Sunshine	Wright Group/McGraw Hill
My Wonderful Aunt, Story Two	M	F	Sunshine	Wright Group/McGraw Hill
Mystery in the Night Woods	M	F	Peterson, John	Scholastic
Mystery of Moody Manor, The	M	F	Dionetti, Michelle	Wright Group/McGraw Hill
Mystery of Pony Hollow, The	N	F	Hall, Lynn	Random House
Mystery of the Cupboard	R	F	Banks, Lynne Reid	Avon Camelot
Mystery of the Dark Old House, The	M	F	Schultz, Irene	Wright Group/McGraw Hill
Mystery of the Missing Dog, The	J	F	Levy, Elizabeth	Scholastic
Mystery of the Missing Leopard, The	Q	F	Leonhardt, Alice	Steck-Vaughn
Mystery of the Pirate Ghost, The	L	F	Hayes, Geoffrey	Random House
Mystery of the Stolen Bike, The	M	F	Brown, Marc	Little, Brown & Co.
Mystery of the Talking Tail, The	M	F	SupaDoopers	Sundance
Myth or Mystery?	Q	F	Weber, Rebecca	Rigby
Mythical Beasts	T	F	Wildcats	Wright Group/McGraw Hill
Nathan and Nicholas Alexander	K	F	Delacre, Lulu	Scholastic
Neighbor From Outer Space, The	N	F	George, Maureen	Scholastic
Nelson the Baby Elephant	J	F	PM Turquoise	Rigby
Never Trust a Cat Who Wears Earrings	N	F	The Zack Files	Grosset & Dunlap
New Kind of Magic, The	P	F	Szymanski, Lois	Avon Camelot
New Light for the Lodge, A	L	F	Smith, Ben	Wright Group/McGraw Hill
Newbery Halloween, A: A Dozen Scary Stories by Newbery Award-Winning Authors	W	F	Greenberg, M.H. & Waugh, C.G.	Delacorte
Newt	J	F	Novak, Matt	HarperTrophy
Nicketty-Nacketty Noo-Noo-Noo	K	F	Cowley, Joy	Mondo
Night of the Ninjas	M	F	Osborne, Mary Pope	Random House
Night Queen's Blue Velvet Dress, The	Q	F	Pair-It Books	Steck-Vaughn
Night Terrors, Stories of Shadow and Substance	Z	F	Duncan, Lois	Aladdin
Nighty-Nightmare	R	F	Howe, James	Avon Camelot
Nine Lives of Adventure Cat, The	L	F	Clymer, Susan	Scholastic
No Flying in the House	P	F	Brock, Betty	Harper Collins
No Jumping On The Bed!	L	F	Arnold, Tedd	Scholastic
No More Monsters for Me!	J	F	Parish, Peggy	HarperTrophy
No Tooth, No Quarter!	K	F	Buller, Jon	Random House
No Way, Winky Blue!	N	F	Jane, Pamela	Mondo
Norman Newman and the Werewolf of Walnut Street	Q	F	Conford, Ellen	Troll
Not Now! Said the Cow	J	F	Bank Street	Bantam Doubleday Dell
Now Listen, Stanley	K	F	Literacy 2000	Rigby
Now You See Me...Now You Don't	N	F	The Zack Files	Grosset & Dunlap
Odder Than Ever	Z	F	Coville, Bruce	Harcourt Inc.

Title	Level	Genre	Author/Series	Publisher/Distributor
Oddly Enough	Z	F	Coville, Bruce	Pocket Books
Oh, Columbus!	K	F	Literacy 2000	Rigby
Old Devil Wind	J	F	Martin, Bill Jr.	Harcourt Brace
Old Enough for Magic	L	F	Pickett, A.	HarperTrophy
Old Meadow, The	S	F	Selden, George	Farrar, Straus and Giroux
Old Recipe Book, The	L	F	Smith, Ben	Wright Group/McGraw Hill
Oliver and Amanda's Halloween	L	F	Van Leeuwen, Jean	Puffin Books
On Fortune's Wheel	Z	F	Voigt, Cynthia	Aladdin
On Friday the Giant	K	F	The Giant	Wright Group/McGraw Hill
On Monday the Giant	K	F	The Giant	Wright Group/McGraw Hill
On Sunday the Giant	K	F	The Giant	Wright Group/McGraw Hill
On the Way to the Moon	O	F	Gold, Becky	Pearson Learning
On Thursday the Giant	K	F	The Giant	Wright Group/McGraw Hill
On Tuesday the Giant	K	F	The Giant	Wright Group/McGraw Hill
On Wednesday the Giant	K	F	The Giant	Wright Group/McGraw Hill
Once upon a Rhyme	M	F	Pacific Literacy	Pacific Learning
Once When I Was Shipwrecked	L	F	Literacy 2000	Rigby
One- Eyed Jake	M	F	Hutchins, Pat	Morrow
Oogly Gum Chasing Game, The	K	F	Literacy 2000	Rigby
Original Adventures of Hank the Cowdog, The	Q	F	Erickson, John R.	Gulf
Oscar Otter	J	F	Benchley, Nathaniel	HarperTrophy
Others See Us	Z	F	Sleator, William	Puffin Books
Outcast of Redwall, The	Z	F	Jacques, Brian	Ace Books
Over Sea, Under Stone	X	F	Cooper, Susan	Simon & Schuster
Owl At Home	J	F	Lobel, Arnold	Harper Collins
Owls in the Family	P	F	Mowat, Farley	Bantam Doubleday Dell
P.W. Cracker Sees the World	Q	F	Yoshizawa, Linda	Steck-Vaughn
Pagemaster, The	P	F	Horowitz, Jordan	Scholastic
Painting Lesson, The	K	F	Pacific Literacy	Pacific Learning
Pandas in the Mountains	M	F	PM Gold	Rigby
Passager: The Young Merlin Trilogy	V	F	Yolen, Jane	Scholastic
Patrick and the Leprechaun	L	F	PM Gold	Rigby
Peanut Butter Gang, The	K	F	Siracusa, Catherine	Hyperion
Perfect the Pig	L	F	Jeschke, Susan	Scholastic
Pete's Story	L	F	Literacy 2000	Rigby
Pets	J	F	Pacific Literacy	Pacific Learning
Phantom Tollbooth, The	W	F	Juster, Norton	Bantam Doubleday Dell
Phantoms Don't Drive Sports Cars	M	F	Dadey, D. & Jones, M. T.	Scholastic
Pie Magic	N	F	Cornell, Laura	Beech Tree Books
Piggle	K	F	Bonsall, Crosby	Harper Collins
Pignocchio	L	F	Pair-It Books	Steck-Vaughn
Pigs Might Fly	R	F	King-Smith, Dick	Scholastic
Pike River Phantom, The	R	F	Wright, Betty	Scholastic
Pioneer Bear	L	F	Sandin, Joan	Random House
Pippi Goes on Board	O	F	Lindgren, Astrid	Puffin Books
Pippi in the South Seas	O	F	Lindgren, Astrid	Puffin Books
Pippi Longstocking	O	F	Lindgren, Astrid	The Penguin Group
Pirate Pie	M	F	Vaughan, Marcia	Pacific Learning
Pirates Don't Wear Pink Sunglasses	M	F	Dadey, D. & Jones, M. T.	Scholastic
Pirates Past Noon	M	F	Osborne, Mary Pope	Scholastic
Planet Boring	P	F	Cook, Nathan	Pacific Learning
Plant That Ate Dirty Socks Goes Up in Space	S	F	McArthur, Nancy	Avon Camelot
Play Ball, Amelia Bedelia	L	F	Parish, Peggy	Harper & Row
Pleasing the Ghost	V	F	Creech, Sharon	Harper Collins
Pocket for Corduroy, A	K	F	Freeman, Don	Scholastic
Polar Bears Past Bedtime	M	F	Osborne, Mary Pope	Random House
Pookie and Joe	K	F	Literacy 2000	Rigby
Pool of Fire, The	V	F	Christopher, John	Aladdin
Poppleton	J	F	Rylant, Cynthia	Scholastic
Poppleton and Friends	J	F	Rylant, Cynthia	Blue Sky Press

Title	Level	Genre	Author/Series	Publisher/Distributor
Poppleton Everyday	J	F	Rylant, Cynthia	Scholastic
Poppleton Forever	J	F	Rylant, Cynthia	Scholastic
Poppleton Has Fun	J	F	Rylant, Cynthia	Scholastic
Poppleton In Fall	J	F	Rylant, Cynthia	Scholastic
Poppleton in Spring	J	F	Rylant, Cynthia	Scholastic
Poppy	S	F	Avi	Avon
Poppy and Rye	S	F	Avi	Avon
Porcupine's Pajama Party	J	F	Harshman, Terry Webb	HarperTrophy
Princess and the Castle, The	J	F	Leonhardt, Alice	Steck-Vaughn
Princess Rosa's Winter	K	F	Hindley, Judy	Wright Group/McGraw Hill
Princess Who Loved to Cook, The	M	F	Cartwright, Pauline	Dominie Press
Princess Who Wanted the Moon, The	M	F	Lane, Sheila and Marion Kemp	Wood Lock Educational
Proof of Magic	N	F	Dionetti, Michelle	Wright Group/McGraw Hill
Proud Taste For Scarlet And Miniver	W	F	Konigsburg, E. L.	Dell
Pterodactyl at the Airport	K	F	Wesley & the Dinosaurs	Wright Group/McGraw Hill
Pumpkin House, The	J	F	Literacy 2000	Rigby
Puppy Who Wanted a Boy, The	L	F	Thayer, Jane	Scholastic
Pushcart War, The	Y	F	Merrill, Jean	Bantam Doubleday Dell
Quackers, the Troublesome Duck	M	F	Ellen, Leslie	Pearson Learning
R is for Radish!	J	F	Coxe, Molly	Random House
Rabbit Catches the Sun	M	F	Sunshine	Wright Group/McGraw Hill
Rabbit Stew	L	F	Literacy 2000	Rigby
Rabbit's Birthday Kite	J	F	Bank Street	Bantam Doubleday Dell
Race to Green End, The	J	F	PM Turquoise	Rigby
Ragweed	U	F	Avi	Avon
Rain Forest Adventure	L	F	Pair-It Books	Steck-Vaughn
Rain Ghost, The	X	F	Kilworth, Garry	Scholastic
Rainbow People, The	V	F	Yep, Lawrence	HarperTrophy
Rainbow Wings	M	F	Nevinski, Margaret	Wright Group/McGraw Hill
Rairarubia	S	F	Adams, W. Royce	Lost Coast Press
Ralph S. Mouse	O	F	Cleary, Beverly	Harper Trophy
Rat's Tale, A	T	F	Seidler, Tor	HarperTrophy
Rats on the Range and Other Stories	O	F	Marshall, James	The Penguin Group
Rats on the Roof and Other Stories	O	F	Marshall, James	The Penguin Group
Raven's Gift	L	F	Books For Young Learners	Richard C. Owen
Real Thief, The	U	F	Steig, William	Farrar, Straus and Giroux
Remarkable Journey of Prince Jen, The	V	F	Alexander, Lloyd	Bantam Doubleday Dell
Rescuers, The	S	F	Sharp, Margery	Dell Publishing
Rescuing Nelson	J	F	PM Turquoise	Rigby
Return to Howliday Inn	P	F	Howe, James	Avon Camelot
Revolutionary War on Wednesday	M	F	Osborne, Mary Pope	Random House
Ring of Endless Light, A	W	F	L'Engle, Madeleine	Dell
Roald Dahl's Revolting Rhymes	P	F	Dahl, Roald	Puffin Books
Robber Pig and the Ginger Bear	M	F	Read Alongs	Rigby
Robber Pig and the Green Eggs	M	F	Read Alongs	Rigby
Rodney, the Surfing Duck	N	F	SupaDoopers	Sundance
Rollo and Tweedy and the Ghost at Dougal Castle	K	F	Allen, Laura Jean	HarperTrophy
Rooster's Gift, The	M	F	Conrad, Pam	HarperCollins
Rosa and Fredo	M	F	SupaDoopers	Sundance
Ruby and the Smoke, The	Y	F	Pullman, Phillip	Laurel-Leaf Books
Runaway Ralph	O	F	Cleary, Beverly	Hearst
Rupert and the Griffin	Q	F	Hillman, Robert	Rigby
Salamandastron	Z	F	Jacques, Brian	Ace Books
Sam and the Firefly	J	F	Eastman, P.D.	Random House
Sam Who Never Forgets	K	F	Rice, Eve	Morrow
Santa Claus Doesn't Mop Floors	M	F	Dadey, D. & Jones, M. T.	Scholastic
Scared Stiff	V	F	Malcolm, Jahnna N.	Scholastic
School Mouse, The	P	F	King-Smith, Dick	Hyperion
Search for Delicious, The	U	F	Babbitt, Natalie	Farrar, Straus and Giroux
Search for the Lost Cave, The	M	F	Schultz, Irene	Wright Group/McGraw Hill

Title	Level	Genre	Author/Series	Publisher/Distributor
Seaward	X	F	Cooper, Susan	Simon & Schuster
Secret Land of the Past	N	F	Schlein, Miriam	Scholastic
Secret of Bunratty Castle, The	Q	F	Vaughan, Marcia	Rigby
Secret of Foghorn Island, The	L	F	Step into Reading	Random House
Secret of NIMH, The	V	F	O'Brien, Robert C.	Scholastic
Secret of the Monster Book, The	M	F	Schultz, Irene	Wright Group/McGraw Hill
Secret of the Old Oak Trunk, The	M	F	Schultz, Irene	Wright Group/McGraw Hill
Secret of the Silver Shoes, The	Q	F	Massie, Elizabeth	Steck-Vaughn
Secret of the Song, The	M	F	Schultz, Irene	Wright Group/McGraw Hill
Selchie's Seed, The	W	F	Levey Oppenheim, Shulamith	Harcourt Brace
Selfish Giant, The	L	F	Literacy 2000	Rigby
Seventh Tower, The: The Fall	W	F	Nix, Garth	Scholastic
Sheeba	L	F	Noonan, Diana	Dominie Press
Sheila Rae, the Brave	K	F	Henkes, Kevin	Scholastic
Shoebag	P	F	James, Mary	Scholastic
Shopping with a Crocodile	L	F	Pacific Literacy	Pacific Learning
Sideways Stories from Wayside School	P	F	Sachar, Louis	Hearst
Silly Tilly's Valentine	K	F	Hoban, Lillian	HarperTrophy
Silly Willy and Silly Billy	J	F	Foundations	Wright Group/McGraw Hill
Silverwing: How One Small Bat Became a Noble Hero	U	F	Oppel, Kenneth	Simon & Schuster
Sing to the Moon	K	F	Story Box	Wright Group/McGraw Hill
Six Voyages of Pleasant Fieldmouse, The	R	F	Wahl, Jan	Tom Doherty
Skeleton On The Bus, The	J	F	Literacy 2000	Rigby
Skeletons Don't Play Tubas	M	F	Dadey, D. & Jones, M. T.	Scholastic
Sky High	L	F	Pair-It Books	Steck-Vaughn
SkyFire	J	F	Asch, Frank	Scholastic
Smallest Tree, The	K	F	Literacy 2000	Rigby
Smartest Bear and His Brother Oliver, The	N	F	Bach, Alice	Bantam Doubleday Dell
Smartest Man in Ireland, The	S	F	Hunter, Mollie	Harcourt Brace
Smokey the Dragon	M	F	Bennett, Jean	Dominie Press
Snot Stew	P	F	Wallace, Bill	Pocket Books
Snow Bright and the Seven Sumos	M	F	SupaDoopers	Sundance
Snow Bright and the Tooth Magician	M	F	SupaDoopers	Sundance
Snow Goes To Town	L	F	Literacy 2000	Rigby
Sock Gobbler and Other Stories, The	M	F	Learning Media	Pacific Learning
Something Soft for Danny Bear	M	F	Literacy 2000	Rigby
Sophie Hits Six	M	F	King-Smith, Dick	Candlewick Press
Sophie in the Saddle	M	F	King-Smith, Dick	Candlewick Press
Sophie Is Seven	M	F	King-Smith, Dick	Candlewick Press
Sophie's Lucky	M	F	King-Smith, Dick	Candlewick Press
Sophie's Snail	M	F	King-Smith, Dick	Candlewick Press
Sophie's Tom	M	F	King-Smith, Dick	Candlewick Press
Space Dog and Roy	L	F	Standiford, Natalie	Random House
Space Dog and the Pet Show	L	F	Standiford, Natalie	Random House
Space Dog in Trouble	L	F	Standiford, Natalie	Random House
Space Dog the Hero	L	F	Standiford, Natalie	Random House
Space Race	J	F	Sunshine	Wright Group/McGraw Hill
Space Rock	L	F	Buller, Jon	Random House
Spell Casters, Phoebe's Fortune	R	F	Warriner, Holly	Aladdin
Spider Kane and the Mystery at Jumbo Nightcrawler's	O	F	Osborne, Mary Pope	Random House
Spider Kane and the Mystery Under the May-Apple	O	F	Osborne, Mary Pope	Random House
Spirit of Hope	N	F	Book Shop	Mondo
Spooky Tail of Prewitt Peacock, The	M	F	Peet, Bill	Houghton Mifflin
Spring Fever!	T	F	Lerangis, Peter	Language for Learning Assoc.
Spy Down the Street, The	M	F	Schultz, Irene	Wright Group/McGraw Hill
Stanley and the Magic Lamp	P	F	Brown, Jeff	HarperTrophy
Stay! Keeper's Story	U	F	Lowry, Lois	Random House
Sterkarm Handshake, The	Z	F	Price, Susan	Scholastic
Straight Line Wonder, The	J	F	Book Shop	Mondo
Stranger Came Ashore, A	U	F	Hunter, Mollie	HarperTrophy

Title	Level	Genre	Author/Series	Publisher/Distributor
Strike Me Down with a Stringbean	L	F	Read Alongs	Rigby
Stuart Little	R	F	White, E.B.	HarperTrophy
Subtle Knife, The	Z	F	Pullman, Philip	Ballantine Books
Summer I Shrank My Grandmother, The	Q	F	Woodruff, Elvira	Bantam Doubleday Dell
Summer in the South, A	Q	F	Marshall, James	Houghton Mifflin
Summer Reading is Killing Me!	N	F	Scieszka, Jon	Puffin Books
Summer Switch	R	F	Rodgers, Mary	HarperTrophy
Sunflower That Went Flop, The	K	F	Story Box	Wright Group/McGraw Hill
Sunset of the Sabertooth	M	F	Osborne, Mary Pope	Random House
Swamp of the Hideous Zombies	M	F	Hayes, Geoffrey	Random House
Swiftly Tilting Planet, A	V	F	L'Engle, Madeleine	Bantam Doubleday Dell
Tales of Amanda Pig	L	F	Van Leeuwen, Jean	Puffin Books
Tales of Olga da Polga, The	P	F	Bond, Michael	Houghton Mifflin
Teach Us, Amelia Bedelia	L	F	Parish, Peggy	Scholastic
Teacher's Pet	L	F	Dicks, Terrance	Scholastic
Teddy Bears Cure a Cold	K	F	Gretz, Susanna	Scholastic
Ten Apples Up on Top	J	F	LaSieg, Theo	Random House
Ten O'Clock Club, The	N	F	Beach York, Carol	Scholastic
Thank You, Amelia Bedelia	L	F	Little Readers	Houghton Mifflin
That Fat Hat	K	F	Barkan, Joanne	Scholastic
That's Really Weird!	K	F	Read Alongs	Rigby
There Is a Carrot in My Ear and Other Noodle Tales	J	F	Schwartz, Alvin	HarperTrophy
Three Blind Mice Mystery, The	L	F	Krensky, Stephen	Bantam Doubleday Dell
Three Sillies, The	L	F	Literacy 2000	Rigby
Three Stories You Can Read to Your Cat	K	F	Miller, Sara Swan	Houghton Mifflin
Three Stories You Can Read to Your Dog	K	F	Miller, Sara Swan	Houghton Mifflin
Through the Garden Door	M	F	Reeves, Barbara	Pearson Learning
Through the Medicine Cabinet	N	F	The Zack Files	Grosset & Dunlap
Tickle-Bugs, The	J	F	Literacy 2000	Rigby
Tigers at Twilight	M	F	Osborne, Mary Pope	Random House
Time for Andrew	S	F	Hahn, Mary	Avon Camelot
Time of Angels, A	W	F	Hesse, Karen	Hyperion
Time Warp Trio: The Knights of the Kitchen Table	P	F	Scieszka, Jon	The Penguin Group
Time Warp Trio: The Not-So-Jolly Roger	P	F	Scieszka, Jon	The Penguin Group
Time Warp Trio: Tut Tut	P	F	Scieszka, Jon	The Penguin Group
Time Warp Trio: Your Mother Was a Neanderthal	P	F	Scieszka, Jon	The Penguin Group
Timothy Whuffenpuffen-Whippersnapper	S	F	Literacy 2000	Rigby
Timothy's Five-City Tour	M	F	Pair-It Books	Steck-Vaughn
Toad for Tuesday, A	O	F	Erickson, Russell E.	Beech Tree Books
Tom, Babette, & Simon	T	F	Avi	Avon
Tom, the Dragon	M	F	New Way Orange	Steck-Vaughn
Tom the TV Cat	J	F	Heilbroner, Joan	Random House
Tom's Midnight Garden	V	F	Pierce, Philippa	HarperTrophy
Tomorrow's Wizard	R	F	MacLachlan, Patricia	Scholastic
Tonight on the Titanic	M	F	Osborne, Mary Pope	Random House
Too Many Mice	J	F	Bank Street	Bantam Doubleday Dell
Too Much Magic	R	F	Sterman, Betsy & Samuel	HarperTrophy
Treasure of Alpheus Winterborn, The	S	F	Bellairs, John	The Penguin Group
Treasure of the Lost Lagoon, The	K	F	Hayes, Geoffrey	Random House
Treasury of Pirate Stories, A	S	F	Bradman, Tony	Kingfisher
Tree by Leaf	V	F	Voigt, Cynthia	Simon & Schuster
Triceratops on the Farm	L	F	Wesley & the Dinosaurs	Wright Group/McGraw Hill
Trickster Ghost, The	O	F	Showell, E.	Scholastic
Triffic the Extraordinary Pig	R	F	King-Smith, Dick	Bantam Doubleday Dell
Trog	M	F	Sunshine	Wright Group/McGraw Hill
Trolls Don't Ride Roller Coasters	M	F	Dadey, D. & Jones, M. T.	Scholastic
Trouble Dolls	P	F	Buffett, Jimmy & Savannah Jane	Harcourt Brace
Trouble with Herbert, The	L	F	Eyles, Heather	Mondo
Troubling a Star	V	F	L'Engle, Madeleine	Dell
Trumpet of the Swan, The	R	F	White, E. B.	Scholastic

Title	Level	Genre	Author/Series	Publisher/Distributor
Tuck Everlasting	U	F	Babbitt, Natalie	Farrar, Straus and Giroux
Turkey That Ate My Father, The	Q	F	Marney, Dean	Scholastic
Turtle Flies South	K	F	Literacy 2000	Rigby
Twiddle Twins' Haunted House, The	L	F	Goldsmith, Howard	Mondo
Twiddle Twins' Music Box Mystery, The	L	F	Goldsmith, Howard	Mondo
Twiddle Twins' Single Footprint Mystery, The	L	F	Goldsmith, Howard	Mondo
Twits, The	P	F	Dahl, Roald	The Penguin Group
Two Foolish Cats	K	F	Literacy 2000	Rigby
Two Silly Trolls	J	F	Jewell, Nancy	HarperTrophy
Tyler Toad and Thunder	M	F	Crowe, Robert	Dutton
Tyrannosaurus the Terrible	L	F	Wesley & the Dinosaurs	Wright Group/McGraw Hill
Uncle Elephant	J	F	Lobel, Arnold	Harper Collins
Unicorns Don't Give Sleigh Rides	M	F	Dadey, D. & Jones, M. T.	Scholastic
Upside-Down Reader, The	L	F	Gruber, Wolfram	North-South Books
Vacation Under the Volcano	M	F	Osborne, Mary Pope	Random House
Vampire Trouble	L	F	Dadey, D. & Jones, M. T.	Scholastic
Vampire Who Came For Christmas, The	Q	F	Curtis Regan, Dian	Bantam Doubleday Dell
Vampires Don't Wear Polka Dots	M	F	Dadey, D. & Jones, M. T.	Scholastic
Velveteen Rabbit, The	Q	F	Williams, Margery	Hearst
Very Strange Dollhouse, A	L	F	Dussling, Jennifer	Grosset & Dunlap
View from Saturday, The	U	F	Konigsburg, E. L.	Atheneum Books
Viking Ships at Sunrise	M	F	Osborne, Mary Pope	Random House
Volcano Goddess Will See You Now, The	N	F	The Zack Files	Grosset & Dunlap
Voyage, The	M	F	Pair-It Books	Steck-Vaughn
Vulpes The Red Fox	T	F	George, Jean Craighead	Puffin Books
Wainscott Weasel, The	T	F	Seidler, Tor	Harper Collins
Wait Till Helen Comes	U	F	Downing Hahn, Mary	Houghton Mifflin
Wake Me in Spring	J	F	Preller, James	Scholastic
Walter the Warlock	M	F	Hautzig, Deborah	Random House
Walter's Worries	L	F	Pacific Literacy	Pacific Learning
Warton and the King of the Skies	O	F	Erickson, Russell E.	Houghton Mifflin
Watership Down	Y	F	Adams, Richard	Avon
Wayside School Gets a Little Stranger	P	F	Sachar, Louis	Avon Camelot
Wayside School is Falling Down	P	F	Sachar, Louis	Avon
Week of the Jellyhoppers, The	R	F	Literacy 2000	Rigby
Well I Never	K	F	Story Box	Wright Group/McGraw Hill
Werewolf Chronicles, The	T	F	Philbrick, R. & Harnett, L.	Scholastic
Werewolves Don't Go To Summer Camp	M	F	Dadey, D. & Jones, M. T.	Scholastic
What Do You Hear When Cows Sing?	J	F	Maestro, Marco & Giulio	HarperTrophy
What Next, Baby Bear?	L	F	Murphy, Jill	Dial
When the Giants Came to Town	L	F	Leonard, Marcia	Scholastic
When the King Rides By	J	F	Book Shop	Mondo
When the Tripods Came	V	F	Christopher, John	Aladdin
When the Volcano Erupted	J	F	PM Turquoise	Rigby
Where Are the Bears?	K	F	Winters, Kay	Bantam Doubleday Dell
Where Did the Maya Go?	P	F	Carroll, Cynthia	Rigby
Where the Wild Things Are	J	F	Sendak, Maurice	Harper & Row
Where to Look for a Dinosaur	O	F	Most, Bernard	Harcourt Brace
Which Way, Jack?	O	F	Yurkovic, Diana Short	Rigby
Which Witch?	S	F	Ibbotson, Eva	Puffin Books
Whipping Boy, The	R	F	Fleischman, Sid	Troll
White Horse, The	K	F	Literacy 2000	Rigby
White Mountain, The	V	F	Christopher, John	Aladdin
Who Sank the Boat?	K	F	Allen Pamela	Coward
Who's a Pest?	J	F	Bonsall, Crosby	HarperTrophy
Who's in Love with Arthur?	M	F	Brown, Marc	Little, Brown & Co.
Why Crocodiles Live in Rivers	M	F	Sunshine	Wright Group/McGraw Hill
Why the Bear's Tail is Short	J	F	Sunshine	Wright Group/McGraw Hill
Wilamina and the Weather Conditions	M	F	Reimer, Luther	Wright Group/McGraw Hill
Wild Willie and King Kyle Detectives	N	F	Joosse, Barbara M.	Bantam Doubleday Dell

Title	Level	Genre	Author/Series	Publisher/Distributor
Wild, Wooly Child, The	J	F	Read Alongs	Rigby
Wind and the Sun and Other Stories, The	J	F	New Way Orange	Steck-Vaughn
Wind in the Door, A	V	F	L'Engle, Madeleine	Bantam Doubleday Dell
Wingman	O	F	Pinkwater, Daniel	Bantam Skylark
Wings	Q	F	Brittain, Bill	HarperTrophy
Winklepoo the Wicked	M	F	Sunshine	Wright Group/McGraw Hill
Wish Giver, The	T	F	Brittain, Bill	HarperTrophy
Witch's Cat	P	F	Chew, Ruth	Scholastic
Witches Don't Do Backflips	M	F	Dadey, D. & Jones, M. T.	Scholastic
Witches of Worm, The	V	F	Snyder, Zilpha K.	Random House
Witches, The	R	F	Dahl, Roald	The Penguin Group
Wizard and Wart at Sea	J	F	Smith, Janice Lee	HarperTrophy
Wizard of Earthsea, A	Z	F	LeGuin, Ursula K.	Bantam Doubleday Dell
Wizard of Oz, The	U	F	Baum, L. Frank	Scholastic
Wizards Don't Need Computers	M	F	Dadey, D. & Jones, M. T.	Scholastic
Wonderful Alexander and the Catwings	N	F	Schindler, S.D.	Scholastic
Woodlanders Begin, The	M	F	Schultz, Irene	Wright Group/McGraw Hill
Worst Witch at Sea, The	P	F	Murphy, Jill	Candlewick Press
Worst Witch Strikes Again, The	P	F	Murphy, Jill	Candlewick Press
Worst Witch, The	P	F	Murphy, Jill	Puffin Books
Wrinkle in Time, A	V	F	L'Engle, Madeleine	Bantom Doubleday Dell
Wrong Way Around Magic	N	F	Chew, Ruth	Scholastic
Wrong-Way Rabbit, The	J	F	Slater, Teddy	Scholastic
Yellow Overalls	L	F	Literacy 2000	Rigby
Yikes! Grandma's a Teenager	N	F	The Zack Files	Grossett&Dunlap
You Are Much Too Small	J	F	Bank Street	Bantam Doubleday Dell
You Can't Catch Me	J	F	Oppenheim, Joanne	Houghton Mifflin
Yuck!	K	F	Little Readers	Houghton Mifflin
Zack's Alligator	K	F	Mozelle, Shirley	HarperTrophy
Zack's Alligator Goes to School	K	F	Mozelle, Shirley	HarperTrophy
Zombies Don't Play Soccer	M	F	Dadey, D. & Jones, M. T.	Scholastic
Abraham's Battle: A Novel of Gettysburg	T	HF	Banks, Sara Harrell	Atheneum Books
Across Five Aprils	Z	HF	Hunt, Irene	Follett
Across the Lines	W	HF	Reeder, Carolyn	Avon Camelot
Adam of the Road	W	HF	Gray, Elizabeth Janet	Scholastic
Addy Learns a Lesson: A School Story	Q	HF	The American Girls Collection	Pleasant Company
Addy Saves the Day: A Summer Story	Q	HF	The American Girls Collection	Pleasant Company
Addy's Surprise: A Christmas Story	Q	HF	The American Girls Collection	Pleasant Company
Adventures of Huckleberry Finn, The	Z	HF	Twain, Mark	Scholastic
Adventures of Tom Sawyer, The	Z	HF	Twain, Mark	Scholastic
After the Dancing Days	W	HF	Rostkowski, Margaret I.	HarperTrophy
After the War	W	HF	Matas, Carol	Aladdin
Ahyoka and the Talking Leaves	S	HF	Roop, Peter and Connie	Beech Tree Books
Ajeemah and his Son	S	HF	Berry, James	HarperTrophy
All Is Well	R	HF	Litchman, Kristin Embry	Bantam Doubleday Dell
Allen Jay and the Underground Railroad	O	HF	Brill, Marlene Targ	Carolrhoda Books
Amos Fortune: Free Man	V	HF	Yates, Elizabeth	Puffin Books
Amy's True Prize	Q	HF	The Little Women Journals	Avon
An Island Far From Home	W	HF	Donahue, John	Carolrhonda Books
Animal Adventures	N	HF	Little House	HarperTrophy
Anna Is Still Here	V	HF	Vos, Ida	Puffin Books
Apprenticeship of Lucas Whitaker, The	U	HF	DeFelice, Cynthia	Avon
April Morning	X	HF	Fast, Howard	Bantam
Ark, The	O	HF	Geisert, Arthur	Houghton Mifflin
At Her Majesty's Request: An African Princess in Victorian England	X	HF	Myers, Walter Dean	Scholastic
Autumn Street	V	HF	Lowry, Lois	Bantam Doubleday Dell
Ballad of Robin Hood, The	P	HF	Literacy 2000	Rigby
Ballad of the Civil War, A	T	HF	Stolz, Mary	HarperTrophy
Bandit Moon	V	HF	Fleischman, Sid	Dell Yearling

Title	Level	Genre	Author/Series	Publisher/Distributor
Barefoot: Escape on the Underground Railroad	S	HF	Edwards, Pamela Duncan	HarperTrophy
Baseball Saved Us	O	HF	Mochizuki, Ken	Scholastic
Bear That Heard Crying, The	P	HF	Kinsey-Warnock, N. & Kinsey, H.	The Penguin Group
Behind Rebel Lines	T	HF	Reit, Seymour	Harcourt Brace
Behind The Bedroom Wall	V	HF	Williams, Laura E.	Milkweed Editions
Ben and Me	S	HF	Lawson, Robert	Little, Brown & Co.
Bess's Log Cabin Quilt	P	HF	Love, D. Anne	Bantam Doubleday Dell
Beth's Snow Dancer	Q	HF	The Little Women Journals	Avon
Betsy and Tacy Go Downtown	Q	HF	Lovelace, Maud Hart	HarperTrophy
Betsy and Tacy Go Over the Big Hill	Q	HF	Lovelace, Maud Hart	HarperTrophy
Betsy-Tacy: 60th Anniversary Edition	Q	HF	Lovelace, Maud Hart	HarperTrophy
Between the Dragon and the Eagle	W	HF	Schneider, Mical	Carolrhoda Books
Beyond the Western Sea, Book II: Lord Kirkle's Money	V	HF	Avi	Avon Camelot
Birchbark House, The	T	HF	Erdrich, Louise	Hyperion
Black Hearts in Battersea	V	HF	Aiken, Joan	Houghton Mifflin
Black-Eyed Susan	Q	HF	Armstrong, Jennifer	Alfred A. Knopf
Blue Door, The	X	HF	Rinaldi, Ann	Scholastic
Borning Room, The	Y	HF	Fleischman, Paul	Harper Collins
Boy's Will, A	S	HF	Haugaard, Erik Christian	Houghton Mifflin
Bracelet, The	R	HF	Uchida, Yoshiko	Philomel Books
Brady	V	HF	Fritz, Jean	Puffin Books
Bright Paddles	P	HF	Downi, Mary Alice	Fitzhenry and Whiteside
Broken Blade, The	T	HF	Durbin, William	Yearling
Bronze Bow, The	U	HF	Speare, Elizabeth George	Houghton Mifflin
Brookfield Days	N	HF	Little House	HarperTrophy
Bull Run	Y	HF	Fleischman, Paul	HarperCollins
Buttons for General Washington	M	HF	Roop, Peter & Connie	Carolrhoda Books
By the Great Horn Spoon!	V	HF	Fleischman, Sid	Little, Brown & Co.
By the Shores of Silver Lake	Q	HF	Wilder, Laura Ingalls	HarperTrophy
Cabin Faced West, The	R	HF	Fritz, Jean	Bantam Doubleday Dell
Caddie Woodlawn	R	HF	Brink, Carol Ryrie	Bantam Doubleday Dell
Caleb's Choice	S	HF	Wisler, Clifton G.	The Penguin Group
Calico Bush	V	HF	Field, Rachel	Simon & Schuster
Calico Captive	S	HF	Speare, Elizabeth George	Yearling
Call Me Francis Tucket	V	HF	Paulsen, Gary	Yearling
Captain Grey	U	HF	Avi	HarperTrophy
Catherine, Called Birdy	U	HF	Cushman, Karen	Clarion
Cay, The	V	HF	Taylor, Theodore	Avon
Changes for Addy	Q	HF	The American Girls Collection	Pleasant Company
Changes For Addy: A Winter Story	Q	HF	The American Girls Collection	Pleasant Company
Changes For Felicity: A Winter Story	Q	HF	The American Girls Collection	Pleasant Company
Changes For Josefina: A Winter Story	Q	HF	The American Girls Collection	Pleasant Company
Changes For Kirsten: A Winter Story	Q	HF	The American Girls Collection	Pleasant Company
Changes For Molly: A Winter Story	Q	HF	The American Girls Collection	Pleasant Company
Changes For Samantha: A Winter Story	Q	HF	The American Girls Collection	Pleasant Company
Charley Skedaddle	U	HF	Beatty, Patricia	Troll
Child in Prison Camp, A	X	HF	Takashima, Shizuye	Tundra Books
Children of the Fire	P	HF	Robinet, Harriette	Aladdin
Children of the Longhouse	S	HF	Bruchac, Joseph	The Penguin Group
Christmas in the Big Woods	J	HF	Wilder, Laura Ingalls	Harper Collins
Circle Unbroken, A	V	HF	Hotze, Sollace	Houghton Mifflin
Cloak of the Wind	O	HF	Voyages in…	Wright Group/McGraw Hill
Clouds of Terror	L	HF	Welsh, Catherine A.	Carolrhoda Books
Come Morning	V	HF	Guccione, Leslil Davis	Lerner Publications
Copper Lady, The	M	HF	Ross, Alice & Kent	Carolrhoda Books
Country Fair	J	HF	Wilder, Laura Ingalls	Harper Collins
Courage of Sarah Noble, The	O	HF	Dalgliesh, Alice	Aladdin
Dance at Grandpa's	J	HF	Wilder, Laura Ingalls	Harper Collins
Dancing with Jacques	P	HF	Voyages in…	Wright Group/McGraw Hill
Daughter of the Mountains	V	HF	Rankin, Louise	The Penguin Group

Title	Level	Genre	Author/Series	Publisher/Distributor
Dawn of Fear	X	HF	Cooper, Susan	Simon & Schuster
Day No Pigs Would Die, A	Z	HF	Peck, Sylvia	Random House
Dear Levi: Letters from the Overland Trail	T	HF	Woodruff, Elvira	Alfred A. Knopf
Deer in the Wood, The	J	HF	Wilder, Laura Ingalls	Harper Collins
Devil's Highway, The	T	HF	Applegate, Stan	Peachtree
Diary of a Pioneer Boy	Q	HF	Massie, Elizabeth	Steck-Vaughn
Door in the Wall, The	U	HF	De Angeli, Marguerite	Bantam Doubleday Dell
Dragon's Gate	W	HF	Yep, Laurence	Harper Collins
Dragonwings	W	HF	Yep, Lawrence	HarperTrophy
Drinking Gourd, The	M	HF	Monjo, F. N.	HarperTrophy
Echohawk	X	HF	Durrant, Lynda	Bantam Doubleday Dell
Farmer Boy	Q	HF	Wilder, Laura Ingalls	HarperTrophy
Farmer Boy Birthday, A	J	HF	Wilder, Laura Ingalls	Harper Collins
Farmer Boy Days	M	HF	Wilder, Laura Ingalls	HarperTrophy
Felicity Learns a Lesson	Q	HF	The American Girls Collection	Pleasant Company
Felicity Saves the Day	Q	HF	The American Girls Collection	Pleasant Company
Felicity's Surprise	Q	HF	The American Girls Collection	Pleasant Company
Fighting Ground, The	V	HF	Avi	HarperTrophy
Fire at the Triangle Factory	P	HF	Littlefield, Holly	Carolrhoda Books
Fire in the Sky	R	HF	Ransom, Candice F.	Carolrhoda Books
Fire! The Beginnings of the Labor Movement	R	HF	Goldin, Barbara Diamond	Puffin Books
First Four Years, The	R	HF	Wilder, Laura Ingalls	HarperTrophy
Flaming Arrows	T	HF	Steele, William O.	Harcourt Brace
Foster's War	V	HF	Reeder, Carolyn	Scholastic
Freedom Crossing	R	HF	Clark, Margaret Goff	Scholastic
Freedom Songs	T	HF	Moore, Yvette	Language for Learning Assoc.
Friendship and the Gold Cadillac, The	S	HF	Taylor, Mildred	Bantam Doubleday Dell
Friendship, The	S	HF	Taylor, Mildred	Puffin Books
Gathering of Days, A: A New England Girl's Journal, 1830-32	U	HF	Blos, Joan	Aladdin
Gentleman Outlaw and Me - Eli, The: A Story of the Old West	T	HF	Hahn, Mary Downing	Avon Camelot
George the Drummer Boy	K	HF	Benchley, Nathaniel	HarperTrophy
Ginger's War	N	HF	Daniel, Lea	Wright Group/McGraw Hill
Girl Who Chased Away Sorrow, The: The Diary of Sarah Nita, a Navajo Girl	T	HF	Turner, Ann	Scholastic
Girl-Son, The	R	HF	Neuberger, Anne E.	Carolrhoda Books
Glory Field, The	X	HF	Myers, Walter Dean	Scholastic
Going to Town	J	HF	Wilder, Laura Ingalls	Harper Collins
Going West	O	HF	Van Leeuwen, Jean	The Penguin Group
Going West	J	HF	Wilder, Laura Ingalls	HarperCollins
Gold Cadillac, The	S	HF	Taylor, Mildred D.	Puffin Books
Gold Dust Kids, The	N	HF	Dionetti, Michelle	Wright Group/McGraw Hill
Gold Fever!	N	HF	Step into Reading	Random House
Good Night, Mr. Tom	Z	HF	Magorian, Michelle	HarperTrophy
Good-Bye, Billy Radish	V	HF	Skurzynski, Gloria	Aladdin
Grace	U	HF	Walsh, Jill Paton	Farrar, Straus and Giroux
Grace's Letter to Lincoln	P	HF	Roop, Peter and Connie	Hyperion
Gratefully Yours	T	HF	Buchanan, Jane	Puffin Books
Great Chicago Fire, 1871, The	Z	HF	Massie, Elizabeth	Pocket Books
Great Expectations	S	HF	Bullseye Step Into Classics	Random House
Guests	T	HF	Dorris, Michael	Hyperion
Hannah of Fairfield	Q	HF	Pioneer Daughters	Puffin Books
Hannah's Fancy Notions: A Story of Industrial New England	R	HF	Ross, Pat	The Penguin Group
Hannah's Helping Hands	Q	HF	Van Leeuwen, Jean	Puffin Books
Hannah's Winter of Hope	Q	HF	Van Leeuwen, Jean	Puffin Books
Happy Birthday, Addy!	Q	HF	The American Girls Collection	Pleasant Company
Happy Birthday, Felicity!	Q	HF	The American Girls Collection	Pleasant Company
Happy Birthday, Josefina!	Q	HF	The American Girls Collection	Pleasant Company

Title	Level	Genre	Author/Series	Publisher/Distributor
Happy Birthday, Kirsten!	Q	HF	The American Girls Collection	Pleasant Company
Happy Birthday, Molly!	Q	HF	The American Girls Collection	Pleasant Company
Happy Birthday, Samantha!	Q	HF	The American Girls Collection	Pleasant Company
Hiroshima	S	HF	Yep, Laurence	Scholastic
Honorable Prison, The	W	HF	Becerra de Jenkins, Lyll	The Penguin Group
House of Dies Drear	V	HF	Hamilton, Virginia	Aladdin
I Am Regina	U	HF	Keehn, Sally	Bantam Doubleday Dell
I Rode a Horse of Milk White Jade	V	HF	Wilson, Diane Lee	HarperTrophy
In a New Land	L	HF	Sunshine	Wright Group/McGraw Hill
In the Year of the Boar and Jackie Robinson	S	HF	Lord, Bette Bao	HarperTrophy
Isabella: A Wish for Miguel	Q	HF	Childhood Journeys	Aladdin
Island of the Blue Dolphins	V	HF	O'Dell, Scott	Bantam Doubleday Dell
Island on Bird Street, The	X	HF	Orlev, Uri	Houghton Mifflin
Jacob's Rescue: A Holocaust Story	Y	HF	Drucker, M. & Halperin, M.	Bantam Doubleday Dell
Jason's Gold	T	HF	Hobbs, Will	William Morrow
Jip His Story	V	HF	Paterson, Katherine	The Penguin Group
Jo's Troubled Heart	Q	HF	The Little Women Journals	Avon
Josefina Learns a Lesson	Q	HF	The American Girls Collection	Pleasant Company
Josefina Saves the Day	Q	HF	The American Girls Collection	Pleasant Company
Josefina's Surprise	Q	HF	The American Girls Collection	Pleasant Company
Joseph: 1861-A Rumble of War	V	HF	Pryor, Bonnie	Avon
Journey to America	U	HF	Levitin, Sonia	Simon & Schuster
Journey to Jo'burg	S	HF	Naidoo, Beverly	HarperTrophy
Journey to Nowhere	T	HF	Auch, Mary Jane	Bantam Doubleday Dell
Journey to the New World	S	HF	Brocker, Susan	Rigby
Journey to Topaz	U	HF	Uchida, Yoshiko	Creative Arts Book Co.
Jump Ship to Freedom	U	HF	Collier, James and Christopher	Bantam Doubleday Dell
Justin Morgan Had a Horse	R	HF	Henry, Marguerite	Scholastic
Katarina	X	HF	Winter, Kathryn	Scholastic
Keep the Lights Burning Abbie	K	HF	Roop, Peter & Connie	Scholastic
Keeping Days, The	Z	HF	Johnston, Norma	Puffin Books
Keeping Room, The	V	HF	Myers, Anna	Puffin Books
King of the Wind	R	HF	Henry, Marguerite	Aladdin
Kirsten Learns a Lesson	Q	HF	The American Girls Collection	Pleasant Company
Kirsten Saves the Day	Q	HF	The American Girls Collection	Pleasant Company
Kirsten's Surprise	Q	HF	The American Girls Collection	Pleasant Company
Lady with the Hat, The	Z	HF	Orlev, Uri	The Penguin Group
Laura and Mr. Edwards	M	HF	Wilder, Laura Ingalls	HarperTrophy
Laura and Nellie	M	HF	Wilder, Laura Ingalls	HarperTrophy
Laura's Ma	M	HF	Wilder, Laura Ingalls	HarperTrophy
Laura's Pa	M	HF	Wilder, Laura Ingalls	HarperTrophy
Let the Circle Be Unbroken	X	HF	Taylor, Mildred D.	The Penguin Group
Letter to Mrs. Roosevelt, A	R	HF	DeYoung, C. Coco	Delacorte Press
Letters From a Slave Girl: The Story of Harriet Jacobs	X	HF	Lyons, Mary E.	Simon & Schuster
Letters from Rifka	S	HF	Hesse, Karen	Puffin Books
Letting Swift River Go	M	HF	Yolen, Jane	Little, Brown & Co.
Light in the Storm, A	T	HF	Hesse, Karen	Scholastic
Lily and Miss Liberty	N	HF	Stephens, Carla	Scholastic
Lily's Crossing	S	HF	Giff, Patricia Reilly	Delacourte Press
Lion to Guard Us, A	P	HF	Bulla, Clyde Robert	HarperTrophy
Listening to Crickets: A Story about Rachel Carson	R	HF	Ransom, Candice F.	Carolrhoda Books
Little Clearing in the Woods	Q	HF	Wilkes, Maria D.	HarperTrophy
Little Farm in the Ozarks	R	HF	MacBride, Roger Lea	HarperTrophy
Little Hawk's New Name	M	HF	Bolognese, Don	Scholastic
Little House Birthday, A	J	HF	Wilder, Laura Ingalls	Harper Collins
Little House by Boston Bay	Q	HF	Wiley, Melissa	HarperTrophy
Little House Farm Days	M	HF	Wilder, Laura Ingalls	HarperTrophy
Little House Friends	M	HF	Wilder, Laura Ingalls	HarperTrophy
Little House in Brookfield	Q	HF	Wilkes, Maria D.	HarperTrophy

Title	Level	Genre	Author/Series	Publisher/Distributor
Little House in the Big Woods	Q	HF	Wilder, Laura Ingalls	HarperTrophy
Little House in the Highlands	Q	HF	Wiley, Melissa	HarperTrophy
Little House on Rocky Ridge	R	HF	MacBride, Roger Lea	HarperTrophy
Little House on the Prairie	Q	HF	Wilder, Laura Ingalls	HarperTrophy
Little Pear	O	HF	Lattimore, Eleanor F.	Harcourt Brace
Little Pear and His Friends	O	HF	Lattimore, Eleanor F.	Harcourt Brace
Little Prairie House, A	J	HF	Wilder, Laura Ingalls	Harper Collins
Little Runner of the Longhouse	K	HF	Baker, Betty	HarperTrophy
Little Town at the Crossroads	Q	HF	Wilkes, Maria D.	HarperTrophy
Little Town in the Ozarks	R	HF	MacBride, Roger Lea	HarperTrophy
Little Town on the Prairie	Q	HF	Wilder, Laura Ingalls	HarperTrophy
Little Women	M	HF	Bullseye	Random House
Log Cabin in the Woods	R	HF	Henry, Joanne Landers	Scholastic
Long Way from Chicago, A	V	HF	Peck, Richard	Puffin Books
Long Way to a New Land, A	L	HF	Sandin, Joan	HarperTrophy
Long Way Westward, The	L	HF	Sandin, Joan	HarperTrophy
Long Winter, The	Q	HF	Ingalls Wilder, Laura	HarperTrophy
Lost at the White House: A 1909 Easter Story	L	HF	Griest, Lisa	Carolrhoda Books
Lotus Seed, The	P	HF	Garland, Sherry	Harcourt Brace
Love from Your Friend, Hannah	Y	HF	Skolsky, Mindy Warshaw	Harper Trophy
Love You, Soldier	R	HF	Hest, Amy	Puffin Books
Lyddie	U	HF	Paterson, Katherine	The Penguin Group
Mare for Young Wolf, A	L	HF	Shefelman, Janice	Random House
Marie: Summer in the Country	Q	HF	Girlhood Journeys	Aladdin
Master Puppeteer, The	X	HF	Paterson, Katherine	Harper Collins
Matchbox, The	S	HF	Literacy 2000	Rigby
Matchlock Gun, The	P	HF	Edmonds, Walter D.	Putnam & Grosset
Meet Addy	Q	HF	The American Girls Collection	Pleasant Company
Meet Felicity	Q	HF	The American Girls Collection	Pleasant Company
Meet Josefina	Q	HF	The American Girls Collection	Pleasant Company
Meet Kirsten	Q	HF	The American Girls Collection	Pleasant Company
Meet Molly	Q	HF	The American Girls Collection	Pleasant Company
Meet Samantha	Q	HF	The American Girls Collection	Pleasant Company
Meg's Dearest Wish	Q	HF	The Little Women Journals	Avon
Megan in Ancient Greece	Q	HF	Korman, Susan	Magic Attic
Midwife's Apprentice, The	X	HF	Cushman, Karen	HarperTrophy
Mieko and the Fifth Treasure	O	HF	Coerr, Eleanor	Bantam Doubleday Dell
Miranda and the Movies	U	HF	Kendall, Jane	Harcourt Brace
Mississippi Bridge	S	HF	Taylor, Mildred	Bantam Doubleday Dell
Moki	Q	HF	Penny, Grace Jackson	Penguin Group
Molly Learns a Lesson	Q	HF	The American Girls Collection	Pleasant Company
Molly Saves the Day	Q	HF	The American Girls Collection	Pleasant Company
Molly's Surprise	Q	HF	The American Girls Collection	Pleasant Company
Moon Bridge, The	W	HF	Savin, Marcia	Scholastic
Morning Girl	S	HF	Dorris, Michael	Hyperion
Mr. Lincoln's Drummer	W	HF	Wisler, G. Clifton	The Penguin Group
Mr. Tucket	U	HF	Paulsen, Gary	Bantam Doubleday Dell
My Brother, My Sister, and I	V	HF	Watkins, Yoko Kawashima	Aladdin
My Brother Sam is Dead	Y	HF	Collier, James and Christopher	Scholastic
My Daniel	T	HF	Conrad, Pam	Harper Trophy
My Hiroshima	T	HF	Morimoto, Junko	The Penguin Group
My Name is Not Angelica	V	HF	O'Dell, Scott	Bantam Doubleday Dell
My Wartime Summers	V	HF	Cutler, Jane	Harper Collins
Natchez Under the Hill	T	HF	Applegate, Stan	Peachtree
Nesting Place, The	K	HF	PM Turquoise	Rigby
Next Spring an Oriole	N	HF	Whelan, Gloria	Random House
Night Birds on Nantucket	V	HF	Aiken, Joan	Houghton Mifflin
Night Crossing, The	O	HF	Ackerman, Karen	Alfred A. Knopf
Night Journey, The	T	HF	Lasky, Kathryn	Puffin Books
Night Journeys	U	HF	Avi	Avon Books

Title	Level	Genre	Author/Series	Publisher/Distributor
Night Music	P	HF	Voyages in…	Wright Group/McGraw Hill
Night the White Deer Died, The	Z	HF	Paulsen, Gary	Dell
Nightjohn	W	HF	Paulsen, Gary	Bantam Doubleday Dell
No Promises in the Wind	Z	HF	Hunt, Irene	Berkley Books
Number the Stars	U	HF	Lowry, Lois	Bantam Doubleday Dell
Of Nightingales That Weep	U	HF	Paterson, Katherine	Harper Collins
Old Tom and the Rogue	M	HF	Wilson, Trevor	Dominie Press
On the Banks of Plum Creek	Q	HF	Wilder, Laura Ingalls	Harper Collins
On the Banks of the Bayou	Q	HF	MacBride, Roger Lea	Harper Collins
On the Way Home	S	HF	Wilder, Laura Ingalls	Harper Collins
On Top of Concord Hill	Q	HF	Wilkes, Maria D.	HarperCollins
Once on this Island	S	HF	Whelan, Gloria	HarperTrophy
One More River	V	HF	Banks, Lynne Reid	Avon Camelot
Onion John	U	HF	Krumgold, Joseph	Harper & Row
Only Earth and Sky Last Forever	Y	HF	Benchley, Nathaniel	Harper Collins
Orphan of Ellis Island, The	S	HF	Woodruff, Elvira	Scholastic
Orphan Train Adventures: Caught in the Act	W	HF	Nixon, Joan Lowery	Bantam Doubleday Dell
Orphan Train Adventures: Circle of Love	W	HF	Nixon, Joan Lowery	Bantam Doubleday Dell
Orphan Train Adventures: Dangerous Promise, A	W	HF	Nixon, Joan Lowery	Dell
Orphan Train Adventures: Family Apart, A	W	HF	Nixon, Joan Lowery	Dell
Orphan Train Adventures: In the Face of Danger	W	HF	Nixon, Joan Lowery	Dell
Orphan Train Adventures: Keeping Secrets	W	HF	Nixon, Joan Lowery	Dell
Orphan Train Adventures: Place to Belong, A	W	HF	Nixon, Joan Lowery	Dell
Orphan Train Children: Aggie's Home	Q	HF	Nixon, Joan Lowery	Yearling
Our Only May Amelia	R	HF	Holm, Jennifer	Harper Collins
Out of the Dust	X	HF	Hesse, Karen	Scholastic
Ox-Cart Man	K	HF	Hall, Donald	Scholastic
Part of the Sky, A	Z	HF	Peck, Robert Newton	Random House
Patrick Doyle is Full of Blarney	O	HF	Armstrong, Jennifer	Random House
Pedro's Journal	Q	HF	Conrad, Pam	Bantam Doubleday Dell
Perilous Road, The	U	HF	Steele, William	Scholastic
Phoebe The Spy	R	HF	Berry Griffin, Judith	Scholastic
Picture of Freedom, A	T	HF	McKissack, Patricia C.	Scholastic
Pioneer Cat	N	HF	Hooks, William H.	Random House
Place in the Sun, A	U	HF	Rubalcaba, Jill	Puffin Books
Pocket Full of Seeds, A	V	HF	Sachs, Marilyn	Scholastic
Pony For Jeremiah, A	R	HF	Miller, Robert H.	Silver Burdett Press
Prairie Songs	Q	HF	Conrad, Pam	HarperTrophy
Quilt Story, The	L	HF	Johnston, T. & de Paola, T.	Scholastic
Rascal	V	HF	North, Sterling	Scholastic
Red Cap	W	HF	Wisler, G. Clifton	The Penguin Group
Riding Freedom	P	HF	Ryan, Pam Munoz	Scholastic
Rifle, The	T	HF	Paulsen, Gary	Dell
River Apart, A	U	HF	Sutherland, Robert	Fitzhenry and Whiteside
Road to Memphis, The	X	HF	Taylor, Mildred D.	The Penguin Group
Roll of Thunder, Hear My Cry	W	HF	Taylor, Mildred D.	The Penguin Group
Root Cellar, The	V	HF	Lunn, Janet	The Penguin Group
Sadako and the Thousand Paper Cranes	R	HF	Coerr, Eleanor	Bantam Doubleday Dell
Sam the Minuteman	J	HF	Benchley, Nathaniel	HarperTrophy
Samuel's Choice	S	HF	Berleth, Richard	Scholastic
Sara Crewe	O	HF	Burnett, Frances Hodgson	Scholastic
Sarah Bishop	X	HF	O'Dell, Scott	Scholastic
Sarah, Plain and Tall	R	HF	MacLachlan, Patricia	HarperTrophy
Sarny: A Life Remembered	W	HF	Paulsen, Gary	Delacorte Press
Second Mrs. Giaconda, The	T	HF	Konigsburg, E. L.	Language for Learning Assoc.
Secret Valley, The	O	HF	Bulla, Clyde Robert	Scholastic
Sees Behind Trees	T	HF	Dorris, Michael	Language for Learning Assoc.
Serpent's Children, The	W	HF	Yep, Laurence	HarperTrophy
Shades of Gray	W	HF	Reeder, Carolyn	Avon Camelot
Sign of the Beaver	T	HF	Speare, Elizabeth George	Bantam Doubleday Dell

Title	Level	Genre	Author/Series	Publisher/Distributor
Silk Route, The	U	HF	Major, John S.	HarperCollins
Sing Down the Moon	T	HF	O'Dell, Scott	Language for Learning Assoc.
Sing for Your Father, Su Phan	W	HF	Pevsner, Stella and Tang, Fay	Bantam Doubleday Dell
Skateway to Freedom	V	HF	Alma, Ann	Orca Book Publishers
Skylark	R	HF	MacLachlan, Patricia	HarperTrophy
Small Wolf	J	HF	Benchley, Nathaniel	HarperTrophy
Snow Treasure	R	HF	McSwigan, Marie	Scholastic
Snow Walker, The	L	HF	Wetterer, M. K. and Charles M.	Carolrhoda Books
Snowshoe Thompson	K	HF	Smiler Levinson, N.	HarperTrophy
So Far From the Bamboo Grove	V	HF	Watkins, Yoko Kawashima	William Morrow
Soldier Boy	T	HF	Burks, Brian	Harcourt Brace
Soldier's Heart	V	HF	Paulsen, Gary	Random House
Song of the Trees	S	HF	Taylor, Mildred	Bantam Doubleday Dell
SOS Titanic	V	HF	Bunting, Eve	Harcourt Brace
Spies on the Devil's Belt	W	HF	Haynes, Betsy	Scholastic
Squanto and the First Thanksgiving	L	HF	Celsi, Teresa	Steck-Vaughn
Stealing Freedom	U	HF	Carbone, Lisa	Random House
Stories From the Days of Christopher Columbus	U	HF	Young, R.A & J. Dockery	August House
Storm at Coldwater Creek	M	HF	Blackaby, Susan	Wright Group/McGraw Hill
Stowaway	W	HF	Hesse, Karen	Simon & Schuster
Sugar Snow	J	HF	Wilder, Laura Ingalls	Harper Collins
Summer of My German Soldier	Z	HF	Greene, Bette	Dell Publishing
Summertime in the Big Woods	J	HF	Wilder, Laura Ingalls	Harper Collins
Survival!: Fire	R	HF	Duey, K. & Bale, K. A.	Aladdin
Sweet Clara and the Freedom Quilt	S	HF	Hopkinson, Deborah	Scholastic
Tales from the Underground Railroad	S	HF	Connell, Kate	Steck-Vaughn
Tar Beach	P	HF	Ringgold, Faith	Crown
That Wild Berries Should Grow	U	HF	Whelan, Gloria	William B. Eerdmans
Theft in Time, A: Timedetectors II	V	HF	Odgers, Darrel & Sally	Rigby
Thunder Rolling in the Mountains	U	HF	O'Dell, Scott & Hall, Elizabeth	Bantam Doubleday Dell
Ties That Bind, Ties That Break	X	HF	Namioka, Lensey	Delacorte Press
Titanic Crossing	R	HF	Williams, Barbara	Scholastic
To Kill a Mockingbird	Z	HF	Lee, Harper	Warner Books
Toliver's Secret	T	HF	Brady, Esther Wood	Alfred A. Knopf
Torn Thread	W	HF	Isaacs, Anne	Scholastic
Treasure Island	Z	HF	Stevenson, Robert Lewis	Scholastic
Treasures in the Dust	U	HF	Porter, Tracey	HarperTrophy
Trojan Horse, The: How the Greeks Won the War	N	HF	Little, Emily	Random House
Trouble River	S	HF	Byars, Betsy	Scholastic
True Confessions of Charlotte Doyle, The	V	HF	Avi	Avon
Tucket's Gold	U	HF	Paulsen, Gary	Bantam
Tucket's Ride	U	HF	Paulsen, Gary	Bantam Doubleday Dell
Turn Homeward, Hannalee	T	HF	Beatty, Patricia	William Morrow
Two Tickets to Freedom: The True Story of Ellen and William Craft	S	HF	Freedman, Florence	Scholastic
Under the Blood-Red Sun	W	HF	Salisbury, Graham	Bantam Doubleday Dell
Undying Glory: The Story of the Massachusetts 54th Regiment	U	HF	Cox, Clinton	Scholastic
Wagon Wheels	K	HF	Brenner, Barbara	HarperTrophy
Wall of Names, A: The Story of the Vietnam Veterans Memorial	O	HF	Donnelly, Judy	Random House
Wall, The	P	HF	Bunting, Eve	Clarion
War Comes to Willy Freeman	U	HF	Collier, J. L., &Collier, C.	Dell Publishing
Watsons Go to Birmingham-1963, The	T	HF	Curtis, Christopher Paul	Bantam Doubleday Dell
Well, The	T	HF	Taylor, Mildred D.	Puffin Books
Who Is Carrie?	W	HF	Collier, J. L. and Collier, C.	Bantam Doubleday Dell
Winter Days in the Big Woods	J	HF	Wilder, Laura Ingalls	Harper Collins
Winter on the Farm	J	HF	Wilder, Laura Ingalls	Harper Collins
Witch of Blackbird Pond, The	W	HF	Speare, Elizabeth George	Bantam Doubleday Dell
Witch of Fourth Street, The	S	HF	Levoy, Myron	Language for Learning Assoc.

Title	Level	Genre	Author/Series	Publisher/Distributor
Wolves of Willoughby Chase, The	V	HF	Aiken, Joan	Bantam Doubleday Dell
Year of Impossible Goodbyes	W	HF	Choi, Sook Nyui	Yearling
Young Joan	X	HF	Dana, Barbara	HarperTrophy
40 Nights To Knowing the Sky	Z	I	Schaaf, Fred	Henry Holt & Co.
52 Days by Camel: My Sahara Adventure	T	I	Raskin, Lawrie	Annick Press
Acid Rain	L	I	Wonder World	Wright Group/McGraw Hill
Adventure In Alaska	O	I	Kramer, S.A.	Random House
Adventures of the Shark Lady	Q	I	McGovern, Ann	Scholastic
African-Americans in the Old West	V	I	Cornerstones of Freedom	Children's Press
African-Americans in the Thirteen Colonies	V	I	Cornerstones of Freedom	Children's Press
Against the Odds	P	I	Layden, Joe	Scholastic
Against the Odds	R	I	Wildcats	Wright Group/McGraw Hill
Alcatraz	V	I	Cornerstones of Freedom	Bantam Doubleday Dell
Alice's Diary, Living With Diabetes	S	I	Gibson, Marie	Pacific Learning
All About Bats	J	I	Ready Readers	Modern Curriculum
All About Cats and Kittens	N	I	Neye, Emily	Grosset & Dunlap
All About Codes	Q	I	Riley, Gail Blasser	Steck-Vaughn
All About Deer	Q	I	Arnosky, Jim	Scholastic
All About Owls	Q	I	Arnosky, Jim	Scholastic
All About Plants	L	I	Home Connection Collection	Rigby
All About Seeds	Q	I	Berger, Melvin	Scholastic
All About Things People Do	K	I	Rice, Melanie & Chris	Scholastic
All Kinds of Animals	O	I	It's Science	Children's Press
All Kinds of Eyes	L	I	Discovery World	Rigby
All Kinds of Flowers	L	I	Turner, Teresa	Steck-Vaughn
All Kinds of Museums	N	I	Ramsey, Joe	Wright Group/McGraw Hill
All Pigs Are Beautiful	N	I	King-Smith, Dick	Candlewick Press
Alligator, The	M	I	Crewe, Sabrina	Steck-Vaughn
Alligators & Crocodiles	U	I	The Untamed World	Steck-Vaughn
Alphabet, The	R	I	Literacy 2000	Rigby
Amaze Us!	T	I	Wildcats	Wright Group/McGraw Hill
Amazing Animal Rescue Team, The	Q	I	Blankenhorn, Rebecca	Steck-Vaughn
Amazing Birds of the Rain Forest	M	I	Daniel, Claire	Steck-Vaughn
Amazing But True Sports Stories	Q	I	Hollander, Phyllis and Zander	Scholastic
Amazing Eggs	J	I	Discovery World	Rigby
Amazing Impossible Erie Canal, The	S	I	Harness, Cheryl	Simon & Schuster
Amazing Journeys	P	I	Literacy 2000	Rigby
Amazing Spiders	Q	I	Eyewitness Juniors	Alfred A. Knopf
Amazing Trains	L	I	Pair-It Books	Steck-Vaughn
American Alligator, The	R	I	Potts, Steve	Capstone Press
American Bison, The	R	I	Potts, Steve	Capstone Press
American Flag, The	N	I	A True Book	Children's Press
American Revolution, The	T	I	Bliven, Bruce Jr.	Random House
American Revolution, The	V	I	Carter, Alden R.	Franklin Watts
An Ancient Heritage: The Arab-American Minority	Z	I	Ashabranner, Brent	Harper Collins
An Indian Winter	U	I	Freedman, Russell	Scholastic
Ancient Greece	S	I	Journey Into Civilization	Chelsea House
Ancient Greeks	Q	I	Worldwise	Grolier
Ancient Romans	Q	I	Worldwise	Grolier
Animal Babies	R	I	Kalman, Bobbie	Crabtree
Animal Champions	O	I	Jones, Teri Crawford	Pearson Learning
Animal Dazzlers: The Role of Brilliant Colors in Nature	T	I	Collard, Susan B. III	Franklin Watts
Animal Friends	N	I	Literacy 2000	Rigby
Animal Homes	K	I	Pair-It Books	Steck-Vaughn
Animal Reports	L	I	Little Red Readers	Sundance
Animal Shelters	N	I	Book Shop	Mondo
Animal Tracks	L	I	Dorros, Arthur	Scholastic
Animals and Their Teeth	K	I	Sunshine	Wright Group/McGraw Hill
Animals and Their Young	N	I	Kratky, Lada Josefa	Hampton-Brown

Title	Level	Genre	Author/Series	Publisher/Distributor
Animals at Work	M	I	Graham, Pamela	Rigby
Animals' Eyes and Ears	K	I	Early Connections	Benchmark Education
Animals in Danger	M	I	Pair-It Books	Steck-Vaughn
Animals on the Move	K	I	Planet Earth	Rigby
Animals Talk, Too	N	I	Literacy 2000	Rigby
Anne Frank: Beyond the Diary	X	I	Van der Rol, R. & Verhoeven, R.	Puffin Books
Annie Oakley	R	I	Wilson, Ellen	Aladdin
Ant	O	I	Chinery, Michael	Troll
Ant Cities	O	I	Dorros, Arthur	HarperCollins
Antarctic Penguins	N	I	PM Animal Facts: Silver	Rigby
Antarctic Seals	N	I	PM Animal Facts: Silver	Rigby
Ants	N	I	Daronco, Mickey & Presti, Lori	Benchmark Education
Apache Indians, The	P	I	Lund, Bill	Capstone Press
Apple Tree, The	J	I	Sunshine	Wright Group/McGraw Hill
Archaeologists Dig for Clues	P	I	Duke, Kate	HarperCollins
Arctic Investigations: Exploring the Frozen Ocean	T	I	Young, Karen Romano	Steck Vaughn
Arctic Life	M	I	Robinson, F.R.	Steck-Vaughn
Arctic Tundra	M	I	Forman, Michael H.	Children's Press
Are We Hurting the Earth?	K	I	Early Connections	Benchmark Education
Arlington National Cemetery	V	I	Cornerstones of Freedom	Bantam Doubleday Dell
Armadillo, The	R	I	Potts, Steve	Capstone Press
Armies of Ants	M	I	Retan, Walter	Scholastic
Around the World in a Hundred Years: From Henry the Navigator to Magellan	V	I	Fritz, Jean	Putnam & Grosset
Art Around the World	M	I	Discovery World	Rigby
Art Around the World	J	I	Early Connections	Benchmark Education
Artists and Their Art	Q	I	Medearis, Michael	Steck-Vaughn
Asli's Story	S	I	Jansen, Adrienne	Pacific Learning
Astronauts	M	I	Deedrick, Tami	Capstone Press
At the Edge of the Sea	M	I	Sunshine	Wright Group/McGraw Hill
At the Water Hole	K	I	Foundations	Wright Group/McGraw Hill
Attack and Defense	Q	I	Weldon Owen	Wright Group/McGraw Hill
Australia	N	I	A True Book	Children's Press
Australia	O	I	Dahl, Michael	Capstone Press
Australia	Q	I	First Reports	Compass Point Books
Auto Mechanics	M	I	Boraas, Tracey	Capstone Press
Autumn	M	I	Pebble Books	Capstone Press
Babe Ruth: One of Baseball's Greatest	R	I	Van Riper, Guernsey	Aladdin
Baby Animal Zoo	O	I	Martin, Ann M.	Scholastic
Baby Whale Rescue: The True Story of J.J.	P	I	Arnold, C. & Hewett, R.	Troll
Back To The Day Lincoln Was Shot!	S	I	Gormley, Beatrice	Scholastic
Backyard Hunter: The Praying Mantis	P	I	Lavies, Bianca	The Penguin Group
Bagels for Kids	O	I	Pacific Literacy	Pacific Learning
Bakers	M	I	Deedrick, Tami	Capstone Press
Bald Eagle Free Again!, The	P	I	Young Readers' Series	Barron's Educational Series
Bald Eagle, The	N	I	A True Book	Children's Press
Bald Eagle, The	R	I	Potts, Steve	Capstone Press
Bald Eagles	Q	I	Wilde, Buck	Rigby
Baseball in the Barrios	P	I	Horenstein, Henry	Harcourt Brace
Baseball Megastars	O	I	Weber, Bruce	Scholastic
Bats	O	I	Gibbons, Gail	Holiday House
Bats	O	I	Holmes, Kevin J.	Capstone Press
Bats	P	I	Literacy 2000	Rigby
Bats	M	I	PM Animal Facts Gold	Rigby
Bats: The Amazing Upside-Downers	S	I	A First Book	Franklin Watts
Battle for Iwo Jima, The	W	I	Cornerstones of Freedom	Children's Press
Battle of Chancellorsville, The	V	I	Cornerstones of Freedom	Children's Press
Battle of the Alamo, The	V	I	Cornerstones of Freedom	Children's Press
Battle of the Little Bighorn, The	V	I	Cornerstones of Freedom	Children's Press
Be a Plant Scientist	L	I	Paul, Michele	Wright Group/McGraw Hill

Title	Level	Genre	Author/Series	Publisher/Distributor
Beacons of Light: Lighthouses	O	I	Gibbons, Gail	Scholastic
Bear Collection, The	N	I	PM Ruby	Rigby
Bear, The	M	I	Crewe, Sabrina	Steck-Vaughn
Bears	O	I	Holmes, Kevin J.	Capstone Press
Beautiful Land: A Story of the Oklahoma Land Rush	S	I	Antle, Nancy	The Penguin Group
Beaver Engineers	N	I	Reeder, Tracey	Wright Group/McGraw Hill
Beaver, The	M	I	Crewe, Sabrina	Steck-Vaughn
Beavers	N	I	Book Shop	Mondo
Beavers Beware!	K	I	Bank Street	Bantam Doubleday Dell
Bee, The	M	I	Crewe, Sabrina	Steck-Vaughn
Beekeeper, The	M	I	Literacy 2000	Rigby
Bees	N	I	A True Book	Children's Press
Bees	O	I	Holmes, Kevin J.	Capstone Press
Beethoven Lives Upstairs	S	I	Nichol, Barbara	Orchard Books
Beginnings of Sports	R	I	PM Nonfiction -Ruby	Rigby
Behind the Scenes	R	I	Literacy 2000	Rigby
Below the Green Pond	N	I	Read All About It	Steck-Vaughn
Best Way to Play, The	K	I	Cosby, Bill	Scholastic
Beyond Belief	Z	I	Steiger, Brad	Scholastic
Beyond the Beyond	Q	I	Wildcats	Wright Group/McGraw Hill
Bicycle Book, The	O	I	PM Nonfiction -Emerald	Rigby
Big Dipper and You, The	Q	I	Krupp, E.C.	Mulberry Books
Big Picture, The	R	I	Bennett, Mary	Pacific Learning
Big Storm, The	Q	I	Hiscock, Bruce	Aladdin
Bighorn Sheep, The	R	I	Mattern, Joanne	Capstone Press
Bill of Rights, The	N	I	A True Book	Children's Press
Bill of Rights, The	V	I	Cornerstones of Freedom	Bantam Doubleday Dell
Billie the Hippo	N	I	Pacific Literacy	Pacific Learning
Bird Behavior: Living Together	M	I	Sunshine	Wright Group/McGraw Hill
Bird's-Eye View, A	K	I	People, Spaces & Places	Rand McNally
Birds and How They Grow	N	I	National Geographic Society	National Geographic Society
Birds At My Feeder	R	I	Kalman, Bobbie	Crabtree
Birds' Nests	J	I	Wonder World	Wright Group/McGraw Hill
Birds of Prey	O	I	Woolley, M. & Pigdon, K.	Mondo
Birds of Prey: A Look at Daytime Raptors	U	I	Collard, Sneed B. III	Franklin Watts
Birds of the City	M	I	Sunshine	Wright Group/McGraw Hill
Bite of the Gold Bug, The: A Story of the Alaskan Gold Rush	S	I	DeClements, Barthe	The Penguin Group
Black Diamond: Story of the Negro Baseball Leagues	Q	I	McKissack, Patricia & Fred	Scholastic
Black Holes	N	I	A True Book	Children's Press
Blast Off!	N	I	Home Connection Collection	Rigby
Blimps	N	I	A True Book	Children's Press
Blue Whales	U	I	The Untamed World	Steck-Vaughn
Boats Afloat	M	I	Sunshine	Wright Group/McGraw Hill
Body Numbers	K	I	Discovery World	Rigby
Book About Planets and Stars, A	R	I	Reigot, Betty Polisar	Scholastic
Book About Your Skeleton, A	M	I	Gross, Ruth Belov	Scholastic
Boomtowns of the West	S	I	Kalman, Bobbie	Crabtree
Boston Tea Party: Rebellion in the Colonies	T	I	Adventures in Colonial America	Troll
Boston Tea Party, The	V	I	Cornerstones of Freedom	Children's Press
Boston Tea Party, The	S	I	We The People	Compass Point Books
Brain	V	I	You And Your Body	Troll
Brand New Butterfly, A	L	I	Literacy 2000	Rigby
Bravest Dog Ever, The: The True Story of Balto	L	I	Standiford, Natalie	Random House
Brazil	N	I	A True Book	Children's Press
Brazil	O	I	Dahl, Michael	Capstone Press
Brazil	Q	I	First Reports	Compass Point Books
Break with Charity, A: A Story About the Salem Witch Trials	X	I	Rinaldi, Ann	Harcourt Brace
Breathing	L	I	Book Shop	Mondo

Title	Level	Genre	Author/Series	Publisher/Distributor
Brendan the Navigator: A History Mystery about the Discovery of America	R	I	Fritz, Jean	The Penguin Group
Brian's Song	Z	I	Blinn, William	Bantam Doubleday Dell
Bridges	N	I	Wildcats	Wright Group/McGraw Hill
Bridging the Gap	Q	I	Miller, Steve	Pacific Learning
Bright Ideas	Q	I	Weldon Owen	Wright Group/McGraw Hill
Brown Bears	K	I	PM Animal Facts: Turquoise	Rigby
Bryce Canyon National Park	N	I	A True Book	Children's Press
Buck Stops Here, The	T	I	Provensen, Alice	Harcourt Brace
Buddy: The First Seeing Eye Dog	M	I	Moore, Eva	Scholastic
Buffalo, The	M	I	Crewe, Sabrina	Steck-Vaughn
Bugs	O	I	Parker, N. W. & Wright, J. R.	Mulberry Books
Bugs and Other Insects	N	I	Kalman, Bobbie	Crabtree
Build, Build, Build	M	I	Sunshine	Wright Group/McGraw Hill
Build It Strong!	M	I	First Science	Children's Press
Building Homes, Building Hope	O	I	Bovez, Marcie	Wright Group/McGraw Hill
Building the Capital City	V	I	Cornerstones of Freedom	Bantam Doubleday Dell
Butterflies	O	I	Holmes, Kevin J.	Capstone Press
Butterflies and Moths	N	I	Kalman, Bobbie	Crabtree
Butterflies of the Sea	L	I	Swartz, Stanley L.	Dominie Press
Butterfly, The	M	I	Crewe, Sabrina	Steck-Vaughn
Butterfly's Life, A	K	I	Burke, Melissa Blackwell	Steck-Vaughn
By Lakes and Rivers	N	I	Animal Trackers	Crabtree
By the Seashore	N	I	Animal Trackers	Crabtree
California	Q	I	Geography Department	Capstone Press
California	T	I	Sea To Shining Sea	Children's Press
California Gold Rush, The	V	I	Cornerstones of Freedom	Children's Press
California Gold Rush, The	T	I	McNeer, May	Random House
California Gold Rush, The	S	I	We The People	Compass Point Books
Camouflage	J	I	Sunshine	Wright Group/McGraw Hill
Can't You Make Them Behave, King George?	R	I	Fritz, Jean	Putnam & Grossett
Canada	O	I	Dahl, Michael	Capstone Press
Canada	Q	I	First Reports	Compass Point Books
Canada Celebrates Multiculturalism	T	I	Kalman, Bobbie	Crabtree
Canada: The Culture	T	I	Kalman, Bobbie	Crabtree
Canada: The Land	T	I	Kalman, Bobbie	Crabtree
Canada: The People	T	I	Kalman, Bobbie	Crabtree
Canoe Diary	O	I	Bishop, Nic	Pacific Learning
Capitol, The	V	I	Cornerstones of Freedom	Bantam Doubleday Dell
Caribou Journey, A	Q	I	Miller, Debbie S.	Little, Brown & Co.
Caribou (Reindeer)	N	I	PM Animal Facts: Silver	Rigby
Carpenters	L	I	Community Workers	Compass Point Books
Cat!	S	I	Kroll, Virginia L.	Dawn
Cat Talk	N	I	Long, Don	Pacific Learning
Catch Me If You Can!: The Roadrunner	M	I	Chukran, Bobbi A.	Wright Group/McGraw Hill
Caterpillars	M	I	Book Shop	Mondo
Caterpillars	P	I	Mini Pets	Steck-Vaughn
Cats	J	I	PM Animal Facts: Orange	Rigby
Cats, Cats, Cats	Q	I	Literacy 2000	Rigby
Cattle	L	I	PM Animal Facts: Purple	Rigby
Caught in a Flash	P	I	Bishop, Nic	Pacific Learning
Caves	M	I	Discovery World	Rigby
Caves	R	I	The Wonders of our World	Crabtree
Caves	R	I	Wood, Jenny	Scholastic
Caves and Caverns	O	I	Gibbons, Gail	Harcourt Brace
Cells	J	I	Wonder World	Wright Group/McGraw Hill
Chasing Tornadoes	P	I	Gold, Becky	Pearson Learning
Chefs	L	I	Community Workers	Compass Point Books
Cherokee Indians, The	P	I	Lund, Bill	Capstone Press
Cheyenne, The	N	I	A New True Book	Children's Press

Title	Level	Genre	Author/Series	Publisher/Distributor
Chicago Winds	K	I	Evangeline Nicholas Collection	Wright Group/McGraw Hill
Chickens	L	I	PM Animal Facts: Purple	Rigby
Chickens Have Chicks	M	I	Animals and Their Young	Compass Point Books
Child's Day, A	T	I	Historic Communities	Crabtree
Children Around the World	M	I	People, Spaces & Places	Rand McNally
Children as Young Scientists	K	I	Early Connections	Benchmark Education
Children of Clay: A Family of Pueblo Potters	S	I	Swentzell, Rina	Lerner Publications
Children of Sierra Leone, The	J	I	Books For Young Learners	Richard C. Owen
Children of the Dust Bowl	Y	I	Stanley, Jerry	Crown Publishers
Children of the Earth and Sky	P	I	Krensky, Stephen	Scholastic
Children of the Wild West	X	I	Freedman, Russell	Clarion Books
Children's Clothing of the 1800's	S	I	Historic Communities	Crabtree
China	N	I	A True Book	Children's Press
China	O	I	Dahl, Michael	Capstone Press
China	Q	I	First Reports	Compass Point Books
China: The Culture	T	I	Kalman, Bobbie	Crabtree
China: The Land	T	I	Kalman, Bobbie	Crabtree
China: The People	T	I	Kalman, Bobbie	Crabtree
Chisholm Trail, The	V	I	Cornerstones of Freedom	Bantam Doubleday Dell
Chocolate!	P	I	Velarde, Linda	Rigby
Chocolate	N	I	What's For Lunch?	Children's Press
Chocolate Flier, The	R	I	Beames, Margaret	Rigby
Christmas: Why We Celebrate It the Way We Do	P	I	Hintz, Martin & Kate	Capstone Press
Circulatory System, The	N	I	A True Book	Children's Press
Cities Around the World	M	I	Pair-It Books	Steck-Vaughn
Cities: The Building of America	Q	I	Thompson, Gare	Children's Press
Cities: Then and Now	O	I	People, Spaces & Places	Rand McNally
City Through the Ages	U	I	Steele, Philip	Troll Associates
Civil Rights Marches	V	I	Cornerstones of Freedom	Children's Press
Close to Home: A Story of the Polio Epidemic	R	I	Weaver, Lydia	Bantam Doubleday Dell
Clothes	O	I	Wonder World	Wright Group/McGraw Hill
Clothes & Crafts in Ancient Egypt	T	I	Balkwill, Richard	Dillon Press
Clothes & Crafts in Ancient Greece	T	I	Steele, Philip	Dillon Press
Clothes & Crafts in Aztec Times	T	I	Dawson,Imogen	Dillon Press
Clothes & Crafts in Roman Times	T	I	Steele, Philip	Dillon Press
Clothes & Crafts in the Middle Ages	T	I	Dawson, Imogen	Dillon Press
Clothes & Crafts in Victorian Times	T	I	Steele, Philip	Dillon Press
Cloud Book, The	N	I	dePaola, Tomie	Scholastic
Clouds	J	I	Early Connections	Benchmark Education
Clouds	N	I	Literacy 2000	Rigby
Clouds, Rain and Fog	K	I	Sunshine	Wright Group/McGraw Hill
Coast to Coast	N	I	People, Spaces & Places	Rand McNally
Colonial Crafts	T	I	Historic Communities	Crabtree
Colonial Life	T	I	Historic Communities	Crabtree
Colonial Times from A to Z	T	I	Kalman, Bobbie	Crabtree
Colonial Town, A: Williamsburg	T	I	Historic Communities	Crabtree
Colorado	T	I	Sea To Shining Sea	Children's Press
Colors of Australia	P	I	Colors of the World	Carolrhoda Books
Colors of Germany	P	I	Colors of the World	Carolrhoda Books
Colors of Ghana	P	I	Colors of the World	Carolrhoda Books
Colors of India	P	I	Colors of the World	Carolrhoda Books
Colors of Kenya	P	I	Colors of the World	Carolrhoda Books
Colors of Mexico	P	I	Colors of the World	Carolrhoda Books
Comanche Indians, The	P	I	Lund, Bill	Capstone Press
Comets	U	I	A First Book	Franklin Watts
Comets and Meteor Showers	N	I	A True Book	Children's Press
Communication	N	I	Literacy 2000	Rigby
Computers Are for Everyone	K	I	Sunshine	Wright Group/McGraw Hill
Congress	N	I	A True Book	Children's Press
Connecticut	T	I	Sea To Shining Sea	Children's Press

Title	Level	Genre	Author/Series	Publisher/Distributor
Constellations	N	I	A True Book	Children's Press
Constitution, The	N	I	A True Book	Children's Press
Constitution, The	V	I	Cornerstones of Freedom	Children's Press
Construction Workers	M	I	Deedrick, Tami	Capstone Press
Contemporary Age, The	R	I	Journey Through History	Barron's Educational Series
Coral	J	I	Marine Life For Yng. Readers	Dominie
Coral Reef	P	I	Habitats	Children's Press
Coral Reefs	Q	I	First Reports	Compass Point Books
Corn: An American Indian Gift	M	I	Pair-It Books	Steck-Vaughn
Corn Is Maize: The Gift of the Indians	O	I	Aliki	Steck-Vaughn
Corvettes	T	I	Gronvall, Kal	Capstone Press
Cotton Plant to Cotton Shirt	L	I	Schaefer, Lola M.	Benchmark Education
Counting Insects	K	I	Early Connections	Benchmark Education
Cow	O	I	Older, Jules	Charlesbridge
Cowboy Trade, The	S	I	Rounds, Glen	Holiday House
Cowboys	T	I	Sandler, Martin W.	HarperTrophy
Cowboys of the Wild West	X	I	Freedman, Russell	Clarion Books
Cows Have Calves	M	I	Animals and Their Young	Compass Point Books
Coyote, The	R	I	Mattern, Joanne	Capstone Press
Crabs	M	I	Wonder World	Wright Group/McGraw Hill
Crabs, Shrimp, & Lobsters	M	I	Marine Life For Yng. Readers	Dominie
Cranes	N	I	Cole, Sally	Wright Group/McGraw Hill
Creatures in the Dark	N	I	Literacy 2000	Rigby
Creatures of the Reef	S	I	Belcher, Angie	Pacific Learning
Creepy Creatures	Q	I	Weldon Owen	Wright Group/McGraw Hill
Crispus Attucks: Black Leader of Colonial Patriots	R	I	Millender, Dharathula H.	Aladdin
Crocodilians	U	I	Short, Joan & Bird, Bettina	Mondo
Crocodilians: Reminders of Age of Dinosaurs	S	I	A First Book	Franklin Watts
Cuba	O	I	Mara, William P.	Capstone Press
Cunning Creatures	K	I	Home Connection Collection	Rigby
Daily Life in a Plains Indian Village: 1868	T	I	Terry, Michael Bad Hand	Clarion
Dancing with Manatees	N	I	McNulty, Faith	Scholastic
Dangerous Animals	R	I	Weldon Owen	Wright Group/McGraw Hill
Day It Rained Forever, The: A Story of the Johnstown Flood	S	I	Gross, Virginia T.	The Penguin Group
Day of the Blizzard	Q	I	Moskin, Marietta	Scholastic
Days of Courage: The Little Rock Story	R	I	Kelso, Richard	Steck-Vaughn
Dear Grandma	M	I	Storyteller Nonfiction	Wright Group/McGraw Hill
Declaration of Independence, The	N	I	A True Book	Children's Press
Declaration of Independence, The	V	I	Cornerstones of Freedom	Children's Press
Delaware	T	I	Sea to Shining Sea	Children's Press
Dentists	M	I	Ready, Dee	Capstone Press
Desert Birds	N	I	A New True Book	Children's Press
Desert Giant: The World of the Saguaro Cactus	L	I	Bash, Barbara	Scholastic
Desert Machine, The	K	I	Sunshine	Wright Group/McGraw Hill
Desert Run, The	P	I	Bonallack, John	Pacific Learning
Deserts	N	I	A True Book	Children's Press
Deserts	Q	I	First Reports	Compass Point Books
Deserts	O	I	Gibbons, Gail	Holiday House
Deserts	N	I	Habitats of the World	Dominie Press
Deserts	R	I	The Wonders of our World	Crabtree
Diary of a Honeybee	L	I	Literacy 2000	Rigby
Digestive System, The	N	I	A True Book	Children's Press
Digging Dinosaurs	P	I	Nayer, Judy	Pearson Learning
Digging Up Tyrannosaurus Rex	P	I	Horner, John & Don Lessem	Crown Publishers
Dinosaur Babies	L	I	Penner, Lucille Recht	Random House
Dinosaur Connection, The	O	I	Wilde, Buck	Rigby
Dinosaur Days	L	I	Milton, Joyce	Random House
Dinosaur Detective	O	I	Wildcats	Wright Group/McGraw Hill
Dinosaur Hunters	L	I	McMullan, Kate	Random House

Title	Level	Genre	Author/Series	Publisher/Distributor
Dinosaur Time	K	I	Parish, Peggy	HarperTrophy
Dinosaurs	K	I	Book Shop	Mondo
Disability Rights Movement, The	W	I	Cornerstones of Freedom	Children's Press
Discovering Jupiter: The Amazing Collision in Space	T	I	Berger, Melvin	Scholastic
Discovering the Past	S	I	Literacy 2000	Rigby
Discovering the Titanic	O	I	Trumbore, Cindy	Pearson Learning
Dive to the Deep Ocean: Voyages of Exploration and Discovery	W	I	Kovacs, Deborah	Steck-Vaughn
Divers' Dream	P	I	Pacific Literacy	Pacific Learning
Do You Like Cats?	K	I	Bank Street	Bantam Doubleday Dell
Doctor's Office, The	K	I	Pebble Books	Grolier, Capstone
Doctors	L	I	Community Workers	Compass Point Books
Doctors	M	I	Ready, Dee	Capstone Press
Dogs	J	I	PM Animal Facts: Orange	Rigby
Dogs at Work	J	I	Little Readers	Houghton Mifflin
Dolphin	L	I	Morris, Robert A.	HarperTrophy
Dolphin, The	P	I	Animal Close-Ups	Charlesbridge
Dolphin's First Day: The Story of a Bottlenose Dolphin	N	I	Zoehfeld, Kathleen Weidnetz	Scholastic
Dolphins!	L	I	Bokoske, S. & Davidson, M.	Random House
Dolphins	O	I	Holmes, Kevin J.	Capstone Press
Dolphins	N	I	Kalman, Bobbie	Crabtree
Dolphins	J	I	Wonder World	Wright Group/McGraw Hill
Douglas Fir	O	I	Davis, Wendy	Children's Press
Down on the Ice	P	I	Alchin, Rupert	Pacific Learning
Down to a Sunless Sea: The Strange World of Hydrothermal Vents	W	I	Madin, Kate	Steck-Vaughn
Dragon Parade: A Chinese New Year Story	O	I	Chin, Steven A.	Steck-Vaughn
Dred Scott Decision, The	X	I	Cornerstones of Freedom	Children's Press
Earth	N	I	A True Book	Children's Press
Earthquake!: A Story of Old San Francisco	S	I	Kudlinski, Kathleen V.	The Penguin Group
Earthquake!: San Francisco, 1906	R	I	Wilson, Kate	Steck-Vaughn
Earthquakes	N	I	A True Book	Children's Press
Earthquakes	O	I	Branley, Franklyn M.	HarperCollins
Earthquakes	T	I	Simon, Seymour	Mulberry Books
Earthquakes	R	I	The Wonders of our World	Crabtree
Earthquakes	R	I	Weldon Owen	Wright Group/McGraw Hill
Earthworms	O	I	Holmes, Kevin J.	Capstone Press
Easter Island: Giant Stone Statues Tell of a Rich and Tragic Past	W	I	Arnold, Caroline	Houghton Mifflin
Eclipses: Nature's Blackouts	T	I	Aronson, Billy	Franklin Watts
Egg To Chick	J	I	Selsam, Millicent E.	HarperTrophy
Eggs and Baby Birds	M	I	Sunshine	Wright Group/McGraw Hill
Eggs, Eggs, Eggs	J	I	Wonder World	Wright Group/McGraw Hill
Eggs, Larvae and Flies	K	I	Sunshine	Wright Group/McGraw Hill
Egypt: The Culture	U	I	Kalman, Bobbie	Crabtree
Egypt: The Land	U	I	Kalman, Bobbie	Crabtree
Egypt: The People	U	I	Kalman, Bobbie	Crabtree
Egytian Town	U	I	Steedman, Scott	Franklin Watts
Electricity	O	I	Winkelman, Barbara Gaines	Wright Group/McGraw Hill
Elephants	N	I	Meadows, Graham & Vial, Claire	Dominie Press
Elephants	K	I	PM Animal Facts: Turquoise	Rigby
Elephants	U	I	The Untamed World	Steck-Vaughn
Ellis Island	N	I	A True Book	Children's Press
Ellis Island	V	I	Cornerstones of Freedom	Children's Press
Emancipation Proclamation, The	V	I	Cornerstones of Freedom	Children's Press
Emergency Vehicles	K	I	PM Plus	Rigby
Encyclopedia of Tiny Creatures	J	I	Discovery World	Rigby
Endangered Animals	N	I	A New True Book	Children's Press
Endangered Desert Animals	R	I	Taylor, Dave	Crabtree

Title	Level	Genre	Author/Series	Publisher/Distributor
Endangered Forest Animals	R	I	Taylor, Dave	Crabtree
Endangered Grassland Animals	R	I	Taylor, Dave	Crabtree
Endangered Island Animals	R	I	Taylor, Dave	Crabtree
Endangered Mountain Animals	R	I	Taylor, Dave	Crabtree
Endangered Ocean Animals	R	I	Taylor, Dave	Crabtree
Endangered Savannah Animals	R	I	Taylor, Dave	Crabtree
Endangered Wetland Animals	R	I	Taylor, Dave	Crabtree
Endurance, Shackleton's Antarctic Expedition	S	I	Marriott, Janice	Pacific Learning
Erosion	M	I	Schaefer, Lola M.	Benchmark Education
Eruption	R	I	Wildcats	Wright Group/McGraw Hill
Eureka! It's an Airplane	S	I	Bendick, Jeanne	Scholastic
Eureka!: Stories of Everyday Inventions	P	I	Literacy 2000	Rigby
Everglades	T	I	George, Jean Craighead	HarperTrophy
Every Body Tells a Story	R	I	Weldon Owen	Wright Group/McGraw Hill
Everybody Cooks Rice	M	I	Dooley, Norah	Scholastic
Everybody Eats Bread	J	I	Literacy 2000	Rigby
Everyday Forces	M	I	Discovery World	Rigby
Everyone Knows About Cars	L	I	Book Shop	Mondo
Everything Changes	L	I	Discovery World	Rigby
Exotic Tropical Fish	L	I	Swartz, Stanley L.	Dominie Press
Experiment with Movement	Q	I	Murphy, Bryan	Scholastic
Experiment with Water	Q	I	Murphy, Bryan	Scholastic
Explorers: Searching for Adventure	M	I	Pair-It Books	Steck-Vaughn
Exploring an Ocean Tide Pool	W	I	Bendick, Jeanne	Henry Holt & Co.
Exploring Freshwater Habitats	P	I	Snowball, Diane	Mondo
Exploring Land Habitats	P	I	Phinney, Margaret Yatsevitch	Mondo
Exploring Saltwater Habitats	P	I	Smith, Sue	Mondo
Exploring Space	R	I	Weldon Owen	Wright Group/McGraw Hill
Exploring the Titanic	Q	I	Ballard, Robert D.	Scholastic
Exploring Tree Habitats	P	I	Seifert, Patti	Mondo
Exploring with Lewis and Clark	O	I	People, Spaces & Places	Rand McNally
Extraordinary Life, An: The Story of a Monarch Butterfly	V	I	Pringle, Laurence	Orchard Books
Extreme Lives	N	I	Wildcats	Wright Group/McGraw Hill
Extreme Sports	R	I	PM Nonfiction -Ruby	Rigby
Extreme Sports	P	I	Wildcats	Wright Group/McGraw Hill
Eye Spy	P	I	Wildcats	Wright Group/McGraw Hill
Fabulous Animal Families	K	I	Home Connection Collection	Rigby
Facing West: A Story of the Oregon Trail	S	I	Kudlinski, Kathleen V.	The Penguin Group
Factory Through the Ages	U	I	Steele, Philip	Troll Associates
Facts and Fun About the Presidents	S	I	Sullivan, George	Scholastic
Families	J	I	Storyteller-Night Crickets	Wright Group/McGraw Hill
Families of the Deep Blue Sea	P	I	Mallory, Kenneth	Charlesbridge Publishing
Famous Animals	Q	I	Literacy Tree	Rigby
Famous Children	O	I	Literacy 2000	Rigby
Fantastic Animal Features	Q	I	Parker, Heather	Steck-Vaughn
Farm Life Long Ago	L	I	Pair-It Books	Steck-Vaughn
Farm Through the Ages	U	I	Steele, Philip	Troll
Farmers	M	I	Ready, Dee	Capstone Press
Feathers and Flight	Q	I	Weldon Owen	Wright Group/McGraw Hill
Festival Fun	N	I	Wildcats	Wright Group/McGraw Hill
Fibers Made by People	M	I	Sunshine	Wright Group/McGraw Hill
Fiesta!	M	I	Festivals and Holidays	Children's Press
Finding the Titanic	Q	I	Ballard, Robert D.	Scholastic
Finding Your Way	R	I	Bonallack, John	Pacific Learning
Fire Fighters	L	I	Community Workers	Compass Point Books
Fire Fighters	M	I	Ready, Dee	Capstone Press
Fire! Fire!	O	I	Wildcats	Wright Group/McGraw Hill
Fire Station, The	J	I	Pebble Books	Grolier, Capstone
Fireflies in the Night	M	I	Hawes, Judy	HarperTrophy

Title	Level	Genre	Author/Series	Publisher/Distributor
First Americans, The	O	I	People, Spaces & Places	Rand McNally
First Book About Africa: An Introduction for Young Readers	Q	I	Ellis, Veronica Freeman	Just Us Books
First Hot-Air Balloons, The	M	I	Moore, Philip	Wright Group/McGraw Hill
First On The Moon	Y	I	Hehner, Barbara	Hyperion/Madison Press
Fish	L	I	Marine Life For Yng. Readers	Dominie
Fish that Hide	L	I	Swartz, Stanley L.	Dominie Press
Five True Dog Stories	M	I	Davidson, Margaret	Scholastic
Five True Horse Stories	M	I	Davidson, Margaret	Scholastic
Flag For Our Country, A	N	I	Spencer, Eve	Steck-Vaughn
Flags	R	I	Pattrick, Steve	Rigby
Flamingos	N	I	Cole, Sally	Wright Group/McGraw Hill
Flicking the Switch	O	I	Pacific Literacy	Pacific Learning
Flies	N	I	A True Book	Children's Press
Flight: The Journey of Charles Lindbergh	R	I	Burleigh, Robert	Putnam & Grosset
Floating and Sinking	J	I	Book Shop	Mondo
Floods	N	I	A True Book	Children's Press
Florida	Q	I	Geography Department	Capstone Press
Flour	K	I	Wonder World	Wright Group/McGraw Hill
Flowers	L	I	Pebble Books	Grolier, Capstone
Flows & Quakes and Spinning Winds	K	I	Home Connection Collection	Rigby
Follow That Fin!: Studying Dolphin Behavior	T	I	Samuels, Amy	Steck-Vaughn
Food and Festivals: Israel	O	I	Randall, Ronne	Steck-Vaughn
Food and Festivals: Italy	O	I	Pirotta, Saviour	Steck-Vaughn
Food & Feasts Between the Two World Wars	T	I	Steele, Philip	Dillon Press
Food & Feasts In Ancient Egypt	T	I	Balkwill, Richard	Dillon Press
Food & Feasts In Ancient Greece	T	I	Steele, Philip	Dillon Press
Food & Feasts In Ancient Rome	T	I	Steele, Philip	Dillon Press
Food & Feasts In the Middle Ages	T	I	Dawson, Imogen	Dillon Press
Food & Feasts In Tudor Times	T	I	Balkwill, Richard	Dillon Press
Food & Feasts With the Aztecs	T	I	Dawson, Imogen	Dillon Press
Food & Feasts With the Vikings	T	I	Martell, Hazel	Dillon Press
Food Journey, The	K	I	Home Connection Collection	Rigby
Forest Community, A	Q	I	Massie, Elizabeth	Steck-Vaughn
Forest Mammals	R	I	Kalman, Bobbie	Crabtree
Forest's Life, A: From Meadow to Mature Woodland	T	I	A First Book	Franklin Watts
Forests	N	I	Habitats of the World	Dominie
Forests	R	I	The Wonders of Our World	Crabtree
Forests, Grasslands, Deserts	M	I	People, Spaces & Places	Rand McNally
Forgotten Heroes, The: The Story of the Buffalo Soldiers	X	I	Cox, Clinton	Scholastic
Fort Life	T	I	Historic Communities	Crabtree
Fort Sumter	V	I	Cornerstones of Freedom	Children's Press
Fossils Alive!	Q	I	Daniel, Claire	Steck-Vaughn
Fossils: Pictures from the Past	Q	I	Daniel, Claire	Steck-Vaughn
Fountains of Life: The Story of Deep-Sea Vents	S	I	A First Book	Franklin Watts
Foxes	M	I	PM Animal Facts: Gold	Rigby
France	O	I	Dahl, Michael	Capstone Press
Free Fall	Q	I	Basalaj, Kathy	Pacific Learning
Freshwater Giants: Hippopatamus, River Dolphins and Manatees	S	I	Perry, Phyllis J.	Franklin Watts
Freshwater Habitats	N	I	Habitats of the World	Dominie Press
Freshwater Pond, A	T	I	Small Worlds	Crabtree
Frog, The	M	I	Crewe, Sabrina	Steck-Vaughn
Frogs	N	I	Book Shop	Mondo
Frogs	K	I	Wonder World	Wright Group/McGraw Hill
Frogs and Toads	P	I	Crabapples	Crabtree
From Cotton Plant to Cotton Shirt	N	I	Schaefer, Lola M.	Benchmark Education
From Cow to Milk Carton	M	I	Miles, Annie	Wright Group/McGraw Hill
From Here to There: Transportation Timelines	P	I	Discovery World	Rigby

Title	Level	Genre	Author/Series	Publisher/Distributor
From Rocks to Sand: The Story of a Beach	J	I	Wonder World	Wright Group/McGraw Hill
Frozen Man	T	I	Getz, David	Henry Holt & Co.
Fun with Fingerprints	M	I	Sokoloff, Myka-Lynne	Wright Group/McGraw Hill
Fur, Feathers, and Flippers: How Animals Live Where They Do	T	I	Lauber, Patricia	Scholastic
Galaxies	N	I	A True Book	Children's Press
Galaxies	T	I	Simon, Seymour	Mulberry Books
Games from Long Ago	T	I	Historic Communities	Crabtree
Garbage Collectors	M	I	Deedrick, Tami	Capstone Press
Gathering: A Northwoods Counting Book	Q	I	Bowen, Betsy	Houghton Mifflin
Gentle Annie: The True Story of a Civil War Nurse	R	I	Shura, Mary Frances	Scholastic
Georgia	Q	I	Geography Department	Capstone Press
Georgia	U	I	LaDoux, Rita C.	Lerner Publications
Georgia	T	I	Sea to Shining Sea	Children's Press
Germany	O	I	Dahl, Michael	Capstone Press
Get on Board: The Story of the Underground Railroad	V	I	Haskins, Jim	Scholastic
Getting To Know Sharks	K	I	Little Books	Sadlier-Oxford
Gettysburg Address, The	V	I	Cornerstones of Freedom	Children's Press
Gettysburg Address, The	T	I	Lincoln, Abraham	Houghton Mifflin
Geysers: When Earth Roars	U	I	A First Book	Franklin Watts
Ghana	O	I	Davis, Lucile	Capstone Press
Giant Pandas	U	I	The Untamed World	Steck-Vaughn
Giants, Monsters & Mythical Beasts	O	I	Literacy 2000	Rigby
Gifts to Make	K	I	Pair-It Books	Steck-Vaughn
Giraffe, The	P	I	Animal Close-Ups	Charlesbridge Publishing
Giraffes	P	I	Crabapples	Crabtree
Giraffes	N	I	Meadows, Graham & Vial, Claire	Dominie Press
Giraffes	O	I	Reeder, Tracey	Wright Group/McGraw Hill
Glaciers	T	I	Gallant, Roy A.	Franklin Watts
Glorious Days, Dreadful Days: The Battle of Bunker Hill	R	I	Kirby, Philippa	Steck-Vaughn
Go-cart Team, The	O	I	PM Nonfiction -Emerald	Rigby
Goats	L	I	PM Animal Facts: Purple	Rigby
Going Lobstering	O	I	Pallotta, Jerry & Bolster, Rob	Charlesbridge Publishing
Going Places	K	I	Early Connections	Benchmark Education
Going to the Bank	J	I	Foundations	Wright Group/McGraw Hill
Going to the City	J	I	People, Spaces & Places	Rand McNally
Going to the Hairdresser	J	I	Foundations	Wright Group/McGraw Hill
Goldfish	J	I	PM Animal Facts: Orange	Rigby
Gorillas	T	I	Burgel, Paul H. & Hartwig, M.	Carolrhoda Books
Gorillas	U	I	The Untamed World	Steck-Vaughn
Gorillas: Gentle Giants on the Forest	L	I	Milton, Joyce	Random House
Grand Canyon Journey, A: Tracing Time in Stone	W	I	A First Book	Franklin Watts
Grand Trees of America: Our State and Champion Trees	T	I	Jorgenson, Lisa	Roberts Rinehart
Grandma's Heart	K	I	Wonder World	Wright Group/McGraw Hill
Grasslands	N	I	A True Book	Children's Press
Grasslands	Q	I	First Reports	Compass Point Books
Gravity: Simple Experiments for Young Scientists	T	I	White, Larry	Millbrook Press
Great Apes, The	S	I	A First Book	Franklin Watts
Great Depression, The	X	I	Cornerstones of Freedom	Children's Press
Great Escapes of World War II	Z	I	Sullivan, George	Scholastic
Great Kapok Tree, The	R	I	Cherry, Lynne	Scholastic
Great Migration, The	R	I	Lawrence, Jacob	HarperCollins
Great Sporting Events	R	I	PM Nonfiction -Ruby	Rigby
Great Wall of China, The	Q	I	Fisher, Leonard Everett	Aladdin
Great White Sharks	U	I	The Untamed World	Steck-Vaughn
Greece: The Culture	U	I	Kalman, Bobbie	Crabtree
Greece: The Land	U	I	Kalman, Bobbie	Crabtree
Greece: The People	U	I	Kalman, Bobbie	Crabtree

Title	Level	Genre	Author/Series	Publisher/Distributor
Greek and Roman Eras, The	R	I	Journey Through History	Barron's Educational Series
Greeks, The	M	I	Footsteps in Time	Children's Press
Green Thumbs	Q	I	Literacy 2000	Rigby
Greg's Microscope	K	I	Selsam, Millicent E.	HarperTrophy
Gristmill, The	T	I	Historic Communities	Crabtree
Grizzly Bear, The	R	I	Potts, Steve	Capstone Press
Grizzly Bears	N	I	Woolley, M. & Pigdon, K.	Mondo
Growing Up	P	I	It's Science	Children's Press
Growing Up in Coal Country	X	I	Bartoletti, Susan Campbell	Houghton Mifflin
Guatemala	O	I	Dahl, Michael	Capstone Press
Guess Who?	L	I	Home Connection Collection	Rigby
Guide Dog, The	K	I	Foundations	Wright Group/McGraw Hill
Guinea Pigs	S	I	Hansen, Elvig	Carolrhoda Books
Guinea Pigs	J	I	PM Animal Facts: Orange	Rigby
Gung Hay Fat Choy	N	I	Behrens, June	Children's Press
Hairy Little Critters	O	I	Wilde, Buck	Rigby
Halloween: Why We Celebrate It the Way We Do	P	I	Hintz, Martin & Kate	Capstone Press
Hand Tools	M	I	Wonder World	Wright Group/McGraw Hill
Hanukkah	N	I	Festivals and Holidays	Children's Press
Happy Accidents!	Q	I	Trussell-Cullen, Alan	Rigby
Have You Seen Birds?	K	I	Oppenheim, J. & Reid, B.	Scholastic
Hawaii	T	I	Sea to Shining Sea	Children's Press
Hawaiian Magic	R	I	Morris, Rod	Pacific Learning
Head For the Hills!	O	I	Walker, Paul Robert	Random House
Heat Is On, The	U	I	Tanaka, Shelley	Firefly Books
Helicopters	N	I	A True Book	Children's Press
Helping the Hoiho	S	I	Literacy 2000	Rigby
Heroes	N	I	Wildcats	Wright Group/McGraw Hill
Hidden World	R	I	Weldon Owen	Wright Group/McGraw Hill
Hide to Survive	L	I	Home Connection Collection	Rigby
High Flying	R	I	Weldon Owen	Wright Group/McGraw Hill
Hippos	K	I	PM Animal Facts: Turquoise	Rigby
History of Machines, The	O	I	McKinnon, Judith	Rigby
Hocus Pocus	M	I	Wildcats	Wright Group/McGraw Hill
Home: A Journey Through America	R	I	Locker, Thomas	Voyageur Books
Home Crafts	T	I	Historic Communities	Crabtree
Homes Are for Living	M	I	Cumpiano, Ina	Hampton-Brown
Honey Bees	M	I	Kahkonen, Sharon	Steck-Vaughn
Horse, of Course, The	Q	I	Elliot-Reep, Tracey	Rigby
Horse Power	O	I	Pacific Literacy	Pacific Learning
Horses	N	I	A New True Book	Children's Press
Horses	P	I	Crabapples	Crabtree
Horses	L	I	PM Animal Facts: Purple	Rigby
Horses Have Foals	M	I	Animals and Their Young	Compass Point Books
Hospitals	L	I	Book Shop	Mondo
Hot Air Balloons	L	I	Pair-It Books	Steck-Vaughn
Hot and Cold Weather	K	I	Sunshine	Wright Group/McGraw Hill
House Through the Ages	U	I	Steele, Philip	Troll Associates
Houses	M	I	Wonder World	Wright Group/McGraw Hill
How a Book is Made	N	I	Aliki	Harper & Row
How a Volcano is Formed	M	I	Wonder World	Wright Group/McGraw Hill
How Animals Move	L	I	Discovery World	Rigby
How Did This City Grow?	M	I	Schaefer, Lola M.	Benchmark Education
How Do Plants Get Food?	L	I	Goldish, Meish	Steck-Vaughn
How Does It Breathe?	K	I	Home Connection Collection	Rigby
How Does It Grow?	L	I	Home Connection Collection	Rigby
How Flexible Are You?	M	I	Marks, Ashley	Wright Group/McGraw Hill
How Goods Are Moved	K	I	People, Spaces & Places	Rand McNally
How I Met Einstein, a Character Comes to Life	S	I	Trussell-Cullen, Alan	Pacific Learning
How Is a Crayon Made?	P	I	Charles, Oz	Scholastic

Title	Level	Genre	Author/Series	Publisher/Distributor
How Kittens Grow	L	I	Selsam, Millicent E.	Scholastic
How My Family Lives in America	O	I	Kuklin, Susan	Aladdin
How Things Work	R	I	Weldon Owen	Wright Group/McGraw Hill
How To Choose a Pet	L	I	Discovery World	Rigby
How To Cook Scones	J	I	Book Shop	Mondo
How To Grow Crystals	P	I	Book Shop	Mondo
How To Make a Kite	M	I	Reeder, Paul	Wright Group/McGraw Hill
How To Make Salsa	J	I	Book Shop	Mondo
How's the Weather?	N	I	Berger, Melvin and Gilda	Ideals Children's Books
Hubble Space Telescope, The	N	I	A True Book	Children's Press
Human Body, The	Q	I	Weldon Owen	Wright Group/McGraw Hill
Humpback Whale, The	S	I	Frahm, Randy	Capstone Press
Hungry, Hungry Sharks	L	I	Cole, Joanna	Random House
Hunting the Horned Lizard	R	I	Bishop, Nic	Pacific Learning
Hurdles and Jumps	M	I	Reeder, Tracey	Wright Group/McGraw Hill
Hurricanes!	P	I	Hopping, Jean	Scholastic
Hurricanes & Tornadoes	R	I	The Wonders of our World	Crabtree
Hyenas	O	I	Holmes, Kevin J.	Capstone Press
I Am A Star: Child of the Holocaust	W	I	Auerbacher, Inge	The Penguin Group
I Love Guinea Pigs	O	I	King-Smith, Dick	Candlewick Press
I Wonder Why Snakes Shed Their Skins and Other Questions About Reptiles	O	I	O'Neill, Amanda	Scholastic
Ibis: A True Whale Story	K	I	Himmelman, John	Scholastic
Ice Mummy: The Discovery of a 5,000-Year-Old Man	P	I	Dubowski, Mark & Cathy East	Random House
Iditarod: Dogsled Race Across Alaska	Q	I	Fuerst, Jeffery B.	Wright Group/McGraw Hill
If You Grew Up with Abraham Lincoln	Q	I	McGovern, Ann	Scholastic
If You Grew Up with George Washington	Q	I	Gross, Ruth Belov	Scholastic
If You Lived 100 Years Ago	Q	I	McGovern, Ann	Scholastic
If You Lived at the Time of Martin Luther King	Q	I	Levine, Ellen	Scholastic
If You Lived at the Time of the American Revolution	Q	I	Moore, Kay	Scholastic
If You Lived at the Time of the Civil War	Q	I	Moore, Kay	Scholastic
If You Lived at the Time of the Great San Francisco Earthquake	Q	I	Levine, Ellen	Scholastic
If You Lived in Colonial Times	Q	I	McGovern, Ann	Scholastic
If you Lived in the Alaska Territory	Q	I	Levinson, Nancy Smiler	Scholastic
If You Lived with the Cherokee	Q	I	Roop, Peter & Connie	Scholastic
If You Lived with the Hopi	Q	I	Kamma, Anne	Scholastic
If You Lived with the Iroquois	Q	I	Levine, Ellen	Scholastic
If You Lived with the Sioux Indians	Q	I	McGovern, Ann	Scholastic
If You Sailed on the Mayflower in 1620	Q	I	McGovern, Ann	Scholastic
If You Traveled on the Underground Railroad	Q	I	Levine, Ellen	Scholastic
If You Traveled West in a Covered Wagon	Q	I	Levine, Ellen	Scholastic
If You Were There in 1492: Everyday Life in the Time of Columbus	U	I	Brenner, Barbara	Aladdin
If You Were There When They Signed the Constitution	Q	I	Levy, Elizabeth	Scholastic
If Your Name was Changed at Ellis Island	Q	I	Levine, Ellen	Scholastic
Illinois	Q	I	Geography Department	Capstone Press
Immigrants	T	I	Sandler, Martin W.	HarperTrophy
Immigrants: Coming to America	R	I	Thompson, Gare	Children's Press
In Danger	M	I	Home Connection Collection	Rigby
In Hiding, Animals Under Cover	L	I	Burke, Melissa Blackwell	Steck-Vaughn
In Search of the Grand Canyon	W	I	Fraser, Mary Ann	Henry Holt & Co.
In Search of the Great Bears	S	I	Literacy 2000	Rigby
In Short: A Collection of Brief Creative Nonfiction	Z	I	Kitchen, J. & Jones, M. P.	W. W. Norton
In the Fast Lane	R	I	Literacy 2000	Rigby
In the News	Q	I	Wildcats	Wright Group/McGraw Hill
In the Path of Lewis & Clark: Traveling the Missouri	V	I	Lourie, Peter	Silver Burdett Press
In the Rain Forest	Q	I	Wildcats	Wright Group/McGraw Hill
Incredible Creatures	P	I	Weldon Owen	Wright Group/McGraw Hill

Title	Level	Genre	Author/Series	Publisher/Distributor
Incredible Places	P	I	Wildcats	Wright Group/McGraw Hill
India	O	I	Dahl, Michael	Capstone Press
Insects	U	I	Bird, Bettina & Short, Joan	Mondo
Insects	J	I	MacLulich, Carolyn	Scholastic
Insects All Around	K	I	Early Connections	Benchmark Education
Insects & Spiders	U	I	World Book Looks at Science	World Book
Insects & Spiders	R	I	Worldwise	Franklin Watts
Inside a Rain Forest	M	I	Pair-It Books	Steck-Vaughn
Into Space	J	I	Momentum Literacy Program	Troll
Inventors	T	I	Sandler, Martin W.	HarperTrophy
Inventors: Making Things Better	M	I	Pair-It Books	Steck-Vaughn
Iowa	T	I	Sea to Shining Sea	Children's Press
Iroquois Indians, The	P	I	Lund, Bill	Capstone Press
Is it a Fish?	K	I	Sunshine	Wright Group/McGraw Hill
Is There Life in Outer Space	O	I	Branley, Franklyn M.	HarperCollins
Isn't It Cool?	R	I	Yurkovic, Diana Short	Rigby
Israel	O	I	Thoennes, Kristin	Capstone Press
It'll Be All Right on the Night!	Q	I	Quinn, Pat	Pacific Learning
It's About Time	M	I	Storyteller Nonfiction	Wright Group/McGraw Hill
It's the Fashion	S	I	Literacy 2000	Rigby
Italy	O	I	Thoennes, Kristin	Capstone Press
Jackie Robinson and the Story of All-Black Baseball	N	I	O'Connor, Jim	Random House
Jaguars	U	I	Green, Michael	Capstone Press
Jamestown Colony, The	V	I	Cornerstones of Freedom	Children's Press
Jamestown Colony, The	S	I	We The People	Compass Point Books
Jamestown: New World Adventure	T	I	Adventures in Colonial America	Troll
Jane's Mansion	N	I	Literacy 2000	Rigby
Japan	N	I	A True Book	Children's Press
Jelly Beans	M	I	Stadler, Charlotte	Benchmark Education Co.
Jokes and Riddles	O	I	Literacy 2000	Rigby
Jupiter	N	I	A True Book	Children's Press
Just a Few Words, Mr. Lincoln	N	I	Fritz, Jean	Putnam
Just Hanging Around	J	I	Storyteller-Night Crickets	Wright Group/McGraw Hill
Kangaroo, The	M	I	Crewe, Sabrina	Steck-Vaughn
Kangaroos	N	I	A New True Book	Children's Press
Kangaroos	K	I	PM Animal Facts: Turquoise	Rigby
Kayaking	Q	I	Lund, Bill	Capstone Press
Keeping Score	J	I	Early Connections	Benchmark Education
Keeping Tadpoles	N	I	Discovery World	Rigby
Keeping Warm! Keeping Cool!	K	I	Sunshine	Wright Group/McGraw Hill
Kenya	O	I	Dahl, Michael	Capstone Press
Kid Heroes of the Environment	Q	I	Dee, Catherine	Scholastic
Kids Can Cook	M	I	Literacy 2000	Rigby
Kids in the Circus	L	I	Robinson, Fay	Wright Group/McGraw Hill
Killer Bees	S	I	Blau, Melinda	Steck-Vaughn
Kitchen, The	T	I	Historic Communities	Crabtree
Kites	N	I	Literacy 2000	Rigby
Kites	O	I	PM Nonfiction -Emerald	Rigby
Klondike Gold Rush, The	S	I	A First Book	Franklin Watts
Knights & Armor	Q	I	Worldwise	Grolier
Koala Is Not a Bear, A	P	I	Crabapples	Crabtree
Koalas	N	I	A New True Book	Children's Press
Kwanzaa	O	I	Chocolate, Deborah M. Newton	Children's Press
Kwanzaa	K	I	Visions	Wright Group/McGraw Hill
La Causa: The Migrant Farmworkers' Story	U	I	deRuiz, Dana Catharine	Steck-Vaughn
Ladybug, The	O	I	Crewe, Sabrina	Steck-Vaughn
Ladybug, The	O	I	Garland, Peter	Rigby
Lamborghinis	U	I	Green, Michael	Capstone Press
Land I Lost, The	P	I	Nhuong, Huynh Quang	HarperTrophy
Land of the Dragons	P	I	Morris, Rod	Pacific Learning

Title	Level	Genre	Author/Series	Publisher/Distributor
Landslides, Slumps, & Creep	U	I	A First Book	Franklin Watts
Laughter Is the Best Medicine	P	I	Literacy Tree	Rigby
Leaders: People Who Make a Difference	R	I	You Are There	Children's Press
Leaping Lizards	M	I	Stadler, Charlotte	Benchmark Education Co.
Leaves	K	I	Pebble Books	Grolier, Capstone
Legendary Places	N	I	Wildcats	Wright Group/McGraw Hill
Let's Build a Playground	O	I	Myers, Edward	Pearson Learning
Let's Get Moving	M	I	Literacy 2000	Rigby
Letter Carriers	L	I	Community Workers	Compass Point Books
Letters from the Sea	S	I	Voyages in Time	Wright Group/McGraw Hill
Lewis and Clark Expedition, The	S	I	We The People	Compass Point Books
Lewis & Clark: Explorers of the American West	S	I	Kroll, Steven	Holiday House
Lexington and Concord	V	I	Cornerstones of Freedom	Children's Press
Liberty Bell, The	V	I	Cornerstones of Freedom	Children's Press
Librarians	M	I	Ready, Dee	Capstone Press
Library of Congress, The	V	I	Cornerstones of Freedom	Children's Press
Life in the City	J	I	Early Connections	Benchmark Education
Life in the Desert	M	I	Pair-It Books	Steck-Vaughn
Life in the Oceans: Animals, People, Plants	T	I	Baker, Lucy	Scholastic
Life in the Rainforests: Animals, People, Plants	T	I	Baker, Lucy	Scholastic
Life of a Miner	T	I	Life in the Old West	Crabtree
Life on a Plantation	T	I	Historic Communities	Crabtree
Light	J	I	Momentum Literacy Program	Troll
Lightning	T	I	Kramer, Stephen	Carolrhoda Books
Lightning	L	I	Pebble Books	Grolier, Capstone
Limestone Caves	N	I	A First Book	Franklin Watts
Limestone Caves	N	I	Davis, Gary	Children's Press
Lincoln Memorial, The	V	I	Cornerstones of Freedom	Children's Press
Lincoln-Douglas Debates, The	W	I	Cornerstones of Freedom	Children's Press
Lions	O	I	Holmes, Kevin J.	Capstone Press
Lions	N	I	Meadows, Graham & Vial, Claire	Dominie Press
Lions	L	I	Pair-It Books	Steck-Vaughn
Lions and Tigers	K	I	PM Animal Facts: Turquoise	Rigby
Little Caribou	N	I	Fox-Davies, Sarah	Candlewick Press
Little Cats	P	I	Crabapples	Crabtree
Living in Space	O	I	Nayer, Judy	Pearson Learning
Living Rain Forest, The	S	I	Bishop, Nic	Pacific Learning
Lizards	L	I	Wonder World	Wright Group/McGraw Hill
Lizards and Salamanders	M	I	Reading Unlimited	Celebration Press
Lizzie's Lizard	L	I	Storyteller Nonfiction	Wright Group/McGraw Hill
Long Ago and Far Away	T	I	Wildcats	Wright Group/McGraw Hill
Long, Long Ago	M	I	Literacy 2000	Rigby
Long Way to Go, A	R	I	O'Neal, Zibby	The Penguin Group
Look at Dogs, A	M	I	Pair-It Books	Steck-Vaughn
Look at Minerals, A: From Galena to Gold	S	I	A First Book	Franklin Watts
Look at Rocks, A: From Coal to Kimerlite	S	I	A First Book	Franklin Watts
Look at Snakes, A	M	I	Pair-It Books	Steck-Vaughn
Look at Spiders, A	M	I	Pair-It-Books	Steck-Vaughn
Look at the Moon	N	I	Book Shop	Mondo
Look Inside	J	I	Storyteller Nonfiction	Wright Group/McGraw Hill
Look What Came from China	O	I	Harvey, Miles	Franklin Watts
Look What Came from Egypt	O	I	Harvey, Miles	Franklin Watts
Look What Came from France	O	I	Harvey, Miles	Franklin Watts
Look What Came from Italy	O	I	Harvey, Miles	Franklin Watts
Look What Came from Mexico	O	I	Harvey, Miles	Franklin Watts
Look What Came from Russia	O	I	Harvey, Miles	Franklin Watts
Look What Came from the United States	O	I	Davis, Kevin	Franklin Watts
Look What I Made!	M	I	Literacy 2000	Rigby
Looking at Animals in Cold Places	O	I	Butterfield, Moira	Steck-Vaughn
Looking at Animals in Hot Places	O	I	Butterfield, Moira	Steck-Vaughn

Title	Level	Genre	Author/Series	Publisher/Distributor
Looking at Animals in the Ocean	O	I	Butterfield, Moira	Steck-Vaughn
Looking at Insects	L	I	Discovery World	Rigby
Looking For Patterns	J	I	Early Connections	Benchmark Education
Looking for Shapes	K	I	Early Connections	Benchmark Education
Looking for the Queen	O	I	Frederick, Shirley	Hampton-Brown
Looking into Space	L	I	Early Connections	Benchmark Education
Lost Tooth, The	J	I	New Way Orange	Steck-Vaughn
Louisiana Purchase, The	V	I	Cornerstones of Freedom	Children's Press
Machines in the Home	N	I	Morrison, Rob	Rigby
Magnet Book, The	T	I	Levine, Shar & Johnstone, Leslie	Sterling
Mail Carriers	M	I	Ready, Dee	Capstone Press
Make a Bottle Orchestra	J	I	Sunshine	Wright Group/McGraw Hill
Make a Cloud, Measure the Wind	M	I	Reimer, Luther	Wright Group/McGraw Hill
Make a Guitar	J	I	Sunshine	Wright Group/McGraw Hill
Make a Shake and a Bakeless Cake	L	I	Cole, Sally	Wright Group/McGraw Hill
Make Masks for a Play	J	I	Sunshine	Wright Group/McGraw Hill
Make Prints and Patterns	K	I	Sunshine	Wright Group/McGraw Hill
Making Pop-ups	O	I	Brian, Janeen	Mondo
Mammals	N	I	Simply Science	Compass Point Books
Mammals of the Sea	Q	I	Weldon Owen	Wright Group/McGraw Hill
Manatee, The	V	I	Silverstein, A. and Nunn, L.	The Millbrook Press
Manatees and Dugongs	M	I	Cole, Sally	Wright Group/McGraw Hill
Many Happy Returns: A Review of Recycling	R	I	Literacy 2000	Rigby
Map Mysteries	M	I	Gard, Stephen	Rigby
Maps and Codes	P	I	Wildcats	Wright Group/McGraw Hill
Maps and Our World	Q	I	Weldon Owen	Wright Group/McGraw Hill
Martial Arts	R	I	Malane, Donna	Pacific Learning
Martin Luther King Day	R	I	Lowery, Linda	Scholastic
Masks	M	I	Literacy 2000	Rigby
Materials and Their Uses	L	I	Discovery World	Rigby
Matter of Conscience, A: The Trial of Anne Hutchinson	U	I	Nichols, Joan Kane	Steck-Vaughn
Maya, The	N	I	A New True Book	Children's Press
Maya, The	S	I	Journey Into Civilization	Chelsea House
Measure Up!	K	I	Early Connections	Benchmark Education
Measuring the Weather	R	I	Gaynor, Bill	Pacific Learning
Measuring Tools	M	I	Daronco, Mickey & Presti, Lori	Benchmark Education
Meat Eaters, Plant Eaters	K	I	Planet Earth	Rigby
Medieval Feast, A	Q	I	Aliki	Harper Collins
Medieval Town	Q	I	Worldwise	Grolier
Meerkats	O	I	Weaver, Robyn	Capstone Press
Meet the Octopus	K	I	Book Shop	Mondo
Memorial Day	K	I	Frost, Helen	Capstone Press
Mercury	N	I	A True Book	Children's Press
Meteorite!: The Last Days of the Dinosaurs	W	I	Norris, Richard	Steck-Vaughn
Meteors: The Truth Behind Shooting Stars	T	I	Aronson, Billy	Franklin Watts
Mexico	O	I	Dahl, Michael	Capstone Press
Mice	O	I	Holmes, Kevin J.	Capstone Press
Mice	J	I	PM Animal Facts: Orange	Rigby
Michigan	Q	I	One nation	Capstone Press
Middle Ages, The	R	I	Journey Through History	Barron's Educational Series
Mighty Mammals	Q	I	Weldon Owen	Wright Group/McGraw Hill
Mini Mammals	R	I	Weldon Owen	Wright Group/McGraw Hill
Mix, Make and Munch	J	I	Home Connection Collection	Rigby
Modern Times	R	I	Journey Through History	Barron's Educational Series
Money Riddles That Count	K	I	Fetty, Margaret	Steck-Vaughn
Mongols, The	S	I	Journey Into Civilization	Chelsea House
Monkeys and Apes	K	I	PM Animal Facts: Turquoise	Rigby
Monsters of the Deep	L	I	Swartz, Stanley L.	Dominie Press
Monticello	V	I	Cornerstones of Freedom	Children's Press

Title	Level	Genre	Author/Series	Publisher/Distributor
Moon, The	U	I	A First Book	Franklin Watts
Moon, The	Q	I	Eye on the Universe	Crabtree
Moon, The	N	I	Literacy 2000	Rigby
Moonwalk: The First Trip to the Moon	O	I	Donnelly, Judy	Random House
Moose, The	R	I	Hemstock, Annie	Capstone Press
More Perfect Union: The Story of Our Constitution	S	I	Maestro, Betsy & Giulio	William Morrow
Mother Sea Turtle	K	I	Foundations	Wright Group/McGraw Hill
Mount Vernon	V	I	Cornerstones of Freedom	Children's Press
Mountain Bike Challenge, The	Q	I	Morgan, Patrick	Pacific Learning
Mountain Gorillas	O	I	Wonder World	Wright Group/McGraw Hill
Mountain Lion, The	O	I	Crewe, Sabrina	Steck-Vaughn
Mountains	S	I	Weitzman, David	Steck-Vaughn
Mummies	M	I	All Aboard Reading	Grosset & Dunlap
Mummies and Their Mysteries	T	I	Wilcox, Charlotte	Carolrhoda Books
Mummies Made in Egypt	R	I	Aliki	Harper Collins
Muscles: Our Muscular System	T	I	Simon, Seymour	HarperTrophy
Mustangs	U	I	Gillespie, Lorrine	Capstone Press
My Body	M	I	Schaefer, Lola M.	Benchmark Education
My Dream of Martin Luther King	R	I	Ringgold, Faith	Crown
My Scrapbook	K	I	Storyteller Nonfiction	Wright Group/McGraw Hill
Mythmakers	T	I	Wildcats	Wright Group/McGraw Hill
National Anthem, The	N	I	A True Book	Children's Press
Native Americans	P	I	Weldon Owen	Wright Group/McGraw Hill
Nature's Celebration	M	I	Literacy 2000	Rigby
Nature's Power	Q	I	Hummer, Patricia K.	Steck-Vaughn
Neptune	N	I	A True Book	Children's Press
Nervous System, The	N	I	A True Book	Children's Press
Netherlands, The	O	I	Dahl, Michael	Capstone Press
Never Bored on Boards	O	I	Literacy 2000	Rigby
New Friends in a New Land: A Thanksgiving Story	N	I	Stamper, Judith Bauer	Steck-Vaughn
New Jersey	Q	I	Kummer, Patricia K.	Capstone Press
New Land: A First Year on the Praire, The	M	I	Reynolds, Marilynn	Orca Book Publishers
New Mexico	S	I	Thompson, Kathleen	Steck-Vaughn
New Year's Around the World	O	I	Trumbore, Cindy	Pearson Learning
New York	Q	I	Geography Department	Capstone Press
New York	S	I	Thompson, Kathleen	Steck-Vaughn
New York City	T	I	Kent, Deborah	Childrens Press
Newborn Animals	J	I	Momentum Literacy Program	Troll
News Flash!	R	I	Hill, Sharon	Pacific Learning
Nez Perce Tribe, The	O	I	Lassieur, Allison	Capstone Press
Nigeria	O	I	Thoennes, Kristin	Capstone Press
Night Lights, A Cruise Around the Solar System	R	I	Hill, David	Pacific Learning
Night Owls, The	M	I	Wonder World	Wright Group/McGraw Hill
Nine True Dolphin Stories	M	I	Davidson, Margaret	Scholastic
North America	Q	I	Petersen, David	Grolier Publishing
North Carolina	T	I	Fradin, Dennis Brindell	Childrens Press
North Carolina	S	I	Portrait of America	Steck-Vaughn
North Star To Freedom	U	I	Gorrell, Gena K.	Random House
Now Is Your Time! The African-American Struggle	Y	I	Myers, Walter Dean	Harper Collins
Nurses	M	I	Ready, Dee	Capstone Press
Ocean Animals	J	I	Early Connections	Benchmark Education
Ocean Detectives: Solving Mysteries of the Sea	W	I	Cerullo, Mary	Steck-Vaughn
Ocean Life	Q	I	Weldon Owen	Wright Group/McGraw Hill
Ocean Life: Tide Pool Creatures	Q	I	Leonhardt, Alice	Steck-Vaughn
Ocean Tide Pool	P	I	L'Hommedieu, Arthur John	Grolier
Oceans	Q	I	First Reports	Compass Point Books
Oceans	Q	I	The Wonders of our World	Crabtree
Octopuses and Squids	O	I	Wonder World	Wright Group/McGraw Hill
Octopuses, Squid, & Cuttlefish	L	I	Marine Life For Yng. Readers	Dominie
Off the Map, The Journals of Lewis and Clark	U	I	Roop, Peter and Connie	Walker and Company

Title	Level	Genre	Author/Series	Publisher/Distributor
Off To Sea: An Inside Look at a Research Cruise	T	I	Kovacs, Deborah	Steck-Vaughn
Ohio	Q	I	Geography Department	Capstone Press
Ohio	S	I	Thompson, Kathleen	Steck-Vaughn
Ojibwa Indians, The	P	I	Lund, Bill	Capstone Press
Olympics and the Mini Olympics, The	N	I	Mack, Rachel	Wright Group/McGraw Hill
On and Off the Road	M	I	Wildcats	Wright Group/McGraw Hill
On Board The Titanic	T	I	Tanaka, Shelley	Hyperion/Madison Press
On Site	S	I	Pollock, John	Mondo
On the Open Plains	J	I	Momentum Literacy Program	Troll
On the Right Track	N	I	Gard, Stephen	Rigby
On With the Show!	M	I	Pair-It Books	Steck-Vaughn
One Day in the Alpine Tundra	P	I	George, Jean Craighead	Harper Collins
One Day in the Desert	P	I	George, Jean Craighead	Harper Collins
One Day in the Tropical Rain Forest	P	I	George, Jean Craighead	HarperTrophy
One Day in the Woods	P	I	George, Jean Craighead	HarperTrophy
One Drop of Water and a Million More	K	I	Book Bank	Wright Group/McGraw Hill
One Giant Leap	S	I	Fraser, Mary Ann	Henry Holt & Co.
Oregon Trail, The	V	I	Cornerstones of Freedom	Children's Press
Our American Flag	O	I	McCloskey, Susan	Wright Group/McGraw Hill
Our Book of Maps	N	I	Discovery World	Rigby
Our Busy Bodies	K	I	Home Connection Collection	Rigby
Our Changing Earth	R	I	Belcher, Angie	Pacific Learning
Our Endangered Planet (Oceans)	W	I	Hoff, M. and Rodgers, M.	Lerner Publications
Our Government	M	I	People, Spaces & Places	Rand McNally
Our Money	J	I	Early Connections	Benchmark Education
Our Planet	R	I	Worldwise	Grolier
Our World of Wonders	Q	I	Canetti, Yanitzia	Steck-Vaughn
Out and About	Q	I	Weldon Owen	Wright Group/McGraw Hill
Outside and Inside Bats	Q	I	Markle, Sandra	Simon & Schuster
Outside and Inside Kangaroos	Q	I	Markle, Sandra	Atheneum
Outside and Inside Sharks	Q	I	Markle, Sandra	Simon & Schuster
Outside and Inside Snakes	Q	I	Markle, Sandra	Simon & Schuster
Outside and Inside Spiders	Q	I	Markle, Sandra	Simon & Schuster
Owls	O	I	Holmes, Kevin J.	Capstone Press
Owls	R	I	Kalman, Bobbie	Crabtree
Owls	M	I	PM Animal Facts: Gold	Rigby
Panama Canal, The	W	I	Cornerstones of Freedom	Children's Press
Parakeets	J	I	PM Animal Facts: Orange	Rigby
Partners	L	I	Home Connection Collection	Rigby
Paul Harvey's The Rest Of The Story	Z	I	Harvey Jr., Paul	Bantam Books
Pawnee Nation, The	O	I	Walters, Anna Lee	Capstone Press
Peanut	Q	I	Selsam, Millicent	William Morrow
Penguin, The	O	I	Crewe, Sabrina	Steck-Vaughn
Penguins	O	I	Holmes, Kevin J.	Capstone Press
Penguins of the Galápagos	P	I	Young Readers' Series	Barron's Educational Series
Pennsylvania	Q	I	Geography Department	Capstone Press
People Are Living Things	K	I	Home Connection Collection	Rigby
People at Work	J	I	Momentum Literacy Program	Troll
People from the Past	R	I	Weldon Owen	Wright Group/McGraw Hill
Peru	O	I	Thoennes, Kristin	Capstone Press
Pet for You, A	K	I	Pair-It Books	Steck-Vaughn
Pet Vet	N	I	Pacific Literacy	Pacific Learning
Pets Need People	M	I	Literacy 2000	Rigby
Philippines, The	O	I	Davis, Lucile	Capstone Press
Photos, Photos	N	I	Wildcats	Wright Group/McGraw Hill
Picking Apples and Pumpkins	L	I	Hutchings, A. & R.	Scholastic
Pigs	L	I	PM Animal Facts: Purple	Rigby
Pigs Have Piglets	M	I	Animals and Their Young	Compass Point Books
Pilgrims of Plimouth, The	T	I	Sewall, Marcia	Simon & Schuster

Title	Level	Genre	Author/Series	Publisher/Distributor
Pilgrims, The	V	I	Cornerstones of Freedom	Children's Press
Pioneer Way, The	Q	I	Kummer, Patricia K.	Steck-Vaughn
Pioneers	T	I	Sandler, Martin W.	HarperTrophy
Pizza for Everyone	K	I	Pair-It Books	Steck-Vaughn
Place Called Heartbreak, A: A Story of Vietnam	U	I	Myers, Walter Dean	Steck-Vaughn
Planets, The	Q	I	Weldon Owen	Wright Group/McGraw Hill
Planets, The	J	I	Wonder World	Wright Group/McGraw Hill
Planning a Birthday Party	N	I	Book Shop	Mondo
Plant Kingdom, The	Q	I	Weldon Owen	Wright Group/McGraw Hill
Platypus	P	I	Short, J., Green, J., and Bird, B.	Mondo
Play Ball!	R	I	Weldon Owen	Wright Group/McGraw Hill
Plumbers	M	I	Boraas, Tracey	Capstone Press
Pluto	N	I	A First Book	Franklin Watts
Pluto	N	I	A True Book	Children's Press
Plymouth Colony, The	S	I	We The People	Compass Point Books
Polar Bear, The	S	I	Hemstock, Annie	Capstone Press
Polar Bears	N	I	PM Animal Facts: Silver	Rigby
Polar Bears	K	I	Wonder World	Wright Group/McGraw Hill
Polar Regions	N	I	Habitats of the World	Dominie Press
Police Officers	L	I	Community Workers	Compass Point Books
Police Officers	M	I	Ready, Dee	Capstone Press
Pompeii...Buried Alive!	N	I	Kunhardt, Edith	Random House
Pony Express, The	V	I	Cornerstones of Freedom	Children's Press
Popcorn Book, The	N	I	dePaola, Tomie	Holiday House
Popcorn Book, The	K	I	Reading Unlimited	Celebration Press
Postcards From France	N	I	Arnold, Helen	Steck-Vaughn
Postcards From Kenya	N	I	Arnold, Helen	Steck-Vaughn
Postcards From South Africa	N	I	Dawson, Zoe	Steck-Vaughn
Postcards From Vietnam	N	I	Allard, Denise	Steck-Vaughn
Potter in Fiji, A	N	I	Wonder World	Wright Group/McGraw Hill
Power Machines	N	I	Robbins, Ken	Henry Holt & Company
Power of Nature, The	K	I	Early Connections	Benchmark Education
Power of Water, The	L	I	Home Connection Collection	Rigby
Powerhouse, Inside a Nuclear Power Plant	Z	I	Wilcox, Charlotte	Carolrhoda Books
Powers of Congress, The	W	I	Cornerstones of Freedom	Children's Press
Powwow Summer: A Family Celebrates the Circle of Life	S	I	Rendon, Marcie R.	Carolrhoda Books
Prehistoric Record Breakers	N	I	Discovery World	Rigby
Prehistory to Egypt	R	I	Journey Through History	Barron's Educational Series
Presidency, The	N	I	A True Book	Children's Press
Presidential Elections	W	I	Cornerstones of Freedom	Children's Press
Presidents' Day	K	I	Frost, Helen	Capstone Press
Project Apollo	N	I	A True Book	Children's Press
Project Gemini	N	I	A True Book	Children's Press
Project Mercury	N	I	A True Book	Children's Press
Prudence	N	I	Raatma, Lucia	Capstone Press
Pueblo Indians, The	P	I	Ross, Pamela	Capstone Press
Pumpkins	M	I	Ray, Mary Lyn	Harcourt Brace
Puppets	P	I	Trussell-Cullen, Alan	Rigby
Puppies, Dogs, and Blue Northers	S	I	Paulsen, Gary	Delacorte Press
Questions and Answers About Forest Animals	P	I	Chinery, Michael	Kingfisher
Questions and Answers About Freshwater Animals	P	I	Chinery, Michael	Kingfisher
Quilt with a Difference, A	N	I	Pacific Literacy	Pacific Learning
Rabbits	N	I	Literacy 2000	Rigby
Rabbits Have Bunnies	M	I	Animals and Their Young	Compass Point Books
Raccoons	M	I	PM Animal Facts: Gold	Rigby
Rain	K	I	Pebble Books	Grolier, Capstone
Rain Forest	R	I	Worldwise	Grolier
Rain Forest, The	Q	I	Fusselman, Fred	Rigby
Rain Forest Tree, A	Q	I	Kite, Lorien	Crabtree

Title	Level	Genre	Author/Series	Publisher/Distributor
Rain or Shine	Q	I	Weldon Owen	Wright Group/McGraw Hill
Rain, Snow, and Hail	J	I	Discovery World	Rigby
Rainbows of the Sea	L	I	Thomas, Meredith	Mondo
Raptors: Hunters in the Sky	R	I	Rauzon, Mark J.	Wright Group/McGraw Hill
Red Means Good Fortune: A Story of San Francisco's Chinatown	S	I	Goldin, Barbara Diamond	The Penguin Group
Reduce, Reuse, and Recycle	K	I	Early Connections	Benchmark Education
Relationships of Living Things	R	I	Atwater, Mary & Baptiste et al	Macmillan/McGraw-Hill
Remember Not To Forget: A Memory of the Holocaust	V	I	Finkelstein, Norman H.	William & Morrow
Remember the Ladies: The First Women's Rights Convention	U	I	Johnston, Norma	Scholastic
Remembering the Big Quake	R	I	Trussell-Cullen, Alan	Pacific Learning
Reptiles and Amphibians	R	I	Weldon Owen	Wright Group/McGraw Hill
Rhinos	O	I	Holmes, Kevin J.	Capstone Press
Rhythm and Shoes	N	I	Pacific Literacy	Pacific Learning
Riches from Nature	K	I	Early Connections	Benchmark Education
Riddle of the Rosetta Stone, The	V	I	Giblin, James Cross	HarperTrophy
Riddles of the Universe	S	I	Bonallack, John	Pacific Learning
River Through the Ages	U	I	Steele, Philip	Troll Associates
Road Goes By, A	J	I	Momentum Literacy Program	Troll
Road Through the Ages	U	I	Steele, Philip	Troll Associates
Rock Climbing	Q	I	Lund, Bill	Capstone Press
Rock Climbing	N	I	Ramsey, Joe	Wright Group/McGraw Hill
Rocks & Minerals	R	I	The Wonders of our World	Crabtree
Rosie the Riveter	Z	I	Colman, Penny	Crown Publishers, Inc.
Round and Round: The Story of Wheels	N	I	McAlister, Margaret	Rigby
Rules	J	I	Early Connections	Benchmark Education
Runaway to Freedom: A Story of the Underground Railway	T	I	Smucker, Barbara	Harper Trophy
Russia	O	I	Thoennes, Kristin	Capstone Press
Salem Days: Life in a Colonial Seaport	T	I	Adventures in Colonial America	Troll
Sam and Kim	O	I	Pacific Literacy	Pacific Learning
San Domingo	R	I	Henry, Marguerite	Scholastic
Sand On The Move: The Story of Dunes	U	I	A First Book	Franklin Watts
Santa Fe Trail, The	V	I	Cornerstones of Freedom	Children's Press
Santa Fe Trail, The	S	I	We The People	Compass Point Books
Saturn	N	I	A First Book	Franklin Watts
Saturn	N	I	A True Book	Children's Press
Save the Everglades	R	I	Stamper, Judith Bauer	Steck-Vaughn
Save the Manatee	N	I	Friesinger, Alison	Random House
Save the Sea Turtles!	M	I	Leonhardt, Alice	Steck-Vaughn
Saving The Yellow Eye	P	I	Darby, John	Pacific Learning
Scaly Things	Q	I	Weldon Owen	Wright Group/McGraw Hill
School Bus Drivers	M	I	Ready, Dee	Capstone Press
School Principals	M	I	Boraas, Tracey	Capstone Press
Science-Just Add Salt	L	I	Markle, Sandra	Scholastic
Sea Otter Rescue: The Aftermath of an Oil Spill	W	I	Smith, Roland	Scholastic
Sea Otters	L	I	Storyteller Nonfiction	Wright Group/McGraw Hill
Sea Turtles	K	I	Marine Life For Yng. Readers	Dominie
Sea Wall, The	K	I	Foundations	Wright Group/McGraw Hill
Seabirds	S	I	A First Book	Franklin Watts
Seals and Sea Lions	N	I	Cole, Sally	Wright Group/McGraw Hill
Searching for Sea Lions	P	I	Westerskov, Kim	Pacific Learning
Seashells	K	I	Marine Life For Yng. Readers	Dominie
Seasons	N	I	A True Book	Children's Press
Seasons	N	I	Simply Science	Compass Point Books
Secret of Kiribu Tapu Lagoon, The	S	I	Literacy 2000	Rigby
Secrets of the Desert	Q	I	Literacy 2000	Rigby
Secrets of the Rain Forest	O	I	Myers, Edward	Pearson Learning
Seed is a Promise, A	O	I	Merrill, Claire	Scholastic

Title	Level	Genre	Author/Series	Publisher/Distributor
Seeds	J	I	Pebble Books	Grolier, Capstone
Self-Discipline	N	I	Raatma, Lucia	Capstone Press
Seminole Indians, The	P	I	Lund, Bill	Capstone Press
Shadow of the Wolf	N	I	Whelan, Gloria	Random House
Shapes of Water, The, Stories About Patterns and Shapes	N	I	Shannan, Gillian and others	Pacific Learning
Sharks	T	I	Simon, Seymour	Harper Trophy
Sharks	L	I	Wonder World	Wright Group/McGraw Hill
Sharks and Rays	L	I	Marine Life For Yng. Readers	Dominie Press
Sharks and Rays	Q	I	Weldon Owen	Wright Group/McGraw Hill
Sheep	L	I	PM Animal Facts: Purple	Rigby
Sheep Have Lambs	M	I	Animals and Their Young	Compass Point Books
Shh! We're Writing the Constitution	T	I	Fritz, Jean	G.P. Putnam's Sons
Ships	L	I	Wonder World	Wright Group/McGraw Hill
Ships at Sea	K	I	PM Plus	Rigby
Shoes Through the Ages	Q	I	Brill, Marlene Targ	Steck-Vaughn
Sideways Arithmetic from Wayside School	S	I	Sachar, Louis	Scholastic
Sierra	Q	I	Siebert, Diane	HarperCollins
Silent Hero, The	O	I	Shea, George	Random House
Silkworms	N	I	Blackburn, Rachel	Wright Group/McGraw Hill
Sioux Indians, The	P	I	Lund, Bill	Capstone Press
Six Things to Make	L	I	Book Shop	Mondo
Skateboarding	O	I	PM Nonfiction -Emerald	Rigby
Skunks	M	I	PM Animal Facts: Gold	Rigby
Sky Watch	Q	I	Weldon Owen	Wright Group/McGraw Hill
Sky's the Limit, The	P	I	Christiansen, Tony	Pacific Learning
Slugs and Snails	N	I	Book Shop	Mondo
Slugs and Snails	P	I	Mini Pets	Steck-Vaughn
Snails	O	I	Holmes, Kevin J.	Capstone Press
Snake, The	O	I	Crewe, Sabrina	Steck-Vaughn
Snakes	K	I	Foundations	Wright Group/McGraw Hill
Snakes!	L	I	Recht Penner, Lucille	Random House
Snakes	J	I	Sunshine	Wright Group/McGraw Hill
Snakes	Q	I	Weldon Owen	Wright Group/McGraw Hill
Snakes	L	I	Wonder World	Wright Group/McGraw Hill
Sneakers	K	I	Sunshine	Wright Group/McGraw Hill
Snowboarding Diary	O	I	PM Nonfiction -Emerald	Rigby
Sod Houses on the Great Plains	N	I	Rounds, Glen	Holiday House
Soil	N	I	Simply Science	Compass Point Books
Solar System, The	N	I	A True Book	Children's Press
Solids, Liquids, Gases	N	I	Simply Science	Compass Point Books
Some Machines are Enormous	J	I	Book Shop	Mondo
Song of the Mantis, The	S	I	Literacy 2000	Rigby
Sound, Heat & Light: Energy at Work	L	I	Berger, Melvin	Scholastic
Sounds	J	I	Early Connections	Benchmark Education
South Korea	O	I	Davis, Lucile	Capstone Press
Space	R	I	Worldwise	Grolier
Space Quest	O	I	Discovery World	Rigby
Space Stations	N	I	A True Book	Children's Press
Space Stations	O	I	Ryan, Cheryl	Wright Group/McGraw Hill
Spanish-American War, The	W	I	Cornerstones of Freedom	Children's Press
Special Effects	M	I	Wildcats	Wright Group/McGraw Hill
Spider Man	M	I	Literacy 2000	Rigby
Spider Relatives	Q	I	Literacy 2000	Rigby
Spider, The	O	I	Crewe, Sabrina	Steck-Vaughn
Spider's Web, A	L	I	Wonder World	Wright Group/McGraw Hill
Spiders	M	I	Book Shop	Mondo
Spiders	O	I	Holmes, Kevin J.	Capstone Press
Spiders	P	I	Mini Pets	Steck-Vaughn
Spirit of St. Louis, The	V	I	Cornerstones of Freedom	Children's Press

Title	Level	Genre	Author/Series	Publisher/Distributor
Sports Bloopers	P	I	Hollander, Phyllis & Zander	Scholastic
Sports for All	Q	I	Weldon Owen	Wright Group/McGraw Hill
Sports Heroes	R	I	PM Nonfiction -Ruby	Rigby
Sports on Wheels	R	I	PM Nonfiction -Ruby	Rigby
Sports Technology	R	I	PM Nonfiction -Ruby	Rigby
Spreading the Word	Q	I	Wildcats	Wright Group/McGraw Hill
Squirrels	N	I	Storyteller Nonfiction	Wright Group/McGraw Hill
Starfish & Urchins	K	I	Marine Life For Yng. Readers	Dominie
Stars	N	I	A True Book	Children's Press
Statue of Liberty, The	N	I	A True Book	Children's Press
Statue of Liberty, The	J	I	Penner, Lucille	Random House
Staying Healthy: Eating Right	O	I	McGinty, Alice B.	Franklin Watts
Stems	K	I	Pebble Books	Grolier, Capstone
Stone Works	K	I	Wonder World	Wright Group/McGraw Hill
Stories in Stone: The World of Animal Fossils	U	I	A First Book	Franklin Watts
Storm Book, The	P	I	Zolotow, Charlotte	Harper Collins
Storms!	L	I	Pair-It Books	Steck-Vaughn
Story of a Book, The	L	I	Reeder, Paul	Wright Group/McGraw Hill
Story of Jeans, The	M	I	Discovery World	Rigby
Story of Small Fry, The	P	I	Vaughan, Marcia	Rigby
Story of the Mayflower Compact, The	T	I	Cornerstones of Freedom	Children's Press
Story of The Persian Gulf War, The	W	I	Cornerstones of Freedom	Children's Press
Story of The Sinking of the Battleship Maine, The	W	I	Cornerstones of Freedom	Children's Press
Story of The Surrender at Yorktown, The	V	I	Cornerstones of Freedom	Children's Press
Story of the White House, The	S	I	Waters, Kate	Scholastic
Story of The Women's Movement, The	V	I	Cornerstones of Freedom	Children's Press
Story of You, The	M	I	Sunshine	Wright Group/McGraw Hill
Storytellers	L	I	Storyteller Nonfiction	Wright Group/McGraw Hill
Street Action	O	I	Wildcats	Wright Group/McGraw Hill
Strike	O	I	Pacific Literacy	Pacific Learning
String Food	K	I	Home Connection Collection	Rigby
String Performers	J	I	Home Connection Collection	Rigby
Sugaring Season (Making Maple Syrup)	S	I	Burns, Diane	Carolrhoda Books
Sugaring Time	S	I	Lasky, Kathryn	Macmillan
Sun	O	I	Vogt, Gregory L.	Capstone Press
Sun, The	N	I	Literacy 2000	Rigby
Sun, The	J	I	Wonder World	Wright Group/McGraw Hill
Sunshine	L	I	Pebble Books	Grolier, Capstone
Supermarket, The	K	I	Pebble Books	Grolier, Capstone
Supreme Court, The	N	I	A True Book	Children's Press
Surprise Party	K	I	Hutchins, Pat	Macmillan
Surprising Swimmers: Nature's Most Amazing Animals	R	I	Fredericks, Anthony D.	NorthWord Press
Survival of Fish, The	M	I	Science	Wright Group/McGraw Hill
Take A Look	N	I	Wildcats	Wright Group/McGraw Hill
Take Care of Our Earth	M	I	Pair-It Books	Steck-Vaughn
Tasmanian Devils	R	I	Morris, Rod	Pacific Learning
Tasmanian Devils	M	I	PM Animal Facts: Gold	Rigby
Taste of Salt: The Story of Modern Haiti	W	I	Temple, Frances	HarperTrophy
Tea	K	I	Wonder World	Wright Group/McGraw Hill
Teachers	M	I	Deedrick, Tami	Capstone Press
Teeth	K	I	Sunshine	Wright Group/McGraw Hill
Telling Stories Through Art	N	I	Reimer, Luther	Wright Group/McGraw Hill
Ten True Animal Rescues	O	I	Betancourt, Jeanne	Scholastic
Tenement Writer, The: An Immigrant's Story	T	I	Sonder, Ben	Steck-Vaughn
Texas	Q	I	Geography Department	Capstone Press
Thailand	O	I	Thoennes, Kristin	Capstone Press
Thanksgiving: Why We Celebrate It the Way We Do	P	I	Hintz, Martin & Kate	Capstone Press
Then and Now	J	I	Discovery World	Rigby
There's No Place Like Home	R	I	Hill, David	Pacific Learning
They Survived Mount St. Helens!	O	I	Stine, Megan	Random House

Title	Level	Genre	Author/Series	Publisher/Distributor
Things Change	M	I	Bourne, Phyllis Montenegro	Hampton-Brown
Things With Wings	J	I	Storyteller Nonfiction	Wright Group/McGraw Hill
Think Like a Scientist	Q	I	Burke, Melissa Blackwell	Steck-Vaughn
Thinking About Ants	L	I	Book Shop	Mondo
This Is My House	L	I	Dorros, Arthur	Scholastic
This Place is Dry	R	I	Cobb, Vicki	Walker and Co.
This Place is Wet	R	I	Cobb, Vicki	Walker and Co.
Those Amazingly Useful Ears	O	I	Frederick, Shirley	Hampton-Brown
Three Days on a River in a Red Canoe	K	I	Williams, Vera B.	Scholastic
Through the Eyes of Your Ancestors: A Step-by-Step Guide to Uncovering Your Family's History	V	I	Taylor, Maureen	Houghton Mifflin
Thunder At Gettysburg	S	I	Gauch, Patricia Lee	Bantam Doubleday Dell
Thunderstorms	N	I	A True Book	Children's Press
Titanic Sinks!, The	T	I	Conklin, Thomas	Random House
Titanic, The	V	I	Cornerstones of Freedom	Children's Press
Titanic, The: Lost. . .and Found	N	I	Donnelly, Judy	Random House
To Be a Slave	Z	I	Lester, Julius	Dial Books
To Fly with the Swallows: A Story of Old California	S	I	deRuiz, Dana Catharine	Steck-Vaughn
To the Moon and Beyond	S	I	Lott, Linda	Wright Group/McGraw Hill
Tomato Picking Day	L	I	Pipher, Tom	Wright Group/McGraw Hill
Tomatoes	M	I	Cole, Sally	Wright Group/McGraw Hill
Tongues: Are for Tasting, Licking, Tricking	L	I	Literacy 2000	Rigby
Tools and Gadgets	T	I	Historic Communities	Crabtree
Top Cat	O	I	Byars, Betsy	The Penguin Group
Tornado	O	I	Byars, Betsy	HarperTrophy
Tornadoes!	N	I	Hopping, Lorraine Jean	Scholastic
Tractor Trailers	N	I	Schaefer, Lola M.	Capstone Press
Train Time	L	I	Baehr, Lisa	Hampton-Brown
Trains on the Rails	K	I	PM Plus	Rigby
Transcontinental Railroad, The	V	I	Cornerstones of Freedom	Children's Press
Transforming Trash	S	I	Quinn, Pat	Pacific Learning
Travelers and Traders	Q	I	Weldon Owen	Wright Group/McGraw Hill
Trees	K	I	Early Connections	Benchmark Education
Trees	J	I	Literacy 2000	Rigby
Trees and Leaves	S	I	Nature Club	Troll
Trees and Plants in the Rain Forest	O	I	Pirotta, Saviour	Steck-Vaughn
Trees Belong To Everyone	L	I	Literacy 2000	Rigby
Triathlon	Q	I	Lund, Bill	Capstone Press
Trip Around the Gulf of Mexico, A	M	I	People, Spaces & Places	Rand McNally
Trojan Horse, The	N	I	Literacy 2000	Rigby
Tropical Rainforests	N	I	Habitats of the World	Dominie Press
Trucks on the Road	K	I	PM Plus	Rigby
True Crimes and How They Were Solved	Z	I	Larsen, Anita	Scholastic
True Story of Balto, The	L	I	Standiford, Natalie	Random House
True-Life Treasure Hunts	N	I	Donnelly, Judy	Random House
Tubes in My Ears: My Trip to the Hospital	K	I	Book Shop	Mondo
Tundra	Q	I	First Reports	Compass Point Books
Turtles	S	I	A First Book	Franklin Watts
Tut's Mummy: Lost and Found	P	I	Donnelly, Judy	Random House
Tutankhamen's Gift	R	I	Sabuda, Robert	Simon & Schuster
TV Reporters	M	I	Boraas, Tracey	Capstone Press
Twelve Dancing Princesses	M	I	Enrichment	Wright Group/McGraw Hill
Twisters and Other Wind Storms	P	I	Wildcats	Wright Group/McGraw Hill
Twisting Up a Storm	R	I	Duksta, Cheryl	Pacific Learning
Two Hungry Hippos	M	I	Adams, Alison	Benchmark Education Co.
Ultimate Field Trip 1: Adventures in the Amazon Rain Forest	S	I	Goodman, Susan E.	Simon & Schuster
Umbrellas	M	I	Sunshine	Wright Group/McGraw Hill
Under the Ground	P	I	Literacy 2000	Rigby

Title	Level	Genre	Author/Series	Publisher/Distributor
Under the Ground	Q	I	Wildcats	Wright Group/McGraw Hill
Underground Railroad, The	V	I	Bial, Raymond	Houghton Mifflin
Underground Railroad, The	V	I	Cornerstones of Freedom	Children's Press
Underwater Animals	Q	I	Weldon Owen	Wright Group/McGraw Hill
United States Holocaust Memorial Museum, The	W	I	Cornerstones of Freedom	Children's Press
Universe, The	Q	I	Pair-It-Books	Steck-Vaughn
Unusual Spiders	N	I	Jensen, Ned	Wright Group/McGraw Hill
Up and Away	Q	I	Weldon Owen	Wright Group/McGraw Hill
Up in the Air	P	I	Wildcats	Wright Group/McGraw Hill
Uranus	N	I	A True Book	Children's Press
Uranus	O	I	Vogt, Gregory L.	Capstone Press
Usborne Book of Inventors, The	W	I	Reid, Struan and Fara, Patricia	Scholastic
Using Nature's Gifts	K	I	People, Spaces & Places	Rand McNally
Using the Library	L	I	Wonder World	Wright Group/McGraw Hill
Vagabond Crabs	J	I	Literacy 2000	Rigby
Vehicles for Fun and Sports	K	I	PM Plus	Rigby
Vehicles in the Air	K	I	PM Plus	Rigby
Venus	N	I	A True Book	Children's Press
Venus	Q	I	Vogt, Gregory L.	The Millbrook Press
Very Special Kwanzaa, A	O	I	Chocolate, Debbi	Scholastic
Veterinarians	L	I	Ready, Dee	Capstone Press
Vicky the High Jumper	K	I	Literacy 2000	Rigby
Vietnam	O	I	Dahl, Michael	Capstone Press
Vietnam Women's Memorial, The	W	I	Cornerstones of Freedom	Children's Press
Vikings, The	S	I	Journey Into Civilization	Chelsea House
Volcanoes	N	I	A True Book	Children's Press
Volcanoes	Q	I	Weldon Owen	Wright Group/McGraw Hill
Volcanoes	Q	I	Worldwise	Grolier
Volcanoes and Earthquakes	T	I	Lauber, Patricia	Language for Learning Assoc.
Wacky Wheels	N	I	Pacific Literacy	Pacific Learning
Walking	M	I	Literacy 2000	Rigby
Walking For Freedom: The Montgomery Bus Boycott	R	I	Kelso, Richard	Steck-Vaughn
War Dog Heroes: True Stories of Dog Courage in Wartime	S	I	Sanderson, Jeannette	Scholastic
War of 1812, The	S	I	A First Book	Franklin Watts
Warthogs	O	I	Holmes, Kevin J.	Capstone Press
Watching Every Drop	M	I	Home Connection Collection	Rigby
Water	J	I	Momentum Literacy Program	Troll
Water	N	I	Simply Science	Compass Point Books
Water for the World	M	I	Home Connection Collection	Rigby
Water Goes Up! Water Goes Down!	K	I	Early Connections	Benchmark Education
Waterhole	K	I	Planet Earth	Rigby
Waves: The Changing Surface of the Sea	J	I	Wonder World	Wright Group/McGraw Hill
Wax Museum	L	I	Cook, Donald	Grosset & Dunlap
We Are All Alike	M	I	Schaefer, Lola M.	Benchmark Education
We Remember the Holocaust	Y	I	Adler, David A.	Henry Holt
We Shall Not Be Moved	Z	I	Dash, Joan	Scholastic
We Use Numbers	J	I	Early Connections	Benchmark Education
We Want Jobs!: A Story of the Great Depression	R	I	Norrell, Robert J.	Steck-Vaughn
Weather	N	I	Literacy 2000	Rigby
Weather	N	I	Simply Science	Compass Point Books
Weather Watch	N	I	Wonders!	Hampton-Brown
Weather Watching	Q	I	Weldon Owen	Wright Group/McGraw Hill
Weather Words and What They Mean	R	I	Gibbons, Gail	Scholastic
Weight Lifting	Q	I	Lund, Bill	Capstone Press
Weird Walkers	R	I	Fredericks, Anthony D.	NorthWord Press
West Virginia: Facts and Symbols	O	I	Feeney, Kathy	Capstone Press
Wetlands	Q	I	First Reports	Compass Point Books
Whale Is Not A Fish, A: And Other Animal Mix-ups	P	I	Berger, Melvin	Scholastic
Whale Tales	N	I	Westerskov, Kim	Pacific Learning

Title	Level	Genre	Author/Series	Publisher/Distributor
Whale, The	O	I	Crewe, Sabrina	Steck-Vaughn
Whales	N	I	Book Shop	Mondo
Whales	O	I	Holmes, Kevin J.	Capstone Press
Whales	N	I	PM Animal Facts: Silver	Rigby
Whales	M	I	Wonder World	Wright Group/McGraw Hill
Whales' Song, The	N	I	Sheldon, Dyan	The Penguin Group
Whales-The Gentle Giants	L	I	Milton, Joyce	Random House
What Am I Made Of?	N	I	Bennett, David	Scholastic
What Are My Chances?	J	I	Early Connections	Benchmark Education
What Can It Be?	N	I	Schaefer, Lola M.	Benchmark Education
What Can You Do with an Elephant House?	R	I	Gaynor, Miriam and Goodwin, A.	Pacific Learning
What Changes Our Earth?	K	I	People, Places & Spaces	Rand McNally
What Do You Think?	O	I	Wildcats	Wright Group/McGraw Hill
What Happens When You Recycle?	K	I	Discovery World	Rigby
What in the World is the World Wide Web?	S	I	Quinn, Pat	Pacific Learning
What Is a Fly?	M	I	Sunshine	Wright Group/McGraw Hill
What Is a Park?	J	I	People, Places & Spaces	Rand McNally
What is a Reptile?	M	I	Now I Know	Troll
What Is Matter?	L	I	Schaefer, Lola M.	Benchmark Education
What Makes a Bird a Bird?	O	I	Garelick, May	Mondo
What Were Castles For?	R	I	Usborne Starting Point History	EDC Publishing
What's Cooking?	Q	I	Cartwright, Pauline	Pacific Learning
What's Inside?	K	I	Wonder World	Wright Group/McGraw Hill
What's It Like to Be a Fish?	L	I	Little Readers	Houghton Mifflin
What's Living at Your Place?	Q	I	Chapman, Bruce	Pacific Learning
What's Missing?	K	I	Book Bank	Wright Group/McGraw Hill
What's Underneath?	K	I	Discovery World	Rigby
When Plague Strikes	X	I	Giblin, James Cross	Harper Collins
Where Do You Live?	N	I	People, Places & Spaces	Rand McNally
Where Does the Wind Go?	M	I	Book Shop	Mondo
Where Jeans Come From	K	I	Ready Readers	Pearson Learning
White Elephants and Yellow Jackets	O	I	Webb, Derek	Rigby
White House, The	V	I	Cornerstones of Freedom	Children's Press
White-Tailed Deer, The	R	I	Zwaschka, Michael	Capstone Press
Who Looks After Me?	M	I	Literacy 2000	Rigby
Who Makes the Rules?	M	I	Schafer, Lola M.	Benchmark Education
Who Shot the President?: The Death of John F. Kennedy	P	I	Donnelly, Judy	Random House
Who Were the First People?	R	I	Usborne Starting Point History	EDC Publishing
Who Were the Romans?	R	I	Usborne Starting Point History	EDC Publishing
Who Were the Vikings?	R	I	Usborne Starting Point History	EDC Publishing
Who's That Stepping on Plymouth Rock?	R	I	Fritz, Jean	Putnam & Grosset
Whoops! It Works!	O	I	Lopez, Orlando	Pearson Learning
Why People Move	K	I	People, Places & Spaces	Rand McNally
Why the Kangaroo Hops	K	I	Sunshine	Wright Group/McGraw Hill
Why the Leopard Has Spots	L	I	Pair-It Books	Steck-Vaughn
Why the Ocean Is Salty	Q	I	Leonhardt, Alice	Steck-Vaughn
Wild and Wooly Mammoths	P	I	Aliki	HarperCollins
Wild Babies	O	I	Simon, Seymour	Harper Collins
Wild Cats	Q	I	Leonhardt, Alice	Steck-Vaughn
Wild Horses	R	I	Wilde, Buck	Rigby
Wild, Wild Wolves	M	I	Milton, Joyce	Random House
Wildfires	N	I	A True Book	Children's Press
Williamsburg	V	I	Cornerstones of Freedom	Children's Press
Wind and Storms	K	I	Sunshine	Wright Group/McGraw Hill
Wind Power	J	I	Pacific Literacy	Pacific Learning
Winter Survival	O	I	Wilde, Buck	Rigby
Winter Woollies	K	I	Storyteller Nonfiction	Wright Group/McGraw Hill
Witch Hunt: It Happened in Salem Village	Q	I	Krensky, Stephen	Random House
Witchcraft of Salem Village, The	U	I	Jackson, Shirley	Random House
Wolf, The	S	I	Dahl, Michael	Capstone Press

Title	Level	Genre	Author/Series	Publisher/Distributor
Wolves	Q	I	Literacy 2000	Rigby
Wolves	N	I	PM Animal Facts: Silver	Rigby
Women's Voting Rights	V	I	Cornerstones of Freedom	Children's Press
Wonderful Eyes	M	I	Science	Wright Group/McGraw Hill
Woods, Irons, and Greens	R	I	Wildcats	Wright Group/McGraw Hill
Words	M	I	Pacific Literacy	Pacific Learning
Working on Water	L	I	Home Connection Collection	Rigby
World of Dogs, The	Q	I	Pair-It-Books	Steck-Vaughn
World of Imagination, A	R	I	Literacy 2000	Rigby
Worms	P	I	Mini Pets	Steck-Vaughn
Wreck Trek	S	I	Belcher, Angie	Pacific Learning
Writer's Work, A	N	I	Wonder World	Wright Group/McGraw Hill
Wyoming: Facts and Symbols	O	I	Dubois, Muriel L.	Capstone Press
Yo-Yo's	O	I	PM Nonfiction -Emerald	Rigby
You Be The Jury	Q	I	Miller, Marvin	Scholastic
You Be The Jury: Courtroom V	Q	I	Miller, Marvin	Bantam Doubleday Dell
You Can Canoe!: A Book of Sporting Activities	O	I	Yurkovic, Diana Short	Rigby
You Can Cook	M	I	Woo, Lornette	Steck-Vaughn
Young Geographers	O	I	People, Spaces & Places	Rand McNally
Your Teeth	J	I	Pebble Books	Grolier, Capstone
Zebras	O	I	Holmes, Kevin J.	Capstone Press
Zebras	N	I	Meadows, Graham & Vial, Claire	Dominie Press
Zeros and Ones	S	I	Wildcats	Wright Group/McGraw Hill
Zoo Keepers	M	I	Deedrick, Tami	Capstone Press
18th Emergency, The	R	RF	Byars, Betsy	Bantam Doubleday Dell
89th Kitten, The	O	RF	Nilsson, Eleanor	Scholastic
Abby	M	RF	Hanel, Wolfram	North-South Books
About The B'nai Bagels	T	RF	Konigsburg, E. L.	Dell
Abracadabra	L	RF	Reading Unlimited	Celebration Press
Absent Author, The	N	RF	Roy, Ron	Random House
Absolutely Normal Chaos	V	RF	Creech, Sharon	HarperTrophy
Absolutely True Story, The: How I Visited Yellowstone Park With the Terrible Rupes	R	RF	Roberts, Willo Davis	Aladdin
Accidental Angel (Secret Sisters)	P	RF	Byrd, Sandra	WaterBrook Press
Adam Joshua Capers: Halloween Monster	N	RF	Smith, Janice Lee	HarperTrophy
Adam Joshua Capers: Kid Next Door, The	N	RF	Smith, Janice Lee	HarperTrophy
Adam Joshua Capers: Monster in the Third	N	RF	Smith, Janice Lee	HarperTrophy
Adam Joshua Capers: Nelson in Love	N	RF	Smith, Janice Lee	HarperTrophy
Adam Joshua Capers: Show-and-Tell War, The	N	RF	Smith, Janice Lee	HarperTrophy
Adam Joshua Capers: Superkid!	N	RF	Smith, Janice Lee	HarperTrophy
Adam Joshua Capers: Turkey Trouble	N	RF	Smith, Janice Lee	HarperTrophy
Addie's Bad Day	J	RF	Robins, Joan	HarperTrophy
Addie's Dakota Winter	T	RF	Lawlor, Laurie	Pocket Books
Adios, Anna	N	RF	Giff, Patricia Reilly	Bantam Doubleday Dell
Adventure of the Buried Treasure, The	L	RF	McArthur, Nancy	Scholastic
Adventures of Ali Baba Bernstein, The	O	RF	Hurwitz, Johanna	Scholastic
Adventures of Granny Gatman, The	L	RF	Meadows, Graham	Dominie Press
After the Goat Man	R	RF	Byars, Betsy	Puffin
After the Rain	Z	RF	Mazer, Norma Fox	Avon Books
Against the Rules	R	RF	Costello, Emily	Dell
Ah Liang's Gift	J	RF	Sunshine	Wright Group/McGraw Hill
Ah-choo!	J	RF	Samuels, Aurora	Sadlier-Oxford
Aldo Ice Cream	O	RF	Hurwitz, Johanna	The Penguin Group
Aldo Peanut Butter	O	RF	Hurwitz, Johanna	The Penguin Group
Alfred the Curious	O	RF	PM Emerald	Rigby
Ali Baba Bernstein, Lost and Found	O	RF	Hurwitz, Johanna	Avon
Alice in Rapture: Sort of	U	RF	Naylor, Phyllis Reynolds	Aladdin
Alice the Brave	U	RF	Naylor, Phyllis Reynolds	Aladdin
Alida's Song	Y	RF	Paulsen, Gary	Random House
Alison Wendlebury	J	RF	Literacy 2000	Rigby

Title	Level	Genre	Author/Series	Publisher/Distributor
Alison's Puppy	K	RF	Bauer, Marion Dane	Hyperion
Alison's Wings	K	RF	Bauer, Marion Dane	Hyperion
All About Me!	J	RF	Pacific Literacy	Pacific Learning
All About Sam	P	RF	Lowry, Lois	Bantam Doubleday Dell
All About Stacy	L	RF	Giff, Patricia Reilly	Bantam Doubleday Dell
All Alone in the Universe	S	RF	Perkins, Lynne Rae	Greenwillow Books
All But Alice	U	RF	Naylor, Phyllis Reynolds	Dell
All For the Better: A Story of El Barrio	R	RF	Mohr, Nicholasa	Steck Vaughn
All-of-a-Kind Family	Q	RF	Taylor, Sydney	Bantam Doubleday Dell
All-Star Fever	M	RF	Christopher, Matt	Little, Brown & Co.
Allie's Basketball Dream	J	RF	Barber, B. & Ligasan, D.	Scholastic
Alligator Alley	M	RF	Schultz, Irene	Wright Group/McGraw Hill
Almost Starring Skinnybones	O	RF	Park, Barbara	Random House
Alroy's Very Nearly Clean Bedroom	N	RF	SupaDoopers	Sundance
Altogether, One at a Time	S	RF	Konigsburg, E.L.	Simon & Schuster
Always My Dad	N	RF	Wyeth, Sharon Dennis	Alfred A. Knopf
Amalia and the Grasshopper	K	RF	Tello, J. & Krupinski, L.	Scholastic
Amazing Maze, The	J	RF	Foundations	Wright Group/McGraw Hill
Amber Brown Goes Fourth	N	RF	Danziger, Paula	Scholastic
Amber Brown is Feeling Blue	N	RF	Danziger, Paula	Scholastic
Amber Brown is Not a Crayon	N	RF	Danziger, Paula	Scholastic
Amber Brown Sees Red	N	RF	Danziger, Paula	Scholastic
Amber Brown Wants Extra Credit	N	RF	Danziger, Paula	Scholastic
Amber Cat, The	P	RF	McKay, Hilary	Simon & Schuster
America Street: A Multicultural Anthology of Stories	R	RF	Mazer, Anne	Persea Books
America's Most Wanted Fifth-Graders	R	RF	Lawrence, Jan and Raskin, Linda	Scholastic
American Dragons: Twenty-Five Asian American Voices	Z	RF	Yep, Laurence	HarperTrophy
American Eyes: New Asian-American Short Stories for Young Adults	Z	RF	Carlson, Lori M.	Ballantine Books
Among the Volcanoes	Y	RF	Castaneda, Omar S.	Bantam Doubleday Dell
Amos Binder, Secret Agent	R	RF	Paulsen, Gary	Bantam Doubleday Dell
An Early Winter	T	RF	Bauer, Marion Dane	Houghton Mifflin
An Island Like You: Stories of the Barrio	Z	RF	Cofer, Judith Ortiz	The Penguin Group
Anastasia, Absolutely	Q	RF	Lowry, Lois	Bantam Doubleday Dell
Anastasia Again!	Q	RF	Lowry, Lois	Bantam Doubleday Dell
Anastasia, Ask Your Analyst	Q	RF	Lowry, Lois	Bantam Doubleday Dell
Anastasia At This Address	Q	RF	Lowry, Lois	Bantam Doubleday Dell
Anastasia At Your Service	Q	RF	Lowry, Lois	Bantam Doubleday Dell
Anastasia Has the Answers	Q	RF	Lowry, Lois	Bantam Doubleday Dell
Anastasia Krupnik	Q	RF	Lowry, Lois	Bantam Doubleday Dell
Anastasia On Her Own	Q	RF	Lowry, Lois	Bantam Doubleday Dell
Anastasia's Chosen Career	Q	RF	Lowry, Lois	Bantam Doubleday Dell
And Grandpa Sat on Friday	K	RF	Marshall, Val & Tester, Bronwyn	SRA/McGraw-Hill
And I Mean it Stanley	J	RF	Bonsall, Crosby	HarperCollins
And One For All	V	RF	Nelson, Theresa	Dell
And Still the Turtle Watched	Q	RF	MacGill-Callahan, Sheila	The Penguin Group
Andy and Tamika	N	RF	Adler, David A.	Harcourt Brace
Angel for Solomon Singer, An	O	RF	Rylant, Cynthia	Orchard Books
Angel Park Hoopstars: Nothing But Net	O	RF	Hughes, Dean	Alfred A. Knopf
Angel Park Hoopstars: Point Guard	O	RF	Hughes, Dean	Alfred A. Knopf
Angel Park Soccer Stars: Backup Goalie	O	RF	Hughes, Dean	Random House
Angel Park Soccer Stars: Defense!	O	RF	Hughes, Dean	Alfred A. Knopf
Angel Park Soccer Stars: Psyched!	O	RF	Hughes, Dean	Random House
Angel Park Soccer Stars: Total Soccer	O	RF	Hughes, Dean	Alfred A. Knopf
Angel Park Soccer Stars: Victory Goal	O	RF	Hughes, Dean	Alfred A. Knopf
Angel's Mother's Boyfriend	O	RF	Delton, Judy	Houghton Mifflin
Angels and Other Strangers	T	RF	Paterson, Katherine	HarperTrophy
Angry Bull and Other Cases, The	O	RF	Simon, Seymour	Avon
Animal, the Vegetable, and John D Jones, The	R	RF	Byars, Betsy	Bantam Doubleday Dell

Title	Level	Genre	Author/Series	Publisher/Distributor
Anna, Grandpa, and the Big Storm	N	RF	Stevens, Carla	The Penguin Group
Annabel the Actress Starring in Gorilla My Dreams	L	RF	Conford, Ellen	Simon & Schuster
Anne of Green Gables	V	RF	Montgomery, L. M.	Scholastic
Annie Bananie Moves To Barry Avenue	L	RF	Komaiko, Leah	Bantam Doubleday Dell
Annie John	Z	RF	Kincaid, Jamaica	Farrar, Straus and Giroux
Annie's Pet	J	RF	Bank Street	Bantam Doubleday Dell
Another Day, Another Challenge	L	RF	Literacy 2000	Rigby
Another Point of View	P	RF	Wildcats	Wright Group/McGraw Hill
Ant City	J	RF	PM Turquoise	Rigby
Appointment with Action	P	RF	Wildcats	Wright Group/McGraw Hill
Are You There God? It's Me, Margaret.	T	RF	Blume, Judy	Bantam Doubleday Dell
Around-the-World Lunch, The	K	RF	Canetti, Yanitzia	Steck-Vaughn
Art Riddle Contest, The	Q	RF	Medearis, Angela Shelf	Steck-Vaughn
Arthur, For the Very First Time	R	RF	MacLachlan, Patricia	Bantam Doubleday Dell
Ask Einstein!	N	RF	Trussell-Cullen, Alan	Pacific Learning
Attaboy, Sam	P	RF	Lowry, Lois	Bantam Doubleday Dell
Aunt Flossie's Hats (and Crab Cakes Later)	M	RF	Howard, Elizabeth	Scholastic
Avion My Uncle Flew, The	Y	RF	Fisher, Cyrus	The Penguin Group
Awfully Short for the Fourth Grade	Q	RF	Woodruff, Elvira	Bantam Doubleday Dell
B-E-S-T Friends	L	RF	Giff, Patricia Reilly	Bantam Doubleday Dell
Baby	T	RF	MacLachlan, Patricia	Language for Learning Assoc.
Baby Grand, the Moon in July, and Me, The	P	RF	Barnes, Joyce Annette	The Penguin Group
Baby Island	P	RF	Brink, Carol R.	Simon & Schuster
Baby-Sitter Burglaries, The	S	RF	Keene, Carolyn	Pocket Books
Baby-Sitters Club: Abby and the Best Kid Ever	O	RF	Martin, Ann M.	Scholastic
Baby-Sitters Club: Abby the Bad Sport	O	RF	Martin, Ann M.	Scholastic
Baby-Sitters Club: Claudia and the Bad Joke	O	RF	Martin, Ann M.	Scholastic
Baby-Sitters Club: Claudia and the Little Liar	O	RF	Martin, Ann M.	Scholastic
Baby-Sitters Club: Claudia and the New Girl	O	RF	Martin, Ann M.	Scholastic
Baby-Sitters Club: Claudia and the Phantom Phone Calls	O	RF	Martin, Ann M.	Scholastic
Baby-Sitters Club: Dawn and Too Many Sitters	O	RF	Martin, Ann M.	Scholastic
Baby-Sitters Club: Dawn's Big Move	O	RF	Martin, Ann M.	Scholastic
Baby-Sitters Club: Dawn's Wicked Stepsister	O	RF	Martin, Ann M.	Scholastic
Baby-Sitters Club: Get Well Soon, Mallory	O	RF	Martin, Ann M.	Scholastic
Baby-Sitters Club: Ghost at Dawn's House, The	O	RF	Martin, Ann M.	Scholastic
Baby-Sitters Club: Good-bye Stacey, Good-bye	O	RF	Martin, Ann M.	Scholastic
Baby-Sitters Club: Hello, Mallory	O	RF	Martin, Ann M.	Scholastic
Baby-Sitters Club: Jessi and the Bad Baby-Sitter	O	RF	Martin, Ann M.	Scholastic
Baby-Sitters Club: Jessi and the Superbrat	O	RF	Martin, Ann M.	Scholastic
Baby-Sitters Club: Jessi Ramsey, Pet-sitter	O	RF	Martin, Ann M.	Scholastic
Baby-Sitters Club: Kristy and the Snobs	O	RF	Martin, Ann M.	Scholastic
Baby-Sitters Club: Kristy's Big Day	O	RF	Martin, Ann M.	Scholastic
Baby-Sitters Club: Kristy's Great Idea	O	RF	Martin, Ann M.	Scholastic
Baby-Sitters Club: Mary Anne and Camp BSC	O	RF	Martin, Ann M.	Scholastic
Baby-Sitters Club: Mary Anne Saves the Day	O	RF	Martin, Ann M.	Scholastic
Baby-Sitters Club Mystery: Beware, Dawn!	O	RF	Martin, Ann M.	Scholastic
Baby-Sitters Club Mystery: Claudia, Clue in the Photograph	O	RF	Martin, Ann M.	Scholastic
Baby-Sitters Club Mystery: Claudia, Mystery at the Museum	O	RF	Martin, Ann M.	Scholastic
Baby-Sitters Club Mystery: Claudia, Recipe for Danger	O	RF	Martin, Ann M.	Scholastic
Baby-Sitters Club Mystery: Dawn, Disappearing Dogs	O	RF	Martin, Ann M.	Scholastic
Baby-Sitters Club Mystery: Dawn, Halloween Mystery	O	RF	Martin, Ann M.	Scholastic
Baby-Sitters Club Mystery: Dawn, Surfer Ghost	O	RF	Martin, Ann M.	Scholastic
Baby-Sitters Club Mystery: Jessi, Jewel Thieves	O	RF	Martin, Ann M.	Scholastic
Baby-Sitters Club Mystery: Kristy, Haunted Mansion	O	RF	Martin, Ann M.	Scholastic
Baby-Sitters Club Mystery: Kristy, Missing Child	O	RF	Martin, Ann M.	Scholastic
Baby-Sitters Club Mystery: Kristy, Missing Fortune	O	RF	Martin, Ann M.	Scholastic
Baby-Sitters Club Mystery: Kristy, Vampires	O	RF	Martin, Ann M.	Scholastic

Title	Level	Genre	Author/Series	Publisher/Distributor
Baby-Sitters Club Mystery: Mallory, Ghost Cat	O	RF	Martin, Ann M.	Scholastic
Baby-Sitters Club Mystery: Mary Anne, Library Mystery	O	RF	Martin, Ann M.	Scholastic
Baby-Sitters Club Mystery: Mary Anne, Secret in the Attic	O	RF	Martin, Ann M.	Scholastic
Baby-Sitters Club Mystery: Mary Anne, Zoo Mystery	O	RF	Martin, Ann M.	Scholastic
Baby-Sitters Club Mystery: Mystery at Claudia's House	O	RF	Martin, Ann M.	Scholastic
Baby-Sitters Club Mystery: Stacey and the Mystery Money	O	RF	Martin, Ann M.	Scholastic
Baby-Sitters Club Mystery: Stacey, Haunted Masquerade	O	RF	Martin, Ann M.	Scholastic
Baby-Sitters Club Mystery: Stacey, Missing Ring	O	RF	Martin, Ann M.	Scholastic
Baby-Sitters Club Mystery: Stacey, Mystery at the Empty House	O	RF	Martin, Ann M.	Scholastic
Baby-Sitters Club Mystery: Stacy, Mystery at the Mall	O	RF	Martin, Ann M.	Scholastic
Baby-Sitters Club Special Edition, The: Readers Request	O	RF	Martin, Ann M.	Scholastic
Baby-Sitters Club: Welcome to the BSC, Abby	O	RF	Martin, Ann M.	Scholastic
Baby-Sitters Little Sister	O	RF	Martin, Ann M.	Scholastic
Baby-Sitters Little Sister: Karen's Big Sister	O	RF	Martin, Ann M.	Scholastic
Baby-Sitters Little Sister: Karen's Dinosaur	O	RF	Martin, Ann M.	Scholastic
Baby-Sitters Little Sister: Karen's Monsters	O	RF	Martin, Ann M.	Scholastic
Baby-Sitters Little Sister: Karen's Mystery Super Special	O	RF	Martin, Ann M.	Scholastic
Baby-Sitters Little Sister (Karen's Stepmother)	O	RF	Martin, Ann M.	Scholastic
Baby-Snatcher	Z	RF	Terris, Susan	Scholastic
Back Home	O	RF	Pinkney, Gloria Jean	The Penguin Group
Back to the Dentist	M	RF	City Kids	Rigby
Back Yard Angel	O	RF	Delton, Judy	Houghton Mifflin
Bad, Badder, Baddest	U	RF	Voigt, Cynthia	Scholastic
Bad Dad List, The	M	RF	Kenna, Anna	Pacific Learning
Bad Day for Ballet	N	RF	Keene, Carolyn	Pocket Books
Bad Day for Benjamin, A	L	RF	Reading Unlimited	Celebration Press
Bad Girls	U	RF	Voigt, Cynthia	Scholastic
Badger in the Basement	Q	RF	Daniels, Lucy	Barron's Educational
Bald Bandit, The	N	RF	Roy, Ron	Random House
Balto and the Great Race	P	RF	Kimmel, Elizabeth Cody	Random House
Barney	P	RF	Literacy 2000	Rigby
Barney's Lovely Lunch	K	RF	Windmill Books	Rigby
Baseball Ballerina	J	RF	Cristaldi, Kathryn	Random House
Baseball Birthday Party, The	J	RF	Prager, Annabelle	Random House
Baseball Fever	O	RF	Hurwitz, Johanna	William Morrow
Baseball Flyhawk	M	RF	Christopher, Matt	Little, Brown & Co.
Baseball Heroes, The	M	RF	Schultz, Irene	Wright Group/McGraw Hill
Baseball in April and Other Stories	U	RF	Soto, Gary	Harcourt Brace
Baseball Pals	M	RF	Christopher, Matt	Little, Brown & Co.
Baseball Pitching Challenge and Other Cases, The	O	RF	Simon, Seymour	Avon
Basket Counts, The	M	RF	Christopher, Matt	Little, Brown & Co.
Bat Bones and Spider Stew	K	RF	Poploff, Michelle	Bantam Doubleday Dell
Battle of Words, A	O	RF	Literacy 2000	Rigby
Be A Perfect Person In Just Three Days!	N	RF	Manes, Stephen	Dell
Beanbag	K	RF	Literacy 2000	Rigby
Beans on the Roof	L	RF	Byars, Betsy	Bantam Doubleday Dell
Bear For Miguel, A	K	RF	Alphin, Elaine Marie	HarperTrophy
Bear's Diet	L	RF	PM Gold	Rigby
Bears' House, The	T	RF	Sachs, Marilyn	Puffin Books
Bears On Hemlock Mountain, The	M	RF	Dalgliesh, Alice	Aladdin Paperback
Bearstone	V	RF	Hobbs, Will	Hearst
Beast and the Halloween Horror	M	RF	Giff, Patricia Reilly	Bantam Doubleday Dell

Title	Level	Genre	Author/Series	Publisher/Distributor
Beast in Ms. Rooney's Room, The	M	RF	Giff, Patricia Reilly	Bantam Doubleday Dell
Beating the Drought	M	RF	Noonan, Diana	Pacific Learning
Beauregard the Cat	M	RF	Book Shop	Mondo
Beauty	V	RF	Wallace, Bill	Holiday House
Bedtime at Aunt Carmen's	K	RF	Ready Readers	Pearson Learning
Bedtime Story, A	K	RF	Book Shop	Mondo
Beetles, Lightly Toasted	Q	RF	Naylor, Phyllis Reynolds	Bantam Doubleday Dell
Beezus & Ramona	O	RF	Cleary, Beverly	Avon
Being Danny's Dog	U	RF	Naylor, Phyllis Reynolds	Aladdin
Belle Prater's Boy	V	RF	White, Ruth	Bantam Doubleday Dell
Ben's Tune	N	RF	PM Ruby	Rigby
Best Bad Thing, The	U	RF	Uchida, Yoshiko	Aladdin
Best Birthday Present, The	K	RF	Literacy 2000	Rigby
Best Clown in Town, The	L	RF	Bradley, Tom	Dominie Press
Best Detective, The	N	RF	Keene, Carolyn	Pocket Books
Best Enemies	P	RF	Leverich, Kathleen	Beech Tree Books
Best Enemies Again	P	RF	Leverich, Kathleen	Alfred A. Knopf
Best Enemies Forever	P	RF	Leverich, Kathleen	William Morrow
Best Older Sister, The	L	RF	Choi, Sook Nyul	Bantam Doubleday Dell
Best Part, The	K	RF	PM Story Books -Silver	Rigby
Best School Year Ever, The	P	RF	Robinson, Barbara	HarperTrophy
Best Teacher in the World, The	K	RF	Chardiet, Bernice	Scholastic
Best Wishes for Eddie	M	RF	Nayer, Judy	Pearson Learning
Best Worst Day, The	L	RF	Graves, Bonnie	Hyperion
Best-Loved Doll, The	L	RF	Caudill, Rebecca	Henry Holt & Co.
Betsy and the Boys	P	RF	Haywood, Carolyn	Harcourt Brace
Better Than TV	J	RF	Miller, Sara Swan	Bantam Doubleday Dell
Beware!	N	RF	Cartwright, Pauline	Pacific Learning
Beyond Providence	X	RF	Schnur, Steven	Harcourt Brace
Beyond the Mango Tree	V	RF	Zemser, Amy Bronwen	HarperTrophy
Bicycle Man, The	P	RF	Say, Allen	Houghton Mifflin
Big Balloon Festival, The	L	RF	PM Gold	Rigby
Big Balloon Race, The	K	RF	Coerr, Eleanor	HarperTrophy
Big Fish, The	M	RF	Yukish, Joe	Kaeden Books
Big Green Caterpillar, The	J	RF	Literacy 2000	Rigby
Big Mama and Grandma Ghana	J	RF	Shelf Medearis, A.	Scholastic
Big Race, The	L	RF	Pattrick, Steve	Rigby
Big Wave, The	Q	RF	Buck, Pearl S.	Scholastic
Biggest Klutz in Fifth Grade, The	V	RF	Wallace, Bill	Simon & Schuster
Bill	J	RF	Sunshine	Wright Group/McGraw Hill
Billy Magee's New Car	J	RF	Foundations	Wright Group/McGraw Hill
Bird in the Basket, The	M	RF	Beveridge, Barbara	Pacific Learning
Bird's-Eye View	J	RF	PM Turquoise	Rigby
Birds of a Feather	N	RF	Literacy 2000	Rigby
Birthday	N	RF	Steptoe, John	Henry Holt & Co.
Birthday Bike for Brimhall, A	K	RF	Delton, Judy	Bantam Doubleday Dell
Birthday Disaster	Q	RF	Literacy 2000	Rigby
Birthday Room, The	V	RF	Henkes, Kevin	William Morrow
Birthday Surprises: Ten Great Stories to Unwrap	R	RF	Hurwitz, Johanna	William Morrow
Black Boy	Z	RF	Wright, Richard	HarperPerennial
Black Gold	R	RF	Henry, Marguerite	Aladdin
Black Pearl, The	W	RF	O'Dell, Scott	Bantam Doubleday Dell
Black Stallion, The	T	RF	Farley, Walter	Language for Learning Assoc.
Black Star, Bright Dawn	V	RF	O'Dell, Scott	Ballantine Books
Black Velvet Mystery, The	N	RF	Keene, Carolyn	Pocket Books
Blackberries in the Dark	N	RF	Jukes, Mavis	Alfred A. Knopf
Blackwater Swamp	T	RF	Wallace, Bill	Language for Learning Assoc.
Bless Me, Ultima	Z	RF	Anaya, Rudolfo	Warner Books
Blind Outlaw, The	P	RF	Rounds, Glen	Scholastic
Bloomability	V	RF	Creech, Sharon	Harper Collins

Title	Level	Genre	Author/Series	Publisher/Distributor
Blossom Promise, A	O	RF	Byars, Betsy	Bantam Doubleday Dell
Blossoms and the Green Phantom, The	O	RF	Byars, Betsy	Dell
Blossoms Meet the Vulture Lady, The	O	RF	Byars, Betsy	Bantam Doubleday Dell
Blubber	T	RF	Blume, Judy	Bantam Doubleday Dell
Blue Heron	W	RF	Avi	Avon
Blue Hill Meadows, The	M	RF	Rylant, Cynthia	Harcourt Brace
Blue Ice	T	RF	Salata, Estelle	Fitzhenry and Whiteside
Blue Ribbon Blues	M	RF	Spinelli, Jerry	Random House
Blue Willow	V	RF	Gates, Doris	Puffin Books
Blue-Eyed Daisy, A	W	RF	Rylant, Cynthia	Simon & Schuster
Blueberries for Sal	M	RF	McCloskey, Robert	Scholastic
Bonanza Girl	T	RF	Beatty, Patricia	Scholastic
Bone Dance	X	RF	Brooks, Martha	Random House
Boodil My Dog	Q	RF	Lindenbaum, Pija	Henry Holt & Co.
Born To Trot	R	RF	Henry, Marguerite	Aladdin
Boundless Grace	M	RF	Hoffman, Mary	Scholastic
Boxcar Children: Amusement Park Mystery, The	O	RF	Warner, Gertrude Chandler	Albert Whitman & Co.
Boxcar Children: Animal Shelter Mystery, The	O	RF	Warner, Gertrude Chandler	Albert Whitman & Co.
Boxcar Children: Basketball Mystery, The	O	RF	Warner, Gertrude Chandler	Albert Whitman & Co.
Boxcar Children: Benny Uncovers a Mystery	O	RF	Warner, Gertrude Chandler	Albert Whitman & Co.
Boxcar Children: Bicycle Mystery	O	RF	Warner, Gertrude Chandler	Albert Whitman & Co.
Boxcar Children: Black Pearl Mystery, The	O	RF	Warner, Gertrude Chandler	Albert Whitman & Co.
Boxcar Children: Blue Bay Mystery	O	RF	Warner, Gertrude Chandler	Albert Whitman & Co.
Boxcar Children: Boxcar Children, The	O	RF	Warner, Gertrude Chandler	Albert Whitman & Co.
Boxcar Children: Bus Station Mystery	O	RF	Warner, Gertrude Chandler	Albert Whitman & Co.
Boxcar Children: Caboose Mystery	O	RF	Warner, Gertrude Chandler	Albert Whitman & Co.
Boxcar Children: Camp-Out Mystery, The	O	RF	Warner, Gertrude Chandler	Albert Whitman & Co.
Boxcar Children: Canoe Trip Mystery, The	O	RF	Warner, Gertrude Chandler	Albert Whitman & Co.
Boxcar Children: Castle Mystery, The	O	RF	Warner, Gertrude Chandler	Albert Whitman & Co.
Boxcar Children: Cereal Box Mystery, The	O	RF	Warner, Gertrude Chandler	Albert Whitman & Co.
Boxcar Children: Deserted Library Mystery, The	O	RF	Warner, Gertrude Chandler	Albert Whitman & Co.
Boxcar Children: Dinosaur Mystery, The	O	RF	Warner, Gertrude Chandler	Albert Whitman & Co.
Boxcar Children: Disappearing Friend Mystery, The	O	RF	Warner, Gertrude Chandler	Albert Whitman & Co.
Boxcar Children: Firehouse Mystery, The	O	RF	Warner, Gertrude Chandler	Albert Whitman & Co.
Boxcar Children: Ghost Ship Mystery, The	O	RF	Warner, Gertrude Chandler	Albert Whitman & Co.
Boxcar Children: Haunted Cabin Mystery, The	O	RF	Warner, Gertrude Chandler	Albert Whitman & Co.
Boxcar Children: Lighthouse Mystery, The	O	RF	Warner, Gertrude Chandler	Albert Whitman & Co.
Boxcar Children: Mike's Mystery	O	RF	Warner, Gertrude Chandler	Albert Whitman & Co.
Boxcar Children: Mountain Top Mystery	O	RF	Warner, Gertrude Chandler	Albert Whitman & Co.
Boxcar Children: Mystery at Snowflake Inn, The	O	RF	Warner, Gertrude Chandler	Albert Whitman & Co.
Boxcar Children: Mystery at the Alamo, The	O	RF	Warner, Gertrude Chandler	Albert Whitman & Co.
Boxcar Children: Mystery at the Dog Show, The	O	RF	Warner, Gertrude Chandler	Albert Whitman & Co.
Boxcar Children: Mystery at the Fair	O	RF	Warner, Gertrude Chandler	Albert Whitman & Co.
Boxcar Children: Mystery Behind the Wall	O	RF	Warner, Gertrude Chandler	Albert Whitman & Co.
Boxcar Children: Mystery Bookstore, The	O	RF	Warner, Gertrude Chandler	Albert Whitman & Co.
Boxcar Children: Mystery Cruise, The	O	RF	Warner, Gertrude Chandler	Albert Whitman & Co.
Boxcar Children: Mystery Girl, The	O	RF	Warner, Gertrude Chandler	Albert Whitman & Co.
Boxcar Children: Mystery Horse, The	O	RF	Warner, Gertrude Chandler	Albert Whitman & Co.
Boxcar Children: Mystery in San Francisco, The	O	RF	Warner, Gertrude Chandler	Albert Whitman & Co.
Boxcar Children: Mystery in the Cave, The	O	RF	Warner, Gertrude Chandler	Random House
Boxcar Children: Mystery in the Old Attic, The	O	RF	Warner, Gertrude Chandler	Albert Whitman & Co.
Boxcar Children: Mystery in the Sand	O	RF	Warner, Gertrude Chandler	Albert Whitman & Co.
Boxcar Children: Mystery in Washington, DC, The	O	RF	Warner, Gertrude Chandler	Albert Whitman & Co.
Boxcar Children: Mystery of the Hidden Beach	O	RF	Warner, Gertrude Chandler	Albert Whitman & Co.
Boxcar Children: Mystery of the Lost Mine, The	O	RF	Warner, Gertrude Chandler	Albert Whitman & Co.
Boxcar Children: Mystery of the Lost Village, The	O	RF	Warner, Gertrude Chandler	Albert Whitman & Co.
Boxcar Children: Mystery of the Missing Cat, The	O	RF	Warner, Gertrude Chandler	Albert Whitman & Co.
Boxcar Children: Mystery of the Mixed-Up Zoo, The	O	RF	Warner, Gertrude Chandler	Albert Whitman & Co.
Boxcar Children: Mystery of the Stolen Music, The	O	RF	Warner, Gertrude Chandler	Scholastic
Boxcar Children: Mystery on Stage, The	O	RF	Warner, Gertrude Chandler	Albert Whitman & Co.

Title	Level	Genre	Author/Series	Publisher/Distributor
Boxcar Children: Mystery on the Train, The	O	RF	Warner, Gertrude Chandler	Albert Whitman & Co.
Boxcar Children: Mystery Ranch	O	RF	Warner, Gertrude Chandler	Albert Whitman & Co.
Boxcar Children: Outer Space Mystery, The	O	RF	Warner, Gertrude Chandler	Albert Whitman & Co.
Boxcar Children: Pizza Mystery, The	O	RF	Warner, Gertrude Chandler	Albert Whitman & Co.
Boxcar Children Return, The	O	RF	Warner, Gertrude Chandler	Scholastic
Boxcar Children: Schoolhouse Mystery	O	RF	Warner, Gertrude Chandler	Albert Whitman & Co.
Boxcar Children: Snowbound Mystery	O	RF	Warner, Gertrude Chandler	Albert Whitman & Co.
Boxcar Children: Soccer Mystery, The	O	RF	Warner, Gertrude Chandler	Scholastic
Boxcar Children Special: The Mystery at Snowflake Inn	O	RF	Warner, Gertrude Chandler	Albert Whitman & Co.
Boxcar Children Special: The Mystery at the Ballpark	O	RF	Warner, Gertrude Chandler	Albert Whitman & Co.
Boxcar Children Special: The Mystery at the Fair	O	RF	Warner, Gertrude Chandler	Albert Whitman & Co.
Boxcar Children Special: The Pilgrim Village Mystery	O	RF	Warner, Gertrude Chandler	Albert Whitman & Co.
Boxcar Children: Surprise Island	O	RF	Warner, Gertrude Chandler	Scholastic
Boxcar Children: Woodshed Mystery, The	O	RF	Warner, Gertrude Chandler	Albert Whitman & Co.
Boxcar Children: Yellow House Mystery, The	O	RF	Warner, Gertrude Chandler	Albert Whitman & Co.
Boy in the Doghouse, A	N	RF	Duffey, Betsy	Simon & Schuster
Boy Who Ate Dog Biscuits, The	N	RF	Sachs, Betsy	Random House
Boy Who Lost His Face, The	R	RF	Sachar, Louis	Alfred A. Knopf
Boy Who Owned the School, The	U	RF	Paulsen, Gary	Bantam Doubleday Dell
Boys Against Girls	S	RF	Naylor, Phyllis Reynolds	Bantam Doubleday Dell
Boys Start the War and the Girls Get Even, The	S	RF	Naylor, Phyllis Reynolds	Bantam Doubleday Dell
Boys Will Be	X	RF	Brooks, Bruce	Hyperion
Brad and Butter Play Ball!	N	RF	Hughes, Dean	William Morrow
Brave As	P	RF	Marriott, Janice	Pacific Learning
Brave Maddie Egg	M	RF	Standiford, Natalie	Random House
Breath of the Dragon	P	RF	Giles, Gail	Bantam Doubleday Dell
Brian's Brilliant Career	P	RF	Literacy 2000	Rigby
Brian's Winter	R	RF	Paulsen, Gary	Bantam Doubleday Dell
Bridge to Terabithia	S	RF	Paterson, Katherine	HarperTrophy
Brighty of the Grand Canyon	R	RF	Henry, Marguerite	Aladdin
Brigid Beware	L	RF	Leverich, Kathleen	Random House
Brigid Bewitched	L	RF	Leverich, Kathleen	Random House
Brigid the Bad	L	RF	Leverich, Kathleen	Random House
Broccoli Tapes, The	S	RF	Slepian, Jan	Scholastic
Broken Bridge, The	Z	RF	Pullman, Philip	Alfred A. Knopf
Broken Window and Other Cases, The	O	RF	Simon, Seymour	Avon
Brown Sunshine of Sawdust Valley	O	RF	Henry, Marguerite	Aladdin
Bud, Not Buddy	T	RF	Curtis, Christopher Paul	Random House
Buffalo Gal	U	RF	Wallace, Bill	Simon & Schuster
Bull Harris and the Purple Ooze	M	RF	SupaDoopers	Sundance
Bully of Barkham Street	R	RF	Stolz, Mary	Harper Trophy
Bungee 70528	O	RF	Belcher, Angie	Pacific Learning
Bunnies in the Bathroom	Q	RF	Baglio, Ben M.	Scholastic
Burning Questions of Bingo Brown	T	RF	Byars, Betsy	Language for Learning Assoc.
Busy Guy, A	K	RF	Rookie Readers	Children's Press
Busybody Nora	N	RF	Hurwitz, Johanna	The Penguin Group
Butterfly Farm Burglar, The	M	RF	Schultz, Irene	Wright Group/McGraw Hill
Button Soup	K	RF	Bank Street	Bantam Doubleday Dell
Bye, Bye, Bali Kai	U	RF	Luger, Harriett	Harcourt Brace
Cabin in the Hills, The	J	RF	PM Turquoise	Rigby
Cake, The	M	RF	Read Alongs	Rigby
Calamity Kate	Q	RF	Deary, Terry	HarperTrophy
Call It Courage	X	RF	Sperry, Armstrong	Aladdin
Call Me Ruth	R	RF	Sachs, Marilyn	Beech Tree Books
Call of the Wild	Y	RF	London, Jack	Signet Classics
Cam Jansen and the Chocolate Fudge Mystery	L	RF	Adler, David A.	Puffin Books
Cam Jansen and the Ghostly Mystery	L	RF	Adler, David A.	Puffin Books
Cam Jansen and the Mystery at the Haunted House	L	RF	Adler, David A.	Puffin Books
Cam Jansen and the Mystery at the Monkey House	L	RF	Adler, David A.	Puffin Books
Cam Jansen and the Mystery of Flight 54	L	RF	Adler, David A.	Puffin Books

Title	Level	Genre	Author/Series	Publisher/Distributor
Cam Jansen and the Mystery of the Babe Ruth Baseball	L	RF	Adler, David A.	Puffin Books
Cam Jansen and the Mystery of the Carnival Prize	L	RF	Adler, David A.	Puffin Books
Cam Jansen and the Mystery of the Circus Clown	L	RF	Adler, David A.	Puffin Books
Cam Jansen and the Mystery of the Dinosaur Bones	L	RF	Adler, David A.	Puffin Books
Cam Jansen and the Mystery of the Gold Coins	L	RF	Adler, David A.	Puffin Books
Cam Jansen and the Mystery of the Monkey House	L	RF	Adler, David A.	Puffin Books
Cam Jansen and the Mystery of the Monster Movie	L	RF	Adler, David A.	Puffin Books
Cam Jansen and the Mystery of the Stolen Corn Popper	L	RF	Adler, David A.	Puffin Books
Cam Jansen and the Mystery of the Stolen Diamonds	L	RF	Adler, David A.	Puffin Books
Cam Jansen and the Mystery of the Television Dog	L	RF	Adler, David A.	Puffin Books
Cam Jansen and the Mystery of the U.F.O.	L	RF	Adler, David A.	Puffin Books
Cam Jansen and the Scary Snake Mystery	L	RF	Adler, David A.	Puffin Books
Camp Big Paw	J	RF	Cushman, Doug	HarperTrophy
Camp Knock Knock	K	RF	Duffey, Betsy	Bantam Doubleday Dell
Camp Knock Knock Mystery, The	K	RF	Duffey, Betsy	Bantam Doubleday Dell
Camping with Claudine	K	RF	Literacy 2000	Rigby
Can Do, Jenny Archer	M	RF	Conford, Ellen	Random House
Can I Have a Dinosaur?	L	RF	Literacy 2000	Rigby
Canada Geese Quilt, The	P	RF	Kinsey-Warnock, Natalie	Bantam Doubleday Dell
Canary Caper, The	N	RF	Roy, Ron	Random House
Candlelight Service	O	RF	Literacy 2000	Rigby
Candy Corn Contest, The	L	RF	Giff, Patricia Reilly	Bantam Doubleday Dell
Cannonball Chris	L	RF	Marzollo, J.	Random House
Car Trouble	L	RF	PM Gold	Rigby
Carole: The Inside Story	R	RF	Bryant, Bonnie	Skylark Books
Cartoonist, The	S	RF	Byars, Betsy	Puffin Books
Case for Jenny Archer, A	M	RF	Conford, Ellen	Random House
Case of Capital Intrigue, The	S	RF	Keene, Carolyn	Pocket Books
Case of Hermie the Missing Hamster, The	N	RF	Preller, James	Scholastic
Case of the Captured Queen	S	RF	Keene, Carolyn	Pocket Books
Case of the Cat's Meow, The	K	RF	Bonsall, Crosby	HarperTrophy
Case of the Christmas Snowman, The	N	RF	Preller, James	Scholastic
Case of the Cool-Itch Kid, The	L	RF	Giff, Patricia Reilly	Bantam Doubleday Dell
Case of the Dangerous Solution, The	S	RF	Keene, Carolyn	Pocket Books
Case of the Dirty Bird, The	O	RF	Paulsen, Gary	Bantam Doubleday Dell
Case of the Disappearing Bones	N	RF	SupaDoopers	Sundance
Case of the Double Cross, The	K	RF	Bonsall, Crosby	HarperTrophy
Case of the Dumb Bells, The	K	RF	Bonsall, Crosby	HarperTrophy
Case of the Elevator Duck, The	M	RF	Berends, Polly Berrien	Random House
Case of the Floating Crime, The	S	RF	Keene, Carolyn	Pocket Books
Case of the Hungry Stranger, The	M	RF	Bonsall, Crosby	HarperTrophy
Case of the Invisible Cat, The	Q	RF	Parker, A.E.	Scholastic
Case of the Lion Dance	U	RF	Yep, Laurence	HarperTrophy
Case of the Nervous Newsboy, The	N	RF	Hildick, E.W.	Sundance
Case of the Sabotaged School Play, The	R	RF	Singer, Marilyn	Bantam Doubleday Dell
Case of the Scaredy Cats, The	K	RF	Bonsall, Crosby	HarperTrophy
Case of the Secret Valentine, The	N	RF	Preller, James	Scholastic
Case of the Spooky Sleepover, The	N	RF	Preller, James	Scholastic
Case of the Stolen Baseball Cards, The	N	RF	Preller, James	Scholastic
Case of the Twin Teddy Bears, The	S	RF	Keene, Carolyn	Pocket Books
Casey's Case	Q	RF	Literacy 2000	Rigby
Casey's Code	Q	RF	Riley, Gail Blasser	Steck-Vaughn
Cassie Binegar	T	RF	MacLachlan, Patricia	HarperTrophy
Cat Ate My Gymsuit, The	U	RF	Danziger, Paula	Putnam & Grosset
Cat Called Tim, A	L	RF	New Way: Literature	Steck-Vaughn
Cat Crazy	O	RF	Baglio, Ben M.	Scholastic
Cat Running	U	RF	Snyder, Zilpha Keatley	Bantam Doubleday Dell
Catch That Pass!	M	RF	Christopher, Matt	Little, Brown & Co.
Catcher With a Glass Arm	M	RF	Christopher, Matt	Little, Brown & Co.
Catcher's Mask, The	M	RF	Christopher, Matt	Little, Brown & Co.

Title	Level	Genre	Author/Series	Publisher/Distributor
Cats of the Night	K	RF	Book Bank	Wright Group/McGraw Hill
Caught by the Sea	N	RF	Keating, Rosemary	Pacific Learning
Ceiling of Stars, A	U	RF	Creel, Ann Howard	Pleasant Company
Center Court Sting	M	RF	Christopher, Matt	Little, Brown & Co.
Centerburg Tales: More Adventures of Homer Price	Q	RF	McCloskey, Robert	Puffin Books
Centerfield Ballhawk	M	RF	Christopher, Matt	Little, Brown & Co.
Chair For My Mother, A	M	RF	Williams, Vera B.	Scholastic
Chalk Box Kid, The	N	RF	Bulla, Clyde Robert	Random House
Challenge at Second Base	M	RF	Christopher, Matt	Little, Brown & Co.
Chang's Paper Pony	L	RF	Coerr, Eleanor	HarperTrophy
Change for Zoe, A	K	RF	Home Connection Collection	Rigby
Change The Locks	S	RF	French, Simon	Scholastic
Changing Times	Q	RF	Treasured Horses Collection	Scholastic
Charlie Is a Chicken	P	RF	Smith, Jane Denitz	HarperTrophy
Charlie Needs a Cloak	J	RF	dePaola, Tomie	Prentice-Hall
Chasing Redbird	V	RF	Creech, Sharon	Harper Collins
Cherries and Cherry Pits	M	RF	Williams, Vera B.	Houghton Mifflin
Chick Challenge	O	RF	Baglio, Ben M.	Scholastic
Chicken in the Middle of the Road	J	RF	Book Shop	Mondo
Chicken Sunday	N	RF	Polacco, Patricia	Scholastic
Child of the Owl	W	RF	Yep, Laurence	HarperTrophy
Child of the Wolves	U	RF	Hall, Elizabeth	Bantam Doubleday Dell
Children of Christmas: Stories for the Season	R	RF	Rylant, Cynthia	Orchard Books
Children of the River	X	RF	Crew, Linda	Bantam Doubleday Dell
Chocolate-Chip Muffins	J	RF	Sunshine	Wright Group/McGraw Hill
Chocolate-Covered Contest, The	S	RF	Keene, Carolyn	Pocket Books
Choosing Up Sides	V	RF	Ritter, John H.	Puffin Books
Christmas Spurs, The	R	RF	Wallace, Bill	Bantam Doubleday Dell
Circle of Gold	R	RF	Boyd, Candy Dawson	Bantam Doubleday Dell
Circus Mystery, The	M	RF	Schultz, Irene	Wright Group/McGraw Hill
City Green	M	RF	DiSalvo-Ryan, DyAnne	Scholastic
Clara and the Bookwagon	K	RF	Levinson, Nancy Smiler	HarperTrophy
Class Clown	O	RF	Hurwitz, Johanna	Scholastic
Class Play, The	J	RF	Little Readers	Houghton Mifflin
Class President	O	RF	Hurwitz, Johanna	Scholastic
Claudine's Concert	L	RF	Literacy 2000	Rigby
Clay Marble, The	V	RF	Ho, Minfong	Farrar, Straus and Giroux
Clocks and More Clocks	J	RF	Hutchins, Pat	Scholastic
Close Call, A	M	RF	Kenna, Anna	Pacific Learning
Clubhouse, The	K	RF	PM Gold	Rigby
Clue at the Zoo, The	L	RF	Giff, Patricia Reilly	Bantam Doubleday Dell
Clue in the Castle, The	M	RF	Schultz, Irene	Wright Group/McGraw Hill
Clue in the Glue, The	N	RF	Keene, Carolyn	Pocket Books
Clue Jr.: The Case of the Chocolate Fingerprints	O	RF	Hinter, Parker C.	Scholastic
Clue of the Gold Doubloons, The	S	RF	Keene, Carolyn	Pocket Books
Clues in the Woods	M	RF	Parrish, Peggy	Bantam
Coach Amos	R	RF	Paulsen, Gary	Bantam Doubleday Dell
Cold As Ice	T	RF	Keene, Carolyn	Pocket Books
Cold Shoulder Road	V	RF	Aiken, Joan	Bantam Doubleday Dell
Come Sing, Jimmy Jo	V	RF	Patterson, Katherine	The Penguin Group
Comeback Challenge, The	M	RF	Christopher, Matt	Little, Brown & Co.
Comeback Dog, The	O	RF	Thomas, Jane Resh	Bantam Doubleday Dell
Concert Night	K	RF	Literacy 2000	Rigby
Connie's Dance	M	RF	Windmill Books	Rigby
Contender, The	Z	RF	Lipsythe, Robert	HarperTrophy
Cookcamp, The	S	RF	Paulsen, Gary	Bantam Doubleday Dell
Cooped Up	K	RF	Pacific Literacy	Pacific Learning
Corey's Christmas Wish	M	RF	Pony Tails	Skylark
Costume Party, The	J	RF	City Kids	Rigby

Title	Level	Genre	Author/Series	Publisher/Distributor
Cottle Street	N	RF	Pulford, Elizabeth	Rigby
Could It Be?	J	RF	Bank Street	Bantam Doubleday Dell
Count Your Money with the Polk Street School	M	RF	Giff, Patricia Reilly	Bantam Doubleday Dell
Counterfeit Tackle, The	M	RF	Christopher, Matt	Little, Brown & Co.
Countess Veronica	Q	RF	Robinson, Nancy K.	Scholastic
Cousins	T	RF	Hamilton, Virginia	Language for Learning Assoc.
Cowpokes and Desperadoes	O	RF	Paulsen, Gary	Bantam Doubleday Dell
Cracker Jackson	T	RF	Byars, Betsy	Puffin Books
CrackerJack Halfback	M	RF	Christopher, Matt	Little, Brown & Co.
Crash	U	RF	Spinelli, Jerry	Alfred A. Knopf
Crazy Fish	T	RF	Mazer, Norma Fox	Avon
Creature from Beneath the Ice and Other Cases, The	O	RF	Simon, Seymour	Avon
Creature of Cassidy's Creek, The	N	RF	PM Emerald	Rigby
Crime At the Chat Café	S	RF	Keene, Carolyn	Pocket Books
Crime for Christmas, A	S	RF	Keene, Carolyn	Pocket Books
Crime in the Queen's Court	S	RF	Keene, Carolyn	Pocket Books
Crowded Dock and Other Cases, The	O	RF	Simon, Seymour	Avon
Cry of the Crow, The	S	RF	George, Jean Craighead	HarperTrophy
Crying Rocks and Other Cases, The	O	RF	Simon, Seymour	Avon
Crystal Unicorn, The	N	RF	PM Emerald	Rigby
Cub in the Cupboard	Q	RF	Baglio, Ben M.	Scholastic
Culpepper's Canyon	O	RF	Paulsen, Gary	Bantam Doubleday Dell
Curse of Being Pharaoh, The	P	RF	Marriott, Janice	Pacific Learning
Cybil War, The	S	RF	Byars, Betsy	Scholastic
Dabble Duck	K	RF	Ellis, Anne Leo	HarperTrophy
Dad's Surprise	J	RF	Foundations	Wright Group/McGraw Hill
Daddy Saved the Day	K	RF	Medearis, Angela Shelf	Rigby
Dance with Rosie	N	RF	Giff, Patricia Reilly	The Penguin Group
Dancing Carl	U	RF	Paulsen, Gary	Aladdin
Danger Guys	N	RF	Abbott, Tony	HarperTrophy
Danger Guys Blast Off	N	RF	Abbott, Tony	HarperTrophy
Danger Guys on Ice	N	RF	Abbott, Tony	HarperTrophy
Danger In Quicksand Swamp	W	RF	Wallace, Bill	Simon & Schuster
Danger on Midnight River	O	RF	Paulsen, Gary	Bantam Doubleday Dell
Danger on Panther Peak	R	RF	Wallace, Bill	Pocket Books
Danger on Parade	T	RF	Keene, Carolyn	Pocket Books
Dangerous Comet and Other Cases, The	O	RF	Simon, Seymour	Avon
Daniel's Dog	K	RF	Bogart, Jo Allen	Scholastic
Daniel's Duck	K	RF	Bulla, Clyde Robert	HarperTrophy
Danny, Champion of the World	T	RF	Dahl, Roald	Language for Learning Assoc.
Danny's Big Jump	L	RF	Reeder, Tracey	Wright Group/McGraw Hill
Danny's Desert Rats	X	RF	Naylor, Phyllis Reynolds	Aladdin
Darcy and Gran Don't Like Babies	K	RF	Cutler, Jane	Scholastic
Dark and Full of Secrets	N	RF	Carrick, Carol	Houghton Mifflin
Dark Side of the Creek, The	M	RF	Harlow, Joan Hiatt	Wright Group/McGraw Hill
Dark Stairs	V	RF	Byars, Betsy	Puffin Books
Day at the Races, A	M	RF	Michaels, Eric	Pearson Learning
Day for J.J. and Me, A	M	RF	Evangeline Nicholas Collection	Wright Group/McGraw Hill
Day I Lost My Bus Pass, The	J	RF	City Kids	Rigby
Day in Town, A	K	RF	Story Box	Wright Group/McGraw Hill
Day of Ahmed's Secret, A	M	RF	Heide, F. P. & Gilliland, J. H.	Scholastic
Day with Wilbur Robinson, A	N	RF	Joyce, William	HarperTrophy
Dayton and the Happy Tree	M	RF	Sunshine	Wright Group/McGraw Hill
Dead Letter	S	RF	Byars, Betsy	Puffin Books
Deadbolts and Dinkles	N	RF	Tapp, Kathy Kennedy	Mondo
Deadly Dungeon, The	N	RF	Roy, Ron	Random House
Dear Diary	P	RF	Literacy 2000	Rigby
Dear Future	Q	RF	Literacy 2000	Rigby
Dear Mr. Henshaw	Q	RF	Cleary, Beverly	HarperCollins

Title	Level	Genre	Author/Series	Publisher/Distributor
Death's Door	V	RF	Byars, Betsy	Puffin Books
December Secrets	L	RF	Giff, Patricia Reilly	Bantam Doubleday Dell
DeDe Takes Charge!	O	RF	Hurwitz, Johanna	Morrow
Definitely Cool	X	RF	Wilkinson, Brenda	Scholastic
Deputy Dan and the Bank Robbers	L	RF	Rosenbloom, Joseph	Random House
Deputy Dan Gets His Man	L	RF	Rosembloom, Joseph	Random House
Desert Treasure	M	RF	Pair-It Books	Steck-Vaughn
Destination Disaster	P	RF	Beale, Fleur	Rigby
Detective Stories	Z	RF	Pullman, Philip	Kingfisher
Devil's Bridge	R	RF	DeFelice, Cynthia	Avon
Diamond Champs, The	M	RF	Christopher, Matt	Little, Brown & Co.
Diamond of Doom, The	M	RF	Schultz, Irene	Wright Group/McGraw Hill
Dicey's Song	W	RF	Voigt, Cynthia	Ballantine Books
Did You Carry The Flag Today, Charley?	N	RF	Caudill, Rebecca	Bantam Doubleday Dell
Different Beat, A	U	RF	Boyd, Candy Dawson	The Penguin Group
Different Dragons	O	RF	Little, Jean	The Penguin Group
Difficult Day, The	J	RF	Read Alongs	Rigby
Dinosaur Days	K	RF	Ready Readers	Pearson Learning
Dinosaur Girl	N	RF	Devereux, Susan	Rigby
Dirt Bike Racer	M	RF	Christopher, Matt	Little, Brown & Co.
Dirt Bike Runaway	M	RF	Christopher, Matt	Little, Brown & Co.
Dirty Socks Don't Win Games	R	RF	Marney, Dean	Scholastic
Disappearing Acts	S	RF	Byars, Betsy	Puffin Books
Disappearing Cookies and Other Cases, The	O	RF	Simon, Seymour	Avon
Disappearing Ice Cream and Other Cases, The	O	RF	Simon, Seymour	Avon
Disappearing Snowball and Other Cases, The	O	RF	Simon, Seymour	Avon
Distant Stars and Other Cases, The	O	RF	Simon, Seymour	Avon
Ditching School	J	RF	City Kids	Rigby
Do The Funky Pickle	U	RF	Spinelli, Jerry	Scholastic
Do You Know Me?	Q	RF	Farmer, Nancy	The Penguin Group
Does Third Grade Last Forever?	O	RF	Schanback, Mindy	Troll
Dog Called Kitty, A	R	RF	Wallace, Bill	Pocket Books
Dog I Share, The	N	RF	Marriott, Janice	Pacific Learning
Dog on Barkham Street, A	R	RF	Stolz, Mary	Harper Trophy
Dog Years	R	RF	Warner, Sally	Alfred A. Knopf
Dog's Best Friend, A	M	RF	Pair-It Books	Steck-Vaughn
Doggy Dare	O	RF	Baglio, Ben M.	Scholastic
Dogs Don't Tell Jokes	O	RF	Sachar, Louis	Alfred A. Knopf
Dogsong	V	RF	Paulsen, Gary	Simon & Schuster
Doing the Dishes	L	RF	City Kids	Rigby
Doll's House, The	R	RF	Godden, Rumer	The Penguin Group
Dollhouse Murders, The	S	RF	Wright, Betty Ren	Scholastic
Dolphin Adventure	P	RF	Grover, Wayne	Beech Tree Books
Dolphin on the Wall, The	K	RF	PM Story Books -Silver	Rigby
Dolphin Treasure	P	RF	Grover, Wayne	Beech Tree Books
Dolphins, The	L	RF	PM Gold	Rigby
Dom's Handplant	L	RF	Literacy 2000	Rigby
Don't Be My Valentine: A Classroom Mystery	J	RF	Lexau, Joan M.	HarperTrophy
Don't Call Me Beanhead!	N	RF	Wojciechowski, Susan	Candlewick Press
Don't Eat Too Much Turkey	J	RF	Cohen, Miriam	Bantam Doubleday Dell
Don't Forget the Bacon	M	RF	Hutchins, Pat	Puffin Books
Don't Split the Pole: Tales of Down-Home Folk Wisdom	S	RF	Tate, Eleanora E.	Bantam Doubleday Dell
Don't Worry	J	RF	Literacy 2000	Rigby
Donald's Garden	K	RF	Reading Unlimited	Celebration Press
Donavan's Word Jar	N	RF	DeGross, Monalisa	HarperCollins
Donna O'Neeshuck Was Chased By Some Cows	L	RF	Grossman, Bill	HarperTrophy
Doorbell Rang, The	J	RF	Hutchins, Pat	Greenwillow
Double Play at Short	M	RF	Christopher, Matt	Little, Brown & Co.
Double Switch	M	RF	Noonan, Diana	Pacific Learning

Title	Level	Genre	Author/Series	Publisher/Distributor
Dr. Jekyll, Orthodontist	N	RF	The Zack Files	Grosset & Dunlap
Dr. MacTavish's Creature	N	RF	PM Emerald	Rigby
Dragon in the Ghetto Caper, The	R	RF	Konigsburg, E.L.	Aladdin
Dream Boat	M	RF	Nagelkerke, Bill	Rigby
Dream Catchers	M	RF	Storyteller-Night Crickets	Wright Group/McGraw Hill
Drew and the Homeboy Question	U	RF	Armstrong, Robb	HarperTrophy
Drylongso	V	RF	Hamilton, Virginia	Harcourt Brace
Duckling Diary	O	RF	Baglio, Ben M.	Scholastic
Ducks Crossing	M	RF	Wilson, Trevor	Pacific Learning
Dunc and Amos and the Red Tattoos	R	RF	Paulsen, Gary	Bantam Doubleday Dell
Dunc and Amos Go to the Dogs	R	RF	Paulsen, Gary	Bantam Doubleday Dell
Dunc and Amos Hit the Big Top	R	RF	Paulsen, Gary	Bantam Doubleday Dell
Dunc and Amos Meet the Slasher	R	RF	Paulsen, Gary	Bantam Doubleday Dell
Dunc and the Greased Sticks of Doom	R	RF	Paulsen, Gary	Bantam Doubleday Dell
Dunc and the Haunted Castle	R	RF	Paulsen, Gary	Bantam Doubleday Dell
Dunc and the Scam Artists	R	RF	Paulsen, Gary	Bantam Doubleday Dell
Dunc Breaks the Record	R	RF	Paulsen, Gary	Bantam Doubleday Dell
Dunc Gets Tweaked	R	RF	Paulsen, Gary	Bantam Doubleday Dell
Dunc's Doll	R	RF	Paulsen, Gary	Bantam Doubleday Dell
Dunc's Dump	R	RF	Paulsen, Gary	Bantam Doubleday Dell
Dunc's Halloween	R	RF	Paulsen, Gary	Bantam Doubleday Dell
Dunc's Undercover Christmas	R	RF	Paulsen, Gary	Bantam Doubleday Dell
Dunkin' Dazza's Daring Dribble	O	RF	SupaDoopers	Sundance
Dunkin' Dazza's Soaring Slammer	O	RF	SupaDoopers	Sundance
E is for Elisa	N	RF	Hurwitz, Johanna	Puffin Books
Eagle Song	S	RF	Bruchac, Joseph	Puffin
Earth to Matthew	U	RF	Danziger, Paula	PaperStar
Earthquake in the Third Grade	N	RF	Myers, Laurie	Clarion
Earthquake Terror	X	RF	Kehret, Peg	Puffin Books
Eat!	M	RF	Kroll, Steven	Hyperion
Ed and Me	L	RF	McPhail, David	Harcourt Brace
Eddie and the Fire Engine	P	RF	Haywood, Carolyn	Beech Tree Books
Edward's Night Light	M	RF	Reading Corners	Dominie
Edwin and Emily	K	RF	Williams, Suzanne	Hyperion
Eenie, Meanie, Murphy, NO!	S	RF	McKenna, Colleen O'Shaunessy	Scholastic
Egypt Game, The	U	RF	Snyder, Zilpha Keatley	Bantam Doubleday Dell
Einstein-Champion of the World	N	RF	Trussell-Cullen, Alan	Pacific Learning
EL Bronx Remembered	Z	RF	Mohr, Nicholasa	Harper Trophy
Elaine and the Flying Frog	M	RF	Chang, Heidi	Scholastic
Elbert's Bad Word	M	RF	Wood, Audrey	Harcourt Brace
Electric Spark and Other Cases, The	O	RF	Simon, Seymour	Avon
Electrifying Cows and Other Cases, The	O	RF	Simon, Seymour	Avon
Eleven Kids, One Summer	O	RF	Martin, Ann M.	Scholastic
Elisa in the Middle	N	RF	Hurwitz, Johanna	The Penguin Group
Eliza the Hypnotizer	M	RF	Granger, Michele	Scholastic
Ellen Tebbits	P	RF	Cleary, Beverly	Dell Publishing
Ellie	Z	RF	Borntrager, Mary Christner	Herald Press
Ellie Brader Hates Mr. G.	R	RF	Johnston, Janet	Pocket Books
Emilio and the River	M	RF	Sunshine	Wright Group/McGraw Hill
Emily and Alice	L	RF	Champion, Joyce	Harcourt Brace
Emily Arrow Promises to Do Better This Year	M	RF	Giff, Patricia Reilly	Bantam Doubleday Dell
Emily at School	L	RF	Williams, Suzanne	Hyperion
Emma	L	RF	Kesselman, Wendy	HarperTrophy
Emma, the Birthday Clown	M	RF	Sunshine	Wright Group/McGraw Hill
Empty Envelope, The	N	RF	Roy, Ron	Random House
Encyclopedia Brown Boy Detective	P	RF	Sobol, Donald J.	Bantam Doubleday Dell
Encyclopedia Brown Carries On	P	RF	Sobol, Donald J.	Bantam Doubleday Dell
Encyclopedia Brown: Case of Pablo's Nose	P	RF	Sobol, Donald J.	Scholastic
Encyclopedia Brown: Case of the Dead Eagles	P	RF	Sobol, Donald J.	Bantam Doubleday Dell
Encyclopedia Brown: Case of the Disgusting Sneakers	P	RF	Sobol, Donald J.	Bantam Doubleday Dell

Title	Level	Genre	Author/Series	Publisher/Distributor
Encyclopedia Brown: Case of the Midnight Visitor	P	RF	Sobol, Donald J.	Bantam Doubleday Dell
Encyclopedia Brown: Case of the Mysterious Handprints	P	RF	Sobol, Donald J.	Bantam Doubleday Dell
Encyclopedia Brown: Case of the Secret Pitch	P	RF	Sobol, Donald J.	Bantam Doubleday Dell
Encyclopedia Brown: Case of the Sleeping Dog	P	RF	Sobol, Donald J.	Scholastic
Encyclopedia Brown: Case of the Slippery Salamander	P	RF	Sobol, Donald J.	Scholastic
Encyclopedia Brown: Case of the Treasure Hunt	P	RF	Sobol, Donald J.	Bantam Doubleday Dell
Encyclopedia Brown: Case of the Two Spies	P	RF	Sobol, Donald J.	Bantam Doubleday Dell
Encyclopedia Brown Finds the Clues	P	RF	Sobol, Donald J.	Bantam Doubleday Dell
Encyclopedia Brown Gets His Man	P	RF	Sobol, Donald J.	Bantam Doubleday Dell
Encyclopedia Brown Keeps the Peace	P	RF	Sobol, Donald J.	Bantam Doubleday Dell
Encyclopedia Brown Lends a Hand	P	RF	Sobol, Donald J.	Bantam Doubleday Dell
Encyclopedia Brown Saves the Day	P	RF	Sobol, Donald J.	Bantam Doubleday Dell
Encyclopedia Brown Sets the Pace	P	RF	Sobol, Donald J.	Bantam Doubleday Dell
Encyclopedia Brown Shows the Way	P	RF	Sobol, Donald J.	Bantam Doubleday Dell
Encyclopedia Brown Solves Them All	P	RF	Sobol, Donald J.	Bantam Doubleday Dell
Encyclopedia Brown Takes the Cake	P	RF	Sobol, Donald J.	Bantam Doubleday Dell
Encyclopedia Brown Takes the Case	P	RF	Sobol, Donald J.	Bantam
Encyclopedia Brown Tracks Them Down	P	RF	Sobol, Donald J.	Bantam Doubleday Dell
Encyclopedia Brown's Book of Strange But True Crimes	P	RF	Sobol, Donald J. & Rose Sobol	Scholastic
Every Living Thing	R	RF	Rylant, Cynthia	Aladdin
Everyone Else's Parents Said Yes	U	RF	Danziger, Paula	PaperStar
Everywhere	R	RF	Brooks, Bruce	Scholastic
Expressway Jewels	M	RF	Evangeline Nicholas Collection	Wright Group/McGraw Hill
Eyes of the Amaryllis, The	V	RF	Babbitt, Natalie	Farrar, Straus and Giroux
Fabulous Freckles	K	RF	Literacy 2000	Rigby
Face to Face	W	RF	Bauer, Marion Dane	Bantam Doubleday Dell
Face-Off	O	RF	Christopher, Matt	Little, Brown & Co.
Facing the Flood	Q	RF	Kleinhenz, Sydnie Meltzer	Steck-Vaughn
Facts and Fictions of Minna Pratt, The	U	RF	MacLachlan, Patricia	HarperTrophy
Fair Day	J	RF	City Kids	Rigby
Falcon, The	N	RF	PM Emerald	Rigby
Falcon's Feathers, The	N	RF	Roy, Ron	Random House
Families Are Different	K	RF	Pellegrini, Nina	Scholastic
Family Dinner	Q	RF	Cutler, Jane	Farrar, Straus and Giroux
Family Tree	S	RF	Ayres, Katherine	Bantam Doubleday Dell
Family Under the Bridge, The	R	RF	Savage Carlson, Natalie	Scholastic
Fancy Feet	L	RF	Giff, Patricia Reilly	Bantam Doubleday Dell
Fangs and Me	N	RF	Gilmore, Rachna	Fitzhenry and Whiteside
Fantastic Water Pot and Other Cases, The	O	RF	Simon, Seymour	Avon
Far-Out Frisbee and Other Cases, The	O	RF	Simon, Seymour	Avon
Fast and Funny	J	RF	Story Box	Wright Group/McGraw Hill
Fast Sam, Cool Clyde, and Stuff	Y	RF	Myers, Walter Dean	Puffin Books
Fastest Ketchup in the Cafeteria and Other Cases, The	O	RF	Simon, Seymour	Avon
Father Water, Mother Woods	V	RF	Paulsen, Gary	Bantam Doubleday Dell
Father's Arcane Daughter	V	RF	Konigsburg, E. L.	Aladdin
Fearless Explorer and Other Cases, The	O	RF	Simon, Seymour	Avon
Felicia the Critic	P	RF	Conford, Ellen	Little, Brown & Co.
Felita	P	RF	Mohr, Nicholasa	Dell
Ferret In The Bedroom, Lizards In The Fridge	T	RF	Wallace, Bill	Language for learning Assoc.
Fifth Grade: Here Comes Trouble	S	RF	McKenna, Colleen O'Shaughnessy	Scholastic
Fig Pudding	R	RF	Fletcher, Ralph	Clarion Books
Fig Pudding	S	RF	McKenna, Colleen	Scholastic
Fight in the Schoolyard, The	K	RF	City Kids	Rigby
Fighting Tackle	M	RF	Christopher, Matt	Little, Brown & Co.
Final Freedom, The	V	RF	Wallace, Bill	Pocket Books
Find A Stranger, Say Goodbye	X	RF	Lowry, Lois	Dell
Finding Buck McHenry	S	RF	Slote, Alfred	Scholastic
Fire in the Hills	Y	RF	Myers, Anna	Puffin Books
Fire in the Wind	U	RF	Levin, Betty	Beech Tree
Firelight Secrets	O	RF	PM Ruby	Rigby

Title	Level	Genre	Author/Series	Publisher/Distributor
First Apple	N	RF	Russell, Ching Yueng	The Penguin Group
First Grade Takes a Test	J	RF	Cohen, Miriam	Bantam Doubleday Dell
Fish Face	M	RF	Giff, Patricia Reilly	Bantam Doubleday Dell
Fish for Sale	K	RF	SupaDoopers	Sundance
Fishy, Flashy Fourth, The	M	RF	Schultz, Irene	Wright Group/McGraw Hill
Five Funny Frights	K	RF	Bauer, Judith	Scholastic
Five-Dog Night, The	P	RF	Christelow, Eileen	Clarion Books
Flora, a Friend for the Animals	J	RF	Sunshine	Wright Group/McGraw Hill
Flower Girls # 1: Violet	L	RF	Leverich, Kathleen	HarperTrophy
Flower Girls # 2: Daisy	L	RF	Leverich, Kathleen	HarperTrophy
Flower Girls # 3: Heather	L	RF	Leverich, Kathleen	HarperTrophy
Flower Girls # 4: Rose	L	RF	Leverich, Kathleen	HarperTrophy
Flowers For Algernon	Z	RF	Keyes, Daniel	Harcourt Brace
Flowers for Mrs. Falepau	M	RF	Book Bank	Wright Group/McGraw Hill
Flunking of Joshua T. Bates, The	Q	RF	Shreve, Susan	Alfred A. Knopf
Flying Fingers	K	RF	Literacy 2000	Rigby
Flying Solo	R	RF	Fletcher, Ralph	Bantam Doubleday Dell
Flying-Saucer People and Other Cases, The	O	RF	Simon, Seymour	Avon
Football Friends	L	RF	Marzollo, J., D. & D.	Scholastic
Football Fugitive	M	RF	Christopher, Matt	Little, Brown & Co.
For The Life of Laetitia	Y	RF	Hodge, Merle	Farrar Straus Giroux
For the Love of Pooch	N	RF	Literacy 2000	Rigby
For the Love of Turtles	N	RF	Palacios, Argentina	Rigby
Forever Amber Brown	N	RF	Danziger, Paula	Scholastic
Forever Friends	X	RF	Boyd, Candy Dawson	Puffin Books
Forged By Fire	Z	RF	Draper, Sharon M.	Aladdin
Forgetful Fran	P	RF	Key, Alexander	Scholastic
Forgotten Hiding Place, The	M	RF	Schultz, Irene	Wright Group/McGraw Hill
Fortune Branches Out, A	R	RF	Mahy, Margaret	Bantam Doubleday Dell
Forty-Three Cats	K	RF	Sunshine	Wright Group/McGraw Hill
Foul Play on the Sidelines	R	RF	Costello, Emily	Dell
Four A's, The	Q	RF	Wildcats	Wright Group/McGraw Hill
Fourth Grade Celebrity	Q	RF	Giff, Patricia Reilly	Bantam Doubleday Dell
Fourth Grade Is a Jinx	P	RF	McKenna, Colleen	Scholastic
Fourth Grade Wizards, The	Q	RF	DeClements, Barthe	The Penguin Group
Fox in the Frost	Q	RF	Baglio, Ben M.	Scholastic
Fox Steals Home, The	M	RF	Christopher, Matt	Little, Brown & Co.
Freckle Juice	M	RF	Blume, Judy	Bantam Doubleday Dell
Freddy's Train Ride	K	RF	Pair-It Books	Steck-Vaughn
Frida María: A Story of the Old Southwest	M	RF	Lattimore, Deborah Nourse	Harcourt Brace
Friends, The	Z	RF	Guy, Rosa	Bantam Doubleday Dell
Friends, The	T	RF	Yumoto, Kazumi	Yearling
Friendship Pact, The	Q	RF	Pfeffer, Susan Beth	Scholastic
Frightful's Mountain	U	RF	George, Jean	Puffin Books
Frindle	R	RF	Clements, Andrew	Aladdin
Frogs of Betts, The	N	RF	SupaDoopers	Sundance
From the Mixed-up Files of Mrs. Basil E. Frankweiler	S	RF	Konigsburg, E.L.	Bantam Doubleday Dell
From the Notebooks of Melanin Sun	Z	RF	Woodson, Jacqueline	Scholastic
Frown, The	K	RF	Read Alongs	Rigby
Fudge	O	RF	Graeber, Charlotte Towner	Simon & Schuster
Fudge-a-Mania	Q	RF	Blume, Judy	Bantam Doubleday Dell
Full House Stephanie	Q	RF	Herman, Gail	Pocket Books
Funny Bananas: The Mystery in the Museum	N	RF	McHargue, Georgess	Dell Publishing
Future-Telling Lady and Other Stories, The	S	RF	Berry, James	HarperTrophy
Fuzz and the Glass Eye	M	RF	Pulford, Elizabeth	Rigby
Gadget War, The	N	RF	Duffey, Betsy	The Penguin Group
Gail & Me	L	RF	Literacy 2000	Rigby
Game for Jamie, A	M	RF	Sunshine	Wright Group/McGraw Hill
Garden of Eden Motel, The	W	RF	Hamilton, Morse	William Morrow

Title	Level	Genre	Author/Series	Publisher/Distributor
Gathering of Flowers, A	Z	RF	Thomas, Joyce Carol	HarperTrophy
General Butterfingers	O	RF	Gardiner, John Reynolds	Puffin Books
Genghis Khan: A Dog Star is Born	L	RF	Sharmat, Marjorie Weinman	Random House
Gentlehands	Z	RF	Kerr, M. E.	Harper Trophy
Gerbil Genius	O	RF	Baglio, Ben M.	Scholastic
Gerbilitis	P	RF	Spinner, S. & Weiss, E.	HarperTrophy
Get A Grip, Pip!	P	RF	Literacy 2000	Rigby
Get On Out of Here, Philip Hall	Y	RF	Greene, Bette	Puffin Books
Getting Cold! Getting Hot!	K	RF	Sunshine	Wright Group/McGraw Hill
Getting Lincoln's Goat	V	RF	Goldman, E. M.	Bantam Doubleday Dell
Getting Rid of Katherine	Q	RF	Wright, Betty Ren	Troll
Ghost Pony, The	O	RF	Betancourt, Jeanne	Scholastic
Ghost Town Treasure	M	RF	Bulla, Clyde Robert	The Penguin Group
Gib Rides Home	V	RF	Snyder, Zilpha Keatley	Bantam Doubleday Dell
Gift for Mama, A	N	RF	Hautzig, Esther	The Penguin Group
Gift of the Girl Who Couldn't Hear, The	U	RF	Shreve, Susan	Beech Tree Books
Gift of the Pirate Queen, The	S	RF	Giff, Patricia Reilly	Yearling
Gift to Share, A	K	RF	Pair-It Books	Steck-Vaughn
Gift-Giver, The	S	RF	Hansen, Joyce	Houghton Mifflin
Gigantic Ants and Other Cases, The	O	RF	Simon, Seymour	Avon
Ginger Brown: The Nobody Boy	L	RF	Wyeth, Sharon Dennis	Random House
Ginger Brown: Too Many Houses	L	RF	Wyeth, Sharon Dennis	Random House
Ginger Pye	U	RF	Estes, Eleanor	Scholastic
Girl Called Al, A	P	RF	Greene, Constance C.	Puffin Books
Girl In the Window, The	U	RF	Yeo, Wilma	Scholastic
Girl Named Disaster, A	X	RF	Farmer, Nancy	The Penguin Group
Girl Who Knew it All, The	Q	RF	Giff, Patricia Reilly	Bantam Doubleday Dell
Girls to the Rescue, Book #3	Q	RF	Lansky, Bruce	Meadowbrook Press
Girls to the Rescue, Book #4	Q	RF	Lansky, Bruce	Meadowbrook Press
Girls to the Rescue, Book #6	Q	RF	Lansky, Bruce	Meadowbrook Press
Gladys and Max Love Bob	M	RF	Book Bank	Wright Group/McGraw Hill
Glass Slipper for Rosie, A	N	RF	Giff, Patricia Reilly	The Penguin Group
Glory Girl, The	S	RF	Byars, Betsy	The Penguin Group
Gluepots	K	RF	Book Bank	Wright Group/McGraw Hill
Go and Hush the Baby	K	RF	Byars, Betsy	Viking
Go Annie, Go!	K	RF	Pacific Literacy	Pacific Learning
Go-cart Day	K	RF	City Kids	Rigby
Goat in the Garden	Q	RF	Baglio, Ben M.	Scholastic
Goblins Don't Play Video Games	M	RF	Dadey, D. & Jones, M. T.	Scholastic
Going Home	T	RF	Mohr, Nicholasa	The Penguin Group
Going Swimming	J	RF	City Kids	Rigby
Gold Dust Letters, The	S	RF	Lisle, Janet Taylor	Avon Camelot
Goliath and the Burglar	L	RF	Dicks, Terrance	Barron's Educational Series
Goliath and the Buried Treasure	L	RF	Dicks, Terrance	Barron's Educational Series
Goliath and the Cub Scouts	L	RF	Dicks, Terrance	Barron's Educational Series
Goliath at the Dog Show	L	RF	Dicks, Terrance	Barron's Educational Series
Goliath at the Seaside	L	RF	Dicks, Terrance	Barron's Educational Series
Goliath Goes to Summer School	L	RF	Dicks, Terrance	Barron's Educational Series
Goliath on Vacation	L	RF	Dicks, Terrance	Barron's Educational Series
Goliath's Birthday	L	RF	Dicks, Terrance	Barron's Educational Series
Goliath's Christmas	L	RF	Dicks, Terrance	Barron's Educational Series
Goliath's Easter Parade	L	RF	Dicks, Terrance	Barron's Educational Series
Golly Sisters Go West, The	K	RF	Byars, Betsy	HarperTrophy
Golly Sisters Ride Again, The	K	RF	Byars, Betsy	HarperTrophy
Gone from Home	W	RF	Johnson, Angela	Alfred A. Knopf
Gone-Away Lake	V	RF	Enright, Elizabeth	Harcourt Inc.
Good As New	L	RF	Douglass, Barbara	Scholastic
Good Dog, Bonita	N	RF	Giff, Patricia Reilly	Bantam Doubleday Dell
Good Grief. . . Third Grade	O	RF	McKenna, Colleen	Scholastic
Good Master, The	S	RF	Seredy, Kate	Scholastic

Title	Level	Genre	Author/Series	Publisher/Distributor
Good-Bye My Wishing Star	S	RF	Grove, Vicki	Scholastic
Good-for-Nothing Dog, The	M	RF	Schultz, Irene	Wright Group/McGraw Hill
Goodbye, Chicken Little	Q	RF	Byars, Betsy	HarperTrophy
Goodbye, Vietnam	V	RF	Whelan, Gloria	Alfred A. Knopf
Goody Hall	V	RF	Babbitt, Natalie	Farrar, Straus and Giroux
Goose on the Loose	Q	RF	Baglio, Ben M.	Scholastic
Goose's Gold, The	N	RF	Roy, Ron	Random House
Grab Hands and Run	V	RF	Temple, Frances	HarperTrophy
Grams, Her Boyfriend, My Family, and Me	U	RF	Derby, Pat	Sunburst
Grandad's Mask	K	RF	PM Turquoise	Rigby
Grandma Mix-Up, The	K	RF	McCully, Emily Arnold	HarperTrophy
Grandma's Pictures of The Past	J	RF	Home Connection Collection	Rigby
Grandmas At Bat	K	RF	McCully, Emily Arnold	HarperTrophy
Grandmas at the Lake	K	RF	McCully, Emily Arnold	HarperTrophy
Grandpa at the Beach	K	RF	Lewis, Rob	Mondo
Grandpa Comes To Stay	K	RF	Lewis, Rob	Mondo
Grandpa's Birthday	J	RF	Literacy 2000	Rigby
Grandpa's Face	Q	RF	Greenfield, Eloise	Putnam & Grosset
Grandpa's Mountain	T	RF	Reeder, Carolyn	Avon Camelot
Granny and the Desperadoes	J	RF	Parish, Peggy	Simon & Schuster
Great Brain at the Academy, The	T	RF	Fitzgerald, John D.	Yearling
Great Brain Does It Again, The	T	RF	Fitzgerald, John D.	Yearling
Great Brain Reforms, The	T	RF	Fitzgerald, John D.	Yearling
Great Brain, The	T	RF	Fitzgerald, John D.	Language for Learning Assoc.
Great Dimpole Oak, The	S	RF	Lisle, Janet Taylor	Puffin Books
Great Genghis Khan Look-Alike Contest, The	L	RF	Sharmat, Marjorie Weinman	Random House
Great Gilly Hopkins, The	S	RF	Paterson, Katherine	Hearst
Great Quarterback Switch, The	M	RF	Christopher, Matt	Little, Brown & Co.
Great Riddle Mystery, The	M	RF	MacClean, James R.	Pearson Learning
Great Wheel, The	U	RF	Lawson, Robert	Scholastic
Greatest Binnie in the World, The	M	RF	Sunshine	Wright Group/McGraw Hill
Green Thumbs, Everyone	N	RF	Giff, Patricia Reilly	Bantam Doubleday Dell
Green with Red Spots Horrible	N	RF	SupaDoopers	Sundance
Grizzly Mistake and Other Cases, The	O	RF	Simon, Seymour	Avon
Growin'	R	RF	Grimes, Nikki	Puffin Books
Growing Up Stories	T	RF	Byars, Betsy	Kingfisher
Guinea Pig Gang	O	RF	Baglio, Ben M.	Scholastic
Gus and Grandpa	J	RF	Mills, Claudia	Sunburst
Gypsy Game, The	U	RF	Snyder, Zilpha Keatly	Yearling
Ha-Ha Party, The	J	RF	Sunshine	Wright Group/McGraw Hill
Hailstorm, The	J	RF	PM Turquoise	Rigby
Hair Party, The	J	RF	Literacy 2000	Rigby
Halloween Horror and Other Cases, The	O	RF	Simon, Seymour	Avon
Hamster Hotel	O	RF	Baglio, Ben M.	Scholastic
Hamster in a Handbasket	Q	RF	Baglio, Ben M.	Scholastic
Hang in there, Oscar Martin!	N	RF	Noonan, Diana	Pacific Learning
Hanged Man, The	Z	RF	Block, Francesca Lia	Harper Collins
Hannah	N	RF	Whelan, Gloria	Random House
Happy Birthday, Anna, Sorpresa!	N	RF	Giff, Patricia Reilly	Bantam Doubleday Dell
Happy Valentine's Day, Miss Hildy!	K	RF	Grambling, Lois	Random House
Hard Drive to Short	M	RF	Christopher, Matt	Little, Brown & Co.
Harriet the Spy	T	RF	Fitzhugh, Louise	Harper Collins
Harris and Me	V	RF	Paulsen, Gary	Bantam Doubleday Dell
Harry and Willy and Carrothead	L	RF	Caseley, Judith	Scholastic
Harry Houdini-Wonderdog!	N	RF	Taylor, William	Pacific Learning
Hat Came Back, The	K	RF	Literacy 2000	Rigby
Hatchet	R	RF	Paulsen, Gary	Aladdin
Haunting of Grade Three, The	O	RF	Maccarone, Grace	Scholastic
Have You Seen Hyacinth Macaw?	R	RF	Giff, Patricia Reilly	Dell
Having a Haircut	J	RF	City Kids	Rigby

Title	Level	Genre	Author/Series	Publisher/Distributor
Haymeadow, The	T	RF	Paulsen, Gary	Dell
He Who Listens	K	RF	Literacy 2000	Rigby
Heather at the Barre	Q	RF	Sinykin, Sheri Cooper	Magic Attic
Heather, Belle of the Ball	Q	RF	Sinykin, Sheri Cooper	Magic Attic
Heather Goes to Hollywood	Q	RF	Sinykin, Sheri Cooper	Magic Attic
Heather Takes the Reins	Q	RF	Sinykin, Sheri Cooper	Magic Attic
Heather's Book	K	RF	Ready Readers	Pearson Learning
Heavy Weight and Other Cases, The	O	RF	Simon, Seymour	Avon
Hedgehog in the Hall	Q	RF	Daniels, Lucy	Barron's Educational
Hello, My Name Is Scrambled Eggs	R	RF	Gilson, Jamie	Pocket Books
Help! I'm a Prisoner in the Library	Q	RF	Clifford, Eth	Scholastic
Helpful Change, A	L	RF	Behr, Alexandra	Hampton-Brown
Helpful Harry and Other Stories	L	RF	New Way: Literature	Steck-Vaughn
Henry	T	RF	Bawden, Nina	Bantam Doubleday Dell
Henry and Beezus	O	RF	Cleary, Beverly	Avon
Henry and Mudge and Annie's Good Move	J	RF	Rylant, Cynthia	Aladdin
Henry and Mudge and the Bedtime Thumps	J	RF	Rylant, Cynthia	Aladdin
Henry and Mudge and the Best Day of All	J	RF	Rylant, Cynthia	Aladdin
Henry and Mudge and the Careful Cousin	J	RF	Rylant, Cynthia	Aladdin
Henry and Mudge and the Forever Sea	J	RF	Rylant, Cynthia	Aladdin
Henry and Mudge and the Happy Cat	J	RF	Rylant, Cynthia	Aladdin
Henry and Mudge and the Long Weekend	J	RF	Rylant, Cynthia	Aladdin
Henry and Mudge and the Sneaky Crackers	J	RF	Rylant, Cynthia	Aladdin
Henry and Mudge and the Snowman Plan	J	RF	Rylant, Cynthia	Aladdin
Henry and Mudge and the Starry Night	J	RF	Rylant, Cynthia	Aladdin
Henry and Mudge and the Wild Wind	J	RF	Rylant, Cynthia	Aladdin
Henry and Mudge Get the Cold Shivers	J	RF	Rylant, Cynthia	Aladdin
Henry and Mudge in Puddle Trouble	J	RF	Rylant, Cynthia	Aladdin
Henry and Mudge in the Family Trees	J	RF	Rylant, Cynthia	Aladdin
Henry and Mudge in the Green Time	J	RF	Rylant, Cynthia	Aladdin
Henry and Mudge in the Sparkle Days	J	RF	Rylant, Cynthia	Aladdin
Henry and Mudge Take the Big Test	J	RF	Rylant, Cynthia	Aladdin
Henry and Mudge: The First Book	J	RF	Rylant, Cynthia	Aladdin
Henry and Mudge Under the Yellow Moon	J	RF	Rylant, Cynthia	Aladdin
Henry and Ribsy	O	RF	Cleary, Beverly	Hearst
Henry and the Clubhouse	O	RF	Cleary, Beverly	Avon
Henry and the Paper Route	O	RF	Cleary, Beverly	Hearst
Henry Huggins	O	RF	Cleary, Beverly	Avon
Henry's Choice	M	RF	Reading Unlimited	Celebration Press
Herbie Jones	N	RF	Kline, Suzy	The Penguin Group
Herbie Jones and Hamburger Head	N	RF	Kline, Suzy	The Penguin Group
Herbie Jones and the Birthday Showdown	N	RF	Kline, Suzy	The Penguin Group
Herbie Jones and the Class Gift	N	RF	Kline, Suzy	The Penguin Group
Herbie Jones and the Dark Attic	N	RF	Kline, Suzy	Puffin Books
Herbie Jones and the Monster Ball	N	RF	Kline, Suzy	The Penguin Group
Here Comes the Strike Out	K	RF	Kessler, Leonard	Harper Trophy
Here's to You, Rachel Robinson	T	RF	Blume, Judy	Bantam Doubleday Dell
Hey, New Kid!	N	RF	Duffey, Betsy	The Penguin Group
Hey World, Here I Am!	S	RF	Little, Jean	HarperTrophy
Hidden Hand, The	M	RF	Schultz, Irene	Wright Group/McGraw Hill
Hiding Places	J	RF	Storyteller-Night Crickets	Wright Group/McGraw Hill
Hill of Fire	L	RF	Lewis, T.P.	Harper Collins
Hit-Away Kid, The	M	RF	Christopher, Matt	Little, Brown & Co.
Ho, Ho, Benjamin, Feliz Navidad	N	RF	Giff, Patricia Reilly	Bantam Doubleday Dell
Holes	V	RF	Sachar, Louis	Random House
Holly & Mac	N	RF	SupaDoopers	Sundance
Home for Diggory, A	K	RF	Pacific Literacy	Pacific Learning
Home in the Sky	K	RF	Baker, Jeannie	Scholastic
Home Sweet Home, Goodbye	R	RF	Stowe, Cynthia	Scholastic
Homecoming	X	RF	Voigt, Cynthia	Ballantine Books

Title	Level	Genre	Author/Series	Publisher/Distributor
Homer Price	Q	RF	McCloskey, Robert	Puffin Books
Hoops	X	RF	Myers, Walter Dean	Bantam Doubleday Dell
Hoopstars: Go to the Hoop!	M	RF	Hughes, Dean	Random House
Hooray for the Golly Sisters!	K	RF	Byars, Betsy	HarperTrophy
Hop to it, Minty!	O	RF	PM Ruby	Rigby
Hope Was Here	W	RF	Bauer, Joan	G.P. Putnam's Sons
Horrible Harry and the Ant Invasion	L	RF	Kline, Suzy	Scholastic
Horrible Harry and the Christmas Surprise	L	RF	Kline, Susy	Scholastic
Horrible Harry and the Drop of Doom	L	RF	Kline, Suzy	Puffin Books
Horrible Harry and the Dungeon	L	RF	Kline, Suzy	The Penguin Group
Horrible Harry and the Green Slime	L	RF	Kline, Suzy	The Penguin Group
Horrible Harry and the Kickball Wedding	L	RF	Kline, Susy	The Penguin Group
Horrible Harry in Room 2B	L	RF	Kline, Suzy	The Penguin Group
Horrible Harry, Moves up to Third Grade	L	RF	Kline, Suzy	Puffin Books
Horrible Harry's Secret	L	RF	Kline, Suzy	The Penguin Group
Horrors of the Haunted Museum	Q	RF	Stine, R. L.	Scholastic
Hot and Cold Summer, The	O	RF	Hurwitz, Johanna	Scholastic
Hot Fudge Hero	L	RF	Brisson, Pat	Henry Holt & Co.
House in the Snow, The	S	RF	Engh, M.J.	Scholastic
House of Wings, The	R	RF	Byars, Betsy	The Penguin Group
House on Walenska Street, The	N	RF	Herman, Charlotte	The Penguin Group
House That Jack's Friends Built, The	J	RF	Pair-It Books	Steck-Vaughn
House that Stood on Booker Hill, The	J	RF	Ready Readers	Pearson Learning
How I Met Archie	M	RF	Kenna, Anna	Pacific Learning
How Much Does This Hold?	K	RF	Coulton, Mia	Kaeden Books
How Much Is That Guinea Pig in the Window?	L	RF	Rocklin, Joanne	Scholastic
How To Be Cool in the Third Grade	N	RF	Duffey, Betsy	The Penguin Group
How To Eat Fried Worms	R	RF	Rockwell, Thomas	Bantam Doubleday Dell
Howling at the Hauntly's	M	RF	Dadey, Debbie & Jones, Marcia	Scholastic
Howling Dog and Other Cases, The	O	RF	Simon, Seymour	Avon
Huberta the Hiking Hippo	L	RF	Literacy 2000	Rigby
Hue Boy	M	RF	Mitchell, Rita Phillips	The Penguin Group
Hundred Dresses, The	O	RF	Estes, Eleanor	Scholastic
Hundred Penny Box, The	P	RF	Mathis, Sharon Bell	Puffin Books
Hurray For Ali Baba Bernstein	O	RF	Hurwitz, Johanna	Scholastic
Hurricane Machine and Other Cases, The	O	RF	Simon, Seymour	Avon
Hushtown: A Peaceful Community	Q	RF	Massie, Elizabeth	Steck-Vaughn
Hypnotized Frog and Other Cases, The	O	RF	Simon, Seymour	Avon
I Am the Cheese	Z	RF	Cormier, Robert	Laurel-Leaf Books
I, Amber Brown	N	RF	Danziger, Paula	Scholastic
I Don't Believe It!	L	RF	Tuer, Judy	Rigby
I Dream	K	RF	Sunshine	Wright Group/McGraw Hill
I Get the Creeps	K	RF	Reading Corners	Dominie
I Hate Camping	M	RF	Petersen, P. J.	The Penguin Group
I Hate Company	M	RF	Petersen, P.J.	The Penguin Group
I Hate English	L	RF	Levine, Ellen	Scholastic
I Hate My Best Friend	L	RF	Rosner, Ruth	Hyperion
I Know a Lady	L	RF	Zolotow, Charlotte	The Penguin Group
I Like Shopping	M	RF	Sunshine	Wright Group/McGraw Hill
I Play Soccer	J	RF	City Kids	Rigby
I Was a Third Grade Science Project	N	RF	Auch, Mary Jane	Yearling
I Was So Mad	J	RF	Mayer, Mercer	Donovan
I Went to the Dentist	K	RF	City Kids	Rigby
I Went to the Movies	J	RF	City Kids	Rigby
I'm No One Else But Me	M	RF	Book Bank	Wright Group/McGraw Hill
Ice Dove and Other Stories, The	M	RF	deAnda, Diane	Arte Publico
Ice Magic	M	RF	Christopher, Matt	Little, Brown & Co.
Iceberg Hermit, The	X	RF	Roth, Arthur	Scholastic
Icy Question and Other Cases, The	O	RF	Simon, Seymour	Avon
If I Forget, You Remember	V	RF	Williams, Carol Lynch	Bantam Doubleday Dell

Title	Level	Genre	Author/Series	Publisher/Distributor
Iggie's House	R	RF	Blume, Judy	Bantam Doubleday Dell
Impossible Bend and Other Cases, The	O	RF	Simon, Seymour	Avon
In a Pickle	M	RF	SupaDoopers	Sundance
In Aunt Lucy's Kitchen	M	RF	Rylant, Cynthia	Aladdin
In the Clouds	M	RF	Literacy 2000	Rigby
In the Dinosaur's Paw	M	RF	Giff, Patricia Reilly	Bantam Doubleday Dell
In the Land of the Polar Bear	J	RF	Robinson, F.R.	Steck-Vaughn
In-Between Days, The	P	RF	Bunting, Eve	HarperTrophy
Incredible Shrinking Machine and Other Cases, The	O	RF	Simon, Seymour	Avon
Indian School, The	P	RF	Whelan, Gloria	HarperTrophy
Indian-Head Pennies and Other Cases, The	O	RF	Simon, Seymour	Avon
Interrupting The Big Sleep	P	RF	Marriott, Janice	Pacific Learning
Invisible in the Third Grade	M	RF	Cuyler, Margery	Scholastic
Ironman	Z	RF	Crutcher, Chris	Laurel-Leaf Books
Island Baby	M	RF	Keller, Holly	Scholastic
Island Keeper	T	RF	Mazer, Harry	Language for Learning Assoc.
Island, The	R	RF	Paulsen, Gary	Bantam Doubleday Dell
It Takes A Village	L	RF	Cowen-Fletcher, J.	Scholastic
It Wasn't My Fault	L	RF	Lester, Helen	Houghton Mifflin
It's a Fiesta, Benjamin	N	RF	Giff, Patricia Reilly	Bantam Doubleday Dell
It's Halloween	K	RF	Prelutsky, Jack	Scholastic
It's Just a Trick	O	RF	Literacy 2000	Rigby
It's New, It's Improved, It's Terrible!	Q	RF	Manes, Stephen	Bantam Skylark
It's Not Easy Being George	S	RF	Smith, Janice Lee	HarperTrophy
It's Not the End of the World	T	RF	Blume, Judy	Dell
Izzy, Willy-Nilly	X	RF	Voigt, Cynthia	Aladdin
J.T.	Q	RF	Wagner, Jane	Bantam Doubleday Dell
Jack's New Power: Stories From a Caribbean Year	W	RF	Gantos, Jack	Sunburst
Jackaroo	Y	RF	Voigt, Cynthia	Scholastic
Jacob Have I Loved	U	RF	Paterson, Katherine	HarperTrophy
Jake and the Copycats	J	RF	Rocklin, Joanne	Bantam Doubleday Dell
Jamaica and Brianna	K	RF	Little Readers	Houghton Mifflin
Jamaica's Find	K	RF	Havill, Juanita	Scholastic
Jar of Dreams, A	R	RF	Uchida, Yoshiko	Aladdin
Jason Kidd Story, The	P	RF	Moore, David	Scholastic
Jazmin's Notebook	Z	RF	Grimes, Nikki	The Penguin Group
Jazz Kid, The	Y	RF	Lincoln Collier, James	The Penguin Group
Jazz, Pizzazz, and the Silver Threads	P	RF	Quattlebaum, Mary	Bantam Doubleday Dell
Jennifer, Hecate, Macbeth, William McKinley, and Me, Elizabeth	R	RF	Konigsburg, E. L.	Yearling
Jennifer, Too	L	RF	Havill, Juanita	Hyperion
Jenny Archer, Author	M	RF	Conford, Ellen	Little, Brown & Co.
Jenny Archer to the Rescue	M	RF	Conford, Ellen	Little, Brown & Co.
Jericho	T	RF	Hickman, Janet	Hearst
Jericho's Journey	U	RF	Wisler, G. Clifton	Penguin Group
Jerry on the Line	R	RF	Seabrooke, Brenda	Puffin Books
Jesse	Y	RF	Soto, Gary	Scholastic
Jigsaw Jones Mystery: The Case of the Christmas Snowman	M	RF	Ruller, James	Scholastic
Jillian Jiggs	J	RF	Gilman, Phoebe	Scholastic
Jim Ugly	Q	RF	Fleischman, Sid	Bantam Doubleday Dell
Jim's Dog Muffins	K	RF	Cohen, Miriam	Bantam Doubleday Dell
Jimmy Lee Did It	J	RF	Cummings, Pat	Lothrop
Jingo Django	V	RF	Fleischman, Sid	Bantam Doubleday Dell
Jo Jo Winnie Again	O	RF	Sachs, Marilyn	Dutton
Job for Giant Jim, A	J	RF	Sunshine	Wright Group/McGraw Hill
Job for Jenny Archer, A	M	RF	Conford, Ellen	Random House
Joe Cocker Spaniel	N	RF	SupaDoopers	Sundance
Joey Pigza Swallowed the Key	T	RF	Gantos, Jack	HarperTrophy
Johnny Long Legs	M	RF	Christopher, Matt	Little, Brown & Co.

Title	Level	Genre	Author/Series	Publisher/Distributor
Jonathan Buys a Present	J	RF	PM Story Books-Turquoise	Rigby
Jordan and the Northside Reps	K	RF	PM Story Books -Silver	Rigby
Jordan's Lucky Day	K	RF	PM Story Books-Turquoise	Rigby
Josephine's Imagination	L	RF	Dobrin, Arnold	Scholastic
Joshua T. Bates	Q	RF	Shreve, Susan	Alfred A. Knopf
Joshua T. Bates in Trouble Again	Q	RF	Shreve, Susan	Alfred A. Knopf
Joshua T. Bates Takes Charge	Q	RF	Shreve, Susan	Alfred A. Knopf
Journey	S	RF	MacLachlan, Patricia	Yearling
Journey Home	V	RF	Uchida, Yoshika	Aladdin
Journey Home, The	S	RF	Holland, Isabelle	Scholastic
Journey Into Terror	U	RF	Wallace, Bill	Simon & Schuster
Journey to an 800 Number	V	RF	Konigsburg, E. L.	Aladdin
Judy Moody	L	RF	McDonald, Megan	Candlewick Press
Julian, Dream Doctor	N	RF	Cameron, Ann	Random House
Julian, Secret Agent	N	RF	Cameron, Ann	Random House
Julian's Glorious Summer	N	RF	Cameron, Ann	Random House
Julie	U	RF	George, Jean Craighead	Harper Trophy
Julie of the Wolves	U	RF	George, Jean Craighead	Harper Collins
Julie's Wolf Pack	U	RF	George, Jean Craighead	HarperTrophy
Jump the Broom	L	RF	Books For Young Learners	Pacific Learning
Jumping Into Nothing	M	RF	Willner-Pardo, Gina	Houghton Mifflin
Junebug	Q	RF	Mead, Alice	Bantam Doubleday Dell
Junie B. Jones and a Little Monkey Business	M	RF	Park, Barbara	Random House
Junie B. Jones and Her Big Fat Mouth	M	RF	Park, Barbara	Random House
Junie B. Jones and Some Sneaky Peeky Spying	M	RF	Park, Barbara	Random House
Junie B. Jones and that Meanie Jim's Birthday	M	RF	Park, Barbara	Random House
Junie B. Jones and the Mushy Gushy Valentine	M	RF	Park, Barbara	Random House
Junie B. Jones and the Stupid Smelly Bus	M	RF	Park, Barbara	Random House
Junie B. Jones and the Yucky Blucky Fruitcake	M	RF	Park, Barbara	Random House
Junie B. Jones Has a Monster Under Her Bed	M	RF	Park, Barbara	Random House
Junie B. Jones Has a Peep in Her Pocket	M	RF	Park, Barbara	Random House
Junie B. Jones Is a Beauty Shop Guy	M	RF	Park, Barbara	Random House
Junie B. Jones Is a Party Animal	M	RF	Park, Barbara	Random House
Junie B. Jones is (almost) a Flower Girl	M	RF	Park, Barbara	Random House
Junie B. Jones Is Not a Crook	M	RF	Park, Barbara	Random House
Junie B. Jones Loves Handsome Warren	M	RF	Park, Barbara	Random House
Junie B. Jones Smells Something Fishy	M	RF	Park, Barbara	Random House
Junior Gymnasts: Katie's Big Move	M	RF	Slater, Teddy	Scholastic
Junkyard Dog, The	N	RF	PM Emerald	Rigby
Just As Long As We're Together	T	RF	Blume, Judy	Bantam Doubleday Dell
Just Call Me Stupid	R	RF	Birdseye, Tom	Puffin Books
Just Juice	Q	RF	Hesse, Karen	Scholastic
Just Plain Cat	O	RF	Robinson, Nancy K.	Scholastic
Just Tell Me When We're Dead!	O	RF	Clifford, Eth	Scholastic
Just Us Women	J	RF	Caines, Jeannette	Scholastic
Justin and the Best Biscuits in the World	P	RF	Pitts, Walter & Mildred	Alfred A. Knopf
Keep Ms. Sugarman in the Fourth Grade	M	RF	Levy, Elizabeth	HarperTrophy
Keep Out, Our Dog Buries What it Can't Eat	P	RF	Beale, Fleur	Pacific Learning
Keep Smiling Through	V	RF	Rinaldi, Ann	Harcourt Brace
Keisha Leads the Way: Magic Attic Club	Q	RF	Reed, Teresa	Magic Attic
Keisha the Fairy Snow Queen: Magic Attic Club	Q	RF	Reed, Teresa	Magic Attic
Keisha to the Rescue: Magic Attic Club	Q	RF	Reed, Teresa	Magic Attic
Keisha's Maze Mystery (Magic Attic)	Q	RF	Benson, Lauren	Magic Attic
Kerry	K	RF	PM Story Books -Silver	Rigby
Kerry's Double	K	RF	PM Story Books -Silver	Rigby
Key to the Playhouse, The	O	RF	York, Carol	Scholastic
Key to the Treasure	N	RF	Parish, Peggy	Bantam Doubleday Dell
Kick, Pass, and Run	J	RF	Kessler, Leonard	HarperTrophy
Kid in the Red Jacket, The	O	RF	Park, Barbara	Random House
Kid Power	P	RF	Pfeffer, Susan Beth	Scholastic

Title	Level	Genre	Author/Series	Publisher/Distributor
Kid Who Only Hit Homers, The	M	RF	Christopher, Matt	Little, Brown & Co.
Kid Who Ran For President, The	T	RF	Gutman, Dan	Language for Learning Assoc.
Kids in Ms. Colman's Class: Author Day	M	RF	Martin, Ann M.	Scholastic
Kilmer's Pet Monster	L	RF	Dadey, D. & Jones, M. T.	Scholastic
Kind of Thief, A	U	RF	Alcock, Vivien	Bantam Doubleday Dell
King Emmett the Second	R	RF	Stolz, Mary	Bantam Doubleday Dell
Kiss the Dust	W	RF	Laird, Elizabeth	The Penguin Group
Kit's Castle	L	RF	Powling, Chris	Wright Group/McGraw Hill
Kitten Crowd	O	RF	Baglio, Ben M.	Scholastic
Kitten in the Cold	Q	RF	Baglio, Ben M.	Scholastic
Kitten That Won First Prize, The	Q	RF	Baglio, Ben M.	Scholastic
Kittens in the Kitchen	Q	RF	Daniels, Lucy	Barron's Educational
Knife, The	N	RF	Cartwright, Pauline	Pacific Learning
Knightly News	P	RF	Kenna, Anna	Pacific Learning
Knitwits	Q	RF	Taylor, William	Scholastic
Knock! Knock!	K	RF	Carter, Jackie	Scholastic
Knots on a Counting Rope	P	RF	Martin Jr., B. & Archambault, J.	Henry Holt & Co.
Know-Nothing Birthday, A	K	RF	Spirn, Michele Sobel	HarperTrophy
Know-Nothings, The	K	RF	Spirn, Michele Sobel	HarperTrophy
Koi's Python	P	RF	Moore, Miriam	Hyperion
Koya DeLaney and the Good Girl Blues	P	RF	Greenfield, Eloise	Scholastic
Kristy and the Walking Disaster	O	RF	Martin, Ann M.	Scholastic
Lamb in the Laundry	Q	RF	Baglio, Ben M.	Scholastic
Lamb Lessons	O	RF	Baglio, Ben M.	Scholastic
Land of the Great Big "No!"	L	RF	Trussell-Cullen, Alan	Dominie Press
Landry News, The	R	RF	Clements, Andrew	Simon & Schuster
Last Look	P	RF	Bulla, Clyde Robert	Puffin Books
Last One In Is a Rotten Egg	J	RF	Kessler, Leonard	HarperTrophy
Later, Gator	R	RF	Yep, Laurence	Hyperion
Lavender	O	RF	Hesse, Karen	Henry Holt & Co.
Lazy Lions, Lucky Lambs	M	RF	Giff, Patricia Reilly	Bantam Doubleday Dell
Leaving Home	Z	RF	Keillor, Garrison	The Penguin Group
Leaving Home: 15 Distinguished Authors Explore Personal Journeys	Z	RF	Rochman, H. & McCampbell, D.	HarperTrophy
Left Behind	L	RF	Carrick, Carol	Clarion Books
Leftovers, The: Catch Flies!	N	RF	Howard, Tristan	Scholastic
Leftovers, The: Fast Break	N	RF	Howard, Tristan	Scholastic
Leftovers, The: Get Jammed	N	RF	Howard, Tristan	Scholastic
Leftovers, The: Reach Their Goal	N	RF	Howard, Tristan	Scholastic
Leftovers, The: Strike Out!	N	RF	Howard, Tristan	Scholastic
Lemonade Trick, The	Q	RF	Corbett, Scott	Scholastic
Lentil	M	RF	McCloskey, Robert	Scholastic
Let's Be Enemies	J	RF	Sendak, Maurice	Harper & Row
Let's Go, Philadelphia!	M	RF	Giff, Patricia Reilly	Bantam Doubleday Dell
Letters from Camp A Mystery	V	RF	Klise, Kate	Harper Trophy
Letters to Julia	W	RF	Holmes, Barbara Ware	HarperTrophy
Liar, Liar, Pants on Fire	O	RF	Korman, Gordon	Scholastic
Library Card, The	R	RF	Spinelli, Jerry	Scholastic
Light at Tern Rock, The	N	RF	Sauer, Julia L.	Scholastic
Lightweight Rocket and Other Cases, The	O	RF	Simon, Seymour	Avon
Like Jake and Me	O	RF	Jukes, Mavis	Alfred A. Knopf
Lilacs, Lotuses, and Ladybugs	L	RF	Evangeline Nicholas Collection	Wright Group/McGraw Hill
Lili the Brave	N	RF	Armstrong, Jennifer	Random House
Lionel and His Friends	K	RF	Krensky, Stephen	Puffin Books
Lionel and Louise	K	RF	Krensky, Stephen	Puffin Books
Lionel at Large	K	RF	Krensky, Stephen	Puffin Books
Lionel In The Fall	K	RF	Krensky, Stephen	Puffin Books
Lionel In The Spring	K	RF	Krensky, Stephen	Puffin Books
Lionel In The Summer	K	RF	Krensky, Stephen	Puffin Books
Lionel In The Winter	K	RF	Krensky, Stephen	Puffin Books

Title	Level	Genre	Author/Series	Publisher/Distributor
Lisa's Diary	L	RF	Pritchett, Jan	Rigby
Listen Children: An Anthology of Black Literature	U	RF	Strickland, Dorothy S.	Bantam Doubleday Dell
Listening in Bed	M	RF	Book Bank	Wright Group/McGraw Hill
Little Adventure, A	J	RF	PM Story Books -Silver	Rigby
Little Black, A Pony	J	RF	Farley, Walter	Random House
Little Firefighter, The	M	RF	Sunshine	Wright Group/McGraw Hill
Little Fireman	J	RF	Brown, Margaret Wise	Harper Collins
Little Icicle	O	RF	Szymanski, Lois	Avon Camelot
Little Lefty	M	RF	Christopher, Matt	Little, Brown & Co.
Little Miss Stoneybrook and Dawn	O	RF	Martin, Ann M.	Scholastic
Little Old Lady Who Danced on the Moon, The	M	RF	Sunshine	Wright Group/McGraw Hill
Little Princess, A	L	RF	All Aboard Reading	Grosset & Dunlap
Little Shopping, A	M	RF	Rylant, Cynthia	Aladdin
Little Soup's Birthday	K	RF	Peck, Robert Newton	Bantam Doubleday Dell
Little Swan	M	RF	Geras, Adele	Random House
Living in the Sky	K	RF	Sunshine	Wright Group/McGraw Hill
Living Up The Street	Y	RF	Soto, Gary	Bantam Doubleday Dell
Llama in the Family, A	O	RF	Hurwitz, Johanna	Scholastic
Llama Pajamas	N	RF	Clymer, Susan	Scholastic
Local News	W	RF	Soto, Gary	Scholastic
Long Shot for Paul	M	RF	Christopher, Matt	Little, Brown & Co.
Long-Lost Friends, The	M	RF	Schultz, Irene	Wright Group/McGraw Hill
Look Out, Washington D.C.!	O	RF	Giff, Patricia Reilly	Bantam Doubleday Dell
Look Who's Playing First Base	M	RF	Christopher, Matt	Little, Brown & Co.
Looking for Dad	M	RF	SupaDoopers	Sundance
Loose Laces	L	RF	Reading Unlimited	Celebration Press
Lost and Found Game, The	M	RF	Nayer, Judy	Pearson Learning
Lost Continent and Other Cases, The	O	RF	Simon, Seymour	Avon
Lost Flower Children, The	Q	RF	Lisle, Janet Taylor	Philomel Books
Lost Hikers and Other Cases, The	O	RF	Simon, Seymour	Avon
Lost in the Forest	K	RF	Robinson, Fay	Wright Group/McGraw Hill
Lost on a Mountain in Maine	R	RF	Fendler, Donn	Peter Smith Publications
Lost Sandals, The	N	RF	Bennett, Jean	Pacific Learning
Love, from the Fifth-Grade Celebrity	Q	RF	Giff, Patricia Reilly	Bantam Doubleday Dell
Love Me, Love My Broccoli	S	RF	Peters, Julie Anne	Avon Camelot
Lucky Baseball Bat, The	M	RF	Christopher, Matt	Little, Brown & Co.
Lucky Last Luke	M	RF	Clark, Margaret	Sundance
Lucky Stars	L	RF	Adler, David A.	Random House
Lucky Stone, The	P	RF	Clifton, Lucille	Bantam Doubleday Dell
Luke's Bully	N	RF	Winthrop, Elizabeth	Puffin Books
Luke's Go-cart	L	RF	PM Gold	Rigby
Lunch at the Joy House Café	K	RF	Blackaby, Susan	Hampton-Brown
Lunchbox Mystery, The	N	RF	Lohans, Alison	Scholastic
M.C. Higgins the Great	X	RF	Hamilton, Virginia	Macmillan
M & M and The Bad News Babies	K	RF	Ross, Pat	The Penguin Group
M & M and the Big Bag	K	RF	Ross, Pat	The Penguin Group
M & M and the Halloween Monster	K	RF	Ross, Pat	The Penguin Group.
M & M and the Haunted House Game	K	RF	Ross, Pat	The Penguin Group
M & M and the Mummy Mess	K	RF	Ross, Pat	The Penguin Group
M & M and the Santa Secrets	K	RF	Ross, Pat	The Penguin Group
M & M and the Super Child Afternoon	K	RF	Ross, Pat	The Penguin Group
Magic Money	L	RF	Adler, David A.	Random House
Magic Moscow, The	P	RF	Pinkwater, Daniel	Aladdin
Magic Squad and the Dog of Great Potential, The	P	RF	Quattlebaum, Mary	Bantam Doubleday Dell
Magic Store, The	J	RF	Sunshine	Wright Group/McGraw Hill
Mailman Mario & His Boris-Busters	L	RF	Parker, John	Dominie Press
Maisie's Race	L	RF	Mawter, Jeni	Wright Group/McGraw Hill
Make A Wish, Molly	O	RF	Cohen, Barbara	Bantam Doubleday Dell
Make Like a Tree and Leave	U	RF	Danziger, Paula	PaperStar
Make Room For Elisa	N	RF	Hurwitz, Johanna	The Penguin Group

Title	Level	Genre	Author/Series	Publisher/Distributor
Make Way For Ducklings	L	RF	McCloskey, Robert	Puffin Books
Making Friends	J	RF	Foundations	Wright Group/McGraw Hill
Making Friends on Beacon Street	M	RF	Literacy 2000	Rigby
Making Lily Laugh!	M	RF	Dreyer, Ellen	Pearson Learning
Mama, Let's Dance	W	RF	Hermes, Patricia	Scholastic
Man From The Sky	S	RF	Avi	BeechTree
Man Out at First	M	RF	Christopher, Matt	Little Brown & Co.
Manatee Winter	K	RF	Zoehfeld, Kathleen Weidnetz	Scholastic
Maniac Magee	V	RF	Spinelli, Jerry	Scholastic
Manly Ferry Pigeon, The	K	RF	Sunshine	Wright Group/McGraw Hill
Marcella	L	RF	Literacy 2000	Rigby
Maria: A Christmas Story	R	RF	Taylor, Theodore	Avon Camelot
Market Day for Mrs. Wordy	K	RF	Sunshine	Wright Group/McGraw Hill
Marrying Malcolm Murgatroyd	T	RF	Farrell, Mame	Sunburst
Martin and the Teacher's Pets	K	RF	Chardiet, B. & Maccarone, G.	Scholastic
Martin and the Tooth Fairy	K	RF	Chardiet, B. & Maccarone, G.	Scholastic
Martin's Mighty Hit	M	RF	Windmill Books	Rigby
Marvelous Treasure, The	M	RF	Sunshine	Wright Group/McGraw Hill
Marvin and the Mean Words	M	RF	Kline, Suzy	PaperStar
Marvin Redpost: A Flying Birthday Cake?	M	RF	Sachar, Louis	Random House
Marvin Redpost: Alone in His Teacher's House	M	RF	Sachar, Louis	Random House
Marvin Redpost (Class President)	M	RF	Sachar, Louis	Random House
Marvin Redpost: Is He a Girl?	M	RF	Sachar, Louis	Random House
Marvin Redpost: Kidnapped at Birth?	M	RF	Sachar, Louis	Random House
Marvin Redpost, Super Fast, Out of Control!	M	RF	Sachar, Louis	Random House
Marvin Redpost: Why Pick on Me?	M	RF	Sachar, Louis	Random House
Mary Marony and the Chocolate Surprise	M	RF	Kline, Suzy	Bantam Doubleday Dell
Mary Marony and the Snake	M	RF	Kline, Suzy	Bantam Doubleday Dell
Mary Marony Hides Out	M	RF	Kline, Suzy	Bantam Doubleday Dell
Mary Marony, Mummy Girl	M	RF	Kline, Suzy	Bantam Doubleday Dell
Mary on Horseback	Q	RF	Wells, Rosemary	Puffin Books
Math Wiz, The	N	RF	Duffey, Betsy	The Penguin Group
Matthew and Tilly	L	RF	Jones, Rebecca C.	The Penguin Group
Matthew Likes to Read	J	RF	Pacific Literacy	Pacific Learning
Matthew's Tantrum	J	RF	Literacy 2000	Rigby
Max	J	RF	Isadora, Rachel	Macmillan
Max Malone and the Great Cereal Rip-off	N	RF	Herman, Charlotte	Henry Holt & Co.
Max Malone Makes a Million	N	RF	Herman, Charlotte	Henry Holt & Co.
Max Malone, Superstar	N	RF	Herman, Charlotte	Scholastic
Max the Man Mountain	Q	RF	McFarlane, Peter	Harper Collins
Maxie, Rosie, and Earl-Partners in Grime	O	RF	Park, Barbara	Random House
Maze, The	V	RF	Hobbs, Will	Morrow Junior Books
McBroom's Wonderful One-Acre Farm	O	RF	Fleischman, Sid	Beech Tree Books
Me and My Little Brain	T	RF	Fitzgerald, John D.	Dell
Me, Mop, and the Moondance Kid	S	RF	Myers, Walter Dean	Bantam Doubleday Dell
Me Too	K	RF	Mayer, Mercer	Donovan
Meanest Thing to Say, The	K	RF	Cosby, Bill	Scholastic
Medal for Molly, A	N	RF	PM Emerald	Rigby
Medal for Nickie, A	M	RF	Sunshine	Wright Group/McGraw Hill
Meet M & M	K	RF	Ross, Pat	The Penguin Group
Meet the Austins	W	RF	L'Engle, Madeleine	Laurel-Leaf Books
Meet the Lincoln Lions Band	L	RF	Giff, Patricia Reilly	Bantam Doubleday Dell
Meg Mackintosh and The Case of the Curious Whale Watch	O	RF	Landon, Lucinda	Secret Passage Press
Meg Mackintosh and The Case of the Missing Babe Ruth Baseball	O	RF	Landon, Lucinda	Secret Passage Press
Meg Mackintosh and The Mystery at Camp Creepy	O	RF	Landon, Lucinda	Secret Passage Press
Meg Mackintosh and The Mystery at the Medieval Castle	O	RF	Landon, Lucinda	Secret Passage Press
Meg Mackintosh and The Mystery at the Soccer Match	O	RF	Landon, Lucinda	Secret Passage Press

Title	Level	Genre	Author/Series	Publisher/Distributor
Meg Mackintosh and The Mystery in the Locked Library	O	RF	Landon, Lucinda	Secret Passage Press
Megan's Balancing Act	Q	RF	Korman, Susan	Magic Attic
Megan's Island	R	RF	Roberts, Willo Davis	Aladdin
Melting Snow Sculptures and Other Cases, The	O	RF	Simon, Seymour	Avon
Messy Bessey's Closet	K	RF	Rookie Readers	Children's Press
Messy Bessey's School Desk	J	RF	Rookie Readers	Children's Press
Middle Moffat, The	T	RF	Estes, Eleanor	Language for Learning Assoc.
Midnight Fox, The	R	RF	Byars, Betsy	Scholastic
Mighty, The	V	RF	Philbrick, Rodman	Scholastic
Mike Swan, Sink or Swim	J	RF	Heiligman, Deborah	Bantam Doubleday Dell
Milo's Great Invention	M	RF	Pair-It Books	Steck-Vaughn
Mina's Spring of Colors	P	RF	Gilmore, Rachna	Fitzhenry & Whiteside
Miracle at the Plate	M	RF	Christopher, Matt	Little, Brown & Co.
Miracles on Maple Hill	R	RF	Sorensen, Virginia	Scholastic
Mischief	M	RF	Pacific Literacy	Pacific Learning
Misha Disappears	K	RF	Literacy 2000	Rigby
Mishmash	N	RF	Cone, Molly	Pocket Books
Miss Geneva's Lantern	P	RF	Book Shop	Mondo
Miss Nelson Has a Field Day	L	RF	Allard, Harry	Scholastic
Miss Nelson is Missing	L	RF	Allard, Harry	Houghton Mifflin
Miss Rumphius	M	RF	Cooney, Barbara	The Penguin Group
Missing Fossil Mystery, The	L	RF	Herman, Emily	Hyperion
Missing May	W	RF	Rylant, Cynthia	Bantam Doubleday Dell
Missing Osprey Nest, The	N	RF	Herman, Emily	Wright Group/McGraw Hill
Missing Pet, The	K	RF	Pair-It Books	Steck-Vaughn
Missing Tooth, The	J	RF	Cole, Joanna	Random House
Missing Will, The	M	RF	Schultz, Irene	Wright Group/McGraw Hill
Misty of Chincoteague	R	RF	Henry, Marguerite	Aladdin
Misty's Twilight	R	RF	Henry, Marguerite	Aladdin
Mitch and Amy	O	RF	Cleary, Beverly	Harper Collins
Moana's Island	M	RF	Sunshine	Wright Group/McGraw Hill
Moccasin Trail	W	RF	McGraw, Eloise	Scholastic
Molly the Brave and Me	K	RF	O'Connor, Jane	Random House
Molly's Pilgrim	M	RF	Cohen, Barbara	Bantam Doubleday Dell
Mom, You're Fired!	O	RF	Robinson, Nancy K.	Scholastic
Mom's Getting Married	K	RF	Sunshine	Wright Group/McGraw Hill
Money Boot, The	N	RF	Russell, Ginny	Fitzhenry and Whiteside
Monkey Island	V	RF	Fox, Paula	Orchard Books
Monster Rabbit Runs Amuck!	M	RF	Giff, Patricia Reilly	Bantam Doubleday Dell
Monsters Next Door, The	L	RF	Dadey, D. & Jones, M. T.	Scholastic
Moonlight on the River	R	RF	Kovacs, Deborah	The Penguin Group
More Adventures of the Great Brain	T	RF	Fitzgerald, John D.	Yearling
More Monsters in School	N	RF	Godfrey, M.	Fitzhenry and Whiteside
More Stories from Grandma's Attic	O	RF	Richardson, Arleta	Chariot Victor Publishing
More Stories Huey Tells	N	RF	Cameron, Ann	Alfred A. Knopf
More Stories Julian Tells	N	RF	Cameron, Ann	Random House
Most Beautiful Place in the World, The	O	RF	Cameron, Ann	Alfred A. Knopf
Most Wonderful Doll in the World, The	O	RF	McGinley, Phyllis	Scholastic
Mostly Michael	Q	RF	Smith, Robert Kimmel	Bantam Doubleday Dell
Mother's Helpers	K	RF	Ready Readers	Pearson Learning
Mountain Bike Mania	O	RF	Belcher, Angie	Rigby
Mouse Magic	O	RF	Baglio, Ben M.	Scholastic
Mouse Rap, The	W	RF	Myers, Walter Dean	HarperTrophy
Moves Make the Man, The	Z	RF	Brooks, Bruce	Harper Trophy
Moving Mama to Town	X	RF	Young, Ronder Thomas	Bantam Doubleday Dell
Mr. Bumbleticker Goes Shopping	J	RF	Foundations	Wright Group/McGraw Hill
Mr. Bumbleticker Goes to the Zoo	L	RF	Foundations	Wright Group/McGraw Hill
Mr. Gumpy's Motor Car	L	RF	Burningham, John	Harper Collins
Mr. Gumpy's Outing	L	RF	Burningham, John	Holt, Henry & Co.

Title	Level	Genre	Author/Series	Publisher/Distributor
Mr. Putter and Tabby Bake the Cake	J	RF	Rylant, Cynthia	Harcourt Brace
Mr. Putter and Tabby Fly the Plane	J	RF	Rylant, Cynthia	Harcourt Brace
Mr. Putter and Tabby Pick the Pears	J	RF	Rylant, Cynthia	Harcourt Brace
Mr. Putter and Tabby Pour the Tea	J	RF	Rylant, Cynthia	Harcourt Brace
Mr. Putter and Tabby Walk the Dog	J	RF	Rylant, Cynthia	Harcourt Brace
Mr. Putter & Tabby Row the Boat	J	RF	Rylant, Cynthia	Harcourt Brace
Mr. Putter & Tabby Take the Train	J	RF	Rylant, Cynthia	Harcourt Inc.
Mr. Putter & Tabby Toot the Horn	J	RF	Rylant, Cynthia	Harcourt Brace
Mrs. Always Goes Shopping	M	RF	Sunshine	Wright Group/McGraw Hill
Mrs. Barnett's Birthday	J	RF	Sunshine	Wright Group/McGraw Hill
Mrs. Jeepers' Batty Vacation	L	RF	Dadey, D. & Jones, M. T.	Scholastic
Mrs. Jeepers in Outer Space	M	RF	Dadey, D. & Jones, M. T.	Scholastic
Much Ado About Aldo	O	RF	Hurwitz, Johanna	The Penguin Group
Muffy's Secret Admirer	M	RF	Brown, Marc	Little, Brown & Co.
Muggie Maggie	O	RF	Cleary, Beverly	Avon Camelot
Music of Dolphins, The	V	RF	Hesse, Karen	Scholastic
Mutt and the Lifeguards	M	RF	Sunshine	Wright Group/McGraw Hill
My Brother, Ant	J	RF	Byars, Betsy	Viking
My Brother is a Superhero	X	RF	Sheldon, Dyan	Candlewick Press
My Brother Louis Measures Worms and Other Louis Stories	T	RF	Robinson, Barbara	HarperTrophy
My Brother, the Spy	N	RF	SupaDoopers	Sundance
My Father	J	RF	Mayer, Laura	Scholastic
My Great-Aunt Arizona	N	RF	Houston, Gloria	HarperCollins
My Life as a Fifth-Grade Comedian	T	RF	Levy, Elizabeth	Harper Trophy
My Mother Got Married (And Other Disasters)	O	RF	Park, Barbara	Random House
My Name is Maria Isabel	N	RF	Ada, Alma Flor	Aladdin
My Name is Yun Jim	N	RF	Murphy, Catherine	Wright Group/McGraw Hill
My New Mom	K	RF	Sunshine	Wright Group/McGraw Hill
My Prairie Summer	M	RF	Pair-It Books	Steck-Vaughn
My Side of the Mountain	U	RF	George, Jean Craighead	The Penguin Group
My Sister Annie	S	RF	Dodds, Bill	Boyds Mills Press
My Sister the Witch	R	RF	Conford, Ellen	Troll
My Sister's Getting Married	K	RF	Foundations	Wright Group/McGraw Hill
My Treasure Garden	J	RF	Book Bank	Wright Group/McGraw Hill
My Two Families	K	RF	PM Story Books -Silver	Rigby
My Weird Mother	M	RF	SupaDoopers	Sundance
Mysterious Green Swimmer and Other Cases, The	O	RF	Simon, Seymour	Avon
Mysterious I.O.U., The	M	RF	Schultz, Irene	Wright Group/McGraw Hill
Mysterious Tracks and Other Cases, The	O	RF	Simon, Seymour	Avon
Mystery of the Blue Ring, The	L	RF	Giff, Patricia Reilly	Bantam Doubleday Dell
Mystery of the Fire in the Sky	Q	RF	Mystery Solvers	Troll
Mystery of the Missing Dog, The	M	RF	Schultz, Irene	Wright Group/McGraw Hill
Mystery of the Missing Malamute, The	M	RF	Kleinhenz, Sydnie Meltzer	Wright Group/McGraw Hill
Mystery of the Phantom Pony, The	N	RF	Stepping Stone	Random House
Mystery of the Three Keys, The	M	RF	Schultz, Irene	Wright Group/McGraw Hill
Mystery of the Tooth Gremlin	L	RF	Graves, Bonnie	Hyperion
Mystery on October Road	O	RF	Herzig, A.C. & Mali, Jane	Scholastic
Mystery Seeds	L	RF	Reading Unlimited	Celebration Press
Mystery Stories	R	RF	Higgins, James	Houghton Mifflin
Nana's in the Plum Tree	M	RF	Pacific Literacy	Pacific Learning
Nana's Kitchen	J	RF	Walton, Darwin McBeth	Steck-Vaughn
Nannies for Hire	M	RF	Hest, Amy	William Morrow
Nasty, Stinky Sneakers	R	RF	Bunting, Eve	HarperTrophy
Nate the Great	K	RF	Sharmat, Marjorie Weinman	Bantam Doubleday Dell
Nate the Great and Me	K	RF	Sharmat, Marjorie Weinman	Random House
Nate the Great and the Boring Beach Bag	K	RF	Sharmat, Marjorie Weinman	Bantam Doubleday Dell
Nate the Great and the Crunchy Christmas	K	RF	Sharmat, Marjorie Weinman	Bantam Doubleday Dell
Nate the Great and the Fishy Prize	K	RF	Sharmat, Marjorie Weinman	Bantam Doubleday Dell
Nate the Great and the Halloween Hunt	K	RF	Sharmat, Marjorie Weinman	Bantam Doubleday Dell

Title	Level	Genre	Author/Series	Publisher/Distributor
Nate the Great and the Lost List	K	RF	Sharmat, Marjorie Weinman	Bantam Doubleday Dell
Nate the Great and the Missing Key	K	RF	Sharmat, Marjorie Weinman	Bantam Doubleday Dell
Nate the Great and the Mushy Valentine	K	RF	Sharmat, Marjorie Weinman	Bantam Doubleday Dell
Nate the Great and the Musical Note	K	RF	Sharmat, Marjorie Weinman	Bantam Doubleday Dell
Nate the Great and the Phony Clue	K	RF	Sharmat, Marjorie Weinman	Bantam Doubleday Dell
Nate the Great and the Pillowcase	K	RF	Sharmat, Marjorie Weinman	Bantam Doubleday Dell
Nate the Great and the Snowy Trail	K	RF	Sharmat, Marjorie Weinman	Bantam Doubleday Dell
Nate the Great and the Sticky Case	K	RF	Sharmat, Marjorie Weinman	Bantam Doubleday Dell
Nate the Great and the Stolen Base	K	RF	Sharmat, Marjorie Weinman	Bantam Doubleday Dell
Nate the Great and the Tardy Tortoise	K	RF	Sharmat, Marjorie Weinman	Bantam Doubleday Dell
Nate the Great Goes Down in the Dumps	K	RF	Sharmat, Marjorie Weinman	Bantam Doubleday Dell
Nate the Great Goes Undercover	K	RF	Sharmat, Marjorie Weinman	Bantam Doubleday Dell
Nate the Great Saves the King of Sweden	K	RF	Sharmat, Marjorie Weinman	Bantam Doubleday Dell
Nate the Great Stalks Stupidweed	K	RF	Sharmat, Marjorie Weinman	Bantam Doubleday Dell
Nelson is Kidnapped	K	RF	PM Story Books -Silver	Rigby
Never Hit a Ghost with a Baseball Bat	O	RF	Clifford, Eth	Scholastic
Never Say Quit	T	RF	Wallace, Bill	Pocket Books
New Bike, The	J	RF	Sunshine	Wright Group/McGraw Hill
New Kid in Town	N	RF	Kroll, Stephen	Avon Camelot
New School, The	J	RF	City Kids	Rigby
Newspaper Kids, The	Q	RF	Phillips, Juanita	Harper Collins
Next Stop, New York City!	O	RF	Giff, Patricia Reilly	Bantam Doubleday Dell
Next Time I Will	K	RF	Bank Street	Bantam Doubleday Dell
Nibble, Nibble, Jenny Archer	M	RF	Conford, Ellen	Little, Brown & Co.
Nice New Neighbors	K	RF	Brandenberg, Franz	Scholastic
Night Flyers, The	W	RF	Jones, Elizabeth McDavid	Pleasant Company
Night of the Chupacabras	Y	RF	Lee, Marie G.	Avon Camelot
Night of the Twisters	U	RF	Ruckman, Ivy	HarperTrophy
Night Swimmers, The	S	RF	Byars, Betsy	Dell
Night Without Stars, A	S	RF	Howe, James	Aladdin
Nightmare	M	RF	Pulford, Elizabeth	Rigby
Nightmare Mountain	X	RF	Kehret, Peg	Puffin Books
Nine Man Tree	Z	RF	Peck, Robert Newton	Random House
Ninjas Don't Bake Pumpkin Pies	M	RF	Dadey, D. & Jones, M. T.	Scholastic
Nissa's Place	Y	RF	LaFaye, A.	Simon & Schuster
No Arm in Left Field	M	RF	Christopher, Matt	Little, Brown & Co.
No Copycats Allowed!	L	RF	Graves, Bonnie	Hyperion
No Dinner for Sally	J	RF	Literacy 2000	Rigby
No Dogs Allowed	O	RF	Cutler, Jane	Farrar, Straus and Giroux
No Fighting, No Biting!	K	RF	Minarik, Else Holmelund	HarperTrophy
No Laughing Matter (Ragged Island Mysteries)	Q	RF	Bensen, Rosie	Wright Group/McGraw Hill
No One is Going to Nashville	O	RF	Jukes, Mavis	Alfred A. Knopf
No Room For a Dog	N	RF	Nichols, Joan Kane	Hearst
No Trouble at All!	M	RF	Powell, Joyce	Rigby
Nobody's Family Is Going to Change	U	RF	Fitzhugh, Louise	Farrar, Straus and Giroux
Noonday Friends, The	R	RF	Stolz, Mary	Scholastic
Norma Jean, Jumping Bean	J	RF	Cole, Joanna	Random House
Nose for Trouble, A	P	RF	Wilson, Nancy Hope	Avon
Not That I Care	V	RF	Vail, Rachel	Scholastic
Not What It Seems	P	RF	Wildcats	Wright Group/McGraw Hill
Not-Just-Anybody Family, The	O	RF	Byars, Betsy	Dell
Not-So-Dead Fish and Other Cases, The	O	RF	Simon, Seymour	Avon
Not-So-Perfect Rosie	N	RF	Giff, Patricia Reilly	The Penguin Group
Nothing But The Truth	U	RF	Avi	Hearst
Nothing But Trouble, Trouble, Trouble	Q	RF	Hermes, Patricia	Scholastic
Nothing to Be Scared About	K	RF	Sunshine	Wright Group/McGraw Hill
Nothing's Fair in Fifth Grade	R	RF	DeClements, Barthe	Scholastic
Obadiah the Bold	N	RF	Turkle, Brinton	The Penguin Group
Obee & Mungedeech	T	RF	Martin, Trude	Aladdin
Obstacles in Our Way	L	RF	McAlister, Margaret	Rigby

Title	Level	Genre	Author/Series	Publisher/Distributor
Odds on Oliver	P	RF	Greene, Carol	Puffin Books
Of Mice and Men	Z	RF	Steinbeck, John	The Penguin Group
Off and Running	S	RF	Soto, Gary	Dell
Oh Boy, Boston!	O	RF	Giff, Patricia Reilly	Bantam Doubleday Dell
Oh, Brother	P	RF	Wilson, Johnnice M.	Scholastic
Ola Shakes It Up	T	RF	Hyppolite, Joanne	Random House
Old Bones	M	RF	Sunshine	Wright Group/McGraw Hill
Old Friends	M	RF	Literacy 2000	Rigby
Old Man and the Bear, The	M	RF	Hanel, Wolfram	North-South Books
Old Red Rocking Chair, The	M	RF	Root, Phyllis	Scholastic
Old Yeller	V	RF	Gipson, Fred	Scholastic
On Guard	R	RF	Napoli, Donna Jo	Puffin Books
On My Honor	S	RF	Bauer, Marion Dane	Bantam Doubleday Dell
On The Far Side Of The Mountain	V	RF	George, Jean Craighead	Puffin Books
On-Line Spaceman and Other Cases, The	O	RF	Simon, Seymour	Avon
Once I Was a Plum Tree	Q	RF	Hurwitz, Johanna	Beech Tree Books
Once Upon a Time in Junior High	U	RF	Norment, Lisa	Scholastic
One Bad Thing About Father, The	M	RF	Monjo, F.N.	HarperTrophy
One Bird	Y	RF	Mori, Kyoko	Ballantine Books
One Fat Summer	Y	RF	Lipsyte, Robert	Harper Collins
One Hundredth Thing about Caroline, The	R	RF	Lowry, Lois	Bantam Doubleday Dell
One in the Middle Is the Green Kangaroo, The	M	RF	Blume, Judy	Bantam Doubleday Dell
One Potato, Tu	T	RF	Pearson, Gayle	Scholastic
One Thing I'm Good At	R	RF	Williams, Karen Lynn	William Morrow
One Who Came Back, The	X	RF	Mazzio, Joann	Houghton Mifflin
One-Eyed Cat	S	RF	Fox, Paula	Bantam Doubleday Dell
Onion Sundaes	L	RF	Adler, David A.	Random House
Onion Tears	Q	RF	Kidd, Diana	William Morrow
Orca Song	K	RF	Armour	Scholastic
Ordinary Miracles	Y	RF	Tolan, Stephanie S.	Morrow
Oscar & Tatiana	N	RF	Literacy 2000	Rigby
Otherwise Known As Sheila the Great	R	RF	Blume, Judy	Bantam Doubleday Dell
Otis Spofford	O	RF	Cleary, Beverly	Avon
Ouch!	L	RF	Noonan, Diana	Dominie Press
Our Baby	J	RF	Foundations	Wright Group/McGraw Hill
Our New Principal	K	RF	City Kids	Rigby
Our Old Friend, Bear	J	RF	PM Story Books -Silver	Rigby
Outrageously Alice	U	RF	Naylor, Phyllis Reynolds	Aladdin
Outside Dog, The	K	RF	Pomerantz, Charlotte	HarperTrophy
Outsiders, The	Z	RF	Hinton, S.E.	The Penguin Group
Owl in the Office	Q	RF	Baglio, Ben M.	Scholastic
Owls in the Garden	L	RF	PM Gold	Rigby
P.S. Longer Letter Later	U	RF	Danziger, P. & Martin, A.	Scholastic
Pack 109	J	RF	Thaler, Mike	Scholastic
Paint Brush Kid, The	M	RF	Bulla, Clyde Robert	Random House
Pajama Party	M	RF	Hest, Amy	William Morrow
Paper Birds, The	K	RF	Foundations	Wright Group/McGraw Hill
Paper Route, The	K	RF	New Way Green	Steck-Vaughn
Parachutes	J	RF	Storyteller-Moon Rising	Wright Group/McGraw Hill
Parakeet Girl, The	J	RF	Sadler, Marilyn	Random House
Parents' Night Fright	K	RF	Levy, Elizabeth	Scholastic
Park's Quest	U	RF	Paterson, Katherine	Puffin Books
Party Games	J	RF	Foundations	Wright Group/McGraw Hill
Paru Has a Bath	J	RF	Pacific Literacy	Pacific Learning
Patches	M	RF	Szymanski, Lois	Avon Camelot
Pearl, The	Z	RF	Steinbeck, John	Penguin Books
Pee Wee Scouts: A Big Box of Memories,	L	RF	Delton, Judy	Bantam Doubleday Dell
Pee Wee Scouts: Bad, Bad Bunnies	L	RF	Delton, Judy	Bantam, Doubleday, Dell
Pee Wee Scouts: Blue Skies, French Fries	L	RF	Delton, Judy	Bantam Doubleday Dell
Pee Wee Scouts: Cookies and Crutches	L	RF	Delton, Judy	Bantam Doubleday Dell

Title	Level	Genre	Author/Series	Publisher/Distributor
Pee Wee Scouts: Fishy Wishes	L	RF	Delton, Judy	Bantam Doubleday Dell
Pee Wee Scouts: Greedy Groundhogs	L	RF	Delton, Judy	Bantam Doubleday Dell
Pee Wee Scouts: Grumpy Pumpkins	L	RF	Delton, Judy	Bantam Doubleday Dell
Pee Wee Scouts: Halloween Helpers	L	RF	Delton, Judy	Bantam Doubleday Dell
Pee Wee Scouts: Lights, Action, Land-Ho!	L	RF	Delton, Judy	Bantam Doubleday Dell
Pee Wee Scouts: Lucky Dog Days	L	RF	Delton, Judy	Bantam Doubleday Dell
Pee Wee Scouts: Moans and Groans and Dinosaur Bones	L	RF	Delton, Judy	Bantam Doubleday Dell
Pee Wee Scouts: Molly for Mayor	L	RF	Delton, Judy	Bantam Doubleday Dell
Pee Wee Scouts on First	L	RF	Delton, Judy	Bantam Doubleday Dell
Pee Wee Scouts on Parade	L	RF	Delton, Judy	Bantam Doubleday Dell
Pee Wee Scouts on Skis	L	RF	Delton, Judy	Bantam Doubleday Dell
Pee Wee Scouts: Peanut-Butter Pilgrims	L	RF	Delton, Judy	Bantam Doubleday Dell
Pee Wee Scouts: Pedal Power	L	RF	Delton, Judy	Bantam Doubleday Dell
Pee Wee Scouts: Piles of Pets	L	RF	Delton, Judy	Bantam Doubleday Dell
Pee Wee Scouts: Rosy Noses, Freezing Toes	L	RF	Delton, Judy	Bantam Doubleday Dell
Pee Wee Scouts: Sky Babies	L	RF	Delton, Judy	Bantam Doubleday Dell
Pee Wee Scouts: Sonny's Secret	L	RF	Delton, Judy	Bantam Doubleday Dell
Pee Wee Scouts: Spring Sprouts	L	RF	Delton, Judy	Bantam Doubleday Dell
Pee Wee Scouts: Teeny Weeny Zucchinis	L	RF	Delton, Judy	Bantam Doubleday Dell
Pee Wee Scouts: The Pee Wee Jubilee	L	RF	Delton, Judy	Bantam Doubleday Dell
Pee Wee Scouts: The Pooped Troop	L	RF	Delton, Judy	Bantam Doubleday Dell
Pee Wee Scouts: Trash Bash	L	RF	Delton, Judy	Bantam Doubleday Dell
Pee Wee Scouts: Tricks and Treats	L	RF	Delton, Judy	Bantam Doubleday Dell
Penny Changes the Day, A	J	RF	Fetty, Margaret	Steck-Vaughn
Perfect Pony, A	O	RF	Szymanski, Lois	Avon Camelot
Peril in the Bessledorf Parachute Factory	U	RF	Naylor, Phyllis Reynolds	Atheneum Books
Pet Parade	O	RF	Giff, Patricia Reilly	Bantam Doubleday Dell
Pet Sitters Plus Five	L	RF	Springstubb, Tricia	Scholastic
Peter the Pumpkin-Eater	M	RF	Scott, Janine	Rigby
Phan's Diary	N	RF	PM Ruby	Rigby
Philip Hall Likes Me. I Reckon Maybe.	Y	RF	Greene, Bette	Puffin Books
Phoenix Rising	W	RF	Hesse, Karen	Penguin Group
Photographic Memory	O	RF	PM Ruby	Rigby
Picked for the Team	L	RF	PM Gold	Rigby
Picking Up Papers	K	RF	City Kids	Rigby
Pickle Puss	L	RF	Giff, Patricia Reilly	Bantam Doubleday Dell
Pierre	K	RF	Sendak, Maurice	Scholastic
Piglet in a Playpen	Q	RF	Baglio, Ben M.	Scholastic
Pigman's Legacy, The	Z	RF	Zindel, Paul	Harper & Row
Pile in Pete's Room, The	K	RF	Sunshine	Wright Group/McGraw Hill
Pinballs, The	S	RF	Byars, Betsy	HarperTrophy
Pine Hollow: Changing Leads	W	RF	Bryant, Bonnie	Bantam Doubleday Dell
Pine Hollow: Conformation Faults	W	RF	Bryant, Bonnie	Bantam Doubleday Dell
Pine Hollow: Reining In	W	RF	Bryant, Bonnie	Bantam Doubleday Dell
Pine Hollow: The Long Ride	W	RF	Bryant, Bonnie	Bantam Doubleday Dell
Pine Hollow: The Trail Home	W	RF	Bryant, Bonnie	Bantam Doubleday Dell
Pinky and Rex	L	RF	Howe, James	Simon & Schuster
Pinky and Rex and the Bully	L	RF	Howe, James	Simon & Schuster
Pinky and Rex and the Double-Dad Weekend	L	RF	Howe, James	Simon & Schuster
Pinky and Rex and the Mean Old Witch	L	RF	Howe, James	Simon & Schuster
Pinky and Rex and the New Baby	L	RF	Howe, James	Simon & Schuster
Pinky and Rex and the New Neighbors	L	RF	Howe, James	Simon & Schuster
Pinky and Rex and the Perfect Pumpkin	L	RF	Howe, James	Simon & Schuster
Pinky and Rex and the School Play	L	RF	Howe, James	Simon & Schuster
Pinky and Rex and the Spelling Bee	L	RF	Howe, James	Simon & Schuster
Pinky and Rex Get Married	L	RF	Howe, James	Simon & Schuster
Pinky and Rex Go to Camp	L	RF	Howe, James	Aladdin
Pirate's Promise	N	RF	Bulla, Clyde Robert	HarperTrophy
Pitching Trouble	N	RF	Kroll, Stephen	Avon Camelot

Title	Level	Genre	Author/Series	Publisher/Distributor
Place to Call Home, A	Y	RF	Koller, Jackie French	Aladdin
Plain Girl	Q	RF	Sorensen, Virginia	Harcourt Brace
Planet of Junior Brown, The	Z	RF	Hamilton, Virginia	Aladdin
Playing Favorites	N	RF	Kroll, Steven	Avon Camelot
Please Don't Be Mine, Julie Valentine!	R	RF	Strasser, Todd	Scholastic
Pocket Full of Acorns, A	L	RF	Beames, Michael	Dominie Press
Ponies at the Point	Q	RF	Baglio, Ben M.	Scholastic
Pony Named Shawney, A	P	RF	Small, Mary	Mondo
Pony on the Porch	Q	RF	Baglio, Ben M.	Scholastic
Pony Pals: A Pony for Keeps	O	RF	Betancourt, Jeanne	Scholastic
Pony Pals: A Pony in Trouble	O	RF	Betancourt, Jeanne	Scholastic
Pony Pals: Detective Pony	O	RF	Betancourt, Jeanne	Scholastic
Pony Pals: Don't Hurt My Pony	O	RF	Betancourt, Jeanne	Scholastic
Pony Pals: Give Me Back My Pony	O	RF	Betancourt, Jeanne	Scholastic
Pony Pals: Good-bye Pony	O	RF	Betancourt, Jeanne	Scholastic
Pony Pals: I Want a Pony	O	RF	Betancourt, Jeanne	Scholastic
Pony Pals: Keep Out, Pony!	O	RF	Betancourt, Jeanne	Scholastic
Pony Pals: Pony to the Rescue	O	RF	Betancourt, Jeanne	Scholastic
Pony Pals, Pony-Sitters	O	RF	Betancourt, Jeanne	Scholastic
Pony Pals: Runaway Pony	O	RF	Betancourt, Jeanne	Scholastic
Pony Pals: The Blind Pony	O	RF	Betancourt, Jeanne	Scholastic
Pony Pals: The Girl Who Hated Ponies	O	RF	Betancourt, Jeanne	Scholastic
Pony Pals: The Lonely Pony	O	RF	Betancourt, Jeanne	Scholastic
Pony Pals: Too Many Ponies	O	RF	Betancourt, Jeanne	Scholastic
Pony Parade	O	RF	Baglio, Ben M.	Scholastic
Pony Tails: Jasmine and the Jumping Pony	P	RF	Bryant, Bonnie	Bantam Doubleday Dell
Pony Tails: Jasmine's Christmas Ride	P	RF	Bryant, Bonnie	Bantam Doubleday Dell
Pony Tails: May Takes the Lead	P	RF	Bryant, Bonnie	Bantam Doubleday Dell
Pony Trouble	L	RF	Gasque, Dale Blackwell	Hyperion
Poopsie Pomerantz Pick Up Your Feet	P	RF	Giff, Patricia Reilly	Dell
Poor Girl, Rich Girl	T	RF	Wilson, Johnniece Marshall	Language for Learning Assoc.
Popcorn Shop, The	J	RF	Low, Alice	Scholastic
Postcard Pest, The	M	RF	Giff, Patricia Reilly	Bantam Doubleday Dell
Postman Pete	J	RF	Book Shop	Mondo
Potato	N	RF	Peirce, Robin	Wright Group/McGraw Hill
Powder Puff Puzzle, The	L	RF	Giff, Patricia Reilly	Bantam Doubleday Dell
Preacher's Boy	T	RF	Paterson, Katherine	Houghton Mifflin
Present From Aunt Skidoo, The	M	RF	Literacy 2000	Rigby
Pretty Good Magic	J	RF	Dubowski, C. E. & Dubowski, M.	Random House
Pride of the Rockets	N	RF	Kroll, Stephen	Avon Camelot
Prince Amos	R	RF	Paulsen, Gary	Bantam Doubleday Dell
Princess Euphorbia	N	RF	SupaDoopers	Sundance
Princess Josie's Pets	L	RF	Macdonald, Maryann	Hyperion
Priscilla and the Dinosaurs	L	RF	Sunshine	Wright Group/McGraw Hill
Private Notebook of Katie Roberts, Age 11, The	P	RF	Hest, Amy	Candlewick Press
Prize for Purry, A	K	RF	Literacy 2000	Rigby
Promise Me the Moon	V	RF	Barnes, Joyce Annette Barnes	The Penguin Group
Puppies in the Pantry	Q	RF	Baglio, Ben M.	Scholastic
Puppy Love	N	RF	Duffey, Betsy	Puffin Books
Puppy Puzzle	O	RF	Baglio, Ben M.	Scholastic
Purple Climbing Days	M	RF	Giff, Patricia Reilly	Bantam Doubleday Dell
Purple Walrus and Other Perfect Pets	O	RF	Wildcats	Wright Group/McGraw Hill
Qillak	M	RF	Jensen, Ned	Wright Group/McGraw Hill
Quake!	T	RF	Cottonwood, Joe	Language for Learning Assoc.
Queen of the Pool	N	RF	PM Emerald	Rigby
Rabbit Race	O	RF	Baglio, Ben M.	Scholastic
Rabble Starkey	T	RF	Lowry, Lois	Bantam Doubleday Dell
Rachel to the Rescue	O	RF	SupaDoopers	Sundance
Rainbow Solution, The	N	RF	Literacy 2000	Rigby
Rainbows All Around	M	RF	Hardin, Suzanne	Pacific Learning

Title	Level	Genre	Author/Series	Publisher/Distributor
Ramona and Her Father	O	RF	Cleary, Beverly	Avon
Ramona and Her Mother	O	RF	Cleary, Beverly	Avon
Ramona Forever	O	RF	Cleary, Beverly	Hearst
Ramona Quimby, Age 8	O	RF	Cleary, Beverly	Hearst
Ramona the Brave	O	RF	Cleary, Beverly	Hearst
Ramona the Pest	O	RF	Cleary, Beverly	Avon
Rats!	O	RF	Cutler, Jane	Farrar, Straus and Giroux
Ready, Set, Go!	K	RF	Pacific Literacy	Pacific Learning
Red and Blue Mittens	M	RF	Reading Unlimited	Celebration Press
Red Dog	U	RF	Wallace, Bill	Simon & Schuster
Red Egg and Ginger	K	RF	SooHoo, Suzanne & Patrick	Rigby
Red Ribbon Rosie	M	RF	Marzollo, Jean	Random House
Red-Tailed Hawk, The	L	RF	Books For Young Learners	Richard C. Owen
Refugees, The	P	RF	Marriott, Janice	Pacific Learning
Rent a Third Grader	O	RF	Hiller, B.B.	Scholastic
Report To the Principal's Office	U	RF	Spinelli, Jerry	Scholastic
Rescue!	J	RF	Sunshine	Wright Group/McGraw Hill
Rescue	O	RF	Wildcats	Wright Group/McGraw Hill
Rescue, The	L	RF	Pacific Learning	Pacific Learning
Return of the Great Brain, The	T	RF	Fitzgerald, John D.	Dell
Return of the Home Run Kid	N	RF	Christopher, Matt	Scholastic
Return of the Third-Grade Ghosthunters, The	M	RF	Maccarone, Grace	Scholastic
Revenge of the Mummy	P	RF	Parker, A.E.	Scholastic
Ribsy	O	RF	Cleary, Beverly	Hearst
Riddle of The Red Purse, The	L	RF	Giff, Patricia Reilly	Bantam Doubleday Dell
Riding to Craggy Rock	J	RF	PM Turquoise	Rigby
Right or Wrong?	O	RF	Wildcats	Wright Group/McGraw Hill
Right Place for Jupiter, The	K	RF	PM Story Books -Silver	Rigby
Righteous Revenge of Artemis Bonner, The	U	RF	Myers, Walter Dean	HarperTrophy
Rip-Roaring Russell	M	RF	Hurwitz, Johanna	The Penguin Group
Ripeka's Carving	J	RF	Literacy 2000	Rigby
Riptide	O	RF	Weller, Frances Ward	Putnam & Grosset
River Rapids Ride, The	L	RF	Sunshine	Wright Group/McGraw Hill
River Rats	O	RF	Belcher, Angie	Pacific Learning
River Runners	M	RF	Belcher, Angie	Rigby
River, The	R	RF	Paulsen, Gary	Dell
Robber, The	M	RF	Sunshine	Wright Group/McGraw Hill
Roller Skates!	J	RF	Calmenson, Stephanie	Scholastic
Rollerama	N	RF	SupaDoopers	Sundance
Rosa's Tonsils	K	RF	Foundations	Wright Group/McGraw Hill
Roses for Renee	J	RF	Evangeline Nicholas Collection	Wright Group/McGraw Hill
Rosie's Big City Ballet	N	RF	Giff, Patricia Reilly	The Penguin Group
Rosie's Nutcracker Dreams	N	RF	Giff, Patricia Reilly	The Penguin Group
Rosie's Story	L	RF	Book Shop	Mondo
Rotating Rollerblades and Other Cases, The	O	RF	Simon, Seymour	Avon
Row, Row, Row Your Boat	J	RF	Bank Street	Bantam Doubleday Dell
Royal Baby-Sitters, The	J	RF	Sunshine	Wright Group/McGraw Hill
Ruby the Copycat	K	RF	Rathman, Peggy	Scholastic
Russell and Elisa	M	RF	Hurwitz, Johanna	The Penguin Group
Russell Rides Again	M	RF	Hurwitz, Johanna	The Penguin Group
Russell Sprouts	M	RF	Hurwitz, Johanna	The Penguin Group
Ryan's Dog Ringo	P	RF	Gibson, Marie	Rigby
Sable	O	RF	Hesse, Karen	Henry Holt & Co.
Sadie and the Snowman	L	RF	Morgan, Allen	Scholastic
Safe Return	Q	RF	Dexter, Catherine	Candlewick Press
Salty Dog	L	RF	Rand, Gloria	Henry Holt & Co.
Sam King and Little Bull	L	RF	Wilson, Trevor	Dominie Press
Sam's Big Clean-up	K	RF	Windmill Books	Rigby
Sam's Glasses	M	RF	Literacy 2000	Rigby
Sam's Solution	K	RF	Literacy 2000	Rigby

Title	Level	Genre	Author/Series	Publisher/Distributor
Samantha Saves the Day	Q	RF	The American Girls Collection	Pleasant Company
Samantha's Surprise	Q	RF	The American Girls Collection	Pleasant Company
Sandwich Hero, The	K	RF	Literacy 2000	Rigby
Sandy's Suitcase	K	RF	Edwards, Elsy	SRA/McGraw-Hill
Saturnalia	W	RF	Fleischman, Paul	Harper Collins
Saving the Park	N	RF	Wilson, Sarah	Pacific Learning
Say "Cheese"	L	RF	Giff, Patricia Reilly	Bantam Doubleday Dell
Say Hola, Sarah	N	RF	Giff, Patricia Reilly	Bantam Doubleday Dell
Scaredy Dog	K	RF	Thomas, Jane Resh	Hyperion
Scary Day, The	N	RF	Bennett, Jean	Pacific Learning
Scary Spiders!	J	RF	Sunshine	Wright Group/McGraw Hill
Schernoff Discoveries, The	T	RF	Paulsen, Gary	Dell
School Mural, The	L	RF	Pair-It Books	Steck-Vaughn
School Vacation	J	RF	City Kids	Rigby
School's Out	N	RF	Hurwitz, Johanna	Scholastic
Schoolyard Mystery, The	L	RF	Levy, Elizabeth	Scholastic
Science Fair Surprise, The	Q	RF	Burke, Melissa Blackwell	Steck-Vaughn
Scorpions	Z	RF	Myers, Walter Dean	HarperTrophy
Scrappers No Easy Out	Q	RF	Hughes, Dean	Aladdin
Scrappers No Fear	Q	RF	Hughes, Dean	Aladdin
Scruffy	K	RF	Parish, Peggy	HarperTrophy
Sea Monsters Don't Ride Motorcycles	M	RF	Dadey, D. & Jones, M. T.	Scholastic
Sea Star	R	RF	Henry, Marguerite	Aladdin
Seat Belt Song, The	K	RF	PM Turquoise	Rigby
Seawall	O	RF	PM Ruby	Rigby
Second Chance	N	RF	Kroll, Stephen	Avon Camelot
Second Grade-Friends Again!	M	RF	Cohen, Miriam	Scholastic
Second Story Sally	N	RF	SupaDoopers	Sundance
Second-Grade Friends	M	RF	Cohen, Miriam	Scholastic
Second-Grade Star	N	RF	Alberts, Nancy	Scholastic
Secondhand Star	L	RF	Macdonald, Maryann	Hyperion
Secret at the Polk Street School, The	M	RF	Giff, Patricia Reilly	Bantam Doubleday Dell
Secret Garden, The	U	RF	Burnett, Frances H.	Scholastic
Secret Hideaway, The	K	RF	PM Gold	Rigby
Secret of the Seal, The	P	RF	Davis, Deborah	Alfred A. Knopf
Secret Secret Passage, The	P	RF	Parker, A. E.	Scholastic
Secret Silver Lining, A (Ragged Island Mysteries)	Q	RF	Bensen, Rosie	Wright Group/McGraw Hill
Secret, The	N	RF	PM Emerald	Rigby
See You in Second Grade	J	RF	Cohen, Miriam	Bantam Doubleday Dell
See You Tomorrow, Charles	J	RF	Cohen, Miriam	Bantam Doubleday Dell
Seedfolks	W	RF	Fleishman, Paul	HarperTrophy
Seeing the School Doctor	K	RF	City Kids	Rigby
Selena Who Speaks in Silence	J	RF	Evangeline Nicholas Collection	Wright Group/McGraw Hill
Seven Kisses in a Row	O	RF	MacLachlan, Patricia	Harper Collins
Seven Treasure Hunts, The	M	RF	Byars, Betsy	HarperTrophy
Seventh Grade Weirdo	S	RF	Wardlaw, Lee	Scholastic
Shadow of a Bull	U	RF	Wojciechowska, Maia	Simon & Schuster
Shadow Over Second	M	RF	Christopher, Matt	Little, Brown & Co.
Shaggy Sheep, The	J	RF	Kratky, Lada Josefa	Hampton-Brown
Shark in School	N	RF	Giff, Patricia Reilly	Bantam Doubleday Dell
Sheepdog in the Snow	Q	RF	Baglio, Ben M.	Scholastic
Shiloh	R	RF	Naylor, Phyllis Reynolds	Bantam Doubleday Dell
Shingo's Grandfather	K	RF	Sunshine	Wright Group/McGraw Hill
Shining Blue Planet and Other Cases, The	O	RF	Simon, Seymour	Avon
Ship in a Bottle, The	M	RF	Herman, Emily	Wright Group/McGraw Hill
Shipwreck Saturday	K	RF	Cosby, Bill	Scholastic
Shoeshine Girl	N	RF	Bulla, Clyde Robert	HarperTrophy
Shooting Star, The	M	RF	PM Gold	Rigby
Shooting Stars	R	RF	Costello, Emily	Dell
Shortest Kid in the World	K	RF	Bliss, Corinne Demas	Random House

Title	Level	Genre	Author/Series	Publisher/Distributor
Shortstop from Tokyo	M	RF	Christopher, Matt	Little, Brown & Co.
Shorty	M	RF	Literacy 2000	Rigby
Show and Tell	K	RF	City Kids	Rigby
Show Me a Snake Hole	L	RF	Frederick, Shirley	Hampton-Brown
Show Time at the Polk Street School	M	RF	Giff, Patricia Reilly	Bantam Doubleday Dell
Show-and-Tell	J	RF	Foundations	Wright Group/McGraw Hill
Sidetrack Sam	K	RF	Literacy 2000	Rigby
Sidewalk Story	N	RF	Mathis, Sharon Bell	The Penguin Group
Sign of the Chrysanthemum, The	U	RF	Paterson, Katherine	HarperTrophy
Silent to the Bone	V	RF	Konigsburg, E. L.	Atheneum
Silent World, A	L	RF	Literacy 2000	Rigby
Silly Willy	M	RF	Book Shop	Mondo
Silver	N	RF	Whelan, Gloria	Random House
Silver and Prince	L	RF	PM Story Books -Silver	Rigby
Simon's Big Challenge	Q	RF	Day, Mark	Steck-Vaughn
Sister	W	RF	Greenfield, Eloise	Harper Collins
Sister Sister Homegirl on the Range	S	RF	Quin-Harkin, Janet	Pocket Books
Sixteen Short Stories by Outstanding Writers	Z	RF	Gallo, Donald R.	Dell
Sixth Grade Can Really Kill You	S	RF	DeClements, Barthe	Scholastic
Sixth Grade Secrets	S	RF	Sachar, Louis	Scholastic
Sixth-Grade Sleepover	R	RF	Bunting, Eve	Scholastic
Skateboard Tough	M	RF	Christopher, Matt	Little, Brown & Co.
Skates of Uncle Richard, The	P	RF	Fenner, Carol	Random House
Skating at Rainbow Lake	J	RF	PM Story Books -Silver	Rigby
Skinny-Bones	O	RF	Park, Barbara	Random House
Skirt, The	N	RF	Soto, Gary	Bantam Doubleday Dell
Sky Dogs	U	RF	Yolen, Jane	Harcourt Brace
Sky Rider	O	RF	Belcher, Angie	Pacific Learning
Sky's the Limit, The	Q	RF	Wildcats	Wright Group/McGraw Hill
Slam!	W	RF	Myers, Walter Dean	Scholastic
Slam Dunk Saturday	M	RF	Marzollo, Jean	Random House
Slim Shorty and the Mules	L	RF	Reading Unlimited	Celebration Press
Slither McCreep and His Brother, Joe	K	RF	Johnston, Tony	Harcourt Brace
Slump, The	N	RF	Kroll, Stephen	Avon Camelot
Smallest Cow in the World, The	K	RF	Paterson, Katherine	HarperTrophy
Smasher	O	RF	King-Smith, Dick	Random House
Smile, The	K	RF	Read Alongs	Rigby
Smoky the Cow Horse	S	RF	James, Will	Scholastic
Snaggle Doodles	M	RF	Giff, Patricia Reilly	Bantam Doubleday Dell
Snake!	M	RF	Sunshine	Wright Group/McGraw Hill
Snowball War, The	K	RF	Chardiet, Bernice	Scholastic
Soccer Cousins	K	RF	Marzollo, Jean	Scholastic
Soccer Mania!	M	RF	Tamar, Erika	Random House
Soccer Sam	M	RF	Marzollo, Jean	Random House
Soccer Stars, Best Friend Face-off	R	RF	Costello, Emily	Dell
Socks	O	RF	Cleary, Beverly	Avon
Solitary Blue, A	W	RF	Voigt, Cynthia	Scholastic
Solo Flyer	L	RF	PM Gold	Rigby
Solo Girl	M	RF	Pinkey, Andrea Davis	Hyperion
Some Dog!	O	RF	PM Ruby	Rigby
Some Friend	R	RF	Warner, Sally	Alfred A. Knopf
Someday a Tree	P	RF	Bunting, Eve	Clarion
Someday Cyril	N	RF	Gershator, Phillis	Mondo
Someone is Following Pip Ramsey	N	RF	Roy, Ron	Random House
Someone to Count On	T	RF	Hermes, Patricia	Language for Learning Assoc.
Something Everyone Needs	J	RF	Ready Readers	Pearson Learning
Something Noise, The	J	RF	Windmill Books	Rigby
Something Queer at the Ball Park	N	RF	Levy, Elizabeth	Bantam Doubleday Dell
Something Queer at the Haunted School	N	RF	Levy, Elizabeth	Bantam Doubleday Dell
Something Queer at the Lemonade Stand	N	RF	Levy, Elizabeth	Bantam Doubleday Dell

Title	Level	Genre	Author/Series	Publisher/Distributor
Something Queer at the Library	N	RF	Levy, Elizabeth	Bantam Doubleday Dell
Something Queer at the Scary Movie	N	RF	Levy, Elizabeth	Hyperion
Something Queer in Outer Space	N	RF	Levy, Elizabeth	Hyperion
Something Queer in the Cafeteria	N	RF	Levy, Elizabeth	Hyperion
Something Queer in the Wild West	N	RF	Levy, Elizabeth	Hyperion
Something Queer Is Going On	N	RF	Levy, Elizabeth	Bantam Doubleday Dell
Something Queer on Vacation	N	RF	Levy, Elizabeth	Bantam Doubleday Dell
Something Upstairs	T	RF	Avi	Language for Learning Assoc.
Something Very Sorry	R	RF	Bohlmeijer, Arno	Putnam & Grosset
Song Lee and the Hamster Hunt	L	RF	Kline, Suzy	The Penguin Group
Song Lee and the Leech Man	L	RF	Kline, Suzy	The Penguin Group
Song Lee In Room 2B	L	RF	Kline, Suzy	The Penguin Group
Song of the Giraffe	O	RF	Jacobs, Shannon K.	Little, Brown & Co.
Sons of Liberty	Y	RF	Griffin, Adele	Hyperion
Sounder	T	RF	Armstrong, William	Scholastic
Soup	Q	RF	Peck, Robert Newton	Bantam Doubleday Dell
Souvenirs	K	RF	Literacy 2000	Rigby
Space Junk	O	RF	Wildcats	Wright Group/McGraw Hill
Space Station Plot and Other Cases, The	O	RF	Simon, Seymour	Avon
Spanish Omelette	L	RF	PM Story Books -Silver	Rigby
Special Gifts	M	RF	Rylant, Cynthia	Aladdin
Special Present, The	L	RF	Cole, Sally	Wright Group/McGraw Hill
Special Ride, The	K	RF	PM Gold	Rigby
Spectacular Stone Soup	L	RF	Giff, Patricia Reilly	Yearling
Speeding Sleigh and Other Cases, The	O	RF	Simon, Seymour	Avon
Speedy Pasta and Other Cases, The	O	RF	Simon, Seymour	Avon
Speedy Snake and Other Cases, The	O	RF	Simon, Seymour	Avon
Speedy Soapbox Car and Other Cases, The	O	RF	Simon, Seymour	Avon
Spencer School Sleepover, The	M	RF	Floyd, Lucy	Wright Group/McGraw Hill
Spider Boy	R	RF	Fletcher, Ralph	Bantam Doubleday Dell
Spirit Quest	S	RF	Sharpe, Susan	Scholastic
Splatter	N	RF	Marriott, Janice	Pacific Learning
Spoiled Rotten	L	RF	DeClements, Barthe	Hyperion
Sports Mysteries: Case of the Basketball Video	P	RF	Edwards, T. J.	Scholastic
Sports Mysteries: Case Of The Missing Pitcher	P	RF	Edwards, T. J.	Scholastic
Spot's First Christmas	J	RF	Hill, Eric	Putnam
Spray-Paint Mystery, The	O	RF	Medearis, Angela Shelf	Scholastic
Spy in the Attic, The	M	RF	Scheffler, Ursel	North-South Books
Spy on Third Base, The	M	RF	Christopher, Matt	Little, Brown & Co.
Squirrels in the School	Q	RF	Baglio, Ben M.	Scholastic
Stacey and the Haunted Masquerade	O	RF	Martin, Ann M.	Scholastic
Stacey and the Missing Ring	O	RF	Martin, Ann M.	Scholastic
Stacey and the Mystery at the Mall	O	RF	Martin, Ann M.	Scholastic
Stacey and the Mystery Money	O	RF	Martin, Ann M.	Scholastic
Stacy Says Good-Bye	L	RF	Giff, Patricia Reilly	Bantam Doubleday Dell
Stage Fright	N	RF	Martin, Ann	Scholastic
Stan the Hot Dog Man	K	RF	Kessler, E.& L.	HarperTrophy
Standing in the Light	T	RF	Osborne, Mary Pope	Scholastic
Star	M	RF	Simon, Jo Ann	Random House
Star Fisher, The	S	RF	Yep, Lawrence	Scholastic
Star Thief	P	RF	Bilbrough, Norman	Pacific Learning
Starring First Grade	J	RF	Cohen, Miriam	Bantam Doubleday Dell
Starring Rosie	N	RF	Giff, Patricia Reilly	The Penguin Group
Stay Away from Simon!	O	RF	Carrick, Carol	Clarion
Staying Nine	O	RF	Conrad, Pam	HarperTrophy
Steal Away...to Freedom	Z	RF	Armstrong, Jennifer	Scholastic
Sticks and Stones, Bobbie Bones	P	RF	Roberts, Brenda C.	Scholastic
Stone Fox	P	RF	Gardiner, John Reynolds	Harper Trophy
Stories Huey Tells, The	N	RF	Cameron, Ann	Alfred A. Knopf
Stories Julian Tells, The	N	RF	Cameron, Ann	Alfred A. Knopf

Title	Level	Genre	Author/Series	Publisher/Distributor
Stories of the North	Y	RF	London, Jack	Scholastic
Storm in the Night	N	RF	Stolz, Mary	Harper Collins
Stormy, Misty's Foal	R	RF	Henry, Marguerite	Aladdin
Strange Clues and Other Cases, The	O	RF	Simon, Seymour	Avon
Strange Museum and Other Cases, The	O	RF	Simon, Seymour	Avon
Stranger at the Window	U	RF	Alcock, Vivien	Houghton Mifflin
Strawberry Hill	Y	RF	LaFaye, A.	Simon & Schuster
Stray, The	R	RF	King-Smith, Dick	Alfred A. Knopf
Streak, The	N	RF	Kroll, Stephen	Avon Camelot
Street Musicians	J	RF	Sunshine	Wright Group/McGraw Hill
Strider	R	RF	Cleary, Beverly	Harper Collins
Striped Ice Cream	N	RF	Lexau, Joan M.	Scholastic
Stumpy's Secret	P	RF	Hager, Mandy	Pacific Learning
Sub, The	P	RF	Peterson, P.J.	Puffin Books
Sugar Cakes Cyril	M	RF	Gershator, Phillis	Mondo
Suki and the Case of the Lost Bunnies	K	RF	Ready Readers	Pearson Learning
Sulky Simon	J	RF	Windmill Books	Rigby
Summer Camp	J	RF	City Kids	Rigby
Summer Life, A	Z	RF	Soto, Gary	Bantam Doubleday Dell
Summer of the Swans, The	U	RF	Byars, Betsy	The Penguin Group
Summer Sands	M	RF	Evangeline Nicholas Collection	Wright Group/McGraw Hill
Summer to Die, A	T	RF	Lowry, Lois	Dell
Sun & Spoon	R	RF	Henkes, Kevin	The Penguin Group
Sunburn	J	RF	City Kids	Rigby
Sunny-Side Up	M	RF	Giff, Patricia Reilly	Bantam Doubleday Dell
Super Amos	R	RF	Paulsen, Gary	Bantam Doubleday Dell
Super Supermarket Plan, The	J	RF	Home Connection Collection	Rigby
Super-tuned!	N	RF	PM Emerald	Rigby
Supercharged Infield	M	RF	Christopher, Matt	Little, Brown & Co.
Superfudge	Q	RF	Blume, Judy	Bantam Doubleday Dell
Supermarket Chase, The	L	RF	Sunshine	Wright Group/McGraw Hill
Supernova	N	RF	PM Ruby	Rigby
Surf's Up	P	RF	Wildcats	Wright Group/McGraw Hill
Surprise Dinner, The	L	RF	PM Gold	Rigby
Surprise Party, The	J	RF	Proger, Annabelle	Random House
Survive!	Q	RF	Wildcats	Wright Group/McGraw Hill
Sweet Memories Still	Q	RF	Kinsey-Warnock, Natalie	Bantam Doubleday Dell
Switcharound	R	RF	Lowry, Lois	Random House
Sydney-Where Biscuits Go Surfing	R	RF	Coy, Michael	Scholastic
Taken by the Wind	M	RF	Wahman, Joe	Wright Group/McGraw Hill
Taking Care of Terrific	S	RF	Lowry, Lois	Dell
Taking Care of Yoki	R	RF	Campbell, Barbara	HarperTrophy
Taking Sides	S	RF	Soto, Gary	Harcourt Brace
Talent Contest, The	K	RF	PM Story Books -Silver	Rigby
Tales from the Homeplace: Adventures of a Texas Farm Girl	S	RF	Burandt, H. and Dale, S.	Bantam Doubleday Dell
Tales of a Fourth Grade Nothing	Q	RF	Blume, Judy	Bantam Doubleday Dell
Talk About a Family	O	RF	Greenfield, Eloise	HarperTrophy
Talking Earth, The	U	RF	George, Jean Craighead	HarperTrophy
Tall Tale and Other Cases, The	O	RF	Simon, Seymour	Avon
Tall Tales	O	RF	PM Emerald	Rigby
Tamika and the Wisdom Rings	O	RF	Yarbrough, Camille	Random House
Tangerine	U	RF	Bloor, Edward	Scholastic
Taste of Blackberries, A	P	RF	Buchanan Smith, Doris	Scholastic
Teacher's Pet	O	RF	Hurwitz, Johanna	Scholastic
Tears of a Tiger	Z	RF	Draper, Sharon M.	Simon & Schuster
Tell Me No Lies	M	RF	Dionetti, Michelle	Wright Group/McGraw Hill
Tent, The	V	RF	Paulsen, Gary	Bantam Doubleday Dell
Terrible Test Mark and Other Cases, The	O	RF	Simon, Seymour	Avon
Tess and Paddy	J	RF	Sunshine	Wright Group/McGraw Hill

Title	Level	Genre	Author/Series	Publisher/Distributor
Then Again, Maybe I Won't	T	RF	Blume, Judy	Language for Learning Assoc.
There's A Boy In The Girls' Bathroom	Q	RF	Sachar, Louis	Alfred A. Knopf
There's a Frog in My Sleeping Bag	R	RF	Clymer, Susan	Scholastic
There's a Hamster in My Lunchbox	R	RF	Clymer, Susan	Scholastic
There's a Hippopotamus Under My Bed	J	RF	Thaler, Mike	Avon
There's a Rainbow in the River	L	RF	Home Connection Collection	Rigby
There's a Ship Outside My Window	O	RF	PM Ruby	Rigby
There's a Tarantula in My Homework	R	RF	Clymer, Susan	Scholastic
There's an Alligator Under My Bed	J	RF	Mayer, Mercer	The Penguin Group
There's an Owl in the Shower	Q	RF	George, Jean Craighead	Harper Collins
There's Something in My Attic	J	RF	Mayer, Mercer	The Penguin Group
These Old Rags	M	RF	Evangeline Nicholas Collection	Wright Group/McGraw Hill
Thief in the Village, A	V	RF	Berry, James	Puffin Books
Thief of Hearts	V	RF	Yep, Laurence	Harper Collins
Things Don't Change Much	L	RF	Rushby, Pamela	Rigby
Third Grade Bullies	N	RF	Levy, Elizabeth	Hyperion
Third Grade Stars	P	RF	Ransom, Candice	Troll
Thirteen	R	RF	Ransom, Candice	Scholastic
This Can't Be Happening at Macdonald Hall	S	RF	Korman, Gordon	Scholastic
Three By the Sea	K	RF	Marshall, Edward	Puffin Books
Three Ducks Went Wandering	K	RF	Roy, Ron	Clarion
Three Investigators, The Mystery of the Fiery Eye	Y	RF	Arthur, Robert	Random House
Three Smart Pals	L	RF	Rocklin, Joanne	Scholastic
Through Grandpa's Eyes	P	RF	MacLachlan, Patricia	HarperTrophy
Throw-Away Pets	N	RF	Duffey, Betsy	Puffin Books
Throwing Shadows	T	RF	Konigsburg, E. L.	Language for Learning Assoc.
Thunder Valley	T	RF	Paulsen, Gary	Bantam Doubleday Dell
Tiger Eyes	W	RF	Blume, Judy	Bantam Doubleday Dell
Tight End	M	RF	Christopher, Matt	Little, Brown & Co.
Till's Christmas	R	RF	Thacker, Nola	Scholastic
Tiltawhirl John	U	RF	Paulsen, Gary	The Penguin Group
Time Apart, A	T	RF	Stanley, Diane	William Morrow
Time Machine and Other Cases, The	O	RF	Simon, Seymour	Avon
Tin Lizzy	M	RF	Windmill Books	Rigby
To JJ From CC	P	RF	Literacy 2000	Rigby
Toby and the Accident	J	RF	PM Turquoise	Rigby
Today I Got Yelled At	J	RF	City Kids	Rigby
Toilet Paper Tigers, The	Q	RF	Korman, Gordon	Bantam Doubleday Dell
Tongue Twister Prize, The	J	RF	Little Books	Sadlier-Oxford
Toning The Sweep	Y	RF	Johnson, Angela	Scholastic
Too Busy for Pets!	K	RF	Sunshine	Wright Group/McGraw Hill
Too Hot to Handle	M	RF	Christopher, Matt	Little, Brown & Co.
Too Many Rabbits	J	RF	Parish, Peggy	Bantam Doubleday Dell
Too Many Steps	J	RF	Foundations	Wright Group/McGraw Hill
Too Many Tamales	M	RF	Soto, Gary	Putnam & Grosset
Too Much Talk and Other Stories	J	RF	New Way: Literature	Steck-Vaughn
Too Much Trouble for Grandpa	J	RF	Sokoloff, Myka-Lynne	Sadlier-Oxford
Too Small Jill	J	RF	Little Books	Sadlier-Oxford
Too Soon to Say Goodbye	S	RF	Kent, Deborah	Scholastic
Tooter Pepperday	L	RF	Spinelli, Jerry	Random House
Toothpaste Millionaire, The	T	RF	Merrill, Jean	Houghton Mifflin
Totara Tree, The	M	RF	Book Bank	Wright Group/McGraw Hill
Touchdown for Tommy	M	RF	Christopher, Matt	Little, Brown & Co.
Tournament Trouble	R	RF	Costello, Emily	Dell
Tracker	T	RF	Paulsen, Gary	Scholastic
Trapped!	O	RF	SupaDoopers	Sundance
Trapped By a Teacher	Q	RF	Duke, Mary Ann	Rigby
Trash Can Band, The	J	RF	Little Books	Sadlier-Oxford
Treasure Hunting	M	RF	Literacy 2000	Rigby
Treasure of El Patrón, The	T	RF	Paulsen, Gary	Bantam Doubleday Dell

Title	Level	Genre	Author/Series	Publisher/Distributor
Treasure on Fraser Street, The	K	RF	Rushby, Pamela	Rigby
Tricksters	M	RF	SupaDoopers	Sundance
Triplet Trouble and the Bicycle Race	L	RF	Dadey, D. & Jones, M. T.	Scholastic
Triplet Trouble and the Class Trip	L	RF	Dadey, D. & Jones, M. T.	Scholastic
Triplet Trouble and the Cookie Contest	L	RF	Dadey, D. & Jones, M. T.	Scholastic
Triplet Trouble and the Field Day Disaster	L	RF	Dadey, D. & Jones, M. T.	Scholastic
Triplet Trouble and the Pizza Party	L	RF	Dadey, D. & Jones, M. T.	Scholastic
Triplet Trouble and the Red Heart Race	L	RF	Dadey, D. & Jones, M. T.	Scholastic
Triplet Trouble and the Runaway Reindeer	L	RF	Dadey, D. & Jones, M. T.	Scholastic
Triplet Trouble and the Talent Show	L	RF	Dadey, D. & Jones, M. T.	Scholastic
Triplet Trouble and the Talent Show Mess	L	RF	Dadey, D. & Jones, M. T.	Scholastic
Trouble with Buster, The	N	RF	Lorimer, Janet	Scholastic
Trouble with Oatmeal, The	O	RF	PM Emerald	Rigby
Trouble with Parents, The	N	RF	SupaDoopers	Sundance
Trouble with Patrick, The	O	RF	Whitaker, Alan	Rigby
Trouble with Tuck, The	R	RF	Taylor, Theodore	Avon
Troublemaker	M	RF	SupaDoopers	Sundance
Trout Summer	T	RF	Conly, Jane Leslie	Scholastic
Trucker	P	RF	Beale, Fleur	Pacific Learning
True Confessions	S	RF	Tashjian, Janet	Scholastic
Tummy Ache	J	RF	Sunshine	Wright Group/McGraw Hill
Turkey Trouble	M	RF	Giff, Patricia Reilly	Bantam Doubleday Dell
Turkeys' Side of It, The	N	RF	Smith, Janice Lee	HarperTrophy
TV Kid, The	R	RF	Byars, Betsy	Puffin Books
TV Time-Out	M	RF	Blackaby, Susan	Wright Group/McGraw Hill
Twilight In Grace Falls	W	RF	Honeycutt, Natalie	Avon
Twinkie Squad, The	S	RF	Korman, Gordon	Scholastic
Two Plus One Goes A.P.E.	L	RF	Springstubb, Tricia	Scholastic
Two Runaways, The	M	RF	Schultz, Irene	Wright Group/McGraw Hill
Ugly Mug	P	RF	Joseph, Vivienne	Pacific Learning
Under the City	K	RF	Sunshine	Wright Group/McGraw Hill
Undercover Tailback	O	RF	Christopher, Matt	Scholastic
Unexpected Treasure	N	RF	Dionetti, Michelle	Wright Group/McGraw Hill
Universal Solvent and Other Cases, The	O	RF	Simon, Seymour	Avon
Up and Away!: Taking a Flight	N	RF	Book Shop	Mondo
Up High in the Mountains	N	RF	Wildcats	Wright Group/McGraw Hill
Ups and Downs of Carl Davis III, The	T	RF	Guy, Rosa	Language for Learning Assoc.
US and Uncle Fraud	S	RF	Lowry, Lois	Houghton Mifflin
Valentine Star, The	M	RF	Giff, Patricia Reilly	Bantam Doubleday Dell
Van Gogh Cafe, The	S	RF	Rylant, Cynthia	Harcourt Brace
Vicar of Nibbleswick, The	O	RF	Dahl, Roald	Puffin Books
Voyage of the Frog, The	S	RF	Paulsen, Gary	Bantam Doubleday Dell
Wacky Jacks	L	RF	Adler, David A.	Random House
Waiting for the Rain	J	RF	Foundations	Wright Group/McGraw Hill
Wake Up, Emily, It's Mother's Day	M	RF	Giff, Patricia Reilly	Yearling
Walk in My World, A	Y	RF	Mazer, Anne	Persea Books
Walk Through a Rainforest, A: Life in the Ituri Forest of Zaire	V	RF	Creech, Sharon	Harper Collins
Walk Two Moons	V	RF	Creech, Sharon	Harper Collins
Walk With Grandpa, A	L	RF	Read Alongs	Rigby
Walkathon, The	K	RF	PM Story Books -Silver	Rigby
Wanderer, The	V	RF	Creech, Sharon	HarperCollins
Wanted...Mud Blossom	P	RF	Byars, Betsy	Dell
War Shirt, The	K	RF	Spang, Bently	Rigby
War With Grandpa, The	S	RF	Kimmel Smith, Robert	Bantam Doubleday Dell
Waste of Space, A	M	RF	SupaDoopers	Sundance
Watch Out, Man-Eating Snake	L	RF	Giff, Patricia Reilly	Bantam Doubleday Dell
Watcher, The	Z	RF	Howe, James	Simon & Schuster
Watching Josh	M	RF	Eaton, Deborah	Wright Group/McGraw Hill
Watching the Whales	L	RF	Foundations	Wright Group/McGraw Hill

Title	Level	Genre	Author/Series	Publisher/Distributor
We Scream for Ice Cream	K	RF	Chardiet, B. & Maccarone, G.	Scholastic
We're Off to Thunder Mountain	L	RF	Book Shop	Mondo
Wedding Day Disaster	M	RF	SupaDoopers	Sundance
West Side Kids: Don't Call Me Slob-o	R	RF	Orgel, Doris	Hyperion
West Side Kids: The Big Idea	R	RF	Schecter, Ellen	Hyperion
West Side Kids: The Pet Sitters	R	RF	Schecter, Ellen	Hyperion
Westing Game, The	V	RF	Raskin, Ellen	The Penguin Group
Wet Day at School, A	J	RF	Sunshine	Wright Group/McGraw Hill
What a Day!	K	RF	Miranda, Anne	Hampton-Brown
What a Great Idea!	L	RF	Shelton, Flip	Rigby
What Do Fish Have To Do With Anything?	W	RF	Avi	Candlewick Press
What Hearts	S	RF	Brooks, Bruce	Language for Learning Assoc.
What Jamie Saw	T	RF	Coman, Carolyn	The Penguin Group
What Joy Found	L	RF	Ready Readers	Pearson Learning
What Kind of Babysitter Is This?	L	RF	Johnson, Dolores	Scholastic
What Shall I Do?	M	RF	Sunshine	Wright Group/McGraw Hill
What Would You Do?	J	RF	Sunshine	Wright Group/McGraw Hill
What's Cooking, Jenny Archer?	M	RF	Conford, Ellen	Little Brown & Co.
What's for Dinner, Dad?	K	RF	Sunshine	Wright Group/McGraw Hill
What's the Matter, Kelly Beans?	N	RF	Enderle, Judith R. & Tessler, S. G.	Candlewick Press
What's the Matter with Herbie Jones?	N	RF	Kline, Suzy	The Penguin Group
When I Broke the Office Window	L	RF	City Kids	Rigby
When I Forgot	N	RF	Marriott, Janice	Pacific Learning
When I Get Bigger	K	RF	Mayer, Mercer	Donovan
When I Was Young and Wild Bill's Secret Wish	P	RF	Miggs, W.B.	Pacific Learning
When My Dad Came to School	M	RF	City Kids	Rigby
When the Circus Came to Town	R	RF	Horvath, Polly	Sunburst
When The Truck Got Stuck!	M	RF	Cowley, Joy	Pacific Learning
When the Water Closes Over My Head	R	RF	Napoli, Donna	Puffin Books
When Tony Got Lost at the Zoo	L	RF	City Kids	Rigby
When Will We Be Sisters?	K	RF	Kroll, Virginia	Scholastic
Where in the World is the Perfect Family?	P	RF	Hest, Amy	The Penguin Group
Where People Live	J	RF	Early Connections	Benchmark Education
Where the Lilies Bloom	Y	RF	Cleavers, Vera and Bill	HarperTrophy
Where the Red Fern Grows	X	RF	Rawls, Wilson	Bantam Doubleday Dell
Where's Tony?	J	RF	City Kids	Rigby
White Bird	N	RF	Bulla, Clyde Robert	Random House
White Fang	Y	RF	London, Jack	Scholastic
Who Killed Mr. Boddy?	P	RF	Parker, A. E.	Scholastic
Who Put That Hair in My Toothbrush?	U	RF	Spinelli, Jerry	Little, Brown
Who Really Killed Cock Robin?	U	RF	George, Jean Craighead	HarperTrophy
Who Stole the Wizard of Oz?	P	RF	Avi	Alfred A. Knopf
Who's Afraid of the Big, Bad Bully?	K	RF	Slater, Teddy	Scholastic
Whose Side Are You On?	Q	RF	Moore, Emily	Bantam Doubleday Dell
Wild Bird and Other Stories of Adventure	O	RF	Belcher, Angie	Pacific Learning
Wild Culpepper Cruise, The	O	RF	Paulsen, Gary	Bantam Doubleday Dell
Wilde Street Club and Molly, The	M	RF	Sunshine	Wright Group/McGraw Hill
Wilde Street Club and the Duck Man, The	M	RF	Sunshine	Wright Group/McGraw Hill
William Problem, The	S	RF	Baker, Barbara	Puffin Books
William's Wheelchair Race	K	RF	Sunshine	Wright Group/McGraw Hill
Williwaw!	V	RF	Bodoff, Tom	Knopf
Wind Blew, The	J	RF	Hutchins, Pat	Puffin Books
Window, The	V	RF	Ingold, Jeanette	Harcourt Brace
Wingman on Ice	M	RF	Christopher, Matt	Little, Brown & Co.
Winter Room, The	U	RF	Paulsen, Gary	Bantam Doubleday Dell
Wish on a Unicorn	T	RF	Hesse, Karen	The Penguin Group
Wolf's First Deer	M	RF	Book Bank	Wright Group/McGraw Hill
Wolfman Sam	O	RF	Levy, Elizabeth	HarperTrophy
Wolfmen Don't Hula Dance	M	RF	Dadey, D. & Jones, M. T.	Scholastic
Woman Hollering Creek	Z	RF	Cisneros, Sandra	Random House

Title	Level	Genre	Author/Series	Publisher/Distributor
Wonder Kid Meets the Evil Lunch Snatcher	M	RF	Duncan, Lois	Little, Brown & Co.
Words	U	RF	Paulsen, Gary	The Penguin Group
Words of Stone	V	RF	Henkes, Kevin	The Penguin Group
Working Cotton	N	RF	Williams, Sherley Anne	Harcourt Brace
World's Best Dog-Walker, The	Q	RF	Zollman, Pam	Steck-Vaughn
World's Greatest Toe Show, The	M	RF	Lamb, Nancy & Singer, Muff	Troll
Wringer	U	RF	Spinelli, Jerry	HarperTrophy
Write Up a Storm with the Polk Street School	M	RF	Giff, Patricia Reilly	Bantam Doubleday Dell
Yang the Eldest and His Odd Jobs	P	RF	Namioka, Lensey	Bantam Doubleday Dell
Yang the Second and Her Secret Admirer	P	RF	Namioka, Lensey	Bantam Doubleday Dell
Yang the Third & Her Impossible Family	P	RF	Namiaka, Lensey	Bantam Doubleday Dell
Yang the Youngest and His Terrible Ear	P	RF	Namioka, Lensey	Bantam Doubleday Dell
Year Mom Won the Pennant, The	M	RF	Christopher, Matt	Little, Brown & Co.
Year of the Sawdust Man, The	Y	RF	LaFaye, A.	Simon & Schuster
Yearling, The	X	RF	Rawlings, Marjorie Kinnan	Simon & Schuster
Yolonda's Genius	V	RF	Fenner, Carol	Aladdin
Yonder	M	RF	Johnston, Tony	The Penguin Group
You Be The Detective	Q	RF	Miller, Marvin	Scholastic
You Be The Detective II	Q	RF	Miller, Marvin	Scholastic
You Can Always Tell Cathy from Caitlin	K	RF	Sunshine	Wright Group/McGraw Hill
You Can't Eat Your Chicken Pox, Amber Brown	N	RF	Danziger, Paula	Scholastic
You Shouldn't Have to Say Good-bye	T	RF	Hermes, Patricia	Scholastic
You're My Nikki	M	RF	Eisenberg, Phyllis Rose	The Penguin Group
You're Out	N	RF	Kroll, Stephen	Avon Camelot
Young Cam Jansen and the Ice Skate Mystery	J	RF	Adler, David A.	Puffin Books
Young Cam Jansen and the Lost Tooth	J	RF	Adler, David A.	Puffin Books
Young Cam Jansen and the Missing Cookie	J	RF	Adler, David A.	Puffin Books
Young Land Lords, The	X	RF	Myers, Walter Dean	The Penguin Group
Young Wolf's First Hunt	M	RF	Shefelman, Janice	Random House
Your Move, J.P.!	R	RF	Lowry, Lois	Random House
Zeely	R	RF	Hamilton, Virginia	Macmillan
Zero's Slider	M	RF	Christopher, Matt	Little, Brown & Co.
Zoe at the Fancy Dress Ball	J	RF	Literacy 2000	Rigby
Zooman Sam	P	RF	Lowry, Lois	Houghton Mifflin
Among the Hidden	Z	SF	Haddix, Margaret Peterson	Aladdin
Boy Who Reversed Himself, The	Y	SF	Sleator, William	Puffin Books
Bozo the Clone	N	SF	The Zack Files	Grosset & Dunlap
Brother To Shadows	Z	SF	Norton, Andre	Avon
CD and the Giant Cat	V	SF	Odgers, Darrel and Sally	Rigby
Computer Nut, The	R	SF	Byars, Betsy	Bantam Doubleday Dell
Cyberspace	S	SF	Wildcats	Wright Group/McGraw Hill
Day in Space, A	L	SF	Lord, Suzanne. & Epstein, Jolie	Scholastic
Disappearing Bike Shop, The	Q	SF	Woodruff, Elvira	Bantam Doubleday Dell
Dreadful Future of Blossom Culp, The	U	SF	Peck, Richard	Bantam Doubleday Dell
Ear, the Eye, and the Arm, The	Y	SF	Farmer, Nancy	Puffin Books
Escape!	N	SF	Cartwright, Pauline	Pacific Learning
ESP TV	R	SF	Rodgers, Mary	HarperTrophy
Forgotten Door, The	T	SF	Key, Alexander	Language for Learning Assoc.
Ghost Cadet	T	SF	Alphin, Elaine Marie	Language for Learning Assoc.
Goldfish Charlie and the Case of the Missing Planet	R	SF	Mazer, Anne	Troll
Great Interactive Dream Machine, The	Y	SF	Peck, Richard	Puffin Books
Harry On Vacation	S	SF	Sheldon, Dyan	Candlewick Press
Iron Giant, The	O	SF	Hughes, Ted	Alfred A. Knopf
Journal, The: Dear Future II	Q	SF	Literacy 2000	Rigby
Journey to the Center of the Earth, A	X	SF	Verne, Jules	Harper Collins
Loose Bolts	O	SF	Neufeld, David	Wright Group/McGraw Hill
Lost in Cyberspace	Y	SF	Peck, Richard	Puffin Books
Lost in Space	M	SF	Pacific Literacy	Pacific Learning
Mad Scientist's Secret, The	P	SF	Miller, Marvin	Scholastic
Max and Me and the Time Machine	T	SF	Greer, Gery and Ruddick, Bob	Harper Trophy

Title	Level	Genre	Author/Series	Publisher/Distributor
Never Hitch a Ride With a Martian!	N	SF	Clark, Tony	Pacific Learning
Night the Heads Came, The	Y	SF	Sleator, William	Puffin Books
No More Magic	R	SF	Avi	Alfred A. Knopf
Number One	J	SF	Pacific Literacy	Pacific Learning
Save the River!	M	SF	Pair-It Books	Steck-Vaughn
Simon and the Aliens	N	SF	SupaDoopers	Sundance
Sleepers, Wake	T	SF	Jacobs, Paul Samuel	Language for Learning Assoc.
Some of the Kinder Planets	U	SF	Wynne-Jones, Tim	The Penguin Group
Starfishers to the Rescue	M	SF	Dreyer, Ellen	Pearson Learning
Strange Creatures	N	SF	Cartwright, Pauline	Pacific Learning
Time Benders	T	SF	Paulsen, Gary	Bantam Doubleday Dell
Time Capsule, The	M	SF	Book Bank	Wright Group/McGraw Hill
Time Warp Trio: 2095	P	SF	Scieszka, Jon	The Penguin Group
Time Warp Trio: Good, the Bad, and the Goofy, The	P	SF	Scieszka, Jon	The Penguin Group
Timedetectors	V	SF	Literacy 2000	Rigby
Timedetectors	N	SF	SupaDoopers	Sundance
Twenty-One Balloons, The	V	SF	DuBois, William	Scholastic
Unbelievable!	K	SF	Shulman, Lisa	Hampton-Brown
Virtual Fred	O	SF	Courtney, Vincent	Random House
Watchers: I.D.	V	SF	Lerangis, Peter	Scholastic
Watchers: Island	V	SF	Lerangis, Peter	Scholastic
Watchers: Lab 6	V	SF	Lerangis, Peter	Scholastic
Watchers: Last Stop	V	SF	Lerangis, Peter	Scholastic
Watchers: Rewind	V	SF	Lerangis, Peter	Scholastic
Watchers: War	V	SF	Lerangis, Peter	Scholastic
Worst Show-and-Tell Ever, The	J	SF	Walsh, Rita	Troll
Zap! I'm a Mind Reader	N	SF	The Zack Files	Grosset & Dunlap
Adventures of Spider, The	R	TL	Arkhurst, Joyce C.	Scholastic
Aesop & Company: With Scenes from His Legendary Life	O	TL	Bader, Barbara	Houghton Mifflin
Aladdin & the Magic Lamp	J	TL	Traditional Tales	Dominie
Androcles and the Lion	L	TL	PM Tales and Plays-Silver	Rigby
Animal Band, The	K	TL	PM Tales and Plays- Purple	Rigby
Ashes for Gold	K	TL	Folk Tales	Mondo
Awumpalema	L	TL	Literacy 2000	Rigby
Baba Yaga	K	TL	Literacy 2000	Rigby
Bank Robbery and Jack and the Beanstalk, The	L	TL	New Way:Literature	Steck-Vaughn
Bear and the Trolls, The	L	TL	PM Tales and Plays-Silver	Rigby
Beauty and the Beast	K	TL	PM Tales and Plays- Gold	Rigby
Beauty and the Beast	K	TL	Sunshine	Wright Group/McGraw Hill
Beowulf	U	TL	Literacy 2000	Rigby
Between Earth and Sky: Legends of Native American Sacred Places	Z	TL	Bruchac, Joseph	Voyager Books
Big Boy	O	TL	Mollel, Tololwa M.	Houghton Mifflin
Big Fish Little Fish	K	TL	Folk Tales	Wright Group/McGraw Hill
Blind Man and the Elephant, The	K	TL	Backstein, Karen	Scholastic
Borreguita and the Coyote	O	TL	Aardema, Verna	Scholastic
Boy Who Cried Wolf, The	K	TL	Aesop's Fables	Dominie
Boy Who Cried Wolf, The	L	TL	Literacy 2000	Rigby
Boy Who Cried Wolf, The	J	TL	Littledale, Freya	Scholastic
Boy Who Cried Wolf, The	K	TL	PM Tales and Plays- Purple	Rigby
Boy Who Went to the North Wind, The	L	TL	Literacy 2000	Rigby
Brave Little Tailor, The	J	TL	PM Tales and Plays Turquoise	Rigby
Bremen-Town Musicians, The	K	TL	Gross, Ruth	Scholastic
Bringing the Rain to Kapiti Plain	J	TL	Aardema, Verna	Scholastic
Buffalo Woman	N	TL	Goble, Paul	Aladdin
Cabbage Princess, The	K	TL	Literacy 2000	Rigby
Cat and Rat	M	TL	Young, Ed	Henry Holt & Co.
Catching the Sun	M	TL	Paul, Michele	Wright Group/McGraw Hill
Chicken Little	L	TL	Traditional Tales & More	Rigby

Title	Level	Genre	Author/Series	Publisher/Distributor
China's Bravest Girl: The Legend of Hua Mu Lan	O	TL	Chin, Charlie	Children's Press
Cinderella	K	TL	Once Upon a Time	Wright Group/McGraw Hill
Cinderella	K	TL	PM Tales and Plays- Gold	Rigby
Cities of Splendor: The Facts and the Fables	R	TL	Landscapes of Legend	Children's Press
City Mouse-Country Mouse	J	TL	Aesop	Scholastic
Coyote in Trouble	L	TL	Beveridge, Barbara	Pacific Learning
Coyote Not-So-Clever	N	TL	Beveridge, Barbara	Pacific Learning
Crafty Jackal	L	TL	Folk Tales	Wright Group/McGraw Hill
Cricket Boy and Other Stories, The	L	TL	New Way: Literature	Steck-Vaughn
Cut From the Same Cloth: American Women of Myth Legend, and Tall Tale	T	TL	San Souci, Robert D.	Puffin Books
Dan the Dunce	J	TL	Tales from Hans Andersen	Wright Group/McGraw Hill
Dick Whittington	L	TL	PM Tales and Plays-Silver	Rigby
Did You Hear Wind Sing Your Name?	N	TL	Book Shop	Mondo
Donkey's Tale, The	J	TL	Bank Street	Bantam Doubleday Dell
Double Trouble	M	TL	Literacy 2000	Rigby
Dragon King's Palace, The	T	TL	Literacy 2000	Rigby
Dragon Prince, The: A Chinese Beauty and the Beast Tale	P	TL	Yep, Laurence	HarperCollins
Drummer Hoff	J	TL	Emberly, Barbara	Prentice-Hall
East of the Sun & West of the Moon	P	TL	Mayer, Mercer	Aladdin
Elves and the Shoemaker,The	K	TL	New Way Orange	Steck-Vaughn
Elves and the Shoemaker, The	J	TL	PM Tales and Plays Turquoise	Rigby
Emperor and the Nightingale, The	L	TL	Literacy 2000	Rigby
Emperor's New Clothes, The	J	TL	Tales from Hans Andersen	Wright Group/McGraw Hill
Er-Lang and the Suns: A Tale from China	M	TL	Folk Tales	Mondo
Fables	N	TL	Lobel, Arnold	Harper Collins
Fables by Aesop	K	TL	Reading Unlimited	Celebration Press
Fabulous Spotted Egg, The	T	TL	Literacy 2000	Rigby
Fair Swap, A	K	TL	PM Story Books -Silver	Rigby
Farmer and His Two Lazy Sons, The	J	TL	Aesop's Fables	Dominie
Farmer in the Soup, The	K	TL	Littledale, Freya	Scholastic
Favorite Greek Myths	Y	TL	Pope, Mary Osborne	Scholastic
Feathery Fables	P	TL	Krueger, Carol	Rigby
Fire and Wind	L	TL	PM Story Books -Silver	Rigby
Fire-Bird, The	U	TL	Literacy 2000	Rigby
Flower of Sheba, The	L	TL	Orgel, Doris & Schecter, Ellen	Bantam Doubleday Dell
Flying Trunk,The	M	TL	Tales from Hans Andersen	Wright Group/McGraw Hill
Flying With the Eagle, Racing the Great Bear Stories from Native North America	U	TL	Bruchac, Joseph	Troll Medallion
Foolish Gretel	O	TL	Armstrong, Jennifer	Random House
Forgotten Princess, The	L	TL	Literacy 2000	Rigby
Fortune's Friend: Tales of Rivalry and Riches	Q	TL	Literacy 2000	Rigby
Fortune-Tellers, The	O	TL	Alexander, Lloyd	Puffin Books
Four Friends and Other Stories, The	L	TL	New Way: Literature	Steck-Vaughn
Fox and the Crow, The	J	TL	Aesop's Fables	Dominie
Fox and The Crow, The	K	TL	Ready Readers	Pearson Learning
Fox and the Little Red Hen	L	TL	Traditional Tales & More	Rigby
Frog Prince, The	K	TL	Tarcov, Edith H.	Scholastic
Frog Princess, The	K	TL	Literacy 2000	Rigby
Frog Who Would Be King, The	N	TL	Walker, Kate	Mondo
Ghosts!: Ghostly Tales from Folklore	J	TL	Schwartz, Alvin	HarperTrophy
Gingerbread Boy, The	L	TL	Galdone, Paul	Clarion
Gingerbread Man, The	J	TL	Traditional Tales & More	Rigby
Girl in the Golden Bower, The	Q	TL	Yolen, Jane	Little, Brown, & Co.
Girl Who Loved the Wind, The	Q	TL	Yolen, Jane	HarperTrophy
Girl Who Married the Moon, The: Tales from Native North America	U	TL	Bruchac, Joseph & Ross, Gayle	Troll Medallion
Golden Goose, The	M	TL	Literacy 2000	Rigby
Golden Goose, The	L	TL	Sunshine	Wright Group/McGraw Hill

Title	Level	Genre	Author/Series	Publisher/Distributor
Goldilocks and the Three Bears	K	TL	New Way: Literature	Steck-Vaughn
Goldilocks and the Three Bears	K	TL	Once Upon a Time	Wright Group/McGraw Hill
Goldilocks and The Three Bears	J	TL	PM Tales and Plays Turquoise	Rigby
Grain of Rice, A	P	TL	Pittman, Helena Clare	Bantam Doubleday Dell
Grasshopper and the Ants	K	TL	Sunshine	Wright Group/McGraw Hill
Gray Heroes Elder Tales from Around the World	Z	TL	Yolen, Jane	Penguin Books
Greatest of All, The: A Japanese Folktale	L	TL	Kimmel, Eric A.	Holiday House
Greedy Goat, The	L	TL	Book Shop	Mondo
Half for You, Half for Me	K	TL	Literacy 2000	Rigby
Hansel and Gretel	K	TL	Enrichment	Wright Group/McGraw Hill
Hare and the Tortoise, The	P	TL	Aesop's Fables	Dominie
Hare and the Tortoise, The	K	TL	Literacy 2000	Rigby
Hare and the Tortoise, The	K	TL	PM Tales and Plays- Purple	Rigby
Headless Horseman, The	L	TL	Standiford, Natalie	Random House
Her Seven Brothers	O	TL	Goble, Paul	Aladdin
Hercules and Other Greek Legends	T	TL	Wildcats	Wright Group/McGraw Hill
House that Jack Built, The	J	TL	Peppe, Rodney	Delacorte
How Fire Came to Earth	K	TL	Literacy 2000	Rigby
How Flamingos Came to Have Red Legs: A South American Folk Tale	M	TL	Jensen, Ned	Wright Group/McGraw Hill
How Grandmother Spider Got the Sun	J	TL	Little Readers	Houghton Mifflin
How the Giraffe Became a Giraffe	M	TL	Sunshine	Wright Group/McGraw Hill
How the Rattlesnake Got Its Rattle	L	TL	Pair-It Books	Steck-Vaughn
How the Tortoise Got His Shell and Other Stories	K	TL	New Way: Literature	Steck-Vaughn
How the Water Got to the Plains	L	TL	Home Connection Collection	Rigby
How Turtle Raced Beaver	J	TL	Literacy 2000	Rigby
Hugo Hogget: Story Based on an Ecuadoran Legend	K	TL	Cumpiano, Ina	Hampton-Brown
I Saw You in the Bathtub	J	TL	Schwartz, Alvin	HarperTrophy
In a Dark, Dark Room	J	TL	Schwartz, Alvin	HarperTrophy
Ishi's: Tale of Lizard	P	TL	Hinton, L. & Roth, S. L.	Farrar Straus Giroux
Jack and the Beanstalk	K	TL	Weisner, David	Scholastic
Jack and the Magic Harp	K	TL	PM Tales and Plays- Gold	Rigby
Jenny and the Cornstalk	L	TL	Pair-It Books	Steck-Vaughn
Johnny Appleseed	K	TL	Moore, Eva	Scholastic
Jump!: The Adventures of Brer Rabbit	T	TL	Harris, Joel Chandler	Harcourt Brace
Keelboat Annie	N	TL	Johnson, Janet P.	Troll
King Midas and the Golden Touch	K	TL	PM Gold	Rigby
King Midas & the Golden Touch	J	TL	Traditional Tales	Dominie
King's Dream and Sammy's New Yellow Sweater, The	L	TL	New Way: Literature	Steck-Vaughn
King's Equal, The	O	TL	Paterson, Katherine	HarperTrophy
Legend of the Bluebonnet, The	O	TL	dePaola, Tomie	Scholastic
Legend of the Hummingbird, The	K	TL	Folk Tales	Mondo
Legend of the Red Bird, The	K	TL	Sunshine	Wright Group/McGraw Hill
Legends	S	TL	Goodman, R., R. Pierce, Betty Jane Wagner	Houghton Mifflin
Lion and the Mouse, The	M	TL	Aesop's Fables	Dominie
Lion and the Mouse, The	J	TL	Little Books	Sadlier-Oxford
Lion and the Mouse, The	K	TL	Pair-It Books	Steck-Vaughn
Lion and the Mouse, The	J	TL	Sunshine	Wright Group/McGraw Hill
Little Brown Jay, The: A Tale from India	K	TL	Claire, Elizabeth	Mondo
Little Red Riding Hood	K	TL	Enrichment	Wright Group/McGraw Hill
Little Red Riding Hood	J	TL	PM Tales and Plays Turquoise	Rigby
Little Tin Soldier, The	M	TL	Tales from Hans Andersen	Wright Group/McGraw Hill
Lon Po Po: A Red-Riding Hood Story from China	S	TL	Young, Ed	Scholastic
Lost Children, The	M	TL	Goble, Paul	Aladdin
Magic Fish, The	L	TL	Littledale, Freya	Scholastic
Magic Porridge Pot, The	L	TL	Sunshine	Wright Group/McGraw Hill
Man Who Kept His Heart in a Bucket, The	S	TL	Levitin, Sonia	The Penguin Group
Man Who Tricked a Ghost, The	N	TL	Yep, Laurence	Troll Medallion
Merlin and the Dragons	U	TL	Yolen, Jane	The Penguin Group

Title	Level	Genre	Author/Series	Publisher/Distributor
Miller Who Tried to Please Everyone, The	Q	TL	Aesop's Fables	Dominie
Min-Yo and the Moon Dragon	N	TL	Hillman, Elizabeth	Harcourt Brace
Miss Mouse Gets Married	K	TL	Folk Tales	Wright Group/McGraw Hill
Mitten, The	M	TL	Brett, Jan	Scholastic
Mollie Whuppie	K	TL	New Way Orange	Steck-Vaughn
Monster from the Sea, The	K	TL	Bank Street	Bantam Doubleday Dell
Moon and the Mirror, The	M	TL	Literacy 2000	Rigby
Mouse and the Elephant, The	J	TL	Little Readers	Houghton Mifflin
Mud Pony, The	M	TL	Reading Rainbow	Scholastic
Mud Pony, The	L	TL	Sunshine	Wright Group/McGraw Hill
Mufaro's Beautiful Daughters: An African Tale	N	TL	Steptoe, John	Scholastic
Myths	S	TL	Goodman, Ronald, Robert Pierce, Betty Jane Wagner	Houghton Mifflin
Native American Stories	Q	TL	Bruchac, Joseph	Fulcrum Publishing
Newf	N	TL	Killilea, Marie	Putnam & Grosset
Nightingale, The	J	TL	Tales from Hans Andersen	Wright Group/McGraw Hill
Not Too Young and Other Stories	L	TL	New Way: Literature	Steck-Vaughn
Novio Boy	X	TL	Soto, Gary	Harcourt Brace
Off To Squintum's/The Four Musicians	N	TL	Collins, Gillian	Mondo
Old Key, The	T	TL	Literacy 2000	Rigby
Old Woman and Her Pig, The: An Old English Tale	K	TL	Litzinger, Rosanne	Harcourt Brace
Old Woman Who Lived in a Vinegar Bottle	M	TL	Douglas, Ann	Mondo
Owl and the Pussy Cat	L	TL	Lear, Edward	Scholastic
Pancake, The	K	TL	Lobel, Anita	Bantam Doubleday Dell
Papagayo the Mischief Maker	N	TL	McDermott, Gerald	Harcourt Brace
People Could Fly, American Black Folktales	W	TL	Hamilton, Virginia	Alfred A. Knopf
Peter and the North Wind	L	TL	Littledale, Freya	Scholastic
Pheasant and Kingfisher	L	TL	Book Shop	Mondo
Pied Piper of Hamelin, The	K	TL	Hautzig, Deborah	Random House
Pied Piper, The	M	TL	Sunshine	Wright Group/McGraw Hill
Pot of Stone Soup, A	L	TL	Ready Readers	Pearson Learning
Princess and the Peas, The	K	TL	Enrichment	Wright Group/McGraw Hill
Princess and the Wise Woman, The	K	TL	Ready Readers	Pearson Learning
Puss-in-Boots	K	TL	PM Tales and Plays- Purple	Rigby
Queen's Parrot, The: A Play	J	TL	Literacy 2000	Rigby
Rapunzel	L	TL	Literacy 2000	Rigby
Respect the Winds	M	TL	Reeder, Paul	Wright Group/McGraw Hill
Return of Rinaldo, the Sly Fox	M	TL	Scheffler, Ursel	North-South Books
Rinaldo the Sly Fox	M	TL	Scheffler, Ursel	North-South Books
Robin Hood and the Silver Trophy	L	TL	PM Tales and Plays-Silver	Rigby
Robinson Crusoe	P	TL	Dolch, E. W. and Marguerite P.	Scholastic
Rough-Faced Girl, The	S	TL	Martin, R. & Shannon, D.	Scholastic
Royal Drum, The	L	TL	Book Shop	Mondo
Rumpelstiltskin	J	TL	Book Shop	Mondo
Rumpelstiltskin	M	TL	Once Upon a Time	Wright Group/McGraw Hill
Rumpelstiltskin	K	TL	PM Tales and Plays- Gold	Rigby
Rumpelstiltskin	J	TL	Traditional Tales	Dominie
Rumpelstiltskin	N	TL	Zelinsky, Paul O.	Scholastic
Samurai's Daughter, The	Q	TL	San Souci, Robert D.	The Penguin Group
Selu and Kana Ti	K	TL	Folk Tales	Mondo
Seven Foolish Fishermen	K	TL	PM Tales and Plays- Gold	Rigby
Seven Stones of Sligo	O	TL	PM Ruby	Rigby
Shady Deal, The: Tales of Cleverness and Cunning	Q	TL	Parkes, Brenda & Stott-Thornton, Janet	Rigby
Singing Drum, The	T	TL	Literacy 2000	Rigby
Six Foolish Fishermen	L	TL	Elkin,Benjamin	Children's Press
Sleeping Beauty	K	TL	Enrichment	Wright Group/McGraw Hill
Sleeping Beauty, The	L	TL	PM Tales and Plays-Silver	Rigby
Sly Fox and Little Red Hen	K	TL	PM Tales and Plays- Purple	Rigby
Snow Daughter, The	L	TL	Sunshine	Wright Group/McGraw Hill

Title	Level	Genre	Author/Series	Publisher/Distributor
Snow White and the Seven Dwarfs	K	TL	PM Tales and Plays- Gold	Rigby
Soap Soup and Other Verses	K	TL	Kuskin, Karla	HarperTrophy
Somewhere	J	TL	Book Shop	Mondo
Stone Soup	J	TL	McGovern, Ann	Scholastic
Stone Soup	J	TL	PM Tales and Plays Turquoise	Rigby
Story, a Story, A: An African Tale	M	TL	Haley, Gail E.	Aladdin
Story of Big Bess Call, The	M	TL	Bovetz, Marcie	Wright Group/McGraw Hill
Story of Hungbu and Nolbu, The	K	TL	Book Shop	Mondo
Story of William Tell, The	M	TL	PM Story Books -Silver	Rigby
Strange Shoe, The	L	TL	PM Tales and Plays-Silver	Rigby
Sun, the Wind, & Tashira, The	J	TL	Folk Tales	Mondo
Sword in the Stone, The	J	TL	Maccarone, Grace	Scholastic
Tale of Peter Rabbit, The	L	TL	Potter, Beatrix	Scholastic
Tale of the Golden Goose, The	L	TL	Behr, Alexandra	Hampton-Brown
Tale of Veruschka Babuschka, The	M	TL	Literacy 2000	Rigby
Teeny Tiny Woman, The	J	TL	Seuling, Barbara	Scholastic
Terrible Fright, A	K	TL	Story Box	Wright Group/McGraw Hill
Terrible Tiger and Sleeping Beauty	L	TL	New Way: Literature	Steck-Vaughn
That's a Laugh: Four Funny Fables	M	TL	Literacy 2000	Rigby
Three Bears, The	K	TL	Galdone, Paul	Clarion
Three Billy Goats Gruff, The	K	TL	Asbjornsen, P. C. & Moe, J. E.	Harcourt Brace
Three Billy Goats Gruff, The	K	TL	Stevens, Janet	Harcourt Brace
Three Little Pigs	L	TL	Galdone, Paul	Houghton Mifflin
Three Little Pigs	L	TL	Once Upon a Time	Wright Group/McGraw Hill
Three Little Pigs, The	L	TL	Marshall, James	Scholastic
Three Wishes, The	L	TL	Book Shop	Mondo
Three Wishes, The	O	TL	Literacy 2000	Rigby
Three Wishes, The	K	TL	Sunshine	Wright Group/McGraw Hill
Thumbelina	K	TL	Tales from Hans Andersen	Wright Group/McGraw Hill
Timber Box, The	M	TL	Enrichment	Wright Group/McGraw Hill
Too Many Babas	K	TL	Croll, Carolyn	HarperTrophy
Too Many Babas	K	TL	Little Readers	Houghton Mifflin
Too Much Noise	J	TL	McGovern, Ann	Scholastic
Touch of Gold and Other Stories, The	M	TL	Lane, Sheila, Marion Kemp	Wood Lock Educational
Town Mouse and Country Mouse	K	TL	PM Tales and Plays- Purple	Rigby
True Story of the Three Little Pigs, The	Q	TL	Scieszka, Jon	Scholastic
Truth About the Moon, The	M	TL	Bess, Clayton	Houghton Mifflin
Ugly Duckling, The	J	TL	PM Tales and Plays Turquoise	Rigby
Weaving Contest, The	O	TL	Literacy 2000	Rigby
What Made Teddalik Laugh	M	TL	Folk Tales	Wright Group/McGraw Hill
Who Pushed Humpty?	K	TL	Literacy 2000	Rigby
Whose Side Are You On?	K	TL	Cisco, Cheyenne	Sadlier-Oxford
Why Coyote Howls at Night	K	TL	Little Books	Sadlier-Oxford
Why Coyote Howls at Night	Q	TL	Moore, Emily	Farrar, Straus and Giroux
Why Rabbits Have Long Ears	L	TL	Literacy 2000	Rigby
Why The Sea Is Salty	L	TL	Literacy 2000	Rigby
Wild Swans, The	L	TL	Tales from Hans Andersen	Wright Group/McGraw Hill
Winged Cat, The: A Tale of Ancient Egypt	U	TL	Lattimore, Deborah Nourse	HarperCollins
Wings	W	TL	Yolen, Jane & Nolan, Dennis	Harcourt Brace
Wish Fish, The	P	TL	Krueger, Carol	Rigby
Woman Who Flummoxed the Fairies, The	O	TL	Forest, Heather	Harcourt Brace
Zomo the Rabbit: A Trickster Tale from West Africa	M	TL	McDermott, Gerald	Harcourt Brace

Professional References

Anderson, T.H., and B.B. Armbruster. 1984. Content area textbooks. In *Learning to read in American schools*, ed. R.C. Anderson, J. Osborn, and R.J. Tierney, 193–224. Hillsdale, NJ: Lawrence Erlbaum Associates.

Anderson, R.C., L. Shirey, P. Wilson, and L. Fielding. 1986. Interestingness of children's reading material. In *Aptitude learning and instructio*, ed. R. Snow and M. Farr. Hillsdale, NJ.

Anderson, R.C., P.T. Wilson, and L.G. Fielding. 1998. Growth in reading and how children spend their time outside of school. *Reading Research Quarterly* 23: 285–303.

Anderson, R.C. 1984. Role of the reader's schema in comprehension, learning, and memory. In *Learning to read in American schools*, ed. R.C. Anderson, J. Osborn, and R.J. Tierney, 243–258. Hillsdale, NJ: Lawrence Erlbaum Associates.

Armbruster, B.B. 1984. The problem of "inconsiderate texts." In *Theoretical issues in reading comprehension*, ed. G.G. Duffy, L.R. Roehler, and J. Mason, 202–217. New York: Longman.

Armbruster, B.B., and T.H. Anderson. 1981. *Content area textbooks*. Reading Education Report NO. 23: Urbana: University of Illinois Center for the Study of Reading.

——— 1985. Frames: Structure for informational texts. In *Technology of text*, ed. D.H. Jonassen, 331–346. Englewood Cliffs, NJ: Education Technology Publications.

Beck, I., E. McCaslin, and M.G. McKeown. 1980. *The rational design of a program to teach vocabulary to fourth-grade students*. Pittsburgh: University of Pittsburgh, Learning Research and Development Center.

Beck, I.L., M.G. McKeown, and E.W. Gromoll. 1989. Learning from social studies. *Cognition and Instruction* 6: 99–158.

Clay, M.M. 2001. *Change over time in children's literacy development*. Auckland, New Zealand: Heinemann.

Davidson, A., P. Wilson, and G. Herman. 1986. *Effects of syntactic connections and organizing cues on text comprehension*. Champaign, IL: Center for the Study of Reading.

Fountas, I.C., and G.S. Pinnell. 2001. *Guiding readers and writers, grades 3–6: Teaching comprehension, genre, and content literacy*. Portsmouth, NH: Heinemann.

——— 1996. *Guided reading: Good first teaching for all children*. Portsmouth, NH: Heinemann.

——— 1999. *Matching books to readers*. Portsmouth, NH: Heinemann.

Fry, E. 1977. Fry's readability graphs: Clarifications, validity, and extension to level 1, *Journal of Reading* 21, 242–252.

Irwin, J.W., and C. A. Davis. 1980. Assessing readability: the checklist approach. *Journal of Reading* 24: 124–130.

New Standards. 1998. *Performance Standards: Volume 1— Elementary School*. National Center on Education and the Economy and the University of Pittsburgh.

Pinnell, G.S., and I.C. Fountas. 1998. *Word matters: Teaching phonics and spelling in the reading/writing classroom*. Portsmouth: NH: Heinemann.

Ruddell, M. R. 1997. *Teaching content reading and writing*, 2nd edition. Boston: Allyn and Bacon.

Scharer, P., J. Williams, and G.S. Pinnell. 2001. Literacy Collaborative: 2001 Research Report. Columbus, OH: The Ohio State University.

Singer, H. 1992. Friendly texts: Description and criteria. In *Reading in the content areas*. 3rd Edition, ed. E. K. Dishner, T.W. Bean, J.E. Readence, and D.W. Moore, 156–168. Dubuque, IA: Kendall/Hunt.

Index